A Rectification Manual

The American Presidency

A Rectification Manual

The American Presidency

Regulus Astrology LLC

Copyright © Regulus Astrology LLC 2008

First Edition, December 17, 2007
Second Edition, October 31, 2008
Third Edition, September 1, 2009
Fourth Edition, March 26, 2023

All rights reserved. No part of this work may be used or reproduced in any manner whatsoever without written permission from the publisher, except in the case of brief quotations embodied in critical articles or reviews.

For errata, please refer to **www.regulus-astrology.com**.

Grateful acknowledgement is made for permission to reprint previously published material:

American Federation of Astrologers: Excerpts on the Moon's aspects and rectification from *Textbook of Astrology*, by Alfred Pearce, reprinted 2006 by the American Federation of Astrologers.

AstroDatabank Company: Birth data including suggested birth times for American Presidents and First Ladies, copyright © 1999-2023.

Astrology House: For permission to include astrological charts calculated by Janus 5.5 software and Janus fonts, copyright © 1998-2023.

Benjamin Dykes/Cazimi Press: Excerpts on directing the SAN and the Lot of Children in revolutions from *Book of Astronomy*, by Guido Bonatti, translated by Benjamin Dykes, copyright © 2007 by Benjamin Dykes.

Elizabeth Bram/Noyes Press: Excerpts on the a planet's bound/dwad placement and the Moon's separation and application from *Ancient Astrology: Theory and Practice*, by Firmicus Maternus, translated by Jean Rhys Bram, copyright © 1975 by Jean Rhys Bram.

Robert Hand and Project Hindsight: Excerpt on the transit of the lord of the Ascendant over the degree on an infortune in the radix from *Opusculum Astrologicum*, by Johannes Schoener, translated and edited by Robert Hand, copyright © 1994 by Robert Hand.

Warburg Institute: Excerpt on transits from *Al-Qabīsī: The Introduction to Astrology*, translated and edited by C. Burnett, K. Yamamoto, and M. Yano, copyright © 2004 by The Warburg Institute and Nino Aragno Editore.

ISBN: 978-0-9801856-0-7 (paper)
ISBN: 978-0-9801856-1-4 (electronic)

CONTENTS

Acknowledgements		vii
Preface		ix
Introduction		xxi
Prerequisites		xxvii
Key		xxviii

Part 1	**DELINEATION**	
Chapter 1	Planets in Signs	3
Chapter 2	Planets in Houses	25
Chapter 3	Physiognomy	39
Chapter 4	Soul	51
Chapter 5	Longevity	67

Part 2	**PREDICTION**	
Chapter 6	The Problem of Under Specification	97
Chapter 7	Temporal Indicators	103
Chapter 8	Planetary Period Methods	127
Chapter 9	Zodiacal Releasing	147
Chapter 10	Directions	159
Chapter 11	Solar Returns: Profections and Time Lords	181
Chapter 12	Solar Returns: Delineation and Prediction	197
Chapter 13	Solar Returns: Hellenistic Lots	237
Chapter 14	Lunar Nodes and Eclipses	261
Chapter 15	Transits	277

Part 3	**RECTIFICATION**	
Chapter 16	Preparing the Event Database	317
Chapter 17	Three Stages of Rectification	325
Chapter 18	Rectification Case Studies	337

Afterword		373
Appendix	The Presidential Database	381
References		761
Index		774

LIST OF FIGURES AND TABLES

FIGURE

1	Shapes of the Face based on Zodiac Signs	42

TABLES

1	Essential Dignities and Assignment of Scores	4
2	Comparison of the Decans (Triplicity) and Dwads, Aries	6
3	Dynamic Activity to the Lot of Death for Various House Systems. Andrew Jackson's Death, 8-Jun-1845	27
4	House Skewness: Ascendant-Midheaven Degree Difference	29
5	Porphyry's Assignment of Zodiac Signs to Body Parts	41
6	Physiognomy Significators	45
7	Correspondences between Aristotle's Soul Levels and Astrological Significators	53
8	Ibn Ezra Victor Model (1507). In-sect triplicity ruler and triplicity decans	54
9	Victor Soul Model	58
10	Kūshyār Ibn Labbān's rating method for Moon and Mercury	60
11	Cognitive Assessment Model: Rulers of Moon and Mercury	62
12	Years of the Planets	75
13	Longevity Model: Predicted vs Actual	79
14	Martin Van Buren: Al-mubtazz Table for Killing Planet	83
15	Arcus Vitae: Model vs Empirical Results	93
16	Lifespan, Midpoint, Syzygy ante Navitatem, and Lunar Phase	105
17	Moon's Separation and Application	115
18	War Events for Presidents with the Moon's application to Mars	116
19	Dorothean Triplicity Rulers	128
20	Firdaria Sequence for Diurnal and Nocturnal Nativities	141
21	Zodiacal Releasing L1 and L2 Time periods, Days	148
22	Zodiacal Releasing for all signs for 2-Nov-1865, Warren Harding	152
23	Delineations for Lot of Spirit's bound placement	157
24	Directing through the Bounds: Ascendant, Theodore Roosevelt	167
25	Directing Through the Bounds: Midheaven, Theodore Roosevelt	176
26	Summary of Annual Time Lords, James Monroe	186
27	Directions/Profections of Lincoln's 1862 Solar Return Ascendant	203
28	Secondary Progressions of Lincoln's 1862 Solar Return Moon	204
29	Monthly and Daily Profections 1862/63, Abraham Lincoln	207
30	Collected Inputs for Lincoln's 1862 Solar Return	210
31	Listing of Historical USA Events following JSC of 21 Oct 1861	213

32	Summary of Solar Return – Lot Examples	242
33	Transits of the Lunar Nodes to the Angles	269
34	Planets and Recommended Orbs	279
35	Events timed by FDR's Mercury transits, 1940-45	292
36	Planets in the 30th or 1st Degrees of Signs	330
37	Comparison of Reported and Proposed Birth Times	383
38	Presidential Birthplace Database	384

ACKNOWLEDGEMENTS

Thanks to Robert Hitt and Henry Weingarten who first introduced me to astrology through the field of finance; to Jeri London, and Ken Negus for basic instruction in prediction and rectification; to Jonathan Pearl for insights in practical application of predictive methods; to Chris Brennan for sharing tenets of Hellenistic astrology; to Ben Dykes for assistance in incorporating the latest research standards in Medieval Astrology; to Perry Havranek for pushing me to document my findings in writing so others might benefit; to Tom Callanan for editorial assistance; to Diana Warwick Zoller for tutoring and my primary teacher Robert Zoller for passing on the tradition of Medieval Predictive Astrology; and most of all to my private clients who have facilitated this research effort.

Practical application of Medieval Predictive Astrology is impossible without accurate and user-friendly designed software. To Mark Griffin of Astrology House, designer of *Janus* software, I owe a special debt of gratitude. Without his choice to include the Regiomontanus method of primary directions, this research project would never have been produced. Thanks also to Rumen Kolev, a tireless researcher of primary directions whose *Placidus* software program greatly simplified testing some of the more arcane primary direction applications.

To my wife and family for allowing me the luxury of endless hours of seclusion while researching and preparing this manuscript, I owe the greatest debt of gratitude.

PREFACE TO THE FOURTH EDITION

Since publication of the 3rd edition in 2009, the revival of traditional astrology has shifted away from late Medieval compilers like Guido Bonatti as championed by Robert Zoller in the early 2000s to the earliest surviving astrological texts from the Hellenistic era. As I write this preface, the first complete English translation of Vettius Valens' *Anthologies* awaits a pickup from the local Amazon package depot. According to Chris Brennan, publication of *The Anthologies* completes the revival of Hellenistic Astrology with all major texts now available in English translation. The years 2020-2023 also mark Saturn's Aquarius Ingress which forms a complete Saturn return measured from initial translations published by Project Hindsight in the mid-1990s which kickstarted the traditional astrology revival in America. It also marks a Saturn return for me personally. With my natal Saturn in the 12th house, time since 2020 has been spent largely in seclusion, collecting, distilling, and codifying my horoscope database and research studies.

The fourth edition represents a substantial rewrite of prior editions. My initial goal was incorporation of **Zodiacal Releasing** within the three-stage model of rectification. This edition adds a side-by-side page comparison of Zodiacal Releasing and Firdaria in the Presidential database so readers can begin to compare the two techniques. As for Firdaria, there is no change to my usage of the Medieval variant of placing the Lunar Nodes between major Mars and Sun periods for nocturnal horoscopes.

For those Hellenistic astrologers familiar with Zodiacal Releasing but new to Firdaria, it may shock to learn that after re-examining rectifications published in ARM 3rd edition with ZR, only three revisions were required based on this technique: to advance the Lot of Spirit three degrees from late Aries to early Taurus for Millard Fillmore and complete revisions for Benjamin Franklin and William McKinley. Said another way, the three-stage rectification approach advocated in this volume has held up well after subjected to Zodiacal Releasing, a technique which I did not use in prior editions. This speaks to the richness of available predictive techniques and warns against overreliance on a single method.

With this book near the limits of allowable page counts for a single volume, addition of nearly 100 pages for Firdaria and Zodiacal Releasing tables required cuts. The chapter on Modern Planets was dropped together with all appendices beyond the now expanded Presidential Database. Deleted appendices are now available for free download on www.regulus-astrology.com. New chapters on Physiognomy and the Soul were added. Chapters on Longevity, Directions, and Case Studies were substantially rewritten. Other additions are marked by ***NEW*** at the beginning of the relevant section.

<u>Modern Planets</u>. At the time of writing the 1st edition, I had almost completely stripped modern planets from my practice. But not quite. The 4th edition retains

only three examples of modern planets (1) the transit of Uranus to MC for the posthumous DNA release confirming descendants of Sally Hemmings were almost certainly descendants of Thomas Jefferson and (2) transits of Uranus to the superior square of Gerald Ford's Midheaven for his accession to both the Vice Presidency and the Presidency and (3) dynamic activity of Uranus for the tragic car accident on 7-Nov-1972 which killed Joe Biden's first wife and daughter. Ford is the best example of the relevance of modern planets as a timer of career milestones in the Presidential database. Natal Uranus is placed in the 10th house of career and promises an unexpected event. The location of the Uranus transit for Ford's accession to Vice President and President was the superior square of the MC degree, e.g., tr Uranus 24LI25 at the 10th positional degree from the MC 24CP25. None of the major time lord techniques indicated Ford rising to high political office (e.g., Firdaria, Zodiacal Releasing, Directing through the Bounds) making the transit of Uranus the key predictive method for the events. The problem with Uranus and other modern planets is that we do not know in advance what type of event they promise. To say that Ford will have an unexpected event which will mark his career is correct, but it is not a prediction. My frank observation is that an obsession with modern planets diverts focus from the tools of traditional astrology which offer better delineation and predictive capabilities for astrology practitioners. If by ignoring modern planets I am to miss a major career event for say, 1 in 50 horoscopes studied, I will pay that price.

Apart from Ford, many other Presidents register major career milestones when transits of the Lunar Nodes and the Victor of the Horoscope reach the exact degree of the superior square of the ASC, MC, Lot of Fortune, or the Lot of Spirit. This is a new finding for the application of transits for rectification.

Alternative angles. Earlier editions included a few dynamic measurements involving the Equatorial Ascendant and the Vertex. Advocated by Martha Lang-Wescott in the 1990s, these derivative angles arise from the same spherical astronomy principles which give us the Ascendant and Midheaven but use a different set of great circles. I am no longer actively using these angles in my current practice but have left a few examples of dynamic activity for the Vertex in this edition. I find Saturn-Vertex directions to be compelling measurements for Woodrow Wilson's stroke and the defeat of the Versailles Treaty in the Senate.

Physiognomy. Focusing on the shape of the face, the proposed model employing the **ruler of the rising decan** is now presented in a standalone chapter. Confirmation bias limits application of the technique in rectification; nevertheless, for certain horoscopes the ruler of the rising decan model can be a decisive rectification tool. Rejecting Leo rising in favor of Virgo rising for George H. W. Bush is one example.

Soul. My research in the last ten years has examined the Victor of the Horoscope which I classify as the **Victor Soul Model**. This is Porphyry's Kurios, the Medieval Almutem Figuris of Robert Zoller, and William Lilly's Lord of the

Geniture. In a separate sample of over 300 horoscopes, I compared Ibn Ezra's model with Porphyry's guidelines for computing this planet. Ibn Ezra's model identified the correct Victor in roughly one-third of the cases which is only slightly better than chance. I now favor Porphyry's guidelines. Identifying the Victor of the Horoscope early on during the rectification process can improve efficiency when choosing the diurnal or nocturnal Firdaria sequence, when ranking the importance of planetary transits, and as a necessary input for longevity computations. A second method of classifying the soul via the Moon, Mercury, and their rulers I tentatively relabel as the **Cognitive Assessment Model**. This is less useful in rectification but helpful in understanding the soul when viewed from a different set of criteria. In particular, the strange mix of success and failure of Richard Nixon's career can be delineated by the interplay between both Victor and Cognitive Assessment Soul Models.

Zodiacal Releasing. As a rectification tool, ZR is useful because the Lots of Fortune and Spirit on which the technique is based require identification of the Sun, Moon, and Ascendant degrees. As such, correctly matching a biographical timeline to ZR time periods can refine the Ascendant degree range. Beyond matching large life chapters to L1 subperiods, the unusual feature of events linked by foreshadowing (FS), loosing of the bond (LB), and completion periods (CP) offer the best application of ZR in rectification because of the low odds such linkages can occur because of chance. In a case study, ZRS is applied to the horoscope of Warren Harding. It confirms the proposed rectification of 9:27:41 AM which is substantially different than the ADB A-rated birth time of 2:30 PM.

Longevity. Prior ARM editions cast doubt on whether major years granted by planets could be adjusted based on the al-kadukhadāh's placement in angular, succedent, or cadent houses. Research favored granting major years no matter what the house placement. This 4th edition goes further and casts doubt on whether the al-kadukhadāh's major years can be modified by middle years (as months) or minor years (as days). Reflecting on the premise that longevity theory is based on the duration of planetary cycles – there is no theoretical justification for middle years of the planets as their average of minor and major years does not correspond to any planetary synodic/sidereal cycle. Recomputing longevity projections without these adjustments yields better results.

Directions. Directing through the Bounds for Theodore Roosevelt has been rewritten for a complete treatment for the Ascendant. Since publication of the 3rd edition, release of Janus software version 5.5 now includes a Distributions module which I applied to the entire Presidential database, though space limitations prevent a full presentation. Surprisingly, my 'absurd' claim of to-the-second rectifications made in prior editions without use of this technique held up under scrutiny when Directing through the Bounds is applied. Reagan is a standout.

Birthplace Location. Over the course of reading biographies and making additions to Presidential chronologies, it came to my attention that Wikipedia has standalone pages dedicated to most Presidential birthplaces which list exact birthplace coordinates. In most cases, an exact street address compared to default coordinates for a city's location in astrological software makes little difference in horoscope calculation. But some do. For Theodore Roosevelt born in the metropolis of New York City, the difference between default coordinates for New York City from astrological software compared to 28 East 20th Street shifted some primary directions nearly a full week. As an author claiming to-the-second rectification is possible, I chose to update all birthplace locations which now vary slightly from Astrodatabank coordinates. A summary list of locations, coordinates, and sources appears at the beginning of the Presidential database.

Revised Rectifications. The horoscope of William McKinley has been my nemesis. The current proposed rectification is much close to the official ADB time. I still have my doubts. Beyond slight changes on account of updated birthplace locations, other revisions including G. Washington (< 1 degree), C. Arthur (< 2 degrees), M. Fillmore (< 3 degrees), J. Polk (< 5 degrees), and J. Buchanan (< 7 degrees). James Madison was shifted by 24 hours to reflect clarification by ADB on exactly which midnight Madison was born. Despite the 24-hour change for Madison's horoscope, the rectified Ascendant was little changed. This reflects the consistency of superior planets for event timing. I am now outside my original claim of 90% accuracy within 30 seconds for the Presidential database. But I am happy with the ability of most of the original rectifications to hold their own when subjected to additional techniques of Directing through the Bounds and Zodiacal Releasing.

Revised Notation. Presentation format for primary directions has been updated to reflect consistency with *America is Born: Introducing the Regulus USA National Horoscope* and other published rectifications. The following primary direction sequence timed Washington's attendance at the 1st Continental Congress beginning 5-Sep-1774 and lasting through October 1774.

| PT | D | Jupiter/Capricorn | P | sin sq Jup (JU) d. => MC | 5-Sep-1774 |
| PT | D | Jupiter/Capricorn | P | sin sq Jup (0) d. => MC | 15-Oct-1774 |

Promissor. This is the planet, aspect, or point which moves with the celestial sphere as the sphere rotates on its axis. Listed in the first row is the sinister square aspect of Jupiter, labeled as 'sin sq Jup (JU).'

Significator. This is the point held fixed on the celestial sphere. Originally, only the Ascendant, Midheaven, Sun, Moon, lot of fortune, and prenatal syzygy were allowable significators. Later authors allowed planets to take on the role of the significator. No matter what is listed as the promissor or significator, any planet or point listed to the *right* of the arrow is held fixed on the celestial sphere. In this example, the significator is the Midheaven, listed by the abbreviation 'MC.'

Distributors and Partners. Abū Ma'shar introduces two new words to primary directions vocabulary. The **distributor** is the Egyptian bound placement of the promissor. Central to Abū Ma'shar's system of distributors and partners, the distributor contributes roughly half the effect of the actual direction by effectively setting the stage for actors to play out roles as partners. The **partner** is nothing more than the grouping of a single promissor and significator. In the example presented above, I abbreviate distributor with 'D' and partner with 'P.'

D = distributor = bound = 'Jupiter/Capricorn'
P = partner = 'sin sq Jup (JU) d. => MC'

Because bounds function differently across signs, bounds need to be identified beyond the planet itself. Stating 'the bound of Jupiter' tells us little because the bound of Jupiter in Capricorn behaves much differently than the bound of Jupiter in Aquarius. *Bounds need identification by both planet and sign.*

Aspect. The type of aspect between the promissor and significator. Either conjunction, sextile, square, trine, or opposition. For this example the abbreviation 'sq' denotes the square aspect.

Dexter/Sinister. For sextile, square, and trine aspects, there are two aspect types to consider. To specify which aspect, the terms dexter (abbreviated 'dex.') and sinister (abbreviated 'sin.') are used. Dexter aspects are found by beginning at the planet and moving against the order of the signs; sinister aspects, vice versa. For this example, 'sin.' is the abbreviation for the sinister aspect of Jupiter. With Jupiter's position at 8LI37, the sinister square aspect of Jupiter is 8CP37. With the bound of Jupiter defined to be the seven degree range from 7CP00'00" to 13CP59'59", the sinister square aspect of Jupiter falls within the bound of Jupiter/Capricorn. Therefore Jupiter/Capricorn is designated the Distributor.

Latitude. Janus offers latitude assignments for both significator and promissor. There are three latitude conditions: zero latitude, the planet's full latitude, or an interpolated latitude based on the method of Bianchini. For zero latitude directions, the number '0' is listed or omitted for the Sun and Nodes where latitude is always zero. For full planet latitude directions, the planet's name is abbreviated. ('SA' = Saturn, 'JU' = Jupiter, 'MA' = Mars, 'SU' = Sun, 'VE' =Venus, 'ME' = Mercury, 'MO' = Moon). For directions which employ the latitude adjustment of Bianchini, 'BI' is listed.

For the first row in this example, '(JU)' denotes the direction is computed with the full latitude of Jupiter. For the second row in this example, '(0)' indicates zero latitude for Jupiter is used to compute the direction. [Note: traditional authors restricted usage of a planet's full latitude for conjunctions and no other dynamic aspect. My usage of full latitude for sextile, square, trine, and opposition aspects is not recognized by traditional authors.]

Direct or Converse. Whether the celestial sphere is moved by direct motion (abbreviated as 'd.') or by converse motion (abbreviated as 'c.') requires identification. For this example, 'd.' indicates direct motion. [Note: traditional authors did not use converse motion which is based on the premise of time moving backwards prior to birth. I continue to use them in my practice.]

The projected event date is listed last. Ptolemy's Key is used to convert the arc of direction to the projected date when the direction is due.

Ptolemy's Key: 1 degree = 1year = 365.2424 days.

Method - Interplanetary directions. Ptolemy and Regiomontanus are two systems for computing interplanetary directions used in this volume. Whatever computation method used for interplanetary directions requires disclosure. I recommend 'PT' for Ptolemy and 'REG' for Regiomontanus.

Distributor Changeovers. When the directed significator changes from one bound to another, the following format is recommended. Added are the words 'Changeover' and 'bound'. Absent is listing of any partner direction. This is the direction which preceded Washington's fatal throat infection by twenty-one days.

| D | Changeover | bound Saturn/Taurus d. → ASC | 23-Nov-1799 |

Future editions. While additional research can uncover more events which are capable of refining published rectifications, it is unlikely that discovery of new predictive methods will substantially advance the tools I advocate for rectification. Therefore, there is a good chance this will be the last edition of ARM.

Refinement of topics raised by *A Rectification Manual* may be better presented in separate volumes. These include: delineation of the bound placement of the Lot of Spirit and the nuances between Firdaria, Zodiacal Releasing, and Directing through the Bounds as the three major time lord systems now under the microscope.

In the grand scheme of things, the issue of whether Directing by Triplicity should divide life into two halves with the 3rd participating triplicity ruler assisting throughout the entire lifetime – or whether the 3rd participating triplicity ruler is assigned to the final third of a tripartite division of years – is the least of my worries. To get to this point it is necessary to grind through event matches to Firdaria, Zodiacal Releasing and Directing Through the Bounds and see if anything is left over which cannot be accounted for by these methods. That is a high hurdle to clear before revisiting Directing by Triplicity.

Dr. H.
Regulus Astrology LLC
November 25, 2022

PREFACE TO THE THIRD EDITION

Since publication of the first edition there has been a resurgence of interest in primary directions among traditional astrologers. Coincident with this movement has been enhancements in software design capable of handling primary directions calculations. The latest edition of Janus software (Version 4.3 released July 20, 2009) introduced a completely revamped primary directions module. In addition to correctly naming the Regiomontanus method (incorrectly labeled Placidus under the Pole in Version 3.0) and fixing some calculation problems for aspects with latitude, Janus 4.3 now includes directions calculated by Ptolemy's method (also referred to as Alchabitius or Placidus-Classic primary directions). Many other promissors and significators have been added as options; for this edition the ability to include the Syzygy Ante Navitatem (SAN) as one of the candidates for the Hīlāj has been helpful in tests of the arcus vitae. Finally, the ability to see both Ptolemy and Regiomontanus primary direction methods with various latitude options on a single screen has improved the speed of rectification by an order of magnitude.

Since the release of Janus 4.3, I have reviewed proposed rectifications from the 1st and 2nd editions and offer the following revisions:

Improved notation style

For those readers having problems comparing directions presented in the book with those generated by software programs, the notation style for primary directions has been changed in order to make these comparisons easier.

22-Jul-1752. *PT. dex. sextile Saturn (l=SA) d. => Moon (l=MO)*.

Calculated for George Washington (p. 422), this direction lists the computed date (22-Jul-1752); method used, Ptolemy (PT) or Regiomontanus (REG); the promissor (sextile Saturn); dexter (dex.) or sinister (sin.) aspect type; latitude assumption for aspects (l=SA); direct (d.) or converse (c.) motion; and the significator (Moon). The absence of any latitude notation means zero latitude is assumed. This notation is compatible with Janus 4.3 and is similar in style to notation presented by primary directions specialist Rumen Kolev.

Definitions. The ***promissor*** positioned to the ***left*** of the arrow is the point or aspect ***moved*** along the celestial sphere. The ***significator*** to the ***right*** of the arrow is the point or aspect ***held fixed*** on the celestial sphere. Direct motion is defined as moving the celestial sphere from east to west in accordance with the diurnal motion of the sky relative to the earth. It is the original and preferred method for primary direction computations. Converse motion is defined as moving the celestial sphere from west to east, a method not introduced until the 19th century. It is not universally accepted among practitioners of primary directions.

Revised rectifications

Within the Presidential database I have made 6 changes. Other than a five second change to Carter, revisions to Arthur, Taft, Truman, Nixon, and Ford represent changes to five of the forty-three horoscopes, or 12% of the original database. These changes are in keeping with the claim made in the 1st edition that the rectified database of American Presidents represented an accuracy level of 30 seconds or less for 90% of the sample. Other than Taft, whose Ascendant I altered to Taurus from Scorpio, the revisions represent minor changes to the original proposed Ascendant. In every case, the revisions move the proposed birth time closer to times presented in the Astrodatabank database. For the First Ladies Database, a substantial number of revisions were made, improving on what were advertised as preliminary rectifications for the 1st edition.

To be sure, some revisions reflect improved accuracy in computation of directions by Janus 4.3. Because of problems in Janus 3.0, approximately 5% of the directions presented in the first two editions were computed incorrectly. And for this reason some readers have raised legitimate questions regarding results presented in the 1st edition. What readers may find of interest is that for as many directions dropped out, just as many new directions were found which yielded results just as accurate as presented in the 1st edition. Some highlights:

Andrew Jackson/Warren Harding. As theorized in the 1st edition, the prenatal Syzygy (SAN) proved muster as the empirical Hīlāj when timing illness and death. For Jackson, incidents of duels and his death were timed by SAN directions including one duel within two days of a SAN direction. For Harding, death was timed by a SAN direction within three days.

William McKinley. Not entirely happy with the Moon-MC direction suggested for the arcus vitae, I indicated McKinley's death was timed by a separate mundane horoscope (see *America is Born: Introducing the Regulus USA National Horoscope*, p. 205). When reviewing McKinley's natal horoscope, a Sun-Saturn direction by Ptolemy's method was found which timed death within 2 days. Keep in mind these directions for Jackson, Harding, and McKinley were computed with the proposed rectifications presented in the 1st edition with no subsequent changes.

Wherever appropriate, references to revised rectifications have been modified throughout the text. Otherwise, the only major change to the text is a rewrite of the Directing through the Bounds example for Theodore Roosevelt's MC based on further research into this technique.

Finally, as an update to the 2008 USA Presidential elections, nativities for Barack Obama, Michelle Obama, and Joe Biden are included. John McCain and Sarah Palin, included in the 2nd edition, have been dropped.

The Three Stages of Rectification

What distinguishes the medieval approach to rectification from modern methods is employment of a richer set of predictive tools. This approach rescues rectification from an underspecified predictive model often restricted to solar arc directions, progressions, and transits. In this preface to the 3rd edition, it is a point worth re-emphasizing. While rectification debates often get caught up in the minutiae of primary directions, I suggest these debates miss the point. Recommended for use in only the third and final stage of rectification after the Ascendant has been fine tuned to within 1-4 degrees of accuracy, primary directions need to be thought of as a 'finishing' tool likened to fine grade sandpaper used to smooth wood after construction is complete. That initial 'construction' is the correct choice of the Ascendant, advocated as the first stage of rectification which relies on robust predictive techniques (e.g., Firdaria, Moon's configuration) as well as understanding the basic configuration of the chart. Primary directions come much later in the process.

Nevertheless, primary directions have been historically used by authors in support of rectifications presented in astrological reference databases such as this one. Emphasizing primary directions when reporting rectification results in *A Rectification Manual* does not mean steps in Stages I & II were not taken; only that primary directions which accurately match the delineation of the promissor and significator are the most succinct way to justify the validity of any rectification. The practical limits of time and space are also relevant; otherwise the book would have taken another 2 years and 2000 pages to complete in order to include the full bevy of Stage I and II steps taken.

Precision

If you are working with an accurate birth time, verified by observation at the time of birth, or accurately rectified, and you are attentive and precise in your calculations you may attain to directions accurate to within 24 hours . . .

Robert Zoller, "More Light on Primary Directions," Sep. 2, 2002, privately published.

My statement that Franklin Roosevelt's rectified Ascendant represents a level of precision which implies accuracy to within a fraction of a second of time has produced some interesting reactions. For skeptics, a common response is to cite authors like Morin who state that uncertainty concerning a direction's timing in a given year (e.g., choosing which single year from a range of years) can be resolved by examining congruity between a direction and a solar return for a particular year. What Morin implies is the inherent imprecision in primary directions requires recourse to the solar return for confirmation; and without that step we are lucky to even get the year of the event correct, much less the month, and in no way the event date within a few days as Zoller or I suggest is possible.

Morin's observation is important; in fact, in approximately one-third of the solar returns studied for the year of death the position of the promissor and significator in the natal arcus vitae was mirrored in the return. Morin's observation is also important for directions involving the Moon which often yield the most inaccurate results of any significator owing to factors which may relate to parallax and disk size. But, for a man living in an era with astronomical tables so inaccurate as to render many published lunar returns with improper Ascendants (not to mention his own errors), for students to rely on Morin as an authority on precision in mathematical astrology is a concept I find amusing. We can do better than stating a 12 month time horizon for a direction's effect. Especially for directions of Mars, Saturn, and the Sun to the Ascendant and Midheaven which produce the most consistently timed events necessary for rectification by primary directions.

Zoller continues...

> *I used to think that Primary Directions pin-pointed specific events in the native's life. I hasten to add, however, that directions often produce a period of time of the character of the Significator and the Promissor during which a number of events happen near each other in time rather than a solitary event. What happens is that we may remember but one event occurring during the time in question . . .*

Having stated that directions can time events within 24 hours, Zoller goes on to state that sometimes more than one event occurs, yet the events are 'near each other.' I agree with this finding and have proposed the *Primary Direction Sequence* in support of the ability of a direction to time events within a discrete time interval. My choice of assigning a full planet's latitude to aspects is non-standard among traditional authors, but represents no less tinkering with latitude than what astrologers like Bianchini, Morin, Montulmo, or Placidus have done in the past. Considering the inaccuracy of astronomical tables used in the Medieval and Renaissance eras, I do not believe pre-1600 authors have the last word on latitude. Only with the availability of personal computer software and accurate astronomical tables such as the Swiss Ephemeris will proper treatment of latitude be found. The *Primary Direction Sequence* represents my solution and I welcome exchanges with other researchers on this method and other approaches.

As I stated in the preface to the 1st edition, the best way to use this book is to pick a single individual, read at least two biographies, construct an event database; then proceed through the recommended three stages of rectification. Check each direction I have listed against life events and see if the delineation of the promissor and significator in the direction matches the specific character of the life event. Only after taking these steps, and testing the proposed rectification against viable alternatives, do we stand to gain from reasoned debate.

===============

America is Born: Introducing the Regulus USA National Horoscope

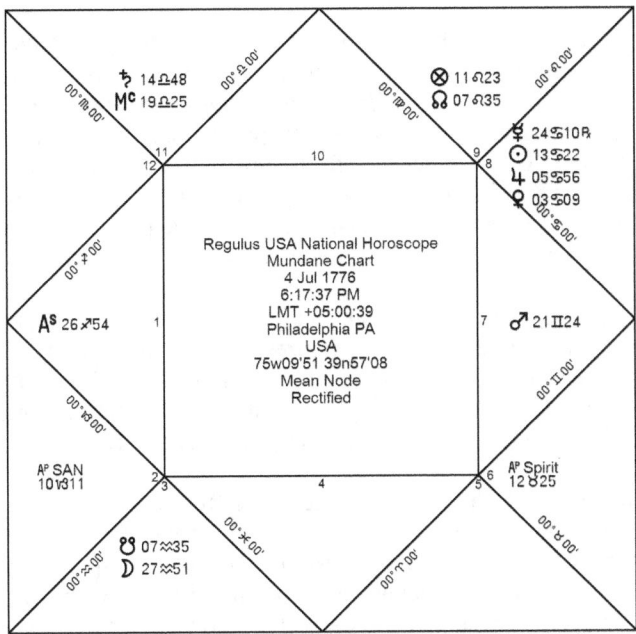

Since publication of the 1st edition of *A Rectification Manual*, I have released my second book which features a newly rectified USA National Horoscope. Of interest for readers of *A Rectification Manual* is the largest empirical study of Directing through the Bounds ever attempted or presented. Besides solidifying the empirical basis of the Egyptian bounds, *America is Born* provides a useful historical guide to the political climate faced by American Presidents and First Ladies during the first 233 years of the American Republic.

Dr. H.
Regulus Astrology LLC
September 1, 2009

PREFACE TO THE FIRST EDITION

For the astrologer. *A Rectification Manual* is intended for astrology students, researchers, and professionals. Because rectification requires mastery of both delineation and prediction, this work assumes completion of a course in delineation and basic familiarity with the most commonly used predictive methods including progressions, transits, and solar arc directions. A prerequisite listing follows the introduction.

Emphasis on Predictive Methods. This work emphasizes predictive methods with an eye to their usefulness in rectification. It is the sophistication of these techniques which distinguishes Medieval Predictive Astrology from modern psychological astrology which de-emphasizes prediction. Yet there is nothing advanced presented in this work because for the medieval astrologer there was no distinction made between introductory and advanced levels of instruction. For example, primary directions were considered part of a practicing astrologer's standard repertoire; not set aside as an optional tool for advanced students.

Extensive Chart Examples. Few surviving medieval texts offer concrete examples of methods applied to actual figures, leaving testing to the modern reader. This work provides dozens of examples which apply predictive methods to figures of American Presidents. It is perhaps the largest single collection of applied medieval predictive techniques for natal charts available today.

How to Use this Book. Choose a single President. Read at least two biographies – one for the subject directly and another for a family member or other significant professional colleague. Create an event database and work sequentially through delineation and prediction techniques outlined in Parts One and Two. After recreating measurements presented in the rectification database, test additional events against the full battery of predictive techniques using examples in this Volume as a guide. There is no better way to learn astrology than to study actual people and past events.

For the Presidential Historian. For those whose primary interest is the American Presidency but are new to astrology, this manual is designed as a springboard to further investigations on both delineation and prediction of life affairs of the Presidents. As instrumental as this manual will serve for that purpose, it remains a complementary text to a course in astrological delineation.

INTRODUCTION

The goal of this work is computation of rectified birth times for all American Presidents within 30 seconds of accuracy for 90% of the forty-three horoscopes studied. In some cases I claim even greater precision, suggesting that Franklin Roosevelt's proposed Ascendant of 20VI57'52" is accurate to the minute and second of zodiacal degree, or within a fraction of a single second.

Such accuracy is unheard of in astrological circles for a simple reason. The modern practice of rectification by transits, progressions, and solar arc directions has been an abysmal failure. Using Ronald Reagan as an example, there have been over 50 different birth times suggested to Astrodatabank, the recognized database leader in documented birth data. Most estimates of Reagan's birth time range from 1:00 a.m. to 11:00 a.m., a variance of ten hours. Even after Reagan's death in 2004, there was a request made on a public astrology website to Joan Quigley (Nancy Reagan's astrologer) to reveal Reagan's *true* birth time. This request was made after publication of several full-length biographies and the opening of the Ronald Reagan Presidential Library in 1991 where literally hundreds of events have been available for study. If practicing astrologers cannot accurately rectify given this abundance of information, then as a rectification tool, modern Western astrology is bankrupt.

The solution is the recovery and application of the richer set of predictive methods practiced in the Medieval Era. What are these methods? Are they useful in rectification? How should they be sequenced and applied in order to compute an accurate rectification? These are the questions addressed by this study.

Proper rectification requires knowing implementation procedures and underlying assumptions for both delineation and prediction. Unfortunately, there is widespread disagreement on the most fundamental astrological tenets ranging from choice of house system to whether or not solar returns should be relocated. Often students take assumptions taught by teachers as given. In my opinion, sufficient time has elapsed since the revival of traditional astrology began in the early 1980s that practitioners need to close ranks on assumptions and methods.

What works? is the single guiding principle to my analytical style. Numerous case studies are provided to support conclusions on these divisive tenets of delineation and prediction. Further tests are suggested in order for others to replicate my findings on a wider sample *or not*. It's an approach designed to fill the void of practical information left by a field which so far has demonstrated more interest in history and theory of astrology. Not that these subjects are unimportant; only that they fall short of identifying which nuts and bolts can be consistently and successfully applied to the practice of natal horoscopy.

As an author, I make no claim of expertise on the history, theory, or transmission of any of the methods presented in this reference manual. My focus is actual life events lived by real people. It is my hope the Presidential Database will spur renewed interest in settling the debate of astrological assumptions among a wider circle of contemporary astrologers.

Organization of this Book

The Rectification Manual is divided into two sections. The first section covers delineation, prediction, and rectification.

Part I includes selected delineation topics. It reinforces the tenet that applied horoscopy is the essence of how *planets* are modified by *signs* and act through *houses*. Minor dignities, modern planets, and choice of house system are introduced. Delineation of the arcus vitae and an introduction to primary directions conclude Part I.

Part II considers all major predictive methods used by medieval astrologers. While not all predictive methods are useful for rectification, in order for events to be properly attributed to the appropriate predictive method, all must be studied. This becomes all the more urgent when it is understood the modern rectification approach limited to transits, progressions, and solar arc directions is grossly under specified.

Part III develops a systematic method of rectification by matching appropriate predictive techniques to uncertain birth data in a three stage process. Proper construction of an event database opens the discussion. Five actual rectification case studies conclude the first section.

The second section opens with an empirical test of bounds, comparing both Egyptian and Ptolemaic versions in Appendix A. Assumptions for two conditions depending on sect are tested in Appendix B: the Lot of Fortune calculation and Firdaria sequence, both for nocturnal nativities.

Appendix C presents rectification details for each American President, a full longevity workup including the solar return for the year of death, and Al-mubtazz tables for the Al-mubtazz Figurae, Significators of the Soul, and the Killing Planet. Rectifications for First Ladies follow in Appendix D. Based on more limited data, proposed birth times for First Ladies are considered trial.

INTRODUCTION   xxiii

Assumptions

Disagreement over choice between Egyptian or Ptolemy's bounds and the Lot of Fortune's computation for nocturnal figures are among the two most jarring dissonances among contemporary traditional astrologers. Appendices A and B present empirical evidence to settle the debate.

Bound: Choose Egyptian bounds. There are two competing sets of bounds. The first is attributed to the Egyptians; the second, developed by Ptolemy. As I suggest in Appendix A, there are two ways to test bounds. First, Directing through the Bounds can be computed for both sets of bounds and compared to life events. I do so in Chapter 10, subjecting Teddy Roosevelt's Ascendant to the Directing through the Bounds procedure. It is a powerful tool which explains his boyhood interest in science as a profession, the relative obscurity of his career and profession through his mid 30's, and his emergence as a national political figure following his appointment as NY City Police Commissioner. It is a sequence of events which cannot be explained by Ptolemy's bounds.

The second method requires expertise in delineation and forces the astrologer to accept Maternus' proposition that planetary behavior cannot be fully explained without considering a planet's bound and dwad. I suggest bounds affect planets through a hidden conjunction between the planet and the planet/sign combination of each bound; similarly for dwads. Chapter 1 opens with an example of Franklin Roosevelt's Moon and proceeds to systematically examine each of Abraham Lincoln's planets this way. Appendix A includes six examples of the Moon in Capricorn which span the entire range of bounds in Capricorn. The influence of competing bounds is compared against individuals signified by the Moon (e.g., mother, wife) and events timed by directions of the Moon to the angles.

Lot of Fortune: Reverse formula for nocturnal figures. Controversy surrounding Ptolemy's *day-only* Lot of Fortune formula is addressed in Appendix B. Of several ways of testing the Lot of Fortune, the two easiest take advantage of the Lot of Fortune's ability to function as the hīlāj and its ability to time concrete events of monetary gain and loss. Appendix B culls from the Presidential and First Ladies Database nativities whose Lot of Fortune either participates or exclusively functions as the hīlāj. What follows for each nocturnal Presidential nativity is a brief Lot of Fortune delineation supplemented with directions for selected Presidents.

Outstanding examples of events timed by Lot of Fortune directions include Matthew Perry's Japan trade mission (M. Fillmore), Secretary of State Seward's Alaskan Purchase (A. Johnson), the McKinley Trade Bill (W. McKinley), the Smoot-Hawley Tariff Bill (H. Hoover), the 1929 stock market crash (H. Hoover), the *Buy War Bonds* campaign (F. Roosevelt), and Reagan's million-dollar contract with Warner Brothers. Perhaps the most damning evidence against Ptolemy's *day-only* Lot of Fortune is two examples for Hoover and Nixon which open Chapter

13's treatment of Hellenistic Lots in Solar Returns. Placement of Hoover's Lot of Fortune in the 1st and Nixon's in the 12th are consistent with Hoover's self-made (1st) fortunes as a mining engineer and Nixon's secret (12th) political slush fund started by wealthy conservative old men. The reverse house positions for Ptolemy's *day-only* formula, placing Hoover's Lot of Fortune in the 12th and Nixon's in the 1st, bear no resemblance to actual life affairs.

Firdaria Sequence for Nocturnal Figures: Insert Nodes between Mars and the Sun. Less contentious is debate surrounding the placement of the North Node and South Node Firdaria periods for nocturnal nativities. This issue is addressed in Appendix B with a discussion of life affairs which confirm Robert Zoller's recommended placement of the Nodes between Mars and the Sun.

House Systems: Use both Whole Sign and Alchabitius Houses. The use of whole sign houses has been reinvigorated by the revival of Hellenistic methods which predate quadrant-based house systems. In Chapter 2, Thomas Jefferson's figure is cited as an excellent example of whole sign houses at work. Delineating Jupiter/Virgo/4th as the endless sprawl of architectural detail at Monticello and Saturn/Leo/3rd as writing about the tyrannical rule of Kings can only be explained by whole sign houses. Directions of Saturn to the angles time events whose effects are also consistent with Saturn in the 3rd by whole signs.

Yet I am not one to discount the applicability of quadrant house systems. It appears that planets may extend their rulership to quadrant defined house cusps from their origins in a whole sign defined house. This is a proposition which I have not taken up elsewhere in the text, yet I have seen a number of cases when the sign on the 8th quadrant house was a significant factor which improved accuracy of determining Killing Planets by al-mubtazz scoring. Which quadrant house system to use is an entirely different question. As suggested in Chapter 2, competing quadrant house systems can be evaluated by testing the accuracy of dynamic activity to lots whose formulas include an intermediate house cusp. Preliminary testing supports Alchabitius houses though Porphyry houses appear statistically similar.

Direct and Converse Motion. Few medieval astrologers advocated converse primary directions computed against the diurnal motion of the sky, yet they appear just as accurate as directions computed by direct motion. The same can be said for solar arc directions computed in converse motion though this usage is not sanctioned by proponents of this technique.

Equatorial Ascendant and Vertex. These derivative angles were not used by medieval astrologers. Promoted in the 20th century by Jayne and Johndro, this study confirms their validity by their ability to time events by primary directions. The Saturn-Vertex direction which timed Woodrow Wilson's stroke and failed passage of the Versailles treaty is a standout. At this point, I am silent on modern attributions of health and fate to these angles.

Oriental/Occidental. There are two definitions of these words used in this text, both mentioned in Chapter 5: *Longevity*. The first definition refers to a planet's position relative to the Sun: if the planet rises before the Sun it is oriental; after the Sun, occidental. These definitions are not universal; some authors (including my teacher Robert Zoller) reverse the nomenclature for Mercury and Venus, the two inferior planets. The reason for this ambiguity appears that inferior planets function better as evening stars rising after the Sun because in this position Mercury and Venus are moving swiftly away from the Sun. The superior planets; Mars, Jupiter, and Saturn, function better as morning stars rising before the Sun. For purposes of this study, the position relative to the Sun for Mercury and Venus appears a key criterion of whether or not the inferior planets can function as the Al-kadukhadāh.

There is a second usage of the oriental/occidental vocabulary which also surfaces in Chapter 5. Dividing the natal figure into four quadrants, the two quadrants comprised of the 4-5-6th and 10-11-12th houses are masculine and oriental. The two quadrants comprised of the 1-2-3rd and 7-8-9th houses are feminine and occidental.

USA Natal Figure. I accept the 4 July 1776 Sagittarius rising natal chart for the USA and have proposed my own rectification with an Ascendant of 26SA54'40" (see *America is Born: Introducing the Regulus USA National Horoscope*). There are several traces of this figure read through Presidential nativities. First and foremost is the Cancer Sun which signifies the President and occurs frequently as one of the angles, luminaries, or Syzygy Ante Navitatem (prenatal New/Full Moon) among Presidential nativities. I suggest in Appendix A that the frequency of Moon in Capricorn in Presidential nativities occurs because the Moon signifies the wife and Capricorn falls seven signs from the Cancer Sun. Finally, though not directly tied to the USA figure but just as important to American political astrology is the frequency of Mars/Leo. Consistently this planet/sign placement signifies a states' right philosophy embodied by the Confederate rebel. Jefferson, Tyler, and Grant are some of the better examples for those who wish to explore this thread further.

Innovations

Directing by Triplicity. In contract to Bonatti who suggests the tripartite division of life is comprised of three divisions of thirty years each, I suggest the division of years is a customized number for each nativity. In addition, for some nativities there is a fourth *end-of-life* period which can be read by the 4th house. See Chapter 7: *Temporal Indicators*.

The Primary Direction Sequence. In my opinion, confusion over treatment of latitude has marred the practical application of primary directions. My proposed solution to the latitude problem recognizes a pair of events can be timed by the direction of either angle to one planet, calculated with and without the planet's full latitude. The probability that a pair of events, often separated by a span of a year or more, can be accurately timed within 72 hours by a corresponding pair of directions is so low the Primary Direction Sequence can be considered the long lost *Holy Grail of Rectification*. It is this tool, more so than any other, which allows precise rectification to the second. See Chapter 10: *Directions*.

Monthly and Daily Profections. I propose monthly and daily profections be computed as 12 and 144 divisions of time between two consecutive solar returns. This is a minor modification of existing practice. See Chapter 12: *Solar Returns: Delineation and Prediction*.

Monthly Profections in Solar Returns. The timing of monthly profections for the natal figure can be used as an overlay technique for timing the promise of the solar return. When a specific natal house is highlighted by profection, so is the same solar return house. See Chapter 11.

Progressed Moon in Solar Returns. I confirm the validity of the return's Moon to time events based on aspects to other return planets computed at the secondary progressed rate. Going further, I resurrect an old debate between Cardin and Morin over the ability of the secondary progressed Moon to time events falling outside the confines of the solar return year proper. I side with Cardin and present evidence the progressed Moon can time events as much as two years outside the return's 365 day active period. See Chapter 12.

Hellenistic Lots in Solar Returns. I confirm the aphorism which states an aspect between Jupiter in a solar return and the natal Lot of Children promises birth of children that year if so promised by the natal figure. I extend this finding to most lots and conclude that affairs signified by any natal lot are strongly activated when aspected by solar return planets. See Chapter 13: *Solar Returns: Hellenistic Lots*.

PREREQUISITES

Before studying this manual, readers should be familiar with:

- Essential nature of planets

- Essential nature of the twelve zodiacal signs

- How the essential dignities of sign and exaltation govern planetary behavior

- Definition of minor dignities: triplicity, bound, decan, 9ths, 12ths (dwads)

- Assignment of life affairs to the twelve houses

- Computation of derived houses

- Definition of derivative angles, e.g., Vertex and Equatorial Ascendant

- Formulas for and computation of Hellenistic Lots

- Calculation of a natal and solar return chart

- Primary and Secondary Motion

- Calculation of progressions

- Direct and Converse Motion

- Solar Arc Directions

- Aspects, antiscia, and contra-antiscia

- Reception, translation of light, and other methods which perfect or deny a planetary configuration.

KEY

♈	AR	Aries
♉	TA	Taurus
♊	GE	Gemini
♋	CA	Cancer
♌	LE	Leo
♍	VI	Virgo
♎	LI	Libra
♏	SC	Scorpio
♐	SA	Sagittarius
♑	CP	Capricorn
♒	AQ	Aquarius
♓	PI	Pisces
♄	SA	Saturn
♃	JU	Jupiter
♂	MA	Mars
☉	SU	Sun
♀	VE	Venus
☿	ME	Mercury
☽	MO	Moon
☊	NN	North Node
☋	SN	South Node
⊗	LOF	Lot of Fortune
	LOS	Lot of Spirit
	SAN	Syzygy Ante Navitatem
	ARM	*A Rectification Manual*
	LOY	Lord of the Year
	LOP	Lord of the Period
	AL	Alchabitius (Quadrant) Houses
	WS	Whole Sign Houses
	d.	Direct (primary) motion
	c.	Converse (primary) motion
	dsa	Direct solar arc direction
	csa	Converse solar arc direction
	BI	Bianchini latitude adjustment
	tr.	Transit
	prog.	Progression
	prof.	Profection (annual rate)
	PT	Ptolemy
	REG	Regiomontanus
	EQ-ASC	Equatorial Ascendant
	VTX	Vertex

I must study politics and war, that our sons may have liberty to study mathematics and philosophy.

Our sons ought to study mathematics and philosophy, geography, natural history and naval architecture, navigation, commerce and agriculture in order to give their children a right to study painting, poetry, music, architecture, statuary, tapestry and porcelain.

John Adams in a letter to Abigail Adams
(May 12, 1780)

PART ONE

Delineation

CHAPTER ONE

Planets in Signs

The core of astrological judgment is based on planets, signs, and houses. Before prediction can take place, modification of a planet's nature by sign and house must be delineated. In this chapter, sign placement is considered. Compared to modern methods which limit dignities to rulership and exaltation, medieval methods considered seven levels of planetary dignity. Of these seven, bound and dwad appear the most important modifiers of planetary behavior.

Chapter Summary

How essential dignities modify planetary behavior. The effects of pure planetary archetypes on human affairs are never observed directly. Planetary influence is substantially modified by sign placement which often results in effects which are at odds with textbook planetary definitions. In addition to sign placement, minor dignities are required to unlock a planet's true qualities.

Impact of Minor Dignities on Planetary Behavior: Bound and Dwad. According to Maternus, understanding a planet's true nature requires delineation of the bound ruler and dwad placement. Compared to dignities of sign, exaltation, and triplicity; bound and dwad are of interest because they further specify a planet's behavior to subsets of the thirty-degree range of a single zodiac sign. Maternus' teaching on the importance of bound and dwad is confirmed by case studies drawn from the Presidential Database.

Case Studies. An examination of Franklin Roosevelt's Cancer Moon reveals the influence of the Moon's placement in the bound of Mars and dwad of Virgo in ways which cannot be explained without these minor dignities. A more comprehensive case study of Abraham Lincoln follows. It introduces the predictive tool of profections as a method for demonstrating the impact of bound and dwad on each natal planet's behavior through actual life events.

NEW Retrograde Planets. Recent research reveals retrograde planets often function as if placed in the opposite sign. This insight is key to understanding the impact of retrogradation on planetary behavior.

How essential dignities modify planetary behavior

<u>Astrology begins with planets</u>. Consider Mars. What is the essential character of Mars, e.g., what is Martian? The Merriam-Webster Collegiate dictionary defines Martian as: (1) of, relating to, or suited for war or a warrior (2) relating to an army or to military life, and (3) experienced in or inclined to war: warlike. Our job in predicting the effects of Mars is complicated by Mars' placement in various zodiacal signs. If Mars is in the sign of Aries or Scorpio where he enjoys rulership, then effects are observed similar to the Martian qualities described by the dictionary entry. Mars in the masculine sign of Aries produces forthright actions; the image of a charging soldier with his sword drawn is apropos. Mars in the feminine sign of Scorpio is more reactive, often motivated by revenge, but nevertheless just as effective as Mars in Aries in dishing out aggression. Placed in other signs, Mars is not as effective.

Discussing planetary behavior in this fashion is made possible by essential dignities which govern a planet's performance. Understanding exactly how a planet will function in each sign is a critical step for prediction and rectification. It is necessary to know what kind of planetary effect to look for when matching actual life events to those predicted by planets in the natal figure.

<u>Seven Levels of Essential Dignities</u>. Since the late 19th century revival led by the British astrologer Alan Leo, western astrological practice has largely limited itself to the dignities of sign and exaltation. By contrast, medieval astrology recognized a total of seven levels of dignity. The first five are assigned numerical scores ranging from +1 to +5 for use in constructing victor tables, a procedure explained in Chapter 5. The navamsas and dwads are not scored.

Table 1. Essential Dignities and Assignment of Scores

Dignity	Score
1. Sign	+5
2. Exaltation	+4
3. Triplicity	+3
4. Bound or Term	+2
5. Decanate (Decan) or Face	+1
6. Navamsa or Novenaria (Novenas) (9th)	n.a.
7. Dwadeshamsa (Dwad) or Duodecimae or Duodecatemorion (12th)	n.a.

It's not my objective to write an exposition on planetary dignities, for which entire books have been written. My point is simpler. The failure of modern astrology to account for any dignities beyond sign and exaltation has introduced significant errors in delineation, prediction, and rectification. It is necessary to reclaim these minor dignities if there is any chance of success in astrological practice. As you will see, some of these dignities are far from *minor* in effect.

Impact of Minor Dignities on Planetary Behavior: Bound and Dwad

Opinion of Maternus. Besides a planet's sign, the dignities of bound and dwad appear important modifiers of planetary behavior. This is the opinion of Firmicus Maternus who included a planet's bound (or "term") and dwad in delineation. For example, at the end of the section on Mars, Maternus (1975, 88) states:

In order to assess the power of Mars more accurately, carefully observe his duodecatemorion and the terms of the duodecatemorion.

Bounds. Maternus makes similar statements at the conclusion of his discussion for every planet. Though both dignities are mentioned by various authors, bounds are cited more frequently than dwads. Many times, the bound ruler is listed as the preferred level of dignity for certain advanced procedures. For instance, instructions for selecting which ruler of the hīlāj as possible al-kadukhadāh often advise testing the bound ruler first – even before considering the sign ruler. It is my opinion that bounds appear to impart their intrinsic quality to any planet placed within their specified degree range. A planet falling in a bound functions like it is on a stage designed by the confines of the bound.

Example: Sun falling in the 24th degree of Aquarius in the bound of Mars can be read as Sun/Aquarius on a stage set by Mars/Aquarius themes. Sometimes the effect is likened to a hidden conjunction between the Sun and Mars which modifies the Sun in ways the Sun's sign placement in Aquarius cannot explain.

Dwads. Dwads appear to have a similar effect as bounds though their influence appears smaller in magnitude. The difference is bounds are signified by a planet in a sign; stated 'the bound of Jupiter in Sagittarius.' Not so with dwads which are signified only by sign; stated: 'the dwad of Sagittarius.' A planet falling in a specific dwad appears to function like it is in that sign[1].

Using the same example, Sun falling in the 24th degree of Aquarius is positioned in the dwad of Scorpio. The combined influence is:

Sun 23AQ19 = Sun/Aquarius + Mars/Aquarius + Sun/Scorpio

Relative Contribution of Bound and Dwad. How to summarize the relative impact of a planet's rulership by sign, bound, and dwad is an open question. Maternus said just to consider them. At present, I am working with the concept that rulership by sign accounts for approximately two-thirds of a planet's effect; rulership by bound, one-quarter; and placement by dwad, one-tenth. These estimates are back-of-the-envelope. They are probably not right but represent a place to start. Others may reach different conclusions and I reserve the right to change them with more research.

---

[1] Maternus says to look at the terms (e.g., bound) of the dwad. This I have not yet tested.

Other Essential Dignities

Triplicity. The impact of triplicity is primarily temporal, with each triplicity ruler ruling a planet/cusp/part for roughly one-third of a person's life set out by the procedure known as Directing by Triplicity (see Chapter 8: *Planetary Period Methods*). In a separate application, triplicity rulers are assigned to specific life affairs as an adjunct delineation tool. For instance, the 1st, 2nd, and 3rd triplicity rulers of the 6th house are assigned to illness, slaves, and the usefulness of slaves respectively in a method attributed to Al-Andarzagar (Alchabitius 2004: 50-55).

Decans. The tripartite division of thirty degrees of each zodiacal sign is known as decanates, abbreviated as decans. Other authors name this dignity *face*. There are two competing sets of decans. The first set is defined by the Chaldean order of planets. It assigns Mars to the first decan of Aries, and continues with the other six planets in descending Chaldean order, repeating the cycle of seven planets until the positions of 36 decans are filled.

Relationship of Decans to Dwads. There is a second set of decans based on the triplicity rulership of signs, not planets. Robert Zoller referred to this set as the decans of Varahamihira. For the sign of Aries, the first Decan is assigned to Aries; the second to Leo; the third to Sagittarius. Decans of the fiery triplicity are selected by order of the signs. Table 2 compares decans and dwads. In this relationship, it is easy to see that both decans and dwads form a fractal relationship to the twelve zodiac signs. Decans recapitulate all the signs by element; dwads form a full fractal of the entire zodiac within each single sign. When evaluating planetary strength in al-mubtazz scoring (see Chapter 5), the decans of Varahamihira are used (replacing Chaldean decans used in the 1st / 2nd editions.)

Table 2. Comparison of the Decans (Triplicity) and Dwads, Aries

Zodiacal Degree	Decan	Dwad
0AR00 – 2AR29	**Aries**	**Aries**
2AR30 – 4AR59	Aries	Taurus
5AR00 – 7AR29	Aries	Gemini
7AR30 – 9AR59	Aries	Cancer
10AR00 – 12AR29	**Leo**	**Leo**
12AR30 – 14AR59	Leo	Virgo
15AR00 – 17AR29	Leo	Libra
17AR30 – 19AR59	Leo	Scorpio
20AR00 – 22AR29	**Sagittarius**	**Sagittarius**
22AR30 – 24AR59	Sagittarius	Capricorn
25AR00 – 27AR29	Sagittarius	Aquarius
27AR30 – 29AR59	Sagittarius	Pisces

Navamsa ('9ths'). The ninth divisions of signs are not emphasized in western medieval astrological literature. They appear to be mentioned almost as a footnote for completeness by collectors of aphorisms.

Case Study: Franklin Roosevelt's Moon

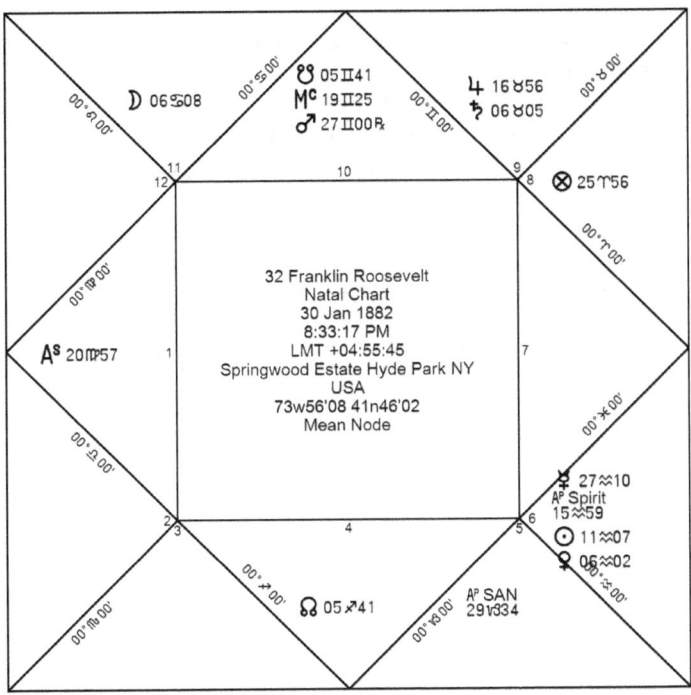

Moon = Moon/Cancer (*sign*) + Mars/Cancer (*bound*) + Moon/Virgo (*dwad*)

Sign. FDR's Moon in Cancer is a good example to demonstrate how bound and dwad modify a planet's sign placement. Franklin Roosevelt's Moon falls at 6CA09. Based on the description of his mother Sara constantly holding him as an infant, breast feeding him for a year, and not allowing him to bathe alone until the age of eight, the Cancer Moon can be confidently assigned to his mother (Black 2003). It is true that Moon in Cancer, its sign of rulership, produced *nurture* which was long lasting in duration. Yet this was not the entire story. Sara Delano Roosevelt had her overbearing side which is puzzling until the Moon's bound ruler is identified: Mars/Cancer.

Bound. Mars in Cancer, sign of his fall, produces timidity instead of any overt aggression. However, when threatened, timidity is replaced by extreme defensiveness to the point of cruelty as the Cancer Mars lashes out in an effort to maintain home turf. Understanding the behavior of Mars in Cancer as bound ruler of FDR's Moon explains why Franklin's relationship with his mother Sara deteriorated after his marriage to Eleanor. Sara Roosevelt felt threatened by another woman and reacted with various schemes in order to maintain control. For starters, Sara held the family's substantial purse strings. Instead of making routine cash outlays to her son, she preferred to be asked for money and gifts as a way of maintaining control.

Dwad. The Moon's bound and dwad position often mirror actual planet placements in the mother's figure. Dwad position is Virgo. Sara Roosevelt (below) has Venus, Moon, and Sun in Virgo. Sara Roosevelt's criticality over his personal affairs (especially Eleanor as wife), and prudishness at the thought of FDR's entrance into the rabble of politics match the Virgo influence.

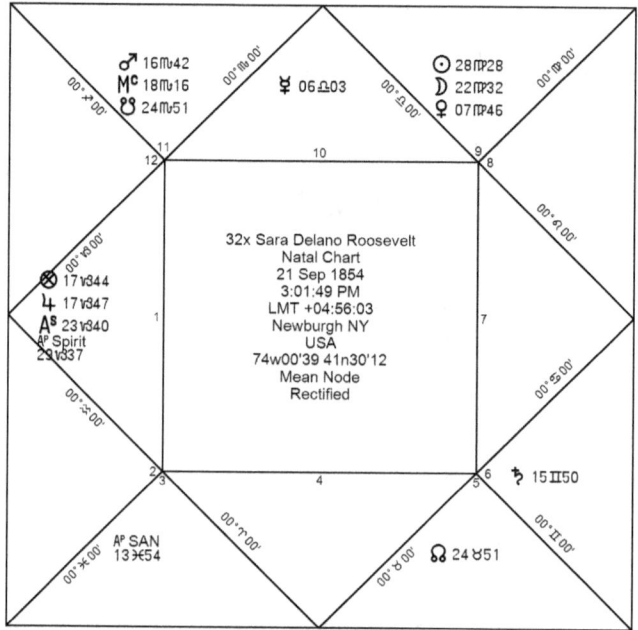

Proposed rectification of Sara Delano Roosevelt: Ascendant = 23CP40'32". **Firdaria Sequence**: Diurnal. Birth of FDR, 30-Jun-1882, Sun-Mercury; FDR elected President, 8-Nov-1932, Mercury-Sun [Note both of these were Sun-Mercury periods]; Death of husband James, 8-Dec-1900, Saturn-Sun; Announcement of FDR's marriage to Eleanor 1-Dec-1904 and marriage 17-Mar-1905, Saturn-Moon; intervention after discovery of FDR's affair with Lucy Mercer, Sep-1918, Mars-Sun. **Moon's configuration**: Moon separates from Jupiter and applies to Sun. Custom delineation: moves away from conservative, provincial neighborhood towards son FDR's participation in politics (Sun in 11th). **Ascendant Profections**: ASC sweeps through Virgo stellium in 9th house for foreign travel from March to November 1862 during 1862 family trip to China. **Lots**: Marriage to James, 7-Oct-1880, dsa Mercury conj L.Marriage of Women a/c Hermes 1SC44; Death of father Warren Delano 17-Jan-1898, trJupiter 10LI13 conj L.Father 11LI02. **Directions**: Death of father Warren Delano 17-Jan-1898, PT opposition Sun d. => ASC 17-Jan-1898 (exact); Death of self, 7-Sep-1941, REG Moon (0) d. => Saturn (SA) 28-Aug-1941.

Case Study: Profecting Abraham Lincoln's Ascendant

<u>Introducing Profections</u>. To demonstrate the influence of sign, bound, and dwad on each planet, I introduce the predictive technique of profections. For starters, this case study computes Ascendant profections to each natal planet by conjunction. These dates are compared to actual life events in order to test the impact of each planet's sign, bound, and dwad.

In Chapter 11: *Solar Returns: Profections and Time Lords*, profections are taken up again from the perspective as a planetary period technique.

Profections: the Rhythm of the Natal Figure

Profections are a type of symbolic direction whose computation bears no relationship to astronomical movement of any kind.

<u>Types</u>. Of profections there are three types: annual, monthly, and daily. Making an analogy to the hour, minute, and second hands of a clock is appropriate though the units are slightly different.

Annual profections move at 30 degrees per year, making a complete circle around the zodiac wheel in 12 years. They constitute a 12-year rhythm or cycle because the same profection occurs every 12 years.

Monthly profections move at 30 degrees per month, making a complete circle around the zodiac in 1 year.

Daily profections move at 30 degrees every 2.5 days, making a complete circle around the zodiac in 1 month.[2]

<u>What is profected?</u> The same significators used in all directional methods: Ascendant, Midheaven, Sun, Moon, Lot of Fortune, and SAN.

<u>How to use profections?</u> Sticking with the profected annual Ascendant is recommended for those new to the technique. It provides the most bang for the buck. Later one can consider profecting other significators at the annual rate and all significators at the faster monthly and daily rates.

NEW <u>Tricks and traps</u>. In my experience, finding event matches to Ascendant profections can be very spotty if working with a limited database. Still, if a horoscope has a stellium or stellia across 2 or 3 adjacent signs, profecting the Ascendant to multiple planets should time a chain of consecutive life events, especially during middle age. If no event matches are found when the profected ASC sweeps through a planetary group, the rectification is likely wrong.

---

[2] Chapter 9 presents a more accurate calculation method for monthly and daily profections.

Profecting Lincoln's Ascendant. Let's start by profecting Lincoln's Ascendant at the annual rate. From Lincoln's birth on 12-Feb-1809 (age 0) to the first birthday 12-Feb-1810 (age 1), imagine the profected Ascendant starting exactly on Lincoln's Ascendant at 29SA45. Now profect the Ascendant by moving it counter clockwise in the direction of the signs at a rate of 1 degree every 12.175 days until it reaches 29CP45 exactly on Lincoln's 1st birthday one year later. Note the Moon's location at 25CP11. The profected Ascendant passed the Moon just before Lincoln's 1st birthday on 18-Dec-1809.

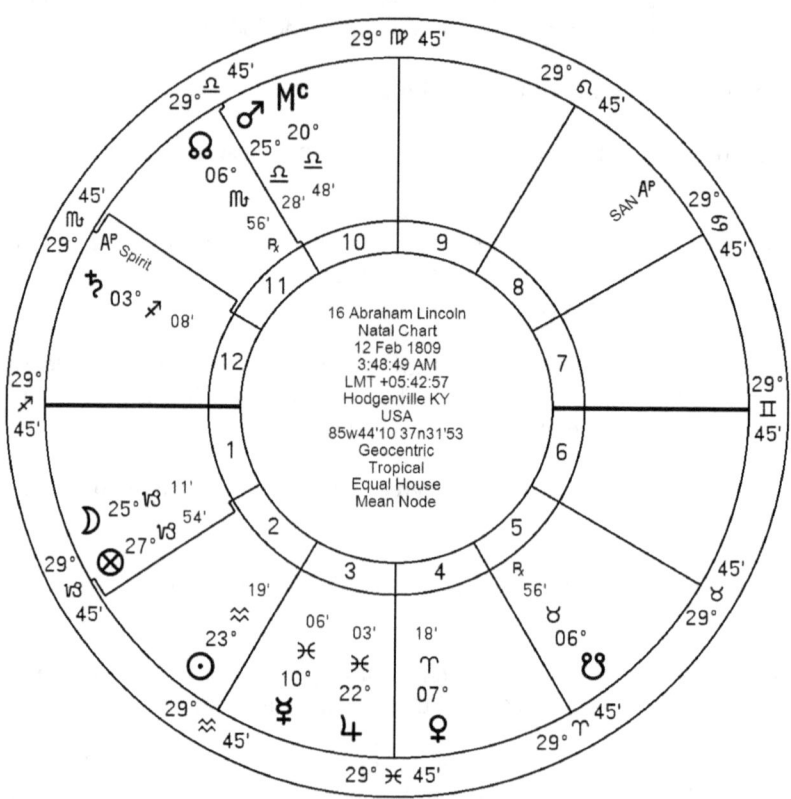

Abraham Lincoln, natal figure, Equal Sign houses.

Language of Profections. To make profection terminology more practical in conversation, say that "Lincoln is having a 1st house year" anytime the profected Ascendant falls between 29SA45 and 29CP45. Note that Lincoln will have a '1st house year' between his 12th and 13th birthday and every 12 years subsequently. Do not say "Lincoln is having a 13th house year." Same for monthly and daily profections. Say "Lincoln is having a 10th house month" or "Lincoln is in a 6th house daily period."

Interpretation. How are profections interpreted? In two ways. First, just like directions, e.g., to time discrete events. The profection: *Ascendant conjunct Moon* is delineated the same as the primary or solar arc direction: *Ascendant conjunct Moon*. Second involves treating profected house positions as active planetary periods. For example, whenever the Ascendant falls in the 1st house by annual, monthly, or daily profection, the individual's physical vitality is brought to focus for the entire period the profected Ascendant remains in the 1st house. The state of the individual's vitality is determined by temperament given by the natal 1st and is modified further by the Ascendant's current bound ruler computed by primary directions, the 1st house of the active solar return, transits in the 1st house, and transiting aspects to ruler of the 1st. As universal significator of the physical body, the Moon also needs consideration as well as the hīlāj, if different. This can be a heady mix. For beginning students, stick with the delineation of the natal 1st house and watch its promise unfold during 1st house annual, monthly, and daily periods. Treat all houses similarly.

Case Study: Profecting Lincoln's Ascendant at the Annual Rate

Objective. The objective of this exercise is to demonstrate the power of bound and dwad to modify planetary behavior above and beyond what can be delineated exclusively by a planet's sign placement. Lincoln's life history was combed for events corresponding to dates computed by Ascendant profections at the annual rate of 30 degrees per year. The case study attempts to match the nature of discovered events to each planet's sign, bound, and dwad.

Minor Aspects and the Seasonality of Profections. Medieval methods did not recognize minor aspects, including the semi-sextile (30 degrees) and quincunx (150 degrees); aspects I use to demonstrate Ascendant profections to Mercury and Mars in the following pages. It is my finding that annual profections impart seasonality to the internal workings of the natal figure because they occur the same date every year. Events seem to occur annually consistent with the profection no matter if the aspect is a standard Ptolemaic aspect or a minor semi-sextile or quincunx aspect. This may happen because the power that event anniversaries hold over people's collective memories. It is the only application of minor aspects that I employ in my practice.

Lincoln: Profected Ascendant conjunct Sun

Lincoln's Sun: Sign, Bound, and Dwad

Sun's Position	23AQ19
Sign ruler	Saturn
Bound	Mars/Aquarius
Dwad	Scorpio

Profection: *Ascendant conjunct Sun*, 26-Nov-1834.
Event: Lincoln seated in Illinois State Legislature, 1-Dec-1834.

Event. Following his first successful election for political office on 4 August 1834, Lincoln took his seat in the Illinois State Legislature on 1-Dec-1834, five days after the *Ascendant conjunct Sun* profection. His 1834 election culminated a process which started on 9-Mar-1832 when Lincoln proposed improved navigability of the Sangamon River as a campaign theme for an earlier unsuccessful bid for the State Legislature.

Sign. Politically, Lincoln sided with Henry Clay's Whig Party which was devoted to internal improvements including canal construction. Canals and their navigability correspond to Aquarius whose glyph signifies the water-bearer.

Bound. Sun falling in the bounds of Mars/Aquarius is a debility and signifies Lincoln's fame marred by a less than humanitarian philosophy. Though history treats Lincoln favorably for his emancipation of slaves, Lincoln's comments on the inferiority of the Negro race placed him closer to a segregationist philosophy than admirers would like to admit. His proposals for the voluntary emigration of emancipated slaves to Liberia closely match a discriminatory philosophy common to a Mars/Aquarius placement. But this was a later issue. At the time of this profection, the Illinois legislature to which Lincoln was elected was known for *log-rolling*, or the passage of special interest legislation at the expense of public welfare (Luthin, 1960, 40). The bound ruler suggests Lincoln participated. Special interest legislation is a form of discrimination which shows the influence of the Mars/Aquarius bound on Lincoln's Sun.

Dwad. The Scorpio dwad adds vitality, intensity, and indefatigability to Lincoln's political fortunes. Lincoln's physical stamina was well-known and garnered the favor (and votes) of working men during his election campaign after he demonstrated his facility with a grain cradle (Luthin, 1960, 37).

Lincoln: Profected Ascendant conjunct Moon

Lincoln's Moon: Sign, Bound, and Dwad

Moon's Position	25CP11
Sign ruler	Saturn
Bound ruler	Saturn/Capricorn
Dwad	Scorpio

Profection: *Descendant conjunct Moon*, 18-Dec-1839
Event: Met future wife Mary Todd, 16-Dec-1839

Event. Lincoln met his wife-to-be two days before the profected Ascendant opposed the Moon. Because the 7th is opposed to the 1st, this measurement is identical to *Descendant conjunct Moon*. Since the 7th cusp is the house of the wife, the descendant/7th cusp is the more operative angle for this event. Mary Todd is signified by Lincoln's Moon.

Sign. Moon in Capricorn seeks wealth and status as an instinctual need. In choosing Mary Todd for his wife, Lincoln saw a wealthy society woman as a useful political tool in order to offset his own low ranking on the social ladder (Garrison, 1993, 32). Todd's lavish spending on clothing and her 1861 White House renovation is a delineation match to the need for status and expensive purchases promised by the Moon in Capricorn.

Bound. Falling in the bound of Saturn/Capricorn means the Moon/Capricorn is effectively conjunct Saturn/Capricorn. Moon-Saturn conjunctions are one of the most difficult emotional combinations, often signifying depression. Mary Todd's fragile emotional state demonstrates the influence of the Moon's placement in the bound of Saturn/Capricorn.

Dwad. Moon in the dwad of Scorpio is a further debility and matches Mary Todd's sensitivity to slights, explosive temper, paranoia, and jealousy commonly found in Moon in Scorpio placements.

Lincoln: Profected Ascendant conjunct Mercury

Lincoln's Mercury: Sign, Bound, and Dwad

Mercury's Position	10PI06
Sign ruler	Jupiter
Bound ruler	Venus/Pisces
Dwad	Cancer

Profection: *Ascendant conjunct Mercury*, 18-Jun-1823
Event: Lincoln's parents joined the Baptist Church, 7-Jun-1823.

Event. On 7-Jun-1823, Lincoln's parents joined the Little Pigeon Creek Baptist Church. Lincoln attended services yet made no effort to officially join the roster of church membership. In fact, after services he was known to gather a group of children around him and parody the sermon. Caught in the act, Lincoln was reprimanded by his father in what was reportedly their most heated disagreement. Whether Mercury is considered a 4th house planet by whole sign houses or as a 3rd house planet ruling the 9th by quadrant houses, the connection between Mercury, father, and religion is clear.

Sign. As the planet of mental process, Mercury does not function as well in water signs where the clarity of reason is clouded by the water element. When in Pisces, the sign of his detriment, Mercury manifests in ways opposite to a reasoned mental process. Often Mercury in Pisces produces a prankster or a joker. This matches Lincoln's parody of church sermons near the time the 1823 profection. Lincoln was also known as a comedian.

Profection: *Ascendant semi-sextile Mercury*, 18-Jun-1846
Event: Lincoln's response to Peter Cartwright, 31-Jul-1846

Event. The influence of Venus/Pisces as bound ruler and Cancer as dwad sign is more evident in a second event. On 31-Jul-1846, Lincoln responded to an attack from political opponent Peter Cartwright who charged Lincoln with infidelity to the Church. Apparently four years earlier Lincoln had stated that 'drunkards were often as honest and generous as church-goers, sometimes more so' (Luthin, 1960, 100). Lincoln's statement fell six weeks after 18 June, the date the profected Ascendant meets Mercury every year on a seasonal basis. Biographer Luthin does not specify the exact date of Cartwright's charges but they predate Lincoln's response of 31 July and are probably near 18 June. In his letter, Lincoln declared his non-membership to any Christian church but claimed he never spoke in disrespect of religion. He described his belief in the *Doctrine of Necessity* which asserts the power of the mind to be subject to a higher power over which humans have no control. In closing his letter, Lincoln opens himself to condemnation should anyone felt insulted by his comments, yet claiming no one was offended rescues himself from self-condemnation (Luthin, 1960: 100-101).

Sign. Lincoln's original comment on the virtue of drunkards in 1842 was probably similar to the style of parody Lincoln made of sermons after his family's church services in 1823. Parody is a form of comedy and matches the placement of Mercury in Pisces.

Bound. The bound of Venus/Pisces imparts self-sacrifice and generosity, qualities Lincoln ascribed to drunkards over regular Churchgoers.

Dwad. Mercury in the dwad of Cancer adds an emotional style of reasoning which is difficult to articulate. Lincoln's letter of 31 July 1846 was the single statement he made on his religious beliefs during his entire lifetime. It's clear he had difficulty putting into words exactly what his religious beliefs were. Lincoln barely scratched out four sentences on the *Doctrine of Necessity* which are not entirely articulate.

Profection: *Ascendant semi-sextile Mercury*, 18-Jun-1860
Event: Publication of Campaign biographies, Jun-1860

Event. Another example of this profection is publication of campaign biographies during June 1860 following his Presidential nomination.

Sign. Pisces is a fertile sign; there were many different biographies printed. Lincoln professed ignorance whenever asked to comment on them by publishers. They contained mostly stories, anecdotes, and humor consistent with Mercury/Pisces.

Dwad. The word *homespun* is also used to describe these campaign biographies; arguably influenced by Mercury falling in the dwad of Mercury/Cancer because Cancer is most closely associated with home, family, and nurture.

Lincoln: Profected Ascendant conjunct Venus

Lincoln's Venus: Sign, Bound, and Dwad

Venus' Position	7AR18
Sign ruler	Mars
Bound ruler	Venus/Aries
Dwad	Gemini

Profection: *Descendant conjunct Venus*, 14-May-1854
Event: Kansas-Nebraska Act signed 26-May-1854

Event. The profection of *Descendant conjunct Venus* on 14-May-1854 arrived during the culmination of debates over the Kansas-Nebraska Act, passed by the House on 22-May; the Senate 25-May, and signed into law on 26-May at 1:10 AM. Stephen Douglas introduced the legislation during January 1854. The central motivation was an accommodation to southern interests to gain support for a newly planned railroad line to the western frontier, originating from a Chicago hub, located in Douglas' home state of Illinois. To induce southern Senators to vote for his plan, Douglas proposed replacing the Missouri Compromise with a plan that allowed the newly-created Kansas and Nebraska territories the right to vote for or against slavery themselves. The net effect was a shift in power towards slaveholding interests. Passage of the Kansas-Nebraska Act radicalized Lincoln against the expansion of slavery in any newly-created territory. This event was a critical event which some historians suggest led directly to Lincoln's capture of the Presidency six years later.

Sign and Bound. Venus in Aries, her sign of detriment, reinforced by placement in the same bound (e.g., Venus/Aries) produces greed and lust. Douglas' financial interests in railroad expansion can be taken as Venus/Aries because of his apparent greediness as the primary cause for the measure.

Dwad. The Gemini dwad adds the theme of communications and short-term travel. Here railroads fit the bill because a railroad track is comprised of a *pair of tracks* which match the duality of Gemini whose glyph is represented by twins.

Venus ruling the 6th of slaves and the 11th of politics tied the Kansas-Nebraska Act to those house affairs. As Mars' ruler, Venus is the cause which triggered Lincoln's own sense of fighting for justice signified by the Mars/Libra placement. Because Venus and Mars are both in detriment, in opposition, and in mutual reception; Lincoln's advocacy against slavery expansion further inflamed political rivals including Douglas which made Lincoln fight even harder. The mutual reception caused a self-reinforcing cycle of viciousness. The profection of the 7th cusp to Venus as the debates culminated tied the Kansas-Nebraska Act to legal matters because legal disputes are assigned to the 7th house.

Lincoln: Profected Ascendant conjunct Mars

Lincoln's Mars: Sign, Bound, and Dwad

Mars' position	25LI28
Sign ruler	Venus
Bound ruler	Venus/Libra
Dwad	Leo

Profection: *Ascendant quincunx Mars*, 22-Dec-1861
Event: Settlement of the Trent Affair, 25-Dec-1861

Event. The Trent Affair is named for the 8-Nov-1861 interception of the Confederacy's two diplomats on the RMS Trent, a British Mail Steamer, en route to Britain. The British considered the actions a threat to their honor and demanded an immediate apology and release of diplomats James Mason and John Slidell. The detention of these two diplomats so angered Britain, who had closer ties to the Confederacy because of the cotton trade, that both militias in Canada (still a British colony) and British troops were activated in preparation for war against the Union. Britain's ultimatum was toned down by Prince Albert and received by Secretary of State Seward on 19-Dec. Lincoln's cabinet met on 25-Dec. Lincoln decided to release the men on the 26th; the decision was announced by Secretary of State Seward on the 27th.

Sign. Mars/Libra in his detriment signifies acts of war which are delayed as long as possible through peacemaking efforts.

Bound. Venus/Libra increases the emphasis on peaceful negotiation.

Dwad. Mars/Leo adds the desire to fight for honor.

The Trent Affair emphasizes the 11th house placement of Mars ruling the 5th and 12th. The 11th is the cabinet; this affair culminated in the Cabinet. Mars in the 11th, or the 5th from the 7th, signifies the diplomats of Confederate open enemies because diplomats are assigned to the 5th and open enemies to the 7th. Mars also rules the 12th of mistakes. Evidence from the Ascendant/North Node profection demonstrates that Lincoln's 12th house is trouble. North Node in 12th ruled by Mars in 11th signifies the mistake of capturing these two diplomats. The episode nearly triggered the entry of Britain into the war against the Union. Mars/Libra shows the urge to fight is delayed by the willingness to let peace have a chance. Prince Albert's intervention and Lincoln's release of the two diplomats show the influence of Mars falling in the bound of Venus/Libra. [Note: one of the two diplomats, James Mason (b. 3-Nov-1798) has Venus/Libra in his nativity.] Britain's outrage at the violation of her honor demonstrates the influence of Mars falling in the dwad of Leo. Mars/Leo is also the universal significator of Confederate rebels in American political astrology.

Lincoln: Profected Ascendant conjunct Jupiter

Lincoln's Jupiter: Sign, Bound, and Dwad

Jupiter's position	22PI03
Sign ruler	Jupiter
Bound ruler	Mars/Pisces
Dwad	Scorpio

Profection: *Ascendant square Jupiter*, 11-Nov-1862
Event: Received list of Sioux condemned to death, 8-Nov-1862

Event. Following the Sioux Uprising on 17-Aug-1862, Lincoln received on 8-Nov-1862 a list of 303 Sioux men condemned to die for charges of rape, pillage, and murder. Lincoln reviewed the list and commuted death sentences for all but 38 men who on 26-Dec were executed in the largest mass execution in American history.

Sign. Jupiter/Pisces shows Lincoln's sympathetic treatment and pardon of most of the men. Jupiter in Pisces is a philosophy of forgiveness.

Bound. Mars in Pisces dilutes the active planet Mars in a cold and wet water sign. Though not technically in detriment, Mars still behaves poorly in Pisces where his behavior often manifests as restless indecision. Following the trials of the Sioux men, there was pressure for immediate application of the death penalty as well as an attempt by a mob to kill them. Yet despite this restlessness, the men were not harmed.

Dwad. Jupiter falling in the dwad of Scorpio adds the ethics of death to the mix. This addition indicates the type of situation Lincoln was faced with the pardon. Scorpio also signifies getting to the bottom of things, or the inside of things – viscerally. Due to the shortage of corpses for medical study, many of the hanged Sioux were taken by medical students for forensic study purposes. Jupiter in the 4th (WS) shows the event dealt with end-of-life and burial.

Lincoln: Profected Ascendant conjunct Saturn

Lincoln's Saturn: Sign, Bound, and Dwad

Saturn's position	3SA08
Sign ruler	Jupiter
Bound ruler	Jupiter/Sagittarius
Dwad	Capricorn

Profection: *Ascendant conjunct Saturn*, 24-Mar-1832
Event: Lincoln demonstrated navigability of Sangamon River, 24-Mar-1832

Event. On 24-Mar-1832, Lincoln successfully piloted the steamship *Talisman* up the Sangamon River to Portland Landing in an effort to demonstrate the navigability of the Sangamon River. He also helped clear brush and other obstructions prior to the steamship's foray. Improvements to navigability of the Sangamon were a central motivation behind Lincoln's announcement to run for Illinois State legislature during the same month of March 1832. That he claimed a river full of brush and obstructions was navigable at all, much less demonstrating his own ability to navigate it, was both a shock and surprise to residents. As a result, Lincoln's political fortunes improved.

Sign. Saturn ruling both his Sun and the 3rd of local transportation is the source of Lincoln's fame and publicity. Saturn signifies height in physiognomy, a trait which undoubtedly helped Lincoln cut back brush over the river. Saturn in Sagittarius brings reality and soberness to the otherwise open-ended sign of Sagittarius. Lincoln was optimistic about prospects for river transport, but realistic about the need for additional state-funded improvements required to support the effort. He demonstrated the sincerity of his campaign platform without overplaying his hand.

Bound. Falling in the bound of Jupiter/Sagittarius, Lincoln's optimism compensates for an otherwise gloomy Saturn in Sagittarius which can sometimes manifest as the denial of the Sagittarian's optimism with a *life of Job* attitude.

Dwad. The effect of the dwad of Saturn/Capricorn is not obvious but was probably felt during a local celebration at the Sangamon Court House following Lincoln's successful navigation efforts. A Court House is one common signification of Saturn/Capricorn because Saturn is height and Capricorn is rocks, a typical construction method of 19th Century Court Houses. Sounds good but in 1832, no such building existed in Vandalia, the site of the Sangamon Court House. Not until 1836 did Vandalia residents erect an elaborate Federal-style brick Court House. This was immediately followed by the more famous Springfield Greek revival Court House made of stone whose cornerstone was laid on 4-Jul-1837. Lincoln's later legal career was framed by court appearances at the Springfield Court House when the Capricorn dwad's influence was unquestionable.

Lincoln: Profected Ascendant conjunct North Node

Lincoln's North Node: Sign, Bound, and Dwad

North Node's position	6SC56
Sign ruler	Mars
Bound ruler	Mars/Scorpio
Dwad	Capricorn

Profection: *Ascendant opposed North Node*, 10-May-1861
Event: Enmity and mistakes through naval warfare, 17-Apr/3-May-1861.

Both examples for the North and South Node Ascendant profections occur during the same time period. I suggest the Ascendant profection to the South Node triggered concurrent events influenced by the North Node.

Event. On 17/18-Apr-1861, as the profected Ascendant moved towards the opposition of the North Node, Confederate President Jefferson Davis announced that any ship owner could apply for *Letters of Marque and Reprisal*. Once obtained, ship owners could operate as privateers in the name of the Confederacy. *Letters of Marque and Reprisal* allowed the search, seizure, and destruction of assets or personnel of the Union's Navy.

Sign and Bound. Mars in Scorpio signifies naval warfare; *reprisal* carries the weight of Scorpio's revengeful side.

Dwad. Dwad of Capricorn, the sign of Mars' exaltation, signifies the Capricorn-type of status granted by the *Letters of Marque and Reprisal*. Capricorn also adds a trumped up, king-of-the-hill, quality to Lincoln's enemies.

The North Node increases affairs of the evil 12th house which spells trouble for Lincoln. On 19-Apr-1861 Lincoln announced a blockage of Southern ports. The Confederate reaction was so violent that when faced by Confederate militia threatening the Norfolk Virginia naval shipyard, Union soldiers decided to blow it up on 20-April rather than risk its surrender. Following these actions, Lincoln announced an enlargement of the US Army by 40% and the US Navy by 250% on 3-May-1861. Lincoln's greater emphasis on naval forces reflects the North Node's placement in Scorpio. Considering that the Civil War was primarily fought on ground, not at sea, Lincoln made a mistake by emphasizing naval recruitment at the expense of the army. Mistakes are one signification of the 12th house.

Lincoln: Profected Ascendant conjunct South Node

Lincoln's South Node: Sign, Bound, and Dwad

South Node's position	6TA56
Sign ruler	Venus
Bound ruler	Venus/Taurus
Dwad	Cancer

Profection: *Ascendant conjunct South Node*, 10-May-1861
Event: Suspended Habeas Corpus, 27-Apr/10-May-1861

Event. As the profected Ascendant moved to the South Node, Lincoln suspended habeas corpus on 27-Apr-1861 along the line of troop movements between Washington D.C. and Philadelphia. On 10-May-1861, he suspended habeas corpus for the Florida coast. As the year progressed Lincoln suspended habeas corpus for the entire United States. If the 7th is the house of open enemies, then the 6th is the house of imprisonment of open enemies which matches the whole sign placement of the South Node.

Sign, Bound, and Dwad. South Node in Taurus, dwad of Cancer, can be delineated as the denial of food (Taurus) and comfort (Cancer). Lincoln's actions were spurred by violence in Baltimore on 19-Apr-1861 after secessionists attacked a group of Union soldiers. Secessionists later burned railroad bridges in order to halt the flow of Union troop movements. As ruler of the South Node, Venus is the cause of the South Node's actions. Venus/Aries in her own bound signifies *love of fire* because Venus is love and Aries is a fire sign. This event was defined by burning bridges. Venus placed in the dwad of Gemini further specifies the type of bridge burned: railroads are a match to Gemini because of their dual tracks.

NEW Retrograde Planets

Traditional aphorisms identify retrogradation as a debility. Planets which are retrograde operate in an erratic fashion when compared to planets in direct motion. Sometimes a repeated action is required to get the job done.

Based on my own research, I came to a different conclusion: retrograde planets act like they are positioned in the opposite sign. The effect varies during the retrograde cycle but appears strongest at both stations and at the inferior conjunction (for Mercury and Venus) and at acronycal rising (for Saturn, Jupiter, and Mars).

Jupiter/Capricorn direct and retrograde: Nixon and Ford

	Planet	Behavior
Richard Nixon	Jupiter/Capricorn	Naked ambition, corruption
Gerald Ford	Jupiter/Capricorn-rx	Public service, anti-corruption

Richard Nixon's Jupiter/Capricorn signified naked ambition which drove him to commit illegal acts during his political career. The planet is also linked to the realpolitik of Henry Kissinger whose Ascendant degree is in the bound of Jupiter/Capricorn[3].

To the very end, Ford naively believed that Nixon's denials on Watergate were the truth. Ford's first sentence of his swearing in address "Our long national nightmare is over" returned the American Presidency to ethical normalcy, an achievement for which the Ford administration is best known.

Jupiter/Libra direct and retrograde: Bush and Trump

	Planet	Behavior
George W. Bush	Jupiter/Libra	Freedom agenda
Donald Trump	Jupiter/Libra-rx	Head-busting militant actions

George W. Bush fervently believed that Operation Iraqi Freedom would bring freedom to the Iraqi people who had lived for decades under Saddam Hussein. Bush makes this clear with his use of the term 'freedom agenda' in his memoir (Bush 2010).

By contrast, Jupiter/Libra-rx in Donald Trump's horoscope shows little evidence of Jupiter/Libra's egalitarian philosophy. While Trump does use the term 'freedom' as recently as June 2022 when he undertook an 'American Freedom

---

[3] Henry Kissinger. 26-May-1923, 10:42:48 PM, CET -01:00, Furth Germany, 10e59, 49n38. Author's rectification.

Tour,' Jupiter's actual behavior replaces egalitarianism with judicial militancy, e.g., with Jupiter/Libra-rx the functional equivalent of Jupiter/Aries. The model can be pushed further with Mars/Leo/1st ruling Trump's re-visioned Jupiter/Aries in the 9th. This means that Trump's own self-styled role as sheriff (Mars ruling the 9th of the law) in turn rules the Judiciary (functional Jupiter/Aries in the 9th). Trump demands the judiciary implement the law in ways he sees fit.

Chapter One: Summary of Findings

Using both Roosevelt and Lincoln as case studies, both bound and dwad modify each planet's behavior by adding their intrinsic nature to a planet's sign position. Lincoln's Sun is a good example. Only through the Sun's placement in the bound of Mars/Aquarius can Lincoln's periodic discriminatory statements about the inferiority of Negroes compared to Whites be understood. So too does the Sun's placement in the dwad of Scorpio add stamina and intensity to Lincoln which is otherwise difficult to identify elsewhere in the natal figure.

Predicting planetary behavior is one of the most important steps in delineation. The influence of bound and dwad helps clarify forces which are often not readily apparent when considering the sign ruler alone. By first delineating each planet by sign, bound, and dwad before jumping to other delineation steps (e.g., aspects, reception, oriental/occidental, fixed stars, etc.), the foundation of delineation is established on a firm footing.

Considering retrograde planet acting like they are functionally positioned in the opposite sign shows promise as a new model of predicting the behavior of retrograde planets in natal astrology.

CHAPTER TWO

Planets in Houses

Assigning planetary effects to specific areas of life through the house system is the second most important step in delineation. Not only is it necessary to know *what* areas of life are assigned to each house, house cusps must be accurately defined to know *through which set of house affairs* does each planet manifest.

Chapter Summary

Brief History of House Systems. The Greek method of whole sign houses predates the introduction of quadrant house systems. Far from an obsolete method of defining houses, the whole sign house system merits the astrologer's attention in delineation, prediction, and rectification.

Why House Systems matter for Rectification. For nativities with skewed Midheavens falling in signs other than ten places from the Ascendant, planets can fall in different houses according to which house system is used. The exclusive focus on quadrant houses at the expense of whole sign houses can lead to large errors in astrological judgment.

Case Study: Thomas Jefferson. Jefferson's Saturn/Leo falls in the 3rd by whole sign houses and in the 4th by the Alchabitius quadrant method of house division. Whether Saturn manifests 3rd or 4th house effects is evaluated by an examination of events timed by Saturn's directions to the angles. For these events, 3rd house effects were dominant, confirming the validity of Saturn's whole sign house placement.

Brief History of House Systems

Greeks originally considered the zodiacal sign on the eastern horizon at birth to define the 1st house. If that were Gemini, then no matter what degree of Gemini rose at birth (e.g., from 0deg 0min to 29deg 59min), any planet in the sign of Gemini was considered in the 1st house. The following sign of Cancer would be the 2nd house, etc. Researchers now refer to this system as the Whole Sign House System (Hand 2000). The zodiacal degree rising on the eastern horizon, now referred to as the Ascendant, was the first step taken to orient the celestial sphere more precisely to the location at time of birth. The Midheaven, or zodiacal degree culminating directly above the birthplace, was added later still. So were intermediate house cusps.

During the heyday of what is considered the Arabic period of astrology, from the 8th to the 11th centuries, the Alchabitius system was a popular system for quadrant house construction. Over time various alternative house systems have been proposed. Today the most used quadrant systems are Porphyry, Campanus, Regiomontanus, Alchabitius, Placidus, and Koch (Reed, 2002).

For this project, both whole sign and Alchabitius houses are used. For reference purposes: Whole sign houses = (WS); Alchabitius houses = (AL).

Why House Systems matter for Rectification

The choice of house system plays an important role in rectification. For if Saturn falls in the 3rd under one method and the 4th under another, does the delineation state the native faces Saturnine influences for his 3rd house of siblings, short-term travel, and communications? (to be confirmed by corroborating events during rectification?) Or do those influences manifest more strongly in ancestry, father, and home signified by the 4th house? Choosing an incorrect house placement for a planet can dangerously lead a rectification astray because it creates faulty delineation of house affairs. If delineation is wrong, prediction and rectification efforts will fail.

<u>First Debate: Which Quadrant House System?</u> "I use Koch." "I stick with Placidus." "I am experimenting with Regiomontanus because I am impressed by William Lilly and his methods." These are the kind of answers given by astrologers if the question of house preference is posed. And if one presses further, usually the testimony of transiting planets setting off events by conjoining house cusps more accurately by *this or that* house system is used as supporting evidence.

<u>Why Transits to House Cusps are a poor methodology.</u> There are multiple problems with testing house cusps with transits. First is the ability of a planet to trigger house affairs when it makes its sign ingress whether or not zero degrees of a sign (WS) falls before, near, or after the respective AL house cusp. Second is the

ability of transiting planets to trigger events when they move from one bound to another within a single sign, just as the significators do when directed through the bounds (see Chapter 10: *Directions*). The dividing line between one bound and another is rarely coincident with a house cusp. Third is the ability of other predictive techniques to trigger house events. These include daily, monthly, and annual profections as well as the solar return. The assumption that planets can trigger house affairs by transiting their cusps falls prey to an under-specification error that gives improper emphasis to transits in the predictive hierarchy.

Test Hellenistic Lots whose formulas include intermediate house cusps. How then can different house systems be evaluated? Because Lots represent customized Ascendants for specific areas of life, I believe that testing transits, progressions, profections, and directions to Hellenistic Lots whose formulas include intermediate house cusps holds promise. Yes, even transits, in the same way that transits to the natal Ascendant can be used as a rectification tool. There are six of these, including the Lot of Death whose formula includes the intermediate 8th house cusp. For the Presidential database, it is also an excellent Lot to test because in nearly all cases death times are recorded. This means that even faster transiting planets, e.g., Moon and Mercury, can be included in the testing methodology.

Software Limitations. To date, I have been unable to access software which can profect or direct Hellenistic Lots[4]. Given the high ranking of profections and directions in the predictive hierarchy, no definitive results are possible until these techniques can be systematically applied. Yet as a place to start, one can note the position of transiting, progressed, and solar arc planets and compare them to the Lot of Death calculated under different house methods. One can also test whether any solar return planets in the year of death aspect the Lot of Death.

Example. Andrew Jackson died on 8-Jun-1845, near 6:00 PM, Nashville, TN. Both transiting Saturn (18AQ52) and Mars (21AQ55) opposed the Lot of Death.

Table 3. Dynamic Activity to the Lot of Death for Various House Systems Andrew Jackson's Death, 8-Jun-1845

Lot of Death	House System	Error to Saturn	Error to Mars
18LE51	Alchabitius	0deg 1min	3deg 4min
17LE32	Porphyry	1deg 20min	4deg 23min
13LE10	Placidus	5deg 42min	8deg 45min
12LE48	Koch	6deg 4min	9deg 7min
16LE27	Regiomontanus	2deg 25min	5deg 28min

This exercise can be repeated for different measurements, making sure to only consider malefics or other killing planets identified by victor tables (see last

---

[4] Janus 5.5 now allows directions with lots.

section of Chapter 5: *Longevity*). Based on a brief survey of transits, progressions, and solar arc directions (both direct and converse for all types), my trial conclusion is that Alchabitius is the most accurate house system, yet in a statistical dead heat with Porphyry. The other house systems registered errors, on average, of between 3 and 7 degrees. These findings are preliminary. As stated before, both a larger data sample and software capable of profecting and directing Hellenistic Lots is required for a definitive answer to the question of optimal house system.

Second Debate: Whole Sign or Quadrant Houses? With whole sign houses, the difference between a planet's house placements can easily be 2 or 3 signs, a discrepancy which increases as latitudes move towards the poles. Table 4 presents the Presidential database sorted by the Ascendant and Midheaven degree difference as a measure of house skewness. The greater the difference from 90, the more likelihood planet placement will differ when comparing whole sign and quadrant house systems. Presidents falling at either the top or bottom of the list have considerable differences in planet placements. For instance, Zachary Taylor's Moon falls in the 3rd by AL and the 5th by WS.

Placement of the MC-IC axis. It's not just the planet placement which is of interest but the placement of the MC – IC axis itself. Robert Hand suggests the Midheaven degree falling into a particular whole sign house elevates that house's importance to the native's career as a general consideration for judgment (Hand 2000, 20-21). For example, with a difference of 64 degrees between his Ascendant and Midheaven, Reagan's Midheaven falls in the 11th house by whole signs. Any President like Reagan who has an *11th house Midheaven* finds his career and social status more strongly defined through politics, friends, and organizations. At a difference of 111 degrees, Jefferson's Midheaven falls in the 9th by whole signs. Jefferson finds himself more of a philosopher-king with a *9th house Midheaven*. Table 4 lists the Midheaven position by whole sign house for those wishing to consider this question further.

Table 4. House Skewness: Ascendant-Midheaven Degree Difference

#	Nativity	Ascendant	Midheaven	Difference Degrees	Midheaven Placement (WS)
46	Joe Biden	14CP39	9SC53	64.77	11th
40	Ronald Reagan	6CP08	1SC21	64.78	11th
12	Zachary Taylor	19CP41	12SC17	67.40	11th
13	Millard Fillmore	14SA16	5LI56	68.33	11th
2	John Adams	10AQ33	1SA52	68.68	11th
16	Abraham Lincoln	29SA45	20LI48	68.95	11th
9	William Harrison	29CP30	20SC28	69.03	11th
11	James Polk	25CP07	15SC18	69.82	11th
29	Warren Harding	14SA14	4LI09	70.08	11th
1	George Washington	9AQ36	28SC58	70.63	10th
8	Martin Van Buren	29AQ55	14SA05	75.83	11th
5	James Monroe	26AQ24	10SA30	75.90	11th
4	James Madison	29SC49	13VI04	76.75	11th
15	James Buchanan	21CA19	3TA53	77.43	10th
17	Andrew Johnson	27SC13	8VI07	79.10	11th
44	Barack Obama	26AQ18	5SA31	80.78	11th
6	John Quincy Adams	6SC48	14LE53	81.92	10th
23	Benjamin Harrison	14PI27	21SA27	83.00	10th
25	William McKinley	29LI08	4LE42	84.43	11th
35	John Kennedy	27LI37	3LE11	84.43	11th
28	Woodrow Wilson	15LI24	17CA30	87.90	10th
39	Jimmy Carter	22LI05	23CA58	88.12	10th
33	Harry Truman	9LI06	10CA14	88.87	10th
42	Bill Clinton	11LI07	12CA06	89.02	10th
37	Richard Nixon	15VI02	13GE38	91.40	10th
32	Franklin Roosevelt	20VI57	19GE25	91.53	10th
41	George H.W. Bush	8VI27	4GE21	94.10	10th
36	Lyndon Johnson	15LE06	10TA10	94.93	10th
30	Calvin Coolidge	3VI50	28TA15	95.58	9th
10	John Tyler	23LE14	17TA15	95.98	10th
21	Chester Arthur	26LE16	17TA58	98.30	10th
45	Donald Trump	15LE59	6TA27	99.53	10th
7	Andrew Jackson	1TA57	19CP30	102.45	9th
43	George W Bush	7LE02	24AR06	102.93	9th
20	James Garfield	26CA39	9AR51	106.80	10th
27	William Howard Taft	10TA36	23CP42	106.90	9th
34	Dwight Eisenhower	22TA41	5AQ02	107.65	10th
38	Gerald Ford	13TA08	24CP25	108.72	9th
19	Rutherford Hayes	14CA11	24PI09	110.03	9th
22/24	Grover Cleveland	12CA40	21PI43	110.95	9th
18	Ulysses Grant	26TA26	5AQ16	111.17	10th
3	Thomas Jefferson	00GE28	9AQ04	111.40	9th
31	Herbert Hoover	2GE06	8AQ03	114.05	9th
26	Theodore Roosevelt	17GE26	22AQ41	114.75	9th
14	Franklin Pierce	3CA15	7PI57	115.30	9th

Case Study: Jefferson's Saturn/Leo: 3rd or 4th house?

With a 9th house Midheaven falling 111 degrees past the Ascendant, Jefferson's nativity yields one of the more interesting tests of quadrant versus whole sign house systems. Saturn/Leo falls in the 4th by AL but the 3rd by WS. By these definitions Saturn falls in *both* houses. But do planets falling in two different houses manifest through each house? Or does one house dominate? Let's test Jefferson's life events against both possibilities.

Delineation of Saturn in Leo

Saturn 29LE04 = Saturn/Leo (sign) + Mars/Leo (bound) + Cancer (dwad)

Leo is the sign of Saturn's detriment where he denies the Sun's positive attributes (think King Arthur), replacing them with totalitarianism. The bound Mars/Leo adds rebellion because of insults to honor. Dwad Cancer adds care and comfort in the home as themes. With Cancer's ruler the Moon and Saturn enemies, the duad placement is problematic. Saturn retrograde means he is rebellious and defiant (Ibn Ezra 1998, 131). **NEW** Recent research suggests Saturn/Leo-rx functions like Saturn/Aquarius, e.g., a rejection of totalitarianism in favor of science.

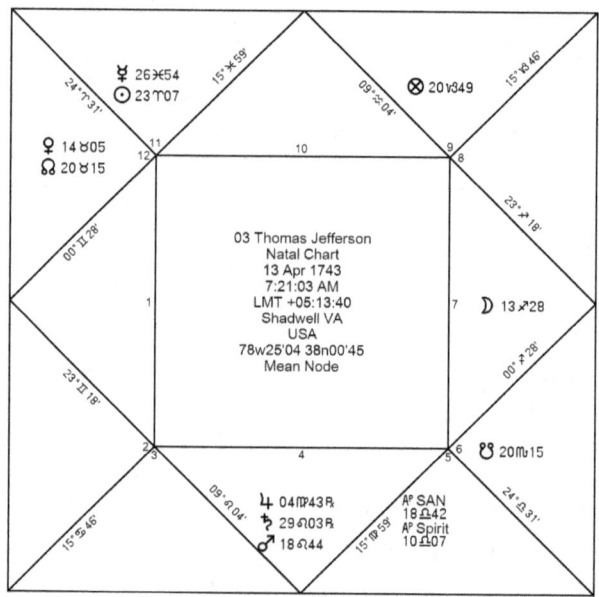

Nativity of Thomas Jefferson, Alchabitius houses.

4th house affairs: Does Saturn or Jupiter predominate?

Let's start with a simple test of 4th house affairs which include home and real estate. Is Jefferson's home better described by Saturn/Leo or Jupiter/Virgo? Visit Jefferson's home Monticello and be astounded by the seemingly endless attention to detail and the sprawling layout created by near-continuous additions made during Jefferson's lifetime. Needless expansion of the detail is characteristic of Jupiter/Virgo not Saturn/Leo. Score one for whole sign houses.

Saturn in Leo ruling the 9th (by *either* AL or WS houses) suggests totalitarian acts promulgated by royalist regimes abroad. Jefferson's best-known foreign travels were time spent abroad in revolutionary France, whose declaration he himself helped to draft. Note that Leo is the sign given to Gaul by Ptolemy; the region now known as France. That he wrote about it; indeed helped foment the French Revolution with his direct contribution to the French Declaration of Independence, emphasizes Saturn/Leo's 3rd house WS placement because writing, communication, and publicity are 3rd house affairs. With either Capricorn (AL) or Aquarius (WS) on the 9th cusp, Saturn rules the 9th under both systems. With either possibility valid, no definitive answer is possible by general delineation of houses.

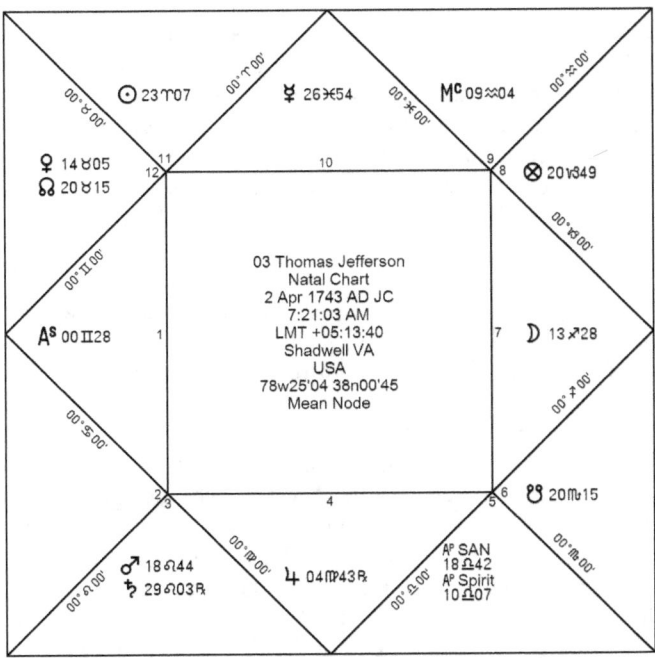

Nativity of Thomas Jefferson, Whole Sign Houses.

Tests of Saturn directed to the Angles

Because there is no better test of planetary behavior than to observe events when planets are directed to the angles, directions of Saturn should demonstrate the delineation of Saturn by both sign and house. If there is any merit to Saturn's whole sign house placement in the 3rd, events timed by primary directions should demonstrate 3rd house and not 4th house types of events.

The following three sets of directions, both direct and converse, list selected Saturn-angle directions. I present a pair of dates for each direction. This pair, a concept formally introduced in Chapter 10 as the *primary direction sequence*, computes two dates with and without latitude of the planet involved, e.g., Saturn.

Set #1: Jefferson attends William & Mary; King George III ascends throne

REG	D	Venus/Leo	P	IC d. => Saturn (0)	21-Nov-1760
REG	D	Venus/Leo	P	IC d. => Saturn (SA)	4-Jan-1762

PT	D	Saturn/Aquarius	P	opposition Saturn (SA) d. => MC	27-Apr-1762
PT	D	Saturn/Aquarius	P	opposition Saturn (0) d. => MC	18-Dec-1762

Thomas Jefferson entered the College of William & Mary on 25-Mar-1760 and graduated during 1762; after college Jefferson read law with George Wythe. At William & Mary, Jefferson studied philosophy and science under the Scotsman William Small who introduced Jefferson to John Locke, Francis Bacon, and Sir Isaac Newton. Locke's influence on Jefferson's political philosophy was substantial. Locke argued that governments achieved legitimacy by consent of the people bound by a social contract which protected the people's natural rights of life, liberty, and estate. If this contract was voided, people were within their rights to rebel against government.

Jefferson's college years paralleled political disruptions between Britain and the American colonies. The death of King George II and King George III's accession on 26-Oct-1760 fell one month prior to the start of the first sequence. The change in leadership marked a shift in British policy which favored increasing taxation on the American colonies, in part to pay for British expenses incurred during the French & Indian War. On 2-Dec-1761, a writ of assistance was issued in Boston. Authorized by Parliament, this law was designed to aid customs officers to enforce tax payments on molasses, rum, and sugar imported from countries other than Britain to the colonies. Customs officers were given power to search any household without cause and without court permission. Colonists considered this act a violation of their freedom. Finally, England declared war on Spain on 2-Jan-1762 (date match to end of the first sequence), who was preparing an alliance with France and Austria.

I submit that these events vindicate Saturn/Leo in the 3rd house by whole signs ruling the 9th house of higher education, philosophy, and foreign affairs. The philosophy of John Locke who warned against tyrannical governments matches the delineation of Saturn in Leo. True enough, with Capricorn on the 9th by AL and Aquarius on the 9th by WS, Saturn will rule the 9th under each house system. Yet Jefferson will spend much time writing, publishing, and receive publicity for the tyranny of Kings later in life. Writing, publishing, and publicity are 3rd house affairs where Saturn resides by WS position. In addition, these 3rd house activities are strongly connected to the 11th house of political alliances through rulership of the Sun. Sun in the 11th by WS is a much better match to this life pattern than Sun in the 12th by AL placement. Furthermore, the death of King George II better fits the whole sign configuration because Saturn is the al-mubtazz of the 5th house, 8th from the 10th, or death of Kings. Saturn does not rule the 5th under AL houses.

Set 2: Colonial Rebellions against Taxation and Arbitrary Police Acts

| PT | D | Saturn/Gemini | P | dex sextile Saturn (SA) d. => ASC | 21-Jan-1769 |
| PT | D | Saturn/Gemini | P | dex sextile Saturn (0) d. => ASC | 25-Nov-1770 |

| REG | D | Jupiter/Leo | P | sin sextile ASC c. => Saturn (0) | 2-Jan-1769 |
| REG | D | Jupiter/Leo | P | sin sextile ASC c. => Saturn (SA) | 30-Jan-1770 |

Between 1768 and 1770 American colonists felt the full force of British demands for taxation through policies viewed as abuses of power. The quartering of British troops in Boston, beginning on 1-Oct-1768 shortly before the start of both sequences, initiated a period of violence which included attacks against loyalist printers John Mein and John Fleeming, Boston, 28-Oct-1769; the Battle of Golden Hill, New York, 19-Jan-1770; the Nassau Street Riot, New York, 20-Jan-1770, arrest of Alexander McDougall of the New York Sons of Liberty for his authorship of a broadside criticizing the NY assembly, 8-Feb-1770; the Boston Massacre, 5-Mar-1770; and the defense by John Adams and acquittal of most of the accused British troops in the Boston Massacre on 3-Dec-1770.

These acts of violence paralleled colonial resistance to taxation under the Townshend Acts of 29-Jun-1767 designed to impose and enforce a new series of external taxes which overruled the authority of colonial legislatures. As the sequence began many colonial legislatures passed Nonimportation laws designed to bypass taxation through consumer boycott of British traded goods. The Townshend Acts were eventually repealed on 12-Apr-1770. Colonies rescinded their Nonimportation laws in response to their victory against the Acts with South Carolina the last colony to abandon their Nonimportation laws on 13-Dec-1770 just after the first sequence ended.

Jefferson's career in the Virginia legislature paralleled these mundane events and the primary direction sequences with his election during Dec-1768 as the second sequence began. The tumultuous events of May-1769 occurred during the interval when both sequences were active. On 16-May, the Virginia House of Burgesses passed a resolution stating their sole authority to levy taxes; on 17-May the House of Burgesses was dissolved by the British Governor; on 18-May the House of Burgesses reconvened, passed a Nonimportation Act, and took steps to see through its implementation.

Both the seemingly unfairness of the taxation and the ruthlessness with which it was enforced enraged the colonists. Later, these events between 1768 and 1770 were considered a *cause célèbre* as continued clashes between Britain and her colonists led towards revolution. They would also become fodder for Jefferson's later justification for independence in his radical writings and publications.

To understand these events and Jefferson's reaction to them, it is helpful to review the delineation of Saturn in Leo:

If the nature of the Sun is power and public recognition which in the sign of Leo rises to the level of intellect, vision, generosity, and splendor; then Saturn in Leo denies this promise by producing what are arguably 'anti-Sun' characteristics.

Tyrannical laws designed to pervert the Sun is the essence of Saturn in Leo which differs from actual physical acts of rebellion signified by Mars in Leo. These effects are a bit tricky to separate in Jefferson's horoscope because not only is Saturn/Leo conjunct Mars/Leo but Saturn/Leo is in the bound of Mars/Leo. Nevertheless, it is fair to say that Jefferson's Saturn in the 3rd WS house matches this set of sequences precisely. That Saturn also rules the 8th house of traded goods – *with Capricorn falling on the 8th exclusively by WS houses* – also strongly comes through in this second set. Furthermore, Jefferson's Lot of Fortune in the 8th ruled both by Saturn (sign) and Mars (exaltation) signifies that Jefferson will profit from writing rebelliously about the impairment of trade. Tyrannical legal actions promulgated by 9th-house-signified imperial political regimes impair trade. Traded goods belong to the 8th house. A king ruling from a foreign country matches a 9th house Midheaven because the King is the angle of the 10th; placed in the 9th he ruled from a foreign country.

Jefferson's list of complaints against King George III, spurred by events during this sequence but written somewhat later, is perhaps the best summary of Saturn/Leo '*anti-Sun*' manifestations ever presented:

1. The king "has refused his assent to laws the most wholesome and necessary for the public good";
2. "he has forbidden his governors to pass laws";
3. "he has refused to pass other laws…unless those people would relinquish the right of representation";
4. "he has dissolved the Representative houses";
5. "he has refused…others to be elected";
6. He has prevented immigration to colonies and new land appropriations;

7. He has refused to assent to laws establishing judiciary powers;
8. He has made judges dependent on his will;
9. He has erected multitudinous new offices;
10. He has kept standing armies in times of peace;
11. He has rendered the military above the civilian authority;
12. He has subjected us to "a jurisdiction foreign to our constitutions" (e.g., Parliament);
13. He has protected usurpers with mock trials;
14. He has cut off colonial trade with the world;
15. He has "imposed taxes on us without our consent";
16. He has deprived us of "trial by jury";
17. He has transported defendants across the sea;
18. He is "taking away our charters & altering fundamentally the forms of our governments";
19. By "suspending our own legislatures." (Jefferson 1950, 425)

Concluding this discussion of the second set of directions, it is difficult to see how Jefferson's participation in 11th house legislative activity (Sun in 11th by whole sign) has anything to do with Mars and Saturn in the 4th.

One of the few events during this time which arguably supports the 4th house placement of Mars/Saturn was a fire at his mother's home that destroyed most of Jefferson's library on 1-Feb-1770. Home belongs to the 4th. Yet considering that most if not all of Jefferson's books (3rd house of learning) were imported from overseas (9th house) makes the 3rd house – 9th house orientation difficult to escape.

Set 3: Recruiting faculty for the University of Virginia

| PT | D | Saturn/Aries | P | dex trine Saturn (SA) d. => MC | 11-Feb-1818 |
| PT | D | Saturn/Aries | P | dex trine Saturn (0) d. => MC | 10-Oct-1818 |

| REG | D | Jupiter/Gemini | P | sin trine MC c. => Saturn (0) | 7-Sep-1823 |
| REG | D | Jupiter/Gemini | P | sin trine MC c. => Saturn (SA) | 20-Sep-1824 |

Both sequences mark disputes over appointment of professors to the University of Virginia.

Thomas Cooper, together with the better-known Joseph Priestley, emigrated from Britain to America in 1794; both were ousted for their sympathies with the French Revolution. Both sought freedom from tyranny for the common people. Priestley's advocacy for Parliamentary Reform triggered a backlash with the Priestley Riots of 1791 when his chapel and home were ransacked and burned. In America, Cooper fought against the Alien & Sedition Acts imposed under John Adams' administration. Both Cooper's agitation against sedition and his relationship with Priestley brought him to Jefferson's attention. Jefferson recommended the Board of Visitors of the University of Virginia to offer Cooper the post of Professor of chemistry and law on 7-Oct-1817.

Both Priestly and Cooper were Unitarians, a sect whose tenets were considered heretical by the Virginia political establishment and some members of the new University's Board of Visitors. These beliefs included denial of the trinity and denial that Jesus died to atone for the sins of mankind. Protests against Cooper's appointment started Feb-1818, as the first sequence began (Bruce 1919, Volume I: 200). Attacks were led by members of religious denominations. Jefferson was able to put Cooper's enemies at bay temporarily; by the spring of 1819 Cooper's appointment was reaffirmed. This was only a temporary hiatus until renewed attacks in late 1819 and early 1820 forced Cooper to resign, hurting Jefferson deeply. Cooper's resignation appears to be marked by the following Moon-Saturn direction which depending on the choice of latitude yields four different dates between late 1819 and spring 1821:

REG	D	Venus/Gemini	P	opposition Moon (0) c. => Saturn (SA)	16-Oct-1819
REG	D	Venus/Gemini	P	opposition Moon (MO) c. => Saturn (SA)	1-May-1820
PT	D	Venus/Gemini	P	opposition Moon (0) c. => Saturn (SA)	2-Jan-1821
PT	D	Venus/Gemini	P	opposition Moon (MO) c. => Saturn (SA)	1-Apr-1821

Cooper's sympathies for the French Revolution and protests against the Alien & Sedition Acts clearly made Cooper an opponent of Saturn-Leo policies. The same perversions of the positive leadership qualities of the Sun by Saturn placed in the Sun-ruled sign of Leo are also evident in religious intolerance espoused by the Virginia elite. Not only the significator of the King, the Sun is also the primary significator of the Spirit. As the King is perverted with Saturn in Leo, so are matters of spirit and religion.

The second sequence in 1824 also dealt with recruitment of professors for the University of Virginia. The chronology is as follows:

23-Nov-1823. Jefferson hired Francis Gilmer to recruit professors from England.
5-Apr-1824. Gilmer received a formal offer from the Board of Visitors.
26-Apr-1824. Gilmer's power of attorney is dated.
8-May-1824. Gilmer set sail from New York for Liverpool
22-Jun-1824. Gilmer left London for Cambridge
LOCK 19-Sep-1824. Gilmer succeeded in engaging four of five professors.

Two elements of Gilmer's trip appear related to significations of Saturn in Leo. First, Gilmer had difficulty in recruiting faculty from either Oxford or Cambridge. Both institutions catered to the 'nobility and the opulent gentry' (Bruce, 361) who could afford their high expenses. Gilmer found it difficult to recruit faculty away from the luxury of financial security and prestige to work for a risky new educational venture in America, considered an undesirable backwater at that time. Gilmer's characterization of the Oxford and Cambridge elite smacks of snobbery.

In landing his first recruit in the 24-year-old George Long, Gilmer found favor with a man for whom elitism held no sway. Long stated: "I have no attachment to England as a country...it is a delightful place for a man of rank and property to live in, but I was not born in that enviable station...If comfortably settled, therefore, in America, I would never wish to leave it" (Bruce 1920, 368). While snobbery and elitism need not rise to the level of the intolerant Saturn in Leo, it is arguably one small step to take from being a snob to the imposition of contentious legal precepts designed to maintain social status of the nobility at the expense of common people.

An astrometerological delineation of Saturn in Leo framed a second problem Gilmer encountered at Oxford whose summer vacation between July and October afforded the locals an escape from the heat. With no such plan for scheduled summer vacation at the University of Virginia, at least one potential recruit dismissed Gilmer's offer because of having to teach during the summer heat. Delineated as an astrometerological signature, Jefferson's Mars-Saturn conjunction signifies hot and dry weather.[5] Saturn's cold-dry nature is heated up in the fiery sign of Leo and accentuates Saturn's dryness. The hot-dry nature of Mars is also intensified in Leo. Whether Mars influences Jefferson's Saturn/Leo by outright conjunction or ruler of Saturn's bound the result is the same: extreme hot and dry weather. Dwad placement of both malefics in water signs adds humidity to the mix and matches Virginia's hot and humid summer climate (duad placements of Mars and Saturn in Pisces and Cancer respectively).

Summary Findings

Planets manifest their nature through houses by both position and rulership. Correctly interpreting the house position is a necessary step in delineation. Otherwise, faulty assumptions enter the rectification process and throw it off.

The example of Jefferson's Saturn in Leo interpreted in the 3rd house by whole sign houses validates the importance of whole sign house placement. Whether or not Saturn generated 3rd house effects 100% of the time I have not proven. This would require an investigation of additional primary directions with the positions of Saturn and the angles reversed as significator and promissor; directions of Saturn to all the other significators (Sun, Moon, Lot of Fortune, SAN), and transits of Saturn to all significators. This is beyond the objective of the current study.

What can safely be concluded is that a planet's whole sign house placement cannot be ignored in delineation, prediction, and rectification.

---

[5] Examples of Mars-Saturn Leo conjunctions timing heat waves include the recent 3-Jun/21-Jul-2006 heat wave and the more serious heat wave of 5-Jun/5-Jul-1976. Note these events were felt strongly in France, ruled by Leo.

CHAPTER THREE

NEW Physiognomy

Definition. Derived from the Greek word φυσιογνωμονικά, physiognomics (more commonly physiognomy) means judging character from bodily features. What the Greeks named physiognomy was practiced long before by the Babylonians as one of their divination methods. Within the Hellenistic tradition, the earliest surviving treatise *Physiognomonics* dates to the 3rd Century BCE and represents the first systematic compilation of physiognomy rules in the West. Like humoural and temperament theory, physiognomy was originally developed by a group of medical-philosophers using an empirical approach based on analogy and observation. Given the fact that not until the 1st Century CE does any surviving astrology text incorporate physiognomy judgments, it appears physiognomy predates astrology as a discipline.

Contemporary relevance. Despite many attempts to link the shape of the face and body to character, none have survived scrutiny. My research focuses on linking the shape of the face and body to the natal horoscope in a model which can be deployed as a rectification tool. Character judgments should be stripped away from physiognomy and reserved for models on the soul (see Chapter 4).

Multiple Systems and Methods. One school of astrological physiognomy is based on the principle of *melothesis*, a doctrine which assigns parts of the body to each of the zodiac signs. In this model the head is assigned to Aries and remaining body parts are assigned to the other eleven zodiac signs moving from head to foot. This is a largely consistent and uninterrupted tradition which dates from the earliest known Hellenistic astrological texts. Beyond *melothesis*, astrological guidelines exist which judge the shape of the body and face by planets, signs, decans, degrees, and fixed stars. A literature review reveals many proposed systems and disagreements among authors to the point there is no consensus on the viability of physiognomy by contemporary astrologers.

The Rising Decan Model. This chapter presents original research which links the sign placement of the ruler of the rising decan to the shape of the face. Planets in cardinal, fixed, and mutable signs are linked to ovate, rectangular/square, and elongated/triangular shapes in a model developed by John Willner (1991).

Melothesis

Porphyry offers one of the earliest lists which assign zodiac signs to body parts. Subsequent authors largely adhere to these correspondences with a few exceptions, e.g., some authors assign Cancer to the belly. See Table 5.

While melothesis assigns the same zodiac signs to the same parts of the body for all humans, what differs is how planets in each sign influence the body part associated with the respective sign. Using the malefic planets as examples, placement of either Mars or Saturn in specific zodiac signs causes harm to the body part assigned to the respective sign. As a delineation step, linking malefic planets to specific body parts is a helpful rectification tool. This improves rectification by focusing on dynamic activity of the relevant planet at the time of an accident/injury/surgery which involves a specific body part.

Dwight Eisenhower. Placement of Mars in Capricorn predicts a knee injury because Capricorn is assigned to the knees and the nature of Mars is to cut, burn, or slice. Eisenhower suffered a knee injury while playing college football. Torn cartilage and/or tendons (most common knee injury) is consistent with the nature of Mars. Eisenhower's Saturn placement in Virgo combines the Saturnian nature of blockage and obstruction with the intestines. Eisenhower suffered from intestinal and bowel obstructions which required surgery.

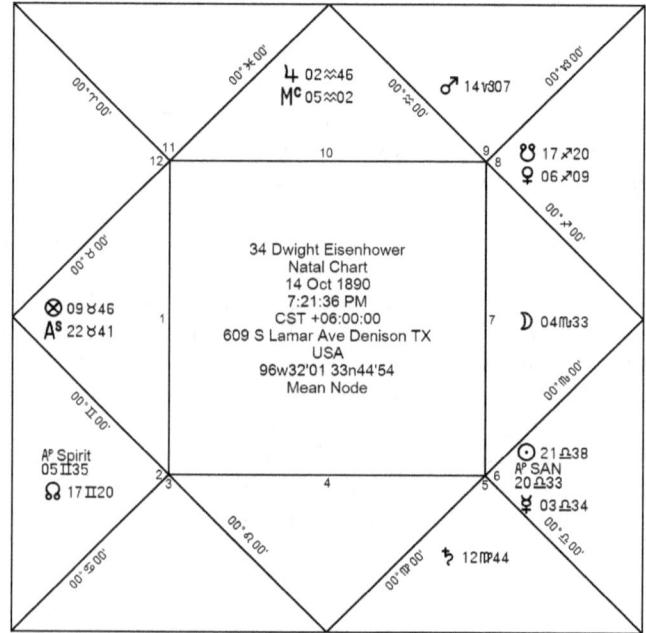

Table 5. Porphyry's Assignment of Zodiac Signs to Body Parts[6]

Zodiac Sign	Body Part
Aries	The head
Taurus	The tendon and the neck
Gemini	The shoulders and upper arms
Cancer	The breast and ribs
Leo	The midriff and the stomach and the belly
Virgo	The abdomen and flanks
Libra	The kidneys and buttocks
Scorpio	The genitals and the hidden and generative places
Sagittarius	The hips (but according to some, also the glands and the bends of the elbow)
Capricorn	The loins and haunches
Aquarius	The legs and ankles
Pisces	The feet

Literature Review

Following publication of the 3rd edition of *A Rectification Manual*, I spent a year researching physiognomy and published a *Working Paper on Astrological Physiognomy: History and Sources* in 2010, revised 2011. What I learned from that project was outside of melothesis, the myriad of systems and methods for linking physical appearance to astrology meant no single system came to dominate the practice. For this reason and the apparent lack of its necessity for astrologers conducting 1-on-1 readings, astrological physiognomy has fallen out of favor and currently occupies the fringes of astrological practice.

Not so 150 years ago when American's most prominent astrologer Luke Broughton actively used physiognomy as a prominent rectification tool for American Presidents, political candidates, and Civil War generals (Broughton 1860-1869). Based on my literature review, the origin of American physiognomy can be traced to Orson Fowler who introduced phrenology in the 1830s. The Fowler's created a family publishing dynasty with titles on self-help subjects (not limited to phrenology) which lasted until the death of Charlotte Fowler Wells in 1901 (Stein 1971). While most associate phrenology with character readings based on bumps on the skull, an examination of actual procedures used during phrenology readings reveals inclusion of multiple factors including a three-fold vital-motive-mental temperament model similar in spirit to the four-fold temperament model used by astrologers. By the turn of the 20th century, the

---

[6] See commentary of Antiochus on Porphyry in *The Astrological Record of the Early Sages, Vol. 2, Definitions and Foundations*, Project Hindsight, Cumberland, MD.: The Golden Hind Press, 2009, p. 117.

medical astrologer Howard Cornell linked the Fowler's three-fold temperament model to the three-fold sign modality (e.g., fixed, mutable, and cardinal) (Cornell 1972). Much later John Willner linked sign modality to the shape of the face.

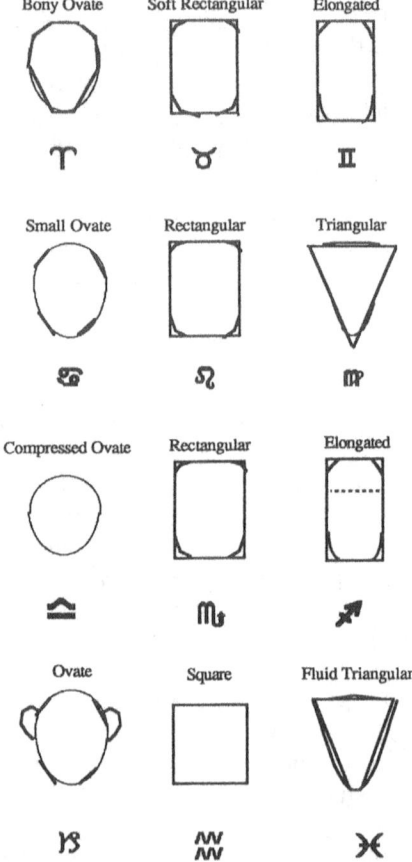

Figure 1. Shapes of the Face based on Zodiac Signs

Source: John Willner, *The Rising Sign Problem: A Series of Essays on the Physical Characteristics and Personality Traits of Individuals for the Twelve Astrological Signs on the Ascendant.* American Federation of Astrologers, 1991, pps. 6-7.

Rising Decan Model

Based on my experiments with these systems, Willner's model works well when applied to the rising decan (not the ASC sign in his usage). Specifically:

1. Identify the Ascendant sign.
2. Identify the Ascendant decan, e.g., which 10 degree decan is on the ASC.
3. Identify the sign ruler of the rising decan.
4. Identify the sign placement of the sign ruler of the rising decan.
5. Link the sign placement to Willner's facial shape model.

In some cases, one need not look beyond the sign of the rising decan itself for the physiognomy significator, e.g., John Tyler (Aries) and Joe Biden (Taurus).

Body or Face?

The proposed model applies to the shape of the face, not the body. Photos of the face are more readily available compared to photos of the physical body for historical subjects. For this reason, I have focused on the shape of the face.

This does not mean that physiognomy of the body is an irrelevant delineation tool for rectification, only that I have not yet tested the material for definitive conclusions. Nevertheless for those who are interested in the body, the Ascendant sign and its occupants are key significators. As a simple example, consider the correlation between Jupiter placed in the Ascendant sign and size of the body. Horoscopes of seven Presidents meet this condition: Tyler, Grant, T. Roosevelt, Taft, Harding, LBJ, and Clinton. The latter five on this list occupy the top tier of Presidents with the highest recorded weight. Tyler is an exception because Jupiter/Leo is retrograde, Mars/Leo is co-present (adds heat), and both planets are ruled by Sun/Aries (adds heat). For Grant, Jupiter/Taurus is co-present with Saturn/Taurus (enemy of Jupiter) and Sun/Taurus (adds heat). Grover Cleveland does not meet the criteria of Jupiter in the Ascendant sign, but the Cancer-Ascendant ruler Moon/Leo is co-present with both Mars/Leo and Jupiter/Leo. Cleveland was one of the largest Presidents by body size.

Usefulness in Rectification

Compared to other rectification techniques reviewed in this book, physiognomy falls prey to confirmation bias more so than other methods. Further research may reduce confirmation bias by applying biometric software to samples sorted by the sign placement of the ruling decan to determine whether Willner's model is true. For example, is the vertical distance between the eyes and the lips smaller for the compressed ovate shape of Libra compared to other cardinal signs as suggested by Willner's sketches? This remains a wide-open topic for astrological research.

Findings

<u>Decan system</u>. Use the decan system based on triplicity by element, sometimes referred to as 'Hindu decans' or the 'decans of Varahamihira' (Chapter 1, Table 2). The more commonly used Chaldean decan system by Medieval astrologers does not work with the proposed physiognomy model.

<u>Age</u>. The human body undergoes significant changes over one's lifespan. One cannot use this tool prior to puberty before hormones exert their genetic influence over body size and facial type. Likewise, decreased metabolism limits the usefulness of this technique for older individuals. Recommendation: limit physiognomy judgments for individuals between the ages of 25 and 45. As a practical matter, this means when conducting rectification for older public figures, one needs to find earlier photographs before using physiognomy for rectification.

<u>Gradation of Effects: Modality</u>. Sign placement of ruler of rising decan in fixed signs gives the best results; cardinal signs, generally so; mutable signs, less so.

<u>Gradation of Effects: Planet</u>. Ranked by Chaldean order, the superior planets (Saturn, Jupiter, Mars) yield physiognomy effects which are more consistent and observable. Either as planet (as ruler of rising decan) or by sign rulership (sign placement of ruler of rising decan). By contrast, inferior planets (Venus, Mercury, Moon) yield physiognomy effects which are less consistent. Ascendants of Cancer (Moon-ruled), Gemini, and Virgo (Mercury-ruled) yield poor results. The relationship between Mercury's trickster nature and individuals who are 'masters of disguise' suggests difficulty in applying physiognomy for Gemini Ascendants.

<u>Influence of Lunar Nodes</u>. Placement of the South Node in the Ascendant sign may invalidate the proposed physiognomy model.

<u>Manifestation beyond shape or the face</u>. Example: The glyph of Sagittarius is classically linked to the Centaur and to horses more generally based on my research. A consistent feature of Sagittarius is long unruly hair akin to a horse's mane. If the sign placement of the ruler of the rising decan is placed in Sagittarius but one observes an individual with short-cropped hair, consider whether the person wears a wig or does so on ceremonial or social occasions (such as Halloween).

Face example: Martin van Buren (Aquarius Ascendant, Libra 3rd decan rising, Venus/Sagittarius ruler of 3rd rising decan). Shape of MVB's face does NOT follow Willner's elongated rectangle for Sagittarius. But MVB DOES HAVE the wild hair of Sagittarius.

Body example: Andrew Johnson, Saturn/Scorpio in 1st house. Saturn/Scorpio signifies national security. During Johnson's political career he was known to remove a pistol from his jacket and place it on a lectern prior to making a speech.

Table 6. Physiognomy Significators

Ascendant: Degree, Sign, Sign ruler, Planets/Nodes Positioned in the Ascendant.
Decan: Sign, Sign ruler, Planets/Nodes Positioned in Decan's sign.

		Ascendant				Decan		
		Degree	**Sign**	**Ruler**	**In**	**Sign**	**Ruler**	**In**
1	George Washington	9AQ36	♒	♄♈	☿	♒	♄♈	☿
2	John Adams	10AQ33	♒	♄♉-rx		♊	☿♏	
3	Thomas Jefferson	00GE28	♊	☿♓		♊	☿♓	
4	James Madison	29SC49	♏	♂♑	☽	♋	☽♏	
5	James Monroe	26AQ24	♒	♄♓		♎	♀♈	
6	John Quincy Adams	6SC48	♏	♂♌		♏	♂♌	
7	Andrew Jackson	1TA57	♉	♀♈	♂	♉	♀♈	♂
8	Martin Van Buren	29AQ55	♒	♄♑		♎	♀♐	☋
9	William Harrison	29CP30	♑	♄♍-rx	♀, ☿	♍	☿ ♑	♄-rx, ☽
10	John Tyler	23LE14	♌	☉♈	♃-rx, ♂	♈	♂♌	☉
11	James Polk	25CP07	♑	♄♊-rx	☋	♍	☿♐	♂
12	Zachary Taylor	19CP41	♑	♄♑	♄	♉	♀♑	☽
13	Millard Fillmore	14SA16	♐	♃♊-rx	♂, ♀, ☿	♈	♂♐	
14	Franklin Pierce	3CA15	♋	☽♌	☋	♋	☽♌	☋
15	James Buchanan	21CA19	♋	☽♑		♓	♃♍-rx	
16	Abraham Lincoln	29SA45	♐	♃♓	♄	♌	☉♒	
17	Andrew Johnson	27SC13	♏	♂♎	♄	♋	☽♉	
18	Ulysses Grant	26TA26	♉	♀♓	♄, ♃, ☉	♑	♄♉	
19	Rutherford Hayes	14CA11	♋	☽♊		♏	♂ ♏	♂, ☿
20	James Garfield	26CA39	♋	☽♊		♓	♃♒	
21	Chester Arthur	26LE16	♌	☉♎	♄	♈	♂♍	
22/24	Grover Cleveland	12CA40	♋	☽♌		♏	♂♌	♄, ☋
23	Benjamin Harrison	14PI27	♓	♃♉		♋	☽♏	♀, ☊
25	William McKinley	29LI08	♎	♀♐		♊	☿♒	
26	Theodore Roosevelt	17GE26	♊	☿♏	♃-rx	♎	♀♐	
27	William Howard Taft	10TA36	♉	♀♌	♃	♍	☿♎	☉, ☋
28	Woodrow Wilson	15LI24	♎	♀♒	☋	♒	♄♋-rx	♂, ♀, ☽
29	Warren Harding	14SA14	♐	♃♐	♃	♈	♂♏	☋
30	Calvin Coolidge	3VI50	♍	☿♋		♍	☿♋	
31	Herbert Hoover	2GE06	♊	☿♌		♊	☿♌	
32	Franklin Roosevelt	20VI57	♍	☿♒		♉	♀♒	♄, ♃
33	Harry Truman	9LI06	♎	♀♋	☊	♎	♀♋	☊
34	Dwight Eisenhower	22TA41	♉	♀♐		♑	♄♍	♂
35	John Kennedy	27LI37	♎	♀♊		♊	☿♉	☉, ♀
36	Lyndon Johnson	15LE06	♌	☉♍	♃	♐	♃♌	
37	Richard Nixon	15VI02	♍	☿♑		♑	♄♉-rx	♃, ☉, ☿
38	Gerald Ford	13TA08	♉	♀♊	♂	♍	☿♌	☋
39	Jimmy Carter	22LI05	♎	♀♌	☉	♊	☿♍	
40	Ronald Reagan	6CP08	♑	♄♉	♂, ☿	♑	♄♉	♂, ☿
41	George H.W. Bush	8VI27	♍	☿♉		♍	☿♉	
42	Bill Clinton	11LI07	♎	♀♎	♃, ♂, ♀	♒	♄♌	
43	George W Bush	7LE02	♌	☉♋	♀, ☿	♌	☉♋	♀, ☿
44	Barack Obama	26AQ18	♒	♄♑-rx	☋	♎	♀♋	
45	Donald Trump	15LE59	♌	☉♊	♂	♐	♃♎-rx	☽, ☋
46	Joe Biden	14CP39	♑	♄♊-rx		♉	♀♏	☽

Selected Examples

George Washington: Impact of illness on shape of face

Proposed rectification: 5:40:41 AM, ASC 9AQ36
AA-rated Astrodatabank record: 10:00 AM, ASC 18TA26

George Washington's Ascendant degree is 9AQ36. The rising sign is Aquarius with sign ruler Saturn/Aries. Mercury occupies the Ascendant sign. Since the Ascendant degree is placed in the first rising decan (00AQ00 to 9AQ59), the rising sign and decan are identical.

Measurements taken by sculptor Jean-Antoine Houdon in the fall of 1785, including a plaster cast of Washington's face, are considered the most accurate of surviving images of Washington.

The rising decan model predicts the shape of Washington's face should be the *bony ovate* assigned to Aries, sign placement of the ruler of the rising decan Saturn/Aries. The width of Washington's lower jaw appears at odds with this delineation until one considers Washington's grim countenance is due to discomfort from ill-fitting dentures installed following extensive tooth decay. Saturn signifies the physical structure of dentures with the straight-line shape of Aries corresponding to the horizontal line across the lips. Aries is assigned to the head and upper jaw and Taurus is assigned to the lower jaw and throat. Though GW had dentures in both upper and lower jaws, the Aries-upper jaw connection is sufficient to identify Saturn/Aries as the physiognomy significator for painful dentures resulting in the arrow-like straight line grimace on his face.

Plaster bust made by Jean-Antoine Houdon, 1786.
Source: Photograph by Daderot - Own work, CC0.
https://commons.wikimedia.org/w/index.php?curid=18118977

CHAPTER 3 – PHYSIOGNOMY   47

John Tyler: Modification by planet placement; decan itself predicts shape of face

Proposed rectification: 2:29:37 PM, ASC 23LE14
DD-rated Astrodatabank record of 5:47 AM is a sunrise chart, ASC 6AR25

John Tyler's Ascendant degree is 23LE14. The rising sign is Leo with sign ruler Sun/Aries. Jupiter/Leo-rx and Mars/Leo occupy the Ascendant sign. The Ascendant degree is placed in the 3rd rising decan of Leo assigned to Aries. Mars/Leo is the ruler of the rising decan.

The rising decan model predicts the shape of Tyler's face should be *rectangular* assigned to Leo, sign placement of the ruler of the rising decan Mars/Leo. Instead, Tyler's face matches the bony ovate shape assigned to Aries.

Tyler's shape of the face (and body) is a better match to Aries, the sign of the rising decan, without resorting to the rising decan's ruler. This may occur because Ascendant lord Sun/Aries is placed in the sign of the rising decan. Since the Sun is exalted in Aries, Sun/Aries appears to reinforce the imprint of Aries on physiognomy without recourse to the sign placement of the rising decan's ruler.

Source: Daguerreotype from Brady-Handy Photograph Collection, Library of Congress.
Public Domain image in the United States.
https://loc.gov/pictures/resource/cwpbh.03576/

Harry Truman: Use of rising decan in rectification; choosing correct rising decan

Proposed rectification: 3:53:11 PM, ASC 9LI06
A-rated Astrodatabank record of 4:00 PM, ASC 10LI30

Harry Truman's Ascendant degree is 9LI06. The rising sign is Libra with sign ruler Venus/Cancer. The North Node occupies the Ascendant sign. Compared to the ADB time, the proposed rectification moves the ASC degree from the 2nd decan of Libra (Aquarius) back to the 1st decan of Libra (Libra).

The rising decan model predicts the shape of Truman's face should be *small ovate* assigned to Cancer, sign placement of the ruler of the rising decan Venus/Cancer. This appears accurate. In addition, the smoothness of the skin and a white paste-like color are all Cancer characteristics. See Friedlander (2009, 73) who also classified Truman as a Cancer type.

For the ADB time, the 2nd Aquarius decan of Libra rises with lord Saturn/Gemini. If correct, Saturn/Gemini should give height or some evidence of Saturn's sharp edges on Truman's face. None are present. Nor is there any evidence of the square shape of Aquarius, the sign of the 2nd rising decan.

Small Ovate

Source: Unknown photograph of Truman as US Senator (1934-1944).
Public Domain image in the United States.

George H. W. Bush: Use of rising decan in rectification; choosing correct Ascendant

Proposed rectification: 11:31:05 AM, ASC 8VI27
B-rated Astrodatabank record: 10:30 AM, ASC 26LE36

George Herbert Walker Bush's Ascendant degree is 8VI27. The rising sign is Virgo with sign ruler Mercury/Taurus. Compared to the ADB time, the proposed rectification advances the ASC degree from the 3rd decan of Leo (Aries) to the 1st decan of Virgo (Virgo).

The rising decan model predicts the shape of Bush's face should be *soft rectangular* assigned to Taurus, sign placement of the ruler of the rising decan Mercury/Taurus. This appears accurate.

For the ADB birth time, the 3rd rising decan of Leo is Aries with lord Mars placed in the fixed sign of Aquarius. According to Willner's model, Aquarius produces a square-shaped face. While there are similarities between squares and rectangles for all fixed signs in Willner's model, Aquarius does not appear a match for Bush based on other Aquarius examples I have reviewed. More generally, Bush lacked the charisma common to Leo rising individuals. I rate physiognomy as a decisive tool which favors Virgo over Leo rising for George H. W. Bush's rectification.

Source: By U.S. Congress - Pocket congressional directory, 1969, Public Domain. https://commons.wikimedia.org/w/index.php?curid=56699605

CHAPTER FOUR

NEW Soul

Definition. Traditional astrology modeled the soul in two ways. Both methods are key delineation steps normally conducted once rectification is complete. Yet if it is possible to identify planetary significators for the soul early on, those planets can help fine tune the rectification process.

Victor Soul Model. The victor soul model is an astrological method which attempts to distill the entire horoscope for an individual into a single planet. This planet best describes the person's major passion and life interest often aligned with career and profession. This planet is Porphyry's *kurios*, the *Almutem Figuris* of the Latin West as taught by Robert Zoller, and William Lilly's Lord of the Geniture.

Cognitive Assessment Model. First introduced by Ptolemy as 'Quality of the Mind' in *Tetrabiblos*, what I provisionally name the Cognitive Assessment Model borrows language from contemporary psychology to assess a person's intuitive and mental faculties. Both Plato and Aristotle recognized the importance of describing the soul in this fashion. Plato's soul typology of 'irrational' and 'calculating' is analogous to Aristotle's 'sensitive' and 'rational' soul divisions. Astrologers linked the Moon and Mercury to the irrational/sensitive and calculating/rational soul divisions in a 1:1 correspondence. William Lilly names this model *Manners* in Christian Astrology (1647).

Usefulness in Rectification. Identification of the Victor of the Horoscope early on allows fine tuning of the rectification process. Choice of Firdaria series, relevant transits, and longevity projections benefit from knowing the Victor. The Cognitive Assessment Model's planetary significators are less useful for rectification, per se; though their impact on the soul needs scrutiny vis-à-vis the Victor Soul Model. In rare cases, the Moon's degree range may be fine-tuned by identifying the appropriate bound ruler in the context of the Cognitive Assessment Model.

NEW Evolution of my Thoughts on Astrology of the Soul

In the first three editions of ARM, I presented three compound scoring tables for the (1) Ruler of the Figure, (2) Significators of the Soul, and (3) Killing Planet. The *Ruler of the Figure*, a.k.a. Robert Zoller's *Almutem Figuris* or what Benjamin Dykes now refers to as the *Victor of the Horoscope* is sometimes used in longevity estimates and therefore a needed input for computing the *Arcus Vitae*. *Significators of the Soul* are equivalent to what William Lilly referred to as *Manners* and were included in prior editions for reference only. The *Killing Planet* was computed as a necessary component for the *Arcus Vitae*. Central to each concept is construction of a compound almuten table[7], where a list of significators relevant to the specific topic is tabulated using the 5-4-3-2-1 scoring system based on five levels of essential dignity advocated by some Medieval astrologers. The highest scoring planet is the 'victor' and considered the significator for the topic in question. Ties between two or more planets are possible. But results are unambiguous given numerical assignment of points.

Like some traditional astrologers who have worked with this approach for twenty years now, I have had less than stellar results for computing the *Victor of the Horoscope* using Ibn Ezra's model as taught by Robert Zoller. For the Presidential database, I found Ibn Ezra's model identified the Victor only 37% of the time, a low level of accuracy consistent with other samples I have investigated. In an unpublished ten-year research project, I compared Ibn Ezra's model with Porphyry's criteria for the victor and found Porphyry's guidelines yielded better results. Compared to Ibn Ezra's method, Porphyry's model offers only guidelines and requires some qualitative judgment. ARM 4th edition presents victor models by Ibn Ezra (for continuity) and Porphyry (my current approach).

Unlike the *Victor of the Horoscope* which can be narrowed down to a single planet and tested as a time lord through a variety of techniques against actual life events, compound scoring tables for *Significators of the Soul* result in many permutations of either one planet or planetary pairs. My current approach rejects the compound scoring method and favors evaluating sign and bound rulers of Mercury and the Moon separately. As the bound ruler for the Moon can change frequently during a 24-hour period, in theory it is possible to use this technique to narrow the Moon's possible degree range based on matching the Moon's bound ruler (jointly with Mercury's bound ruler) to lists of behaviors. For ARM 4th edition, I provisionally introduce the phrase *Cognitive Assessment Model* to describe this analytical approach for the Moon and Mercury.

Finally, the Killing Planet's compound scoring tables are retained. I continue to achieve good results with these tables and so cannot entirely throw them out. Al-mubtazz table construction for Killing Planets is presented in Chapter 5.

---

[7] The Arabic term *al-mubtazz* and its Latinized version *almuten* means 'winner.'

Astrological approaches to the Soul[8]

Victor Soul Model. Within traditional astrology, two separate models exist for delineating the soul. The first tradition draws from the *kurios* model of Porphyry, works its way through the *Almutem Figuris* of the Latin West, and concludes with William Lilly's *Lord of the Geniture*. Simply put, this model attempts to distill the entire horoscope for an individual into a single planet. This planet best describes the person's major passion and life interest which is often aligned with career and profession. The linkage between this concept and Plato is indirect. It is possible to link Plato's description of the soul as recounted in Plato's *Myth of Er* with the Neoplatonic philosopher Porphyry's astrological model for matching the horoscopic planet to the daimon referenced in the *Myth of Er*. Compared to the *Cognitive Assessment Model* discussed next, the *Victor Soul Model* has been transmitted unevenly through the western astrological tradition. Ibn Ezra gives an exact formula for computing the planet; Porphyry gives only guidelines which require judgment on a case-by-case basis. Going forward, I have chosen to adopt the term *Victor of the Horoscope* for this planet.

Cognitive Assessment Model. The second approach to the soul was formalized in Ptolemy's *Tetrabiblos* (c. 2nd Century AD) as 'Quality of the Mind.' Compared to the Victor Soul Model, Ptolemy's astrological delineation of the Moon, Mercury, and their rulers remains little changed in the western astrological tradition. Ptolemy's 'Quality of the Mind' is identical to what William Lilly names 'Manners' in *Christian Astrology* (1647 AD). The model derives from Aristotle's tripartite soul model for plants, animals, and humans. Based on the notion that all living things were ensouled, Aristotle argued that plants and animals also had souls, not just humans. Plants are capable of sustaining growth and existence through use of the *vegetative* soul. The animal kingdom's capacity for motion, sensation and desire is sustained through the *sensitive* soul. Finally, the human capacity for reason and judgment is due to the *rational* soul. This system was nested, so that plants had vegetative soul alone, animals had vegetative and sensitive souls, and humans possessed all three soul levels. The following linkage was made between Aristotle's soul model and the horoscope:

Table 7. Correspondences between Aristotle's Soul Levels and Astrological Significators

Living Being	Soul Level	Function	Astrological Significators
Plant	Nutritive	Growth/Reproduction	Ascendant + Ruler
Animal	Sensitive	Locomotion/Perception	Moon + Ruler
Human	Rational	Thought	Mercury + Ruler

---

[8] This section is based in part on *Working Paper – Astrology and the Soul: History and Sources*. Regulus Astrology LLC, 2012.

Implementing the Victor Soul Model

Method I: Ibn Ezra

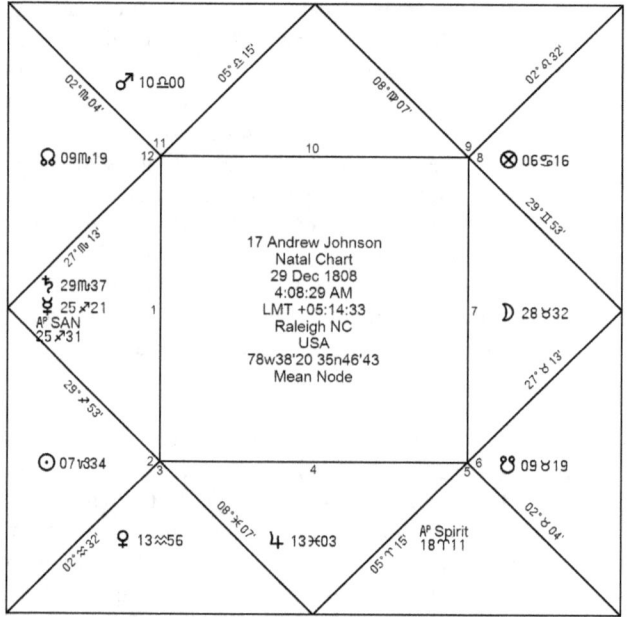

Nativity of Andrew Johnson, Alchabitius houses.

Table 8. Ibn Ezra Victor Model (1507)
In-sect triplicity ruler and triplicity decans

	Position	☉	☽	☿	♀	♂	♃	♄
Sun	07 CP 34		3			4	2	6
Moon	28 TA 32	7			5	2		1
Asc	27 SC 13	1				8		2
Lot of Fortune	06 CA 16		6			5	4	
Syzygy	25 SA 31	1					8	2
Oriental						2	0	3
Houses			6	10	6	3	8	9	12
Score		0	7	27	6	8	29	23	26

Rulership: *sign=5; exaltation=4; in-sect triplicity=3; bound=2; decan/face=1*
Houses: *H1=12; H10=11; H7=10; H4=9; H11=8; H5=7; H2=6; H8=5; H9=4; H3=3; H12=2; H6=1*
House system: *Alchabitius semi-arc with 5-degree offset rule*
Superiors – Oriental: *helical rising to sextile=3; sextile to square=2; square to 1st station=1*

Table 8 presents computations for the Victor of the Horoscope for President Andrew Johnson. This is a model which awards points based on essential dignities of the Sun, Moon, Ascendant, Lot of Fortune, and the Prenatal Syzygy, points for the oriental solar phase of superior planets, and points for house position. The planet with the highest score is the Victor of the Horoscope according to Ibn Ezra.

Since publication of the 3rd edition of ARM, I conducted tests on a total of 12 different variations of Ibn Ezra's model for over 300 horoscopes. I considered both 1507 and 1485/1537 models, the former which awards points for solar phase (shown below) and the latter which awards points for the planetary day and hour ruler (prior ARM editions). I computed house position by Whole Sign and Alchabitius semi-arc house systems and considered two decan systems: Chaldean and Triplicity. Finally, unlike prior ARM editions which awarded 3 points for each triplicity ruler, I limited awarding points to the first triplicity ruler as suggested by Dykes (Hermann of Carinthia, 2011). Of the twelve models tested, the following parameter choices yielded the best results:

- Ibn Ezra 1507 model (solar phase for superior planets)
- In-sect triplicity ruler
- Triplicity Decans
- Alchabitius semi-arc house system with 5-degree offset rule.

Choice of quadrant houses over whole sign houses yielded only marginally better results which are unlikely to be statistically significant.

Debate on the Merit of Victor Tables

After experimenting with victor tables in the last twenty years, I join skeptical voices within practicing traditional astrologers on the efficacy of this method which proliferated at the end of the Medieval period. As early as 2007, Dykes raised two questions (Bonatti, 2007, lxxxiv – lxxxvi):

1. Do planets each receive a score of +1 or should the 5-4-3-2-1 scaled system be applied where planets in their own sign are assigned +5; exaltation, +4; etc.,?

2. Is the al-mubtazz approach intended for multiple significators or is the method intended for single planets or points? Based on the rarity of compound al-mubtazz tables in Bonatti's *Book of Astronomy* and other sources, Dykes questions whether certain medieval astrologers used the technique.

The more common complaint reserved for Ibn Ezra's victor model is the lumping of essential dignities ("quality") and house position ("quantity") into a single numerical model. Why? Because it is impossible to compute a single numerical value for items unequal in function or importance, e.g., one cannot add 5 apples and 3 oranges and say the result is 8 'appanges.'

Method II: Porphyry's Expanded Criteria

The primary difference between Ibn Ezra and Porphyry's method for determining the Victor of the Horoscope is Porphyry's guidelines to break the process into two stages: (1) identify possible candidates and (2) rank the candidates. In this way, Porphyry avoids criticism levied at Ibn Ezra's approach which lumps both *quality* and *quantity* ratings into a single numerical score.

Stage I: Identify candidates for the Victor[9]

MC – Sign ruler of the MC if ruler is angular
MC – Planet positioned near MC degree
MC – Planet next carried to MC degree by primary motion
ASC – Sign ruler
ASC – Planet in ASC sign and bound
Moon – Sign ruler
LOF – Sign ruler
SAN – Bound ruler
Planets rising, setting, or stationing within 7 days of birth

Stage II: Rank candidates

Solar phase
Essential dignities
House position
Reception

Finally, luminaries are not candidates for the Victor in Porphyry's model. Instead, their relationship with the Victor is used as a criterion for eminence. Specifically, when the Victor receives the sect light and is the same planet used as the longevity significator (see Chapter 5, Al-kadukhadāh), eminence is predicted.

Operationalizing tests of Porphyry's Model. When designing templates to identify and rank victor candidates, one of the first things I noticed was Porphyry's instruction to consider only the bound rulership of the SAN whereas sign rulership was considered for all other candidates. I speculate that Porphyry's choice of bound for the SAN may have been motivated by more accurate astronomical observations for the SAN relative to other significators, e.g., it might have been more difficult to reliably determine the bound placement for the ASC, MC, Moon, and LOF when compared to the SAN. For this and other reasons, I chose to cast my net wide by allowing greater freedom in choosing victor candidates. I considered planets positioned in any degree of the whole sign for the ASC and MC as well as sign, bound, and dwad rulership for each of the

---

[9] Schmidt and Holden offer slightly different translations of Porphyry's text. See Schmidt (2009) and Porphyry (2009). What follows is my own distillation of both translations.

significators to which I added the Lot of Spirit. In addition to steps listed for ranking, I added angularity relative to the Lots of Fortune and Spirit, whether the Moon separated from or applied to the victor candidate, configuration with the Lunar Nodes, and whether the candidate was the day or hour ruler.

Tentative Research findings[10]. Factors which favor a planet as victor:

Stage I: sign rulership (as expected)
Stage I: bound rulership (for all significators, not just SANS, as suspected)
Stage I: planets positioned in ASC or MC whole sign house (as expected)
Stage II: planets angular to the ASC (as expected)
Stage II: planets to which the Moon applies (as suspected)
Stage II: planets conjunct the North Node (as suspected)

Surprisingly, whether a planet was oriental or occidental of the Sun had no bearing on whether the planet was the Victor. Also surprising was the inconsistent importance of essential dignities for the Victor of the Horoscope.

Perhaps the biggest surprise was the ability of the Victor of the Horoscope to identify key life periods based on its rulership of Firdaria Major or Minor time periods. These results were at least as, and sometimes better, than results for peak career periods predicted by Zodiacal Releasing. This result was so consistent it has now changed how I use Firdaria as a Stage I rectification tool.

Victor Results for American Presidents. Presented in Table 9 are quantitative results for Ibn Ezra's model and qualitative results for Porphyry's model for the Victor of the Horoscope. For the sample of 46 Presidents, Ibn Ezra's formula agreed with my assessment of Porphyry's model for only 17 or 37% of the sample. Since there is roughly a 20% chance for any of the five planets (Mercury, Venus, Mars, Jupiter, Saturn) to be the victor; these findings for Ibn Ezra's model are only slightly better than chance. As discussed in the Presidential database, reasonable people may disagree on my choices for Victor of the Horoscope. Mars/Libra or Saturn/Scorpio for Andrew Johnson; Mars/Gemini-rx or Jupiter/Taurus for Franklin Roosevelt; and Mercury/Virgo or Jupiter/Leo for Lyndon Johnson are easily debated. Even if a few of my choices are incorrect (likely), it is unlikely that enough of my victor choices using Porphyry's approach will be overturned necessary to rescue the poor performance of Ibn Ezra's model.

Presentation in the Presidential Database. Each Presidential entry includes two choices for the Victor Soul Model: (1) the Ibn Ezra approach as presented in Table 8 for Andrew Johnson and (2) Porphyry's Expanded criteria which includes a list of attributes considered when choosing the victor.

---

[10] Regulus Astrology LLC, *Reclaiming the Soul in Traditional Astrology*, presentation for the Astrological Society of Princeton, January 8, 2022.

Table 9. Victor Soul Model

	President	Ibn Ezra	Porphyry	Agree
1	G. Washington	♀/♓	♂/♏	
2	J. Adams	♄/♉-rx	♄/♉-rx	*
3	T. Jefferson	♄/♌-rx	♄/♌-rx	*
4	J. Madison	♂/♑	♂/♑	*
5	J. Monroe	♄/♓	♃/♐-rx	
6	J. Q. Adams	♀/♍	♃/♍	
7	A. Jackson	♀/♈	♂/♉	
8	M. van Buren	♃/♑	♃/♑	*
9	W. Harrison	☿/♑	♂/♋-rx	
10	J. Tyler	☿/♓	♂/♌	
11	J. Polk	♀/♏	♀/♏	*
12	Z. Taylor	♂/♏	♂/♏	*
13	M. Fillmore	♂/♐, ☿/♐	♃/♊-rx	
14	F. Pierce	♃/♏	♃/♏	*
15	J. Buchanan	♀/♊	♃/♍-rx	
16	A. Lincoln	♂/♎	♂/♎	*
17	A. Johnson	♂/♎	♄/♏	
18	U. Grant	♀/♓	♄/♉	
19	R. Hayes	♂/♏, ☿/♏	♃/♊-rx	
20	J. Garfield	♂/♏	♄/♍	
21	C. Arthur	☿/♏	♂/♍	
22/24	G. Cleveland	♃/♌-rx	♂/♌	
23	B. Harrison	♃/♉	♂/♍	
25	W. McKinley	♂/♏	♃/♒	
26	T. Roosevelt	♂/♑	♂/♑	*
27	W. Taft	♃/♉-rx	♃/♉-rx	*
28	W. Wilson	♄/♋-rx, ☿/♑	♃/♈	
29	W. Harding	♀/♎	♀/♎	*
30	C. Coolidge	☿/♋	☿/♋	*
31	H. Hoover	☿/♌	♄/♒-rx	
32	F. Roosevelt	♂/♊-rx	♃/♉	
33	H. Truman	♀/♋	♂/♌	
34	D. Eisenhower	♀/♐	♃/♒	
35	J. Kennedy	☿/♉	♃/♉	
36	L. Johnson	☿/♍	☿/♍	*
37	R. Nixon	♄/♉-rx, ♂/♐	♀/♓	
38	G. Ford	♃/♑-rx	♃/♑-rx	*
39	J. Carter	♄/♏	♀/♌	
40	R. Reagan	♄/♉	♂/♑	
41	G. H. W. Bush	☿/♉	☿/♉	*
42	B. Clinton	♄/♌	♃/♎	
43	G. W. Bush	♀/♌	♀/♌	*
44	B. Obama	☿/♌	♃/♒-rx	
45	D. Trump	♄/♋	♃/♎-rx	
46	J. Biden	♀/♏	♀/♏	*

Implementing the Cognitive Assessment Model

In the chapter heading *Of the Quality of the Soul*, Ptolemy introduces a set of guidelines for judging the soul. After considering modality, sect, solar phase, house position, dignity, and aspect; he devotes the bulk of the chapter to descriptions of the soul based on lists sorted by planets which have dominion over the Moon and Mercury (Ptolemy, 1940, III.13). What Ptolemy means by 'dominion' is not explicitly stated. Many medieval astrologers implementing Ptolemy's guidelines have used tables which tally points for rulers of the Ascendant, Moon, and Mercury. Included in ARM editions 1-3 were tables labeled as *Significators of the Soul* which evaluated the Ascendant, Moon, and Mercury by the standard medieval 5-4-3-2-1 point system.

Al-mubtazz Table for George Washington[11]:

		☉	☽	☿	♀	♂	♃	♄	Al-mubtazz
ASC	9AQ01			3	2		3	5,3,1	♄
☽	14CP24	3			3,2,1	4,3		5	♂
☿	6AQ24			3,2			3	5,3,1	♄

Computing this table makes many assumptions. Most important is the planet which has the highest total score of essential dignities for the significator's specific degree has 'dominion' over that significator. For Washington, Mars has dominion over the Moon; Saturn has dominion over the Ascendant and Mercury. Some authors summed the entire table without the individual significator breakdown as shown above.

Uselessness of Victor Tables

Beyond problems already cited for victor tables, victor tables for implementing Ptolemy's soul model have this additional flaw:

When two planets have dominion over the Moon and Mercury, there is no 1:1 correspondence between the two planets and the Moon and Mercury. Taking Washington as an example, Mars has dominion over the Moon; Saturn has dominion over Mercury. We refer to Ptolemy's descriptions for Saturn-Mars to describe Washington's soul. But! What if the rulership occurs in the reverse order so that Saturn has dominion over the Moon and Mars has dominion over Mercury? We use Ptolemy's identical list for Saturn-Mars. But wait! Since the Moon signifies intuition and Mercury signifies reason, wouldn't delineation of the soul differ if these rulers were reassigned to the other respective planet? *Certainly so!* The failure of this approach to make such a distinction is indicative of its sloppy construction.

---

[11] For the revised rectification of ASC 9AQ36 in the 4th edition, computations are the same.

Rip off the Bandaid: What are really delineating in Ptolemy's Soul Model?

Sometimes another author provides a better description of the method than the original proponent of the technique. Here is what Kūshyār Ibn Labbān has to say:

The conditions of the soul are divided into that which is intellectual and that which is moral. As for the intellectual, Mercury is in charge of it; as for the moral, the Moon is in charge of it. Thus according to the strength or weakness of the two planets and their beneficence and maleficence there occur condition in these two matters, so that a man is between the intelligent man and the prophet <on one side> and the ignorant and the fool <on the other> (Labbān 1997, 183).

Table 10: Kūshyār Ibn Labbān's rating method for the Moon and Mercury.

	Intellect - Mercury	Morality - Moon
Bonified	Intelligent	Prophet
Maltreated	Ignorant	Fool

Simply put, how well bonified or how poorly maltreated are Mercury and the Moon determines where a natal horoscope falls on this four-quadrant table. The result is how the soul is judged according to Ptolemy's soul model. Implied in this approach is separate treatment for the Moon and Mercury, a choice I agree with. And as implied here, a straight-up Hellenistic delineation of how many ways the Moon and Mercury are bonified or maltreated may give us a more consistent way of evaluating the Ptolemy's soul model rather than clumsy attempts with victor tables. Note the absence of the Ascendant in Labbān's statement. Perhaps the Ascendant need not be considered for assessing the soul. Perhaps the Ascendant should be reserved for temperament models as the way to assess qualities of hot, cold, wet, and dry as inputs for medical astrology.

Why the term Cognitive Assessment Model? Truth be told in my initial 4th edition revision, I went so far as to rename the Victor Soul Model the "Platonic Soul Model" and Ptolemy's Soul Model the "Aristotelian Soul Model" based on linkages cited earlier. That is, until I reread the first nine chapters of Plato's Republic presented prior to the Myth of Er. It turns out Plato also proposed the soul be divided into 'irrational' and 'calculating' portions in a manner similar to Aristotle's 'sensitive' and 'rational' soul divisions (Plato, Book IV, section 439d). So Aristotle does not hold the monopoly on this method of soul classification. My provisional choice of 'Cognitive Assessment Model' reflects contemporary psychological parlance for the scope of Ptolemy's original model. In practice, what this model does is to delineate the Moon and Mercury as significators for the strength/weakness of a person's intuitive and mental faculties. Lilly named this delineation 'manners.' Contemporary job recruiters screen and classify job applicants with these parameters in mind.

Findings

Ptolemy's original soul model has many permutations:

Saturn, Saturn-Jupiter, Saturn-Mars, Saturn-Venus, Saturn-Mercury;
Jupiter, Jupiter-Mars, Jupiter-Venus, Jupiter-Mercury;
Mars, Mars-Venus, Mars-Mercury; Venus, Venus-Mercury; Mercury.

Each of these single planets or planetary pairs has its own laundry list of descriptions for the soul many of which are difficult to confirm based on known biographical details or subject to confirmation bias if small but rare personality traits are taken out of context. Because of this subjectivity in variable measurement, I rate the odds of developing successful statistical tests for the Cognitive Assessment Model based on Ptolemy's list of single planets or planetary pairs as very low.

Nevertheless the following qualitative observations should prove useful:

- Porphyry's guidelines disallow either luminary to be Victor of the Horoscope. Follow the same rule. Should either Sun or Moon be the ruler for Moon or Mercury, choose the Sun or Moon's bound ruler for the relevant planetary significator rather than the Sun or Moon directly.

- Replace compound almuten tables with two simple lists for the Moon and Mercury's sign and bound rulers. Keep these lists separate.

- Sign rulers often register a first impression of manners; bound rulers are more subtle and may take further inquiry to assess their influence or presence.

- When sign and bound rulers of the Moon and Mercury are identical, outward appearance matches internal design, e.g., what you see is what you get.

- When sign and bound rulers differ; especially if one set are benefics and another is malefic, outward appearance does not and may have no bearing on internal design, e.g., the true character of the person cannot be judged on first impression or even after a few meetings.

- The Moon's configuration is important, especially the planet to which the Moon applies. As demonstrated in Chapter 7 *Temporal Indicators*, the Moon's configuration delineates a significant life pattern which I suggest also impresses itself upon the native's manners.

- Fixed stars show promise in determining whether the native is good or evil. Consider whether benefic or malefic stars are co-present with bound rulers, sign rulers, the Moon, and Mercury for this delineation.

Table 11. Cognitive Assessment Model: Rulers of the Moon and Mercury

	President	Moon	Mercury	Sign rulers		Bound rulers	
1	G. Washington	14CP23	6AQ24	♄	♄	♀	☿
2	J. Adams	25AR53	28SC16	♂	♂	♄	♄
3	T. Jefferson	13SA28	26PI54	♃	♃	♀	♂
4	J. Madison	22SC50	29AQ32	♂	♄	♃	♄
5	J. Monroe	7CP40	21TA54	♄	♀	♃	♃
6	J. Q. Adams	20CP23	9LE56	♄	☉=>♃	♀	♀
7	A. Jackson	24VI01	3AR32	☿	♂	♂	♃
8	M. van Buren	25SA28	24SC25	♃	♂	♄	♄
9	W. Harrison	17VI18	28CP11	☿	♄	♃	♂
10	J. Tyler	27VI33	13PI55	☿	♃	♂	♃
11	J. Polk	27CA53	1SA20	☽=>♄	♃	♄	♃
12	Z. Taylor	3TA47	29SC02	♀	♂	♀	♄
13	M. Fillmore	5GE24	26SA18	☿	♃	☿	♂
14	F. Pierce	29LE04	29SC44	☉=>♃	♂	♂	♄
15	J. Buchanan	11CP48	14TA12	♄	♀	♃	♃
16	A. Lincoln	25CP11	10PI06	♄	♃	♄	♀
17	A. Johnson	28TA32	25SA21	♀	♃	♂	♄
18	U. Grant	26CA29	18AR31	☽=>♄	♂	♄	☿
19	R. Hayes	8GE35	4SC58	☿	♂	♃	♂
20	J. Garfield	1GE26	00SA50	☿	♃	☿	♃
21	C. Arthur	3CP15	7SC03	♄	♂	☿	♀
22/24	G. Cleveland	17LE18	5PI12	☉=>♂	♃	♄	♀
23	B. Harrison	12SC25	1VI09	♂	☿	☿	☿
25	W. McKinley	6AQ32	28AQ04	♄	♄	☿	♄
26	T. Roosevelt	16CA34	2SC55	☽=>☿	♂	☿	♂
27	W. Taft	27LE38	16LI38	☉=>♂	♀	♂	♃
28	W. Wilson	00AQ45	18CP46	♄	♄	☿	♀
29	W. Harding	00TA08	17SC36	♀	♂	♀	☿
30	C. Coolidge	29GE45	23CA55	☿	☽=>♄	♄	♃
31	H. Hoover	7LE12	00LE01	☉=>☿	☉=>☿	♀	♃
32	F. Roosevelt	6CA08	27AQ10	☽=>♂	♄	♂	♄
33	H. Truman	4SC56	1GE16	♂	☿	♂	☿
34	D. Eisenhower	4SC33	3LI34	♂	♀	♂	♄
35	J. Kennedy	17VI32	20TA35	☿	♀	♃	♃
36	L. Johnson	9VI04	10VI18	☿	☿	♀	♀
37	R. Nixon	20AQ01	00CP00	♄	♄	♂	☿
38	G. Ford	3SA55	16LE08	♃	☉=>♃	♃	♄
39	J. Carter	13SC36	21VI10	♂	☿	☿	♂
40	R. Reagan	14TA05	21CP33	♀	♄	♃	♀
41	G. H. W. Bush	17LI47	29TA23	♀	♀	♃	♂
42	B. Clinton	20TA33	7LE37	♀	☉=>♂	♃	♀
43	G. W. Bush	16LI42	9LE49	♀	☉=>☿	♃	♀
44	B. Obama	3GE36	2LE22	☿	☉=>♄	☿	♃
45	D. Trump	20SA37	8CA45	♃	☽=>☿	☿	♀
46	J. Biden	2TA36	21SC44	♀	♂	♀	♃

Note: (1) When the sign ruler is either Sun or Moon, the respective bound lord of the Sun or Moon is substituted for the sign ruler, e.g., ☉=>♃. (2) Shaded boxes indicate when sign and bound rulers are identical for the Moon and Mercury.

Selected Examples

George Washington: When Bound rulers differ from Sign rulers

Planet	Degree	Sign Ruler	Bound Ruler
☽	14CP23	♄	♀
☿	6AQ24	♄	☿

Based on sign rulers, Saturn alone is the significator for the Cognitive Assessment Model. Physiognomy informs us that Saturn/Aries is responsible for the grimace Washington wears on his face on account of ill-fitting dentures. If Saturn/Aries alone, we would expect meetings with Washington to be frosty, austere sessions, and laced with anti-British remarks since mundane choreography rules assign Britain to Aries. Actual accounts of meetings with Washington at Mount Vernon differ with Washington entertaining in the high style of a Virginia planter (Venus/Pisces) offering up learned conversations about real estate, business opportunities, and wartime intelligence (Mercury/Aquarius). Without the bound rulers, we would not anticipate this type of social engagement at Mount Vernon.

James Monroe: When Bound rulers better signify morality than Sign rulers

Planet	Degree	Sign Ruler	Bound Ruler
☽	7CP40	♄	♃
☿	21TA54	♀	♃

In describing his colleague James Monroe, Thomas Jefferson is reported to have said that "if you turned his soul inside out there would not be a spot on it." Based on sign rulers, Saturn and Venus are planetary significators for the soul. Testimony of the bound rulers is different with Jupiter alone the significator. Jefferson's comment suggests Jupiter/Sagittarius-rx as the greater benefic is the better significator for the Cognitive Assessment Model.

James Polk: When Bound rulers are identical to Sign rulers

Planet	Degree	Sign Ruler	Bound Ruler
☽	27CA53	☽ => ♄	♄
☿	1SA20	♃	♃

Polk is an example where sign and bound rulers yield identical significators. If correct, then Polk's public manner should be identical to his private manner. Polk is described as an introvert with few friends who nevertheless forced himself to interact with others and was well-liked. Polk is one of the few Presidents who outlined his goals, achieved them, and died shortly after leaving office. Polk had no ulterior political motives which appears a delineation match to 'what you see is what you get.'

Richard Nixon: When Victor and Cognitive Assessment Models differ

Planet	Degree	Sign Ruler	Bound Ruler
☽	20AQ01	♄	♂
☿	00CP00	♄	☿

For many historians, Nixon remains an enigma. How is it possible that a man who ushered in détente with China and Russia was simultaneously unraveling on the domestic front with Watergate? How could a man who successfully drew down US South Vietnam military deployments from over 500,000 in 1968 when he took office to negligible levels when he left office in 1974 be at such odds with anti-war activists during his Presidency?

The negotiation strategy of détente, or peace negotiations generally, is a delineation match to Venus/Pisces placed in the 7th house of open enemies and legal disputes. I favor Venus/Pisces as the Victor of the Horoscope citing Nixon's longevity of 82 years a match to Venus' major years and the ability of Venus as Major and Minor Firdaria rulers to outline key career milestones.

But! *And this is the key But!* the Cognitive Assessment Model gives much different results. Saturn rules both Moon and Mercury by sign, is the planet to which the Moon applies, and overcomes the Moon at the superior square. Saturn/Taurus-rx functions like Saturn/Scorpio in the opposite sign which signifies paranoia over national security concerns which sabotaged Nixon's Presidency. "National security" are words Nixon used repeatedly in the last year of his presidency (Woodward and Bernstein, 1976). Nixon believed his tapes would never be released because of national security concerns.

As cognitive significators, bound lords Mars and Mercury are linked to lying, deceit, and criminal activity. Nixon's secret negotiations with South Vietnam via back-channel Anna Chennault were purposely designed to thwart a peace deal under negotiation by the LBJ administration in 1968 prior to the November 1968 election contest. Nixon wanted credit for the peace deal himself and was willing to subvert peace negotiations by elongating the war until after the 1968 election. He achieved that objective.

Among American Presidents, the horoscope of Richard Nixon offers an excellent example of the interplay between the two soul models described in this chapter. The main takeaway is to distinguish what each model offers on its own and not try to force a round peg into a square hole. For Nixon this means not to gloss over his heavy-handed use of Presidential power while elevating Nixon as peacemaker. It also means not to ignore his successful opening of China and Vietnam troop drawdown despite the fact he operated the White House as a criminal enterprise.

George W. Bush. When Victor and Cognitive Assessment Models differ

Planet	Degree	Sign Ruler	Bound Ruler
☽	16LI42	♀	♃
☿	9LE49	☉ => ☿	♀

While at Yale, Bush was a cheerleader. He was also a successful business promoter with the Texas Rangers professional baseball team his best effort. Promotion and marketing is signified by Venus-Mercury as sign rulers of the Moon and Mercury.

Operation Iraqi Freedom was driven by Bush's desire to grant the Iraqi people freedom from the dictatorship of Saddam Hussein. Without the Jupiterian influence on planetary significators via bound rulership of the Moon, Bush's desire to promulgate Operation Iraqi Freedom is less obvious unless we peel back the sign rulers and examine the bound rulers.

Donald Trump: How the Moon's degree position can be narrowed by its bound position in the context of the Cognitive Assessment Model.

Planet	Degree	Sign Ruler	Bound Ruler
☽	20SA37	♃	☿
☿	8CA45	☽ => ☿	♀

With Mercury in the sign of Cancer, instead of taking the Moon as Mercury's sign ruler, substitute the Moon's bound ruler – Mercury.

Donald Trump's horoscope is one of the few examples where the Moon's bound position differs for the ARM proposed rectification when compared to Astrodatabank. As such, the Cognitive Assessment Model is useful for refining the Moon's position for rectification purposes.

For the AA-rated birthtime of 10:54 AM, the Moon's degree is 21SA12 placed in the bound of Saturn. The ARM 4th edition proposed rectification of 9:42:46 AM places the Moon's degree at 20SA37 in the bound of Mercury. As Moon placed in the bound of Saturn is associated with depression, the reported Moon's position is unlikely. If this observation is correct, then the Moon's degree range cannot be in the bound of Saturn/Sagittarius (21deg 00min to 25deg 59min).

Usefulness in Rectification

Victor Soul Model

Delineation of the soul usually occurs once a rectification is complete as some inputs for the soul depend on an exact birth time. Nevertheless, if the *Victor of the Horoscope* can be identified early on, then the rectification process can be fine-tuned with better results.

Firdaria. Major life events will occur when the *Victor of the Horoscope* is either the major or minor Firdaria ruler. The same can be said for Firdaria periods ruled by either luminary if the Sun or Moon is placed in the bound of the victor. As choice of Firdaria series requires knowing only whether the horoscope is diurnal or nocturnal, it is a very robust rectification step. Identifying the victor increases odds of choosing the correct diurnal or nocturnal Firdaria time lord series.

Transits. Once the *Victor of the Horoscope* is determined, transits will prove helpful in confirming signs for the ASC, MC, Lot of Fortune, and Lot of Spirit. At least some major life events will be timed by transits of the Victor to the exact degree of these four significators OR to the 10th position from one of these significators. Likewise, transits of the victor to the ASC or MC which do NOT coincide with major life events suggests either the Victor choice is incorrect or the rectification is wrong.

Arcus Vitae. As an alternative to the al-kadukhadāh (see Chapter 5).

Cognitive Assessment Model

If there is a question over which bound the Moon resides, competing bound rulers may offer guidance to the Moon's degree in the context of the Cognitive Assessment Model. This technique may be useful when there is no birth time available. For birth times which are generally accurate and only need fine tuning, it is unlikely this technique will be relevant as a rectification tool.

The better application is understanding the interplay of both soul models. Especially for cases like Richard Nixon when they give different results. Given the usefulness of the *Victor of the Horoscope* in refining rectification results, one does not want to make the mistake of improperly classifying a planet as the Victor of the Horoscope when in fact that planet may be better modeled as one of the planetary significators in the second Cognitive Assessment Model.

CHAPTER FIVE

Longevity

Current ethical standards prohibit the forecast of death for a living individual. Nevertheless, understanding the hīlāj-killing planet model is of great significance for accurate delineation and prediction of incidents of illness for the living. In this regard, the material has practical value for the contemporary practicing astrologer.

Chapter Summary

Definitions and Basic Framework. The following terms are defined: hīlāj, al-kadukhadāh, killing planet, arcus vitae, and al-mubtazz table.

The Hīlāj. Basic principles for choice of hīlāj are presented. The recommended checklist includes contributions from both Alchabitius and Bonatti.

The Al-kadukhadāh. A recommended al-kadukhadāh computation model is presented. Empirical findings from the Presidential Database are compared to the model and demonstrate many variations and exceptions. Compared to theory, the most important finding appears to be the contribution of a planet's major years even when the al-kadukhadāh falls in a succedent or cadent house. *NEW* Unlike major years, middle years have no theoretical basis and do not appear relevant in modifying a planet's major years to fine tune longevity projections.

Constructing Al-mubtazz Tables: Nuts and Bolts. The Al-mubtazz Table assigns points to multiple significators to determine which planet is the most relevant significator for a specific life activity. Tables are constructed for the Killing Planet.

The Arcus Vitae. The arc of direction which joins the hīlāj and the killing planet nearest to the al-kadukhadāh longevity projection is the arcus vitae, or *arc of life*. The modus operandi is primary directions, for which a brief outline is given. Among the more interesting findings is support for the ability of sextile and trine aspects to kill, the dominance of 8th house resident Nodes as killers, the accuracy of both Ptolemy and Regiomontanus methods for interplanetary directions, and a negligible ability for solar arc directions to time death.

!WARNING!

The techniques described in this section are among the most powerful and revered in Medieval Predictive Astrology. They are also dangerous in the hands of the inexperienced and dilettante. Study of these techniques may lead one to contemplate one's own longevity and that of family members and friends. For those new to the study of astrology this is not recommended without serious study of the subject, meditation, and consultation with one's religious or spiritual advisors. These techniques are not foolproof and do not work in all cases. It is easy to make a mistake, especially if studying them for the first time. Yet they are not tricks or parlor games. Those readers not comfortable with ramifications of the arcus vitae should skip this chapter.

For those that continue, treat this subject in accordance with the respect it deserves. The passing of a President, especially if death occurs during an active term, is a time of national mourning. You are advised to recall that millions of people have grieved over the events you are about to study. Above all remember that natal charts signify the lives of real people who have walked this earth and left their mark. Putting yourself in the shoes of a forensic medical professional as he prepares to make his first incision is an appropriate image to consider.

=============

Introduction

It may strike the reader that discussing the primary direction which times death in a chapter on delineation is out of place. Yet the arcus vitae is not just any direction. It is a direction which joins the hīlāj ('giver of life') to the killing planet after the native's longevity projection has expired. The longevity measure is known as the al-kadukhadāh ('giver of years'). To compute the arcus vitae correctly, it is necessary to first identify the hīlāj, the killing planet, and the al-kadukhadāh. All these preliminary steps require delineation.

<u>Controversy and Practical Application</u>. The arcus vitae ("arc of life") is a mathematical computation of life expectancy which directs the killing planet to the hīlāj by primary direction. Because this technique is greatly revered by medieval predictive astrologers, it demands full treatment in any rectification study. Ever so today, the arcus vitae functions as a lightning rod in the free-will/deterministic debate for its stark assumption that one's death can be computed by a mathematical equation.

Importance in Rectification. Some traditional rectifications have been based solely on the arcus vitae. Anybody can claim to rectify a chart with one measurement and in some cases achieve great accuracy. While I highlight the arcus vitae in this chapter, it is one of many directions used in this study to compute a rectified birth time.

Limits to Theory. Nor do I claim the ability to predict the arcus vitae for any individual in advance with absolute certainty. The results I present here have been computed as ex-post exercises which demonstrate the proper application of astrological technique. Why the difficulty in the technique's ex-ante accuracy? Though the theory works fairly well, there remain several holes in it. For example, suppose one selected the Moon as hīlāj and Mars as the killing planet. In practice, one might find the Ascendant, not the Moon, is the actual significator attacked at death. And instead of Mars as the killing planet, it's possible to find either Mars' ruler or a planet aspecting Mars as the actual killer. The discrepancy between *actual* versus *theoretical* hīlāj's and killing planets introduce permutations which are further multiplied by the inclusion of converse as well as direct primary directions. The bottom line is there may be multiple directions within a five to ten-year period that can be considered as the ex-ante arcus vitae.

Natal figures subject to Mundane forces. Because natal charts are subject to mundane figures for cities, states, countries, and the world; death from war, famine, or natural disasters can supersede longevity measures based purely on natal techniques. One cannot live out his full lifespan if he is swallowed into the earth during an earthquake.

Ethics. Even if I could rule out mundane influences and accurately predict death to a specific time period, I would not make such a prediction publicly for ethical reasons. Why? Words have great power and a public prediction may cause death in accordance with the prediction. This is unethical and is the position taken by most if not all Codes of Ethics issued by contemporary astrological organizations.

Usefulness in Timing Illness. With this ethical dilemma, why study the arcus vitae method at all? Because during a single lifespan, there may be as many as 20 or 25 directions of various killing planets to the hīlāj or Ascendant, only one of which times death. The others time illnesses and other impediments to the physical body. Their identification and prediction are of great interest to both the practicing astrologer and client who, working as a team, may select remedies or agree on lifestyle changes which may help to ameliorate any potential medical problems in advance.

Definitions

<u>Hīlāj, Haylag, Hyleg, Apheta</u>. Hīlāj means *Giver of Life* and is the planet or point from which one's life journey begins.

The hīlāj is a sensitive point for health. When attacked dynamically by malefics or killing planets, illness or death results. Suppose the hīlāj is the Moon. Every time Mars afflicts the Moon there will be some type of illness or physical stress because it is the nature of Mars to generate heat and anger which can manifest as fevers or discord. If not for male natives, then these Mars-signified effects occur for other Moon-signified persons in the native's life such as mother, wife, or daughter.

Not all natal figures have a hīlāj. Those that don't fall into categories Bonatti labels as the first, second, and third species or distinction (Bonatti 2007, 1123). They correspond to babies born dead, those which cannot be nourished, and those who do not survive childhood. Figures with both a hīlāj and al-kadukhadāh are classified by Bonatti as the fourth species. They are the focus of this study.

<u>Al-kadukhadāh, Kadhudah, Alcocoden</u>. Al-kadukhadāh means *Giver of Years* and corresponds to the primary measure of longevity established at birth.

The al-kadukhadāh is a *ballpark* number, easily off by 3-5 years even if calculated correctly. Compared to the choice of hīlāj for which differences among authors are relatively minor; there is a much wider difference of opinion on calculation of the al-kadukhadāh. In empirical testing, it shows many departures from theory and requires frequent judgment calls. The previously computed *Victor of the Horoscope* sometimes functions as the al-kadukhadāh though no rules exist which seek an order of preference for either significator.

<u>Killing Planet, Anareta, Cutter, Significator of Death</u>. The killing planet signifies the planet which causes death.

The killing planet is the planet which is most conducive to causing illness and death. It may be any planet in the figure, whether or not the planet exercises dominion on the 4th or 8th houses by position or rulership. Even luminaries under certain conditions can cause illness and death. There also may be more than one killer. Calculation of killing planets is made using an al-mubtazz table.

<u>Arcus Vitae</u>. The *Arc of Life* predicts the date of death by directing the killing planet or one of its aspects to the hīlāj using primary directions.

During a single lifespan, there are many different directions of the killing planet to the hīlāj. In youth these directions yield illness not death. Once the al-kadukhadāh longevity projection has expired, the next computed arcus vitae is considered the theoretical ex-ante arcus vitae.

HĪLĀJ

Rules for choosing the Hīlāj vary yet bear some common principles. They are:

- Of the five possible hīlāj's: Sun, Moon, Lot of Fortune, Ascendant, SAN; the luminaries are preferred. As one moves down the list from the luminaries to the SAN the life force weakens. If there is no hīlāj, the infant will not survive childhood. *NEW* The only exception to prioritization of luminaries are horoscopes when the SAN is also an eclipse. Based on recent research, for these cases the SAN takes priority over other possible hīlāj candidates.

- Sect is important. Sun is preferred in diurnal nativities; Moon for nocturnal.

- Position is important. Ptolemy calls these places *hīlājical positions*. The hīlāj is required to be in angular or succedent house. Cadent houses are inappropriate positions for the hīlāj. The Sun in the 9th and the Moon in the 3rd are the only exceptions to the cadent rule. This is because the Sun and Moon are in their respective houses of joy, a minor dignity.

- Sign sex is important for the luminaries. Sun is preferred as hīlāj when in either masculine signs or in masculine quadrants. The two masculine quadrants are the 10-11-12th houses and the 4-5-6th houses; also known as the two *oriental* quadrants. Likewise the Moon is preferred as hīlāj when in either feminine signs or feminine quadrants. Feminine quadrants are the 1-2-3rd houses and the 7-8-9th houses; also known as the two *occidental* quadrants. Sex is ignored when considering the Ascendant, Lot of Fortune, or SAN as a potential hīlāj.

- The hīlāj must be aspected by one of its rulers, ideally the al-kadukhadāh. When this condition is not met the tentative hīlāj is rejected and one moves down the hierarchy of possible hīlāj's until one finds a candidate that aspects the al-kadukhadāh.

It's been my experience that both Ptolemy, who limits hīlājical positions to the 1st, 7th, 9th, 10th, and 11th houses, and Bonatti who further allows the Moon in 3rd and Sun in 9th, are both too restrictive in allowable hīlājical positions. In my opinion, Alchabitius comes closer to the mark with his more extensive list of allowable hīlājical positions for the luminaries (Alchabitius 2004, 111-115). While still not perfect, Alchabitius' rules appear better at defining hīlājical positions for luminaries. Bonatti's rules for selecting the hīlāj appear to work well when the hīlāj is the Ascendant, Lot of Fortune, or SAN (Bonatti 2007, 1133-1134). The following guidelines for hīlāj selection combine the best of both authors.

Rules for Choosing the Hīlāj When Figure is Diurnal

Special Rule #1: When a possible hīlāj is found, check to see if one of its rulers aspects the hīlāj and can function as the al-kadukhadāh. If not, then continue down the hīlāj checklist until a suitable hīlāj/al-kadukhadāh combination is found.

Special Rule #2: When the hīlāj falls within a succedent house by quadrant houses yet a cadent house using whole sign houses; judgment is required whether or not the hīlāj is still allowed.

1st choice: Sun is preferred and will be the hīlāj if found in these positions:

House	Sex of Sign	Special
1st	M or F	Not more than 5 degrees above 1st cusp
10th	M or F	
11th	M or F	
7th	M only	
8th	M only	
9th	M only	

2nd choice: If the Sun fails the above criteria, choose the Moon if it is found in:

House	Sex of Sign	Special
1st	M or F	Not more than 5 degrees behind 1st cusp
2nd	M or F	
3rd	M or F	
7th	M or F	Not more than 5 degrees below 7th cusp
8th	M or F	
4th	F only	
5th	F only	
10th	F only	
11th	F only	

If neither Sun nor Moon fall in these hīlājical positions, then choose from the Ascendant, Lot of Fortune, or Syzygy Ante Nativitatem (SAN). For these three hīlājical positions, sex of sign can be either masculine or feminine. If Lot of Fortune or SAN, these positions must fall in angular or succedent houses.

If the SAN is conjunctional (follows New Moon with Moon in 1st or 2nd quarter), choose the hīlāj from these choices in order of priority.	If the SAN is preventional (follows Full Moon with Moon in 3rd or 4th quarter), choose the hīlāj from these choices in order of priority.
3rd Choice: Ascendant	**3rd Choice**: Lot of Fortune
4th Choice: Lot of Fortune	**4th Choice**: Ascendant
5th Choice: SAN - Conjunctional Degree	**5th Choice**: SAN – Preventional Degree

If the Ascendant fails to be the hīlāj and both Lot of Fortune and SAN are in cadent houses, the figure does not have a hīlāj.

CHAPTER 5 – LONGEVITY

Rules for Choosing the Hīlāj When Figure is Nocturnal

Special Rule #1: When a possible hīlāj is found, check to see if one of its rulers aspects the hīlāj and can function as the al-kadukhadāh. If not, then continue down the hīlāj checklist until a suitable hīlāj/al-kadukhadāh combination is found.

Special Rule #2: When the hīlāj falls within a succedent house by quadrant houses yet a cadent house using whole sign houses; judgment is required whether or not the hīlāj is still allowed.

1st choice: Moon is preferred and will be the hīlāj if found in these positions:

House	Sex of Sign	Special
1st	M or F	Not more than 5 degrees behind 1st cusp
2nd	M or F	
3rd	M or F	
7th	M or F	Not more than 5 degrees below 7th cusp
8th	M or F	
4th	F only	
5th	F only	
10th	F only	
11th	F only	

2nd choice: If the Moon fails the above criteria, choose the Sun if it is found in:

House	Sex of Sign	Special
4th	M or F	
5th	M or F	
7th	M or F	Not more than 5 degrees below 7th cusp
1st	M only	
2nd	M only	

If neither Sun nor Moon fall in these hīlājical positions, then choose from the Ascendant, Lot of Fortune, or Syzygy Ante Nativitatem (SAN). For these three hīlājical positions, sex of sign can be either masculine or feminine. If Lot of Fortune or SAN, these positions must fall in angular or succedent houses.

If the SAN is conjunctional (follows New Moon with Moon in 1st or 2nd quarter), choose the hīlāj from these choices in order of priority.	If the SAN is preventional (follows Full Moon with Moon in 3rd or 4th quarter), choose the hīlāj from these choices in order of priority.
3rd Choice: Ascendant	**3rd Choice**: Lot of Fortune
4th Choice: Lot of Fortune	**4th Choice**: Ascendant
5th Choice: SAN - Conjunctional Degree	**5th Choice**: SAN – Preventional Degree

If the Ascendant fails to be the hīlāj and both Lot of Fortune and SAN are in cadent houses, the figure does not have a hīlāj.

AL-KADUKHADĀH

Like the hīlāj, rules vary. This checklist is based on Bonatti (2007, 1137-1139).

- Choose the planet with the highest dignities in the position of the hīlāj as the trial al-kadukhadāh. Double check whether the trial al-kadukhadāh aspects the hīlāj. Inferior planets which rise or set with respect to the Sun are acceptable. In addition to Ptolemaic aspects, consider antiscion and contra-antiscion. If no aspect is found, choose the planet with the second highest dignities in the position of the hīlāj, moving down the list of all planets with dignity in the position of the hīlāj, e.g., sign, exaltation, triplicity, bound, and decan; from highest to lowest measured by dignity scoring. Consider also the Victor.

- Once found, compute the al-kadukhadāh's projection by using the Years of the Planets table. Assign the al-kadukhadāh its major years.

- When the Sun is in Leo or Aries; or the Moon is in Cancer or Taurus; either luminary often functions as both hīlāj and al-kadukhadāh.

- A planet found 3 degrees before or 5 degrees after the 1st or 10th cusps participates. It often supercedes the previously selected al-kadukhadāh altogether.

- First adjustment for Nodes: The North Node adds 25% to the al-kadukhadāh's major years when conjunct; the South Node deducts 25% when conjunct. Use a 12-degree orb.

- Second adjustment for benefics Venus and Jupiter: (1) When a benefic aspects the al-kadukhadāh by trine or sextile and receives the al-kadukhadāh; the benefic adds its minor years. (2) When a benefic aspects the al-kadukhadāh by trine or sextile but does NOT receive the al-kadukhadāh, the benefic may add its minor years but the addition of years is less likely. (3) When a benefic aspects and receives the al-kadukhadāh by square or opposition, the benefic also adds its minor years and as many days as his major years. (4) When a benefic aspects the al-kadukhadāh by trine or sextile and is impeded, it will add as many months as its minor years.

- Third adjustment for malefics Mars and Saturn: (1) When malefics are conjunct, square, or opposed to the al-kadukhadāh; the malefic deducts its minor years. (2) If these conditions occur but the malefic is fortunate and strong; the malefic deducts only one-third of its minor years. (3) If malefics aspect the al-kadukhadāh by trine or sextile and receive the al-kadukhadāh; the malefic deducts its minor years. (4) Likewise if conditions in (3) apply but the malefic is fortunate and strong, the malefic deducts only one-third of its minor years.

Table 12. Years of the Planets

	Minor	Middle	Major	Maximum
Saturn	30	43.5	57	265[12]
Jupiter	12	45.5	79	426
Mars	15	40.5	66	284
Sun	19	69.5	120	1461
Venus	8	45	82	1151
Mercury	20	48	76	461
Moon	25	66.5	108	520

Findings

Aspect. Must the al-kadukhadāh aspect the hīlāj? Most authors require this but not all. Some state that a highly dignified planet can function as al-kadukhadāh without aspect; yet this is a minority opinion. For this study, in nearly every case an aspect between the hīlāj and al-kadukhadāh was found. Casting the net fairly wide, my definition of aspect is based on any aspect using whole sign houses. I have not considered moiety of orb at this stage. Aspects by antiscion and contra-antiscion are included. In only rare cases will this condition not be met by some hīlāj - al-kadukhadāh combination.

A special case is no aspect between inferior planets and the Sun when the Sun is the hīlāj and Mercury or Venus are considered possible al-kadukhadāhs. If *aspect* is restricted to Ptolemaic aspects beginning with the 60 degree sextile, then Mercury or Venus can only function as al-kadukhadāhs when co-present with the Sun because their orbits limit their maximum distance from the Sun to 28 and 48 degrees respectively so can never reach a sextile aspect. In my view this is too restrictive. Consider Mercury or Venus when they rise or set relative to the Sun.

Position. Much ink has been spilled on the assignment of an al-kadukhadāh's major, middle, and minor years based on the planet's placement in angular, succedent, or cadent houses. The typical instruction is for angular planets to grant their major years; succedent, middle years; and cadent, minor years. Some authors have taken this much further, attempting to translate the distance between – say the 10th and 11th house cusps – as a proportional adjustment made between major and middle years (Montulmo 1995, Part 2:1-9). Evidence from this sample suggests that not only are these kinds of adjustments overkill but more shockingly that the al-kadukhadāh grants its major years no matter if it is placed in a succedent or cadent house. This occurs in virtually every case! This finding marks a significant departure from theory and bears further study.

---

[12] Earlier editions listed Saturn's greatest years as 256, not 265. Saturn's 1.0352 synodic cycle means it makes 256 synodic cycles for every 265 sidereal years. The numeraire for the Years of the Planets table is years, not synodic cycles. The correct number is 265. This error is present in many astrological texts including Robert Zoller's Diploma Course.

If these findings hold up the question arises how could these authors have been so wrong? My speculation is the rules for assigning years based on angularity date from eras when the average lifespan was far less than for the late 20th century in western countries. In this situation, astrologers must have consistently found actual lifespans falling below al-kadukhadāh projections and started making wholesale adjustments to the method to fit the average longevity of their era. In their day, adjustments for angularity may have had merit. My findings have to be taken in light of the relatively advanced quality of life measures in the United States compared to other countries. In the present era (2007) longevity measures of mid to high 70s in the developed world contrast with measures as low as 40 in some developing countries. And the average lifespan by country is not static. For instance, Russia's average lifespan has declined recently. *NEW* USA average lifespan also declined during COVID.

My point is that using this sample taking anything other than major years for an al-kadukhadāh cannot be justified. Rules for taking middle or minor years if the al-kadukhadāh is succedent or cadent may be appropriate for countries and eras when persistent warfare, natural disasters, diseases, and poor medical care reduce average measures of longevity.

Combustion. Most authors consider the hīlāj or al-kadukhadāh invalid if it is combust the Sun. Some make the distinction that if the planet is past the Sun's conjunction and moving away from the Sun the situation is not as dire. There are several examples which support combust planets in these situations. LBJ is one, with both Moon/Mercury combust the Sun yet both passing empirical tests for the hīlāj/al-kadukhadāh combination. Both are past the conjunction to the Sun.

Planets on the 1st and 10th cusps. Bonatti's instruction to make planets near the 1st and 10th cusps *participate* with the al-kadukhadāh is a critical insight that greatly simplified al-kadukhadāh computations for about 20% of the examples studied. In these cases I found these angular planets did not just *participate*, they *overruled* the computed al-kadukhadāh. In a few cases I found the 3 degree before and 5 degree after cutoff a bit too tight; allowing an additional degree tolerance made a difference in some cases.

Adjustments from Nodes. Authors agree that the South Node within 12 degrees of an al-kadukhadāh reduces years by 25%; they disagree on whether the North Node can add years. This sample supports claims that the North Node increases years. An exception is when the North Node is conjunct the Moon. In this case the North Node does not add years; in fact it appears to disqualify the Moon as hīlāj completely. When the Nodes are one of several bodies aspecting the al-kadukhadāh, authors do not specify the order of mathematical operations. This sample supports making the Nodal adjustment first, then adding or subtracting years as a second step. Finally, it is possible the Nodes add or subtract years by antiscia but this is a tentative finding.

Adjustments from Benefics and Malefics. Bonatti's rules for adding/subtracting years for benefics and malefics are based on three criteria: (1) whether the planet receives the al-kadukhadāh, (2) whether the aspect is a sextile/trine or square/opposition, and (3) essential dignity. Planets which are fortunate and strong add/subtract minor years as years; planets less fortunate modify by other permutations from the Years of the Planets table, such as modifying by middle years as months.

NEW _Recent research suggests making adjustments using anything other than minor years cannot be substantiated._ We must step back and consider that minor and major years are based on astronomical cycles which suggest once the wheel is turned the cycle is over. For this reason, I reject middle years on theoretical grounds because as the average of minor and major years they have no astronomical basis. If there are additional adjustments to be made, then partitioning major years into halves or quarters is probably the better approach. Working with a larger sample, I have seen a few incidences where solar types live 60 years (1/2 Sun's major 120 years) and lunar types lived 54 or 27 years (½ or ¼ of the Moon's major 108 years).

NEW _Of Bonatti's criteria for adjustments, the most important appears to be reception_. Planets are more likely to add or subtract years if they receive the al-kadukhadāh. For minor dignities as Bonatti defines them (triplicity, bound, decan), his requirement that two of three minor dignities must occur before judging reception appears incorrect. There are examples of reception by triplicity and decan which DO NOT modify years as well as examples of reception by bound alone which DO modify years. The primacy of the bounds continues to pervade my research to the point I now consider reception is possible by bound rulership alone, in the same manner as reception by sign or exaltation.

NEW _When the al-kadukhadāh receives the aspecting planet, the aspecting planet will not modify years_. Malefic planets which are received by the al-kadukhadāh may cause an injury that maims but does not kill. Benefic planets which are received by the al-kadukhadāh may not add years.

Adjustment accuracy from malefic/benefic planets. Adjustments from malefics seldom fail, especially with the malefic is in square or opposition aspect to the _al-kadukhadāh_. Adjustments from benefics are less consistent. It is also possible for accidental malefics/benefics to reduce/add years. For instance, a benefic planet which is placed in or rules a bad house and ranks as a high scoring killing planet may function as an accidental malefic and reduce years. Mercury rarely adds or subtracts years no matter if Mercury is judged an accidental malefic or benefic.

Adjustments from Luminaries. Authors vary on whether aspects from the Sun or Moon can add or subtract years. Evidence from this sample suggests the luminaries rarely add or subtract years with John Tyler a possible example.

Choice of Victor of the Horoscope over Al-kadukhadāh. It is a bit galling to read and study these rather complicated al-kadukhadāh calculations and then find an author concluding his section on the al-kadukhadāh with the seemingly tossed-off statement: *Some prefer the Victor of the Horoscope*. Which in a matter of words means all of the computational hijinks are wasted efforts. ***NEW*** This is no small matter. For the Presidential database, 21 of 39 (54%) of the sample meets this condition (See Table 13). This is why this 4th edition presents the Victor of the Horoscope prior to the Arcus Vitae.

When people live shorter than the al-kadukhadāh projection. In his treatise on Lots, Bonatti states that when the Lot of Life is afflicted, lifespan is reduced. Examples in this study include Grant and LBJ. There is no rule for quantifying the reduction in lifespan. In addition, whenever the South Node falls in the natal Ascendant, the native is prone to physical weakness. This is an additional consideration for judgment when considering longevity.

When people live longer than the al-kadukhadāh. Just because an individual lives longer than the al-kadukhadāh projection, it doesn't mean the al-kadukhadāh projection is incorrect. It may mean the person's physical body begins to deteriorate and quality of life rapidly declines. In the extreme category is Andrew Jackson who lived to the age of 78, outliving his al-kadukhadāh projection by 29 years. After the age of 49, his body was racked with pain daily, suffering the effects of bullets and shrapnel from prior duels and battles causing infections and other complications. Gerald Ford and George H. W. Bush are the two other outliers which lived significantly longer than the al-kadukhadāh projection. Benefics in the 4th house (end-of-life) may be responsible for this effect but this observation needs more testing.

Unusual cases. Finally there are unusual cases which are very confusing to judge. (1) The first category occurs when the SAN is an eclipse. John Adams, John Quincy Adams, Warren Harding, Barack Obama, and Donald Trump fall in this category. It appears when the SAN is an eclipse, the SAN and its bound ruler function as the hīlāj/al-kadukhadāh pair. (2) The second category occurs when the hīlāj falls in a non-allowed cadent house. (3) The third category is cases with more than one functional hīlāj. (4) The fourth category includes cases where the rules do not work; yet their rarity does not warrant changing the rules. No matter how well a set of rules is designed, no system works 100% of the time.

Table 13. Longevity Model: Predicted vs Actual

	President	Victor	Al-kadukhadāh	Projection	Actual	Diff
1	G. Washington	♂	♂	♂ (66)	67.8	1.8
2	J. Adams	♄	♀	♀ (82)	90.7	8.7
				Alt: ♄ (30 * 3) = 90		
3	T. Jefferson	♄	☉	☉ (120) - ♄ (30) - ♂ (15) = 75	83.2	8.2
4	J. Madison	♂	♂	♂ (66) + ♃ (12) + ♀ (8) = 86	85.3	-0.7
5	J. Monroe	♃	♃	JU (79)	73.2	-5.8
6	J. Q. Adams	♃	♀	♀ (82)	80.6	-1.4
7	A. Jackson	♂	♃	♃ (79) - ♄ (30) = 49	78.2	**29.2**
8	M. van Buren	♃	♀	♀ (82)	79.6	-2.4
9	W. Harrison	♂	♂	♂ (66)	68.1	2.1
10	J. Tyler	♂	☉	♂ (66)	71.8	5.8
				Alt: ♂ (66) - ♃ (12) + ☉ (19) = 73		
11	J. Polk	♀	♄	♄ (57)	53.6	-3.4
				Alt: ½ of Moon's 108 yrs = 54		
12	Z. Taylor	♂	♂	♂ (66)	65.6	-0.4
13	M. Fillmore	♃	♃	♃ (79) - ♂ (15) = 64	74.2	10.2
14	F. Pierce	♃	♃	♃ (79) - ♂ (15) = 64	64.9	0.9
				Alt: ♄ (57) + ♀ (8) = 65		
15	J. Buchanan	♃	♀	♀ (82)	77.1	-4.9
16	A. Lincoln	♂	♄	♄ (57)	56.2	-8.8
17	A. Johnson	♄	♂	♂ (66)	66.6	0.6
18	U. Grant	♄	♄	♄ (57) + ♀ (8) + ♃ (12) - ♂ (15) = 62	63.2	1.2
19	R. Hayes	♃	♃	♂ (66) + ♀ (8) = 74	70.3	-8.7
20	J. Garfield	♄	♂	♂ (66) * ☋ (-25%) = 49.5	49.8	0.3
21	C. Arthur	♂	♄	♄ (57)	57.1	0.1
22/24	G. Cleveland	♂	♂	♂ (66) + ♃ (12) = 78	71.3	-6.7
23	B. Harrison	♂	♂	♂ (66)	67.6	1.6
25	W. McKinley	♃	♄	♄ (57) * ☊ (1.25) – ♂ (15) = 56.25	58.6	2.35
26	T. Roosevelt	♂	♂	♂ (66)	60.2	-5.8
27	W. Taft	♃	♃	♃ (79) + ♀ (8) - ♂ (15) = 72	72.5	0.5
28	W. Wilson	♃	♃	♃ (79) + ☊ (+25%) - ♄ (30) = 68.75	67.1	-1.65
29	W. Harding	♀	☽	MO (108) * ☋ (-25%) - ♄ (30) = 51	58.7	7.7
30	C. Coolidge	☿	☿	☿ (76) - ♄ (30) = 46	60.5	**14.5**
				Alt: ½ of Sun's 120 yrs = 60		
31	H. Hoover	♄	☉	☉ (120) - ♄ (30) = 90	90.2	0.2
32	F. Roosevelt	♃	♂	♂ (66)	63.2	-2.8
33	H. Truman	♂	♀	♀ (82)	88.6	6.6
34	D. Eisenhower	♃	♃	♃ (79)	78.5	-0.5
35	J. Kennedy	♃	♃	♃ (79) - ♄ (30) = 49	46.5	-2.5
36	L. Johnson	☿	☿	☿ (76) - ♂ (15) = 61	64.4	3.4
37	R. Nixon	♀	♀	♀ (82)	81.3	-0.7
38	G. Ford	♃	♃	♃ (79) - ♂ (15) = 64	93.5	**29.5**
40	R. Reagan	♂	♂	♂ (66) + ♀ (8) + ♃ (12) = 86	93.3	7.3
41	G. H. W. Bush	☿	☿	☿ (76) - ♂ (15) + ♀ (8) = 69	94.5	**25.5**

Notes. (1) Cases when the Victor and al-kadukhadāh are identical are shaded. (2) Difference between projected and actual longevity was less than 1 year for 10 examples; less than 3 years for 20; and less than 8 years for 30. Total sample size is 39. The largest outliers are A. Jackson, C. Coolidge, G. Ford, and G. H. W. Bush all of whom substantially lived longer lives than predicted by the longevity model. That two of these four were born in the 20th century suggests access to improved medical care may allow longer lifespans compared to Presidents born in earlier epochs.

Additional Notes for Table 13

1	G. Washington	Venus does not add years with a separating trine and reception by diurnal triplicity.
3	T. Jefferson	Sun's reception of Mars mitigates Mars' ability to reduce years, allowing for a longer lifespan.
5	J. Monroe	Saturn's square too wide to reduce years; separating trine from Mars does not receive Jupiter so does not reduce years.
6	J. Q. Adams	Saturn's square too wide to reduce years.
7	A. Jackson	After 1818 (age 51) was in continuous pain until death.
10	J. Tyler	Failing as al-kadukhadāh, the Sun still adds years.
11	J. Polk	If moiety rules are ignored, wide aspects from Jupiter (+12) and Mars (-15) yield 54 years which is a better fit.
12	Z. Taylor	Venus does not add years with a wide applying aspect and reception by diurnal triplicity.
13	M. Fillmore	No major career milestones after age 64.
14	F. Pierce	While Jupiter receives Mars by nocturnal triplicity and decan this reception does not mitigate Mars' deduction of years.
16	A. Lincoln	Venus separates from Saturn by trine aspect but does not receive Saturn so does not add minor years. Jupiter receives by a wide square aspect but does not add minor years despite receiving Saturn by sign and bound.
17	A. Johnson	Venus does not add years with a separating trine and reception by sign.
19	R. Hayes	Health declined after age 66. Venus receives Mars only by diurnal triplicity whereas Mars receives Venus by bound; this limits the ability of Venus to add quality years.
21	C. Arthur	Jupiter does not add years with an applying trine and reception by triplicity and decan.
22, 24	G. Cleveland	Square aspect from Saturn is mitigated by Mars' rulership of Saturn. Dialing the longevity estimate back 30 years finds Cleveland at age 48 in the year 1885. Eight years later GC did have surgery to remove cancer from his mouth; it is possible cancer started in 1885. It maimed but did not kill him.
23	B. Harrison	Harrison lived Mars' 66 major years. Saturn is co-present with Mars and should deduct 30 minor years; Mars' reception of Saturn by bound appears to nullify this deduction. Likewise, Venus should add 8 minor years by sextile aspect and reception of Mars by triplicity and decan but does not. Mars' reception of Venus by triplicity and decan may nullify Venus' ability to add years.
28	W. Wilson	The wide sextile from Venus and Mars to Jupiter does not modify years. Note Jupiter receives both planets by bound.
29	W. Harding	The solution allows the Moon in the 6th house by whole sign houses (a normal disqualifier) and in the 5th by quadrant houses.

CHAPTER 5 – LONGEVITY 81

30	C. Coolidge	Coolidge lived longer. Actual longevity of 60.5 years is about half the Sun's major 120 years. While Venus and Mars are co-present, they are on the other side of the Sun relative to Mercury's position. It is unclear if Venus and Mars can modify years in this configuration.
32	F. Roosevelt	This solution is based on Mars' position near the MC degree as the al-kadukhudhah with Mars granting 66 major years and no modifications.
33	H. Truman	While Jupiter is co-present with and receives Venus by exaltation, the configuration is too wide (25 degrees) for Jupiter to add years.
34	D. Eisenhower	Mercury does not add years by separating trine and receiving Jupiter by participating triplicity and bound; Venus does not add years by separating sextile without reception.
35	J. Kennedy	Proposed solution from earlier editions focused entirely on planets in the 8th house with JU (79) - MA (15) - ME (20) = 46 which appeared accurate. The 4th edition solution makes better use of reception in accordance with recent findings: Saturn's sextile aspect deducts years with Saturn's reception of Jupiter by bound and decan; Mars co-present with Jupiter - but received by Jupiter - maims but does not kill. Age 46 less Mars' 15 minor years yields age 34, the year 1951 when JFK was given the last rights for the 2nd time.
36	L. Johnson	Mercury's reception of Mars should mean that Mars' 15-year deduction maims but does not kill. Yet cardio incidents began in 1970 the year following the projection given by ME - MA.
37	R. Nixon	Jupiter does not add years by trine and reception by sign and decan.
38	G. Ford	Ford left the Presidency six months prior to the longevity projection. In a separating trine, Mars receives Jupiter by exaltation but Jupiter receives Mars by bound suggesting deduction of Mars' minor years yields an injury which maims but does not kill. No injuries were reported but the following year the family staged an intervention for his wife Betty Ford's substance abuse. It is possible that Mars signifies stress from his wife's recovery.
40	R. Reagan	Jupiter conjunct South Node is highly afflicted and speaks to the low quality of Jupiter's addition of 12 years. Dialing back Jupiter's addition takes Reagan back to 1985, the year after his son Ron Jr suspected the onset of Alzheimer's in 1984.
41	G. H. W. Bush	A tennis accident at age 61 when Bush was knocked unconscious in a fall shows the deduction of Mars' 15 minor years from Mercury's major 76 years (76-15=61). But Bush lived much longer. Jupiter/4th, end-of-life, may be responsible.

KILLING PLANET

NEW The killing planet is the final piece of the puzzle required before computing the Arcus Vitae. Readers may be surprised by my inclusion of compound scoring tables for this purpose after I denigrated them in the prior chapter. But in this application, compound scoring tables for the killing planet avoid a criticism previously levied at Ibn Ezra's model for the Victor of the Horoscope: here there is no attempt to mix quality and quantity scores, e.g., there are no points for house position. While the other limitations of compound scoring tables still apply, results for this small sample of 39 American Presidents are sufficiently robust to justify their use.

NEW Specifically: for 29 or 75% of the sample, one of the killing planets timed death as a component of the arcus vitae. For those 29 examples, only 10 killing planets were 8th house occupants or rulers. Said another way, if one relied solely on 8th house occupants or sign rulers to identify the planet most likely to be triggered at the time of death using primary directions, one would have failed to identify the correct planet for roughly half the horoscopes studied.

Schoener's Significator List for Al-Mubtazz Scoring Tables (Schoener 2001, 41)

- Relevant house cusp
- Sign ruler of house cusp
- Co-significator (such as Moon/Venus for wife or Mars for brothers)
- Ruler of Co-significator
- Relevant lot
- Ruler of lot
- Relevant Triplicity ruler(s) of the house

Recommended Significator List for Al-mubtazz Table for Killing Planet

- Ascendant
- Ruler of the Ascendant
- Part of Death (Saturn + 8th cusp − Moon)
- Ruler of Lot of Death
- 8th House Cusp[13]
- Ruler of 8th House Cusp
- Triplicity ruler of 8th House Cusp
- Any Planets or Nodes on the 8th House (Whole Sign placement)
- If diurnal: Position 8 signs from the Sun and ruler of this position
- If nocturnal: Position 8 signs from the Moon and ruler of this position

---

[13] Some authors prefer 4th or 7th house significators. I have not formally tested the difference. The above significator list works reasonably well for this sample.

Example: Martin Van Buren

Shown below as Table 14, the first three columns list the significators and their zodiacal degree. The remaining seven columns - one for each planet and luminary - score each zodiacal degree according to five levels of essential dignity. The levels and scores are: Sign Rulership, +5; Exaltation, +4; Triplicity, +3; Bound, +2; Decan, +1.

Starting with the first row, consider the Ascendant degree: 29AQ55.

<u>What planet rules 29AQ55 by sign?</u> **Saturn**. Saturn in fact rules all degrees of Aquarius. Saturn is assigned a score of +5. Note '5' in Saturn's column.

<u>What planet rules 29AQ55 by exaltation?</u> **No planet**. You will note the absence of the number '4' in the first row of the table.

<u>What planets rule 29AQ55 by triplicity?</u> Aquarius belongs to the Airy triplicity, whose rulers are **Saturn, Mercury, and Jupiter**. Note that *each* and *every* triplicity ruler is assigned a score of +3. You will see three '3's in the first row.

<u>What planet rules 29AQ55 by bound?</u> **Saturn**. Saturn is assigned a +2.

<u>What planet rules 29AQ55 by decan?</u> **Mars**. Mars is assigned a +1.

Continue this procedure, row by row; when finished, sum by column. The planet with the highest score is the al-mubtazz (literally 'winner') for the question at hand; here the planet most conducive to Martin Van Buren's death. Note there may be more than one planet with high scores as in this case for Van Buren.

Table 14. Martin Van Buren: Al-mubtazz Table for Killing Planet

			☉	☽	☿	♀	♂	♃	♄
ASC		29AQ55			3		1	3	5,3,2
Rul ASC	♄	1CP19		3	2	3	4,3	1	5
L.Death		11LI57			3,2	5		3	4,3,1
Rul L.Death	♀	6SA33	3		1			5,3,2	3
H8 Cusp		6LI06		1	3,2	5		3	4,3
Rul H8	♀	6SA33	3		1			5,3,2	3
T-Rul H8	♄	1CP19		3	2	3	4,3	1	5
8th from ☉		13CA46		5,3	2,1	3	3	4	
Rul 8th fr ☉	☽	25SA28	3				2	5,3	3,1
TOTAL			9	15	22	19	20	**43**	**45**

Both Jupiter and Saturn are high scoring killers for Van Buren. In the 1861 solar return preceding death, Jupiter and Saturn appear together in the 4th house end-of-life. Mercury as 8th house ruler did not appear in the 4th; only the killing planets.

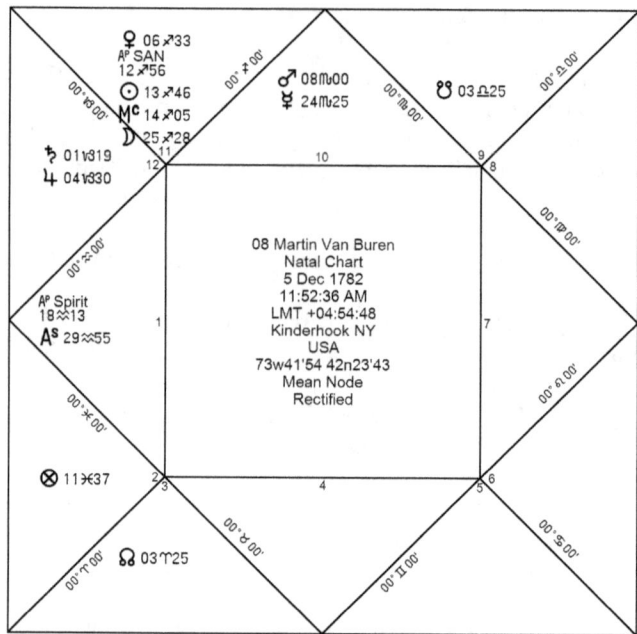

Nativity of Martin Van Buren.

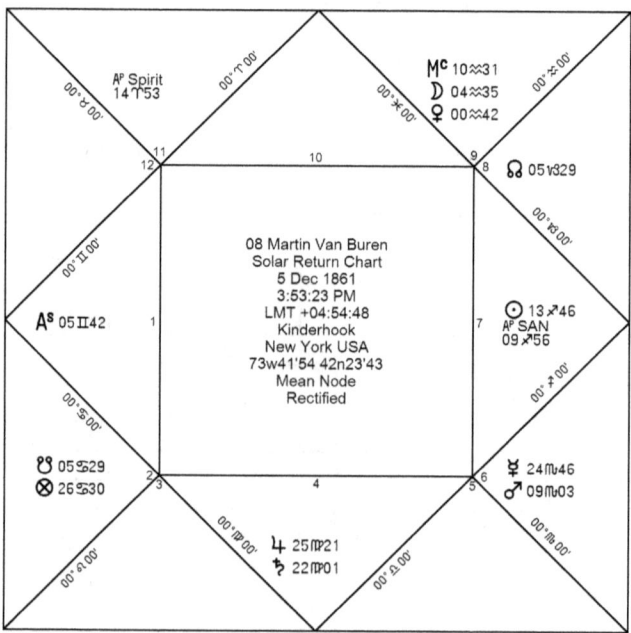

1861 Solar Return of Martin Van Buren preceding death.

SIDEBAR: PRIMARY DIRECTIONS

The arcus vitae ("arc of life") is a mathematical computation of life expectancy which directs the killing planet to the hīlāj by primary direction. As primary directions are a specialized predictive technique new to some readers, I give a conceptual crash course in primary directions helpful to understand the arcus vitae model.

Example: George Washington. Consider Washington with the Sun in the 2nd; Mercury in the 1st, Moon in 12th, and North Node in the 11th.

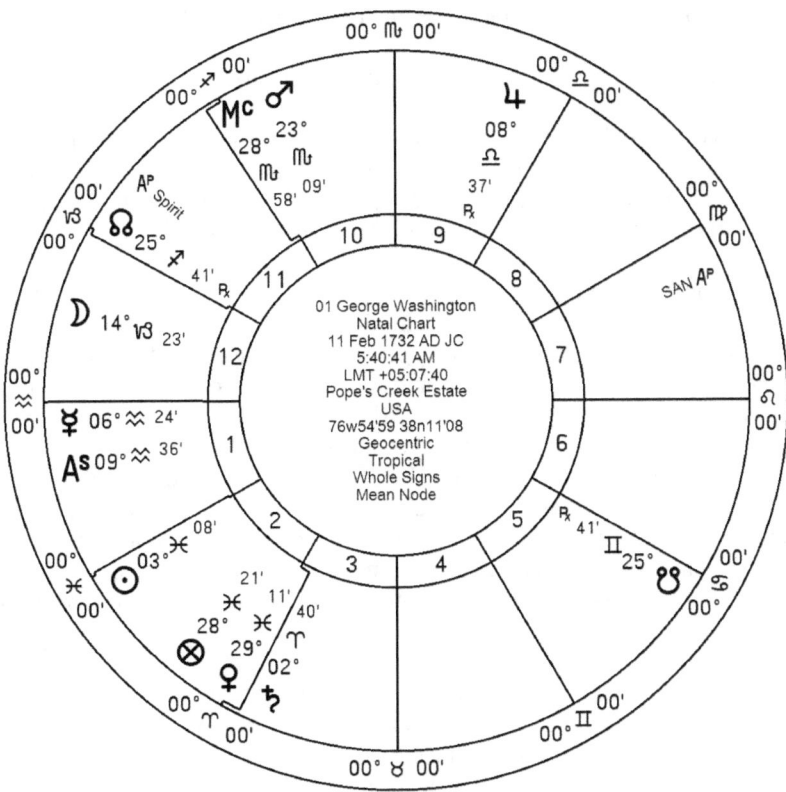

Nativity of George Washington, Alchabitius houses.

Diurnal Motion. Remember the natal chart is a snapshot of the sky at birth and as the day progresses planets move clockwise: from the position of the Ascendant (1st house), they rise in the eastern sky, culminate directly above the birthplace in the Midheaven, and pass out of sight after they set on the western horizon (7th house). This is what is known as *diurnal motion* and is the basis of all primary directions which asks three kinds of questions (here using Washington as an example):

1. When will the Sun, below the horizon in the 2nd house, be visible on the eastern horizon at sunrise?

2. Assuming the position of natal Mercury in the 1st is *frozen* at birth, when will the Sun in the 2nd rise and meet the position of Mercury?

3. When will the North Node culminate at the Midheaven?

The answers to these questions are computed as arcs of direction measured in degrees and minutes. Using a key of 1 degree = 1 year, the arc of direction is converted into a future date corresponding to an event whose nature is predicted by the combined delineation of the two points directed and their aspect.

Significators and Promissors. The point *frozen* at birth is named the *significator*. A planet or aspect moved in diurnal motion is named the *promissor*. Promissors indicate, or *promise* some type of accident, good or bad, lying dormant until the promissor or its aspect meets a significator by primary motion. Washington's Mercury promises an airborne illness like smallpox because Mercury is in an air sign conjunct the antiscion of Mars. Fever is a general signification of Mars; Mars ruling the 3rd of siblings ties fevers to siblings; Mars ruling the 3rd in the 10th ties fevers to death of siblings. When Washington's Sun, hīlāj and significator of health, rose to meet Mercury by conjunction, he took a trip with his half-brother Lawrence to Barbados (who contracted tuberculosis), contracted smallpox on the trip, and later returned to Virginia where he sadly learned of Lawrence's death the following year.

If you studied this example carefully, you saw that Mercury was held *frozen* and the Sun was moved by primary motion to meet Mercury. This makes Mercury the significator and the Sun the promissor. Historically only the Ascendant, Midheaven, Sun, Moon, Lot of Fortune, and SAN were treated as significators; only the planets, excluding the luminaries, were treated as promissors. Empirical testing shows it doesn't matter whether promissors are treated as significators, vice versa. A second historical preference for directing planets only in direct motion, (e.g., 'directing direct') also doesn't hold up. Directing by converse motion works just as well which is a very controversial statement made by me disputed by many traditional astrologers.

Computation. The calculation of arcs of direction takes a bit of work only because the earth rotates on its own axis, currently tilted at 23deg 26min relative to the Sun, a measure known as obliquity. In fact, if the obliquity were zero, all primary directions could be computed in right ascension, greatly simplifying the entire process. But this is not so. Reality dictates that primary directions require trigonometry to account for the obliquity of the earth's axis relative to the Sun.

Directions of the Ascendant and Midheaven. Because of obliquity, the first listed direction – Sun conjunct Ascendant – must be computed by what is known as *oblique ascension*. The last listed direction – North Node conjunct MC – is computed in what is termed *right ascension*. Both oblique and right ascension are terminology that belongs to a more detailed discussion of primary directions which I will save for a different time and place. What the beginning student should know is there is little debate among authors on the choice of oblique and right ascension for Ascendant and Midheaven primary directions respectively. Authors differ only on the treatment of latitude. I present my own solution to the latitude problem in Chapter 10: *Directions*.

Interplanetary Directions. It is the second of Washington's three directions - Mercury conjunct Sun - which falls into the category of interplanetary directions over which much ink has been spilled. *Interplanetary directions* are a classification reserved for directions which do not include either Ascendant or Midheaven as significator or promissor. For example, all Sun-planet, Moon-planet, and Lot of Fortune-planet directions are considered interplanetary directions. Defining what constitutes an aspect for planets which never actually meet because of differences in declination requires assumptions which vary widely from author to author. Ptolemy proposed a proportional solution which Alchabitius includes in his *Introduction to Astrology*. Alchabitius' book was so popular that this method of primary directions was known as the Alchabitius method during most of the medieval period. Results in this study confirm the accuracy of these directions, abbreviated as **PT** for Ptolemy.

Computation method of Interplanetary Directions. Beyond Ptolemy's method, Regiomontanus introduced his own method of primary directions during the Renaissance. It was taken up by other astrologers including Argoli, Morin, and Lilly (Kolev 2003). For this study, Regiomontanus is abbreviated as **REG**. Of the two methods, I have had success with both methods. Given the small sample size, there is insufficient evidence to favor either method by Ptolemy or Regiomontanus based on the present study. I continue to use both directional methods of Ptolemy and Regiomontanus in my professional practice.

COMPUTING THE ARCUS VITAE

Step 1. Identify the hīlāj. This is the significator, or planet/point which is held fixed as the rest of the horoscope planets and aspects are rotated clockwise in diurnal motion.

Step 2. Identify the killing planet(s). Killing planets are promissors which are most conducive for illness, injury, and death. Killing planets and their aspects are what actually move when computing primary directions. When they meet the hīlāj, this is the arcus vitae.

Step 3. Use the longevity projection as a milestone. Directions of killing planets to the hīlāj prior to the al-kadukhadāh longevity calculation time illness and injury, and sometimes for the native's family, not the native directly.

Step 4. Additional permutations. Begin with classical rules of direct motion. Additional permutations of primary directions are possible, e.g., converse motion and switching places between significators and promissors.

FINDINGS

<u>When many directions kill</u>. For some nativities, the direction of the high scoring killing planet to the hīlāj is very accurate. Grover Cleveland's arcus vitae joins Venus to the Sun by square aspect in a primary direction which kills within 16 days. There are no other nearby alternate directions. This is an open and shut case. It is also the exception. More common is the case of Ulysses Grant where three different sets of directions progressively weakened Grant until death.

Most striking is the case of John Quincy Adams who suffered a stroke on 20-Nov-1847. After a partial recovery he did not die until the following February.

> *Is the Ascendant conjunct Mercury direction of 22-Nov-1847 which timed his stroke within two days the arcus vitae?*

OR

> *Is the Moon conjunct Ascendant direction of 23-Feb-1848 which times death the exact day the official arcus vitae?*

Adams stated himself that for all practical purposes that he was functionally dead after the November 1847 stroke.

It appears for relatively long-lived individuals a series of directions which progressively weaken the physical body cause death. Trying to single out a specific direction as the *official* arcus vitae becomes somewhat academic.

<u>When the hīlāj directed to the Ascendant can kill</u>. Bonatti (2007, 1141-1142) states that Hīlāj - Ascendant directions can kill. This rule applies to the Sun and Moon when either luminary is the Hīlāj. The theory behind Bonatti's rule is sect-based and identifies diurnal/nocturnal transitions when either luminary loses sect status as a time of weakness which can cause death. By diurnal motion, the Moon loses its sect status as it rises at the Ascendant degree where it is blinded by the Sun's light. Therefore, Moon-ASC directions are possible killers. Likewise, at the Descendant degree, the Sun loses its status when it moves below the horizon; therefore, Sun-DSC directions are possible killers. For the Presidential database, there are five of these examples: John Quincy Adams, Martin Van Buren, Ulysses Grant, John F. Kennedy, and George H. W. Bush. [Note there are some variations in this set: Martin Van Buren dies with an ASC-Sun direction not a DSC-Sun direction]. Ultimately, there is no explanation of conditions when Hīlāj - Ascendant directions take precedence over Killing Planet - Hīlāj directions when computing the ex-ante arcus vitae. This means that once the al-kadukhadāh longevity calculation expires, this is another category of directions that is necessary to identify.

When the Nodes Kill. Because the Nodes have no dignity[14], they cannot by definition be selected as a killing planet using the al-mubtazz technique. Still, whenever they appear in the 8th house they are elevated to the primary killer in a majority of cases in this study. The effect occurs for the 8th house defined by both whole sign and Alchabitius semi-arc houses.

When trines and sextile kill. In theory, only directions by conjunction, square, or opposition should kill. This is because a killing planet and hīlāj work *side-by-side* in a conjunction, are *confrontational* (nature of Mars) in a square aspect, and are *destructive* (nature of Saturn) in the opposition aspect.

Yet Ptolemy states sextiles can kill in signs of long ascension and trines can kill in signs of short ascension (Ptolemy 2002, 92-93). Here is his logic: Suppose the Ascendant falls in Aries, a sign of short ascension. Now suppose killing planet Mars is located in the 2nd house. Because the Aries Ascendant moves so quickly, a theoretical arcus vitae like converse Ascendant *square* Mars might occur at a relatively young age – say 20 or 25 – well before the al-kadukhadāh's longevity estimate in this hypothetical example. Yet the direction of converse Ascendant *trine* Mars – occurring say at age 90 or 95 – which matches the al-kadukhadāh projection is the direction which causes death. A similar argument can be made for reasons why sextiles can kill in signs of long ascension.

Ptolemy's reasoning is sound, confirmed by arcus vita formed by sextile or trine aspects comprising approximately one-third of the thirty-nine cases studied. It's also quite a blow to some 20th Century astrological schools which assert that major life events are exclusively timed by hard aspects and their harmonics.

Interplanetary Directions. Both methods by Ptolemy and Regiomontanus were used to compute interplanetary directions. A review of arcus vitae measurements reveals no dominance among either method for yielding the most accurate arcus vitae. In fact, for some nativities both methods produced directions which could conceivably be argued as the empirical arcus vitae. Clearly both methods work. Whether or not Ptolemy or Regiomontanus directions may yield more consistent results is a question better suited for a larger data sample.

Solar Arc Directions. I also considered the modern solar arc direction method in arcus vitae computation. Only in a few cases did solar arc directions qualify as potential arcus vitae measurements. Examples: William Henry Harrison and Calvin Coolidge. Yet even for Harrison, there were also other primary directions computed by the arcus vitae method at the time of death. I conclude that solar arc directions are rare dynamic measurements for timing death, found perhaps in only in 2-3% of cases I have encountered over the last twenty years of research.

---

[14] Except for the North Nóde in Gemini and the South Node in Sagittarius, the significance of which I pass over for the moment.

Recapitulation of the Arcus Vitae in the Solar Return preceding Death. In roughly one-third of the cases studied, the empirical arcus vitae was recapitulated in the solar return. For example, Mars was found near the IC of William Henry Harrison's 1841 solar return computed for the year of death. By primary direction, a similarly configured Mars - IC direction was one of two which accurately timed death. This kind of recapitulation appears one factor which greatly increases the odds of death during a particular year. This is a consistent finding of traditional authors like Morin who teach that when there is uncertainty regarding the timing of a primary direction that a similar configuration found in a solar return shows the actual year when the direction will be felt. I agree with Morin, but believe that better rectification and more precise computation means primary directions need not be mirrored in the return for their promise to unfold in any particular year. The promise of primary directions can be fulfilled independently of solar returns. For this reason, I suggest directions rank higher than solar returns in the predictive hierarchy.

NEW Directing Significators through the Bounds. Formally introduced in Chapter 10, Directing through the Bounds is a refinement of primary directions methodology which incorporates directing the significators through the bounds in addition to any aspects made with planets. Since publication of the 3rd edition of ARM in 2009, Janus software added a module for Directing through the Bounds, named 'Distributions' in its Version 5.5. Applying this module for the first time to the Presidential database revealed four examples of Ascendant Distributor changeovers which timed death. Two other close cases for the Moon and SAN Distributors were also noteworthy.

| D | Changeover | bound Saturn/Taurus d. => ASC | 23-Nov-1799 |

George Washington. Precedes death on 14-Dec-1799 by 21 days. This measurement was used to adjust the ASC from 9AQ01'14" to 9AQ36'49" for the 4th edition.

| D | Changeover | bound Saturn/Gemini d. => ASC | 19-Jun-1826 |

John Adams. Precedes death on 4-Jul-1826 by 15 days.

| D | Changeover | bound Mars/Aries d. => SAN (full latitude) | 3-Mar-1848 |

J. Q. Adams. Follows death on 23-Feb-1848 by 8 days. JQA's SAN was a lunar eclipse.

| D | Changeover | P | Bound Saturn/Aries d. => ASC | 2-Jul-1850 |

Zachary Taylor. Precedes death by 7 days.

| D | Changeover | P | Bound Saturn/Capricorn => Moon (MO) | 11-May-1901 |

Benjamin Harrison. Follows death by 59 days.

| D | Changeover | Bound Saturn/Taurus => ASC | 27-May-2004 |

Ronald Reagan. Precedes death by 9 days.

Suffice it to say this is another style of primary directions which needs to be added to the standard arcus vitae methodology.

MODEL EFFICACY

The following table compares model-derived hīlāj(s) and killing planet(s) to the empirical arcus vitae observed near the time of death. In other words, having taken time to delineate the hīlāj and killing planet, how likely is it that a primary direction linking these two planets/points would approximate the day of death?

Table 15 presents model results for the arcus vitae model.

When more than one hīlāj is identified, this is usually indicative of a secondary hīlāj which demonstrated dynamic activity during times of illness or injury based on empirical data in addition to the theoretical hīlāj based on templates presented in this chapter.

More than one killing planet means that total scores for several planets were very close to another when ranking them using the al-mubtazz table approach.

The final column shows the empirical arcus vitae observed at death. Ideally one of the components in each of the first two columns should be combined in a primary direction which times death. How did the model fare?

- How often was the hīlāj correctly identified? **31/39 or 79%**
- How often was a killing planet correctly identified? **29/39 or 74%**
- How often was the killing planet the high scoring killing planet? **19/39 or 49%**
- How often was the hīlāj and killing planet identified jointly? **24/39 or 62%**

Exceptions to model-derived hīlāj/killing planet combinations are:

• <u>Hīlāj-Ascendant directions</u>. John Quincy Adams, Martin van Buren, Ulysses Grant, John F. Kennedy, and George H. W. Bush.

• <u>Killing Planet-Ascendant directions</u>. (Killing Planet identified correctly but ASC was not identified as hīlāj during delineation). Thomas Jefferson, John Quincy Adams, John Tyler, James Buchanan, Theodore Roosevelt.

• <u>Nodes as killers</u>. James Madison, Andrew Johnson, Chester Arthur, Benjamin Harrison, William McKinley, Warren Harding, Calvin Coolidge, Harry Truman.

• <u>Distributor Changeovers</u>. George Washington, John Adams, John Quincy Adams, Zachary Taylor, Benjamin Harrison, Ronald Reagan.

• <u>Other exceptions</u>. (Killing Planet directed to the MC). William Henry Harrison, James Garfield. Both individuals died in office.

Table 15. Arcus Vitae: Model vs Empirical Results

	President	Hīlāj	Killing Planets	Empirical Arcus Vitae
1	G. Washington	☉	♄, ♃, ♀	☽ c. => ♄
				ASC Distributor ♄/♉
2	J. Adams	☉	♂	♂ c. => ☉
				☿ d. => MC
				ASC Distributor ♄/♊
3	T. Jefferson	☉	♃, ♂, ☿	ASC c. => ♂
4	J. Madison	☉	♂	☉ d. => ☊
5	J. Monroe	☽	♄, ♃, ♀	♄ c. => ☽
				ASC c. => ☿
6	J. Q. Adams	SAN	☿, ♄	ASC d. => ☿
				ASC c. => Moon
				SAN Distributor ♂/AR
7	A. Jackson	SAN	♀, ♂	SAN d. => ♀
8	M. van Buren	☉	♄, ♃	ASC d. => ☉
9	W. Harrison	LOF	☿, ♂	♂ d. => MC
				☿ d. => LOF
10	J. Tyler	☉	♀, ♂, ♃	☉ c. => Mars
				♃ d. => ASC
11	J. Polk	LOF	♃, ☿	♄ d. => LOF
12	Z. Taylor	☽	♂, ♀	☽ d. => Mars
				ASC Distributor ♄/AR
13	M. Fillmore	ASC/☉	♃, ☿	☿ d. => ☉
14	F. Pierce	☽/LOF	♂, ♀	♀ c. => LOF
				☽ d. => ♀
15	J. Buchanan	☉	☿, ♂, ♃	♃ d. => ASC
16	A. Lincoln	☽	♃, ♄, ♀	♀ d. => ☽
				☽ d. => ♄
17	A. Johnson	☉/LOF	♄, ♃, ♂	☉ d. => ☊
				LOF d. => ☋
18	U. Grant	☉/☽	♀, ☽	☽ d. => ASC
				☉ d. => ♃
				☉ c. => ♀
19	R. Hayes	☉/LOF	♀, ☽, ♂	LOF c. => ♂
				♂ c. => ☉
				☉ c. => ♀
20	J. Garfield	☉/LOF	☿, ♃, ♄	☿ d. => MC
21	C. Arthur	☉/LOF	♂, ♀, ♃	☋ d. => ☉
				☋ d. => LOF
22	G. Cleveland	☉	♀	♀ d. => ☉
23	B. Harrison	☽	☿, ♀	☽ c. => ♀
				☽ c. => ☊
				☽ Distributor ♄/♑
25	W. McKinley	☉	♄, ☿, ♃	☋ d. => ☉
26	T. Roosevelt	☽	♄, ♂, ♃	♃ c. => ASC
				♄ d. => ☽

Table 15 - *Continued*

27	W. Taft	☽	♀	♀ c. => ☽
28	W. Wilson	☉	♄, ☿	LOF d. => ☿
				☉ c. => ♄
29	W. Harding	☉/SAN	♂, ♀, ♃	☋ d. => SAN
				☉ c. => ♃
30	C. Coolidge	☉	☽, ♀, ♂	**solar arc** ☉ square ☋
31	H. Hoover	☉	♄, ♃	♄ d. => ☽
				♃ d. => ☉
32	F. Roosevelt	☽	♄, ♀, ☿	♄ d. => ☽
33	H. Truman	☽	☽, ♃, ♀	☿ d. => ☉
				☽ d. => ☋
34	D. Eisenhower	ASC	♃, ♄	♃ d. => ASC
35	J. Kennedy	LOF	♀, ☽	LOF c. => ♀
				ASC d. => ♂
				DSC c. => ☉
36	L. Johnson	☽	☿, ♃, ♀	☽ d. => ♄
37	R. Nixon	LOF	♂, ♄	LOF d. => ♄
38	G. Ford	☽	♃	♃ c. => ☽
				☽ d. => ♄
40	R. Reagan	Sun/LOF	☽, ♀, ♂	ASC Distributor ♄/ ♉
41	G. H. W. Bush	Sun/LOF	♄, ♂	ASC d. => ♂
				☉ c. => ASC

PART TWO

Prediction

CHAPTER SIX

The Problem of Under Specification

This Chapter opens a comprehensive survey of predictive methods used by practicing medieval astrologers. Because rectification assumes life events are timed by the promise of the natal figure, it is important to know *what* methods time *which* events. This requires understanding the interplay of competing techniques. Some methods are not useful for rectification; nevertheless, it is important to understand them all. Proper rectification requires the correct assignment of events to the appropriate predictive method. Understanding the nuts and bolts of each method is the goal of Part II.

Under Specification. Chapters 6-15 describe and illustrate each major predictive method using examples from the Presidential Database. When one considers the vast array of methods ranging from planetary periods to solar returns, it is no wonder why the modern rectification approach relying on transits, progressions, and solar arc directions has been lacking. There is a simple reason for this. As medieval methods fell out of favor, remaining tools like transits have been forced to pick up the slack. This problem has a name: *under specification*. It means that events are improperly attributed to various predictive techniques because the modern predictive toolbox is incomplete. With the rediscovery of medieval methods, there is no reason to continue forcing square pegs into round holes.

Andrew Jackson's House Fire. As a jumpstart to Part II, this Chapter opens with a detailed look at a major life event. Traditional methods including Directing through the Bounds (Chapter 10) and Hellenistic Lots (Chapter 13) are included. My objective in introducing these methods in this introductory example is to underscore the difference between modern and traditional predictive methods. Feel free to skip or return to this Chapter after reading all of Part II.

Case Study: Andrew Jackson's House Fire

A chimney fire destroyed much of the Hermitage, Andrew Jackson's Nashville, Tennessee estate, on 13-Oct-1834. This is one of many events used to refine Jackson's birth time to 7:52:55 AM; Ascendant = 1TA57'35" for this rectification project. As a case study, I will backtrack and first assume that rectification has confirmed a Taurus Ascendant for Jackson. In Chapter 17: *Three Stages of Rectification*, I assign the Ascendant selection to Stage I of the rectification process. In Stage II, events are tested to narrow down the angles to within 1-4 degrees of accuracy. The chimney fire is one such event. It and others are used to determine the exact degrees found on the angles by testing transits, progressions, and solar arc directions – at least that is the modern approach.

House Fire: Delineation. Because delineation precedes prediction, the first step is to assess what planets are the sources of Jackson's house fire read through his natal chart. The second step is to review dynamic measurements of these planets at the time of the house fire.

Mars. Because Mars signifies fire, Mars is the first suspect. In addition, other planets in fire signs may also contribute. To begin: do Mars or other planets in fire signs occupy or rule the 4th house or afflict the 4th house ruler?

Technically we do not know the sign on the 4th cusp. Should the true Ascendant be 16TA55 or later, the MC-IC axis will change to Aquarius-Leo. To cover both possibilities, both Cancer and Leo must be considered as possible signs on the 4th house cusp. *If Cancer*, look to Cancer's ruler the Moon because Cancer contains no planets. Mars receives the Moon by exaltation and harms the Moon. Mars/Taurus generally signifies explosions and does not appear to match the nature of a chimney fire which tends to spread slowly. However Mars/Taurus is in generosity with Venus/Aries which links Mars to Venus. Venus in a fire sign in the 12th house of secrets should be considered because the nature of chimney fires is hidden. Things hidden are signified by either combust planets or planets in the 12th house. Jackson has no planets combust, but Venus falls in the 12th. Because Mercury is conjunct Venus, Mercury also may be involved. *If Leo*, South Node in the fire sign of Leo signifies loss to real estate. Lord Sun in the 11th signifies that solar-signified friends, groups, organizations, are the cause.

Rounding up the suspects:

Moon. Afflicted and rules a possible Cancer 4th house (QS)
Mars. Afflicts the Moon and is the universal significator of fire
Venus. Connected to Mars by generosity, in a fire sign, and in the 12th house
Mercury. Conjunct Venus and may participate as a conspirator
South Node. Placement in the Leo 4th house (WS)
Sun. Ruler of the South Node and 4th house (WS)

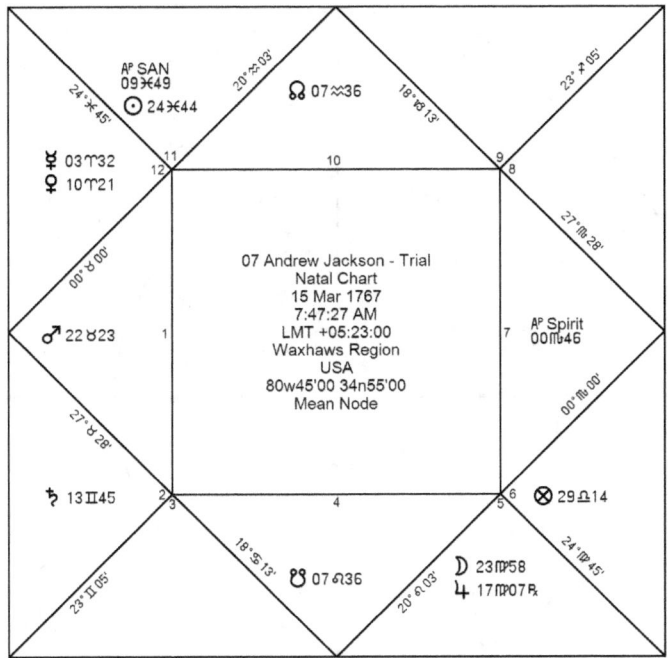

Testing the House Fire: Modern Approach

Once the Ascendant sign is confirmed, the goal of Stage II rectification is to narrow the Ascendant and Midheaven to between 1 and 4 degrees of accuracy. To proceed, the dynamic placement of the suspects is evaluated on the date of the house fire. For this exercise, I use a four-wheel quad module which presents, from inside to out: natal, solar arcs, progressions, and transits. Ideally there will be some measurements which cluster in Cancer or Leo. Clusters of multiple measurements, say transiting Mars at 15 Cancer and progressed Moon at 16 Cancer, might suggest the true position of the 4th cusp is between 15-16 degrees of Cancer. This step is taken to confirm the degree area of the IC; an exercise repeated with many other events.

I make no suggestion that Jackson's figure can be rectified with this house fire alone. My objective in this presentation is to see how far the envelope can be pushed by relying on progressions, transits, and solar arc directions. Next the exercise is repeated drawing from the full arsenal of methods available to the medieval predictive astrologer.

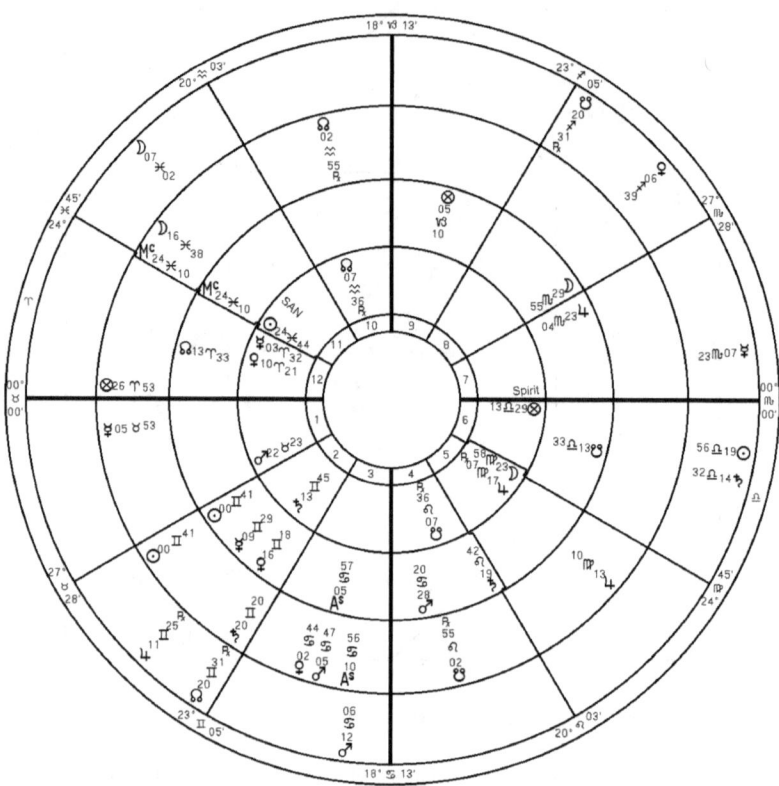

Tying the suspect list to the scene of the crime:

Planet	Measurement	Position
Mars	Transit	12CA01
Mars	Progressed	5CA47
Mars	Solar Arc	28CA20
Venus	Progressed	2CA44
South Node	Solar Arc	13LI33
Moon	Progressed	29SC55

At this point, under all methods Mars falls in the sign of Cancer, suggesting Cancer on the 4th cusp of home and real estate. Notice dsa South Node 13LI33 squares trMars 12CA01 within 2 degrees. Also see trSaturn 14LI30 forms a square aspect with trMars 12CA01. Saturn did not make the suspect list, but probably still plays a role because of the square aspect to Mars. Mars-Saturn in hard aspect is always a difficult configuration. So a *cluster* of dynamic measurements is identified falling between 12-15 degrees of cardinal signs. This suggests the IC might be 12-15 Cancer. The second possibility is 28-29 degrees Cancer because of dsa Mars 28CA20 and progressed Moon 29SC58. Finally, progressed Mars and Venus are within 2-5 Cancer, another possible degree range. As for measurements activating the Moon, except for trNodes square the Moon within 5 degrees, there is no dynamic activity to the Moon of interest.

Using modern methods of rectification which assume this fire should be timed by dynamic activity to the angles (here the 4th) or the Moon, the exercise is now complete. It is repeated for a wider array of events to determine if either 12-15, 28-29, or 2-5 degrees of Cancer is confirmed as a possible IC. The IC's degree is then chosen on a *best fit* basis from all events tested.

Testing the House Fire: Medieval Predictive Astrology

Considering the complete array of predictive methods, the solution to timing Jackson's house fire requires the use of Hellenistic Lots and Directing through the Bounds. Without these methods, the house fire cannot be predicted.

Converse Measurements. It's been my practice to complement direct measurements with converse measurements because events are occasionally shown through converse and not by direct motion.[15] There is no documented use of converse measurements in traditional astrology; accordingly, my usage here is unusual, even heretical for some in the tradition.

Adding some converse measurements to the Suspect list:

Planet	Motion	Measurement	Position
Mars	Direct	Transit	12CA01
Mars	Direct	Progressed	5CA47
Mars	Direct	Solar Arc	28CA20
Venus	Direct	Progressed	2CA44
South Node	Direct	Solar Arc	*13LI33****
Moon	Direct	Secondary Progressed	29SC58
Moon	*Converse*	Solar Arc	*15CA45****
Mars	*Converse*	Solar Arc	*14PI10****

---

[15] Writing this 4th edition in 2022, I currently use converse solar arc and primary directions. I no longer use converse transits though there are a few examples of converse transits which remain in this book from earlier editions.

Lots. Rechecking Jackson's figure for converse measurements, I discover two additional observations: csa Moon 15CA45 and csa Mars 14PI10. Compared to dsa South Node 13LI33 both Moon and Mars converse solar arc directions form an antiscia relationship. Do these three measurements work as a unit to time the house fire? It's at this point I will let the cat out of the bag. Based on the final rectification, these measurements formed tight aspects to the Lot of Real Estate 15LI32 and its antiscion 14PI28:

dsa South Node conj. Lot of Real Estate, error = 2 deg 1min
csa Moon square Lot of Real Estate, error = 13 minutes
csa Mars conj. antiscion of Lot of Real Estate, error = 18 minutes

The earlier assumption that 12-15 cardinal was correct, except it applied to a Lot and not the 4th house cusp! Because Lots represent *customized Ascendants* for a specific life area, they are especially helpful in rectification.

Directing through the Bounds. This method supplies the missing link of dynamic activity to the 4th cusp itself. Of the many predictive methods recently uncovered, few appear more significant than Directing through the Bounds which dynamically moves the significators through the Egyptian bounds by primary motion. Recalling comments on bounds in Chapter 1, I stated that bounds impart their own intrinsic quality to whatever planet falls within their confines. The same can be said for any significator (e.g., the IC) which moves through the bounds.

On 13-Oct-1834, Andrew Jackson's directed 4th cusp fell at 28VI35, falling in the bound of Saturn/Virgo, defined as the two-degree range between 28deg00min and 28deg59min of Virgo. The position of the directed 4th cusp at 28VI35 meant the bound had changed from Mars/Virgo about seven months previously. Understanding the nature of both these bounds and the evolution of chimney fires helps explain why the fire started in the fall of 1834.

The nature of Mars is hot and dry; in the cold and dry earth sign of Virgo, dryness is emphasized. The nature of Saturn is cold and dry, both qualities emphasized by Virgo. Saturn's nature is destruction by compression and breakage unlike Mars which burns. Chimneys are constructed with bricks and mortar. Chimney fires happen after mortar is fatigued by repeated applications of heat; finally cracking and revealing exposed flammable materials, usually wood or plaster. It is the agency of Mars/Virgo, acting as the directed 4th cusp moved through its bound; that caused mortar fatigue by heat. Yet the actual crumbling of the mortar did not occur until the directed 4th cusp moved into the bound of Saturn/Virgo because it is Saturn's nature to destroy through cracking. Why did the fire not occur as soon as the directed 4th cusp entered the bound of Saturn/Virgo on 28-Mar-1834? Because seasonally, no fires were lit after the warmth of spring arrived. The fire lit on 13-Oct-1834 was probably one of the first fires lit in the fall season.

CHAPTER SEVEN

Temporal Indicators

Sometimes a particular event or activity changes *over time* or *as one gets older*. Implied in these statements is a temporal change in life affairs which has no precise date or time. This chapter discusses three predictive methods which are designed to identify these long-term temporal shifts.

Chapter Summary

Conjunctional and Preventional Births. The degree of the New or Full Moon immediately prior to birth is known as the Syzygy Ante Navitatem ("SAN"). It joins the Ascendant, Midheaven, Sun, Moon, and Lot of Fortune as one of the six principal significators which are directed and profected. If after a New Moon, the natal chart is called *conjunctional*. If after a Full Moon, the natal chart is called *preventional*. Applied as a temporal indicator, conjunctional nativities manifest higher levels of activity during the first half of life; preventional figures, during the second half.

Moon's Separation and Application. In horary astrology, the planet from which the Moon separates shows events in the past; the planet to which the Moon applies shows events in the future. When applied to natal astrology, the interpretation is slightly different. The separating planet bears influence during early life; the applying planet, during later years. The Moon's configuration is one of the most important aspect combinations which indicate the flow of energy through the overall natal chart.

Multiple Planets in a single Sign. When two or more planets fall in a single sign, there is an implied sequence in each planet's temporal influence on house affairs. The first planet in a sign marks its influence and is followed by each successive planet, ordered from lowest to highest by zodiacal degree. Should the sign ruler participate in the stellium, its influence is relatively constant.

CONJUNCTIONAL AND PREVENTIONAL BIRTHS

Use of SAN in natal astrology. Besides its use as a possible hīlāj, one of the principal significators, and one input for computing the victor, little survives as to the use of the SAN in natal astrology. Here Bonatti (2007, 1403) provides a hint:

> *But the degree of the conjunction is directed for generally knowing ahead of time and for considering, all the aforesaid up to the middle of the native's life (if he nativity were conjunctional). Whence if it were well disposed, it will increase the signification of those things signifying good, and will decrease what is signified by those signifying evil. If however it were badly disposed, it will increase the signification of those things signifying evil, and will take away from what is signified by those signifying good. You could say the same about the degree of the prevention after the middle of life (if the nativity were preventional).*

Though Bonatti is talking about employing the SAN in primary directions, it is possible to glean from his reasoning the conjunctional degree is analogous to the first half of life, as is the Moon in her waxing phase. The preventional degree is analogous to the second half of life, as is the waning Moon. It is a small jump from this analogy to the notion that individuals born after a New Moon demonstrate higher levels of activity earlier than those born after a Full Moon. Stated differently, conjunctional figures demonstrate accelerated development before middle age. In contrast, those with preventional figures do not come into their own until after middle age. This is the opinion of Robert Zoller who suggests individuals with conjunctional figures are *early bloomers*; those with preventional figures, *late bloomers* (Zoller 2002, Chapter 16).

No implication for 'Good' or 'Bad' Affairs. Be aware there is nothing *good* or *bad* implied about how individuals may develop. A conjunctional figure which is unusually stressed will manifest difficulties early on. The most that can be said for these individuals is that life should not materially deteriorate after middle age because all the skeletons should be out of the closet. The opposite scenario applies for preventional figures. Hints of crisis before midlife may become full-blown disasters after midlife if so promised.

Evaluating the Presidential Database. Table 16 summarizes birth date, lifespan, midpoint of lifespan, SAN's degree, lunar phase, and whether the figure is conjunctional or preventional.

In what follows, the early/late bloomer proposition is evaluated for all Presidential nativities.

Table 16. Lifespan, Midpoint, Syzygy ante Navitatem, and Lunar Phase

	President	Birth	Span	Midpoint	SAN	Qtr	Type
1	G. Washington	22-Feb-32	67.8	15-Jan-66	21LE33	4th	Prev.
2	J. Adams	30-Oct-35	90.7	28-Feb-81	22LI14	2nd	Conj.
3	T. Jefferson	13-Apr-43	83.2	21-Nov-84	18LI42	3rd	Prev.
4	J. Madison	15-Mar-51	85.3	3-Nov-93	21VI09	3rd	Prev.
5	J. Monroe	28-Apr-58	73.2	29-Nov-94	3SC09	3rd	Prev.
6	J. Q. Adams	11-Jul-67	80.6	31-Oct-07	18CP58	3rd	Prev.
7	A. Jackson	15-Mar-67	78.2	25-Apr-06	9PI49	2nd	Conj.
8	M. van Buren	5-Dec-82	79.6	26-Sep-22	12SA56	1st	Conj.
9	W. Harrison	9-Feb-73	68.1	8-Mar-07	19LE05	3rd	Prev.
10	J. Tyler	29-Mar-90	71.8	18-Feb-26	25PI24	2nd	Conj.
11	J. Polk	2-Nov-95	53.6	22-Aug-22	4TA37	3rd	Prev.
12	Z. Taylor	24-Nov-84	65.6	14-Sep-17	21SC17	2nd	Conj.
13	M. Fillmore	7-Jan-00	74.2	5-Feb-37	4CP56	2nd	Conj.
14	F. Pierce	23-Nov-04	64.9	29-Apr-37	24TA56	3rd	Prev.
15	J. Buchanan	23-Apr-91	77.1	10-Nov-29	28LI33	3rd	Prev.
16	A. Lincoln	12-Feb-09	56.2	15-Mar-37	11LE22	4th	Prev.
17	A. Johnson	29-Dec-08	66.6	13-Apr-42	25SA31	2nd	Conj.
18	U. Grant	27-Apr-22	63.2	8-Dec-53	00TA57	1st	Conj.
19	R. Hayes	4-Oct-22	70.3	25-Nov-57	7AR12	3rd	Prev.
20	J. Garfield	19-Nov-31	49.8	17-Oct-56	26TA44	3rd	Prev.
21	C. Arthur	5-Oct-29	57.1	27-Apr-58	4LI39	1st	Conj.
22/24	G. Cleveland	18-Mar-37	71.3	3-Nov-72	16PI06	2nd	Conj.
23	B. Harrison	20-Aug-33	67.6	30-May-67	22LE27	1st	Conj.
25	W. McKinley	29-Jan-43	58.6	20-May-72	9LE32	4th	Prev.
26	T. Roosevelt	27-Oct-58	60.2	30-Nov-88	28AR56	3rd	Prev.
27	W. Taft	15-Sep-57	72.5	9-Dec-93	11PI34	4th	Prev.
28	W. Wilson	29-Dec-56	67.1	17-Jul-90	5CP51	1st	Conj.
29	W. Harding	2-Nov-65	58.7	15-Mar-95	26LI18	2nd	Conj.
30	C. Coolidge	4-Jul-72	60.5	3-Oct-02	00CP08	4th	Prev.
31	H. Hoover	10-Aug-74	90.2	14-Sep-19	5AQ50	4th	Prev.
32	F. Roosevelt	30-Jan-82	63.2	4-Sep-13	29CP34	2nd	Conj.
33	H. Truman	8-May-84	88.6	30-Aug-28	5TA46	2nd	Conj.
34	D. Eisenhower	14-Oct-90	78.5	3-Jan-30	20LI33	1st	Conj.
35	J. Kennedy	29-May-17	46.5	23-Aug-40	29TA23	2nd	Conj.
36	L. Johnson	27-Aug-08	64.4	8-Nov-40	3VI15	1st	Conj.
37	R. Nixon	9-Jan-13	81.3	30-Aug-53	16CP33	1st	Conj.
38	G. Ford	14-Jul-13	93.5	3-Apr-60	11CA36	2nd	Conj.
40	R. Reagan	6-Feb-11	93.3	5-Oct-57	9AQ24	1st	Conj.
41	G. H. W. Bush	12-Jun-24	94.5	17-Sep-82	11GE44	2nd	Conj.

George Washington: Preventional, Midpoint = 15-Jan-1766. Before midlife, Washington was a surveyor and fought during the French and Indian Wars. His life was relatively undistinguished before 1765 when he was elected to the House of Burgesses. He witnessed conflict with Britain over taxation in 1765 with the Stamp Act's passage and its repeal in 1766. Following the imposition of the Townshend Act in 1767, Washington presented resolutions opposing taxation on 7-May-1769. Conflict over taxation directly led to the American Revolution with Washington taking a leading role after midlife.

John Adams: Conjunctional, Midpoint = 25-Feb-1781. Adams' role as signer of the Declaration of Independence in 1776, writer of the Massachusetts State Constitution in 1779, and his strained foreign diplomatic efforts culminating with his Dutch Mission of 1780-1782 established patterns for the rest of his life. He considered the Massachusetts State Constitution one of his life's greatest achievements. All of these events occurred prior to midlife. His later Presidential term was considered weak. In addition, his post-Presidential correspondence with Jefferson did not break new ground; it was a purposeful revisiting of themes from Adams' early days.

Thomas Jefferson: Preventional, Midpoint = 21-Nov-1784. Jefferson's departure for France on 5-Jul-1784 opened a new world for him as a diplomat and later as witness to the French Revolution. In France, Jefferson was exposed to new ideas which he would eventually translate into the formation of the new Republican Party. The timing of his Presidency coincided with the shift of the Jupiter-Saturn conjunction into the earthy triplicity. This conjunction, triggering Jefferson's Jupiter/Virgo/4th house, marked numerous changes including the expansion of the United States with the Louisiana Purchase. With regard to the exact life midpoint, note that Jefferson's French Mission in the fall of 1782 was cancelled because of a peace treaty. Not until Jefferson passed his life's midpoint did he travel to France for the first time.

James Madison: Preventional; Midpoint = 3-Nov-1793. On first glance, the fact that Madison's role as the *Father of the Constitution* – signed 1787 before midlife – appears to invalidate the theory that Madison should make his mark later. And yet Madison's 3-Jan-1794 introduction of Congressional measures relating to trade; asserting the commercial power of the United States because of raw materials exports to Europe, tells another story. From this point on, Madison would be deeply involved with issues of trade, neutrality, and impressments which would culminate under his wartime Presidency against Britain with the War of 1812. These were new themes for Madison which would ultimately have as much impact on the early Republic as did his work on the Constitution.

James Monroe: Preventional; Midpoint = 29-Nov-1794. The 19-Nov-1794 conclusion of the Jay Treaty favoring the British triggered a period of political upheaval for Monroe whose preference for the French was unwelcome by Washington and other Federalists. Not until Jefferson's election in 1800 did political winds shift towards Monroe. He would serve as Governor of Virginia, as Minister to France where he (with Livingston) negotiated the Louisiana Purchase, as Secretary of War under Madison, and as President where his Monroe Doctrine continues to influence American Foreign Policy to the present day.

John Quincy Adams: Preventional; Midpoint = 31-Oct-1807. Under Jefferson's term, the Senate passed the Embargo Act on 18-Dec-1807; John Quincy Adams helped write the legislation. Regulation of trade is a theme he would return to as President with his signing of the infamous Tariff of Abominations in 1828. More importantly, by supporting the Embargo Act, Adams broke with his constituents of the Federalist Party which included his parents as members. Before midlife his development was dominated by both parents. His support of the Embargo Act of 1807 marks a break with the past. After midlife he achieved recognition as Secretary of State and *Old Man Eloquent* in his post-Presidential Senatorial career though his Presidency was largely a failure.

Andrew Jackson: Conjunctional; Midpoint = 25-Apr-1806. In the early 1800s, Jackson built a sizeable political organization in Tennessee. His disputes with both Governor-to-be Sevier over his wife Rachel and a separate argument with Charles Dickinson who Jackson killed in a duel on 30-May-1806 culminated at Jackson's life midpoint. One major natal placement – ruler of the 1st in the 12th – manifested early in Jackson's youth when he was captured and tortured by the British. His universal hatred of Indians also marked his early development. After 1806, Jackson's life was a variation on these themes.

Martin Van Buren: Conjunctional; Midpoint = 26-Sep-1822. Van Buren's role in creating the Democratic Party during the years 1817-1821 was his life's most important accomplishment. Following his 1821 election, his active political life as Senator and President was the logical extension of the party he created prior to midlife.

William Harrison: Preventional; Midpoint = 8-Mar-1807. Though Harrison's role in fraudulently negotiating away much Indian land predates midlife, the rise of Tecumseh following the solar eclipse of 16-Jun-1806 predicted by Tecumseh's brother (a.k.a. the 'Prophet') had a greater influence on Harrison's career. Harrison would later defeat Tecumseh at the Battle of Thames River on 5-Oct-1813; an event which would play a prominent role in his 1840 Presidential election some twenty-seven years later.

John Tyler: Conjunctional; Midpoint = 18-Feb-1826. Tyler's 20-Feb-1819 speech on the floor of the House stating the Bank of the United States was unconstitutional was a key life event which would similarly mark his Presidency. His 10-Dec-1825 election to the Virginia Governorship for a one-year term – a position mostly ceremonial – marked his life midpoint. As President, Tyler would have little political power following his veto of the Bank of the United States.

Both of these themes – holding a ceremonial office and hatred of central banking – were fully developed before midlife.

James Polk: Preventional; Midpoint = 22-Aug-1822. Polk's engagement to Sarah Childress in 1822 and his election to Congress in the fall of 1824 opened new chapters in his life. His expansionist policies including settlement of the Oregon question and the acquisition of territory through the Mexican War are for what Polk is remembered. Both occurred after midlife.

Zachary Taylor: Conjunctional; Midpoint = 14-Sep-1817. Taylor's early military career was marked by victories, facilitating appropriate food and supplies for his troops during periods of organizational disarray, and conflict with superiors over promotion and rank. These patterns would continue throughout his almost fifty years as a career military professional. His Presidency offered nothing new and was considered a failure.

Millard Fillmore: Conjunctional; Midpoint = 5-Feb-1837. By midlife Fillmore was known as a distinguished lawyer in western New York. The balance of his political life was a variation on legalistic themes including the Missouri Compromise of 1850 signed during his Presidential term.

Franklin Pierce: Preventional; Midpoint = 29-Apr-1837. Prior to midlife, Pierce carved out a minor role as a New Hampshire politico in the shadow of his father. Pierce's election to the Senate in 1837 together with death of both parents during 1838-1839 opened the national political stage to Pierce and propelled his subsequent rise to the Presidency.

James Buchanan: Preventional; Midpoint = 10-Nov-1829. Buchanan's October 1828 re-election to the House as a Democrat, following four terms as a Federalist, marked his successful transition to the new Democratic Party united under Andrew Jackson. This election solidified Buchanan's reputation as Pennsylvania's leading Democrat. This was the foundation of his remaining political career which led to the Presidency.

Abraham Lincoln: Preventional; Midpoint = 15-Mar-1837. If there is any accuracy of life's midpoint marking a distinct shift in activity one need look no further than Lincoln who on 15-Mar-1837 moved to Springfield to begin his law practice. This immediately followed his 1st attack against slavery on 3-Mar-1837 when he protested an anti-abolitionist resolution. After this time Lincoln's level of activity increased dramatically.

Andrew Johnson: Conjunctional; Midpoint = 13-Apr-1842. By 1840, Johnson was a wealthy businessman with interests in his own tailor shop and real estate. Politically he adhered to the strict Jackson party line on the limited role of central government; a philosophy which would later influence his decisions on Reconstruction. He was also openly criticized as a *brigand*. Similar comments would mar his publicity as President. All of these patterns were fully in place by midlife.

Ulysses Grant: Conjunctional; Midpoint = 8-Dec-1853. Grant began his career at West Point in 1839. After military exploits during the Mexican War which brought Grant to the attention of his superiors, Grant's military career faded by midlife as peacetime demobilization left Grant among the few remaining members of a skeleton Army. He started drinking heavily and resigned his army commission on 11-Apr-1854. Grant's rise to the Presidency after midlife is directly tied to the recapitulation of his natal Jupiter-Saturn conjunction in Taurus at age 60. This is an example of a mundane configuration which overrides theory regarding conjunctional births. Without the Jupiter-Saturn conjunction in his figure, Grant would have probably died a broken man.

Rutherford Hayes: Preventional; Midpoint = 25-Nov-1857. Though Hayes' nomination speech for Fremont as Republican Presidential Candidate during June 1856 did not lead to Fremont's election, it did open doors for Hayes in the Republican Party. Hayes' subsequent Civil War service, his efforts at civil service reform as President, his involvement with prison reform, and the education of Freedman were accomplishments which marked the second half of his life.

James Garfield: Preventional; Midpoint = 17-Oct-1856. Garfield's graduation from Williams College on 7-Aug-1856 opened the world of academia to him where he was first appointed to Professor of Latin and Greek at Hiram College the same year. He was quickly promoted to College President in 1857. He spoke as a preacher in Great Awakening revivals and won an important debate on Darwinism, taking the Intelligent Design viewpoint. Active participation in Civil War military service, in Congress, and as President demonstrates accelerated development after midlife.

Chester Arthur: Conjunctional; Midpoint = 27-Apr-1858. Arthur's college days were marked by partying and pranks. As he approached midlife, he moved to New York in 1856 and became entrenched in Thurlow Weed's political machine. Arthur's remaining political life was marked by the aggressive tactics of local politics, a pattern established during his first two years in New York prior to 1858.

Grover Cleveland: Conjunctional; Midpoint = 3-Nov-1872. By 1872, Cleveland had carved out a well-defined political niche in Buffalo, New York. While still at the city-level, Cleveland had already earned a reputation as an honest law enforcer first as Assistant District Attorney and later as Sheriff. He rode these themes to a position of national prominence following midlife when the popularity of reform movements made Cleveland's no-nonsense style valuable at the ballot box.

Benjamin Harrison: Conjunctional; Midpoint = 30-May-1867. Harrison's successful law career was interrupted by riding Lincoln's coattails to an elected political office in 1860 following his adoption of an anti-slavery platform.

Harrison served in the Civil War with distinction and was present at the fall of Atlanta. After demobilization, Harrison returned to his legal practice where he achieved his greatest legal victory in the successful prosecution of a widely publicized double homicide in 1869. The remainder of his life was marked by his legal expertise, an area developed before midlife. His 1898 post-Presidential assignment as Venezuela's representative in a border dispute with British Guyana is another variation of legal expertise acquired before midlife.

William McKinley: Preventional; Midpoint = 20-May-1872. Following his marriage to Ida Saxton in 1871, the death of his two daughters during 1873 and 1875 caused his wife to suffer tremendous psychological distress. His marriage – now to an invalid – would strongly mark McKinley's post mid-life period all the way to the Presidency. He achieved sympathy from the public because of his tender care for his wife's condition. Politically, McKinley won his first seat in the House in 1876 and begun to specialize in the tariff the following year. Interest in the tariff and corporate trusts were new themes for McKinley which would mark the balance of his political life.

Theodore Roosevelt: Preventional; Midpoint = 30-Nov-1888. Roosevelt's 1889 appointment to the Civil Service Commission by Grover Cleveland gave Roosevelt the platform to gain a reputation as a reformer through propaganda. Before this time, Roosevelt had suffered extreme loss with the death of his wife and mother in 1884. Roosevelt's life between 1884 and 1889 was largely spent as a pilgrimage in the Dakota Badlands. Up to 1888 his life was relatively undistinguished. Roosevelt's rise to national political fame can be dated to his Civil Service appointment, just after midlife.

William Howard Taft: Preventional; Midpoint = 9-Dec-1893. Taft's 1892 resignation from the position as U.S. solicitor general to become a US circuit judge marked an increase in life activity and purpose. His eventual goal of Chief Justice of the Supreme Court was achieved following stints as Governor of the Philippines under McKinley, Secretary of War under Theodore Roosevelt, and as President. All these activities followed midlife.

Woodrow Wilson: Conjunctional; Midpoint = 17-Jul-1890. Wilson's 1890 appointment to Princeton University as professor of jurisprudence and history marked the culmination of his academic career at midlife.

Wilson's later prominence during World War I and its aftermath was tied to his Jupiter-Saturn square without which he would have likely remained functioning at the local or regional political level. Wilson's *Peace without Victory* speech of 22-Jan-1917 epitomized his role in the mundane wave; the speech was timed by the recapitulation of Wilson's natal Jupiter/Aries – Saturn/Cancer square.

Warren Harding: Conjunctional; Midpoint = 15-Mar-1895. With the printing of the Industrial Edition of the Marion Star newspaper on 15-Jun-1895, a 32-page supplement with pictures of local buildings and landmarks, Harding firmly established himself as the editor and publisher of one of Ohio's leading newspapers. His *bloviations* on the editorial page, frequent trips to Battle Creek Sanitarium for depression, and marriage to Florence King were all key life patterns established by midlife. His election to the State Senate in 1899 and subsequent political life were variations on these existing themes.

Calvin Coolidge: Preventional; Midpoint = 3-Oct-1902. Coolidge's appointment as Clerk of Courts on the death of the incumbent in 1903 and his 1904 chairmanship of the Northhampton Republican City Committee laid the political groundwork which would later propel him to national politics. As with his 1903 appointment, he would assume the Presidency after the death in office of a sitting elected political leader.

Herbert Hoover: Preventional; Midpoint = 14-Sep-1919. Hoover's accomplishments are so many that one questions with a fortune made from mining engineering and volunteer service as head of the Belgium Food Relief effort (ending September 1919 at midlife) whether Hoover should qualify as a conjunctional nativity. But his figure is preventional. It appears that Hoover's rise and fall as President, together with the start of the Hoover Dam's construction in 1930, represents a sufficient departure from affairs prior to midlife to qualify Hoover as a Preventional figure.

Franklin Roosevelt: Conjunctional; Midpoint = 4-Sep-1913. By midlife, FDR followed his cousin Theodore Roosevelt's playbook by first winning a seat to the New York Assembly followed by a stint as Assistant Secretary of the Navy. Roosevelt's political machinations, together with his hawkish stance in response to the 1914 Vera Cruz incident, were patterns FDR carried with him the remainder of his life. Roosevelt's stature as wartime President and world statesman is attributed to the unique placement of his Jupiter-Saturn conjunction in the 9th house of foreign affairs; without which he never would have rode the mundane wave of WWII.

Harry Truman: Conjunctional; Midpoint = 30-Aug-1928. By 1928, Truman served in the military during WWI, had run a haberdashery business, and as elected judge achieved a no-nonsense reputation later epitomized by his placard *The Buck Stops Here* which he carried to the White House.

Dwight Eisenhower: Conjunctional; Midpoint = 3-Jan-1930. By midlife, Eisenhower's military career was marked by his work in military logistics and procurement published during 1930-1931. His subsequent career, ranging from his success at D-Day to his final Presidential speech warning of the power of the military-industrial complex was a direct outgrowth of his military expertise in logistics achieved prior to midlife.

John F. Kennedy: Conjunctional; Midpoint = 23-Aug-1940. Kennedy's active sex life and physical ailments were patterns established early in life. More important to understanding his role in American history was publication of his honors thesis *Why England Slept* during August 1940. Acclaimed at the time, but criticized by a later generation of historians as a work filled with errors, Kennedy came to the conclusion that Germany's domination of air power had forced a weak Britain to appease Hitler at Munich in 1938. In an argument made by biographer Perret (1995: 85-86), Kennedy's bias – fully developed by midlife – later convinced himself that there truly was a *missile gap* between the US and Russia. The missile gap scare accelerated the cold war nuclear arms race and arguably led to the Cuban Missile Crisis of 1962 for which Kennedy was a principal player.

Lyndon Johnson: Conjunctional; Midpoint = 8-Nov-1940. FDR's appointment of Johnson to manage Democratic Congressional campaigns on 9-Oct-1940 placed LBJ on the national political stage. This event was the culmination of LBJ's life up to that point. Prior to 1940, LBJ had garnered exceptional political skills as a workaholic in Senator Kleburg's Congressional office, an aggressive experimenter and implementer of social programs as Texas administrator for FDR's National Youth Administration, and as an effective dealmaker for local constituents – particularly his efforts in supplying electricity through the Rural Electric Administration. After 1940, LBJ's national political career was a variation on themes developed prior to midlife.

Richard Nixon: Conjunctional; Midpoint = 30-Aug-1953. Nixon's aggressive political tactics against opponents funded by off-the-record political contributions from powerful conservatives established his political modus operandi prior to midlife. His wildly successful *Checkers* speech of 23-Sep-1952, when he turned accusations of campaign finance irregularities into a political boon, marked for many years the most widely seen television event in American history. With *Checkers,* Nixon truly made his mark by midlife.

Gerald Ford: Conjunctional; Midpoint = 3-Apr-1960. During Ford's World War II military service, his philosophy moved from Midwestern isolationism to an interventionist foreign policy doctrine. His knack for fiscal conservatism combined with military experience landed Ford as chair of the Army subcommittee on Defense Appropriations during Eisenhower's Presidential tenure in the 1950s. By 1960, Ford's transformation as a fiscal conservative with an interventionist philosophy backed by a strong military was complete. His later years and extensive post-Presidency revealed no new major life themes.

Ronald Reagan: Conjunctional; Midpoint = 5-Oct-1957. Reagan's early stint in radio broadcasting established his skills as the *Great Communicator.* His acting career added comfort in appearing on the political stage. His conservative political views, marked by anti-Communist testimony against fellow actors/actresses, were firmly established prior to midlife. Reagan achieved national name recognition with his position as host of General Electric Theatre in the mid-1950s. Together with his marriage to Nancy Davis, in 1952; Reagan's development was complete by midlife.

George H. W. Bush: Conjunctional; Midpoint = 5-Sep-1971. Early years witnessed a steady sequence of career events which marked the bulk of GHWB's professional life. They include: WWII service, oil drilling, political elections: two unsuccessful Senate bids and two successful House elections, and his first political appointment as UN Ambassador. While success in the First Gulf War was an outstanding accomplishment of GHWB's Presidential term occurring after midlife, arguably the pattern of public service through elected office and political appointments was firmly established prior to midlife. GHWB states his life in public service was based on his family's belief that those gifted with health, money, and intellectual competence should give back to society. For public service, GHWB was an 'early bloomer.'

Conjunctional and Preventional Births: Summary of Findings

Vindication of Early-Late Bloomer Development Pattern. These findings support the thesis that conjunctional nativities assert their influence prior to midlife; preventional nativities, after midlife. Exceptions to the rule for Ulysses Grant, Woodrow Wilson, and Franklin D. Roosevelt are attributed to the overriding importance of mundane Jupiter-Saturn aspects which connect these individuals to world affairs, without which I suggest the second half of their lives would have been considerably less active.

Usefulness in Rectification. For individuals born a few hours before or after either a New or Full Moon, this technique may prove helpful for rectification. Be aware that only until one passes life's midpoint will sufficient data accumulate in order to judge when the individual made their mark. For these cases, especially for historical figures for which the entire life story is known, the technique can be useful. But the probability of a practicing astrologer encountering this situation is rather low. Consider it a useful, but rare method in the rectification toolbox.

For further Study. Of all significators, very few aphorisms survive regarding the usage of the Syzygy Ante Navitatem. For conjunctional figures, Bonatti instructs the SAN should be directed to time events during the first one-half of life; for Preventional figures; the latter one-half of life. This instruction remains untested and may prove difficult to falsify based on the ability of other planetary period methods to time major life events.

MOON'S SEPARATION AND APPLICATION

Application to Natal Astrology. On initial glance, the inclusion of topics like application and separation, the transfer, collection, or deprivation of light; and refranation appear out of place in natal astrology texts. But Abū Ma'shar, Bonatti, Ibn Ezra, and others include them not as horary rules mistakenly placed in a natal text, but as fundamental tools to analyze the interaction among planets once individually delineated. Given the infinite number of planetary configurations, it is easy to get lost in the details of every possible configuration. Traditional authors recognized the Moon's separation and application as one of the most important planetary configurations. For this reason, the Moon is the focus of this section. A more complicated example of Mercury rounds out the discussion.

Predictive Capability. Unlike horary where the separating planet shows a past event relative to the time when the horary question is posed, the separating planet in natal astrology shows events early in life which over time are replaced by events signified by the planet to which the Moon applies.

Moon's Application to Malefics. When the Moon applies to malefics, the general signification is calamity (Saturn) or warfare (Mars). Most Presidents whose Moon applies to Saturn are ranked as failures by historians. All Presidents whose Moon applied to Mars fought wars either during or prior to their Presidential Terms.

Presidential Greatness. Washington, Lincoln, and Franklin D. Roosevelt consistently rank as the greatest USA Presidents. Maternus' aphorisms for the Moon's configuration with Mars, Jupiter, and Saturn are successful in predicting effective Presidential leadership.

Moon's Application to Malefics

Quite often when facing a new predictive method for the first time I wish to see whether the influence of malefics is clearly demonstrated. Such is the power of malefics that if one encounters active malefics in a predictive method but no sign of adversity; then either the method does not work, the event remains unknown to the researcher, or the chart is incorrect. Only when the zodiacal state of malefics configured as accidental benefics do malefics avoid calamity. Yet even when malefics are accidental benefics, gains in these special cases are not freely bestowed because they are usually accompanied by struggle. Bottom line: when the Moon applies to malefics, the individual should encounter problems as they age.

Sources for aphorisms. Both Maternus (1975) and Pearce (1970) provide aphorisms for the Moon's separation and application.

Table 17. Moon's Separation and Application

	President	Separates	Applies	Sect	SAN	
1	G. Washington	♃	♂	N	Preventional	
2	J. Adams	♂	VOC (M) ☉ (H)	D	Conjunctional	SE
3	T. Jefferson	♃	♂	D	Preventional	
4	J. Madison	♂	☉	N	Preventional	
5	J. Monroe	♄	☉	N	Preventional	
6	J. Q. Adams	☉	VOC (M) ♂ (H)	D	Preventional	LE
7	A. Jackson	♂	☉	D	Conjunctional	
8	M. van Buren	☉	VOC (M) ♄ (H)	D	Conjunctional	
9	W. Harrison	♄	♀	N	Preventional	
10	J. Tyler	♀	♄	D	Conjunctional	
11	J. Polk	♀	♂	D	Preventional	
12	Z. Taylor	♀	♂	D	Conjunctional	
13	M. Fillmore	n.a.	♄	N	Conjunctional	
14	F. Pierce	♃	☿	N	Preventional	
15	J. Buchanan	☉	♄	D	Preventional	LE
16	A. Lincoln	♃	♂	N	Preventional	
17	A. Johnson	♃	♄	N	Conjunctional	
18	U. Grant	♀	VOC (M) ♄ (H)	D	Conjunctional	
19	R. Hayes	♃	☉	N	Preventional	
20	J. Garfield	☿	♄	N	Preventional	
21	C. Arthur	n.a.	☿	N	Conjunctional	SE
22/24	G. Cleveland	♄	VOC (M) ☿ (H)	D	Conjunctional	
23	B. Harrison	♃	♀	N	Conjunctional	
25	W. McKinley	♃	☉	N	Preventional	LE
26	T. Roosevelt	☉	♂	N	Preventional	
27	W. Taft	♂	VOC (M) ♃ (H)	D	Preventional	LE
28	W. Wilson	n.a.	♃	N	Conjunctional	
29	W. Harding	n.a.	♄	D	Conjunctional	SE
30	C. Coolidge	♃	VOC (M) ♂ (H)	N	Preventional	
31	H. Hoover	♂	♄	N	Preventional	
32	F. Roosevelt	♄	♃	N	Conjunctional	
33	H. Truman	♀	♂	D	Conjunctional	SE
34	D. Eisenhower	♃	♄	N	Conjunctional	
35	J. Kennedy	♀	♂	D	Conjunctional	
36	L. Johnson	☉	☿	N	Conjunctional	
37	R. Nixon	n.a.	♄	N	Conjunctional	
38	G. Ford	n.a.	♀	N	Conjunctional	
39	J. Carter	♄	☿	D	Conjunctional	
40	R. Reagan	♃	☉	N	Conjunctional	
41	G. H. W. Bush	♀	☉	D	Conjunctional	
42	B. Clinton	☿	☉	D	Preventional	
43	G. W. Bush	☉	♃	D	Conjunctional	SE
44	B. Obama	☿	☉	N	Preventional	
45	D. Trump	♃	☉	D	Conjunctional	SE
46	J. Biden	n.a.	♂	D	Conjunctional	

Application to Saturn. Such is the negativity of the Moon's application to Saturn that most individuals with this configuration suffered failed Presidencies. In Table 17, there are nine horoscopes with applications to Saturn a/c medieval criteria and another two if out-of-sign aspects are allowed under Hellenistic criteria (adding Martin van Buren and Ulysses Grant). Of this group, nine are rated below average in the 2021 C-SPAN Presidential Historians Survey with the bulk at the bottom of the list[16]. The biggest exception is Dwight Eisenhower's Saturn/Virgo/5th which elevated him through Saturn's discrimination applied to military logistics, deployment, and tank warfare. For Eisenhower, Saturn/Virgo functioned as an accidental benefic.

Application to Mars. Listed below are nine Presidents whose nativities feature the Moon's application to Mars. In every case each of these Presidents was involved in warfare either prior to or while serving office.

Table 18. War Events for Presidents with the Moon's application to Mars

President	Conflict
G. Washington	Revolutionary War (1776-1783)
	Whiskey Rebellion (1791-1794)
T. Jefferson	First Barbary War (1801-1805)
	Undeclared Naval War versus Britain (1805-1809)
J. Polk	Mexican War (1846-1848)
Z. Taylor	Mexican War (1846-1848)
A. Lincoln	Civil War (1861-1865)
T. Roosevelt	Spanish American War (1898)
H. Truman	Korean War (1950-1953)
J.F. Kennedy	Vietnam War (1959-1975)
J. Biden	Iraq War – Obama administration (2008-16)
	Russia-Ukraine Conflict (2022-?)

James Madison's horoscope, with Moon separating from Mars and applying to the Sun, produces identical results (War of 1812). Moon applies to an out-of-sign Mars aspect under Hellenistic criteria for John Quincy Adams (civil unrest following accusation of stolen election) and Calvin Coolidge (early 1920s Communist Red Scare). Not every signification of Mars is tied to warfare.

- Trust Busting. Theodore Roosevelt's Trust-Busting days are tied to Mars/Capricorn/8th because Mars signifies fights; Capricorn, established wealth; 8th house, trusts as investment vehicles.

---

[16] C-SPAN. Presidential Historians Survey, 2001.
Available online: https://www.c-span.org/presidentsurvey2021/?page=overall
Accessed 3-Mar-2023.

- MacArthur termination. Truman's Mars/Leo (bound of Saturn/Leo) signified Truman's opposition to General Douglas MacArthur's prima donna (Leo) personality and military insubordination. Truman fired him.

- Bullet through the throat. For Kennedy, Mars/Taurus/8th of death signified assassination through gunfire. The first of two bullets punctured his throat. Taurus is assigned to the throat.

However strong this correspondence, the Moon need not apply to Mars for Presidents to be involved in warfare. Wilson (World War I), Franklin Roosevelt (World War II), George Herbert Walker Bush (Gulf War), and George W. Bush (Operation Iraqi Freedom) are exceptions. Jupiter-Saturn aspects tied Wilson, Roosevelt, and George W. Bush to global conflict, as did Roosevelt's elevated Mars/10th. I suggest that George H.W. Bush's wartime Presidency is tied to the partile conjunction between his natal Sun and the position of Mars found in the Regulus USA National Horoscope cast for 4-Jul-1776.

Testing Maternus' Aphorisms for Presidential Greatness

No matter what group of Presidential historians is surveyed, Presidents Washington, Lincoln, and Franklin Roosevelt routinely top presidential rankings. Do Maternus guidelines give any indication of this ranking?

Washington & Lincoln: Moon separates from Jupiter and applies to Mars.
Both figures are Preventional and nocturnal.

> *If in a nocturnal chart the waxing Moon, moving away from Jupiter, is carried toward Mars, great power is predicted: control of great states and regions. But it also indicates anxieties and dangers. The natives will not be free from afflictions and illnesses but will be the type who endure these things easily, especially if Mars is found in important houses of the chart. But if Mars is in dejected houses, this indicates skills pertaining to fire. The natives themselves are low-class and humble; suffer illnesses and afflictions and often an evil death.*

> *But if the waxing Moon is moving away from Jupiter toward Mars by day, the natives will be exposed, be slaves, or wretched beggars. They will suffer illness and afflictions, slavery which is like captivity, and lose their life in a violent death.*

> *If it is a nocturnal chart, the natives will be famous and important, Mars found in important houses will make leaders or judges entrusted with the highest power. But Mars in dejected houses will make soldiers or athletes who make a living for themselves by fire or sword; or he will make physicians or surgeons.*

> *The waning Moon in this situation wastes paternal and maternal inheritance, destroys the parents when the native is young, and imposes the burden of extreme beggary. Some suffer bitter pain; some become slaves, sometimes captives, often dying a violent death, especially if Mars is on one of the angles or its anaphora or catafora. For then the effects we have described will be much stronger.* Maternus (1975, 124-125).

Evaluation. While crude, these cookbook aphorisms still offer valuable guidance. It's clear that Maternus favored nocturnal nativities; most likely because Mars is in sect when nocturnal. Both Washington and Lincoln have nocturnal nativities, a point in their favor. Maternus' reasoning behind differences behind conjunctional and preventional figures is less obvious, as is the translation. Maternus does not favor preventional figures (e.g., waning Moon). Lincoln died a violent death, one of Maternus' indications; yet Washington's fate was not as bad.

Note Jefferson with the same Jupiter-Mars configuration – but a diurnal figure – is not ranked as highly because Mars is out-of-sect. His undeclared naval war with Britain was considered a disaster.

Franklin Roosevelt: Moon separates from Saturn and applies to Jupiter
Figure is conjunctional and nocturnal.

> *If the waxing Moon, moving away from Saturn; comes into aspect with Jupiter or is moving toward Jupiter, the natives will be wealthy, generous, famous, noble, ruling great people or great estates. To some is allotted large inheritance, to others treasure, to still others important gifts.* Maternus (1975, 123).

Evaluation: Roosevelt's biography could be summarized by the words 'wealthy, generous, famous, noble, and ruling great estates.' Highly accurate.

Usefulness in Rectification

The Moon's separation from and application to planets is a valuable rectification tool but only for certain configurations. On days when the Moon makes either few or no new aspects the technique is limited. On days when the Moon makes several aspects, choosing which planet the Moon separates from and applies to can help narrow the birth time to a discrete block of time, say 3 or 4 hours, from the day's 24-hour range. To confidently match life events to a specific configuration of the Moon, one needs to understand life patterns of the individual. Because some of these long-term trends may not be apparent until at least middle age, this technique is probably not suitable for younger individuals with limited history.

Case Study: Rectifying Pierce with the Moon's Aspects

Let's take the figure for Franklin Pierce set for 12:00 Noon; birth time unknown.

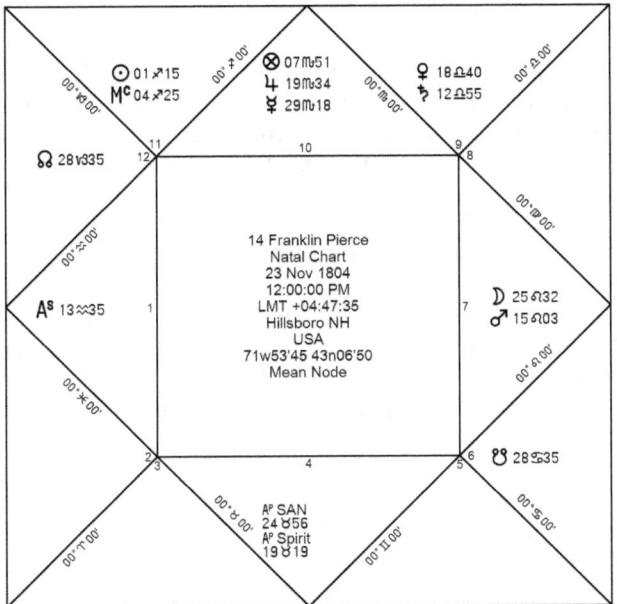

The Moon is in Leo. Consider the date and time of all the Moon's aspects made following her Leo ingress and any other aspects made during 23 November:

Aspect	Date	Time
Moon Ingress Leo	21 November	2:59 PM
Moon sextile Saturn	22 November	1:15 PM
Moon conjunct Mars	22 November	4:47 PM
Moon sextile Venus	22 November	10:26 PM
Moon square Jupiter	23 November	1:04 AM
Moon square Mercury	23 November	7:50 PM
Moon Ingress Virgo	23 November	8:09 PM
Moon square Sun	23 November	11:21 PM
Moon sextile Jupiter	25 November	9:35 AM

Our job in using the Moon's separation and application as a rectification tool is to match life patterns to one of the possible Moon's configurations. Because there is no question of Pierce's actual birth date of 23 November, the first possible combination is the Moon's separation from Venus and application to Jupiter which implies a birth time between 12 midnight and 1:04 AM on 23 November. The process moves down the list until a match is found.

As practical as this approach is, there are two other procedures I prefer to employ before identifying the Moon's separation and application. The first is to choose the Moon's sign based on evidence from the native's mother, wife, daughter(s), and/or appearance/temperament. The second is Firdaria (see Chapter 8: *Planetary Period Methods*).

Choosing the Moon's sign. Pierce's mother had a distinct taste for flashy clothing (Degregorio 2001, 198). Pierce himself was also known for his handsome appearance. Both observations are consistent with a Leo Moon. If correct, this step knocks out any possible birth time after 8:09 PM when the Moon makes its Virgo Ingress.

Whether the figure is diurnal or nocturnal. The Planetary Period Method known as Firdaria requires the choice of either a diurnal or nocturnal figure (e.g., whether or not the Sun is above or below the horizon). Proper choice of the figure's sect eliminates 12 hours – on average – from consideration as possible birth times. For this reason it is an extremely powerful and robust tool. For those new to Firdaria, I suggest jumping ahead to the Firdaria section in Chapter 8 before continuing with this example based on Franklin Pierce.

My choice for the Firdaria's nocturnal series (e.g., Sun below horizon) is based on two correspondences between life affairs and planetary periods. The first is a match between the South Node period and Pierce's serious battlefield injuries sustained August 1847 while serving in the Mexican War. The second dates his rise to the national political stage following the onset of his major Sun period beginning 23-Nov-1848.

Choice of the nocturnal series eliminates all times when the Sun is above the horizon from consideration. For this example: 7:08 AM – 4:24 PM is ruled out.

What's left? Excluding 7:08 AM – 4:24 PM and 8:09 PM – 12:00 AM leaves the following possible birth times for 23 November 1804:

12:00 AM – 7:08 AM   *or*   4:24 PM – 8:09 PM.

Computing possible configurations of the Moon for these two time slots yields four choices:

Possible Birth Time	Moon's Configuration
12:00 AM – 1:04 AM	Moon separates from Venus and applies to Jupiter
1:04 AM – 7:08 AM	Moon separates from Jupiter and applies to Mercury
4:24 PM – 7:50 PM	Moon separates from Jupiter and applies to Mercury
7:50 PM – 8:09 PM	Moon separates from Mercury and is void of course

Matching life affairs to the Moon's configuration.

Step 1. *Cite aphorisms by Maternus and Pearce for all possible Moon configurations. Understand the logic behind the aphorisms. [Note: the figure is nocturnal and preventional.]*

Moon separates from Venus and applies to Jupiter.

> *If the waning Moon is moving from Venus toward Jupiter, this will provide financial help from individual women; and fame and good fortune will be passed on from parents to natives at an early age; some will receive an inheritance, others will discover means for the greatest profit or hold honored office in temples.* Maternus (1975, 129).

> *If the Moon decreases [editor's note: and separates from Venus and apply to Jupiter], it signifies gain by the good friendship of ladies, happiness, attainment of property or of an honourable office in the Church.* Pearce (1970, 76).

Comment: Both aphorisms take Venus as the universal significator of women. The aphorisms assign good fortune, inheritance, and property to Jupiter. In addition, Maternus assigns holding an *honored office in temples* which Pearce modifies to an *honourable office in the Church*. These statements emphasize Jupiter's professional signification as a priest. Assuming both planets are in positive zodiacal state, there is a flow from women to happiness, wealth, and wisdom expressed professionally through the priesthood.

Moon separates from Jupiter and applies to Mercury.

> *If the Moon is waning in this situation [editor's note: moving from Jupiter toward Mercury], the natives seek their livelihood from literature, from teaching, business, or from granaries. Some obtain some kind of inheritance; others make discoveries; others refuse to return what has been entrusted to them so that from this treachery they lay the foundation for a fortune.* Maternus (1975, 125-126).

> *If the Moon separates from Jupiter and applies to Mercury, she signifies judges, collectors of money, interpreters of law, religious and fortunate persons.* Pearce (1970, 74).

Comment: If Jupiter is happiness, wealth, wisdom, and the priesthood; then the movement from Jupiter to Mercury suggests business and/or written/verbal activities follow whatever Jupiter bestows. Maternus' mention of treachery exemplifies Mercury's nature as the trickster.

Moon separates from Mercury and is void of course.

> *The waning Moon in this situation [editor's note: moving away from Mercury toward nothing], indicates illness from body humors or serious dangers from water; some she injures in mind, some in speech, others in the ears; but all these are illiterate; others will prophesy, but in temples; some become guardians of temples and still others servants or assistants in temples.* <u>Maternus</u> (1975, 133-134).

<u>Pearce</u>: no aphorism supplied.

<u>Comment</u>: With the Moon leaving Mercury void of course, Maternus gives the idea of a babbling idiot running amok, a prescient soothsayer wandering temple halls dishing out advice to anyone who will listen, or individuals whose end-use is in the employment of others (e.g., not self-starters or business owners). Which alternative depends on Mercury's zodiacal condition.

Step 2. *Adapt the themes of each aphorism to Franklin Pierce's figure by incorporating the state of each planet.*

Venus/Libra. Signifies a pleasant, harmonizing, *fair value* quality to matters of love, money, and art.

Jupiter/Scorpio. Philosophy/teaching of war, crime, and intense ethical decisions.

Mercury/Scorpio. Lying, deceit, and communications tinged with revenge ever so because Mercury's ruler – Mars/Leo – fights for honor. Incensed messages.

<u>Possible interpretations</u>:

Moon moving from Venus/Libra to Jupiter/Scorpio suggests sound finances provide funds for study of philosophy/teaching of war, etc., and a professional career based on the same significations of Jupiter.

Moon moving from Jupiter/Scorpio to Mercury/Scorpio signifies the bestowal of philosophy/wisdom is dissipated through ill-mannered communications. This is not too dissimilar from Maternus' cookbook statement that those with this configuration *refuse to return what has been entrusted to them so that from this treachery they lay the foundation for a fortune* (cited above).

Moon moving from Mercury/Scorpio to void of course. Mental illness is ruled out because two conditions for mental illness (no Moon-Mercury aspect and the presence of a Mercury-Saturn hard aspect) are not met (Schoener 1996, 134). The best delineation for Pearce's configuration is incensed speech finds no outlet.

CHAPTER 7 – TEMPORAL INDICATORS

Step 3. *Determine the closest match between possible Moon configurations and Pierce's actual life.*

Moon moves from Venus to Jupiter?

If Venus signifies a woman, there is no evidence that Pierce was materially helped by either his mother or his wife. His youth was dominated by his father who was a Revolutionary War hero. His father did help establish Pierce's law office by building the office and supplying funds for legal books. Maternus does indicate that good fortune will be passed on from parents to natives (e.g., not just from women). So the evidence is mixed for this configuration.

Moon moves from Jupiter to Mercury?

Pierce did study and practice law in his early professional life before politics. His Presidency was marred by several incidents consistent with the Mercury/Scorpio placement. The Ostend Manifesto, presented by Pierce's ambassadors, stated that Spain should sell Cuba to the United States; if they disagreed, then America would take Cuba by force. This warlike message tinged with threats and revenge is a classic Mercury/Scorpio statement. Pierce's decision to send the slave Anthony Burns back to Virginia in accordance with the Fugitive Slave Act was another act consistent with Mercury/Scorpio.

These incidents are sufficient to confirm the Moon's separation from Jupiter to Mercury. There is no need to consider the Moon's separation from Mercury to void of course. There is no evidence that Pierce made incendiary messages to anyone who would listen *without effect*. Incendiary messages *were most definitely the effect* and appear to have dissipated his warlike philosophy.

Step 4. *Narrow the possible birth time to the range from the Moon's separation of Jupiter to the application of Mars.*

That calculation has already been made: the birth time should fall within the range of 4:24 PM to 7:50 PM. This makes Pierce's Ascendant range fall between 1GE27 and 20CA39. His Ascendant is either Gemini or Cancer. From here other techniques are employed to narrow the range of the Ascendant.

Jumping ahead, the final rectification places 3CA15 on the Ascendant, with both Jupiter and Mercury falling in the 5th house (WS). One signification of Jupiter/Scorpio/5th was discussions/teaching/learning of war while as a child listening to stories of his father's fellow comrades from the Revolutionary War. The Pearce household was a busy place because it was also a tavern which housed travelers. Placement in the 5th of entertainment means Pearce acquires this wisdom in a tavern which is a 5th house signification. Mercury/Scorpio/5th signifies incensed communications carried out by his diplomatic team, with the Ostend Manifesto the best example. Ambassadors are assigned to the 5th house.

Beyond the Moon: other planetary configurations

For all the attention paid to the Moon's applications and separations as an indicator of temporal change, planets besides the Moon can apply to and separate from other planets in the same way the Moon does.

As one example of Mercury's separation and application, consider this unusual configuration in Herbert Hoover's figure: Mercury separates from the sextile of Venus and applies to the conjunction of Jupiter. Based on whole sign houses, some would argue that technically Mercury does not separate from Venus because they are both in different signs. I submit that the out-of-sign separation from Venus is valid because Venus will make her Libra Ingress before Mercury perfects its sextile aspect to Jupiter. This happens because Venus moves faster than Mercury. Also, Venus falls in Jupiter's contra-antiscion.

What does it mean? As a mining engineer, Hoover was famous for buying poorly managed, undervalued mining properties and turning them around into successful business ventures. Mercury signifies Hoover's business expertise, Venus/Virgo signifies an undervalued – literally *fallen value* – property, Venus/Libra signifies a fairly valued property, Jupiter/Libra signifies mining profits because it falls in the 5th, or 2nd from the 4th (money from things buried). Mercury is the agency which extracts *fair value* from *fallen value* properties by the application of business expertise. Mercury delivers *fair value* to Hoover's pocketbook.

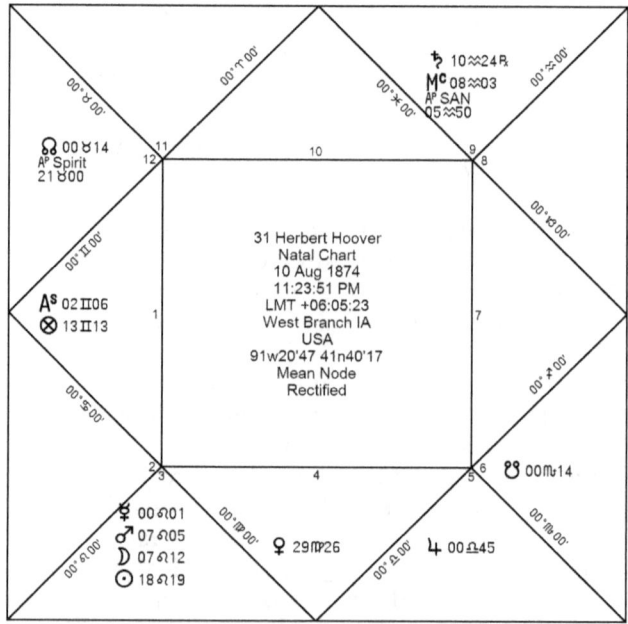

MULTIPLE PLANETS IN A SINGLE SIGN

When two or more planets fall in a single sign, there is an implied sequence in each planet's temporal influence on house affairs. How does the method work? The first planet in a sign exerts its influence over house affairs before any other. Each successive planet influences house affairs corresponding to its position in the house. Planets are ordered based on their zodiacal degrees, from lowest to highest. An exception: should the stellium include the sign ruler, the sign ruler's influence may be relatively constant compared to other planets in the stellium.

Example: Herbert Hoover. 4th House Stellium: Mercury-Mars-Moon-Sun

Mercury/Leo signifies Hoover's business acumen in mining engineering which dominated his early professional life.

Mars/Leo. Following the outbreak of World War I on 3-Aug-1914, Hoover in Europe abandoned his mining career in order to help stranded Americans in Europe find their way home. Shortly thereafter he began his tenure as head of the Belgium Food Relief Commission. Both actions are consistent with the heroic delineation of Mars/Leo.

Moon/Leo. Hoover's tenure as Commerce Secretary under both Harding and Coolidge is marked by a need for fame through communications, committees, and press conferences. Coolidge nicknamed Hoover "The Wonder Boy." This is consistent with the Moon/Leo/3rd (QS) placement. On several occasions, Hoover presciently raised alarms about the credit quality of foreign bonds sold to the American public – most of which would eventually default later under his term as President. Concern about credit quality is also consistent with Hoover's pro-gold *hard money* philosophy which during his Presidential term was widely considered a contributor to deflation and depressed economic activity. Moon/Leo/4th (WS) can be delineated as the need for gold in the ground as the stable foundation for American monetary policy. It is consistent with concerns for credit quality and Hoover's resistance to inflationary monetary policies during his Presidential term.

Sun/Leo. Sun signifies the King. Hoover did serve a term as President. Either the Sun and Moon overlap their influences during his Presidential term, or Sun/Leo signifies his post-Presidential activities as leader of the opposition political party because Sun in the 4th is 7th from the 10th. During the era of Democratic dominance beginning with FDR, Hoover was nicknamed the 'Chief' and expressed frequent views in opposition to the sitting President. In addition, his theories of Presidential Power, formally written as conclusions of both Hoover Commissions under Truman and Eisenhower, are consistent with the power of the Sun/Leo to act in final years. True also is the Sun/Leo's power as ruler over the entire stellium. From his early mining days Hoover quickly became head, chair, or President for every organization with which he was involved.

Example: Calvin Coolidge: 11th House Stellium: Mars-Venus-Sun-Mercury

Mars/Cancer signifies timid behavior unless threatened. At the outset of his political career, Coolidge was noted for the lack of hostility towards members of opposing political parties. In his mind, gaining a vote from the opposition party was really worth two: one less for the opposition and one more for his party. He went out of his way not to upset the opposition. Moon/Gemini – the *flip-flop* position of the Moon - rules Mars/Cancer and suggests Coolidge said whatever was necessary to maintain his popularity with voters.

Venus/Cancer signifies consumerism and is the universal significator of the Progressive Era which brought voting rights for women to America. [Note: for the Regulus USA National Horoscope, Venus/Cancer/8th rules the 5th house of voting.] His tenure as President of the State Senate in Massachusetts politics was marked for his support of progressive political causes, including women's suffrage. This stance was unusual for a Republican politician.

Sun/Cancer signifies his political fortunes as an American President because Coolidge's natal Sun is conjunct the USA natal Sun.

Mercury/Cancer signifies writing and is consistent with his syndicated newspaper column *Calvin Coolidge Speaks* written after his Presidency.

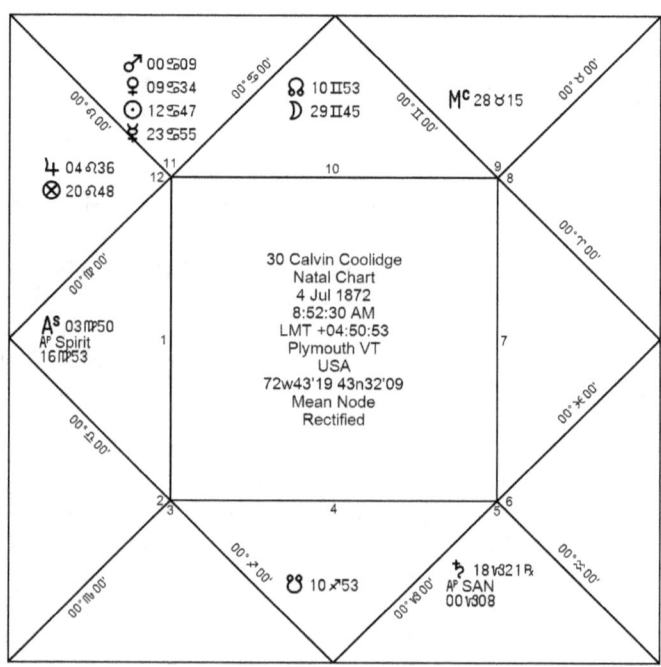

CHAPTER EIGHT

Planetary Period Methods

Planetary period methods mark the most significant departure from modern predictive methods which yield only discrete days for events to occur. The common thread of these techniques is the power of planets to act when they rule time. Think of all the planets as audience participants in any game show. When called forward to bid on prizes, the planet called moves from the audience to center stage and actively controls events. Just as a contestant may generate 15 minutes of television time, a planet ruling time will contribute a chapter to the native's life for a time period with themes consistent with its natal delineation.

Chapter Summary

<u>Directing by Triplicity</u>. This method divides life into three sections. The active triplicity ruler corresponding to the element of any cusp, lot or planet exerts its influence – for better or worse – during its assigned one-third section of life. The effects of triplicity rulers on the Ascendant and Midheaven are most evident and can be used to confirm the signs on the angles during rectification. Tests from the Presidential database suggest the Division of Years is a customized number for each nativity. Following the completion of each of the three divisions, there appears to be an additional end-of-life period read by the 4th house.

<u>Firdaria</u>. The Firdaria method is a fixed 75-year cycle. Because of the different series for diurnal and nocturnal nativities, Firdaria is among the most robust rectification tools when the birth time is unknown. Choice of either diurnal or nocturnal sequence eliminates – on average – 12 hours of the 24-hour day from consideration as a potential birth time.

<u>Planetary Days and Hours</u>. In the moment-by-moment timing of events, the signification of each natal planet is more likely to be felt on days or during hours the planet rules. Day and hour rulers can be used to confirm planet placement in specific houses for some rectification cases.

DIRECTING BY TRIPLICITY

The Method

Directing by Triplicity divides life into three sections, assigning three triplicity rulers to each one-third section of life. In this system, the relative strength of each triplicity ruler influences each house, cusp, planet, or lot of the same triplicity - for better or worse - during the specific one-third section of life when active. This is one of the oldest planetary period methods presented by Hellenistic astrologers Dorotheus and Valens though Valens takes a slightly different approach. Instead of partitioning life into three sections, Valens divides life into two halves. The first and second triplicity rulers are assigned to the first and second halves of life respectively; the third triplicity ruler assists throughout. Writing as of 2022, research by Benjamin Dykes currently supports Valens' partition (*Carmen Astrologicum 2017*). In his Diploma of Medieval Astrology course, Zoller taught Dorotheus' tripartite division; an approach supported by this research project and assumed for the balance of this chapter. Further research is required to settle this debate.

Table 19. Dorothean Triplicity Rulers

Element	Diurnal Sequence	Nocturnal Sequence
Fire	☉, ♃, ♄	♃, ☉, ♄
Earth	♀, ☽, ♂	☽, ♀, ♂
Air	♄, ☿, ♃	☿, ♄, ♃
Water	♀, ♂, ☽	♂, ♀, ☽

<u>Definitions</u>. Taking the set of fiery triplicity rulers as an example, the first ruler – named the *diurnal triplicity ruler* – is the Sun. The second ruler – named the *nocturnal triplicity ruler* – is Jupiter. The final ruler – named the *participating triplicity ruler* – is Saturn. The *diurnal sequence* is used for diurnal nativities. For nocturnal nativities, the order of the first two rulers is reversed. As listed in the third column of Table 19, this set is referred to as the *nocturnal sequence*. The final participating ruler is the same for both diurnal and nocturnal horoscopes.

<u>Defining the Division of Years</u>. From a practical perspective, the major problem in application of this technique is defining the partitions from early to middle to final years. Research findings from the Presidential Database suggest the tripartite division of years is customized for each nativity. In every case a major life event can be identified which marks an obvious transition from either early to middle or from middle to final years. Key dates marking changeovers can be used as mathematical plugs to determine start and end dates for other periods.

<u>End-of-life</u>. After three divisions of life have timed out, it appears a fourth division exists for some nativities. The 4th period activates the end-of-life delineation read from the 4th house. *This is a new finding.*

Directing by Triplicity: George Washington.

It is generally recognized by biographers that George Washington's acceptance of the command of the Continental Army on 16-Jun-1775 was the key life event which led inevitably to his Presidency. Assuming that each one-third section of life is equal in days and 16-Jun-1775 marked the beginning of final years; start and end dates of early, middle, and final years can be worked out.

Division of Years: Computation

Step 1. *Based on a key life event, choose a single date which is a logical choice for the start of middle or final years.*

For Washington, choose his acceptance of command of the Continental Army on 16-Jun-1775 as the start of final years.

Step 2. *Compute the elapsed time from the date of birth to the chosen life event.*

16-Jun-1775 to 22-Feb-1732 (N. S.) = 7,910 days.

Step 3. *Assuming each one-third division of life comprises an equal number of days, compute the length of each division.*

7,910 days is the elapsed time from birth to the start of final years. This is equivalent to stating that 7,910 days = 2/3rd of life. If 7,910 days is the sum of the first two divisions of life, then each single division is computed as 7,910 divided by 2 = 3,955 days. Total lifespan is 3,955 * 3 = 11,865 days.

Step 4. *Convert length of each section in days to dates*:

Early years begin: 22-Feb-1732
Middle years begin: 19-Oct-1753 (22-Feb-1732 + 3,955 days)
Final years begin: 16-Jun-1775 (22-Feb-1732 + 7,910 days)

When Final Years run out. Taking the calculation one step further, one sees that Washington's final years end on 10-Feb-1797 yet he lived longer to 14-Dec-1799:

End-of-Life begins: 10-Feb-1797 (22-Feb-1732 + 11865 days)

What happened to Washington on 10-Feb-1797? Following his Farewell Address of 19-Sep-1796 and inauguration of John Adams as President on 4-Mar-1797, Washington retired to his Mount Vernon home. This is a close match to 10-Feb-1797 read as the start of his 4th house *end-of-life*.

The next step is to apply the technique.

Directing by Triplicity: George Washington

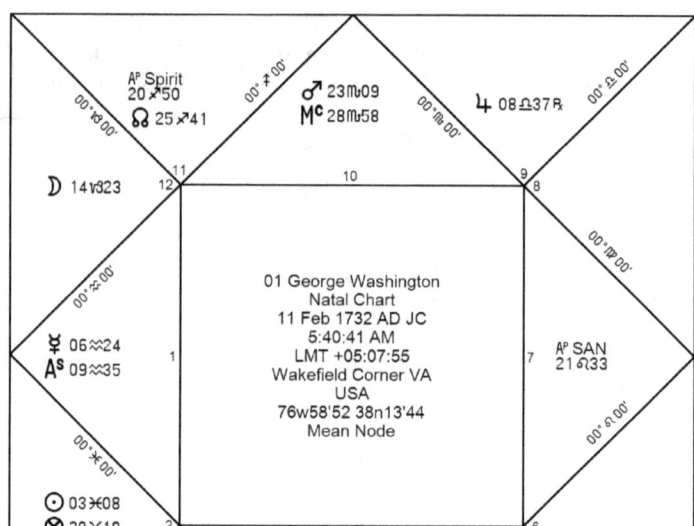

Early Years [Empirical: 22-Feb-1732 to 18-Oct-1753]

Ascendant – Nocturnal triplicity ruler: Mercury
Midheaven – Nocturnal triplicity ruler: Mars

Ascendant. Mercury and Mars as triplicity rulers of the Ascendant and Midheaven in early years are self-reinforcing because they are partile conjunct by antiscia. Mercury/Aquarius signifies Washington's early interests in surveying. Mercury's signification of writing combined with the fixed air sign of Aquarius is consistent with marking straight lines *through the air* as a method of fixing land boundaries.

Midheaven. Mars as Midheaven triplicity ruler marks Washington's reputation by the death of his half-brother Lawrence because Mars ruling the 3rd of siblings placed in the 10th brings death to his sibling. The war-God Mars signifies Washington's military career which did not fully develop until much later. How else then, did Mars mark Washington's Midheaven in early years? I suggest Washington's reputation for excellence in horsemanship as a youth is tied to Mars because Mars as the 3rd triplicity ruler of the 12th is assigned to riding animals by Al-Andarzagar's method.

Middle years [Empirical: 18-Oct-1753 to 15-Jun-1775]

Ascendant – Diurnal triplicity ruler: Saturn
Midheaven – Diurnal triplicity ruler: Venus

Ascendant. What empirical evidence exists to support the changeover from early to middle years on 18-Oct-1753? With the Ascendant ruler shifting from Mercury to Saturn, Washington's primary motivation should change from surveying to whatever is signified by Saturn. This should be a change for the worse because Saturn/Aries is in fall. Saturn will interfere with Washington's primary motivation in middle years.

Saturn/Aries signifies obstructions to warfare whose highest function for Washington was the defensive tactic of guerilla warfare used successfully against the British during the Revolutionary War. But that came later. He first had to experience guerrilla tactics directly in the French and Indian War before he could put them to use later. Washington was sworn in as a major in the Virginia militia on 1-Feb-1753 and on 31-Oct-1753 was ordered by Virginia Governor Dinwiddle to send a message to the Indians to stop encroachment on the Ohio territory. Falling just 13 days past the 18-Oct-1753 calculated start of middle years, Washington's mission to the Indians was a key event which led to the outbreak of the French and Indian War, his defeat suffered at the Battle of the Wilderness, and his December 1758 resignation from the military. These difficulties match one signification of Saturn in Aries as a frustrated soldier.

Midheaven. After Washington resigned his commission, he married Martha Custis and started living the life of a Virginia planter – signified by Venus/Pisces ruling the 4th of lands. In her exaltation, Venus marked Washington's reputation as a member of the landed gentry surrounded by the finest luxuries money could buy. From clothing to dogs, horses, tobacco, and furnishings, Washington acquired the very best for Mount Vernon.

Final years [Empirical: 16-Jun-1775 to 10-Feb-1797]

Ascendant – Participating triplicity ruler: Jupiter
Midheaven – Participating triplicity ruler: Moon

Ascendant. As suggested in the Division of Years calculation, Washington's acceptance of command of the Continental Army triggered the changeover to final years. How so, considering military command is signified by Mars and not Jupiter? Remember that Mars' close conjunction to the Midheaven means Mars *always and everywhere* marks Washington's career and social status over and above any predictive method including Directing by Triplicity. By saying Jupiter rules Washington's Ascendant in final years, the Directing by Triplicity method means that Washington finds another outlet for his Ascendant's primary motivation through Jupiterian activities in final years. Moreover, since Jupiter is in much better condition than Saturn; Washington will find greater happiness and fulfillment in final years compared to middle years. What are these Jupiterian activities? Jupiter in the 9th ruling the 11th and 2nd suggests foreign alliances and foreign sources of money driven by an egalitarian philosophy. Washington's alliance with the Marquis de La Fayette is the most famous example. *NEW* Based on recent research, retrograde planets behave as positioned in the opposite sign. In this case, Jupiter/Libra-rx functions as Jupiter/Aries. Washington resorts to a military alliance with France to achieve his political objectives, after rejecting the ineffectiveness of Jupiter/Libra's egalitarianism in colonial jurisprudence.

Midheaven. Washington's military success in final years was marred by the condition of his troops which were poorly supplied, malnourished, and badly clothed. As a result, soldiers threatened mutiny on 25-May-1790 because they had not been paid for months and were underfed. This is consistent with the traditional aphorism that the ruler of the 6th in the 12th signifies slave revolts because the Capricorn Moon in her detriment cannot supply nourishment.

This *slave revolt* theme carried over to Washington's Presidential years as the source of the Hamilton-Jefferson feud and the Whiskey Rebellion. Moon in Capricorn's need for money signified Hamilton's desire for centralized national banking. Hamilton's National Bank and the Whiskey Rebellion are linked because the 1794 Whiskey Rebellion was in direct response to Hamilton's 1791 excise tax on distilled spirits, in turn designed to pay off the national debt funded by Hamilton's National Bank. These actions were abhorrent to Jefferson and are the source of the Hamilton-Jefferson feud. If this analysis is correct, then Washington's Moon ruling the MC in final years is one cause of the American two-party political system: Federalists (Hamilton/Washington) and the Republican-Democratic Party (Jefferson/Madison/Monroe).

More Directing by Triplicity Examples

James Madison. Mars, participating ruler of the earth triplicity, rules the MC in final years. This confirms the dominant influence of military conflict on Madison's career and reputation in final years. The War of 1812 was referred to as "Mr. Madison's War" by contemporary press accounts.

Richard Nixon. How a man whose Cold War obsession with Communism led to détente with China and Russia in the early 1970s is explained by Saturn and Venus as triplicity rulers for Nixon's middle years. Nixon's recklessness and naked ambition which led to the Watergate scandal is consistent with Mars/Sagittarius and Jupiter/Capricorn ruling final years.

George Herbert Walker Bush. His 1997 parachute jump is an excellent example of a dramatic launch to his end-of-life period.

Franklin Roosevelt. Included in Chapter 15's Case study on FDR's War Years.

CHAPTER 8 – PLANETARY PERIOD METHODS 133

Directing by Triplicity: James Madison

```
MC 13♍04          AP Spirit
AP SAN            26♋25
21♍09

                                    ☊ 16♊59
                  04 James Madison
                     Natal Chart
                   5 Mar 1751 AD JC
                    11:20:04 PM
☽ 22♏50             LMT +05:08:45           ♃ 06♉10
AS 29♏49         Belle Grove Port Conway VA
                        USA
                 77w11'18 38n10'45
                     Mean Node

♄ 13♐30                              ♀ 11♈03
☊ 16♐59                              ⊗ 03♈14

    ♂ 11♑47    ☿ 29♒32    ☉ 26♓15
```

Early Years [Empirical: 15-Mar-1751 to 24-Jan-1780]

Ascendant – Nocturnal triplicity ruler: Mars
Midheaven – Nocturnal triplicity ruler: Moon

   Ascendant. Mars/Capricorn/3rd ruling the 1st and 6th grants ambition for learning to satisfy Madison's Scorpio Ascendant's need for visceral intensity. Because Mars also rules the 6th of illness, studies cause illness. This delineation matches Madison's stint at Princeton which compressed a four-year program of study into two years. Madison suffered physical burnout in April 1772.

   Midheaven. Moon ruling the 9th ties reputation in early years to higher education and religion. He attended both the College of William and Mary and Princeton University. Presbyterian minister John Witherspoon was Princeton's President at the time, a strong advocate of religious freedom and supporter of the Scottish Enlightenment. Though not placed directly in the 9th house, the Moon does rule the 9th and applies to Mars which signifies hatred of organized religion. Madison's ideas on religious freedom date from these early years, a philosophy which marked his reputation in 1776 as a delegate to the Virginia Convention. Madison revised a key clause on religious freedom, striking the word "toleration" to leave the phrase "free exercise of religion" unencumbered by the possibility that "tolerated" religious practices might ever be subject to discrimination (Ketchum 1990, 72-73).

Middle years [Empirical: 25-Jan-1780 to 6-Dec-1808]

Ascendant – Diurnal triplicity ruler: Venus
Midheaven – Diurnal triplicity ruler: Venus

<u>Ascendant and Midheaven</u>. Venus rules both angles in middle years. Venus/Aries in detriment is weak. By AL houses, Venus rules and weakens the King's money in the 11th. As middle years started, he composed his famous essay on Money where he correctly made the connection between currency stability and confidence in government (Winter 1779/1780). Madison took his seat in the Continental Congress on 18-Mar-1780 during the midst of an inflationary currency collapse which gave rise to the phrase *not worth a Continental*. Similar concerns with currency marked his entry into the very first session of Congress on April 1789. As the first order of business, Madison moved that Congress establish a revenue system so America could transact business.

Final years [Empirical: 7-Dec-1808 // 28-Jun-1836 // 19-Oct-1837]

Ascendant – Participating triplicity ruler: Moon
Midheaven – Participating triplicity ruler: Mars

Madison's election to President on 7-Dec-1808 (age 57y 8m 23d) is the logical start of final years and the plug for the division of years.

<u>Ascendant</u>. From Jefferson, Madison inherited an undeclared naval war with Britain. Jefferson's failed embargo tactics kept the embers of war very much alive. Madison's outrage over British impressments of American seamen matches the Scorpio Moon ruling the 9th of foreign policy. By AL houses, Moon/Scorpio/12th damages the Moon by exaggerating the true significance of its intuitive style; here the need to stew and engender resentment about impressments (e.g., a variation of 12th house imprisonment) because Scorpio is the military water sign.

<u>Midheaven</u>. He was known as a wartime President; the War of 1812 was nicknamed "Mr. Madison's War." Moon as ASC ruler ruled by Mars as participating MC triplicity ruler in final years connects Madison's outrages over impressments with the necessity of warfare against Britain.

The strong dignity of Mars shows Madison's success in final years which provided a foundation for an idyllic retirement. He did not live out final years.

Directing by Triplicity Example: Richard Nixon

```
                    MC 13♊38        ♄ 27♉29℞

    ⊗ 14♌24                  10              ☊ 07♈14

                    37 Richard Nixon
                    Natal Chart
                    9 Jan 1913
                    9:23:46 PM
    AS 15♍02        PST +08:00:00              ♀ 03♓28
                    18001 Yorba Linda Blvd CA
                    USA
                    117w49'05 33n53'22
                    Mean Node
                    Rectified

    ☋ 07♎14                                    ☽ 20♒01
    AP Spirit
    15♎40
                                    ☉ 19♑23
                                    AP SAN
                                    16♑33
                    ♂ 29♐44          ♃ 01♑40
                                    ☿ 00♑00
```

Stephen Ambrose partitioned his 3-volume Nixon biography by the years 1962 and 1972/73. A reasonable start to final years marked by triplicity rulers Mars and Jupiter (significators for lying and naked ambition) is the infamous Watergate break-in of 17-Jun-1972. Making this assumption and dividing the length between birth and 17-Jun-1972 by two; the date of 28-Sep-1942 is generated. This falls in the middle of Nixon's WWII service and is near the time of a crucial shift in his wartime experience.

Early Years [Empirical: 9-Jan-1913 to 27-Sep-1942]

Ascendant – Diurnal triplicity ruler: Moon
Midheaven – Diurnal triplicity ruler: Mercury

<u>Ascendant</u>. Moon in Aquarius ruling the Ascendant in early years shows humanitarian concerns as a basic instinct. In the 6th house it is tied to employees. Nixon is remembered at both Whittier and Duke as one with very liberal views on social issues and civil rights. He ran and won for President of the Duke Law School in his senior year on a ticket with a handicapped friend running as Secretary. During Winter/Spring 1935/1936 Nixon volunteered much of his spare time to a legal clinic helping poor white and blacks through the local District Attorney's office.

Midheaven. Mercury ruling the MC in early years ties his reputation as an ace debater at Whittier College, a law student at Duke, a lawyer back home in California, and as a bureaucrat at the Office of Price Administration after World War II broke out.

Middle years [Empirical: 28-Sep-1942 to 16-Jun-1972]

Ascendant – Nocturnal triplicity ruler: Venus
Midheaven – Nocturnal triplicity ruler: Saturn

Ascendant/Midheaven. On 31-May-1943, Nixon disembarked from San Francisco for a naval assignment in the South Pacific. While on Bougainville during mid-December 1943, Nixon survived a heavy attack in an air raid bunker which decimated their camp and his tent. The most basic delineation of Saturn/Taurus/9th is destruction of the earth including agricultural goods grown in the soil. As a political aspirant, Nixon knew the value of military service. By placing himself near enemy fire and risk of death, the incident at Bougainville qualified as political resume fodder. Taurus also is the sign of capitalism. Saturn in Taurus hinders capitalist pursuits and in the 9th of philosophy is arguably the source of Nixon's anti-Communist stance which defined his political reputation in middle years. Yet Venus in Pisces disposing Saturn shows a compassionate and sacrificial outcome to Nixon's anti-Communist philosophy. One example is the Marshall Plan, designed as a generous financial partnership with the vanquished Axis powers. Following the Marshall Plan's announcement, Nixon was asked to travel to Europe with other Senators to view the utter destruction signified by Saturn/Taurus. Upon his return and lobbying of his constituents, the Marshall Plan passed and aid was doled out. As middle years culminated, the Venus-Saturn combination formed the basis of détente with Communist China and Russia. Nixon's visit to China on 22-Feb-1972 and the successful SALT I Russian Treaty signed 26-May-1972 mark his highest efforts in making peace with the world's two largest Communist powers.

Final years [Empirical: 17-Jun-1972 // 22-Apr-1994 // 6-Mar-2002]

Ascendant – Participating triplicity ruler: Mars
Midheaven – Participating triplicity ruler: Jupiter

Ascendant/Midheaven. Undoubtedly the lying-spying-naked ambition which marked Nixon's downfall was in play prior to the discovery of the Watergate Break-in on 17-Jun-1972. Nevertheless, Nixon's reputation was not tied to these characteristics until after the break-in. Jupiter/Capricorn in detriment signifies naked ambition. As ruler of Mars/Sagittarius, significator of blusterous aggression, Jupiter is the source and result of Nixon's reckless behavior. Because of his desire for a landslide re-election, orders to spy and lie are given. The result is further self-aggrandizement.

Division of Years/End-of-Life Example: George H.W. Bush

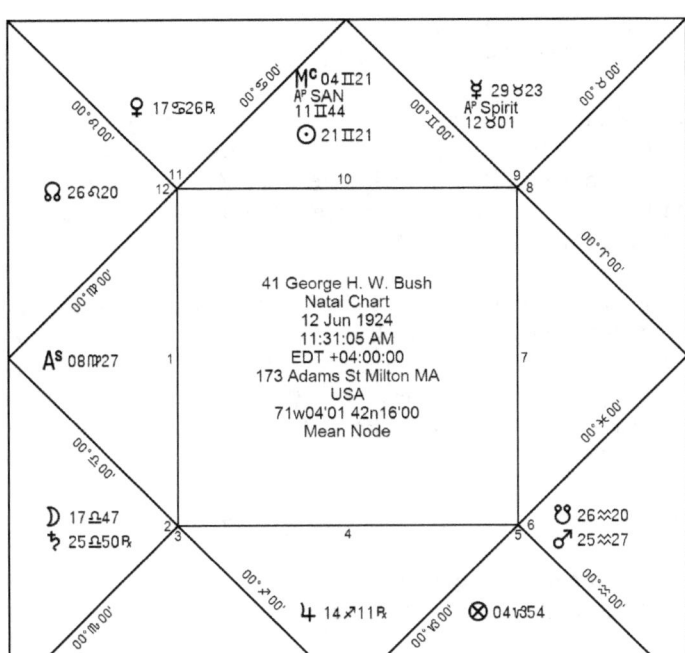

George H.W. Bush's 25-Mar-1997 parachute jump is one of the most dramatic examples of the onset of end-of-life read by the 4th natal house.

Jupiter in Sagittarius, the sign of flight, falls in the 4th natal house of real estate. For this event, I suggest Jupiter signifies a *parachute jump with successful landing* (e.g., on the land/ground = 4th house). Retrograde means the activity is repeated. In fact, the 1997 jump was widely perceived as an attempt to exorcise remaining demons from his 2-Sep-1944 World War II parachute jump. The 1944 jump was made from a combat plane, damaged in a firefight with the Japanese. Tragically two of Bush's crewmates were never found.

Assuming the 1997 parachute jump marks the plug for the start of end-of-life:

Early Years: 12-Jun-1924 to 14-Sep-1948
Middle Years: 15-Sep-1948 to 18-Dec-1972
Final Years: 19-Dec-1972 to 24-Mar-1997
End-of-life: ***25-Mar-1997*** to 30-Nov-2018.

Now let's test this division of years against Bush's chronology.

Early Years [Empirical: 12-Jun-1924 to 14-Sep-1948]

Ascendant – Diurnal triplicity ruler: Venus
Midheaven – Diurnal triplicity ruler: Saturn

Ascendant. Venus/Cancer/11th ruling Ascendant in early years indicates eating comfort food among friends. While this 11th house delineation is not readily specified by biographers, Bush's nickname *Fatty McGee McGaw* given by his father when he was a pudgy toddler matches the presumable effects of living a posh lifestyle as a child.

Midheaven. Saturn/Libra/2nd received by Venus matches Bush's involvement in fundraising for the United Negro College Fund (UNCF) while a senior at Yale. Saturn/Libra can be delineated as a structure with an egalitarian purpose; in the 2nd it is specified to financial concerns. The 2nd is also the 11th from the 4th, or groups/organizations of his father. Prescott Bush later served as his state's chairman of the UNCF.

Middle years [Empirical: 15-Sep-1948 to 18-Dec-1972]

Ascendant – Nocturnal triplicity ruler: Moon
Midheaven – Nocturnal triplicity ruler: Mercury

Ascendant. Moon/Libra/2nd ruling ASC in middle years is delineated as eagerness to please friends and organizations through financial activities. Mutual reception between Moon/Libra in the 2nd and Venus/Cancer ruling the 11th of good fortune perfects the promise of both houses. Bush was a successful oilman and made most of his money during middle years.

Midheaven. The day following his 1948 Yale graduation, Bush moved to Odessa, Texas to begin his career as an oilman. Mercury in Taurus combines Mercury's universal significator as business affairs with natural resources whose domain is the earth sign of Taurus. Placement in the 9th house shows that Bush's relocation was in part a pilgrimage, even an escape, from his East Coast parents. Eventually Bush's oil company activities would encompass offshore drilling, with *offshore* filling out another 9th house signification.

Final years [Empirical: 19-Dec-1972 to 24-Mar-1997]

Ascendant – Participating triplicity ruler: Mars
Midheaven – Participating triplicity ruler: Jupiter

Ascendant. Mars/Aquarius conjunct South Node in the 6th is a complicated configuration. The same configuration appears in Carter's 5th house (see Chapter 14: *Lunar Nodes and Eclipses*). Mars/Aquarius/6th signifies employees or Bush's own service to Saturn/Libra New World Order financial concerns because Saturn rules Mars (see rectification for New World Order delineation of Saturn/Libra). Mars/Aquarius fights against the Aquarian principle of universality in a discriminatory manner. As demonstrated in the rectification, Mars directions timed activities of the Nicaraguan contras. South Node destroyed the effectiveness of the contras as demonstrated by the eventual unraveling of what later became known as the Iran Contra Affair. Another delineation of Mars/Aquarius/6th conjunct the South Node, ruling the 5th by exaltation and the 8th by sign, is a real estate tax dodge that failed. 5th is money from real estate, 8th is taxes, and Mars in 6th is the tax accountant. In 1984, Bush was forced to pay back taxes on the sale of his Houston home, the proceeds of which were used to purchase additional land around his Walker's Point residence in Maine. This deduction was disallowed by the IRS, demonstrating the ability of the South Node to diminish Mars' strength.

Midheaven. Start of final years on 19-Dec-1972 immediately followed Bush's 20-Nov-1972 acceptance of the Chair of the Republican National Committee. This followed Nixon's reelection victory and Nixon's request that all political appointees resign after the election. Bush did not want this position, which would effectively devolve into leading the opposition party (4th as 7th from the 10th) with Nixon's fall from grace under Watergate. During the Carter administration, Bush worked as a volunteer fundraiser for various charities which matches one Jupiter/4th house signification as the bestowal of a generous financial legacy. He also formed an alliance with businessmen and policy makers from Asia, Europe and the U.S. known as the Trilateral Commission, showing Jupiter's connection to the 11th house as exaltation ruler.

During his Presidential term, Bush made *Family Values* an important tenet of his public reputation in final years, always punctuating White House photography with family portraits packing in as many children and grandchildren as possible.

End-of-Life [Empirical: 25-Mar-1997 to 30-Nov-2018]. See prior discussion.

Accuracy of Division of Years. With further research, there is probably a more accurate computation of division of years. For instance, the exact date of Bush's move to Odessa during May 1948 is arguably the better start for middle years. That's three months earlier than the suggested 15-Sep-1948 start date. If true, that would move up the start of end-of-life by six months. Perhaps September 1996 corresponded with Bush's actual decision to make the 25-Mar-1997 parachute jump. Whatever error may exist in the proposed Division of Years, for a planetary period technique with 20+ years as its measure, a few months of error is immaterial to the robustness of the method.

FIRDARIA (Firdar, Fridaries, Alphradar)

Firdaria is a planetary period technique which gives planets the ability to act. When planets are main or subperiod Firdaria rulers, their natal promise manifests in houses they occupy or rule. This means Firdaria rulers extend their dominion as time lords to multiple house topics making it easier to match their effects with events supplied by biographical chronologies. For a given Firdaria subperiod, at least *one* notable event should occur which matches topics related to houses where the Firdaria ruler is positioned or rules. Keep in mind, we are interested in how to rectify a horoscope – not to explain every life event.

Compared to Directing by Triplicity, where the Division of Years appears a customized measurement for each nativity, specification of Firdaria main and subperiods is completely defined within a fixed 75-year cycle.

Debate: Position of Nodes in Nocturnal Series

Table 20 lists both Diurnal and Nocturnal series for the start date of 1-Jan-2000. Starting at a century mark makes it easy to see at which age a certain period starts. For instance, the Venus main period starts at age 10 for the Diurnal series. While there is no dispute on the construction of the diurnal series, there has been debate on the placement of the Nodes for the nocturnal series. As confirmed by Benjamin Dykes (Abū Ma'shar al-Balhi 2020), the Nodes should fall at the end of the nocturnal sequence, as they do for the diurnal. By contrast, Bonatti stated the Nodes should be placed between Mars and the Sun for the nocturnal Firdaria series which is the system taught by Robert Zoller in his Diploma of Medieval Astrology course. Research originally presented in earlier editions of *A Rectification Manual* (Appendix B) [now extracted and published separately on www.regulus-astrology.com] confirms the Bonatti variant for the nocturnal Firdaria series. Writing in 2022, this is not a widely held view among astrologers.

Usefulness in Rectification

For birth times recorded *near sunrise* and *near sunset*, the exercise of matching life events to main periods for either diurnal or nocturnal Firdaria series is an excellent way to establish whether the Sun was above or below the horizon at birth. For unknown birth times, Firdaria is especially valuable because in most cases the choice of the diurnal or nocturnal series is reasonably obvious. Choosing whether the Sun falls above or below the horizon early in the rectification process is a great help because it eliminates, on average, 12 of 24 hours of the day from birth time choices. **NEW** For births very close to sunrise or sunset use the midpoint of the Sun's disk crossing the horizon to define the chart sect.

For individuals 45 and older, the best way to choose between the diurnal or nocturnal series is to look for evidence of Saturn starting as the main period ruler at age 40 which would support the diurnal series. Or look for a 3 year – 2 year

Table 20. Firdaria Sequence for Diurnal and Nocturnal Nativities

Diurnal Main Period	Diurnal Subperiod	Date	Nocturnal Main Period	Nocturnal Subperiod	Date
Sun	Sun	1 Jan 2000	Moon	Moon	1 Jan 2000
	Venus	6 June 2001		Saturn	15 April 2001
	Mercury	9 Nov 2002		Jupiter	28 July 2002
	Moon	15 April 2004		Mars	10 Nov 2003
	Saturn	18 Sep 2005		Sun	21 Feb 2005
	Jupiter	22 Feb 2007		Venus	6 June 2006
	Mars	27 July 2008		Mercury	19 Sep 2007
Venus	Venus	1 Jan 2010	Saturn	Saturn	1 Jan 2009
	Mercury	23 Feb 2011		Jupiter	29 July 2010
	Moon	15 April 2012		Mars	23 Feb 2012
	Saturn	6 June 2013		Sun	19 Sep 2013
	Jupiter	29 July 2014		Venus	15 April 2015
	Mars	19 Sep 2015		Mercury	10 Nov 2016
	Sun	9 Nov 2016		Moon	7 June 2018
Mercury	Mercury	1 Jan 2018	Jupiter	Jupiter	1 Jan 2020
	Moon	10 Nov 2019		Mars	18 Sep 2021
	Saturn	19 Sep 2021		Sun	6 June 2023
	Jupiter	29 July 2023		Venus	22 Feb 2025
	Mars	6 June 2025		Mercury	9 Nov 2026
	Sun	16 April 2027		Moon	28 July 2028
	Venus	21 Feb 2029		Saturn	15 April 2030
Moon	Moon	1 Jan 2031	Mars	Mars	1 Jan 2032
	Saturn	15 April 2032		Sun	1 Jan 2033
	Jupiter	28 July 2033		Venus	1 Jan 2034
	Mars	10 Nov 2034		Mercury	1 Jan 2035
	Sun	22 Feb 2036		Moon	1 Jan 2036
	Venus	6 June 2037		Saturn	1 Jan 2037
	Mercury	19 Sep 2038		Jupiter	1 Jan 2038
Saturn	Saturn	1 Jan 2040	North Node	N Node	1 Jan 2039
	Jupiter	28 July 2041	South Node	S Node	1 Jan 2042
	Mars	22 Feb 2043	Sun	Sun	1 Jan 2044
	Sun	18 Sep 2044		Venus	5 June 2045
	Venus	14 April 2046		Mercury	10 Nov 2046
	Mercury	10 Nov 2047		Moon	14 April 2048
	Moon	6 June 2049		Saturn	18 Sep 2049
Jupiter	Jupiter	1 Jan 2051		Jupiter	22 Feb 2051
	Mars	18 Sep 2052		Mars	28 July 2052
	Sun	6 June 2054	Venus	Venus	1 Jan 2054
	Venus	23 Feb 2056		Mercury	22 Feb 2055
	Mercury	9 Nov 2057		Moon	15 April 2056
	Moon	29 July 2059		Saturn	6 June 2057
	Saturn	14 April 2061		Jupiter	29 July 2058
Mars	Mars	1 Jan 2063		Mars	19 Sep 2059
	Sun	1 Jan 2064		Sun	10 Nov 2060
	Venus	1 Jan 2065	Mercury	Mercury	1 Jan 2062
	Mercury	1 Jan 2066		Moon	10 Nov 2063
	Moon	1 Jan 2067		Saturn	18 Sep 2065
	Saturn	1 Jan 2068		Jupiter	29 July 2067
	Jupiter	1 Jan 2069		Mars	7 June 2069
North Node	N Node	1 Jan 2070		Sun	15 April 2071
South Node	S Node	1 Jan 2073		Venus	22 Feb 2073
Sun	Sun	1 Jan 2075	Moon	Moon	1 Jan 2075

consecutive periods of increase and decrease signified by the Nodes followed by a delayed period of fame beginning at age 44. These middle age years from 39 to 44 often define a *mid-life crisis* and are usually evident from life events.

For younger individuals who have passed teenage years, the best way to choose between the diurnal and nocturnal series is to look for evidence of musical or artistic expression between ages 10-18 which would support Venus as the main period ruler in the diurnal series. [***NEW*** Be patient! sometimes these talents do not emerge until the final Venus-Sun subperiod.] For the nocturnal series, look for events which would support Saturn as the main period ruler between ages 9-20. Usually the difference in life history between diurnal or nocturnal series is stark during teenage years. Remember to always consider the relative strength of the specific planet before judging the effects of Firdaria periods. While musical or artistic expression is one outlet for Venus ruling the diurnal series during teenage years; keep in mind that a poorly placed Venus in Aries, Virgo, or Scorpio can signify substance abuse or sexual promiscuity.

NEW The interplay between the *Victor of the Horoscope* and Firdaria is another way to match life events to Firdaria periods. If it can be determined which planet is the Victor of the Horoscope based on general delineation principles without recourse to house position, then look for career highlights when the victor is either Major or Minor Firdaria ruler. The victor's Firdaria periods will not highlight every major career event, but they should highlight enough events that if we sit back in a counterfactual exercise and erase all life events which occur during victor-ruled Firdaria periods, we would remove so much of an individual's key life milestones we would effectively erase the individual in question. <u>My findings suggest victor-ruled Firdaria periods time peak career events in the same manner as do Zodiacal Releasing periods which are angular from the LOF</u>.

Rectification Example: George Washington

Douglas Freeman (1968) cites 10:00 a.m. for George Washington's birth time; taken from a family Bible. I disagree and propose a 5:40:41 a.m. birth time which shifts the Sun below the horizon compared to Freeman's 10:00 a.m. time. Firdaria was one of the first reasons why I rejected the 10:00 a.m. birth time.

For Washington, compare differences between nocturnal and diurnal series:

Nocturnal	Main Periods
Moon	22 Feb 1732
Saturn	22 Feb 1741
Jupiter	22 Feb 1752
Mars	22 Feb 1764
North Node	22 Feb 1771
South Node	22 Feb 1774
Sun	22 Feb 1776
Venus	22 Feb 1786
Mercury	22 Feb 1794

Diurnal	Main Periods
Sun	22 Feb 1732
Venus	22 Feb 1742
Mercury	22 Feb 1750
Moon	22 Feb 1763
Saturn	22 Feb 1772
Jupiter	22 Feb 1783
Mars	22 Feb 1795

CHAPTER 8 – PLANETARY PERIOD METHODS 143

Washington: Examining the years 1772-1776; ages 39-43

Saturn. Does Saturn best describe life between 1772 and 1783? Without knowing the actual house positions at this point, limit this analysis to Saturn's universal significations. Saturn/Aries, in fall, signifies obstacles to fighting and for Washington best describes his defensive guerilla war tactics used against the British during the Revolutionary War. Because the war occurred during Saturn's major Firdaria period in the diurnal series, this is one vote for the diurnal series.

What about Saturn as descriptor of his teenage years between 1741 and 1752 were the Firdaria series nocturnal? Washington's father died in 1743, leaving his older half-brother Lawrence as a surrogate father figure whose military activities served as a model for young Washington. As the Saturn period ended, Lawrence contracted tuberculosis; Washington traveled with Lawrence to Barbados and contracted smallpox; as the Saturn period closed, Washington recovered but Lawrence died. The smallpox episode occurred between 29-Jul-1750 and 22-Feb-1752, a Major Saturn and Moon subperiod. Saturn and Moon are square in the figure. Illnesses and periods of grief often mark Moon-Saturn Firdaria periods, whether or not the Moon is the actual hīlāj because the Moon's universal signification includes the physical body. The correspondence between Washington's illness during the Saturn-Moon Firdaria as well as the loss of two male family figures in what would be a major Saturn period for the nocturnal series is a possible match.

At this point I am at a draw.

Sun. Does the Sun best describe life between 1776 and 1786? If the nocturnal sequence were correct, then the major Sun period should show a delayed period of fame starting at age 44 following the five-year set of Nodal periods. I say *delayed* because in selected cases events during the North Node Firdaria period between ages 39-42 are often so strong that they may be confused with the onset of lasting fame and fortune.

Did Washington achieve fame between 1776 and 1786? Following his appointment as Commander in Chief on 15-Jun-1775, GW achieved considerable fame during the Revolutionary War. Score one for the nocturnal series. But let's not be so hasty. Sun in Pisces, lord Jupiter/Libra-rx and al-mubtazz Venus/Pisces, signifies fame from both aggressive military tactics and luxury goods. Is this delineation correct? Considering Washington helped secure an alliance with the French and retired to the luxury of Mount Vernon by the end of the period; yes, the Sun period does make sense. In addition, Jupiter is also the universal significator of noble men. As the principal manifestation of the American-French alliance, Marquis de La Fayette (and his military assistance) best signifies Jupiter and one source of Washington's fame during this period.

Consider the alternative: did the Sun rule Washington's first ten years between 1732 and 1742 were the diurnal sequence correct? Because the Sun is the universal significator of the father, usually natives with diurnal figures experience a childhood where the father leaves a greater mark than the mother. For Washington, this was not the case. His father was essentially absent. Instead his early years were dominated by his icily cold mother Martha Ball Washington who is undoubtedly signified by the Moon in Capricorn (Rejai & Phillip 2000, 13).

Considering the Sun, two elements favor the nocturnal series: Washington's fame during the Revolutionary War and the stronger influence of his mother relative to his father during his first decade of life.

North Node and South Node. <u>Did Washington's life match a period of increase and decrease corresponding to the North Node and South Node for the periods 1771-74 and 1774-76 respectively?</u> If so, this would favor the nocturnal Firdaria series and complete this exercise. Shortly after the onset of Washington's North Node period on 22-Feb-1771, the Committees of Correspondence were formed in the colonies. While Washington was no literary activist like Jefferson, the period nonetheless benefited him because political alliances solidified following the repeal of both Stamp and Townshend Acts. Success was relatively short-lived as the British quickly tired of colonists' demands and imposed the first Coercive Act on 31-Mar-1774 just after the onset of Washington's South Node period on 22-Feb-1774. The period between 1774 and 1776 was marked by divisive relations with the British who broke off diplomatic relations prior to the Revolutionary War. These events match the tempo of increase and decrease suggested by the three-year North Node and two-year South Node Firdaria periods.

Together with events from the Sun's major period, the weight of the evidence favors the nocturnal Firdaria series for Washington. By making this choice, Washington's Sun is placed below the horizon. Diurnal hours between 6:47 AM sunrise and 5:41 PM sunset are excluded from consideration in the rectification.

Revisiting the Nodes and Saturn in Washington's rectified figure.

The final rectification places the North Node in the 11th of political alliances which matches the formation of the Committees of Correspondence. The South Node falls in the 5th house of ambassadors and legates. This placement matches failed negotiations with the British.

Reviewing the earlier Saturn main period for the nocturnal series during 1741-1752, Saturn falls in the 3rd of siblings and is the logical significator of Washington's half-brother Lawrence. He died during the Saturn-Moon subperiod as the major Saturn period completed. Saturn's nature is to grant with difficulty, deny, delay, or to destroy. His half-brother died at the end of Saturn's period.

PLANETARY DAYS AND HOURS

The principle that *planets have power to act when they rule time* filters down to specific days of the week and hours during each day. There is an astrological correspondence between planets and days of the week: Sunday/Sun; Monday/Moon; Tuesday/Mars; Wednesday/Mercury; Thursday/Jupiter; Friday/Venus; Saturday/Saturn. Lincoln's cabinet meetings were held Tuesdays and Fridays (Guelzo 2004: 130). With Mars placed in the 11th of political organizations ruled by Venus, the connection between Tuesday/Mars and Friday/Venus is obvious. Such combination is consistent with both these planets' influence on the 11th house because for a President the 11th signifies his cabinet and Lincoln met with his cabinet on those days. This provides additional confidence the basic configuration of Lincoln's figure is correct; otherwise Mars by position and Venus by rulership would influence other life affairs.

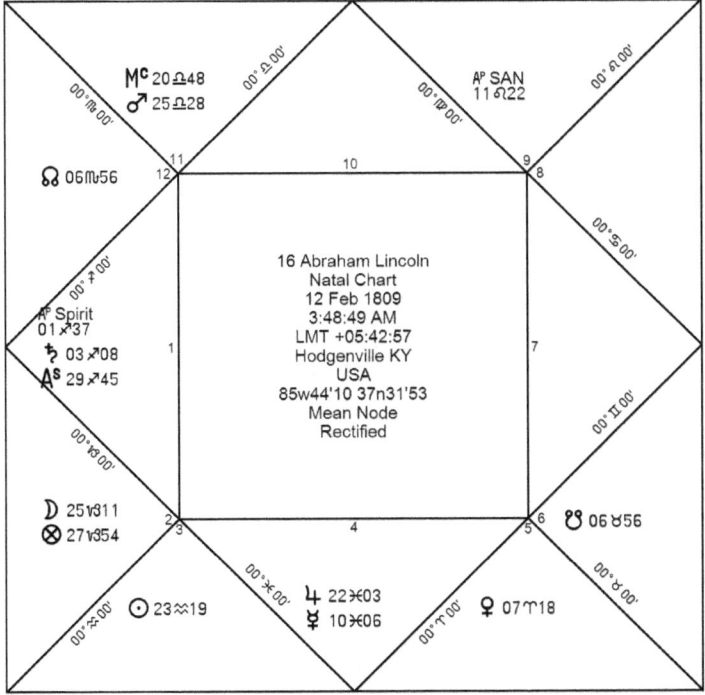

This approach can be refined further by matching the timing of life events to the day's subdivisions by the system of planetary hours.

Usefulness in Rectification. The practicality of using planetary days and hours in rectification is limited by the obvious need for detailed data; the likes of which would require access to personal diary records. Because of this limitation, for most cases, planetary days and hours are an impractical rectification tool.

CHAPTER NINE

NEW Zodiacal Releasing

Zodiacal Releasing ("ZR"). The Hellenistic time lord technique introduced by Vettius Valens has increased in popularity following the revival of Hellenistic Astrology (Valens 2022 Book 4). As a rectification tool, ZR joins the class of planetary period techniques which purport to divide life into discrete units of time likened to chapters of a book. Three other time lord techniques with similar function are Directing by Triplicity, Firdaria, and Directing through the Bounds. Whether one technique prevails OR whether each technique creates different books with different chapters and unique book covers is an open question. Research for ARM and other projects favors the latter interpretation.

Usefulness in Rectification. ARM 4th edition presents results for Zodiacal Releasing from Spirit ("ZRS") because the Lot of Spirit, sometimes referred to as the Lot of the Sun, is the appropriate lot to consider for Sun-signified Kings or Presidents. The most salient aspects of ZR for rectification are: (1) the ability of L1 periods to divide life into major chapters, (2) for the signs of GE, CA, LE, VI, CP, and AQ to link events between Foreshadowing and Loosing of the Bond subperiods (adding Completion periods for CP and AQ), and (3) the ability to outline higher levels of professional activity for signs angular from the Lot of Fortune.

Confirmation of ASC, LOF, LOF degree. By matching a ZR sequence to a chronology, ZR confirms sign placement of Lots of Spirit and Fortune. Since the Ascendant degree is necessary to compute Spirit and Fortune, knowing the correct sign placements for the Lots narrows the allowable Ascendant degree range. In a case study, ZR is applied to Warren Harding to confirm the ASC, LOF, and LOS.

Delineation of bound placement of the Lots. In the current revival of the technique, missing is delineation of sign and bound placement for the Lots. As one example, I propose Theodore Roosevelt's Lot of Spirit in the bound of Saturn/Aquarius is responsible for his passion for science in ways which cannot be delineated with the later ADB birth time which places the Lot of Spirit in Pisces.

ZODIACAL RELEASING

Similar to other Planetary Period Methods, Zodiacal Releasing divides biographical events into chapters of a book. In contrast to Planetary Period Methods, Zodiacal Releasing is sign-based not planet-based. As a rectification tool the obvious question is this: how is it possible that multiple techniques (Planetary Period Methods, Zodiacal Releasing, and Directing through the Bounds/next chapter) are capable of dividing life events into chapters of a book? Does one technique prevail? Or do the techniques create different books with alternate chapter partitions and unique book covers? Writing in 2022 this remains an open question. The side-by-side presentation of Firdaria and Zodiacal Releasing for each President in the 4th edition is designed to stimulate discussion on this 'known unknown' in the contemporary practice of traditional astrology.

Mechanics. Valens (2022 Book 4) is the sole source for Zodiacal Releasing. Inputs for the technique require computation of the Lots of Spirit and Fortune. As these lots are based on the degree positions of the Ascendant, Sun, and Moon these items are assumed. Application of Zodiacal Releasing to other lots is possible and requires known degree positions for all respective lot components.

Lots. Identify sign positions of the Lots of Spirit and Fortune. Choose the Lot of Spirit to create life chapters for fame and career. Choose the Lot of Fortune for financial affairs and other topics specific to Fortune. Since *A Rectification Manual* presents results for Presidents, the balance of this section will focus on the Lot of Spirit as this lot is also known as the Lot of the Sun. Since the Sun is the universal significator for Kings, Presidents, and other Heads of State, the Lot of Spirit is the appropriate lot to examine for American Presidents.

Periods. Like Firdaria, Zodiacal Releasing works like a fractal which runs in sequences. L1 periods are measured in years and assume 360 days per year. L2 periods assume 30 days per month and are based on the same unit used for years.

Table 21. Zodiacal Releasing L1 and L2 Time periods, Days

Sign	Period	Days-yr	L1-Days	Days-mo	L2-Days
♈	15	360	5400	30	450
♉	8	360	2880	30	240
♊	20	360	7200	30	600
♋	25	360	9000	30	750
♌	19	360	6840	30	570
♍	20	360	7200	30	600
♎	8	360	2880	30	240
♏	15	360	5400	30	450
♐	12	360	4320	30	360
♑	27	360	9720	30	810
♒	30	360	10800	30	900
♓	12	360	4320	30	360

Release the Lots. Choose the sign where the Lot of Spirit is positioned. Suppose the sign is Scorpio. Then the first chapter of life lasts 15 years. Subsequent chapters are created by counting in the order of the signs, e.g., 12 years for Sagittarius is the next chapter; 27 years, Capricorn; 30 years, Aquarius, etc., In this example which releases from Scorpio, by the time Aquarius is completed the individual is 15 + 12 + 27 + 30 = 84 years old. This set of chapters which count planetary periods *by years* are referred to as 'L1' periods. The second set of chapters which count planetary periods *by months* are referred to as 'L2' periods. *A Rectification Manual* limits ZR presentation to L1 and L2 periods. At least another two fractal subperiods can be computed.

Trick #1. When the Moon is either near its New Moon or Full Moon phase, it is possible that both Lots of Spirit and Fortune will be positioned in the same sign. If this condition applies, Valens instructs to release from the next zodiac sign, counting in the order of the signs. My own tests confirm this rule.

Trap #1. There are rare conditions where it may be appropriate to flip the lots, e.g., instead of releasing from the Lot of Fortune for financial activities, release the Lot of Fortune for fame and fortune in ways normally done using the Lot of Spirit. Conditions like eclipses may be a variable in favor of flipping the lots. My tests are not definitive in this regard and writing as of 2022 I find few exceptions to Valens' guidelines.[17] Based on rectifications presented in ARM 4th edition, only for William McKinley did I flip the lots. Yes McKinley's pre-natal syzygy was a lunar eclipse BUT other horoscopes with eclipses in the Presidential sample did not demonstrate the need to flip the lots. This question requires further research.

Trick #2. Setting aside the question of whether to release from either Lot of Spirit or Lot of Fortune, much less flip the lots, can and should we release from other lots? The answer is yes. While preparing the 4th edition, I found it possible to match a chronology of the Mexican War to Zodiacal Releasing for James Polk's horoscope using the Lot of Courage (Mars). In a second private client example, I found it possible to match the client's career history to Zodiacal Releasing from the Lot of Victory (Jupiter). Jupiter ruled the Ascendant, was powerfully placed, and was the Victor of the Horoscope. Releasing from the Lot of Spirit gave no obvious results for this client's chronology. Releasing from other lots beyond Spirit and Fortune remains a wide-open research question. At the same time I would not recommend straying beyond the 7 hermetic lots for ZR testing at this stage in the revival of Hellenistic astrology.

---

[17] Recently the astrologer Patrick Watson raised this issue for Donald Trump. For an Astrodatabank AA-rated birthtime of 10:54 AM the Lot of Spirit and Fortune are placed in Aquarius and Pisces respectively. Watson makes a strong argument to flip the lots for Trump and release from the Lot of Fortune in Pisces for his professional and political career. I agree to release from Pisces but for a different reason: my proposed Trump rectification 9:42:46 AM places both lots in Aquarius. Reverting to Valens, I release from the following sign of Pisces since both lots are in Aquarius.

Foreshadowing (FS), Loosing of the Bond (LB), and Completion (CP) periods. One of the most unusual features of zodiacal releasing is so bizarre that its mere existence may allow for the technique to be falsified to meet the demands of scientific inquiry by the likes of Karl Popper.

Returning to the fractal concept for L2 subperiods, what happens when an L1 period lasts longer than the sum of all L2 subperiods? (6,330 days) This condition applies for the following signs: GE (7,200 days), CA (9,000 days), LE (6,840 days), VI (7,200 days), CP (9,720 days), and AQ (10,800). One presumes to begin a second cycle of L2 subperiods in the order of signs. But in a moment likened to a glitch in the matrix, a trap door in the roulette wheel opens and the ball disappears and reappears on the other side of the roulette wheel. The gods strike!

Let's consider an L1 Aquarius period with L2 subperiods:

AQ	2-Nov-65	
PI	20-Apr-68	
AR	15-Apr-69	
TA	9-Jul-70	
GE	6-Mar-71	
CN	26-Oct-72	
LE	*15-Nov-74*	*(FS) Foreshadowing Period (hints for Loosing of the Bond)*
VI	7-Jun-76	
LI	28-Jan-78	
SC	25-Sep-78	
SA	19-Dec-79	
CP	13-Dec-80	
LE	*3-Mar-83*	*(LB) Loosing of the Bond. The Gods strike!*
VI	23-Sep-84	
LI	16-May-86	
SC	11-Jan-87	
SA	5-Apr-88	
CP	31-Mar-89	
AQ	*19-Jun-91*	*(CP) Completion Period*
PI	5-Dec-93	
AR	30-Nov-94	
PI	**29-May-95**	

LB occurs on 3-Mar-83 when instead of continuing in the order of the signs from prior Capricorn period (CP) to the expected Aquarius period (AQ), the opposite sign of Leo (LE) appears as the ball emerges on the opposite side of the roulette wheel.

The **FS** period 15-Nov-74 usually gives hints for **LB** starting 3-Mar-83.

Only for the signs of Capricorn and Aquarius does enough time elapse for the original L1 sign to appear at the L2 level. This is called the Completion period (**CP**).

Zodiacal Releasing from Spirit: Warren Harding

Harding is a good example for ZR because both Lots of Spirit and Fortune are in the same sign. Also among 20th century Presidents ARM's proposed rectification of 9:27:41 AM varies substantially from the A-rated birthtime of 2:30 PM which we know was actually used historically in astrology readings conducted by astrologer Marcia Champney for First Lady Florence Harding.

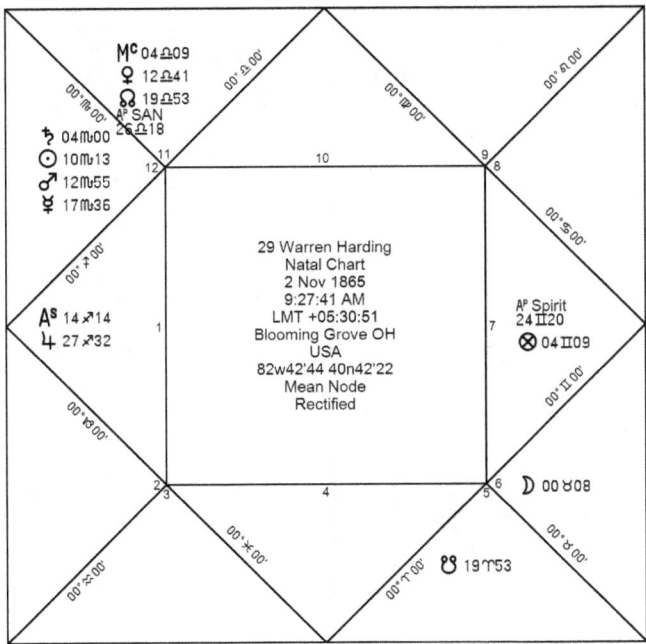

Step 1. Compute the lots and determine the starting sign for releasing.

Lot of Fortune = 4GE09; Lot of Spirit = 24GE20
Both lots are placed in Gemini, begin releasing from next sign of Cancer.

Step 2. Compute the L1 and L2 periods.

The following two pages compute L1 and L2 periods for all possible releasings. Releasing for Cancer (ARM rectification) and Libra (ADB) can be compared.

Step 3. Compare chronologies to ZR periods.

Look for major events which shift the career at L1 periods. Test linkages between Foreshadowing and Loosing of the Bond L2 subperiods as appropriate. Evaluate whether L2 periods angular from the Lot of Fortune are more active.

Table 22. Zodiacal Releasing for all signs for 2-Nov-1865, Warren Harding.

						↓ ARM					
AR	2-Nov-65	TA	2-Nov-65	GE	2-Nov-65	CN	2-Nov-65	LE	2-Nov-65	VI	2-Nov-65
TA	26-Jan-67	GE	30-Jun-66	CN	25-Jun-67	LE	22-Nov-67	VI	26-May-67	LI	25-Jun-67
GE	23-Sep-67	CN	20-Feb-68	LE	14-Jul-69	VI	14-Jun-69	LI	15-Jan-69	SC	20-Feb-68
CN	15-May-69	LE	11-Mar-70	VI	4-Feb-71	LI	4-Feb-71	SC	12-Sep-69	SA	15-May-69
LE	4-Jun-71	VI	2-Oct-71	LI	26-Sep-72	SC	2-Oct-71	SA	6-Dec-70	CP	10-May-70
VI	25-Dec-72	LI	24-May-73	SC	24-May-73	SA	25-Dec-72	CP	1-Dec-71	AQ	28-Jul-72
LI	17-Aug-74	**GE**	**21-Sep-73**	SA	*17-Aug-74*	CP	*20-Dec-73*	AQ	*18-Feb-74*	PI	*14-Jan-75*
SC	14-Apr-75	CN	14-May-75	CP	12-Aug-75	AQ	9-Mar-76	PI	6-Aug-76	AR	9-Jan-76
SA	7-Jul-76	LE	2-Jun-77	AQ	30-Oct-77	PI	26-Aug-78	AR	1-Aug-77	TA	3-Apr-77
CP	2-Jul-77	VI	24-Dec-78	PI	17-Apr-80	AR	21-Aug-79	TA	25-Oct-78	GE	29-Nov-77
AQ	20-Sep-79	LI	15-Aug-80	AR	12-Apr-81	TA	13-Nov-80	GE	2-May-79	CN	22-Jul-79
TA	**15-Aug-80**	SC	12-Apr-81	TA	6-Jul-82	GE	11-Jul-81	CN	11-Feb-81	LE	10-Aug-81
GE	12-Apr-81	SA	*6-Jul-82*	SA	*3-Mar-83*	CP	*3-Mar-83*	AQ	*3-Mar-83*	PI	*3-Mar-83*
CN	3-Dec-82	CP	1-Jul-83	CP	26-Feb-84	AQ	21-May-85	**VI**	**25-Jul-84**	AR	26-Feb-84
LE	22-Dec-84	AQ	18-Sep-85	**CN**	**20-Jul-85**	PI	7-Nov-87	LI	17-Mar-86	TA	21-May-85
VI	15-Jul-86	PI	6-Mar-88	LE	9-Aug-87	AR	1-Nov-86	SC	12-Nov-86	**LI**	**20-Jul-85**
LI	6-Mar-88	AR	1-Mar-89	VI	1-Mar-89	TA	25-Jan-90	SA	5-Feb-88	SC	17-Mar-86
GE	**4-Jul-88**	TA	25-May-90	LI	22-Oct-90	**LE**	**24-Jun-90**	CP	30-Jan-89	SA	10-Jan-87
CN	24-Feb-90	SA	*20-Jan-91*	SC	19-Jan-91	VI	15-Jan-92	AQ	20-Apr-91	CP	4-Jun-88
LE	15-Mar-92	CP	*15-Jan-92*	SA	11-Sep-92	LI	6-Sep-93	PI	*6-Oct-93*	AQ	23-Aug-90
VI	6-Oct-93	**CN**	**8-Jun-93**	CP	*6-Sep-93*	SC	4-May-94	AR	1-Oct-94	PI	8-Feb-93
LI	29-May-95	LE	28-Jun-95	AQ	25-Nov-95	SA	28-Jul-95	TA	25-Dec-95	**SC**	**8-Jun-93**
SC	24-Jan-96	VI	18-Jan-97	PI	13-May-98	CP	22-Jul-96	GE	21-Aug-96	SA	1-Sep-94
SA	*18-Apr-97*	LI	10-Sep-98	AR	8-May-99	AQ	*10-Oct-98*	CN	13-Apr-98	CP	27-Aug-95
CP	13-Apr-98	SC	8-May-99	TA	31-Jul-00	PI	28-Mar-01	LE	2-May-00	AQ	14-Nov-97
AQ	1-Jul-00	SA	31-Jul-00	GE	28-Mar-01	AR	23-Mar-02	PI	*23-Nov-01*	PI	2-May-00
PI	18-Dec-02	CP	*26-Jul-01*	CP	*18-Nov-02*	TA	16-Jun-03	AR	18-Nov-02	AR	27-Apr-01
AR	13-Dec-03	AQ	14-Oct-03	AQ	5-Feb-05	GE	11-Feb-04	TA	11-Feb-04	TA	21-Jul-02
TA	7-Mar-05	PI	1-Apr-06	PI	25-Jul-07	CN	3-Oct-05	**LI**	**11-Apr-04**	GE	18-Mar-03
SA	*2-Nov-05*	AR	27-Mar-07	AR	19-Jul-08	AQ	*23-Oct-07*	SC	7-Dec-04	CN	7-Nov-04
CP	28-Oct-06	TA	19-Jun-08	TA	12-Oct-09	**VI**	**16-Mar-09**	SA	2-Mar-06	LE	27-Nov-06
CN	**21-Aug-08**	GE	14-Feb-09	**LE**	**11-Mar-10**	LI	6-Nov-10	CP	25-Feb-07	**SA**	**21-Aug-08**
LE	10-Apr-10	CP	*7-Oct-10*	VI	2-Oct-11	SC	4-Jul-11	AQ	15-May-09	CP	16-May-09
VI	1-Nov-11	AQ	25-Dec-12	LI	24-May-13	SA	26-Sep-12	PI	1-Nov-11	AQ	4-Jun-11
LI	23-Jun-13	PI	13-Jan-15	SC	19-Jan-14	CP	21-Sep-13	**SC**	**29-Feb-12**	PI	20-Nov-13
SC	18-Feb-14	AR	7-Jun-16	SA	14-Apr-15	AQ	10-Dec-15	SA	24-May-13	AR	15-Nov-14
SA	14-May-15	**TA**	**31-Aug-17**	CP	8-Apr-16	PI	*28-May-18*	CP	19-May-14	TA	8-Feb-16
CP	*8-May-16*	LE	**28-Jan-18**	AQ	*27-Jun-18*	AR	23-May-19	AQ	6-Aug-16	GE	5-Oct-16
AQ	27-Jul-18	VI	12-Aug-19	PI	13-Dec-20	TA	15-Aug-20	PI	19-May-14	CN	28-May-18
PI	12-Jan-21	LI	12-Apr-21	AR	8-Dec-21	GE	12-Apr-21	AR	18-Jan-20	**CP**	**18-Jan-20**
AR	7-Jan-22	SC	8-Dec-21	TA	3-Mar-23	CN	3-Dec-22	TA	12-Apr-21	AQ	7-Apr-22
TA	2-Apr-23	SA	3-Mar-23	GE	29-Oct-23	LE	22-Dec-24	GE	8-Dec-21	PI	23-Sep-24
GE	28-Nov-23	CP	26-Feb-24	CN	20-Jun-25	PI	*15-Jul-26*	CN	31-Jul-23	AR	18-Sep-25
CP	*20-Jul-25*	AQ	*16-Jun-26*	AQ	*10-Jul-27*	AR	10-Jul-27	LE	19-Aug-25	TA	12-Dec-26
AQ	8-Oct-27	PI	1-Nov-28	**VI**	**1-Dec-28**	TA	2-Oct-28	SA	12-Dec-26	GE	9-Aug-27
PI	26-Mar-30	AR	27-Oct-29	LI	24-Jul-30	**LI**	**1-Dec-28**	CP	7-Dec-27	*CN*	*31-May-29*
AR	21-Mar-31	TA	20-Jan-31	SC	21-Mar-31	SC	29-Jul-29	AQ	24-Feb-30	LE	20-Apr-31
TA	13-Jun-32	GE	17-Sep-31	SA	13-Jun-32	SA	22-Oct-30	PI	12-Aug-32	VI	10-Nov-32
LE	**10-Nov-32**	CN	9-May-33	CP	8-Jun-33	CP	17-Oct-31	AR	7-Aug-33	LI	3-Jul-34

Table 22 presents all possible releasings for Harding's birthdate. This is a compressed version of a more legible spreadsheet I use when studying ZR for horoscopes with unknown birthtimes. Start of L1 periods are in bold. FS, LB, and CP periods are underlined and in italics. Shaded dates are L2 periods from LB until the next L1 period begins.

L1 Cancer (double-outlined columns 7 and 8).

L2 Capricorn **FS** 20-Dec-73: WH's father purchased a local newspaper during Summer 1875; WH worked as a printer.
L2 Capricorn **LB** 3-Mar-83: WH assumes editorship position of Marion STAR newspaper purchased by his father, May-1884.
Events for Capricorn FS and LB are linked. √

At the end of L1 Capricorn (Nov-1889 to early 1890, WH suffered a breakdown and recovered at Kellogg's Battle Creek Sanitarium. √

CHAPTER 9 – ZODIACAL RELEASING   153

Table 22 - *Continued*

↓	ADB															
LI	2-Nov-65	SC	2-Nov-65	SA	2-Nov-65	CP	2-Nov-65	AQ	2-Nov-65	PI	2-Nov-65
SC	30-Jun-66	SA	26-Jan-67	CP	28-Oct-66	AQ	21-Jan-68	PI	20-Apr-68	AR	28-Oct-66
SA	23-Sep-67	CP	21-Jan-68	AQ	15-Jan-69	PI	9-Jul-70	AR	15-Apr-69	TA	21-Jan-68
CP	17-Sep-68	AQ	10-Apr-70	PI	4-Jul-71	AR	4-Jul-71	TA	9-Jul-70	GE	17-Sep-68
AQ	6-Dec-70	PI	26-Sep-72	AR	28-Jun-72	TA	26-Sep-72	GE	6-Mar-71	CN	10-May-70
PI	24-May-73	AR	21-Sep-73	TA	21-Sep-73	GE	24-May-73	CN	26-Oct-72	LE	29-May-72
SC	21-Sep-73	TA	15-Dec-74	GE	19-May-74	*CN*	*14-Jan-75*	*LE*	*15-Nov-74*	VI	20-Dec-73
SA	15-Dec-74	GE	12-Aug-75	CN	9-Jan-76	LE	2-Feb-77	VI	7-Jun-76	LI	12-Aug-75
CP	10-Dec-75	CN	3-Apr-77	**CP**	**31-Aug-77**	VI	26-Aug-78	LI	28-Jan-78	SC	8-Apr-76
AQ	27-Feb-78	LE	23-Apr-79	AQ	19-Nov-79	LI	17-Apr-80	SC	25-Sep-78	SA	2-Jul-77
PI	15-Aug-80	**SA**	**15-Aug-80**	PI	7-May-82	SC	13-Dec-80	SA	19-Dec-79	**AR**	**31-Aug-77**
AR	10-Aug-81	CP	10-Aug-81	AR	2-May-83	SA	8-Mar-82	CP	13-Dec-80	TA	24-Nov-78
TA	3-Nov-82	AQ	29-Oct-83	TA	25-Jul-84	*CN*	*3-Mar-83*	*LE*	*3-Mar-83*	GE	22-Jul-79
GE	1-Jul-83	PI	16-Apr-85	GE	22-Mar-85	LE	22-Mar-85	VI	23-Sep-84	CN	13-Mar-81
CN	20-Feb-85	AR	11-Apr-87	*CN*	*12-Nov-86*	VI	13-Oct-86	LI	16-May-86	LE	2-Apr-83
LE	12-Mar-87	TA	4-Jul-88	LE	1-Dec-88	LI	4-Jun-88	SC	11-Jan-87	VI	23-Oct-84
SA	**4-Jul-88**	GE	1-Mar-89	VI	24-Jun-90	SC	30-Jan-89	SA	5-Apr-88	LI	15-Jun-86
CP	29-Jun-89	CN	22-Oct-90	LI	14-Feb-92	SA	25-Apr-90	CP	31-Mar-89	SC	10-Feb-87
AQ	17-Sep-91	**CP**	**13-Jun-92**	SC	11-Oct-92	*CP*	*20-Apr-91*	*AO*	*19-Jun-91*	SA	5-May-88
PI	5-Mar-94	AQ	1-Sep-94	SA	4-Jan-94	**AQ**	**13-Jun-92**	PI	5-Dec-93	CP	30-Apr-89
AR	28-Feb-95	PI	17-Feb-97	*CN*	*30-Dec-94*	PI	30-Nov-94	AR	30-Nov-94	AQ	19-Jul-91
TA	23-May-96	AR	12-Feb-98	LE	18-Jan-97	AR	25-Nov-95	**PI**	**29-May-95**	**TA**	**13-Jun-92**
GE	18-Jan-97	TA	8-May-99	VI	11-Aug-98	TA	17-Feb-97	AR	23-May-96	GE	8-Feb-93
CN	10-Sep-98	GE	3-Jan-00	LI	2-Apr-00	GE	15-Oct-97	TA	16-Aug-97	CN	1-Oct-94
CP	**2-May-00**	*CN*	*25-Aug-01*	SC	28-Nov-00	CN	7-Jun-99	GE	13-Apr-98	LE	20-Oct-96
AQ	21-Jul-02	LE	14-Sep-03	SA	21-Feb-02	*LE*	*26-Jun-01*	CN	4-Dec-99	VI	13-May-98
PI	6-Jan-05	VI	6-Apr-05	*CP*	*16-Feb-03*	VI	17-Jan-03	LE	23-Dec-01	LI	3-Jan-00
AR	1-Jan-06	LI	27-Nov-06	**AQ**	**11-Apr-04**	SC	8-Sep-04	VI	16-Jul-03	**GE**	**2-May-00**
TA	27-Mar-07	SC	25-Jul-07	PI	28-Sep-06	SC	6-May-05	LI	7-Mar-05	CN	23-Dec-01
GE	22-Nov-07	SA	17-Oct-08	AR	23-Sep-07	SA	30-Jul-06	SC	2-Nov-05	LE	12-Jan-04
CN	*14-Jul-09*	*CN*	*12-Oct-09*	TA	16-Dec-08	CP	25-Jul-07	SA	26-Jan-07	VI	4-Aug-05
LE	3-Aug-11	LE	1-Nov-11	GE	13-Aug-09	*LE*	*12-Oct-09*	**AR**	**27-Mar-07**	LI	27-Mar-07
VI	23-Feb-13	VI	24-May-13	CN	5-Apr-11	VI	5-May-11	TA	19-Jun-08	SC	22-Nov-07
LI	16-Oct-14	LI	14-Jan-15	*LE*	*24-Apr-13*	LI	25-Dec-12	GE	14-Feb-09	*SA*	*14-Feb-09*
SC	13-Jun-15	SC	11-Sep-15	VI	15-Nov-14	SC	22-Aug-13	CN	7-Oct-10	CP	9-Feb-10
SA	5-Sep-16	SA	4-Dec-16	LI	7-Jul-16	SA	15-Nov-14	LE	26-Oct-12	AQ	29-Apr-12
CN	*31-Aug-17*	*CP*	*29-Nov-17*	SC	4-Mar-17	*CP*	*10-Nov-15*	VI	19-May-14	PI	16-Oct-14
LE	20-Sep-19	**AQ**	**23-Jan-19**	SA	28-May-18	*AO*	*28-Jan-18*	LI	9-Jan-16	AR	11-Oct-15
VI	12-Apr-21	PI	11-Jul-21	CP	23-May-19	PI	16-Jul-20	SC	5-Sep-16	TA	3-Jan-17
LI	3-Dec-22	AR	6-Jul-22	*LE*	*10-Aug-21*	AR	11-Jul-21	SA	29-Nov-17	*SA*	*31-Aug-17*
SC	31-Jul-23	TA	29-Sep-23	VI	3-Mar-23	**PI**	**7-Jan-22**	CP	24-Nov-18	CP	26-Aug-18
SA	23-Oct-24	GE	26-May-24	LI	23-Oct-24	AR	2-Jan-23	AQ	11-Feb-21	**CN**	**18-Jan-20**
CP	*18-Oct-25*	CN	16-Jan-26	SC	20-Jun-25	TA	27-Mar-24	**TA**	**7-Jan-22**	LE	6-Feb-22
AQ	**12-Dec-26**	*LE*	*5-Feb-28*	SA	13-Sep-26	GE	22-Nov-24	GE	4-Sep-22	VI	30-Aug-23
PI	30-May-29	VI	28-Aug-29	CP	8-Sep-27	CN	15-Jul-26	CN	26-Apr-24	LI	21-Apr-25
AR	25-May-30	LI	20-Apr-31	*AQ*	*26-Nov-29*	LE	3-Aug-28	LE	16-May-26	SC	17-Dec-25
TA	18-Aug-31	SC	16-Dec-31	PI	14-May-32	VI	24-Feb-30	VI	7-Dec-27	SA	12-Mar-27
GE	14-Apr-32	SA	10-Mar-33	AR	9-May-33	LI	17-Oct-31	LI	29-Jul-29	*CP*	*6-Mar-28*
CN	5-Dec-33	CP	5-Mar-34	**PI**	**5-Nov-33**	SC	13-Jun-32	GE	26-Nov-29	AQ	25-May-30

So far the event match to Cancer is consistent with theory, not with releasing from Libra based on the later 2:30 PM ADB birthtime. (ZR from Libra presented in first two columns of Table 22 on the current page fails to offer any matches).

L1 Leo (still referring to Table 22, prior page, columns 7-8)

L2 Aquarius **FS 10-Oct-98**: First WH electoral victory in Ohio Senate.
L2 Aquarius **LB 23-Oct-07**: Endorsed Foraker, then Taft for President. WH was endorsed for the US Senate but did not run.
Both Aquarius FS and LB link key periods of WH's political career. √

The changeover from L1 Leo to L1 Virgo occurs 16-Mar-1909. During this transition, WH, his wife Florence, and his mistress Carrie Phillips took a Mediterranean cruise between 4-Feb-1909 and 30-Apr-1909. Notable purchases during the cruise included a half-size marble bust of a female nude and another marble bust of a naked dancing girl both bought by WH. Not to be outdone,

Harding's wife Florence purchased a marble-clothed statue of "Priscilla the Puritan Girl." The delineation match of these statues to the sign depiction of L1 Virgo (often depicted as a naked maiden) is one of those rare in-your-face delineation matches which cannot be ignored. Immediately prior to the cruise in early 1909, WH reorganized the Marion STAR newspaper by offering 25% of its capital stock to employees. This is a significant change in business operations we should expect to see at L1 changeovers. √√√

Again, so far so good. Both linkages between L2 Aquarius FS and LB periods are clear. Significant transitional events occur at the L1 changeover.

L1 Virgo

While Virgo is a long enough period to include FS and LB periods, WH dies before the L2 Pisces LB occurs. Therefore, I will look at angular signs from the LOF and make a qualitative judgment whether life events are more active for signs which are angular from Fortune according to ZR theory [see box below].

First consider L1 Virgo itself is 4th from LOF positioned in Gemini. This means at the L1 level, this L1 Virgo period should be more active than the two prior L1 Cancer and Leo periods. As WH ran an unsuccessful Ohio Gubernatorial campaign and successful campaigns for the US Senate and the Presidency, the chronology DOES match theory that L1 Virgo should be very active. √

L2 Virgo **LOF4 16-Mar-1909:** Unsuccessful Ohio Gubernatorial election.
L2 Sagittarius **LOF7 26-Sep-1912:** Requested Japanese diplomatic post from President Taft, but it was unavailable.
L2 Pisces **LOF10 28-May-1918:** Death of Roosevelt left a void in the Republican Party which led to Harding's presidential nomination during L2 AR.
L2 Gemini **LOF1 12-Apr-1921:** Notable events during Presidency: Washington Disarmament Conference of 12-Nov-1921; Teapot Dome scandal unfolds, 1922; Labor strike and loss of life known as the Herrin Massacre, 21-Jun-1922.

Note on Angular signs from the Lot of Fortune

When we speak of 'LOF angles' or whether a sign is 'angular form Fortune' what is meant? For Warren Harding, the Lot of Fortune is positioned in Gemini. Gemini can be relabeled LOF 1 (1st house if we turn the chart so the LOF is treated as a functional Ascendant). In sequence, LOF 4 is Virgo; LOF 7, Sagittarius; LOF 10, Pisces. Just as the MC is the 10th house from the Ascendant and ranked as a critical horoscopic point, the 10th sign from the Lot of Fortune is delineated in a similar manner. Whether or not the sign of LOF 10 is bonified or maltreated is one factor that can determine whether an individual will have a successful or failed career.

Though the activity level is reasonable during times when ZR highlights L2 signs which are angular from the LOF, missed are Harding's 1914 election to the US Senate (L2 Capricorn) and his 1920 election to the Presidency (L2 Taurus) which is disappointing. X

What is consistent about the performance of L2 subperiods is the influence of the Lunar Nodes which bonify Capricorn and Libra (10th from Capricorn housing the North Node and Venus/Libra which is the victor of the horoscope) and maltreat Cancer and Aries (10th from Cancer housing the South Node). WH is elected to the US Senate during L2 Capricorn and dies while President during L2 Cancer.

Recall earlier L2 Capricorn events under L1 Cancer were favorable and marked WH's early rise as a newspaper editor. For WH's final years, L2 Capricorn again times a significant career milestone but at a much higher operating level (under the influence of L1 Virgo with Virgo in the angular 4th sign from the Lot of Fortune.) Death under L2 Cancer is consistent with Cancer the sign of the 8th house of death ruled by an afflicted Moon applying to the opposition of Saturn. Both the Moon and Saturn are out-of-sect in a diurnal horoscope.

Following my own tricks and traps, is it possible that using the ADB birthtime of 2:30 PM, another Hermetic Lot placed in Cancer could yield this same set of chapters? I checked and no, there are no Hermetic Lots in Cancer (at any degree) for the A-rated birthtime of 2:30 PM. The proposed rectification is confirmed by ZR. √√√

Beyond Harding: A Miscellany of other ZR Presidential Observations

L1 periods which closely defined start/end of Presidential terms or other major shifts in national politics:

Start: John Adams (3 months), John Quincy Adams (post-presential election to Congress, 3 months), Van Buren (1 month), Hayes (3 months), Theodore Roosevelt (Vice-Presidential nomination, 3 months), Kennedy (1 month).
End: Tyler (withdrew Presidential bid in 1844, 2 months), Fillmore (Lost Whig Presidential nomination which ended political career, 3 months), Grant (end of Presidency, 8 months), Arthur (abruptly ended opposition to Civil Service Reform by signing Pendleton Act, 1 month), Nixon (named Watergate co-conspirator, 1 month).

L2 FS-LB connections which are notable:
Washington, Madison, Monroe, Jackson, Pierce, Lincoln, Johnson, Garfield, McKinley, Taft, Wilson, Harding, Hoover, Truman, Eisenhower, G. H. W. Bush, Clinton, Obama.

Cases where ZR was unimpressive as timer of Presidential Elections:
Coolidge, Ford.

Usefulness in Rectification

As presented, zodiacal releasing purports to identify discrete periods of time when career milestones are more likely to occur. For rectification purposes this is the primary interest in the technique. Specifically:

- Do major life chapters conform to partitions defined by L1 periods?

- For GE, CA, LE, VI, CP, and AQ can similar life events link Foreshadowing and Loosing of the Bond periods; adding Completion periods for CP and AQ?

- Do L2 periods show higher levels of activity for signs angular from fortune?

If the answer to these questions is yes, then Zodiacal Releasing confirms the sign placement of the Lots of Spirit and Fortune. Since the Ascendant degree is one component necessary to compute Spirit and Fortune, knowing the correct sign placements for the Lots narrows the allowable Ascendant degree range.

Omitted from this chapter is a discussion of how to delineate each sign with Hellenistic techniques so the quality of events for a specific ZR subperiod can be predicted in advance. While these are necessary steps prior to a client natal reading they are not completely necessary for rectification. This is another reminder that rectification is not designed to explain all life events, rectification is a process designed to create an accurate birth time model so that proper delineation and prediction steps can be taken as a next step.

For further research: What do the Lots Actually Mean?

Absent from contemporary ZR discussions is the meaning of the Lots of Fortune and Spirit not just in the signs but in the bound subdivisions of each sign.

Consider Theodore Roosevelt as an example. Comparing the ADB (7:45 PM) and the ARM proposed rectification (7:15:59 PM), the Lot of Spirit shifts from 7PI10 to 29AQ42. While we know changing signs for the LOS alters the sign where the Lot is released, we haven't discussed what it actually means for TR as a person for the different sign placements, much less the bound placements.

My work suggests the Lot of Spirit's bound placement is a key delineation step necessary to unlock a hidden feature central to career and life purpose. For Roosevelt, LOS in the bound of Saturn/Aquarius makes him a scientist, data collector, and an idealogue. He is not afraid to combat the rugged individualism of Leo commonly found among American businessmen with top-down command and control regulations for the benefit of the greater society. Roosevelt is this way because the Lot of Spirit is placed in the bound of Saturn/Aquarius and we can make these types of statements based on the Lot of Spirit's placement in the bound of Saturn/Aquarius without recourse to the Lot's rulers. Both sign and bound rulers indicate methods that TR will use to achieve a Saturn/Aquarius-signified Lot of Spirit. For TR, the sign and bound ruler of the lot are the same: Saturn/Leo which signifies TR's 'bully pulpit' leadership style when undertaking political reform. It also signifies heroic manly activities including big game hunting and safari adventures. Some of TR's hunting trophies are displayed in the Mammals Hall of the Museum of Natural History, New York City, which shows the unlikely connection between highly publicized big game trophy hunts and a scientific interest in animal life. Not only did TR have strong ties to the Museum of Natural History; as President, TR established the US Forest Service and dozens of bird reservations, national monuments, national parks, and game preserves. Writing in 2022, diving deeper into the delineation of the Lot of Spirit by its bound placement and bound rulers is a brand-new research topic for astrologers.

Try repeating this exercise with Lot of Spirit in the bound of Venus/Pisces for Roosevelt's ADB time. I just don't think it makes any sense.

For a minority of American Presidents, I delineate the Lot of Spirit in this fashion. Often one must read multiple biographies and personal correspondence to see evidence of the Lot of Spirit functioning in the manner I have described. A few highlights in Table 23.

Table 23. Delineations for Lot of Spirit's bound placement.

President	LOS	Bound	Ruler	Observations
George Washington	20SA52	☿♐	☿♒	LOS in the bound of Mercury/Sagittarius makes Washington a land speculator with lord Mercury/Aquarius signifying his surveying skills as a driving force.
John Adams	21LE32	☿♌	☿♏	LOS in bound of Mercury/Leo makes Adams a humanist though lord Mercury/Scorpio means he uses a biting tongue and trenchant legal arguments to achieve his aims.
Andrew Jackson	2SC41	♂♏	♂♉	LOS in bound of Mars/Scorpio makes Jackson a tenacious brawler who uses open conflict with enemies (Lord Mars/Taurus in the 1st ruling the 7th) as a method to achieve martial revenge.
James Polk	4TA37	♀♉	♀♏	LOS in bound of Venus/Taurus makes Polk interested in accumulating land. Venus/Scorpio signifies lust for land as a driving influence for territorial acquisition.
FDR	15AQ59	♃♒	♃♉	LOS in bound of Jupiter/Aquarius with Jupiter/Taurus as Victor signifies FDR's humanitarian philosophy epitomized by his 6-Jan-1941 Four Freedoms speech.
Joe Biden	9LE43	♀♌	♀♏	LOS in bound of Venus/Leo makes Biden a lover of peace, love, vitality, politics, and entertainment. Bound lord Venus/Scorpio at superior conjunction recognizes pain and suffering of Venus in detriment as a social norm worth recognizing via Biden's role as 'comforter-in-chief' be it his presence at funerals or his support of the *Violence Against Women Act*, his signature legislative achievement as Senator. Biden uses his role as 'comforter-in-chief' (Venus/Scorpio) to achieve LOS (bound Venus/Leo) objectives. In mundane astrology, Leo is assigned to Europe which makes Biden 'love' NATO and other European interests with LOS in bound of Venus/Leo.

CHAPTER TEN

Directions

Chapter Summary

Primary Directions: Standalone. Prior to the first English translation of Directing Through the Bounds (Abū Ma'shar al-Balhi 1999), the few astrologers and software companies who worked with primary directions in the 20th century added minor aspects, modern planets, and converse motion in what can be characterized as a free-for-all. Stripped of any relationship to the Egyptian bounds, this approach yielded so many event permutations that it is impossible to ignore the role of confirmation bias in assigning the 'correctness' of an event match to a specific primary direction. In ARM 1st edition, I proposed the *Primary Direction Sequence* to cut this Gordian knot. The *Primary Direction Sequence* is comprised of a set of dates, each computed with permutations of zero and full latitude for the significator and promissor. Dates generated by sequences time the start and end of a series of events which historically have been attributed to a direction's orb of influence. Because the odds are very low that two separate events, often a year apart or more, could be precisely timed by a pair of primary directions; sequences are the long-lost *Holy Grail of Rectification*. *NEW*: Critics of my proposal point to the fact the planet's full latitude was not considered by traditional authors when computing primary directions. Those traditional authors who considered latitude adjustments used a method by Bianchini whose effect is to maintain the position of all aspects on a single great circle using spherical geometry principles. This is a technical concept which is beyond the scope of this book. Readers should note since the 3rd edition I have found no evidence that Bianchini latitude adjustments consistently outperform a full planet's latitude.

Primary Directions: Directing through the Bounds. Because directions can time major life events accurately within 24 hours, they are rightly placed at the top of the predictive hierarchy. Not just directions of the significators to planets are of interest. Movement of the significators through the Egyptian bounds forms another set of life chapters which complement other Planetary Period Methods.

NEW: For Theodore Roosevelt, a complete set of event matches is presented for Directing the Ascendant through the Bounds.

Solar Arc Directions gained popularity in the 20th century for their ease of computation in contrast to primary directions which fell out of favor for their mathematical complexity. In what I consider a rush to judgment, some traditional astrologers having rediscovered primary directions no longer consider solar arc directions worthy of consideration. Research conducted for this book details solar arc directions are very effective in timing life events comparable to events timed by primary directions; however, their effectiveness appears greater for horoscopes with a Leo emphasis (ASC sign, ASC ruler or planets in Leo). Likewise, for horoscopes which emphasize Libra or Aquarius (signs of the Sun's fall and detriment) and with no planets in Leo, solar arc directions seldom register events which appear on biographical timelines.

Linkage between Solar Arc and Primary Directions. When researching the horoscope of Woodrow Wilson, I discovered an unusual connection between directions for the same set of significators when computed by both solar arc and primary directions. The solar arc direction timed a mundane event between WWI combatants; the same primary direction timed Wilson's face-to-face meeting with those same individuals at the Paris Peace Conference. The ability of the same set of significators to generate linked events when computed by both directional systems is mathematically a very low probability. Today I rank this linkage with the Primary Direction Sequence as another *Holy Grail of Rectification*. ARM 4th edition includes an example for Joe Biden: that a Sun-MC direction by solar arc timed the Montreal spree shooting by Marc Lepine and the same Sun-MC direction by primary direction timed passage of the *Violence Against Women Act*. The events are linked because Lepine's victims were primarily women which so disgusted Biden that he launched a study on the incidence of violence against women under the auspices of the Senate Judiciary Committee. The result was the *Violence Against Women Act* which was Biden's signature legislative achievement.

Usefulness of Directions in Rectification

In the three-stage approach to rectification I advocate in Part III of this manual, solar arc directions and transits can be introduced in Stage II to narrow the Ascendant degree range to between 1 and 4 degrees using dynamic activity to the Hellenistic Lots and angles. But the full gamut of directions is reserved for Stage III rectification only when the unknown Ascendant has been narrowed to a one-to-four-degree range. Once a limited degree range is identified, the tools introduced in this chapter – the Primary Direction Sequence, Directing through the Bounds, Solar Arc directions, and the linkage between Solar Arc and Primary Directions – are the most sophisticated techniques available to achieve the elusive 'to-the-second' rectified horoscope.

Chapter 10 – Directions

The Free-For-All to Garner 'Maximum Hits' for birth time rectification

Or How I Developed the PRIMARY DIRECTIONS SEQUENCE

Prior to the first English translation of Directing through the Bounds made in 1999, the few astrologers and software vendors who calculated primary directions did so without consideration of the bound placement of the Distributor. Many incorporated modern planets and minor aspects to the point where so many directions were computed that with the benefit of confirmation bias, virtually any life event could be explained by a computed primary direction not more than a few days away from the actual event.

When I first started this project in 2005, I used an early version of Janus software which turned out to use Placidus-under-the-Pole as a calculation method which is only an approximation for some directions which involve planetary aspects. The 1st edition of ARM included some of these Placidus-under-the-Pole directions. Following the 1st edition, I worked with Janus software developer Mark Griffin to revise the software's primary directions module which as it stands is one of the most versatile on the market. The current Version 5.5 released in 2021 adds the Distributions module whose output appears later in this Chapter.

While writing ARM, I first stripped out minor aspects and minor planets. Then I began to observe that I could link the start and end of a series of similar events to the same primary direction computed with and without the full latitude of the planet. I found these results consistent and developed the following thesis:

Definition: *Primary Direction Sequence*

A set of dates, computed with all latitude combinations between significator and promissor, which defines a sequence of events listed in chronological order.

For Ascendant-planet and Midheaven-planet directions, a pair of dates is computed. The first direction is computed with the full latitude of the planet. The second direction assumes the planet has zero latitude.

Because the Sun has zero latitude, only a single direction is computed for the Sun.

For interplanetary directions, four dates are computed:

(1) zero latitude of significator and zero latitude of promissor,
(2) zero latitude of significator and full latitude of promissor,
(3) full latitude of significator and full latitude of promissor, and
(4) full latitude of significator and zero latitude of promissor.

Findings of other researchers. Two other researchers of primary directions note similar findings. Rumen Kolev computes a pair of Sun - Mars directions for Adoph Hitler's figure which bracket Hitler's decline during 1908-1910 culminating with homelessness (Kolev 2005[?]: 23). The difference in Kolev's approach is that one direction is computed using direct motion; the other, converse. Under my definition, while allowing both direct and converse directions, I do not mix direct and converse motion within a single sequence. Jerry Makransky also reported that interchanging the significator and promissor for mundane conjunctions and oppositions in the Campanus and Regiomontanus systems yielded a pair of events or time periods which were linked in some way (McKransky 1998). Though I did not perform the exact types of directions that Makransky describes, it appears my findings are similar in spirit.

NEW: Evaluating the Primary Direction Sequence. Two main criticisms emerged following publication of the $1^{st} - 3^{rd}$ editions on my thesis. (1) Except for directing conjunctions of planets to significators with full latitude of the planet, the full latitude was never used for planetary aspects. Either zero latitude was used, and if latitude were considered, the method of Bianchini was most frequently applied (Gansten 2009). The implication is that my proposed primary direction sequence picks up phantom events which can be explained by rectification errors or a lengthy orb of influence from a single direction. (2) Converse primary directions which are based on minutes prior to birth, conceived as time moving backwards, were never used by traditional practitioners of primary directions. They were first introduced by Alan Leo in the late 19th century under the influence of the Theosophical Society and were thought to identify past-life influences through the theory of karma.

NEW: Incorporating Bianchini latitude adjustments. By adding Bianchini latitude adjustments, a third date can be computed for sextile, trine, and opposition aspects. Consider the third date another possible event timer for the primary direction sequence. In these cases, a series of three date/three events can be identified as the primary direction sequence.

NEW: Latitude adjustments for interplanetary directions. Recent research suggests that significators should be directed with their full latitude. This is particularly evident when directing the Moon through the bounds. If this tentative finding proves correct then the four possible interplanetary directions listed in the Primary Directions Sequence definition box on the prior page can be cut in half, e.g., eliminating (1) and (2) but keeping (3) and (4).

Case Study: Theodore Roosevelt

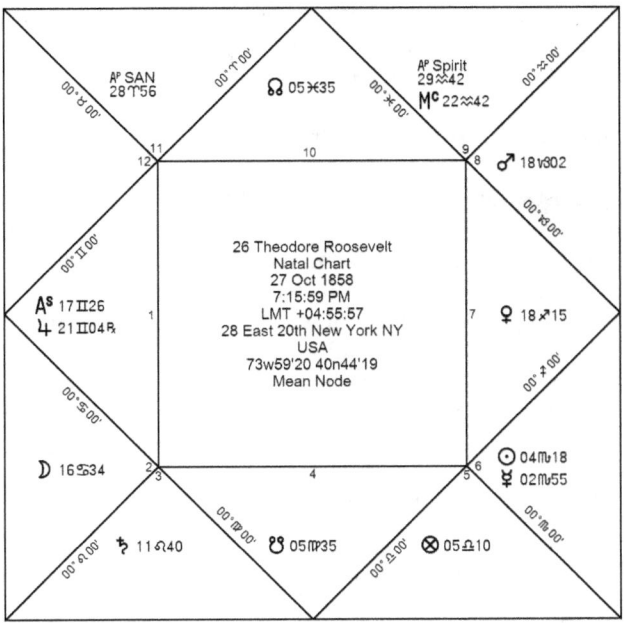

Reviewing Roosevelt's timeline for the first time in 2006, one of the standout events of his life was his ill-fated third-party Presidential bid in 1912 which ended splitting the Republican Party and giving Democratic Nominee Woodrow Wilson the election. During the summer of 1912, he stated "I feel as strong as a bull moose" which quickly morphed into the Bull Moose Party as the moniker for his progressive political party. The delineation match to this statement is Saturn/Leo in the 3rd house of short-term travel and publicity with both of those life affairs consistent with a political campaign. Saturn/Leo signifies a strong man, often athletic and autocratic in political style. Included in the Presidential database is the following primary direction sequence used to time peak activity of Roosevelt's challenge to Taft:

| REG | D | Mars/Gemini | P | sinister trine MC c. => Saturn (0) | 30-May-1912 |
| REG | D | Mars/Gemini | P | sinister trine MC c. => Saturn (SA) | 9-Jun-1912 |

LOCK This sequence comprises the climax of delegate selection when Roosevelt nearly garnered sufficient delegate seats to secure a victory. Roosevelt's strong showing in President Taft's home state of Ohio on 22-May gave Roosevelt a temporary surge in popularity. As the sequence closed, Roosevelt's luck had run out as he was unable to outmaneuver the Republican National Party. See New York Times "48 More Votes Awarded to Taft; Roosevelt's Contests Collapse," June 9, 1912, p. 1.

This type of primary direction is not sanctioned by traditional authors because (1) it is computed by converse motion and (2) aspects of significators (here sinister trine MC) were never used in the position of the significator or promissor when constructing a primary direction. Yet this is the type of primary direction sequence which peppers the Presidential database.

Locking Down a Rectification with Primary Direction Sequences

Low odds against a random finding. The value in primary direction sequences is based on the extremely low odds of finding pairs of events, sometimes months or years apart, which match start and end dates for a primary direction sequence. It's fairly easy to find close matches of individual directions to a smattering of events. But matching several pairs of events to sequences of Ascendant and Midheaven directions is a low probability mathematical feat which increases odds the rectification is correct. I use the notation *LOCK* to signify either Sun-angle directions or primary direction sequences with outstanding accuracy. These *locked-down* directions capture the *AHA!* moments of the rectification process.

DIRECTING THROUGH THE BOUNDS

A New Paradigm for Primary Directions. The revival of Hellenistic and Medieval astrology in the last 20 years has uncovered a more sophisticated implementation of primary directions known as Directing through the Bounds. There are two main differences between a standard primary directions printout which lists a smashup of planets, angles, lots and this more formal procedure known as Directing through the Bounds. Both are computed with primaries, but

1. Directing through the Bounds is computed for a single significator such as the Ascendant. Other possible significators are the Midheaven, Sun, Moon, Lot of Fortune, Lot of Spirit, and the SAN. These reports are computed independently so that one will not see, for example, a mix of ASC and MC directions in a single event listing.

2. Beyond the two planets/points which form the primary directions, Directing through the Bounds adds the Egyptian bound placement of the Significator to the equation. Known as the 'Distributor,' the bound placement of the Significator refines the type of event which occurs at the time of the primary direction.

Terminology. In 1999, Project Hindsight made the first English translation of this technique choosing the term "Circumambulations" as the best match from Hellenistic sources (Abū Ma'shar 1999: 1-40). In 2008, I published *American is Born: Introducing the Regulus USA National Horoscope* which includes a complete set of mathematical instructions for Directing the Ascendant through the Bounds. Applied to the 4-Jul-1776 proposed birthdate of the United States of America, *America is Born* presents the most complete application of Directing

Through the Bounds published in the modern era (Regulus 2008). In that book I used the following vocabulary: "Abū Ma'shar's Theory of Distributors and Participators," "Directing Through the Bounds," "Distributors," and "Participators." In 2019 Benjamin Dykes published the first complete English translation from Arabic sources and used the terms "Distributions," "Distributors," and "Partners" (Abū Ma'shar 2019). In all cases these slight differences in vocabulary refer to the same technique. I will use Dykes' vocabulary for this text. Since publication of ARM 3rd edition, Janus 5.5 added a "Distributions" module which has increased facility in testing Directing through the Bounds for the Presidential database.

Application of the Technique. Using the Ascendant as an example, Abū Ma'shar names the bound ruler the *Distributor* and the most recent planet aspecting the significator by primary direction the *Partner*. Further classifying Distributors and Partners as benefics or malefics, he then proceeds to outline every possible permutation. For example, moving from the bound of a benefic to another benefic is good; from the bound of a benefic to a malefic is bad; from the bound of one malefic to another malefic is quite bad. Then he overlays the benefic/malefic status of the Partner. So if there has been a change of one benefic bound to another benefic, yet the Partner is a malefic; there is a degradation of the effect. For every change in Distributor and Partner a new planetary period is established. The joint influence of Distributor and Partner influences the Ascendant in ways which can be explained and predicted.

Theodore Roosevelt: Directing Through the Bounds: Ascendant

The proposed rectified birth time of 7:15:59 PM corresponds with an Ascendant degree of 17GE26'30". Falling between the degree range of 17GE00'00" and 23GE59'59", the Ascendant is placed in the bound of Mars/Gemini. This makes Mars the Distributor for the period between TR's birth and 7-Jun-1865 when the Distributor changes from Mars to Saturn. My research shows not just the planet but the planet's sign is key to understanding the behavior of the Distributor; in this case, I prefer to say the Distributor is Mars/Gemini.

Ascendant Distributions

Mars/Gemini ASC Distribution. Birth to 6-Jun-1865.
Saturn/Gemini ASC Distribution. 7-Jun-1865 to 26-Oct-1871.
Mars/Cancer ASC Distribution. 27-Oct-1871 to 24-Aug-1879

Choosing the Ascendant as the significator for Directing through the Bounds, the expectation is this technique should identify changes in the physical body. TR is a good example of this with both Mars/Gemini and Saturn/Gemini consistent with his thin physique plagued by asthma. Gemini is assigned to the lungs, arms, and hands. The malefic bounds of Gemini interfere with lung capacity since the double-bodied air sign of Gemini is assigned to the lungs. Once the Distributor changed to Mars/Cancer on 27-Oct-1871, his physique changed from a gangly-Gemini appearance to a more full-bodied Cancer appearance. Biographers date the physical transformation to 6-Sep-1870 when his father imposed a strict physical fitness regimen after his father lost patience with his asthma attacks.

By the summer of 1872, Roosevelt's body mass had changed so rapidly he quickly outgrew his clothes. Asthma attacks diminished at this time (McCullough 1981, Chapter 5). The Distributor changeover from Saturn/Gemini to Mars/Cancer shifts the Distributor from one malefic to another. While Abū Ma'shar considers this transition difficult, TR's asthma condition did begin to improve after the Distributor changeover to Mars/Cancer on 27-Oct-1871. The malefic nature of Mars/Cancer appears consistent with the harsh physical regimen imposed by his father deemed necessary to change his physique.

Venus/Cancer Distribution. 25-Aug-1879 to 21-Aug-1886

Continuing with Distributors, what events occurred which correspond to the changeover from Mars/Cancer to Venus/Cancer on 25-Aug-1879? TR met his first wife-to-be Alice Lee on 18-Oct-1878 while a Harvard upperclassman. His marriage proposal made 20-Jun-1879 was rejected; but following a lunch TR organized in the honor of Alice Lee and her family at the Porcellian Club on 22-Nov-1879, Alice Lee accepted TR's marriage proposal on 25-Jan-1880. Note the rejected marriage proposal occurs during the Mars/Cancer distribution and the accepted marriage proposal occurs during the Venus/Cancer distribution after TR organized a Venusian-type social event. The Venus/Cancer distribution continues for 7 more years until 22-Aug-1886. During this eventful time, Alice Lee contracted the fatal kidney ailment known as Bright's disease and died two days after giving birth to their daughter also named Alice Lee. Just days before the end of the Venus/Cancer Distribution the New York Times reported TR's engagement to Edith Carow. This demonstrates the ability of Venus/Cancer as Distributor to pick up the effects of natal Venus/Sagittarius in the 7th house of marital partner. Sagittarius is a double bodied sign and TR begins the two significant relationships of his life during the Venus/Cancer Distribution.

Mercury/Cancer Distribution. 22-Aug-1886 to 9-Nov-1893

Following the changeover to Mercury/Cancer on 22-Aug-1886, the Great Blizzard of winter 1886/1887 occurred which led to TR's decision to sell his Dakota cattle operation. In financial astrology, the sign of Cancer is a poor sign for new investments and is associated with profit taking. This Distribution picks up the influence of natal Mercury/Scorpio combust in the 6th house to which cattle are assigned. A second major life event during this distribution is the theme of Civil Service Reform taken up by TR following his 13-May-1889 appointment to the Civil Service Commission by President Grover Cleveland. Significations of Mercury/Cancer include propaganda because the Moon-ruled sign of Cancer is

Table 24. Directing through the Bounds : Ascendant, Theodore Roosevelt

```
Date                Distributor     Partner
27 Oct 1858         ♂
14 Aug 1859         ♂               ☍ ♀    (0)
10 Jun 1862         ♂               ☌ ♃    (0)
22 Mar 1863         ♂               ☌ ♃    (JU)
27 Nov 1864         ♂               ☍ ♀    (VE)
07 Jun 1865         ♄
27 Oct 1871         ♂ ♋
16 May 1874         ♂               dex △ ☿  (ME)
17 Jan 1875         ♂               dex △ ☿  (0)
19 May 1875         ♂               dex △ ☿  (BI)
02 Aug 1876         ♂               dex △ ☉  (0)
25 Aug 1879         ♀
22 Aug 1886         ☿
20 Jan 1887         ☿               ☌ ☽    (MO)
13 Nov 1890         ☿               ☍ ♂    (BI)
30 Nov 1890         ☿               ☌ ☽    (0)
13 Sep 1892         ☿               ☍ ♂    (0)
09 Nov 1893         ♃
16 Jun 1894         ♃               ☍ ♂    (MA)
01 Jul 1902         ♄
07 Jul 1907         ♃ ♌
29 Sep 1910         ♃               dex □ ☿  (ME)
19 Mar 1911         ♃               dex □ ☿  (0)
15 Dec 1912         ♃               dex □ ☉  (0)
10 Feb 1915         ♀
27 Jun 1921         ♄
23 Dec 1921         ♄               ☌ ♄    (SA)
05 May 1922         ♄               ☌ ♄    (0)
```

Technical Notes: Table is output of Janus 5.5, Distributions module. All latitude options are presented for Partners (software allows choice of one latitude option per report run). The final column is my own addition and shows the latitude used in computing participating primary directions. For zero latitude, (0) is used. By definition the Sun always has zero latitude. For planets two additional latitude assumptions are used. (BI) stands for the Bianchini latitude adjustment. Note that square aspects using Bianchini's method have zero latitutde. The balance of latitude assumptions use the full latitude of the planet and are noted by a two character abbreviation for each respective planet: (SA, JU, MA, VE, ME, and MO).

TR died on 6-Jan-1919. The purpose of showing the additional data rows are to highlight that by primary motion, the participating direction of Saturn DOES NOT occur prior to TR's death (1921-22); however the same measurement by solar arc direction DOES occur prior to death during his 3rd party presidential bid in 1912.

assigned to the public-at-large and Mercury signifies speech. To wit: "Roosevelt's work as Civil Service Commissioner marked his first prolonged exercise of extraordinary gifts as propagandist" (Pringle 1931, 123). The linkage to combust Mercury/Scorpio in the 6th occurs because employees (and labor in a mundane horoscope) are assigned to the 6th and Mercury/Scorpio signifies the spoils system made possible by financial assessments or statements of political loyalty from political appointees. As Commissioner, TR's major dispute was with US Postmaster General John Wanamaker who replaced ~30,000 postal workers which led to inefficiency at the Post Office. TR won this legal battle.

Jupiter/Cancer Distribution. 9-Nov-1893 to 30-Jun-1902

At this point with Ascendant Distributors we are well beyond discussing changes in the physical body. Often Ascendant Distributions identify themes which are related to overall life purpose, not just the condition of the physical body. For TR, this distribution coincided with TR's interest in philosophy, a Jupiter-signified topic; specifically, the philosophy of Americanism. Immediately prior to the Jupiter/Distribution, the historian Frederick Jackson Turner linked American philosophy to western expansion in a thesis first presented at the Chicago World's Fair (1-May to 30-Oct-1893) and published the following year. Biographer Morris states TR spent most of 1893-1895 working out his own version of Americanism inspired by Jackson's thesis (Morris 1979, 367). Publication of *American Ideals* (1897) was one example of TR's output during the Jupiter Distribution as well as the final two volumes of *The Winning of the West* (1894 and 1896). How does this distribution pick up natal Jupiter/Gemini/rx/1st? Functionally, Jupiter/Gemini-rx acts like Jupiter/Sagittarius placed in the 7th house, the angle of the West, a possible linkage to Turner's thesis on the American West. In my view, the better linkage to Americanism is linkage of the Jupiter/Cancer distributor for TR to the Regulus USA National Horoscope, Sagittarius rising with lord Jupiter placed in the same sign of Cancer as TR's Ascendant Distributor active when TR wrote on the philosophy of America.

Saturn/Cancer Distribution. 1-Jul-1902 to 6-Jul-1907

The next distributor changeover occurs 1-Jul-1902 during the first year of TR's Presidency. Thirteen days later, TR learned of the court martial of General Jake Smith in Manila, Philippines, based on Smith's advocacy of killing women and children. TR refused the lenient recommendation of the Philippine military tribunal and fired Smith. Smith's actions exemplify an overzealous Saturn-signified command and control attitude towards the Cancer-signified populace. William Howard Taft was already in the Philippines a year earlier as military Governor and would oversee the Philippines as Secretary of War, picking up oversight of Cuba on 29-Sep-1906 towards the end of the Saturn/Cancer Distribution. Taft is linked to the Distribution because he has natal Saturn/Cancer. TR's Taft/Cuba assignment invoked the Platt Amendment (1901) itself a Saturn/Cancer document of unequal American control over Cuba which among other things established American rights to the Guantanamo Bay Naval Base (opened 1903). During the early phases of America's post-911 War on Terror, Guantanamo was used as a detention facility for terrorists under the GWB administration by the newly formed Homeland Security department. By transit the Homeland Security department was launched shortly before Saturn's Cancer Ingress 4-Jun-2003. This consistency of significators across techniques increases the odds that I am choosing the correct events from TR's chronology to match the Saturn/Cancer Distribution for Guantanamo's creation in 1903 and its renewed use during Saturn's 2003 Cancer Ingress. One last issue deserves mention at the conclusion of the Saturn/Cancer Distribution because its reversal is directly linked to the subsequent Distributor changeover. During 1907, a wave of anti-immigrant race riots occurred along the Pacific Coast, mostly directed against Japanese. As a consequence, the Immigration Act of 1907 limited Japanese immigration to the United States. Anti-immigration is characteristic of Saturn/Cancer which consistently generates isolationist political movements, often with an anti-immigration component.

Jupiter/Leo Distribution. 7-Jul-1907 to 9-Feb-1915

In the week leading up to the Distributor changeover from Saturn/Cancer to Jupiter/Leo on 7-Jul-1907, TR decided to gather all US naval vessels and embark on a global diplomatic tour later nicknamed "The Great White Fleet" (16-Dec-1907 to 22-Feb-1909). Among its stops was Japan, purposely included to ease tensions with Japan after the 1907 Pacific Coast Race Riots and the Immigration Act of 1907. The tour was wildly successful as a signal to the world that America was now a world power (Leo). Pomp and ceremony accompanied each port visit (Leo) without any fearful tinge of militarism (Jupiter). Reception of the Great White Fleet in Japan was successful and diminished diplomatic tensions with Japan. The balance of the Jupiter/Leo Distribution covers the end of TR's Presidency and his failed 3rd party presidential bid for the Progressive Party. As the Jupiter/Leo Distribution concluded, TR published a collection of 12 articles during the last week of January 1915. *America and the World War* attacked the Wilson administration's WWI neutrality and argued for intervention. One chapter title "The Peace of Righteousness" picks up the functional placement of natal Jupiter/Gemini-rx as Jupiter/Sagittarius/7th. My mundane research classifies the planet/sign combination of Jupiter/Sagittarius as the philosophy (Jupiter) of righteousness (Sagittarius). Of the three fire signs, Sagittarius is the least focused and often results in collateral damage; part and parcel of the "consequences be damned" attitude of Sagittarius.

Venus/Leo Distribution. 10-Feb-1915 to death.

The changeover from Jupiter/Leo to Venus/Leo on 10-Feb-1915 which remained active until TR's death should be less dramatic than the prior changeovers since both Distributors are benefics. A possible delineation match (and I am not 100% confident on this event match) is TR's success in a libel suit launched against him by Republican William Barnes Jr. During July 1914, TR accused Barnes of political corruption and his involvement with a conspiracy with Tammany Hall leader Charles Francis Murphy to block progressive reforms. Barnes sued TR for libel. The trial held 19-Apr to 22-May-1915 dismissed all charges against TR. This event is a possible delineation match if Venus/Leo is delineated as social (Venus) reputation (Leo). Linkage between this event and natal Venus/Sagittarius in the 7th of open enemies and legal conflicts is possible, but Venus ruling the 12th of enemies may be the better delineation match.

Ascendant Partner Directions

Next Partner Directions are added as the final layer to fill out the Directing through the Bounds procedure. Here are some Tricks and Traps:

Trick. The Distributor adds its intrinsic nature to any significator which dynamically passes through its degree range by primary motion. As a result, the significator is predisposed to actions consistent with the symbolism of the Distributor's planet/sign combination. As we have also seen, the Distributor adds another layer of delineation to the event by picking up the zodiacal state of the natal planet which matches the Distributor. Said another way, the Distributor predisposes the Significator (here the ASC for TR) to specific types of actions in the manner a stage is set prior to the arrival of actors. Certain stage sets are more conducive to certain actions than others. This narrows the types of possible events each Partner can manifest, above and beyond its own zodiacal state. For Roosevelt, the transition from Saturn/Cancer to Jupiter/Leo was dramatic with the Great White Fleet used as a soft power political tool to end Japanese resentment over American anti-immigration policies. Transitioning from Saturn to Jupiter, Roosevelt was less likely to continue or double down on anti-immigration policies. Though the Immigration Act of 1907 was not lifted, the tone changed after the Ascendant Distributor changed to Jupiter/Leo on 7-Jul-1907.

Trap. In theory a Partner Direction imparts its influence on the Ascendant starting from the exact date of direction up until the next Participating Direction takes over. The difference between two consecutive directions creates a planetary period in the same manner that the Distributor does from the time the directed Ascendant starts and concludes its passage over the respective bound. There is one problem with this assumption. Except for the Sun which has zero latitude, any planet with latitude can generate two or three distinct dates when computing Partner Directions. This occurs because there are three possible latitude assumptions for planetary aspects: zero latitude, Bianchini's latitude adjustment, and the full latitude of the planet; the latter of which is supported by my own research but not recognized by traditional authorities. In practice this means that two or three Partner Directions may collectively as a group constitute the start or end of a planetary period. It is messy. If these observations are correct, then be careful if by using only the zero-latitude assumption for Partner Directions if no event is found for the opening pages of a chapter as the technique purports to create. It is possible the omission of an earlier computed Partner Direction with a different latitude assumption marks the better start of the chapter. In particular, I would guard against deploying the modern concept from transit theory that the effects of a Partner Direction begin before the computed date because the notion from transit theory that an exact transit has an orb of influence before and after the exact transit date. My research suggests that primary directions create distinct events with zero forewarning before arrival. Any findings to the contrary are most likely due to incorrect rectification or the failure to integrate other predictive techniques. We need to be careful of letting the techniques speak for themselves without overworking them beyond the original intent of the author. If we do, we need to be clear how and why we have done so.

Notation: For the balance of this section, I will revert to the primary directions notation used in the Presidential database to improve readability. These are the same directions which appear in Table 24.

PT	D	Mars/Gemini	P	opposition Venus (0) d. => ASC	14-Aug-1859
PT	D	Mars/Gemini	P	Jupiter (0) d. => ASC	10-Jun-1862
PT	D	Mars/Gemini	P	Jupiter (JU) d. => ASC	22-Mar-1863
PT	D	Mars/Gemini	P	opposition Venus (VE) d. => ASC	27-Nov-1864

This set of participating directions occurs between age 1 and 6 during Civil War years. It is usually impossible to find exact date matches for biographical subjects at this age; yet for TR it is possible to make two generalizations for these Partner Directions.

Venus/Sagittarius/7th ruling the 5th and 12th signifies ebullient, goofy, and free-spirited behavior which is competitive, involves other children in play, and occasionally gets TR into trouble.

Jupiter/Gemini-rx/1st ruling the 7th and 10th signifies intellectual curiosity which often manifests in reading books. It is also possible that Jupiter/Gemini-rx ruling the 10th coincided with Teedie's awareness of differing pro-Union and pro-Confederacy views held by his parents and family.

Generally speaking, the best delineation match of these Partner Directions is that Teedie's behavior was rambunctious and bookish at the same time. Without asthma and other health problems indicated by the Directed Ascendant in bounds of malefics, Teedie might have been merely physically active without so much time to read so many books. He alternated between periods of vigorous outside activity and time spent inside.

Not identified by this technique is Teedie's collection of small animals which formed his own upstairs zoo. It can be attributed to Ascendant lord Mercury combust in the 6th house of small animals. Lord Mercury/Scorpio is combust which means many of these animals died or were otherwise subject to taxidermy procedures prior to display. Note that Mercury is the nocturnal triplicity of air signs, including the Gemini ascendant. Therefore Directing by Triplicity is a reasonable explainer for his youthful passion as a zoologist. Ascendant lord Mercury/Scorpio combust in the 6th house of illness is another indicator of physical illness beyond Mars/Gemini and Saturn/Gemini as Ascendant Distributors through the age of 13.

PT	D	Mars/Cancer	P	dexter trine Mercury (ME) d. => ASC	16-May-1874
PT	D	Mars/Cancer	P	dexter trine Mercury (BI) d. => ASC	17-Jan-1874
PT	D	Mars/Cancer	P	dexter trine Mercury (0) d. => ASC	19-May-1875
PT	D	Mars/Cancer	P	dexter trine Sun d. => ASC	2-Aug-1876

In spring 1874, TR's father rented a plantation-style residence at Oyster Bay which was later the location for TR's permanent residence. Natal Mercury's rulership of the 4th whole sign of father, family, and real estate connect the Mercury Partner Directions to the family move organized by his father who also supervised activities for his children during their first Oyster Bay summer. At this time, TR began to study intensely for a period of 18 months until he passed his Harvard entrance exam held July 1875. This date is a close match to the final Mercury Partner Direction listed as 19-May-1875. In this way the collective set of three Mercury Partner Directions from 16-May-1874 to 19-May-1875 corresponds with the final 12 months of an 18-month study program. Combust Mercury/Scorpio/6th is a delineation match to intense study which caused some illness. He complained of eye fatigue. Besides studying, TR also continued his physical exercise regimen to improve his health while he studied. On 27-Sep-1876, TR left home for Harvard six weeks after the Sun Participating Direction. He reports his asthma completely disappeared at this time. The Sun always signifies vitality no matter what sign and house it occupies. It is possible to interpret the Sun's partner direction as increased vitality from literally 'burning up' the illness signified by Mercury. Also as an event of honor for successfully passing the Harvard entrance exam and traveling to Harvard to begin his collegiate studies.

PT	D	Mercury/Cancer	P	Moon (MO) d. => ASC	20-Jan-1887
PT	D	Mercury/Cancer		opposition Mars (BI) d. => ASC	13-Nov-1890
PT	D	Mercury/Cancer	P	Moon (0) d. => ASC	30-Nov-1890
PT	D	Mercury/Cancer	P	opposition Mars (0) d. => ASC	13-Sep-1892
PT	D	Mercury/Cancer	P	opposition Mars (MA) d. => ASC	16-Jun-1894

Partner Directions for the years 1887-1894 are among the most consequential in TR's chronology prior to his assumption of the Presidency in 1901. In the first of three biographical volumes on TR, biographer Edmund Morris splits the years 1858-1901 into two parts: 1858-1886 and 1887-1901. Morris labels the brutal winter weather which killed off most cattle in the North Central Plains as the 'Winter of the Blue Snow: 1886-1887" (Morris 1979). Which is when the Partner Directions begin.

While the annual seasonal snowfall began 13-Nov-1886, it was preceded by strange atmospheric effects and animal behaviors which suggested an unusual winter ahead. TR had already observed overgrazing in the last few years which bode ill for the long-term health of the cattle industry in the Dakotas. Eight days after the first Moon conj ASC direction, a 72-hour blizzard let loose on 28-Jan-1887 at TR's Dakota cattle property. The time between the blizzard and 2-Mar-1887 when Chinook winds brought warm weather and the spring melt, TR lost over 50% of his cattle herd. Aggregate industry losses were 80%. Upon his return to New York City after his European honeymoon, TR announced to sister Bamie that he would exit the cattle business.

Death of his sister-in-law Anna Hall Roosevelt (17-Dec-1892) and his brother Elliott from alcoholism (14-Aug-1894) follows each of the last two Mars directions by 2-3 months. Elliott's behavior was erratic prior to death. In control of Elliott's finances during this time, TR was very involved with his brother's affairs. The Moon-Mars opposition in the 2nd of wealth and 8th of debt proved difficult for TR. By year-end 1893, TR was in debt to the tune of $2,500.

Besides closing the chapter on his Dakota cattle ranching operations and the deaths of two family members, the Moon-Mars opposition did begin something as well: it timed the start of TR's political identity as a reformer not afraid to take on established pockets of wealth and power if the public interest could be improved. President Cleveland appointed TR to the Civil Service Commission on 13-May-1889 a post he served until his May-1895 appointment as NYC Police Commissioner. I suggest these Mars directions ranging from 1890 to 1894 collectively function as one unit which turned TR into a political reformer on the national stage. Moon/Cancer signifies the care and protection of females, food and water supplies, and more generally the public interest in mundane figures. Mars/Capricorn signifies an opposition to corporate trusts and centralized government power, first seen for this project in the horoscope of James Madison who was an anti-Federalist.

What I find compelling on linking the Moon-Mars opposition in TR's horoscope to civil service reform and the larger Progressive Movement which began under his Presidency is the similarity between the Moon-Mars opposition in TR's natal and a similar configuration in the 1901 Jupiter-Saturn conjunction. In that figure the Moon separates from Mars and applies to the Jupiter-Saturn conjunction. The great trusts created during the Robber Baron era came under scrutiny during TR's Presidency. Occurring 6-10 years prior to the 1901 JSC, TR's Moon-Mars Ascendant directions allowed TR to develop his credibility as a reformer so when he advanced to the national stage he was ready to use those tools to great effect. By 1901, the world stage was ready for TR's type of reform politics. The close similarity between these two horoscopes suggests that without linkage to the 1901 JSC, TR would not have ascended to the Presidency in 1901.

174   A RECTIFICATION MANUAL

<u>Linkage between Moon/Cancer – Mars/Capricorn opposition aspect in Theodore Roosevelt's natal horoscope and the Jupiter-Saturn conjunction of 1901.</u>

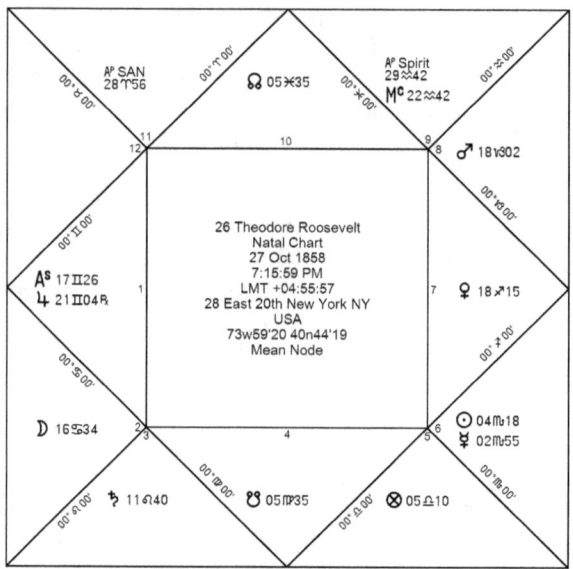

Theodore Roosevelt, Natal Horoscope, Whole Sign Houses

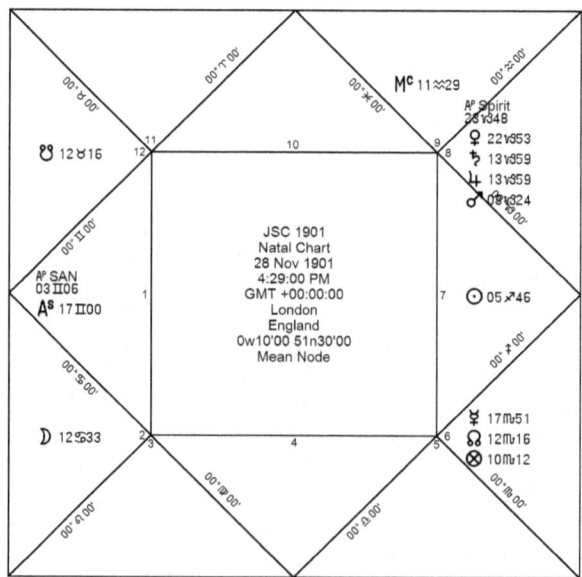

1901 Jupiter Saturn Conjunction, London, Whole Sign Houses

PT	D	Jupiter/Leo	P	dexter square Mercury (ME) d. => ASC	29-Sep-1910
PT	D	Jupiter/Leo	P	dexter square Mercury (0) d. => ASC	19-Mar-1911
PT	D	Jupiter/Leo	P	dexter square Sun d. => ASC (0)	15-Dec-1912

The final set of Partner Directions begins a few months after TR returned from his post-Presidential year-long African Safari on 18-Jun-1910. As another match to the chapters of a book concept, biographer Morris begins the third volume of his TR biography in 1910.

Both Mercury directions time caustic (Scorpio) political comments (Mercury) which were supported by TR's own sense of moral authority (Jupiter/Leo). TR's political split from his hand-appointed successor Taft occurred during these Partner Directions. The final direction timed an anti-climactic Presidential nomination by the Progressive Party for TR. Following these directions, TR renewed his writing career which he needed for income.

On 27-Sep-1910, TR addressed delegates at the New York Republican Convention in a speech designed to promote his role as Convention Chair. His competitor was William Barnes Jr. TR stated (Morris 2010, 114):

We are against the degrading alliance which adds strength to the already powerful corrupt boss and to the already powerful corrupt head of big business.

On 23-Mar-1911, TR addressed the University of California, Berkeley on the Panama Canal (Morris, 2010, 134):

The Panama Canal I naturally take an interest in, because I started it...If I had acted strictly according to precedent, I should have turned the whole matter over to Congress; in which case, Congress would be ably debating it at this moment, and the canal would be fifty years in the future.

What followed was increasingly caustic political rhetoric against President Taft including a February 1912 address "A Charter of Democracy" whereby TR advocated for the recall of judges and judicial decisions on constitutional questions. This led to a showdown with Taft and TR's launch of his failed 3rd party 1912 Presidential bid which split Republicans and allowed Democratic contender Woodrow Wilson to win. In the rectification notes for TR I present one Saturn-MC primary direction sequence by converse motion and an ASC-Saturn solar arc direction as timers of TR's 1912 election bid. This consequential campaign was not identified by Directing through the Bounds for any significator – ASC, MC, Sun, Moon, LOF, LOS.

The final Participating direction timed TR's 1916 Presidential nomination by the National Progressive Party in Chicago on 10-Dec-1912. But it was anti-climactic.

Table 25. Directing Through the Bounds: Midheaven, Theodore Roosevelt

```
Date              Distributor    Partner
27 Oct 1858       ♂
20 Jan 1861       ♄
11 Nov 1865       ♀  ♓
03 Jun 1868       ♀              sin △ ☿     (ME)
25 Aug 1868       ♀              sin △ ☿     (0)
05 Oct 1868       ♀              sin △ ☿     (BI)
14 Dec 1869       ♀              sin △ ☉
03 Mar 1877       ♃
21 Nov 1879       ♃              dex △ ☽     (MO)
19 Nov 1880       ☿
31 May 1881       ☿              dex △ ☽     (0)
08 Mar 1882       ☿              dex △ ☽     (BI)
12 Oct 1882       ☿              sin ⁎ ♂     (0)
20 Dec 1882       ☿              sin □ ♀     (0)
01 Mar 1883       ☿              sin ⁎ ♂     (BI)
19 Jul 1883       ☿              sin ⁎ ♂     (MA)
29 Aug 1883       ♂
27 Oct 1884       ♂              sin □ ♀     (VE)
29 Jul 1885       ♂              dex □ ♃     (0)
03 Nov 1885       ♂              dex □ ♃     (JU)
07 Dec 1891       ♄
07 Oct 1893       ♃  ♈
11 Apr 1899       ♀
12 Apr 1904       ♀              dex △ ♄     (SA)
01 Jul 1904       ♀              dex △ ♄     (0)
10 Aug 1904       ♀              dex △ ♄     (BI)
20 Oct 1904       ☿
05 Jul 1907       ☿              dex □ ☽     (MO)
14 Jan 1909       ☿              dex □ ☽     (0)
12 Sep 1909       ☿              sin △ ♀     (BI)
31 May 1910       ☿              sin □ ♂     (0)
09 Aug 1910       ☿              sin △ ♀     (0)
28 Feb 1911       ☿              sin □ ♂     (MA)
26 Mar 1912       ♂
22 May 1912       ♂              sin △ ♀     (VE)
30 Mar 1913       ♂              dex ⁎ ♃     (0)
16 May 1913       ♂              dex ⁎ ♃     (BI)
01 Jul 1913       ♂              dex ⁎ ♃     (JU)
05 Dec 1916       ♄
```

Provided for reference, here are two carryover notes from prior ARM editions on TR's MH Distributions: (1) The 25-Mar-2912 MC Distributor Changeover to Mars/Aries occurred one month after TR's entry to the Presidential race on 22-Feb-1912. TR's reputation was marked by his militant zeal for political reform. (2) The subsequent MC Distribution Changeover to Saturn/Aries preceded TR's failed requests made to President Woodrow Wilson to recruit and lead a division on infantry in Europe. TR's reputation suffered harm after this ploy which matches the delineation of Saturn/Aries as frustration (Saturn) of war (Mars).

Usefulness in Rectification

My second book, *America is Born* (2008) took a year to write and applies the Directing Through the Bounds technique to the Ascendant. The work was demanding and required construction of an extensive database the likes of which is not practical for most astrology clients. Nevertheless it does not mean the technique does not work, it's just difficult to deploy in practice.

Such is the power of Ascendant Distributors to partition an event database into chapters, I stated in *America is Born* that the 4-Jul-1776 *Regulus USA National Horoscope* rectification could stand based entirely on Ascendant Distributors without recourse to any planet-significator directions. For some, this is an outlandish claim; for me, it speaks to the power of the technique. Perhaps the most important takeaway for the revival of traditional astrology among contemporary astrologers is awareness of not one but at least three major techniques which can divide life into chapters. For Firdaria and ZR users, if one gets stuck on a significant new chapter of life affairs which cannot be explained by either technique, compute ASC Distributors and see if a Distributor changeover explains the new chapter. Then look to Distributors of the MC, Sun, Moon, LOF, and LOS.

At this point what can we say about the differences between Firdaria, Zodiacal Releasing, and Directing through the Bounds?

Firdaria is a planet-based system with major and minor period rulers. There are either 1 or 2 planets active at one time. Because planets influence signs where they are positioned and where they rule, there are so many signs activated by Firdaria rulers, I have found it relatively easy to match either diurnal or nocturnal Firdaria ruler sequences, even with limited event databases. Firdaria remains my 'go-to' as the first planetary period method to rule out broad periods of time from further consideration as possible birth times.

Zodiacal Releasing is a sign-based system. While one can make a similar argument that signs either containing or at least ruled by planets light up multiple signs in the horoscope, my research shows the effects of ZR are more limited but no less powerful than other planetary period methods. The ZR sign relationship I find most valuable is the linkage between the active ZR sign and the sign which is 10th from the current sign. In this interpretation, configuration of the 10th sign is more important to the outcome of the current sign in question, rather than the rulers of the current sign. Especially when either Node is in the 10th sign.

Directing Through the Bounds is a significator-based system. The specific planet/sign combination of the Distributor as well as the zodiacal state of the active Distributor in the natal horoscope yields events which are more specific in nature than characterized by Firdaria or Zodiacal Releasing because there are multiple levels of delineation at work.

PROGRESSIONS AND SOLAR ARC DIRECTIONS

Progressions in Brief. Compared to primary directions based on the diurnal movement of planets rising in the east and setting in the west; secondary progressions are based on the clockwise motion of planets through the degrees of the zodiac. Calculation of secondary progressions assumes that one day corresponds to one year of life. For example, the secondary progressed chart for age 24 is computed by examining planet positions 24 days after birth. Together with transits, secondary progressions make up the two most popular types of predictive techniques in contemporary use, assuredly because of their ease in calculation relative to primary directions.

Emphasis on Progressed Moon and Sun. Because outer planets' speed is so slow, much of this technique is focused on the faster moving progressed Moon and Sun. This research project confirms the validity of the secondary progressed Moon, primarily used as one of three methods to time the promise of the solar return (See Chapter 12: *Solar Returns: Delineation and Prediction*). The progressed Sun as the base measurement for the solar arc method of directing also has merit. Aspects made by progressions of planets to the significators occur so rarely they are not emphasized in my approach to rectification or prediction. Such is the power of other medieval techniques including Firdaria and Profections that I publicly admit to computing only a handful of progressed charts in the last few years. They are not a mainstay of my practice. ***NEW***: Since publication of this book in 2007 I have not computed a single progressed chart: I only use the progressed Sun as the basis for solar arcs.

Solar Arc Directions. In the solar arc method of directing, the distance between the natal Sun and the progressed Sun, for a given date, is named the *Solar Arc*. This solar arc distance is added to each planet or body in the natal figure. It is approximately 1 degree per year but the most reliable key known as *True Solar Arc* deploys the exact speed of the sun which varies from 57'05" and 1 01'10" depending on the season and hemisphere. Aspects between these adjusted planet positions and natal significators are computed and delineated just as for primary directions. For instance, Mars square Ascendant by solar arc is interpreted the same way as Mars square Ascendant by primary direction. For more on the history of this technique see Gadek (2017) and Saunders (1996).

Relationship between Solar Arc and Primary Directions. While computing Dwight Eisenhower's rectification, it struck me quite odd the direction of *ASC opposed Mars* timed formation of the US/UK combined Chiefs of Staff following the Pearl Harbor attack *by solar arc* yet the same *ASC opposed Mars* timed Eisenhower's own response to the attack through his own travel and military operations during WWII *by primary direction*.

Woodrow Wilson's figure showed a similar configuration for the outbreak of WWI. For Wilson, an *ASC opposed Mars* timed Archduke Ferdinand's assassination *by solar arc* and the same *ASC opposed Mars* timed Wilson's failed negotiations at the Paris Peace talks of 1919 *by primary direction*.

Observations from Eisenhower, Wilson, and other Presidential nativities led me to the following proposition:

Proposition: The Relationship between Solar Arcs and Primary Directions

Primary directions time the direct effects of planetary behavior for the native. While the effects are similar, solar arc directions time more public manifestations of the same planetary behavior for which the native may be only an indirect participant.

Public events timed by solar arc directions may directly draw the native into similar events timed later by primary directions. The reverse order, events first timed by primary directions; later by solar arcs, is also possible.

It also may be true that solar arcs, unlike primary directions, have a more public manifestation generally, whether or not the same type of event is mirrored in primary directions at some other time. One example is Franklin Roosevelt's contraction of polio on 10-Aug-1921. This was closely timed by the solar arc direction of Ascendant opposed Sun on 27-Aug-1921. Sun/Aquarius in detriment in the 6th house of illness ruling the 12th of confinement signifies illness from poor circulation in the shanks/legs. It is consistent with polio. While an error of 17 days may be acceptable for many in timing this event, I suggest the Sun's direction to the 7th cusp by solar arc direction has more of a public manifestation because this solar arc timed the exact date of the first public news release of his polio illness on 27-Aug-1921. For emphasis: it did not time actual onset of illness, just its public announcement.

Redux: Theodore Roosevelt

The origins of TR's actual 3rd party run date from his statement that "I am strong as a Bull Moose" timed by the following solar arc direction:

<u>18-Jun-1912</u>. *dsa ASC conj. Saturn*.

I mention this ASC-Saturn solar arc direction because the same measurement calculated by primary direction does not occur until after TR's death (23-Dec-1921, Saturn's full latitude; 5-May-1922, zero latitude). Any astrologer working exclusively with primary directions, perhaps trying to direct Saturn to the Ascendant by primary motion for the Bull Moose comment (reasonable to me!) would fail in their approach. In my view, the solar arc is the better measurement.

Usefulness in Rectification

Solar arc directions are highly useful in rectification, especially considering their relative ease of use compared to primary directions. As Stage II tools, dynamic activity of solar arcs and transits to Hellenistic Lots is helpful to narrow the Ascendant to a one-to-four-degree range. As Stage III tools, they can also help finalize the exact degree and minute of the Ascendant in the final stage of rectification.

Solar arc directions work especially well for horoscopes with a strong Leo emphasis (ASC, ASC ruler, Planets in Leo). Likewise, for horoscopes which emphasize Libra or Aquarius (signs of the Sun's fall and detriment), solar arcs seldom register events which appear on biographical timelines.

The possibility of linking events to the same set of significators by both primary and solar arc directions is so low that these types of relationships should be sought out whenever possible. Looking back since 2008, I am tempted to assign these linkages as another Holy Grail of rectification after the Primary Direction Sequence.

CHAPTER ELEVEN

Solar Returns: Profections and Time Lords

In this first of three chapters on solar returns, the interaction of the profected annual Ascendant and the solar return is considered. The house position of the profected Ascendant elevates the themes of that specific house for the year. The relative strength of time lords in the solar return compared to the natal is one indication of the goodness of the year.

Chapter Summary

<u>Ability of Profections to Highlight Life Affairs</u>. Identification of the profected Ascendant's house position is one of the simplest methods to narrow the range of possibilities when preparing an annual forecast. If the profected Ascendant falls in the 9th house, then delineation of the natal 9th house will identify themes encountered during the year. One is more likely to make a pilgrimage, take a career sabbatical, or travel when the profected Ascendant moves to the 9th house. The same can be said for affairs of all other houses. Because profections follow a 12 year repeating cycle, this delineation step generates the same promise every 12 years.

<u>Interaction between Annual Profections and the Solar Return</u>. While the promise of the year can be read exclusively through the relevant natal house, profections may used in tandem with the solar return. The solar return adds themes which modify but do not obliterate the natal promise. The integration of profections and the return is accomplished through evaluation of two time lords: the Lord of the Year ('LOY'), named for the sign ruler of the profected Annual Ascendant and the Lord of the Period ('LOP'), named for a cycled planetary hour.

<u>Case Study: James Monroe's 9th House Years</u>. For the years 1778, 1790, and 1802, Monroe's life affairs are evaluated. While the relative strength of both LOY and LOP show natal 9th house affairs modified for better or worse, delineation of the return's 9th house appears a critical delineation step which cannot be ignored.

Profections as a Planetary Period Method

Ability of Profections to Highlight Life Affairs. Chapter 1: *Planets in Signs* mentioned profections could be used in two ways. First to time specific events by computing exact dates when profections of natal significators perfect their aspects to natal planets. Second to define planetary periods as a method of highlighting life affairs specified by houses. Let's turn to the second method and investigate James Monroe's 9th house affairs as a case study.

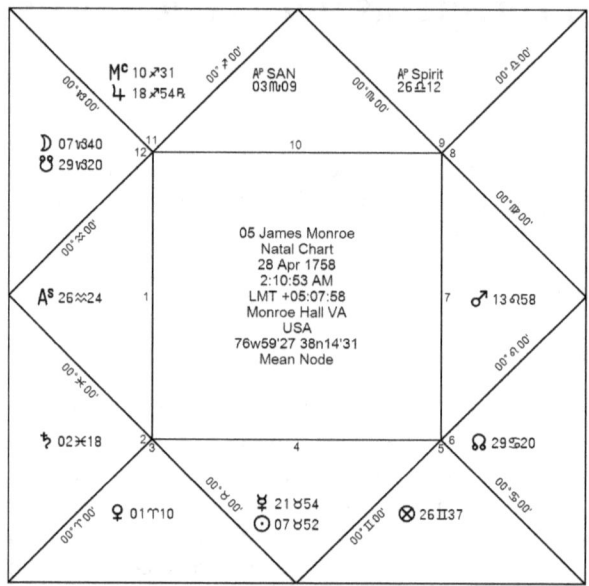

Terminology. 28-Apr-1766 is Monroe's 8th birthday. On this date, the Profected Annual Ascendant moving at a rate of 30 degrees per year reached 26LI24 which fell in his 9th house by whole signs. On Monroe's 20th birthday, it returned to this exact position on 28-Apr-1778 and did do so every 12 years thereafter until death. Between 28-Apr-1766 and 28-Apr-1767, the Profected Annual Ascendant moved through Monroe's 9th house. During this one year period, say *"Monroe is having a 9th house profected year."* The sign ruler of the Profected Annual Ascendant is called the *Lord of the Year ('LOY')*.

Changeover of Lord of the Year? 30 degrees per year works out to 12.175 days per single degree. Beginning at 26LI24, the profected Ascendant changed signs to Scorpio about two months after his 8th birthday. At this time did the LOY change to Mars? It's a reasonable question and one answered in the affirmative by Lilly (2004, 720). Yet there is no evidence that medieval writers suggested such a changeover, nor do I find any empirical evidence that the LOY should be changed midyear. It's my opinion the LOY remains the same for the entire year.

How profections highlight House Affairs. For Monroe's 9th house year, affairs of the 9th house are elevated in importance for the entire year. Position of the Profected Annual Ascendant as it moves through the 9th house effectively turns this discrete event timing method into a quasi-planetary period technique. It is one of the simplest and most accurate ways to focus the upcoming year's events on a specific area of life when making an annual client forecast.

If promised, during *9th house years*, individuals are more likely to travel overseas, study philosophy, concern themselves with religious practice, or take a career sabbatical in that year compared to any other. Of course an individual with an afflicted 9th house will either not travel, or will travel with impediments.

Delineating James Monroe's 9th House

General Delineation Method. Lord of Year is Venus. She applies to her ruler Mars by trine but before the aspect perfects, Mars moves into Virgo. The first and only aspect Venus makes is the trine of Jupiter. True Mars does perfect its trine to Jupiter before it leaves Leo raising the possibility that Jupiter returns the effects of Mars to Venus in what is called *return of light*. If so, Mars will tend to interfere with Venus' ability to perfect her trine to Jupiter. Evidence from the 1802 solar return timing the Louisiana Purchase suggests Mars' interference is ephemeral.

Venus in the cardinal sign of Aries is active. In the sign of her detriment Venus signifies lust, greed, sadism, love of weaponry, and love of warfare. Placement in bound of Jupiter/Aries ameliorates the condition by adding Jupiter's expansionist philosophy to an otherwise debilitated Venus. Presence of Jupiter means the worst of Venus/Aries' behavior (e.g., sadism) can be nixed. Dwad of Aries is the same influence as the sign placement and adds nothing new. Placement in the 3rd means Monroe's siblings, short-term travels, communications, and publicity influence Monroe's 9th house affairs by rulership.

Mars in Leo seeks to hoard fame and protect honor from heroics; military and otherwise. Placement in the bound of Saturn/Leo degrades Mars by introducing anti-Sun totalitarian themes (see Chapter 2: *Planets in Houses* for a discussion of Jefferson's Saturn/Leo). Dwad of Capricorn adds ambition and a trumped-up perception of Martian ability and status. Mars falling in the 7th house by whole signs, a common placement for military professionals, means Monroe faces open enemies with the styles incorporated by Mars' sign, bound, and dwad.

Jupiter in Sagittarius is the *too much is not enough* philosophy which in the 11th house pervades Monroe's political alliances and later relations with Congress. Placement in the bound of Mercury/Sagittarius reinforces Jupiter with pie-in-the-sky analysis, statements, or other rhetoric which makes Jupiter overoptimistic. Jupiter in the dwad of Cancer, sign of his exaltation, adds home, care, and nurture to Jupiter's significations.

Putting it all together. As ruler of Venus, Mars is the cause of Venus' problems. This means that Monroe's difficulties with 3rd house affairs (e.g., bad publicity, etc.,) are caused by 7th house conflicts (e.g., open enemies, etc.,). Despite these difficulties which Mars imposes by rulership, Venus still meets with success because she applies to Jupiter by trine. A few possible delineations:

Example 1. Legal disputes with open enemies over honor give Monroe a bad reputation as a greedy, lustful man. Yet these disputes do not derail him from acquiring political alliances.

Example 2. Love of warfare and weaponry causes Monroe to make short-term trips where he purchases collectible weaponry. His seller is a former military serviceman interested in preserving his honor by having his firearms passed on to a fellow Revolutionary War fighter who has achieved national political office.

Example 3. Siblings die a fiery death in battle against open enemies. Monroe receives compensation from the Government (Jupiter in 11th is King's money).

As to effects in the 9th house, because Venus rules the 9th, any variation of the Venus-Mars-Jupiter configuration will be found as the underlying cause of 9th house affairs. Foreign travel is not taken on a whim, it originates from this configuration.

Wrapup: Monroe's 9th house. The delineations just presented are endless and only represent ex-ante possibilities. Properly completed, the delineation of Monroe's 9th house should include delineation of relevant lots including the Lot of Spirit, Lot of Faith, and Lot of Hīlāj all necessary to judge Monroe's religious beliefs. I leave this exercise incomplete because it goes beyond what is required to demonstrate profections as a period technique.

Profections as a Standalone Method. The themes just delineated (and other permutations thereof) will appear each time Monroe has a 9th house profected year. While the basic themes remain, the storyboard they support will be slightly different each time. How so? For this answer, turn to the Lord of the Year.

Interaction between Annual Profections and the Solar Return

All authors consider the solar return a secondary modification to the natal figure which remains the primary life influence. Never does the solar return obliterate the natal. Yet the solar return may show events which are substantially better or worse than what is promised by the natal. How can the influence of the solar return be evaluated? First to recognize that effects of the solar return or any other predictive technique are additive. Solar returns do not *blend* their influences with the natal figure. Second to identify the LOY, LOP and other time lords and compare their relative strength in both natal and solar return figures.

CHAPTER 11 – SOLAR RETURNS: PROFECTIONS AND TIME LORDS

Time Lords. As ruler of the profected Ascendant's sign, the *Lord of the Year* is the single most important time lord to consider when evaluating house affairs for a given year. Here are the steps required to make this evaluation:

For Monroe's 9th house years:

1. Identify the Lord of the Year. LOY = Venus
2. What is the promise of Venus based on her natal planetary strength?
3. What is the promise of Venus based on planetary strength in the solar return?
4. Compare Venus in the solar return to Venus in the natal.
5. If the planetary strength of Venus in the return is better, say that Venus' natal promise will be complemented by events signified by Venus in the return.
6. If the planetary strength of Venus in the return is worse, say that Venus' natal promise will be degraded by events signified by Venus in the return.

Not withstanding the importance given to the Lord of the Year by many authors including Abū Ma'shar who ranks the LOY as the 1st of 19 considerations when evaluating solar returns (Abū Ma'shar 1999: viii-ix), there are other time lords to consider. Besides triplicity and Firdaria lords, Distributors and Partners; there is another time lord intended to be evaluated side-by-side the LOY on an annual repeating cycle. It is based on planetary hours.

Lord of the Circle or of the Orb of the Signs. This phrase is how Bonatti describes the name for the time lord based on planetary hours (2007, 1408). Burnett, Yamamoto, and Yano translate Alchabitius' name for the same time lord as *Lord of the Period* (Alchabitius 2004, 133). In this study, I refer to this time lord as *Lord of the Period* ('LOP') according to Alchabitius' convention. To underscore its importance, Alchabitius indicates that some practitioners used the LOP exclusively, dropping the LOY all together. What information the LOP provides in addition to the LOY is not specified by any translations I have seen to date. Writing in 2007, purpose and effect of the LOP vis-à-vis the LOY remains a missing puzzle piece to the medieval predictive hierarchy.

LOP Procedure. The method relies on two items: the planetary hour at birth and the Chaldean order of planets. The first year is assigned to the planetary hour at birth and functions with similar effect to the LOY. For Monroe the LOP for his first year is Saturn because Saturn was the hour ruler at birth. Each subsequent LOP is determined by cycling through the Chaldean order of planets: Saturn, Jupiter, Mars, Sun, Venus, Mercury, and the Moon. After seven years the cycle repeats. For Monroe, these time lords are summarized in Table 26. As to its effects, the LOP is evaluated in an identical fashion to the LOY: compare its zodiacal state in the solar return relative to the natal and pass judgment.

Table 26. Summary of Annual Time Lords, James Monroe

Start Date	End Date	Year	Age	Profected Ascendant	LOY	LOP
28-Apr-58	27-Apr-59	1		26AQ25	Saturn	Saturn
28-Apr-59	27-Apr-60	2	1	26PI25	Jupiter	Jupiter
28-Apr-60	27-Apr-61	3	2	26AR25	Mars	Mars
28-Apr-61	27-Apr-62	4	3	26TA25	Venus	Sun
28-Apr-62	27-Apr-63	5	4	26GE25	Mercury	Venus
28-Apr-63	27-Apr-64	6	5	26CA25	Moon	Mercury
28-Apr-64	27-Apr-65	7	6	26LE25	Sun	Moon
28-Apr-65	27-Apr-66	8	7	26VI25	Mercury	Saturn
28-Apr-66	27-Apr-67	9	8	26LI25	Venus	Jupiter
28-Apr-67	27-Apr-68	10	9	26SC25	Mars	Mars
28-Apr-68	27-Apr-69	11	10	26SA25	Jupiter	Sun
28-Apr-69	27-Apr-70	12	11	26CP25	Saturn	Venus
28-Apr-70	27-Apr-71	1	12	26AQ25	Saturn	Mercury
28-Apr-71	27-Apr-72	2	13	26PI25	Jupiter	Moon
28-Apr-72	27-Apr-73	3	14	26AR25	Mars	Saturn
28-Apr-73	27-Apr-74	4	15	26TA25	Venus	Jupiter
28-Apr-74	27-Apr-75	5	16	26GE25	Mercury	Mars
28-Apr-75	27-Apr-76	6	17	26CA25	Moon	Sun
28-Apr-76	27-Apr-77	7	18	26LE25	Sun	Venus
28-Apr-77	27-Apr-78	8	19	26VI25	Mercury	Mercury
28-Apr-78	27-Apr-79	9	20	26LI25	Venus	Moon
28-Apr-79	27-Apr-80	10	21	26SC25	Mars	Saturn
28-Apr-80	27-Apr-81	11	22	26SA25	Jupiter	Jupiter
28-Apr-81	27-Apr-82	12	23	26CP25	Saturn	Mars
28-Apr-82	27-Apr-83	1	24	26AQ25	Saturn	Sun
28-Apr-83	27-Apr-84	2	25	26PI25	Jupiter	Venus
28-Apr-84	27-Apr-85	3	26	26AR25	Mars	Mercury
28-Apr-85	27-Apr-86	4	27	26TA25	Venus	Moon
28-Apr-86	27-Apr-87	5	28	26GE25	Mercury	Saturn
28-Apr-87	27-Apr-88	6	29	26CA25	Moon	Jupiter
28-Apr-88	27-Apr-89	7	30	26LE25	Sun	Mars
28-Apr-89	27-Apr-90	8	31	26VI25	Mercury	Sun
28-Apr-90	27-Apr-91	9	32	26LI25	Venus	Venus
28-Apr-91	27-Apr-92	10	33	26SC25	Mars	Mercury
28-Apr-92	27-Apr-93	11	34	26SA25	Jupiter	Moon
28-Apr-93	27-Apr-94	12	35	26CP25	Saturn	Saturn
28-Apr-94	27-Apr-95	1	36	26AQ25	Saturn	Jupiter

Table 26 – *Continued.*

Start Date	End Date	Year	Age	Profected Ascendant	LOY	LOP
28-Apr-95	27-Apr-96	2	37	26PI25	Jupiter	Mars
28-Apr-96	27-Apr-97	3	38	26AR25	Mars	Sun
28-Apr-97	27-Apr-98	4	39	26TA25	Venus	Venus
28-Apr-98	27-Apr-99	5	40	26GE25	Mercury	Mercury
28-Apr-99	27-Apr-00	6	41	26CA25	Moon	Moon
28-Apr-00	27-Apr-01	7	42	26LE25	Sun	Saturn
28-Apr-01	27-Apr-02	8	43	26VI25	Mercury	Jupiter
28-Apr-02	27-Apr-03	9	44	26LI25	Venus	Mars
28-Apr-03	27-Apr-04	10	45	26SC25	Mars	Sun
28-Apr-04	27-Apr-05	11	46	26SA25	Jupiter	Venus
28-Apr-05	27-Apr-06	12	47	26CP25	Saturn	Mercury
28-Apr-06	27-Apr-07	1	48	26AQ25	Saturn	Moon
28-Apr-07	27-Apr-08	2	49	26PI25	Jupiter	Saturn
28-Apr-08	27-Apr-09	3	50	26AR25	Mars	Jupiter
28-Apr-09	27-Apr-10	4	51	26TA25	Venus	Mars
28-Apr-10	27-Apr-11	5	52	26GE25	Mercury	Sun
28-Apr-11	27-Apr-12	6	53	26CA25	Moon	Venus
28-Apr-12	27-Apr-13	7	54	26LE25	Sun	Mercury
28-Apr-13	27-Apr-14	8	55	26VI25	Mercury	Moon
28-Apr-14	27-Apr-15	9	56	26LI25	Venus	Saturn
28-Apr-15	27-Apr-16	10	57	26SC25	Mars	Jupiter
28-Apr-16	27-Apr-17	11	58	26SA25	Jupiter	Mars
28-Apr-17	27-Apr-18	12	59	26CP25	Saturn	Sun
28-Apr-18	27-Apr-19	1	60	26AQ25	Saturn	Venus
28-Apr-19	27-Apr-20	2	61	26PI25	Jupiter	Mercury
28-Apr-20	27-Apr-21	3	62	26AR25	Mars	Moon
28-Apr-21	27-Apr-22	4	63	26TA25	Venus	Saturn
28-Apr-22	27-Apr-23	5	64	26GE25	Mercury	Jupiter
28-Apr-23	27-Apr-24	6	65	26CA25	Moon	Mars
28-Apr-24	27-Apr-25	7	66	26LE25	Sun	Sun
28-Apr-25	27-Apr-26	8	67	26VI25	Mercury	Venus
28-Apr-26	27-Apr-27	9	68	26LI25	Venus	Mercury
28-Apr-27	27-Apr-28	10	69	26SC25	Mars	Moon
28-Apr-28	27-Apr-29	11	70	26SA25	Jupiter	Saturn
28-Apr-29	27-Apr-30	12	71	26CP25	Saturn	Jupiter
28-Apr-30	27-Apr-31	1	72	26AQ25	Saturn	Mars
28-Apr-31	27-Apr-32	2	73	26PI25	Jupiter	Sun

Case Study: Monroe's 9th House Profected Years

All events are taken from Ammon (1971).

James Monroe Solar Return, 20th birthday

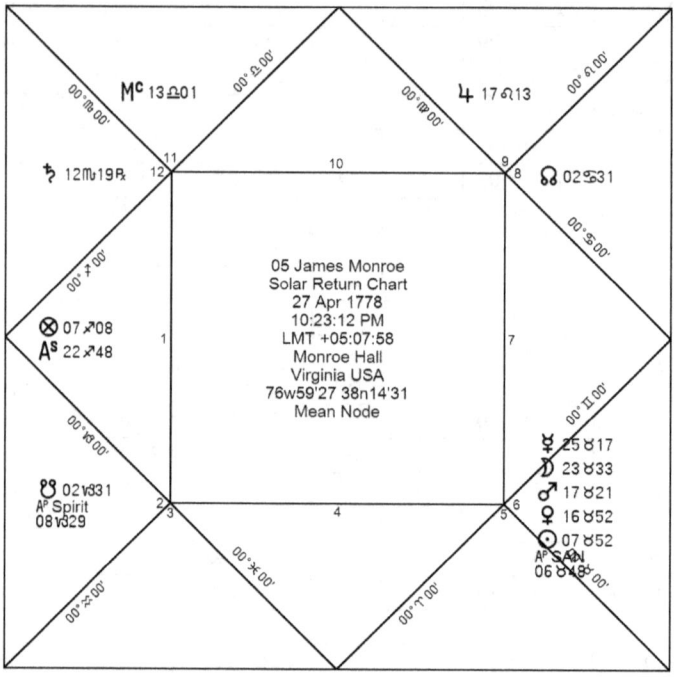

LOY = Venus
LOP = Moon

Events: As the year opened, Monroe served as military aide to Lord Sterling, one of Washington's brigade commanders. It is late spring following the notoriously difficult winter at Valley Forge. On 6-May-1778, Washington celebrated the recent French treaty with parades, pomp, and an abundance of food and alcohol. This was a major celebration. Washington resolved a dispute with Charles Lee by giving him command of the army. Unfortunately Lee botched the Battle at Monmouth Court House resulting in his court-marshal. During late summer 1778, Monroe socialized in the home of Mrs. Theodosia Prevost (later Mrs. Aaron Burr) where his affections towards a young lady were not returned. Out of boredom, Monroe quit his position with Sterling after an unsuccessful attempt to land a Foreign Service position. His next efforts to fight on the front lines with the militia were also unsuccessful. As the year closed, he planned to raise his own troops for service in the Southern theatre.

Event match to 9th house affairs - general. Three 9th house affairs dominated Monroe's life during his 20th year.

- The 6-May-1778 party celebrated the French Alliance which is signified by Jupiter in Leo, the sign of France.

- Monroe attempted to find a foreign diplomatic post.

- Monroe quit his job as Stirling's aide and started a career sabbatical.

All three events belong to the 9th, with Jupiter/Leo in the 9th ruling the return's Ascendant and an additional force behind Monroe's interest in 9th house affairs.

Event match to 9th house affairs – natal. Monroe's love of war driven by the desire to fight open enemies in defense of honor is the correct variant of the Venus-Mars-Jupiter configuration which explains his desire to raise his own regiment for the Southern front.

Relative zodiacal state of LOY and LOP. LOY Venus in her own sign, separating from the opposition of Saturn and applying to the square Jupiter is much improved over her natal zodiacal state; yet the close conjunction to Mars is a debility, especially with Mars' higher relative latitude to Venus. LOP Moon in Taurus applying to Mercury is considerably improved over the natal Moon/Capricorn/12th. Both LOY and LOP are in improved condition.

Influence of Relative zodiacal state of LOY and LOP. Venus' separation from Saturn and application to Jupiter match the *night and day* change from the winter at Valley Forge (Saturn/Scorpio/12th) to the French alliance and celebration (Jupiter/Leo/9th). Moon/Taurus/6th matches Monroe's romantic interest in an unnamed woman at the Prevost house, probably a servant given placement in the 6th. As the source of entertainment and food, Mrs. Prevost herself is probably signified by Venus.

Given the improved zodiacal state of both LOY and LOP and Jupiter's placement in the 9th, why did Monroe find himself at year's end chasing his dream to raise his own regiment of troops? How did the strength of Jupiter/Leo/9th fail Monroe? My answer is that Jupiter's ruler, the Sun, is afflicted by Saturn to which he applies by opposition. Though separating from the rest of the planets in the Taurus stellium, Saturn still opposes the entire complex. But it is the applying Sun-Saturn opposition, with the Sun ruling the 9th, which appears to thwart Monroe's plans for a Foreign Service position leaving the pursuit of his own regiment as his fallback career strategy.

James Monroe Solar Return, 32nd birthday

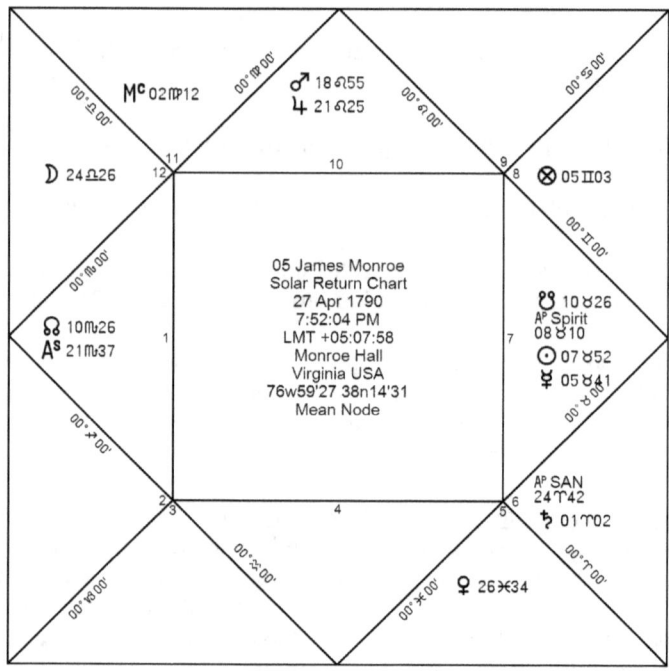

LOY = Venus
LOP = Venus

Events. The year began with Monroe's discovery he had narrowly missed election to the Senate by one vote. Still essentially on sabbatical from political life, he is nevertheless reluctantly pushed to run for the Senate in the fall of 1790. He won the election easily as a moderate candidate positioned between anti-federalists and extreme federalist factions. After the election, he settled as many of his active legal cases as possible before returning to Philadelphia in November. The Senate's legislative session was relatively quiet; yet Monroe's presence was marked by service on many committee assignments. He did vote against the bill to charter the Bank of the United States but the measure easily passed both Houses. His more controversial proposal was to end the wall of privacy surrounding Senate proceedings. Monroe felt that bodies operating in secret eventually succumbed to the enlargement of their own power at the expense of public welfare. Only an open-door policy, as was practiced by the House, would guard against such abuses. The measure was strongly voted down. (It passed later in 1794). Following adjournment in March 1791, Monroe was angry to find on his return home that his younger brother had married the daughter of a family in Charlottesville whose lower relative social status would be an impediment to his brother's future success.

Event match to 9th house affairs – natal. Monroe's anger at his brother's marriage is an example of the standalone influence of natal Venus-Mars-Jupiter configuration on Monroe's affairs this year. First is Monroe's anger described as an insult to his honor which is signified by Mars/Leo. This anger is routed to Venus through the Sun in the following manner: Mars/Leo is ruled by Sun/Taurus/4th in turn ruled by Venus/Aries/3rd. Ammon states that part of Monroe's anger towards his younger brother stemmed from the unlikelihood that his brother, with this particular marriage, would ever be able to offer Monroe's own family a safe haven in the event Monroe's finances deteriorated. (Ammon 1971: 85) Sun/Taurus in the 4th of retirement disposed by Venus/Aries shows end-of-life affairs marred by financial problems because Venus is the universal significator of money and in detriment is one measure of financial distress. So this Sun-Venus configuration triggers Monroe's anger towards his sister-in-law, another signification of the same Venus/Aries who as ruler of the 9th on the 3rd cusp signifies the brother's wife (7th from the 3rd).

A second event tied to the promise of the natal 9th is a 9th house lot activated by a solar return planet. Though I did not delineate the Lot of Spirit earlier, it is required to explain Monroe's measure to make the Senatorial proceedings public. Monroe's Lot of Spirit falls at 26LI12 in the natal 9th which is less than 2 degrees from the return's Moon/Libra. As Chapter 13 demonstrates, whenever solar return planets aspect Hellenistic Lots, affairs signified by lots are activated that year. Lot of Spirit in the air sign of Libra signifies value placed on knowledge. Libra's cardinality means information is spread widely. In the sign of Libra, knowledge is used to balance competing viewpoints in an egalitarian manner. Moon in the return's 12th of secrets matches Monroe's need to end the veil of secrecy over Senatorial proceedings for the public's benefit. Moon separating from Jupiter and void of course means he is not successful in passing this measure.

Relative zodiacal state of LOY and LOP. Venus/Pisces is in the sign of her exaltation and though she widely aspects both Sun and Mercury by sextile, by moiety of orb Venus is feral. Disposed by Jupiter/Leo angular in the 10th, Venus is in better zodiacal state than in the natal. She is also in the house of her joy.

Influence of Relative zodiacal state of LOY and LOP. I take Venus/Pisces as the primary signification of Monroe's success at the ballot box because she is placed in the 5th house of elections. Why is Venus successful in getting Monroe elected to the Senate? Because of her ruler Jupiter. Natal Jupiter/Sagittarius/11th signifies optimistic friends and political alliances which ameliorate hostility from open enemies because Jupiter transits to the natal 7th house on the day of the solar return and softens the harshness of natal Mars/Leo/7th. What this means is that anti-federalists like Patrick Henry (signified by Mars/Leo/7th of open enemies) are defused by Jupiter. The Mars/Jupiter conjunction falling in the 10th of the return marks Monroe's career/reputation for the better and allows him an easy electoral victory.

James Monroe Solar Return, 44th birthday

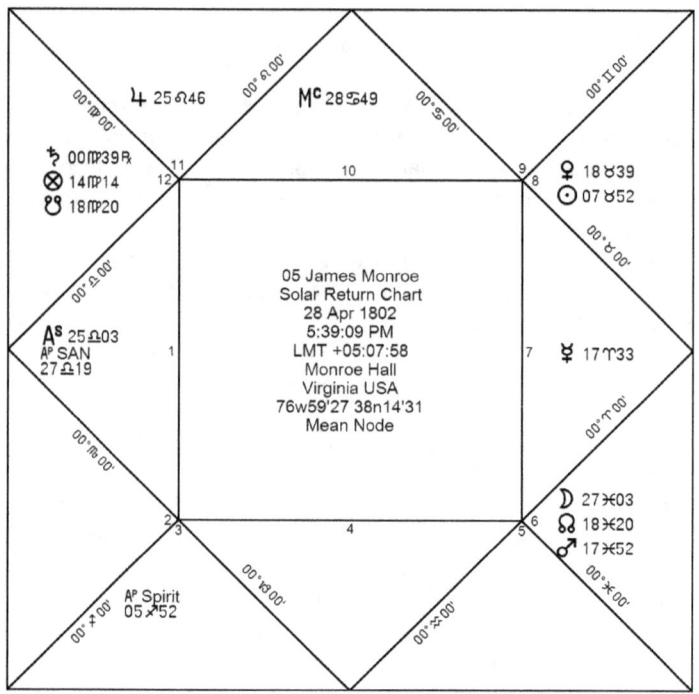

LOY = Venus
LOP = Mars

Events. Monroe's third and final year as Virginia Governor, from December 1801 to December 1802 overlaps both 1801 and 1802 returns. The year 1802 was marked by rumors of local slave revolts following a renewed uprising in Haiti. Monroe supported the preemptive decision made by the Norfolk mayor to call out the militia but made no orders himself for a statewide summons of militia. Because of high personal debts, Monroe decided to practice law in Richmond in lieu of another low-paying political position. He also planned trips to the West to survey his real estate properties and a New York trip to facilitate a reunion on his wife's side of the family. In January 1803, Jefferson gave Monroe notice that he had been nominated and confirmed as envoy to France to assist Robert Livingston in purchasing the mouth of the Mississippi River from France for use as a navigable port. This most famous trip would culminate with the Louisiana Purchase treaty signed by Monroe on 29-Apr-1803, the start of his following solar return, a 10th house profected year. Between January and April, Monroe suffered fallout with Livingston over Livingston's maneuvers to claim full credit for the Treaty. On arrival in France, Monroe also suffered a back ailment and was confined to bed for a short period.

Event match to 9th house affairs - general. Monroe's plans for a legal career following his three-year service as Virginia Governor are consistent with the *falling away* delineation of the 9th from the 10th which often times career sabbaticals. Both his aborted travel plans and subsequent trip to France highlight the importance of travel to Monroe's return.

Event match to 9th house affairs – natal. What would culminate in the Louisiana Purchase began on 16-Oct-1802 when Spanish officials operating the port of New Orleans suspended trade concessions with Americans. This disruption of trade so incensed businessmen that Federalist factions clamored for war as a method of dividing Jefferson's support among Western voters. The signification of Venus/Aries as *love of war* falling in the natal 3rd house of publicity matches the Federalist's agitation for war at home because Venus rules the natal 4th of homeland. As 9th house ruler, Venus is also the cause of Monroe's trip to France. As the ruler and cause of Venus' events, Mars/Leo signifies the insult to America's honor following the revocation of US trade concessions in New Orleans. As the ruler and result of Venus' events, Mars/Leo/7th signifies 7th house legal opposition over the Louisiana Purchase because it violated a strict constructionist interpretation of the Constitution which forbade Jefferson from signing the treaty without approval from Congress. Yet the treaty is successful because Mars is an impediment which only temporarily disrupts the application of Venus to Jupiter by trine. Monroe makes successful political alliances in the end.

Relative zodiacal state of LOY and LOP. LOY Venus in Taurus, sign of her rulership, moving fast after her superior conjunction with the Sun, is in far better zodiacal state than natal Venus. Mars/Pisces/6th ruled by Jupiter/Leo/11th is also in better zodiacal state than the natal. Both planets are in their houses of joy.

Influence of Relative zodiacal state of LOY and LOP. The Sun/Venus Taurus combination falls in the return's 8th, highlighted by profection in the final month of the return and times Monroe's negotiations with France. The Louisiana Purchase is funded largely by debt, an 8th house signification. By position in the 6th, Mars/Pisces most likely signifies Virginia slaves and their restless indecision after receiving word of the Haiti uprising.

More salient to rumors of a Virginia slave uprising is Mercury, lord of the 12th of rumors, in the 7th of legal conflict. Mars/6th rules Mercury/7th, confirming Mars as the significator of slaves because it is their restless activity which triggers rumors of possible revolts. Because slave revolts are signified by the ruler of the 6th in the 12th – with this condition not met in the return – Monroe faces no actual revolt. Mercury also rules the 9th house of travel and as the significator of rumors carries his influence to the machinations of both Talleyrand and Livingston during the Louisiana Purchase Treaty negotiations. Jupiter in Leo, sign of France, in the 11th of alliances confirms a successful Treaty.

Summary Findings for Monroe Study

Importance of return's 9th house. The zodiacal state of both LOY and LOP do appear to modify each return, for better or worse, relative to their natal condition. So too does the placement of the profected Ascendant in the 9th house accurately elevate the importance of 9th house affairs to Monroe's life for these years. Yet the recommendation that 9th house affairs can be fully judged by both the return's LOY and LOP appears incomplete. Just as important to 9th house affairs is the return's 9th house configuration, by planet placement and rulership, whether or not said planets function as LOY or LOP. Consider:

1778 return. Jupiter/Leo/9th as the significator of Washington's successful alliance with France delivers Monroe from the ordeal of winter at Valley Forge. Sun as lord of the 9th applying to Saturn by opposition cuts off Monroe's chances for a foreign service post. Neither Jupiter, Sun, nor Saturn are LOY or LOP yet their collective impact on the year is substantial.

1790 return. Moon/Libra/12th ruling the 9th conjunct natal Lot of Spirit moved Monroe to seek the elimination of Senate secrecy to further public legislative dialog. As the measure which most defined his first Senate term, it is a critical action which defined Monroe's 9th house of philosophy in 1790. Yet LOY is Venus.

1802 return. Mercury/Aries/7th ruling both 9th and 12th as significator of rumored slave revolts and the maneuvers of Talleyrand and Livingston has as much to say about the year as either Venus or Mars.

A Final Observation on Profections

Profections versus Directions. Traditional authors often instruct students to profect or direct *this or that* significator to make successful predictions. At this point, can anything be said regarding differences between profections or directions as predictive methods?

Difference in Magnitude of Event? In theory, there is no difference between the magnitude of event that can be caused by either profection or direction. Despite the fact that most traditional authors reserve superlatives for directions, profections generate events of similar importance as profections of Abraham Lincoln's profected Ascendant in Chapter 1 attest. Events including taking his seat in the Illinois State Legislature, meeting his wife-to-be Mary Todd, and suspension of habeas corpus during the Civil War rank as major life events; the magnitude of which one might normally associate with primary directions.

Directions more Consistent than Profections. If there is any difference in profections compared to directions, it appears that profections *can* but *do not always* time events as significant as primary directions consistently do. The twelve year embedded cycle of events timed by profections appears subject to greater modification by other predictive methods. On the other hand, effects of primary directions can be delineated and predicted solely on the disposition of the significator and promissor in the natal figure without recourse to any other technique. In this way, primary directions are more robust and occupy a higher rung on the predictive hierarchy in my opinion.

Usefulness in Rectification

In theory, profections are very useful in rectification; in practice I did not use them in this study because no software program includes a profection rectification module. While it's easy to create a rough and ready spreadsheet module to compute profections for an iterated Ascendant, the real challenge for astrological software vendors is to create a multi-window rectification system which utilizes both directions and profections.

My recommendation would be four windows: (1) directions of the Ascendant through the bounds with aspects to promissors, (2) directions of the Midheaven through the bounds with aspects to promissors, (3) Ascendant profections computed at the annual rate with conjunctions to promissors, and (4) transits to the angles. It will take this type of combined system before profections can be used effectively in rectification.

CHAPTER TWELVE

Solar Returns: Delineation and Prediction

A Rich Predictive Tool. The solar return, or *birthday chart* is a snapshot of the current position of transiting planets taken at the exact moment the Sun returns to its natal degree each year. In my opinion, it is one of the richest predictive tools available because it offers great specificity in defining events which cannot be read by the natal figure.

A Limited Rectification Tool. Because traditional authors consider solar returns subordinate to the natal, they are of limited use in rectification. Without knowing and delineating the natal figure first, trying to rectify events timed by the solar return is virtually impossible.

Chapter Summary

Solar Return Assumptions: Precession and Relocation. This book's research confirms non-precessed returns cast for the natal birthplace. Methods to test the validity of precession and relocation are discussed.

Solar Return Delineation. Of the four steps in solar return delineation, the most important is to treat the return as a transit to the natal figure. Superposition of the return's house positions further specifies transit effects to life areas during the return. These steps properly subordinate the return to the natal figure.

Solar Return Prediction. There are three ways to time the promise of the solar return: (1) direct and profect the return's Ascendant to return planets and their aspects, (2) progress the return's Moon at the secondary rate to return planets and their aspects, and (3) overlay timing of natal monthly profections on the return's house positions.

Case Study: Lincoln in 1862. As a comprehensive case study, Lincoln's 1862 solar return is delineated and timed by these three methods of solar return prediction. A special delineation method is applied to the Jupiter-Saturn conjunction which appears in this return.

Solar Return Assumptions: Precession and Relocation

Two solar return calculation assumptions remain disputed topics. The first is whether precession should be accounted for. Second is whether the birth location, residence location at the time of the return, or actual physical presence at the time of the return (if different – e.g., if one is on a trip), should be used for calculation. It's important to state first that there is no evidence that solar returns were precessed or relocated by astrologers who originally developed the technique. While there are some advocates for relocation during the Renaissance (Jean-Baptiste Morin as one example), they are relatively late figures. The bottom line is the burden of proof for precession and relocation lies with modern-day challengers; not with practitioners using non-precessed birthplace returns specified by originators of the solar return technique.

My findings confirm adjustments for precession and relocation are not necessary. What follows will demonstrate methods I used to reach this conclusion and a process for those wishing to conduct further tests on a wider sample. For starters, consider the overall configuration of the return taking note of signs of planets and houses where they fall. Is the configuration consistent with the events of the year? For the Presidential Database, a consistent finding for solar returns of the year of death is that killing planets most commonly fall in the 1st, 4th, 7th, or 8th houses and afflict the luminaries or hīlāj. This is consistent with the 1st house signifying the physical body; the 4th, end-of-life; the 7th, an allusion to old age because it is the angle of the Western sky where the Sun sets; and the 8th, death itself. The pairing of killing planets and the luminaries or hīlāj in these houses by position or rulership predisposes the year to illness or death.

No matter what the major events of the year: marriage, birth of a child, career change, etc., configuration of solar return planets by house placement or rulership should clearly confirm the events of the year. Suppose the ruler of the 1st applies to the ruler of the 7th. Then increased sexual activity and possible marriage is indicated for that year. If instead elevated financial and investment activity dominate the affairs of that year, then that pair of planets probably rules the 2nd and 8th houses, not the 1st and 7th. Either the birth time is wrong or the use of precession or relocation has incorrectly altered house cusps.

Debate: Precession. Because differences between non-precessed and precessed figures are magnified as one gets older, studying solar returns for the year of death is an excellent way to test precession. As just stated, killing planets afflict the hīlāj for solar returns in years of illness or death. Because the Moon is also a significator of the physical body whether or not it is the actual hīlāj, the Moon is usually afflicted in returns whose years coincide with illness or death. An exception occurs when the afflicted Moon signifies harm to someone besides the native, such as the mother, wife, sister, or daughter. A test for precession can be constructed based on the accuracy of either non-precessed and precessed solar return Moons to closely aspect malefics in returns for years of illness or death.

Consider the tightness of the aspect. In addition, consider whether the Moon translates to a high scoring killing planet, no matter if the aspect is a sextile or trine. Study which assumption yields more consistent results and pass judgment.

Debate: Relocation. The validity of relocation can be tested by evaluating the general configuration of the chart as well as the ability of either directed or profected ascendants to accurately time events. Take Eisenhower as an example. He was born in Denison, TX, was in Washington, D.C. for his 1968 solar return, and died there on 29-Mar-1969 at 12:35 PM.

Death was caused by a combination of factors. Eisenhower was moved to Walter Reed Army Medical Center during May 1968 following an April 1968 heart attack. He had a long history of problems following his first heart attack in 1955. Prior to death, Eisenhower had emergency surgery for the removal of scar tissue from the intestine on 23-Feb-1969. He suffered pneumonia following surgery. He rallied briefly but died from congestive heart failure. Jupiter is the universal significator of both heart disease and pneumonia. Mars/Virgo combines cutting (Mars) and the intestines (Virgo) and signifies his intestinal surgery. Based on these delineations, Mars and Jupiter are Eisenhower's killers in the solar return.

By configuration of the chart, Mars and Jupiter in the 7th of the Denison location is more consistent with theory which predicts the positions of killing planets in the return's 1st, 4th, 7th, or 8th houses. Mars and Jupiter located in the 5th of the Washington location are not. For the Denison return, Jupiter also opposes the Ascendant within five degrees, a relationship mirrored by the Jupiter conjunct Ascendant arcus vitae computed from the natal figure.

Location	Direction	Arc	Projection
Denison	Mars conj. ASC, lat=Mars	162deg 8min	28 March 2:44 AM
Denison	Jupiter conj. ASC, lat=Jup	173deg 33min	8 April 4:55 PM
Washington	Mars conj. ASC, lat=Mars	141deg 39min	7 March 6:59 AM
Washington	Jupiter conj. ASC, lat=Jup	153deg 35min	19 March 10:48 AM

Testing Ascendant directions against Eisenhower's death on 28-Mar-1969 yields mixed results. The first direction closely times death within 10 hours, yet by delineation is a better match to intestinal surgery because Mars signifies cutting. The second Jupiter direction, ideally timing death by heart failure complicated by pneumonia, is too late. What may tip the evidence in support of the first Mars direction is Mars' closer alignment to the Sun-Saturn opposition by antiscion/contra-antiscion.

Consider also Grant, Harding, Hoover, JFK, Nixon, and Reagan as case studies because of variance between birthplace and death locations. The last four feature directions timing death in the return within 48 hours. Most impressive is *d. LOF conj. Mars* for JFK which timed assassination within *minutes* based on his natal Brookline, MA birth location despite his assassination in Dallas, TX.

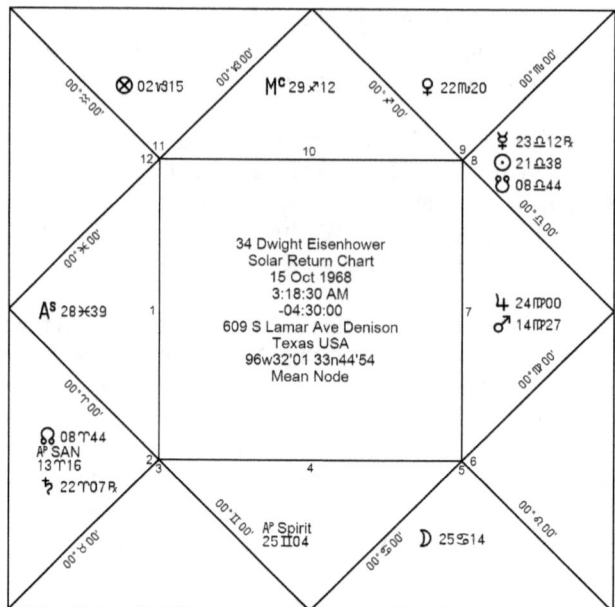

Dwight Eisenhower, 1968 Solar Return, Natal Coordinates

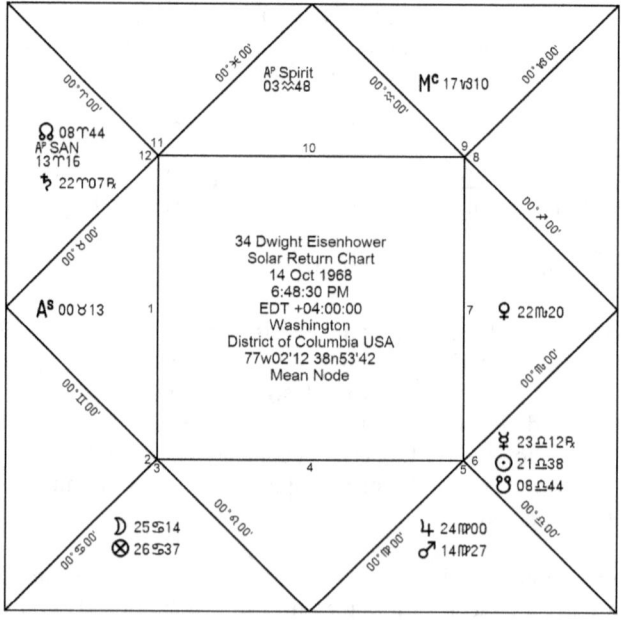

Dwight Eisenhower, 1968 Solar Return, Relocated Coordinates

Solar Return Delineation

Because delineation precedes prediction, any discussion of predictive methods for solar returns must necessarily begin with delineation. From what is currently available, Abū Ma'shar (1999) and Morin (2002) are the two traditional sources of most value. Of the two, Abū Ma'shar's treatment is more comprehensive yet contains no examples. It is also an incomplete translation. What Morin lacks in technique is made up by examples. Consulting both authors, what follows is my distillation of the most important steps for solar return delineation.

Solar Returns: Four Key Steps

Step 1. *Consider the solar return first as a transit snapshot to the natal figure. Next superimpose the return's house positions to clarify which set of house affairs those transits impact for the year.*

This is the most important step which distinguishes traditional from modern methods which tend to analyze the return on a standalone basis. Step One has three parts:

1. Delineate each planet in the natal figure. Suppose a natal figure has Mercury/Gemini in the 4th house. One delineation might be a father or male relative who is a writer or journalist. Or that the native himself has research interests in genealogy.

2. Determine the meaning of the planet's transit through every house for the natal figure. Suppose on the day of the solar return that Mercury was in Scorpio, placing its transit in the natal 9th house. If Mercury/Gemini signified the father as journalist, placement of Mercury/Scorpio in the 9th might mean the father writes about a murder in a foreign land. Or he might travel to a Scorpio-ruled country. Or it might mean the native while researching his own family's genealogy uncovers a deceased relative who was murdered or poisoned in a foreign country.

3. Overlay the solar return's house position on the transiting planet to clarify which life area the natal transit will impact for the solar return year. Suppose the transit of Mercury to the natal 9th house falls in the return's 3rd house of siblings, writing, and publicity. Perhaps the father's article or the native's genealogy research causes a dispute between the native and his siblings. Perhaps the native himself receives publicity for regaling a local reporter about his father's exploits and travels that year. Or perhaps his neighbors make inflammatory remarks about either the native or his father's activities.

Consistent among solar return theorists is the notion that the solar return cannot predict some event which is not promised by the natal figure. What these three steps accomplish is the proper subordination of the solar return to the natal figure.

These rules work a majority of time. Still there are exceptions. One cannot completely discount the standalone method. Suppose the Moon in the natal figure of a male signifies the wife. There are examples where the Moon in a solar return does not signify the wife. Lincoln's 1862 return is one. In these exceptions, the Moon can be considered a co-ruler of the return's Ascendant, borrowing a technique from horary astrology. The Moon can also be considered on a standalone basis.

The second exception is mundane events (e.g., Jupiter-Saturn conjunction, Mars-Saturn conjunction, and eclipses) which can introduce new themes for the return which were not present at the time of birth. These mundane events must first be considered independently before delineating their impact on the return.

Step 2. *Evaluate the Distributors and Partners for each Significator.*

As stated in Chapter 10: *Directions*, the Egyptian bounds impart their intrinsic nature to each significator when the significator passes through a bound by primary direction. In practical predictive work, it appears that the current Distributor predisposes certain types of behavior/events which otherwise might not occur. For example, if Mars predisposes the native to illness and is found in the return's Ascendant; whether or not an illness is predicted that year may depend on the Ascendant's Distributor and Partner. If the directed Ascendant falls in the bound of a benefic during the return's active period, then some protection is afforded against illness. (As one example, see the FDR case study in Chapter 15: *Transits*.)

Step 3. *Employ Annual Profections and Rulers of Time to elevate a select number of life areas to be emphasized for the year.*

The house position of the profected annual Ascendant and the strength of the Lord of the Year and Lord of the Period are valuable tools to focus the promise of the solar return. The position of the profected Ascendant in a particular house automatically elevates those house affairs in importance for the year. The strength of the rulers indicates how the return will modify the natal promise for better or worse. Besides LOY and LOH, Firdaria major and subperiod rulers should be examined in the return. (See Chapter 11: *Solar Returns: Profections and Time Lords*.)

Step 4. *Examine aspects between solar return planets and natal Hellenistic Lots. Such aspects can trigger the promise of the natal lot, especially when that lot pertains to house affairs highlighted by profection.*

The power of solar return planets to activate natal lots is so strong that I devote an entire chapter to this technique. See Chapter 13 for details.

Now on to predicting the promise of the solar return.

Solar Return Prediction

There are three methods to predict the promise of the solar return:

- Directions/Profections of the solar return Ascendant. This is the primary method emphasized by medieval authors.
- Secondary Progressed Moon. This method dates from the era of Placidus who invented secondary progressions.
- Monthly Profections. Solar return houses are highlighted according to the active house identified by natal monthly profections. *This is a new finding.*

Solar Return Prediction: Directions/Profections of the Ascendant

Medieval authors constantly admonish students to profect and direct the significators. What can be said for the natal chart also applies to timing the promise of the solar return. Omar of Tiberias (1997, 26-49) is one source for solar return timing methods. He quotes several authorities who suggest the return's Ascendant should either be profected at the rate of 59deg 8min per day or alternatively directed by oblique ascension. One author cited by Omar recommends directing the Midheaven for kings and rulers. The reader is left with the impression the labor intensive efforts of computing additional directions for the Midheaven are only a worthwhile exercise for someone as important as the King. Omar makes no conclusion as to whether profections or directions are preferred. While the differences can be minor, they are not negligible. For example, the direction of the Ascendant to the South Node in Lincoln's 1862 return occurs on 28 August by primary direction or 25 September by profection, a difference of almost a month. Differences between profections and directions are magnified during the middle of a year's return.

Table 27. Directions/Profections of Lincoln's 1862 Solar Return Ascendant

Directed Ascendant	Direction	Profection	Difference
Conjunct Mars	31 March	22 March	-9 days
Conjunct North Node	7 April	29 March	-9 days
Conjunct Sun	23 May	19 May	-4 days
Conjunct Mercury	29 May	6 June	+8 days
Conjunct Venus	3 June	9 June	+6 days
Conjunct South Node	28 August	25 September	+28 days
Conjunct Moon	24 September	16 October	+22 days
Conjunct Saturn	4 December	13 December	+9 days
Conjunct Jupiter	10 December	18 December	+8 days

As with profections and directions of the natal figure, in theory all significators can be profected and directed in the solar return: Ascendant, Midheaven, Sun, Moon, Lot of Fortune, and SAN. In practice this produces an unwieldy number of measurements. I suggest directing the Ascendant to the conjunction of each planet, to all aspects of the Lord of the Year, and to limit treatment of other significators to conjunctions calculated by profections. Many of these measurements yield events so subtle – such as timing an email or a phone conversation – that unless one is keeping a very careful daily diary it's difficult to test the relative accuracy of directions versus profections. Another issue is what key to use. Compared to natal primary directions, where the key of 1 degree = 1 year is recommended, the key of 1 day = 59deg 8min is theoretically preferred in solar returns – because at this rate 360 degrees will be consumed over one year. Yet many of the solar returns examined for this study confirm the validity of the 1 day = 1 degree key. For the moment, I have not reached a conclusion on which key works best.

Solar Return Prediction: Secondary Progressed Moon

The solar return's Moon, when progressed at the secondary rate, times events signified by return planets with great accuracy. It is a method recommended by modern astrologers including Shea (1999). In using this technique, I make no distinction between the specific aspect made by the progressed Moon to other solar return planets; e.g., whether or not the return's Moon aspects by sextile, square, or trine. The solar return Moon is considered a timer which sets off the promise of other return planets.

Usually only a few planets are triggered by the progressed Moon during the year. For example, only the progressed Moon's sextile to Jupiter occurs during Lincoln's actual 1862 solar return year. More events can be timed by considering the progressed Moon's aspects outside the solar return year proper. Note the Moon at 23CA25 made four different aspects which calculated by progression occurred during the years 1860-1861 (See Table 28 below). The ability of the progressed Moon to time events outside of the solar return year proper is a radical notion, but not new. In his Book 23 on Revolutions, Jean Baptiste-Morin dismisses a similar notion by Cardin as an absurdity (Morin 2002, 99-107). My research suggests that Cardin was on the right track.

Table 28. Secondary Progressions of Lincoln's 1862 Solar Return Moon

Date	Progressed Moon	Respective Solar Return Year
22-May-1860	conjunct South Node	1860
28-Feb-1861	trine Mercury	1861
23-May-1861	trine Venus	1861
11-Dec-1861	sextile Saturn	1861
25-Apr-1862	sextile Jupiter	1862

Of the four progressed Moon aspects predating Lincoln's 1862 solar return, the three 1861 projected measurements all match events consistent with the return's delineation. See documentation at the end of this Chapter for details.

CHAPTER 12 – SOLAR RETURNS: DELINEATION AND PREDICTION   205

Solar Return Prediction: Monthly Profections

<u>Solar returns modify the natal promise</u>. Solar return theory states that solar returns modify but do not obliterate the promise of the natal figure. What this means is that house by house, the solar return modifies the natal promise. For Lincoln, 1862 marked a 6th house profected year. Sixth house affairs are elevated in importance. As one step of delineating the year, the sixth house of the natal is read. Next the sixth house of the solar return is read. The promise of houses in both natal and return is synthesized. While the sixth is the most important, the exercise can be continued house by house around both figures.

<u>Align natal and solar return figures by houses, not signs</u>. This sounds easy enough, yet there are no software programs which allow two figures to be aligned *by house* in a biwheel chart format for comparison. Most (if not all) biwheel charts are constructed so that zodiacal signs are in alignment, not house positions. Only when the solar return's Ascendant is the same sign as the natal chart will a biwheel chart directly align respective houses for each chart. In all other cases, natal and return houses will be proximally mismatched. *NEW* For whole sign houses this problem disappears.

<u>Application of monthly profections of natal to the return</u>. Taking the step of aligning the solar return and the natal by houses, the application of monthly profections of the natal to the solar return becomes evident. Here's how it works:

<u>Lincoln's 1862 return</u>. For Lincoln, 1862 was a 6th house year because the profected natal ascendant moving at the rate of 30 degrees per year reached 29TA45 on 12-Feb-1862, which fell in Lincoln's 6th house (WS). Because monthly profections divide the year into 12 sections, the period starting on Lincoln's 12-Feb-1862 birthday lasting roughly 30 days to 12-Mar-1862 highlighted issues of the 6th house. From 12-March to 12-April, the 7th house, etc., until the period 12-Jan-1863 to 12-Feb-1863 highlights the 5th house and closes out his 53rd year.

Recall these monthly calculations are derived from profecting the *natal Ascendant* by 30 degrees per month. But there is no reason why they cannot be applied to the *solar return*. Just as the period 12-Feb to 12-Mar-1862 highlights affairs in the *natal 6th house*; because the solar return is effectively an overlay on the natal figure, it will also highlight affairs in the *solar return 6th house* simultaneously. Likewise, the period 12-Mar to 12-Apr-1862 will highlight the 7th house for both the natal and solar return figures.

The same can be said for daily profections.

Next is presented the recommended method for computing monthly and daily profections. It is a slight departure from 30 day and 2 ½ day periods for monthly and daily profections recommended by traditional authors.

Calculation of Monthly and Daily Profections

Because the date and time of the actual solar return varies as much as a day from the actual birthday, there is the question of whether one should start measuring profections from the date of the solar return or from the date of the actual birthday. Taking Lincoln's 1862 solar return as an example:

Date and time of actual birthday: 12-Feb-1862 3:48:55 AM
Date and time of solar return: 12-Feb-1862 12:22:16 AM

These two times differ by 3 hours 26 minutes. This is relatively minor but for years immediately preceding leap years, the difference can be up to a full day until the leap year adjustment realigns both solar return and actual birth dates. For daily profections with a purported active period of 2 ½ days, a one-day uncertainty of their starting time introduces up to 40% error of their effective period.

Through personal observations recorded in a daily diary for two years, I concluded that monthly and daily profections should be started from the time of the solar return, not the actual birthday. The length of the year, as defined by the difference in time between two consecutive solar returns, is evenly divided by 12 to determine starting times for monthly profections; and by 12 again for daily profections. It's not quite the 30-day period advocated for monthly profections nor the 2 ½ day period for daily profections, but I have found it more accurate.

Example: Lincoln's 53rd year, described by his 12 Feb 1862 solar return

Date and time of 1862 solar return: 12-Feb-1862 12:22:16 AM
Date and time of 1863 solar return: 12-Feb-1863 6:16:32 AM

The following three pages list Lincoln's complete monthly and daily profections for his 1862 solar return year. The subsequent return analysis demonstrates the application of monthly profections. The detail offered by daily profections is too tedious for our purposes. As a practical predictive tool, daily profections are best applied in customized calendar/appointment books along with other measurements like transits. Those who have worked with daily profections recognize simple but powerful applications, such as avoiding making significant decisions during the ~2.5 days each month when the profected daily Ascendant falls in the 12th house.

Note: The sheer enormity of data required to test monthly and daily profections makes this recommended calculation method difficult for others to independently verify. For those interested in doing so, Presidential appointment books and diaries offer the level of detail required for such tests. FDR's daily Presidential appointment book, minute by minute, now available online at the Hyde Park library, is one such tool. Other Presidential Libraries offer similar tools. Harry Truman's 1947 diary is available online (www.trumanlibrary.org).

Table 29. Monthly and Daily Profections 1862/63, Abraham Lincoln

Monthly House	Monthly Profected Time Period	Profected Monthly Ascendant Position	Daily Profected Time Period	Daily House
6	2/12/62 12:22 AM	29TA45	2/12/62 12:22 AM	6
			2/14/62 1:14 PM	7
			2/17/62 2:07 AM	8
			2/19/62 2:59 PM	9
			2/22/62 3:52 AM	10
			2/24/62 4:44 PM	11
			2/27/62 5:37 AM	12
			3/1/62 6:29 PM	1
			3/4/62 7:21 AM	2
			3/6/62 8:14 PM	3
			3/9/62 9:06 AM	4
			3/11/62 9:59 PM	5
7	3/14/62 10:51 AM	29GE45	3/14/62 10:51 AM	7
			3/16/62 11:44 PM	8
			3/19/62 12:36 PM	9
			3/22/62 1:29 AM	10
			3/24/62 2:21 PM	11
			3/27/62 3:14 AM	12
			3/29/62 4:06 PM	1
			4/1/62 4:59 AM	2
			4/3/62 5:51 PM	3
			4/6/62 6:43 AM	4
			4/8/62 7:36 PM	5
			4/11/62 8:28 AM	6
8	4/13/62 9:21 PM	29CA45	4/13/62 9:21 PM	8
			4/16/62 10:13 AM	9
			4/18/62 11:06 PM	10
			4/21/62 11:58 AM	11
			4/24/62 12:51 AM	12
			4/26/62 1:43 PM	1
			4/29/62 2:36 AM	2
			5/1/62 3:28 PM	3
			5/4/62 4:21 AM	4
			5/6/62 5:13 PM	5
			5/9/62 6:05 AM	6
			5/11/62 6:58 PM	7
9	5/14/62 7:50 AM	29LE45	5/14/62 7:50 AM	9
			5/16/62 8:43 PM	10
			5/19/62 9:35 AM	11
			5/21/62 10:28 PM	12
			5/24/62 11:20 AM	1
			5/27/62 12:13 AM	2
			5/29/62 1:05 PM	3
			6/1/62 1:58 AM	4
			6/3/62 2:50 PM	5
			6/6/62 3:42 AM	6
			6/8/62 4:35 PM	7
			6/11/62 5:27 AM	8

Table 29 - *Continued*

Monthly House	Monthly Profected Time Period	Profected Monthly Ascendant Position	Daily Profected Time Period	Daily House
10	6/13/62 6:20 PM	29VI45	6/13/62 6:20 PM	10
			6/16/62 7:12 AM	11
			6/18/62 8:05 PM	12
			6/21/62 8:57 AM	1
			6/23/62 9:50 PM	2
			6/26/62 10:42 AM	3
			6/28/62 11:35 PM	4
			7/1/62 12:27 PM	5
			7/4/62 1:20 AM	6
			7/6/62 2:12 PM	7
			7/9/62 3:04 AM	8
			7/11/62 3:57 PM	9
11	7/14/62 4:49 AM	29LI45	7/14/62 4:49 AM	11
			7/16/62 5:42 PM	12
			7/19/62 6:34 AM	1
			7/21/62 7:27 PM	2
			7/24/62 8:19 AM	3
			7/26/62 9:12 PM	4
			7/29/62 10:04 AM	5
			7/31/62 10:57 PM	6
			8/3/62 11:49 AM	7
			8/6/62 12:42 AM	8
			8/8/62 1:34 PM	9
			8/11/62 2:26 AM	10
12	8/13/62 3:19 PM	29SC45	8/13/62 3:19 PM	12
			8/16/62 4:11 AM	1
			8/18/62 5:04 PM	2
			8/21/62 5:56 AM	3
			8/23/62 6:49 PM	4
			8/26/62 7:41 AM	5
			8/28/62 8:34 PM	6
			8/31/62 9:26 AM	7
			9/2/62 10:19 PM	8
			9/5/62 11:11 AM	9
			9/8/62 12:04 AM	10
			9/10/62 12:56 PM	11
1	9/13/62 1:48 AM	29SA45	9/13/62 1:48 AM	1
			9/15/62 2:41 PM	2
			9/18/62 3:33 AM	3
			9/20/62 4:26 PM	4
			9/23/62 5:18 AM	5
			9/25/62 6:11 PM	6
			9/28/62 7:03 AM	7
			9/30/62 7:56 PM	8
			10/3/62 8:48 AM	9
			10/5/62 9:41 PM	10
			10/8/62 10:33 AM	11
			10/10/62 11:25 PM	12

Table 29 - *Continued*

Monthly House	Monthly Profected Time Period	Profected Monthly Ascendant Position	Daily Profected Time Period	Daily House
2	10/13/62 12:18 PM	29CP45	10/13/62 12:18 PM	2
			10/16/62 1:10 AM	3
			10/18/62 2:03 PM	4
			10/21/62 2:55 AM	5
			10/23/62 3:48 PM	6
			10/26/62 4:40 AM	7
			10/28/62 5:33 PM	8
			10/31/62 6:25 AM	9
			11/2/62 7:18 PM	10
			11/5/62 8:10 AM	11
			11/7/62 9:03 PM	12
			11/10/62 9:55 AM	1
3	11/12/62 10:47 PM	29AQ45	11/12/62 10:47 PM	3
			11/15/62 11:40 AM	4
			11/18/62 12:32 AM	5
			11/20/62 1:25 PM	6
			11/23/62 2:17 AM	7
			11/25/62 3:10 PM	8
			11/28/62 4:02 AM	9
			11/30/62 4:55 PM	10
			12/3/62 5:47 AM	11
			12/5/62 6:40 PM	12
			12/8/62 7:32 AM	1
			12/10/62 8:25 PM	2
4	12/13/62 9:17 AM	29PI45	12/13/62 9:17 AM	4
			12/15/62 10:09 PM	5
			12/18/62 11:02 AM	6
			12/20/62 11:54 PM	7
			12/23/62 12:47 PM	8
			12/26/62 1:39 AM	9
			12/28/62 2:32 PM	10
			12/31/62 3:24 AM	11
			1/2/63 4:17 PM	12
			1/5/63 5:09 AM	1
			1/7/63 6:02 PM	2
			1/10/63 6:54 AM	3
5	1/12/63 7:47 PM	29AR45	1/12/63 7:47 PM	5
			1/15/63 8:39 AM	6
			1/17/63 9:31 PM	7
			1/20/63 10:24 AM	8
			1/22/63 11:16 PM	9
			1/25/63 12:09 PM	10
			1/28/63 1:01 AM	11
			1/30/63 1:54 PM	12
			2/2/63 2:46 AM	1
			2/4/63 3:39 PM	2
			2/7/63 4:31 AM	3
			2/9/63 5:24 PM	4
7	2/12/63 6:16 AM	29GE45	2/12/63 6:16 AM	7

Case Study: Abraham Lincoln's 1862 Solar Return

Table 30. Collected Inputs for Lincoln's 1862 Solar Return

Directing by Triplicity: Final years	Ascendant ruler	Saturn
	Midheaven ruler	Jupiter
	6th house ruler	Mars

Firdaria	Main Period	Sun since 12-Feb-1853
	Subperiod	Mars since 9-Sep-1861

Significator	Directed Position	Distributor (Bound Lord)	Partner (Last direction – directing 'direct')
Ascendant	1PI44	Venus/Pisces	square Saturn since 25-Oct-1860 (sequence to 16-Jan-1863)
Midheaven	13SA38	Venus/Sag	square Mercury since 9-May-1858
Sun	1TA37	Venus/Taurus	opposed Mars since 22-May-1851 (sequence to 16-Oct-1853) Calc method: Pole
Moon	29PI30	Saturn/Pisces Jupiter/Aries as of 13-Jun-1862	trine Saturn since 10-May-1857 (sequence includes 2-Jul-1860 to 23-Aug-1862) Calc method: Pole

Time Lords	
Lord of Year (sign ruler of annual profected Ascendant – cycles of 12)	Venus
Lord of the Period (planetary hour ruler – cycles of 7)	Venus
Victor of Return (by QS I make a judgment call and take Mars over Saturn because Mars rules the Ascendant.)	Mars

Moon's Application and Separation, Phase, and Chart Sect
Moon separates from sextile of Saturn and applies to sextile of Jupiter
Moon is waxing, 2nd quarter, figure is nocturnal

Configuration of Natal and Return Angles
Return's Ascendant falls in natal 12th
Natal Ascendant falls in return's 2nd

Planet Ingresses and Returns	
Return's Moon 23CA25	Opposes natal Moon 25CP11
Return's Mercury 11PI24	Returns to same natal sign and bound
Return's Venus 14PI17	Ingresses to place of natal Jupiter
Return's Mars 25SA01	Ingresses to place of natal Saturn and natal ASC
Return's Jupiter 25VI56	Opposes natal Jupiter and falls in natal MC
Return's Saturn 21VI14	Squares natal Saturn and falls in natal MC

Notable Configurations
Mercury-Venus // Mars // Jupiter-Saturn t-square dominates the figure
Moon translates Jupiter-Saturn conjunction in natal MC falling in return's 11th
Mars translates Saturn to Jupiter

CHAPTER 12 – SOLAR RETURNS: DELINEATION AND PREDICTION

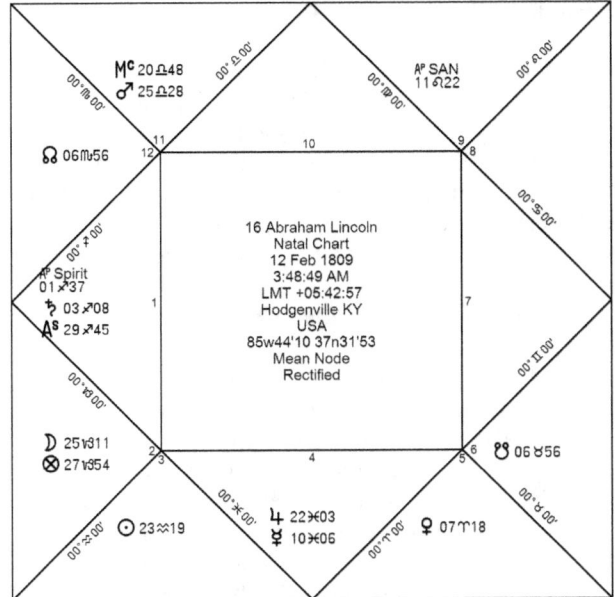

Abraham Lincoln, natal figure, Whole Sign houses.

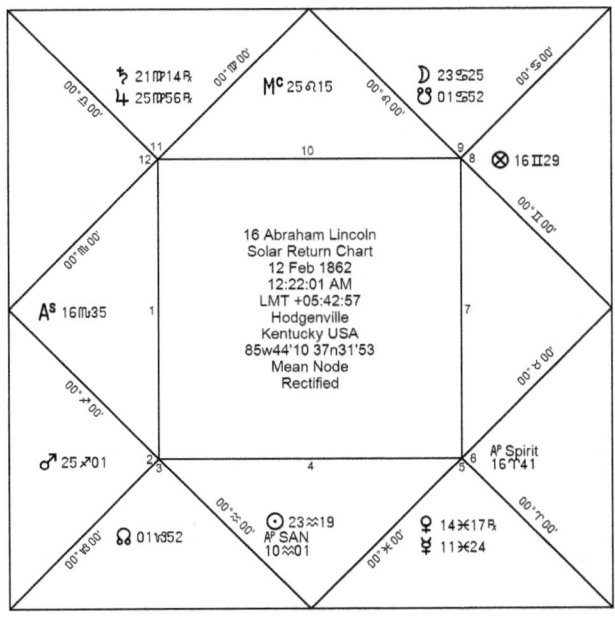

Abraham Lincoln, 1862 solar return, Alchabitius Houses.

Delineating Lincoln's 1862 Solar Return

The figure is dominated by the Jupiter-Saturn conjunction which as a transit falls in the natal 10th (WS) and the return's 11th. As a mundane configuration, this conjunction introduces new themes not previously present. As a consequence the recommended procedure for solar return analysis needs to be modified. The procedure of considering Jupiter & Saturn's natal placement, their transits to the natal figure, and their placement in solar return houses is suspended. Instead, the Jupiter-Saturn conjunction will be considered as an independent figure.

Jupiter-Saturn conjunction as a Mundane Figure

According to Medieval theory, each Jupiter-Saturn conjunction signifies a new breath of God's will transmitted through prophets to the people.[18] These new ideas directly impact world affairs through political change. God's will imparted at the conjunction can also be considered a *thesis*. Roughly five years later, the thesis is challenged at the first Jupiter-Saturn square; referred to as the *Fortitude of the Sword* by Abū Ma'shar. At the opposition, the original thesis is turned on its head by its *anti-thesis*. The waning Jupiter-Saturn square is *The Final Battle* where both sides dispute the thesis for the last time. By the time of the next Jupiter-Saturn conjunction, issues raised by the original thesis are resolved.

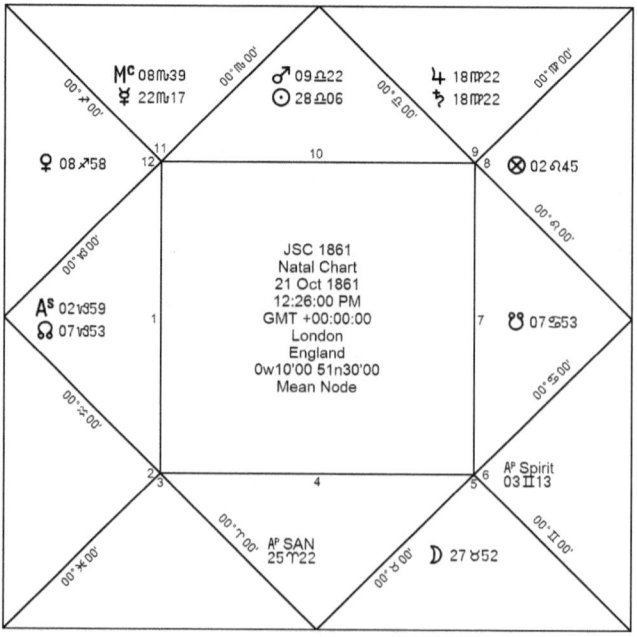

---

[18] This section is based on notes from private sessions and the 1st Intensive on Mundane Astrology presented by Robert Zoller, January 2004, Vancouver B.C.

An Empirical Event Study of the Jupiter-Saturn Conjunction of 21-Oct-1861

There are two ways to study this conjunction. The first relies on the benefit of hindsight by studying events during the years 1861-1881. Based on this approach, two major themes were Emancipation/Reconstruction and Western Expansion, aided by the Homestead Act and the Transcontinental Railroad's construction.

Table 31. Listing of Historical USA Events following JSC of 21 Oct 1861

JU-SA	Date	Events
Conjunction	21-Oct-1861	**Emancipation and Reconstruction**: Lincoln relieved General Fremont from command on 2-Nov following his unauthorized Emancipation Proclamation of 11-Sep. He replaced the aging General Winfield Scott with George McClellan as Commander of the Union Army on 31-Oct. During November Lincoln considered compensating Delaware for emancipation of its slaves. **Western Expansion**: During October 1861, railroad promoter Theodore Judah traveled to Washington D.C. to lobby for the Central Pacific Railroad Company. A year earlier he discovered Donner Pass as a practical solution for the transcontinental railroad route.
Waxing Square	16-Mar-1867	**Emancipation and Reconstruction**: Between 2-Mar and 19-Jul, Radical Republicans in Congress passed the first three Reconstruction Acts over President Johnson's veto. They imposed martial law on southern states to guarantee rights for emancipated slaves known as *freedmen*. Under the protection of 20,000 Federal troops, 700,000 freedmen and 6,000 whites registered to vote. **Western Expansion**: On 21-Dec-1866, Sioux Warriors ambushed Captain William Fetterman in the Powder River Basin, a pristine hunting area threatened by the railroad's expansion. On 27-Aug-1867, Cheyenne Warriors destroyed track, burned a work train, and killed most of a work crew in the same area.
Opposition	21-Aug-70 5-Nov-1870 24-Jun-1871 19-Mar-1872 11-Apr-1872	**Emancipation and Reconstruction**. Democratic-led white supremacists regained control of state legislatures and began to peel away layers of protection accorded by Reconstruction. Examples: 4-Aug-1870 (North Carolina); 8-Nov-1870 (Missouri). On 22-May-1872, Congress passed the Amnesty Act which allowed Southerners previously barred from running for public office to do so. **Western Expansion**: On 3-Oct-1870, Secretary of Interior Jacob Cox was pressured to resign through Congressional influence of robber barons. He had advocated the restraint of natural resource usage. On 1-Mar-1872, Congress created Yellowstone National Park after demands for conservation of this natural resource.
Waning Square	22-Dec-1875 17-Mar-1876 13-Oct-1876	**Emancipation and Reconstruction**. The contested Presidential election between Samuel Tilden and Rutherford Hayes occurred on 7-Nov-1876. Hayes was eventually selected following compromise measures to the South. In April 1877 he ordered remaining Federal troops out of the South, ending Reconstruction. **Western Expansion**. During October 1875, the 2nd Sioux War erupted after the Sioux tribe refused to sell their land. The Indian victory at the Battle of the Little Big Horn on 25-Jun-1876 was their last; it triggered a massive extermination and resettlement campaign.

This event listing is by no means complete. I have left out the railroad strikes of the late 1870s which are tied to the larger cycle of railroad investment dating from the Transcontinental Railroad proposal made October 1861. Still, I believe the event list adequately marks major turning points for the themes of *Emancipation/Reconstruction* and *Western Expansion*.

Delineating the Jupiter-Saturn Conjunction of 21-Oct-1861

The second way to study the conjunction is to delineate it from the ground up. The recommended two-step process first begins by considering macro issues of the conjunction's placement in larger cycles of Great, Middle, and Small conjunctions, which regions/themes will be emphasized, and whether the forces of expansion or contraction will prevail. The second step takes a micro approach and builds the conjunction's delineation one planet at a time.

Step 1. Macro Delineation

Abū Ma'shar (2005) classified Jupiter-Saturn conjunctions into three types: Great, Middle, and Small. Great conjunctions are defined as the first of three Jupiter-Saturn conjunctions in Aries which happen every ~720 years. Middle conjunctions occur every ~240 years when the sign of the conjunction changes from one triplicity to another. Small conjunctions occur every ~20 years and are signified by the most recent Jupiter-Saturn conjunction.

Great Conjunction. There is some debate whether the Great Conjunction for the current era is the 18-Dec-1603 conjunction in Sagittarius or the conjunction of 17-May-1702 in Aries. Supporters of the 1603 conjunction cite the changeover from the water to fiery triplicity giving its importance. I side with Abū Ma'shar because Aries is a cardinal sign and signifies greater action than the mutable sign Sagittarius. Empirically the birth of religious prophets and their impact on society can be evaluated to test which conjunction should be considered the *Great*. The birth of Roger Williams (circa 1603, date unknown) supports the importance of the 1603 conjunction. His philosophy of separation of church and state was new and an important challenge to New England Puritans without which America might have evolved with a state-supported religion. Still I suggest that the births of John Wesley (17-Jun-1703) and Jonathan Edwards (5-Oct-1703) for Christians; together with Muhammed Ibn Abdul Wahhab (b. 1703) for Muslims and Israel ben Eliezer (c. 1698) for Jews vindicate the empirical importance of the 1702 conjunction. There were some inklings of the Enlightenment prior to 1702, but it didn't really take hold until the 18th century. The year 1702 also marked the beginning of the War of Spanish Succession which triggered dramatic upheavals in Europe, more important than the 1606 settlement of Jamestown to world history, in my opinion. St. Petersburg, Russia also dates from 1703.

Principal themes of the Enlightenment are independence from political tyranny, preference for scientific thought, and materialism.

Middle Conjunction. Marking the changeover from fire to earth signs, the 17-Jul-1802 Jupiter-Saturn conjunction at 5VI07 is the Middle conjunction. The changeover marked the end of the Federalist Era and the beginning of the Republican-Democratic Party led by Thomas Jefferson as its standard bearer. Jefferson himself has Jupiter/Virgo in the 4th cusp of his natal figure. At 4VI43, Jefferson's Jupiter is partile conjunct the 1802 Jupiter-Saturn conjunction, allowing him to ride the mundane wave. Under his administration the Louisiana Purchase was consummated, doubling the size of the United States.

Small Conjunction. The 21-Oct-1881 conjunction is the Small conjunction. It is the second in Virgo and revisits themes of the 1802 conjunction by its focus on settlement of lands acquired through the Louisiana Purchase during the Middle conjunction.

Virgo-Earth Triplicity. The mere fact that both Middle and Small conjunctions are in the sign of Virgo is an important macro issue. Earlier I suggested that the Small Conjunction in Virgo signified settlement of the Great Plains through Western Expansion because one of Virgo's significations is sown crops. Farming of sown crops was a principal activity of settlers; if not for direct human consumption, then as a feedstock for cattle.

But there is a second reason why Virgo as a member of the earth triplicity is important. To each of the four quadriplicities – fire, air, earth, and water – Abū Ma'shar assigned a region of the world. The earth quadriplicity is assigned to the West. Any Jupiter-Saturn conjunction falling in any of the earth triplicity rulers is said to indicate a shift in power to the West (Abū Ma'shar 2000 Vol. 1, 31). What does he mean by West? In effect, Abū Ma'shar picks a single point on the earth and names that place the center. Ptolemy's earliest cartography defined the Canary Islands (off the coast of Spain) as the longitudinal divide between East and West; and made the equator the division between North and South. At other junctures in history, places like Constantinople and the Berlin Wall have been considered dividing lines between the East and West. More generally, America is defined as a Western country despite that America has both a West and an East coast. Similarly the nations of the Orient including China and Japan have traditionally been referred to as Eastern countries.

Importance for Lincoln's Return. Why is it important that Virgo is assigned to the West? For a solar return for a national leader like Lincoln, it further specifies the actions of the conjunction to leaders of Western countries including Lincoln. He is more likely to *ride the mundane wave* relative to some other head of state in an Eastern country. This justifies reading the Jupiter-Saturn conjunction for Lincoln's return with the full gamut of mundane significations; instead of simply transits of Jupiter and Saturn to his natal figure.

Evaluating relative forces of Contraction/Expansion. As one measure of whether the forces of contraction or expansion prevailed for conjunctions, relative latitude was evaluated. The planet with the higher latitude dominates. This is a broad brush-stroke of conjunction delineation which considers both Jupiter and Saturn as competing elements of growth and destruction. For the 1861 Small Conjunction, Jupiter's latitude = 1n01'37"; Saturn's latitude = 1n49'09". Saturn has the higher latitude indicating its strength over Jupiter during the conjunction's era. Saturn's higher relative latitude is the first indication that destruction will prevail following the conjunction.

Bound and Dwad. My own suggestion is to consider the bound and dwad placement of the conjunction at this macro level of analysis. Arguably, conjunctions falling in the bounds or dwads of malefics should be more difficult than conjunctions falling in the bounds or dwads of benefics. In this case, for 18VI22, bound = Jupiter/Virgo; dwad = Aries. Both influences further degrade the conjunction. Jupiter/Virgo is already in detriment; in the bound of his detriment accentuates these tendencies. Together with the conjunction to Saturn, Jupiter/Virgo is arguably an accidental malefic. Both Jupiter and Saturn in the dwad of Aries are also very polarizing influences; Jupiter/Aries is the archetype of military expansion; Saturn/Aries denies, delays, or destroys military activity.

Step 2. Micro Delineation

These first steps of macro delineation are important. Knowing this conjunction emphasizes a shift in power to the West, that it will revisit issues raised between 1800-1820, and that destruction will prevail are helpful facts which will shape the details of the delineation. For instance, because Saturn's higher latitude is one indication that destruction will prevail following this conjunction, the analytical bias will lean towards a *half-empty* delineation rather than one that is *half-full*.

At this stage, the strength of each planet is evaluated. Unusual aspect patterns, translations of light, etc., are considered in the final synthesis.

Saturn/Virgo. From a psychological perspective, Saturn is peregrine in the sign of Virgo probably because Virgo is sufficiently detail oriented that it does not need the heavy handedness of Saturn to exert further control. When it does, it often results in an overkill of excessive criticality. True there are some applications where this is useful; for instance, redundant operational procedures for a nuclear power plant or massive wartime logistical feats. But in general excessive criticality occurs with this placement.

A blunter physical delineation of Saturn/Virgo is pillage of the Midwest and Great Plains because Saturn destroys the Virgo-signified agricultural land. I suggest the principal significator of Saturn/Virgo for this era was the locomotive steam engine. Why? To the Indians, the image of a tall, black, iron machine partitioning their buffalo hunting grounds captures both Saturn (tall, black, iron, destructive) and Virgo (plains filled with grass). The steam engine was also very similar in appearance to military tanks, also signified by Saturn/Virgo for Dwight Eisenhower whose Army career was strongly influenced by logistics of tank warfare.

Jupiter/Virgo. The dominant psychological characteristic of Jupiter/Virgo is an excessive expansion of detail at the expense of the larger, more profound issues which Jupiter best handles in other signs where he has some dignity. In Virgo, a common manifestation for Jupiter is legalese, or long-winded legal documents which fail to treat a matter with true wisdom. I suggest that legal documents including both the Emancipation Proclamation[19] and the Homestead Act are primary significators of legalese for this era.

Mercury/Scorpio. Because Mercury rules the conjunction, he should be considered next. Mercury is the universal significator of business affairs and all things written. Because all Mercury-Mars combinations include debate and lying as their primary characteristics, Mercury in Mars' sign of Scorpio signifies unscrupulous business practices and contracts. Following on the heels of Saturn's higher relative latitude to Jupiter, this is the second indication that this conjunction will prove destructive.

Venus/Sagittarius. As a significator of fashion, Venus/Sagittarius is a dandy. Her dress is stylish, comical, and in the extreme that of a court jester. As a monetary significator, Venus/Sagittarius is inflationary because Venus is money and Sagittarius' nature is to expand. Ruled by Jupiter/Virgo, her cause is poorly worded legal documents which allow Venus to profit. She is the very embodiment of the gaudiness with which historians would later use to define the era as the *Gilded Age*. The antics of Jim Fisk (together with Jay Gould) defined Fisk as the archetypal free-wheeling financial speculator of this era. Fisk got his start by selling shoddy merchandise to the government for inflated prices (Sandburg 1939, vol. 1, 422). Stories of Civil War soldiers wearing uniforms which decomposed during the first rain stem from the interaction of Jupiter (poorly worded legal documents), Mercury (unscrupulous business practices), and Venus (inflated profits) in this conjunction.

Mars/Libra. Mars/Libra is in detriment and avoids fighting at all costs. He may try to fight for peace or simply can't make up his mind. For this figure, Venus/Sagittarius is the cause of his inability to fight. How so? Considering the numerous tales of disintegrating coats, inoperable firearms, and useless horses; it should come as no surprise that General McClellan frequently cited the lack of adequate supplies as a principal reason why he did not deploy his troops more actively. This is not the thread that most historians have used to justify McClellan's delays. If this delineation is correct, then McClellan's reputation comes off a little less tarnished.

---

[19] See Guelzo (2004) for characterization of the Emancipation Proclamation as legalese.

Sun/Libra. As the universal significator of the King, Sun in Libra is in his fall, making him a 'nice guy – trying to please all people' who is an ineffective leader and decision maker. In the bound of Mars/Libra accentuates the King's inability to lead because he himself is tied closely to generals unwilling to fight.

Moon/Taurus. Moon in Taurus needs to hoard land, food, money, and all other Taurus-signified items including cattle. Moon's placement in the bound of Mars/Taurus is a debility. Moon's placement in dwad of Aries adds a headstrong determination to the mix. Finally, Moon separates from the opposition of Mercury and is void of course.

I suggest Moon/Taurus signifies western settlers who took advantage of the Homestead Act to acquire land. As has been widely documented, there were numerous manipulations of that law. They included incidents of large land tracts consolidated by controlling interests through legal loopholes (contrary to the Homestead Act's intent to favor the small family farmer). In many cases this was aggravated by the relatively low fertility of arid land in the Great Plains which required more than 160 acres per family to raise cattle. In any case, Moon in the bound of Mars/Taurus degrades the normally strong Taurus Moon with financial loss. Moon void of course suggests western settlers were stuck with tracts of unusable land.

Venus/Sagittarius rules the Moon. Both as the source and the cause of the Moon's effects, I suggest that Jim Fisk-type characters enticed settlers to travel west with wildly inflated promises of riches. They also probably acted as buyers of land tracts from unsuccessful settlers and may have been agents behind the consolidation of large land tracts. As an alternate delineation which emphasizes her monetary attributes, Venus/Sagittarius signifies inflationary monetary policies. Those homesteaders who did not sell their lands were later crushed by the economic depression of 1873-1879. Economic distress directly led to their demands for inflationary monetary policies through the free-silver populist movement which took hold during the next Small Conjunction.

North Node/Capricorn signifies gains in accumulated wealth and status acquired through Saturn-signified destruction of western lands.

South Node/Cancer signifies loss to environmental quality by ruinous farming and cattle operations of Homestead Act settlers. Environmental degradation would not be substantially reversed until Theodore Roosevelt – with a strong Cancer Moon – became President in 1901. His efforts at trust busting, conservation, and expansion of National Parks marked the shift from the Gilded Age to the Progressive Era.

Synthesis of the 1861 Jupiter-Saturn Conjunction

The era is marked by the free-wheeling pursuit of land and wealth. Business dealings are unscrupulous. Harmed parties have little recourse in the court system because legal documents are poorly worded and favor the dishonest. Environmental degradation is a significant consequence. Leadership of the King and his army is weak and unable to exert control.

This delineation focused on the theme of Western Expansion, not Emancipation. The connection between the two arose because Southerners had long opposed the Homestead Act; they feared it would dilute the relative standing of slavery as a modus operandi of agricultural production in America. This was a constant fear since the days of the Lincoln-Douglas debates over the Kansas-Nebraska Act. By this conjunction, these issues came to a head.

Now back to Lincoln.

Jupiter-Saturn conjunction in Lincoln's return

For Lincoln, the Jupiter-Saturn conjunction falls in the return's 11th of political organizations. For a President the 11th house also includes his Cabinet and the nation's currency as special significations. Based on the delineation of the conjunction, emancipation and westward expansion should dominate Lincoln's Cabinet relations this year. Yet for Lincoln, there will be slight differences from the conjunction's delineation because (1) the conjunction falls in the bound of Mars/Virgo not Jupiter/Virgo, (2) both planets are retrograde, and (3) Mercury/Pisces rules the conjunction. What do these differences mean for Lincoln?

Falling in the bound of Mars/Virgo increases the destructiveness of the conjunction because it adds Mars' strife. As one signification, crops should be looted or burned. As another, Mars/Virgo debases the currency through increased wartime expenditures because the 11th house is the king's money. Both planets retrograde impart a rebellious and defiant nature to the conjunction. It also means that emancipation and westward expansion are issues that Lincoln will have to deal with his Cabinet on repeated occasions. As ruler, Mercury/Pisces alters the conjunction primarily through mutual reception with Jupiter/Virgo. Mercury/Pisces is a good-natured jokester and storyteller. While good for joking around, it is an inappropriate combination with legal affairs of the type which Jupiter is attempting to work out. Mercury in Jupiter's sign of Pisces is optimistic yet not capable of handling details which mar legal paperwork by the lack of specificity. Mercury's joking can also trigger criticism because as ruler he is the cause of the over-critical Saturn/Virgo.

<u>Reversion to Recommended Procedure</u>. Having delineated the Jupiter-Saturn conjunction in Lincoln's solar return 11th house, it's time to revert to the

recommended procedure for solar return planet delineation. First consider each planet's natal delineation; second consider each solar return planet as a transit to the natal chart; third how the solar return's house placement in the return ties its effects to specific areas of life.

Mars/Sagittarius. Mars/Libra in Lincoln's natal 11th house signifies generals like George McClellan who delay fighting at all costs. Recall that McClellan was appointed by Lincoln at the time of the 21-Oct-1861 Jupiter-Saturn conjunction which also featured Mars/Libra. McClellan is Mars/Libra in both figures.

The transit of natal Mars/Libra to Sagittarius falls in Lincoln's 1st natal house. This could be an illness because this is a 6th house profected year and Mars signifies fevers. Yet the directed Ascendant falling in the bounds of Venus/Pisces – a benefic – affords Lincoln some protection from illness. Because of McClellan's prominence as a player in the larger Jupiter-Saturn conjunction, it is probably a safe bet to treat the Mars transit of Lincoln's natal Ascendant as disputes with McClellan and other ineffective military generals.

Placed in the 2nd house of the return, Mars means arguments with generals over financial matters. What kind of financial matters? Because 1862 marked a 6th house profected year, I believe that derived houses are required to unlock Mars' signification. Beginning with the 6th house of slaves, 9 houses later falls in the 2nd. Because the 9th is long distance travel, pilgrimage, and the house of God, interpreting the 9th as freedom/emancipation makes sense. The 9th from the 6th, or 2nd by derived houses, signifies emancipation of slaves. Mars in a financial house means expenditures. In fact, Lincoln's consideration of the gradual emancipation of slaves with compensation to each state ("compensated emancipation") was a dominant theme for the entire year. He considered this a cheaper alternative than war and considerably less bloody. Its importance to the year is confirmed by Mars' rulership over the return's Ascendant. Mars is also the return's al-mubtazz.

Venus/Pisces. For Lincoln's natal figure, Venus/Aries in the 5th opposed to Mars/Libra in the 11th signifies Lincoln's disputes with both diplomats (5th house parties) and his cabinet/generals (11th house) over slavery issues because Venus rules the 6th house of slaves.

Venus' Pisces Ingress places transiting Venus in Lincoln's natal 4th house of family and real estate. For a President, the 4th is also a general significators of the homeland. The 4th is also the *end-of-the matter* and suggests that this year will mark the *endgame* for the slavery issue. Venus/Pisces in the return's 5th of diplomacy indicates a conciliatory attitude towards slaves in the homeland. Note Lincoln's Ascendant distributor is also Venus/Pisces which reinforces his conciliatory behavior this year.

Mercury/Pisces. Mercury makes a return to its natal sign and bound. As a jokester and storyteller, his effects will be felt strongly this year. Conjunct Venus in the 5th, also the house of entertainment, Lincoln will experience songs filled with humorous anecdotes. Because Mercury rules and is the cause of Saturn/Virgo's rebelliousness and defiance, this entertainment will bring Lincoln criticism.

Moon/Cancer. For Lincoln, natal Moon/Capricorn signifies his wife Mary. Falling in the 9th house is inconsistent with Mrs. Lincoln's activities during 1862 which opened with the death of her son Willie from bilious fever. For several months she remained a recluse in her room; after which she began to minister to injured soldiers as therapy. If the Moon/Cancer were Todd, the Moon should apply to a planet in or ruling the 12th house because this is the logical place to find injured soldiers. The 12th house also signifies death of children. This configuration does not occur so Mary Lincoln is disqualified as the return's Cancer Moon.

This leaves the return's Cancer Moon open to delineation as a female traveler. Since the Moon translates Saturn to Jupiter, she is probably involved in legal maneuvers in response to some type of criticism or other act of destruction signified by Saturn/Virgo.

North Node/Capricorn. North Node in natal 12th harms Lincoln because it gives power to enemies. It also increases mistakes made by Mars/Libra-signified generals because Mars rules the natal North Node. Transiting the natal 2nd house of finance and falling in the return's 3rd of short-term travel it indicates Lincoln will be taking short-term trips to visit generals in the field. Disputes over financial issues, including expenses and the compensated emancipation of slaves will mark those visits.

South Node/Cancer. Natal South Node in 6th harms Lincoln's health and slaves; it also denies food and comfort to open enemies imprisoned under martial law, timed by profecting the Ascendant at the annual rate (see Chapter 1).

Transit of the South Node to natal 8th (WS) harms foreign trade, a theme recapitulated because the South Node falls in the return's 9th of foreign affairs. One delineation is Lincoln's suspension of habeas corpus and imposition of martial law raised eyebrows among trading partners. Either trading partners objected on human rights grounds or they considered martial law an act of desperation which diminished the status of the Union cause in foreign capitals.

Synthesis of Lincoln's 1862 Solar Return

Sun. The return has two prominent configurations. First is the Sun ruling the 10th in its detriment placed in the 4th. By definition, the Sun's degree position is identical to that in the natal figure. Confirmed by the profected Ascendant conjunct Sun measurement in Chapter 1, natal Sun in 3rd signifies fame from speaking and communications. Sun in Aquarius tied Lincoln's early political career to improved navigation, later one part of Henry Clay's *American System*. Saturn/Sagittarius ruling the Sun grants the Sun sober judgment and is a benefit to the Sun in the natal figure. In the solar return the configuration is different. Anytime the ruler of the 10th is in fall/detriment in the 4th of the return, career problems will mar the year. This is problematic because Lincoln himself is the President or 10th house 'King.' The source of his infamy is the overly critical Saturn/Virgo in the 11th of alliances, Cabinet, and Congress.

T-Square. The second primary configuration is the Jupiter/Saturn – Mars – Mercury/Venus t-square involving five of the return's nine planets/Nodes, of which the Jupiter/Saturn conjunction is the dominant member. Mercury and Venus jointly can be read as the *cause* of the conjunction. Mercury-signified failed peace negotiations, poor wartime intelligence, and comical musical entertainment are the cause of Congressional criticism. Conjunct Mercury, Venus adds her conciliatory measures of forgiveness, reinforcing Venus/Pisces as the Distributor of directed Ascendant. Unfortunately for Lincoln, Congress was in no mood for reconciliation with the South.

Mars translates Jupiter-Saturn conjunction. Mars is the first facilitator of the conjunction because he translates Saturn to Jupiter. As Mars' ruler, Jupiter is also the source and outcome of Mars' effects. Take McClellan. Besides disputes with McClellan over the reluctance of McClellan's willingness to engage in hostilities, Lincoln argued with McClellan over the emancipation of slaves. McClellan had little interest in the slavery issue. With Jupiter/Virgo as the significator of the Emancipation Proclamation, Lincoln's arguments with McClellan over emancipation indeed confirm Jupiter as the source of Mars' effects. And yet because Jupiter shows the outcome as well as the source, emancipation will happen despite McClellan. How does Mars/Sagittarius facilitate this? Because the return modifies the natal promise. Mars/Sagittarius as significator of Lincoln's generals means that generals take on the qualities of Mars/Sagittarius for the 1862 return year. Compared to Mars/Libra, Mars/Sagittarius is more aggressive, more forceful, and occasionally more effective. Even McClellan acted more aggressive a few times, including at Antietam. Victory at Antietam allowed Lincoln to proclaim the Emancipation Proclamation. When McClellan backtracked to inactivity, Lincoln replaced McClellan with Burnside who was also not effective, but at least was willing to fight. Burnside was later replaced with 'Fighting Joe' Hooker whose personal description is a textbook delineation of Mars/Sagittarius. Other newly promoted Mars/Sagittarius-signified generals *ruled* by the Jupiter-signified Emancipation Proclamation undoubtedly aided emancipation by facilitating slaves in various ways – something that McClellan (still returning fugitive slaves to their masters in 1862) had no interest.

Moon translates Jupiter-Saturn conjunction. The Moon is the second facilitator of the conjunction because she is the second planet which translates Saturn to Jupiter. The Moon's separation from Saturn and application to Jupiter is a combination favored by Maternus. (Recall the discussion of this configuration in FDR's figure as one indication supporting Presidential Greatness. See Chapter 7: *Temporal Indicators*.) True enough Jupiter/Virgo in Lincoln's figure has a number of debilities which degrade its expected effects relative to Maternus' cookbook aphorisms. Still, the Moon moving from the greater malefic to the greater benefic is a step in the right direction. Based on the zodiacal state of Jupiter and Saturn in Lincoln's 1862 return, the configuration can be delineated this way: *after initially facing criticism from poor intelligence and failed peace attempts, Lincoln's efforts will gravitate towards a legalistic framework which is marred by an over emphasis of details.* As the agency of translation, Moon in the cardinal water sign of Cancer keeps Lincoln actively engaged in his legal maneuvers despite their limitations.

Problems with generals and emancipation of slaves were primary issues Lincoln faced during his 1862 solar return year. It is safe to focus the synthesis of the return on these two issues, leaving other minor details of the year to emerge as each planet's effects are uncovered in tests against actual life events.

Timing the Promise of Lincoln's 1862 Solar Return

The ability to test projected dates based on the three methods of timing solar returns: (1) directed/profected Ascendant, (2) solar return progressed Moon, and (3) monthly profections method requires research above and beyond what is available in even the best biographies. Access to primary sources including letters, diaries, journals, or detailed chronologies is required.

Three references were helpful for evaluating Lincoln's 1862 solar return. First is Lincoln's actual letters, published as *The Collected Works of Abraham Lincoln*, edited by Roy P. Basler (1953). Volume 5 contains the relevant references for Lincoln's 1862 solar return. Second is *The Civil War Day by Day, An Almanac 1861 – 1865*, edited by E. B. Long (1971) provided many battle details which are otherwise difficult to find gathered in a single space. Within the broader Lincoln literature, *Lincoln's Emancipation Proclamation* by Allen C. Guelzo (2004) was invaluable in tracing the progress of slavery emancipation in Lincoln's mind through the course of the 1862 solar return.

Lincoln's 1862 Return: Timing Saturn's Effects

Monthly Profection	11th house – position	14-Jul-1862 to 13-Aug-1862
	3rd house – rulership	12-Nov-1862 to 13-Dec-1862
	4th house – rulership	13-Dec-1862 to 12-Jan-1863
Progressed Moon	Sextile Saturn	11-Dec-1861
Directed Ascendant	Conjunct Saturn	4-Dec-1862
Profected Ascendant	Conjunct Saturn	13-Dec-1862

Progressed Moon. On 9-Dec-1861, two days before the progressed Moon sextile Saturn measurement, the Senate established the *Joint Committee on the Conduct of the War*. Officially, this was designed to critically examine military leaders and their campaigns; in reality the Committee was designed to hold General McClellan's feet to the fire for inaction since his 1-Nov-1861 appointment as Commander of the Union Army. McClellan was not particularly interested in Emancipation; in fact, fugitive slaves continued to be arrested under his command (Guelzo 2004, 69-70). This event matches the criticality of Saturn/Virgo falling in the 11th house of organizations which for Lincoln included his Cabinet and Congress.

Directed/Profected Ascendant. Both measurements of the directed and profected Ascendant conjunct Saturn on 4 & 13-Dec accurately timed Lincoln's Annual Message to Congress on 1-Dec-1862 as Congress reconvened. The session to 23-Dec was stormy and marked by widespread criticism of the Emancipation Proclamation both by newly elected Democrats but also by Radical Republicans who feared that Lincoln's failure to immediately emancipate the slaves on 22-Sep meant he might backtrack on the entire measure. Radical Republicans considered the extreme measure of withholding supplies for troops and allowing the country to fall into anarchy, if necessary, to make sure Lincoln stayed the course (Guelzo 196). There was also a Cabinet crisis when Seward and Chase threatened to resign.

Monthly Profections.

11th House: 14-Jul to 13-Aug-1862. The same type of anarchy considered by the Radical Republicans in Dec-1862 was also in play during Lincoln's 11th house profected month beginning 14-Jul. This was the exact date that the 2nd Confiscation Act was brought before Lincoln, which he signed on 16-Jul. It was designed by the Radical Republicans intended as a harsh measure against the South.

3rd House: 12-Nov to 13-Dec-1862. On 14-Nov, Lincoln gave approval to Burnside's proposal to capture the Confederate capital at Richmond. This would lead directly to Burnside's disastrous loss at Fredericksburg on 13-Dec as Lincoln's Saturn-ruled 4th house profected month started.

4th House: 13-Dec-1862 to 12-Jan-1863. As to the accuracy to the date and hour of monthly profections, Confederate General James Longstreet reported the fog lifted at 10:00 a.m. at Fredericksburg, 43 minutes after the beginning of Lincoln's Saturn-ruled 4th house profected month which started at 9:17 a.m. (Longstreet 1997). This was also the same day that Lincoln's profected Ascendant conjoined Saturn. Fredericksburg was also marked by the same kind of anarchy and destruction that permeated both the Second Confiscation Act and the willingness of Radical Republicans to withhold troops and supplies in December even if anarchy resulted. On 12-Dec, Burnside's Army looted, ransacked, and destroyed most of Fredericksburg before the primary battle started on 13-Dec.

Influence of Mercury. As Saturn's ruler, Mercury/Pisces also influenced both Congressional opposition to Lincoln during December and Burnside's disastrous loss at Fredericksburg. Radical Republicans threatened to withhold supplies from Union armies because of Lincoln's delay in making the Emancipation Proclamation effective. As the universal significator of negotiation, Mercury is further tied to negotiation in Lincoln's 1862 return by placement in the 5th house of diplomacy. Mercury in the sign of Jupiter's rulership, in mutual reception with Jupiter/Virgo, infuses Lincoln's complicated legalistic maneuvers with a sense of optimism that Congress found puzzling. Even at this late date, Lincoln still held out some hope that his proposal of compensated emancipation would be taken up; allowing states to avoid the fate of emancipation with no compensation (Guelzo 193-196).

Mercury is also evident in the disastrous losses at Fredericksburg; both in the looting before the battle on the 12th and the battle itself on the 13th. Amidst the pillaging was a comic scene of soldiers parading the streets wearing looted clothing of the style worn during the Federal Era.

Mercury/Pisces also signifies faulty intelligence and planning. Because of a logistical error, pontoons required for a river crossing failed to arrive in time, costing Burnside valuable time and allowing General Lee to fortify his men. This delay was a major reason why Fredericksburg was such a slaughter. Note the obvious connection between the water sign of Pisces, the water needed to be crossed with pontoons, and failed intelligence which prevented proper deployment.

Lincoln's 1862 Return: Timing Jupiter's Effects

Monthly Profection	11th house – position	14-July-62 to 13-Aug-1862
	2rd house – rulership	13-Oct-62 to 12-Nov-1862
	5th house – rulership	12-Jan-63 to 12-Feb-1863
Progressed Moon	Sextile Jupiter	25-Apr-1862
Directed Ascendant	Conjunct Jupiter	10-Dec-1862
Profected Ascendant	Conjunct Jupiter	18-Dec-1862

Progressed Moon. The Moon sextile Jupiter progression of 25-Apr matches the Union victory at New Orleans; yet on first glance it does not seem related to the delineation of Jupiter/Virgo as legalese. If there is any connection between Jupiter/Virgo ruled by Mercury/Pisces and New Orleans it may lie with ruler Mercury/Pisces. The combination of darkness, smoke, and mortar firing provided cover for Union ships as they passed Confederate forces (Long 1971, 203). Mercury/Pisces signifies confused intelligence which, if correctly delineated here, aided the Union.

The better event match based on the delineation of Jupiter/Virgo as legalese is Lincoln's 11-Apr signature on a bill to emancipate slaves in the District of Columbia. In addition, during Apr-1862 Congress passed a resolution stating the Federal Government would cooperate with any state which adopted Lincoln's proposed plan for gradual and compensated emancipation. Lincoln's approval of the Homestead Act on 20-May was the second piece of legislation which corresponded to the delineation of Jupiter/Virgo as legalese. While 20-May is not 25-Apr, I suspect that additional research may validate 25-Apr as a critical date in preparing the Homestead Act for passage. This needs further investigation.

Directed/Profected Ascendant. On 10-Dec by direction, Lincoln suspended the order of General Schofield issued on 28-Aug for the assessment of $500,000 from Secessionists and Southern sympathizers for a single county in Missouri over which Schofield held control (Lincoln 1953, 548). Lincoln rejected the order based on six legal doubts ranging from the vagueness of defining the persons to be assessed to conflicts with other laws including the Confiscation Act and – if the assessment were to be considered a tax – the Constitution itself. What perfect example of legalese!

On 18-Dec by profection, Lincoln listened to complaints against Seward made by the Radical Republicans. They accused Seward of muting anti-slavery agitation and elevating the importance of saving the Union in Lincoln's mind as a priority over emancipation. On 19-Dec Lincoln suffered the worst case of depression since assuming the office of the Presidency as Seward submitted his resignation (Luthin 1960: 360). During the next 48 hours, Lincoln's maneuverings between his

Cabinet and the *Senate Committee on the Conduct of the War* resulted in the additional resignation of Treasury Secretary Chase. However, Lincoln refused to accept both resignations of Seward and Chase and the crisis passed. As a match to the Ascendant conjunct Jupiter/Virgo by profection, the influence of legalese; combined with Mercury/Pisces' jocular, good-natured, and optimistic attitude, triggered the ire of the Radical Republicans because they were in no mood for measures which diluted chances for immediate emancipation. By Dec-1862, Lincoln's continued advocacy for the gradual compensated emancipation of slaves was considered too meek a measure. The Radical Republicans wanted more.

Monthly Profections.

11th House: 14-Jul to 13-Aug-1862. On 22-Jul-1862, Lincoln announced his intent to emancipate all the slaves to his Cabinet. This was a significant event during an 11th house profected month; whose house contained the Jupiter-Saturn conjunction. The preliminary draft of the Emancipation Proclamation Act was marked by legalese, in part to stave off future attempts by the Supreme Court under Taney to overturn the Act.

2nd House: 13-Oct to 12-Nov-1862. Other than Lincoln's appointment of David Davis to the position of Associate Justice of the US Supreme Court on 17-Oct-1862, initial research efforts did not uncover any other events consistent with Jupiter's rulership over Lincoln's 2nd house profected month. As a match to the Davis appointment, Jupiter/Virgo can be delineated as a constitutional lawyer. Natal figures of Thomas Jefferson and James Buchanan are other examples where the legal delineation of Jupiter in Virgo matches professional interests.

5th House: 12-Jan to 12-Feb-1863. No events found.

Lincoln's 1862 Return: Timing Mars's Effects

Monthly Profection	6th house – rulership	12-Feb-62 to14-Mar-1862
	1st house – rulership	13-Sep-62 to 12-Oct-1862
	2nd house – position	13-Oct-62 to 12-Nov-1862
Directed Ascendant	Conjunct Mars	31-Mar-1862
	Sextile Mars	24-Apr-1862
	Square Mars	13-Jun-1862
	Trine Mars	2-Jul-1862
	Opposed Mars	21-Aug-1862
	Trine Mars	2-Nov-1862
	Square Mars	9-Dec-1862
	Sextile Mars	15-Jan-1863
Profected Ascendant	Conjunct Mars	22-Mar-1862

Monthly Profections.

6th house: 12-Feb to 14-Mar-1862. The month opened with Grant's victory at Fort Donelson on 16-Feb, the date when Grant uttered his famous statement "No terms except unconditional and immediate surrender." On 6-Mar, Lincoln sent a message to Congress outlining his proposal for the gradual compensated emancipation of slaves. As the profected month closed, Lincoln met with representatives from border states to discuss his compensated emancipation plan on 10-Mar. On 11-Mar, Lincoln took over McClellan's role as Chief of Staff following his criticized evacuation of Manassas.

1st house: 13-Sep to 12-Oct-1862. As the month began, McClellan's men found Lee's battle plans by accident. As a result, McClellan scored a Union victory at Antietam and allowed Lincoln to announce the Emancipation Proclamation on 22-Sep-1862.

2nd house: 13-Oct to 12-Nov-1862. This month Lincoln made three significant changes to his military staff: Grant was given control of the Dept. of Tennessee on 16-Oct; Rosecrans replaced Buell on 23-Oct; and Burnside replaced McClellan on 5-Nov.

Union victories and the elimination of weak generals during these profected months speak well on Mars' behalf to aid Lincoln during this return. As delineated, Mars in the 2nd, 9th from the 6th, signifies compensated emancipation which marks the 6th house profected month. A Union victory during the 1st house profected month allowed Lincoln to announce the Emancipation Proclamation from a position of strength. Rosecrans, known for his debate of religious doctrine and a proneness to impulsive bouts of anger, typifies the Mars/Sagittarius trait.

Compared to Mars/Libra-signified generals in Lincoln's natal figure, it appears that Mars/Sagittarius in Lincoln's 1862 solar return signified Lincoln's replacement of ineffective Mars/Libra generals with more aggressive Mars/Sagittarius generals. In the case of Burnside, who was *not* a Mars/Sagittarius type, he was eventually replaced by 'Fighting Joe Hooker' on 25-Jan-1863 whose frank manner and reputation for aggressive fighting are consistent with Mars/Sagittarius.

Directed/Profected Ascendant. Both 22-Mar (profection) and 31-Mar (direction) measurements time two key events which broke the logjam of legislation to emancipate slaves in Washington DC. Introduced by Wilson in Dec-1861, the bill had been stymied by Garrett Davis whose amendment required forced colonization for all emancipated. On 24-Mar, Vice-President Hamlin broke a tie which stripped Davis' amendment. On 1-Apr, moderate Republicans endorsed the emancipation plan which picked up momentum. Separately, on 2-Apr, the Senate passed Lincoln's 6-Mar bill which recommended gradual compensated emancipation for border and southern states (Guelzo 95,96).

Other events which match the delineation of Mars/Sagittarius:

30-Apr-1862. *ASC sextile Mars*. On 1-May-1862, General Benjamin Butler assumed military command of New Orleans. Earlier in the war Butler was a commander at Fort Monroe, VA where he refused to return fugitive slaves to their owners because he classified them as contraband under international law. Presumably, this facilitated the road to freedom for those slaves under his guardianship.

13-Jun-1862. *ASC square Mars*. Lincoln considered the slavery issue while on vacation. It is suggested that he showed a first draft of the Emancipation Proclamation to Vice President Hamlin on 18-Jun.

3-Jul-1862. *ASC trine Mars*. On 4-Jul, Congressman Sumner suggested that Lincoln free the slaves and use them as Union troops.

21-Aug-1862. *ASC opposed Mars*. Horace Greeley's 20-Aug editorial asked Lincoln to emancipate slaves according to the new Confiscation Act, stop listening to the Border States, start making the army fight, and stop the army from arresting fugitive slaves.

2-Nov-1862. *ASC trine Mars*. No event match.

9-Dec-1862. *ASC square Mars*. No event match

16-Jan-1863. *ASC sextile Mars*. Burnside's *Mud March* of 21-Jan resulted in his replacement by 'Fighting Joe' Hooker on 25-Jan.

Lincoln's 1862 Return: Timing the Sun's Effects

Monthly Profection	10th house – rulership	13-Jun-62 to 14-Jul-1862
	4th house – position	13-Dec-62 to 12-Jan-1862
Directed Ascendant	Conjunct Sun	23-May-1862
	Opposed Sun	30-Oct-1862
Profected Ascendant	Conjunct Sun	19-May-1862

Sun/Aquarius/4th in detriment ruling the MC shows a diminished reputation. Saturn/Virgo/11th as the cause means critical political alliances are to blame.

Directed/profected Ascendant. Lincoln's 19-May (profection) revocation of General Hunter's Military Emancipation Order brought Lincoln widespread criticism and loss of prestige from Radical Republicans who favored immediate emancipation.

On 20-May Lincoln signed the Homestead Act into law. Other than the Sun's tie to real estate because of its 4th house placement, it is unclear how the Homestead Act matches the delineation of the Sun. Despite the importance of both the Homestead Act and the Transcontinental Railroad to Western Expansion, most Lincoln biographers give these issues little weight when discussing 1862.

On 22/23-May (direction), Lincoln visited the army at Fredericksburg. See the 4th house monthly profection (below) for the connection.

The 30-Oct ASC opposed Sun direction immediately preceded political losses during midterm elections on 4 November.

Monthly Profections.

10th house: 13-Jun to 14-Jul-1862. This was a weak period for the Administration. During this month, Lee successfully fought McClellan during the Seven Days' Battles, ending McClellan's Peninsular Campaign with a resounding defeat. On 11-Jul, Lincoln ended his four-month experiment as Commander-in-Chief with the appointment of Henry Halleck for the position.

4th house: 13-Dec-1862 to 12-Jan-1863. The month opened with the disastrous loss at Fredericksburg and continued with the Cabinet crisis. The Emancipation Proclamation went into force on 1-Jan-1863. What is curious about the Sun's connection to Fredericksburg is that Lincoln visited Fredericksburg earlier in the year during 22/23-May when the directed Ascendant conjoined the Sun. The actual Battle of Fredericksburg occurred exactly as the profected 4th house began. The 4th house contained the Sun.

Lincoln's 1862 Return: Timing Venus's Effects

Monthly Profection	7th house – rulership	14-Mar-1862 to 13-Apr-1862
	12th house – rulership	13-Aug-62 to 13-Sep-1862
	5th house – position	12-Jan-63 to 12-Feb-1863
Progressed Moon	Trine Venus	23-May-1861
Directed Ascendant	Conjunct Venus	6-Jun-1862
Profected Ascendant	Conjunct Venus	9-Jun-1863

Directed/Profected Ascendant. On 4-Jun Lincoln signed two pardons for soldiers. This event falls slightly before the direction (6-Jun) and profection (9 June). Venus/Pisces/5th ruling the 12th shows forgiveness for the imprisoned.

Monthly Profections. No major events found.

Progressed Moon. As the first conspicuous Union casualty of the Civil War, the death of Lincoln's friend, law student, and campaign aide Elmer Ellsworth was a blow to Lincoln. Ellsworth was a colonel of a group of National Guard Cadets, who wore Zouave uniforms (same as worn by colonial French troops) and led his unit to national recognition as a drill team.

Following Virginia's officially date of succession on 23-May-1861, Ellsworth led troops uncontested down the streets of Alexandria the next day. He spotted a Confederate flag flying above the Marshall House Inn. After cutting it down and making his way down the stairs, Ellsworth was shot in the chest by the hotel's infuriated owner on 24-May. I suggest this event was timed by progressed Moon trine Venus on 23-May.

Delineating Venus/Aries as Ellsworth

Venus/Aries/5th of Lincoln's natal figure: Earlier I suggested that natal Venus/Aries in the 5th opposed to Mars/Libra in the 11th signified Lincoln's disputes with both diplomats (5th house parties) and his cabinet/generals (11th house) over slavery issues because Venus ruled the 6th house of slaves. That it does. But Venus wears more than one hat. In this case, Venus/Aries ruling the 11th of friends, the 6th of employees, and positioned in the 5th of entertainment reveals Ellsworth as a friend, an employee, and as a source of entertainment through maneuvers of Ellsworth's drill team.

Venus/Pisces Ingress as a transit to Lincoln's natal 4th house: This transit signified Ellsworth's death because Venus is a friend and the 4th is the end-of-the matter. Placement in Pisces tinges Ellsworth's death with sacrifice. Ellsworth received status as a martyr following his death.

Influence of transiting Venus/Pisces on Lincoln's solar return 5th house: Ellsworth's death was useful in recruiting a significant number of soldiers to the Union cause. I suggest that recruiting is a 5th house affair because the 5th is the house of diplomacy (ambassadors and legates).

Synastry: If there is any doubt over the signification of Venus as Ellsworth, two synastry connections should convince even the diehard skeptic. First is the obvious connection between Lincoln's natal Venus which at 7AR18 falls in the same sign and bound as Ellsworth's own natal Venus at 11AR29. Second is Ellsworth's Ascendant 17PI41 conjunct Venus in Lincoln's return at 14PI17. In this speculative rectification, I suggest that the solar arc direction of Venus (ruler of Ellsworth's 8th of death) to the Ascendant as a possible arcus vitae.

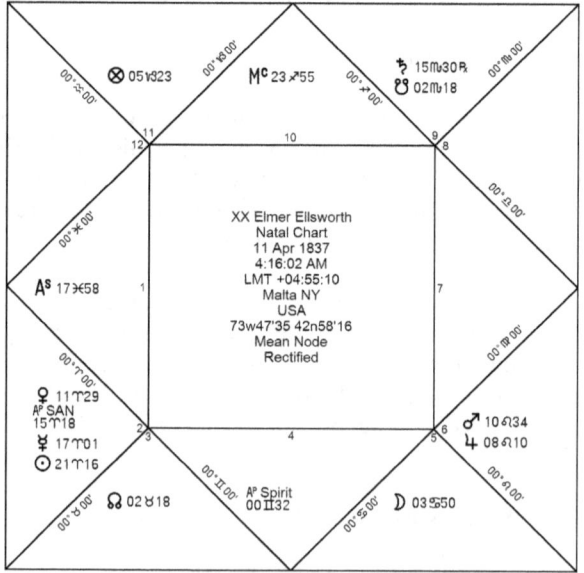

Natal figure, Colonel Elmer Ephraim Ellsworth.

Trial Rectification of Ellsworth figure: Configuration of Ascendant: Pisces rising, seeks emotional security through 6th house bold military cadets signified by the Ascendant's sign ruler Jupiter and triplicity ruler Mars conjunct in the 6th. Exalted ruler Venus/Aries signifies the art of war exemplified by military drill team routines; Mercury/Aries adds marching. At Civil War outbreak, *REG dex. square MC d.* => Mars (l=MA), 16-Apr-1861; at death 24-May-1861, csa Venus conj. ASC, trMars conj Moon, trSaturn opposed Lot of Death, trVenus and trMercury conj Lot of Hīlāj.

Lincoln's 1862 Return: Timing Mercury's Effects

Monthly Profection	8th house – rulership	13-Apr-62 to 14-May-1862
	11th house – rulership	14-Jul-62 to 13-Aug-1862
	5th house – position	12-Jan-63 to 12-Feb-1863
Progressed Moon	Trine Mercury	28-Feb-1861
Directed Ascendant	Conjunct Mercury	4-Jun-1862
Profected Ascendant	Conjunct Mercury	6-Jun-1862

Progressed Moon. Former President John Tyler wrote an editorial on 17-Jan-1861 suggesting a Washington Peace Conference as a last-ditch effort to avoid conflict between the North and South. The Conference, with Tyler as its head, convened from 4-Feb to 2-Mar-1861. Anticipating Congressional rejection of the southern position on 2-Mar, Tyler denounced the results of the Convention on 28-Feb-1861 (exact date of progression).

Directed/Profected Ascendant. In early June, excerpts from Lincoln's letters show his attempts at micromanaging his ineffective generals. This occurred during the four-month period that Lincoln served as Commander-in-Chief. Micromanaging is a Jupiter/Virgo signification; together with Mercury/Pisces, it is hampered by confused intelligence. As one example, in letter to McClellan dated 3-Jun (one day prior to date of direction), Lincoln expressed worry about continuous rains which could have allowed the enemy to cross a communications line (Lincoln 1953, 257). Besides confusing communications, Mercury/Pisces signifies *wind + rain* from an astrometerological perspective.

Monthly Profections.

<u>8th house: 13-Apr to 14-May-1862</u>. No events found.

<u>11th house: 14-Jul to 13-Aug-1862</u>. On 14-Jul, border state representatives refused Lincoln's appeal for compensated emancipation.

<u>5th house: 12-Jan to 12-Feb-1862</u>. On 4-Feb the Illinois legislature urged Congress to issue an armistice, arrange for a peace convention, and named five commissioners who were prepared to travel to Washington for their proposed Peace Convention. Illinois reasoned that both preservation of the Constitution and restoration of the Union demanded the Emancipation Proclamation be withdrawn. Not only did this event occur during a 5th house profected month where Mercury resides by position, but the event was timed by the directed Ascendant trine Mercury on 5-Feb. The similarity between this event and Tyler's failed Peace Convention of Feb-1861 - both timed by Mercury in this return - is remarkable.

Lincoln's 1862 Return: Timing the Moon's Effects

Monthly Profection	9th house – position + rulership	14-May-62 to 13-Jun-1862
Directed Ascendant	Conjunct Moon	23-Sep-1862
Profected Ascendant	Conjunct Moon	16-Oct-1862

Directed/Profected Ascendant. Two events are candidates for the 23-Sep direction. First, on 24-Sep, Lincoln wrote a letter of introduction to be taken by Unitarian clergyman, orator, and statesman Edward Everett for his European mission taken as a private citizen. As the most prominent orator of the time, Everett had made many speeches in support of the Union cause across the North. He would carry a similar message to European capitals.

The second possible event is the announcement of the Emancipation Proclamation on 22-Sep-1862. The Proclamation included specific language which encouraged voluntary colonization of freed slaves in North America and elsewhere. Moon in the 9th of foreign lands is a match for colonization. Placement in the sign of Cancer means Lincoln genuinely felt that slaves would be better cared for in places outside the United States.

I was unable to determine an event match for the profection of 16-Oct-1862.

Monthly Profection

<u>9th house: 14-May to 13-Jun-1862</u>. A possible event match for this profection is Congressional approval of the Morrill Land-Grant College Act on 2-Jul-1862. This legislation provided federal land grants to colleges that taught agricultural and mechanical arts. Most likely, Congressional debate during this 9th house profected month included discussions on the Morrill Land-Grant Act passed on 2-Jul in the following month. This delineation requires additional research for confirmation.

Lincoln's 1862 Return: Timing the North Node's Effects

Monthly Profection	3rd house – position	12-Nov-62 to 13-Dec-1862
Directed Ascendant	Conjunct North Node	7-Apr-1862
Profected Ascendant	Conjunct North Node	29-Mar-1862

In Lincoln's natal figure, North Node/Scorpio/12th ruled by Mars/Libra/11th signifies mistakes from generals who are reluctant to fight. As a transit to the natal 2nd house, North Node/Capricorn signifies increased financial problems with his military. Placed in the 3rd house of the return, Lincoln both makes short-term trips and receives bad publicity from these financial disputes.

Monthly Profection: 3rd House: 12-Nov to 13-Dec-1862. On 22-Nov-1862, Lincoln expressed shock at General Banks' demands for excessive supplies following his appointment to replace Butler's command in New Orleans.

Directed/Profected Ascendant. In a 9-Apr letter to McClellan, Lincoln rebuts McClellan's complaints over insufficient troop levels and orders him to act.

Lincoln's 1862 Return: Timing the South Node's Effects

Monthly Profection	9th house – position	14-May to 13-Jun-1862
Progressed Moon	Conjunct South Node	22-May-1860
Directed Ascendant	Conjunct South Node	28-Aug-1862
Profected Ascendant	Conjunct South Node	25-Sep-1862

Progression. No events found. This progression followed Lincoln's nomination for President on 18-May-1860.

Directed/Profected Ascendant. Pope's defeat during the Second Battle of Bull Run during 26/30-Aug corresponds with the directed Ascendant conjunct South Node. Part of Pope's defeat was blamed on recently released soldiers from McClellan's command who were said to have ignored and/or delayed orders to fight. How this event can be signified by South Node in Cancer is not clear. The better match is the profection on 25-Sep which fell one day after Lincoln expanded the suspension of habeas corpus for 'all Rebels and Insurgents' arrested by the military. In Chapter 1, the annual profection of Ascendant conjunct South Node timed his first suspension of habeas corpus.

Monthly Profection: 9th House (position): 14-May to 13-Jun-1862. This was one of the worst months of 1862. It included McClellan's poor performance against Stonewall Jackson at the Battle of Fair Oaks and the imbroglio over Hunter's unilateral Emancipation Proclamation cancelled on 19-May.

Lessons Learned: Lincoln's 1862 Solar Return

As with every delineation, there are events not predicted which occur, events predicted which do not occur, or predicted events which occur some *other* time.

Death of Willie Lincoln. Lincoln's third son Willie died of bilious fever on 20-Feb-1862. Venus, ruler of the 12th (death of children) falling in the 5th of children is one indication of Willie's death. The second is Mercury in the same 5th house partile conjunct the contra-antiscion of the Lot of Children 18AR41/11VI19. This configuration promises Willie's death because Mercury (significator of boys) is joined with Venus (ruler of the 12th and death of children).

Activities of Mary Lincoln. Willie's death was a severe blow to Mary Lincoln who spent two months in isolation following the loss of her third son. Later in the year she spent time visiting military hospitals, delivering flowers to soldiers, and engaging in other volunteer work. If Mary Lincoln is not the Moon in Lincoln's return, how are her activities shown? I suggest her grief is shown by Saturn/Pisces as the Moon's Distributor at the time of Willie's death. On 13-Jun-1862, the Moon's Distributor changed to Jupiter/Aries. This is the approximate time when Mary Lincoln started her outreach activities.

Blasphemy at Antietam. An event promised, but not timed by any of the methods cited above, occurred during Lincoln's 1/4-Oct-1862 visit to the headquarters of the Army of the Potomac and battlefields in the Antietam area. Facing so many dead soldiers, Lincoln asked his friend Ward Hill Lamon to perform a melancholy song; a request filled by an irreverent tune by the black French singer and banjo player John 'Picayune' Butler. Lincoln's engagement in this entertainment on the battlefield was considered an act of blasphemy for which he was later criticized. This event is the perfect match to the Mercury/Venus Pisces conjunction in the 5th as songs; with Venus ruling the 12th of sorrow and Mercury ruling Saturn in the 11th of criticism.

Western Expansion. Both the Homestead Act and the Transcontinental Railroad, themes delineated through the Jupiter-Saturn conjunction, were not emphasized by biographers I consulted. However this does not mean these issues were not a focus of Lincoln during 1862. Remember not all events are reported. The direction of Ascendant conjunct Saturn in early Dec-1862 timed his Annual Message to Congress on 1-Dec-1862 for which he received criticism for his apparent commitment to compensated emancipation at this late date. One account does mention briefly that Lincoln's message included comments on the Transcontinental Railroad. If so, that would confirm Saturn's ties to the Transcontinental Railroad, for which I have delineated as the steam-spewing black steam engine slicing, destroying, and partitioning the American Great Plains.

CHAPTER THIRTEEN

Solar Returns: Hellenistic Lots

Lots as customized Ascendants. Because Lots are calculated points which usually include the Ascendant as an input, they represent a customized Ascendant for a specific area of life. Of all delineation tools, they are the most helpful in rescuing rectification from errors of under specification. Not all major life events are timed by dynamic activity to the angles.

Chapter Summary

Hellenistic Lots. For event timing, Lots are either directed or profected to promissors, just as the Ascendant or any other significator. A second method involves aspects of solar return planets to natal Lots.

Usefulness in Rectification. Because the Ascendant is usually one component of a lot's formula, the iterative testing of aspects between solar return planets and the degree of natal Lots simultaneously refines the natal Ascendant.

Lot Examples. A set of sixteen solar return examples is presented. Lot examples include fortune, spirit/faith, accidents, parents, siblings, marriage, and children.

Reference. Ramsay Wright's translation of Al-Biruni (1934, 283-295) was for many years the primary source of Lots for traditional astrologers. Bonatti's treatment of lots elucidates Al-Biruni's laundry list by giving insights on lot construction and application. See Zoller (1980) and Dykes (2007, 1040-1106). Another recent source is Meira Epstein's translation of Ibn Ezra's *Beginning of Wisdom* (Ezra 1998, 139-155).

Lots in Prediction

There are two primary methods of timing events with Lots. First is to direct or profect Lots in the same manner as the Ascendant and other significators. The second method is to examine whether a particular Lot is activated by a solar return. With regard to children:

> *Moreover he [Abu 'Ali al-Khayyat] said if Jupiter or Venus, in a revolution of years, were to arrive at the place of the Part of Children (or were to aspect it from a square aspect or the opposition), it signifies he is going to have children at that time (but Jupiter has greater signification in children) (Bonatti 2007, 1264).*

This statement by Abu 'Ali al-Khayyat is a key insight. Such is the power of solar return planets to activate natal Lots by aspect I believe this aphorism can be generalized further to virtually any Lot.

It is true that Lots can be set off by profections, directions, progressions, and transits. Solar return planet aspects are not their exclusive timers. Yet when solar return planets *do* aspect natal Lots, life affairs signified by the respective Lot are almost always brought to focus during the year.

Usefulness in Rectification

Lots are highly useful in rectification. Because most Lots include the Ascendant in their calculation, refining a Lot's position by either dynamic activity or solar return planet configuration simultaneously optimizes the Ascendant.

This chapter exemplifies the power of solar return planets to set off natal Lots. In many cases, the aspect is within 1-2 degrees of accuracy. Study the examples carefully and note that many times the solar return planet aspects the part's antiscion and not the lot directly. Use antiscia and contra-antiscia consistently. They are not advanced tools which need be reserved for unusual circumstances.

Lot Examples

What follows are sixteen solar returns which feature solar return planets activating natal Lots by aspect. Demonstrating these connections is the sole objective of this chapter. Though some solar return details are included, such as the sign of the profected Ascendant and the identification of the Lord of the Year, these are secondary. Full delineation of each return is not sought nor offered.

This research project makes the assumption the Lot of Fortune calculation should be reversed for nocturnal figures.

Overview of Hellenistic Lot Examples

Lots of Fortune. Herbert Hoover (#1) and Richard Nixon (#2)

Both Hoover and Nixon are nocturnal nativities. Consider their respective *Lots of Fortune*. They are an interesting pair because Hoover's LOF falls in the 1st; Nixon's falls in the 12th. If Ptolemy's incorrect *day-only* formula were used, Hoover's LOF would fall in the 12th and Nixon's in the 1st. There is an enormous difference when delineating the LOF in these two houses. The secrecy and illicitness of Nixon's political slush fund matches the 12th house LOF placement. Hoover's profits from his own actions as a business owner are demonstrated by the LOF placed in his 1st house.

Lot of Spirit/Lot of Faith. Franklin Pierce (#3) and James Garfield (#4)

For these two nocturnal nativities, I identify solar return planets aspecting one or both lots in years of religious conversion. There is no debate on calculation of the *Lot of Faith*, but it needs to be included with the *Lot of Spirit* for completeness. From my research, conversion is usually timed by some combination of dynamic activity to both lots. The Pierce example is also an excellent demonstration of the accuracy of the Mean Node compared to the True Node (see Chapter 14: *Lunar Nodes and Eclipses* for further discussion). There is a solar arc measurement which joins the North Node to the Lot of Spirit by 7 minutes of degree on the date of his baptism in the Episcopal Church.

Accidents. George H. W. Bush (#5) and George W. Bush (#6)

Bonatti lists two lots which use Mars and Saturn in their computation. The first *Lot of Illness according to Hermes* is listed as a 6th house lot. The second *Lot of Secret Enemies* is listed as a 12th house lot. Curiously, the sect adjustment is recommended only for the 6th house lot and not the second 12th house lot. This produces the strange result that for diurnal nativities both lots yield the same mathematical result. It appears something is amiss here. In my opinion, it is better to calculate two lots for all nativities covering both permutations of Mars & Saturn. For the moment I am referring to these parts as the *Lot of Illness/Accidents (1) and (2)*. It would be helpful to the literature if these names were standardized. Janus 5.5 refers to them as the *Lot of Infirmities and accidents and of inseparable vices* and the *Lot of Secret Enemies*.

Parents. William Howard Taft (#7)

For each parent, there exist two lots. For the father, *Lot of the Father* and *Lot of Death of the Father*. Likewise for the mother. Lots confirm the death of Taft's father using the 1890 return.

Grandparents. Benjamin Harrison (#8)

The *Lot of Grandfather* should prove helpful in rectifying nativities of younger individuals for whom few significant events exist. In some cases, the death of a grandparent ranks among the top 5 or 6 major life events for young children. Bonatti and Al-Biruni list two different formulas for the same lot. Although I have not made extensive tests of both lots, this example supports Bonatti's formula which is based on the Sun's ruler and Saturn, sidestepping the 2nd house cusp which Al-Biruni uses. Benjamin Harrison's grandfather was President William Harrison who died in office on 4-Apr-1841 following his Mar-1841 inauguration.

Siblings. Andrew Jackson (#9) and Richard Nixon (#10)

Of the more valuable family lots used in rectification of the Presidential Database was the *Lot of Death of Siblings*. The literature shows two formulas for this lot, with Abū Ma'shar, Ibn Ezra, and Bonatti subtracting the Sun from the MC. In empirical tests I could find no support for Al Biruni's variant which subtracts the Sun from the 3rd cusp + 10 degrees.

Marriage. John Adams (#11) and William Henry Harrison (#12)

There are many marriage lots beginning with Valens who uses Sun & Venus for males and Moon & Mars for females. From my experience these combinations proposed by Valens better time acts of sexual intercourse rather than marriage. I consider three marriage lots for this study. The first *Lot of Marriage* includes the 7th house cusp and Venus as its components. It appears to time love matches with sexual overtones more frequently than the next two lots attributed to Hermes. *The Lots of Marriage of Men and Women according to Hermes* includes both Venus and Saturn in their construction. The inclusion of Saturn in the Hermetic formulas appears to impart a degree of stability in marriage.

Be aware that sometimes these lots are activated in returns for years when a future spouse is met or when engagement commitments are made. This lot activation by the solar return may not be the year a marriage takes place.

Adultery. Grover Cleveland (#13)

Before his Presidential bid, Cleveland had an affair and an out-of-wedlock birth. This became a campaign issue. Mars in the solar return conjunct the *Lot of Adultery* in the 10th house of the return sets up the scandal during the campaign. Bonatti names this lot the *Lot of Intelligence and ease of marriage*. I believe Ibn Ezra is closer to the mark with the description *Lot of Adultery in Marriage*.

Special Note!! The public discussion of sexual preference and sexual activities of political figures can easily devolve into a tawdry affair better suited for tabloid journalists. While the sophistication of medieval techniques allows both delineation of sexual preference and prediction of sexual activity, let me state that attempts to publicly disseminate these results is not recommended for sitting political figures, much less than for the dead whose reputation is often policed by admirers and family descendants. I think a period of at least 100 years after death is required to discuss these matters openly without fear of reprisal. It's taken about that length of time before discussion of Jefferson's affair with his slave Sally Hemings to gain an air of public acceptability, though scorn is still directed to researchers of this topic from some circles.

Children. Amy Carter (#14) and Patti Davis (#15)

Both births of Amy Carter and Patti Davis are viewed from the perspective of their father's solar returns. In addition to the *Lot of Children* emphasized by Bonatti in his aphorism which opened this chapter, the *Lot of Sons* and *Lot of Daughters* cannot be overlooked. There are examples where these lots and *not* the *Lot of Children* are aspected in the solar return for years when children are born.

Death of Children. Ronald Reagan (#16)

Unlike the existence of lots for death of parents, there is no *Lot of Death of Children*. If this example proves representative, malefics in the solar return afflicting the *Lot of Children, Lot of Sons*, and/or *Lot of Daughters* are sufficient to induce harm to children. Keep in mind that harm need not be death. Malefics can cause illness, accidents, or verbal abuse. This example views the birth of a stillborn child by Jane Wyman from the perspective of her husband Ronald Reagan's solar return.

Table 32. Summary of Solar Return – Lot Examples.

#	Nativity	Lot	Event	Date
1	Herbert Hoover	Fortune	Smoot Hawley Act	17-Jun-1930
2	Richard Nixon	Fortune	Checkers Speech	23-Sep-1952
3	Franklin Pierce	Spirit/Faith	Baptism	3-Dec-1865
4	James Garfield	Spirit/Faith	Conversion	3-Mar-1850
5	George H. W. Bush	Accidents	Parachute Jump	2-Sep-1944
6	George W. Bush	Accidents	Bike Accident	7-Jul-2005
7	William Taft	Parents	Death of Father	21-May-1891
8	Benjamin Harrison	Grandparents	Death of Grandfather	4-Apr-1841
9	Andrew Jackson	Siblings	Death of Sibling	After Apr-1781
10	Richard Nixon	Siblings	Death of Sibling	7-Mar-1933
11	John Adams	Marriage	Marriage	27-Oct-1764
12	William Harrison	Marriage	Marriage	22-Nov-1795
13	Grover Cleveland	Adultery	Negative Publicity	Summer 1884
14	Jimmy Carter	Children	Birth of Amy Carter	19-Oct-1967
15	Ronald Reagan	Children	Birth of Patti Davis	22-Oct-1952
16	Ronald Reagan	Children	Stillborn Child	26-Jun-1947

Suggestions for Studying Lot Examples:

- Each solar return example is presented in biwheel format: natal (inner wheel); solar return (outer wheel). Solar Return Ascendant (ASC) and Midheaven (MC) are so labeled in the outer wheel. Intermediate house cusps for solar returns are not presented.

- Familiarize yourself with the lot's placement and delineation in the natal figure.

- Delineate the solar return based on principles outlined in Chapters 11 and 12.

- Focus on aspects between solar return planets and natal lots as a method of further refining delineation techniques found in Chapters 11 and 12.

Lot Calculation Example: Richard Nixon

Name of Lot	Formula	Sect	Lot	Antiscion
Death of Siblings	MC – Sun + ASC	Yes	20AR47	9VI13

Step 1. *Calculate lots based on **natal figures** found in the Presidential database.* Each of the following examples displays natal lot calculations and a Solar Return figure. Though Bonatti indicates a second set of lots can be calculated from the solar return, this is *not* the procedure followed here.

Step 2. *Convert zodiacal degrees of each component to a 360 degree scale.*

Item	Position	360 Degree Conversion
MC	13GE38	73deg 38min
Sun	19CP23	289deg 23min
ASC	15VI02	165deg 02min

Step 3. *Determine whether a sect adjustment is required.*

Nixon's figure is nocturnal. Sect adjustments are a consideration for nocturnal figures. If the Sect box is marked YES (which is the case here) reverse the first two components in the formula; e.g., revised formula = Sun – MC + ASC.

Step 4. *Compute the formula.*

For this step, first calculate Sun - MC. Next add this difference to the Ascendant.

[Sun - MC] + ASC =

[289deg 23min – 73deg 38min] + 165deg 02min =

215deg 45min + 165deg 02min = 380deg 47min //subtract 360deg// 20deg 47min

Lot of Death of Siblings = **20AR47**

Antiscion of Lot of Death of Siblings = **9VI13**

Special Note: Be careful to add or subtract degrees if the 0 Aries Point is crossed. An adjustment of 360 degrees may be required. Example ~ Compute the distance from 20 Pisces to 10 Aries. 20 Pisces is 350 degrees; 10 Aries is 10 degrees. 10deg – 350deg is a negative number. Need to add 360deg to the terminal point 10 Aries before making the subtraction. (10deg + 360deg) – 350deg = 20 degrees.

1. Fortune – Herbert Hoover

Name of Lot	Formula	Sect	Lot	Antiscion
Lot of Fortune	Moon – Sun + ASC	Yes	13GE13	16CA47

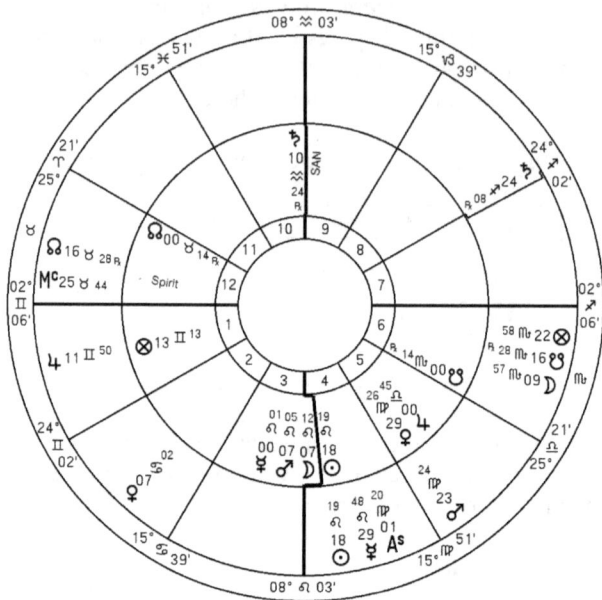

Event: Hoover signed the Smoot-Hawley tariff legislation on 17-Jun-1930.

Natal: Lot of Fortune in 1st ruled by Mercury in the 4th ties Hoover's finances to the gold mining business. He was a self-made successful millionaire.

Profection: 8th house year. 8th house is investments, stock market, and foreign trade. All influenced Hoover's life this year. LOY is Saturn.

Return: LOY Saturn is partile conjunct the natal 8th house cusp 24SA02 (AL). Saturn/Sagittarius signifies tariff legislation infused with a sober judgment of the issue. Hoover's initial proposal included flexible tariffs (up to 50% higher *OR* lower) with the goal of offsetting *either* higher domestic costs *or* lower international costs of production. As Saturn's ruler, Jupiter/Gemini signifies the flexible tariff philosophy. Return's Jupiter is conjunct natal LOF. The final legislation Hoover signed included high fixed tariffs for agricultural goods mandated by Congress. Return's Mars/Virgo, ruling natal 11th of political alliances including Congress falls in the return's 1st ruling the 8th of trade. Mars signifies a tax on foreign agricultural products because Virgo is the sign of sown crops. The return's LOF is heavily afflicted by the South Node and Mars by rulership. The return's South Node is partile trine the antiscion of natal LOF.

2. Fortune – Richard Nixon

Name of Lot	Formula	Sect	Lot	Antiscion
Lot of Fortune	Moon – Sun + ASC	Yes	14LE24	15TA36

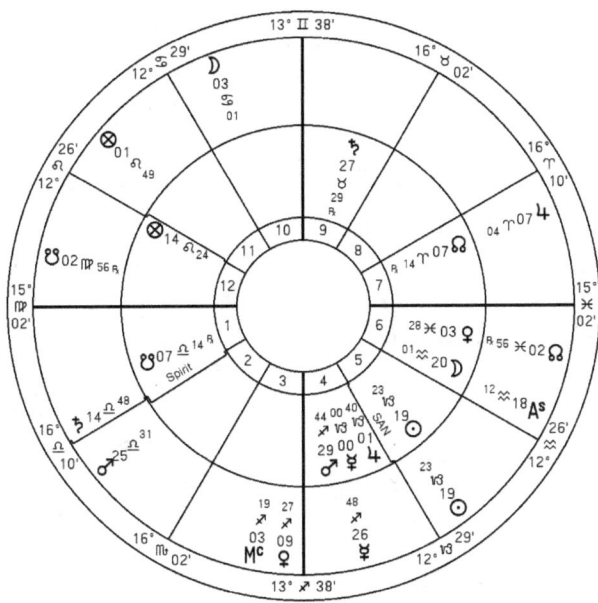

Event: On 23-Sep-1952, Richard Nixon made his televised *Checkers* speech to defend charges of conflict of interest from an unreported campaign fund.

Natal: Lot of Fortune in 12th shows money from secret and illegal dealings. Lord Sun/Capricorn/5th shows wealthy old men interested his election success.

Profection: 4nd house year. LOY is Jupiter. Fund was started in 1950 which was a 2nd house year.

Return: Return's LOF recapitulates the Leo placement found in the natal. For the return, LOF in 7th signifies enmity from fortunes because LOF ruler Sun is placed in the 12th of mistakes and illegality. But the story ends well. Moon applies to LOY Jupiter. Compared to natal Jupiter/Capricorn in his fall, LOY Jupiter/Aries is stronger. By transit Jupiter is conjunct North Node in natal 8th of partner's money and amplifies contributions from the public Nixon received following his Checkers speech. Jupiter falls in the return's 3rd which gives Nixon favorable publicity. Jupiter disposes Venus/Sagittarius which transits the natal 4th house, emphasized by profection. Both the return's Venus and Jupiter form a grand trine with natal LOF which is the key solar return planet – natal Hellenistic Lot link which guaranteed Nixon success this year.

3. Spirit/Faith – Franklin Pierce

Name of Lot	Formula	Sect	Lot	Antiscion
Lot of Spirit	Sun – Moon + ASC	Yes	0AR47	29VI13
Lot of Faith	Mercury – Moon + ASC	Yes	2AR35	27VI25

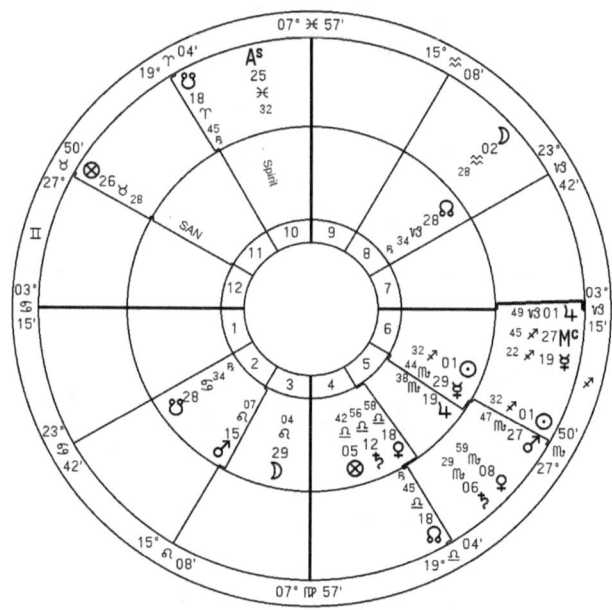

Event: Franklin Pierce was baptized on 3-Dec-1865 (Episcopal Church).

Natal: Both lots in Aries fall in the natal 11th of political alliances and are ruled by Mars/Leo (significator of pro-southern states rights philosophy). Note Pierce's religious conversion occurred only after his health was ruined and the outbreak of the Civil War showed the futility of his philosophy.

Profection: 2nd house year. LOY Sun, universal significator of spirit, falls in the return's 10th house (WS), within 2 degrees of the return's 9th house cusp (AL).

Return: Moon falls in natal 9th and sextiles both lots. Sun's ruler Jupiter occupies the superior square aspect of both lots.

Dynamic: csa North Node 00AR40 is partile conjunct Lot of Spirit on day of conversion (7 minutes error!). dsa Sun 00LI39 opposed the same lot.

Transits: On 3-Dec-1865 trMercury 2CP28 just passed the superior square to the Lot of Faith. The following day, Moon translated Mercury to Jupiter 4CP14.

4. Spirit/Faith – James Garfield

Name of Lot	Formula	Sect	Lot	Antiscion
Lot of Spirit	Sun – Moon + ASC	Yes	1AQ03	28SC57
Lot of Faith	Mercury – Moon + ASC	Yes	27CP15	2SA45

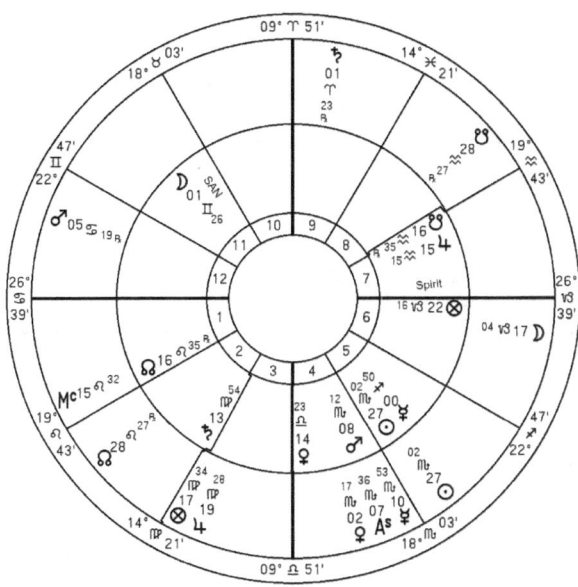

Event: On 3-Mar-1850, James Garfield converted to the Disciples of Christ.

Natal: Pisces on the 9th cusp, Lord Jupiter conjunct South Node within a degree and disposed by Saturn is afflicted and blocks 9th house affairs. Until the return.

Profection: 7th house year. Lot of Faith on the natal 7th cusp activated by position.

Return: With the antiscion of the Lot of Spirit conjunct the Sun, it is tricky to distinguish the impact of the return's Nodes square the Lot of Spirit's antiscion and the Sun. Recall that the Lot of Spirit is also known as the Lot of the Sun because the Sun is the universal significator of the soul. Return's Saturn, who in the natal disposes 9th house ruler Jupiter, is sextile the Lot of Spirit in the return.

Dynamic: csa Jupiter and South Node at 26CP51 and 28CP11 respectively conjunct the Lot of Faith.

Return & Transits: In the return, Moon separates from Mercury and applies to Jupiter. The same configuration exists on 3-Mar-1850, the exact date of his conversion, with tr. Mercury partile conjunct natal Jupiter.

5. Accidents – George H. W. Bush

Name of Lot	Formula	Sect	Lot	Antiscion
Illness/Accidents (1)	Saturn – Mars + ASC	Yes	8TA50	21LE10
Illness/Accidents (2)	Mars – Saturn + ASC	Yes	8CP04	21SA56

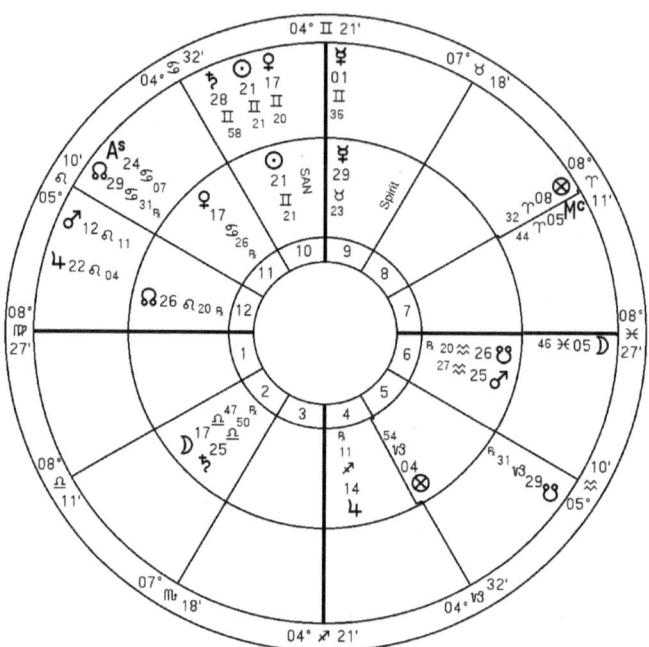

Example: On 2-Sep-1944, George H. W. Bush was shot down in an air raid over the island of Chichi Jima, nearly died, and lost two crewmates. Yet he survived after making a successful parachute jump.

Natal: Jupiter/Sagittarius/4th shows a success in flight because Jupiter is the greater benefic and Sagittarius is the sign of flight. Jupiter positioned in the 4th means parachute jumps result in successful landings on the ground.

Profection: 9th house year. LOY = Venus falls in return's 12th of mistakes, enemies, and imprisonment. Note the first Lot of Illness/Accidents at 8TA49 is partile conjunct the profected Ascendant at 8TA27 on the day of the solar return.

Return: Jupiter transits the natal 12th and falls in the return's 2nd. Note also Jupiter rules the return's 9th in a 9th house profected year. Jupiter conjunct the antiscion of the Lot of Illness/Accidents allows Bush to evade capture from the Japanese via a successful parachute jump. This underscores the power of benefics to release the evil of dangerous lots.

6. Accidents – George W. Bush

Name of Lot	Formula	Sect	Lot	Antiscion
Illness/Accidents (1)	Saturn – Mars + ASC	Yes	19VI50	10AR10
Illness/Accidents (2)	Mars – Saturn + ASC	Yes	24GE14	5CA46

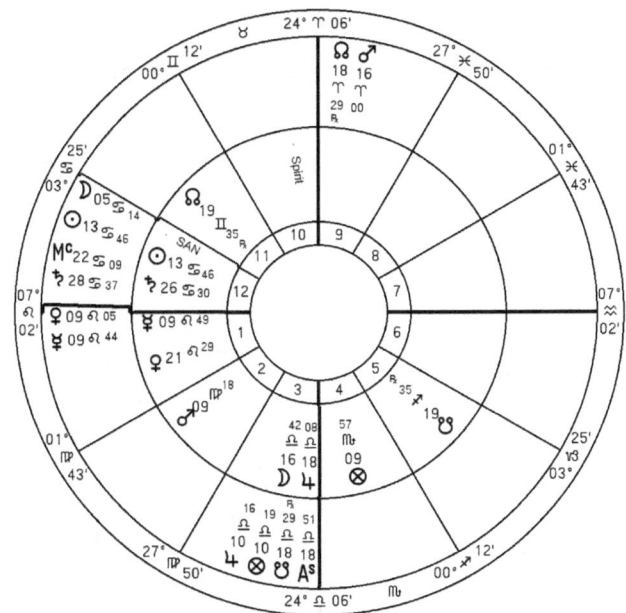

Example: On 7-Jul-2005, while exercising at a G-8 meeting, George W. Bush fell off his bicycle while exercising. On the same day, London was racked with a multiple bombing of the transportation system. Hurricane Katrina also marked the year as did negative publicity for extraordinary rendition of enemy combatants.

Natal: In mundane astrology, Saturn/Cancer signifies floods.

Profection: 12th house year. LOY is the Moon.

Return: This is an unusual return because the natal Jupiter-Saturn square is recapitulated. It is amplified by the Nodes and Mars which form a t-square. 12th house delineations are often difficult because they remain hidden to the public. The combination of a Saturn return and the natal 12th placed angular on the return's 10th for all to see shows revelations of an otherwise secret house. Moon applies to Jupiter/Libra in both natal and return. However the return's Jupiter is diminished by the South Node. Moon, little light in her final waning hours, is partile conjunct the antiscion of the 2nd Lot of Illness/Accidents. As natal hilaj, the Moon conjunct this lot promises an accident and problems with enemies.

7. Parents – William Taft

Name of Lot	Formula	Sect	Lot	Antiscion
Lot of the Father	Saturn – Sun + ASC	Yes	7CA57	22GE03
Lot of Death of Father	Jupiter – Saturn + ASC	Yes	20CA35	9GE25

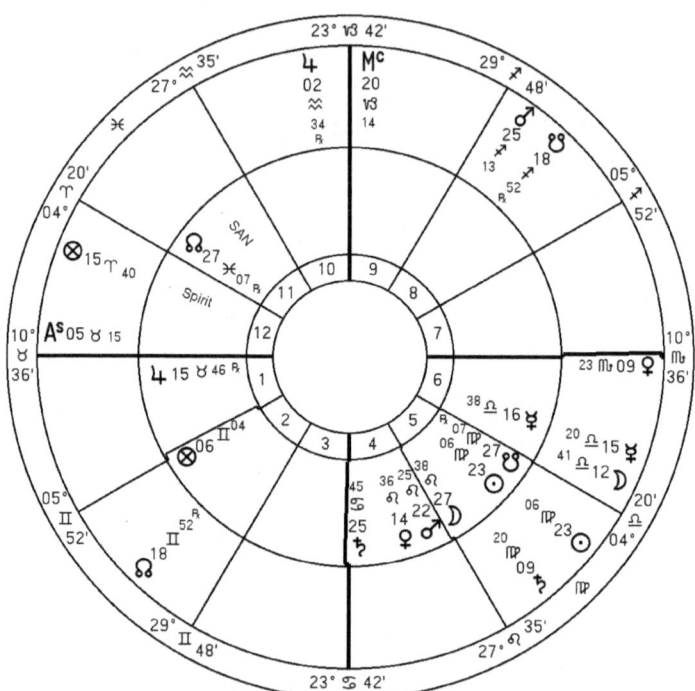

Event: On 21-May-1891, William Taft's father died.

Profection: 10th house year. LOY = Sun.

Return: The position of the natal angles is recapitulated which brings additional focus to the Sun falling in the 5th of both natal and return. Sun is also LOY. The 11th house is 8th from the 4th and signifies death of the father. 11th house ruler Saturn is conjunct the Sun. The t-square established by the Nodes, Mars, Sun, and Saturn in mutable signs aspect the antiscia of both lots.

Most telling is Lot of Death of the Father 20CA35; partile conjunct the 4th cusp of the father in the return.

8. Grandparents – Benjamin Harrison

Name of Lot	Formula	Sect	Lot	Antiscion
Grandfather - Bonatti	Saturn – Lord Sun + ASC	Yes	15AQ04	14SC56

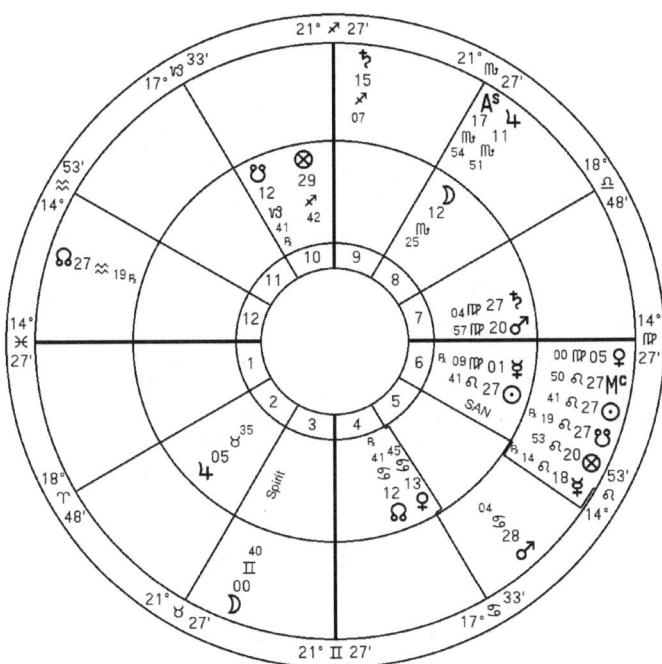

Event: On 4-Apr-1841, Benjamin Harrison's grandfather William Henry Harrison died shortly after his Presidential inauguration.

Profection: 8th house year. LOY is Venus.

Return: The first indication of death is the return's South Node partile conjunct the Sun. At this point it is uncertain if the father or grandfather has problems. Derived houses refine the choice. If father is the 4th, then grandfather (father's father) is 4th from the 4th, or the 7th house. Death of grandfather is 8th from the 7th, or the 2nd house.

In the return, Saturn in the 2nd is partile sextile to the Lot of Grandfathers. Jupiter is lord of the 2nd. Both Jupiter and the return's Ascendant are conjunct the antiscion of the same lot. At time of death, trNorth Node 15AQ04 is partile conjunct the Lot of Grandfather with trSun conjunct the 2nd natal cusp.

9. Siblings – Andrew Jackson

Name of Lot	Formula	Sect	Lot	Antiscion
Siblings	Jupiter – Saturn + ASC	No	5LE19	24TA41
Death of Siblings	MC – Sun + ASC	Yes	26AQ42	3SC18

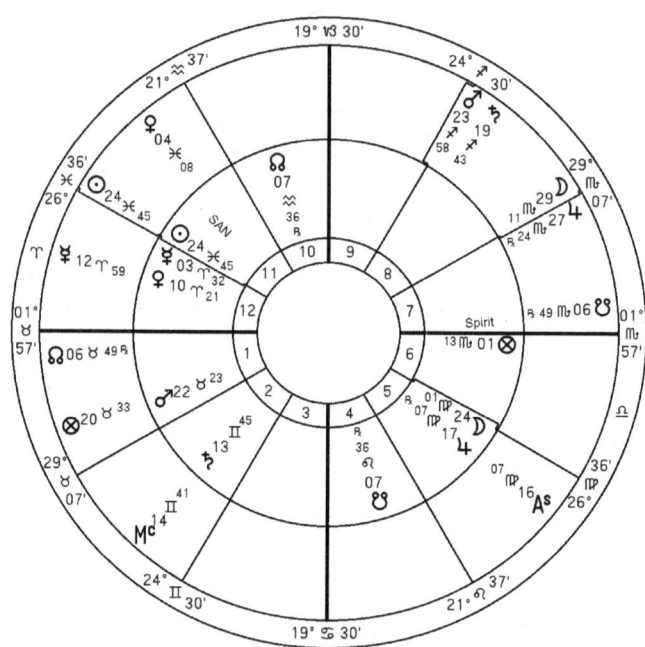

Events: Following capture and torture, Andrew Jackson's brother Robert was released from captivity, contracted smallpox, and died after April 1781. Jackson suffered a head wound while in captivity. His mother died in the fall of 1781.

Profection: 3rd house year. This highlights siblings. LOY is the Moon.

Return: The return's South Node 6SC49 falling in the 3rd of siblings conjunct the antiscion of the Lot of Death of Siblings (~4 degrees) spells trouble. Mars, lord of the 3rd, is conjunct Saturn in the 4th. Because Capricorn rules the natal 10th (death of siblings), both its primary rulers – Saturn by sign and Mars by exaltation – in the return's 4th suggest a bad ending to the years' events.

Comparing the return to the natal, see that tr. Mercury, lord of the natal 3rd, falls in the natal 12th of imprisonment conjunct Venus/Aries which signifies the sadistic treatment at the hands of the British soldiers. Also note the return's MC 14GE41 is conjunct natal Saturn 13GE45. This is bad for Jackson's mother and his brother. Recall the 10th signifies both the mother and death of siblings (8th from the 3rd).

10. Siblings – Richard Nixon

Name of Lot	Formula	Sect	Lot	Antiscion
Siblings	Jupiter – Saturn + ASC	No	19AR16	10VI44
Death of Siblings	MC – Sun + ASC	Yes	20AR47	9VI13

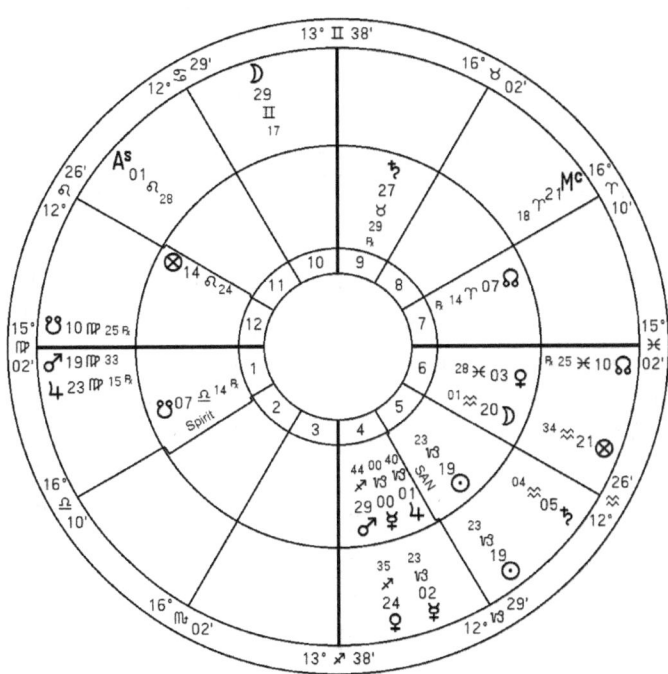

Event: Richard Nixon's brother Harold died on 7-Mar-1933.

Natal: Mercury conjunct Mars joins the lord of the 10th (Gemini) and the lord of the 3rd (Scorpio). This configuration suggests the early death of siblings.

Profection: 3rd house year. LOY is the Moon.

Return: Mercury returns to its natal sign and rules the 3rd of siblings (QS). Mercury applies to Mars, 10th house lord, with reception. 10th signifies death of siblings because it is 8th from the 3rd. This configuration could be delineated as aggressive (Mars) verbal (Mercury) sparring with office co-workers (Mercury in 6th). But it is the contact between solar return planets and natal lots which further specify the Mercury-Mars configuration to the death of Nixon's brother. The return's South Node is conjunct antiscion of Lot of Siblings within 12 minutes of degree.

11. Marriage – John Adams

Name of Lot	Formula	Sect	Lot	Antiscion
Marriage	7th cusp – Venus + ASC	No	4SC28	25AQ32
Mar. Men - Hermes	Venus – Saturn + ASC	No	1LE39	28TA21

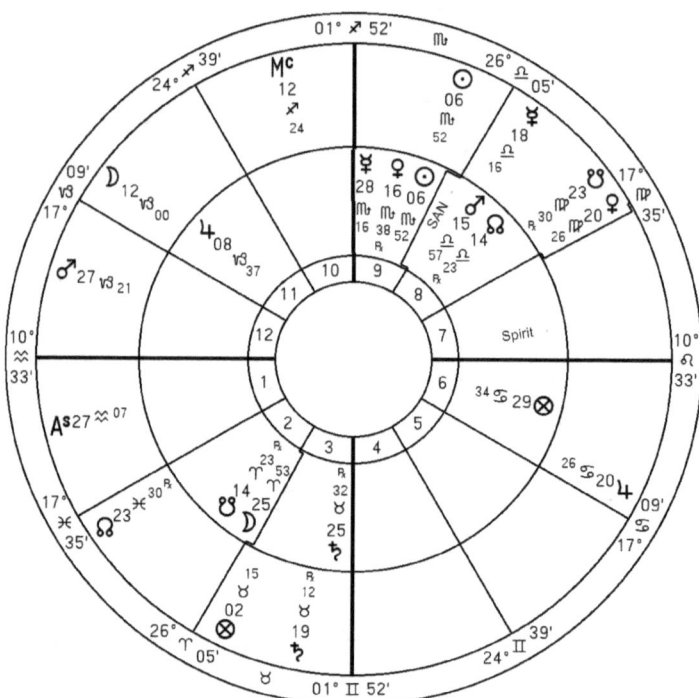

Event: John Adams married Abigail Smith on 27-Oct-1764.

Natal: Venus opposed Saturn suggests emotional coldness and difficulty with women. Compare this placement to Venus and Saturn in the return.

Profection: 6th house year. LOY is the Moon.

Return: Angles of the natal figure are recapitulated and this marks Adam's first Saturn return. Saturn, lord of the 1st, widely opposes the Sun, lord of the 7th. The natal Venus/Saturn opposition is ameliorated in the return by trine.

The return's Ascendant is partile conjunct the antiscion of the Lot of Marriage. Here the Lot aspects not a solar return planet, but a solar return angle. This is an interesting variation of the rule that solar return planets must aspect natal Lots to trigger their effects.

12. Marriage – William Henry Harrison

Name of Lot	Formula	Sect	Lot	Antiscion
Marriage	7th cusp – Venus + ASC	No	6LE54	24TA06
Mar. Men - Hermes	Venus – Saturn + ASC	No	10GE27	19CA33

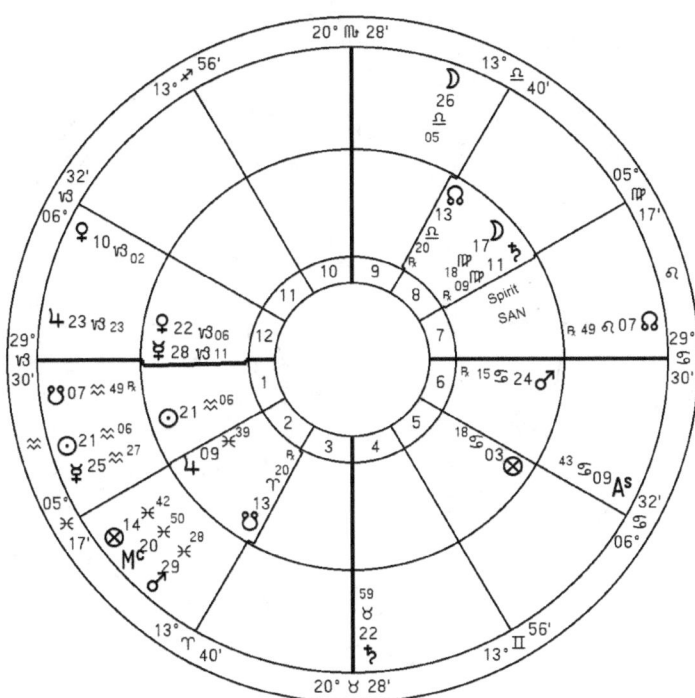

Event: William Henry Harrison married Anna Tuthill Symmes on 22-Nov-1795.

Profection: 9th house year. LOY is the Moon.

Return: Venus on the 7th cusp, Venus applies by trine to 7th house ruler Saturn with mutual reception by trine, and the North Node's conjunction to the Lot of Marriage all favor marriage in 1795.

Transits: On the wedding day, transiting Saturn 11GE02 and Venus 9SA34 aspect the Lot of Marriage of Men a/c Hermes by conjunction and opposition.

13. Adultery – Grover Cleveland

Name of Lot	Formula	Sect	Lot	Antiscia
Adultery[20]	Moon – Sun + Venus	No	1LE33	28TA27

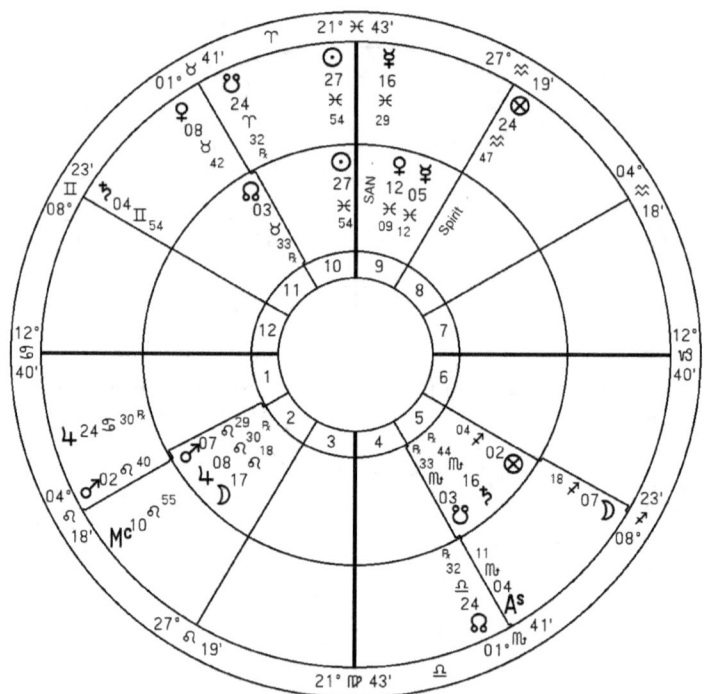

Event: During Cleveland's 1st Presidential Campaign, it was discovered that Cleveland sired an illegitimate child in 1874. Opponents made fodder of this event with the campaign ditty "Ma, Ma, where's my Pa?" (Nevins 1933, 177).

Profection: 12th house year. LOY is Mercury.

Return: Mars at 2LE40 in the return's MC is conjunct the Lot of Adultery just over one degree. LOY Mercury, ruler of the natal 12th house of rumors, is placed in the 5th house of children for the return.

---

[20] Ibn Ezra names this the Lot of Adultery in Marriage. Bonatti names it the Lot of Intelligence and Ease of Marriage. My research confirms Ibn Ezra's characterization.

14. Children – Jimmy Carter

Name of Lot	Formula	Sect	Lot	Antiscion
Children	Saturn – Jupiter + ASC	Yes	9VI34	20AR26
Sons	Jupiter – Moon + ASC	No	22SC54	7AQ06
Daughters	Venus – Moon + ASC	No	1LE47	28TA13

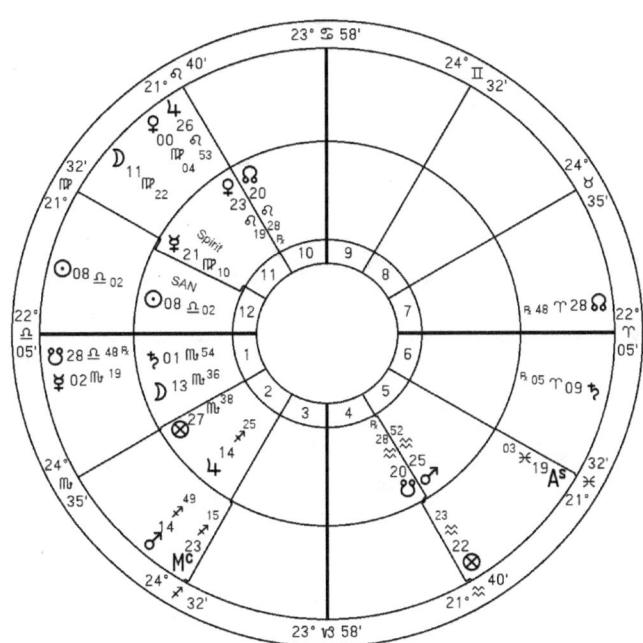

Event: Jimmy Carter's fourth child, Amy, was born on 19-Oct-1967.

Profection: 8th house year. LOY is Venus.

Return: Both return's Venus and Moon are in Virgo with srMoon 11VI22 conjunct the L.Children within two degrees. srMoon also rules the return's 5th of children. Born just 17 days after Carter's solar return, trVenus moves within a degree of the L.Children on the day of birth.

Note the fact that both Moon and Venus are in the barren sign of Virgo does not deny Carter children. The return's Ascendant is Pisces, a fertile sign.

There is another minor measurement which may not be relevant: srJupiter 26LE53 is square the anticision of the L.Daughters.

15. Children – Ronald Reagan

Name of Lot	Formula	Sect	Lot	Antiscion
Children	Saturn – Jupiter + ASC	Yes	19CA03	10GE57
Sons	Jupiter – Moon + ASC	No	5CA47	24GE13
Daughters	Venus – Moon + ASC	No	25LI44	4PI16

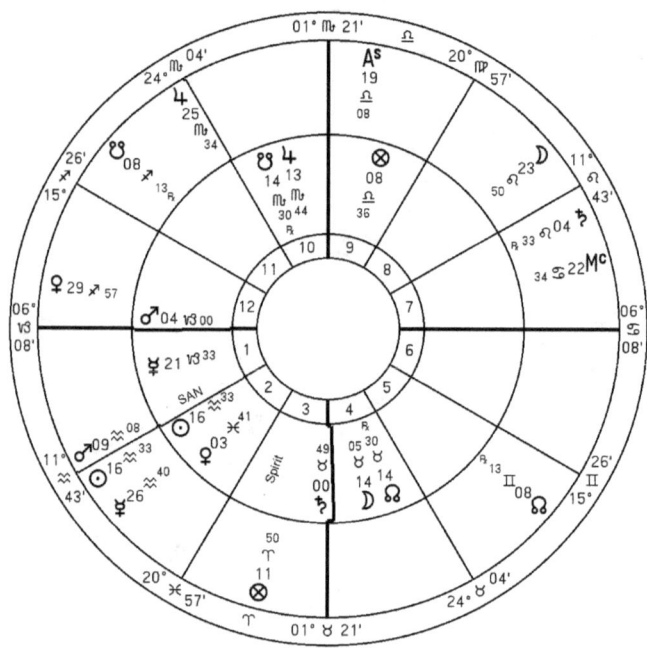

Event: First wife Jane Wyman gave birth to a stillborn child on 26-Jun-1947.

Profection: 1st house year. LOY is Saturn. LOP is Mercury.

Return: *NEW* Mercury rules the 12th and is placed in the 5th. Since the 12th is the 8th from the 5th, or death of children, ruler of the 12th in the 5th results in the death of children. By primary directions, the return's directed Ascendant meets Mercury on 24-Jun-1947 two days before death.

Venus rules natal 5th of children and transits to natal 12th for the return. The return's Venus and Lunar Nodes fall in the Gemini/Sagittarius axis which picks up the antiscion of both Lots of Children and Sons.

16. Children – Ronald Reagan

Name of Lot	Formula	Sect	Lot	Antiscion
Children	Saturn – Jupiter + ASC	Yes	19CA03	10GE57
Sons	Jupiter – Moon + ASC	No	5CA47	24GE13
Daughters	Venus – Moon + ASC	No	25LI44	4PI16

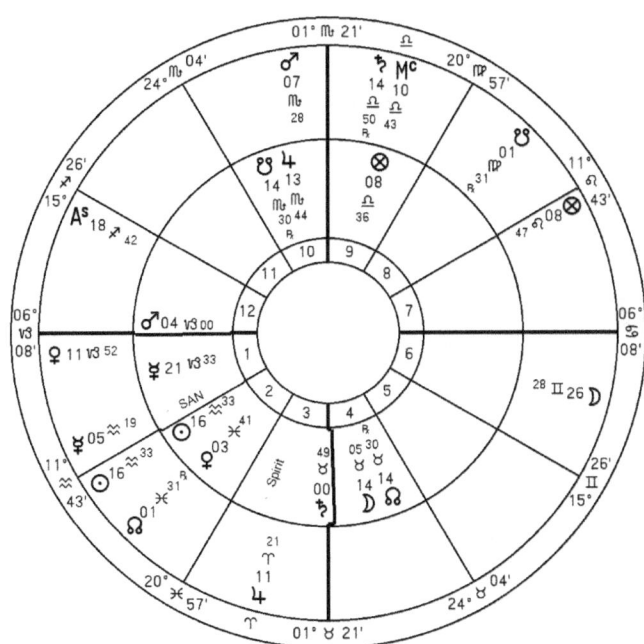

Event: Birth of Patti Davis on 22-Oct-1952

Profection: 6th house year. LOY is Mercury.

Return: Ascendant Lord Jupiter falls in the return's 5th of children (WS) and sextiles the antiscion of the Lot of Children. North Node 1PI31 is conjunct the antisicion of the Lot of Daughters within 3 degrees.

Other Reagan children:

1940 return (birth of Maureen 4-Jan-1941) North Node 23LI57 conjunct the Lot of Daughters 25LI44 within 2 degrees.

1958 return (birth of Ron Jr. on 20-May-1958) Jupiter and North Node fall in the 5th, with North Node 5SC28 trine Lot of Sons 5CA47.

CHAPTER FOURTEEN

Lunar Nodes and Eclipses

Eclipses are one of the most powerful predictive tools in all branches of astrology. They signify both beginnings and endings. Endings may be dramatic. Originally developed as a predictive tool in mundane astrology, many eclipse principles are directly applicable to natal astrology. Eclipses follow an 18.6 year cycle based on the time it takes for the Lunar Nodes to transit 360 degrees of the zodiac. Because eclipses are special cases of New and Full Moons which fall near the Lunar Nodes, the Chapter begins with the Nodes.

Chapter Summary

Lunar Nodes. The first debate of whether the Nodes signify gain/loss or increase/decrease is settled in favor of the increase/decrease effect. The second debate surrounding choice over the Mean or True Node calculation assumption is settled in favor of the Mean Node. This finding is confirmed by the ability of directions of the Mean Node to more accurately time events when compared to the True Node. Transits of the Lunar Nodes to the angles are one of the most accurate rectification methods because they time events which connect the native to the world-at-large for which a public record likely exists.

Eclipses. Because rules for judging the effects of eclipses on nativities are scant relative to rules for their application in mundane astrology, the best tactic is to apply mundane guidelines to natal astrology. Eclipses exert great power when conjunct natal significators. Despite the ability of eclipses to trigger major life events, two factors limit their usefulness in rectification. First, proximity to the exact degree of each significator need not be precise for eclipse effects to occur. This limits the ability of eclipses to define an angle's specific degree in rectification's reverse engineering approach. Second, eclipse effects are often triggered subsequent to the actual eclipse date. If not actively testing eclipses side-by-side other rectification tools; it is easy to miss identification of a prior eclipse as the cause behind a specific event.

LUNAR NODES

North Node (Ascending Node, Dragon's Head, Caput Draconis, Caput)
South Node (Descending Node, Dragon's Tail, Cauda Draconis, Cauda)

Definition. What are the Nodes? The Lunar Nodes are mathematical calculations which mark the two positions where the Moon's orbit crosses the ecliptic. The North Node occurs where the Moon moves from South to North in its orbit; the South Node, vice versa.

There are two debates surrounding Lunar Nodes in contemporary practice. First is whether the Nodes signify gain/loss or increase/decrease. Second is whether the True or Mean calculation assumption should be used.

Debate: Do Nodes signify gain/loss or increase/decrease?

Consider Al Biruni's opinion:

> *Many astrologers attribute a definite nature to the ascending and descending nodes, saying that the former is warm and beneficent and denotes an increase in all things, and the latter cold, maleficent, and accompanied by a diminution of influences. It is related that the Babylonians held that the ascending node increases the effects of both beneficent and maleficent planets, but it is not every one who will accept these statements, for the analogy seems to be rather farfetched (Al-Biruni 1934, 233-234).*

Though Al Biruni casts doubt on the ability of the North Node to increase effects of both benefics and malefics by conjunction, Abū Ma'shar has no qualms about such interpretation. In fact, Abū Ma'shar goes further to state the South Node functions as a benefic when conjunct malefics (e.g., two negatives make a positive) and the South Node destroys the power of a benefic by conjunction (Abū Ma'shar 1994, 57).

Example: Jimmy Carter's 1962 Election Campaign

As a test case, consider Carter's figure with Mars conjunct South Node in the 5th. As detailed in the rectification, the Mars-Ascendant direction timed Carter's 1962 election victory against Georgia segregationists following the Supreme Court's decision in *Baker v. Carr* to enforce the 'One Man, One Vote' rule (Carter 1992). For Carter, Mars/Aquarius signifies segregationists because they fight against the Aquarian principle of inclusion. The South Node diminishes Mars' power by conjunction. I suggest this configuration impacted Carter's election process because elections are a 5th house affair. Both these significations of Mars and the South Node were evident in Carter's 1962 victory timed by the Mars direction.

What happened? After manipulating the election process directly and challenging Carter after his victory, the segregationists eventually faded away. They gave up. These results match the spirit of Abū Ma'shar's statement that the tail is a benefic when conjunct a malefic; restating the mathematical axiom that two negatives make a positive. The difference in Carter's example is for the time period of six weeks before the segregationists went away, Carter experienced malicious violation of civil rights at the hands of segregationists. For Carter's example, there was a temporal condition which had to be satisfied before the power of the malefic was diminished.

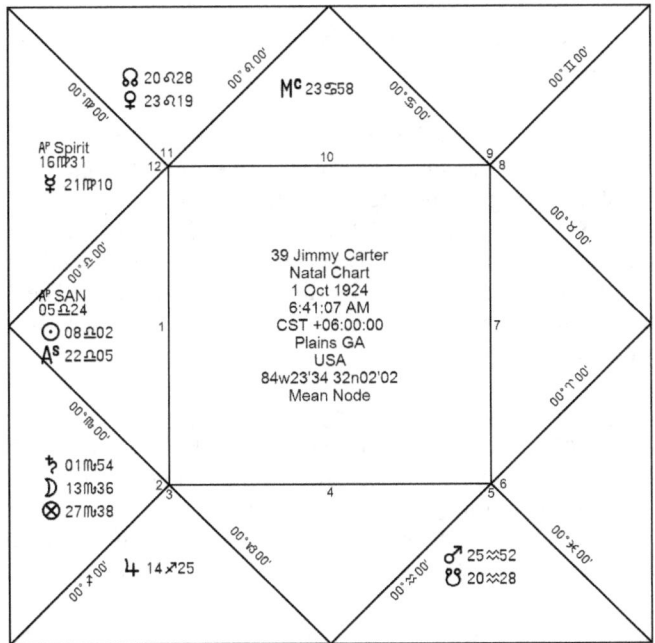

Debate: Use Mean or True Node for Node's position?

There is a slight difference between the Lunar Node's *true* mathematical position and its *average* or *mean* position. Historically the mean position was used. Only with the advent of astrological software since the mid-1980s has the Lunar Node's true position ever been an option. What is the difference? Basically the true position wobbles around the mean position like a sine wave ebbs and flows around its midline. Periodically the true and mean positions are identical. Their maximum difference is roughly 1 ½ degrees. Considering that uncertainty of one degree in the actual Node's position produces a forecast difference of approximately one year when using directions, the choice between the mean and true position is not trivial.

It is very easy to test the relative merit of either assumption by comparing the accuracy of directions to the angles using both mean and true positions. Simply perform this test on a wide sample and render judgment. Based on the Presidential Database, the mean position consistently beat the true position when evaluating directions and transits to the angles against actual life events.

Hoover's Lunar Nodes: a Rosetta Stone for the Mean/True Node debate?

North Node position (True Node): 29AR29
North Node position (Mean Node): 00TA14

South Node position (True Node): 29LI29
South Node position (Mean Node): 00SC14

Because the calculated position for Herbert Hoover's mean and true Lunar Node positions fall in different signs, their delineation by sign should offer an important clue for solving the debate. Consider the North Node. First, what does the North Node signify in the 12th? Because the 12th is the house of enemies, mistakes, confinement, and hospitalization; those affairs will be increased/accentuated because of the North Node's placement. The North Node increases the evil of a bad house. The Node's sign and ruler specify the cause of 12th house problems.

Delineation 1. North Node in Taurus ruled by Venus/Virgo signifies fraud, a *fall in value*, out-of-favor investments, poorly run business operations, and the lack of Venus-signified foodstuffs because Venus in Virgo is in detriment and fall. Because of the unusual configuration with Mercury and Jupiter, in most cases Hoover can harness his business expertise to surmount these difficulties. (See Chapter 7: *Temporal Indicators* for a review of this configuration).

Delineation 2. North Node in Aries ruled by Mars/Leo signifies hospitalization from Mars/Leo-signified heroics. Why? Mars/Leo gives Hoover courage in dangerous situations where he is prone to making mistakes and receiving injuries. This is the Hoover, who while trapped in Peking during the Boxer Rebellion, asked for a rifle and once holding it lost all fear. With the tendency of Mars/Leo individuals to run towards the fire, it's not difficult to see how Hoover's attraction to danger could cause 12th house problems were the North Node in Aries.

There are three ways to test which delineation is correct: (1) examine life events during the Node's Firdaria periods, (2) review events timed by Nodal returns, and (3) consider events timed by directions of the Nodes to the angles.

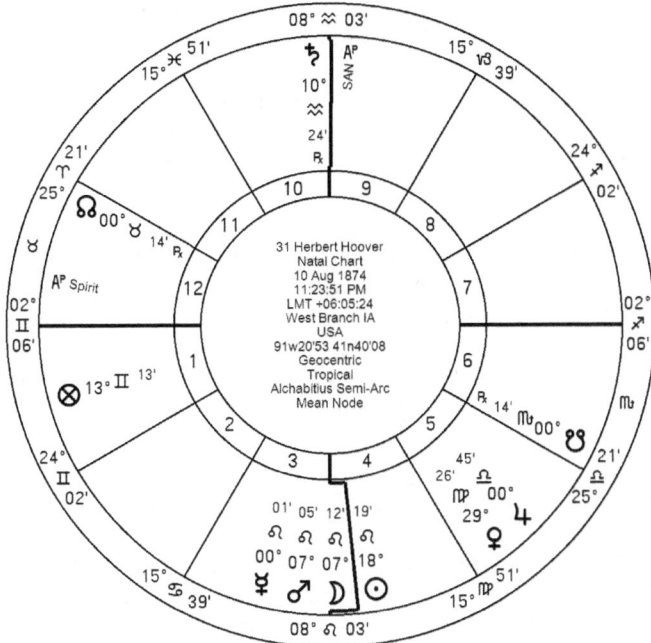

North Node Firdaria Period: 10-Aug-1913 to 9-Aug-1916. At this time World War I broke out and Hoover agreed to head the Belgian Food Relief Efforts on 19-Oct-1914. Hoover's decision to take the post was also timed by a MC-Nodal direction (See Direction of Nodes to the Angles, next page).

In my opinion, Belgians living under German occupation should be assigned to the 12th house because confinement is a 12th house affair. Their numbers were in the millions, confirming the power of the North Node to increase the affairs of a bad house. As ruler, Venus shows the cause: unavailability of foodstuffs because Venus is in her fall. Yet Hoover overcomes these privations because of his unusual Mercury-Venus-Jupiter configuration.

Nodal Return: 14-Jun-1930. After the Senate passed the Conference Tariff Report on 13 June, the stock market started to decline on 16 June when it was rumored Hoover would sign the infamous Smoot-Hawley Tariff legislation which he did on 17-Jun-1930. The legislation included provisions for high fixed tariffs on imported agricultural products to support the domestic agricultural industry, suffering from declining prices. Recall that one signification of Venus/Virgo is a fall in price. Because Virgo is the sign of sown crops, Venus/Virgo is further specified to low prices for agricultural goods. In these situations, Hoover's normal modus operandi was to use his own business skills to stage a recovery in value.

In this case, he sought fairness in tariffs because Jupiter, to which Mercury applies, rules the 8th of trade (QS). He argued for flexible tariff provisions, read through Jupiter/Gemini in Hoover's 1929 solar return (see Chapter 13), but had to accept Congressional demands for high fixed tariffs on farm products to get the legislation passed. This was considered one of the worst mistakes of his Presidency. Passage of the Smoot-Hawley tariff legislation set off a trade war which aggravated declines in business activity.

The role that undervalued agricultural products played in Hoover's mistake by signing the Smoot-Hawley tariff legislation vindicates the North Node's placement in Taurus, not Aries.

Direction of Nodes to the Angles. Consider the following direction of converse MC trine North Node, with two dates calculated for each Nodal assumption:

Herbert Hoover	True Node 29AR27	Mean Node 00TA14
PT dex trine NN c. => MC	3-Sep-1915	29-Oct-1914

Both directions time Hoover's involvement with the World War I Belgium Food Relief Commission. He agreed to head the Commission on 19-Oct-1914, a close match for the mean position assumption. The 3-Sep-1915 date is less significant; Hoover had made a successful plea to the Germans to maintain the relief programs earlier on 5-Aug-1915.

This finding is consistent with activity during the North Node's Firdaria period and its 1930 return. Each of these three evaluation methods support the Lunar Node's mean position as the correct calculation assumption.

More Evidence Favoring the Mean Node over True Node

For Benjamin Harrison, Theodore Roosevelt, and George W. Bush, there is no ambiguity over the Node's sign placement. But directions to the angles vary as much as two years. These examples favor the Mean Node's ability to more accurately time events which match the Node's delineation by sign and house.

Benjamin Harrison	True Node 11CP07	Mean Node 10CP05
PT SN c. => ASC	29-Nov-1878	17-Jun-1880
REG ASC d. => SN	5-Feb-1885	16-Mar-1887

South Node in 11th diminishes political activity. Using the true position, the Republicans lost legislative elections in the fall of 1878, matching the timing of the converse direction on 29-Nov-1878; yet in January 1885 Harrison began his final two years of service in the Senate which saw his prominence rise. His start in the Senate is inconsistent with the direct true node direction calculated for 5-Feb-1885. A far better match is the end of his Senate career on 3-Mar-1887, an error of 11 days from the direct mean node direction. Also, his 8-Jun-1880 decision at the

Republican National Convention to persuade the Indiana delegation to switch support from himself to Garfield as Presidential candidate is a better match to the mean node direction of 17-Jun-1880.

Theodore Roosevelt	True Node 6PI52	Mean Node 5PI35
REG dex. sextile MC d. => NN	7-Jan-1897	20-Jun-1898

On the date of the Lunar Node's true direction, Roosevelt found himself between his election as Vice President and inauguration in March 1898. No event matches were found for the True Node calculation for 7-Jan-1897. On 22-Jun-1898, two days after the Lunar Node's mean direction, Roosevelt landed in Cuba with the Rough Riders. He made his famous ride up the San Juan Hill a few days later on 1 July. As one of the most famous and memorable acts committed by a President in America's history, the Lunar Node's mean position captured the tremendous publicity potential of this event.

George W. Bush	True Node 20GE35	Mean Node 19GE35
REG MC c. => NN	5-Nov-1994	20-Dec-1993
PT NN d. => MC	12-Dec-2003	16-Nov-2002

On the surface, Bush's election as Governor of Texas on 8-Nov-1994 and the capture of Saddam Hussein on 13-Dec-2003 speak well for the Lunar Node's true position. Yet it's unclear how the North Node in the 11th of politics relates to Saddam. Better is Bush basking in his glow following the successful Republican midterm elections held 5-Nov-2002. He appeared on the cover of Time magazine following this victory. Also a better fit is Queen Elizabeth II's bestowal of knighthood on his father on 22-Dec-1993, two days from the converse direction using the Lunar Node's mean position. Mercury rules the North Node in the 11th; placed in the royal sign of Leo on Bush's Ascendant, Mercury signifies his father's reputation because the 1st is the 10th from the 4th.

Directions and Transits of the Lunar Nodes

The examples just presented were events timed by primary directions. Next are events timed by transits. There is an important difference. Because eclipses occur when New and Full Moons fall close to the Lunar Nodes, any mention of Nodes transiting the angles necessarily implies that eclipses have or will shortly fall in the signs of the angles. Not so for directions of the Nodes to the angles which may occur at any time regardless of current eclipse activity.

Because eclipses signify beginnings and endings, their impact on political careers can be substantial. It appears the Lunar Nodes' contribution to eclipse effects arises because the Nodes have an intrinsic public nature. By *public nature* I mean the Nodes act as a transmitter or connector between an individual and the world-at-large. If there is any support for this connection among traditional authors, it can first be seen in the Moon's universal signification of the public in mundane astrology. As another example from natal astrology, delineation of the Moon in the 10th usually signifies a career tied to the public and can signify widespread fame under certain conditions.

It appears that whenever the Nodes aspect the Ascendant or Midheaven by direction or transit, they open a channel between an individual and the public. At these times the individual's actions become known by a larger circle of participants. Said in a different way, the public experiences vicariously the individual's own life affairs whenever the Nodes and eclipse cycles connect the individual to the public. At all other times, an individual lives out their own life. Nobody outside the native's sphere of influence seems to notice.

Usefulness in Rectification

Transits of the Nodes to the angles are extremely valuable for rectification. First because they often time significant events which connect the individual to the world-at-large for which a public record is likely to exist. This is an important observation for rectifying figures for which little data is available. From what *does* survive, it is highly likely at least some of the events are timed by Lunar Nodes transits to the angles.

Second they can narrow the unknown angle position to within a single degree. Why? Because the transiting Nodes move very slowly – only a few minutes of degree each day - unlike a fast-moving planet like Mercury which may move a full degree or more over the course of a single day. This difference becomes critical for rectification because for most events the astrologer knows only the day and not the time. Trying to rectify events timed by Mercury's transits to the angles is impossible if the exact time and day of the event is unknown. Because the Nodes move so slowly, the time of day doesn't matter; making the Nodes a more robust rectification tool.

Table 33. Transits of the Lunar Nodes to the Angles

President	Transit Date	Transit	Actual	Event
G. Washington	12-May-1789	NN conj MC	30-Apr / 29-May	Presidential Inauguration / Held first public reception
J. Adams	19-Mar-1789	NN conj MC	4-Feb / 13-Apr	Elected Vice President / Departed home for Inauguration
T. Jefferson	6-Jun-1776	SN conj MC	7-Jun	Appointed to committee to draft Declaration of Independence. South Node conj MC = 'King is deposed'
T. Jefferson	14-Apr-1789	NN conj DSC	6/26/-Apr	Account book showed record of clothing purchases made for slave Sally Hemings; speculation their relationship dated from this time.
J. Madison	14-Apr-1793	NN conj MC	22-Apr	George Washington Neutrality Statement.
J. Monroe	16-Jun-1803	NN conj ASC	2-May / 24-Jun	Louisiana Purchase signed / Audience with Napoleon
J.Q. Adams	5-Jul-1790	NN conj ASC	15-Jul	Sworn into practice as lawyer in Boston.
A. Jackson	24-Dec-1823	NN conj MC	3-Dec	Arrived Washington DC to begin Senatorial duties.
M. van Buren	2-Jul-1840	NN conj ASC	4-Jul	Independent Treasury Act
W. Harrison	6-Nov-1803	NN conj ASC	3-Nov	Signed treaty with Fox and Sauk Tribes for Wisconsin.
J. Polk	9-Sep-1823	NN conj ASC	Sep	Entered TN state legislature, First public office.
Z. Taylor	24-Jan-1835	NN conj MC	13-Jan / 3-Feb	Orders written for Rio Grande. Rcvd orders to advance to Rio Grande (leadup to Mexican War).
F. Pierce	17-Jan-1854	NN 10th fr MC	23-Jan	Stephen Douglas introduced Kansas-Nebraska legislation.
A. Johnson	31-Dec-1867	NN conj MC	12-Dec / 13-Jan	Told why suspended Stanton. Senate refused Stanton's removal.
U. Grant	3-Apr-1873	NN conj ASC	4-Mar	Second Presidential Inauguration.
R. Hayes	22-Jun-1876	NN conj MC	15-Jun	Presidential Nomination.
J. Garfield	18-Jan-1857	NN conj MC	Ear-1857	Preached at Great Awakening Revivals in Ohio.
C. Arthur	31-Dec-1882	SN conj MC	27-Dec	Pendleton Reform Passed Senate.
G. Cleveland	12-Nov-1870	NN conj ASC	Nov	Elected Sheriff of Erie County.
B. Harrison	27-Aug-1862	NN conj MC	Aug	Joined Union Army.
W. McKinley	10-Feb-1893	SN conj LOF	17-Feb	Financial losses threatened bankruptcy and end of politics.
T. Roosevelt	6-Feb-1878 / 2-Feb-1900	SN conj IC / SN conj ASC	9-Feb / 6-Feb	Death of father. / Stated would not run for VP.
W. Taft	25-Jun-1921	NN 10th fr MC	30-Jun	Named Chief Justice.
W. Wilson	23-Feb-1917	SN conj MC	25-Feb	Received Zimmerman letter
W. Harding	31-Nov-1918	SN conj DSC	11-Nov	Wife ill - kidney inflammation.
C. Coolidge	12-Sep-1919	SN conj MC	11-Sep	Called out National Guard to assume control in Police strike.

Table 33 - *Continued*

President	Transit Date	Transit	Actual	Event
H. Truman	6-Nov-1940	NN conj ASC	5-Nov	Won Senate Election.
Eisenhower	29-Feb-1944	SN conj MC	End-Feb	Aerial bombings of Germany began. South Node in Sagittarius, sign of flight.
	22-Jul-1952	NN 10th fr ASC	11-Jul	Presidential nomination.
	20-Jun-1953	NN conj MC	19-Jun	Execution of Rosenbergs.
J. Kennedy	10-Aug-1961	SN trine MC	13-Aug	Construction of Berlin Wall began.
	14-Nov-1962	NN conj MC	6-Nov	Teddy Kennedy elected to Senate; followed increased reputation after Cuban Missile Crisis 16-28 Oct.
L. Johnson	3-Apr-1962	NN conj ASC	10-Apr	Hailed by JFK and Congressional Leaders on 25 years of political service.
R. Nixon	26-Oct-1946	NN conj MC	2-Nov	House election victory.
	27-Sep-1974	SN conj MC	Fall	Fallout after resignation, illness.
G. Ford	25-May-1948	NN conj ASC	Jun	Announced bid for House Seat.
J. Carter	28-May-1977	NN conj ASC	22-May	Made Human Rights foreign policy speech at Notre Dame.
	28-Jul-2000	NN conj MC	30-Jul	Observed Venezuelan elections.
R. Reagan	30-Jul-1981	NN 10th fr MC	29-Jul	Won approval for tax cuts.
	18-Nov-1982	SN conj ASC	10-Nov	USSR leader Brezhnev died.
GHW Bush	8-Jun-1942	NN conj ASC	12-Jun	Enlisted in Navy.
	19-Dec-1988	SN conj ASC	9-Dec	Regulators seized assets of son Neil Bush's Silverado Savings & Loan.
B. Clinton	30-Aug-1968	SN conj ASC	22-Aug	Witnessed Grant Park violence at DNC.
	18-Mar-1992	SN conj LOF	16-Mar	HRC "could have stayed home and baked cookies" comment.
G. W. Bush	25-Jul-2000	SN 10th fr MC	24-Jul	Selected Dick Cheney as VP.
B. Obama	5-Aug-1989	NN conj ASC	Ear-Aug	Played basketball with Craig Robinson as part of Michelle's due diligence on Barack as partner.
	29-Jan-2003	SN conj MC	22-Jan	Chicago *Defense* stated "Obama has no relationship with the Black community and is a product of the white lakefront community. He is a white liberal in blackface."
	20-May-2012	NN conj MC	9-May	Announced support for gay marriage.
D. Trump	16-Feb-1990	SN conj ASC	11-Feb 16-Feb	Separated from Ivana Trump. NY Post headline "Best Sex I Ever Had" with Marla Maples, described as media circus.
	8-Jun-1999	NN conj ASC	8-Jun	Divorce proceedings finalized with Marla Maples.

ECLIPSES

Eclipses are special cases of New and Full Moons which fall close enough to the Lunar Nodes that the light of either luminary is truncated. Medieval authors left few rules for interpreting eclipse effects on nativities. What they did leave stated eclipses falling on the Ascendant, luminaries, hīlāj, or Nodes were dangerous. Surviving aphorisms tended to make a distinction between the tightness of the aspect, reserving dire predictions of death for only those cases when the eclipse degree was partile conjunct to one of the significators or Nodes.

The best tactic is to apply mundane astrology eclipse rules to natal astrology. The most important points appear to be the following:

- Effects of lunar eclipses are mild when compared to solar eclipses.

- Effects of lunar eclipses are often felt immediately, lasting one month for each hour of the eclipse's duration.

- Effects of solar eclipses are often delayed, triggered by the subsequent transit of a planet (usually a malefic like Mars) to the eclipse degree. They last one year for each hour of the eclipse's duration.

- Eclipse effects also depend on their totality (fraction of light truncated). Total eclipses are more powerful than partial eclipses.

- Eclipse rules include guidelines for tying eclipse effects to a geographical location by country-sign correspondences, a procedure more formally known as *choreography*. Also to classes of beings by the significations of signs (e.g., eclipses in Pisces affect fish). These rules do not appear as crucial when applying eclipse methodology to natal figures. As long as the eclipse degree closely contacts a significator or Lunar Node, an effect should occur. Example: an individual with a Pisces Ascendant has a solar eclipse falling on their Ascendant. The individual is not a *fish,* yet should still experience an interruption of physical vitality from eclipse effects.

In addition:

- All aphorisms state that eclipses influence planets, parts, or cusps they contact by conjunction. There is no mention of effects by any other aspect.

- *North Node eclipses* occur when the eclipsed luminary is conjunct the North Node; *South Node eclipses*, vice versa. Because the Nodes increase or decrease; eclipse delineation must take this factor into account.

Example One. 30-Oct-1845 Annular Total Solar Eclipse and James Polk

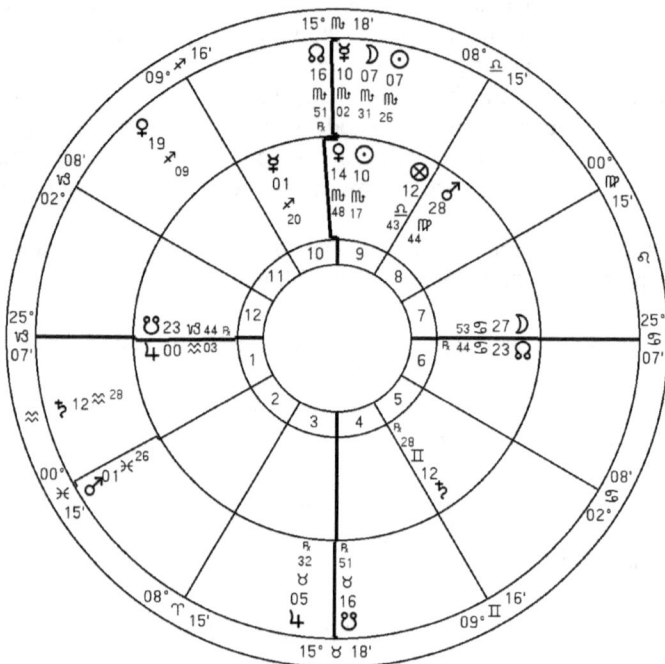

This is a good example of a North Node eclipse which elevated both Polk and Taylor through the Mexican War. Taylor's figure has the same angles as Polk.

Date	Transit	Actual	Event
10-May-1845	Mars square SE	28-May-45	Secretary of War Marcy notified Zachary Taylor of high probability movement of troops to Texas. Actual order issued 15-Jun-1845.
18-Feb-1846	Mars opp. SE	24-Feb-46	Taylor issued preliminary order for troops to march from Corpus Christi to Matamoras. Actual march began 1 March.
22-May-1846	Mars trine SE	23-May-46	Mexico officially declared war against US
9-Jul-1846	Mars sq. SE	7/9-Jul-46	California theatre: Commodore Sloat landed at Monterrey and claimed possession of California for the United States. Ordered capture of Sonoma and San Francisco.
25-Nov-1846	Mars conj. SE	25-Nov-46	Colonel Kearney entered Southern California and won victories at San Pascual on 6-Dec and at San Diego on 12-Dec.
20-Feb-1847	Mars sex. SE	23-Feb-47	Taylor defeated Santa Anna at Buena Vista.
20-Aug-1847	Mars opp. SE	18-Aug-47	Winfield Scott chalked up final victories in war: Contreas, 18-Aug; Churubusco, 19-Aug; Molino Del Ray, 8-Sep; entered Mexico City, 13-Sep.
6-Nov-1848	Mars conj. SE	7-Nov-47	Taylor won election to US Presidency.

CHAPTER 14 – LUNAR NODES AND ECLIPSES

Example Two. 18-Aug-1849 Total Solar Eclipse and Zachary Taylor

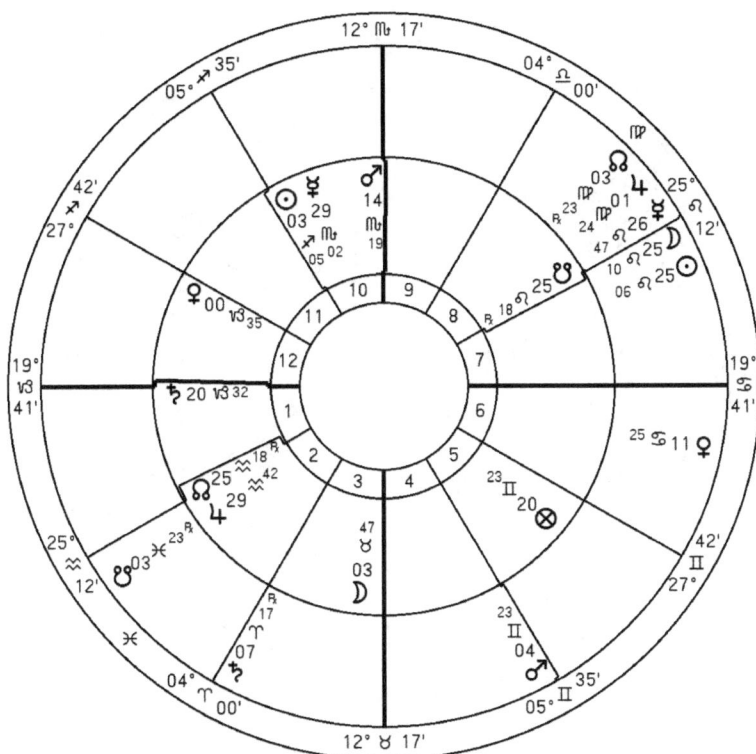

Eclipse rules state a solar eclipse partile conjunct the South Node causes death. Taylor died on 9-Jul-1850, less than one year after this eclipse.

Example Three. 26-May-1854 Annual Solar Eclipse and Franklin Pierce

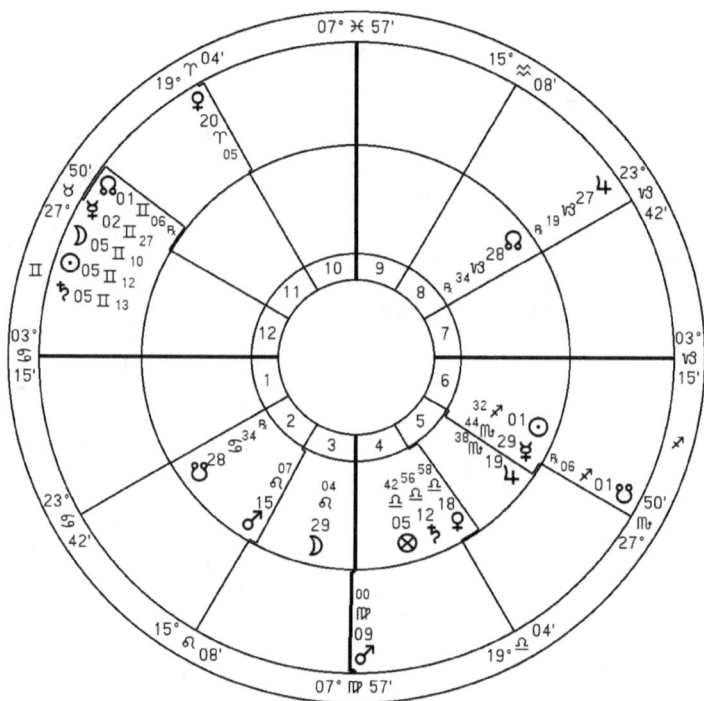

This eclipse falls hours after the Senate passed the Kansas-Nebraska Act at 1:10 AM on 26-May-1854. This action terminated the Missouri Compromise, marred Pierce's Presidency, and was a major step towards the Civil War. It was also the event which led Lincoln to actively challenge Stephen Douglas on slavery expansion. It was a pivotal moment which led Lincoln to the Presidency.

For Franklin Pierce, the eclipse fell in the 12th house of enmity. Pierce's signature of the Kansas-Nebraska Act on 30-May led to his downfall as President. Eclipse Lord Mercury rules the Saturn-Mars square, with Mars conjunct the 4th cusp. This configuration signifies an error in decision making which is the cause of civil unrest. Note the partile conjunction of the South Node to Pierce's Sun. Traditional aphorisms do not mention this type of contact – they focus only on the conjunction between the actual eclipse degree and natal significators. Still this contact must have intensified Pierce's problems.

Example Four. 18-Sep-1857 Solar Eclipse and James Buchanan

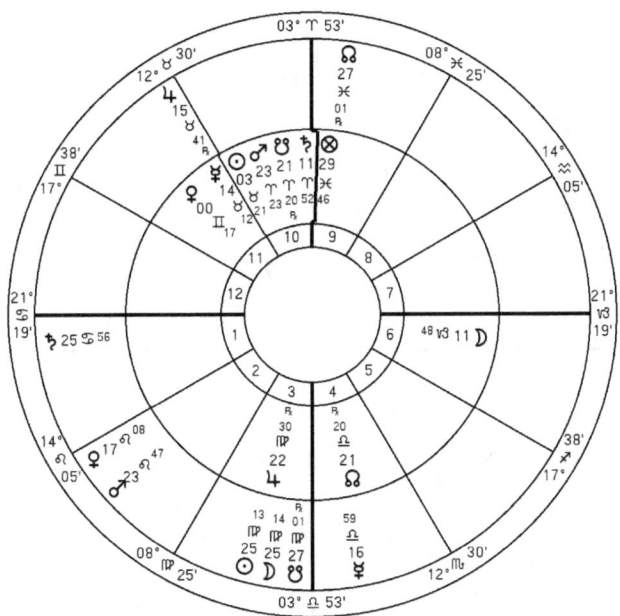

While marking the end of the Bleeding Kansas saga dating from Franklin Pierce's administration, Buchanan's decision to support Kansas' legal process in passing the Lecompton Constitution was considered a disaster. This is a South Node eclipse in the 4th conjunct natal Jupiter. It wipes away Buchanan's legal abilities. Note eclipse effects are timed primarily by Mercury and Venus.

Date	Transit	Actual	Event
19-Oct-1857	Venus conj. SE	19-Oct-1857	Kansas Governor Robert Walker reported massive voter fraud at the Lecompton Convention which supported Kansas as a slave state. Buchanan sided with Lecompton vote.
7-Dec-1857	Merc. conj. SE	8-Dec-1857	Buchanan told Congress he would be bound to submit whatever Constitution voted on by Kansas residents to Congress
		9-Dec-1857	Stephen Douglas opposed the Lecompton Constitution.
30-Dec-1857	Venus sq. SE	21-Dec-1857 4-Jan-1858	Vote on Lecompton Constitution Lecompton Constitution was rejected
12-Mar-1858	Venus opp. SE	23-Mar-1858	Senate voted to accept; House rejected.
20-Mar-1858	Merc. opp. SE	1-Apr-1858	House asked for new vote
24 May 1858	Venus sq. SE	19 May 1858	Marais Massacre of Kansas Free Soilers by Missouri pro-slavery forces.

Example Five. 3-Oct-1986 Total Solar Eclipse and Ronald Reagan

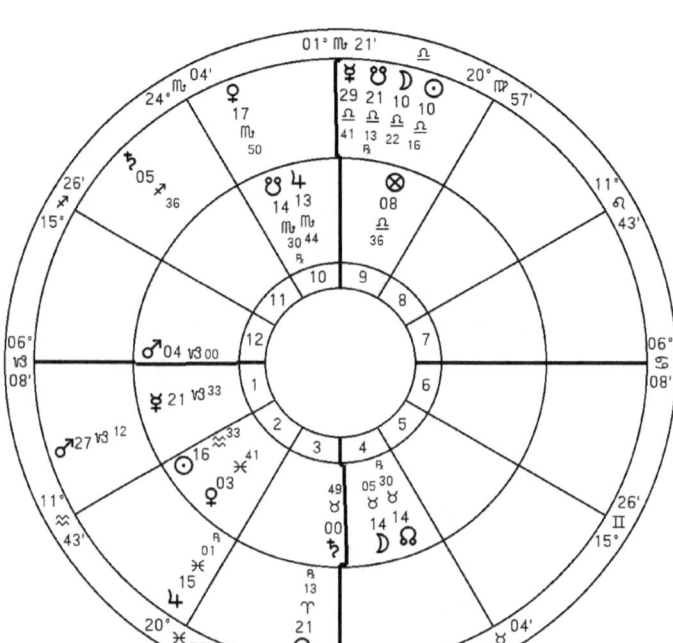

Immediately following the 3-Oct-1986 eclipse, one of the US covertly-funded contra operatives was shot down over Nicaragua on 5-Oct. The eclipse almubtazz, Saturn in Sagittarius, signifies the fall from a horse. It also signifies an airplane crash because Sagittarius has the modern signification of flight. Saturn falls in Reagan's 12th of covert activity. The eclipse also falls within 2 degrees of Reagan's Lot of Fortune, a plausible Hīlāj (see rectification). This means the eclipse should have caused Reagan health problems. It did. Eclipse ruler Venus/Scorpio indicates problems with the reproductive system. Reagan had prostate surgery on 5-Jan-1987; several cancerous polyps in his colon were also discovered and removed.

Usefulness in Rectification. Because eclipse effects may be timed by subsequent transits, I do not recommend using eclipses for rectification. At best they may help confirm signs on the angles if eclipses in certain signs consistently time major life events. At the same time, there are far easier methods of confirming signs on the angles.

CHAPTER FIFTEEN

Transits

The word transit, derived from the Latin *trans-ire*, 'to go across,' refers to times when the current position of a planet or its rays crosses the same zodiacal degree held by a planet or point at some prior moment. Natal figures are the most common benchmark for which transits are measured. Solar returns and eclipse charts are other types of figures for which transits have application. By far transits are the most common method of prediction used by contemporary practitioners.

Chapter Summary

What Aspect and Orb? Transits which conjoin natal planets, parts, or cusps are preferred. Transiting planets begin to manifest their effects as soon as they enter another planet's sign. Action takes place when both transiting and transited planets meet within their moiety of orb.

Planetary Returns. Transiting planets manifest effects strongly when they return to their own sign. The configuration of other transiting planets at the same time must also be taken into consideration as modifiers to a planetary return. When two or more planets return to their own natal sign, the significance of the transit is increased. If a natal aspect repeats, the condition is known as a *Planetary Aspect Recapitulation*.

Transits of Planets to Different Planets, Cusps, or Parts. Transiting planets mix their own natal significations with other planets, cusps, or parts they meet by conjunction or aspect. The importance of the event, for good or bad, is modified by the power of both transiting and transited planets when they rule time.

Case Study: Franklin Roosevelt's War Years. Schoener states the Ascendant Lord's transit over malefics in the natal figure is modified by the strength of malefics in the active solar return. Tests confirm this aphorism when applied to the transits of Mercury over Roosevelt's natal Saturn and Mars during 1940-1944.

Medieval usage of Transits

Medieval predictive astrologers used transits, but placed their predictive ability below other techniques including planetary period methods, primary directions, and solar returns. The main difference between transit usage in the medieval era is the subjugation of transits to planetary period methods. Transiting planets which rule time have greater power to act than transiting planets which do not. Neglecting this consideration is one reason why predictions of some transits fail.

What aspect?

> *The most powerful indications of the planets are at the transits of one of them over the other at conjunction. As for at oppositions and quadratures, their indication is less in manifestation and weaker in influence (Alchabitius 2004, 135).*

This is the opinion of Alchabitius writing in his *Introduction to Astrology*, the most popular textbook used by European universities in the Middle Ages. Note he fails to make any mention of sextiles or trines, not to mention minor aspects. This omission is probably due to the benefic nature of many sextile and trine transits which time pleasant yet unremarkable events not easily identified or remembered by the native.

Why has the list of transiting aspects proliferated over time? The addition of minor aspects, such as the semisquare (45deg) and sesquiquadrate (135deg), appears directly correlated to the loss of other predictive methods. Transits have been forced to *fill in* as causal agents for events which could not be predicted after older techniques such as profections, directions, Firdaria, and Zodiacal Releasing fell out of favor. In my opinion, the resulting overuse of transits has played a large role in the under specification of modern predictive methods.

How best to apply transiting aspects as transits are redeployed within the context of a more sophisticated predictive hierarchy? My current practice is to employ transiting conjunctions to the principal significators: Ascendant, Midheaven, Sun, Moon, Lot of Fortune, and SAN (if hīlāj). To this list I add both 4th and 7th cusps. Second, I consider transiting oppositions and squares to the Sun, Moon, and hīlāj (if different). Third I consider transiting conjunctions of time lords to any natal planet. Fourth I consider planetary returns and planetary aspect recapitulations. ***NEW*** *Transits of the victor to the angles are often significant.*

What orb?

Another assumption often overlooked is the time period when transits are effective. The basic principle is whenever a planet makes a sign ingress; its effects are felt by any other planets in that sign. This principle dates from Hellenistic usage of whole sign houses. If the analogy is taken that a natal chart is comprised of 12 rooms with each room occupying 30 degrees of an exclusive sign, the transiting planet can be considered a visitor who at each sign Ingress announces his entry by opening a door, entering the room, and closing the door behind him. At this point the visiting planet can see everyone in the room at once. Yet contact does not occur – at least the type of contact that produces effects – until the visitor gets close enough to another person in the room signified by a resident natal planet. *Close enough* is defined when the orbs of both planets meet, a measure formally known as *moiety of orb*.

Understanding Moiety. Let's take an example. Suppose Mars falls at 15 degrees of Sagittarius. Everything (e.g., planet, lot, and cusp) that falls between 11 and 19 degrees of Sagittarius is within Mars' orb of influence. That's because Mars has an 8-degree orb of influence, or four degrees on either side of its position. Assigning 8 degrees to Mars is an assumption taken from Al-Biruni (1934, 255) whose recommended orbs are listed here[21]:

Table 34. Planets and Recommended Orbs.

Planet	Orb (degrees)
Saturn	9
Jupiter	9
Mars	8
Sun	15
Venus	7
Mercury	7
Moon	12

Next suppose the Sun falls at 28 Sagittarius. Its orb of 15 degrees means the Sun's orb of influence falls between 20deg 30min of Sagittarius and 5deg 30min of Capricorn. While Mars is in the same sign as the Sun and sees him, using the analogy of people seeing and greeting people in the same room, at 15 degrees of Sagittarius Mars is still too far away to physically contact the Sun. Not until Mars passes 16SA30 will he be sufficiently near the Sun to manifest his effects as a transiting planet.

To calculate the moiety for any two planets, simply add the orbs for both planets and divide by two. For this example, add the orb for Mars (8 deg) to the Sun's orb (15 deg) and divide by two (8+15)/2 = 11deg 30min. Working back from the Sun's position at 28 Sagittarius: 28SA – 11deg 30min = 16SA30. This is the degree and minute of Sagittarius that Mars must reach before the transit begins to manifest its effects.

---

[21] Bonatti uses the same list. Slight variation is found from author to author.

Applying aspects are more important. Applying and separating aspects are treated differently for predictive purposes. Applying aspects are more important. Some say once the aspect is mathematically exact the separating aspect has no power. Others say the transit remains in effect as long as the degree range remains in aspect. By ignoring the minutes, this rule allows transits to remain active for a few days after the aspect perfects. I have yet to reach a conclusion on when separating aspects lose their effects. Since transits are not emphasized in rectification, for our purposes it doesn't matter.

Planetary Returns

Solar Return. The first and easiest type of transit to understand is when any transiting planet returns to its own natal position. The most famous type is the solar return which occurs when the Sun returns to its exact degree and minute found at birth once each year. Such is the power of the Sun's return that an entire predictive methodology has evolved around casting a figure for the solar return.

Based on the principle that planets begin to manifest their returns as soon as they make their sign ingress, effects of the solar return begin to manifest immediately after the Sun's ingress to the natal Sun sign.[22] This may occur prior to the actual birth date. Consider two individuals with their Suns at 1 and 14 degrees of the same sign. For the first individual, effects of the solar return should begin on the birth date. For the second, the return's effects may start as much as two weeks prior to the actual birth date.

Saturn and Jupiter returns. Saturn and Jupiter returns are often characterized as times of challenge and reward though it is necessary to judge the strength of the natal planet before making any prediction for the return. Should Jupiter prove an accidental malefic by delineation, then the 12-year cycle of Jupiter's return will bring on bad effects not good.

Modification by other transiting planets. In addition to considering the strength of each planet before predicting its effects for the return, one cannot overlook the configuration of other transiting planets. Should natal Venus promise the accumulation of luxury goods, but at the time of Venus' return Saturn is square Venus, Saturn will interfere no matter how bountiful is the natal promise of Venus. Luxury goods may be defaced or stolen in this situation.

Jupiter Scorpio Ingress: 2005/06. A recent example of a benefic planetary return ruined by malefics was Jupiter's Scorpio Ingress on 25-Oct-2005 lasting through 24-Nov-2006. For most of this period, Jupiter was afflicted either by the opposition of Mars/Taurus or the square of Saturn/Leo. Though there were periods when the transiting Jupiter-Mars opposition and the transiting Saturn-Mars square

---

[22] Occasionally much earlier based on the solar return's progressed Moon making aspects to other solar return planets. See Lincoln's case study in Chapter 9 for further details.

were outside their official moieties; because of the stubbornness of their fixed sign placements and both malefics in signs of their detriment, from what I observed Jupiter's Scorpio Ingress was essentially ruined for the entire twelve months. This meant that many individuals with Jupiter/Scorpio configured for gain in the natal chart instead found diminished benefits during their 2005/06 Jupiter return.

Planetary Aspect Recapitulations

When more than one planet makes its natal return, the effects are elevated in importance. Suppose a natal figure has Mercury opposed Jupiter. Whenever transiting Mercury opposes transiting Jupiter the natal Mercury-Jupiter opposition is activated. This is a variation of Carter's *Law of Excitation*, a theory developed to explain activation of natal aspects by transits and progressions. (See Blaschke 1998, 6-9 for further discussion). There are three levels of aspect recapitulation, each with progressively greater effects. The first is an aspect recapitulation in any group of signs. The second is an aspect recapitulation in signs of the same quadriplicity as the natal aspect. In the third case, the transiting aspect repeats the identical signs as found in the natal figure. In the example section which follows, a Mercury-Jupiter opposition prior to Millard Fillmore's death recapitulates the same natal opposition by quadriplicity.

Transits of Planets to other Natal Planets and Significators

Next consider the transit of a planet through other signs aspecting other planets or points in the figure. By far this is the most common situation because planetary returns comprise only $1/12^{th}$ of a transiting planet's life. When a planet enters a new sign – formally we say "Venus makes its Aquarius Ingress on 3-Jan-2007 10:31 PM EST" – there is a mixing of effects.

Influence of natal condition. No matter where the transiting planet falls, it carries some of its natal delineation by sign and house with it. For example, suppose Venus signifies the native's wife; Mercury, a younger brother. The transit of Venus in the 9th house may indicate the native's wife is traveling in a foreign country. Transit of Mercury in the 9th might mean a younger brother is traveling to college or that the native himself is pursuing research in a university library if Mercury has any dignity in the Ascendant. Transit of Mars in the 9th might mean illness causing a trip cancellation if Mars rules the 6th or legal problems abroad if Mars rules the 7th. These types of permutations are endless.

Modification from other transiting planets. This restates the earlier comment about planetary returns, taking Jupiter's 2005 Scorpio Ingress as one example where aspects from Mars and Saturn substantially modified Jupiter's effects. That was an example of a planetary return, but the same principle applies for transits to other planets. Individuals with natal planets besides Jupiter in Scorpio were affected differently by Jupiter's 2005/06 transit, as compared to prior Jupiter Scorpio Ingresses.

When planets rule time. Effects of transits are felt more strongly when the transiting planet rules time by any Planetary Period method.

Modification of significators by Distributors and Partners. When the transited body is one of the six principal significators: Ascendant, Midheaven, Sun, Moon, LOF, or SAN; transit effects are modified by the active Distributor and Partner. Suppose Saturn in the natal 6th is delineated as illness. Transits of Saturn to the natal Ascendant may not mark incidences of illness if at the time of the transit the directed Ascendant falls in the bounds of a benefic. In this case, the benefic influence of the Ascendant's Distributor may be strong enough to ward off effects of a malefic transit.

Influence of transited planet's condition in the solar return. A second way transited planets can be modified depends on the configuration of the transited planet in the active solar return. This aphorism comes from Schoener (1996, 94-95). It is tested in a comprehensive case study on Franklin Roosevelt's WWII years at the end of this chapter.

List of Transit Examples

Example One: Millard Fillmore; Transits preceding death
Planetary Aspect Recapitulation: Mercury opposed Jupiter

Example Two: Coolidge and Boston Police Strike
Planetary Return: Jupiter/Leo returns to its position in natal 12th
Transit to Angle: South/North Nodes aspect MC/IC axis
Transit to Angle: Saturn to Ascendant
Transit to Angle: Mercury to Ascendant

Example Three: FDR and Germany's Invasion of the Low Countries
Planetary Return: Saturn/Taurus/9th
Planetary Return: Mars/Gemini/10th
Transit to Planet: Mercury to Saturn

Example Four: Nixon and Chambers in the Pumpkin Patch
Planetary Aspect Recapitulation: Mercury-Mars-Jupiter stellium.
Lunar Phase: New Moon conjunct 4th cusp.

Example Five: Gerald Ford nominated for Vice President
Planetary Return: Mars/Taurus
Transit to Planet: Venus to Moon
Transit to Angle: Uranus to 10th position from Midheaven

Example Six: Clinton Global Initiative
Planetary Return: Jupiter/Libra/1st and Saturn/Leo/11th
Transit to Angle: South Node to Ascendant
Transit to Planet: Saturn to Mercury

Example One: Millard Fillmore; Transits preceding death

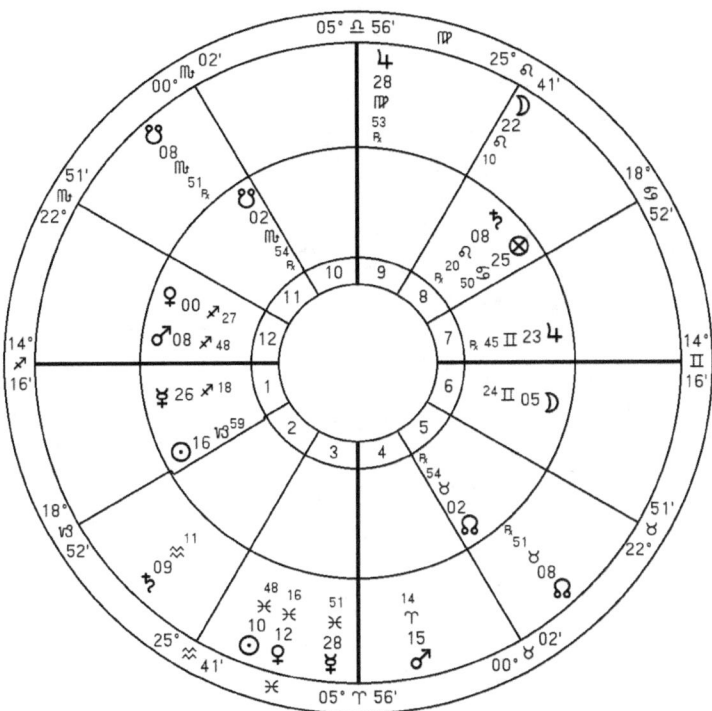

Planetary Aspect Recapitulation: Mercury opposed Jupiter

The outer wheel depicts transits on 1-Mar-1874 prior to Fillmore's death on 8-Mar-1874. As delineated in the rectification section, both Mercury and Jupiter are Fillmore's high-scoring killing planets. In the natal, both Mercury and Jupiter are opposed in the 1st-7th house axis in mutable signs. For this event, the aspect is recapitulated in the 4th-10th houses in mutable signs.

The phrase *opening the doors* describes the case when an inferior planet applies to a superior planet when positioned in opposite houses. (Alchabitius 2004, 137). It is applicable here.

For Fillmore, another example of this identical Mercury-Jupiter recapitulation occurred during the Missouri Compromise negotiations of March 1850; signed during early September. This specific aspect cropped up several times during this study. For other examples, see Jefferson's natal figure and Lincoln's 1862 return (Chapter 12: *Solar Returns: Delineation and Prediction*).

Example Two: Coolidge and Boston Police Strike, 9-Sep-1919, 5:45 PM

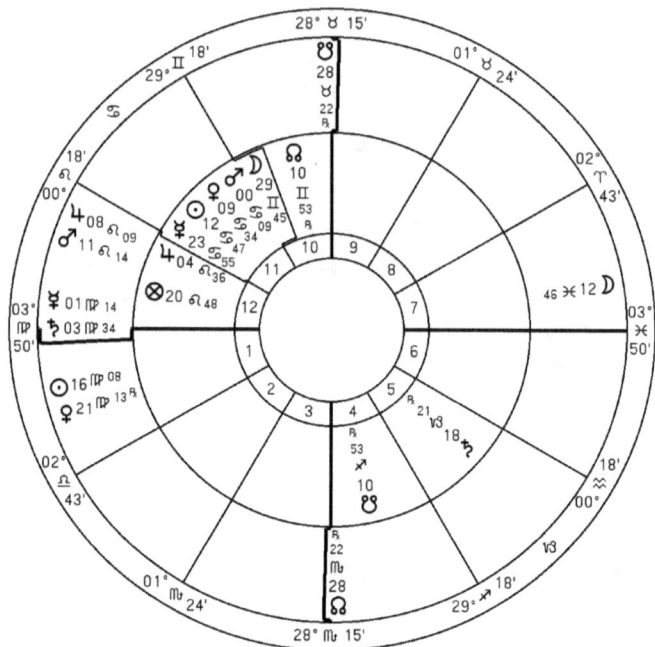

Planetary Return: Jupiter/Leo returns to its position in natal 12th
Transit to Angle: South/North Node aspects MC/IC axis
Transit to Angle: Saturn to Ascendant
Transit to Angle: Mercury to Ascendant (exact 11 September)

The Boston Police strike starting 9-Sep-1919, 5:45 pm and Coolidge's response to call the National Guard to replace strikers on 11-Sep were his five minutes of fame which brought Coolidge to national attention. Jupiter/Leo/12th ruled by Sun/Cancer/11th signifies the proud police officers interested in wages because Sun is in the 11th of king's money. Jupiter's rulership of South Node in Sagittarius in natal 4th shows the police as cause of civil unrest. Transit of South Node to Coolidge's MC marks his career by the disruption to civil unity. Between 9 and 11 September when Coolidge called out the National Guard, there were several incidents of crimes reported in Boston which irritated citizens and Coolidge. Saturn/Capricorn rules the 6th of employees and labor unions. When Mercury transited the Ascendant on 11-Sep, Coolidge telegrammed labor leader Samuel Gompers saying: "There is no right to strike against the public safety by anybody, anywhere, anytime" (Sobel 1998, 144). This most famous sound bite was publicized nationwide and led directly to his nomination for Vice President the following year.

Example Three: FDR and Germany's Invasion of the Low Countries

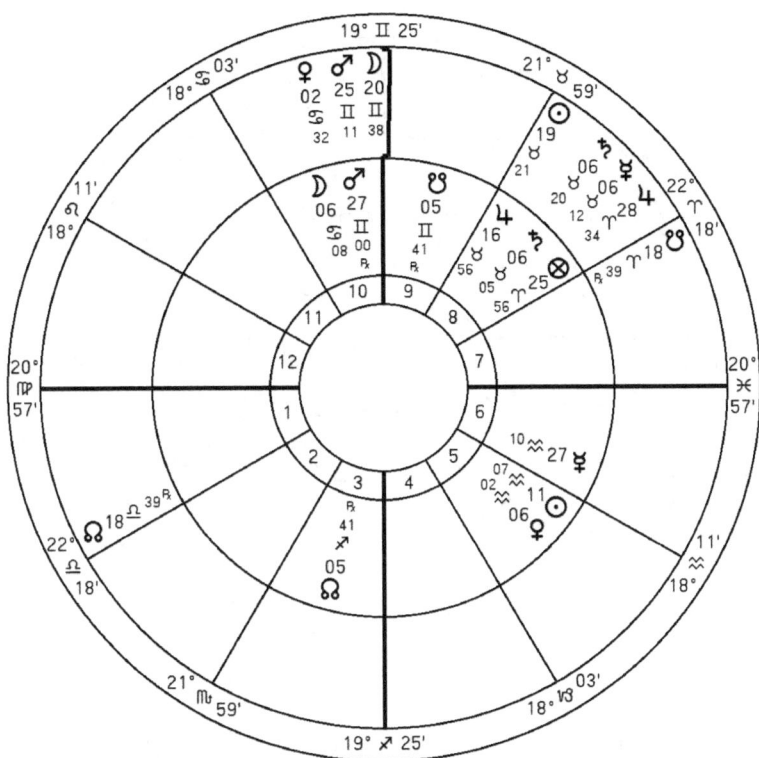

Planetary Return: Saturn/Taurus/9th
Planetary Return: Mars/Gemini/10th
Transit to Planet: Mercury to Saturn

This figure, cast for bombs dropped by the Germans over Brussels at 5:20 a.m. on 10-May-1940 marked Germany's invasion of the Low Countries. Saturn/Taurus/9th signifies destruction to land, food, and financial institutions in foreign countries. This was among the accomplishments of Hitler's invasion of Western Europe.

Mars/Gemini/10th is incendiary firepower and matches Blitzkrieg battle tactics used by the Germans in their invasion. Mars/Gemini is also FDR's own professional significator as a wartime President, activated further by this event. As Ascendant ruler, Mercury signifies Roosevelt himself. The transit of the Ascendant ruler over Saturn brings FDR in direct involvement with the tragedy signified by Saturn/Taurus in the 9th of foreign lands. This specific transit is detailed in the FDR study which concludes this chapter.

Example Four: Nixon and Chambers in the Pumpkin Patch

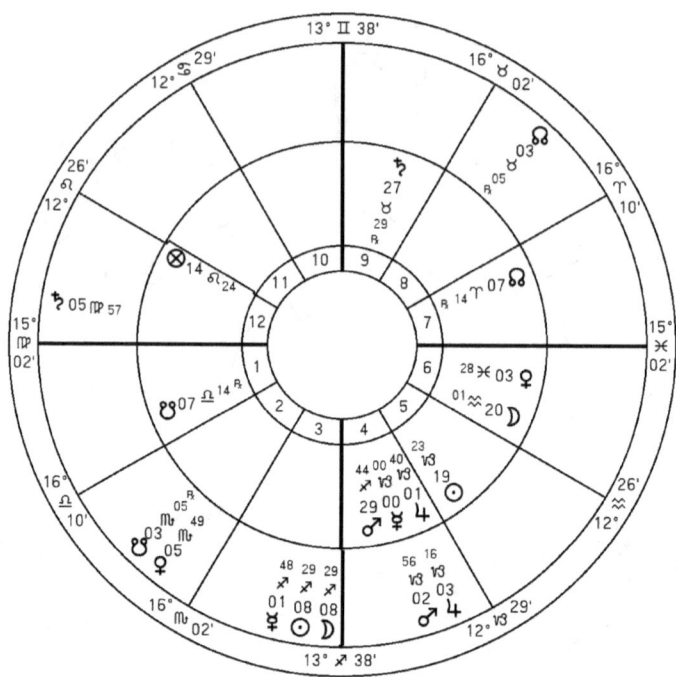

Planetary Aspect Recapitulation: Mercury-Mars-Jupiter stellium.
Lunar Phase: New Moon conjunct 4th cusp.

One of the more controversial events in Richard Nixon's rise to political power was his McCarthy era prosecution of Alger Hiss based on evidence supplied by Whittaker Chambers. The New Moon of 30-Nov-1948 marked an important turn of events for Nixon in this case. A few days before, Mars in late Sagittarius and Jupiter in early Capricorn both made their natal returns. With the New Moon, Mercury ingressed to the sign of natal Mars. For Nixon, the natal Mars-Mercury-Jupiter stellium combines the principles of naked ambition (Jupiter/Capricorn), blusterous aggression (Mars/Sagittarius), and methodical planning (Mercury/Capricorn).

On 1-Dec-1948, Chambers told Nixon of additional evidence previously withheld. Chambers had hidden two rolls of film in a hollowed-out pumpkin in his yard, retrieved them on 2-Dec-1948, and handed them over to Nixon who used them in a sensational attack against Hiss. Though not technically buried, I suggest that film concealed in an outdoor vegetable patch matches the 4th house signification of things buried; triggered by this New Moon in Nixon's 4th house.

NEW Ex. Five: Gerald Ford VP nomination, 12-Oct-1973

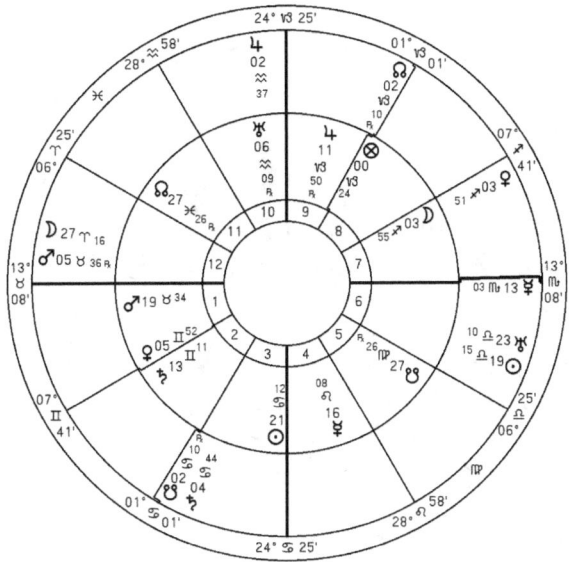

Planetary Return: Mars/Taurus
Transit to Planet: Venus to Moon
Transit to Angle: Uranus to 10th position from Midheaven

Gerald Ford was the only Vice President or President who was not elected to either office. Upon the resignation of Spiro Agnew as Vice President, Richard Nixon appointed him VP. Upon the resignation of Richard Nixon as President, Ford succeeded him as President. Research since ARM 3rd edition reveals the importance of planets and the Nodes transiting the 10th positional degree of the ASC, MC, LOF, and LOS as key timers of events. Jupiter is Ford's Victor of the Horoscope and its transit to the 10th house does help Ford professionally but this is not specific enough to predict elevation to a national office. Nor did Jupiter rule by Firdaria time lord nor did ZRS show a subperiod angular from the Lot of Fortune or any type of loosing of the bond. In fact, prior to his VP nomination, Ford was considering retirement.

Transiting Uranus makes 3 passes to the 10th degree of the MC: 1-Nov-1973, 20-May-1974, and 13-Aug-1974. On 1-Nov-1973 he began Senate confirmation hearings for VP; he was sworn in as President on 9-Aug-1974 four days before the 3nd pass of trUranus. While we cannot predict in advance the nature of the event timed by Uranus because its behavior is erratic, it is true that natal Uranus/10th predicted an unexpected event would mark his career/reputation. The promise was timed precisely TWICE with trUranus reaching the 10th positional degree of the MC (e.g., 24LI25 is 10th from 24CP25).

Example Six: Clinton Global Initiative, 15/17-Sep-2005

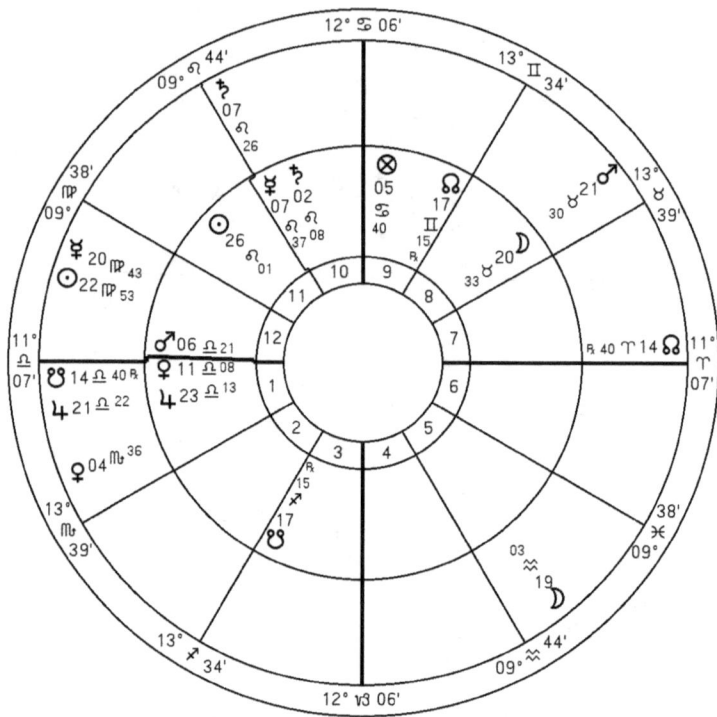

Planetary Return: Jupiter/Libra/1st and Saturn/Leo/11th
Transit to Angle: North Node to Descendant
Transit to Planet: Saturn to Mercury
Transit to Planet: Mars to Moon

In President Clinton's largest post-Presidential act to date, on 15-Sep-2005 he opened a three-day conference where he sought and received pledges of several billion dollars to fund initiatives in energy and climate change, global public health, poverty alleviation, and the mitigation of religious and ethnic conflict. Jupiter/Libra/1st ruling 3rd and 6th signifies Clinton's egalitarian efforts at philanthropy. Emphasis on public health resonates with Jupiter's position in the 1st of physical vitality and rulership of the 6th of illness. Saturn's return signifies both religious intolerance and political totalitarianism. Saturn's transit to natal Mercury/Leo brings home these themes to Clinton's Mercury-signified friends who are sympathetic to his cause. Natal Mars ruling the 7th in the 1st shows Clinton attracting partners based on the theme of social justice delineated by Mars in Libra. The transit of Mars to natal Moon in 8th of partner's money shows 7th house partners investing their funds in Clinton's initiative.

Case Study: Franklin Roosevelt's World War II Years

Courage under fire is the principal reason why Washington, Lincoln, and Franklin Roosevelt consistently rank as Presidential Greats when queried by historians (Lee and Taranto, 2004, 253). In this case study of World War II events, the types of obstacles faced by Franklin Roosevelt will be examined through the lens of a specific application of transits.

Schoener's aphorism on transits of the Ascendant ruler. Schoener's *Opusculum Astrologicum* concludes with specific rules detailing how transits should be ranked among the predictive hierarchy. In one rule, he provides an example of how transit effects are modified by the zodiacal state of the transited planet in the active solar return.

> *The transit of the lord of the Ascendant of the Nativity over the degree of an infortune in the radix makes the native unfortunate on that day according to the position of the infortune in the house of the revolution, especially if that infortune has dominion in the year. For example, Saturn in the radix was in 19 degrees of Cancer in the tenth house with Libra ascending in the radix. And in the revolution Saturn placed itself in the twelfth. When therefore Venus, the lady of the Ascendant in the nativity, came by transit to 19 Cancer, the native was captured, etc. (Schoener 1996, 94-95).*

Here Schoener inserts two conditions before considering the effects of the transit. First is *position of the infortune in the active solar return*. Second if the infortune *has dominion in the year*. Schoener is unspecific about what kind of *dominion*, yet because he uses *year*, it is probably a safe assumption to assume Schoener is talking about any malefic who rules the sign of the profected Ascendant (LOY). The power of malefics should also be stronger when they rule time as Firdaria main or subperiod rulers, or from any other time lord method.

Design of Case Study. With Mercury as Roosevelt's Ascendant ruler, the transit of the Ascendant ruler over Mars and Saturn happens once each year. The years 1940-1944 yield five solar returns and ten events to consider. Because of the limit of space and time, I make no attempt to fully delineate each solar return. Though this detracts from what is possible with a complete workup of each return, my goal is to delineate malefics in the return and understand how they modify Mercury's transit each year. To this end the analysis of solar returns is commissioned.

Because delineation precedes prediction, the study begins with a brief overview of Franklin Roosevelt's natal figure.

Franklin Roosevelt: Delineation in Brief

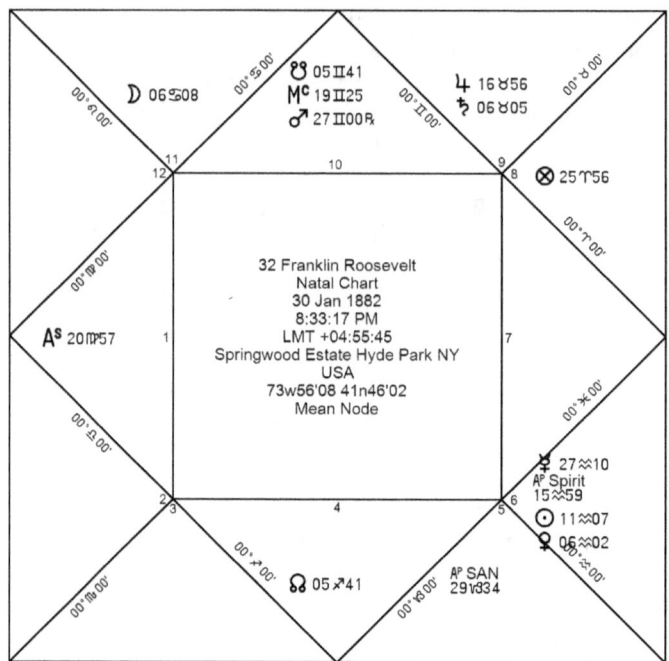

Ascendant-Mercury-Mars. Virgo rising grants FDR the need for discrimination and precision largely satisfied through the employment of Mercury-signified individuals. They are smart, scientific, and optimistic because Mercury in the bound of Saturn/Aquarius is the signature for a scientist; Mercury's position in the dwad of Sagittarius is optimistic. They are the *Brain Trust*. Mars/Gemini/10th is Roosevelt's professional significator. Separating from yet received by Mercury, Roosevelt takes recommendations of his Brain Trust as an input; then he proceeds to manipulate them for his own purposes not only as a risk taker in New Deal experiments but later as wartime President. He receives criticism for his professional activity because Mars is elevated and South Node occupies the 10th. Mercury-ruled South Node damages his reputation because some Brain Trust recommendations are overly optimistic and prove unworkable.

Sun. Fame is marred by polio because Sun/Aquarius/6th in his detriment signifies poor circulation in the legs because Aquarius rules the shins. Sun ruling the 12th means he suffers confinement from this condition. Sun in the sign opposed to Leo, the sign of Kings and gold; Roosevelt is no politician who seeks the limelight. Sun, Mercury, and Venus all in the humanitarian sign of Aquarius signify FDR's strong ties with labor issues and the working class because they fall in the 6th of employees which for a President signifies labor issues generally.

Saturn-Jupiter. Born following the 1st of three Saturn-Jupiter conjunctions in Taurus on 18-Apr-1881, Roosevelt's own life rides the wave of world affairs because of this conjunction. When it returns during 1940-1941, FDR is head of the free world during World War II. Saturn and Jupiter represent the forces of contraction and expansion for Taurus-signified things. These include money, banking, finance, real estate, and food. He faces these issues in foreign countries because this conjunction is placed in the 9th of foreign affairs. Malefics in the 9th house consistently define foreign conflicts for all Presidential nativities.

Saturn-Jupiter & the Moon. Two chart configurations indicate Roosevelt will have success in foreign conflicts. First is the placement of Jupiter and Saturn in the sign of Taurus. At 16TA56, Jupiter follows Saturn at 6TA05. The abundance of Jupiter/Taurus, in his own bound, follows the scarcity imposed by Saturn because Jupiter's degree is higher than Saturn's. This satisfies the temporal rule that planets with higher degrees take on increased prominence as the individual ages. The second indication of success is the Moon's separation from Saturn and application to Jupiter. Not only does the Moon's separation from Saturn show that Roosevelt leaves scarcity behind as he ages, but the Cancer Moon in the 11th of alliances gives Roosevelt a personal stake in facilitating the transformation.

Venus-Saturn. Venus/Aquarius square Saturn/Taurus surfaces primarily as restrictions placed on foreign financial assistance to Britain and France imposed by post-WWI Neutrality Acts. These were passed in reaction to the disgust felt by Congress at war-profiteering activities of American companies whose sole objective in selling arms to both sides of the conflict was financial. Were it not for the mutual reception by rulership, this configuration might have kept Roosevelt's hands tied when he wished to aid Britain and France after Hitler's rise to power. Yet he was able to loosen the restrictions on Neutrality Acts before Pearl Harbor. After that they were a moot point.

Venus/Aquarius also signified FDR's wife Eleanor and female workers idealized by the advertising icon *Rosy the Riveter*. Both Eleanor (through travels) and female factory workers (through wartime production) aided FDR's foreign affairs. I also suggest that this square is the crux of FDR's anti-business egalitarian philosophy because Venus/Aquarius imparts fairness about financial matters – reinforced by the anti-business reaction following Saturn/Taurus-signified financial losses of the Great Depression. This square is the signature which formed the New Deal alternative to profit maximization and the concentration of wealth which defined the Roaring 1920s.

Lot of Fortune in 8th ruled by Mars/Gemini signifies FDR's emphasis on war bonds because the 8th is the house of debt. FDR's sales job in encouraging the public to buy bonds to support the war effort exemplifies Mars' ability to deceive. Purchasing fixed rate bonds during a wartime inflationary boom was a terrible investment. Sun ruling LOF by al-mubtazz, opposite the sign of Leo which rules gold also shows FDR's abhorrence of gold. He made gold investments illegal.

FDR: Examination of Mercury Transits to Mars and Saturn, 1940-1944

<u>Restatement of Schoener's Thesis</u>. If Mercury as Ascendant Lord signifies Roosevelt, the objective of this exercise is to determine the specifics of Roosevelt's misfortune each time the transit of Mercury passed over natal Mars and Saturn. Schoener states the condition of Mars and Saturn in the active solar return effectively modifies the natal promise of Mars and Saturn. By delineating Mars and Saturn in the return, it should be possible to make a better prediction for the specific misfortune FDR encountered each time these malefics were transited. Schoener also indicates the magnitude of these transits depends on whether either malefic rules time, presumably as Lord of the Year.

Table 35. Events timed by FDR's Mercury transits, 1940-45

Source: Black (2003)

Date	Transit	Event
9-May-1940	Saturn	10-May-1940. Germany invaded low countries. 10-May-1940. Churchill became UK Prime Minister.
3-Jun-1940	Mars	29-May-1940. FDR reactivated Council of National Defense. 28-May – 4-Jun-1940. French and British evacuated Dunkirk. Churchill speech on 4 June: 'We shall go on to the end...' 17-Jun-1940. FDR fired Sec. War Woodring after he refused to transfer B-17s to Britain.
1-May-1941	Saturn	2/10-May-1941. FDR ill with hypertension and iron deficiency from bleeding hemorrhoids. 5-May-1941. British ejected Italians from Ethiopia.
27-May-1941	Mars	20-May-1941. British/Greeks evacuated Crete. 24-May-1941. German ship Bismarck sunk British cruiser Hood, shock to Churchill, Bismarck sunk in retaliation on the 27$^{th.}$ 27-May-1941. FDR declared state of emergency.
23-Apr-1942	Saturn	18-Apr-1942. Doolittle raid on Tokyo. 28-Apr-1942. FDR presented economic stabilization package during a Fireside Chat radio broadcast.
10-Jul-1942	Mars	10/14-Jul-1942. Row between FDR and Joint Chiefs who suggested abandoning European front for Japan if England did not commit to a cross channel landing (e.g., D-Day) for 1943.
15-Apr-1943	Saturn	13-Apr-1943. FDR dedicated Jefferson Memorial. 13-Apr-1943. FDR left for 16-day tour of military facilities. 15-Apr-1943. Departure of first contingent of African American soldiers from Tuskegee Airfield to North Africa.
4-Jul-1943	Mars	20/22-Jun-1943. Race riots in Detroit. 5-Jul-1943. Hitler launched tank offensive against Russians at Kursk; disaster for Hitler. 10-Jul-1943. Allies began assault on Sicily.
7-Apr-1944	Saturn	9-Apr/7-May 1944 FDR traveled to Baruch's South Carolina estate for extended period of recuperation following a poor medical checkup on 27-Mar-1944.
25-Jun-1944	Mars	20-Jun-1944. Eisenhower squashed Churchill's Italian plan. 23-Jun-1944. Russians launched offensive against Germans. 28-Jun-1944. Churchill exploded over changes to Italian plan, threatened to resign as Prime Minister.

Organization of Time Lords

Schoener implies if the Lord of the Year is a malefic, then the transit of the Ascendant ruler over said malefic will prove more harmful to the native than in other years when the malefic does not rule time. Though an important time lord, the Lord of the Year is not the only way planets can rule time. As these chapters have demonstrated, planets can rule time in the following ways:

- Directing by Triplicity

- Firdaria: Main and Subperiod rulers

- Primary Directions: Distributors and Partners

- Lord of the Year (12 year cycle of sign ruler of annual profected Ascendant)

- Lord of the Period (7 year cycle of planetary hour rulers)

In addition to looking at the influence of the Lord of the Year, other time lord systems are evaluated. Taking a stab at the full spectrum of time lords is one way to tackle the difficult question of establishing the appropriate hierarchy of predictive methods. As present, the order and relative importance of competing predictive methods remains an open question.

Of the many questions that arise with this kind of case study, consider:

- How are the effects of the Lord of the Year felt compared to the Lord of the Period in the solar return?

- Do Firdaria main and subperiod rulers extend their power to the solar return, or are their effects felt purely through planets in their natal configurations?

- How do triplicity rulers interact with Firdaria main period rulers? For example, when the triplicity ruler of the Ascendant is Saturn and the Firdaria main period ruler is Jupiter, how are these effects mixed – and is the interpretation any different if Jupiter rules by triplicity and Saturn by Firdaria?

These are important questions for which definitive answers do not exist. It is hoped that this case study will provide a starting point for further research into structuring the predictive hierarchy.

Directing by Triplicity

Ascendant: Virgo/Earth/Nocturnal: Moon, Venus, Mars
Midheaven: Gemini/Air/Nocturnal: Mercury, Saturn, Jupiter

Division of Years: Roosevelt's election to the NY State Assembly on 8-Nov-1910 began his political career and middle years. Projecting this partition yields the start of final years on 17-Aug-1939 and end-of-life on 25-May-1968. Start of final years on 17-Aug-1939 timed the exact date FDR received the report of Germany and Russia's alliance and preceded Hitler's invasion of Poland on 1-Sep-1939 by two weeks. These events effectively launched his final years as a wartime President. He did not live out final years.

Early Years (30-Jan-1882 – 7-Nov-1910). Moon and Mercury rule the ASC and MC in early years. Consider participation by Mars as the Moon's bound ruler. Moon/Cancer signifies care and comfort from FDR's overprotective mother Sara during FDR's youth. Mercury and Mars both in air signs in a tight trine, signify FDR's interest in writing (as newspaper editor at Harvard), debate (starting at Groton), and a legal profession. The separation of Mercury from Mars weakens the effectiveness of the combination and is responsible for FDR's lackadaisical attitude toward his law practice.

Middle Years (8-Nov-1910 – 16-Aug-1939). FDR launched his political career in New York with his entry into middle years. While many events transpired these 29 years, I suggest that Venus and Saturn as triplicity rulers elevated both FDR's polio illness and his purchase and renovation of the hot springs at Warm Springs, Georgia as a rehabilitation center for polio victims as his two primary life affairs. This is because Saturn in the 9th of travel ruling the 6th of illness is in mutual reception to Venus in the 6th of illness ruling the 9th of travel. Trips to Warm Springs were pilgrimages taken to recuperate.

Final Years (17-Aug-1939 ~ 12-Apr-1945 (actual) ~ 25-May-1968).
Mars/Gemini-rx/10th ruling the Ascendant in final years shows FDR's use of deceit and trickery as a wartime President. Consider also that Mars/Gemini-rx functions like Mars placed in the opposite sign of Sagittarius; a delineation match to FDR's ability to ramp up military aircraft production which helped secure the Allied WWII victory. (Note: Sagittarius = air travel). Jupiter/Taurus as MC ruler shows restoration of global economic security marking career and reputation in final years. Moon applying to Jupiter accentuates the emphasis on abundance as well as the mutual reception by exaltation between the Moon and Jupiter.

Influence of Triplicity Rulers on Mercury's transit of Mars and Saturn. Mars and Jupiter rule the angles in final years. Mars signifies conflict faced as a wartime President; Jupiter shows a favorable outcome over time. Jupiter functions as the light at the end of the tunnel and undoubtedly helped FDR maintain his composure during setbacks timed by difficult Mercury transits.

Primary Directions: Distributors and Partners

Distributors

Ascendant Distributor: Mars/Scorpio from 12-Dec-1931 to 21-Dec-1940
Ascendant Distributor: Venus/Scorpio from 22-Dec-1940 to death

In general, with a transit of Mercury to either Mars or Saturn, incidents of 6th house problems are expected because (1) Saturn rules the 6th and (2) Mercury as 6th house occupant is afflicted by the separation from Mars. These incidents should include illness, pets, servants, and labor issues. If the Ascendant's Distributor has any modifying impact on Mercury's transits to either Mars or Saturn, more examples of problematic 6th house affairs should occur when the directed Ascendant either changes from the bound of a benefic to a malefic or is simply in the bound of a malefic. For FDR, the directed Ascendant fell in the bound of Mars/Scorpio from the onset of his Presidential term until late 1940 when it moved to the bound of Venus/Scorpio. While Mars is a malefic, the Distributor Mars/Scorpio is powerfully placed in his own sign and functions as an accidental benefic in Scorpio. The opposite is true for the benefic Venus who functions as an accidental malefic in Scorpio which is the sign of her detriment.

The striking observation from testing Roosevelt's Mercury transits from 1931 to 1940 when the directed Ascendant fell in the bounds of Mars/Scorpio is that FDR suffered no major health problems when the transit of Mercury passed over either Mars or Saturn during those years. Instead employee and labor problems predominated, including the death of FDR's close friend and political advisor Lewis Howe who died on Mercury's transit of Saturn in 1936. I attribute the lack of physical problems (at least those publicly written about) due to the tremendous stamina that the directed Ascendant in Mars/Scorpio offered FDR in those years.

As soon as the directed Ascendant moved to the bound of Venus/Scorpio, the very first time Mercury transited Saturn, FDR fell ill with hypertension and iron deficiency as a complication from bleeding hemorrhoids (2/10-May-1941).

The second primary health crisis during this period followed the Tehran Conference with Churchill and Stalin on 1-Dec-1943. Roosevelt suffered from the flu and other maladies after Christmas 1943. He was so weak in the spring of 1944 that after a dismal medical checkup on 27-March he traveled to South Carolina on 9-April spending a month to recuperate. The trip was timed by the transit of Mercury to Saturn on 7-Apr-1944. Saturn in the 9th of travel ruling the 6th of illness signifies both foreign conflict as the cause of stress/illness and travel to recuperate as the result because the ruler of the house shows both the source and outcome of its affairs. An additional signification of Venus/Scorpio is poison. It was rumored Roosevelt was poisoned at the Tehran Conference; but this has not been substantiated. Venus/Scorpio as Distributor lends credence to that rumor.

Partner Directions

PT	D	Venus/Libra	P	dex trine Mercury (ME) d. => ASC	28-Sep-1928
PT	D	Venus/Libra	P	dex trine Mercury (0) d. => ASC	27-Apr-1928
PT	D	Mars/Scorpio	P	dex square Venus (0) d. => ASC	30-Sep-1939
PT	D	Mars/Scorpio	P	dex square Venus (VE) d. => ASC	27-Apr-1940
PT	D	Venus/Scorpio	P	opposition Saturn (0) d. => ASC	20-Oct-1939
PT	D	Venus/Scorpio	P	sinister trine Moon (0) d. => ASC	17-Nov-1939
PT	D	Venus/Scorpio	P	opposition Saturn (SA) d. => ASC	28-Feb-1941
PT	D	Venus/Scorpio	P	sinister trine Moon (MO) d. => ASC	24-Apr-1941

In following Abū Ma'shar's method of Distributors and Partner to the letter, the most recent planet aspected by the directed Ascendant needs identification. Such planet should further specify events timed by the transit of Mercury to Mars and Saturn because the Partner adds its signification to the Mercury-ruled Ascendant, just as the Distributor does.

Mercury trine Ascendant

During mid-March 1932, FDR was advised to form his Brain Trust of advisors. This event occurred midway between 1928 and 1939/40, the planetary period established by Mercury as Partner until Venus took over during 1939/40.

Effect on Mercury transits. During this time, many Mercury transits to Saturn and Mars timed difficulties with New Deal programs instigated by the Brain Trust. These included the Supreme Court's ruling of the NIRA as unconstitutional on 27-May-1935, one day after Mercury transited Mars.

Venus square Ascendant/Saturn opposed Ascendant

Because Venus and Saturn are square with mutual reception, their effects should be considered jointly. These directions timed FDR's success in dismantling WWI Neutrality Acts which prohibited the US from selling arms to foreign belligerents. The revised act allowed France and the UK to purchase arms from the US, as long as they used their own ships and paid cash, making *cash and carry* the moniker for the 1939 Act. How did Venus and Saturn signify the loosening of the prior Neutrality Acts? Venus/Aquarius/6th is a humanitarian US worker who receives the Saturn/Taurus/9th war-torn foreign party. Wearing a second hat, Venus in the 10th from the 9th signifies foreign governments who bring cash (Venus) in ships (Aquarius=water bearer) to satisfy business contracts (bound of Mercury=written documents) for arms (dwad of Aries=armaments). Saturn/Taurus/9th, the war-torn foreign countries, gladly receive arms from US workers. The mutual reception effectively means war torn foreign countries can extricate themselves from their devastation because their governments have sufficient cash and are willing to travel via ship to obtain arms and other supplies for rebuilding.

Treating the Moon as co-ruler of the Ascendant, the Moon's separation from Saturn to Jupiter also shows FDR's role in passing the *cash and carry* Neutrality Act of 1939. Moon/Cancer/11th signifies FDR's care for allies. Moon's translation from Saturn to Jupiter shows restoration of financial stability over time. Not only financial stability and agricultural fertility, Jupiter in Taurus signifies worker's goods because Jupiter rules the 7th, 2nd from the 6th. While internationally traded goods are usually signified by the 8th house, in this case it appears that the 7th house is more appropriate because during the Neutrality Act, private parties, not the American government, were the primary participants in arms deals with Europe. Assigning traded goods to the 7th emphasizes that traded goods are 6th house *worker's goods* and not 7th house products of *business partnerships* which is the more common relationship.

Effect on Mercury transits. The change in Partner from Venus/Saturn to the Moon occurs so quickly that only the 1940 events can be isolated to test for the impact of the *cash and carry* Neutrality Act on Mercury's transits. Both 9-May-1940 and 3-Jun-1940 Mercury transits of Saturn and Mars were among the signal events of WWII. Germany's invasion of the Low Countries on 10-May and the fall of France on 22-June marked two fateful bookends to the 1940 pair of Mercury transits. FDR's response was a request that Congress raise airplane production from 12,000 to 50,000 per year to support European allies; a proposal ridiculed by some. How FDR's request, made on 16-May with Mercury positioned at 20TA, is modified by Venus/Saturn as partners is not obvious until Venus/6th is delineated as a female worker. Calls for increased wartime production were met with women, *à la Rosie the Riveter* once American men were mobilized to fight following Pearl Harbor a year later. The availability and willingness of American women to produce goods for war-torn allies makes them participate in this set of transits.

Moon trine Ascendant

Moon/Cancer/11th signifies FDR's care for alliances and is best signified by his relations with Winston Churchill, in particular the Atlantic Charter issued by both men on 14-Aug-1941 at Newfoundland during this sequence. This is the famous document which included *Freedom from Want and Fear* as one of eight points, an apt description of the Moon's effects in the sign she rules.

Effect on Mercury Transits. After 1941, FDR spent much time working closely with Winston Churchill as an ally. Many of Mercury's transits during this period timed events marked by Allies; the most famous being Mercury's transit to Mars on 25-Jun-1944 when Churchill threatened to resign after Eisenhower rejected Churchill's Italian invasion plans in favor of a second French landing.

Firdaria

Next consider how Firdaria main and subperiod rulers impact Mercury's transits.

Main Period Ruler	Subperiod Ruler	Date
Venus	Venus	31-Jan-1936
Venus	Mercury	24-Mar-1937
Venus	Moon	15-May-1938
Venus	Saturn	7-Jul-1939
Venus	Jupiter	27-Aug-1940
Venus	Mars	19-Oct-1941
Venus	Sun	10-Dec-1942
Mercury	Mercury	31-Jan-1944

Saturn subperiod: 7-Jul-1939 to 26-Aug-1940

Mercury transited Saturn on 9-May-1940, the day before Germany invaded the Low Countries. This was among the worst days of the entire conflict; for Americans, second only to Pearl Harbor.

Mars subperiod: 19-Oct-1941 to 9-Dec-1942

Mercury transited Mars on 10-Jul-1942. On this date the Joint Chiefs delivered to FDR a paper stating that unless the U.K. committed to a cross channel landing in 1943 (e.g., D-Day), that the US should de-emphasize the European theatre and refocus efforts on Japan. FDR was shocked at these plans and told Marshall to travel to London with Harry Hopkins, giving them one week to smooth over relations with the U.K.

Evaluation. Are these events timed by Mercury's transits more problematic when compared to other transits when Saturn or Mars were not Firdaria rulers?

In the first case, a qualified yes. Hitler's invasion of the Low Countries was also timed by FDR's 2nd Saturn return and a Mars return. Without the coincident Saturn and Mars returns, the effects would not have been as serious.

In the second case, a definite yes. Threats from top ranking military officials to abandon a close ally would roil any President. Yet this event appears below the level of maliciousness compared to Mercury's 1944 transit of Mars when Churchill threatened to resign. Though malefics were not Firdaria rulers during 1944, Mars had power to act because he was Lord of the Year.

Considering both 1940 and 1942 events when Saturn and Mars ruled time by Firdaria and the 1944 event when Mars was Lord of the Year, it does appear that Mercury's transits produced greater evil when malefics ruled time.

Franklin Roosevelt: 1940 Solar Return

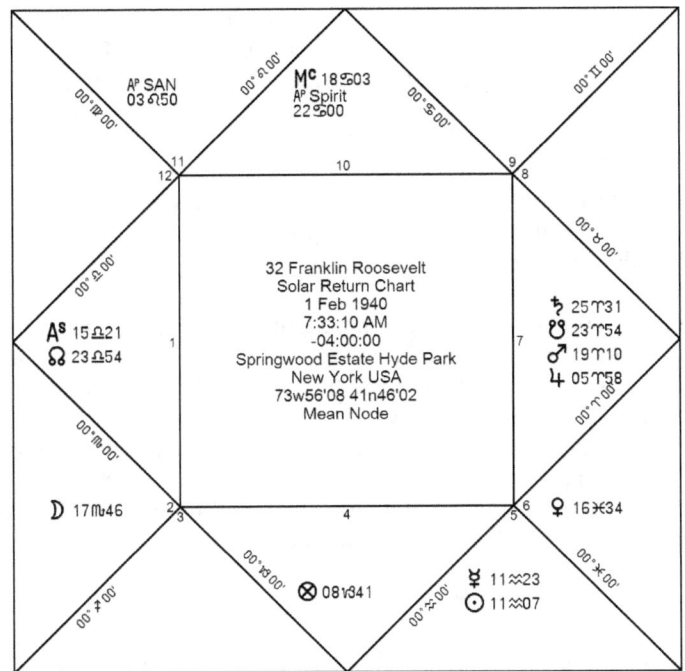

Solar Return statistics

Date: 1-Feb-1940

Age: 58

<u>Firdaria Lords</u>: Venus/Saturn; changed to Venus/Jupiter on 26-Aug-1940

<u>Profected Annual Ascendant</u>: 11th House

<u>Lord of Year</u>: Moon

<u>Lord of Period</u>: Jupiter

<u>Return Al-mubtazz</u>: Saturn

<u>Moon</u>: separates from trine of Venus and is void of course; Moon's ruler is Mars

Return Ascendant falls in natal 2nd; Natal Ascendant falls in return 12th

Delineating Mars and Saturn in the 1940 return.

The Saturn-South Node-Mars-Jupiter stellium in Aries dominates the figure. These transits fall in FDR's natal 8th of foreign trade and return's 7th of business partnerships. Foreign trade is highlighted because the return's Saturn is partile conjunct natal Lot of Fortune in the 8th of traded goods. The return's Saturn and Mars rule the return's Lot of Fortune in the 4th.

Saturn/Aries signifies obstructions to warfare; *Mars/Aries* signifies the opposite.
South Node/Aries diminishes both Saturn and Mars' qualities.
Jupiter/Aries signifies advising/teaching/philosophy of war.

This is a tricky configuration to sort out. An important clue is found when on 2 July, the starting date of the 4th house monthly profection, FDR was forced to sign a measure prohibiting arms sales to Britain unless the Dept. of Defense stated the arms were non-essential items. This action was taken because there had been a significant depletion of US ammunition stockpiles. The Saturn/South Node/Mars stellium marred FDR's attempts to facilitate the export of armaments to Britain and France (stellium falling in natal 8th of foreign trade) and business contracts thereof (stellium falling in return's 7th of business partnerships).

Influence of the return's Mars and Saturn on Mercury's transit

It appears the return's Saturn/Aries conjunct natal Lot of Fortune accentuated the devastation of Hitler's invasion of the Low Countries on 10-May-1940, timed by Mercury's transit over natal Saturn, because the return's Saturn/Aries obstructed arms sales to Britain and France, without which they became easier prey for the Germans.

That FDR requested increased aircraft production on 16-May as an alternative course was timed by progressed Moon square Mars/Sagittarius on 17-May based on the following 1941 return. Sagittarius is the sign of flight; Mars in that sign signifies military aircraft. Remember natal Mercury falls in the dwad of Sagittarius, making FDR himself interested in aircraft and prone to optimistic statements like the one he made on 16-May calling for an *increase in airplane production from 12,000 to 50,000 units annually*. FDR's firing of Secretary of War Woodring on 17-June for failure to transfer aircraft to Britain places transiting Mercury well beyond the conjunction of Mars on 3-June, but the issue probably started around 3-June. Woodring's dismissal dealt with aircraft and demonstrates the influence of Mars on Mercury's transit, though from the 1941 return.

As to this 1940 return, the inability of FDR to directly export arms underlies the entire affair; this is signified by Mars conjunct the South Node. In this way, Mars modified Mercury's transit.

Franklin Roosevelt: 1941 Solar Return

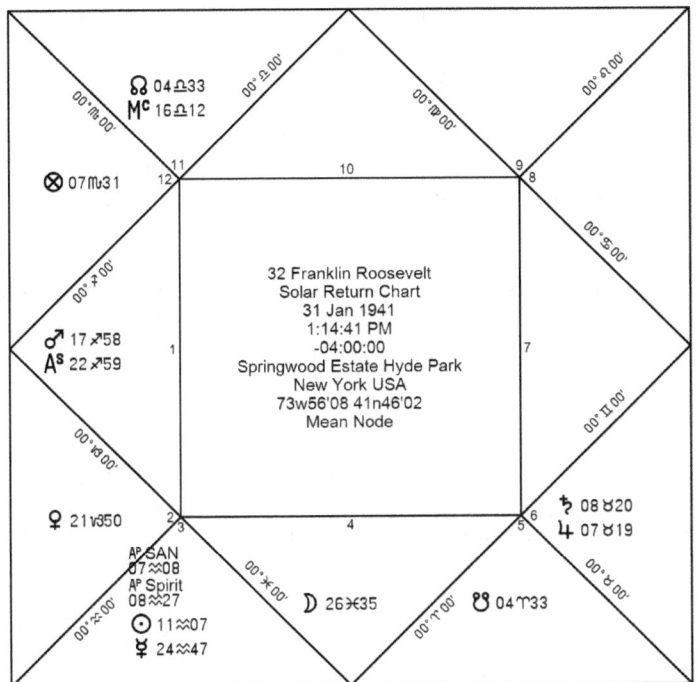

Solar Return statistics

Date: 31-Jan-1941

Age: 59

<u>Firdaria Lords</u>: Venus/Jupiter; changes to Venus/Mars on 17-Oct-1941

<u>Profected Annual Ascendant</u>: 12th House

<u>Lord of Year</u>: Sun

<u>Lord of Period</u>: Mars

<u>Return Al-mubtazz</u>: Jupiter

<u>Moon</u>: separates from trine of Venus and is void of course; Moon's Lord is Jupiter

Return Ascendant falls in natal 4th; Natal Ascendant falls in return 10th

Delineating Mars and Saturn in the 1941 return

Saturn returns to his natal sign and bound. He rules the natal 6th of illness and is placed directly in the same 6th house (WS) in the return. Saturn's placement in the return predisposes FDR to illness this year.

Mars/Gemini-rx in natal 10th functions as though placed in the opposite sign of Sagittarius in the 4th. This can be delineated as domestic military aircraft production. Mars/Sagittarius placed in the return's 1st whole sign house makes domestic aircraft production one of FDR's primary motivations for 1941.

As stated in the 1940 return discussion, the 1941 solar return's progressed Moon activated this Mars by square on 17-May-1940, triggering FDR's proposal to increase domestic aircraft production from 12,000 to 50,000 units per year.

Influence of the return's Mars and Saturn on Mercury's transit

Mercury's transit of Saturn on 1-May-1941 sets off a period of illness from hypertension and iron deficiency from bleeding hemorrhoids. Saturn's rulership of natal 6th and Saturn's placement in the return's 6th predisposed FDR to illness for this Mercury transit.

As Mercury transited Mars on 27-May-1941, FDR declared a *State of Unlimited National Emergency*. This action was apparently triggered by nervousness following the destruction of the British cruiser *Hood* by Germany's *Bismarck* battleship. Though the *Bismarck* was disabled shortly thereafter, the ease with which Germany destroyed the *Hood* on the heels of the evacuation of Crete struck fear among the Allies. While this transit of Mercury over Mars did not trigger any events related to domestic aircraft production (at least none mentioned by Black); declaring a state of emergency is consistent with Mars/Sagittarius acting in a blustering manner. The functional placement of Mars in natal 4th ties FDR's bluster to the homeland; e.g., *national* emergency; placement in the return's 1st adds this warlike agitation to FDR's primary motivation for the year.

Influence of other time lords on Mercury's transit

12th house year emphasizes secret enemies, self-undoing, and confinement. LOY Sun/Aquarius/6th of illness ruling the 12th of confinement signifies FDR's confinement in a wheelchair because of polio. By this time, FDR had lived with polio for 20 years so this was nothing new. Yet during this particular year, FDR's suffered from bleeding hemorrhoids, undoubtedly aggravated by constant sitting and lack of movement. The 12th house signification of fear probably added to FDR's decision to declare a state of emergency following British losses at sea.

Franklin Roosevelt: 1942 Solar Return

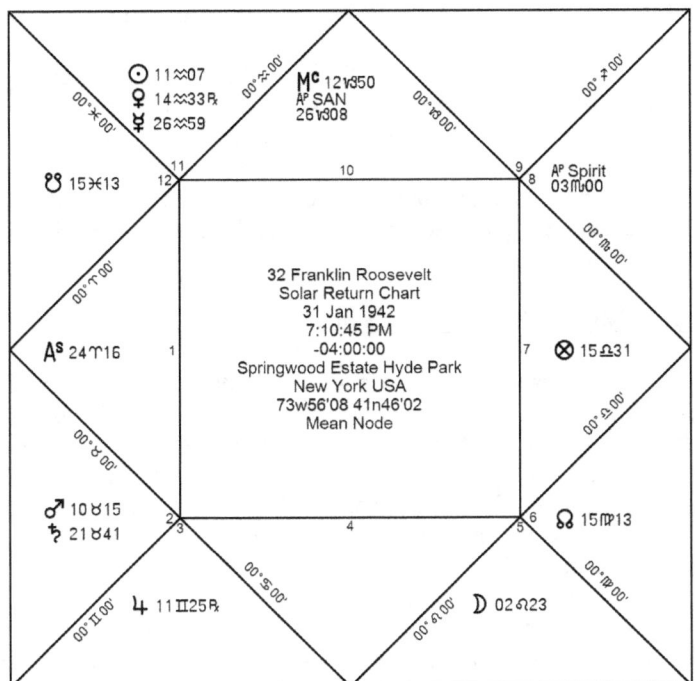

Solar Return statistics

Date: 31-Jan-1942

Age: 60

<u>Firdaria Lords</u>: Venus/Mars; changes to Venus/Sun 8-Dec-1942

<u>Profected Annual Ascendant</u>: 1st House

<u>Lord of Year</u>: Mercury

<u>Lord of Period</u>: Sun

<u>Return Al-mubtazz</u>: Saturn

<u>Moon</u>: applies to square of Mars

Return Ascendant falls in natal 8th; Natal Ascendant falls in return 6th

Delineating Mars and Saturn in the return

If natal Saturn/Taurus/9th signifies destruction of resources and financial difficulties abroad, then those problems are brought home this year by Saturn's placement in the return's 2nd of wealth. Saturn/Taurus diminishes resources and causes inflation because of supply reductions. Saturn also rules the 11th of alliances and squares Mercury who is fearful of resource scarcity.

Mars/Taurus/2nd ruling the 1st and 8th made FDR worry about the stock and bond markets which are both 8th house affairs. Taurus is the sign of wealth and money; Mars in Taurus damages wealth.

Influence of the return's Mars and Saturn on Mercury's transit

On 28-Apr-1942, FDR presented his seven-point Economic Stabilization Program in a Fireside Chat. It included wage and price controls, a call for the public to invest in bonds, commodity rationing, and the discouragement of private debt. This speech followed Mercury's transit of Saturn on 23-April when these proposals were likely being finalized. The influence of the return's Saturn/Taurus/2nd signifying a contraction of wealth from resource scarcity is clear on Mercury's transit of natal Saturn.

Mercury's transit of natal Mars on 10-Jul-1942 triggered a row between FDR and the Joint Chiefs who proposed that America should focus war efforts on the Pacific theater if the English did not commit to a cross-channel landing (e.g., D-Day) by 1943. This followed Britain's 8-July announcement that they would drop plans for a diversionary landing in France known as Operation Sledgehammer. This triggered an explosion of rage by Chief of Staff Marshall.

An explosion of anger is the style of Mars/Taurus; in this return, triggered by the weak Venus/Aquarius/11th – retrograde and combust. Retrograde planets are rebellious and defiant; here in the 11th of alliances placed in Aquarius the sign of the water bearer, Venus signifies Britain's unwillingness to make a cross-channel landing and Mars is Marshall's rage; both planets are square in the figure and there is a dispute. This dispute was an underlying factor behind FDR's shock at Marshall's plan to virtually abandon the European theatre on 10-Jul-1942 when transiting Mercury passed over natal Mars.

Influence of Lord of the Year on Mercury's transit

In a 1st house profected year, LOY Mercury returns to its same sign and bound. Compared to natal Mercury, oriental and swift, the return's Mercury is moving slow at its first station. This made Roosevelt more fearful this year. His decision making is marred by the feeling of being on edge. Saturn, significator of resource scarcity, receives Mercury; it is the source of Roosevelt's fear this year and caused him to overreact with an austere economic stabilization plan.

Franklin Roosevelt: 1943 Solar Return

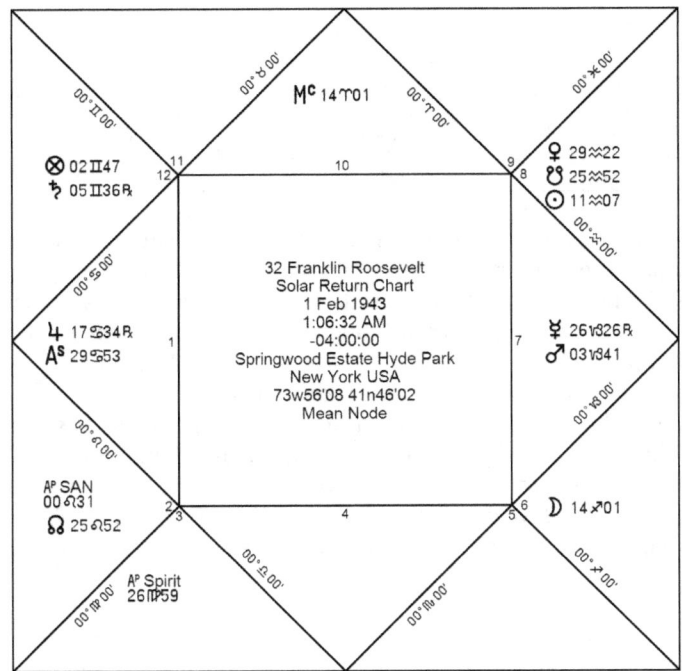

Solar Return statistics

Date: 1-Feb-1943

Age: 61

Firdaria Lords: Venus/Sun; changed to Mercury/Mercury on 30-Jan-1944

Profected Annual Ascendant: 2nd House

Lord of Year: Venus

Lord of Period: Venus

Return Al-mubtazz: Jupiter (WS)

Moon: separates from sextile of Sun and is void of course; Moon's Lord is Jupiter

Return Ascendant falls in natal 11th ; Natal Ascendant falls in return 3rd

Delineating Mars and Saturn in the 1943 return

Antiscia are required to unlock this return's promise:

Planet	Position	Antiscion	Contra-antiscion
Saturn	5GE36	24CA24	24CP24
Mercury	26CP26	3SA34	3GE34
Ascendant	29CA56	00GE04	00SA04

Saturn falls in Mercury's contra-antiscion and the Ascendant's antiscion. Saturn and Mercury are in generosity by sign. They powerfully drive the figure. Now what does this Saturn signify? First consider natal Saturn in 9th signifies destruction of resources and banking crises in foreign lands. Next consider for this return, Saturn has moved from its natal sign of Taurus in FDR's 9th to the sign of Gemini and falls in FDR's natal 10th. The devastation of the world war marks FDR's career. How so? The return places Saturn in the 12th. 12th House is secret enemies but also hidden knowledge. I suggest that Saturn/Gemini signifies scientists, most of them European war refugees, who immigrated to the United States. In their commitment to develop nuclear weapons to destroy Adolph Hitler, they marked FDR's natal 10th house of career through the 1943 return's 12th house of covert activity.

An important clue to confirm Saturn as a nuclear physicist is to study what happened when the progressed Moon opposed Saturn earlier on 1-Jul-1942. During June 1942, Robert Oppenheimer convened a summer study session at the University of California where a group of physicists confirmed the feasibility of a fission bomb. On 17-Jun-1942, FDR approved a pilot plan to construct one or two reactors. These events fell very close to the 1-Jul-1942 date.

In addition to the general signification of Saturn/Gemini as a scientist, I suggest these scientists have nuclear research interests because Saturn's antiscion at 24CA24 falls at a hot degree area which has been associated with many subsequent nuclear events, such as the Sun's position at 23CA32 at the time of the successful Alamogordo test on 16-Jul-1945.

If Saturn signifies the scientists, then Mercury signifies the research. Mercury/Capricorn's al-mubtazz is Mars/Capricorn which adds a military emphasis to research. Both Saturn and Mercury retrograde means there will be setbacks causing steps to be repeated. This is confirmed by timing setbacks in the Manhattan Project during July and December; months highlighted by the monthly profection technique which recognizes Mercury and Saturn's influence by position.

House of Monthly Profection	Date	1943 Return	Event
2	1/31/1943 16:11		
3	3/3/43 2:40 AM	ME-rules	Researchers arrive at Los Alamos,
4	4/2/43 1:10 PM		
5	5/2/43 11:40 PM	MA-rules	
6	6/2/43 10:09 AM		
7	7/2/43 8:39 PM	ME-pos MA-pos SA-rules	Oppenheimer reports need for 3x as much fissionable material as originally thought.
8	8/2/43 7:09 AM	SA-rules	Groundbreaking for Hanford, Washington site takes place,
9	9/1/43 5:38 PM		
10	10/2/43 4:08 AM	MA-rules	
11	11/1/43 2:38 PM		
12	12/2/43 1:07 AM	SA-pos ME-rules	First Alpha racetrack is shut down due to maintenance problems.
1	1/1/44 11:37 AM		

Start of construction of the Hanford Washington site during August 1943, an 8th house profected month, is interesting because the site was selected because of proximity to the Columbia River basin and access to cheap hydroelectric power. FDR's Sun is tied to hydro power because his Sun falls in Aquarius which is the sign of the water bearer. As shown in the rectification, this delineation is confirmed by his fame achieved for a hydroelectric power proposal before the New York Assembly on 12-Mar-1929 timed by a Sun-DSC primary direction. Sun in the 8th of return, house of government debt, shows the connection between hydroelectric power and the financing of atomic research.

Mars/Gemini/10th in the natal figure signifying FDR's professional significator of manipulated intelligence, risk taking, and wartime president, moves to Capricorn the sign of his exaltation. Powerfully placed in the return's 7th, a common natal placement for military leaders, FDR achieved victory in 1943. This is confirmed by Allied successes during May, July, and October 1943; months where Mars exerted its influence by position or rulership as specified by monthly profections.

May 1943: Allies won Battle of Tunisia, took 275,000 prisoners;
July 1943: Allies began assault on Sicily and Rome;
October 1943: Liberation of Naples from Axis occupation kicked off month and is followed by many other gains in Italy.

Influence of the return's Mars and Saturn on Mercury's transit

Immediately prior to Mercury's transit of Saturn on 15-Apr-1943, FDR left for a sixteen-day tour of military facilities. Saturn in the natal 9th is in the house of travel. While the public record of FDR's trip makes no mention of trips to Manhattan Project sites; Saturn as the significator of scientists conducting covert nuclear research should have influenced FDR's trip by the inclusion of visits and/or meetings related to the Manhattan Project. Because 12th house planets are hidden and often difficult to delineate, it is hard to confirm whether this assertion is true. Black (2003) makes no mention of it. Unfortunately with most 12th house planets, the full story is often never known.

As Mercury transited Mars on 4-Jul-1943, the Allies were gearing up for what would be a successful assault on Italy, beginning with Sicily. As stated above, the powerfully placed Mars in the 1943 return guaranteed Allied success.

Influence of Lord of the Year on Mercury's transit

LOY Venus in all likelihood signified the 1st contingent of African American soldiers from the Tuskegee Airfield deploying to North Africa on 15-April, the exact day of Mercury's transit of Saturn. Eleanor was instrumental in pushing FDR to integrate the US Armed Forces. She personally arranged a 27-September 1940 meeting between FDR and the NAACP which resulted in some small steps taken to integrate African Americans. This Tuskegee group of fighter pilots was the most celebrated example.

As the original force behind the creation of this group, Eleanor – signified by Venus – left her mark on this Mercury transit.

Franklin Roosevelt: 1944 Solar Return

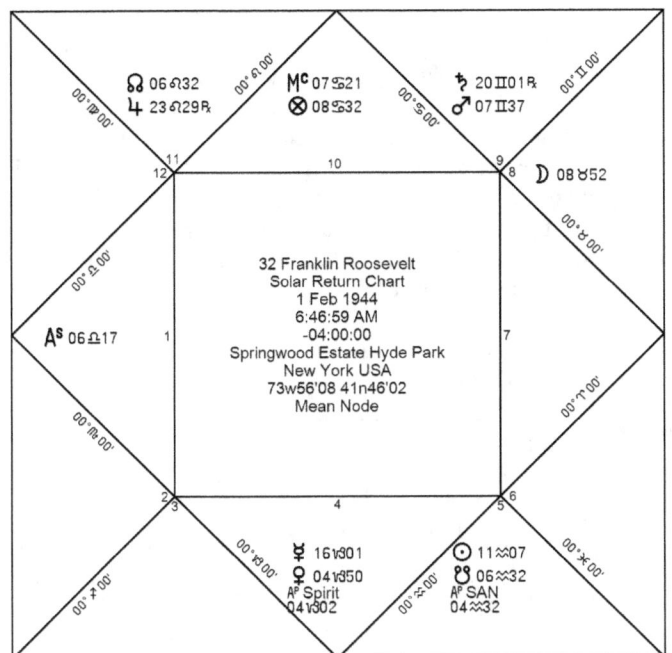

Solar Return statistics

Date: 1-Feb-1944

Age: 62

Firdaria Lords: Mercury/Mercury; changed to Mercury/Moon on 9-Dec-1945

Profected Annual Ascendant: 3rd House

Lord of Year: Mars

Lord of Period: Mercury

Return Al-mubtazz: Saturn

Moon: separates from trine of Venus and applies to square of Sun

Return Ascendant falls in natal 2nd ; Natal Ascendant falls in return 12th

Delineating Mars and Saturn in the 1944 return

Just as in the 1943 return, Saturn and Mercury are similarly configured in Gemini and Capricorn, conjunct widely by contra-antiscia and in generosity. Events listed for Mercury's transits of Mars and Saturn do not mention nuclear physicists (nor did the 1943 event listing), yet the Manhattan Project was active during this time. As one example of a Saturn-signified émigré acting his part during the 1944 return, Klaus Fuchs arrived at Los Alamos on 14-Aug-1944. He would prove to be the primary conduit for passing secrets of the Manhattan Project to the Russians. August 1944 was a 9th house profected month, the very same house that contains Saturn for the return. Saturn is interested in secrets because of his connection to Mercury who rules the 12th of secrets.

House of Monthly Profection	Date	1944 Return	Event
3	1/31/1944 21:51		
4	3/2/44 8:21 AM	ME-pos SA-rules	Aerial bombing of Germany FDR bad health checkup,
5	4/1/44 6:50 PM	SA-rules	FDR trip for recuperation.
6	5/2/44 5:20 AM		
7	6/1/44 3:50 PM	MA-rules	6 June. Operation Overlord, *D-Day* invasion of Northern France.
8	7/2/44 2:19 AM		
9	8/1/44 12:49 PM	MA-pos SA-pos ME-rules	12 August. FDR made ill-conceived speech to ship workers in Alaska with severe winds. 14 August. Fuchs arrived at Los Alamos. 15 August. Operation Dragoon, invasion of Southern France.
10	8/31/44 11:19 PM		
11	10/1/44 9:48 AM		
12	10/31/44 8:18 PM	ME-rules	FDR successful election to 4th term, included travel in open car in 40-degree temperatures as a statement of FDR's vitality to the press.
1	12/1/44 6:48 AM		
2	12/31/44 5:17 PM	MA-rules	Battle of the Bulge/German retreat.

To explain why Mercury's transit of Saturn on 7-Apr-1944 triggered FDR's month-long forced recuperation following an extended period of ill health, it first makes sense to check the return for indications of physical stress. Hīlāj Moon in the 8th of death applying to the Sun – both afflicted by aspects to the Nodes – predisposed FDR to illness this year. So does Saturn who rules natal 6th of illness and by transit to the natal 10th marked his career by Saturn/Gemini's scrutinizing style of investigation. Together with Mercury/Capricorn which signifies a methodical mental process but one that tends towards depression and Mars/Gemini's incendiary tendencies, the Saturn-Mercury-Mars configuration undoubtedly took a toll on FDR's health. One can imagine that strategy sessions discussing how to properly corral the incendiary firepower of Allied forces prior to landings in France. Though he didn't yet know about the infiltration of Klaus Fuchs, this same Saturn-Mercury-Mars configuration shows that maintaining the secrecy of the Manhattan Project was never far from Roosevelt's mind. Balancing Operation Overlord and Dragoon on one hand and the secrecy of the Manhattan Project on the other would tax anyone's physical vitality. For Roosevelt in a weakened condition, it pushed him to the very limits of physical existence.

Saturn's placement in the 9th by position and rulership of the 4th and 5th signifies illness and travel for FDR. This delineation is confirmed by health problems witnessed during 4th, 5th, and 9th house monthly profected periods.

With respect to Mars, the largest military operations in the European theatre were launched in 7th house and 9th house profected months when Mars exerted his influence by position or rulership, just as Mars did in the 1943 return.

Operation Overlord (*D-Day*) = 7th house profected month ruled by Mars

Operation Dragoon = 9th house profected month where Mars is active by position.

Why did the return's Mars/Gemini mean success for Overlord and Dragoon? First consider Mars/Gemini makes his natal return and is tied to Mercury/Capricorn in the 4th. Lord Mercury 16CP01 disposes both Saturn and Mars, is partile conjunct the Mars/Saturn midpoint of 13GE47 by contra-antiscion, and is in mutual reception with Saturn. I suggest the methodical nature of Mercury/Capricorn was very effective in planning the logistics of foreign military operations signified by both Mars and Saturn in the 9th house. This Mars-Saturn-Mercury configuration is similar to the 1943 return which was also successful for Roosevelt. Whereas the 1943 return emphasized covert research by Saturn/Gemini's placement in the 12th; for 1944 military strategy is more overt because Saturn and Mars are in the 9th of foreign lands. Mercury in the 4th suggests the strategy dealt with the end-game because the 4th house signifies the end of the matter.

One major source of difficulty for FDR in 1944 was disagreement with Churchill over Operation Dragoon designed to complement Operation Overlord with a southern landing in France. Churchill favored a different strategy that would have pushed Allied forces more towards Eastern Europe than the strategy to deploy in Southern France. Though Operation Dragoon was a success, the ability of Stalin to outmaneuver the Allies in control of Poland and other Eastern European nations post-Yalta did vindicate Churchill's concerns over the vulnerability of Eastern Europe at the hands of Russia.

Can FDR's favoritism for France be shown by the 1944 return? Yes for three reasons. First is Jupiter's transit to Leo which falls in the return's 11th of alliances. According to mundane choreography, France is assigned to Leo; England to Aries. Jupiter's placement in Leo elevates France as an ally in 1944. Second the North Node/Leo in the same 11th house amplifies the importance of France. Third because Mars falls in the bound and decan of Jupiter. Jupiter/Leo receives Mars/Gemini in the return. This means that France has more claims over Roosevelt's Mars/Gemini-signified military deployment than does England. Note that Mars/Gemini in the natal falls in the dwad of Aries which is England's sign. So France is not only emphasized in the return, but there is a shift *from* England *to* France read through the minor dignities of Mars's placement in the return relative to the natal figure.

If there is any doubt that the Jupiter-North Node/Leo/11th configuration favored France for 1944, consider the progressed solar return Moon squared the Nodes on 30-Nov-1943; the exact date during the Teheran Conference that Churchill, Roosevelt, and Stalin agreed that Operation Overlord would start by 1-Jun-1944. Yet another example of the accuracy of the Lunar Node's mean position.

Influence of the return's Mars (LOY) and Saturn on Mercury's transit

Immediately following Mercury's transit of Saturn on 7-Apr-1944, FDR took a sojourn to Bernard Baruch's South Carolina estate for an extended period of recuperation. Though this was technically a domestic trip, not foreign travel, this trip does meet the 9th house signification of *falling away from one's career*. If healthy, the 9th house might time a research-type sabbatical; if ill, a recuperation. As stated earlier, Saturn's configuration predisposed FDR to illness this year because of stress from the all-consuming military planning sessions for Operation Overlord and Dragoon. He also tended to overtax himself in public, such as the 12-Aug-1944 disastrous outdoor speech marred by high winds; Roosevelt's performance was so poor that rumors began to circulate whether he could sustain another political campaign in the fall of 1944.

Mercury's transit over Mars on 25-Jun-1944 timed Churchill's explosion over changes to his Italian plan and his threatened resignation as Prime Minister on 28 June. As already identified, 1944 marked a 3rd house profected year ruled by Mars. With a malefic as LOY, the expectation for a nasty confrontation was met. As stated above, the return's Mars/Gemini in the bound and decan of Jupiter predisposed FDR towards France. Together with the Jupiter-North Node/Leo/11th configuration which also favored France, there is no way that FDR would have acceded to Churchill's demands. Mars' preference towards France clearly marked Mercury's transit of natal Mars on 25-Jun-1944.

Summary of Roosevelt Transit Study

In my opinion, the power of Mars and Saturn in each return to modify effects witnessed by Mercury is uncannily accurate. Based on this case study, I rate Schoener's recommendations as one of the most significant insights on how to properly forecast transits that I have uncovered to date.

Still there remain limits on the efficacy of this case study. They are:

Event Data. This analysis was based primarily on events recorded by one biographer. While comprehensive, Black (2003) did not include many details of the War Bond campaign, one of the principal delineations of Mars/Gemini ruling the Lot of Fortune in the 8th house of debt. Items like this need to be considered. In addition, events surrounding the Manhattan Project included in the discussion of the 1943 return were pulled from a limited public access chronology. A more thorough investigation of the Manhattan Project's history might lead to somewhat different conclusions.

Analysis of other Significators. Mercury also rules Roosevelt's Midheaven. Distributors and Partners for the MC should be considered. In addition, to evaluate the full range of health matters, Distributors and Partners for the Moon (as hīlāj) should be analyzed.

Natal Planet Configuration. Jupiter falls so close to Saturn in Roosevelt's figure that events timed by Mercury's transits to Saturn are sometimes difficult to separate from Mercury's transits to Jupiter. I may not have attributed the events correctly.

Finishing this limited study makes one appreciate the work performed by Presidential scholars, whose research for a single subject may span ten years or longer. Yet while any astrological study will fall short of the full range of life's events, it remains a testament to the power of medieval predictive astrology that many significant events during 1940-1945 were accurately captured by a few simple rules.

Usefulness in Rectification. The Roosevelt case study demonstrates how solar returns modify the effect of transits when the Ascendant lord transits a malefic planet. Theoretically, this technique can be used to confirm the signs on angles and house cusps by application of its rules. Because there are many other easier methods to accomplish this task, I do not consider transits of the Ascendant Lord an effective rectification technique.

PART THREE

Rectification

CHAPTER SIXTEEN

Preparing the Event Database

Because of the *Garbage-In* → *Garbage-Out* rule, constructing the event database requires great care. Unlike some modern approaches which require a comprehensive life history to confirm psychological development, a rectification method based on medieval predictive astrology is simpler. With as few as ten or fifteen events it is possible to rectify a natal chart. Event types most conducive to timing by medieval techniques are emphasized in database construction.

Chapter Summary

Preferred Events for Data Collection. Because Mars always leaves his mark, Martian events are preferred. Saturn-signified events are not far behind. The emphasis on gathering events marked by Mars and Saturn in no way denies the influence of benefics during a person's lifetime. Yet events marked by malefics are the first to be remembered and usually the first to be told. Events of notoriety and other events impacting family members are also emphasized.

Inclusion of Mundane Affairs in an Individual Event Database. Results of this study support the ability of natal figures for political leaders to time mundane events; yet it is easy to read mundane events into a natal figure where none exist, especially for a sitting political figure. For national political leaders, rectification should be based on events prior to their arrival on the national stage.

Choosing and Reading Biographies. A non-partisan work containing accurately timed dates is the first prerequisite for choosing a biography. Of additional interest are biographies based on access to material recently discovered or declassified. Besides culling as many dates as possible, qualitative information on the native's temperament, manners, Moon's significations, wealth, philosophy, and identification of life's major turning points all complement a purely event-driven database.

Introduction to Rectification

Historical Methods

During the Medieval Era, three approaches to rectification were taken: Animodar, Pre-Natal Epoch, and Accidents of the Native.

Animodar. In this technique, the Ascendant or Midheaven, whichever is closer, is made the degree of the al-mubtazz of the Syzygy Ante Navitatem (SAN). A recent statistical study of this technique demonstrated its purported results are not distinguishable from random birth times (Ventura, 2009).

Pre-Natal Epoch. Sometimes referred to as the *Trutine of Hermes*, the *Pre-Natal Epoch* method assumes the position of the Ascendant and Moon are transposed from conception to birth. Because the moment of conception is generally not verifiable by actual event records, this method is not falsifiable.

Accidents of the Native. The word *Accidents* is taken to mean the full range of events that happens during a lifetime and does not have purely malefic connotations. Rectification by accidents is a purely empirical approach which matches actual life events to dates determined by specific predictive methods.

Working with an empirical approach, I have chosen *Accidents of the Native* as the preferred rectification method.

Late Victorian Approach to Rectification

Writing at the turn of the 20th century, two noted astrologers gave the following advice for rectifying birth times:

Alfred John Pearce, in his Textbook of Astrology (1911, 203-204), wrote:

> *Several methods have been propounded for rectifying approximate times of birth. The only true process is by computing arcs of primary direction for past events of importance – such as serious accidents, dangerous illness, death of father or mother, emigration, etc., - and comparing the arcs of such directions as may fall due near the periods of such events and harmonise with the nature of them...*
>
> *It is usually found that directions of Mars afford the most reliable means of rectifying an uncertain estimate of the birth-moment; especially in the case of an acute fever, or an accident causing much loss of blood, or necessitating a surgical operation, or the sudden death of a parent.*

The date of marriage if already entered upon, will sometimes be useful to this end, especially in the case of a real love-match, of happy and advantageous nature; in such case a direction of Venus may fall a little earlier than the arc of marriage, thereby accounting for the fascination leading up to the engagement and wedding.

W. J. Simmonite, in The Arcana of Astrology (1890, 282), wrote:

The best directions by which to rectify the estimated time of birth are those of the M.C. to Mars or the Sun, the Sun to parallels of Mars or the angles, as their effects do generally answer very closely to the time of direction. Marriage, accident, and death of parents, are safe events by which to rectify.

Locking down a birth time with events marked by malefics or the Sun. Other than the ability of the Moon to time marriage (not just Venus), I agree with Pearce and Simmonite's assertion that primary directions to the angles are the most reliable rectification method. As demonstrated in the Presidential database, primary directions of Mars, Saturn or the Sun to the angles are the most common directions used to *lock down* to-the-second rectified birth times.

Primary Directions are only one of many possible rectification techniques. Where I differ from Pearce and Simmonite is the apparent exclusivity assigned to primary directions as a rectification tool. As presented in Chapter 17: *Three Stages of Rectification*, a richer mix of techniques is recommended. From planetary period methods to Hellenistic Lots, there are multiple tools which can narrow the Ascendant to within 1-4 degrees of accuracy. It is at this point in the process where I believe primary directions are appropriate. In my opinion, to begin rectification with primary directions, especially when a birth time is unknown, is akin to a surgeon using a scalpel when the patient has not had clothing removed, much less been shaved or washed.

Emphasize events signified by malefics and the Sun in database construction. Pearce and Simmonite indicate the importance of events marked by Mars, Saturn, and Sun for rectification purposes. If these types of events are such reliable rectification inputs, then logically it makes sense to emphasize these events when constructing an event database. Taking these in turn, let's look at events marked by malefics and events of notoriety; not only for the individual but for other family members.

Preferred Events for Data Collection

<u>Events Marked by Malefics</u>. Because Mars always leaves his mark, events of a Martian nature are preferred. These include marital and legal disputes, home fires and burglaries, accidents, surgeries, illness, and death. Criminal activity, arrest, trial, and incarceration dates are also valuable though they are sometimes of Saturn's nature. Compiling this kind of list is akin to preparing a crime report for the evening news. This is not to deny the occurrence of pleasure, joy, and triumph in anyone's life. However, like the evening news, events of a malefic nature have always been emphasized in collective memories, whether by a living client or those presented by a biographer written later. They are the first to be remembered and – unless unusually traumatic – the first to be told.

<u>Events of Fame or Notoriety</u>. Not just a career change but any event with a public connection is helpful. Events where the individual gains publicity or notoriety are also excellent choices when assembling an event database. While this category typically includes dates of major career changes, the more important thread is any type of event which connects the individual to the community. This can mean an art gallery opening, any mention in the public media, a publication date or book tour, making speeches to large audiences, or receiving recognition in front of many people. Even the date a person was interviewed by a television crew can prove valuable.

<u>Both the Sun and Lunar Nodes can time publicity</u>. Public events are timed by two methods. First are directions of the Sun to the angles. Second are transiting aspects or directions of the Lunar Nodes to the angles. While the literature has focused mostly on Sun directions, there are relatively few of these during a single lifetime. More frequent are transits of the Lunar Nodes to the angles. As demonstrated in Chapter 14, the Lunar Nodes time events which connect the native to the world-at-large for which public records are likely to exist.

<u>Events Impacting Family Members</u>. Seldom do astrologers request events for family members other than death of parents or close relatives. Virtually any incident involving a family member is fodder for rectification testing, especially if the subject with unknown birth time is younger and has few events of their own available for testing.

<u>Events other than death can be timed by Lots of Death</u>. Family events can be used in conjunction with relevant lots, including the Lot of Mother, Lot of Father, Lot of Siblings, and Lots of Death for either Parents or Siblings. I will reiterate a comment made in Chapter 13 to not shy away from lots which include *death* in their naming. In some cases injuries and accidents occur when these lots are active, not death.

<u>Using children's events to rectify parental figures</u>. The reverse is also true: events of the children can help rectify the parent's figure. Birth and premature

death of children are always marked through parental figures. But it is possible to time other more subtle events.

Including Mundane Affairs in an Event Database for Individual Nativities

Q. Can a natal chart time mundane events? For heads of state and anyone who plays a role in mundane events, the question arises whether to include mundane affairs when trying to rectify the chart of a person. The answer to this question depends on the validity of the theory that one can time mundane affairs through a natal figure. Traditional authors are largely silent on this issue, preferring ingresses and other methods for mundane prediction. One exception is Ptolemy's recommendation to consider the angles and luminaries for a ruler's natal figure as one outlet for eclipses to manifest (Ptolemy 1822, 61). The 30-Oct-1845 solar eclipse in the natal Midheaven for James Polk and Zachary Taylor tied these two leaders directly to the Mexican War. This is one example which supports Ptolemy's argument (see Chapter 14: *Lunar Nodes and Eclipses*).

A. Yes, but don't let mundane events overly skew a rectification. The conclusion of this study reaches further and confirms the connection between charts of American Presidents and world affairs. The ability of Mars in the figures of Polk, Wilson, and Eisenhower to time events surrounding the Mexican War, WWI, and WWII respectively is an astounding feat of mundane synchronicity achieved by timing directions of Mars to the angles for natal figures. Still, one should not let mundane events skew the rectification process early on. It is easy to be swayed by reading mundane events into a political leader's figure where none exist. My recommendation is to base rectifications for national politicians primarily on family events or on political events leading up to service in a national office. To this end, there are a number of Presidential biographers who stop short of the Presidency. Sellers (1966), Morris (1990), and McCullough (2001) are examples. For cradle-to-grave biographies, one can also simply cut off the event database following nomination to national office.

Examples of Mundane Events read through Presidential nativities. For those who wish to push the envelope on the inclusion of mundane events in the event database for political leaders, I have two suggestions. First is to consider protests, riots, and civil wars which can be timed by transits or directions of malefics to the 4th house cusp. Second is harm to or assassination of the President (usually the sitting President; occasionally a former President) which can be timed by transits or directions of malefics, planets in the 5th, or planets ruling the 5th house; to the 10th house cusp which signifies the King. In addition, because the Sun signifies the King, sometimes directions of malefics to the Sun time the death of the head of state. Franklin Roosevelt's death read through Lyndon Johnson's Sun is one example of this type of direction. Third, delineate the 4th house as the opposition party because the 4th is 7th from the 10th, house of the King. For example, Mercury/Leo/4th signifies Gerald Ford's Minority Speakership of the House.

What type of biography to choose for a Rectification project?

The importance of accurately-dated events, a non-partisan tone, and recently uncovered facts. The first and foremost requirement for choosing a biography is finding one littered with dates. Second is finding a biography which is not overly partisan. Third is a biography based on access to private papers, letters, or official documents which have been unavailable to the public. Frequently a group of papers or documents is found or declassified some years after a President's death. This usually spurs increased interest in the President's life and often a new biography. Research of this type is also likely to help uncover the subtleties of delineation which can be difficult to crack if one limits research to relatively sanitized biographies which populate the internet.

Treat the bias of memoirs with caution. Presidential memoirs and autobiographies of any kind should be treated cautiously. Often they are useful for providing dates considered too tedious for most biographers to include. I rate Eisenhower's memoirs highly in this regard; for example it's difficult to find the critical events and dates of the Suez Crisis better summarized in a single source. However, most memoirs are limited by their biased selectivity which highlights events favorable to the author. Generally, what is left out is of greater interest. Campaign biographies are another type of book unique to studying the American Presidency. Unless working with Presidential candidates (whose campaign biographies are often the only background available to the general public), campaign biographies are to be avoided at all costs.

How to Read a Biography for a Rectification Project

In addition to gathering as many events as possible, there are several types of purely descriptive data which are helpful to gather when reading biographies.

Temperament and Manners. Look for succinct statements of personality and the individual's mental process. All good biographers take time away from the chronology of their subject's life to comment on personality, character, and mental style. These observations are helpful to confirm the Ascendant sign and inputs for the Cognitive Assessment Model.

Moon's significations (Mother and/or Wife). Gain enough understanding of the Moon, usually significator of the Mother or Wife, so that the Moon's sign, bound, and dwad can be established early on. Determining the degree of the Moon is one of the first steps taken in rectification and this descriptive data can help confirm it.

Wealth and Philosophy. Gather evidence which can support the sign and house placement of both the Lot of Fortune and Lot of Spirit. Environmentalists often have their Lot of Spirit in Virgo or Cancer; capitalists in Taurus or Capricorn; politicians in Aries or Leo; intellectuals in Gemini or Libra. With the Lot of Fortune, evidence showing the house placement is usually more evident than sign position. For example, does the individual obtain easy credit because of his own integrity? (LOF in 1st – Herbert Hoover). Does the individual use banks and debt as their primary financial vehicle? (LOF in 8th – Franklin Roosevelt). Does the individual use secret methods to finance activities? (LOF in 12th – Richard Nixon).

Identify Major Life Events. Always watch for events which biographers describe as turning points in life. Sometimes they are referred to as *signal dates* or are similarly emphasized. Frequently biographers organize their work into chapters or sections based on these major events. They can be used to confirm planetary periods like those used in Directing by Triplicity, Firdaria, Zodiacal Releasing, and Directing through the Bounds.

Firdaria periods are usually easy to match against major life events. Even before starting to read a biography, I like to determine the correct Firdaria Sequence by performing a few simple tests. Having the correct Firdaria Sequence in hand allows me to read a biography and cross reference events to the Firdaria periods simultaneously. Sometimes I literally hold the book I am reading in one hand and a printout of Firdaria periods in the other. Reading a biography in this manner allows me to match Firdaria periods to life events while I read; as a result, I gain an increased awareness of planetary behavior in action. In every case, I learn valuable information about planetary rulership, which houses are stressed, and which houses are relatively care-free. Often a preliminary figure with correct signs on the angles can be made purely by the understanding achieved by matching life patterns to Firdaria periods obtained while reading a biography.

The End Result

The final event database contains a chronological list of events, dates, event descriptions, qualitative descriptions of parents, wife, siblings, and children; and insights to the person's appearance, manners, financial activities, and philosophy and/or religious practice. I suggest collecting this data in a computer spreadsheet where it can be sorted and otherwise manipulated. Depending on the level of detail in the biography written, one should easily generate a list of 100 dates. Multivolume and single volume biographies more than 1000 pages may yield upwards of 300 events. Together with written commentary, the size of spreadsheets can range from 700 up to 2000+ rows. For this study, the Presidential Database includes well over 50,000 rows of event data and biographical notes.

CHAPTER SEVENTEEN

The Three Stages of Rectification

Rectification is best thought of as a mathematical optimization problem. A common feature of all optimizations is sensitivity to initial conditions. What this means is the correct solution is more likely to be achieved if initial parameters are reasonably close to the final solution before the optimization begins. The same principle applies to rectification. A three-stage rectification method is proposed which matches each technique to a commensurate level of robustness appropriate for each rectification stage.

Chapter Summary

Stage I: Determine the Ascendant Sign. Planetary period techniques, including Firdaria and Zodiacal Releasing, are relatively robust methods which allow large blocks of time to be culled from the day of birth. Determination of the Moon's sign and her separation from and application to other planets is another robust method which can significantly narrow the birth time range. Once the Ascendant is narrowed to a few possible signs, physiognomy and general delineation techniques are used to narrow the Ascendant choice to a single sign.

Stage II: Determine the Ascendant's range within 1-4 degrees. Both physiognomy and dynamic measurements to the angles further specify the Ascendant to a range of ten degrees or less. It is at this point when lots are deployed to narrow the Ascendant's range to 4 degrees or less. Iterating Ascendant Profections is also useful at this stage.

Stage III: Determine the exact Degree and Minute of the Ascendant. Primary directions, primary direction sequences, and solar arc directions are the *scalpels* of the rectification toolbox designed to finalize the Ascendant's exact degree and minute. Confirmation of a suitable arcus vitae is the final rectification step.

A Miscellany of Tricks and Traps concludes the chapter. It includes a discussion for choosing *magical times* for conducting rectification projects.

Treating Rectification as a Mathematical Optimization

Sensitivity to initial conditions. Above all one must consider rectification a mathematical optimization process. Like all optimizations, rectification is sensitive to initial conditions. Consider a vast moonscape filled with craters, pits, and hidden tunnels as an analogy to the rectification problem. Each surface depression or opening represents a possible rectification solution. Many holes may appear promising yet only one will lead to the correct answer which lies below the surface, connected to the surface by some optimal path. The process itself is like throwing a ball across the moonscape and hoping it lands in the correct hole. With the permutations of transits, progressions, directions, and their different mathematical aspects, it is easy to find at least *some fit* for any hole. The trick then is to start near the *optimal* hole by identifying the correct crater from the outset. One is less likely to go astray if the starting point is reasonably close. One simply can't see the right hole if it is in some other out-of-sight crater 1000 or 3000 feet away. Finding *some* event matches for a particular time may cause too much time spent in the wrong place – literally throwing the ball round and around the surface of the wrong crater!

Proper attribution of planetary behavior to life events requires accurate delineation. For example, suppose one observes a client's punctuality, tidiness of dress, and attention to detail. These are the characteristics of Virgo. Suppose the trial chart has no planets in Virgo so Virgo is assumed a trial Ascendant. Some event matches are found consistent with a Virgo Ascendant and a trial time is computed. But has the rectification really started in the *correct crater*? Suppose that the detail of Virgo manifests through the dwad position of the Moon or Sun in Virgo? Then the rectification has fallen victim to the trap of anchoring, sticking with some initial notion which unfairly biases the entire rectification. How to avoid anchoring? Delineation, Delineation, Delineation!

The Rectification Process in Brief

The proposed three stage rectification progressively resolves the choice of birth time to the exact degree and minute of the zodiac rising on the Eastern horizon at birth. Both the Ascendant and Midheaven are the two most important angles for use in rectification.

Stage I: Determine the Ascendant Sign. The goal of Stage I is to correctly choose the Ascendant sign through testing robust planetary period techniques, identifying the Moon's configuration, and by creating a figure whose planet placement is consistent with life patterns, and physiognomy.

Stage II: Determine the Ascendant's range within 1-4 degrees. Narrowing the Ascendant to a tight range is the most time-consuming part of the rectification process. Physiognomy of the rising decan, lots, and Ascendant Profections are recommended tools for this stage.

Stage III: Determine the exact Degree and Minute of the Ascendant. Primary directions, primary direction sequences, and solar arc directions are tools used to fine tune the Ascendant. Identification of a suitable arcus vitae provides final confirmation of the rectified Ascendant.

Where does one begin?

Depending on the quality of birth data, the practicing astrologer may choose to begin the rectification process with any one of the three stages. What types of birth data does the astrologer face? In general, four types of data are encountered:

1. Date but no time. This is relatively common for historical figures, older generations still living, or individuals who by reason of immigration, warfare, or other displacement no longer have access to official birth times.

2. Date and approximate time of day, such as *late at night, sunrise, or before lunch*. Biographers often provide these indications for historical subjects, saving astrologers from working completely blind.

3. Date and exact - but suspicious - birth certificate time. Just because the time of 1:15 PM or 3:00 AM appears on a birth certificate does not mean it is accurate. Whenever birth times are rounded to the nearest 10, 15, 30 or 60 minute interval, one has good reason to be suspicious that for whatever reason the exact birth time was not recorded. What kind of reasons? Incorrect clock settings, insufficient nursing staff on duty, lack of attentiveness by nursing staff and complications at birth which demand immediate medical attention are the most common causes for incorrect birth time notations. In virtually all cases rounded times are off, in some cases as much as 20 or 30 minutes based on my experience!

4. Date and exact birth certificate time. When one finds 2:23 PM or 5:51 PM recorded on a birth certificate, one can be reasonably certain that a nurse was watching the clock. There is still room for error, but it is generally very small. From my experience, these observations are often slightly late by 0-90 seconds.

Caution: When Mercury is Retrograde or Combust. Irrespective of whether a birth time is rounded or not; whenever Mercury is retrograde or combust one must be suspicious of the birth time. The ability of Mercury retrograde periods to disrupt communications is common knowledge among even armchair astrologers. Yet few have made the connection between Mercury–retrograde and errors in recording birth times. The same can be said for times when Mercury is near the Sun, making his actions hidden. In one case, I rectified an *official* birth time of 5:32 AM to 5:22:30 AM. It appears the official birth time should have been 5:23 AM but someone transposed the digits from 5:23 to 5:32. The additional difference between 5:23:00 and 5:22:30 is within the normal range of error for an accurate birth time. Mercury was under the sunbeams in this example.

What is the _True_ Birth Time? So what actually constitutes the birth time? I have personally never witnessed a live birth. From what other astrologers have reported, while the birth process is generally quite fast, there remains an interval of time between the appearance of the head, the first breath, and the severing of the umbilical cord; any one of which can be argued as the true birth time. I can only state that empirical events timed by directions to the angles are the only decisive proof of the empirical birth time. What this means is not until an individual has lived for 5, 10, or even 15 years might there be sufficient evidence using primary directions to determine the _true_ birth time.

Choosing the Initial Rectification Stage. For the first three types of data – day but no time, day but approximate time, and day with exact but suspicious time - I recommend beginning with Stage I rectification procedures. For the fourth type of data – date and exact birth certificate time – one may immediately jump in with primary directions, primary direction sequences, and solar arc directions as outlined in Stage III. Even for these cases, some Stage II lot testing is still recommended. Confirmation of sign placements for both Lots of Spirit and Fortune using Zodiacal Releasing is especially helpful to confirm the recorded birth time before jumping into directions.

One Shortcut worth Trying First

Illness/Death of native or female family members. Before introducing Stage I, let me mention one shortcut which for about 5% of cases studied was able to achieve an Ascendant accurate within 1 degree in just a few minutes of work. If the event database contains 4-6 events including one or more major illnesses and/or death for the native, mother, grandmother, wife, sister, and/or daughter; often the Moon's position can be accurately determined because most of these events are timed by afflictions to the Moon. For illnesses and/or death of the native, this occurs whether or not the Moon is the actual hīlāj because the Moon is a universal significator of the physical body. For illnesses of other female family members, this guideline works because female family members are often read through the Moon in the native's figure. Even when females are signified by Venus, not the Moon, the stress of family illnesses often marks the native's own Moon indirectly.

Determine the Moon's trial degree. Measurements like these, even if just a transit, can often provide a clue to the Moon's true degree. With these types of events in hand, I use the quad-wheel software function to examine dynamic planet positions for each event[23]. Test events using the quad-wheel, noting degree positions of planets which are most likely cause of the affliction. See if a common degree can be used for the Moon's trial position. South Node transits are very useful in this step.

---

[23] Default settings in Janus 5.5 for the dynamic quad-wheel are (from in to out): natal, solar arcs, progressions, and transits. I replace the progressions wheel with converse solar arc directions.

Stage I: Determine the Ascendant Sign

Correct Day and Year. As obvious as it sounds, there are some instances when even the birthday of a historical figure is in question. Woodrow Wilson gave his birthday as 28 December even though the family Bible recorded 29 December 12:45 AM as the birth time. The latter proved accurate in testing. A variation of this problem occurs for births occurring *near midnight*. Compared to James Madison's official birthday of 6-Mar-1751 O.S. occurring near midnight, my proposed rectification is 5-Mar- 1751 O.S., 11:20:04 PM, just shy of midnight. In these cases, I believe some flexibility must be allowed for a day either side of the official birth date. Finally there are examples of outright lies. Out of sheer vanity, Chester Arthur, born 5-Oct-1829, changed his birth year to 1830 sometime between 1870 and 1880. The birth year of 1829 is correct (Reeves 1975, 5).

Firdaria: Establishing the Sun's position above or below the horizon. Because Firdaria sequences differ for diurnal and nocturnal births, they effectively divide the day into two halves. Matching major life periods to either the diurnal or nocturnal sequence is usually so evident that it makes sense to begin with a Firdaria sequence comparison when the birth time is unknown. There is no better way to cull invalid blocks of time. Choosing a diurnal sequence leaves only times between sunrise and sunset for consideration, a reduction on average of 50% of the hours of the day; for the nocturnal sequence, vice versa.

NEW Behavior of malefic planets as a clue to sect. The central role of Firdaria in my approach agrees with the Hellenistic doctrine of the importance of sect; however, Firdaria is a medieval astrological technique to arrive at the correct chart sect. Within the Hellenistic tradition, the out-of-sect malefic generates effects which are more difficult than the in-sect malefic. While I did not compare this difference in malefic behavior during research for this book, it remains another tool which can be used to narrow the sect of the chart. Specifically, if life events suggest that Mars is behaving poorly and generating worse effects relative to Saturn, the chart sect is probably diurnal when Mars is the out-of-sect malefic; vice versa for Saturn.

Getting the Planets in the correct signs. For most cases this step involves choosing the Moon's correct sign; yet other planets, usually Mercury, Venus, or the Sun, may be positioned at the 30th or 1st degree of a sign and need to be double checked. For the Presidential database, this condition was met in 7 of 45 cases. Table 36 considers planets in the 30th or 1st degrees of signs with actual zodiacal degree positions taken from proposed rectifications. Delineation of the planet in the actual sign is contrasted with the planet in the adjacent sign. In some cases, such as Hoover where the Ingress of Mercury to Leo confirms a birth time no earlier than 10:27 p.m., much of the day's hours can be dismissed as rectification possibilities.

Table 36. Planets in the 30th or 1st Degrees of Signs

President	Planet	Delineation Notes
G. Washington	Venus 29PI11	Interest in luxury goods is Venus/Pisces not the lust of Venus/Aries.
F. Pierce	Mercury 29SC44	Vindictive diplomats (e.g., Ostend) are Mercury in Scorpio not Sagittarius.
J. Buchanan	Venus 00GE15	Reputation as entertainer and as writer of frequent correspondence matches Venus/Gemini as love of talk.
J. Garfield	Mercury 00SA50	Dreaminess and accidents from falling (including falling overboard 14 times during a canal boat ride at age 16) is Mercury in Sagittarius not Scorpio.
C. Coolidge	Mars 00CA09	Coolidge's delayed yet eventual forceful response during the Boston Police Strike matches Mars/Cancer not Mars/Gemini which would make Coolidge much more of a risk taker and debater.
H. Hoover	Mercury 00LE01	Earliest profession in gold mine management is Mercury in Leo not Cancer

Moon's Sign and Aspects. With an average motion of 13.2 degrees per day and 30 degrees in each zodiacal sign, the odds of two possible Moon signs for a single day are high. There are two methods to narrow the Moon's degree range.

Delineation. Identify the Moon's sign, bound, and dwad. See Chapter 1: *Planets in Signs* for the theoretical basis for this approach.

Prediction. Match the Moon's separation and application to long-term patterns of life development. Use aphorisms by Maternus, Pearce, and others as a baseline. Remember to customize their observations to the nativity at hand by respecting the actual zodiacal state of each planet involved in the Moon's configuration. Chapter 7: *Temporal Indicators* includes a case study for Franklin Pierce's Moon position using this approach.

Basic Configuration of the Chart. The effects of benefics and malefics placed in houses are so strong that their effects are hard to miss. Good health yet a childless marriage? Not if the trial rectification shows Jupiter in the 5th. Try moving Jupiter to the 6th house and see if a malefic moves to the 5th by position or rulership. More so than any other rectification method, matching the basic configuration of the chart to the native's life requires expertise in delineation. The Jupiter-5th-children is but one example. There are endless others. A military leader? Look for Mars in the 7th or 10th. Wealthy? Look for the Lot of Fortune ruled and aspected by strong benefics. Multiple marriages? Look for a mutable sign on the 7th cusp. No religious affiliation? Look for Mars in or ruling the 9th house. Good health? Watch for Venus, Jupiter, or the North Node in the 6th house. Even the Lot of Fortune in the 6th can ameliorate the effects of an empty house ruled by a malefic. The possibilities are endless.

NEW Stage I/II Tools

Zodiacal Releasing. If the techniques described so far fail to elicit a trial Ascendant sign, test ZR sequences against life events to find an event match. Notice that matching life events to ZR L1 periods does not confirm the Ascendant sign, only the Lot of Spirit. If L1 period matches are prominent, use ZR to confirm the Lot of Fortune by identifying more active life/career periods for a specific LOF sign placement that would make LOF angles match the chronology. At this point there is still no guarantee of getting the correct Ascendant sign, but one should be close, if not correct, in most cases.

Conversely, if prior Stage I techniques confirm the Ascendant sign, then wait until Stage II to deploy ZR to confirm sign placements for LOF and LOS. At this point in Stage II, it may be worthwhile to investigate the bound placement of LOF and LOS to further narrow the Ascendant degree range. Ability to match the correct bound placement for LOF and LOS requires an in-depth understanding of the individual in question.

Physiognomy. As presented in Chapter 3, physiognomy is best suited to choosing the correct rising decan once the Ascendant sign is confirmed. However, since the 1st decan is the same as the rising sign, individuals born with an Ascendant degree in the 1st ten degrees of any sign can benefit from physiognomy as a Stage I rectification tool. Cited in Chapter 3 was George H. W. Bush whose soft rectangular facial shape was a delineation match to Mercury/Taurus as ruler of the rising sign and 1st rising decan of Virgo. There will be some cases like Bush where physiognomy can be a decisive Stage I rectification tool. Otherwise, reserve physiognomy for Stage II.

Remember physiognomy judgments are best made for individuals who are somewhere between puberty and menopause. As stated in Chapter 3, for older individuals I recommend finding photographs of the face and body between the ages of 25 and 45.

Stage II: Determine the Ascendant's range within 1-4 degrees

Entering Stage II with only the Ascendant sign known, there are two steps to further specify the Ascendant's range. The first step narrows the Ascendant to a range of ten degrees or less using physiognomy and dynamic measurements to the angles. The second step makes use of lots and profections to narrow the Ascendant's range to within 1-4 degrees.

Dynamic Measurements to the Angles. If unable to confidently secure the rising decan through physiognomy, one can check for transits, progressions, and solar arc directions to the angles. This is the approach recommended by most contemporary sources including Tyl (2001). As demonstrated with Andrew Jackson's chimney fire which opened Part II, this approach falls flat if measurements relate to a lot and not one of the angles. Still one cannot entirely ignore insights from this method.

Recalling the ability of the Lunar Nodes to connect the native to the public, I recommend emphasizing transits of the Lunar Nodes to the angles to time major life events. In some cases, Nodal transits allow refinement of the Ascendant to within a few minutes of degree during Stage II rectification. These moments are rare but they do occur.

NEW Consider transits to the 10th positional degree of the ASC, MC, LOF, and LOS with the same importance as transits to the ASC, MC, LOF, and LOS directly. Transit of Uranus to the 10th positional degree from the MC for Gerald Ford is a good example. Jupiter's transit to the 10th positional degree from the Lot of Spirit for Barack Obama's 27-Jul-2004 DNC convention speech is a more recent example of the power of this type of transit to usher momentous life changes.

Hellenistic Lots. Testing events against lots is the bread and butter of Stage II rectification. It is best to have the Ascendant narrowed to ten degrees or less before testing lots; otherwise one feels as if looking for a needle in a haystack. The ability of the eye and brain to iterate differences between planet positions and lots is compromised if the differences are too great. Consider trying to iterate which Ascendant minimizes the error of these three observations:

4 degrees between Jupiter and the antiscion of the Lot of Marriage,
3 degrees from the square of Mars and the Lot of Illness/Accidents,
5 degrees between Saturn and the contra-antiscion of the Lot of Death.

Now reconsider the same exercise if the 4, 3, and 5 degree differences were instead 15, 22, and 25. This case with wider measurements is virtually impossible for the brain to iterate much less sort out.

For this study, the most common events tested against lots were:

Accidents, Illness, and Death of Parents and Siblings
Marriage and death of Spouse
Birth and Death of Children
Accidents and Surgeries
Real Estate: purchases, sales, loss (fire or theft)
Native's Death

See Chapters 10 and 13 for examples of both solar return planet aspects and dynamic activity to lots which can narrow the Ascendant to 1-4 degrees.

Profected Ascendant. Because the profected Annual Ascendant moves 30 degrees per year, its movement of 12.175 days per one degree is sufficiently robust for Stage II rectification. Because the profected Ascendant aspects the same planets on the same date every year, I recommend watching for anniversary events with similar planetary significations. This exercise requires an extensive database of events to spot these periodic repetitions. One example is James Garfield whose Ascendant profection to Mars on 8 April each year timed:

12-Apr-1861. Profected Ascendant sextile Mars. Outbreak of Civil War.
6/7-Apr-1862. Profected Ascendant square Mars. Battle of Shiloh.
14-Apr-1865. Profected Ascendant opposed Mars. Lincoln assassination.

Note the ability of the profected Ascendant to time these events with an error of 6 days or less implies an Ascendant accurate to 30 minutes of degree.

To confess, because of the nonexistence of any software which includes profections in their rectification module, I did not use iterations of the Profected Ascendant for this rectification project. Had software allowed, my story here would differ. Until such software is developed, one can either create a customized spreadsheet model or simply train the eye to calculate the profected Ascendant's position without the aid of software.

Stage III: Determine the exact Degree and Minute of the Ascendant

Primary Directions. Starting with *directing direct*, begin to test primary directions against the event database. Here are a few tips to consider:

Focus on directions of the Sun, Mars, and Saturn to the Ascendant and Midheaven. Chapter 16: *Preparing the Event Database* opened with observations by Pearce and Simmonite which emphasized the consistency of these directions for rectification. It's a point which cannot be overemphasized.

Planets close to the Midheaven are most likely to signify parental events in youth. These include death or divorce of either parent and/or changes in living location.

When planets are angular (any angle – 1st, 4th, 7th, or 10th), events of interest are most likely to occur when the directed planet aspects the angle by sextile or trine, depending on whether the angle is in a sign of long or short ascension. Because the modern psychological assumption that *development requires a hard aspect to occur*, many practicing astrologers discount the ability of soft aspects to time events through directions. As explained in Chapter 10: *Directions*, this notion is completely false. Sextiles and trines can cause havoc - even death - just as well as any hard aspect. Ignore them at your peril!

Primary Direction Sequences. In my opinion, the discovery of primary direction sequences is the most significant technical advancement reported by this study. The odds that a pair of events, often a year apart of more, can be timed by the same direction computed with and without latitude are so low that primary direction sequences can effectively *lock down* a rectified birth time to within a fraction of a single second of time. This level of accuracy is unheard of in astrological circles yet possible with primary direction sequences.

The trick in confirming primary direction sequences is to first discard any notion the *orb* surrounding a primary direction to the angles may last several months or a year. This is not correct. Replace this notion with the recognition that directions to the angles for a reliably timed birth chart can trigger actual events within a few days, often within 24 hours. Any continued effects after a primary direction, mistakenly ascribed to some kind of *orb*, are properly attributed to the elapsed time between the first and last direction defined by the primary direction sequence. Once the sequence is kicked off from an initial event, often similar events continue to occur until the last direction closes the sequence.

NEW Directing through the Bounds. With the advent of Janus Version 5.5, one can deploy the Distributions module to test a series of event matches against a set of Distributors. Focus on the Ascendant but consider all significators as fair game. Study the example for Theodore Roosevelt's Ascendant given in Chapter 10. Focus on Distributor changeovers from benefics to malefics, vice versa; as well as changeovers from malefics to malefics.

Solar Arc Directions. Solar arc directions are just as accurate as primary directions, yet they routinely show better performance for horoscopes with a strong Leo emphasis. The ASC, ASC ruler, or any planet in Leo usually give the horoscope a Leonine quality which generates public events captured by solar arc directions. Likewise for horoscopes with a heavy Aquarius or Libra emphasis (with the Sun in detriment or in fall) solar arcs do not work particularly well.

Consider the proposition presented in Chapter 10: *Directions* which links public events timed by solar arc directions to events of a more personal nature by primary direction. The low odds of this type of linkage, if it can be documented, greatly increase the odds of an accurate rectification. They have been helpful in 'locking down' Joseph Biden's horoscope.

Arcus vitae. The last word in any rectification project is confirmation of the arcus vitae. Be aware that there are many exceptions to theory in choice of hīlāj and killing planets.

A Miscellany of Tricks and Traps

<u>All events are not recorded</u>. Even the most carefully constructed databases omit events which would otherwise be helpful for rectification. Why? Two reasons. First, the event may not have been recorded for reasons including embarrassment, secrecy, or sloppy record keeping. Second, the event may have occurred but was not mentioned by a biographer. It may have been manifested through other people read through the individual's figure. This is very common for the Moon which can signify the grandmother, aunt, mother, wife, sister, or daughter. If not reported by the biographer, there is no way to confirm the direction.

<u>Attack multiple events with a variety of rectification techniques</u>. Avoid the error of anchoring a rectification on two or three events based on familiar or favorite techniques. Employ the full battery of predictive methods to confirm a rectification. Directions and transits to the angles are helpful but not the end of the story. As stated time and time again, lots are more accurate. Do solar return planets highlight lots? Do transits and solar arc directions highlight a relevant lot and *not* an angle?

<u>When planets are hidden</u>. Effects of planets are often hidden when either combust or in the 12th house. In my experience, significations of 12th house planets are especially difficult to observe when testing directions against even well-constructed event databases.

Jefferson is a good example. I delineate Venus/Taurus/12th as his slave mistress Sally Hemings whose rumored identity was settled only by DNA evidence released in 1998, a full 172 years following Jefferson's death. Only because Jefferson was a public figure did scrutiny cause the truth to be known. For lesser figures, the significations of 12th house planets may be forever hidden. Even some individuals cannot identify nor understand planets in the 12th, even when confronted with their delineation by an astrologer in a private counseling session. This is especially true when 12th house planets do not rule the Ascendant's sign, triplicity, bound, or dwad nor aspect the Ascendant's ruler.

<u>Universal significations of Sun and Moon</u>. Remember because the Moon signifies the physical body and Sun the spirit, dynamic measurements to the Moon can time illness whether or not the Moon is the hīlāj. In cases where the Sun is the true hīlāj, afflictions to a combination of the Sun, Moon, or Ascendant can time physical illness and death.

<u>Focus on directions to the Ascendant and Midheaven</u>. Avoid paralysis of working with too many significators. Focus on the Ascendant and Midheaven. After refining a birth time to a range of a few minutes, only at this point introduce other significators such as the Lots of Fortune and Spirit or alternative angles like the Equatorial Ascendant or Vertex.

Let it rest. After making a trial rectification, let it rest overnight. See if it holds up after a good night's sleep and a cup of morning coffee. If working with a living client, identify directions due in the next year which can be monitored to test the rectification on an out-of-sample basis.

Magical times. Recently an entire book was written on connections between the time established for an astrological consultation and dynamic measurements between natal figures of both the astrologer and client (Sellars & Newman 2000).

Can the same be said for rectification? Are astrologers driven to study and research certain figures, be they clients or historical personages, based on the position of currently transiting planets? I answer in the affirmative. This from the experience of comparing times when I *locked down* a rectification to the natal figure studied at that time.

The most common connections I witnessed were between transiting planets and the figure's Moon or Mercury. Even the writing of this book was partly timed by Mercury transits. I completed Chapter 15's case study of Franklin Roosevelt at War during the Mercury Aquarius Ingress of January 2007, a Mercury return for FDR. During the following Mercury Pisces Ingress of February 2007, I completed most of Chapter 12's study of Lincoln's 1862 solar return – also a Mercury return for Lincoln. When Mercury went retrograde, I paused on that chapter, and completed it during March when Mercury made its last pass through Pisces after its direct station. *NEW* For the current 4th edition, I completed the writeup for George Whitefield in the following chapter on an exact Jupiter/Aries return to his natal figure.

Another valuable method for choosing *magical times* for the study of historical figures is to make use of the New Moon's sign position. Several rectification cases were started following New Moon's whose sign matched the sign of the final Ascendant, Moon, or Sun position for the nativity studied.

The future. Research in traditional astrology continues. It takes time for software to catch up with research findings and methods. Some valuable predictive methods, like profections, are difficult to use in rectification unless one has the facility to design an iterative rectification spreadsheet. Stay abreast of new research and advances in astrological software.

CHAPTER EIGHTEEN

Rectification Case Studies

ARM 4th edition presents a complete revision of rectification case studies. The original design of this chapter incorporated multiple objectives: (1) to include religious leaders and philosophers in a horoscope collection following the tradition of Medieval and Renaissance horoscope collections, (2) to flesh out themes of the 18th century Jupiter-Saturn conjunctions in Aries as a necessary backdrop for the American Revolution, and (3) to give more examples of Stage I and Stage II rectification techniques which are largely omitted in the Presidential database for reasons of space.

Unfortunately, the original chapter was written in a rush with my process violating my own instructions outlined in Chapter 16: Preparing the Event Database. While I did compile brief chronologies, I did not read any full-length biographies and results suffered. Unlike rectifications presented in the Presidential database most of which have held up under scrutiny from additional techniques, none of the trial rectifications for this chapter's rectification studies have proven their merit.

In a strange combination of embarrassment and clarity, for the three horoscopes which I presented incorrect dates based on confusion between Julian and Gregorian calendar for birth dates prior to 1752, all three of those horoscopes yield the same rising sign despite the difference of 11 calendar days between the two date systems. This I attribute to the consistency and importance of the Stage I technique: Configuration of the Chart.

John Locke: Jupiter/Taurus/11th ruling the 6th and 9th signifies patronage by the Earl of Shaftesbury (11th), travels and philosophy tied to the Earl (9th), and the Earl's near death from a liver abscess (6th = 8th from the 11th, death of friend)

Jonathan Edwards: Mercury/Scorpio ruling the 8th of death signifies death from a failed smallpox inoculation. Sun/Libra/9th is consistent with his reputation as the most prominent 18th century colonial theologian.

Charles Whitefield: Jupiter/Aries/9th is a delineation match to Whitfield's nickname as the 'Grand Itinerant.'

All these configurations, specifically the location of planets in a specific house and rulership of other houses, remain consistent for several days either side of the actual birth date. Revisiting these three case studies reveals Configuration of the Chart a very robust Stage I rectification technique. This key takeaway may be worth the price of failed rectifications in early editions.

Rectification case studies for John Wesley and Benjamin Franklin presented in prior editions were computed for the correct date but did not stand up to further scrutiny. Recent insights on the behavior of the Moon conjunct South Node configuration (for Wesley) and application of Zodiacal Releasing (for Wesley and Franklin) were key steps taken to revise the rectifications.

Spreadsheets with complete chronologies for John Locke, John Wesley, Jonathan Edwards, George Whitefield, and Benjamin Franklin are available for free download on the research tab of my website. https://regulus-astrology.com/research.html. These include solar arc and primary directions used in Stage III to compute the final rectified Ascendant. For reasons of space, they are omitted from this chapter.

John Locke (29-Aug-1632 OS to 28-Oct-1704 OS)

Of Interest. Influential Enlightenment philosopher.

Britain. Locke's lifetime coincided with the 17th century English Civil Wars. He studied medicine, wrote philosophy tracts, and played a role in the 1689 Glorious Revolution by supporting William of Orange. Locke's lifespan overlaps that of three prominent English astrologers William Lilly (1602-1681), John Gadbury (1627-1704), and John Partridge (1644 – c. 1714).

America. Locke's *Second Treatise on Government* was reprinted in America in 1773 in the years immediately preceding the July 4, 1776 Declaration of Independence written primarily by Thomas Jefferson. Direct textual linkages exist between Locke's *Second Treatise on Government* and the Declaration. Locke's *Treatise* can also be linked to Thomas Paine's *Common Sense* (1776).

Astrology. Locke's epistemological work *An Essay on Human Understanding* sheds light on the configuration of Locke's natal Moon.

Chronologies

Liberty Fund Network. Listing of 40-50 key dates (by year).
https://oll.libertyfund.org/page/chronology-of-john-locke-s-life

John Locke Resources. Operated by John Attig, State College, PA.
https://openpublishing.psu.edu/locke/chron/index.html#toc

Regulus Astrology LLC. Composite Chronology. See Research Tab.
https://regulus-astrology.com/research.html

Biographical Comments

Other than his father's death, there are few available family dates. Locke did not marry nor have children. Locke's political fortunes were closely tied to Anthony Ashley Cooper, initially known as The Lord Ashley and later the 1st Earl of Shaftesbury so named by King Charles II. Ashley's eventual split from Charles II made Ashley a direct enemy of the state and Locke an indirect enemy of the state for his association with Ashley. As a result, Locke fled England for France in 1675. Locke left England for similar reasons under the rule of James II in 1683 and spent six years in Holland before returning in 1689 for the coronation of William of Orange. The dates of Lord Ashley's political activities and Locke's overseas travels are well documented. Less well known are Locke's early academic activities prior to his association with Lord Ashley.

Stage I. Determine the Ascendant Sign

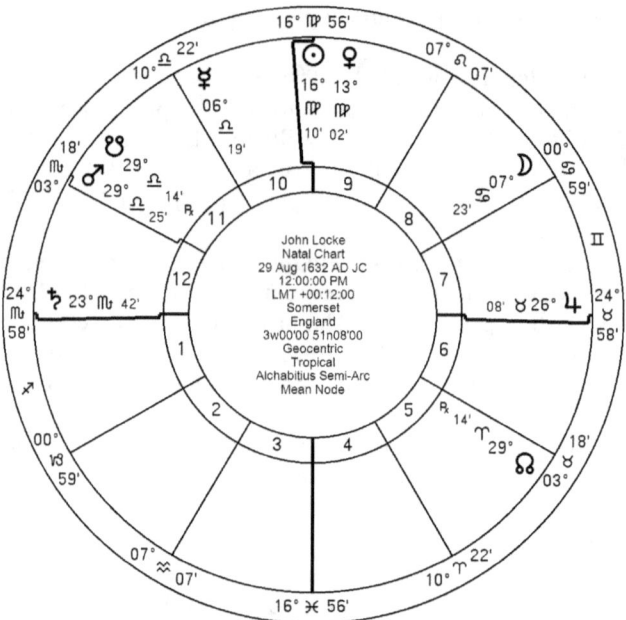

John Locke. *Trial Noon Horoscope for unknown birth time.*

All sources agree Locke was born on 29-Aug-1632 in Somerset, England. As England did not adopt the Gregorian calendar until 1752, the entirety of Locke's chronology is compiled using the Julian calendar.

➢ Match Significations of the planets with biographical details.

Jupiter/Taurus most likely signifies Lord Ashley. Jupiter is the universal significator of noble men and Ashley qualifies. Locke's medical skills facilitated a risky surgery on Ashley's liver (Jupiter-ruled) and saved Ashley's life. Locke was also involved in real estate and commercial speculations, some of which involved the Carolina colony in the New World for which Ashley was involved.

Saturn/Scorpio signifies national security and at first glance is a reasonable delineation match to the English state security apparatus which opposed Ashley. Note that Jupiter separates from Saturn which diminishes Saturn's ability to harm.

Moon stays in Cancer the entire day. Moon/Cancer is the likely significator for Locke's epistemology of sensory perception.

Mercury/Libra and Venus/Virgo in generosity (mutual reception by sign without aspect) shows Mercury advocating for Venusian objects which have fallen out of favor or are otherwise damaged. This configuration may link Locke to religious tolerance but there may be other economic significations which are not obvious from a first review of his chronology.

> Use Firdaria to choose the horoscope's diurnal or nocturnal sect.

The following event matches favor the nocturnal Firdaria sequence:

Major Saturn (1641-1652). English Civil War (1642-1651) during teenage years with Locke's father fighting on the side of the Parliamentarians is a better match to Saturn's national security theme than Major Venus period for teenage years. What little survives of Locke's biographical details offers no Venusian hints during this time.

Major Jupiter (1652-1664). Match to Oxford induction (1652), Oxford degrees (1656, 1658) and faculty appointment to the Censorship of Moral Philosophy (1663) as the major Jupiter period ends. For the diurnal sequence, Major Mercury is a close overlap to Major Jupiter for the nocturnal series. As most students enter university in their 20s, it can be difficult to choose between diurnal and nocturnal Firdaria sequences for university years. What favors Jupiter for Locke is that he immediately took on a Lecturer position after graduation and was promoted on two separate occasions. Teaching is a Jupiterian profession.

Major Mars (1664-1671). Not an obvious match as Locke begins his association with Lord Ashley in 1666 who is signified by Jupiter, not Mars. Given Mars' weakness in the natal horoscope (Mars/Libra sign of detriment closely conjunct the South Node), it may be that Mars is so weak that he cannot deliver many notable events during Mars-ruled planetary periods.

North Node (1671-1674). During this time, Locke invests in the Royal Africa Company (slave trade) and a land development company in the Bahamas. Lord Ashley is named the 1st Earl of Shaftesbury; soon after Shaftesbury established the Council for Trade and Foreign Plantations. Locke is sworn in as the Secretary to the Council for Trade in 1673.

South Node (1674-1676). Locke unwinds business dealings begun during the North Node period: shares in the Royal Africa Company are sold in 1675; shares in the Bahamas investment are sold in 1676; and the Council of Trade and Foreign Plantations for which he served as Secretary was abolished by early 1675. To my eye, this increase in affairs during the North Node period and decrease in those same affairs during the South Node period are the most powerful event matches which confirm the nocturnal series so far.

Sun-Saturn (16-May-1682 to 19-Oct-1683). Locke fled to Holland on 8-Sep-1683 after suspicion he was involved in the Rye House Plot against Charles II. Saturn/Scorpio signifies the national security apparatus. Also compelling for this choice is the inconsistency of the Jupiter Major Firdaria period beginning 29-Aug-1683 were the Firdaria series diurnal. While there is a case to be made for Jupiter's separation from Saturn a match to the diurnal series – with Jupiter signifying Locke's ability to leave the country - the overall tenor of the period is Saturnian.

Conclusion: Horoscope is nocturnal.
Birthtime range is 12:00 AM – 5:29 AM or 6:23 PM to 12:00 AM.

> Use Moon's Configuration to choose morning or evening nocturnal hours.

Time	Moon	Sect	Configuration
12:00 AM	1CA24	N	Moon applies to Mercury Moon in bound of Mars/Cancer
5:29 AM	4CA08	D	Sunrise
9:34 AM	6CA10	D	Moon separates from Mercury and applies to Venus
11:13 AM	7CA00	D	Moon enters bound Venus/Cancer
6:23 PM	10CA35	N	Sunset
11:11 PM	13CA00	N	Moon enters bound Mercury/Cancer
12:00 AM	13CA24	N	Moon separates from Mercury and applies to Venus

If morning nocturnal hours, the Moon is in the bound of Mars/Cancer and applies to Mercury.

If evening nocturnal hours, the Moon is either in bound of Venus/Cancer or Mercury/Cancer; the Moon separates from Mercury and applies to Venus.

The fact that Locke's major works were published late in life (1689/1690) and after that time he continued to write new works and revise old ones favors the Moon's application to Mercury. Mercury signifies writing, an activity Locke did more of as he aged, not less were the Moon's separation from Mercury to Venus the Moon's correct configuration.

Conclusion: Choose morning nocturnal hours. Locke was born between 12:00 AM and 5:29 AM with the Moon's degree position between 1CA24 and 4CA08. The possible Ascendant degree range is 16CA52 to 15VI49. The Ascendant sign is Cancer, Leo, or Virgo.

> Use Configuration of the Chart to match life themes to houses.

As a philosopher opposed to the divine right of Kings signified by Sun-ruled Leo, a Leo Ascendant is highly unlikely. This leaves either Cancer or Virgo.

For Cancer rising, Jupiter/Taurus appears in the 11th house and rules the 6th and 9th houses. I favor this configuration because:

1. Jupiter/Taurus signifies the 1st Earl of Shaftesbury.
2. Placement in the 11th ties Locke to a political alliance with Shaftesbury.
3. Rulership of the 9th ties Locke to a career in teaching, philosophy, and foreign travel tied to Shaftesbury. Locke made two foreign trips to France and Holland as escapes from the state security apparatus when Shaftesbury fell out of favor.
4. Rulership of the 6th of illness ties Locke to Shaftesbury's life-threatening liver abscess for which Locke oversaw a successful surgical intervention saving Shaftesbury's life. While the 6th is the house of illness and one of the bad houses; strictly speaking the 6th is Locke's illness, not Shaftesbury's illness. However, by derived houses see that the 6th house (Sagittarius) is 8 signs from the 11th house (Taurus) which signifies the death of a friend or political alliance. This derived house delineation appears the better match to life affairs as Shaftesbury faced a life-threatening illness. Jupiter also rules the liver.

> Confirm Ascendant sign with Physiognomy

My research on physiognomy so far shows that Moon and Mercury-ruled Ascendant signs are the least reliable for physiognomy as a rectification tool. Therefore with Cancer the trial Ascendant sign, I am circumspect on the relevance of physiognomy for Locke's rectification. At the very least I want to see some consistency between the Ascendant and physiognomy as well as to rule out any blatant contradictions.

There are two observations which are consistent with Cancer rising.

Judith Hill (1997, 58-59) identifies two Cancer types of faces which depend on whether the Moon is New or Full. Locke's Moon is just past the waning square and therefore closer to the next New Moon. Based on Hill, Locke is a dead ringer for Hill's Type 2 Cancer New Moon. Abundant hair and "a long, narrow face with a sad, dreamy and somewhat woe-begone expression" is spot on.

Locke's ill-health is also consistent with the Moon itself placed in the 1st house. This delineation match does not require the Moon to be in a particular sign; only its position in the 1st house. By diurnal motion, when the Moon rises on the eastern horizon it loses its status as the sect leader. Psychologically and physically, the effect is akin to a rude awakening of bedsheets ripped off one's body at sunrise. Sudden daylight is a shock to the system with Moon placed in the 1st associated with physical weakness. Locke met this condition. The Moon in the 1st is also associated with prophecy; as if the Moon has accumulated a full night's worth of intuitive insights which are momentarily transferred to the active consciousness just after sunrise before the rays of the Sun become bright enough to obliterate them.

Overall these observations are consistent with Cancer rising. I will return to physiognomy as a Stage II rectification tool to further refine the Ascendant.

Before we proceed, note as the day begins at midnight on 29-Aug-1632 the rising degree is 16CA52. This simplifies the rectification project: the allowable Ascendant degree range is from 16CA52 to 29CA59.

Stage II. Determine the Ascendant's range within 1-4 degrees.

➤ <u>Use physiognomy to choose the correct rising decan.</u>

If the second decan of Cancer rises, the Ascendant is 16CA52 to 19CA59.
If the third decan of Cancer rises, the Ascendant is 20CA00 to 29CA59.

According to the rising decan model proposed in Chapter 3, the sign placement of the ruler of the rising decan should correspond to the face.

The second decan of Cancer is Scorpio with ruler Mars placed in the sign of Libra. In Willner's model, Libra corresponds to the compressed ovate.

The third decan of Cancer is Pisces with ruler Jupiter placed in the sign of Taurus. In Willner's model, Taurus corresponds to the soft rectangle.

Are either of these observations a delineation match or conversely a blatant contradiction? Certainly the narrow, willow-like face is a blatant mismatch to

Jupiter/Taurus ruling the 3rd rising decan of Cancer. This leaves the 2nd decan with Mars/Libra the physiognomy significator. Does Locke's facial shape match the compressed ovate of Libra? If it does it is not obvious to me. This doesn't necessarily mean the 2nd decan is not correct, only that we can't use Willner's model to support it. Note that Mars is partile conjunct the South Node. This conjunction obliterates Mars and may account for Mars' inability to function as a physiognomy significator. Recall from Stage I something similar was observed during the major Mars Firdaria period: no obvious delineation matches.

In some examples, the sign of the rising decan itself (here Scorpio), not the ruler of the rising decan (Mars), is the better delineation match. Prior ARM editions cited observations by Anrias (1970, 76) that the prominent nose, intensity in the eyes, dark eyebrows, firmness in the chin, and a close-set mouth all match Scorpio characteristics of the second decanate of Cancer. Of these features, the prominent nose is the most striking feature of Locke's face. If correct, the 2nd rising Cancer decan assigned to Scorpio is the rising decan.

Conclusion: Ascendant degree range is 16CA52 to 19CA59.

Stage III: Determine the exact Degree and Minute of the Ascendant

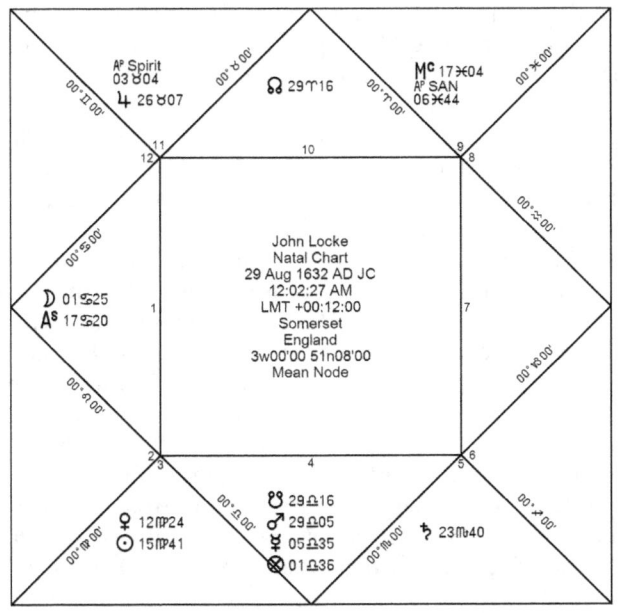

John Locke. *Final proposed rectification:* ASC 17CA20'51"

John Wesley (17-Jun-1703 OS to 2-Mar-1791 NS)

Of Interest. Religious leader.

Britain and America. Founder of Methodist religious sect and leading preacher of the First Great Awakening.

Chronologies

Regulus Astrology LLC. Composite Chronology. See Research Tab.
https://regulus-astrology.com/research.html

Wesley's timeline is drawn primarily from Stephen Tompkins' biography (2003) published by the religious specialty publisher William B. Eerdmans.

Biographical Comments

John Wesley was born into a large family whose head, Samuel Wesley, was a minister of the Church of England. His rescue at age six from the burning rectory on 9-Feb-1709 made a strong impression; Wesley considered himself a child of Providence following the escape. He followed in his father's footsteps by choosing the ministry as a profession. Wesley first studied at the Charterhouse School in London and later at Christ Church College, Oxford. After ordination as a deacon on 19-Sep-1725, he served in his father's parish a few years before returning to Oxford on 22-Nov-1729.

The origins of Methodism can be traced to Wesley's stint at Oxford beginning in 1729. His younger brother Charles, also at Oxford and preparing for the ministry, started the *Holy Club* whose membership included his brother John and the soon-to-be famous evangelist, George Whitefield. The name *Methodist* was given to club members because of their methodical habits. Following Oxford, John Wesley's first mission was in the American colony of Georgia, where he spent the years 1735-1738 attempting to convert Indians to Christianity. The mission was a failure. Though some scholars suggest Wesley was converted during 1725, it appears that 24-May-1738 was more significant to the development of his religious philosophy. It was on this date during a Moravian meeting that he discerned the connection between faith and forgiveness. This changed his life forever. Shortly after, George Whitefield convinced Wesley to preach an open-air sermon in Bristol, which he did with reluctance on 2-Apr-1739. His sermon met with success and launched his preaching career which included an estimated 40,000 sermons during his lifetime.

Wesley later split with Whitefield over the issue of predestination, taking the view that people could achieve salvation by their faith alone. He met with considerable criticism amongst the established Church of England and faced mob violence on several occasions.

His marriage on 17/18-Feb-1751 was considered a failure. His wife left him after fifteen years. Other dates of interest: ordination to Priesthood, 22-Sep-1728; death of father, 5-Apr-1735; death of mother, 30-Jul-1742; illness-near death, Jun-1775; death, 2-Mar-1791.

Stage I. Determine the Ascendant Sign

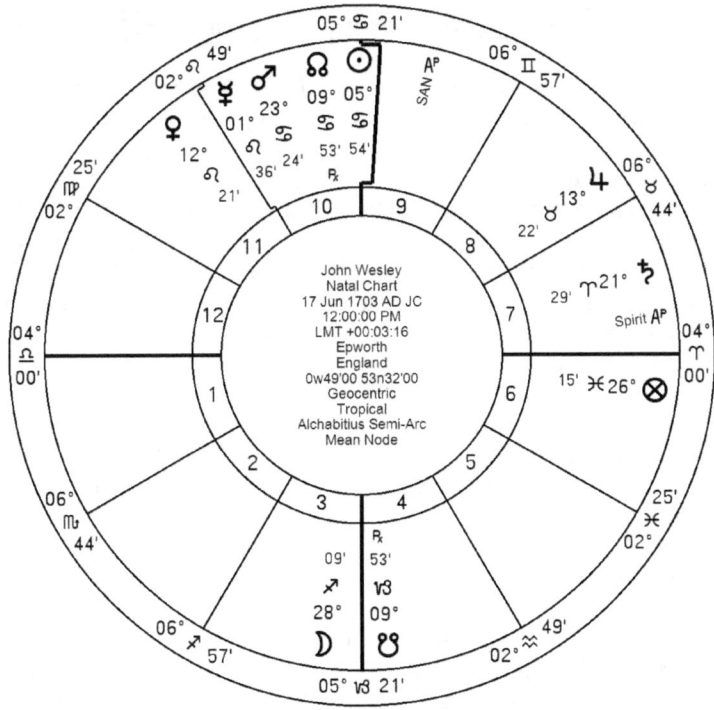

John Wesley. *Trial Noon Horoscope for unknown birth time.*

➤ Match Significations of the planets with biographical details.

Notable configurations are the Mars-Saturn and the Mercury/Venus-Jupiter square aspects. Both planetary groups are in aversion; e.g., they do not see each other. From a religious doctrinal point-of-view, Wesley's abandonment of predestination in favor of faith as a steppingstone to religious perfection is consistent with Mercury and Venus placed in the optimistic sign of Leo overcome by Jupiter at the superior square. His opponents who believed in predestination, e.g., George Whitefield, are signified by one or both malefics.

> Use Moon's Configuration to narrow the Ascendant degree range.

Time	Moon	Sect	Configuration
12:00 AM	20SA34	N	Moon separates from Venus and applies to Saturn Moon in bound Mercury/Sagittarius
12:41 AM	21SA00	N	Moon enters bound Saturn/Sagittarius
1:23 AM	21SA27	N	Moon separates from Saturn and is VOC
3:39 AM	22SA53	D	Sunrise
8:35 AM	26SA00	D	Moon enters bound Mars/Sagittarius
2:55 PM	00CP00	D	Moon enters bound Mercury/Capricorn
8:25 PM	3CP28	N	Sunset
12:00 AM	5CP43	N	Moon applies to Sun, bound Mercury/Capricorn

Moon's sign is either Sagittarius or Capricorn. The term *Methodist* derives from practices of the Holy Club established at Oxford. Routine activities of prayer, fasting, financial donations, prison visits, and communion were thought excessive by observers, e.g., too 'methodical.' Astrologically, methodical is a Capricorn signification and suggests the Moon is in Capricorn, not Sagittarius. If so, the Moon is closely conjunct the South Node which is a debility. My research suggests the Moon conjunct South Node overemphasizes its Capricorn sensitivity beyond what is necessary for the Moon's normative intuitive channels. This is consistent with public comments about the Holy Club's activities as excessive.

If correct, birth time is 2:55 PM or later. Moon transits the bound of Mercury/Capricorn from 2:55 PM to midnight and applies to the Sun. There are no other possible refinements to the birth time using the Moon's configuration.

> Use Firdaria to choose the horoscope's diurnal or nocturnal sect.

Major Jupiter (1723-1735). Jupiter signifies preaching and is most likely Wesley's victor. Match to ordination as deacon (19-Sep-1725), ordination as priest (22-Sep-1728), participation in the Holy Club (after 22-Nov-1729), and introduction to George Whitefield through the Holy Club (1733). Father died during Jupiter-Saturn subperiod (25-Apr-1735).

Major Mars (1735-1742). In my view Major Mars is the most striking delineation match to the nocturnal Firdaria series compared to Major Moon (1734-1743) were the series diurnal. Four months after the start of Major Mars, JW left for the Georgia colony in America. In the company of Moravians he quickly became aware of how poor was his level of faith. He was also involved in a love triangle which led to arrest and financial penalties which JW avoided by fleeing the colony and returning to England. While JW did experience his religious conversion on 24-May-1738 (Mars-Venus subperiod) and did form the Methodist sect on 24-Dec-1739 (Mars-Moon subperiod), the period was still marred by the split from Whitefield during Winter 1740/41 during the Mars-Saturn subperiod, consistent with delineation of malefics as JW's enemies.

North Node (1742-1745). Match to promulgation of "The General Rules of the United Societies" designed to unite and integrate operations of various religious societies run under the Methodist banner, 1743.

South Node (1745-1747). While personal attacks against JW and Methodists occurred at various times not exclusive to the South Node period, just one month after the start of the South Node period, JW narrowly escaped a mob attack (Jul-1745). During Britain's war against France, Methodists were lumped together with French Catholics and other foreigners as objects of enmity and scorn. The last battle on British soil against the French occurred at Culloden (April-1746). This event was the high-water mark of Methodist persecution consistent with the ability of the South Node to time loss.

Sun-Saturn (1753-1754). A life-threatening illness required six months of recovery during the Saturn subperiod (Oct-1753 to Mar-1754).

Conclusion: Overall evidence favors the nocturnal series. This limits the allowable birth time range from 8:25 PM to 12:00 AM. Ascendant sign is either Capricorn, Aquarius, Pisces, or Aries.

> Use Configuration of the Chart to select Ascendant sign.

Keeping with the theme that Saturn is Wesley's primary nemesis and both malefics work against him, it is unlikely that Aries (Mars-ruled with Saturn by position) is an allowable Ascendant sign. And while Saturn rules both Capricorn and Aquarius, Capricorn is the significator for the methodical practices of the Methodist faith and is more congruent with Wesley. The ideological fixed air sign of Aquarius does not appear a match. Are we down to Capricorn or Pisces as allowable Ascendant signs?

If Wesley's victor is Jupiter, one is drawn to Pisces for the sign's association with Christianity. However, by whole sign houses Pisces rising makes Scorpio the 9th of religion ruled by malefic Mars. It also makes Virgo the 7th of the spouse ruled by the optimistic Mercury/Leo. Both configurations are inconsistent with JW's religious beliefs and his failed marriage.

If Capricorn rises, see first that Jupiter rules the 12th; consistent with the Holy Club's initial mission to the imprisoned. Mars/Cancer is placed in the 7th of the spouse. Jupiter/Taurus occupies the 5th ruled by Venus/Leo. JW experienced plenty of sex, just not so much with his wife.

Conclusion: Choose Capricorn as the tentative rising sign.

> Use physiognomy to confirm the rising sign.

With only a few available portraits and no actual photographs to review, I am reluctant to give much weight to physiognomy as a rectification tool for John Wesley. Nevertheless, the prominent chin does appear to outline the ovate shape of Capricorn in John Willner's sign-based facial-shape model. At the very least, this drawing is not *inconsistent* with Capricorn as a rising sign.

Stage II. Determine the Ascendant's range within 1-4 degrees.

For Capricorn rising and a nocturnal horoscope, the earliest allowable Ascendant degree is opposite the Sun's position, after sunset. This narrows the possible Ascendant degree range to 6CP15 to 29CP59. Within three degrees of the Full Moon, both Lots of Fortune and Spirit will be a few degrees apart opposite the Ascendant.

Birth time	8:25 PM	9:43 PM
Ascendant	6CP15	29CP59
Lot of Fortune	9CA01	1LE59
Lot of Spirit	3CA29	27CA59

For most of the time both lots are in Cancer which means Zodiacal Releasing from Spirit begins from the following sign of Leo. Not until 9:37 PM does the Lot of Fortune advance from Cancer to Leo, leaving the Lot of Spirit in Cancer. In that narrow slot of time from 9:37 PM to 9:43 PM ZRS would begin from Cancer since both lots are in different signs allowing us to revert to the basic rule of releasing directly from the sign of the Lot of Spirit as given in the natal horoscope. In what follows, I present an event match consistent with ZRS from Leo. While this will shave only 6 minutes from a possible birth time range, sometimes we just have to take whatever a technique offers.

CHAPTER 18 – RECTIFICATION CASE STUDIES

> ➢ Use Zodiacal Releasing from Spirit to confirm the sign placement of the Ascendant, Lot of Fortune, and Lot of Spirit.

L1 Leo 17 Jun 1703. O.S.		
L1 Virgo 09 Mar 1722		1722, Read *Health and Long Life* by Dr. Cheyne, Proscribed strict moderation in food and drink, supported by sleep and exercise.
L2 Pisces 21 May 1731	FS	31-Aug-1731, JW and William Morgan decided the Holy Club should make cash gifts to those needy people targeted by their outreach; Feb-1732, William Morgan went mad, delivering the Holy Club a severe blow.
L2 Aries 15 May 1732	LOF10	26-Aug-1732, death of William Morgan, many blamed the Holy Club for Morgan's death; 9-Dec-1732, negative newspaper coverage on the Holy Club's fanaticism; 1733 (no exact date), George Whitefield joined the Holy Club.
L2 Pisces 08 Jul 1739	LB	11-Nov-1739, first preached at Foundary; later bought/renovated building which was center of Methodism in London; 24-Dec-1739, formed Methodist Societies.
L2 Aries 02 Jul 1740	LOF10	16-Jul-1740, members of Fetter Lane Society decided JW should no longer preach there; 24-Dec-1740, George Whitefield wrote letter of protest against JW's anti-predestination views; Jun-1741, preached in Leichestershire, beginning of network of Methodist societies.
L1 Libra 24 Nov 1741		Winter 1741/42, fell seriously ill; stoned between the eyes near Whitechapel but felt no pain, wiped away the blood, and continued to preach; 28-May-1742, traveled to Newcastle for first time, extension of preaching tours.
L1 Scorpio 13 Oct 1749		
L1 Sagittarius 06 Aug 1764. N.S.		
L1 Capricorn 04 Jun 1776		1776, spoke against American Revolution with result that 50% of Northern members dropped out but a large revival in Virginia caused members to surge over 400%
L2 Cancer 16 Aug 1785	FS	1787, American Methodists asserted independence over JW's instructions for conventions and other matters; renamed themselves the Methodist Episcopal Church of America.

For L1-Virgo, striking are linkages between L2-Pisces and L2-Aries before and after loosing the bond. Especially L2-Aries, with Saturn/Aries the significator for predestination theology espoused by George Whitefield. With the Lot of Fortune in Cancer, all cardinal signs are angular from Fortune, very active, and with Aries 10th from Fortune, especially climactic with Whitefield.

Conclusion: Both Lots of Fortune and Spirit are in Cancer. This narrows the possible birth time range to between 8:25 PM and 9:37 PM corresponding to an Ascendant degree range of 6CP15 to 27CP56.

> Identify sensitive degrees by investigating dynamic activity to angles and lots for key life events.

This rectification approach seeks to identify common degree areas for a wide number of life events. This is the bread and butter of modern rectification approaches. I deploy it here after refining the rectified Ascendant to just over 21 degrees. Commonly thought to identify degrees of either the Ascendant or Midheaven, this approach may also identify common degree areas for specific lots.

Two of the most striking events in Wesley's chronology are surviving a house fire at the age of 6 which left him a sense of destiny and attacks levied by George Whitefield against Wesley over predestination during winter 1740/1741. For these two events I see:

Date	Event	Measurement
9-Feb-1709	House fire	dsa Mars 29CA01
24-Dec-1870	Whitefield letter	tr Mars 29CA41

With natal Mars/Cancer, the latter marks a Mars return, the former a solar arc with Mars remaining very active on a dynamic basis in Cancer. My suspicion is these measurements will fall very close to the Descendant degree; however, because the Lots of Fortune and Spirit are so close to the Descendant degree, it is difficult to know whether this dynamic activity tags the LOF, LOS, or the DSC. Still if I am correct about this dynamic activity occurring close to the DSC, this suggests the DSC is late Cancer making the ASC late Capricorn.

Other measurements used to fine tune sensitive degrees. Note dynamic activity to the 10th position of selected lots. This type of measurement is a refinement I present for the first time in ARM 4th edition.

Date	Event	Measurement
19-Sep-1725	Ordination as Deacon	trNorth Node 29AR22 10th from LOF
25-Jun-1744	1st Methodist Conference	trNorth Node 27AR00 10th from LOF/DSC.
10-Feb-1751	Slipped on ice; Sprained ankle	trJupiter 29AR50 conj 12th house Lot of Accusation, Exile, and Injury
8-Oct-1781	Death of wife	trVenus 12CP conj L.Marriage

Conclusion : These observations are consistent with an Ascendant in the last 1-4 degrees our degree range: e.g., 23CP56 – 27CP56. Stage II is closed.

Stage III: Determine the exact Degree and Minute of the Ascendant

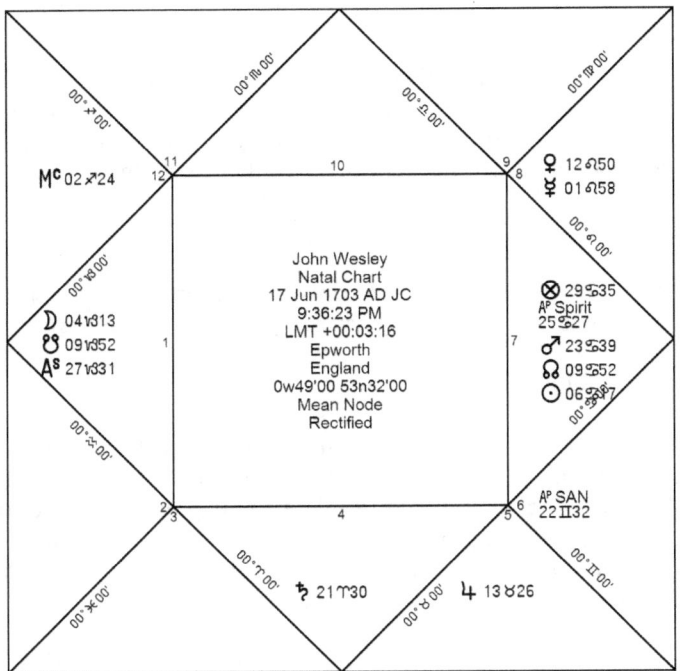

John Wesley. *Final proposed rectification:* ASC 27CP31'10"

See 'Rectification Case Studies' for directions used to finalize the Ascendant degree, available for download: https://regulus-astrology.com/research.html

For Stage III Rectification with directions, a standout measurement is the following primary direction I propose to time Wesley's Aldersgate experience of 24-May-1738 AD JC, 8:45 PM, about 28 Aldersgate Street, London, UK.

| REG | D | Mercury/Libra | P | sin sq North Node d. => Lot of Spirit | 23-May-1738 |

Celebrated today each year by the Methodist Church, this is the event when Wesley felt his heart 'strangely warmed.' It is one of the best documented cases of a born-again Christian conversion experience. For the event chart (not shown), the Moon separates from Mars/Aries and applies to Jupiter/Aries. As will be shown with the horoscope of George Whitefield, Jupiter/Aries is the astrological significator for the born-again experience called forth by the 1702 Jupiter-Saturn conjunction in Aries.

Jonathan Edwards (5-Oct-1703 OS to 22-Mar-1758 NS)

Of Interest

Britain and America. Leading New England revivalist preacher of the First Great Awakening. Spoke fire and brimstone sermons in the Calvinist tradition. Theologian whose written record spans 18,000 pages in 26 volumes published by Yale. Incorporated emerging scientific worldview into theology.

Chronologies

The Jonathan Edwards Center of Yale University offers a comprehensive biographical timeline. http://edwards.yale.edu/research/chronology

Biographical Comments

Jonathan Edwards was the leading American revivalist preacher during the First Great Awakening. His theology was Calvinistic. During times of revival, Edwards' preaching elicited public displays of religious fervor never before witnessed during the conversion process. His connections with George Whitefield's New England visit of 1740 are of interest to students tracing mundane cycles of religious leaders and movements.

Edwards studied at Yale for two years and was appointed tutor on 21-May-1724. He was ordained to the ministry on 15-Feb-1727 and appointed to assistant pastor for a Northampton church led by his maternal grandfather Solomon Stoddard. On the unexpected death of Stoddard on 11-Feb-1729, Edwards took the helm of the Northampton parish. Edwards was a successful family man, marrying Sarah Pierpont on 20-Jul-1726. The couple raised a large family of 11 children, all of whom survived infancy to adulthood which was very rare for the 18th century.

The Northampton community underwent two major revivals associated with Edwards: 1733-1735 and 1740-1741, the latter associated with George Whitefield's New England trip. In the mid-1740s, a reaction set in against Edwards from religious quarters who considered the revivals of 1740-1741 excessive. Edwards eventually ran amok of his congregation following his reversal of the Half-Way Covenant espoused by Solomon Stoddard which had loosened requirements for church membership. Edwards demanded formal tests of faith prior to receiving benefits of church membership. After his congregation rejected this process, Edwards was dismissed on 22-Jun-1750.

In his last years, Edwards took up an Indian Mission at Stockbridge on 19-May-1751. In his final position, he was installed as President of Princeton University on 16-Feb-1758 but died a few weeks later following complications from an unsuccessful smallpox vaccine.

Stage I. Determine the Ascendant Sign

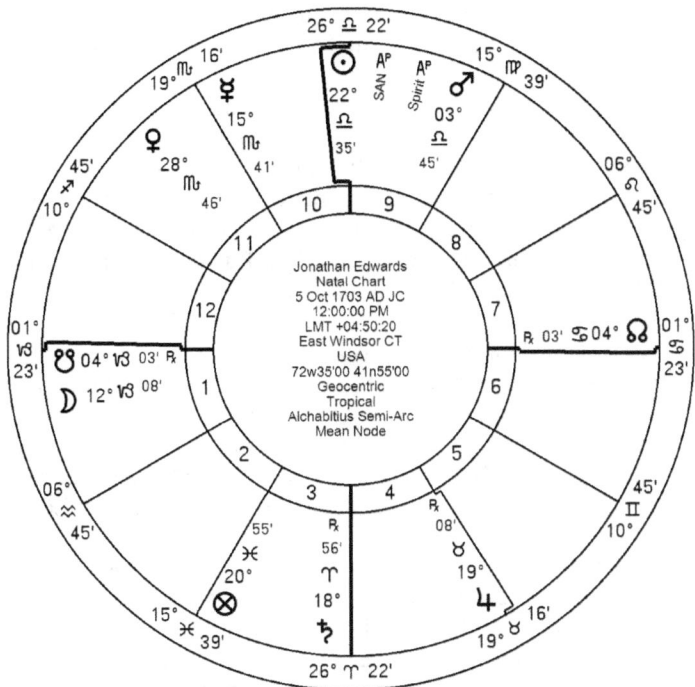

Jonathan Edwards. Trial Noon Horoscope for unknown birth time.

Edwards was born under the Julian Calendar. With the changeover to the Gregorian Calendar in 1752 six years prior to his death in 1758, the bulk of his chronology is based on Julian Calendar dates.

➢ Match Significations of the planets with biographical details.

Born four months after John Wesley, the Nodes remain in the Cancer-Capricorn axis with the Moon coincidentally conjunct the South Node. By this time both Jupiter and Saturn are now retrograde. The Nodes, Moon, Sun, Mars, and Saturn are placed in cardinal signs. See that Saturn makes its heliacal appearance which increases its power to act from a solar phase perspective. The remaining planets of Mercury, Venus, and Jupiter form an opposition in the fixed signs of Taurus and Scorpio. Together with the retrogrades, placement of Mercury and Venus in the caustic sign of Scorpio differs markedly from the optimistic placement of Mercury and Venus in Leo for the horoscope of John Wesley.

While Venus/Scorpio and Mars/Libra are in generosity (in each other's sign but without aspect), this is a difficult configuration as both planets are in detriment. Based on observations from my practice, this configuration often yields lengthy simmering disputes which erupt in violent emotional outbursts.

Edwards is best known for leading and observing religious revivals characterized by displays of extreme emotion, e.g., screams, shouts, and unusual physical movements including rolling on the floor. The Venus-Mars configuration is the best delineation match for this feature of Edwards' ministry with Venus/Scorpio the significator for emotional excess. Venus is also the Sun's sign and bound ruler tying Edward's reputation to public emotional displays witnessed during the Northampton revivals.

Saturn/Aries-retrograde at heliacal rising suggests a turn against the strictures of Saturn/Aries-signified predestination. This is a delineation match to the Half-Way Covenant espoused by his grandfather Solomon Stoddard designed to loosen rules for church membership necessary to grow his parish. Later, Edwards rejected the Half-Way Covenant which resulted in termination by his congregation. I conclude Saturn is a planet which works against Edwards.

Mercury is the universal significator of writing; placement in the sign of Scorpio adds depth, intensity, and a return to first principles. Edwards wrote extensively, with Yale publishing his collected works in 26 volumes of over 18,000 pages. This is something to keep in mind as Edwards had a complex set of theological beliefs which changed over time. Even reading a full-length biography is unlikely sufficient to generate enough clarity to match his complete theology to natal horoscope planets. We should aim for the big pieces, which is my attempt here, remembering that the goal of this exercise is to rectify a horoscope with an unknown birthtime, not to match every life event to the natal horoscope by either static delineation or dynamic events.

> Use Firdaria to choose the horoscope's diurnal or nocturnal sect.

In the prior example of John Wesley, I started with the Moon's Configuration because the Moon had two possible sign choices for the day of birth: Sagittarius or Capricorn. For Edwards, the Moon stays in Capricorn the entire day of birth so I will begin with Firdaria to determine the chart sect.

The following key life events yield event matches for the diurnal sequence:

Venus/Scorpio as significator for emotional revivals yields two event matches:

Mercury-Venus. (25-Nov-1732 to 3-Oct-1734). First revival under Edwards begins June 1734. Preached and published the sermon "A Divine and Supernatural Life" which described a genuine conversion experience.

Moon-Venus. (9-Mar-1741 to 21-Jun-1742). Another revival started, Spring 1741, following visit of George Whitefield the prior fall. Preached and published the sermon "Sinners in the hands of an Angry God," 8-Jul-1741.

Assign Jupiter/Taurus-rx to Edward's preaching and ministerial life.

Venus-Jupiter. (1-May-1718 to 22-Jun-1719). Began undergraduate studies at Yale. Initially studied with tutor Samuel Johnson, returned home after dissatisfaction with Johnson, returned to Yale after Johnson left. The interruption of his Yale studies is consistent with Jupiter retrograde.

Mercury-Jupiter. (1-May-1727 to 9-Mar-1729). Married, 28-Jul-1727; Became senior pastor at Northampton after death of maternal grandfather Solomon Stoddard, 11-Feb-1729.

Moon-Jupiter. (1-May-1737 to 12-Aug-1738). Dedicated new meetinghouse, 25-Dec-1737; Published "A Faithful Narrative of the Surprising Work of God," 1737; Old meetinghouse pulled down, 5-May-1738.

Saturn-Jupiter. (1-May-1745 to 25-Nov-1746). Son Jonathan born, 26-May-1745; Fortifications built to protect against Indian attacks, May/Sep-1746.

Jupiter-Jupiter. (4-Oct-1754 to 21-Jun-1756). Published "Freedom of the Will," Dec-1754; Published "End for Which God Created the World" and "On the Nature of True Virtue," 1755.

Jupiter-Mars. (22-Jun-1756 to 9-Mar-1758). Father died, 27-Jan-1758; Assumed Presidency of Princeton University, 16-Feb-1758.

Jupiter-Sun. (10-Mar-1758 to 25-Nov-1759). Died from complications of smallpox inoculation, 22-Mar-1758.

By inspection, it appears Jupiter is the victor of the horoscope. To restate the importance of Firdaria in rectification, Edwards' horoscope is a good example of just how well Firdaria main and subperiods call forth the power of planets to act. Combining victor delineation with Firdaria in rectification, I approach Firdaria as a counterfactual exercise: If Jupiter is indeed the victor, were we to eliminate all life events which occurred during time periods when Jupiter ruled time as major or minor Firdaria lord, would we still have Jonathan Edwards the pastor and theologian?, or would his life be so stripped of key events that we would not be discussing him right now.

Assumption of his grandfather's Northampton church, construction of a new meetinghouse, publication of theological works on freedom, his appointment to President of Princeton University, and his unexpected death from a smallpox vaccination all occur during Jupiter-ruled Firdaria main or subperiods. Biographical essays consistently include these chronological details. Without them, I argue we would not have Jonathan Edwards.

Ergo, the Firdaria sequence is diurnal.

➤ Use Moon's Configuration to narrow the birth time range.

Time	Moon	Sect	Configuration
12:00 AM	5CP03	N	Moon separates from Mars and applies to Mercury Moon in bound Mercury/Capricorn
3:18 AM	7CP00	N	Moon enters bound Jupiter/Capricorn
6:17 AM	8CP46	D	Sunrise
3:10 PM	14CP00	D	Moon enters bound Venus/Capricorn
5:13 PM	15CP12	N	Sunset
6:36 PM	16CP01	N	Moon separates from Mercury and applies to Saturn
11:30 PM	18CP54	N	Moon separates from Saturn and applies to Jupiter
11:49 PM	19CP05	N	Moon separates from Jupiter and applies to Sun
12:00 AM	19CP11	N	Moon separates from Jupiter and applies to Sun

If the figure is diurnal, the Moon separates from Mars and applies to Mercury for all diurnal birth times. The only difference is the Moon's bound placement in either Jupiter (between 6:17 AM and 3:10 PM) or Venus (3:10 PM to 5:13 PM). Based on biographical details I have uncovered so far, I am unable to choose between Jupiter or Venus for the Moon's bound placement.

For Edwards, the Moon's Configuration will not advance the rectification beyond what Firdaria has demonstrated so far.

➤ Test Moon's Degree based on events for Moon-signified persons.

For a diurnal horoscope, the Moon's degree range is 8CP46 to 15CP12. Can we narrow this degree range based on dynamic activity to the Moon for events regarding Moon-signified persons? Consider the following events: marriage (2-Jul-1727), death of sister Jerusha (22-Dec-1729), death of sister Elisabeth (21-Sep-1733), death of sister Lucy (21-Aug-1736), death of daughter Jerusha (14-Feb-1748), Edward's own death (22-Mar-1758), posthumous deaths of daughter Esther (7-Apr-1758) and his wife Sarah (2-Oct-1758).

For five events, solar arc directions are clustered in the 13-14 degree area.

Date	Event	Measurement
21-Aug-1736	Death of sister Lucy	csa Mercury 13LI24
14-Feb-1748	Death of daughter Jerusha	dsa Venus 13CP23
22-Mar-1758	Death of Edwards	dsa Jupiter 13CA58
7-Apr-1758	Death of daughter Esther	dsa Jupiter 14CA01
2-Oct-1758	Death of wife Sarah	dsa Jupiter 14CA31

Chapter 18 – Rectification Case Studies

Suppose the Moon's degree is 13CP40. This yields ASC=Aquarius, LOF = Taurus, and LOS = Scorpio. With misses for several of the earlier events, I consider this finding provisional.

> Confirm the Lots of Spirit and Fortune with Zodiacal Releasing.

The following table shows positions for the Ascendant, Lot of Fortune, and Lot of Spirit for the sweep of diurnal motion from sunrise to sunset.

Diurnal Figure	Sunrise	Noon	Sunset
Ascendant	22LI21	1CP23	22AR48
Lot of Fortune	8CP46	26PI55	15CA12
Lot of Spirit	5LE58	11LI50	00AQ24

Let us focus on the Lot of Spirit: it ranges from Leo to Aquarius. Can we match L1 ZR periods for any of the seven possible Lot of Spirit placements? Leo, Virgo, Libra, Scorpio, Sagittarius, Capricorn, or Aquarius?

To make this comparison, I use a spreadsheet which lists L1 and L2 periods for all possible sign placements for a given date. It is available for free download from the research tab of www.regulus-astrology.com.

Let us start with the provisional finding from the Moon's trial degree of 13CP40 which corresponds to the Lot of Spirit in Scorpio. At this stage of rectification, our interest is the ability of L1 periods and FS-LB-CP subperiods to subdivide a biographical chronology into distinct chapters.

L1 Scorpio 5-Oct-1703 O.S.		
L1 Sagittarius 18-Jul-1718		Oct-1718, enrolled at Yale.
L1 Capricorn 16-May-1730		(just prior) 11-Feb-1729, Northampton pastor. (just prior) 26-Apr-1730, daughter Jerusha born.
L2 Capricorn 16-May-1730		8-Jul-1731, preached "God Glorified in the Work of Redemption."
L2 Cancer 28-Jul-1739	FS	17-Oct-1740, George Whitefield visitation; 1741-1742, revival; 8-Jul-1741, preached "Sinners in the Hands of an Angry God" at Enfield.
L2 Cancer 14-Sep-1747	LB	8-Oct-1747, David Brainerd died (love interest of daughter Jerusha); 14-Feb-1749, daughter Jerusha died; 19-Jun-1748, father-in-law John Stoddard died; Dec-1748, Edwards rejected Half-Way Covenant by refusing admission of new church member.
L2 Capricorn 12-Nov-1755 N.S.		18-Nov-1755, large earthquake.
L1 Aquarius 05-Jan-1757 N.S.		24-Sep-1757, death of Rev. Aaron Burr; 16-Feb-1758, assumed Presidency of Princeton University; 22-Mar-1758, died from complications of smallpox inoculation.

The standout delineation match for Zodiacal Releasing from the Lot of Spirit in Scorpio is the ability of L1-Capricorn to identify the rise and fall of Edwards' preaching career at Northampton. It is true the start of L1 on 16-May-1730 was a year late compared to his accession to Northampton senior pastor on the death of his grandfather Solomon Stoddard on 11-Feb-1729, but the Whitefield visitation during L2-Cancer foreshadowing is linked to L2-Cancer loosing of the bond because Whitefield's insistence on predestination ultimately led to Edwards' rejection of Stoddard's Half-Way Covenant and his dismissal from Northampton after the loosing of the bond from Capricorn to Cancer.

From a ZR perspective, the Cancer-Capricorn axis is turbocharged by position of the Lunar Nodes and the Moon. Accordingly we should expect striking life events to occur during FS and LB subperiods with the ZR technique.

Capricorn: Moon/South Node conjunct Capricorn. This signifies the over-reliance of duty and hierarchy in an intuitive/emotional soul context. Moon-signified people assign too much value to "going through the motions." This is the starting point. The ending point is 10 signs away in Libra which contains the Sun and Mars. Focusing on the Sun as fame, Edwards begins with a duty-burdened congregation and revives their souls via emotional revivals signified by Venus/Scorpio which rules the Sun by sign and bound. More people are drawn to religion. While Capricorn starts badly, it ends well because of the Sun's placement in Libra 10 signs away in the sign of the superior square.

Cancer: North Node/Cancer. Sign and bound lords are Moon/Capricorn and Mars/Libra respectively. The North Node increases affairs of the sign/house it is placed. We have not chosen the Ascendant sign so we don't know which house the North Node will occupy. But the increase in its house affairs is due to Moon-signified people "going through the motions" buffeted by a weak-willed Mars/Libra. The ending point is 10 signs away in Aries which contains Saturn/Aries-rx. With Saturn already delineated as his grandfather Stoddard's Half-Way Covenant (something Edwards ultimately rejects), placement of Saturn/Aries-rx at the superior square of the North Node predicts affairs of the North Node's sign will end badly. They do. Edwards rejected his grandfather's Half-Way Covenant and was dismissed from his Northampton parish.

Consider also the birth of his daughter Jerusha immediately prior to the start of L1-Capricorn and her death at L2-Cancer LB. Her birth and death mirrors Edward's rise and fall as Northampton's senior pastor.

Ergo, Lot of Spirit is in Scorpio.

This choice refines the birth time range to 1:14 PM to 2:49 PM.
The corresponding Lot of Fortune range is 10AR to 12TA.
The corresponding Ascendant range is 20CP to 21AQ.

To choose between Aries and Taurus for the Lot of Fortune's sign with ZR, it is appropriate to compare the level of career activity for cardinal and fixed signs as either L1 major or L2 subperiods. Before we start, consider if LOF were Aries, then the Moon/South Node Capricorn configuration occupies the superior square to Aries, or the 10th from the LOF which if correct should time Edward's lifetime career peaks. If LOF were Taurus, then Aquarius occupies 10th from the LOF.

At this point, it should be obvious to anyone that I choose the LOF in Aries making Capricorn 10th from LOF. As the previous discussion attests, Edwards' career as Northampton senior pastor occurred during L1 Capricorn which should be the case if Capricorn were 10th from LOF. His appointment as Princeton University President just after the shift to L1 Aquarius was not a career peak as he quickly died and was unable to institute any plans for the University.

Ergo, Lot of Fortune is in Aries.

This choice refines the birth time range to 1:14 PM to 2:16 PM.
The corresponding Ascendant range is 20CP to 9AQ.

> Use Configuration of the Chart to select Ascendant sign.

Is the Ascendant sign Capricorn or Aquarius? While physiognomy may be useful here and in prior ARM editions I made the case for Aquarius rising based on physiognomy, upon further consideration I do not consider a limited number of highly stylized paintings suitable documentary evidence necessary for a physiognomy judgment. I therefore revert to configuration of the chart.

The following observations favor Aquarius rising:

- Interest in science from a young age favors the fixed air sign of Aquarius.
- The Moon/South Node Capricorn configuration moves to the 12th house which among other things signifies death of children. His daughter Jerusha did die during L1-L2 Capricorn-Cancer (LB).
- Sun/Libra moves to the 9th house of God. He was a priest and theologian.
- Gemini moves to the 5th house of children. He had eleven, all of whom survived to adulthood. Scorpio is a fruitful sign for children. If the 5th is Gemini, Mercury/Scorpio applies to Jupiter/Taurus-rx. This is consistent.
- Mercury also rules the 8th house of death which is a bad house. Placed in the sign of Scorpio associated with poison, Mercury's rulership of the 8th is consistent with Edward's death from a smallpox inoculation.

Ergo, the Ascendant degree range is 00AQ00 to 9AQ12. Stage I is complete.

Stage II. Determine the Ascendant's range within 1-4 degrees.

> Use Dynamic Measurements to the Angles to refine the Ascendant degree.

The Victor of the Horoscope is Jupiter. As Jupiter is a slower moving planet, transits to the angles highlight major life affairs (for final rectified time):

Jupiter conj ASC: 31-Mar-1724, 8-Jul-1724, 20-Nov-1724: Elected tutor at Yale, 21-May-1724; Traveled to New Haven to begin tutorship, **Jun-1724**.

Jupiter conj ASC: 6-Mar-1736, 25-Aug-1736, 19-Oct-1736; Birth of daughter Lucy, ****31-Aug-1736****; Completed short account of late revivals which was republished widely in Europe, **6-Nov-1736**.

Jupiter conj DSC: 23-Sep-1741, 14-Jan-1742, 20-May-1742. Delivered "Distinguishing Marks of the Work of the Spirit of God", **10-Sep-1741**; wife Sarah undergoes series of religious ecstasies, ****19-Jan-1742****.

Jupiter conj LOF: 11-Jun-1750, 19-Oct-1750, 28-Jan-1751. Dismissed from Northampton, ****22-Jun-1750****; Called to Stockbridge, **22-Feb-1751**.

Stage III: Determine the exact Degree and Minute of the Ascendant

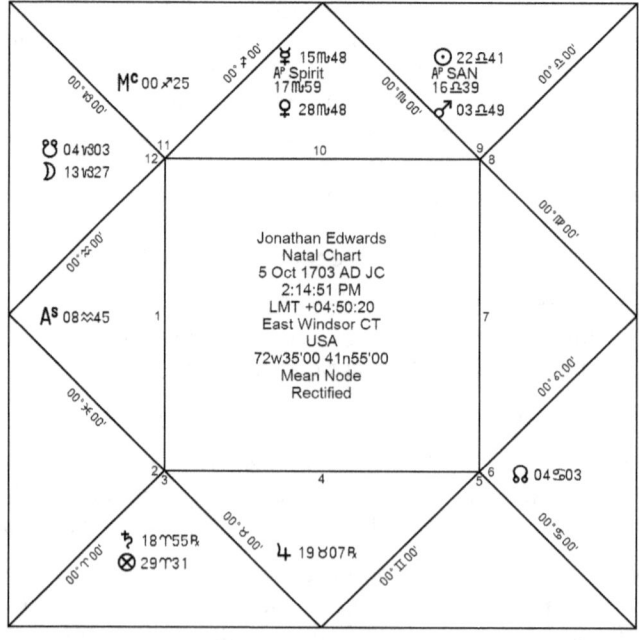

Jonathan Edwards. *Final proposed rectification: ASC 8AQ45'39"*

George Whitefield (16-Dec-1717 OS to 30-Sep-1770 NS)

Of Interest

Britain and America. Leading Methodist revival preacher of the First Great Awakening. Advocate of the 'New Birth' or 'born-again' conversion experience. Preached to over 10 million persons during his career.

Chronologies

Regulus Astrology LLC. Composite Chronology. See Research Tab. https://regulus-astrology.com/research.html

Dates are drawn from Harry S. Stout's *The Divine Dramatist* (1991) and Peter Choi's *George Whitefield: Evangelist for God and Empire* (2018) both published by William B. Eerdmans. Also recommended is J. D. Dickey's *American Demagogue: The Great Awakening and the Rise and Fall of Populism* (2019) published by Pegasus Books.

Biographical Comments

George Whitefield was the leading Evangelical Methodist preacher during the 1st Great Awakening. Though John Wesley is known as the founder of Methodism, George Whitefield delivered more converts to the church than any other. During his approximately 24 years in Britain and 9 years in America, he is estimated to have spoken to ten million people. His booming voice carried far. He routinely spoke to crowds of 10,000 or more without amplification, a claim confirmed by the skeptical Benjamin Franklin who made scientific crowd measurements. Whitefield made 13 transatlantic trips via sea and was the most traveled preacher in world history up to his time.

He was born into a family of poverty, his father died at the age of two, and after a bout of childhood measles Whitefield suffered from *squint eyes* or eyes which looked perpetually crossed. He entered Oxford at age 17 and there met John Wesley who invited him to join the Holy Club. His conversion occurred during Spring 1735. Wesley left Oxford in May 1735 to recuperate for nine months after an illness. Returning to Oxford in March 1736, Whitefield was ordained a deacon on 20-Jun-1736. He immediately began to draw large crowds in England as he launched his preaching career.

His first American trip, urged by John Wesley, was during spring 1738. He was ordained a priest in the Church of England on 14-Jan-1739. Soon after he was met by opposition in the established church which opposed the hysteria among crowds to which he preached. He was denounced by the Bishop of London on 1-Aug-1739 just before he left for America on 14-Aug-1739 for one of his most successful trips. His arrival in Savannah on 10-Jan-1740 was quickly followed by laying the cornerstone for an orphanage on 25-Mar-1740. During his New England stint, he stayed with Jonathan Edwards during October 1740. Whitefield returned to England on 14-Mar-1741. He made many more trips which were alternately marred by illness or violence from open enemies. Besides having to endure garbage thrown at himself by unruly crowds, he was physically attacked and beaten in 1744 and barely escaped death from mob violence during his 1756 stay in Ireland. He split with John Wesley on the matter of predestination during 1741 (Whitefield believed in it; Wesley did not).

Whitefield married Elizabeth James on 14-Nov-1741; she predeceased him on 9-Aug-1768. They had one son John, born 4-Oct-1743, who died at age four months. Whitefield died during his last trip to America, exhausted from demands of preaching, on 30-Sep-1770.

Stage I. Determine the Ascendant Sign

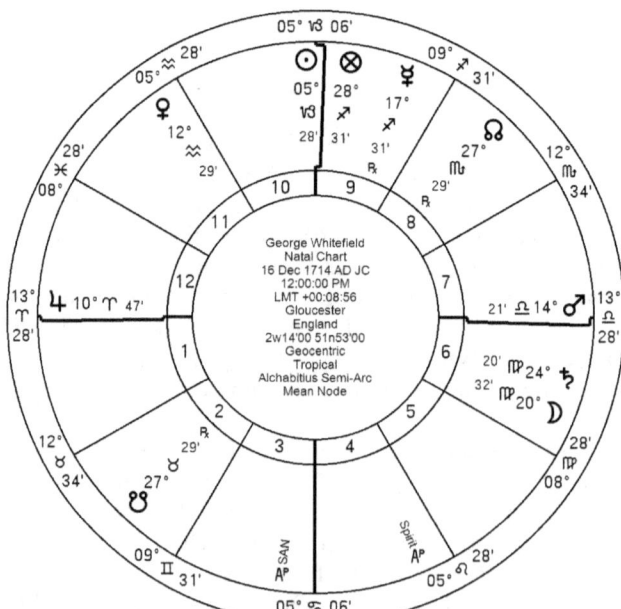

George Whitefield. *Trial Noon Horoscope for unknown birth time.*

> Match Significations of the planets with biographical details.

The mundane Jupiter-Saturn synodic cycle yields three conjunctions in Aries: 21-May-1702 (6AR36), 18-Mar-1762 (12AR21), and 19-Jun-1821 (24AR38). Whitefield was born one Jupiter cycle following the 1702 JSC with both

Jupiter placements for the 1702 JSC and Whitefield in the bound of Venus/Aries. So far we have seen evidence of doctrinal disputes with Wesley's Saturn/Aries signifying conflict with Whitefield over predestination and Edward's Saturn/Aries-retrograde signifying conflict with his grandfather Solomon Stoddard's Half Way Covenant.

Now we find Jupiter/Aries in Whitefield's horoscope. What does it signify? Simply put Jupiter/Aries is the significator for Christian evangelism with the born-again conversion experience a common tenet. When we read in a letter from Whitefield to Benjamin Colman that "surely our Lord intends to put the whole world in a Flame" (Stout 1991, 117) we know the fiery triplicity is at work in Whitefield's ministry.[24] Beyond Jupiter, Saturn/Virgo at the superior square of Mercury/Sagittarius-rx is a delineation match to the established church hierarchy's disapproval over Whitefield's open-air preaching to the masses and other doctrinal issues.

Mars/Libra ruling but separating from Jupiter/Aries is tricky to delineate but makes more sense when we see by degree that Venus separates from Jupiter and applies to Mars. A further investigation reveals that Venus will retrograde before perfecting the trine aspect to Mars. In any case, what does this configuration mean? Venus/Aquarius is a delineation match to the ecumenical appeal of the born-again conversion experience across multiple Christian sects. Venus' application to Mars bonifies Mars/Libra's anti-establishment impulse. Both actions of Mars and Venus accentuate Jupiter/Aries' New Birth signification, creating a reinforced chain of rulership: Venus in her own bound rules Mars by sign and Jupiter by bound; Mars rules Jupiter by sign.

Finally, beyond Whitefield's preaching style, Mercury/Sagittarius-rx is the probable significator for orphaned children with Mercury the significator of youth and retrogradation the debility which describes their orphaned status.

> Use Firdaria to choose the horoscope's diurnal or nocturnal sect.

The following events favor the nocturnal Firdaria sequence:

<u>Major Jupiter.</u> (16-Dec-1734 to 15-Dec-1746 O.S.) Supplies accurate bookends to Whitefield's born-again conversion experience in 1735 and the end of the first intercolonial revival in 1746. This correlation is so precise that it will be hard to shake off Firdaria's testimony in favor of a nocturnal nativity.

---

[24] For Whitefield, the combination of Jupiter/Aries (preaching the new birth) and Mercury/Sagittarius-rx (over-the-top presentation style) is similar to the combination of Aries rising and Mars/Sagittarius for the 20th century revivalist Billy Graham. 7-Nov-1918, 4:02:21 PM, Charlotte, NC. Author's rectification.

Mars-Jupiter. (26-Dec-1752 to 25-Dec-1753 N.S.) Fourth American trip. Not as dramatic as Major Jupiter.

Sun-Jupiter. (17-Feb-1766 to 23-Jul-1767) Raised 12,000 pounds to fund Dartmouth College from Feb/1766 to Jul/1767. This appears a precise match.

Conclusion: Horoscope is nocturnal. Possible birth times are prior to 8:15 AM and after 3:48 PM.

➤ Use Moon's Configuration to choose morning or evening nocturnal hours.

Time	Moon	Sect	Configuration
12:00 AM	14VI23	N	Moon separates from Sun and applies to Mercury Bound Venus/Virgo
4:54 AM	17VI00	N	Moon enters bound Jupiter/Virgo
6:01 AM	17VI35	N	Moon separates from Mercury and applies to Saturn
8:15 AM	18VI40	D	Sunrise
12:55 PM	21VI00	D	Moon enters bound Mars/Virgo
3:48 PM	22VI25	N	Sunset
7:39 PM	24VI20	N	Moon separates from Saturn and is VOC
12:00 AM	26VI29	N	Moon separates from Saturn and is VOC

There are three possible Moon configurations for a nocturnal horoscope:

Moon separates from Sun and applies to Mercury (morning)
Moon separates from Mercury and applies to Saturn (morning/evening)
Moon separates from Saturn and is VOC (evening)

Do any of these make sense?

The first emphasizes Whitefield's preaching and commitment to his Georgia orphanage as primary life themes. *True.*
The second shows Whitefield encountering more criticism and regulatory oversight from establishment religious leaders as life progressed. *True.*
The final configuration suggests a very bleak life pattern for Whitefield, especially with Saturn the out-of-sect malefic. *Appears too extreme.*

While normally I like to choose a single Moon's configuration based on this Stage I rectification technique, sometimes the results are ambiguous. Nonetheless if these observations are correct, we can still shave off over 4 hours from consideration (7:39 PM to 12:00 AM) which is no small matter.

➤ Use Configuration of the Chart to match life themes to houses.

For morning nocturnal hours, possible Ascendants are Libra, Scorpio, Sagittarius, and Capricorn to the Sun's position of 5CP19.

For evening nocturnal hours, the Ascendant range is 4CA36 to 18LE44.

Based on the core delineation tenet that Christian evangelism is signified by fire signs, I am first drawn to Sagittarius rising (for morning nocturnal hours) and Leo rising (for evening nocturnal hours). Of the two choices, Leo rising places Jupiter/Aries in the 9th house of God, travel, pilgrimage, and philosophy. Whitefield's nickname of "The Grand Itinerant" is also a perfect delineation match to Jupiter ("Grand") and the 9th house ("Itinerant" = travel). By most accounts he was one of, if not the single most traveled individual in the entire 18th century. As for Leo rising, Whitefield was a rock star of his time. People would literally run from their farm chores to be in his presence and hear him speak. In prior ARM editions, I incorrectly mapped this feature to Moon/Aries based on an incorrect Gregorian Calendar birth date. Revisiting Whitefield with Leo rising and Moon/Virgo, I believe it reasonable for Leo rising alone to account for his celebrity level of popularity.

Conclusion: Ascendant degree range is Leo (00LE00 to 18LE44)

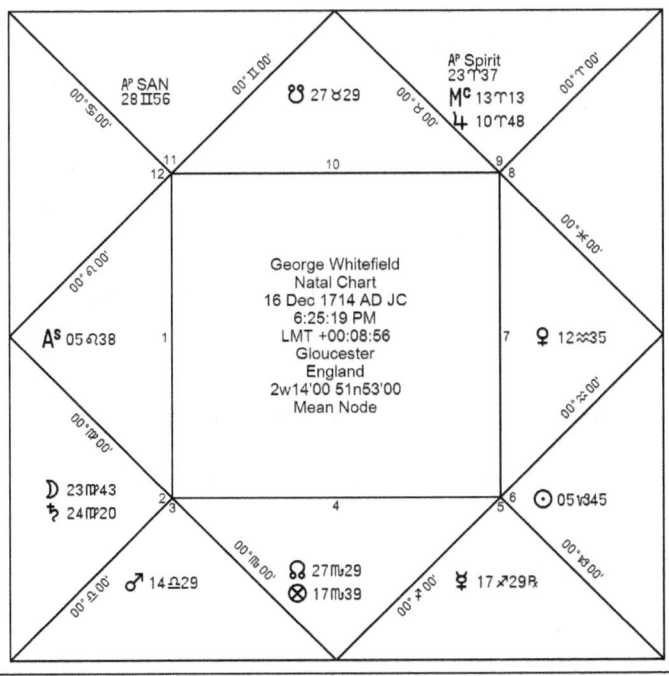

George Whitefield. *Final proposed rectification: ASC 5LE38'28"*

Benjamin Franklin (6-Jan-1705 OS to 17-Apr-1790 NS)

Of Interest

America. Leading publisher, inventor, businessman, diplomat, and public intellectual of colonial America. Initially pro-British, he broke with the British and favored revolution. Less well-known is Franklin's covert diplomatic role in arranging acquisition of weapons and cash for colonial revolutionaries. An early abolitionist who sided with the Quakers in their opposition to slavery.

Chronologies

Regulus Astrology LLC. Composite Chronology. See Research Tab.
https://regulus-astrology.com/research.html

Benjamin Franklin Historical Society
http://www.benjamin-franklin-history.org/timeline/

The Electric Ben Franklin is sponsored by the Independence Hall Association.
https://www.ushistory.org/franklin/info/timeline.htm

Biographical Comments

Any capsule biography of Benjamin Franklin is an oxymoron given the scope and depth of his interests. For those new to Franklin, the National Park Service created a resume based on Franklin's life and career. It highlights his most important accomplishments.
https://www.nps.gov/inde/learn/historyculture/people-franklin-resume.htm

Available Birth Data

Records from Old South Church, Boston, state Franklin was baptized on Sunday morning, the same day as his birth. Born just a few blocks away from his family's church, it was relatively easy for his family to take their newborn to church for baptism.

Revised Rectification

Prior editions of ARM featured a trial rectification of 1:43:14 PM, ASC 16GE11 which has not held up under further scrutiny. In addition to records stating he was born in the morning, my prior choice of Gemini rising as a delineation match to Franklin's intellectual curiosity was faulty. The proposed Aquarius Ascendant with Mercury as occupant is another Ascendant consistent with intellectual curiosity. Aquarius is a fixed air sign; Mercury/Aquarius-retrograde tinkers with intellectual axioms and rules.

Stage I. Determine the Ascendant Sign

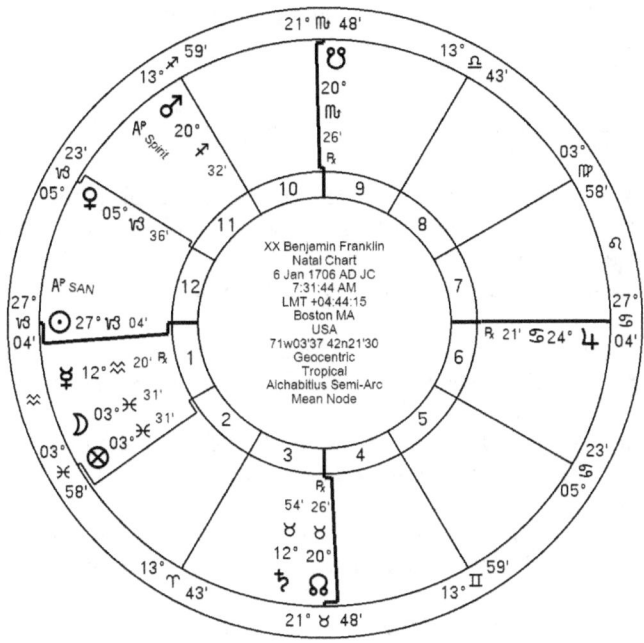

Benjamin Franklin. *Trial Noon Horoscope for sunrise birth time.*

➤ Match Significations of the planets with biographical details.

Two superior planets stand out for their solar phase. Mars is oriental, past the sunbeams, and approaches the waxing sextile which is the most powerful solar phase. Mars is also the bound lord of the Sun. Fire was an important theme for Franklin. He organized the Union Fire Company of Philadelphia, invented the Franklin stove, invented the lightning rod to prevent building fires, and proposed the first Philadelphia fire insurance company. Politically, Mars/Sagittarius signifies righteous indignation capable of turning Franklin against Britain. Jupiter at acronycal rising is also a standout. With Jupiter/Cancer-rx functioning like Jupiter/Capricorn, Jupiter is the likely significator for the British, colonial Loyalists, and potentially his son William Franklin who led the colonial Loyalists. William and his father Benjamin were later estranged, a deep loss. Venus/Capricorn applying to Saturn/Taurus, mutual reception by sign, signifies Franklin's practical application of science for public benefit. As significator of electricity, Mercury/Aquarius-rx matches Franklin's electricity experiments with the famous kite experiment transmitting an electrical charge from a kite to a Leyden jar for storage. Mercury/Aquarius-rx functions like Mercury/Leo, the fixed fire sign which stores the light/brilliance of electricity for practical use.

➤ Use Firdaria to choose the horoscope's diurnal or nocturnal sect.

Birth records state Franklin was born and baptized in the morning but do not specify whether birth was before or after sunrise. The following events favor the diurnal Firdaria sequence:

Major Mercury (6-Jan-1724 O.S. to 4-Jan-1737). Became printer, 1724.

Major Jupiter (16-Jan-1757 N.S. to 15-Jan-1769). Happiest five years of his life are described as his years in England between 1757 and 1762. Note with the delineation of Jupiter/Cancer-rx as colonial Royalists that Franklin had not yet split from the British while Major Jupiter was active.

Major Mars (16-Jan-1769 to 16-Jan-1776). Approach to Revolutionary War. Franklin's earlier diplomatic success in reigning in the Stamp Act (1766) was not repeated. Dispute with Britain over Franklin's leak of the Hutchinson papers led to his public humiliation before the Privy Council on 29-Jan-1774. This was a key life event which led Franklin to break with the British.

Major North Node (17-Jan-1776 to 16-Jan-1779). Named Commissioner to the French Court, helped negotiate an alliance with France during 1778.

Major South Node (17-Jan-1779 to 15-Jan-1781). Dispute with John Adams.

Conclusion: Figure is diurnal. Birth time range is 7:31 AM to 12:00 Noon. The corresponding Ascendant degree range is 27CP04 – 14TA27. Possible Ascendant signs are Capricorn, Aquarius, Pisces, Aries, and Taurus.

➤ Use Moon's Configuration to narrow the birth time range.

Time	Moon's Degree	Sect	Configuration
7:31 AM	3PI31	D	Sunrise, Moon applies to Venus
11:15 AM	5PI47	D	Moon separates from Venus and applies to Saturn
12:00 PM	6PI14	D	Noon

In prior ARM editions, I delineated Saturn/Taurus as the practical application of science for mankind and favored the Moon's separation from Venus and application to Saturn. Venus/Capricorn in mutual reception with Saturn/Taurus does link the two planets closely and makes it difficult to determine how the Moon's application to Venus, or the Moon's separation from Venus and application to Saturn might produce a distinctly different set of life themes which makes it possible to choose one configuration over the other. As ZRS analysis shows below, the Moon's application to Venus proves the better configuration, despite my initial observations.

CHAPTER 18 – RECTIFICATION CASE STUDIES   371

> Use Zodiacal Releasing to narrow the Ascendant degree range.

Franklin is a rectification case study where ZR was decisive in narrowing the possible Ascendant degree range to two possible rising signs.

L1 Capricorn 06 Jan 1706 O.S.		
L2 Cancer 20 Mar 1715	FS	Sep-1715, attended George Brownell's English school.
L2 Cancer 07 May 1723	LB	25-Sep-1723, broke apprenticeship with brother James; sailed for New York, then Philadelphia 24-Dec-1724, arrived in London with financial backing from PA Governor Sir William Keith whose promise of financial aid was fraudulent.
L2 Capricorn 24 Jun 1731		1-Jul-1731, founded Library Company of Philadelphia; 3-Sep-1731, sponsored his journeyman Thomas Whitmarsh as printing partner in South Carolina.
L1 Aquarius 17 Aug 1732		
L2 Leo 30 Aug 1741	FS	No events found.
L2 Leo 16 Dec 1749	LB	19-Jul-1790, proposed design for lightning rod; 7-Feb-1751, lobbied for funding for first hospital in Philadelphia; Apr-1751, published *Experiments and Observations on Electricity, made at Philadelphia in America*.
L2 Aquarius 14 Apr 1758 N.S.		Summer/Fall 1758, UK scientific trip, met James Watt and Joseph Priestly among other scientists and philosophers; 1759, received two honorary doctorates from University of St. Andrews and Oxford respectively.
L1 Pisces 24 Mar 1762		Mixed period which featured overturning Britain's Stamp Act (elevating Franklin's public stature) but infuriating the British by leaking the Hutchinson letters (diminishing Franklin's status in eyes of the British).
L1 Aries 20 Jan 1774		
L2 Aries 20 Jan 1774		29-Jan-1774, accused of stealing the Hutchinson letters, blamed for entire colonial rebellion 'in the Cockpit' before the British Privy Council, key life event which radicalized BF against Britain. The American Revolution followed shortly thereafter. During L2 Capricorn (LOF10), Franklin proposed the "Great Compromise" at the Constitutional Convention on 3-Jul-1787.
L1 Taurus 02 Nov 1788		17-Apr-1790, died.

Decisive in favor of LOS in Capricorn are the two loosing of the bonds to Cancer (broke apprenticeship with brother) and Leo (ended printing career and started scientific experiments). "In the Cockpit" nine days after L1-Aries is also a decisive major life event which radicalized Franklin against the British.

Conclusion: Lot of Spirit in Capricorn refines the Ascendant degree range to 6AQ45 to 7PI29. The Ascendant sign is either Aquarius or Pisces.

➤ Use Configuration of the Chart to choose Ascendant sign.

The following observations favor Aquarius rising:

South Node/Scorpio/10th ruled by Mars/Sagittarius/11th signifies a diminished career and reputation from political alliances, organizations, and individuals who are fractious and violent. The Hutchinson letter affair (timed by dynamic activity of Mars) timed Franklin's humiliation before the British Privy Council on 29-Jan-1774. Two days later the British fired Franklin from his position as Deputy Postmaster General in America.

Sun/Capricorn/12th (Sun in the bound of Mars) with Mars/Sagittarius/11th signifies infamy and secret arms deals with Silas Deane and Beaumarchais in France as the revolution broke out. The configuration also signifies fame from municipal firefighting organizations.

Mercury/Aquarius-rx/1st in the house of his joy is consistent with Franklin's intellectual curiosity.

Conclusion: The Ascendant range is 6AQ45 to 29AQ59. Stage I complete.

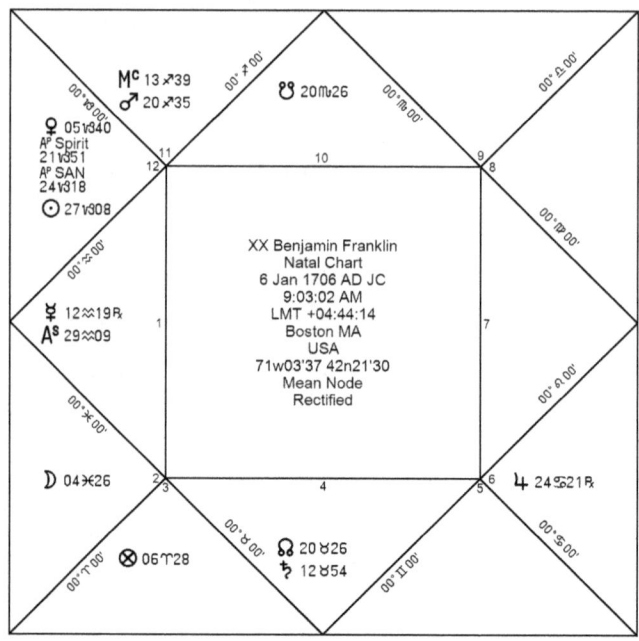

Benjamin Franklin. *Final proposed rectification: ASC 29AQ09'55"*

Afterword

"Charts continue to work after death."

Jeri London

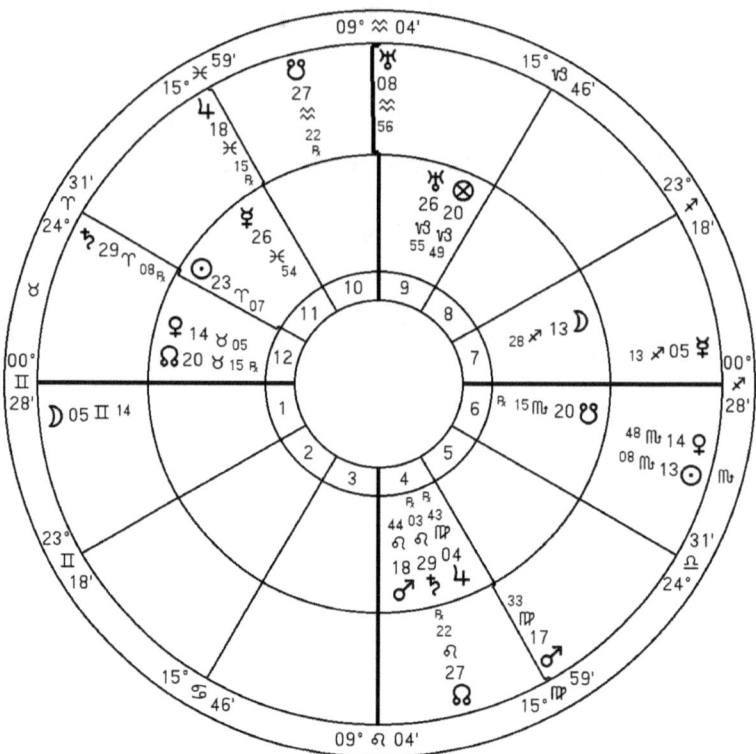

Thomas Jefferson. On 5-Nov-1998, the scientific journal *Nature* published DNA findings on Thomas Jefferson's descendants. For some, this settled the controversial issue that Jefferson fathered children by his alleged slave mistress Sally Hemings. For others, the debate remains an open question.

Measurements (outer wheel = transits). Transit of Uranus conjuncts the MC three times: 4-Feb-1998, 22-Sep-1998, and 13-Nov-1998. Moon separates from Mercury and applies to Mars.

Delineation. Natal Uranus 8th/9th QS/WS does not appear an obvious cause of this event unless its conjunction to the Lot of Fortune, read as Lot of the Moon or Marriage, is taken into consideration. Uranus' antiscia is also within 3 degrees of the 7th house cusp of the spouse. Natal Venus/Taurus/12th is Hemings. For the event, Sun-Venus at her superior conjunction denotes judgment of scandal according to the Mayan system (Scofield 1994). Moon's separation from Mercury to Mars/Virgo shows the critical response to the DNA findings.

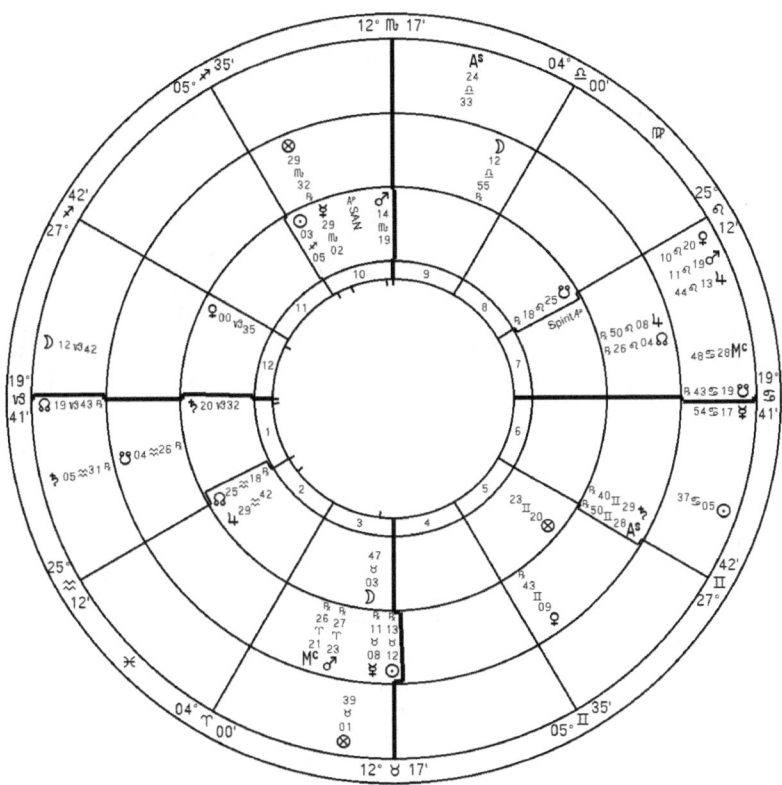

Zachary Taylor. In order to settle a historical debate on whether Taylor died from arsenic poisoning, his body was exhumed on 18-Jun-1991 and tested for arsenic on 22-June. Findings released on 27-Jun-1991 were negative.

Measurements (middle wheel = converse solar arc). csa Sun 12TA13 is only 4 minutes of degree from the natal IC on 27-June, the day tests were released.

Delineation. The 4th house signifies the end-of-the-matter generally and the grave specifically. An apt delineation for the Sun moved dynamically to the 4th cusp is: "May his soul rest in peace."

Measurements (outer wheel = transits). trNorth Node is within 2 minutes of degree of an exact conjunction to the Ascendant degree. Transits of Lunar Nodes to the Angles (ASC, MC, LOF, LOS) connect the native to the world-at-large with events which are knowable by the public and useful for rectification.

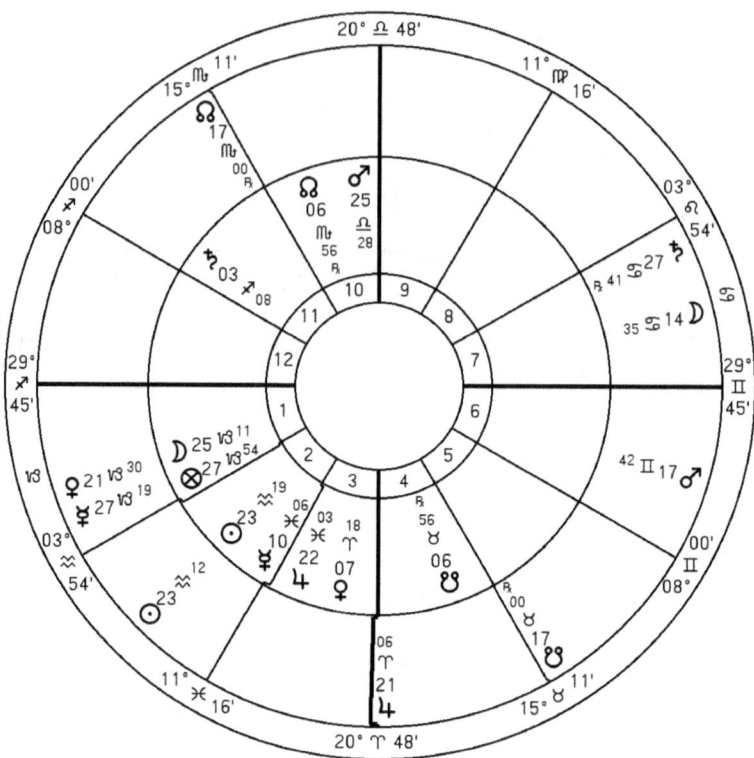

Abraham Lincoln. On 12-Feb-1976, Daniel Boorstin, historian and Librarian of Congress, opened a sealed box containing items held in Lincoln's pockets at the time of his assassination. After Lincoln's death, they were held by Lincoln's son Robert Todd Lincoln. The box had been sealed for 111 years. Display of these artifacts renewed the public's interest in Lincoln.

Measurements (outer wheel = transits). Venus applies to Jupiter, Jupiter conjunct IC; Mercury conjunct Lot of Fortune.

Delineation. Relics and artifacts are 4th house items. By whole signs, Lincoln's natal Mercury and Jupiter fall in the 4th. Natal Venus/Aries/5th signifies Lincoln's son who controlled the artifacts because Venus rules both Mercury and Jupiter by exaltation. On the day of the box opening, Venus sextiles Jupiter; who as the greater benefic falling on the 4th appears to ameliorate the ability of natal Venus to hide artifacts. Mercury appears to signify the relics themselves or news surrounding their release. Conjunct LOF, Mercury indicates that Lincoln *profits* from the public's increased interest.

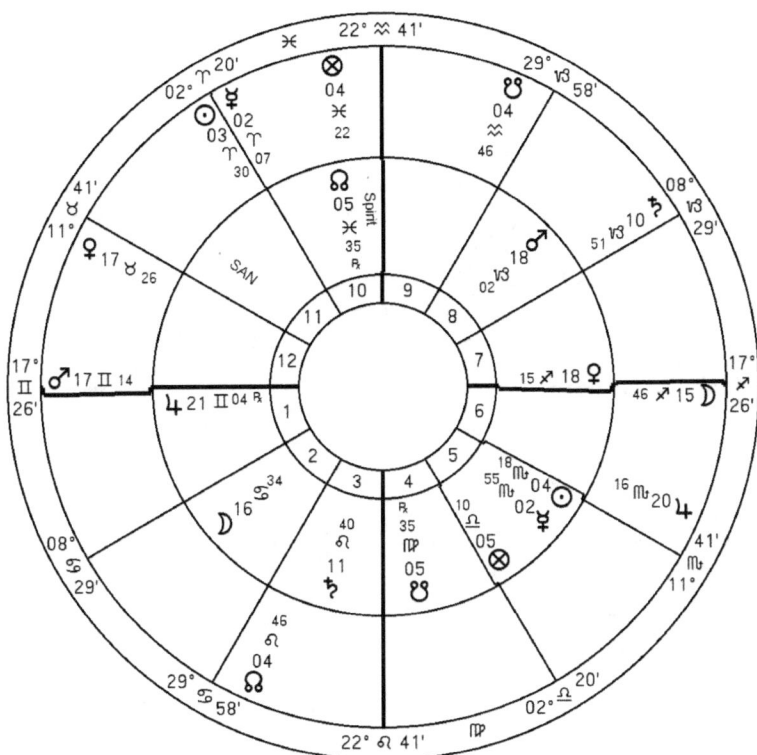

Theodore Roosevelt. On 26-Jun-2006, TIME magazine honored TR with a cover story entitled, "The Making of America—Theodore Roosevelt—The 20th Century Express" (Lacayo, 2006). In assessing Roosevelt's greatest legacy, the article begins with a discussion of his economic policies including the breakup of monopolies, passage of the Pure Food and Drug Act, and implementation of meat-inspection and industrial-safety laws.

Measurements (outer wheel = solar arc directions). The natal Moon-Mars opposition moves to the ASC-DSC axis. Lot of Fortune conjunct North Node.

Delineation. Natal Moon/Cancer demands purity generally; in the 2nd house as relates to financial dealings. Natal Mars/Capricorn/8th fights corporate trusts. Mars' rulership of the 6th of slaves ties Roosevelt's trust-busting activities to protection of the labor class.

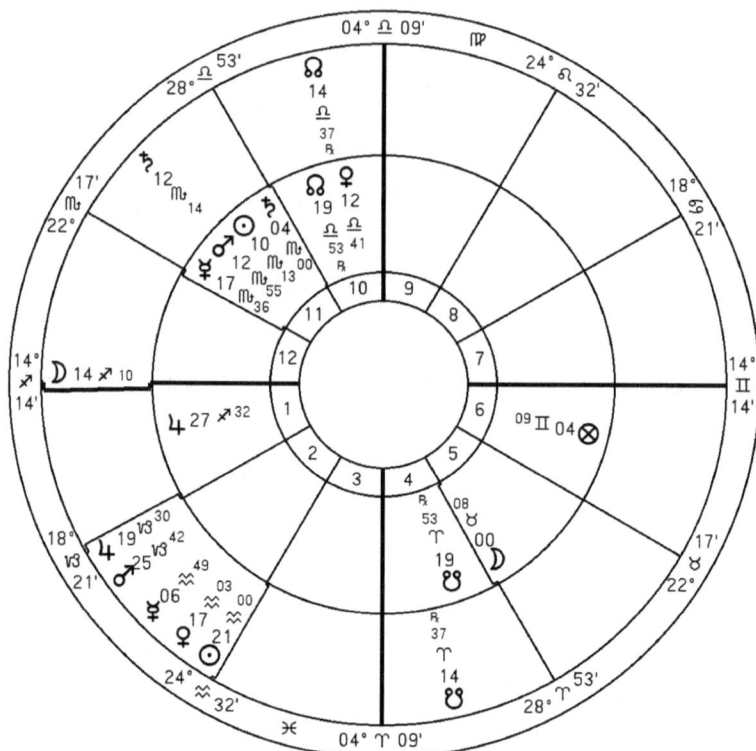

Warren Harding. On 20-Feb-1965, the Harding family paid the debts of the Phillips estate to control recently discovered love letters between Harding and Carrie Phillips (Russell 1968, 659).

Measurements (outer wheel = progressed). Progressed Moon conjunct ASC.

Delineation. Moon rules the 8th house of death, debt, and inheritance. Harding's lover Carrie Phillips can be delineated as Moon/Taurus in the 5th of romance ruling the 8th of debts. Affairs are settled when the progressed Moon reaches the Ascendant.

The Presidential Database

Organization of the Presidential Database

Each entry in the Presidential Database is comprised of nine pages:

Page One: Natal Figures

Two horoscopes: (1) Traditional medieval square format with whole sign houses and (2) modern round format with Alchabitius semi-arc houses.

Page Two: Selected Model Results

Moon's configuration, results for Cognitive Assessment and Victor Soul Models, and a Victor Table for computing Killing Planets.

Pages Three-Four: ZRS, Firdaria, and Directing through the Bounds

NEW Side by side presentation of ZR and Firdaria is designed to facilitate comparison between both techniques. For a subset of horoscopes, highlights from Directing through the Bounds are included. Because of space limitations, it is impossible to list all periods for all techniques. Properly delineated and matched to event examples would detail at least 100 pages per horoscope. *Remember the goal of this volume is to match enough life events to predictive techniques to compute a rectified horoscope, the goal is NOT to match every life event to a technique.* With this in mind, ZR lists L1 periods; foreshadowing (FS), loosing of the bond (LB), and completion periods (CP) as appropriate; and selected L2 subperiods which are angular from the LOF. Firdaria lists major and minor periods which match the Victor of the Horoscope. Given the key role to the Victor in the native's soul, one should approach these proposed Firdaria event matches in a counter-factual framework, e.g., should the sum of Firdaria periods ruled by the Victor be excluded from the biographical timeline, would anything be left of the native's timeline to justify his role as President? If the answer is no, this supports the choice of Firdaria sequence. It also suggests that victor-ruled Firdaria periods are capable of identifying career highlights as important as ZR proposes to identify through signs which are angular from the Lot of Fortune. The side-by-side presentation of ZR and Firdaria is designed to stimulate this mode of thinking.

Pages Five-Seven: Transits, Profections, and Directions

Presentation of transits, solar arc directions, primary directions, and primary direction sequences. There is some variation in presentation; for instance, profections are listed for James Garfield but not for most horoscopes. Entries proceeded by the designation *LOCK* are considered central to the precision of the proposed rectification. Because of their importance, most of the discussion is reserved for primary direction sequences. Presenting comprehensive rectifications in a small space poses a difficult balancing act. In the interest of both economy and the desire to present a comprehensive database for forty-five individuals, I have chosen to omit detailed explanations for all directions. More in the style of a workbook, the reader is left to delineate each measurement.

Pages Eight-Nine: Longevity Study (omitted for living Presidents)

Death: Date, time, and cause of death.

Hīlāj and Al-kadukhadāh: Theoretical choice based on rules outlined in Chapter 5: *Soul*. Empirical Hīlāj and Al-kadukhadāh, if different, are presented.

Victor of the Horoscope: Results of Porphyry's guidelines are presented in summary form. Omitted are the complete set of steps taken to choose the Victor. Templates comprising over 100 rows of spreadsheet data are too voluminous to include in this volume.

Killer(s): Results of the victor scoring method from page 2 are listed.

Natal Arcus Vitae: One or more measurements are proposed.

Solar Return for Year of Death: Whole sign format. Return data and discussion follows. If identified, primary directions to time death from the solar return itself are included. None of these were used during rectification. They are provided for information only.

Table 37. Comparison of Reported and Proposed Birth Times

	President	Birth	Reported (ADB)	Proposed	Proposed ASC
1	G. Washington	22-Feb-32	10:00 AM	5:40:41 AM	9AQ36'49"
2	J. Adams	30-Oct-35	unknown	1:24:50 PM	10AQ33'15"
3	T. Jefferson	13-Apr-43	unknown	7:21:04 AM	00GE28'50"
4	J. Madison	16-Mar-51	Midnight	11:20:04 PM	29SC49'46"
5	J. Monroe	28-Apr-58	unknown	2:10:52 AM	26AQ24'46"
6	J. Q. Adams	11-Jul-67	unknown	1:51:46 PM	6SC48'56"
7	A. Jackson	15-Mar-67	unknown	7:52:55 AM	1TA57'35"
8	M. van Buren	5-Dec-82	unknown	11:52:36 AM	29AQ55'59"
9	W. Harrison	9-Feb-73	unknown	5:52:47 AM	29CP29'58"
10	J. Tyler	29-Mar-90	unknown	2:29:37 PM	23LE14'18"
11	J. Polk	2-Nov-95	Noon	12:03:33 PM	25CP07'49"
12	Z. Taylor	24-Nov-84	unknown	10:22:33 AM	19CP41'56"
13	M. Fillmore	7-Jan-00	unknown	5:14:53 AM	14SA16'50"
14	F. Pierce	23-Nov-04	unknown	6:27:41 PM	3CA15'18"
15	J. Buchanan	23-Apr-91	unknown	10:07:52 AM	21CA19'37"
16	A. Lincoln	12-Feb-09	Sunrise	3:48:49 AM	29SA45'51"
17	A. Johnson	29-Dec-08	At night	4:08:29 AM	27SC13'52"
18	U. Grant	27-Apr-22	~6:00 AM	6:10:57 AM	26TA25'55"
19	R. Hayes	4-Oct-22	9-10 PM	10:45:25 PM	14CA11'52"
20	J. Garfield	19-Nov-31	2:00 AM	8:42:49 PM	26CA39'30"
21	C. Arthur	5-Oct-29	Sunrise	2:07:17 AM	26LE16'20"
22/24	G. Cleveland	18-Mar-37	11:32 AM	11:45:28 AM	12CA40'02"
23	B. Harrison	20-Aug-33	Unknown	7:26:19 PM	14PI27'14"
25	W. McKinley	29-Jan-43	11:32 PM	11:53:01 PM	29LI08'58"
26	T. Roosevelt	27-Oct-58	7:45 PM	7:15:59 PM	17GE25'30"
27	W. Taft	15-Sep-57	8:00 PM	8:02:29 PM	10TA36'29"
28	W. Wilson	29-Dec-56	12:45 AM	12:44:25 AM	15LI24'44"
29	W. Harding	2-Nov-65	Morning/2:00 PM	9:27:41 AM	14SA14'58"
30	C. Coolidge	4-Jul-72	9:00 AM	8:52:30 AM	3VI50'39"
31	H. Hoover	10-Aug-74	Midnight	11:23:51 PM	2GE06'39"
32	F. Roosevelt	30-Jan-82	8:45 AM	8:33:17 PM	20VI57'56"
33	H. Truman	8-May-84	4:00 PM	3:53:11 PM	9LI06'46"
34	D. Eisenhower	14-Oct-90	Afternoon/Evening	7:21:36 PM	22TA41'24"
35	J. Kennedy	29-May-17	3:00 PM	3:39:16 PM	27LI37'02"
36	L. Johnson	27-Aug-08	Sunrise	4:44:37 AM	15LE06'39"
37	R. Nixon	9-Jan-13	9:35 PM	9:23:45 PM	15VI02'38"
38	G. Ford	14-Jul-13	12:43 AM	12:43:02 AM	13TA08'39"
39	J. Carter	1-Oct-24	7:00 AM	6:41:07 AM	22LI05'23"
40	R. Reagan	6-Feb-11	Early morning	4:54:08 AM	6CP08'21"
41	G.H.W. Bush	12-Jun-24	11:45 AM	11:31:05 AM	8VI27'43"
42	B. Clinton	19-Aug-46	8:51 AM	9:17:32 AM	11LI07'26"
43	G.W. Bush	6-Jul-46	7:26 AM	7:25:40 AM	7LE02'13"
44	B. Obama	4-Aug-61	7:24 PM	7:51:34 PM	26AQ18'16"
45	D. Trump	14-Jun-46	10:54 AM	9:42:46 PM	15LE59'24"
46	J. Biden	20-Nov-42	8:30 AM	11:36:28 AM	14CP39'13"

Table 38. Presidential Birthplace Database

Coordinates designated 'Wiki' are directly obtained via the relevant Wikipedia link. Coordinates designed 'GoogleMaps' are manually taken from GoogleMaps based on the location. GoogleMaps coordinates are highly sensitive to the cursor position.

11-Feb-1732 JC	George Washington, Popes Creek, VA
	Birthplace home burned down on 25-Dec-1779. Foundation outlines were discovered years later and preserved.
	Address: 1732 Popes Creek Road, Colonial Beach, Virginia
	Coordinates: Wiki
	38n11'8"
	76w54'59"
	https://en.wikipedia.org/wiki/George_Washington_Birthplace_National_Monument
	https://www.presidentsusa.net/washingtonbirthplace.html
19-Oct-1735 JC	John Adams, Braintree, MA
	Braintree birthplace home survives in its original location. Braintree was later incorporated into Quincy.
	Address: 133 Franklin Street, Quincy, Massachusetts
	Coordinates: Wiki
	42n14'21"
	71w0'13"
	https://en.wikipedia.org/wiki/John_Adams_Birthplace
	https://www.presidentsusa.net/jadamsbirthplace.html
2-Apr-1743 JC	Thomas Jefferson, Shadwell plantation, Albemarle County, VA
	Shadwell plantation is currently marked by a Virginia Historical Marker.
	Address: 2450 Richmond Road, Charlottesville, Virginia
	Coordinates: Wiki
	38n00'45"
	78w25'4"
	https://en.wikipedia.org/wiki/Shadwell,_Virginia
	https://www.presidentsusa.net/jeffersonbirthplace.html
16-Mar-1751	James Madison, Belle Grove plantation, Port Conway, VA
	Born at Belle Grove, Port Conway, Virginia. Plantation is named for Madison's mother.
	Address: 17200 James Madison Parkway, Port Conway, Virginia
	Coordinates: GoogleMaps
	38n10'45"
	77w11'18"
	https://en.wikipedia.org/wiki/Belle_Grove_(Port_Conway,_Virginia)
	https://www.presidentsusa.net/madisonbirthplace.html
28-Apr-1758	James Monroe, Westmoreland, VA
	Family Home Site located near Oak Grove and Colonial Beach, Westmoreland County, Virginia. Discovered in 1976.
	Address: 4460 James Monroe Highway, Colonial Beach, Virginia
	Coordinates: Wiki
	38n14'31"
	76w59'27"
	https://en.wikipedia.org/wiki/James_Monroe_Family_Home_Site
	https://www.presidentsusa.net/monroebirthplace.html

11-Jul-1767	**John Quincy Adams, Braintree, MA**	
	Address: 141 Franklin Street, Quincy, Massachusetts	
	Braintree birthplace home survives in its original location. Braintree was later incorporated into Quincy. JQA was born in a separate house adjacent to the home where his father John Adams was born.	
	Coordinates: Wiki	
	42n14'21"	
	71w0'15"	
	https://en.wikipedia.org/wiki/John_Quincy_Adams_Birthplace.	
	https://www.presidentsusa.net/jqadamsbirthplace.html	
15-Mar-1767	**Andrew Jackson, Waxhaw settlement, SC**	
	Address: Waxhaws Region of North and South Carolina. Historical markers along the border of both North and South Carolina each claim they were born in their respective state. When queried on his birthplace by James H. Witherspoon of South Carolina in 1824, AJ said: As to the question asked, I with pleasure answer, I was born in South Carolina, as I have been told at the plantation whereon James Crawford lived about one mile from the Carolina road and of the Waxhaw Creek, left that State in 1784, was born on the 15 of March in the year 1767.	
	Coordinates: Wiki	
	34n55'32"	
	80w44'45"	
	https://en.wikipedia.org/wiki/Waxhaws	
5-Dec-1782	**Martin Van Buren, Kinderhook, NY**	
	No house survives but the site is marked by a historical marker.	
	Address: 46 Hudson Street, Kinderhook, New York	
	Coordinates: Wiki	
	42n23'30"	
	73w41'40"	
	https://www.presidentsusa.net/vanburenbirthplace.html	
9-Dec-1773	**William Henry Harrison, Berkeley Plantation, Charles City County, VA**	
	Berkeley Plantation no longer survives but the site is marked by a historical marker.	
	Address: 12602 Harrison Landing Road, Charles City, Virginia	
	Coordinates: Wiki	
	37n19'18"	
	77w10'54"	
	https://en.wikipedia.org/wiki/Berkeley_Plantation	
	https://www.presidentsusa.net/whharrisonbirthplace.html	
29-Mar-1790	**John Tyler, Greenway Plantation, Charles City County, VA**	
	The Greenway home survives but is a private residence.	
	Address: 10920 John Tyler Memorial Highway, Charles City, Virginia	
	Coordinates: Wiki	
	37n21'15"	
	77w6'6"	
	https://en.wikipedia.org/wiki/Greenway_Plantation	
	https://www.presidentsusa.net/tylerbirthplace.html	
2-Nov-1795	**James K Polk, Pineville, NC**	
	A reconstructed log cabin, site of James Polk's birthplace, resides at the President James K. Polk Historic Site.	
	Address: 12031 Lancaster Highway, Pineville, North Carolina	
	Coordinates: Wiki	
	35n4'40"	
	80w52'54"	
	https://en.wikipedia.org/wiki/President_James_K._Polk_Historic_Site	
	https://www.presidentsusa.net/polkbirthplace.html	

24-Nov-1784	**Zachary Taylor, Montebello estate, Barboursville, Orange County, VA**	
	Historical marker commemorates birthplace, approx. location of Montebello estate	
	Address: 7350 Spotswood Trail, Barboursville, Virginia	
	Coordinates: hmdb.org	
	38n9'14"	
	78w14'54"	
	https://www.hmdb.org/m.asp?m=30181	
	https://www.presidentsusa.net/taylorbirthplace.html	
7-Jan-1800	**Millard Fillmore, near Locke Township, Cayuga County, NY**	
	There is a pavilion and a historical marker at the site of a log cabin where Fillmore was born.	
	Address: just west of the intersection of Fillmore and Salt roads, Moravia, New York	
	Coordinates: GoogleMaps	
	42n41'34"	
	76w20'8"	
	https://www.presidentsusa.net/fillmorebirthplace.html	
23-Nov-1804	**Franklin Pierce, Hillsboro, NH**	
	Pierce was born in a log cabin near the Franklin Pierce Homestead. Site of former log cabin is now the Franklin Pierce Lake.	
	Address: Franklin Pierce Lake, Hillsborough County, New Hampshire	
	Coordinates: Wiki	
	43n5'54"	
	71w57'10"	
	https://en.wikipedia.org/wiki/Franklin_Pierce_Lake	
	https://www.presidentsusa.net/piercebirthplace.html	
23-Apr-1791	**James Buchanan, near Cove Gap, PA**	
	Birthplace was named Stony Batter and purchased a/c instructions by his niece Harriet Lane Johnston in 1907	
	Address: 2831 Stony Batter Road, Cove Gap, Pennsylvania	
	Coordinates: Wiki	
	39n52'15"	
	77w57'14"	
	https://en.wikipedia.org/wiki/Buchanan%27s_Birthplace_State_Park	
	https://www.dcnr.pa.gov/StateParks/FindAPark/BuchanansBirthplaceStatePark/Pages/default.aspx	
	https://www.presidentsusa.net/buchananbirthplace.html	
12-Feb-1809	**Abraham Lincoln, LaRue County south of Hodgenville, KY**	
	The log cabin was located on Sinking Spring Farm.	
	Address: 2995 Lincoln Farm Road, Hodgenville, Kentucky	
	Coordinates: Wiki	
	37n31'53"	
	85w44'10"	
	https://www.nps.gov/abli/index.htm	
	https://en.wikipedia.org/wiki/Abraham_Lincoln_Birthplace_National_Historical_Park	
	https://www.presidentsusa.net/lincolnbirthplace.html	
29-Dec-1808	**Andrew Johnson, Raleigh, NC**	
	The home in which Andrew Johnson was born, a small one-story house originally a kitchen, has been moved several times and is located currently in Mordecai Historic Park near downtown Raleigh. The original location of the home is marked by a historic marker.	
	Address: 123 Fayetteville Street, Raleigh, North Carolina	
	Coordinates: GoogleMaps	
	35n46'43"	
	78w38'20"	
	https://www.ncpedia.org/andrew-johnson-birthplace	
	https://www.presidentsusa.net/ajohnsonbirthplace.html	

27-Apr-1822	**Ulysses S. Grant, Point Pleasant, OH**
	Grant birthplace is located in Point Pleasant, Monroe Township, Ohio. Original location, never moved.
	Address: 1551 State Route 232, Point Pleasant, Ohio
	Coordinates: Wiki
	38n53'39"
	84w13'58"
	https://www.ohiohistory.org/visit/browse-historical-sites/u-s-grant-birthplace/
	https://en.wikipedia.org/wiki/Grant_Birthplace
	https://www.presidentsusa.net/grantbirthplace.html
4-Oct-1822	**Rutherford B. Hayes, Delaware, OH**
	Birthplace demolished. Historical Marker erected at what is now a gas station.
	Address: 17 East William Street, Delaware, Ohio
	Coordinates: GoogleMaps
	40n17'56"
	83w4'1"
	https://www.atlasobscura.com/places/the-rutherford-b-hayes-birthplace-gas-station-delaware-ohio
	https://www.presidentsusa.net/hayesbirthplace.html
19-Nov-1831	**James Garfield, Orange, OH**
	Garfield was born in a log cabin in Orange township, now Moreland Hills, Ohio. Historical marker and a log cabin mark the birthplace. Not sure if log cabin is reconstructed.
	Address: 4350 S.O.M. Center Road, Moreland Hills, Ohio
	Coordinates: GoogleMaps
	41n26'12"
	81w26'38"
	https://mhhsohio.org/visit/
	https://www.northeastohiomuseums.org/museum-listings/d-k/james-a-garfield-birthsite-park
	https://www.presidentsusa.net/garfieldbirthplace.html
5-Oct-1829	**Chester A. Arthur, Fairfield, VT**
	In 1903 a granite monument was unveiled at the spot believed to be the birthplace. Ultimately the birthplace location could not be confirmed based on historical records. Therefore Fairfield, Vermont remains the approximate default birth location.
	Address: Fairfield, Vermont default city coordinates
	Coordinates: Janus 5.0 software for Fairfield, VT
	44n48'07"
	72w56'46"
	https://historicsites.vermont.gov/chester-arthur
	https://www.presidentsusa.net/arthurbirthplace.html
8-Mar-1837	**Richard Cecil Cleveland, Caldwell NJ**
	Home known as the Caldwell Presbyterian Church Manse where Cleveland's family lived when his father was the local priest. Remains standing.
	Address: 207 Bloomfield Avenue, Caldwell, New Jersey
	Coordinates: Wiki
	40n50'13"
	74w16'19"
	https://en.wikipedia.org/wiki/Grover_Cleveland_Birthplace
	https://presidentcleveland.org/
	https://www.presidentsusa.net/clevelandbirthplace.html

20-Aug-1833	Benjamin Harrison, North Bend, OH	
	Born on farm established by Grandfather William Henry Harrison, original house no longer exists but a historical marker was erected in 2003.	
	Address: Symmes & Washington Avenues, North Bend, Ohio	
	Coordinates: GoogleMaps	
	39n9'2"	
	84w44'44"	
	https://www.presidentsusa.net/bharrisonbirthplace.html	
29-Jan-1843	William McKinley, Niles, OH	
	The original home no longer exits but a replica was built on the birthplace location 2002/2003.	
	Address: 40 South Main Street, Niles, Ohio	
	Coordinates: Wiki	
	41n10'47"	
	80w45'56"	
	https://en.wikipedia.org/wiki/McKinley_Birthplace_Home_and_Research_Center	
	https://www.mcklib.org/BirthplaceHome	
	https://www.presidentsusa.net/mckinleybirthplace.html	
27-Oct-1858	Theodore Roosevelt Jr., New York City, NY	
	A replica of the original house was constructed on the original location in 1921.	
	Address: 28 East 20th Street, New York, New York	
	Coordinates: Wiki	
	40n44'19"	
	73w59'20"	
	https://en.wikipedia.org/wiki/Theodore_Roosevelt_Birthplace_National_Historic_Site	
	https://www.presidentsusa.net/trooseveltbirthplace.html	
15-Sep-1857	William Howard Taft, Cincinnati, OH	
	Original home exists.	
	Address: 2038 Auburn Avenue, Cincinnati, Ohio	
	Coordinates: Wiki	
	39n7'11"	
	84w30'31"	
	https://en.wikipedia.org/wiki/William_Howard_Taft_National_Historic_Site	
	https://www.presidentsusa.net/taftbirthplace.html	
29 Dec 1856	Woodrow Wilson, Staunton, VA	
	Original home known as The Manse exists and is part of a museum.	
	Address: 20 North Coalter Street, Staunton, Virginia	
	Coordinates: Wiki	
	39n9'1"	
	79w4'9	
	https://en.wikipedia.org/wiki/Woodrow_Wilson_Presidential_Library	
	https://www.presidentsusa.net/wilsonbirthplace.html	
2-Nov-1865	Warren Gamaliel Harding, Blooming Grove, OH	
	The town nor the house survive but a historical marker exists on the site.	
	Address: 6297 Ohio Route 97, Blooming Grove, Ohio	
	Coordinates: GoogleMaps	
	40n42'22"	
	82w42'44"	
	https://en.wikipedia.org/wiki/Blooming_Grove,_Ohio	
	https://www.hmdb.org/m.asp?m=183843	
	https://www.presidentsusa.net/hardingbirthplace.html	

4-Jul-1872	John Calvin Coolidge, Plymouth Notch, VT
	Home and family farm complex still exists.
	Address: 3780 Route 100A, Plymouth, Vermont
	Coordinates: Wiki
	43n32'09"
	72w43'20"
	https://en.wikipedia.org/wiki/Coolidge_Homestead
	https://www.presidentsusa.net/coolidgebirthplace.html
10-Aug-1874	Herbert Hoover, West Branch, IA
	Home still exists.
	Address: Downey and Penn Streets, West Branch, Iowa
	Coordinates: Wiki
	41n40'8"
	91w20'53"
	https://en.wikipedia.org/wiki/Herbert_Hoover_National_Historic_Site
	https://www.presidentsusa.net/hooverbirthplace.html
30-Jan-1882	Franklin Delano Roosevelt, Hyde Park, NY
	Born in Springwood Estate, Hyde Park, which still exists.
	Address: 4097 Albany Post Road, Hyde Park, New York
	Coordinates: Wiki
	41n46'2"
	73w56'8"
	https://en.wikipedia.org/wiki/Home_of_Franklin_D._Roosevelt_National_Historic_Site
	https://www.presidentsusa.net/fdrbirthplace.html
8-May-1884	Harry Truman, Lamar, MO
	Address: 1009 Truman Street, Lamar, Missouri
	Coordinates: Wiki
	37n29'37"
	94w16'16"
	https://en.wikipedia.org/wiki/Harry_S_Truman_Birthplace_State_Historic_Site
	https://www.presidentsusa.net/trumanbirthsite.html
14-Oct-1890	Dwight Eisenhower, Denison, TX
	Address: 609 South Lamar Avenue, Denison, Texas
	Coordinates: GoogleMaps
	33n44'54"
	96w32'1"
	https://www.thc.texas.gov/historic-sites/eisenhower-birthplace-state-historic-site
	https://www.presidentsusa.net/eisenhowerbirthplace.html
29-May-17	John F Kennedy, Brookline, MA
	Address: 83 Beals Street Brookline, MA
	Coordinates: Wiki
	42n20'49"
	71w07'24"
	https://en.wikipedia.org/wiki/John_Fitzgerald_Kennedy_National_Historic_Site
	https://www.presidentsusa.net/jfkbirthplace.html
27-Aug-08	Lyndon Baines Johnson, near Stonewall, TX
	A reconstructed house exists on the original site.
	Address: Lyndon B. Johnson National Historic Park, Highway 290 East at Park Road 49, Stonewall, Texas
	Coordinates: Wiki
	30n14'27"
	98w37'27"
	https://en.wikipedia.org/wiki/Lyndon_B._Johnson_National_Historical_Park
	https://www.presidentsusa.net/ljohnsonbirthplace.html

9-Jan-13	**Richard Nixon, Yorba Linda, CA**	
	Original house exists on original location.	
	Address: 18001 Yorba Linda Boulevard, Yorba Linda, California	
	Coordinates: Wiki	
	33n53'22"	
	117w49'5"	
	https://en.wikipedia.org/wiki/Birthplace_of_Richard_Nixon	
	https://www.presidentsusa.net/nixonbirthplace.html	
14-Jul-13	**Leslie Lynch King Jr., Omaha, NE**	
	Address: 3202 Woolworth Avenue, Omaha, Nebraska	
	Coordinates: Wiki	
	41n14'43"	
	95w57'35"	
	https://en.wikipedia.org/wiki/Gerald_R._Ford_Birthsite_and_Gardens	
	https://www.presidentsusa.net/fordbirthsite.html	
1-Oct-24	**Jimmy Carter, Plains, GA**	
	Address: 225 Hospital Street, Plains, Georgia	
	Coordinates: Wiki	
	32n2'16"	
	84w23'23"	
	https://en.wikipedia.org/wiki/Lillian_G._Carter_Nursing_Center	
	https://www.presidentsusa.net/carterbirthplace.html	
6-Feb-11	**Ronald Reagan, Tampico, IL**	
	Site is a 2nd floor apartment in the Graham Building, 19-th century commercial building, still standing.	
	Address: 111 South Main Street, Tampico, Illinois	
	Coordinates: Wiki	
	41n37'52"	
	89w47'9"	
	https://en.wikipedia.org/wiki/Birthplace_of_Ronald_Reagan	
	https://www.presidentsusa.net/reaganbirthplace.html	
12-Jun-24	**George Herbert Walker Bush, Milton, MA**	
	Private residence not open to public, outside historical marker.	
	Address: 173 Adams Street, Milton, Massachusetts	
	Coordinates: GoogleMaps	
	42n16'00"	
	71w4'1"	
	https://www.presidentsusa.net/ghwbushbirthplace.html	
19-Aug-46	**William Jefferson Clinton, Hope, AR**	
	Julia Chester Hospital, closed in 1955 and later demolished. Brazzel Oakcrest Funeral Home built on location. Historical Marker in front of funeral home identifies it as Clinton's birthplace.	
	Address: 1001 South Main Street, Hope, Arkansas	
	Coordinates: GoogleMaps	
	33n39'36"	
	93w35'19"	
	https://www.presidentsusa.net/clintonbirthplace.html	
	The following link is not his birth location, but is the house he lived in after returning from the hospital.	
	https://en.wikipedia.org/wiki/President_William_Jefferson_Clinton_Birthplace_Home_National_Historic_Site	

6-Jul-46	George Walker Bush Jr., New Haven, CT	
	Birth location is Grace-New Haven Hospital, now known as Yale-New Haven Hospital	
	Address: 20 York Street, New Haven, Connecticut	
	Coordinates: Wiki	
	41n18'14"	
	72w56'10"	
	https://en.wikipedia.org/wiki/Yale_New_Haven_Hospital	
	https://www.presidentsusa.net/gwbushbirthplace.html	
4-Aug-61	Barack Hussein Obama II, Honolulu, HI	
	Born at Kapi'olani Maternity & Gynecological Hospital (now called Kapi'olani Medical Center for Women & Children)	
	https://en.wikipedia.org/wiki/Kapiolani_Medical_Center_for_Women_and_Children	
	Coordinates: Wiki	
	21n17'59"	
	157w50'0"	
14-Jun-46	Donald J. Trump, Jamaica, Queens, NY	
	Address: 8900 Van Wyck Expressway, New York, New York	
	Jamaica Hospital, now known as Jamaica Hospital Medical Center	
	Coordinates: Wiki	
	40n42'1"	
	73w48'57"	
	https://en.wikipedia.org/wiki/Jamaica_Hospital_Medical_Center	
	https://www.presidentsusa.net/trumpbirthplace.html	
20-Nov-42	Joseph Robinette Biden Jr., Scranton, PA	
	St. Mary's Hospital, 930 Hickory Street, Scranton, PA	
	Coordinates: GoogleMaps	
	41n23'40"	
	75w39'21"	

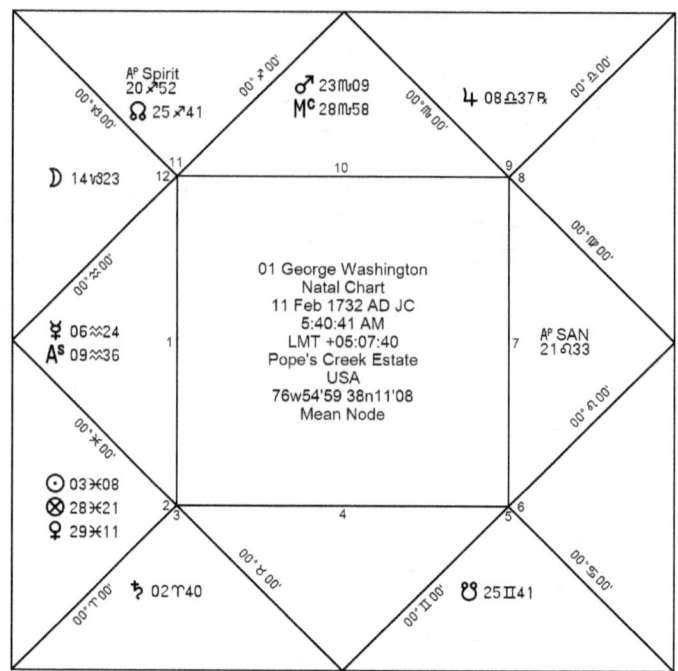

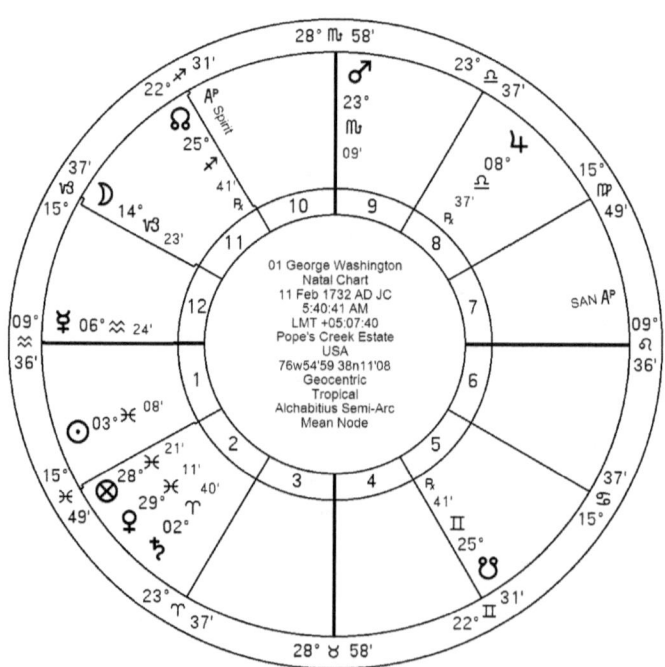

1. GEORGE WASHINGTON

Moon's Configuration

Moon separates from **Jupiter** and applies to **Mars**, nocturnal, preventional. Prenatal syzygy is 21LE33. Eclipse? No.

Cognitive Assessment Model (Rulers of Moon and Mercury)

Sign rulers: **Saturn** (both)
Bound rulers: **Venus, Mercury**

Victor Soul Models

Ibn Ezra Victor Model (1507), in-sect triplicity ruler, triplicity decans.

	Position	☉	☽	☿	♀	♂	♃	♄
Sun	03 PI 08				6	3	6	
Moon	14 CP 23		3		3	4		5
Asc	09 AQ 36			3	2			6
Pars Fortuna	28 PI 21				4	6	5	
Syzygy	21 LE 33	5		2		1	3	
Oriental						1	1	0
Houses		12	2	12	6	4	5	6
Score		17	5	17	**21**	19	20	17

Porphyry's Expanded Victor Model (2022)

Mars rules MC by sign; LOF by bound. Sect: of favor. Solar phase: oriental waxing square to 1st station. Position: 10th from ASC, conjunct MC. Dignity: sign and nocturnal triplicity. Moon applies to Mars.

Victor Table for Killing Planets

			☉	☽	☿	♀	♂	♃	♄
ASC		9AQ36			3	2		3	5,3,1
Rul ASC	♄	2AR40	4,3				5,1	3,2	3
L.Death		4SA06	3					5,3,2,1	3
Rul L.Death	♃	10LI59			3,2	5,1		3	4,3
H8 Cusp		15VI49		3	5,4	3,2	3		1
Rul H8	☿	6AQ24			3,2			3	5,3,1
T-Rul H8	☽	14CP23		3		3,2,1	4,3		5
8th from ☽		14LE23	5,3					3,1	3,2
Rul 8th fr ☽	☉	3PI08		3		4,3,2	3	5,1	
TOTAL			18	9	22	**28**	19	**35**	**42**

2007 Proposed Rectification: 5:38:57 AM, ASC 9AQ01'14"
2022 Revised Rectification: 5:40:41 AM, ASC 9AQ36'49"

Of the first fifteen Presidents, George Washington is one of three with a recorded birthtime. A family bible entry states the birthtime was 10 AM. This corresponds to an Ascendant of 18TA26. The proposed rectification is four hours earlier making the horoscope nocturnal, not diurnal.

ZRS. Lots of Fortune 28PI21 and Spirit 20SA52 yield matches to key life events using Zodiacal Releasing from Spirit. Lot of Spirit in the bound of Mercury/Sagittarius made Washington a land speculator with lord Mercury/Aquarius signifying surveying skills as a driving force.

L1 Sagittarius 11 Feb 1732 O.S.		12-Apr-1743, unexpected death of father.
L1 Capricorn 10 Dec 1743 O.S.		Increased family responsibilities following death of father. led to survey work.
L2 Cancer 3 Mar 1753 N.S.	FS	28-May-1754, triggered start of French and Indian War with Battle of Jumonville Glen.
L2 Cancer 20 Apr 1761 LB	LB	10-Feb-1763, treaty of Paris ended French and Indian War.
L2 Capricorn 7 Jun 1769	CP	12-Apr-1770, repeal of Townshend Revenue Act, except for tea.
L1 Aquarius 1 Aug 1770		2-Nov-1772, Boston established Committee of Correspondence.
L2 Leo 14 Aug 1779	FS	10-Jul-1780, French troops arrived at Newport.
L2 Leo 30 Nov 1787 LB	LB	30-Apr-1789, Presidential Inauguration.
L2 Aquarius 17 Mar 1796	CP	19-Sep-1796,\. Farewell address and retirement.
L2 Aries 29 Aug 1799		14-Dec-1799, Death 10-11PM, few hours after start of L3 Cancer.
L1 Pisces 25 Feb 1800		

Directing through the Bounds. Based on this technique, the rectification was revised. For the 9AQ01'14" Ascendant, the distributor changeover to Saturn/Taurus (throat problems) was about 4 months too late based on Washington's death from a throat infection. The revised time also gives a near perfect match to GW's military career dating from the Stamp Act.

Date	ASC Distributor	Event
28-Aug-1746 O.S.	Venus/Pisces (00PI)	1747, formal education ended. plans for naval career thwarted by Mother, went into surveying.
23-May-1765 N.S.	Jupiter/Aries (00AR)	22-Mar-1765, colonial protests following passage of Stamp Act drew GW into politics and military career.
5-Feb-1784	Venus/Taurus (00TA)	14-Jan-1784, Congress ratified final Peace Treaty with Britain; Washington resumed life as gentleman farmer.
23-Nov-1799	Saturn/Taurus (22TA)	14-Dec-1799, died from throat infection.

1. GEORGE WASHINGTON

Firdaria – Mars major and minor Periods

Firdaria according to Bonatti	Life Event
Julian Calendar	
Moon **Mars** 21 Dec 1735	No events found.
Saturn **Mars** 03 Apr 1744	No events found.
Gregorian Calendar	
Jupiter **Mars** 09 Nov 1753	12-Dec-1753, GW's demand from Gov Dinwiddle that the French cease encroachment upon Ohio country is rejected; 1754, start of French & Indian War; Mar-1754, commissioned as lieutenant colonel in Virginia militia; 27-May-1754, defeated French troops in skirmish; 4-Jul-1754, surrendered Fort Necessity; 9-Jul-1755, defeated in Battle of the Wilderness, General Braddock mortally wounded and died.
Mars 7 years Age 32 to 39	
Mars Mars 21 Feb 1764	May-1764; reports reached Virginia that British planned tax on colonists to defray wartime costs and pay for future protection.
Mars Sun 21 Feb 1765	1765 (no exact date), GW elected to Virginia House of Burgesses; 22-Mar-1765, Stamp Act passed.
Mars Venus 21 Feb 1766	18-Mar-1766, Stamp Act repealed.
Mars Mercury 21 Feb 1767	29-Jun-1767, Townshend Revenue Act passed.
Mars Moon 21 Feb 1768	
Mars Saturn 21 Feb 1769	Apr-1769, met with George Mason and others to plan boycott of British goods; 17-May-1769, Virginia House of Burgesses is dissolved.
Mars Jupiter 21 Feb 1770	12-Apr-1770, Townshend Revenue Act repealed except for tax on tea.
Sun **Mars** 17 Sep 1784	No events found.
Venus **Mars** 09 Nov 1791	26-Nov-1791, convened 1st official cabinet meeting; 15-Nov-1791, Bill of Rights ratified; 1792, Republican Party created in opposition to Federalist Party; 2-Oct-1792, failed to mediate differences between Hamilton and Jefferson.

Mars as Victor. Mars' periods include GW's (1) role in launch of French and Indian War, (2) entry in politics and radicalization against the British, and (3) formation of first cabinet, creation of the Federalist Party, and inability to mediate the Hamilton/Jefferson feud which launched the two-party system.

Transits

<u>28-May-1776</u>. *tr South Node conj ASC*. Traveled to Philadelphia to consult with Congress on military strategy (ahead of defeat in New York), late-May-1776.

<u>21-Jan-1780</u>. *tr South Node conj MC*. British General Clinton's 8000-man army landed in Charleston, SC, 1-Feb-1780

<u>12-May-1789</u>. *tr North Node conj MC*. Presidential Inauguration, 30 April. Held first public reception 29-May-1789.

Solar Arc Directions

<u>27-Jul-1758</u>. *csa NN conj MC*.
<u>25-Nov-1758</u>. *dsa MC conj NN*.
   Elected to Virginia House of Burgesses, 24-Jul-1758.
   Awarded Honorary brevet rank of Brigadier General for battle at Fort Duquesne, 25-Nov-1758 (date of battle).

<u>26-Jun-1775</u>. *csa ASC conj NN*.
<u>7-May-1776</u>. *dsa NN conj ASC*.
   Appointed Commander in Chief of Continental Army, 15-Jun-1775.
   Arrived NYC after success in Boston, 13-Apr-1776.

<u>13-Dec-1776</u>. *csa Moon conj MC*.
<u>15-Nov-1777</u>. *dsa MC conj Moon*.
   Low troop morale, end-1776; *The American Crisis* published by Thomas Paine "These are times which try men's souls," 19-Dec-1776.
   Thomas Conway offered to resign after conspiracy revealed, 16-Nov-1777.

<u>15-Oct-1781</u>. *csa MC conj Jupiter*.
<u>30-Nov-1782</u>. *dsa Jupiter conj MC*.
   Final offensive against Cornwallis began: Hamilton's charge; 14-Oct-1781.
   Preliminary Treaty of Paris signed, 30-Nov-1782.

1. GEORGE WASHINGTON

Primary Directions

REG	D	Venus/Pisces	P	Sun d. => Merc (ME)	23-Sep-1751 JC
PT	D	Venus/Pisces	P	Sun d. => Merc (ME)	27-Dec-1751 JC
PT	D	Merc/Aquarius	P	dex sex Sat (SA) d. => Moon (MO)	12-Jul-1752 JC

Accompanied stepbrother Lawrence to Barbados on 28-Sep-1751 (ill from smallpox) where GW contracted the same; GW recovered by December; stepbrother Lawrence died 26-Jul-1752.

REG	D	Saturn/Scorpio	P	MC d. => NN	29-Oct-1762

Became vestryman of Truro Parish, position held for 22 years, Oct-1762.

PT	D	Venus/Aries	P	opp Jup (JU) d. => ASC	16-Nov-1768

British negotiated two Indian treaties which reopened the Ohio Country to settlers, ushering in a frenzied wave of real estate speculation, late-1768.

PT	D	Venus/Aries	P	sin sex Merc (0) d. => ASC	9-Apr-1769

Wrote letter to George Mason, reasons for supporting boycott, 5-Apr-1769.

REG	D	Venus/Aquarius	P	ASC d. => NN	12-Jul-1775
PT	D	Venus/Aquarius	P	ASC d. => NN	9-Oct-1776

Took command of Continental Army at Cambridge, 2-Jul-1775.
General Howe's force left New York City, 12-Oct-1776.
Compare these events to the solar arc pairs for same time period.

PT	D	Jupiter/Capricorn	P	sin sq Jupiter (0) c. => Sun	3-May-1778

Learned of French Treaty, late April-1778.

PT	D	Venus/Capricorn	P	Moon (0) d. => MC	8-Jan-1781

Mutiny of Pennsylvania Troops, 1 to 10-Jan-1781.

PT	D	Saturn/Libra	P	opp Saturn (0) c. => MC	10-Jun-1786

Nathaniel Greene died following stroke, 19-Jun-1786.

PT	D	Saturn/Virgo	P	opp Venus (0) c. => MC	19-Aug-1789

Death of mother, 25-Aug-1789; rcvd news, 1-Sep-1789.

REG	D	Mars/Leo	P	dex sq MC d. => SN	6-Mar-1791

1st Internal Revenue Law, taxed distilled spirits, 3-Mar-1791.

PT	D	Jupiter/Aries	P	Sat (0) d. => Moon (0)	15-Feb-1795

Alexander Hamilton resigned as Treasury Secretary, 31-Jan-1795

Primary Direction Sequences

PT	D	Venus/Capricorn	P	Moon (0) c. => ASC.	21-Jan-1754
PT	D	Venus/Capricorn	P	Moon (MO) c. => ASC.	15-Sep-1755

LOCK Sequence timed inception of the French and Indian War. Sequence began with GW handing British Governor Dinwiddle the French Captain's negative response to British demands that the French should vacate territory claimed by England, 16-Jan-1754. Dinwiddle commissioned GW as Lieutenant Colonel in the Virginia militia but was unsuccessful with the 4-Jul-1754 surrender of Fort Necessity and his defeat in the Battle of the Wilderness on 9-Jul-1755. As the sequence marched to its conclusion, Dinwiddle offered to make GW the supreme commander of all military forces in Virginia on 14-Aug-1755, GW lost an election contest for the House of Burgesses on 10-Dec-1755, and GW ended the year in a dispute of military rank with John Dagworthy as the sequence concludes. Moon/Capricorn/12th is a delineation match to these events because the Moon/Capricorn signifies GW's military ambitions which were thwarted because of errors (12th house placement).

PT	D	Jupiter/Capricorn	P	sin sq Jup (JU) d. => MC	5-Sep-1774
PT	D	Jupiter/Capricorn	P	sin sq Jup (0) d. => MC	15-Oct-1774

One of seven to attend 1st meeting of Continental Congress beginning 5-Sep-1774 and lasting through Oct-1774.

PT	D	Saturn/Taurus	P	opp Mars (MA) d. => LOF	10-Jan-1773
PT	D	Saturn/Taurus	P	opp Mars (0) d. => LOF	14-Mar-1774

Sequence broadly timed British interference with traded goods, GW's conversion to the patriot cause, and his appearance in military garb as the 2nd Continental Congress convenee. In March 1773, GW supported the VA House of Burgesses' decision to form a Committee of Correspondence to harmonize defensive measures with other colonies. On 18-Mar-1774, Lord North introduced the Port Bill which restricted trade in the Port of Boston until damages from the Boston Tea Party were paid.

PT	D	Jupiter/Gemini	P	dex trine Jupiter (JU) d. => LOF	17-Mar-1787
PT	D	Jupiter/Gemini	P	dex trine Jupiter (0) d. => LOF	6-Jun-1788

LOCK Sequence began with a 19-Mar-1787 letter from Henry Knox stating if the Constitutional Convention were successful, it would be highly honorable to GW. In the opinion of biographer Chernow, this letter cinched GW's decision to attend the convention (Chernow 523). Second direction occurs during midpoint of Constitution's ratification; also a financial milestone for payment of all personal back taxes.

1. GEORGE WASHINGTON

Longevity: 67y 9m 22d

Death: 14-Dec-1799, ~10:20 pm, Mount Vernon, Virginia, at home. Following a property inspection conducted on horseback during bad winter weather on 12-Dec, GW awoke on 13-Dec around 2:00 a.m. with a swollen sore throat and was diagnosed with inflammatory quinsy, a complication of tonsillitis. Washington failed to respond to purges and bleeding.

Hīlāj: **Sun**. Sun is within 25 degrees below the horizon in the 1st (QS) or in the 2nd (WS). Sun in feminine sign tests well as the Hīlāj, in variance with the rules. His smallpox episode between September and December 1751 was timed by a Mercury - Sun primary direction. His high fever, probably malaria, during May-Sep 1761 was timed by a Saturn-Sun solar arc direction. Finally, the Sun was afflicted in the 1790 solar return which preceded a major illness during May 1790.

Al-kadukhadāh: **Mars**. In the place of the Sun, Mars is the high scoring ruler; Mars is also the Victor of the Horoscope. Mars grants 66 major years. Venus separates by trine aspect, receives Mars by diurnal triplicity, and should add 8 minor years but does not. Sticking with Mars' major years is the simplest model for Washington's longevity.

Victor of the Horoscope: **Mars**
Killing Planets: **Saturn (42), Jupiter (35), Venus (28)**

Arcus Vitae:

| D | Changeover | bound Saturn/Taurus d. => ASC | 23-Nov-1799 |

| PT | D | Venus/Capricorn | P | Moon (MO) c. => Sat (SA) | 10-Jan-1800 |

How the Solar Return foretold Washington's last ride. Gemini rising and Lord of Year Mercury/Aquarius in the 9th makes Washington intellectually curious, seeking an outlet in surveying trips. Mercury in the fixed air sign signifies surveying (think 'fixed lines' drawn through the air). Mercury also disposes Moon/Virgo/4th which signifies the need for details about his property. Result: his curiosity about surveys triggers the need to examine his property. Saturn/Cancer in the 2nd signifies financial loss from flood/hail damage; specifically, the cold/wet winter storm on 12 December. Moon separating from the sextile of Saturn to VOC means Washington is cold and soaking wet at home yet he does not change clothes. Moon also rules by exaltation the Mars-Jupiter-North Node Taurus stellium in the 12th. Taurus is the throat; Mars/Taurus signifies infection; Jupiter/Taurus signifies swelling; North Node/Taurus amplifies the condition. Washington can barely breathe because his throat is swollen so badly.

1799 Solar Return for year of Death

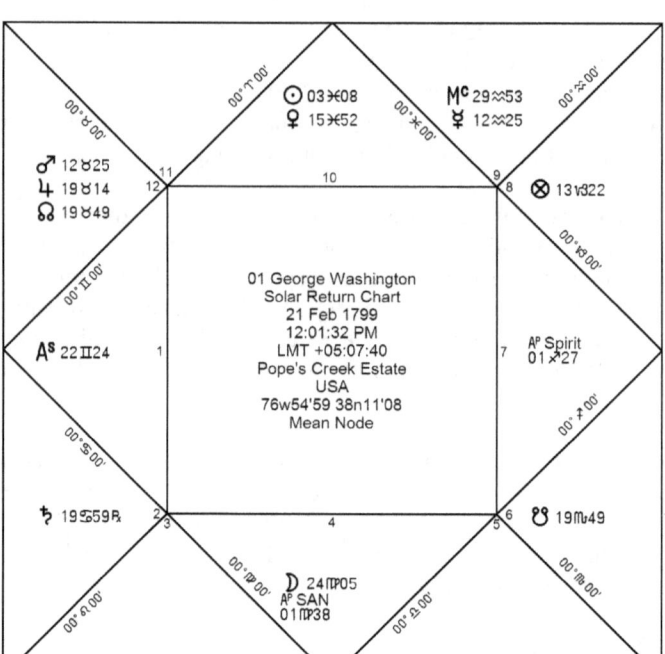

Ascendant Distributor: Saturn/Taurus since 23-Nov-1799
Profected Ascendant: 9VI36, 8th house; SR Victor: Mercury
Lords: LOY – Mercury; LOP – Moon
Firdaria: Mercury – Jupiter
Moon: separates from sextile of Saturn to void of course
Return Ascendant falls in natal 5th; Natal Ascendant falls in return's 9th

Washington died in an 8th house profected year with LOY Mercury returning to his natal sign and closely aspecting the natal Ascendant by conjunction. The natal Mercury-Mars square by antiscia is replicated by a direct square in the return. Moon separates from high-scoring killer Saturn (ruler of the return's 8th) and is void of course.

| PT | D | Jupiter/Pisces | P | Venus d. => ASC | 11-Dec-1799 |

Timed death within 3 days. May be related to Washington's willingness to be bled by attending physicians. Venus (blood disorders) + Pisces (sacrifice) = bloodletting.

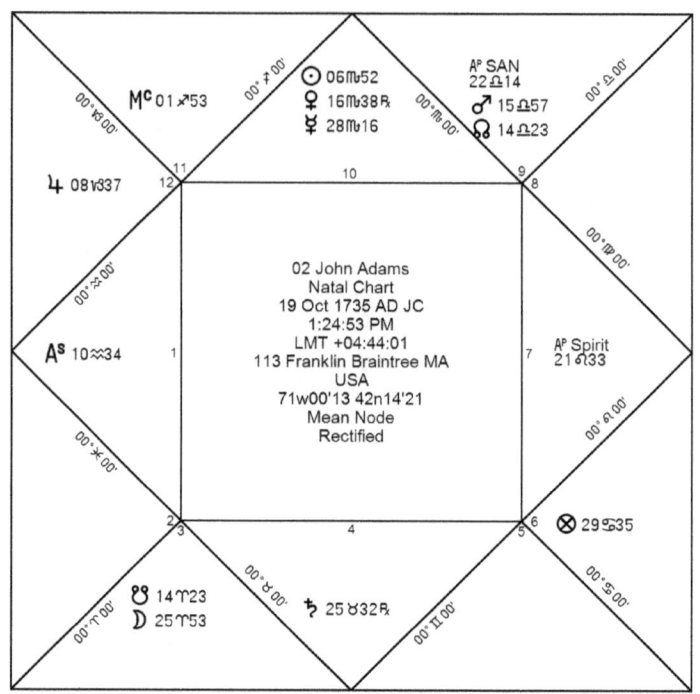
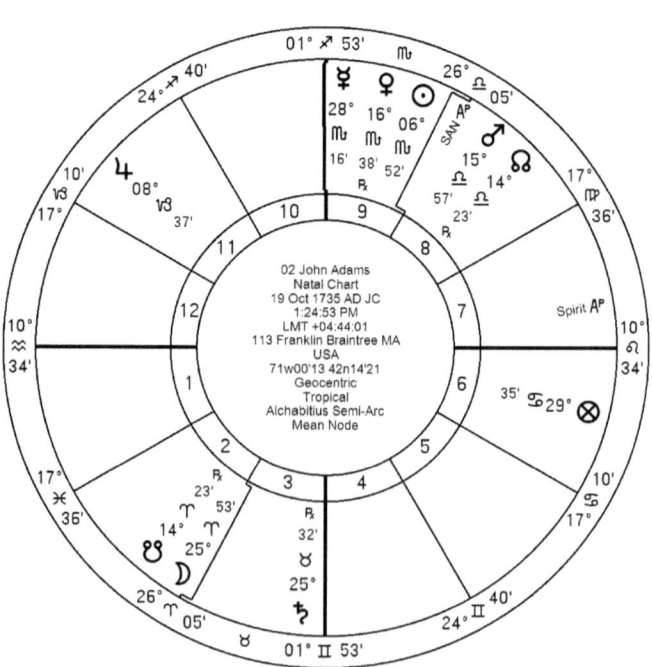

2. JOHN ADAMS

Moon's Configuration

Moon separates from **Mars** and is **VOC** (Medieval) or applies to the **Sun** (Hellenistic), diurnal, conjunctional.
Prenatal syzygy is 22LI14. Eclipse? **YES**. Annular Total Solar Eclipse.

Cognitive Assessment Model (Rulers of Moon and Mercury)

Sign rulers: **Mars** (both)
Bound rulers: **Saturn** (both)

Victor Soul Models

Ibn Ezra Victor Model (1507), in-sect triplicity ruler, triplicity decans.

	Position	☉	☽	☿	♀	♂	♃	♄
Sun	06 SC 52				3	8		
Moon	25 AR 53	7				5	1	2
Asc	10 AQ 34			1	2			8
Pars Fortuna	29 CA 35		5		3		5	2
Syzygy	22 LI 14 (SE)			1	7			7
Oriental						3	0	1
Houses		4	3	11	4	5	8	3
Score		11	8	13	19	21	14	**23**

Porphyry's Expanded Victor Model (2022)

Saturn rules the ASC by sign; Moon and LOS by bound. Sect: of favor. Solar phase: oriental retrograde to acronycal rising. Position: 4th from the ASC, 10th from LOS. Dignity: bound and decan. Alternate: Mercury.

Victor Table for Killing Planets

			☉	☽	☿	♀	♂	♃	♄
ASC		10AQ34			3,1	2		3	5,3
Rul ASC	♄	25TA32		4,3		5,3	3		2,1
L.Death		17LI14			3	5		3,2	4,3,1
Rul L.Death	☽	25AR53	4,3				5	3,1	3,2
H8 Cusp		17VI36		3	5,4	3	3	2	1
Rul H8	☿	28SC16		3,1		3	5,3		2
T-Rul H8	♀	16SC38		3	2	3	5,3	1	
8th from ☉		6GE52			5,3,1			3,2	3
Rul 8th fr ☉	☿	28SC16		3,1		3	5,3		2
TOTAL			7	21	27	27	**35**	20	**32**

2007 Proposed Rectification: 1:23:43 PM, ASC 10AQ10'51", Quincy
2022 Proposed Rectification: 1:24:50 PM, ASC 10AQ33'15", Braintree

Astrodatabank reports a C-rated birth time of 2:57 AM, original source not known, with 24 Virgo rising. I favor an early afternoon time with Aquarius rising as do other rectifiers (Noel Tyl 2AQ and Isaac Starkman 28AQ). This 4th edition revised rectification reflects a slight change in birth location from Quincy, MA to Braintree, MA as well as a slight tweak in dynamic activity between the Nodes and the angles.

ZRS. Releasing from the Lot of Spirit 21LE32 yields key chapter's in Adam's life including his standalone legal career (L1-Virgo), revolutionary career (L1-Libra), diplomatic career (L1-Scorpio), Presidency (L1-Sagittarius), and post-Presidency reconciliation with Jefferson (L1-Capricorn). LOS in bound of Mercury/Leo makes Adams a humanist though lord Mercury/Scorpio means he uses a biting tongue and trenchant legal arguments to achieve his aims.

L1 Leo 19 Oct 1735		
L1 Virgo 22 Jul 1754		12-Oct-1755, wrote prophetical letter on his life and US Revolution to classmate Nathan Webb; 21-Aug-1756, began legal career with apprenticeship with attorney James Putnam.
L2 Pisces 03 Oct 1763	FS	May-1764, first reports reached Virginia that British Parliament planned a tax on colonists to defray wartime costs and pay for future protections.
L2 Pisces 20 Nov 1771	LB	1772, business was prosperous. appeared in over 200 Superior Court Cases incl for John Hancock.
L1 Libra 08 Apr 1774		31-Mar to 22-Jun-1774, Coercive Acts passed - signaled economic point of no return as key milestone towards revolution.
L1 Scorpio 25 Feb 1782		26-Feb-1782, defended request for Dutch loan which led directly to Dutch loan and Treaty of Commerce. active politically. 4-Feb-1789, elected Vice President.
L1 Sagittarius 08 Dec 1796		4-Mar-1797, Presidential Inauguration.
L1 Capricorn 07 Oct 1808		17-Oct-1809, Benjamin Rush dreamed that Adams and Jefferson will write and reconcile their differences; 1-Jan-1812, wrote first letter to TJ.
L2 Cancer 19 Dec 1817	FS	28-Oct-1818, death of wife Abigail.
L2 Cancer 05 Feb 1826	LB	4-Jul-1826, died.

2. JOHN ADAMS

Firdaria – Saturn major and minor periods

Firdaria according to Bonatti	Life Event
Julian Calendar Dates	
Sun **Saturn** 06 Jul 1741	1741, started school and studied math, reading, and religion.
Venus **Saturn** 24 Mar 1749	1947, prepared for Harvard admission with tutor Joseph Marsh.
Gregorian Calendar Dates	
Mercury **Saturn** 17 Jul 1757	1758, concluded apprenticeship with James Putnam and moved to Braintree.
Moon **Saturn** 11 Feb 1768	Spring 1769, successfully defended colonial seamen on charges of justifiable homicide when naval officer was killed while trying to impress them.
Saturn 11 years Age 40 to 51	
Saturn Saturn 30 Oct 1775	8-Feb-1776, arrived Philadelphia; 2-Jul-1776, voted for Independence.
Saturn Jupiter 26 May 1777	27-Nov-1777, appointed Minister to France; 6-Feb-1778, French Alliance before JA even left Boston; 8-May-1778, presented to Louis XVI.
Saturn Mars 21 Dec 1778	2-Aug-1779, returned to Braintree; 30-Oct-1779, completed draft of Massachusetts Constitution; 9-Feb-1780, arrived Paris.
Saturn Sun 17 Jul 1780	27-Jul-1780, left for Holland after relationship with Vergennes was in tatters; 16-Sep-1780, Congress authorized JA to negotiate for Dutch loan; 4-May-1781, presented proposal to the Hague; 23-Nov-1781, news of victory at Yorktown reached JA.
Saturn Venus 11 Feb 1782	19-Apr-1782, recognized as ambassador by the Dutch; 11-Jun-1782, received Dutch loan; 8-Oct-1782, signed Treaty of Commerce at the Hague; 30-Oct-1782, negotiations with Britain began; 3-Sep-1783, signed Treaty of Paris.
Saturn Mercury 08 Sep 1783	7-Aug-1784, JA reunited with wife Abigail in Paris.
Saturn Moon 03 Apr 1785	26-Apr-1785, JA named Minister to Court of St. James; 1-Jun-1784, audience with the King.
Jupiter **Saturn** 10 Feb 1797	4-Mar-1797, Presidential Inauguration; 18-Oct-1797, XYZ Affair; 18-Jun/14-Jul-1798, Alien & Sedition Acts passed; 4-Oct-1798, learned on Gerry's return from Paris the French wanted peace.
Mars **Saturn** 31 Oct 1803	12-Jul-1804, Hamilton died after duel.
Sun **Saturn** 17 Jul 1816	7-Jul-1817, President Monroe visited JA for dinner; 18-Aug-1817, son JQA returned home from overseas, happy time.
Venus **Saturn** 04 Apr 1824	9-Feb-1825, son JQA elected President; 4-Mar-1825, JQA Inauguration.

Saturn as Victor. Saturn/Taurus-rx behaves like it is positioned in the opposite sign, Saturn/Scorpio, the significator for national security. As Firdaria ruler, Saturn highlighted early education, successful defense of sailors on justifiable homicide (with naval impressment also a Saturn/Scorpio signification), time as a founder of America from the 1776 Declaration throughout his ministerial appointments to France, Holland, and England; and the beginning of his Presidential term. Adams' push for the Alien & Sedition Acts of 1798 tarnished his Presidential term. Paranoia and control of political opposition is consistent with Saturn's functional placement as Saturn/Scorpio.

Transits

21-Aug-1756. *tr North Node 10th from MC*. Signed contract with attorney James Putnam, 21-Aug-1756.

7-Aug-1770. *tr North Node conj MC*. Midway between Boston Massacre of 5-Mar-170 and Adams' defense of British soldiers 3-Dec-1770.

19-Mar-1789. *tr North Node conj MC*. Midway between VP election 4-Feb-1789 and his departure for NYC on 13-Apr-1789 for the Inauguration.

9-Jul-1798. *tr South Node conj MC*. Criticism surrounding passage of Alien and Sedition Acts; four separate Acts between 18-Jun-1798 and 14-Jul-1798.

1-Aug-1813. *tr South Node conj ASC*. Tragic final days of daughter Nabby who died from reoccurrence of breast cancer, 15-Aug-1813.

Solar Arc Directions

22-Nov-1777. *dsa MC sq Nodes*
11-Oct-1778. *csa Nodes sq MC*
   Appointed Minister to France by Congress, 27-Nov-1777.
   Presented to King Louis XVI, 8-May-1778.

24-Mar-1781. *dsa Mars conj MC*
3-Apr-1782. *csa MC conj Mars*
   Completed 16-page memo asking for Dutch alliance, 18-Apr-1781.
   Recognized as ambassador by the Dutch, 19-Apr-1782.

3-Oct-1782. *dsa North Node conj MC*
6-Nov-1783. *csa MC conj North Node*
   Signed Treaty of Commerce at The Hague, 8-Oct-1782.
   Signed Treaty of Paris, 3-Sep-1783.
   Death of father-in-law, 17-Sep-1783.

2-Jan-1799. *dsa Saturn conj LOF*
28-Nov-1800. *csa LOF conj Saturn*
   US Navy victory against French with capture of L'Insurgente, 9-Feb-1799.
   Notified of death of son Charles, 3-Dec-1800.
   Presidential electors convened, 3-Dec-1800.
   Notified of loss to Jefferson and Burr's tie vote, few days later.

22-May-2001. *dsa Sun 29CA36'24" conj Lot of Fortune 29CA34'17"*
   Published, *John Adams* by David McCullough.

2. JOHN ADAMS

Primary Directions

| REG | D | Mercury/Aquarius | P | sin sq Sun d. => Jupiter (0) | 24-May-1761 |

Death of father, 25-May-1761.

| REG | D | Jupiter/Sagittarius | P | MC d. => North Node | 7-Feb-1771 |
| PT | D | Jupiter/Sagittarius | P | MC d. => North Node | 8-Apr-1774 |

Defended British soldiers who committed Boston Massacre, 3-Dec-1770.
Elected to Colonial legislature, 1771 (no exact date).
Coercive Acts passed after Boston Tea Party, 31-Mar/22-Jun-1774.
This pair of MC-North Node directions increased JA's public stature and reputation in the years leading up to the Revolution of 1776.

| PT | D | Jupiter/Capricorn | P | Jupiter (JU) d. => MC | 20-Jun-1775 |

Battle of Bunker Hill, 17-Jun-1775; Jupiter/Cap/12th signifies Tory enemies.
Death of Mother-in-law, 1-Oct-1775; Jup rules 11th; 8th from 10th from 7th.

| REG | D | Jupiter/Libra | P | North Node d. => LOF | 8-Nov-1782 |

Started British negotiations, 30-Oct-1782.
Preliminary peace treaty signed with British, 30-Nov-1782.

| PT | D | Mercury/Taurus | P | sin tr Jupiter (JU) d. => ASC | 9-Feb-1789 |

Received 34 votes behind Washington's 69 at first meeting of electors making JA the Vice President, 4-Feb-1789.

| PT | D | Mars/Taurus | P | opp Merc (BI) d. => ASC | 30-Sep-1799 |

Learned that son Charles disappeared, was bankrupt, faithless, and an alcoholic, 30-Sep-1799.

| PT | D | Saturn/Taurus | P | Saturn (0) d. => ASC | 8-Nov-1800 |

Received word that French Treaty was signed on 8-Oct-1800, 7-Nov-1800.

| REG | D | Saturn/Aries | P | Moon (MO) d. => Jupiter (JU) | 1-Oct-1813 |

Death of daughter Nabby from breast cancer, 15-Aug-1813. Jupiter in 12th is 8th from the 5th or death of children. Jupiter shows growth; in Capricorn Jupiter is in detriment and shows excessive/unwanted growth which is cancerous. Permutations of Moon-Jupiter directions range from 21-Sep-1812 to 6-Feb-1814.

Primary Direction Sequences

PT	D	Saturn/Aries	P	Moon (0) d. => ASC	31-Oct-1780
PT	D	Saturn/Aries	P	Moon (MO) d. => ASC	2-Jan-1782

This sequence forms bookends to Adams' negotiations with the Dutch.
Congressional authorization for JA to seek Dutch loan, 16-Sep-1780.
JA completed memo asking for Dutch loan, 16-Apr-1781.
JA recognized by the Dutch as ambassador, 19-Apr-1781.
Presented proposal at the Hague, 4-May-1781.
News of Cornwallis' surrender at Yorktown reached JA, 23-Nov-1781.
JA doubled down on request for Dutch loan after Yorktown, early 1782.
Delineation: JA's memo was published in English, French, and Dutch and widely circulated through newspapers in Europe. Moon/Aries shows forthright emotions; this memo was considered rash because its distribution occurred prior to Adam's formal recognition. Traditional protocol required ambassadors to wait in the country until the King chose to recognize them. Moon's placement in 3rd house shows publicity.

REG	D	Venus/Leo	P	DSC c. => Mars (0)	2-Jul-1780
REG	D	Venus/Leo	P	DSC c. => Mars (MA)	5-Aug-1781

Concurrent with the Moon - ASC direction, this sequence timed a diplomatic break with French minister Vergennes and backstabbing by fellow Minister Benjamin Franklin. Franklin was upset at Adams' blunt diplomacy after JA stood up for American interests in frank meetings with Vergennes 16/21-Jun-1780. After JA left for Holland on 27-Jul-1780, Vergennes broke his relations with JA. A week later Franklin wrote a letter to Congress with negative comments on JA. This led to Congressional revocation of JA's ministerial position on 15-Jun-1781 which JA learned on 24-Aug-1781. He promptly became ill for six weeks including one five-day period when he lapsed into a coma. This was one of his most serious illnesses and shows the action of high scoring killing planet Mars when aspecting the Ascendant by opposition.

PT	D	Saturn/Virgo	P	dex sextile Merc (0) c. => MC	5-Mar-1797
PT	D	Saturn/Virgo	P	dex sextile Merc (BI) c. => MC	31-Aug-1797
PT	D	Saturn/Virgo	P	dex sextile Merc (ME) c. => MC	25-Feb-1798

Sequence timed key events in the XYZ Affair which was one of the most important episodes during the Adams Presidency.
JA learned that the French refused to see Minister to France Charles Pinckney who was appointed by Washington, 13-Mar-1797.
"Coup of 18 Frictidor" propelled anti-Americans into power, 4-Sep-1797.
John Marshall and Elbridge Gerry joined Pinckney in Paris for renewed attempts at peace negotiations by JA, 18-Oct-1797.
JA learned the French refused to see Pinckney, Marshall, and Gerry after the American envoys refused to pay bribes, 4-Mar-1798.

2. JOHN ADAMS

Longevity, 90y 8m 4d

Death: 4-Jul-1826, about 6:00 PM, Quincy, MA, at home. John Adams spent most of his final days in bed, both he and Thomas Jefferson exchanged some final correspondence. Both died on Independence Day.

Hīlāj: **Sun**. Sun in a feminine sign tests well as the empirical hyleg at variance with the rules.

Al-kadukhadāh: **Venus**. This is a difficult case to work out the proper Hīlāj - Al-kadukhadāh combination because most planets have little or no dignity. When the prenatal syzygy is an eclipse, often the bound lord usurps other candidates as the al-kadukhadāh. If so, Venus grants 82 major years which takes JA to 1817 the year before his wife Abigail died. The final 8 years of his life were unremarkable. One can also make the case with Saturn as al-kadukhadāh since Adams lived just past 3x Saturn's 30 minor years.

Victor of the Horoscope: **Saturn (primary), Mercury (alternate)**

Killing Planets: **Mars (35), Saturn (32)**

Arcus Vitae:

REG	D	Merc/Cancer	P	dex sq Mars (MA) c. => Sun	18-Feb-1824
REG	D	Merc/Cancer	P	dex sq Mars (0) c. => Sun	21-Sep-1824

D	Changeover	bound Saturn/Gemini d. => ASC	19-Jun-1826

PT	D	Saturn/Aquarius	P	sin sq Mercury (0) d. => MC	5-Jul-1826

PT	D	Merc/Cancer	P	dex sq Mars (MA) c. => Sun	1-Mar-1831
PT	D	Merc/Cancer	P	dex sq Mars (0) c. => Sun	2-Aug-1831

The theoretical Mars-Sun arcus vitae is early (by Regio) or late (by Ptolemy).

Most accurate is the changeover in Ascendant Distributor from Mars/Gemini to Saturn/Gemini two weeks before death. See George Washington for a similar pattern. For Adams, Saturn was transiting Gemini at the time of death, same sign as the Ascendant Distributor.

Most accurate direction timing death was a Mercury-MC direction; these are rare, ideally the MC involves career and social status, not matters of health as it does in this example.

1825 Solar Return for year of Death

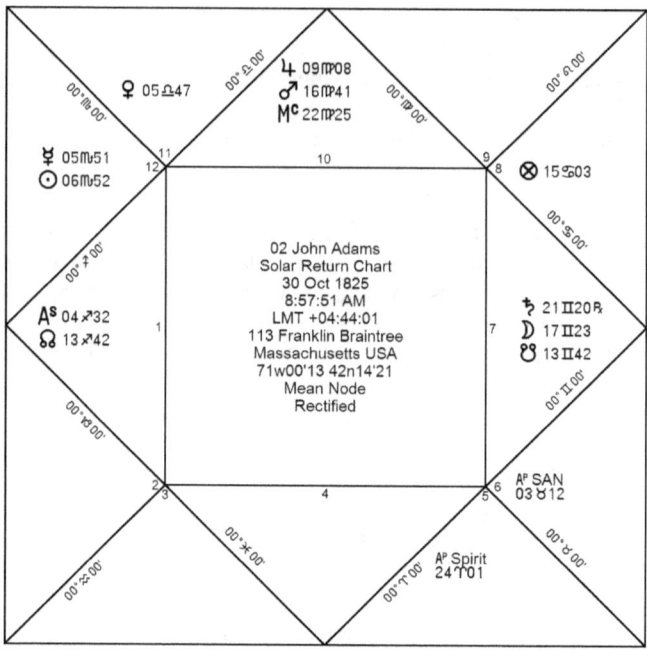

Ascendant Distributor: Saturn/Gemini since 19-Jun-1826
Profected Ascendant: 10LE33, 7th house, SR Victor: Mars
Lords: LOY – Sun; LOP – Mercury
Moon: separates from square of Mars and applies to conjunction of Saturn
Firdaria: Major – Venus; Subperiod – Jupiter
Return Ascendant falls in natal 11th (WS).

Moon is besieged by South Node and Saturn, separates from Mars and applies to Saturn both of which are high scoring killers. As the return's Victor and the most elevated planet in the figure, Mars is given ample power to act. The Moon - South Node - Saturn stellium is doubly emphasized because it falls in the 7th in a 7th house profected year.

Lord of Year Sun is cadent in the 12th is afflicted by Mercury, the 3rd high scoring killing planet after Mars and Venus; Mercury is given power to act by ruling both the profected 7th house cusp and Mars which is the killer.

| PT | D | Venus/Virgo | P | Mars d. => ASC | 20-Jul-1826 |

Directed ASC of the solar return reaches Mars two weeks after JA's death.

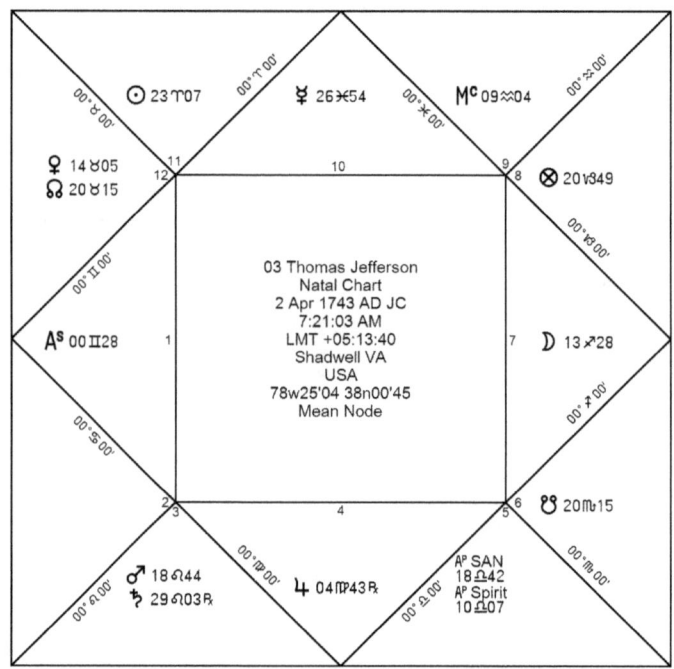
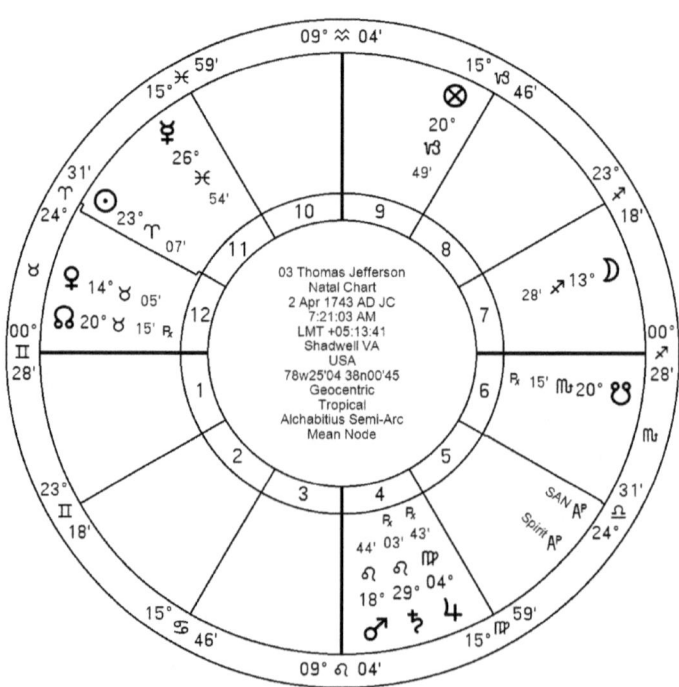

3. THOMAS JEFFERSON

Moon's Configuration

Moon separates from **Jupiter** and applies to **Mars**, diurnal, preventional. Prenatal syzygy is 18LI42. Eclipse? No.

Cognitive Assessment Model (Rulers of Moon and Mercury)

Sign rulers: **Jupiter** (both)
Bound rulers: **Venus, Mars**

Victor Soul Models

Ibn Ezra Victor Model (1507), in-sect triplicity ruler, triplicity decans.

	Position	☉	☽	☿	♀	♂	♃	♄
Sun	23 AR 07	7				7	1	
Moon	13 SA 28	3			2	1	5	
Asc	00 GE 28			8				3
Pars Fortuna	20 CP 49			1	5	4		5
Syzygy	18 LI 42				5		2	8
Oriental						0	0	0
Houses		2	10	8	2	9	9	9
Score		12	10	17	14	21	17	**25**

Porphyry's Expanded Victor Model (2022)

Saturn rules MC and LOF by sign. Sect: of favor. Solar phase: occidental, opposition to 2nd station. Dignity: participating triplicity. Debility: detriment. Comment: Saturn/Leo-rx rejects the totalitarian divine right of Kings in favor of scientific enlightenment signified by Saturn/Aquarius in the opposing sign.

Victor Table for Killing Planets

			☉	☽	☿	♀	♂	♃	♄
ASC		00GE28			5,3,2,1			3	3
Rul ASC	☿	26PI54		3		4,3	3,2,1	5	
L.Death		8VI53		3	5,4,1	3,2	3		
Rul L.Death	☿	26PI54		3		4,3	3,2,1	5	
H8 Cusp		23SA18	3,1					5,3	3,2
Rul H8	♃	4VI43		3	5,4,2,1	3	3		
T-Rul H8	☉	23AR07	4,3				5,2	3,1	3
8th from ☉		23SC07		3,1		3	5,3	2	
Rul 8th fr ☉	♂	18LE44	5,3		2			3,1	3
TOTAL			19	16	**35**	24	**33**	31	14

2007 Proposed Rectification: 7:21:04 AM, ASC 00GE28'50"

Astrodatabank reports an untimed birthdate of 2-Apr-1743 AD JC. Starkman proposed a similar rectified time of 8:51:08 AM also with Gemini rising.

The rectification continues to stand up well with Lots of Fortune and Spirit yielding good results with Zodiacal Releasing. By configuration of the chart, the most salient delineation of Venus/Taurus/12th as a secret love interest remains consistent with TJ's hidden relationship with his slave Sally Hemmings. As featured in Chapter 2, house placements of the Mercury/Jupiter opposition and the Mars/Saturn conjunction vary by choice of house system. TJ's horoscope remains a fertile study for behavior of planets in either whole sign or quadrant house systems.

ZRS. LOS 10LI07, bound Mercury/Libra, makes TJ an egalitarian thinker who uses a professional career as writer and philosopher to achieve this objective. LOF 20CP49 in the 8th of debt provides Jefferson financial advantages in matters of debt. Though below the surface, this theme is apparent when considering L1 Capricorn L2 Cancer (LB) timed conflicts over Jay's Treaty including unresolved debt issues between British royalists and American revolutionaries; also L1 Capricorn L2 Capricorn (CP) which featured TJ's use of debt instruments to secure the Louisiana Purchase.

L1 Libra 02 Apr 1743		
L1 Scorpio 19 Feb 1751		1751, studied Latin, Greek, and French with Rev. William Douglas.
L1 Sagittarius 13 Dec 1765		19-Mar-1786, Britain repealed Stamp Act; 30-Mar-1786, began entries in his 'Garden Book' on systematic observations of plant life - last entry Autumn 1824.
L1 Capricorn 11 Oct 1777		6-Feb-1778, US and France signed treaties with French choosing to support the Revolution; 1-Jun-1779, elected Governor of VA.
L2 Cancer 23 Dec 1786	FS	TJ in France most of this time in the period leading up to the French Revolution.
L2 Cancer 09 Feb 1795	LB	14-Aug-1795, GW signed Jay's Treaty with Britain which attempted to resolved unsettled issues between France and Britain after the revolution; Oct-1795, met with JM and both opposed ratification of Jay's Treaty; 7-Dec-1796, won election as Vice President.
L2 Capricorn 30 Mar 1803	CP	2-May-1803, Louisiana Purchase signed; Feb-Mar-1804, completed Jefferson Bible.
L1 Aquarius 23 May 1804		4-Mar-1805, Inauguration of 2nd term found TJ increasingly dogmatic, intolerant, and rigid.
L2 Leo 05 Jun 1813	FS	15-Jul-1813, letter from John Adams stating it would be a shame for them to die without having explained themselves to each other. Correspondence lasted 3 years.
L2 Leo 21 Sep 1821	LB	
L2 Scorpio 01 Aug 1825		4-Jul-1826, died.

3. THOMAS JEFFERSON

Firdaria – Saturn major and minor periods

Firdaria according to Bonatti	Life Event
Venus **Saturn** 15 Sep 1756	17-Aug-1757, death of father; soon after enrolled with Rev James Maury, classics scholar, gained access to Maury's library.
Mercury **Saturn** 29 Dec 1764	22-Mar-1765, Stamp Act passed; 30-May-1765, witnessed Patrick Henry's speech against Stamp Act; 30-Mar-1766, began 'Garden Book' diary.
Moon **Saturn** 26 Jul 1775	22/31-Jul-1775, drafted Congressional draft resolutions in response to Lord North's reconciliation proposal; 1-Oct-1775, returned to Philadelphia and served on various Congressional Committees; 7-Jun-1776, headed committee to draft the Declaration of Independence; 4-Jul-1776, Declaration of Independence signed; 8-Oct-1776, appointed Commissioner to France.
Saturn 11 years Age 40 to 51	
Saturn Saturn 12 Apr 1783	6-Jun-1783, appointed by VA legislature to head VA delegation to Confederation Congress; 23-Dec-1783, present for GW's ceremonial resignation as Commander-in-Chief; 7-May-1784, appointed with JA and BF to negotiate treaties with European nations; 1-Aug-1784, arrived Le Havre, France.
Saturn Jupiter 06 Nov 1784	10-May-1785, succeeded BF as ambassador to France; 17-Jan-1786, Virginia adopted TJ's Ordinance of Religious Freedom after re-introduction by JM; 11-Mar-1786, JA presented TJ to King George III.
Saturn Mars 03 Jun 1786	22/25-Aug-1786, Shay's Rebellion began; 4-Feb-1787, Shay's Rebellion put down; May/Sep-1787, JM kept TJ abreast of Constitutional Convention; TJ urged JM to add bill of rights and to limit the number of terms a President can serve.
Saturn Sun 29 Dec 1787	Jul/Sep-1788, present for riots in France which preceded the French Revolution; 30-Apr-1789, GW Inauguration; Jun-1789, with Lafayette, TJ drafted a French charter of rights which was the basis for the French Declaration of Rights which Lafayette presented to the National Assembly in July; 14-Jul-1789, storming of the Bastille.
Saturn Venus 25 Jul 1789	26-Aug-1789, French Revolution: Declaration of the Rights of Man and the Citizen released; 26-Sep-1789, named Secretary of State; 21-Mar-1790, arrived in NY to take up Secretary of State responsibilities; Summer-1790, Hamilton/Jefferson divide began to surface.
Saturn Mercury 19 Feb 1791	25-Feb-1791, GW signed bill for Bank of United States following TJ's report of 15-Feb-1791; 31-Oct-1791, Republican newspaper *National Gazette* formed.
Saturn Moon 15 Sep 1792	2-Oct-1792, GW failed to mediate Hamilton/Jefferson split; 21-Jan-1793, execution of Louis XV in France; Apr/Jul-1793, Genet affair; 22-Apr-1793, GW issued neutrality proclamation; 31-Dec-1793, finished term as Sec State after informing GW of his plans to resign on 31-Jul-1793.
Jupiter **Saturn** 26 Jul 1804	Nov-1804, Re-elected President; 16-Jan-1806, Sec State Madison reported on British impressment of American sailors.
Mars **Saturn** 13 Apr 1811	1-Jan-1812, JA began correspondence with TJ.
Sun **Saturn** 30 Dec 1823	Apr-1924, prepared instructions for recruiting faculty for University of Virginia in Europe.

Transits

6-Jun-1776. *tr South Node conj MC*. Appointed to committee to draft Declaration of Independence, 7 June. This action harmed the King.

7-Feb-1786. *tr Saturn conj MC*. Virginia legislature adopted TJ's Ordinance of Religious Freedom after re-introduction by James Madison, 17-Jan-1786.

14-Apr-1789. *tr North Node conj DSC*. Account book showed record of clothing purchases for slave Sally Hemings 6/26-Apr-1789; speculation that their relationship dated from this time.

29-Jun-1800. *tr Saturn conj IC*. A false report that TJ is dead published in a Baltimore newspaper, 30 June.

6-Jan-1809. *tr Saturn conj DSC*. TJ pushed Embargo Enforcement Act through Congress, 9 January.

Solar Arc Directions

19-Dec-1781. *csa Saturn opposed LOF*.
13-Oct-1782. *dsa LOF opposed Saturn*.
TJ absolved for cowardly actions taken June 1781 when he and his family fled when facing British capture instead of securing the Virginia statehouse for an orderly transition of power as his term ended, 15-Dec-1781.
Death of wife Martha, 6-Sep-1782.
Depression lifts, after mid-Oct-1782.

28-Apr-1796. *csa Sun sq ASC*.
28-Oct-1797. *dsa ASC square Sun*.
Private letter to Philip Mazzei written 24-Apr-1796 complaining about rise of a Federalist political faction is subsequently reprinted causing a fracture of political relations with George Washington.
XYZ affair created anti-French sentiment and harmed Republican politics, 18-Oct-1797.

10-Jul-1813. *csa MC sq Saturn*.
9-Jan-1816. *dsa Saturn sq MC*.
John Adams writes TJ asking to begin correspondence, 15-Jul-1813.
Letter to Charles Thomson mentioned correspondence with JA plus plans for compiling what will be known as the Jefferson Bible, 9-Jan-1816.

3. THOMAS JEFFERSON

Primary Direction Sequences

REG	D	Saturn/Scorpio	P	sin sq Saturn (0) d. => Vertex	20-Feb-1766
REG	D	Saturn/Scorpio	P	sin sq Saturn (SA) d. => Vertex	13-Jan-1768

LOCK Passage of the Stamp Act on 22-Mar-1765 was a milestone leading to war. On 13-Feb-1766 Ben Franklin warned use of military power to enforce the Stamp Act might lead to open revolution. Repeal of the Stamp Act on 18-Mar-1766 brought only temporary relief as the Townshend Acts passed 29-Jun-1767 levied more taxes. As this sequence culminated, Sam Adams composed a circular letter on 11-Feb-1768 addressed to colonial assemblies calling for rebellion.

PT	D	Venus/Pisces	P	opp Jup (JU) d. => LOF	24-Nov-1789
PT	D	Venus/Pisces	P	opp Jup (0) d. => LOF	18-Feb-1790

LOCK TJ arrived in Norfolk after spending five years in Europe to learn that he had been appointed Secretary of State, 23-Nov-1789.

TJ reluctantly accepted appointment to State; he had hoped to devote his time to Monticello and private affairs, 14-Feb-1790.

REG	D	Venus/Scorpio	P	dex sq MC d. => Saturn (SA)	7-Sep-1798
REG	D	Venus/Scorpio	P	dex sq MC d. => Saturn (0)	1-Jun-1800

LOCK The arrest of Benjamin Franklin's grandson on charges of sedition on 12-Sep-1798 marked a defining moment for both Jefferson and Madison who now consulted on ways to block the Alien & Sedition Acts during meetings held September-October 1798. The result was Jefferson's *Kentucky Resolutions* and Madison's *Virginia Resolutions* which rejected the Alien & Sedition Acts as unconstitutional. The end of the sequence was marred by Federalist attacks on Jefferson's belief in deism during the Presidential campaign of 1800.

PT	D	Saturn/Aquarius	P	opp Saturn (0) c. => ASC	9-Mar-1804
PT	D	Saturn/Aquarius	P	opp Saturn (SA) c. => ASC	24-Mar-1806

The House vote to impeach Justice Chase on 12-Mar-1804 opened this sequence. But it is Aaron Burr's duel with Hamilton on 11-Jul-1804, Burr's escapade as a British spy, and word of Burr's treason reaching Jefferson during Spring 1806 which filled out the balance of the sequence.

PT	D	Mercury/Aries	P	dex trine Mars (MA) d. => MC	10-Jan-1808
PT	D	Mercury/Aries	P	dex trine Mars (0) d. => MC	19-Jan-1809

Embargo Acts against Britain: 1st signed on 22-Dec-1807, 2nd Act signed on 9-Jan-1808, Enforcement Act passed on 9-Jan-1809. Repealed 1-Mar-1809.

Longevity, 83y 2m 21d

Death: 4-Jul-1826, 12:50 AM; Monticello, Virginia, at home. Jefferson suffered from poor health with an enlarged prostate, rheumatism, and chronic diarrhea in his final months. His last two days were spent in and out of consciousness.

Hīlāj: **Sun**. Figure is diurnal; Sun is preferred and in an Hīlājical position in the 11th house by whole signs.

Al-kadukhadāh: **Sun**. In his exaltation in mutual reception with Mars, Sun trumps all other candidates for Al-kadukhadāh. Sun grants 120 major years. Jefferson lived considerably shorter than this projection; deducting years for trines from both Saturn and Mars is the only way to approximate his actual longevity. Saturn receives the Sun as participating triplicity ruler which appears to be sufficient for Saturn to deduct his 30 minor years. Saturn may also deduct years because the Sun's applying aspect to Saturn aspect is a tight 6-degree orb. Mars receives the Sun and deducts 15 minor years for a net projection of 75yrs. Jefferson lived longer but at age 75 he founded the University of Virginia, after which his career achievements diminished in relative importance compared to what came before. The Sun's mutual reception with Mars by sign also mitigates the ability of Mars to reduce vitality allowing Jefferson to live beyond 75 years.

Sun (120) – SA (30) – MA (15) = 75 years.

Victor of the Horoscope: **Saturn**

Killing Planets: **Mercury (35), Mars (33), Jupiter (31)**

Arcus Vitae:

| REG | D | Mercury/Gemini | P | ASC c. => Mars (MA) | 27-Jun-1826 |
| PT | D | Mercury/Gemini | P | ASC c. => Mars (MA) | 14-Sep-1826 |

No Mars-Sun directions occur near Jefferson's death. The Regiomontanus direction, with latitude, is the most precise Mars-Ascendant measurement.

1826 Solar Return for year of Death

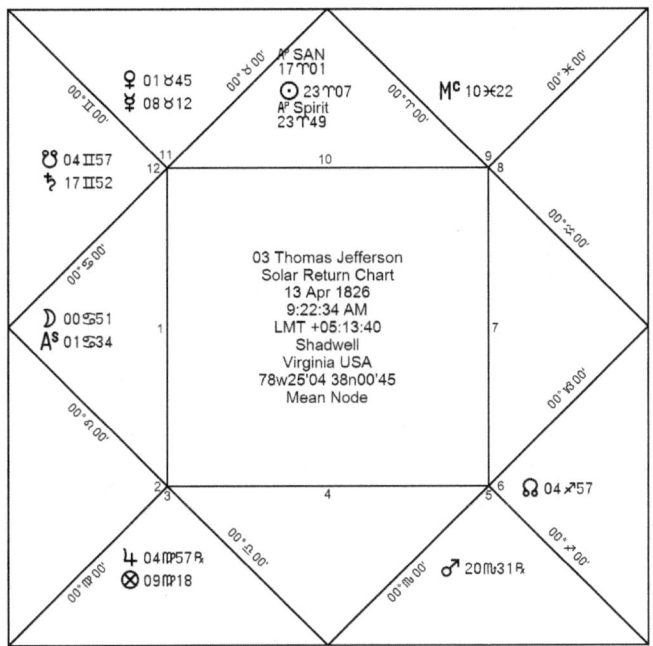

Ascendant Distributor: Saturn/Leo since 16-Dec-1820
Profected Ascendant: 00TA28, 12th House; SR Victor: Mars
Lords: LOY – Venus; LOP – Saturn
Moon: applies to sextile of Venus
Firdaria: Major – Sun; Subperiod – Jupiter
Return Ascendant falls in natal 2nd; Natal Ascendant falls in return's 12th

The Hīlāj Sun's antiscia falls at 6VI53 which is conjunct Jupiter, the third high-scoring killing planet whose power to act is increased by his partile return to his natal degree. Jupiter also falls near the 4th cusp. Moon conjunct Ascendant is notable because aphorisms state that Hīlāj-Ascendant combinations can kill.

In this 12th house year, Saturn and South Node in the return's 12th are emphasized, considering their transit to the natal Ascendant. Return Saturn opposes natal Moon within 4 degrees. Return's victor is Mars. He is the high scoring killing planet and opposes secondary killer Mercury. Mars at 20SC31 opposes natal Lot of Illness at 20TA09.

| PT | D | Venus/Virgo | P | sin trine Mercury (0) d. => ASC | 4-Jul-1826 |

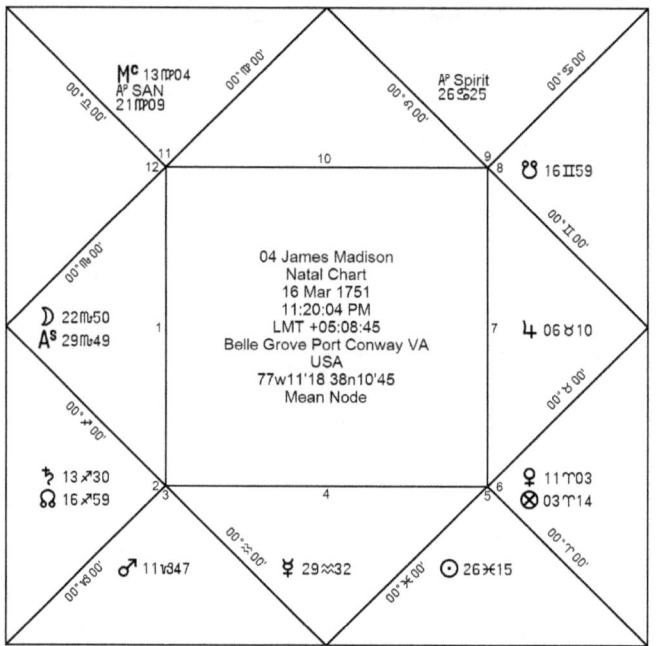
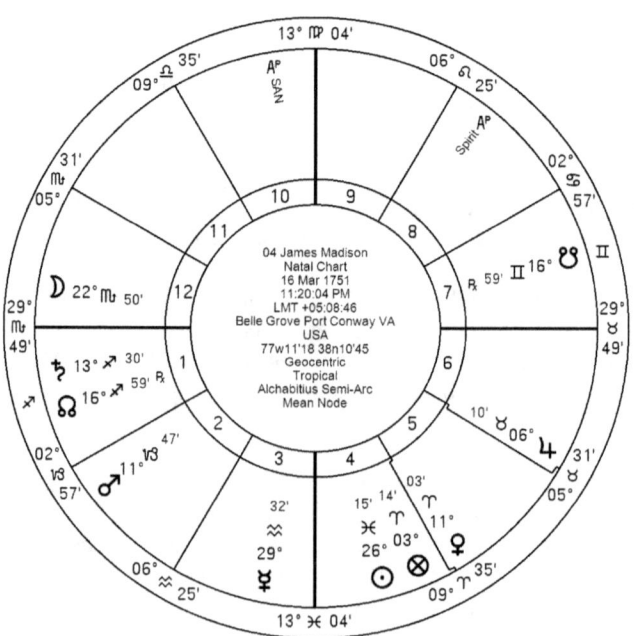

4. JAMES MADISON

Moon's Configuration

Moon separates from **Mars** and applies to the **Sun**, nocturnal, preventional. Prenatal syzygy is 21VI09. Eclipse? No.

Cognitive Assessment Model (Rulers of Moon and Mercury)

Sign rulers: **Mars, Saturn**
Bound rulers: **Jupiter, Saturn**

Victor Soul Models

Ibn Ezra Victor Model (1507), in-sect triplicity ruler, triplicity decans.

	Position	☉	☽	☿	♀	♂	♃	♄
Sun	26 PI 15				4	6	5	
Moon	22 SC 50		1			8	2	
Asc	29 SC 49		1			8		2
Pars Fortuna	3 AR 14	4				6	5	
Syzygy	21 VI 09			3	9	1	2	
Oriental						2	0	1
Houses		9	2	3	7	6	1	12
Score		13	7	12	8	38	13	15

Porphyry's Expanded Victor Model (2022)

Mars rules the ASC, Moon, and LOF by sign; Sun and SAN by bound. Sect: out of favor. Solar phase: oriental – waxing square to 1st station. Position: 10th from LOF, 7th from LOS. Dignity: exaltation, participating triplicity.

Victor Table for Killing Planets

			☉	☽	☿	♀	♂	♃	♄
ASC		29SC49		3,1		3	5,3		2
Rul ASC	♂	11CP47		3		3,1	4,3	2	5
L.Death		23CA37		5,3		3	3	4,2,1	
Rul L.Death	☽	22SC50		3		3	5,3	2,1	
H8 Cusp		2CA57		5,3,1		3	3,2	4	
Rul H8	☽	22SC50		3		3	5,3	2,1	
T-Rul H8	♂	11CP47		3		3,1	4,3	2	5
H8 Occupants	SN	17GE02			5,3		2,1	3	3
8th from ☽		22GE50			5,3	1	2	3	3
Rul 8th fr ☽	☿	29AQ32			3	1		3	5,3,2
TOTAL			0	33	19	25	51	30	28

2007 Proposed Rectification: 4-Mar-1751 AD JC, Ascendant 29SC47'31"
2022 Proposed Rectification: 5-Mar-1751 AD JC, Ascendant 29SC49'46"

Astrodatabank reports a B-rated birthtime at midnight 5-Mar-1751 JC or 16-Mar-1761 GC. In 2007 when ARM was written, ADB's pictured horoscope for Madison assumed birth was midnight 'the last of the 4th but the beginning of the 5th'. Recently ADB added notes which stated the birthdate was 'the last of the 5th but the beginning of the 6th'. Both dates compute the Moon in Scorpio with both Lots of Spirit and Fortune in the same signs of Cancer and Aries respectively. Whatever the date, physiognomy suggests the birth time was before midnight shifting the midnight Ascendant sign of Sagittarius back to Scorpio. Madison's widow's peak (Scorpio) and white hair parted at the midline (Cancer) suggest the 3rd decan of Scorpio rises (Cancer).

ZRS. LOS 26CA25 in the bound of Saturn/Cancer signifies Madison's concern for homeland security.

L1 Cancer 04 Mar 1751		
L2 Capricorn 02 May 1759	FS	Moved into new family house.
L2 Capricorn 13 Jul 1768	LB	Summer-1768, Witherspoon accepted Presidency of College of New Jersey; Summer-1769, Madison departed for College of New Jersey.
L1 Leo 04 Nov 1775		25-Apr-1776, voted to represent Orange County at Williamsburg General Convention.
L2 Aquarius 20 Feb 1784	FS	12-May-1784, served as Orange County delegate to Virginia Assembly, 1784-1786.
L2 Aquarius 04 Mar 1793	LB	Dec-1793, TJ presented *Report on the Privileges and Restrictions on the Commerce of the United States in Foreign Countries* on which he and JM had worked for two years; 3-Jan-1794, JM introduced Congressional measures related to trade; 19-Apr-1794, GW selected John Jay to negotiate trade differences with Britain.
L1 Virgo 27 Jul 1794		19-Nov-1794, John Jay signed Treaty with England; 24-Jun-1795, Senate ratified Jay's Treaty. Treaty attempted to negotiate trade differences with Britain but left no mention of eliminating naval impressments.
L2 Pisces 09 Oct 1803	FS	Jun-1804, Royal Navy captain impressed American seamen in NY harbor.
L2 Pisces 26 Nov 1811	LB	1-Apr-1812, Congress approved JM's proposed 60 day trade embargo against Britain; 19-Jun-1812, Madison declared war against Britain.
L1 Libra 14 Apr 1814		25-Apr-1814, British extended blockade to New England; overall the British expanded their war against the US after Napoleon abdicated on 6-Apr-1814; 21-Oct-1814, first British peace offer signaled last phase of war.
L1 Scorpio 03 Mar 1822		
L2 Leo 22 Aug 1835		28-Jun-1836, died.

Firdaria – Mars major and minor periods

Firdaria according to Bonatti	Life Event
Moon **Mars** 22 Jan 1755	19-Aug-1755, Braddock's defeat in French and Indian war forced some pioneer families back east.
Saturn **Mars** 07 May 1763	No events found.
Jupiter **Mars** 30 Nov 1772	16-Dec-1773, Boston Tea Party; subsequently JM witnessed Baptist preachers jailed in Culpeper which radicalized him to freedom of religion. 13-May-1774, JM learned of British decision to close port of Boston as punishment in response to Boston Tea Party.
Mars 7 years Age 32 to 39	
Mars Mars 15 Mar 1783	18-Apr-1783, Congress approved assumption of state debts in financial plan submitted by Madison on 6-Mar-1783; 25-Oct-1783, last appeared as delegate to Congress; Dec-1783, returned home after away for 4 years.
Mars Sun 14 Mar 1784	12-May-1784, served as Orange County delegate to Virginia Assembly (to 1786).
Mars Venus 15 Mar 1785	Jun-1785, wrote *Memorial and Remonstrance against Religious Assessments*, 22-Jan-1786, proposed adoption of Jefferson's *Bill for Establishing Religions Freedom*.
Mars Mercury 15 Mar 1786	Aug-1786, attended Annapolis Convention; Nov-1786, opposed proposal for Virginia to issue its own paper money.
Mars Moon 15 Mar 1787	3-May-1787, arrived Philadelphia for Constitutional Convention; 29-May-1787, Randolph presented Madison's Virginia Plan; 16-Jul-1787, Convention adopted 'Great Compromise,' 17-Sep-1787, final form of Constitution approved; 28-Sep-1787, Constitution sent to states for ratification; 22-Nov-1787, Madison's first contribution to the Federalist Papers.
Mars Saturn 14 Mar 1788	25-Mar-1788, addressed local Virginians on Constitution prior to ratification vote; 25-Jun-1788, Virginia ratified constitution; 2-Feb-1789, won election to 1st Congress in a race against James Monroe.
Mars Jupiter 15 Mar 1789	8-Apr-1789, proposed Congress establish a revenue system to enable nation to pay its debts and meet expenses of government; 4-May-1789, announced intention to introduce a Bill of Rights.
Sun **Mars** 11 Oct 1803	June-1804, Royal Navy captain impressed some seamen from an American vessel in New York harbor; this was an issue that eventually led to War of 1812.
Venus **Mars** 02 Dec 1810	4-Mar-1811, Bank of United States dissolved; 4-Nov-1811, 'War Hawk' Congress convened, Henry Clay and John Calhoun took office; Dec-1811, Congress passed measures to increase military personnel and armaments.
Mercury **Mars** 19 Aug 1820	No events found.
Moon **Mars** 22 Jan 1830	1830, began to suffer from rheumatism and fever.

Transits

<u>4-Aug-1787</u>. *tr North Node 10th from LOF*. 'Great Compromise' adopted at Constitutional Convention, 16 July.

<u>26-Apr-1789</u>. tr. *North Node conj ASC*. GW Inauguration, 30 April.

<u>15-Apr-1793</u>. *tr North Node conj MC*. GW Neutrality Statement, 22-Apr.

<u>16-Aug-1798</u>. *tr South Node conj ASC*. Followed passage of Alien & Sedition Acts (18-Jun to 14-Jul) and meeting with TJ to plan their response, 2-Jul.

<u>10-Nov-1810</u>. *tr South Node conj LOF*. A victim of slow speed of diplomatic messages, JM realized his 2-Nov-1810 prohibition of trade against England was based on erroneous assumptions; yet chose not to rescind the 2-Nov-1810 order, early-Nov-1810.

Solar Arc Directions

<u>13-Aug-1798</u>. *dsa MC trine Mercury*.
Began writing legislative response to Alien & Sedition Acts, Summer and Fall-1798 following passage of the Fourth Act on 14-Jul-1798.

LOCK <u>22-Dec-1798</u>. *dsa Sun trine MC*.
Virginia Legislature adopted resolutions submitted by JM against the Alien & Sedition Acts, 24-Dec-1798.

LOCK <u>7-Dec-1808</u>. *dsa ASC sextile Sun*.
Elected President, 7-Dec-1808.

<u>6-Jan-1812</u>. *csa MC opposed Mars*.
<u>22-Dec-1813</u>. *dsa Mars opposed MC*.
Congress passed Army bill enlarging army to 25,000, 10-Jan-1812.
British laid waste to East Niagara River area, 20-Dec-1813.

Notable Ascendant Distributions

D	Changeover	bound Mercury/Capricorn d. => ASC	9-Oct-1786
D	Changeover	bound Mars/Capricorn d. => ASC	9-May-1812
D	Changeover	bound Mercury/Aquarius d. => ASC	17-Oct-1815

Returned home after originally scheduled September 1786 Annapolis Convention was cancelled; spent time on additional research in preparation for Constitutional Convention, 1787.
Renominated for President, 18-May-1812; War declared, 19-Jun-1812; Treaty of Ghent ratified, 17-Feb-1815 (Mars/Capricorn distribution better match to length of war than Mars-MC solar arc directions above.)

4. JAMES MADISON

Primary Direction Sequences

PT	D	Mars/Sagittarius	P	dex sex Merc (0) d. => ASC	7-Apr-1786
PT	D	Mars/Sagittarius	P	dex sex Merc (BI) d. => ASC	26-Jan-1787
PT	D	Mars/Sagittarius	P	dex sex Merc (ME) d. => ASC	22-Nov-1787

LOCK This sequence best encapsulates Madison's significant role in crafting the Constitution of the United States.

Note: his historical title as 'father of the Constitution' is a delineation match to Mercury in the 4th house of the father.

Received and began to study literary cargo of books on history, politics, and commerce sent by Jefferson from Paris, Spring/Summer-1786.

Stopped by Mount Vernon for visit with George Washington on way to New York, 25-Jan-1787. (Note Mercury/Aquarius is Washington's victor).

Madison's first contribution to Federalist Papers (#10) written to advocate passage of Constitution by the states, 22-Nov-1787.

| PT | D | Jupiter/Capricorn | P | Mars (0) d. => ASC | 29-Jan-1799 |
| PT | D | Jupiter/Capricorn | P | Mars (MA) d. => ASC | 11-Aug-1799 |

The revised rectification advances these directions by about six months. Instead of timing Madison's anti-Federalist cooperation with Jefferson following passage of the Alien & Sedition Acts of 1798, early 1799 can be delineated as the revival of his political career with election to the Virginia Legislature on 24-Apr-1799. With Mars/Capricorn the victor, we should expect Madison to find his political voice when Mars rises by primary motion. The year 1799 was the penultimate year prior to the 1800 Presidential Election which, after a tie-breaking vote in the House of Representatives on 17-Feb-1801, sent Jefferson to the White House.

| PT | D | Jupiter/Pisces | P | IC d. => Mars (MA) | 11-Jul-1804 |
| PT | D | Jupiter/Pisces | P | IC d. => Mars (0) | 21-Oct-1804 |

Aaron Burr killed Alexander Hamilton in a duel, 11-Jul-1804. Hamilton was the most prominent member of the Federalist Party, signified by Capricorn. For this reason, Mars/Capricorn directed to the IC is a good delineation match to Hamilton's death.

Emergence of John Randolph as enemy of Republican Party, 1804/05.

Longevity, 85y 3m 13d

Death: 28-Jun-1836, after 6:00 A.M., Montpelier estate, Virginia, at home. Died in bed after being served breakfast by his niece. Madison was in ill health in his final years, confined to bed the last six months of his life.

Hīlāj: **Sun**. Figure is nocturnal and Moon is preferred; yet Moon falling 7 degrees back from the Ascendant in the 12th exceeds the recommended 5 degree cutoff. Sun in 5th qualifies and sextiles the Al-kadukhadāh Mars.

Al-kadukhadāh: **Mars**. Whether Moon or Sun is the Hīlāj, Mars is the Al-kadukhadāh. Mars grants 66 major years. Instead of adjusting years by considering the antiscia from Saturn and North Node which I advocated in prior editions, a less complicated solution adds Jupiter's 12 minor years by trine aspect, receiving Mars by bound. Venus adds 8 minor years by square aspect, receiving Mars by triplicity and decan.

MA (66) + JU (12) + VE (8) = 86 years.

Consider without Venus' addition longevity is reduced to 78 years. This coincides with the onset of rheumatism in the fall of 1829 which signaled a significant stepdown in physical vitality.

Victor of the Horoscope: **Mars**

Killing Planet: **Mars (51)**

Arcus Vitae:

REG	D	Mars/Pisces	P	Sun d. => North Node	5-Nov-1834
PT	D	Mars/Pisces	P	Sun d. => North Node	15-Mar-1837

Nodes in the 2nd-8th house axis kill by position. Death occurs between the same direction computed by Regiomontanus and Ptolemy's method.

1836 Solar Return for year of Death

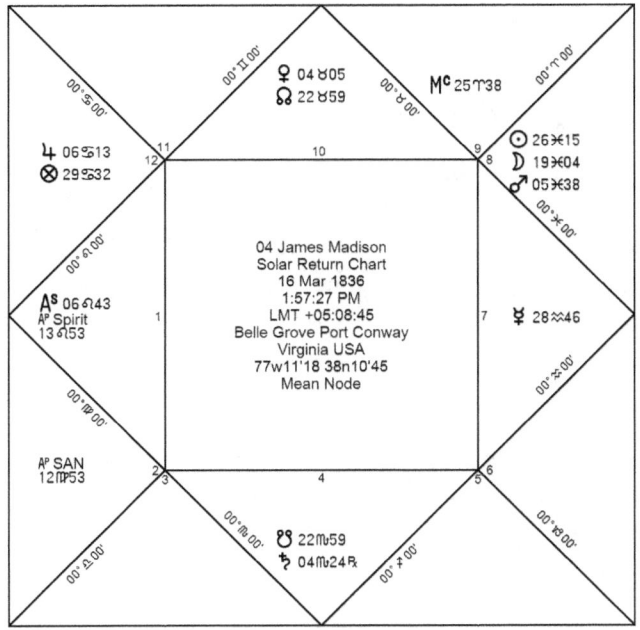

Ascendant Distributor: Saturn/Aquarius since 24-Sep-1834
Profected Ascendant: 29SA49, 2nd house; SR Victor: Venus
Lords: LOY – Jupiter; LOP – Sun
Moon: separates from trine of Jupiter and applies to the Sun.
Firdaria: Major – Saturn; Subperiod – Saturn
Return Ascendant falls in natal 9th

Both luminaries in the 8th house of death are a bad sign as well as the Moon's final hours in her last quarter. Moon's separation from Jupiter and application to the Sun intensifies the activity of Jupiter, an effect similar to combustion. Jupiter's rulership of the 8th of death is problematic.

The solar return directed Ascendant reached the 4h cusp on 29-Jun-1836 the day after death.

428 · A Rectification Manual

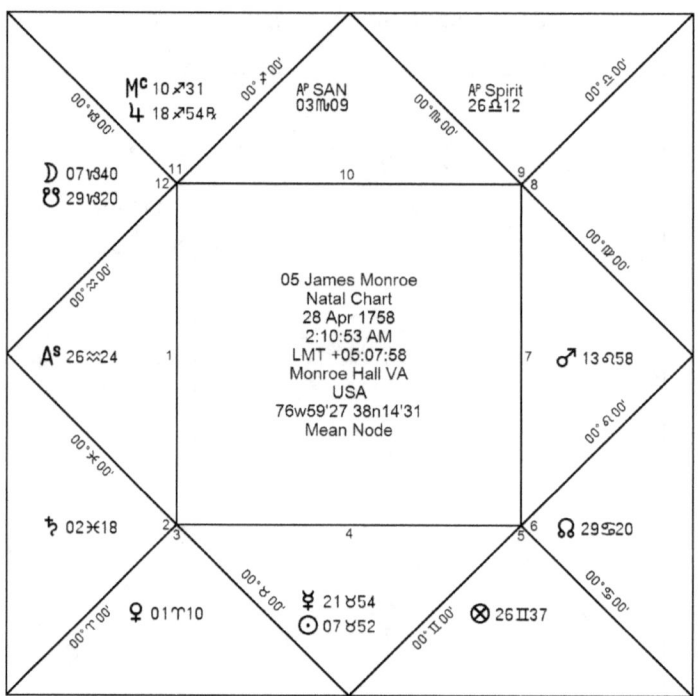

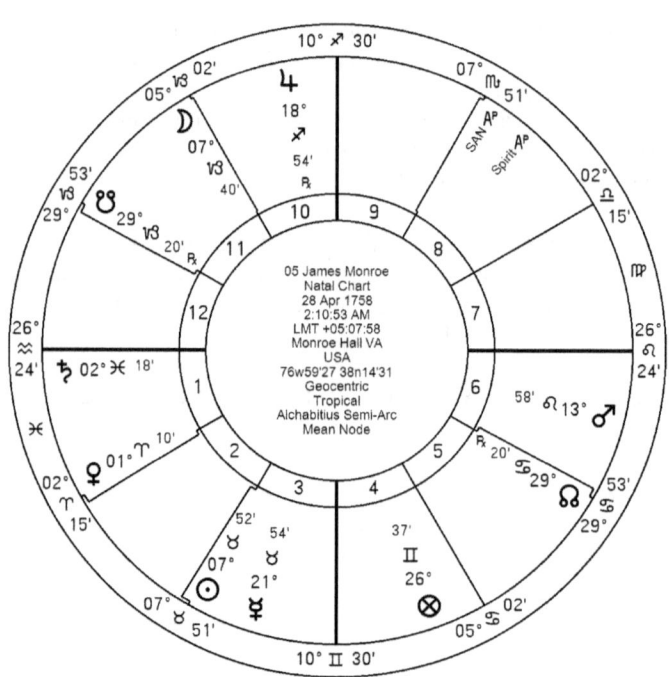

5. JAMES MONROE

Moon's Configuration

Moon separates from **Saturn** and applies to the **Sun**, nocturnal, preventional. Prenatal syzygy is 3SC09. Eclipse? No.

Cognitive Assessment Model (Rulers of Moon and Mercury)

Sign rulers: **Saturn, Venus**
Bound rulers: **Jupiter** (both)

Victor Soul Models

Ibn Ezra Victor Model (1507), in-sect triplicity ruler, triplicity decans.

	Position	☉	☽	☿	♀	♂	♃	♄
Sun	07 TA 52		7		8			
Moon	07 CP 40		3			4	2	6
Asc	26 AQ 24			3	1			7
Pars Fortuna	26 GE 37			8				3
Syzygy	03 SC 09					11		
Oriental						0	1	2
Houses		3	8	3	6	1	11	12
Score		3	18	14	15	16	14	**30**

Porphyry's Expanded Victor Model (2022)

Jupiter rules the MC by sign; MC and Moon by bound. Sect: out-of-favor. Solar phase: oriental retrograde to acronycal rising. Position: 7th from LOF; House of Joy. Dignity: sign and nocturnal triplicity.

Victor Table for Killing Planets

			☉	☽	☿	♀	♂	♃	♄
ASC		26AQ24			3	1		3	5,3,2
Rul ASC	♄	2PI18		3		4,3,2	3	5,1	
L.Death		26SC53		3,1		3	5,3		2
Rul L.Death	♂	13LE58	5,3					3,1	3,2
H8 Cusp		2LI15			3	5,1		3	4,3,2
Rul H8	♀	1AR10	4,3				5,1	3,2	3
T-Rul H8	♄	2PI18		4,3		5,3	3	2	1
8th from ☽		7LE40	5,3,1			2		3	3
Rul 8th fr ☽	☉	7TA52		4,3	1	5,3,2	3		
TOTAL			24	21	7	**39**	23	26	**33**

2007 Proposed Rectification: 2:10:53 AM, ASC 26AQ25'07"
2022 Proposed Rectification: 2:10:52 AM, ASC 26AQ24'46"

Astrodatabank reports a C-rated birthtime of 1:52:18 AM citing D.C. Doane's *Horoscopes of US Presidents*. ADB's time, Starkman's rectification of 2:05:02 AM, and my proposed time of 2:10:52 AM all yield late Aquarius rising.

ZRS. With his early Presidency nicknamed the 'Era of Good Feelings,' it should come as no surprise that Monroe's Lot of Spirit 26LI12 is placed in the sign and bound of Venus. Though fissures developed at the end of his second term, Monroe nevertheless presided over the 1820 Missouri Compromise which postponed the slavery debate for thirty years. Highlights from Monroe's L1 periods include L1-Scorpio, military service; L1-Sagittarius, launch of political career under tutelage of Jefferson; L1-Capricorn, Rivalry between Jefferson's Democratic-Republican Party and the Federalist Party; L1-Aquarius, National and personal financial crises.

L1 Libra 28 Apr 1758		
L1 Scorpio 17 Mar 1766		1776, entered Campbell Academy; 1774, inherited family property after death of both parents; Uncle Jones (Judge) a mentor; 1776-1778, Revolutionary War service.
L1 Sagittarius 28 Dec 1780		Spring 1780, slightly ahead of L1 Sagittarius, Monroe began relationship with Jefferson as legal and political mentor; Spring-1782, elected to VA House of Delegates; 1783-1786, member Continental Congress, distinguished service while on numerous committees, gained functional experience in foreign affairs, land boundary issues, and the limits of the Articles of Confederation; 1788, turned against Constitution for its excessive Federal powers; 1790, won Senate seat.
L1 Capricorn 26 Oct 1792		Beginning of Jefferson and Hamilton rivalry. Fall 1792, Monroe wrote articles favorable to Jefferson published in the *National Gazette*.
L2 Cancer 08 Jan 1802	FS	12-Jan-1803, Envoy Extraordinary to France; 2-May-1803, Louisiana Purchase signed.
L2 Cancer 25 Feb 1810	LB	16-Jan-1811, elected Governor of Virginia; 2-Apr-1811, named Secretary of State under Madison.
L2 Capricorn 14 Apr 1818	CP	24-Feb-1819, Adams-Onis Treaty ratified whereby Spain renounced claims on Florida; set western borders of Louisiana Territory.
L1 Aquarius 08 Jun 1819		Jun-1819, beginning of Panic of 1819; 6-Mar-1820, Missouri Compromise signed.
L2 Leo 20 Jun 1828	FS	Late-1828 or 29, injured right wrist in fall from horse; Rives Committee recommended Congress pay Monroe additional $60K for past claims.
L2 Virgo 11 Jan 1830		21-Sep-1830, death of son-in-law; 23-Sep-1830, death of wife; ear-Feb-1831, House approved grant of $30K based on Rives report, 4-Jul-1831, death.

Firdaria – Jupiter major and minor periods

Firdaria according to Bonatti	Life Events
Moon **Jupiter** 22 Nov 1760	No events found.
Saturn **Jupiter** 22 Nov 1768	No events found.
Jupiter 12 years Age 20 to 32	
Jupiter Jupiter 27 Apr 1778	6-May-1778, GW celebrated recently signed treaty with France with large party at Valley Forge; 28-Jun-1778, participated in Battle of Monmouth, last military engagement.
Jupiter Mars 14 Jan 1780	Spring-1780, moved to Richmond to study law with TJ.
Jupiter Sun 01 Oct 1781	Spring-1782, elected to House of Delegates, Continental Congress.
Jupiter Venus 19 Jun 1783	13-Dec-1783, seated as Virginia's rep in Confederation Congress; 14-Jan-1784, Treaty of Paris ratified.
Jupiter Mercury 06 Mar 1785	8-May-1785, Land Ordinance of 1785 passed; Aug-1785, toured the West and encountered hostility of western interests towards the east; 16-Feb-1786, married Elizabeth Kortright; 18-Aug-1786, made proposal for dealing with Spanish and commercial navigation of the Mississippi River; 13-Oct-1786, returned to Virginia after completing service in Continental Congress.
Jupiter Moon 22 Nov 1786	5-Dec-1786, birth of daughter Eliza; late-1787, brother's bankruptcy complicated personal finances; Jun-1788, attacked Electoral College among other features of the Constitution during Richmond ratifying convention.
Jupiter Saturn 09 Aug 1788	Oct-1788, purchased estate in Albemarle, present site of University of Virginia.
Mars **Jupiter** 27 Apr 1796	13-Jun-1796, notified by Pickering of GW's displeasure of his handling of French attitudes in response to Jay's Treaty; ear-Jul-1796; GW instructed Pickering to notify JM of his recall; 30-Dec-1796, ended diplomatic post; delayed return until Spring 1797 because of weather.
Sun **Jupiter** 19 Jun 1809	Oct-1809, withdrew from public life to focus on Albemarle plantation; Apr-1810, made speech stating loyalty to Richmond Republicans in bid to rehabilitate his political reputation; May-1810, received by President Madison and others in the administration on friendly terms.
Venus **Jupiter** 22 Nov 1816	4-Dec-1816, elected President; 4-Mar-1817, Inauguration; 12-Jul-1817, "Era of Good Feelings" coined by Boston newspaper; 26-Dec-1817, First Seminole War began.
Mercury **Jupiter** 23 Nov 1825	21-May-1826, Congress agreed to reimburse JM $29,513 for past services.

Jupiter as Victor. Major Jupiter included the start of Monroe's Revolutionary War service, his Continental Congress service, and concludes with his role in the Jay Treaty. Subsequent minor Jupiter periods timed his political rehabilitation, election as President, and receipt of Congressional funds for past services unpaid.

Transits

16-Jun-1803. *tr North Node conj ASC.* Louisiana Purchase signed 2-May; Audience with Napoleon, 24-Jun-1803.

14-March, 9-April, and 22-Oct-1817. *tr Jupiter conj MC.*
Inauguration 4-Mar; *Era of Good Feelings* proclaimed on 12-Jul-1817.

22-Sep-1830. *tr Saturn conj DSC.* Death of wife, 23-Sep-1830.

Solar Arc Directions

9-Feb-1786. *csa Moon conj MC.*
29-Jun-1786. *dsa MC conj Moon.*
Marriage, 16-Feb-1786.
Need for income to support family drove JM to a law career in the months following these directions.

5-Jun-1794. *csa Moon square Saturn.*
25-Jan-1795. *dsa Saturn square Moon.*
Sailed for France with family in tow, 18-Jun-1794.
Secured release of American prisoners in France, Feb-1795.
Saturn signifies prisoners because Saturn rules the 12th of prisoners; bonification by Jupiter at the superior square signifies prisoner release.

LOCK 15-Sep-1806. *csa Mars trine ASC.*
LOCK 31-Oct-1807. *dsa ASC trine Mars.*
Death of British minister Fox signaled increased difficulties in negotiation, 13-Sep-1806. Left Britain after unsuccessful diplomatic mission, Nov-1807.

16-Oct-1813. *csa Moon conj Saturn.*
3-Apr-1815. *dsa Moon conj Saturn.*
Both directions outlined key events in the War of 1812 which favored the USA. Battle of Thames River and death of Tecumseh, 5-Oct-1813; Monroe appointed interim Secretary of War following the burning of Washington DC, 27-Aug-1814; Monroe surprised Congress with request of 100,000 men, 17-Oct-1814; News of Treaty of Ghent reaches USA, 11-Feb-1815; Monroe resigned from War Department in bad health and required six months to recover, 16-Mar-1815. Delineation: Moon/Capricorn/12th makes a cognitive error by overemphasizing the importance of troop numbers. Saturn/Pisces establishes defensive barriers around bodies of water and is consistent with USA naval victories at Lake Champlain and the Great Lakes which cut off British offensives to the USA mainland. These naval victories occurred shortly after Monroe took over as Secretary of War. Resignation because of illness is a traditional Saturn-Moon dynamic measurement.

Primary Directions

| REG | D | Mercury/Libra | P | dex sq Moon (0) c. => MC | 9-Mar-1820 |

White House wedding of daughter marred by sister's meddling, 9-Mar.

| REG | D | Saturn/Scorpio | P | dex sq ASC d. => Mars (MA) | 1-Jan-1824 |

Fight with Georgia Senators on Indian removal, January 1824.

Primary Direction Sequences

| PT | D | Jupiter/Capricorn | P | Moon (0) c. => ASC | 1-Feb-1799 |
| PT | D | Jupiter/Capricorn | P | Moon (MO) c. => ASC | 16-Dec-1800 |

As Virginia Governor, JM dealt with a large slave revolt in the fall of 1800. Moon ruling 6th in the 12th signifies slave revolts. More precise to the timing of the sequence is the birth of his only son James Spence during May 1799, his death on 28-Sep-1800, and his wife's subsequent depression.

| PT | D | Mercury/Taurus | P | dex sq Mars (MA) d. => ASC | 13-May-1805 |
| PT | D | Mercury/Taurus | P | dex sq Mars (0) d. => ASC | 25-Oct-1807 |

LOCK This sequence timed difficulties Monroe faced on diplomatic missions to Spain and Britain. On 12-May, Monroe and Pinkney made their final offer to Spain in their attempts to have Spain cede Florida to the US. They were unsuccessful because Spain was loyal to Napoleon who had no interest in ceding Florida. The subsequent mission to Britain, obtaining a few concessions but failing to eliminate the practice of impressments, was considered such a failure by Jefferson that the Treaty was never submitted to the Senate. Monroe left Europe in Nov-1807. The above solar arc pair of Mars trine ASC generates similar dates and picks up the death of British minister Fox which led to the diplomatic failure as Fox's replacement was not as friendly to Monroe.

| PT | D | Mercury/Gemini | P | sin sq Saturn (0) d. => ASC | 11-May-1822 |
| PT | D | Mercury/Gemini | P | sin sq Saturn (SA) d. => ASC | 3-Dec-1823 |

LOCK This sequence timed many of the critical events culminating with the proclamation of the Monroe Doctrine. Monroe called for US recognition of new Latin American Republics on 8-Mar-1822; Congress appropriated $100,000 for South American ambassadors on 4-May; JM received Manuel Torres as charge d'affaires for the newly recognized state of Columbia; Britain proposed a joint Anglo-US alliance against European intervention in the Americas on 20-Aug-1823; after conferring with the Cabinet on the Monroe Doctrine during November it was proclaimed as the sequence ended on 2-Dec-1823. Saturn in Pisces has a polarizing hands-off quality which for Monroe is caused by an exaggerated 'too much is not enough' wish for America's territorial expansion by political alliances (Jupiter/Sagittarius/11th).

Longevity, 73y 2m 6d

Death: 4-Jul-1831, approx. 3:15 PM, New York City, NY. Monroe died of heart failure following many months of a nagging cough, suspected a symptom of tuberculosis.

Hīlāj: **Moon**. Figure is nocturnal; Moon is preferred and qualifies on the 11th cusp in a feminine sign. Moon also conjoins her bound ruler Jupiter by antiscia. 12th whole sign placement raises questions yet the Moon tests well as empirical Hīlāj. If not the Moon, then LOF in the 4th opposed Jupiter.

Al-kadukhadāh: **Jupiter**. Whether the Moon or Lot of Fortune is the Hīlāj, Jupiter is the Al-kadukhadāh. Jupiter gives his 79 major years. The square from Saturn is too wide to deduct years. Mars trines but does not receive Jupiter so he cannot deduct years. Monroe lived fewer years.

Victor of the Horoscope: **Jupiter**

Killing Planet: **Venus (39), Saturn (33)**

Arcus Vitae:

REG	D	Jupiter/Aries	P	Venus (VE) d. => Moon (MO)	15-Aug-1827
REG	D	Jupiter/Aries	P	Venus (0) d. => Moon (MO)	7-Mar-1829

The theoretical Venus-Moon arcus vitae timed Monroe's illness in final years suspected to be pulmonary tuberculosis. He also had a fever in spring 1829. Same sequence by Ptolemy is late.

REG	D	Mars/Scorpio	P	dex tr Sat (SA) c. => Moon (MO)	26-Jun-1831
REG	D	Mars/Scorpio	P	dex tr Sat (0) c. => Moon (MO)	16-Sep-1831
REG	D	Mars/Scorpio	P	dex tr Sat (BI) c. => Moon (MO	26-Oct-1831

Saturn is the second high scoring killer. Same sequence by Ptolemy is early.

PT	D	Saturn/Aquarius	P	ASC c. => Mercury (ME)	3-Jul-1831

Though not a high scoring killer, Mercury rules the 8th of death (WS).

1831 Solar Return for year of Death

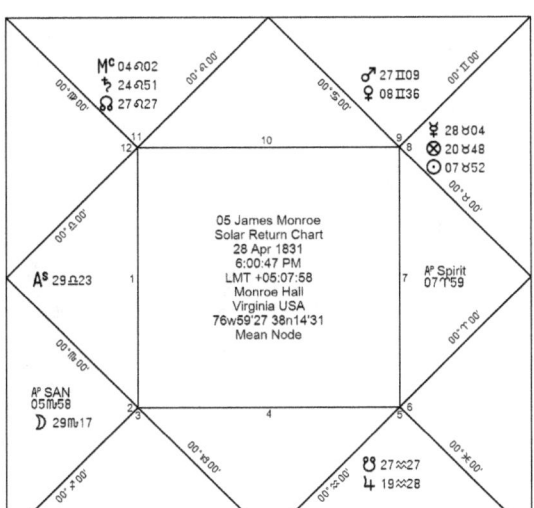

Ascendant Distributor: Venus/Gemini since 3-Feb-1831
Profected Ascendant: 26PI25, 2nd House; SR Victor: Venus
Lords: LOY – Jupiter; LOP – Sun
Firdaria: Mercury-Venus
Moon: separates from opposition to Mercury and is void of course
Return Ascendant falls in natal 8th; Natal Ascendant falls in return's 5th

This is a 2nd house profected year. Natal 2nd has Saturn by position and is ruled by Jupiter. Both are square. In the return, Jupiter conjunct South Node and Saturn conjunct North Node are opposed. Lord of the Year and benefic Jupiter is weakened by the South Node; high-scoring killing planet Saturn is strengthened by the North Node. South Node falling in the natal Ascendant weakens the physical body as does Saturn falling near the 7th cusp. Saturn afflicts the Moon by square and conjoins the Sun by antiscia. Sun-Mercury conjunction in natal 4th is replicated in the return's 8th (WS).

The following direction falls two days after death, it links the high scoring killing planet to the solar return Ascendant.

| PT | D | Saturn/Sagittarius | P | sin tr Sat (0) d. => ASC | 6-Jul-1831 |

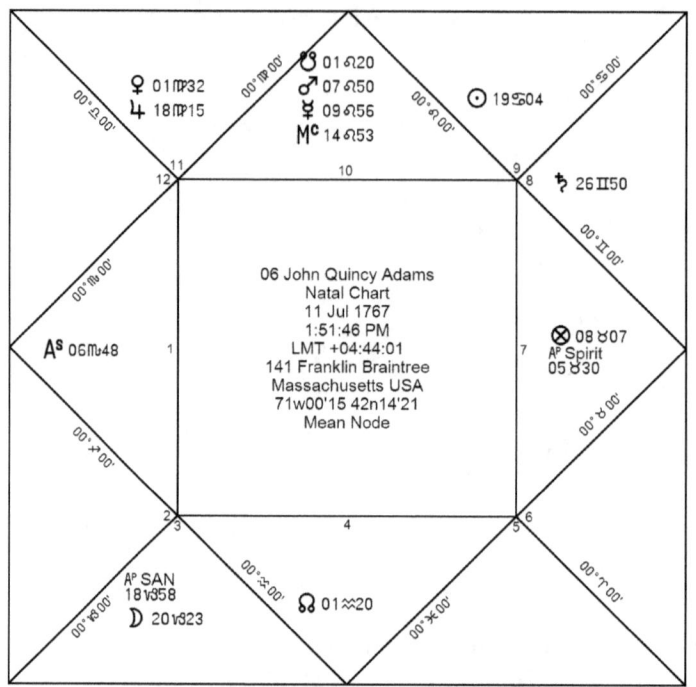
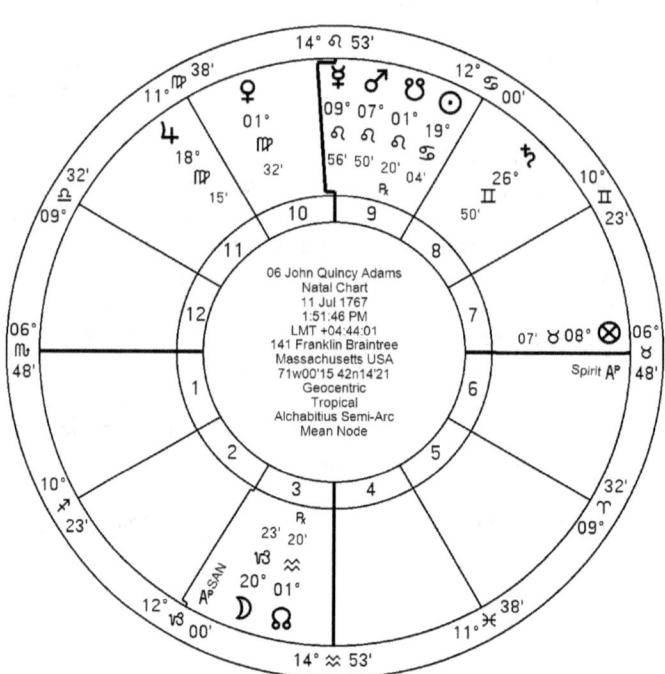

6. JOHN QUINCY ADAMS

Moon's Configuration

Moon separates from the **Sun** and is **VOC** (Medieval) or applies to **Mars** (Hellenistic), diurnal, preventional.
Prenatal syzygy is 20CP23. Eclipse? **YES**. Appulse Lunar Eclipse.

Cognitive Assessment Model (Rulers of Moon and Mercury)

Sign rulers: **Saturn, (Sun)/Jupiter**
Bound rulers: **Venus** (both)

Victor Soul Models

Ibn Ezra Victor Model (1507), in-sect triplicity ruler, triplicity decans.

	Position	☉	☽	☿	♀	♂	♃	♄
Sun	19 CA 04		5		3	1	6	
Moon	20 CP 23			1	5	4		5
Asc	06 SC 48				3	8		
Pars Fortuna	08 TA 07		4	2	9			
Syzygy	18 CP 58 (LE)				6	4		5
Oriental						0	0	3
Houses		4	3	11	11	4	8	5
Score	0	4	12	14	37	21	14	18

Porphyry's Expanded Victor Model (2022)

Jupiter rules the Sun by bound. Sect: of-favor. Solar phase: occidental sextile to sinking. Position: House of Joy (WS). Dignity: bound. Debility: detriment.

Victor Table for Killing Planets

			☉	☽	☿	♀	♂	♃	♄
ASC		6SC48		3		3	5,3,2,1		
Rul ASC	♂	7LE50	5,3,1			2		3	3
L.Death		16SC50		3	2	3	5,3	1	
Rul L.Death	♃	18VI15		3	5,4	3	3	2	1
H8 Cusp		10GE23			5,3	1		3,2	3
Rul H8	☿	9LE56	5,3,1			2		3	3
T-Rul H8	♄	26GE50			5,3			3	3,2,1
Planets in H8	♄	26GE50			5,3			3	3,2,1
8th from ☉		19AQ54			3,1			3,2	5,3
Rul 8th fr ☉	♄	26GE50			5,3			3	3,2,1
TOTAL			18	9	47	14	22	28	**36**

2007 Proposed Rectification: 1:51:49 PM, ASC 6SC49'06", Quincy
2021 Proposed Rectification: 1:51:46 PM, ASC 6SC48'56", Braintree

Astrodatabank reports a C-rated birthtime of 11:00 AM, accuracy in question, citing *Horoscopes of US Presidents* by D. C. Doane. The strongest Stage I criteria in support of the proposed rectification is the configuration of the chart favoring Scorpio rising. (1) Sun/9th shows fame is tied to foreign travel. JQA traveled at an early age, unusual for the time, and was highly successful as a foreign diplomat. (2) Sun's bound lord is Jupiter placed in the 11th of politics and rules the 5th of diplomacy. (3) Saturn/Gemini/8th shows restraint of trade harms traded good (reading the 8th as 2nd from the 7th, or other people's moveable wealth). The Tariff of Abominations is a delineation match.

ZRS. LOS 5TA30 in the sign and bound of Venus placed in the 7th suggests partnerships, open enemies, and spousal interests in real estate, art, and other tangible assets were a driving feature of Adam's life purpose. He did engage in successful negotiations which significantly expanded US lands. With both LOF and LOS in Taurus, ZRS begins from Gemini. L1-Cancer: start of his legal career, marriage, and first overseas travels; L1-Leo: political career while his political party held sway - Secretary of State under James Monroe and his Presidency which ended two weeks prior the L1-Leo – L2-Aquarius loosing of the bond; L1-Virgo: Congressional career as anti-slavery advocate.

L1 Gemini 11 Jul 1767		
L2 Sagittarius 24 Apr 1776	FS	2-Jul-1776, Father John Adams voted for Independence.
L2 Sagittarius 08 Nov 1784	LB	26-Apr-1785, Father John Adams appointed Minister to England; 17-Jul-1785, JQA returned from Europe for America and studied with a tutor prior to admission to Harvard.
L1 Cancer 28 Mar 1787		Jun-1787, graduated from Harvard.
L2 Capricorn 15 May 1795	FS	Early-1796, romance with Louisa Johnson, her father lost money eliminating chances for a dowry; 29-Jun-1797, Married Louisa.
L2 Capricorn 27 Jul 1804	LB	Summer 1804, studied Supreme Court decisions during Congressional recess.
L1 Leo 18 Nov 1811		19-Jun-1812, US declared war on Britain; 25-Jun-1812, Napoleon invaded Russia; 15-Sep-1812, sudden death of daughter Louisa Catherine.
L2 Aquarius 05 Mar 1820	FS	1821, son G. W. Adams graduated from Harvard and began reading law; 1822, Report on Weights and Measures; Congress gave consent to recognize newly liberated Latin American countries.
L2 Aquarius 18 Mar 1829	LB	30-Apr-1829, son GW Adams committed suicide; 3-Sep-1829, son Charles Francis married Abigail Brown Brooks.
L1 Virgo 10 Aug 1830		Nov-1830, elected to Congress.
L2 Pisces 22 Oct 1839	FS	
L2 Pisces 09 Dec 1847	LB	21-Feb-1848, suffered major stroke; 23-Feb-1848, death.

Firdaria – Jupiter major and minor periods

Firdaria according to Bonatti	Life Event
Sun **Jupiter** 01 Sep 1774	17-Jun-1775, witnessed Battle of Bunker Hill
Venus **Jupiter** 04 Feb 1782	Traveled to Russia, Sweden, Netherlands.
Mercury **Jupiter** 04 Feb 1791	1791 (no date), published pro-Federalist essays *Letters of Publicola* in response to Thomas Paine's *Rights of Man*.
Moon **Jupiter** 05 Feb 1801	4-Sep-1801, returned to Philadelphia after extended time in Europe; 4-Apr-1802, elected to Massachusetts state Senate.
Saturn **Jupiter** 05 Feb 1809	27-Jun-1809, Senate confirmation as Minister to Russia; 23-Oct-1809, arrived St. Petersburg.
Jupiter 12 years Age 51 to 63	
Jupiter Jupiter 11 Jul 1818	20-Oct-1818, Convention of 1818 settled border dispute with Britain; 22-Feb-1819, Adams-Onis Treaty established western boundary of Louisiana Purchase - greatest diplomatic feat of his lifetime.
Jupiter Mars 29 Mar 1820	
Jupiter Sun 15 Dec 1821	1822 (no date), Report on Weights and Measures.
Jupiter Venus 02 Sep 1823	2-Dec-1823, Monroe Doctrine, written mostly by JQA; 9-Feb-1825, elected President.
Jupiter Mercury 20 May 1825	6-Dec-1825, delivered controversial State of Union speech.
Jupiter Moon 05 Feb 1827	17-Mar-1827, closed American ports to British goods; 19-May-1828, signed Tariff of Abominations.
Jupiter Saturn 23 Oct 1828	3-Mar-1829, left White House night before Andrew Jackson inauguration.
Mars **Jupiter** 11 Jul 1836	No events found.

Jupiter as Victor. As Firdaria subperiod ruler, Jupiter timed JQA's witness of the Battle of Bunker Hill, his entry into politics, and some of his key foreign trips. As Firdaria major period ruler, Jupiter timed the Adams-Onis Treaty and the Monroe Doctrine – two of his highlights as Secretary of State – and his Presidential election.

Transits

<u>5-Jul-1790</u>. *tr North Node conj ASC.*
Sworn into practice as lawyer in Boston, 15-Jul-1790.

<u>19-May-1828</u>. *tr Jupiter-rx conj ASC.*
Signed Tariff of Abominations, 19-May.

<u>21-Dec-1831</u>. *tr North Node conj MC.*
Began term in Congress, 5-Dec-1831.

Primary Directions

| REG | D | Saturn/Leo | P | MC d. => Mars (0) | 8-Jun-1774 |

Intolerable Acts, Quartering Act, 2-Jun-1774.
Note: In earlier editions, I mistakenly listed this direction as timing JQA's witness of the Battle of Bunker Hill the following year. However, there was sufficient upheaval in Boston during 1774 for this direction to be a delineation match.

| REG | D | Jupiter/Aquarius | P | IC d. => Moon (MO) | 2-Aug-1790 |

Mother opposed romance with Mary Frazier, early August.

Primary Direction Sequences

The following sequences timed key events in the Adams-Onis Treaty which secured Florida from the Spanish and the Panic of 1819.

| PT | D | Mercury/Sagittarius | P | sin sq Jupiter (JU) d. => ASC | 1-Oct-1818 |
| PT | D | Mercury/Sagittarius | P | sin sq Jupiter (0) d. => ASC | 31-Dec-1819 |

| REG | D | Jupiter/Virgo | P | Jupiter (0) d. => Sun | 23-May-1820 |
| REG | D | Jupiter/Virgo | P | Jupiter (JU) d. => Sun | 14-Mar-1821 |

| PT | D | Mars/Scorpio | P | ASC d. => Jupiter (JU) | 22-Jun-1818 |
| REG | D | Mars/Scorpio | P | ASC d. => Jupiter (JU) | 7-Apr-1821 |

Panic of 1819. The 11th house of the king's money, or nation's currency, contains both Venus and Jupiter in Virgo, the sign of their detriment. Lord Mercury is doubly afflicted by the conjunction to Mars and the South Node. For Adams, 11th house affairs are weak. Jupiter in Virgo in the 11th is delineated as a rabid overexpansion of currency by both state-run banks and the Second Bank of the United States. Lord Mercury, afflicted in gold's sign of Leo, shows that unstable gold contracts underlie the banking system, making it extremely vulnerable to disruptions. When it is learned the Panic of

1819 was caused by multiple factors including (1) the overexpansion of business/credit during the post War of 1812 *Era of Good Feelings* during Monroe's first term, (2) the requirement that the Bank of the United States (BUS) repay its foreign loans granted to fund the Louisiana Purchase in gold specie, (3) the subsequent deflationary forced loan liquidation policies of the BUS necessary to shrink their outstanding loans in concert with an outflow of gold, and (4) the negative impact of these deflationary policies on the nation's business activity, all the pieces fall into place. The influence of Jupiter/Virgo on the overexpansion of business and credit can be traced to its placement in Thomas Jefferson's 4th house as a signature for the Louisiana Purchase itself. The BUS's payment of gold specie to foreign governments to settle loans matches Mercury/Leo's placement in the 10th house of the King. That Mercury is afflicted shows the resulting instability to the banking system as gold is sent abroad to European governmental lenders. The first Jupiter-Ascendant sequence timed the most severe effects of the panic with settlement of the Louisiana Purchase in specie on 21-Oct-1818 one fundamental trigger for a deflationary crash. The final Jupiter-Ascendant sequence timed the full range of the panic with silver moving to a premium in Jun-1818 as the sequence started and passage of a debt relief bill on 28-Feb-1821 as the sequence closed. Ammon (1971) is a good source for the Panic of 1819.

Florida/Andrew Jackson. John Quincy Adams was a strong proponent of Andrew Jackson's unauthorized military activities in Florida. They culminated with the expulsion of the Spanish governor and soldiers after Jackson's 24-May-1818 attack on Pensacola. The third set of Jupiter directions opens at a time when Jackson's escapades forced the Monroe administration to deal with a potentially explosive foreign policy crisis. See that Jupiter/Virgo in JQA's 11th house of alliances is replicated by Jupiter/Virgo in Andrew Jackson's 5th house of diplomacy. Jupiter/Virgo can be read as Andrew Jackson in JQA's figure. This is confirmed by Monroe's appointment of Jackson as Governor of the territory of Florida on 15-Apr-1821, a match to the final direction.

Florida/Adams-Onis Treaty. Adams' first treaty for the acquisition of Florida from Spain on 22-Feb-1819 was mired in technical problems which were not solved until a mid-1820 Spanish Revolution produced a change in political winds. The final treaty was ratified by the Senate on 22-Feb-1821; the entire period matches the 2nd Jupiter-Sun sequence.

| REG | D | Saturn/Gemini | P | Saturn (SA) d. => LOF | 6-Jan-1827 |
| REG | D | Saturn/Gemini | P | Saturn (0) d. => LOF | 10-Mar-1828 |

LOCK Timed events leading to the Tariff of Abominations. Saturn/Gemini/8th regulates business ventures by the imposition of high fees/tariffs on 8th house traded goods. The first protectionist bill was introduced on 10-Jan-1827; debate on competing proposals began on 4-Mar-1828.

Longevity, 80y 7m 14d

Death: 23-Feb-1848, 7:15 PM. Adams collapsed while rising to make a speech in Congress on 21-Feb-1848; he went into a coma and died two days later in a small room located off the main floor of the House of Representatives. Adam's death was preceded by a significant stroke on 20-Nov-1847. While the 1847 incident did not kill him, Adams himself stated that from that day, "I date my decrease and consider myself for being for every useful purpose to myself and to my fellow creatures as dead."

Prior ARM editions selected Jupiter as al-kadukhadāh with Jupiter as bound lord of the Sun. Recent research favors the SAN as hīlāj when the hīlāj is an eclipse. For these cases the bound lord of the eclipse degree tests well as the al-kadukhadāh.

Hīlāj: **SAN**. JQA was born 14-15 hours following a lunar eclipse.

Al-kadukhadāh: **Venus**. The SAN 18CP58 is placed in the bound of Venus.

Venus grants 82 major years.

Victor of the Horoscope: **Mars**

Killing Planet: **Mercury (47), Saturn (36)**

Arcus Vitae:

PT	D	Mars/Scorpio	P	ASC d. => Merc **(ME)**	**22-Nov-1847**
PT	D	Mars/Scorpio	P	ASC d. => Merc (0)	21-Mar-1848

First stroke, 20-Nov-1847.

REG	D	Mars/Scorpio	P	ASC c. => Moon (0)	20-Sep-1847
REG	D	Mars/Scorpio	P	ASC c. => Moon **(MO)**	**23-Feb-1848**

Second stroke, 21-Feb-1848.
Death, 23-Feb-1848.

Note for primary directions students: the significator computed using its full latitude is the more accurate direction for each pair. Anecdotally I am seeing more evidence that planetary significators should be computed using their full latitude, especially the Moon.

D	Changeover	bound Mars/Aries d. => SAN (full latitude)	**3-Mar-1848**

This is one of the few examples where I have seen the SAN yield a longevity measurement using Directing the Bounds.

1847 Solar Return for year of Death

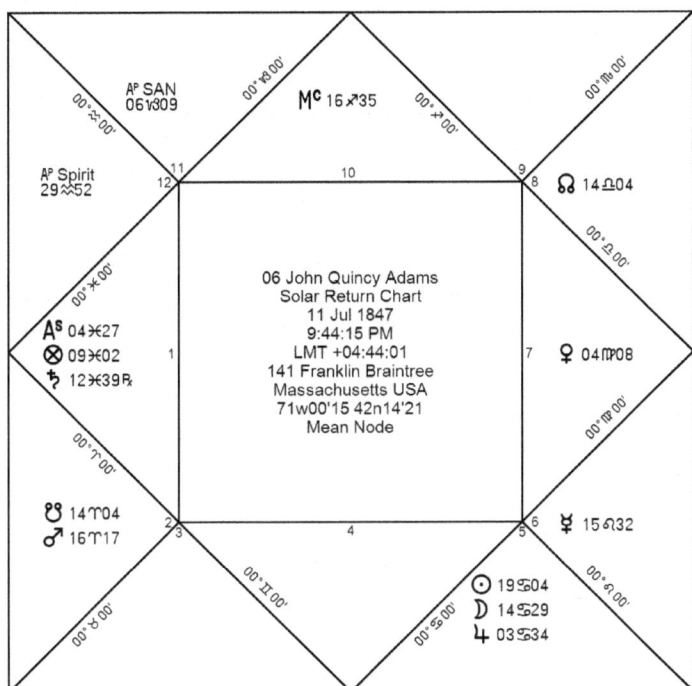

Ascendant Distributor: Venus/Capricorn since 25-Sep-1847
Profected Ascendant: 6CA48, 9th House; SR Victor: Venus
Lords: LOY – Moon; LOP – Sun
Firdaria: Jupiter - Moon
Moon: separates from trine of Saturn and applies to square of Mars.
Return Ascendant falls in natal 5th.

This return's Moon is very weak. The Moon is configured with both malefics by aspect, is square the Nodes, and is in the waning 4th quarter combust the Sun. The Moon's debilities are destructive to Adams this year because Moon is LOY and Firdaria subperiod ruler.

While the solar return Ascendant directions did not time death, the return's directed Moon did yield this precise direction for death:

REG	D	Jupiter/Pisces	P	Saturn (SA) d. => Moon (MO)	223deg 37min

Death on 23-Feb-1848: 226.9 days or 223deg 39min following his return.

444 · A RECTIFICATION MANUAL

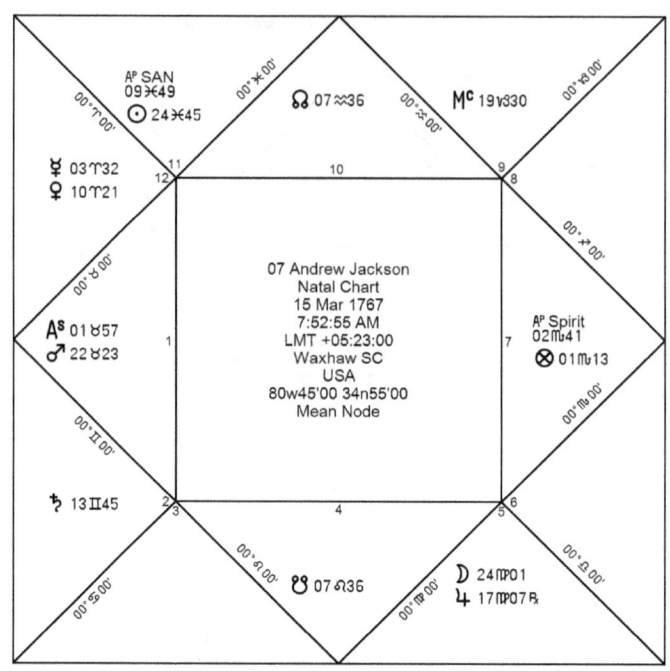

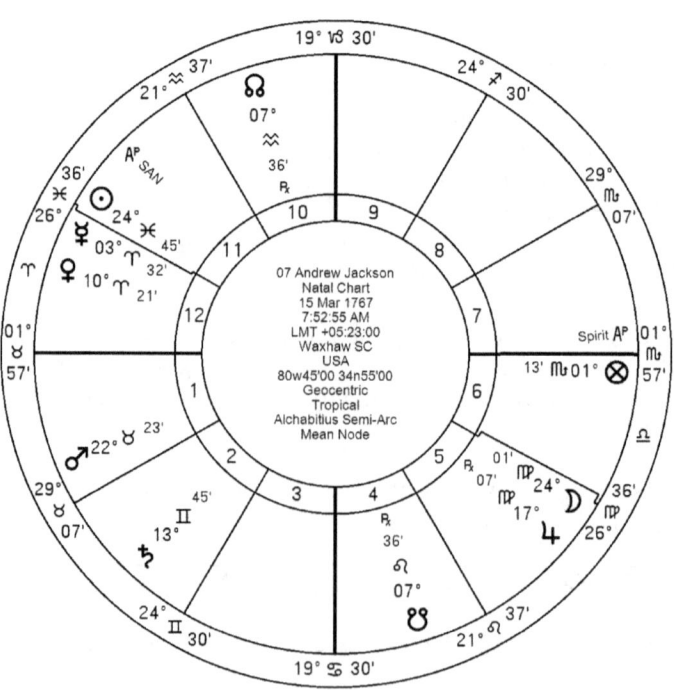

7. ANDREW JACKSON

Moon's Configuration

Moon separates from **Mars** and applies to the **Sun**, diurnal, conjunctional. Prenatal syzygy is 9PI49. Eclipse? No.

Cognitive Assessment Model (Rulers of Moon and Mercury)

Sign rulers: **Mercury, Mars**
Bound rulers: **Mars, Jupiter**

Victor Soul Models

Ibn Ezra Victor Model (1507), in-sect triplicity ruler, triplicity decans.

	Position	☉	☽	☿	♀	♂	♃	♄
Sun	24 PI 45				7	3	5	
Moon	24 VI 01			9	4	2		
Asc	01 TA 57		4		11			
Pars Fortuna	01 SC 14				3	8		
Syzygy	09 PI 49				9		6	
Oriental						0	0	0
Houses		2	1	2	2	12	7	6
Score		0	2	5	11	**36**	25	18	6

Porphyry's Expanded Victor Model (2022)

Mars rules Lots of Fortune and Spirit by sign; both luminaries and both lots again by bound. Sect: out-of-favor. Solar phase: occidental sextile to sinking. Position: Angular in ASC, 7th from LOF and LOS. Dignity: participating triplicity. Debility: detriment. Generosity with Venus. Moon's separation.

Victor Table for Killing Planets

			☉	☽	☿	♀	♂	♃	♄
ASC		1TA57		4,3		5,3,2,1	3		
Rul ASC	♀	10AR21	4,3,1			2	5	3	3
L.Death		18LE51	5,3		2			3,1	3
Rul L.Death	☉	24PI45		3		4,3	3,2,1	5	
H8 Cusp		29SC07		3,1		3	5,3		2
Rul H8	♂	22TA23		4,3		5,3	3		2,1
T-Rul H8	♀	10AR21	4,3,1			2	5	3	3
8th from ☉		24LI45			3,1	5,2		3	4,3
Rul 8th fr ☉	♀	10AR21	4,3,1			2	5	3	3
TOTAL			32	21	6	**42**	35	21	24

2007 Proposed Rectification: 7:52:55 AM, ASC 1TA57'35"

Astrodatabank reports a DD-rated birthtime of 7:35:57 AM from *Horoscopes of US Presidents* by Doane with an unverified source. Compared to an Ascendant of 25AR49 for the ADB time, the proposed rectification features a slightly later Ascendant degree in early Taurus which places Ascendant lord Venus/Aries in the 12th. By configuration of the chart, this is a textbook delineation match to torture during imprisonment; in Jackson's case, nearly having his head split in two by a sword-wielding British soldier.

ZRS. LOS 2SC41 in the sign and bound of Mars makes Jackson a tenacious brawler who uses open conflict with enemies (Lord Mars/Taurus in the 1st ruling the 7th) as a method to achieve his spiritual objectives. ZR Highlights: L1-Capricorn timed his Revolutionary War service and start of his legal/political career at the state level. L1-Aquarius elevated Jackson's political career to the national level. His Presidential nomination occurred during an L1-Aquarius – L2-Leo loosing of the bond with Leo 10th from LOF. L1-Pisces witnessed Jackson passing the baton to Martin van Buren.

L1 Sagittarius 15 Mar 1767		
L1 Capricorn 11 Jan 1779		1779, fought for Americans during the revolution; later captured and wounded during captivity as POW.
L2 Cancer 24 Mar 1788	FS	Spring-1788, moved to Jonesborough and obtained license to practice law; 12-Aug-1788, fought duel with Avery, both shots thrown away; 26-Oct-1788, arrived Nashville.
L2 Cancer 11 May 1796	LB	1-Jun-1796, Tennessee statehood signed by George Washington; 1797, elected to US Senate; Apr-1798, resigned senate seat.
L2 Capricorn 29 Jun 1804	CP	24-Jul-1804, resigned as judge; 4-Aug-1804, purchased Hermitage property.
L1 Aquarius 23 Aug 1805		1805/1807, participated in Aaron Burr conspiracy; 30-May-1806, killed Charles Dickinson in duel.
L2 Leo 05 Sep 1814	FS	25-Oct-1814, began invasion of Florida; 8-Jan-1815, won Battle of New Orleans.
L2 Leo 22 Dec 1822	LB	1-Oct-1823, elected to US Senate; 3-Dec-1823, arrived Washington for Senate term; 4-Mar-1825, nominated for President; 16-Mar-1824, President Monroe awarded Medal voted by Congress for victory at New Orleans.
L2 Sagittarius 25 Jan 1828		End-1828, elected President.
L2 Aquarius 09 Apr 1831	CP	24-Mar-1832, Creek Indian tribe removal agreement; 6-Apr-1832, Black Hawk War to 2-Aug-1832; 10-Jul-1832, vetoed bank bill; 14-Jul-1832, signed Tariff of 1832; 10-Dec-1832, issued Proclamation to the people of South Carolina; 11-Mar-1833, South Carolina repealed its Nullification Ordinance; 1-Oct-1833, Deposit removal began.
L1 Pisces 19 Mar 1835		May-1835, demanded Martin van Buren's Presidential nomination as self-appointed successor.
L2 Libra 26 Dec 1844		death, 8-Jun-1845.

Firdaria – Mars major and minor periods

Firdaria according to Bonatti	Life Event
Sun **Mars** 09 Oct 1775	
Venus **Mars** 30 Nov 1782	Dec-1782, after British evacuated Charleston, AJ returned to Waxhaw after winning a craps bet for which he risked his horse.
Mercury **Mars** 17 Aug 1792	10-Sep-1792, appointed judge advocate for Davidson County militia.
Moon **Mars** 22 Jan 1802	5-Feb-1802, elected Major General of Tennessee militia; sold Hunter's Hill property; 16-Feb-1802, formed business partnership with Thomas Watson and John Hutchings.
Saturn **Mars** 06 May 1810	No events found.
Jupiter **Mars** 01 Dec 1819	15-Apr-1821, appointed and confirmed Governor of Florida Territory; 1-Jun-1821, resigned Army Commission.
Mars 7 years Age 63 to 70	
Mars Mars 15 Mar 1830	13-May-1830, initiated break with Calhoun; 28-May-1830, signed Indian Removal bill; 21-Feb-1831, read Calhoun out of the party.
Mars Sun 15 Mar 1831	7-Apr-1831, Cabinet shakeup; Jan-1832, submitted to operation for bullet removal.
Mars Venus 15 Mar 1832	24-Mar-1832, Creek Indian tribe agreed to removal; 6-Apr-1832, Black Hawk War to 2-Aug-1832; 10-Jul-1832, vetoed bank bill; 14-Jul-1832, signed Tariff of 1832; 10-Dec-1832, issued Proclamation to the people of South Carolina; 11-Mar-1833, South Carolina repealed its Nullification Ordinance.
Mars Mercury 15 Mar 1833	6-May-1833, assaulted by Robert Randolph; 26-Jun-1833, notified Treasury to remove deposits in a move away from national banking; Dec/1833-Mar/1834, resisted appeals to restore deposits.
Mars Moon 15 Mar 1834	28-Mar-1834, censured by Senate; 21-Apr-1834, proposed currency and banking reforms; 13-Oct-1834, Hermitage burned; 30-Jan-1835, escaped assassination attempt.
Mars Saturn 15 Mar 1835	29-May-1835 to 15-Jan-1836, diplomatic conflict with France; 18-Dec-1835, Second Seminole War began.
Mars Jupiter 15 Mar 1836	23-Mar-1836, declared Cherokee removal treaty in force; May/Jun-1836, Cherokee Indian Trail of Tears; 23-Jun-1836, signed deposit bill; 11-Jul-1836, signed Specie Circular.

Mars as Victor. Missing major life events from Mars' Firdaria periods are AJ's 8-Jan-1815 victory at the Battle of New Orleans and his Presidential election in the fall of 1828. But Mars' periods do identify AJ's appointment as judge, election as Major General of the Tennessee militia, and his election as Governor of the Florida Territory. The Major Mars period begins one year into AJ's two term Presidency and includes events for which the AJ Presidency is most remembered: Indian removal legislation culminating in the Cherokee Trail of Tears; political split with Calhoun and his cabinet shakeup; South Carolina nullification crisis; and the bank war. Mars/Taurus in generosity with Venus/Aries, both in detriment, is one of the most hostile configurations towards banking that I have observed in all of astrology.

Directing through the Bounds

Date	ASC Distributor	Event
10-Jan-1789	Mercury/Gemini (00GE)	Moved to Nashville a few months prior to start of the Gemini distribution on 26-Oct-1788. Rise of legal career.
8-Jun-1818	Mars/Cancer (00CA)	2-Jun-1818, declared Seminole War over and returned to Tennessee, ending active-duty military career. Note: Mars/Cancer signifies defense of home and property and is not a favored significator for offensive warfare.

Transits

<u>24-Dec-1823</u>. *tr North Node conj MC.*
Arrived in Washington to begin Senatorial duties, 3-Dec-1823.

<u>7-Jul-1833, 13-Oct-1833, and 23-Feb-1834</u>. *tr Jupiter conj ASC.*
This series of transits timed Jackson's decision to move deposits to "Pet Banks" on 26-Jun-1833; the date that deposits started to transfer on 1-Oct-1833; and his resistance to the Senate to restore deposits from Dec-1833 culminating with the Senate's censure on 28-Mar-1834. Jupiter rules both 8th and 11th (WS) and is tied to banking and currency issues.

Solar Arc Directions

<u>26-Jul-1821</u>. *csa MC trine Sun.*
<u>25-Feb-1823</u>. *dsa Sun trine MC.*
Received Florida from Spain after end of Seminole War, 17-Jul-1821.
Nominated for President by Tennessee legislature, 20-Jul-1822.
Declined Mexican post after surge in Presidential bid, 14-Mar-1823.

<u>14-May-1824</u>. *csa Jupiter opposed MC.*
Voted for Tariff of 1824, 13-May-1824.

<u>9-Feb-1825</u>. *csa Mars opposed Moon.*
House of Representatives selected JQA as President, 9-Feb-1825.

<u>15-Apr-1830</u>. *dsa Mars sextile Moon.*
Competing toasts with John C. Calhoun at Jefferson birthday dinner began split with Calhoun, 13-Apr-1830.

<u>12-Jul-1836</u>. dsa *Jupiter trine Sun.*
Signed Specie Circular, 11-Jul-1836.

Primary Directions

PT	D	Jupiter/Taurus	P	sin trine MC d. => VE (VE)	10-Jan-1794

Marriage, 18-Jan-1794.

| PT | D | Venus/Cancer | P | sin square Venus (0) d. => ASC | 24-Jan-1830 |

Asked Cabinet to end conspiracy against Eaton; 25-Jan-1830.

| PT | D | Mars/Pisces | P | Sun d. => MC | 6-Apr-1831 |

LOCK Mass Cabinet resignation as Eaton affair culminated. Sun/Pisces in 11th signifies a Cabinet sacrifice, 6-Apr-1831.

| PT | D | Mars/Pisces | P | opp Moon (MO) d. => MC | 15-Jan-1832 |

Van Buren's English Mission rejected by Senate; 25-Jan-1832.

| REG | D | Jupiter/Cancer | P | sin trine Sun d. => Mars (MA) | 31-Aug-1832 |

Ordered military preparations after SC nullification threats; Sep-1832.

Primary Direction Sequences

| PT | D | Venus/Aries | P | Venus (VE) d. => ASC | 14-Aug-1780 |
| PT | D | Venus/Aries | P | Venus (0) d. => ASC | 4-Sep-1781 |

LOCK This sequence contained most of Jackson's Revolutionary War service beginning with the Battle of Hanging Rock, 1-Aug-1780; his capture and head/hand wounds by British soldiers, Apr-1781; death of his brother Robert of smallpox, ~Apr/May-1781, and death of mother, Autumn 1781. Note ruler of the Ascendant in the 12th house shows Jackson in confinement/jail. Venus/Aries shows the sadistic attack by the British officer which would have split his head had not Jackson broken the blow of the sword with his hand.

| PT | D | Mars/Aquarius | P | dex sq Mars (0) c. => ASC | 1-Jul-1813 |
| PT | D | Mars/Aquarius | P | dex sq Mars (MA) c. => ASC | 26-Jun-1814 |

This sequence contained all the events of the first Creek Indian War starting with the Battle of Burnt Corn on 21-Jul-1813 [Jackson does not participate]. Jackson first led troops against the Creeks on 7-Oct-1813. Numerous engagements followed which culminated with his first major battle victory at Horseshoe Bend, 27-Mar-1814. Sequence also contained mass desertion of troops Nov-1813 // Jan-1814 and the execution of John Woods on 14-Mar-1814. Finally, Jackson was commissioned a major general in the US Army on 28-May-1814.

| PT | D | Jupiter/Scorpio | P | opp Mars (MA) c. => MC | 5-Feb-1828 |
| PT | D | Jupiter/Scorpio | P | opp Mars (0) c. => MC | 8-May-1828 |

LOCK This sequence timed the climax of the Tariff of Abominations which John Quincy Adams signed into law as an act of spite against Congress. On 31-Jan-1828 Jacksonian forces introduced high tariff proposals; Adams signed the legislation on 19-May-1828.

Longevity, 78y 2m 24d

Death: 8-Jun-1845, about 6:00 p.m. Hermitage, Nashville, at home. Jackson died from tuberculosis but suffered from other illnesses. Death was expected.

Hīlāj: **SAN**. Chart is diurnal and Sun in the 11th qualifies yet is questionable when looking at both the quality of and aspects to possible Al-kadukhadah's. This is a problem which runs throughout every possible Hīlāj/Al-kadukhadāh combination. This is a rare figure with the SAN as Hīlāj. Empirical evidence:

| PT | D | Mars/Aquarius | P | dex sq Mars (0) c. => SAN | 16-Feb-1781 |
| PT | D | Mars/Aquarius | P | dex sq Mars (MA) c. => SAN | 3-Nov-1781 |

A prisoner of war, Jackson suffered a head wound from a sword (April 1781), his brother Robert (also in captivity) died of smallpox which Jackson also caught; his mother Elizabeth died in the fall of 1781.

| PT | D | Sat/Taurus | P | dex trine Mars (0) c. => SAN (SAN) | 28-May-1806 |

Duel, 30-May-1806. Left a bullet lodged near his heart for the rest of life.

| PT | D | Venus/Cancer | P | sin trine SAN (SAN) d. => Mars (0) | 24-Feb-1813 |
| PT | D | Venus/Cancer | P | sin trine SAN (SAN) d. => Mars (MA) | 6-Dec-1813 |

Duel, 4-Sep-1813. Shattered left shoulder.

Al-kadukhadāh: **Jupiter**. Jupiter rules both Sun and SAN, aspects both by opposition, and is in his own bound despite in detriment. Jupiter grants 79 major years. Saturn overcomes Jupiter by superior square aspect and deducts 30 years. Net projection is 49 years, or 15-Mar-1816. This followed Jackson's duels and two major battle victories which left him on the verge of physical collapse. Following the 1818 Florida campaign he did not expect to live long and planned on retiring permanently. After Florida, he suffered continuous pain until death.

Victor of the Horoscope: **Mars**

Killing Planets: **Venus (42), Mars (35)**

Arcus Vitae:

| PT | D | Venus/Cancer | P | sin trine SAN (SAN) d. => Venus (VE) | 19-Jan-1845 |
| PT | D | Venus/Cancer | P | sin trine SAN (SAN) d. => Venus (0) | 1-Mar-1846 |

Death, 8-Jun-1845.

Also: Consider the role of Venus as killing planet in solar returns for 1781, 1806, 1813, and 1845. In each return Venus makes her Pisces Ingress, same sign as the SAN (9PI49) with positions in both 1813 and 1845 returns (8PI48 in both cases) within a degree of the natal SAN itself.

1845 Solar Return for year of Death

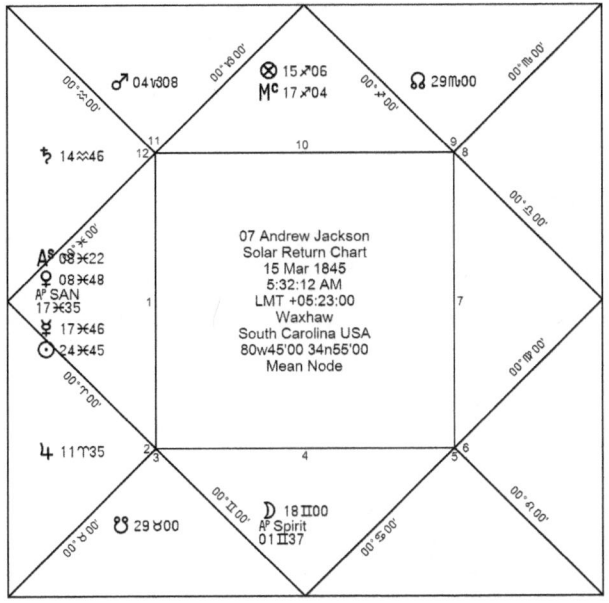

Ascendant Distributor: Jupiter/Cancer since 3-Mar-1840
Profected Ascendant: 1SC57, 7th House; SR Victor: Venus
Lords: LOY – Mars; LOP – Mercury
Firdaria: Major – Sun; Subperiod – Mercury
Moon separates from square of Mercury and applies to square of Sun
Return Ascendant falls in natal 11th ; natal Ascendant falls in return's 3rd.

High scoring killing planet Venus is partile conjunct the return's Ascendant. Venus rules the 8th of death in the return. Secondary killer Mars squares the Sun's antiscia within 2 degrees. Both killing planets afflict either the Sun or Ascendant. The return's Ascendant falls only 1 degree away from natal SAN.

Compared to death on 8-Jun-1856, the closest Venus-ASC direction is early by three weeks.

| PT | D | Jupiter/Gemini | P | sin square Venus (0) d. => ASC | 20-May-1845 |

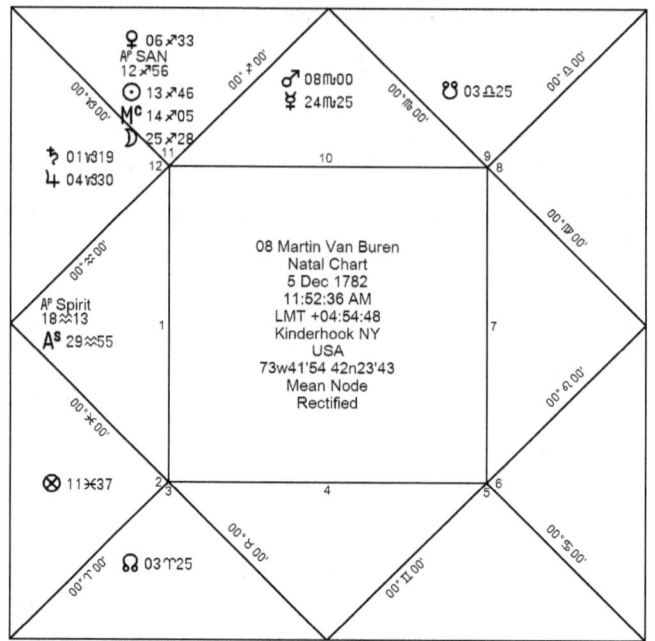

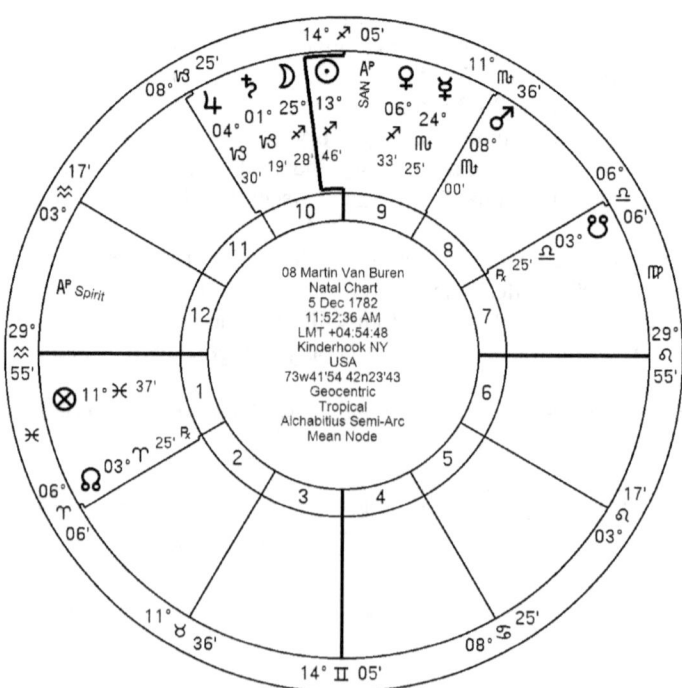

8. MARTIN VAN BUREN

Moon's Configuration

Moon separates from the **Sun** and is **VOC** (Medieval) or applies to **Saturn** (Hellenistic). Prenatal syzygy is 12SA56. Eclipse? No.

Cognitive Assessment Model (Rulers of Moon and Mercury)

Sign rulers: **Jupiter, Mars**
Bound rulers: **Saturn** (both)

Victor Soul Models

Ibn Ezra Victor Model (1507), in-sect triplicity ruler, triplicity decans.

	Position	☉	☽	☿	♀	♂	♃	♄
Sun	13 SA 46	3	1		2		5	
Moon	25 SA 28	3					5	3
Asc	29 AQ 55		1					10
Pars Fortuna	11 PI 37				9		6	
Syzygy	12 SA 56	3	1		2		5	
Oriental						3	0	0
Houses		11	11	4	4	4	8	11
Score	0	20	14	4	17	7	**29**	24

Porphyry's Expanded Victor Model (2022)

Jupiter rules the MC, Sun, Moon, LOF and Syzygy by sign; rules the Lot of Spirit by bound. Sect: of favor. Solar phase: occidental sextile to sinking. Debility: fall. At the bending of the Nodes.

Victor Table for Killing Planets

			☉	☽	☿	♀	♂	♃	♄
ASC		29AQ55			3	1		3	5,3,2
Rul ASC	♄	1CP19		3	2	3	4,3		5,1
L.Death		11LI57			3,2	5		3	4,3,1
Rul L.Death	♀	6SA33	3					5,3,2,1	3
H8 Cusp		6LI06			3,2	5,1		3	4,3
Rul H8	♀	6SA33	3					5,3,2,1	3
T-Rul H8	♄	1CP19		3	2	3	4,3		5,1
8th from ☉		13CA46		5,3	2	3	3,1	4	
Rul 8th fr ☉	☽	25SA28	3,1					5,3	3,2
TOTAL			10	14	19	21	18	**43**	**48**

2007 Proposed Rectification: 11:52:36 AM, ASC 29AQ55'57"
2022 Proposed Rectification: 11:52:36 AM, ASC 29AQ55'59"

Astrodatabank reports an X-rated date without time. Doane's rectification of 7:28:12 AM is unsourced. By configuration of the chart, the most important element that supports the proposed rectification is placement of the Jupiter/Saturn conjunction in Capricorn in the 12th whole sign house. Capricorn signifies both Federalist and Whig parties. Politically, MVB is known for his alliance with Andrew Jackson and his role in creating the Democratic Party from the ashes of Jefferson's Democratic-Republican Party. If Capricorn is the enemy, then MVB's Sagittarius stellium in the 11th whole sign house of political alliances (10th quadrant house) shows the way forward with a new political regime. This change is best shown with ZRS. L1-Gemini, angular from LOF, timed MVB's most active political period. L2-Sagittarius (foreshadowing) timed creation of the Democratic Party and L2-Sagittarius (loosing of the bond) timed his Presidential Nomination. Sagittarius is 10th from the Lot of Fortune, the predicted peak period using ZR methodology.

L1 Pisces 05 Dec 1782		
L1 Aries 03 Oct 1794		1796, became law clerk; 1798, switched political affiliation from Federalist to Democratic-Republican party; 1805-1806, became active in local Kinderhook politics; 20-Feb-1808, appointed to first public office, surrogate of Columbia County.
L1 Taurus 17 Jul 1809		Increased political reach from Kinderhook to NY State; Apr-1812, elected NY State Senate; 4-Jul-1812, began term in NY State Senate; 17-Feb-1815, appointed NY State Attorney General, still holding senate seat; Apr-1816, moved to Albany and formed "Albany Regency" informally known as the Bucktails.
L1 Gemini 05 Jun 1817		Period is defined by MVB's creation of the new Democratic party out the embers of Jefferson's Democratic-Republican Party; 1817-1824, period marked by rivalry with NY Governor DeWitt Clinton.
L2 Sagittarius 20 Mar 1826	FS	26-Sep-1827, committed the Bucktails and the Regency to Andrew Jackson which some historians argue is the official beginning of the Democratic Party.
L2 Sagittarius 04 Oct 1834	LB	20/22-May-1835, Nominated for President.
L1 Cancer 20 Feb 1837		4-Mar-1837, Presidential Inauguration
L2 Capricorn 09 Apr 1845	FS	8-Aug-1845, Wilmot Proviso introduced banning the extension of slavery into territory acquired in the Mexican War; MVB eventually took the anti-slavery position with his April-1848 'Barnburner Manifesto' but was unsuccessful as Presidential candidate for the Free Soil Party.
L2 Capricorn 21 Jun 1854	LB	21-Jun-1854, began work on his autobiography while vacationing in Sorrento, Italy. He never finished the book but it was published in 1920 and is widely read today by scholars.
L1 Leo 12 Oct 1861		24-Jul-1862, Death.

Firdaria – Jupiter Major and Minor periods

Firdaria according to Bonatti	Life Event
Sun **Jupiter** 26 Jan 1790	No events found.
Venus **Jupiter** 01 Jul 1797	1798 (no date), defected from the Federalist Party to the Jeffersonian-Democrats.
Mercury **Jupiter** 02 Jul 1806	21-Feb-1807, married Hannah Hoes; 20-Feb-1808, appointed to 1st public office.
Moon **Jupiter** 02 Jul 1816	(No specific date), formed 'Albany Regency' party, also known as the Bucktails; Apr-1817, campaigned against DeWitt Clinton's NY Gubernatorial race.
Saturn **Jupiter** 02 Jul 1824	2-Nov-1824, opponent DeWitt Clinton elected Governor of NY; 9-Feb-1825, John Quincy Adams selected President; MVB had backed the unsuccessful candidate William Crawford.
Jupiter 12 years Age 51 to 63	
Jupiter Jupiter 05 Dec 1833	16-Dec-1833, presided over Senate for 1st time; 28-Mar-1834, Senate censures AJ over BUS deposit removal; Apr-1834, Henry Clay formed the Whig Party; 20/22-May-1835, nominated for President.
Jupiter Mars 23 Aug 1835	23-Jun-1836, Deposit Act adopted; 11-Jul-1836, AJ issued Specie Circular; 7-Dec-1836, elected President, 13-Feb-1837, NYC Flour Riot; 10-May-1837, Panic of 1837 began with banks suspending gold convertibility.
Jupiter Sun 11 May 1837	5-Sep-1837, Special Message to Congress on creating specie backed currency and an Independent Treasury system to counter the depression; 5-Jan-1838, issued 1st Neutrality Proclamation on Canadian border violence; 21-Nov-1838, issued 2nd Neutrality Proclamation.
Jupiter Venus 27 Jan 1839	12-Feb-1839, Aroostook War broke out in Maine; 24-Aug-1839, slave ship Amistad seized off Long Island; 14-Apr-1840, mocked for spending and tastes which hurt reputation; 5-May-1840, renominated for President by Democratic Party; 4-Jul-1840, Independent Treasury Act signed into law.
Jupiter Mercury 14 Oct 1840	Oct/Dec-1840, lost election to WHH; 13-Mar-1841, left Washington DC; Feb/May-1842, made extensive trip through Southern states; 13-Aug-1841, Whigs repealed the Independent Treasury act.
Jupiter Moon 02 Jul 1842	28-Jul-1842, returned home; Nov-1842, Democrats gained control of Congress.
Jupiter Saturn 19 Mar 1844	27-Apr-1844, wrote newspaper letter opposing Texas annexation; 27-May-1844, James Polk nominated as Democratic Presidential candidate; Aug-1845, declined appointment as minister to Britain.
Mars **Jupiter** 06 Dec 1851	Nov-1852, returned to Democratic Party and supported Franklin Pierce for President.

Transits

<u>20-Nov-1821</u>. *tr North Node conj ASC*.
Arrived Washington DC to take up Senate seat, 5-Nov-1821.

<u>2-Jul-1840</u>. *tr North Node conj ASC*.
Independent Treasury Act, 4-Jul-1840.

<u>3-Jun-1844</u>. *tr North Node conj MC*.
Democratic Convention convened. James Polk received nomination after MVB failed to win two-thirds of the delegates, 29-May-1844.

Solar Arc Directions

<u>14-May-1837</u>. *dsa Jupiter conj. ASC*.
<u>25-Jan-1838</u>. *csa ASC conj Jupiter*.
Panic of 1837 on 10-May spurred MVB to call special session of Congress, 15-May-1837. No specific event for 2nd direction but NY bankers announced on 17-Apr-1838 they would resume specie payments in May-1838. At a minimum, the time during this solar arc pair coincided with the harshest initial phase of the Panic of 1837 and its aftermath.

<u>4-Jul-1840</u>. *dsa Saturn conj. ASC*.
<u>14-Apr-1841</u>. *csa ASC conj Saturn*.
Independent Treasury Act, 4-Jul-1840.
Departed Washington after Harrison Inauguration, 13-Mar-1841.
Death of President Harrison, 4-Apr-1841.
Whig party repealed the Independent Treasury Act, 13-Aug-1841.

Primary Directions

| PT | D | Venus/Taurus | P | sin trine Saturn (SA) d. => ASC | 12-Apr-1817 |

Death of father, 8 April.

| REG | D | Jupiter/Aquarius | P | sin sextile MC d. => Saturn (SA) | 2-Dec-1824 |

Disputed election between Jackson and Adams. Saturn/Capricorn/12th signifies the pro-bank & pro-internal improvement Federalist Party as a secret enemy.

| PT | D | Saturn/Taurus | P | opp Mercury (ME) d. => ASC | 27-Aug-1831 |

MVB sailed to England on 16-Aug-1831 for his appointment as minister. Mercury falls in the 9th of travel by QS; alternatively Mercury rules the 5th of emissaries by WS.

Primary Direction Sequences

| REG | D | Venus/Sagittarius | P | Sun d. => Mars (MA) | 28-Oct-1812 |
| REG | D | Venus/Sagittarius | P | Sun d. => Mars (0) | 26-May-1813 |

LOCK This sequence followed MVB's election to the NY State Senate and timed MVB's hawkish war sentiment. It also timed struggles faced by then President James Madison with major losses at Niagara Falls (13-Oct/ 28-Nov) and at the Battle of Queenstown Heights (13-Oct) as the sequence began. As the sequence concluded, Britain extended their naval blockade to cover additional states on 26-May. Mars/Scorpio/9th (QS) signifies naval warfare with foreign parties.

| REG | D | Venus/Sagittarius | P | MC d. => Mars (MA) | 20-Feb-1813 |
| REG | D | Venus/Sagittarius | P | MC d. => Mars (0) | 18-Sep-1813 |

LOCK Like the prior sequence this direction timed MVB's war radicalization which eventually led to the passage of his conscription bill in the NY legislature during Sep-1814. Also like the prior sequence, these directions timed key events in the war. On 22-Feb, the British captured Ogdensburg in retaliation for the US raid on Brockville on 6-Feb. Retaliation matches the revengefulness of Mars in Scorpio. The end of the sequence timed two successful US military victories: Perry's famous naval victory of 10-Sep and the Battle of Thames River on 5-Oct when the Indian Chief Tecumseh was killed. Mars in the water sign of Scorpio signifies naval warfare and matches Perry's win at sea.

| PT | D | Venus/Sagittarius | P | Moon (MO) c. => ASC | 12-Apr-1831 |
| PT | D | Venus/Sagittarius | P | Moon (0) c. => ASC | 6-May-1837 |

LOCK On 7-Apr-1831 Secretary of War John Eaton resigned from Andrew Jackson's cabinet, triggering one of the most complete cabinet reshuffles in American history. By April 8 all but one cabinet member remained. Moon in 11th (WS) signifies a change in the President's cabinet generally. Jupiter rules the Moon and is conjunct the Moon by antiscia. Jupiter signifies Secretary of War Eaton and Moon signifies his wife Peggy O'Neale. The cabinet shakeup is triggered by Peggy O'Neale's previous adulterous activity which Washington society considered scandalous. Most of the cabinet could not abide Eaton because of his marriage to this woman. Van Buren saw this issue as a weakness in Jackson's cabinet and offered to resign, yet Eaton beat him to the punch. The 11th house also signifies currency (King's money) and on 10-May-1837 banks suspended specie payment in response to the Panic of 1837. Jupiter is also involved in this event, conjunct the ASC by solar arc direction (see above); here Jupiter/Capricorn/12th signifies fraudulent and corrupt lending practices which grew directly from Andrew Jackson's banking policies.

Longevity, 79y 7m 17d

Death: 24-Jul-1862, ~2:00 AM, Lindenwald estate, Kinderhook, NY. Martin Van Buren died of a heart attack at home in the company of his sons. He had suffered from an attack of bronchial asthma in recent months and was weak.

Hīlāj: **Sun**. Figure is diurnal. Sun is preferred and qualifies in the 10th/11th.

Al-kadukhadāh: **Sun**. Sun within one degree of the MC qualifies the Sun as Al-kadukhadāh. Sun grants 120 major years, malefics are in aversion and cannot deduct years, Venus is co-present and receives the Sun and adds 8 minor years for a net projection of 128 yrs. Clearly the criteria of Sun conjunct the MC degree as al-kadukhadāh does not work in this case.

Venus. As the Sun's bound lord, allow Venus to grant 82 major years which is a close fit to actual longevity. Note that MVB was born slightly after a new Moon with Venus also the bound lord of the SAN degree 12SA56. Further, note that Venus is 10th from the Lot of Fortune 11PI37 which is also placed in the bound of Venus. These are important testimonies for Venus.

Jupiter as Victor of the Horoscope is also possible given MVB lived only 7 months after Jupiter's 79 major years. If so, neither Saturn co-present or Mars in a sextile aspect with reception by exaltation reduces years.

Victor of the Horoscope: **Jupiter (primary), Venus (alternate).**

Killing Planets: **Saturn (48), Jupiter (43)**

Arcus Vitae:

| PT | D | Saturn/Aquarius | P | ASC d. => Sun | 14-Aug-1862 |

Death, 24-Jul-1862, error = 21 days.

This is an example of Hīlāj-Ascendant directions which kill.

This direction is echoed in the return with the Sun placed in the 7th in opposition to the return's Ascendant.

Also note csa Saturn 11LI47 conj. Lot of Death at 11LI56, an error of 8 weeks. Saturn is the high scoring killing planet.

Consider also the role of South Node as a killer for its position close to the 8th cusp by Alchabitius houses in the natal horoscope. For the 1862 solar return, the North Node appears in the 8th house and at time of death the North Node 23SA15 has just transited the Moon 25SA28 and applies to the Sun 13SA46.

1861 Solar Return for year of Death

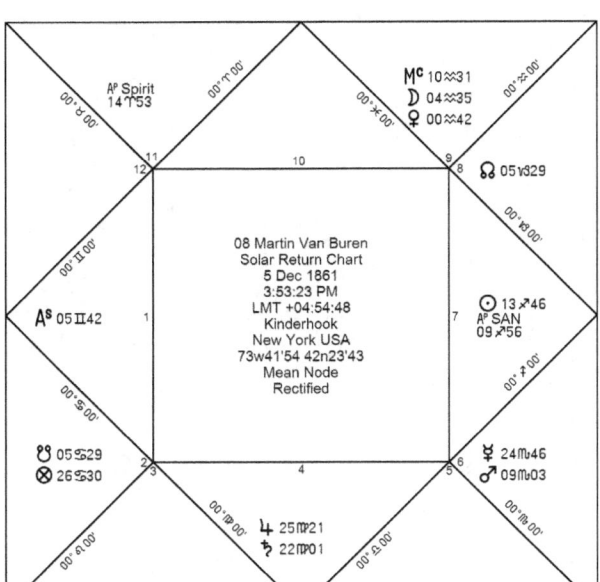

Ascendant Distributor: Saturn/Gemini since 17-Jun-1860.
Profected Ascendant: 29VI55, 8th House; SR Victor: Jupiter
Lords: LOY – Mercury, LOP – Mars
Firdaria: Major – Sun; Subperiod – Moon
Moon separates from conjunction of Venus to square of Mars
Return Ascendant falls in natal 3rd; Natal Ascendant falls in return's 9th.

Death occurs in an 8th house profected year. Both LOY Mercury and LOP Mars make returns to their natal positions, increasing their power to act, and fall in the return's 6th house of illness. Mercury is also ruler of the return's Ascendant in Gemini, the sign of the lungs. Mercury ruling the 1st (lungs) in the 6th (illness) is consistent with Van Buren's asthma problems. Asthma is also indicated by the directed Ascendant in the bound of Saturn/Gemini.

High scoring killing planets Jupiter and Saturn fall in the natal 4th of end-of-life and the Hīlāj Sun falls in the angle of the West.

| PT | D | Venus/Sagittarius | P | Sun d. => ASC | 28-Jul-1862 |

The solar return Ascendant direction is four days late. It does recapitulate the natal arcus vitae primary direction.

460 — A RECTIFICATION MANUAL

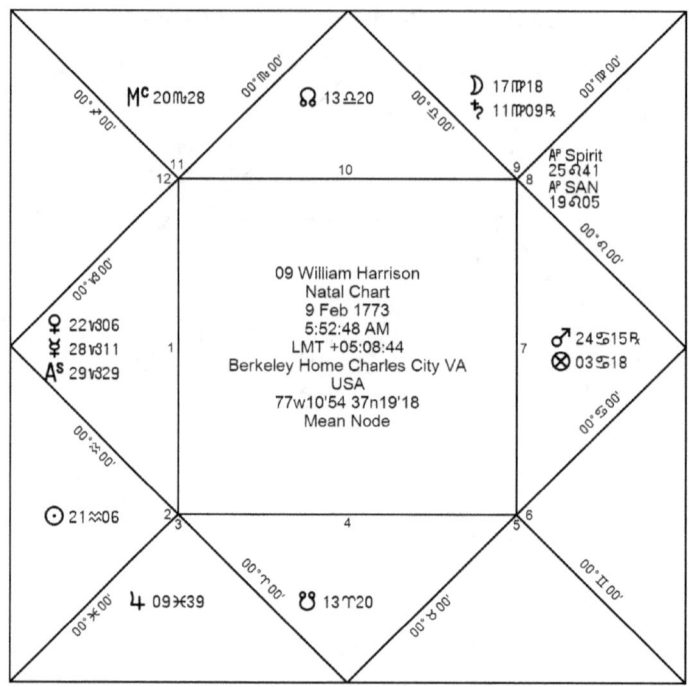

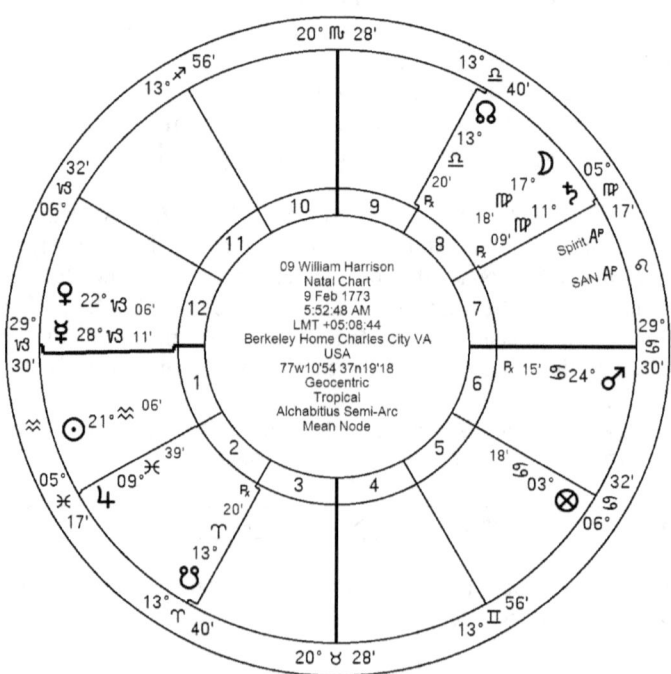

9. WILLIAM HARRISON

Moon's configuration

Moon separates from **Saturn** and applies to **Venus**, nocturnal, preventional. Prenatal syzygy is 19LE05. Eclipse? No.

Cognitive Assessment Model (Rulers of Moon and Mercury)

Sign rulers: **Mercury, Saturn**
Bound rulers: **Jupiter, Mars**

Victor Soul Models

Ibn Ezra Victor Model (1507), in-sect triplicity ruler, triplicity decans.

	Position	☉	☽	☿	♀	♂	♃	♄
Sun	21 AQ 06			3	1	2		5
Moon	17 VI 18		3	9			2	1
Asc	29 CP 29		3	1		6		5
Pars Fortuna	03 CA 17		6			5	4	
Syzygy	19 LE 05	5			2			4
Oriental						0	0	1
Houses		12	5	12	2	1	6	5
Score	0	17	17	27	3	14	16	17

Porphyry's Expanded Victor Model (2022)

Mars rules the MC by sign; the ASC, Sun, Lot of Fortune and Lot of Spirit by bound. Sect: of favor. Solar phase: occidental opposition to 2nd station. Position. 7th from ASC, co-present with Lot of Fortune. Dignity: nocturnal triplicity. Debility: fall.

Victor Table for Killing Planets

			☉	☽	☿	♀	♂	♃	♄
ASC		29CP29		3	1	3	4,3,2		5
Rul ASC	♄	11VI09		3	5,4	3,2	3		1
L.Death		29LE08	5,3				2,1	3	3
Rul L.Death	☉	21AQ06			3	1	2	3	5,3
H8 Cusp		5VI16		3	5,4,2,1	3	3		
Rul H8	☿	28CP11		3	1	3	4,3,2		5
T-Rul H8	☽	17VI20		3	5,4	3	3	2	1
8th from ☽		17AR20	4,3,1		2		5	3	3
Rul 8th fr ☽	♂	24CA15		5,3		3	3	4,2,1	
TOTAL			16	23	37	21	40	18	26

2007 Proposed Rectification: 5:52:47 AM, ASC 29CP29'58"

Astrodatabank reports a DD-rated conflicting/unverified birth time of 10:38:52 AM from Doane's *Horoscopes of US Presidents*.

Given the duration of his Presidency was a single month, Harrison's contribution to American history stems from his role as Indiana territorial governor and military general in battles against Native Americans roughly between the Louisiana Purchase and the War of 1812. As a Stage I rectification tool, match of the major Mars Firdaria period (1805-1812) to WHH's active military career favors the nocturnal Firdaria series.

Lot of Spirit 25LE41 in the bound of Mars/Leo grants Harrison a martial spirit reinforced by Mars/Cancer-rx as the victor of the horoscope.

ZRS. LOF 3CA17 makes the cardinal signs angular from Lot of Fortune. Cardinal signs are loaded with Aries/South Node; Cancer/Mars; Libra/North Node; and Capricorn Mercury/Venus. This is a grand square in cardinal signs. L1-Libra brings forth WHH's military victories against the Native American prophet Tenskwatawa at the Battle of Tippecanoe on 7-Nov-1811 and his older brother Tecumseh at the Battle of the Thames on 5-Oct-1813.

Mutable signs are cadent from LOF. See that during L1-Sagittarius WHH loses the Presidential election as the Anti-Masonic Party candidate against Martin Van Buren. This shows consistency of ZR across both MVB and WHH's horoscopes: MVB's horoscope has a Sagittarius stellium which is 10th from LOF – MVB won the Presidency under a Sagittarius ZR period in his own horoscope. WHH loses to MVB under a Sagittarius ZR period in his own horoscope. When WHH advances to L2-Aries, a cardinal sign, he wins the election but dies in office after a month. South Node in Aries (10th from LOF) shows WHH's bad outcome.

L1 Virgo 02 Nov 1791		
L2 Pisces 14 Jan 1801	FS	[4 Days before start of period] 10-Jan-1801, sworn in as Governor in territorial capital at Vincennes.
L2 Pisces 03 Mar 1809	LB	30-Sep-1809, concluded Treaty of Fort Wayne where tribes sold 3 million acres to US; condemned by Tecumseh.
L1 Libra 21 Jul 1811		27-Jul-1811, another meeting between Tecumseh and WHH; 7-Nov-1811, Battle of Tippecanoe, WHH victory.
L1 Scorpio 09 Jun 1819		Overall difficult period for political fortunes and personal finance.
L1 Sagittarius 22 Mar 1834		16-Dec-1835, nominated for President by Anti-Masonic Party; 7-Dec-1836, lost election to Martin Van Buren; 6-Dec-1839, nominated for President by the Whig Party.
L2 Aries 15 Nov 1840		2-Dec-1840, officially declared President by Electoral College; 4-Mar-1841, inauguration; 4-Apr-1841, death.

Firdaria – Mars major and minor periods

Firdaria according to Bonatti	Life Event
Moon **Mars** 19 Dec 1776	No events found.
Saturn **Mars** 02 Apr 1785	No events found.
Jupiter **Mars** 28 Oct 1794	Feb-1795, General Wayne recommended WHH be promoted to Captain.
Mars 7 years Age 32 to 39	
Mars Mars 09 Feb 1805	29-Jul-1805, delivered 1st Annual Message to Indiana General Assembly; 21-Aug-1805, completed treaty negotiations with four different tribes for land.
Mars Sun 10 Feb 1806	16-Jun-1806, Solar Eclipse predicted by the Prophet, brother of Tecumseh, convinced many of the Prophet's power.
Mars Venus 10 Feb 1807	1807/1808, continued as Governor of Indiana Territory; opposed movement to divide territory into two parts, Indiana and Illinois.
Mars Mercury 10 Feb 1808	3-Feb-1809, bill to carve out Illinois from Indiana Territory passed Congress; WHH opposed.
Mars Moon 09 Feb 1809	30-Sep-1809, concluded Treaty of Fort Wayne whereby several tribes sold 3 million acres to the US, southern Indiana region; condemned by Tecumseh.
Mars Saturn 10 Feb 1810	12-Aug-1810, In an agitated state, Tecumseh met with WHH at Vincennes; WHH avoided immediate conflict by calming down Tecumseh.
Mars Jupiter 10 Feb 1811	7-Nov-1811, Battle of Tippecanoe; 18-Dec-1811, President Madison commended WHH on performance in Battle of Tippecanoe.
Sun **Mars** 06 Sep 1825	Senate service.
Venus **Mars** 28 Oct 1832	13-Feb-1833, supported AJ's rejection of South Carolina's nullification; favored of AJ's Force Bill; 4-Jul-1833, Independence Day address - opposed nullification on one side and abolitionism and emancipation through colonization on the other; favored strong central government and internal improvements.

Mars as Victor. WHH's Major Mars period contains the beginning and end of WHH's conflict with Tecumseh culminating with the Battle of Tippecanoe which was used as a tagline in WHH's successful 1840 Presidential campaign: "Tippecanoe and Tyler too."

Transits

6-Nov-1804. *tr North Node conj ASC.*
Signed treaty with Fox and Sauk tribes for land in region now known as Wisconsin, 3 November.

8-Nov-1811. *tr Mars conj ASC.*
Battle of Tippecanoe, 7-Nov-1811.

3-May-1836. *tr South Node conj MC.*
Sent letter outlining positions on distribution, internal improvements, and he Bank of the United States to the *Niles Weekly Register* for publication.

Solar Arc Directions

13-Mar-1791. *csa ASC trine Saturn.*
27-Apr-1791. *dsa Saturn trine ASC.*
Prior to death of father, WHH studied medicine with Dr. Benjamin Rush at the Medical School of Pennsylvania, early 1791.
Saturn = serious study; Virgo = details, medicine, rx = interrupted.
Death of father spurred decision to join Army, 24-Apr-1791.
Saturn is eight signs from the Sun.

6-Apr-1825. *csa Moon conj Mars.*
11-Apr-1826. *dsa Mars conj. Moon.*
Elected US Senate and succeeds AJ as chair of military affairs, Feb-1825.
Death of Daughter Lucy, 7-Apr-1826.

22-Dec-1828. *csa Moon trine MC.*
16-Feb-1830. *dsa MC trine Moon.*
  LOCK Departed for Columbia, 10-Nov-1828.
Returned to New York, 5-Feb-1830.
This solar arc pair forms bookends to travel to Columbia where WHH served as minister to Columbia. Moon/Virgo/9th (WS) = travel.

Primary Directions

| REG | D | Saturn/Pisces | P | sin sex ASC d. => Sun | 30-May-1798 |

LOCK Appointed Land Office Registrar, 1 June.

| REG | D | Saturn/Pisces | P | sin sex Mercury (ME) d. => Sun | 10-Jun-1798 |
| PT | D | Mars/Cancer | P | LOF c. => Mars (MA) | 5-Jul-1798 |

Appt. Secretary of Northwest Territory by President John Adams, 28 June.

| PT | D | Mars/Pisces | P | dex trine Mars (0) d. => ASC | 22-Jul-1811 |

Second confrontation with Tecumseh, 27 July.

| PT | D | Mercury/Pisces | P | opp Moon (BI) d. => Venus (VE) | 20-Dec-1812 |

Requested official investigation into his conduct following charges of profiteering in purchase of supplies in order to clear his name, 20-Dec-1812. Note Venus acts as 12th house planet.

| PT | D | Mars/Aries | P | sin sq Venus (0) d. => ASC | 17-Nov-1828 |

Departed for Columbia, 10-Nov-1828. Venus rules 9th of travel (QS).

| REG | D | Jupiter/Virgo | P | Moon (MO) c. => MC | 23-Aug-1833 |

Birth of grandson Benjamin Harrison and future President of US, 20-Aug-1833. 9th house is grandchildren (5th from 5th). Note his grandson inherits an interest in Latin American affairs, e.g., Venezuelan border dispute.

| REG | D | Saturn/Aries | P | sin sq ASC d. => Mercury (ME) | 27-Dec-1833. |

Large celebration of 45th anniversary of Cincinnati settlement, 26-Dec-1833. A large party which had so much alcohol the subsequent 47th anniversary party was dry. Mercury rules the 5th of pleasure.

Primary Direction Sequences

| REG | D | Jupiter/Scorpio | P | MC d. => Moon (0) | 9-Oct-1817 |
| REG | D | Jupiter/Scorpio | P | MC d. => Moon (MO) | 13-Jul-1819 |

As an 8th house planet (QS), the Moon signifies an interest in banking and investments. The start of the sequence followed the founding of the Cincinnati branch of the Bank of United States in May-1817 with Harrison's approval, and criticism of his directorship at the same Bank during the summer of 1819 prior to his run for Ohio State Senate. As a 9th house planet (WS), the sequence also followed the founding of Christ Church, 18-May-1817, for which WH served on the vestry. As ruler of the 6th house of slaves (QS), it timed the initiation of a slave purchase for his son on 8-Jul-1819.

| REG | D | Venus/Virgo | P | Saturn (0) d. => LOF | 11-Feb-1830 |
| REG | D | Venus/Virgo | P | Saturn (SA) d. => LOF | 18-Mar-1832 |

This sequence timed difficulties with finance, including settling outstanding debts of his son John Cleeves, the death of same John Cleeves (30 Oct 1830), and a serious flood which damaged farm operations (March/April 1832). By quadrant houses, Saturn in the 8th of debt rules the 12th house of death of children as well as children's debts. Saturn also afflicts the Moon by conjunction. As the Moon ruled the LOF, Saturn's affliction of the Moon also harms LOF.

Longevity, 68y 1m 23d

Death: 4-Apr-1841, 12:30 AM, Washington, D.C. Harrison's lengthy inauguration speech on a cold and rainy 4-Mar-1841 is considered a contributing cause to his fatal pneumonia. Other accounts report that he became ill on 27-Mar-1841 and quickly succumbed to pneumonia. His death was so rapid that his wife was unable to travel to be with him when he died.

Hīlāj: **LOF?** Figure is nocturnal and Moon is preferred. Placement in 8th (QS) is allowable; her 9th (WS) placement is not. Sun/2nd/masculine sign appears promising but is feral, making no aspects to possible Al-kadukhadah's. Figure is preventional; LOF is third choice for Hīlāj after the luminaries. Angular in the 7th (WS) and trine the Al-kadukhadāh Jupiter in his own sign qualifies the LOF as Hīlāj.

Al-kadukhadāh: **Jupiter**. If LOF is Hīlāj, then Al-kadukhadāh Jupiter grants 79 major years; Saturn deducts 30 minor years by opposition, Venus adds 8 minor years by a wide sextile receiving Jupiter by bound, Mars by trine only receives by triplicity and may deduct years. Net is $79 - 30 + 8 = 57$yrs, or 42yrs if Mars deducts years. This is incorrect.

Alternate: The better solution is to assign the al-kadukhadāh to **Mars** since Mars is the Victor of the Horoscope. Mars grants 66 major years and Harrison lived only 2 years longer.

Victor: **Mars**

Killing Planets: **Mars (40), Mercury (37)**

Arcus Vitae:

| PT | D | Saturn/Capricorn | P | opp Mars (MA) d. => MC | 17-Jun-1840 |
| PT | D | Saturn/Capricorn | P | opp Mars (0) d. => MC | 30-Mar-1841 |

LOCK This sequence opens just after the death of Harrison's son Benjamin on 9-Jun-1840, the 5th child he lost to death during his lifetime. Mars is the Al-mubtazz of the 12th cusp of death of children.

| REG | D | Saturn/Virgo | P | dex trine Merc (0) d. => LOF | 12-Apr-1841 |

LOCK Similar timing to above sequence. Both Mars and Mercury are the high scoring killing planets. This direction joins Mercury and the Hīlāj. Mercury/Capricorn signifies speech and is a direct match to the role of his lengthy inaugural speech filled with classical Roman and Greek allusions as a contributing cause to Harrison's fatal pneumonia.

1-Apr-1841. *csa MC conj Saturn*, error = 3 days.
4-Apr-1841. *dsa MC conj Mercury*, exact day of death.

1841 Solar Return for year of Death

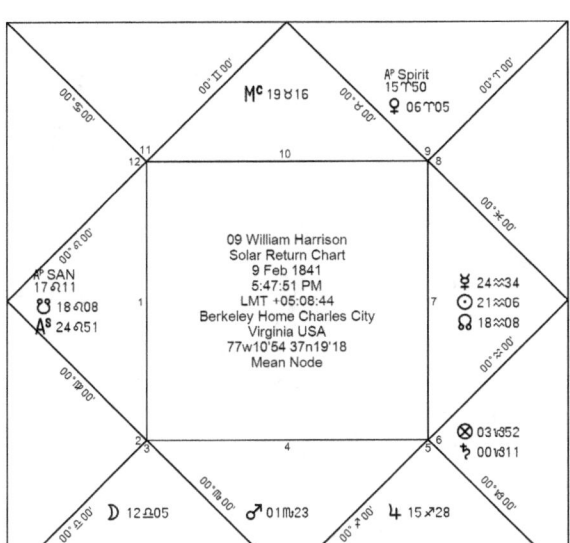

Ascendant Distributor: Mercury/Taurus since 6-Aug-1839
Profected Ascendant: 29VI29, 9th house; SR Victor: Saturn
Lords: LOY – Mercury; LOP – Moon
Firdaria: Mercury-Jupiter
Moon: separates from opposition of Venus and applies to sextile of Jupiter
Return Ascendant falls in natal 7th; natal Ascendant in return's 6th.

High scoring killing planets Mars and Mercury fall in the return's 4th and 7th. Mars' placement in the 4th recapitulates the natal Mars-IC direction which timed death. Moon applies to Jupiter who rules the return's 8th. Return's Victor Saturn conjuncts the return's LOF; both oppose natal LOF.

By far the most dangerous contacts are the return's Moon conjunct natal North Node within a degree and the return's South Node conjunct the natal preventional degree within a degree. This Moon-Node-Preventional degree relationship is further amplified by the 5-Feb-1841 lunar eclipse which at 17LE11 fell within 2 degrees of the preventional degree.

No solar return Ascendant directions involving high scoring killing planets found near death on 4-Apr-1841.

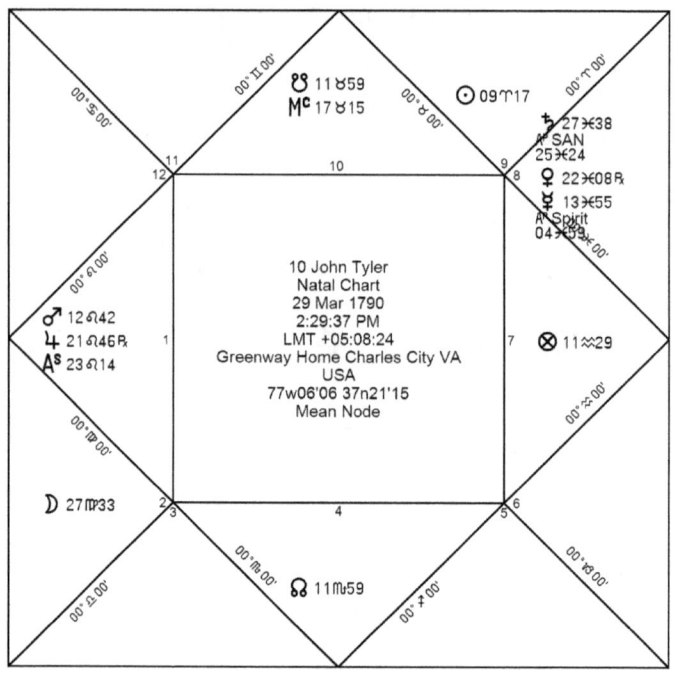
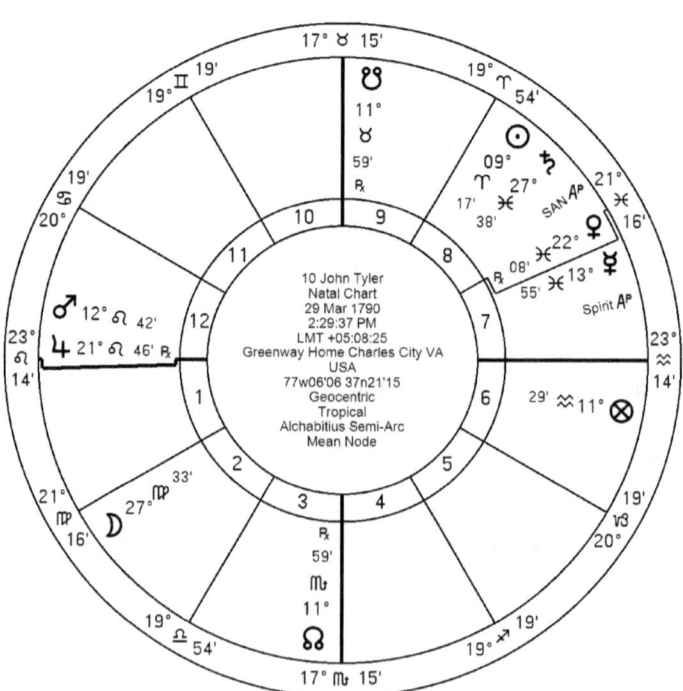

Moon's Configuration

Moon separates from **Venus** and applies to **Saturn**, diurnal, conjunctional. Prenatal syzygy is 25PI24. Eclipse? No.

Cognitive Assessment Model (Rulers of Moon and Mercury)

Sign rulers: **Mercury, Jupiter**
Bound rulers: **Mars, Jupiter**

Victor Soul Models

Ibn Ezra Victor Model (1507), in-sect triplicity ruler, triplicity decans.

	Position	☉	☽	☿	♀	♂	♃	♄
Sun	09 AR 17	7			2	6		
Moon	27 VI 33			9	4	2		
Asc	23 LE 14	8		2		1		
Pars Fortuna	11 AQ 29			1	2			8
Syzygy	25 PI 24					7	3	5
Oriental						0	0	0
Houses		5	6	10	5	2	12	5
Score		0	20	6	**22**	20	14	17	13

Porphyry's Expanded Victor Model (2022)

Mars rules the Sun by sign; the Moon and syzygy by bound. Sect: out-of-favor. Solar phase: occidental from 2nd station to waning square. Position: Angular in ASC, 7th from Lot of Fortune. Mars and Sun in mutual reception by sign. At the bending of the Nodes.

Victor Table for Killing Planets

			☉	☽	☿	♀	♂	♃	♄
ASC		23LE14	5,3		2		1	3	3
Rul ASC	☉	9AR17	4,3			2	5,1	3	3
L.Death		21VI21		3	5,4	3,1	3,2		
Rul L.Death	☿	13PI55		3,1		4,3	3	5,2	
H8 Cusp		21PI16		3		4,3	3,2,1	5	
Rul H8	♃	21LE46	5,3		2		1	3	3
T-Rul H8	♀	22PI08		3		4,3	3,2,1	5	
☿ in 8th	☿	13PI55		3,1		4,3	3	5,2	
♀ in 8th	♀	22PI08		3		4,3	3,2,1	5	
♄ in 8th	♄	27PI38		3		4,3	3,2,1	5	
8th from ☉		9SC17		3		3,2	5,3,1		
Rul 8th fr ☉	♂	12LE42	5,3					3,1	3,2
TOTAL			31	26	13	**53**	52	47	14

2007 Proposed Rectification: 2:29:37 PM, ASC 23LE13'59"
2007 Proposed Rectification: 2:29:37 PM, ASC 23LE14'18"

Astrodatabank reports a DD-rated Conflicting/unverified birth time.

ZRS. JT's political career matches chapters outlined by L1 levels: L1-Aries, state politics; L1-Taurus, national politics – House; L1-Gemini, Whig party formation and his expulsion from; L1-Cancer, anti-establishment politician.

L1 Pisces 29 Mar 1790		
L1 Aries 26 Jan 1802		1802, entered William & Mary; 1811, began law practice and seated in Virginia House of Delegates.
L1 Taurus 08 Nov 1816		17-Dec-1816, entered US House of Representatives.
L1 Gemini 27 Sep 1824		1824, appointed to Board of Visitors of William & Mary College, served until death; 9-Feb-1825, John Quincy Adams selected President which triggers formation of the Whig Party (Adams/Clay), a splinter group from the Democratic-Republican Party whose residual members are taken over by pro-Jackson forces, 10-Dec-1825, Elected VA Governor.
L2 Sagittarius 12 Jul 1833	FS	10-Sep-1833, announced plans to suspend the government's deposits in the Bank of the US; 14-Apr-1834, Whig Party formally adopted its name; JT involved in creation of.
L2 Aries 07 Mar 1840		4-Apr-1841, ascended to Presidency after death of WHH.
L2 Taurus 31 May 1841		1-Jun-1841, addressed special session of Congress; 16-Aug and 9-Sep-1841, vetoed both Bank of the United States bills; 11-Sep-1841, all cabinet members resigned except for Daniel Webster; 13-Sep-1841, expelled from Whig Party.
L2 Sagittarius 26 Jan 1842	LB	25-Mar-1842, decried deficit and called for higher tariffs; 9-Aug-1842, vetoed permanent tariff bill because JT thoughts tariffs too high.
L1 Cancer 14 Jun 1844		26-Jun-1844, second Marriage to Julia Gardner; 20-Aug-1844, withdrew from Presidential bid to favor Polk.
L2 Capricorn 01 Aug 1852	FS	2-Nov-1852, Winfield Scott's loss to Franklin Pierce signaled end of Whig Party's influence.
L2 Capricorn 13 Oct 1861	LB	Nov-1861, Chosen to the Confederate House of Representatives; 12-Jan-1862, Died.

Firdaria – Mars major and minor periods

Firdaria according to Bonatti	Life Events
Sun **Mars** 24 Oct 1798	No events found.
Venus **Mars** 16 Dec 1805	1806 (no date), read Adam Smith's *Wealth of Nations*.
Mercury **Mars** 03 Sep 1815	17-Dec-1916, entered US House of Representatives.
Moon **Mars** 05 Feb 1825	9-Feb-1825, John Quincy Adams selected President; 10-Dec-1825, elected Governor of Virginia, one year term, more of a ceremonial position.
Saturn **Mars** 21 May 1833	24-Feb-1834, spoke in Senate against AJ's deposit removal proposal; 28-Mar-1834, voted to censure AJ; Apr-1834, involved in forming Whig Party bringing together all Jackson foes including Anti-Masons, Southern states' rights Democrats, National Republicans, and supporters of Henry Clay; 14-Apr-1834, Whig name formally adopted as name of new party.
Jupiter **Mars** 16 Dec 1842	10-Jan-1843, resolution for impeachment defeated in the House; May/Sep-1843, many opponents removed from office and replaced by supporters; 27-Apr-1844, submitted treaty with Texas for annexation to the Senate; 28-May-1844, Polk nominated for President.
Mars 7 years Age 63 to 70	
Mars Mars 29 Mar 1853	Sep-1853, sold Kentucky property.
Mars Sun 30 Mar 1854	1854 (no date), supported Kansas-Nebraska Act. attacked Know-Nothings for their opposition to Catholic Church; expressed approval of Catholic noninvolvement in slavery issue in contrast to Protestant denominations which were split over slavery.
Mars Venus 30 Mar 1855	No events found.
Mars Mercury 29 Mar 1856	17-Jun-1856, supported Buchanan without special enthusiasm.
Mars Moon 29 Mar 1857	Spring-1857, entertained some hope of being the Democratic nominee in 1860, convinced of the need for a moderate Southerner in office; 16-Oct-1857, John Brown's raid aroused fears of slave uprisings among JT and his neighbors.
Mars Saturn 30 Mar 1858	No events found.
Mars Jupiter 30 Mar 1859	No events found.

Mars as Victor. Mars/Leo includes Tyler's 1825 election as Governor of Virginia, his involvement in formation of the Whig Party, his political survival as President after a failed impeachment attempt, and submission of the Texas annexation treaty to the Senate during active political years. During retirement, Major Mars echoed prior political themes but without leaving any legacy of importance. Not included in this listing is the North Node Firdaria period (1860-1863) with Mars/Leo ruling the North Node in Scorpio. At this time, Tyler led a last ditch failed Peace Conference to head off the Civil War. Tyler was subsequently elected to the Confederate House of Representatives. Beginning with Thomas Jefferson, Mars/Leo has signified the philosophy of states' rights in American political history.

Solar Arc Directions

12-May-1836. *csa Sun opposed ASC.*
23-Jul-1837. *dsa ASC opposed Sun.*
   Resigned Senate seat rather than follow instructions from VA for expunction of AJ's censure, 29-Feb-1836.
   Elected as Whig to VA House of Delegates, 26-Apr-1838.
   Note the time between these two directions he is out of political office.

15-Jun-1836. *csa Saturn conj LOF.*
27-Aug-1837. *dsa LOF conj Saturn.*
   AJ signed Deposit Act, 23-Jun-1836; Specie Circular, 11-Jul-1836.
   Fall-1837. Panic of 1837 in full swing.
   Saturn/Pisces is deflationary; placed in 8th ties Saturn to investments.

16-Nov-1839. *csa MC conj Saturn.*
1-Apr-1841. *dsa Saturn conj MC.*
   JT nominated for VP at Whig Convention, 4-Dec-1839.
   Became President on death of President William Harrison, 4-Apr-1841.

26-Apr-1845. *csa MC conj Venus.*
27-Dec-1846. *dsa Venus conjunct MC.*
   No event found for first direction.
   Started financial partnership to develop Kentucky property following October 1846 survey results.

Primary Directions

| REG | D | Jupiter/Taurus | P | MC c. => Sun | 3-Jul-1832 |

Infamy for opposing renewal of charter for Bank of United States. JT voted against, 11-Jun; President Jackson vetoed legislation, 10-Jul.

| REG | D | Jupiter/Taurus | P | MC c. => Sun | 3-Dec-1840 |

LOCK Won election for Vice-President, 2-Dec-1840.

| PT | D | Mars/Pisces | P | Venus (0) c. => MC | 1-Apr-1842 |

Called for upward revision of tariff duties, 25 March.

| PT | D | Saturn/Gemini | P | sin sq Saturn (0) c. => ASC | 3-Dec-1856 |

Suffered major illness, November-December 1856.

Primary Direction Sequences

| PT | D | Saturn/Gemini | P | sin sq Saturn (0) d. => MC | 21-Nov-1832 |
| PT | D | Saturn/Gemini | P | sin sq Saturn (SA) d. => MC | 5-Dec-1832 |

LOCK This sequence timed the South Carolina Nullification crisis of 1832-1833. On 24-Nov South Carolina nullified the Tariff of 1832 and threatened secession if the federal government attempted to use force to collect tariffs. On 10-Dec, President Jackson issued his *Proclamation to the People of South Carolina* warning South Carolina that no state can secede from the Union.

| REG | D | Jupiter/Virgo | P | sin trine MC d. => Mars (0) | 28-Sep-1832 |
| REG | D | Jupiter/Virgo | P | sin trine MC d. => Mars (MA) | 19-Apr-1834 |

Tyler considered Jackson's handling of the South Carolina Nullification crisis a virtual *military despotism*. After the spring of 1833, Tyler drifted towards Henry Clay's position as the Whig Party is created. The Whig name is formally adopted on 14-Apr-1834 after Clay mentioned it in a Senate speech.

| PT | D | Mars/Pisces | P | Saturn (SA) c. => MC | 16-May-1836 |
| PT | D | Mars/Pisces | P | Saturn (0) c. => MC | 9-Mar-1837 |

This sequence timed the promulgation of Jackson's policies designed to squash lending/land speculation and kill off the Bank of the United States. Both the Deposit Act (Surplus Revenue Act) adopted on 23-Jun-1836 and the Specie Circular of 11-Jul-1836 had deflationary effects. As the sequence ended, Jackson published his farewell address on 4-Mar-1837 condemning monopolies, speculation, and paper currency.

| REG | D | Mars/Aries | P | dex trine ASC d. => Mercury (0) | 1-Mar-1837 |
| REG | D | Mars/Aries | P | dex trine ASC d. => Mercury (ME) | 23-Oct-1837 |

LOCK This sequence timed the financial Panic of 1837 whose cause stemmed from credit contraction. Mercury/Pisces in the 8th of debt signifies problems with borrowing. Martin Van Buren took office 4 March just after the sequence began; 10 May marked the official panic day; on 12 October Congress authorized issuance of treasury notes to restore system liquidity as the sequence ended.

Longevity, 71y 9m 19d

Death: 18-Jan-1862, 12:15 AM, Exchange Hotel, Richmond, Virginia.

Hīlāj: **Sun**. Figure is diurnal and Sun/9th/masculine sign qualifies.

Al-kadukhadāh: If **Sun/Aries** in the sign of its exaltation and located in its 9th house of joy trumps all other planets as the Al-kadukhadāh, then the Sun grants 120 major years. Mars trines the Sun, receives by sign rulership, and should deduct 15 minor years. Jupiter also trines the Sun without reception and should add 12 minor years without reception. The net projection of 117 years is too long.

Consider **Mars** as Victor of the Horoscope. Mars grants 66 major years. We either stop there and say Tyler lived slightly longer. OR treat Jupiter as an accidental malefic (as it rules the 8th of death) reducing its 12 minor years and adding the Sun's minor 19 years by trine aspect.

MA (66) – JU (12) + SU (19) = 73 years.

While this is technically closer, this solution may be too convoluted. If correct, this is one of the few examples I have seen when the luminaries add years.

Victor of the Horoscope: **Mars**

Killing Planets: **Venus (53), Mars (52), Jupiter (47)**

Arcus Vitae:

REG	D	Jupiter/Gemini	P	sin sextile Sun c. => Mars (MA)	20-May-1860
REG	D	Jupiter/Gemini	P	sin sex Sun c. => Mars (0)	10-Jan-1862

PT	D	Venus/Libra	P	sin sextile Jupiter (JU) d. => ASC	16-Sep-1861
PT	D	Venus/Libra	P	sin sextile Jupiter (0) d. => ASC	15-Feb-1862

The first sequence captured Lincoln's Presidential nomination on 18-May-1860, includes Taylor's last-ditch Peace Conference on 20-Jan-1861, the Civil War outbreak, and 12-Jan-1862 (date he was reported seriously ill six days prior to death). Second sequence joined the ruler of the 8th to the Ascendant.

10. JOHN TYLER

1861 Solar Return for year of Death

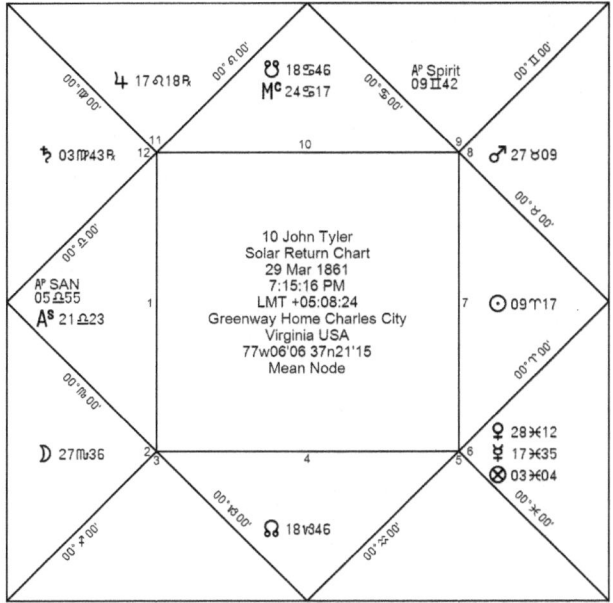

Ascendant Distributor: Venus/Libra since 6-Mar-1861
Profected Ascendant: 23CA54, 12th house; SR Victor: Venus
Lords: LOY – Moon; LOP – Jupiter
Firdaria: North Node
Moon: separates from opposition of Mars and applies to trine of Venus
Return Ascendant falls in natal 3rd; Natal Ascendant falls in return's 11th.

Hīlāj Sun is square the Nodes. High scoring planet Venus returns to its natal sign and rules the 8th of death. After Venus as high scoring killer, next in rank is Mars placed in the return's 8th and Jupiter which recapitulates its natal sign and bound. See Jupiter is sextile the return's Ascendant which recapitulates the natal arcus vitae (see prior page). The Moon translates Mars to Venus; a deadly combination considering Mars and Venus are high scoring killers and both emphasize the 8th by position and rulership.

Jupiter in the 11th ruling the 3rd is delineated as a group/organization causing short-term travel. Tyler arrived at Richmond on 10 January to attend a Confederate Conference and is joined by wife on 12 January who dreamed of Tyler succumbing to an illness which caused her to change plans and travel to be with her husband on short notice.

| PT | D | Saturn/Leo | P | Jupiter (0) d. => ASC | 8-Jan-1862 |

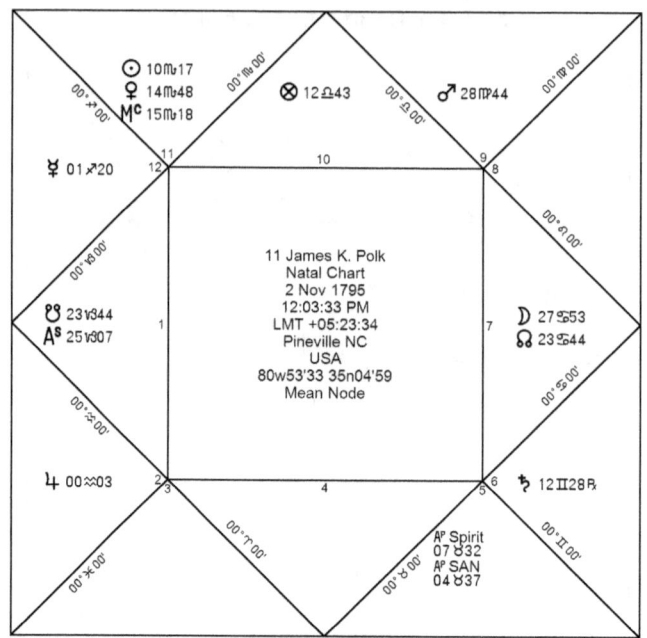

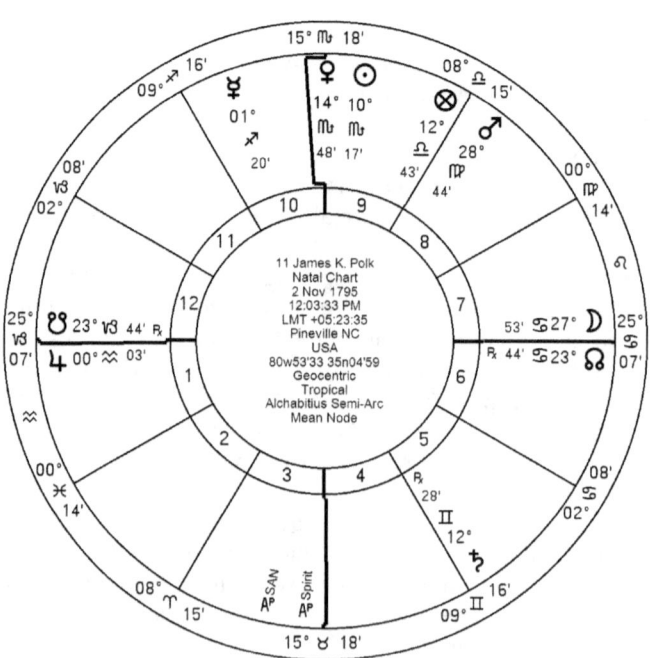

Moon's Configuration

Moon separates from **Venus** and applies to **Mars**, diurnal, preventional Prenatal syzygy is 4TA37. Eclipse? No.

Cognitive Assessment Model (Rulers of Moon and Mercury)

Sign rulers: **(Moon)/Saturn, Jupiter**
Bound rulers: **Saturn, Jupiter**

Victor Soul Models

Ibn Ezra Victor Model (1507), in-sect triplicity ruler, triplicity decans.

	Position	☉	☽	☿	♀	♂	♃	♄
Sun	10 SC 17				5	5	1	
Moon	27 CA 53		5		3		5	2
Asc	25 CP 07			1	3	4		7
Pars Fortuna	12 LI 43			2	5			8
Syzygy	04 TA 37		4		11			
Oriental						3	0	1
Houses		4	10	11	11	5	12	7
Score	0	4	19	14	**38**	17	18	25

Porphyry's Expanded Victor Model (2022)

Venus rules the Lot of Fortune, Lot of Spirit, and syzygy by sign; the Sun, Lot of Spirit, and syzygy by bound. Sect: out-of-favor. Solar phase: occidental direct combust. Position: conj MC degree. Dignity: diurnal triplicity. Debility: detriment. Moon's separation.

Victor Table for Killing Planets

			☉	☽	☿	♀	♂	♃	♄
ASC		25CP07		3	1	3	4,3		5,2
Rul ASC	♄	12GE28			5,3	2,1		3	3
L.Death		14CA50		5,3	2	3	3,1	4	
Rul L.Death	☽	27CA53	3					5,3,2,1	3
H8 Cusp		00VI15		3	5,4,2,1	3	3		
Rul H8	☿	1SA20	3					5,3,2,1	3
T-Rul H8	♀	14SC48		3	2	3	5,3	1	
8th from ☉		10GE17			5,3	1		3,2	3
Rul 8th fr ☉	☿	1SA20	3					5,3,2,1	3
TOTAL			9	17	**33**	16	22	**46**	22

2007 Proposed Rectification: 12:20:17 PM, ASC 29CP52'04"
2022 Proposed Rectification: 12:03:33 PM, ASC 25CP07'49"

Astrodatabank records an A-rated birth time of Noon, from memory. The revised rectification is within 4 minutes of Noon.

The rectification continues to delineate Mars/Virgo as the significator for the Mexican War with Virgo assigned to many Latin American countries as well as land acquired by the US through the Louisiana Purchase and the Mexican War. These acquisitions follow the change in triplicity for the Jupiter-Saturn conjunctional cycle to Virgo in the Jefferson administration which laid the groundwork for US western expansion.

The prior rectification made use of Uranus/Virgo in addition to Mars/Virgo for timing the Mexican War. Revising the rectification in 2021, I recognized that Uranus led me astray and threw those measurements out.

This rectification is a good example of the solar arc – primary direction hypothesis which links the same measurement computed by two different methodologies. Study carefully the similarity between Venus-LOF directions for his entry to the state legislature (primary) and his subsequent election to the House of Representatives (solar arc). In addition, compare the MC-North Node direction which timed his selection as Democratic Presidential candidate (primary) to victories and the conclusion of the Mexican War (solar arc). Finally, the use of transits to the angles was notable for Polk (trMars conj IC for diplomatic actions to end the Mexican War; trVenus conj IC for his final illness and death). Both should be studied.

ZRS. ZR is less impressive for Polk compared to many other Presidents for the failure of the L1-Cancer // L2-Capricorn LB to lift him to the Presidency. What is interesting is his announcement of the California gold discovery 5 days before the start of L1-Leo, as gold is a Sun-ruled commodity.

L1 Taurus 02 Nov 1795		
L1 Gemini 22 Sep 1803		
L2 Sagittarius 06 Jul 1812	FS	1813, started formal education.
L2 Sagittarius 20 Jan 1821	LB	1821, successful in local law practice; chosen Captain in local militia.
L1 Cancer 09 Jun 1823		Sep-1823, entered TN state legislature for two years.
L2 Capricorn 27 Jul 1831	FS	1832, provided legislative support for Jackson's bank war.
L2 Capricorn 07 Oct 1840	LB	Aug-1841, lost Gubernatorial re-election bid.
L2 Aquarius 26 Dec 1842		14-Nov-1844, elected President, ran as Jackson protégé, "Young Hickory."
L1 Leo 29 Jan 1848		[early by 5 days] 24-Jan-1848, gold discovered in California; 2-Feb-1848, Treaty of Guadalupe Hidalgo signed ending Mexican War; 15-Jun-1849, died.

Firdaria – Venus major and minor periods

Firdaria according to Bonatti	Life Event
Sun **Venus** 07 Apr 1797	No events found.
Venus 8 years	
Venus Venus 02 Nov 1805	1806 (No date), family moved to Tennessee.
Venus Mercury 25 Dec 1806	1807 (no date), Maury County, TN organized at the instigation of the Polk family.
Venus Moon 15 Feb 1808	No events found.
Venus Saturn 08 Apr 1809	No events found.
Venus Jupiter 30 May 1810	No events found.
Venus Mars 22 Jul 1811	No events found.
Venus Sun 11 Sep 1812	12-Sep-1812, surgery to remove stones in urinary tract; most likely left JP impotent.
Mercury **Venus** 24 Dec 1824	9-Feb-1825, JQA selected President; 4/5-Aug-1825, elected to House as Jackson loyalist.
Moon **Venus** 08 Apr 1833	Oct-1833, lost bid for Speaker of the House; Dec-1833, selected Chairman House Ways and Means Committee; 30-Dec-1833, made speech in favor of deposit removal; Jun-1834, acted as administration voice within the House via Chair of House Ways and Means Committee.
Saturn **Venus** 15 Feb 1842	Jun/Jul-1842, lobbied for VP slot in next election; Aug-1843, defeated 2nd time in TN Gubernatorial race "darkest hour of my political life."

Venus as Victor. While Venus did not time Polk's Presidential election or the Mexican War, as a time lord Venus did time Polk's initial election to the House of Representatives, his subsequent selection as Chair of the House Ways and Means Committee from which he pushed the Jackson administration's controversial deposit removal program, and his second consecutive Tennessee Gubernatorial loss after which he doubled down in his efforts to achieve high national office. In early years, Venus-Sun timed the excruciating surgery to remove stones from his urinary tract performed without anesthesia.

Venus/Scorpio signifies Polk's lust for land which was a driving influence for territorial acquisition. Venus rules the LOS 7TA32 in the bound of Venus/Taurus which signifies land directly.

Transits

9-Sep-1823. *tr North Node conj ASC.*
Entered Tennessee state legislature, first political office, Sep-1823.

24-Dec-1828. *tr North node conj LOF.*
Followed Jackson's presidential election, 3-Dec-1828; and assistance from Jackson for Polk's move from Nashville to Washington in the weeks after.

8-Aug-1836. *tr South Node conj MC.*
Death of sister Naomi Tate, 6-Aug-1836.

29-Nov-1845. *tr North Node conj MC.*
Outlined Polk Doctrine in 1st Annual Message to Congress, 2-Dec-1845.

20-Sep-1847. *tr Mars conj IC.*
30-Sep-1847. *tr Mars-rx conj IC.*
25-Jan-1848. *tr Mars conj IC.*
Trist wrote Polk explaining his Mexican negotiations, 19-Sep-1847.
JP recalled Trist because he exceeded diplomatic instructions, 4-Oct-1847.
Trist wrote Buchanan that final terms had been agreed to, 25-Jan-1848.

Solar Arc Directions

23-Aug-1812. *dsa Moon sq Venus.*
16-Oct-1812. *csa Venus sq Moon.*
Surgery without anesthesia removed stones in urinary tract, 12-Sep-1812.

12-Aug-1827. *dsa LOF conj Venus.*
12-Feb-1828. *csa Venus conj LOF.*
Re-elected to House of Representatives by wide margin, Aug-1827.
Death of father, JP inherited responsibilities for property and care for younger siblings, 5-Nov-1827.
Note: The first solar arc direction can be linked to the same direction computed by primary directions Fall-1823 when he entered TN legislature.

25-Sep-1846. *dsa North Node sextile MC.*
25-Dec-1847. *csa MC sextile North Node.*
LOCK Mexican War victory at Battle of Monterey, 21/25-Sep-1846.
Peace negotiations began in town of Guadalupe Hidalgo, 30-Dec-1847.

3-Dec-1848. *dsa Mercury conj ASC.*
Last annual message, JP announced California gold discovery, 5-Dec-1848.

11. JAMES K. POLK

Primary Directions

| PT | D | Mercury/Scorpio | P | Venus (0) d. => LOF | 30-Jun-1823 |
| PT | D | Mercury/Scorpio | P | Venus (VE) d. => LOF | 30-Oct-1823 |

Entered TN legislature and served for 2 years, political stance against banking interests consistent with Venus/Scorpio, Sep-1823.
See possible linkage to above solar arc directions Aug-1827/Feb-1828.
Married Sarah Childress, 1-Jan-1824

PT	D	Venus/Virgo	P	dex sex Venus (0) d. => Moon (0)	19-Jan-1831
REG	D	Venus/Virgo	P	dex sex Venus (VE) d. => Moon (0)	30-May-1831
PT	D	Venus/Virgo	P	dex sex Venus (VE) d. => Moon (0)	26-Aug-1831

Death of brother Frank Ezekiel of acute alcoholism, 21-Jan-1831.
Death of brother Marshall Tate, 12-Apr-1831.
Death of brother John Lee, 28-Sep-1831.
Death of siblings is 8th from the 3rd, or 10th; Venus in 10th is relevant.

| PT | D | Mars/Virgo | P | sin sextile North Node c. => MC | 30-May-1844 |

LOCK Selected Democratic Presidential candidate, 29-May-1844.
Note the same solar arc direction computed for 25-Dec-1847 timed the start of negotiations for ending the Mexican War.

| REG | D | Venus/Capricorn | P | dex sex MC c. => Sun | 2-Sep-1845 |
| PT | D | Venus/Capricorn | P | dex sex MC c. => Sun | 24-Apr-1846 |

JP ordered ZT to regard any attempt by Mexican forces to cross the Rio Grande as "the commencement of hostilities," 26-Aug-1845.
Mexican War began, 24/26-Apr-1846.

REG	D	Mars/Sagittarius	P	sin sq Mars (0) d. => Sun	13-Nov-1845
REG	D	Mars/Sagittarius	P	sin sq Mars (MA) d. => Sun	29-Dec-1845
PT	D	Mars/Sagittarius	P	sin sq Mars (0) d. => Sun	23-Feb-1846
PT	D	Mars/Sagittarius	P	sin sq Mars (MA) d. => Sun	26-Mar-1846

JP authorized John Slidell to negotiate with Mexico for land, 7-Nov-1845.
Mexican President overthrown by General Paredes, 31-Dec-1845.
Slidell gave Mexico peace ultimatum, 1-Mar-1846.
Mexico refused to respond to Slidell's peace ultimatum, 16-Mar-1846.

| REG | D | Jupiter/Cancer | P | DSC c. => Sun | 3-Nov-1893 |

Remains moved to Tennessee Capitol, 19-Sep-1893 (posthumous).

| PT | D | Venus/Capricorn | P | sin sex MC d. => North Node | 25-Mar-2017 |

TN State Senate approved resolution for Polk remains to be moved from the grounds of the TN Capitol, 27-Mar-2017 (posthumous).

Longevity, 53y 7m 12d

Death: 15-Jun-1849, 4:40 PM, Polk Place, Nashville Tennessee, at home. Following Taylor's inauguration on 4-Mar, Polk went on a southern tour and likely contracted cholera in New Orleans on 21-Mar. After a reoccurrence of diarrhea and vomiting on 3-Jun, Polk failed to respond to opiates. He died quietly on the afternoon of 15-Jun-1849.

Hīlāj: **LOF**. By quadrant houses, Sun in 9th (QS) is disallowed because of placement in feminine sign, but acceptable in the 11th by whole sign houses. Moon in Cancer, her sign of rulership, angular the 7th, appears the obvious choice yet her close conjunction to the North Node appears to eliminate her from consideration as hīlāj. Empirical testing supports the LOF as the true hīlāj. Note the LOF is angular in the 10th by whole signs (see also Reagan's figure with a LOF/Libra/10th functioning as hīlāj).

Al-kadukhadāh: **Saturn**. Saturn in his triplicity is the Al-mubtazz of the LOF and trines within 1 degree. Saturn grants his 57 major years. He lived slightly fewer years. It is unlikely the trine from Jupiter and the square from Mars can respectively add and subtract years as the aspects are outside moiety of orb. If these moiety violations are allowed, then Jupiter adds 12 minor years; Mars deducts 15 minor years for a net projection of 54 years which is accurate.

Alternatively, allow the Cancer Moon in her own sign amplified by the North Node to function as both Hīlāj and Al-kadukhadāh. See that Polk lived just under one-half of the Moon's 108 major years (54yrs).

Victor of the Horoscope: **Venus**.

Killing Planets: **Jupiter (46), Mercury (33)**

Arcus Vitae:

Transits. *trVenus to the IC* on 21-Mar, 25-May, and 13-Jun-1849 corresponds with his 21-Mar trip through New Orleans where he is thought to have been exposed to cholera, severe recurrence of diarrhea and vomiting on 3-Jun, and death on 15-Jun-1849. At the same time, trMars and trSaturn both in Aries were opposed to natal Lot of Fortune though aspects did not perfect at death. With a Saturn opposed LOF primary direction near the time of death, trSaturn opposed natal Lot of Fortune is a relevant measurement.

| REG | D | Venus/Sagittarius | P | opp Saturn (SA) d. LOF | 13-Jul-1849 |

1848 Solar Return for year of Death

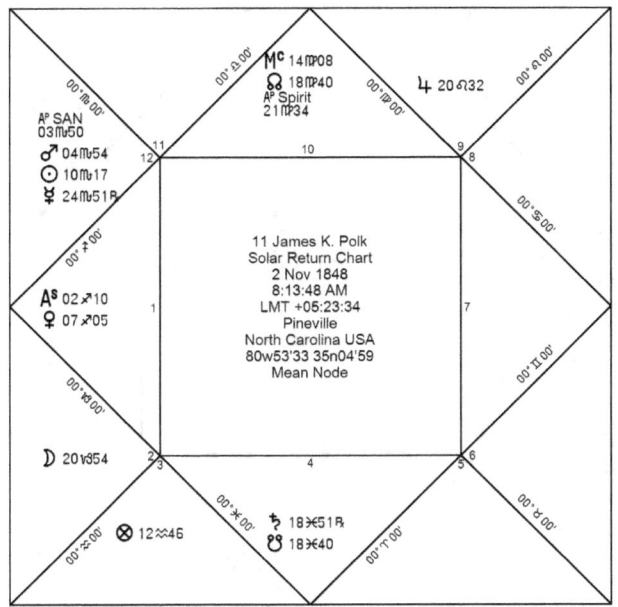

Ascendant Distributor: Venus/Aries since 2-Nov-1846.
Profected Ascendant: 25GE07, 6th House; SR Victor: Mars
Lords: LOY- Mercury; LOP – Mars
Firdaria: Jupiter-Mars
Moon separates from sextile of Saturn; applies to sextile of Mercury
Return Ascendant falls in natal 12th; natal Ascendant falls in return's 2nd.

Polk meets death in a 6th house profected year. Natal 6th contains Saturn and is ruled by LOY Mercury. Mercury appears in both natal 12th and return 12th. Both are weak placements yet Mercury's zodiacal state in the return is far worse. Retrograde, combust, ruled by Mars who with Mercury jointly besieges the Sun. Sun applies to Mercury which is the second high scoring killer and LOY. Moon separates from Saturn and applies to Mercury. Both luminaries are afflicted by malefics through aspect or translation. The Moon is further damaged by conjunction with the natal South Node. Hīlāj LOF is opposed by high-scoring killer Jupiter.

No obvious Ascendant directions found at time of death from the solar return.

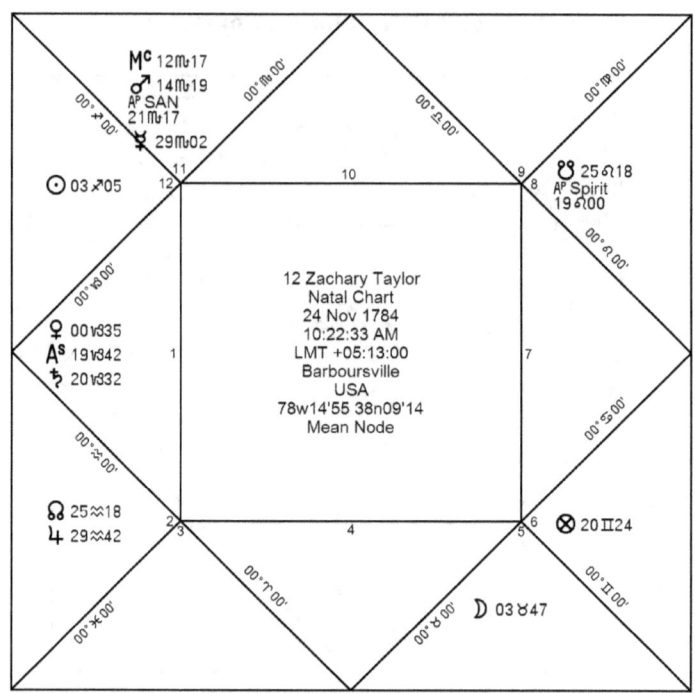

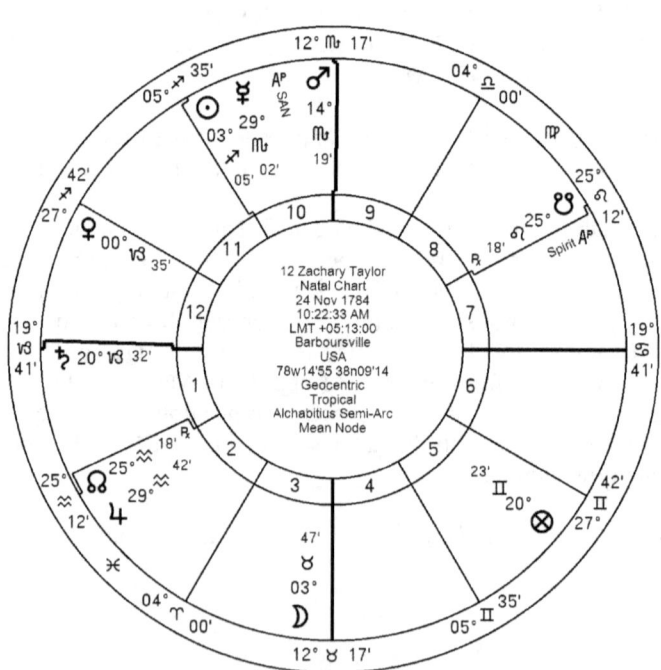

Moon's Configuration

Moon separates from **Venus** and applies to **Mars**, diurnal, conjunctional. Prenatal syzygy is 21SC17. Eclipse? No.

Cognitive Assessment Model (Rulers of Moon and Mercury)

Sign rulers: **Venus, Mars**
Bound rulers: **Venus, Saturn**

Victor Soul Models

Ibn Ezra Victor Model (1507), in-sect triplicity ruler, triplicity decans.

	Position	☉	☽	☿	♀	♂	♃	♄
Sun	03 SA 05	3					8	
Moon	03 TA 47		4		11			
Asc	19 CP 42				6	4		5
Pars Fortuna	20 GE 24			5		2		4
Syzygy	21 SC 17		1		3	5	2	
Oriental						3	0	0
Houses		8	3	11	2	11	6	12
Score		0	11	8	16	22	**25**	16	21

Porphyry's Expanded Victor Model (2022)

Mars rules the MC and syzygy by sign; the Lot of Fortune by bound. Sect: out-of-favor. Solar phase: oriental rising to waxing sextile. Position: conjunct MC. Dignity: sign and nocturnal triplicity. Moon's application.

Victor Table for Killing Planets

			☉	☽	☿	♀	♂	♃	♄
ASC		19CP41		3		3,2,1	4,3		5
Rul ASC	♄	20CP32		3	1	3,2	4,3		5
L.Death		11TA578		4,3	2,1	5,3	3		
Rul L.Death	♀	00CP35		3	2	3	4,3		5,1
H8 Cusp		25LE12	5,3				2,1	3	3
Rul H8	☉	3SA05	3				5,3,2,1	3	
T-Rul H8	☉	3SA05	3				5,3,2,1	3	
8th Occupants	SN	25LE18	5,3				2,1	3	3
8th from ☉		3CA05		5,3,1		3	3,2	4	
Rul 8th fr ☉	☽	3TA49		4,3		5,3,2,1	3		
TOTAL			22	32	6	**36**	38	32	28

2007 Proposed Rectification, Ascendant 19CP54'40" Montebello
2022 Proposed Rectification, Ascendant 19CP41'56" Barboursville

Astrodatabank reports a C-rated birth time of 10:56:51 AM with original source unknown. The proposed rectification is slightly earlier.

The 2022 rectification was revised based on a slight change in birth location. Taylor was born at the Montebello estate with Barboursville the closest town. Changing the location a few miles can alter ASC or MC primary directions a few days. For Taylor, it is an exercise worth pursuing as Directing through the Bounds shows death following the changeover of the ASC distributor from Mars to Saturn by seven days. See also George Washington, John Adams, and Ronald Reagan who also died after a similar ASC distributor changeover.

ZRS. LOF in Gemini means mutable ZR periods should be most active; this bears out with L1-Virgo timing early career milestones and L1-Sagittarius timing Mexican War victories. During L1-Libra he moved around to many posts but saw little action; this changes with L1-Scorpio with the Blackhawk and Seminole conflicts for which he is a direct participant. Presidential inauguration is two weeks prior to the start of L1-Sagittarius // L2-Aquarius.

L1 Leo 24 Nov 1784		
L1 Virgo 18 Aug 1803		Began military service in 1808; no event matches found for start of L1-Virgo in 1803.
L2 Pisces 29 Oct 1812	FS	31-Oct-1812, Brevet promotion to Major following Battle of Fort Harrison on 3/4-Sep-1812 which was first land victory against Indians in War of 1812.
L2 Pisces 16 Dec 1820	LB	12-Dec-1820, much jockeying for remaining officer positions after Secretary of War Calhoun introduced legislation to reduce the army to 6,000 men; 16-Aug-1821, formally joined 7th Infantry as 2nd in command, moved to Southwest following Adams-Onis Treaty.
L1 Libra 05 May 1823		Posted at Louisville, New Orleans, Fort Snelling, and Fort Howard. Recruiting position at Louisville; little offensive military activity during Libra period.
L1 Scorpio 24 Mar 1831		Blackhawk and Seminole Indian conflicts dominated the early phase of L1-Scorpio.
L1 Sagittarius 04 Jan 1846		13-Jan-1846, Secretary of War Marcy ordered ZT to advance troops to Rio Grande; Apr-1835, Thornton's ambush began Mexican War; battle victories at Palo Alto and Resaca del la Palma; 30-May-1846, promoted to Major General; 20/24-Sep-1846, victory at Monterrey and ordered armistice; 11-Oct-1846, President Polk canceled armistice; 24-Nov-1846, Polk chose General Scott to lead forces to Veracruz.
L2 Aquarius 19 Mar 1849		5-Mar-1849, Inauguration (2 weeks before start of L2-Aquarius); 9-Jul-1850, Death.

12. ZACHARY TAYLOR

Firdaria – Mars major and minor periods

Firdaria according to Bonatti	Life Event
Sun **Mars** 21 Jun 1793	No events found.
Venus **Mars** 12 Aug 1800	No events found.
Mercury **Mars** 01 May 1810	30-Nov-1810, promoted to Army Captain; 10-Jul-1811, took command of Fort Knox; 6-Mar-1832, ordered to form company at Louisville and travel to Fort Harrison, Indiana.
Moon **Mars** 04 Oct 1819	Winter 1820, traveled to new command in Madisonville, LA postponed because of river ice; Mar-1820, reached Madisonville and found malnourished and badly supplied troops; ZT remedied that situation.
Saturn **Mars** 17 Jan 1828	Early-1838, last of service at New Orleans; 1-May-1828, left New Orleans for Fort Snelling anticipating Indian conflict; 10-Jan-1829, death of father; 12-Jul-1829, transferred command of Fort Snelling to John Gale, traveled to Fort Howard to attend Indian Council; 18-Jul-1829, assumed command of Fort Howard and had men build new fort described as an imposing structure.
Jupiter **Mars** 12 Aug 1837	12-Aug-1837, took leave of Army after finished service on upper Mississippi; moved to Florida to combat Seminoles; formulated 'squares plan' of defensive fortifications.
Mars 7 years Age 63 to 70	
Mars Mars 25 Nov 1847	5-Dec-1847, left New Orleans which closed career as an active field soldier; 9-Jun-1848, nominated for President; 7-Nov-1848, elected President.
Mars Sun 24 Nov 1848	No events found.
Mars Venus 25 Nov 1849	9-Jul-1850. Death.

Mars as Victor. Mars' periods highlighted key episodes in Taylor's military service including his 'squares plan' of defensive fortifications during the Seminole War of the 1830s. As Major Firdaria ruler, Mars timed Presidential nomination, victory, and death in office.

Compare to George Washington with Mars/Scorpio also conjunct the MC. Both were generals.
Both lifespans were near Mars' 66 major years.

Transits

13-Apr-1834. *tr Jupiter conj IC*, Formation of Whig Party, 14-Apr-1834.

6-Dec-1836; 25-May-1837; 31-Aug-1837. *tr Saturn conj MC*. The culmination of career assignments while spent on the upper Mississippi. On 30-Nov-1836, Taylor took command at Jefferson Barracks near St. Louis; on 30-May he resumed command at Fort Crawford; on 18-Jul he left Fort Crawford for New Orleans.

24-Jan-1846. *tr North Node conj MC*. Taylor received orders to advance to the Rio Grande on 3-Feb; orders were written on 13-Jan-1846.

POSTHUMOUS

3-Apr-1974. *tr Mars conj LOF*.
Boyhood home hit by tornado, required 4 ½ years restoration, 3-Apr-1974.

27-Jun-1991. *tr North Node conj ASC*.
No arsenic found in tests conducted on exhumed body to put to rest rumors of death by poison, 27-Jun-1991.

Solar Arc Directions

7-Jan-1824. *dsa ASC conj Jupiter*.
Appointed superintendent of recruiting (J rules 3rd of publicity), Jan-1824.

12-Jul-1831. *dsa Sun conj Saturn*.
31-Mar-1832. *csa Saturn conj Sun*.
Ordered to return to Louisiana 11-July, assumed command 8-Aug-1831.
Became Colonel of 1st infantry on death of Colonel Morgan, 4-Apr-1832.

3-May-1838. *dsa Nodes sq ASC*.
10-Apr-1839. *csa ASC sq Nodes*.
ZT formally received command of Florida, 15-May-1838.
General Macomb arrived to bring Florida war to conclusion, 4-Apr-1839.

20-Feb-1849. *dsa Mars conj. ASC*.
14-Jun-1850. *csa ASC conj Mars*.
This solar arc pair spanned most of his presidency (5-Mar-49 to 9-Jul-50). Cholera outbreak from Dec-1848 to Aug-1849 opened the period and North-South contention over Texas and slavery concluded the period. On 13-Jun-1850, ZT threatened to take the field if Texans didn't back down from threats to use force to exert claims over part of New Mexico.

12. ZACHARY TAYLOR

Primary Directions

| REG | D | Mercury/Scorpio | P | MC c. => Sun | 17-May-1808 |

LOCK Appointed Lieutenant in 7th infantry, 3-May-1808.
Accepted appointment, 6-Jun-1808.

| PT | D | Venus/Capricorn | P | ASC d. => Sun | 11-Jul-1835 |

Marriage of daughter Sarah Knox to Jefferson Davis, 17-Jul-1835

| PT | D | Mercury/Capricorn | P | Venus (0) d. => MC | 12-Sep-1835 |

Death of daughter Sarah Knox from malaria after both Sara and husband Jefferson Davis contracted malaria in August, 15-Sep-1835.

| PT | D | Jupiter/Aries | P | sin trine Sun d. => ASC | 30-Nov-1836 |

LOCK First major command at Jefferson Barracks, 30-Nov-1836.

Primary Direction Sequences

| REG | D | Jupiter/Capricorn | P | sin sex MC d. => Merc (ME) | 29-Jun-1832 |
| REG | D | Jupiter/Capricorn | P | sin sex MC d. => Merc (0) | 6-Jul-1832 |

LOCK This sequence timed two specific incidences of angry speech and legal problems, consistent with Mercury in Scorpio. On 22 June, ZT was involved in an angry dispute with militia who rebelled after he gave orders to continue marching when the men were exhausted. On 9 July Congress prohibited the entry of liquor into Indian Territory. That same month Taylor's Captain Jouett confiscated banned liquor from the American Fur Company but faced a lawsuit in response. Taylor made his frustration known to the War Department on their weakness in supporting officers in the field when their actions clashed with local groups.

| REG | D | Mercury/Aries | P | sin sq ASC d. => Saturn (SA) | 22-Mar-1846 |
| REG | D | Mercury/Aries | P | sin sq ASC d. => Saturn (0) | 8-May-1846 |

Sequence timed ZT's arrival to Rio Grande and first battle success.
On brink of attack from Mexican patrol, Mexicans faded, 15/20-Mar-1846.
Defeated Mexicans at Palo Alto (8-May) and Resaca de la Palma (9-May).

| REG | D | Mars/Aries | P | sin sq Saturn (0) d. => ASC | 27-Aug-1847 |
| REG | D | Mars/Aries | P | sin sq Saturn (SA) d. => ASC | 14-Oct-1847 |

Administration embraced ZT's suggestion that northern forces remain on defensive in addition to diverting troops to General Scott, 15-Jul-1847.
ZR requested 6 months leave, 4-Oct-1847; approved, 6-Nov-1847.

Longevity, 65y 7m 14d

Death: 9-Jul-1850, 10:30 PM, Washington, D.C. Taylor died in office of cholera contracted after eating contaminated food; some sources suggest a bowl of cherries and ice milk. This followed his attendance at a party for the then-under-construction Washington Monument, an interesting backdrop for death of a President.

Hīlāj: **Moon**. Sun is preferred in a diurnal figure yet is disqualified by position in the 12th (WS). Moon/feminine in either 3rd/5th QS/WS qualifies.

Al-kadukhadāh: **Mars**. Though the Moon in the sign of her exaltation qualifies her as double duty for both Hīlāj and Al-kadukhadāh, both Saturn and Mars within three degrees of the angles are better candidates. Both planets are in the sign of rulership. Mars as Victor of the Horoscope tips the scales to Mars. Mars' 66 major years are very close to actual longevity. Note the wide sextile from Venus does not add years with reception by diurnal triplicity. Neither does Saturn's square *in mundo* deduct years. Mercury, who is co-present with Mars and receives Mars by bound also has no effect on longevity. Since Mars receives Mercury this is not surprising.

Victor of the Horoscope: **Mars**

Killing Planets: **Mars (38), Venus (36)**

The natal Moon's configuration strongly suggests that illness from tainted food will result in illness/death. Moon/Taurus (need/instinct to eat) separating from Venus and applying to Mars signifies tainted food (Venus in 12th imparts hidden/secret qualities to her) and contraction of a fever (nature of Mars).

Arcus Vitae:
The theoretical arcus vitae is a direction of either Mars or Venus to the Moon.

| REG | D | Mercury/Virgo | P | sin trine Moon (MO) c. => Mars (MA) | 26-Jul-1850 |

The above direction is the closest to death. What I find compelling about this direction is at the time of death trMars 2VI24 is within a degree of the partner of the directions, e.g., position of sinister trine Moon is 3VI47.

More precise is the following pair of Ascendant directions:

| PT | D | Mars/Aries | P | sin square Saturn (0) d. => ASC | 27-Aug-1847 |
| PT | D | Saturn/Aries | P | Changeover from bound of Mars to Saturn | 2-Jul-1850 |

This sequence begins with the Ascendant Distributor in the bound of a malefic, with a participating malefic direction; then the Distributor changes from the bound of one malefic (Mars) to another (Saturn), error = 7 days.

1849 Solar Return for year of Death

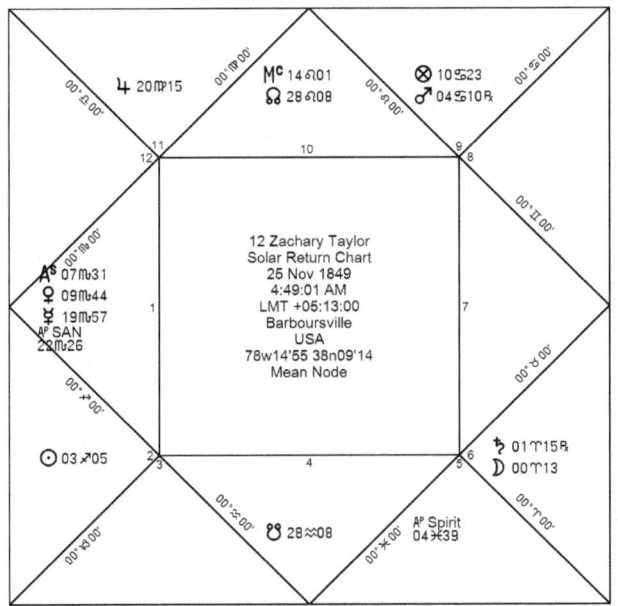

Ascendant Distributor: Changeover to Saturn/Aries 2-Jul-1850.
Profected Ascendant: 19GE42, 5th house; SR Victor: Jupiter
Lords: LOY – Mercury; LOP – Venus
Firdaria: Mars-Venus
Moon: applies to conjunction of Saturn
Return Ascendant falls in natal 10th, Natal Ascendant falls in return's 3rd.

In a fifth house profected year, natal 5th cusp 5GE35 conjunct the return's 8th cusp 10GE32 (not shown) ties entertainment to Taylor's death. Hīlāj Moon is afflicted both by conjunction to Saturn and square aspect to high-scoring killer Mars who receives her. Venus, the second high-scoring killer, falls in the return's Ascendant with Mercury LOY, both ruled by Mars. While Venus/Scorpio is capable of signifying poisoned food independently, if the story is accurate that Taylor died following consumption of eating a bowl of cherries and ice milk, then Mars in Cancer (Cancer = milk/dairy) appears to show the source of the poison, not improperly washed cherries as suggested by some historians. Venus in the hoarding sign of Scorpio may signify the rapid absorption of tainted milk into the cherries themselves. Finally, LOY Mercury rules the 8th of death in the return.

PT	D	Venus/Cancer	P	dex trine Venus (0) d. => ASC	30-Jun-1850
PT	D	Jupiter/Cancer	P	dex trine Mercury (0) d. => ASC	12-Jul-1850

A RECTIFICATION MANUAL

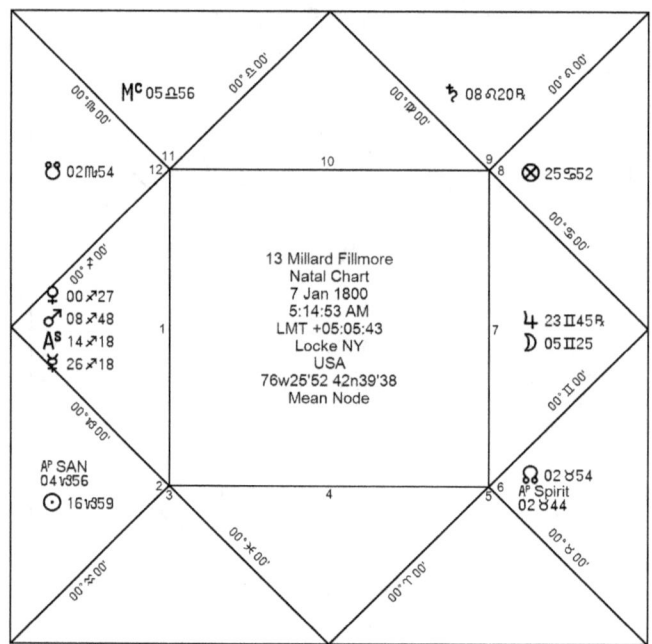

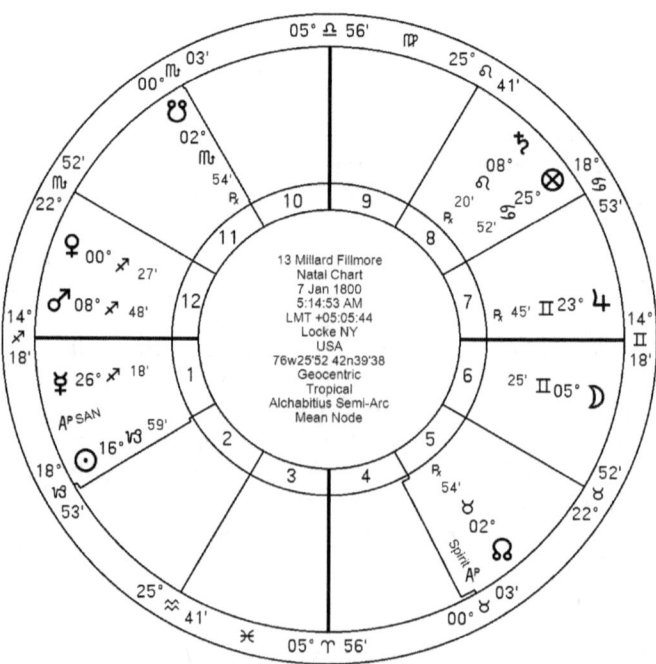

Moon's Configuration

Moon applies to **Saturn**, nocturnal, conjunctional.
Prenatal syzygy is 4CP56. Eclipse? No.

Cognitive Assessment Model (Rulers of Moon and Mercury)

Sign rulers: **Mercury, Jupiter**
Bound rulers: **Mercury, Mars**

Victor Soul Models

Ibn Ezra Victor Model (1507), in-sect triplicity ruler, triplicity decans.

	Position	☉	☽	☿	♀	♂	♃	♄
Sun	16 CP 59		3		3	4		5
Moon	05 GE 24			11				
Asc	14 SA 16			2		1	8	
Pars Fortuna	25 CA 50		5			3	7	
Syzygy	04 CP 56		3	2		4		6
Oriental						3	0	1
Houses		6	1	12	2	12	10	5
Score		6	12	**27**	5	**27**	25	17

Porphyry's Expanded Victor Model (2022)

Jupiter rules the ASC by sign; Lot of Fortune by bound. Sect: out-of-favor. Solar phase: occidental opposition to 2nd station. Position: 7th from ASC. Dignity: participating triplicity. Debility: detriment; Mutual reception with Mercury by sign.

Victor Table for Killing Planets

			☉	☽	☿	♀	♂	♃	♄
ASC		14SA16	3			2	1	5,3	3
Rul ASC	♃	23GE45			5,3		2	3	3,1
L.Death		21VI48		3	5,4	3,1	3,2		
Rul L.Death	☿	26SA18	3,1				2	5,3	3
H8 Cusp		18CA52		5,3	2	3	3,1	4	
Rul H8	☽	5GE31			5,3,2,1			3	3
T-Rul H8	♂	8SA49	3					5,3,2,1	3
8th from ☽		5CP24		3	2	3	4,3		5,1
Rul 8th fr ☽	♄	8LE20	5,3,1			2		3	3
TOTAL			19	14	**32**	14	21	**40**	25

2007 Proposed Rectification: 5:00:47 AM, ASC 11SA24'37"
2021 Proposed Rectification: 5:14:53 AM, ASC 14SA16'50"

Astrodatabank reports a C-rated birth time of 5:50:24 AM, rectified from approximate time citing Doane's *Horoscopes of US Presidents*. The revised rectification advances the LOS from Aries to Taurus, a better match to life affairs considering his post-presidential advocacy in formation of the Buffalo Fine Arts Academy as well as home entertaining with his second wife.

ZRS. LOS 2TA44, sign and bound lord Venus/Sagittarius, yields good results for ZR. Fillmore's active political career is entirely timed by the L1-Cancer period with Capricorn foreshadowing timing Fillmore's nurture of the Whig Party for which he would become the standard bearer after the death in office of Zachary Taylor. Note L2-Capricorn loosing of the bond timed Fillmore's political losses, not gains; he became President during L2-Pisces which is somewhat irregular based on ZR methodology.

L1 Taurus 07 Jan 1800		
L1 Gemini 27 Nov 1807		
L1 Cancer 14 Aug 1827		25-Feb-1828, birth of son Millard; Summer-1828, met Thurlow Weed, editor and political boss during NY anti-Masonic conventions; Fall-1828, elected to NY Assembly.
L2 Capricorn 01 Oct 1835	FS	1835, spent time out of office building the Whig Party; Nov-1836, elected as Whig candidate for House of Representatives, 2nd of two non-consecutive terms; opposed President Van Buren's sub-treasury proposal (considered deflationary); Fall-1837, Whigs captured NY Assembly.
L2 Capricorn 12 Dec 1844	LB	After losing Whig VP nomination via Thurlow Weed's machinations and losing the NY Gubernatorial race in fall 1844, MF helped found the University of Buffalo and became its first chancellor.
L2 Pisces 18 Aug 1849		10-Jul-1850, sworn in as President after death of Taylor.
L1 Leo 04 Apr 1852		16/21-Jun-1852, lost Whig Presidential nomination to General Winfield Scott.
L2 Aquarius 21 Jul 1860	FS	6-Nov-1860, supported Stephen Douglas for President; 12-Apr-1861, Civil War, thereafter supported Lincoln in order to preserve the Union.
L2 Aquarius 03 Aug 1869	LB	Summer-1869, accidental meeting with Thurlow Weed led to brief reconciliation.
L2 Scorpio 14 Apr 1873		8-Mar-1874, death.

13. MILLARD FILLMORE

Firdaria – Jupiter major and minor periods

Firdaria according to Bonatti	Life Event
Moon **Jupiter** 04 Aug 1802	No events found.
Saturn **Jupiter** 04 Aug 1810	No events found.
Jupiter 12 years Age 20 to 32	
Jupiter Jupiter 08 Jan 1820	No events found.
Jupiter Mars 25 Sep 1821	No events found.
Jupiter Sun 13 Jun 1823	No events found.
Jupiter Venus 28 Feb 1825	5-Feb-1826, married Abigail Fillmore.
Jupiter Mercury 16 Nov 1826	25-Apr-1828, birth of son Millard Powers Fillmore.
Jupiter Moon 03 Aug 1828	Summer-1838, met political boss Thurlow Weed.
Jupiter Saturn 21 Apr 1830	2-May-1831, death of mother.
Mars **Jupiter** 07 Jan 1838	No events found.
Sun **Jupiter** 28 Feb 1851	25-Apr-1851, made proclamation against Southerners wishing to annex Cuba; 5-Jun-1851, *Uncle Tom's Cabin* published as a serial, radicalized public against slavery; 25-Jul-1851, gold is discovered in Oregon; 22-Oct-1851, urged Americans against further military exploits in Mexico; 1/6-Jun-1852, Democrats nominated Franklin Pierce for President.
Venus **Jupiter** 03 Aug 1858	No events found.
Mercury **Jupiter** 04 Aug 1867	No events found.

Jupiter as Victor. Among all Presidents, Fillmore is the least written about and offers the fewest events for constructing a timeline. As Fillmore was a protégé of the political boss Thurlow Weed in his early political career, a chronology for Weed should help fill in the blanks for Fillmore's timeline – a project for future research.

As the chronology stands, Jupiter does identify Fillmore's initial meeting with Weed during the Jupiter-Moon subperiod.

The Sun-Jupiter period, which astronomically highlights Jupiter's retrograde motion, does in fact pick up the bulk of Fillmore's Presidential term. He was sworn in on 10-Jul-1850 on the death of Zachary Taylor.

Transits

8-Oct-1850. *tr Jupiter conj MC*.
  Compromise of 1850 passed, 20-Sep-1850.

12-Jan-1853. *tr Jupiter conj ASC*.
  Authorized Matthew Perry to seek trade relations with Japan, 24-Nov-1852.
  Washington Territory formed after separation from Oregon, 2-Mar-1853.
  Authorized Pacific Railroad Surveys, 1853 (no exact date). Eventually led to Transcendental Railroad construction after Civil War.

16-Aug-1854. *tr Saturn opposed ASC*.
  Death of daughter Mary Abigail "Abby" Fillmore, 26-Jul-1854.

10-Jan-1863. *tr North Node conj ASC*.
  Buffalo Fine Arts Academy opening exhibition, 23-Dec-1862.

24-Mar-1969. *tr Venus 25AR56rx and tr Saturn 25AR29 10th from LOF*.
  NYT reported 10,000 Millard Fillmore letters found which revealed "a deep personal relationship" between Fillmore and social reformer Dorothea Dix.

Solar Arc Directions

19-Mar-1853. *csa Saturn opposed ASC*.
1-Jun-1853. *dsa ASC conj Saturn*.
  President Franklin Pierce's appointment of Catholic James Campbell to postmaster general triggered formation of the anti-immigrant "Know Nothing" party, 4-Mar-1853.
  Wife Abigail Fillmore caught cold at Franklin Pierce's Inauguration, 4-Mar.
  Wife Abigail Fillmore died, 30-Mar-1853.
17-Sep-1856. *csa MC conj Saturn*.
9-Dec-1856. *dsa Saturn conj MC*.
  Whigs nominated Fillmore for President, 17-Sep-1856.
  Fillmore lost Presidential election, ended political career, 5-Nov-1856.

Lots

5-Feb-1826. *csa North Node 6AR19 conj L.Marriage.Men (Hermes) 6AR23*.
  Marriage to Abigail Powers.
10-Feb-1858. *csa Moon 6AR24 conj L.Marriage.Men (Hermes) 6AR23*.
  Marriage to Caroline Carmichael McIntosh.

Primary Directions

PT	D	Mercury/Aquarius	P	dex sq North Node d. => ASC	11-Nov-1848

Elected Vice President, 7-Nov-1848.

Delineation of Saturn/Leo-rx as the Know Nothing Party

The Know Nothing Party emerged following the collapse of the Whig Party after Whig Presidential candidate Winfield Scott lost to Franklin Pierce in the 1852 Presidential election. The high-water mark for the party was the 1854 election cycle when it nearly swept the entire Massachusetts legislature, its most impressive national electoral victory. In 1856 while Fillmore was on vacation in Europe, the newly formed American National Party comprised of Know Nothing proponents nominated him for President on 22-Feb-1856. He was nominated a 2nd time by the remnants of the Whig Party on 17-Sep-1856. His loss to James Buchanan on 5-Nov-1856 ended his political career and saw a rapid decline of the Know Nothing movement which split into pro and anti-slavery factions. Anti-slavery Know Nothings merged into the new Republican Party under Lincoln; pro-slavery Know Nothings dissolved once the Civil War began.

The Know Nothing Party was an anti-immigrant backlash movement following a surge in Irish immigrants during the potato famine between 1845 and 1852. Most were Catholic which added fears of subversion of the US political system by the Pope who would somehow exercise his papal objectives via his Catholic subjects. As recently as JFK's 1960 successful Presidential bid, the conspiratorial fear of Catholic subversion of American democracy has been a national political theme.

In *American is Born, Introducing the Regulus USA National Horoscope*, I delineated the Ascendant distributor Jupiter/Leo as a pro-Catholic signature active during the early 1950s when the Catholic Church reached its highest influence in 20th century American life with the popularity of parochial schools and media personalities like Bishop Fulton Sheen. Compared to Jupiter/Leo, as a religious significator Saturn/Leo adds a command-and-control element to matters of religious faith. Accordingly, Saturn/Leo-retrograde rejects Saturn/Leo themes which is consistent with the Know Nothing's rejection of 'Popery', the catch-all term used in 1850s popular media.

My recent research shows retrograde planets act like they are placed in the opposite sign; in this case, Aquarius. Legislation passed by the Know Nothing-dominated Massachusetts legislature in 1855 is consistent with Saturn/Aquarius: idealistic reforms of all types including opposition to slavery, women's rights, industry regulation, measures to support the working-class, public-school textbooks, and the promotion of libraries.

By solar arc, direction of Saturn/Leo-rx to the DSC timed formation of the Know Nothing Party; direction to the MC timed Fillmore's Presidential nomination and unsuccessful bid as a Know Nothing candidate.

Longevity, 74y 2m 0d

Death: 8-Mar-1874, 11:10 PM, Buffalo, NY, at home. Other than suffering from obesity from over consumption of food, Fillmore suffered no apparent critical health incidents until shortly before his death. He suffered an initial stroke on his left side 13-Feb while shaving. After a partial recovery of affected muscles, a second stroke on 26-Feb proved fatal as his ability to swallow was affected. He fell unconscious and died on 8-Mar.

Hīlāj: **ASC or Sun**. Moon is preferred in a nocturnal figure though she is technically disqualified by exceeding the 5-degree cutoff rule below the 7th cup. Sun/Capricorn/2nd is acceptable but is feral with no aspect to any traditional planet. For a conjunctional figure, next choice is the Ascendant with both sign and bound lords angular, Jupiter and Venus respectively.

Al-kadukhadāh: **Jupiter**. Bound lord of both the Ascendant and the Sun is Venus which is angular. If Venus, then Venus grants 82 major years and Mars deducts 15 minor years by conjunction for a net of 67 years. He lived longer.

As victor, Jupiter is the better empirical choice. Jupiter grants 79 major years; Mars deducts 15 minor years by opposition aspect with reception by bound.

JU (79) – MA (15) = 64 years

This projection takes Fillmore to March 8, 1864 which is about the time he made a conciliatory speech on post-Civil War treatment of the Confederacy. Coming in the final days of the war, Fillmore was labeled a traitor and a Copperhead. Between 1864 and his death ten years later there were no major events on his timeline.

Victor of the Horoscope: **Jupiter**

Killing Planets: **Jupiter (40), Mercury (32)**

Arcus Vitae:

| PT | D | Mars/Aries | P | sin tr Mercury (0) d. => Sun | 26-Feb-1874 |

This is the most logical primary direction for death as it joins Mercury, significator of strokes, with the Sun as empirical Hīlāj.

13. MILLARD FILLMORE

1874 Solar Return for year of Death

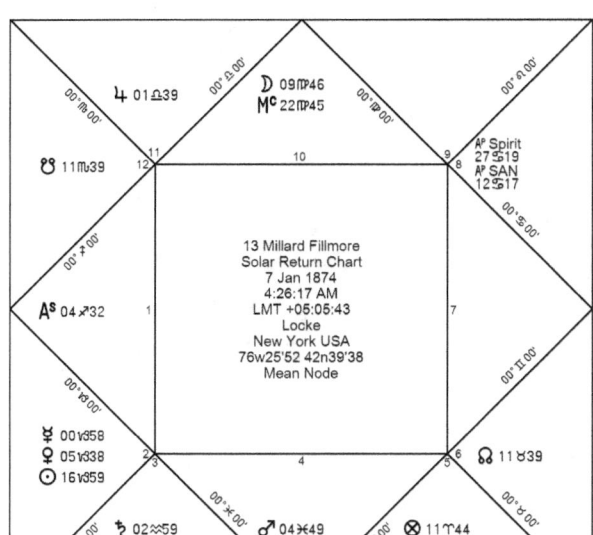

Ascendant Distributor: Venus/Pisces since 19-Jun-1867.
Profected Ascendant: 14AQ16, 3rd house; SR Victor: Mars
Lords: LOY – Saturn; LOP – Sun
Firdaria: Mercury-Venus
Moon separates from trine of Venus and applies to trine of Sun
Natal and Return Ascendant both Sagittarius.

Mercury, significator of strokes, makes his Capricorn ingress just before the solar return is cast. In the natal, Mercury and Jupiter are in opposition aspect in mutable signs. In the return, Mercury and Jupiter are in square aspect with Jupiter overcoming Mercury. By transit at time of death, Mercury and Jupiter recapitulate the natal opposition aspect in mutable signs on 1-Mar between his second stroke on 28-Feb and death 8-Mar-1874.

Jupiter and Mercury are the high scoring killing planets.

Death is timed by a solar return Ascendant direction to Jupiter.

| PT | D | Mercury/Aquarius | P | sin trine Jupiter d. => ASC | 8-Mar-1874 |

14 Franklin Pierce

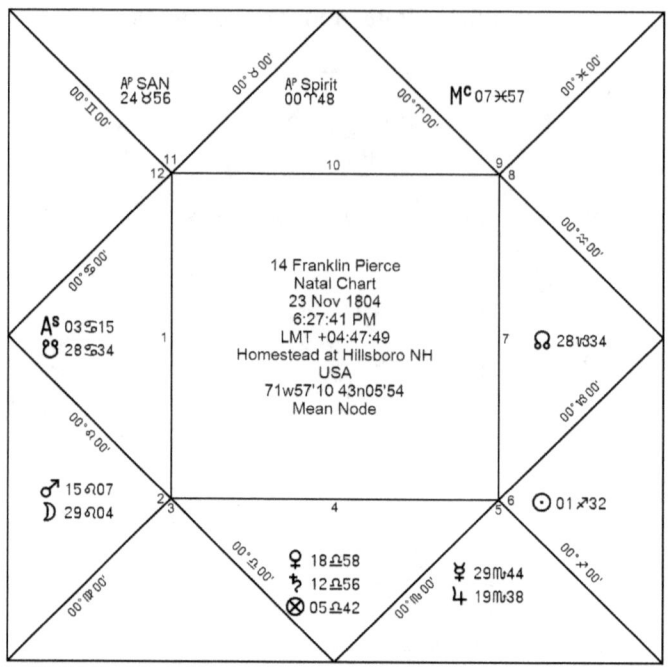

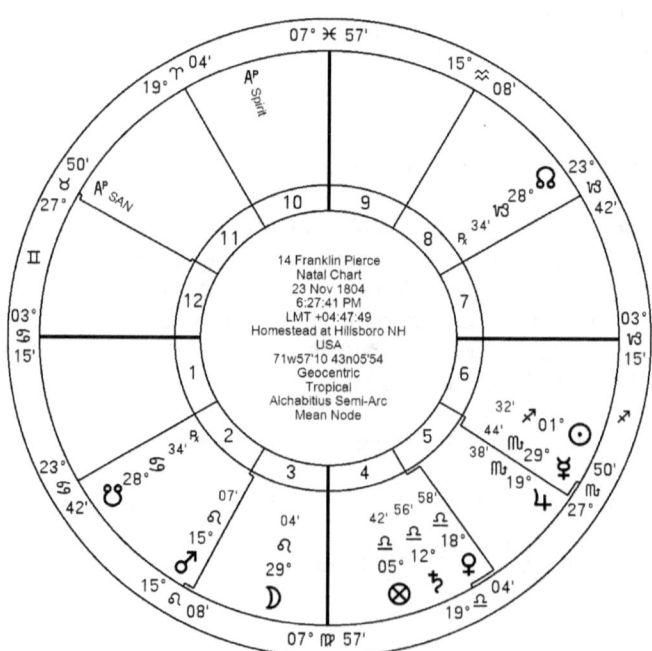

Moon's Configuration

Moon separates from **Jupiter** and applies to **Mercury**, nocturnal, preventional. Prenatal syzygy is 24TA56. Eclipse? No.

Cognitive Assessment Model (Rulers of Moon and Mercury)

Sign rulers: **(Sun)/Jupiter, Mars**
Bound rulers: **Mars, Saturn**

Victor Soul Models

Ibn Ezra Victor Model (1507), in-sect triplicity ruler, triplicity decans.

	Position	☉	☽	☿	♀	♂	♃	♄
Sun	01 SA 32						11	
Moon	29 LE 04	5				3	3	
Asc	03 CA 15		6			5	4	
Pars Fortuna	05 LI 42			3	6			6
Syzygy	24 TA 56			7	5			3
Oriental						1	0	3
Houses		1	3	1	7	3	7	9
Score		0	6	16	4	18	12	**25**	21

Porphyry's Expanded Victor Model (2022)

Jupiter rules the MC and Sun by sign; the Sun and Lot of Spirit by bound. Sect: out-of-favor. Solar phase: oriental under the sunbeams. Dignity: bound and decan. Moon's separation.

Victor Table for Killing Planets

			☉	☽	☿	♀	♂	♃	♄
ASC		3CA15		5,3,1		3	3,2	4	
Rul ASC	☽	29LE05	5,3				2,1	3	3
L.Death		7PI34		3		4,3,2	3	5,1	
Rul L.Death	♃	19SC38		3		3	5,3	2,1	
H8 Cusp		23CP42		3	1	3	4,3		5,2
Rul H8	♄	12LI56			3,1	5		3	4,3,1
T-Rul H8	☽	29LE05	5,3				2,1	3	3
8th from ☽		29PI04		3		4,3	3,1	5	2
Rul 8th fr ☽	♃	19SC38		3		3	5,3	2,1	
TOTAL				16	24	6	**33**	**41**	30	23

2007 Proposed Rectification: 6:27:37 PM, ASC 3CA15'15"
2022 Proposed Rectification: 6:27:41 PM, ASC 3CA15'18"

Astrodatabank reports an X-rated birth date without time. The 2007 rectification holds up well with ZRS. L1-Gemini timed Pierce's local/statewide political career; L1-Cancer timed his brief military service in the Mexican War which he successfully marketed in the 1852 Presidential race. L2-Capricorn (FS) saw him voted out of office and L2-Capricorn (LB) timed threats of mob violence following Lincoln's assassination.

L1 Aries 23 Nov 1804		
L1 Taurus 06 Sep 1819		
L1 Gemini 26 Jul 1827		Sep-1827, admitted to the bar; 11-Mar-1828, elected moderator of Hillsborough's town meetings; Mar-1828, began his 1st term in court; early-1829, elected to State Senate.
L2 Sagittarius 09 May 1836	FS	May-1836, newly elected Governor Isaac Hill resigned Senate seat, leaving it open; Dec-1836, Pierce elected to Senate term beginning March 1837.
L2 Sagittarius 23 Nov 1844	LB	12-Jan-1845, political ally John Hale wrote letter stating he would oppose Texas annexation despite instructions from state Democratic Party; 12-Feb-1845, FP convened NH Democratic state convention to rescind Hale's nomination for re-election to the House; Mar-1845, Hale retained enough popularity to deny the Democrat's favored candidate from gaining enough votes to win House election; Apr-1845, law partnership with Asa Fowler ended; 5-Jun-1845, famous debate between Hale and Pierce; both men held their own but slight edge to Hale; Nov-1845 elections repeated results of March with Hale obtaining enough votes to deny the state Democratic party candidate victory.
L1 Cancer 12 Apr 1847		13-May-1847, left home for military service in Mexican War; 27-Jun-1847, arrived in Vera Cruz; 10-Aug-1847, began march to Mexico City; 19-Aug-1847, serious injury at Battle of Contreras; 28-Dec-1847, returned home.
L2 Libra 14 Jul 1852		2-Nov-1852, defeated General Winfield Scott to win Presidency; 6-Jan-1853, death of 3rd son Benjamin in train accident; 3-Mar-1853, Presidential Inauguration.
L2 Capricorn 30 May 1855	FS	5-Jun-1855, Know Nothing party formed; 2-Jul-1855, Kansas territorial legislature passed laws institutionalizing slavery, one trigger for *Bleeding Kansas* conflict; 23-Oct-1855, Topeka Constitution; 21-May-1856, "Sack of Lawrence;" 2/5-Jun-1856, Democrats nominated James Buchanan; 4-Nov-1856, Buchanan won Presidency.
L2 Capricorn 10 Aug 1864	LB	14-Apr-1865, Lincoln's Assassination triggered angry mob surrounding FP's house, FP disbursed the crowd with a speech.
L2 Pisces 16 Apr 1869		8-Oct-1869, died.

14. FRANKLIN PIERCE

Firdaria – Jupiter major and minor periods

Firdaria according to Bonatti	Life Events
Moon **Jupiter** 20 Jun 1807	No events found.
Saturn **Jupiter** 20 Jun 1815	No events found.
Jupiter 12 years Age 20 to 32	
Jupiter Jupiter 23 Nov 1824	Fall-1824, studied law while ran post office; Jun-1826, Father nominated Governor.
Jupiter Mars 11 Aug 1826	Mar-1827, Father elected Governor; Sep-1827, FP admitted to the bar.
Jupiter Sun 28 Apr 1828	4-Jul-1828, made notable speech but reporter failed to note down the subject; Jan-1829, jump in legal business; Early-1829, moderator at town meeting; elected to State Senate same day father is re-elected as Governor; May-1829, appointed Justice of the Peace.
Jupiter Venus 15 Jan 1830	No events found.
Jupiter Mercury 03 Oct 1831	No events found.
Jupiter Moon 20 Jun 1833	10-Nov-1834, marriage to Jane Pierce; 18-Feb-1835, bilious attack.
Jupiter Saturn 08 Mar 1835	2-Feb-1836, birth of 1st son Franklin who died three days later.
Mars **Jupiter** 23 Nov 1842	14-Nov-1843, death of 2nd son Frank Robert Pierce from typhus.
Sun **Jupiter** 15 Jan 1856	21-May-1856, *Sack of Lawrence* triggered Bleeding Kansas civil conflict; 2/5-Jun-1856, Democrats nominated James Buchanan; 4-Nov-1856, Buchanan won Presidency.
Venus **Jupiter** 20 Jun 1863	No events found.

Jupiter as Victor. Pierce's Major Jupiter period timed legal studies, admission to the bar, and entry to political office. At the same time his father is nominated, elected, and re-elected as Governor of New Hampshire.

As minor Firdaria lord, Jupiter did time Pierce's final year of his Presidency. It included the outbreak of civil conflict in Kansas, e.g., 'Bleeding Kansas,' for which his Presidency is remembered.

Note both Jupiter-Sun and Sun-Jupiter periods timed peak periods for Franklin Pierce's political career.

Transits

20-Jun-1826. *tr Jupiter conj IC*.
Father nominated for NH Governorship, Jun-1826.

4-Apr-1841. *tr Saturn conj DSC, 1st station 11-Apr.*
Death in office of President William Henry Harrison, 4-Apr-1841.

2-Apr-1847; 24-Sep-1847; 25-Dec-1847. *tr Saturn conj MC*.
Mexican War service: appointed Brigadier General on 3-Mar; injured at Battle of Contreras, 19-Aug-1847; returned home on 28-Dec-1847.

16-Dec-1853. *tr Jupiter conj DSC*.
US and Mexico signed Gadsen purchase treaty, 30-Dec-1853.

17-Jan-1854. *tr North Node 10th from MC*. Stephen Douglas introduced Kansas-Nebraska legislation, 23-Jan-1854.

Solar Arc Directions

5-Feb-1836. *dsa Sun opposed ASC*.
10-Jun-1836. *csa ASC opposed Sun*.
   LOCK Death of 1st son, 5-Feb-1836; beginning of interest in religion. John Page chosen to fill unexpired Senate seat, Jun-1836; suggested implicit agreement by the legislature for FP to take full term Senate seat, Dec-1836.

19-Apr-1839. *dsa MC opposed Saturn*.
20-Sep-1839. *csa Saturn opposed MC*.
   Death of Father, 1-Apr-1839.
   Quit alcohol, 1839 (no exact date).

20-Jan-1846. *dsa ASC conj Mars*.
27-Aug-1846. *csa Mars conj ASC*.
   LOCK Taylor ordered to advance to banks of Rio Grande on 13 January, received orders 3 February.
   FP declined President Polk's offer of Attorney General; FP saw opportunity to garner wartime credentials for political purposes instead, 27-Aug-1846.

10-Jan-1853. *dsa Venus square MC*.
   Witnessed death of son Benjamin in train accident, 6-Jan-1853.
   Venus rules 12th (QS).

7-Aug-1854. *dsa Mars conj LOF*.
   Hit by hardboiled egg thrown by enraged South Carolinian, 7-Aug-1854.

14. FRANKLIN PIERCE

Primary Directions

| PT | D | Jupiter/Aries | P | sin trine Sun d. => MC | 4-Sep-1826 |

Father nominated NH Governor, Jun-1826.
Father elected NH Governor, Mar-1827.

| PT | D | Mercury/Capricorn | P | DSC d. => Jupiter (JU) | 4-Apr-1846 |
| PT | D | Mercury/Capricorn | P | DSC d. => Jupiter (0) | 14-Feb-1847 |

Period leading up to and including FP's appointment in the infantry, 15-Feb-1847, where he is charged to recruit a regiment from New England.

| REG | D | Venus/Cancer | P | sin trine MC c. => Mars (MA) | 23-Feb-1847 |

Passage of Benton Bill confirmed Pierce as Brigadier General, 3-Mar-1847.

| REG | D | Venus/Pisces | P | MC d. => North Node | 23-Nov-1853 |

Death of New Hampshire Senator Charles G. Atherton whom FP had chosen to be his agent in the Senate, 15-Nov-1853.

Primary Direction Sequences

| PT | D | Saturn/Leo | P | Mars (MA) d. => ASC | 4-May-1855 |
| PT | D | Saturn/Leo | P | Mars (0) d. => ASC | 18-Dec-1856 |

This sequence contained most of the brutal events of *Bleeding Kansas* including the Pawnee Convention of 2-Jul-1855, the Wakarusa War (21-Nov-1854 to 7-Dec-1855), the *Sack of Lawrence* on 21-May-1856, John Brown's retaliatory raid at Pottawotamie Creek on 24-May-1856, Charles Sumner's *Crime Against Kansas* speech in the Senate during 19/20-May-1856, and Preston Brooks' 22-May-1856 attack on Sumner when he beat Sumner unconscious on the floor of the Senate.

| PT | D | Mars/Cancer | P | ASC c. => Moon (0) | 30-Nov-1863 |
| REG | D | Mars/Cancer | P | ASC c. => Moon (MO) | 21-May-1864 |

LOCK This mix of PT and REG directions timed the death of Pearce's wife on 2-Dec-1863 and his close friend, the author Nathanial Hawthorne, on 19-May-1864. After the death of his wife, Pierce started to drink alcohol again heavily.

Longevity, 64y 10m 14d

Death: 8-Oct-1869, 4:35 AM, Concord, New Hampshire, at home. Pierce died from liver cirrhosis, a side effect of alcoholism. Pierce had stopped drinking towards the end of his life; yet started again following the death of his wife in 1863. His health deteriorated during the summer of 1869. He took to bed in September and passed in and out of consciousness in his final days.

Hīlāj: **Moon/LOF**. Figure is nocturnal. Moon in $2^{nd}/3^{rd}$/masculine qualifies. There is some evidence that the LOF also functions as the Hīlāj. In addition to the 7-Aug-1854 Mars-LOF solar arc direction which timed an angry southerner throwing a hardboiled egg at Pierce (which under slightly difference circumstances could have marked an assassination attempt), the Venus-LOF direction (see below) is a potential arcus vitae.

Al-kadukhadāh: **Jupiter**. In the place of the Moon, triplicity ruler Saturn scores the highest in essential dignities yet does not aspect. Moon separates from the square of Jupiter who in his own bound rules the Moon by triplicity. Jupiter grants his 79 major years. Mars squares Jupiter and deducts 15 minor years.

JU (79) – MA (15) = 64 years.

While Jupiter receives Mars by nocturnal triplicity and decan, this reception does not mitigate Mars' deduction of years.

Note: South Node falling in natal Ascendant weakens the physical body.

Victor of the Horoscope: **Jupiter**

Killing Planets: **Mars (41), Venus (33)**

Arcus Vitae:

REG	D	Mercury/Cancer	P	dex sq Venus (VE) c. => LOF	14-Apr-1868
REG	D	Mercury/Cancer	P	dex sq Venus (0) c. => LOF	16-Jul-1869

With alcoholism the principal cause of death, Venus is the logical killing planet. Any Venus - Hīlāj combination is a plausible killing direction.

PT	D	Mars/Sagittarius	P	sin trine Moon (0) d. => Venus (0)	7-Oct-1869

This is the last of multiple Moon trine Venus directions dating back to 1864 which joins one of the high scoring killers to the Moon as Hīlāj. This set of directions conforms to Pierce's resumption of drinking alcohol following his wife's death in 1863 which ultimately led to his death.
See also tr. Mars conj. DSC at death.

14. FRANKLIN PIERCE

1868 Solar Return for year of Death

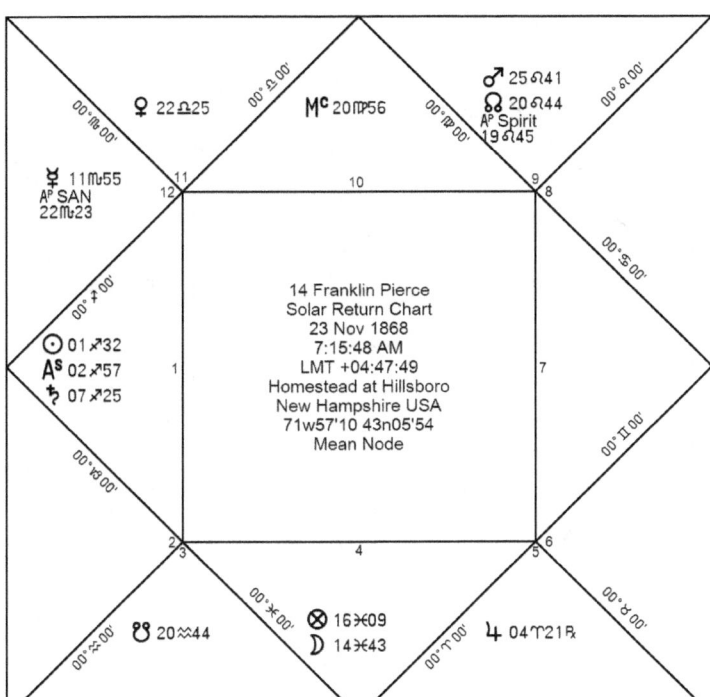

Ascendant Distributor: Mars/Leo since 24-Jul-1868.
Profected Ascendant: 3SC24, 5th House; SR Victor: Jupiter
Lords: LOY - Mars; LOP – Venus
Firdaria: Mercury-Moon
Moon separates from trine of Mercury and is void of course.
Return Ascendant falls in natal 6th; natal Ascendant falls in return's 8th.

Saturn, ruler of the natal 8th, falls in the return's Ascendant and afflicts both luminaries in the return. Both high-scoring killing planets Venus and Mars return to their natal sign positions, increasing their power to act. Return Mars at 25LE41 is closely conjunct natal Moon at 29LE04. Return Venus (22LI25) is conjunct the antiscia of the Lot of Death (7PI33/22LI27).

| PT | D | Venus/Libra | P | Venus (0) d. => ASC | 30-Sep-1869 |
| PT | D | Venus/Libra | P | sin sextile Mars (0) d. => ASC | 5-Oct-1869 |

At the time of these two directions, Pierce was mostly in bed, by 7-Oct he was in an out of consciousness before dying the morning of 9-Oct-1869.

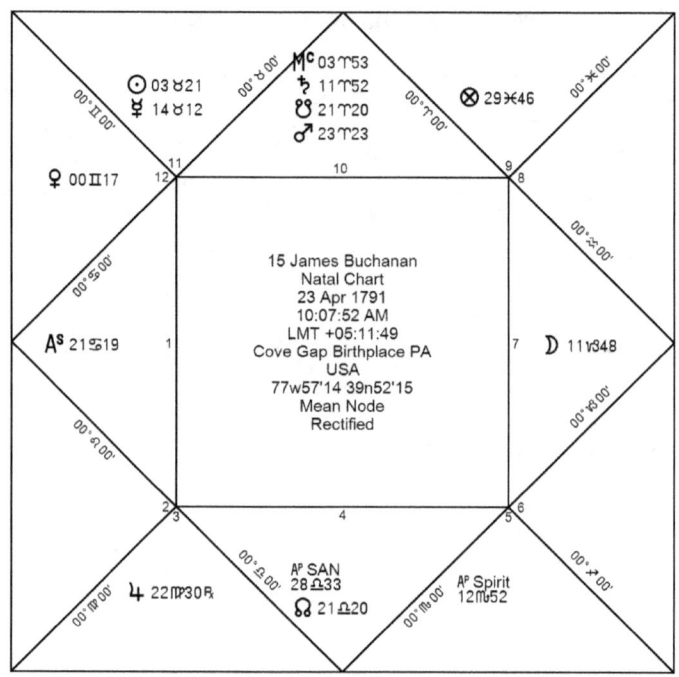
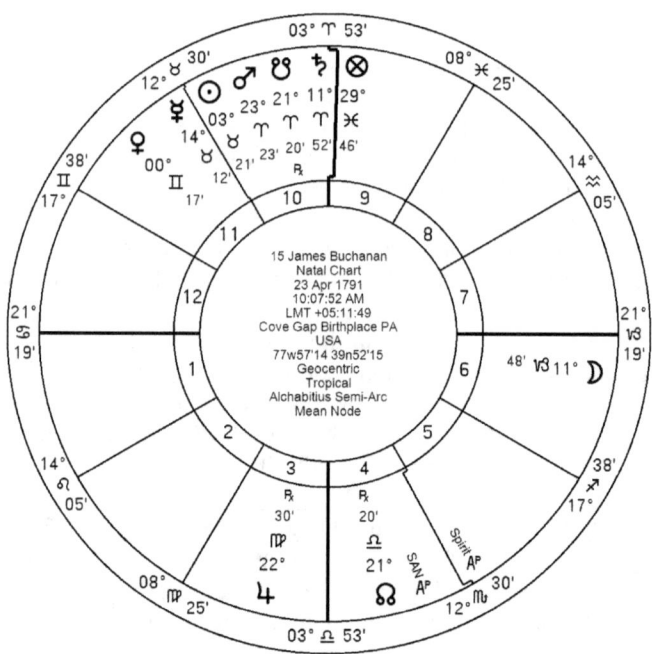

15. JAMES BUCHANAN

Moon's Configuration

Moon separates from the **Sun** and applies to **Saturn**, diurnal, preventional. Prenatal syzygy is 28LI33. Eclipse? **YES**. Partial Lunar Eclipse.

Cognitive Assessment Model (Rulers of Moon and Mercury)

Sign rulers: **Saturn, Venus**
Bound rulers: **Jupiter** (both)

Victor Soul Models

Ibn Ezra Victor Model (1507), in-sect triplicity ruler, triplicity decans.

	Position	☉	☽	☿	♀	♂	♃	♄
Sun	03 TA 21		4		11			
Moon	11 CP 48				4	4	2	5
Asc	21 CA 19		5		3		7	
Pars Fortuna	29 PI 46				7	1	5	2
Syzygy	28 LI 33 (LE)			1	5	2		7
Oriental						0	0	3
Houses			8	10	8	8	11	9	11
Score		0	8	19	9	**38**	18	23	28

Porphyry's Expanded Victor Model (2022)

Jupiter rules the Lot of Fortune by sign; the MC, ASC, and Moon by bound. Sect: in-favor. Solar phase: occidental opposition to 2nd station. Position: 7th from Lot of Fortune. Debility: detriment. Jupiter/Virgo-rx is a delineation match to Buchanan's vacillating decisions as a diplomat, Supreme Court contender, and President.

Victor Table for Killing Planets

			☉	☽	☿	♀	♂	♃	♄
ASC		21CA19		5,3		3	3	4,2,1	
Rul ASC	☽	11CP48		3		3,1	4,3	2	5
LOD		14TA09		4,3	1	5,3	3	2	
Rul LOD	♀	0GE17			5,3,2,1			3	3
H8 Cusp		14AQ05			3,1			3,2	5,3
Rul H8	♄	11AR52	4,3,1			2	5	3	3
T-Rul H8	♄	11AR52	4,3,1			2	5	3	3
8th fr ☉		3SA21	3					5,3,2,1	3
Rul 8th fr ☉	♃	22VI30		3	5,4	3,1	3,2		
TOTAL			19	21	**25**	23	**28**	**36**	25

2007 Proposed Rectification, 9:34:09 AM, ASC 14CA18'02", Mercersburg
2022 Proposed Rectification, 10:07:52 AM, ASC 21CA19'37", Cove Gap

Astrodatabank reports an X-rated date without time. The 2022 revision advances the time by half an hour, maintaining the same signs for the Ascendant, LOF, and LOS. MC degree moves from Pisces to Aries. The change was motivated by moving the LOS from the bound of Mar/Scorpio (unlikely) to Mercury/Scorpio (though bound of Jupiter/Scorpio cannot be ruled out).

Configuration of the chart remains the most important rectification tool in support of Cancer rising. Buchanan's professional career as a lawyer and traveling diplomat are consistent with Jupiter as the victor of the horoscope; with Cancer rising Jupiter is in the 3rd ruling the 9th of foreign affairs which houses the Jupiter-ruled Lot of Fortune. The fact that Jupiter is in aversion to the dominant configuration of Saturn-South Node-Mars in the 10th house is a delineation match to Buchanan's real-life aversion between himself and the militancy of the Polk administration and militant factions of the Democratic Party which broke up under his administration. The second delineation match concerns Mercury/Taurus – Venus/Gemini in generosity with both planets in and ruling the 11th/12th. This is consistent with Buchanan's friendship and political alliance with William R. King, rumored to be Buchanan's homosexual partner. The linkage between friendship (11th) and rumor (12th) is obvious with this configuration. Compare to Thomas Jefferson with Venus/Taurus/12th the significator of his secret love interest Sally Hemings.

ZRS

L1 **Scorpio** 23 Apr 1791		
L1 **Sagittarius** 04 Feb 1806		
L1 **Capricorn** 03 Dec 1817		Summer 1819, engaged to Ann Coleman; 9-Dec-1819, Ann Coleman died, rumored suicide.
L2 Cancer 14 Feb 1827	FS	4-Feb-1828, made anti-Adams speech in House, served as start of re-election campaign; early-Oct-1828, won re-election to House, demonstrated Amalgamation plan on uniting Jackson Federalists and Jackson Democrats was a success.
L2 Cancer 03 Apr 1835	LB	Winter 1836, re-elected to Senate; 7-Dec-1836, Martin Van Buren elected as President but JB did not receive any significant position in the administration.
L1 **Aquarius** 14 Jul 1844		4-Dec-1844, James Polk elected President.
L2 Leo 27 Jul 1853	FS	Aug-1853, diplomatic mission to UK failed to secure agreement over Honduras or Nicaragua; 18-Oct-1854, participated in Ostend Manifesto on annexation of Cuba for the security of slavery.
L2 Libra 09 Oct 1856		4-Nov-1856, won Presidential Election.
L2 Capricorn 25 Aug 1859		1860, failed to be renominated for President.
L2 Leo 12 Nov 1861	LB	15-Dec-1862, attempt made to censure JB in the Senate (check 1861 or 1862).
L2 Capricorn 11 Dec 1867		1-Jun-1868, death.

Firdaria – Jupiter major and minor periods

Firdaria according to Bonatti	Life Event
Sun **Jupiter** 14 Jun 1798	No events found.
Venus **Jupiter** 18 Nov 1805	No events found.
Mercury **Jupiter** 18 Nov 1814	Autumn-1814, won first election to PA legislature; 1-Feb-1815, spoke against conscription bill in favor of volunteer bill; Dec-1815, returned to PA legislature and sat on Judiciary and Banking committees.
Moon **Jupiter** 18 Nov 1824	9-Feb-1825, John Adams selected President; subsequently JB formed 'Amalgamation' political organization.
Saturn **Jupiter** 18 Nov 1832	18-Dec-1832, near the end of his Russian mission, JB rcvd surprise announcement that Russian Emperor signed the commercial treaty that was the focus of Buchanan's mission.
Jupiter 12 years Age 51 to 63	
Jupiter Jupiter 23 Apr 1842	No events found.
Jupiter Mars 09 Jan 1844	17-Feb-1845, accepted Polk's offer of Secretary of State; Summer-1845, unsuccessful negotiations with UK over Oregon and Mexico over Texas.
Jupiter Sun 27 Sep 1845	Late-September-1834, asked Polk to let him quit Secretary of State position and be appointed to Supreme Court, Polk nominated Woodward instead; 13-May-1846, Congress approved Polk's War Declaration against Mexico; 27-Jul-1846, JB offered to negotiate with Mexico for Texas; 26-Feb-1847, Polk agreed to JB's proposal for settling Oregon at 49th parallel; 13-Apr-1847, JB proposed Mexican deal for up to $15 million; 12-Jun-1847, Senate approved Oregon Treaty signed 15-Jun-1847 (start of next Jupiter-Venus period).
Jupiter Venus 15 Jun 1847	Aug-1847, JP proposed extending Missouri Compromise line westward; 19-Feb-1848, JP presented Treaty of Guadalupe Hidalgo negotiated by Nicholas Trist to President Polk; 22-May-1848, Baltimore convention nominated Cass for President, ending JB's chances that year; 7-Nov-1848, Taylor elected President.
Jupiter Mercury 02 Mar 1849	15-Jun-1849, Polk died, after this JB actively sought the Presidency; 9/12-Sep-1850, Missouri Compromise.
Jupiter Moon 18 Nov 1850	19-Nov-1850, JB wrote letter on his opinion of Missouri Compromise which constituted his opening bid for the 1852 Presidential race.
Jupiter Saturn 05 Aug 1852	Autumn-1852, JP suffered from worst bilious attack of his lifetime immediately prior to the election; 2-Nov-1852, Pierce elected President; 1-Apr-1853, Pierce asked JB to accept Mission to England; Summer/Fall-1853, While in England unable to secure any negotiations with Britain to leave Honduras or Nicaragua - anticipating conflict over the Panama Canal under Theodore Roosevelt years later.
Mars **Jupiter** 23 Apr 1860	23-Apr-1860, Democratic Party abandoned Stephen Douglas as candidate; no nominee chosen; 20-Nov-1860, asked for clarification of legal powers of the President under secession; 3-Dec-1860, Annual Message - JB stated the South had no legal right to secede from the Union, yet neither did the Federal Government have the basis to prevent such action; 20-Dec-1860, South Carolina seceded; 12-Apr-1861, Civil War began.

Transits

31-May-1844. *tr Jupiter conj LOF*.
Multiple transits of Jupiter direct and retro to MC and LOF.
8-Feb-1845. *tr Jupiter conj MC*.
   James Polk selected as Democratic Presidential nominee, 29-May-1844.
   James Polk invited Buchanan to be Secretary of State, 17-Feb-1845.

7-May-1856. *tr Jupiter conj LOF*.
Multiple transits of Jupiter direct and retro to MC and LOF.
16-Jan-1857. *tr Jupiter conj MC*.
   Started front porch Presidential campaign, May-1856.
   Elected President, 4-Nov-1856.
   Traveled to Washington to finalize cabinet, 27-Jan/3-Feb-1857.

Parents

11-Jun-1821. *dsa Venus 29GE23 conj L.Father 29GE50* for death of father.
   Venus rules the 11th, death of the father.

14-May-1833. *trMars 21CA conj ASC, tr Jup conj S.Node* for death of mother.
   Mars rules the 5th (death of mother). SN/10th signifies harm to mother.

Solar Arc Directions

13-Sep-1820. *csa ASC conj Jupiter*.
25-Feb-1821. *dsa Jupiter conj ASC*.
12-May-1821. *csa Sun conj MC*.
31-Oct-1821. *dsa MC conj Sun*.
   These two direction pairs are a reasonable delineation match to JB's first Congressional election victory during Fall-1820 and the intervening period of newfound fame up until he left for Washington DC in late-Nov-1821.

7-Jan-1834. *csa Sun trine ASC*.
11-Dec-1834. *dsa ASC trine Sun*.
   No event found for first direction.
   LOCK Elected to US Senate, 6-Dec-1834; seated 15-Dec-1834.

4-Apr-1863. *csa MC trine Jupiter*.
15-Sep-1865. *dsa Jupiter trine MC*.
   No event found for first direction.
   LOCK Elders of Presbyterian church admitted JB to the church making him eligible for communion, 23-Sep-1865. Jupiter rules the 9th of religion.

15. JAMES BUCHANAN

Primary Directions

| PT | D | Mercury/Virgo | P | sin trine Sun d. => ASC | 26-Apr-1844 |

Texas annexation treaty submitted to the Senate by JT, 27-Apr-1844.
This action by President Tyler effectively blew away Presidential contenders Henry Clay and Martin Van Buren who had only recently said they would not support Texas annexation. In response to Tyler's action, there was a brief boomlet for JB to run for President but it didn't last.

Primary Direction Sequences

| REG | D | Jupiter/Cancer | P | ASC d. => Jupiter (0) | 11-Jul-1854 |
| REG | D | Jupiter/Cancer | P | ASC d. => Jupiter (JU) | 19-Oct-1854 |

JB interested in buying Cuba from the Spanish, nothing happened, 1854.
JB and other American European ministers met in Ostend, Belgium and published the Ostend Manifesto, 18-Oct-1854. Stated the US needed to annex Cuba for the security of slavery and that if Spain refused to sell the island, then Cuba should be taken by force. Shows the influence of Jupiter placed in the bound of Mars on the militant tone of JB's diplomacy.

PT	D	Mercury/Taurus	P	sin trine Moon (MO) d. => LOF	8-Dec-1829
PT	D	Mercury/Taurus	P	sin trine Moon (0) d. => LOF	12-Jun-1831
PT	D	Mercury/Taurus	P	sin trine Moon (BI) d. => LOF	4-Mar-1832

21st Congress convened, Dec-1829.
Beginning in Spring-1830, Calhoun's political power eroded which revived the influence of JB and his political alliance known as the Amalgamators.
JP accepted appointment as Russian diplomat, 12-Jun-1831.
Senate confirmation, 12-Jan-1832
Left Washington in preparation for Russian trip, 21-Mar-1832.

PT	D	Jupiter/Gemini	P	sin sextile Saturn (0) d. => MC	5-Feb-1858
PT	D	Jupiter/Gemini	P	sin sextile Saturn (BI) d. => MC	5-Apr-1858
PT	D	Jupiter/Gemini	P	sin sextile Saturn (SA) d. => MC	1-Jun-1858

JB's Lecompton message sent to Congress, 2-Feb-1858.
Senate voted to accept Kansas as slave state; House asked for Kansas to vote again on the state constitution, 23-Mar-1858.
House amended Kansas bill to provide for new vote, 1-Apr-1858.
Lecompton Constitution rejected in 3rd vote, 2-Aug-1858.
This primary direction sequence coincides with one section of the larger unsuccessful attempt by JB to resolve the Kansas slavery question. Saturn/Aries works to stop conflict; the distributor Jupiter/Gemini/12th links Saturn to an illegal judicial act.

Longevity, 77y 1m 9d

Death: 1-Jun-1868, ~8:30 AM, Lancaster, PA, Wheatland estate, at home. Buchanan died of pneumonia and inflammation of the lining of the heart following recurring attacks of rheumatic gout. He took to bed in May 1868 and anticipated his death.

Hīlāj: **Sun**. Chart is diurnal and Sun in 11th qualifies.

Al-kadukhadāh: **Venus**. As bound ruler of the Sun, in generosity with Mercury, moving fast as an evening star, just past 20 degrees from the Sun; Venus is the Al-kadukhadāh. Venus grants her 82 major years. Actual longevity was slightly less.

This figure is a good example of an inferior planet functioning as Al-kadukhadāh to the Hīlāj Sun when technically Venus is not in 'aspect.' By position, Venus occidental and out of the sunbeams is sufficient for Venus to qualify as Al-kadukhadāh.

Victor of the Horoscope: **Jupiter**

Killing Planets: **Jupiter (36), Mars (28), Mercury (25)**

Arcus Vitae:

PT	D	Mars/Virgo	P	Jupiter (0) d. => ASC	15-May-1868

JB fell ill during May 1868 with a cold and added complications. He died the first day of the following month of June.

Jupiter is the high scoring killing planet.

1868 Solar Return for year of Death

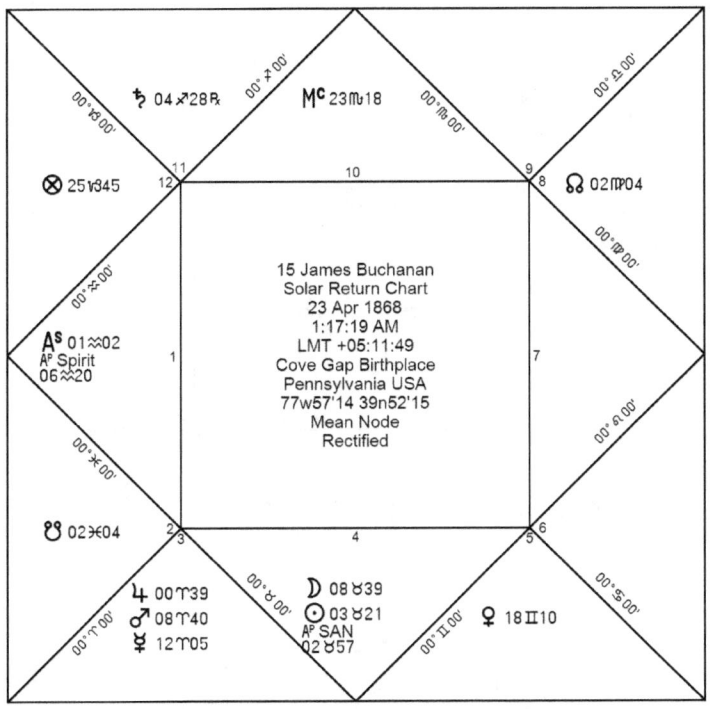

Ascendant Distributor: Mars/Virgo since 27-Jun-1866
Profected Ascendant: 21SA19, 6th House; SR Victor: Venus
Lords: LOY – Jupiter; LOP – Sun
Firdaria: Sun-Venus
Moon: separates from conjunction of Sun and is void of course
Return Ascendant falls in natal 8th

What is striking about this return is that the three high scoring killing planets form a stellium and transit natal 10th: Mercury, Mars, and Jupiter.

| PT | D | Jupiter/Aries | P | Jupiter (0) d. => ASC | 2-Jun-1868 |

This direction recapitulates the arcus vitae.

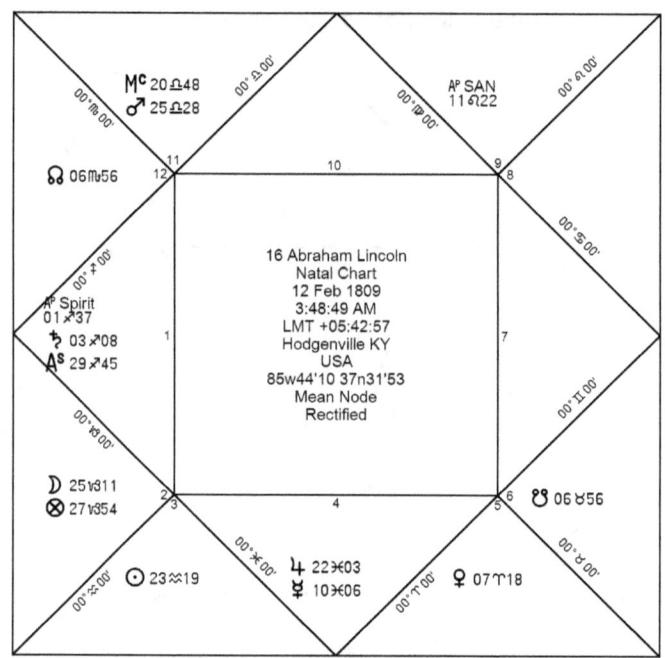

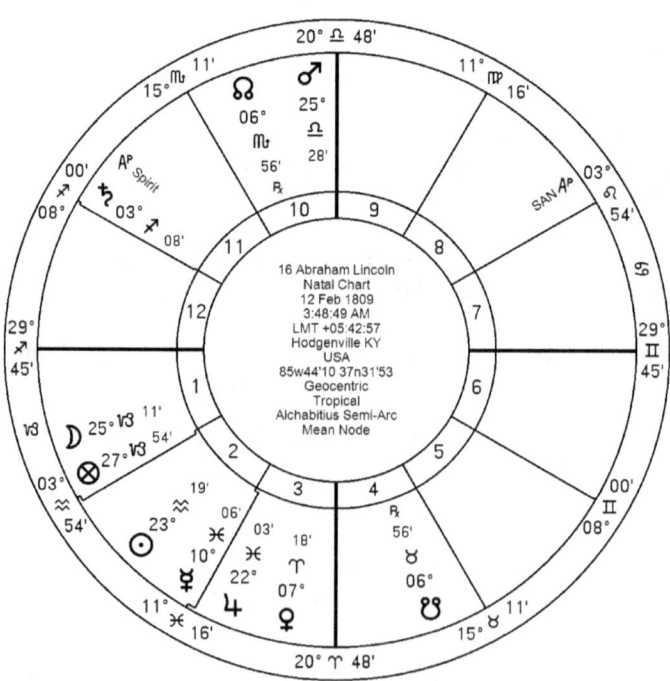

16. ABRAHAM LINCOLN

Moon's Configuration

Moon separates from **Jupiter** and applies to **Mars**, nocturnal, preventional. Prenatal syzygy is 11LE22. Eclipse? No.

Cognitive Assessment Model (Rulers of Moon and Mercury)

Sign rulers: **Saturn, Jupiter**
Bound rulers: **Saturn, Venus**

Victor Soul Models

Ibn Ezra Victor Model (1507), in-sect triplicity ruler, triplicity decans.

	Position	☉	☽	☿	♀	♂	♃	♄
Sun	23 AQ 19			3	1	2		5
Moon	25 CP 11		3	1		4		7
Asc	29 SA 45	1				2	8	
Pars Fortuna	27 CP 54		3	1		6		5
Syzygy	11 LE 22	5					4	2
Oriental						1	0	2
Houses		6	12	3	3	11	3	2
Score	0	12	18	8	4	**26**	15	23

Porphyry's Expanded Victor Model (2022)

Mars rules the ASC, Sun, and Lot of Fortune by bound. Sect: in-favor. Solar phase: oriental square to 1st station. Position: 10th from Lot of Fortune. Debility: detriment; mutual reception with Venus by sign. Moon's application. Conjunct North Node.

Victor Table for Killing Planets

			☉	☽	☿	♀	♂	♃	♄
ASC		29SA45	3,1				2	5,3	3
Rul ASC	♃	22PI03		3		4,3	3,2,1	5	
L.Death		11GE51			5,3	1		3,2	3
Rul L.Death	☿	10PI06		3,1		4,3,2	3	5	
H8 Cusp		3LE54	5,3,1					3,2	3
Rul H8	☉	23AQ19			3	1	2	3	5,3
T-Rul H8	♃	22PI03		3		4,3	3,2,1	5	
8th from ☽		25LE11	5,3				2,1	3	3
Rul 8th fr ☽	☉	23AQ19			3	1	2	3	5,3
TOTAL			21	10	14	**26**	24	**42**	28

2007 Proposed Rectification: 3:48:55 AM, ASC 29SA45'20"
2022 Proposed Rectification: 3:48:49 AM, ASC 29SA45'51"

Astrodatabank reports a B-rated birth time of sunrise which equates to 8:54 AM. The proposed rectification is five hours earlier. It continues to hold up with ZRS and Directing through the Bounds.

The application of Moon to the superior square of Mars is a linchpin of Stage I rectification techniques. If this configuration is correct, the birth time cannot be after 4:18 AM. Primary directions of the Moon and the sinister square of Mars to the Ascendant are crucial in locking down the time. Under various latitude assumptions, the Moon directed to the Ascendant times the death of his sister as well as his intent to run for political office (also a lawsuit for nonpayment of debt which is what one would expect with Moon/Capricorn in detriment ruling the 8th of debt). The square of Mars directed to the Ascendant timed his encounter with chained slaves which haunted him for many years as well as his first political victory. See discussion next page which links Moon's application to Mars with emancipation of slaves.

ZRS. With LOF in Capricorn, cardinal sign, L1-Capricorn period works like clockwork by linking FS, LB, and CP periods. L1-Aquarius is less impressive but does pick up Sun/Aquarius and the Nodes in fixed signs.

L1 Sagittarius 12 Feb 1809		
L1 Capricorn 11 Dec 1820		1821 (no date), increased workload on AL and strain on relations with father after Dennis Hanks moved away.
L2 Cancer 22 Feb 1830	FS	15-Mar-1830, family moved to north bank of Sangamon River; Summer 1830, made 1st political speech on Sangamon River improvements for transportation; left home with cousin and stepbrother to seek his fortune; 1831, worked as pilot for flatboats on Mississippi River; 9-Mar-1832, announced Candidacy for State Legislature.
L2 Cancer 11 Apr 1838	LB	6-Aug-1838, re-elected to IL legislature for 3rd time; 23-Sep-1839, began law practice on 8th Judicial Circuit which he continued until his Presidential nomination; 16-Dec-1839, met Mary Todd.
L2 Capricorn 29 May 1846	CP	May-1846, announced candidacy for US House of Representatives; won race; 4-Mar-1847, Oath of Office.
L1 Aquarius 23 Jul 1847		6-Dec-1847, took seat on Congress; 22-Dec-1847, asked to be shown the 'spot' where the Mexican War started, implying that Polk engineered the Mexican War without provocation.
L2 Leo 04 Aug 1856	FS	4-Nov-1856, James Buchanan elected President; 6-Mar-1857, Dred Scott decision.
L2 Scorpio 14 Jun 1860		6-Nov-1860, elected President.
L2 Leo 20 Nov 1864	LB	31-Jan-1865, House approved 13th Amendment to end slavery; ratified Dec 1865; 14-Apr-1865, assassinated.

16. ABRAHAM LINCOLN

Firdaria – Mars major and minor periods

Firdaria according to Bonatti	Life Event
Moon **Mars** 21 Dec 1812	No events found.
Saturn **Mars** 05 Apr 1821	1821 (no date), increased workload on AL and strain on relations with father after Dennis Hanks moved away.
Jupiter **Mars** 31 Oct 1830	Mar-1831, left home for good; first position piloting flatboat down Mississippi River to New Orleans; 9-Mar-1832, announced candidacy for State Legislature; 21-Apr-1832, elected captain of New Salem volunteers for Black Hawk War.
Mars 7 years Age 32 to 39	
Mars Mars 11 Feb 1841	14-May-1841, ended partnership with J. Stuart and started one with S. Logan; 1-Feb-1842, New Bankruptcy law provided many cases for law practice.
Mars Sun 12 Feb 1842	22-Sep-1842, proposed duel with J. Shields averted by friends; 4-Nov-1842, married Mary Todd.
Mars Venus 12 Feb 1843	1-Aug-1843, Son Robert Lincoln Todd born; 16-Jan-1844, purchased house in Springfield business district.
Mars Mercury 12 Feb 1844	9-Dec-1844, W. Herndon admitted to the Bar; firm of Lincoln & Herndon organized soon after.
Mars Moon 11 Feb 1845	No events found.
Mars Saturn 12 Feb 1846	3-Aug-1846, won House Seat as Whig party member.
Mars Jupiter 12 Feb 1847	4-Mar-1847, took oath of office; 22-Dec-1837, presented resolution requesting JP inform the house whether the 'spot' on which American blood was first shed in Mexican War was within territory claimed by Mexico.
Sun **Mars** 08 Sep 1861	11-Sep-1861, ordered Fremont to revoke Fremont's Emancipation Act; 1-Nov-1861, McClellan appointed General of Union Army; 11-Mar-1862, McClellan relieved of command; 17-Sep-1862, Antietam Union victory; 22-Sep-1862, Emancipation Proclamation announced; 1-Jan-1863, Emancipation Proclamation into force.

Mars as Victor. Mars' periods included AL's departure from home, his first political campaign for the Illinois State legislature, formation of Lincoln & Herndon legal practice, and his election to the House. During AL's tenure as President, the Sun-Mars period timed the Union victory at Antietam which AL required before announcing the Emancipation Proclamation.

Mars/Libra made Lincoln a reluctant military leader. The connection to emancipation occurs because the 2nd is 9th from the 6th which I delineate as long-term travel/freedom (9th) for slaves (6th). Moon/Capricorn/2nd applies to Mars/Libra which receives the Moon by exaltation and overcomes it. AL is a reluctant wartime president who freed the slaves.

Transits

16-Jan-1844. *tr Saturn conj LOF.*
Purchased house for $1,200 in Springfield business district from Rev Charles Dresser; Saturn in 12th is 4th from 9th or priest's real estate. Exact.

18-Jul-1850. *tr Saturn conj IC.*
Death of President Zachary Taylor 9-Jul; Lincoln gave eulogy 25-Jul.

17-May-1860. *tr Mars conj Moon.*
Presidential nomination, 18-May.

Solar Arc Directions

18-Aug-1835. *dsa Saturn conj ASC.*
Death of Ann Rutledge, betrothed; Saturn rules 2nd (death of wife), 21-Aug.

Primary Directions

| REG | D | Mars/Pisces | P | Jupiter (JU) d. => Sun | 22-Feb-1831 |

Frozen feet from ice break required one month recuperation, Feb-1831; Note: Jupiter/Pisces signifies large feet and Sun/Aquarius signifies poor circulation in the calves/ankles.

| REG | D | Mars/Aries | P | IC d. => Jupiter (JU) | 22-Mar-1831 |

Left home for good; took flatboat to New Orleans; Mar-1831.

| REG | D | Venus/Pisces | P | sin sq Saturn (SA) d. => LOF | 29-Apr-1834 |

Legal judgment against Lincoln for loan nonpayment, 26-Apr.

| REG | D | Venus/Capricorn | P | sin sq MC c. => Sun | 8-Apr-1837 |

Moved to Springfield to begin law practice, 15-Mar.

| REG | D | Jupiter/Aries | P | sin trine Saturn (0) d. => LOF | 26-Jan-1856 |

Made opening argument in rehearing of the famous tax case, Illinois Central RR v. McLean County, Illinois & Parke. Lincoln won, 16-Jan-1856.

| PT | D | Mars/Aquarius | P | Sun d. => ASC | 26-May-1856 |

Gave 'best speech of life' at Illinois Republican Convention, 29-May.

| REG | D | Jupiter/Sagittarius | P | dex sq Merc (ME) d.=> MC | 16-May-1858 |

Cleared client murder conviction with Farmer's Almanac anecdote, 7-May.

16. ABRAHAM LINCOLN   521

Primary Direction Sequences

| PT | D | Venus/Capricorn | P | Moon (MO) d. => ASC | 20-Jan-1829 |
| PT | D | Venus/Capricorn | P | Moon (0) d. => ASC | 20-Apr-1834 |

LOCK Death of sister; 20-Jan-1829.
Van Bergen sued AL for nonpayment of debt, Apr-1834.
Note: Moon/Capricorn/2nd ruling 8th of debt shows debt problems.
Announced candidacy for state legislature, 19-Apr-1834.

| PT | D | Saturn/Capricorn | P | sin square Mars (MA) d. => ASC | 12-Sep-1831 |
| PT | D | Saturn/Capricorn | P | sin square Mars (0) d. => ASC | 21-Jul-1834 |

LOCK Witnessed a dozen Negroes chained together during steamboat to Louisville with Joshua Speed, 8-Sep-1831. Later wrote "that sight was a continual torment to me."
Won first political race for seat in State Legislature, 4-Aug-1834.
If these two directions in fact link these two events, this supports a thesis that Lincoln's abhorrence of slavery is an underlying political motivation from his earliest days.

| REG | D | Jupiter/Libra | P | MC c. => Saturn (SA) | 7-Aug-1858 |
| REG | D | Jupiter/Libra | P | MC c. => Saturn (0) | 4-Oct-1859 |

LOCK This sequence timed Lincoln's famous encounter with Stephen Douglas beginning with Lincoln's invitation to Douglas for the debates written on 24-Jul-1858; all Lincoln-Douglas debates August-October; and Lincoln's loss to Douglas announced on 5-Jan-1859. Lincoln continued to speak during the balance of 1859, but it was not until this sequence concluded did Lincoln receive an invitation on 12-Oct-1859 to speak in New York City. Once Saturn lifted, his fortunes improved.

PT	D	Jupiter/Leo	P	dex trine ASC c. => Mars (0)	29-Sep-1861
REG	D	Jupiter/Leo	P	dex trine ASC c. => Mars (0)	28-Apr-1862
PT	D	Jupiter/Leo	P	dex trine ASC c. => Mars (MA)	6-Oct-1862
REG	D	Jupiter/Leo	P	dex trine ASC c. => Mars (MA)	9-May-1863

LOCK This set of ASC-Mars directions is a reasonable delineation match to AL's difficulties with General McClellan whose ineffectiveness in military offensives is consistent with the inability of Mars/Libra to fight.
Conflict between Winfield Scott and McClellan, 27-Sep-1861.
McClellan criticized for excessive parades and shows, 12-Oct-1861.
McClellan failed to initiate offensive against Confederates at Yorktown as late as 3-May-1862 after AL had ordered two attacks. On 4-May-1862, McClellan discovered Confederates had vanished. After victory at Antietam on 17-Sep-1862, AL ordered McClellan to aggressively fight the enemy in early Oct-1862. After McClellan dawdled, AL fired him 5-Nov-1862. The NY Herald published testimony before the Joint Committee on Conduct of the War demonstrating McClellan's incompetence, 28-Apr-1863.

Longevity, 56y 2m 2d

Death: Following a mortal gunshot delivered by the assassin John Wilkes Booth at the Ford Theatre on 14-Apr-1865 at 10:15 PM, Lincoln died the next morning at 7:22 AM in the Peterson House, Washington, DC.

Hīlāj: **Moon**. Moon is preferred in a nocturnal nativity and falls in the 2nd house which is an allowable position.

Al-kadukhadāh: **Saturn**. Saturn is both bound and sign ruler of the Moon. Saturn has dignity of triplicity and conjoins the Moon by antiscia. Saturn grants 57 major years. Venus separates from Saturn by trine aspect but does not receive Saturn so does not add minor years. Jupiter receives by a wide square aspect but does not add minor years despite receiving Saturn by sign and bound.

Victor of the Horoscope: **Mars**

Killing Planet: **Jupiter (42), Saturn (28), Venus (26)**

Arcus Vitae:

REG	D	Venus/Aries	P	Venus (VE) d. => Moon (MO)	25-Jan-1865
REG	D	Venus/Aries	P	Venus (0) d. => Moon (MO)	18-Apr-1865

The actor John Wilkes Booth is signified by Venus. The anger/sadism of Venus/Aries is caused by her dispositor Mars/Libra. On 11-Apr, Booth heard Lincoln state that he was in favor of granting suffrage to freed slaves. Booth turned to a man named Lewis Powell and urged Powell to shoot the president on the spot. Powell refused. Booth vowed that it would be the final speech Lincoln would ever make. Mars/Libra/11th can be delineated as Lincoln's hopes/wishes for social justice achieved through Black voting rights. Mars disposes Venus/Aries/5th which signifies the actor Booth in the theatre as a 5th house entertainment. My research also shows elections are a 5th house affair. Lincoln's desire to grant voting rights is a direct match.

REG	D	Saturn/Capricorn	P	Moon (MO) d. => Saturn (SA)	5-Jan-1862
REG	D	Saturn/Capricorn	P	Moon (0) d. => Saturn (SA)	3-Jun-1866

The Moon-Saturn directions join the hīlāj with the 2nd high scoring killer. It's possible that Saturn is a delineation match to the diagnosis of Lincoln with MEN2B, a rare genetic disorder in which long bones and nerve cells grow excessively (Sotos, 2008). Without treatment, thyroid cancer results.

16. ABRAHAM LINCOLN

1865 Solar Return for year of Death

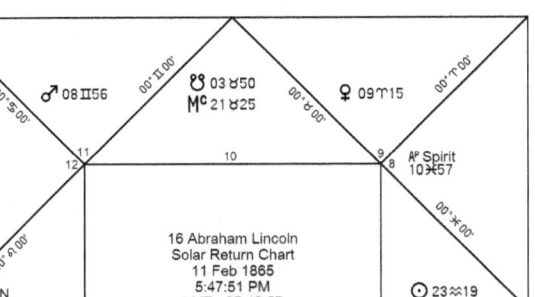

Ascendant Distributor: Venus/Pisces since 19-Dec-1860
Profected Ascendant: 29LE45, 9th House; SR Victor: Saturn
Lords: LOY – Sun; LOP – Saturn
Firdaria: Venus-Mercury
Moon: separates from sextile of Saturn and applies to square of Mars
Return Ascendant falls in natal 8th/9th QS/WS.

The Union won the Civil War during this return and Lincoln was assassinated shortly thereafter. South Node in the 10th signifies *the king is deposed* in mundane figures; it matches Lincoln's demise. Hīlāj Moon's translation from one malefic to another is a major affliction. The Sun is afflicted by a wide antiscia from Saturn and falls in the 7th house, the angle of the West. Both luminaries are afflicted. As the significator for Booth, Venus/Aries is given power to act by returning to her own sign and bound. Venus is also found in the return's 9th house which is emphasized in this 9th house year.

| PT | D | Mercury/Libra | P | opp Venus (0) d. => ASC | 5-Apr-1865 |

This direction is 10 days early.

524 A RECTIFICATION MANUAL

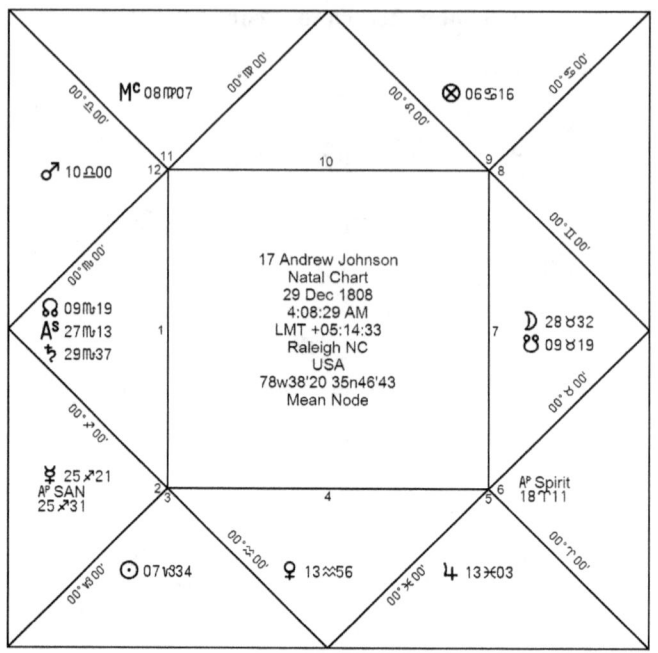

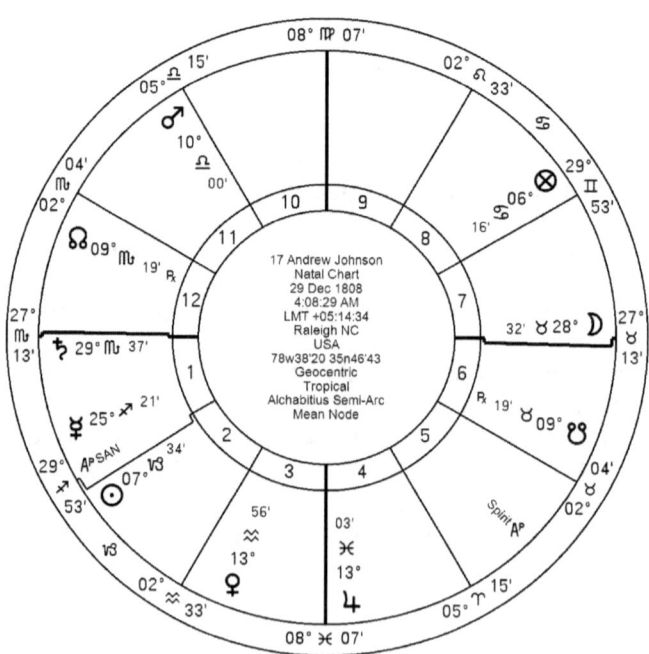

Moon's Configuration

Moon separates from **Jupiter** and applies to **Saturn**, nocturnal, conjunctional. Prenatal syzygy is 25SA31. Eclipse? No.

Cognitive Assessment Model (Rulers of Moon and Mercury)

Sign rulers: **Venus, Jupiter**
Bound rulers: **Mars, Saturn**

Victor Soul Models

Ibn Ezra Victor Model (1507), in-sect triplicity ruler, triplicity decans.

	Position	☉	☽	☿	♀	♂	♃	♄
Sun	07 CP 34		3			4	2	6
Moon	28 TA 32		7		5	2		1
Asc	27 SC 14		1			8		2
Pars Fortuna	06 CA 16		6			5	4	
Syzygy	25 SA 31	1					8	2
Oriental						2	0	3
Houses			6	10	6	3	8	9	12
Score		0	7	27	6	8	**29**	23	26

Porphyry's Expanded Victor Model (2022)

Saturn rules the Sun by sign; the ASC and syzygy by bound. Sect: out-of-favor. Solar phase: oriental rising to waxing sextile. Position: Angular in the ASC. Dignity: bound. Moon applies to Saturn. Conjunct North Node.

Victor Table for Killing Planets

			☉	☽	☿	♀	♂	♃	♄
ASC		27SC13		3,1		3	5,3		2
Rul ASC	♂	10LI00			3,2	5		3	4,3,1
L.Death		00CP58		3	2	3	4,3		5,1
Rul L.Death	♄	29SC37		3,1		3	5,3		2
H8 Cusp		29GE53			5,3			3	3,2,1
Rul H8	☿	25SA31	3,1					5,3	3,2
T-Rul H8	☿	25SA31	3,1					5,3	3,2
8th from ☽		28SA33	3,1				2	5,3	3
Rul 8th fr ☽	♃	13PI03		3,1		4,3	3	5,2	
TOTAL			12	15	15	21	28	**37**	**37**

2007 Proposed Rectification: 4:08:28 AM, ASC 27SC13'48"
2022 Proposed Rectification: 4:08:29 AM, ASC 27SC13'52"

Astrodatabank reports a C-rated (accuracy in question) birth time of 12:34 AM, Ascendant 13LI23. The proposed rectification is a morning nocturnal figure with late Scorpio rising.

ZRS. LOS 18AR11, bound Mercury/Aries/6th (WS) makes Johnson an advocate for the poor white working class (assigning this group to the 6th house of labor). LOF 6CA16 in the 9th WS house grants Johnson an element of luck in legal matters of which the best example is his 26-May-1868 acquittal of impeachment charges arguably timed by tr Jupiter 7AR27 10th from the LOF. Revisiting many rectifications for the 4th edition has shown that the 10th positional degree from either LOF or LOS are legitimate activations of these lots capable of timing major life events. LOF in Cancer makes cardinal signs angular from LOF. For Johnson, this makes L1-Cancer and all cardinal signs reliable timers of key career events. These include Johnson's accession to the Presidency under L2-Aries which is 10th from LOF.

L1 **Aries** 29 Dec 1808		
L1 **Taurus** 12 Oct 1823		24-Jun-1824, ran away from apprenticeship as tailor; eventually settled in Greenville, TN, married on 17-Dec-1827, and established a favorable reputation as tailor.
L1 **Gemini** 31 Aug 1831		Period began immediately after Nat Turner slave rebellion 21/23-Aug-1831. The rebellion motivated TN to call for a constitutional convention to disenfranchise blacks (held 1834). This backdrop proved fertile for Johnson who started a rapid political ascent in local and state politics.
L2 Sagittarius 14 Jun 1840	FS	1840, selected Presidential elector for TN which gave him more publicity.
L2 Sagittarius 29 Dec 1848	LB	Fall-1849, won reelection to House in higher margin of victory than in 1847.
L1 **Cancer** 18 May 1851		25-Jul-1851, made impassioned plea for Homestead legislation; Fall-1852, lost House re-election race because of gerrymandering.
L2 Capricorn 05 Jul 1859	FS	22-Jun-1860, Homestead act vetoed by Buchanan; 18/19-Dec-1860, made "Union must be preserved" speech; 27-Jul-1861, Senate speech in favor of Presidential war powers raises popularity.
L2 Aries 05 Mar 1865		Reputation sullied after drunken inauguration speech prior day 4-Mar-1865; 15-Apr-1865, assumed Presidential office after Lincoln assassination; 29-May-1865, granted amnesty to Southerners who took loyalty oath; 4-Dec-1865, Congressional session of Radical Republicans began, Johnson broke with Congress after this point.
L2 Capricorn 15 Sep 1868	LB	3-Nov-1868, Grant elected President.
L2 Aries 17 May 1874		26-Jan-1875, won election for Senator from TN; 31-Jul-1875, death.

Firdaria – Saturn major and minor periods

Firdaria according to Bonatti	Life Event
Moon **Saturn** 12 Apr 1810	No events found.
Saturn 11 years Age 9 to 20	
Saturn Saturn 29 Dec 1817	8-Nov-1818, apprenticed to learn tailor's trade.
Saturn Jupiter 26 Jul 1819	
Saturn Mars 19 Feb 1821	
Saturn Sun 16 Sep 1822	
Saturn Venus 12 Apr 1824	24-Jun-1824, ran away from apprenticeship; settled in Laurens, SC where AJ worked in a tailor shop for two years.
Saturn Mercury 07 Nov 1825	Sep-1826, returned to Greenville, TN to settle down.
Saturn Moon 04 Jun 1827	17-Dec-1727, marriage and time of business prosperity.
Jupiter **Saturn** 12 Apr 1839	1839 (no date), elected to TN state legislature.
Mars **Saturn** 29 Dec 1845	27-Mar-1846, introduced Homestead Bill.
Sun **Saturn** 15 Sep 1858	1-Feb-1859. House passed its version of Homestead Bill, Senate version tabled; 20-Dec-1859, AJ reintroduced Homestead Bill.
Venus **Saturn** 03 Jun 1866	13-Jun-1866, Congress passed 14th Amendment which established citizenship for African Americans among other measures; July-1866, three Radical Republican members of AJ's cabinet resigned; Aug/Sep-1866, AJ's campaign tour prior to midterm elections a failure, included infamous harangue where AJ compared himself to Judas; Mar-1867, Congress passed 1st and 2nd Reconstruction Acts in veto overrides; 26-Jun-1867, Judiciary Committee met to consider impeachment charges but could not develop a case.
Mercury **Saturn** 15 Sep 1874	26-Jan-1875, elected to Senate, Tennessee; 31-Jul-1875, died.

Saturn as Victor. Saturn periods include his early years of apprenticeship as tailor; marriage; establishment of home and start of real estate investments; and political debut in the Tennessee state legislature. Later as member of the House of Representatives, AJ attempted unsuccessfully to introduce the Homestead Bill on multiple occasions; two incidents of which were timed by Saturn as minor Firdaria ruler. Finally passed in 1862 under the Lincoln administration, the Homestead Bill made land acquisition affordable for AJ's constituents, many of them poor members of the white working class. Saturn rules the 4th house of real estate (WS). As President, the minor Saturn period timed a heated period of conflict with the Radical Republicans over reform measures which threatened AJ's white working-class supporters by leveling the playing field with newly freed African American slaves. The 1866/67 Saturn period provided fodder for AJ's subsequent impeachment trial.

Transits

10-Nov-1860. *tr Saturn conj MC.*
29-Jan-1861. *tr Saturn-rx conj MC.*
28-Jul-1861. *tr Saturn conj MC.*
Advocated resolutions declaring secession unconstitutional at the Greeneville, TN convention, 24-Nov-1860.
Made famous national unity speech which caused TN to vote against secession, 5/6-Feb-1861.
Made three-hour address 27-Jul-1861 in Senate asking for Presidential War Powers after Bull Run Confederate victory (21-Jul) threatened safety of Washington D.C. AJ's popularity surged following this speech.

23-Nov-1864. *tr North Node sextile MC.*
Re-elected Vice President, 8-Nov-1864.

23-Nov-1867. *tr Saturn conj ASC.* Judiciary Committee voted for impeachment proceedings 22-Nov. In the Cabinet meeting of 30-Nov, Johnson declared his intent to fight a legal maneuver that proposed to remove the President prior to the trial as unconstitutional.

31-Dec-1867. *tr North Node conj MC.* First impeachment attempt failed, 5/7-Dec; Informed Senate of reasons why he suspended Stanton as Secretary of War, 12-Dec; Senate refused to support Johnson's removal of Stanton who returned to the War Department, 13-Jan.

Solar Arc Directions

12-Nov-1857. *dsa Sun square MC.*
Elected to Senate, 8-Oct.

6-Oct-1865. *dsa Saturn sextile ASC.*
Brother William accidentally shot himself while hunting/died, 24-Oct-1865.

12-Apr-1866. *dsa Mars square MC.*
Senate overrode Johnson's veto of Civil Rights Act of 1866, 6-Apr-1866. Made a controversial interview with the *London Times*, 16 April.

13-Aug-1867. *dsa MC sextile Sun.*
Johnson suspended Stanton and replaced him with Grant during Congressional recess, 12 August.

8-Sep-1868. *dsa Sun opposed MC.*
Directions of the Sun to the IC time periods of spiritual crisis. This direction occurs between the time Democrats failed to renominate AJ in favor of Horatio Seymour on 9-Jul-1868 and Grant's election on 3-Nov-1868.

17. ANDREW JOHNSON

Primary Directions

| PT | D | Venus/Scorpio | P | dex sextile Sun d. => MC | 8-Jun-1864 |

LOCK Nominated for VP on ticket with Abraham Lincoln, 8-Jun.

Primary Direction Sequences

Delineation of Johnson's fight with the Radical Republicans

Saturn/Scorpio signifies paranoia and is the mundane signature for national security. For Johnson, Saturn/Scorpio/1st matches his opposition to increased Federal control of Civil Rights over state affairs because Saturn/Scorpio individuals are paranoid of Federal control over virtually anything. For the source of Saturn's paranoia, look to ruler Mars/Libra. Mars ruling the 6th in the 12th (WS) signifies slave revolts; Mars ruling the 5th in the 11th (QS) signifies Radical Republicans interested in voting rights for Freedmen. Saturn is paranoid because of rebellious slaves and politicians. Why do these groups revolt? Look to Mars' ruler, Venus. Venus/Aquarius seeks fair and pleasant social behavior, a signature for integration through Civil Rights. But Venus also signified Johnson's own political base of Workers and Mechanics whose rights (read 'fairness') he championed against those of big business. Because Radical Republicans wanted Freedman to have the same rights as Johnson's own political base, Johnson felt threatened.

| PT | D | Mercury/Libra | P | Mars (0) c. => ASC | 19-Sep-1866 |
| PT | D | Mercury/Libra | P | Mars (MA) c. => ASC | 20-Apr-1867 |

This sequence follows race riots in New Orleans on 30-Jul-1866 (variation of slave revolt) and Johnson's own poorly conceived campaign tour when he complained that the people considered him Judas. Republicans swept midterm elections and the first impeachment measures were taken in Jan-1867. The first two Reconstruction Acts were passed over Johnson's vetoes in Mar-1967.

| PT | D | Venus/Cancer | P | dex sq Mars (MA) c. => MC | 16-Sep-1867 |
| PT | D | Venus/Cancer | P | dex sq Mars (0) c. => MC | 20-Nov-1867 |

Following Johnson's replacement of Secretary of War Stanton (a Radical Republican) with Ulysses Grant on 12-Aug-1867, the Judiciary Committee voted for impeachment 22-Nov-1867.

| REG | D | Mars/Scorpio | P | sin trine LOF c. => Mercury (0) | 21-Nov-1866 |
| REG | D | Mars/Scorpio | P | sin trine LOF c. => Mercury (ME) | 29-Mar-1867 |

LOCK Timed negotiations for the purchase of Alaska conducted by Secretary of State William Seward. The purchase was ridiculed for what was considered worthless territory and nicknamed *Seward's Folly,* a delineation match to the overoptimistic Mercury/Sagittarius. The treaty was signed on 30-Mar-1867 and passed by the Senate in early April.

Longevity, 66y 7m 1d

Death: While visiting his daughter, Johnson had a stroke on 28-Jul-1875 around 4:00 p.m. which paralyzed one side. He asked for no medical care, sensing the end. He died on 31-Jul-1875, ~2:00 AM, in Carter County, TN.

Hīlāj: **Sun/LOF**. Moon is preferred in a nocturnal figure and should qualify in the 7th. Conjunction to South Node by 19deg 14min is wide enough that the South Node should not interfere with the Moon's ability to function as hīlāj, yet it appears the South Node *does* interfere, knocking out the Moon as potential hīlāj. Empirically, directions to the Sun and LOF accurately time illness and death.

Al-kadukhadāh: **Mars**. Mars forms a t-square with LOF and Sun. Mars receives the LOF by bound and the Sun by exaltation. While Mars itself is in detriment, note Mars is received by Venus which improves Mars' dignity rating. If Mars is the al-kadukhadāh, then Mars grants 66 major years. Venus should add 8 minor years by trine aspect with reception by sign for a net projection of 74 years. Empirically, Venus does not add years with Johnson living just beyond Mars' 66 major years.

Victor of the Horoscope: **Saturn**

Killing Planets: **Saturn (37), Jupiter (37), Mars (28)**

Arcus Vitae:

PT	D	Jupiter/Capricorn	P	Sun d. => North Node	9-Jul-1875
REG	D	Mars/Cancer	P	LOF d. => South Node	24-Jul-1875

Based on these measurements, either the Sun or LOF can be argued as the empirical hīlāj. Evidence from the primary direction sequence which timed near death in 1873 (see next) adds credence to the LOF as hīlāj.

Incident of Near Death:

On 29-Jun-1873, Johnson nearly died from cholera. By transit there is a Moon-Jupiter conjunction in Leo square natal Moon, one of two occasions which suggest the Moon's ability to function as hīlāj (for the other, see the solar return of year of death – next page). By direction, the incident occurred during the following primary direction sequence:

PT	D	Venus/Aries	P	sin square LOF c. => Saturn (SA)	20-Oct-1872
PT	D	Venus/Aries	P	sin square LOF c. => Saturn (0)	7-Oct-1873

1874 Solar Return for year of Death

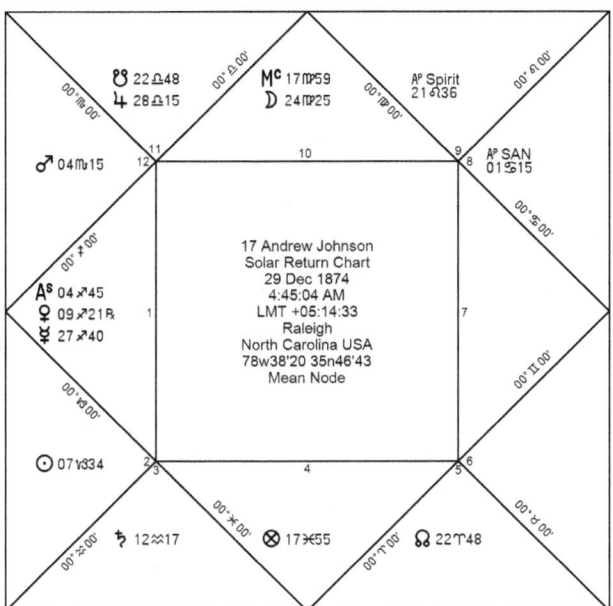

Ascendant Distributor: Mars/Capricorn since 1-Apr-1873.
Profected Ascendant: 27TA13, 7th House; SR Victor: Moon (bound lord Mars)
Lords: LOY – Venus; LOP – Jupiter.
Firdaria: Mercury-Saturn
Moon: separates from square of Venus and applies to square of Mercury
Return Ascendant falls in natal 2nd; natal Ascendant falls in return's 12th.

Johnson died from a stroke, the cause of which is Mercury. Mercury is not the high-scoring killing planet yet rules the natal 8th (WS). In the return Mercury is given power to act in the following ways: he returns to his same natal sign, he rules the return's 7th house in a 7th house profected year, and he falls in the angular 1st house. Hīlāj Moon separates from Venus and applies to Mercury who also receives her by sign.

| PT | D | Saturn/Cancer | P | dex square Jupiter (0) d. => ASC | 25-Jul-1875 |
| PT | D | Jupiter/Leo | P | dex square Mars (0) d. => ASC | 2-Aug-1875 |

Stroke (28-Jul) and Death (31-Jul) fall between these two Ascendant directions which activate Jupiter and Mars, the high scoring killing planets after Saturn.

532   A RECTIFICATION MANUAL

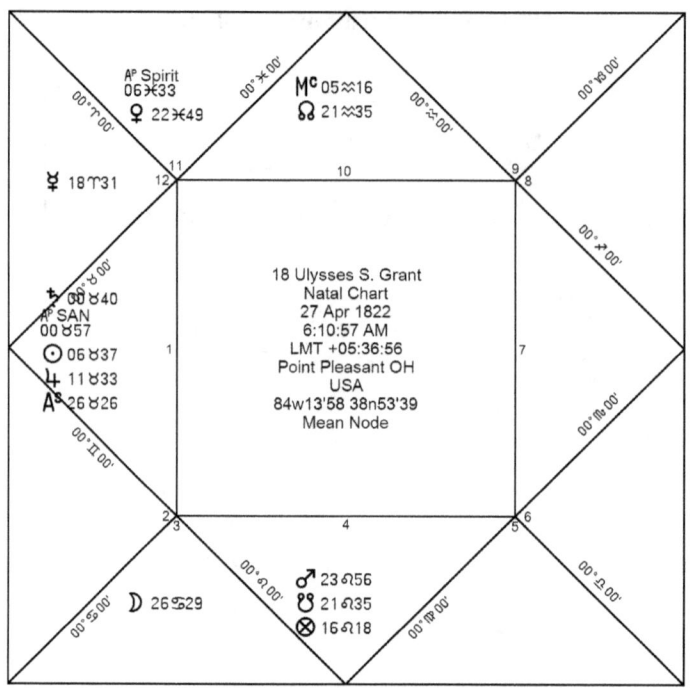

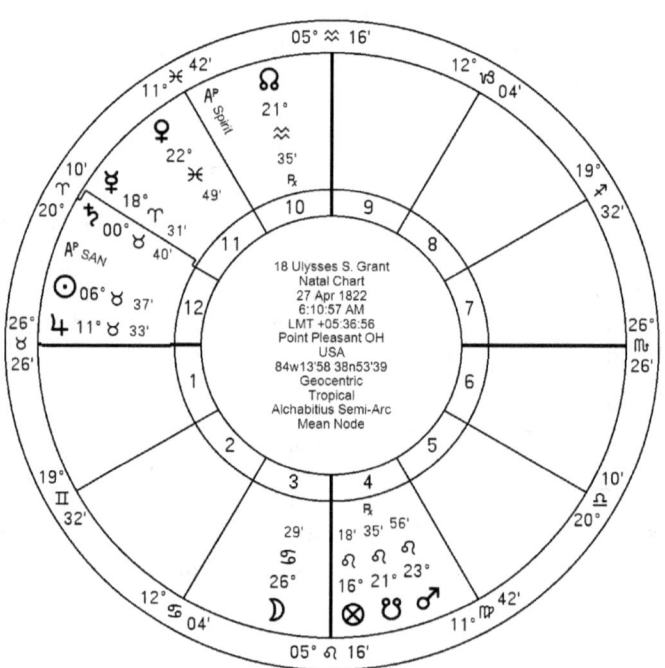

Moon's Configuration

Moon separates from **Venus** and is **VOC** (Medieval) or applies to **Saturn** (Hellenistic), diurnal, conjunctional.
Prenatal syzygy is 00TA57. Eclipse? No.

Cognitive Assessment Model (Rulers of Moon and Mercury)

Sign rulers: (**Moon**)/**Saturn, Mars**
Bound rulers: **Saturn, Mercury**

Victor Soul Models

Ibn Ezra Victor Model (1507), in-sect triplicity ruler, triplicity decans.

	Position	☉	☽	☿	♀	♂	♃	♄
Sun	06 TA 37		4		11			
Moon	26 CA 29		5		3		5	2
Asc	26 TA 26		4		8			3
Pars Fortuna	16 LE 18	8					1	2
Syzygy	00 TA 57		4		11			
Oriental						0	0	0
Houses			2	3	2	8	9	2	2
Score		0	10	20	2	41	9	8	9

Porphyry's Expanded Victor Model (2022)

Saturn rules the MC by sign; the ASC, Moon, and Lot of Fortune by bound. Sect: in-favor. Solar phase: oriental combust. Position: Angular in 1st and 10th from the Lot of Fortune.

Victor Table for Killing Planets

			☉	☽	☿	♀	♂	♃	♄
ASC		26TA25		4,3		5,3	3		2,1
Rul ASC	♀	22PI49		3		4,3	3,2,1	5	
L.Death		23VI43		3	5,4	3,1	3,2		
Rul L.Death	☿	18AR31	4,3,1	2			5	3	3
H8 Cusp		19SA32	3		2		1	5,3	3
Rul H8	♃	11TA33		4,3	2,1	5,3	3		
T-Rul H8	☉	6TA37		4,3		5,3,2,1	3		
8th from ☉		6SA37	3					5,3,2,1	3
Rul 8th fr ☉	♃	11TA33		4,3	2,1	5,3	3		
TOTAL			14	34	19	46	29	27	12

2007 Proposed Rectification: 6:10:57 AM, ASC 26TA25'55"

Astrodatabank reports an A-rated birth time of 6:00 AM. The proposed rectification is a few minutes later.

ZRS. LOS 6PI33 is unusual for a military man. For Grant, it is a delineation match to fair treatment of Confederate prisoners at war's end. The configuration may be one factor which predisposes Grant towards alcoholism; but never an angry drunk, only a silly foolish drunk. LOF 16LE18 in the bound of Saturn/Leo/4th ruled by victor Saturn/Taurus shows Grant's luck on the battlefield (4th/real estate).

L1 Pisces 27 Apr 1822		
L1 Aries 23 Feb 1834		No major event found immediately after start of L1 but the period included the start of his military career from West Point to success in the Mexican War as well as marriage to Julia Dent.
L1 Taurus 06 Dec 1848		President Polk's 5-Dec-1848 announcement of California's gold discovery led to Grant reinforcing a small garrison in California and bringing soldiers and a few hundred civilians from New York City via Panama to California. Overall L1-Taurus was a challenging time for Grant's military career, a common plight for many military men during peacetime. By the end of the period, Grant and his family moved into a property named 'Hardscrabble' which lived up to its name for the impossibility of making a living from the land.
L1 Gemini 25 Oct 1856		Grant reached his financial nadir during L1-Gemini when he had to pawn his watch on 23-Dec-1857 to buy family Christmas gifts. During LOF angular periods, Grant's fortunes rose with the outbreak of the Civil War, his victory over Lee, and his Presidential election.
L2 Sagittarius 09 Aug 1865	FS	Oct-1865, Grants moved into Washington DC house after successful nationwide tour; Nov/Dec-1865, toured the South; 25-Jul-1866, appointed to newly created rank of General of the Armies of the United States.
L2 Aquarius 22 Oct 1868		3-Nov-1868, elected President; 24-Sep-1869, gold corner broken; 1870/1871 KKK Enforcement Acts, Dept Justice created; Federal Election Law passed.
L2 Sagittarius 23 Feb 1874	LB	22-Apr-1874, vetoed bill to increase greenbacks; 15-Sep-1874, puts down New Orleans rebellion by the White League; 14-Jan-1875, Congress passed Specie Resumption Act.
L1 Cancer 12 Jul 1876		L1-Cancer coincides with the end of his national political career. On 5-Dec-1876 he sent his final annual message to Congress. After a successful globetrotting trip 1877-1879, Grant hoped to be renominated as President in 1880 but that did not occur.
L2 Capricorn 29 Aug 1884	FS	Nov-1884, throat cancer detected; 23-May-1885, Vol 1 of memoirs published; 23-Jul-1885, death.

Firdaria – Saturn major and minor periods

Firdaria according to Bonatti	Life Event
Sun **Saturn** 13 Jan 1828	No events found.
Venus **Saturn** 30 Sep 1835	No events found.
Mercury **Saturn** 13 Jan 1844	Feb-1844, met Julia Dent for first time; May-1844, regiment ordered to LA; Apr-1845, asked Julia's parents for consent for engagement; Sep-1845, sailed for Texas and promoted to 2nd Lieutenant prior to outbreak of Mexican War.
Moon **Saturn** 09 Aug 1854	Summer 1855, family moved to another farm on the Dent estate after living for a year in same house as Julia's parents.
Saturn 11 years Age 40 to 51	
Saturn Saturn 26 Apr 1862	11-Jul-1862, after conflicts with General Halleck, UG ordered to command army at Corinth as Halleck ordered back to Washington; 1-Jan-1863, Emancipation Proclamation into force; May/Jul-1863, victories at Jackson and Vicksburg.
Saturn Jupiter 21 Nov 1863	23/25-Nov-1863, victory at Battle of Chattanooga; 3-Mar-1864, received commission as Lieutenant General; 8-Mar-1864, met Lincoln in Washington; 1/3-Jun-1864, large losses at Battle of Cold Harbor; 15-Jun-1864, siege of Petersburg began; 9-Apr-1865, Robert E. Lee surrender; 14-Apr-1865, Lincoln assassination.
Saturn Mars 17 Jun 1865	Nov/Dec-1865, made Southern tour and recommended lenient reconstruction policy to AJ; 25-Jul-1866, appointed to General of the Armies of the United States.
Saturn Sun 12 Jan 1867	14-Jan-1868, broke with AJ by resigning and siding with Sec of War Stanton; 21-May-1868, nominated for President.
Saturn Venus 08 Aug 1868	3-Nov-1868, elected President; 24-Sep-1869, gold corner broken in Black Friday selloff; 10-Jan-1870, submitted Santo Domingo annexation treaty but unable to get confirmed; 3-Feb-1870, 15th Amendment granting African American suffrage is ratified.
Saturn Mercury 05 Mar 1870	31-May-1870 to 20-Apr-1871, three enforcement acts passed aimed to curb KKK activity; 22-Jun-1870, Dept of Justice created; 28-Feb-1871, Federal Election Law passed.
Saturn Moon 30 Sep 1871	22-May-1872, Amnesty Act signed; 5-Sep-1872, Credit Mobilier scandal; 5-Nov-1872, re-elected President.
Jupiter **Saturn** 09 Aug 1883	24-Dec-1883, fell on ice and confined to bed; 6-May-1884, Grant and Ward business operated by his son went bankrupt; Nov-1884, throat cancer detected; 27-Feb-1884, signed contract with Mark Twain to write his memoirs.

Saturn as Victor. Saturn/Taurus signifies UG's father's profession as a tanner and UG's brief stint working in the tannery. It also signifies UG's Civil War battlefield nickname as the 'butcher,' his consistent failures as a businessman, and death from throat cancer. Saturn's Major Firdaria period, age 40-51, outlines the most succinct period of career success from the Civil War to his first term as President. Saturn also timed his literary contract with Mark Twain to publish his memoirs, the most important event of his post-Presidency considering Grant's memoirs consistently rate as the best Presidential memoirs ever written.

Transits

<u>22-Jun-1853</u>. *tr Saturn conj ASC*.
<u>14-Dec-1853</u>. *tr Saturn-rx conj ASC*.
<u>8-Mar-1854</u>. *tr Saturn conj ASC*.
 Arrived at Fort Vancouver, Oregon, 30-Sep-1852. Developed melancholy from long separation from his family, started drinking alcohol and contemplated resignation from the Army.
 Notice of promotion to Captain on death of officer, 30-Sep-1853.
 Resigned Army same day as received official commission, 11-Apr-1854.

<u>12-Aug-1859</u>. *tr Saturn conj LOF*.
 Submitted unsuccessful application for St. Louis County Engineer, 15-Aug.

<u>14-Feb-1869</u>. *tr North Node conj LOF*.
 Presidential Inauguration, 4-Mar-1869.

<u>3-Apr-1873</u>. *tr North Node conj ASC*.
 Second Presidential Inauguration, 4-Mar-1873.

<u>6-May-1884</u>. *tr Sun 10th from LOF, tr Mars conj LOF, tr Jupiter conj Moon*.
 Grant and Ward business bankruptcy, 6-May-1884.

Solar Arc Directions

<u>9-Dec-1860</u>. *csa ASC conj Mercury*.
<u>10-Sep-1861</u>. *dsa Mercury conj. ASC*.
 LOCK Quick change in tactics with occupation of Paducah prevented Confederates from consolidating their defenses in Kentucky. Mercury/Aries signifies military strategy and rapid decision making, 6-Sep.

<u>19-May-1864</u>. *csa MC trine Mars*.
<u>9-Apr-1865</u>. *dsa Mars trine MC*.
 LOCK Battle of Spotsylvania, 8/20-May.
 LOCK Surrender of Robert E. Lee at Appomattox, 9-Apr.

<u>11-Feb-1883</u>. *csa Moon conj ASC*.
<u>19-Nov-1884</u>. *dsa ASC conj. Moon*.
 Slipped on ice in front of NYC home, 24-Dec-1883.
 Moon/Cancer (water) in bound of Saturn (cold) creates ice.
 Developed pleurisy while confined in bed, Jan-1884.
 Began dictating Memoirs, Nov-1884.
 Note that Moon-Ascendant directions are an acceptable arcus vitae and all of these events were related to ill health, including the start of his memoirs whose purpose was to raise funds for support of his surviving family after his expected death from throat cancer.

18. ULYSSES S GRANT

Primary Directions

| REG | D | Mercury/Gemini | P | sin trine MC d. => Saturn (SA) | 13-May-1846 |

Taylor won Battle of Palo Alto and Grant found himself in the line of fire for the 1st time, 8-May.

| PT | D | Mercury/Capricorn | P | dex trine Sun c. => MC | 28-Sep-1852 |

Arrived in Fort Vancouver 30-Sep, unhappy with family separation; Sun acts as 12th house planet.

| PT | D | Mars/Cancer | P | sin sextile Sun d. => ASC | 26-Jul-1861 |

LOCK Made Captain, 31-Jul.

| PT | D | Saturn/Sag | P | sin trine Mars (0) c. => MC | 24-Jul-1866 |

Made General of Armies, 25-Jul. Compare to similar Mars trine MC solar arc directions for 19-May-1864 and 9-Apr-1865.

| PT | D | Mercury/Aquarius | P | MC c. => Sun | 25-Jun-1885 |
| REG | D | Mercury/Aquarius | P | MC d. => Jupiter (0) | 26-Jun-1885 |

Favorable reception following Volume 1 of Memoirs published on 23-May.

Primary Direction Sequences

| PT | D | Mars/Gemini | P | dex sextile Mars (MA) d. => ASC | 23-Apr-1845 |
| PT | D | Mars/Gemini | P | dex sextile Mars (0) d. => ASC | 21-Sep-1847 |

LOCK This sequence timed the Mexican War conflict. On 28-May-1845 President Polk issued the order to send a detachment of troops under Zachary Taylor to the Mexican border. Grant's actual movements trail this order but are directly impacted by it. Grant was dispatched to New Orleans during Jul-1845, to Corpus Christi during Sep-1845 and reached the border during Mar-1846 in time for the outbreak of War on 23-Apr-1846. The war ended with the surrender of Mexico City 13/14-Sep-1847 with Grant's actions at San Cosme Garita on 13-Sep recognized favorably by his superiors.

| REG | D | Saturn/Aquarius | P | dex sq ASC d. => Saturn (0) | 4-Feb-1863 |
| REG | D | Saturn/Aquarius | P | dex sq ASC d. => Saturn (SA) | 2-May-1865 |

LOCK Assuming personal command of the Vicksburg expedition over protests of General McClernand on 30-Jan-1863 marked a pivotal shift in the Vicksburg campaign (won 4-Jul-1863). Grant's reputation as a 'butcher', a Saturn/Taurus trait, was largely responsible for his military success between 1863 and 1865. [Note: this delineation is consistent with the Saturn/Taurus - meatpacking industry connection identified in *America is Born* (p. 120)]. The sequence closed with Lee's surrender at Appomattox on 9-Apr and Sherman's surrender on 24-Apr-1865.

Longevity, 63y 2m 27d

Death: 23-Jul-1885, ~8:00 A.M., Mount McGregor, New York. In spring 1884 Grant noted pain in his throat but was not diagnosed with terminal throat cancer until November 1884. During April 1885, Grant's throat cancer ruptured an artery in his neck. After this event, Grant was unable to swallow much food and steadily lost weight until cancer overcame him.

Hīlāj: **Sun/Moon**. Sun/1st/feminine sign qualifies by WS but not by QS where he falls more than 5 degrees beyond the Ascendant in the 12th. Despite this disqualification, empirical findings in both arcus vitae and the solar return preceding death support the Sun as the Hīlāj. This is an exception to the 5-degree cutoff rule. Moon/Cancer/3rd also appears to participate as Hīlāj.

Al-kadukhadāh: **Venus or Moon**. If the Sun is Hīlāj, then Venus as bound lord and in a wide trine is the Al-kadukhadāh. If the Moon is Hīlāj, then she in her own sign is also the Al-kadukhadāh. Neither Venus granting 82 major years nor Moon granting 108 major years give good results. Two lots suggest a short lifespan. First, the conjunction of Jupiter 11TA33 to the Lot of Life at 15TA52 appears a debility given Jupiter's rulership of the 8th house and his power to time death as a killing planet. In addition, the South Node 22LE09 is conjunct the Lot of Hīlāj at 21LE57. **Finally, consider Saturn/Taurus as the victor.** Saturn grants 57 years. Venus adds 8 years by sextile aspect with reception by sign. Jupiter is co-present and adds 12 minor years. Mars in a wide out-of-moiety square aspect with no reception deducts 15 years.

SA (57) + VE (8) + JU (12) - MA (15) = 62 years.

Projection of 62 years is a good estimate for the arrival of throat cancer.

Victor of the Horoscope: **Saturn**

Killing Planets: **Venus (46), Moon (34)**

Arcus Vitae:

PT	D	Saturn/Cancer	P	Moon (0) d. => ASC	11-Apr-1885

Joins hīlāj to the Ascendant. Ruptured artery in neck during Apr-1885.

REG	D	Mercury/Aquarius	P	dex sq Sun d. => Jupiter (0)	29-May-1884
REG	D	Mercury/Aquarius	P	dex sq Sun d. => Jupiter (JU)	11-May-1885

Joins the natal 8th house ruler with the hīlāj.

REG	D	Mercury/Capricorn	P	dex trine Sun c. => Venus (VE)	19-Nov-1884
REG	D	Mercury/Capricorn	P	dex trine Sun c. => Venus (0)	19-May-1885

Joins the high scoring killing planet with the hīlāj.

1885 Solar Return for year of Death

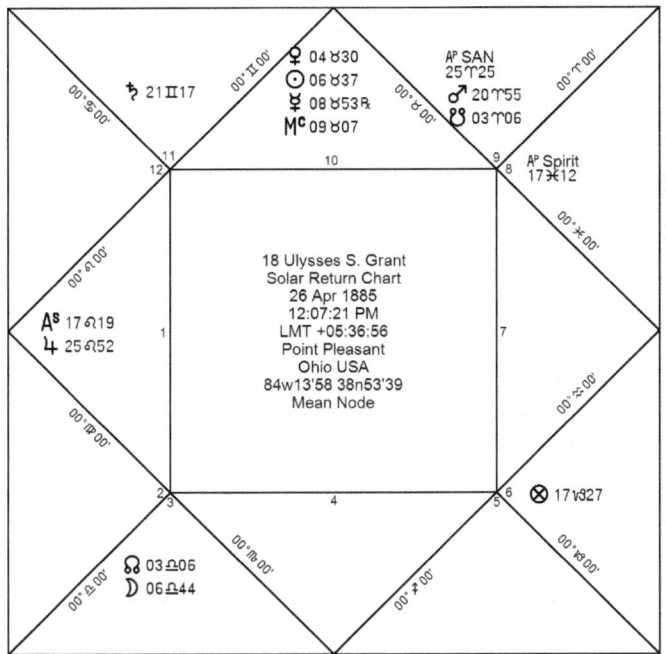

Ascendant Distributor: Saturn/Cancer since 2-Sep-1884
Profected Ascendant: 26LE25, 4th House; SR Victor: Sun (bound lord Venus)
Lords: LOY – Sun; LOP – Saturn
Firdaria: Mars-Mars
Moon: applies to trine of Saturn
Return Ascendant falls in natal 4th; natal Ascendant falls in return's 10th.

The 4th house end-of-life is doubly emphasized by a profected 4th house year and the return's Ascendant falling in the natal 4th house. Moon is afflicted by the North Node. High scoring killer Venus is the Al-mubtazz of the return's 8th and afflicts the Sun by conjunction. Jupiter lord of the 8th of death in both natal and return falls in the return's Ascendant and afflicts the Sun by antiscia.

| PT | D | Venus/Libra | P | sinister trine Jupiter d. => ASC | 22-Jul-1885. |

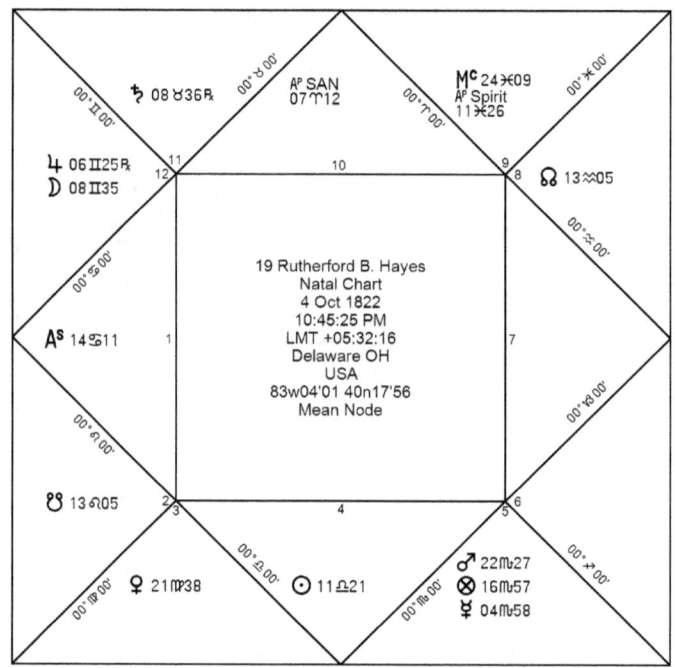
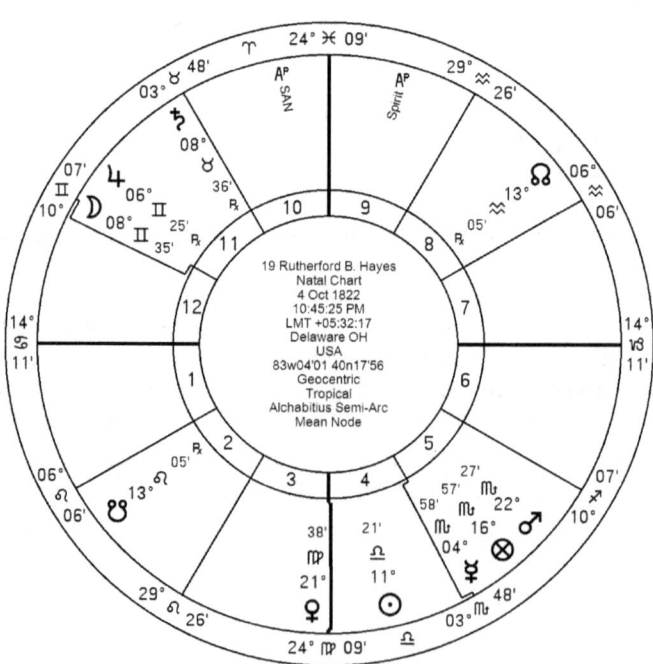

Moon's Configuration

Moon separates from **Jupiter** and applies to the **Sun**, nocturnal, preventional. Prenatal syzygy is 7AR12. Eclipse? No.

Cognitive Assessment Model (Rulers of Moon and Mercury)

Sign rulers: **Mercury, Mars**
Bound rulers: **Jupiter, Mars**

Victor Soul Models

Ibn Ezra Victor Model (1507), in-sect triplicity ruler, triplicity decans.

	Position	☉	☽	☿	♀	♂	♃	♄
Sun	11 LI 21			5	5			5
Moon	08 GE 35			9		2		
Asc	14 CA 11		5	2		4	4	
Pars Fortuna	16 SC 57			2		8	1	
Syzygy	07 AR 12	4			2	6	3	
Oriental						0	1	1
Houses		9	2	7	9	7	2	8
Score	0	13	7	**25**	16	**25**	13	14

Porphyry's Expanded Victor Model (2022)

Jupiter rules the MC and Lot of Spirit by sign; the Moon by bound. Sect: out-of-favor. Solar phase: oriental retrograde to acronycal rising. Dignity: participating triplicity and bound. Debility: detriment. Moon's separation.

Victor Table for Killing Planets

			☉	☽	☿	♀	♂	♃	♄
ASC		14CA11		5,3	2	3	3,1	4	
Rul ASC	♃	8GE35			5,3,1			3,2	3
L.Death		6CP06	3	2	3	4,3			5,1
Rul L.Death	♄	8TA36	4,3	2		5,3,1	3		
H8 Cusp		6AQ06			3,2			3	5,3,1
Rul H8	♄	8TA36	4,3	2		5,3,1	3		
T-Rul H8	☿	4SC58	3			3	5,3,2,1		
8th Occupants	NN	13AQ05			3,1			3,2	5,3
8th from ☽		8CP35	3			3	4,3	2	5,1
Rul 8th fr ☽	♄	8TA36	4,3	2		5,3,1	3		
TOTAL				**38**	**28**	**39**	**38**	**19**	**32**

2007 Proposed Rectification: 10:45:08 PM, ASC 14CA08'10"
2022 Revised Rectification: 10:45:25 PM, ASC 14CA11'52"

Astrodatabank reports a 9:30 PM birth time with a late Gemini Ascendant based on the eyewitness account of Uncle Sardis who recounted the birth time was possibly 9 to 10 PM in the evening. This recollection was made many years later when Hayes was President. Hayes recorded the same information in his diary.

The 2007 proposed rectification holds up well with ZRS from Pisces which implies a birth time of 9:55 PM or later which shifts the Ascendant degree to early Cancer. The 4th edition revised rectification was a slight tweak based on a few directions. In addition to ZR, the Stage I technique of Configuration of the Chart has aged well with Hayes' interest in prison reform consistent with Moon and Jupiter placed in the 12th.

ZRS. Most striking about releasing LOS from Pisces is the onset of L1 Cancer on 19-Dec-1876 between the time of the disputed election of 1876 and its resolution in Hayes' favor on 2-Mar-1877. As further validation of this ZR structure, for L1-Cancer at the start of Hayes' Presidency, both L3 Capricorn FS and LB subperiods precisely timed the firing and termination of Chester Arthur from the New York Custom House which was central to Hayes' efforts in Civil Service Reform.

L1 Pisces 04 Oct 1822		
L1 Aries 02 Aug 1834		4-Oct-1834, enrolled in Norwalk Seminary chosen by Uncle Sardis. completed education and began law career during L1-Aries. took interest in national political elections. decided to move to Cincinnati at period's end.
L1 Gemini 03 Apr 1857		4-Oct-1858, made campaign speech for Republicans. during L1-Gemini, RH won political office first as Cincinnati solicitor before interrupting his political career for Civil War service. Upon return he was elected Ohio Governor 3 times and President as L1 closed.
L2 Sagittarius 16 Jan 1866	FS	Congressional session featured disputes between Radical Republicans and President Andrew Johnson with veto overrides.
L2 Sagittarius 02 Aug 1874	LB	2-Jun-1875, nominated for OH Governor 3rd time.
L2 Capricorn 28 Jul 1875		Nov-1875, won re-election to Governor; 16-Jun-1865, won Republican Presidential Nomination; 7-Nov-1876, Presidential election results are disputed.
L1 Cancer 19 Dec 1876		29-Jan-1877, Electoral Commission Act established; 2-Mar-1877, election resolved in Hayes' favor; 5-Mar-1877, Presidential swearing in ceremony.
L2 Cancer 19-Dec-1876		
L3 Capricorn 24-Aug-1877	FS	6-Sep-1877, fired Chester Arthur from Custom House position but Arthur refused to resign.
L3 Capricorn 31-May-1878	LB	11-Jul-1878, suspended Arthur from Custom House.
L2 Capricorn 05 Feb 1885	FS	Feb-1885, financial problems eclipse other concerns.
L2 Gemini 27 Aug 1892		17-Jan-1893, death.

Firdaria – Jupiter major and minor periods

Firdaria according to Bonatti	Life Event
Moon **Jupiter** 01 May 1825	20-Jan-1826, drowning death of brother Lorenzo while ice skating.
Saturn **Jupiter** 01 May 1833	4-Jun-1834, began 5-month family trip to New England to visit relatives; Fall-1834, entered Norwalk Seminary chosen by Uncle Sardis.
Jupiter 12 years Age 20 to 32	
Jupiter Jupiter 04 Oct 1842	17-Oct-1842, began reading law with Thomas Sparrow; Aug-1843, enrolled Harvard Law School.
Jupiter Mars 21 Jun 1844	Fall-1844, last term Harvard; Spring-1845, opened law practice in Lower Sandusky, Ohio.
Jupiter Sun 10 Mar 1846	1-Apr-1846, entered partnership with Ralph Buckland; 6/8-Jul-1847, Met Lucy Webb - wife-to-be.
Jupiter Venus 26 Nov 1847	1848/1849, multiple trips with Uncle Sardis; 6-Apr-1849, arrived in Cincinnati, decided to relocate there.
Jupiter Mercury 13 Aug 1849	24-Dec-1849, left Columbus to move to Cincinnati; early 1850, attended newly formed Cincinnati Literary Society; 2-Mar-1850, made first speech to literary club; late-May-1850, heard Ralph Waldo Emerson speak at literary club.
Jupiter Moon 01 May 1851	13-Jun-1851, RH and LW mutually confessed their love and sealed private engagement; 26-Nov-1852, attended Henry Lecount's execution, an accused murderer and client of RH; 30-Dec-1852, Married Lucy Web.
Jupiter Saturn 16 Jan 1853	Jan-1853, successfully defended man accused of poisoning his family before the Supreme Court of Ohio "greatest triumph of my professional life," 1853, defended many African Americans on pro bono basis for cases arising under the Fugitive Slave Act.
Mars **Jupiter** 04 Oct 1860	6-Nov-1860, AL elected President; 11-Feb-1861, RH talked directly with AL; 7-Jun-1861, received Civil War military commission.
Sun **Jupiter** 25 Nov 1873	26-Nov-1873, Uncle Sardis moved out of Spiegal Grove and gave estate to RH; 21-Jan-1874, Sardis died; 25-Mar-1875, Ohio Republican Caucus called on RH to run a 3rd time for Governor.
Venus **Jupiter** 30 Apr 1881	May-1881, Post Office Star Route fraud scandal broke; Oct-1881, anonymous leak to media stated RH had known about Star Route fraud and failed to shut it down; 18-May-1822, RH active in Slater Fund, educational venture, date is 1st meeting.
Mercury **Jupiter** 30 Apr 1890	4/6-Jun-1890, attended Mohonk conference on education, housing, and crime; 5-May-1891, adopted Ohio State University resolution for building construction projects; Nov-1891, met with Slater Fund agent Curry, inspected schools in 6 southern states, found evidence of wasteful spending.

Jupiter as Victor. Jupiter/Gemini ruling the 9th in the 12th ties matters of the law to the imprisoned. His greatest legal victory (Jupiter-Saturn) was the successful defense of a man accused of poisoning his family. As Firdaria lord, Jupiter timed no period of RH's Presidency, though the Star Route post office fraud revealed after he left office was linked to his Presidency. Interest in education reform, especially his work with the Slater Fund, is a delineation match to Jupiter ruling the 9th of education in the 12th of fraud (Slater Fund accused of wasteful spending).

Transits

3-Mar-1867. *tr South Node conj MC*
40th Congress convened and planned to challenge Presidential authority over Reconstruction, 4-Mar.

22-Jun-1876. *tr North Node conj MC.*
Nominated for President, 16-Jun; Tilden Democratic nomination, 27-Jun.

17-Feb-1877. *tr North Node conj LOS.*
Electoral commission awarded Florida to RH, 8-Feb; Louisiana, 16-Feb; Oregon, 23-Feb; election resolved in RH favor, 2-Mar-1877.

31-Dec-1877. *tr Jupiter conj DSC.*
RH and wife Lucy renewed wedding vows on 25th anniversary, 30-Dec.

Solar Arc Directions

17-Nov-1852. *dsa Saturn conj Moon.*
Present at execution of murderer Hayes was unable to acquit, 26-Nov.

22-Jun-1858. *dsa Moon conj ASC.*
Birth of 3rd child Rutherford Platt Hayes, 24-Jun; wife Lucy ill to August.

20-Nov-1864. *csa Mars conj Sun.*
Promoted to Brigadier General, 9-Dec.

LOCK 6-Apr-1867. *dsa MC conj Saturn.*
LOCK 19-May-1868. *csa Saturn conj MC.*
Hayes family returned to Fremont where Uncle Sardis was ill with pneumonia, 10-Apr-1867; impeachment vote against Johnson, 16-May-1868; death of former President Buchanan, 1-Jun-1868.

26-Dec-1877. *dsa Venus conj LOF.*
RH and wife Lucy renewed wedding vows on 25th anniversary; high point of White House social events for Hayes' entire Presidency, 30-Dec-1877.

6-Feb-1888. *dsa Saturn conj ASC.*
Wife's church burned to the ground. Hayes helped rebuild it, 6-Feb-1888.

Primary Directions

PT	D	Venus/Leo	P	sin sextile Jupiter (0) d. => ASC	13-Apr-1850
PT	D	Venus/Leo	P	sin sextile Jupiter (BI) d. => ASC	17-Aug-1850
PT	D	Venus/Leo	P	sin sextile Jupiter (JU) d. => ASC	20-Dec-1850

Made first speech to Cincinnati Literary Society, 2-Mar-1850.

Ralph Waldo Emerson visited Cincinnati with appearance before Cincinnati Literary Society, late-May-1850.

| PT | D | Saturn/Leo | P | dex sextile Sun d. => ASC | 17-Jul-1856 |

Death of sister Fanny, complications from childbirth, 16-Jul.
Sun rules 10th by exaltation (8th from the 3rd); Venus/3rd rules Sun.

| PT | D | Mars/Scorpio | P | Mercury (ME) d. => IC | 23-Jul-1861 |

Union losses at Manassas (Bull Run) hurt morale, 22-Jul.
Guerilla attacks by Confederate forces, 17/18-Aug.

| PT | D | Jupiter/Aquarius | P | North Node c. => MC | 1-Nov-1861 |

Promoted to Lieutenant Colonel of 23rd regiment, 2-Nov-1861.

Primary Direction Sequences

| REG | D | Saturn/Gemini | P | sin square MC d. => Saturn (SA) | 18-Oct-1862 |
| REG | D | Saturn/Gemini | P | sin square MC d. => Saturn (0) | 11-Apr-1865 |

| PT | D | Saturn/Gemini | P | sin square MC d. => Saturn (SA) | 11-Jul-1864 |
| PT | D | Saturn/Gemini | P | sin square MC d. => Saturn (0) | 21-Jul-1866 |

First sequence immediately follows injury from musket ball which struck his left arm above the elbow on 14-Sep-1862. Distributor Saturn/Gemini harms the arms and placed in the 12th signifies confinement and hospitalization. On 5-Oct-1862, RH left for home and spent October and November recuperating. The 12-Apr-1865 direction times the end of the war and Lincoln's 15-Apr-1865 assassination.

Second sequence is arguably linked to Andrew Johnson whose natal victor Saturn/Scorpio functions in a similar manner to Hayes' Saturn/Taurus-rx. Johnson wrote letter of acceptance for the Vice-Presidency, 2-Jul-1864. Congress overrode Johnson's veto of the Freeman's Bill, 16-Jul-1866

PT	D	Jupiter/Taurus	P	dex trine Venus (VE) d. => MC	10-Dec-1876
PT	D	Jupiter/Taurus	P	dex trine Venus (0) d. => MC	4-May-1877
PT	D	Jupiter/Taurus	P	dex trine Venus (BI) d. => MC	15-Jul-1877

Senate President received electoral certificates from each state, 6-Dec. From this time to the time the election is decided, there were attempts by RH's political alliances to bribe election officials.

Treasury Secretary Sherman appointed John Jay to head investigation into fraud at the New York customhouse, 23-Apr-1877.

'Great Railroad Strike' began after Baltimore & Ohio cuts pay, 16-Jul-1877.

Longevity, 70y 3m 15d

Death: 17-Jan-1893, 11:00 PM, Fremont, OH, Spiegal Grove, at home.

Hīlāj: **Sun/LOF**. Figure is nocturnal and Moon is preferred yet disqualified by her placement in the 12th. Sun in 4th qualifies and tests well empirically. Wartime injuries (14-Sep-1862 & 19-Oct-1864) consistently show Mars dynamically afflicting the Sun by either transit or solar arc. At death a tight Mars-Saturn opposition afflicts the Sun with transiting Saturn a little more than a degree past the Sun. Arcus vitae also favors the Sun.

Yet the LOF appears to participate with the Sun as Hīlāj. A closer look at the interplay of Mars, Venus, and the Nodes in each respective solar return prior to wartime injuries shows the LOF activated by aspect.

Al-kadukhadāh: **Jupiter**. If the Sun is the hīlāj, participating triplicity lord Jupiter in his bound closely trines the Sun, is the al-kadukhadāh, and grants 79 major years. Malefics are inconjunct and cannot deduct years. 79 is too long.

Mars. If LOF is the hīlāj, then Mars is the al-kadukhadāh and Mars grants 66 major years. Venus may add 8 minor years by sextile aspect; however Venus receives Mars only by diurnal triplicity whereas Mars receives Venus by bound. Cases when al-kadukhudhah receives the additive planet argue against addition of years, or low quality if any years are added. Age 66 takes Hayes to the year 1888 when he first had a mild attack of diabetes which returned in 1891. During 1890 he observed symptoms of a small stroke. This is clear evidence of a decline in vitality after Hayes exceeded Mars' 66 major years.

MA (66) + VE (8) = 74 years.

Victor of the Horoscope: **Jupiter**

Killing Planets: **Venus (39), Mars (38), Moon (38)**

Arcus Vitae:

REG	D	Saturn/Leo	P	dex square LOF c. => Mars (MA)	19-Jan-1892
REG	D	Saturn/Leo	P	dex square LOF c. => Mars (0)	20-Jun-1892

This sequence includes a serious case of poison ivy in April 1892.

REG	D	Jupiter/Cancer	P	dex trine Mars (0) c. => Sun	16-Jan-1893
REG	D	Jupiter/Cancer	P	dex trine Mars (MA) c. => Sun	30-Apr-1893

Death occurred 1 day after the start of this sequence.

PT	D	Venus/Cancer	P	dex sq Sun c. => Venus (0)	20-Mar-1893
PT	D	Venus/Cancer	P	dex sq Sun c. => Venus (VE)	25-Aug-1893

Joins the high scoring killing planet to the Hīlāj. A bit late.

1892 Solar Return for year of Death

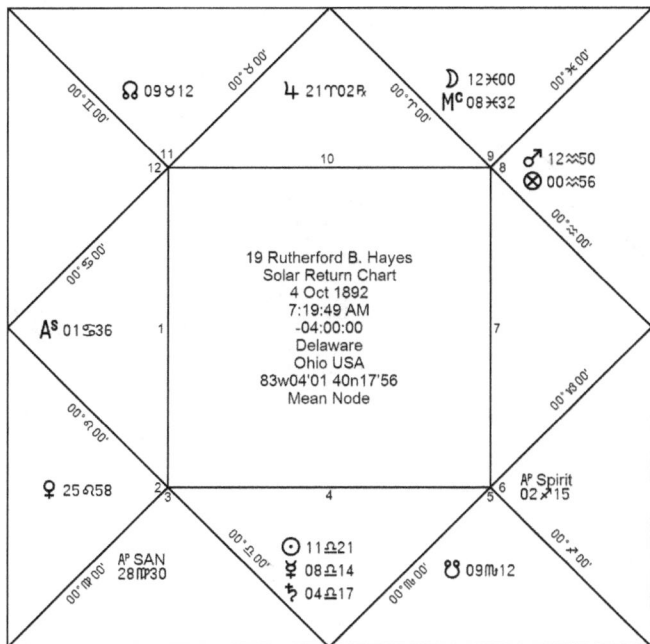

Ascendant Distributor: Venus/Virgo since 4-Mar-1889
Profected Ascendant: 14TA11, 11th house; SR Victor: Jupiter
Lords: LOY – Venus; LOP – Moon
Firdaria: Mercury-Mars
Moon makes no aspects; she is feral
Return Ascendant matches natal Ascendant.

Hīlāj Sun falls in the end-of-life 4th house and is afflicted by a Mercury-Mars trine both of whom are high-scoring killers and rule time by Firdaria. LOF in 8th is also negative considering the LOF participates as Hīlāj.

The Mars trine Sun arcus vitae is recapitulated by position in the return.

Saturn, lord of the 8th in both natal and return, brings additional testimony to death. In the natal position Saturn falls 8 signs from the Sun which increases his testimony as a killer. The return's North Node at 8TA11 makes a partile conjunction to natal Saturn, increasing its power to act by transit at the time of the return. At death, tr Saturn conjoins the Sun; tr Mars opposes the Sun.

No relevant solar return Ascendant directions were found.

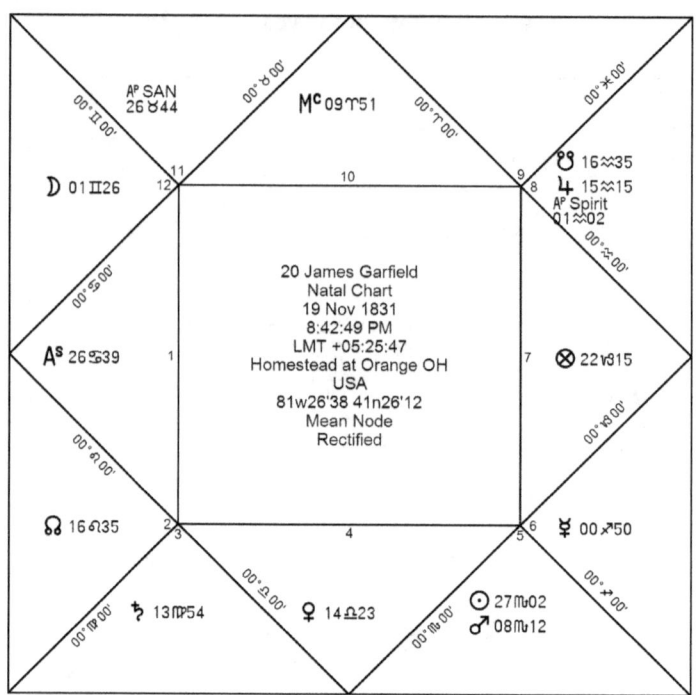
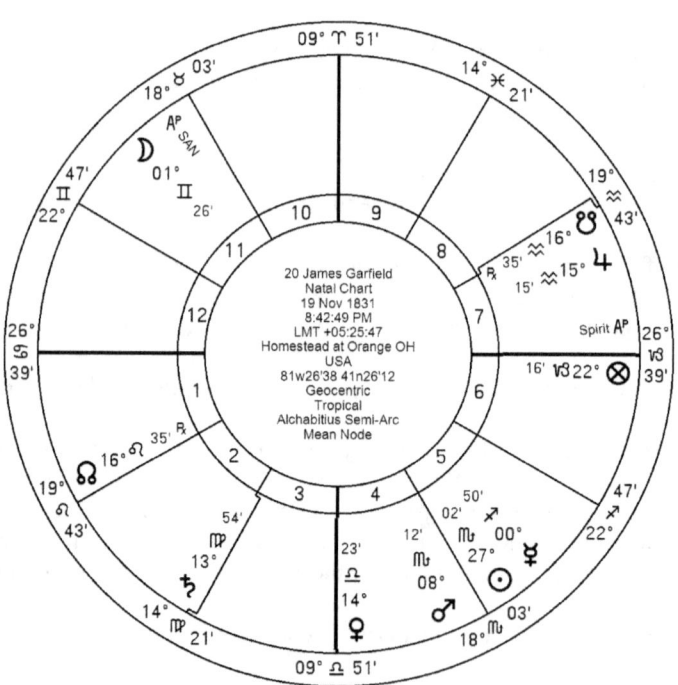

Moon's Configuration

Moon separates from **Mercury** and applies to **Saturn**, nocturnal, preventional. Prenatal syzygy is 26TA44. Eclipse? No.

Cognitive Assessment Model (Rulers of Moon and Mercury)

Sign rulers: **Mercury, Jupiter**
Bound rulers: **Mercury, Jupiter**

Victor Soul Models

Ibn Ezra Victor Model (1507), in-sect triplicity ruler, triplicity decans.

	Position	☉	☽	☿	♀	♂	♃	♄
Sun	27 SC 02	1				8		2
Moon	01 GE 26			11				
Asc	26 CA 39		5			3	5	2
Pars Fortuna	22 CP 15		3	1		4		7
Syzygy	26 TA 44		7		5			3
Oriental						3	0	2
Houses		7	8	7	9	9	5	3
Score		0	7	24	19	14	**27**	10	19

Porphyry's Expanded Victor Model (2022)

Saturn rules the Lot of Fortune and Lot of Spirit by sign; the ASC, Sun, Lot of Fortune, and syzygy by bound. Sect: out-of-favor. Solar phase: oriental waxing sextile to square. Dignity: decan. Moon's application.

Victor Table for Killing Planets

			☉	☽	☿	♀	♂	♃	♄
ASC		26CA39	5,3		3	3	4,1	2	
Rul ASC	☽	1GE26			5,3,2,1			3	3
L.Death		3GE11			5,3,2,1			3	3
Rul L.Death	☿	00SA50	3					5,3,2,1	3
H8 Cusp		19AQ43			3,1			3,2	5,3
Rul H8	♄	13VI54		3	5,4	3,2	3		1
T-Rul H8	☿	0SA50	3					5,3,2,1	3
♃ in 8th	♃	15AQ15			3,1			5,2	5,3
SN in 8th	SN	16AQ35			3,1			3,2	5,3
8th from ☽		1CP26		3	2	3	4,3		5,1
Rul 8th fr ☽	♄	13VI54		3	5,4	3,2	3		1
TOTAL			6	17	**54**	16	16	**48**	46

2007 Proposed Rectification: 8:42:50 PM, ASC 26CA40'04"
2022 Proposed Rectification: 8:42:49 PM, ASC 26CA39'30"

Astrodatabank reports an A-rated birthtime of 2:00 AM, from memory, with an Ascendant of 28VI. The proposed rectification varies considerably in time and structure with different sign placements for both Moon and Mercury. Mercury/Scorpio and Moon/Taurus in the ADB record varies from Mercury/Sagittarius and Moon/Gemini in the proposed rectification. Getting planets in the correct sign is a Stage I rectification tool. Usually this applies to the Moon but it can apply to other planets. In Chapter 17, I cite biographical evidence of Garfield's dreaminess and accidents including falling overboard 14 times during a canal boat ride at age 16 as evidence favoring Mercury in Sagittarius not Scorpio. Literary interests and indecisiveness are consistent with Moon/Gemini. As for Cancer rising with Ascendant lord Moon/Gemini/12th, I can think of no better delineation match than Garfield's early Civil War experience when he repeatedly left the battlefield to find solace talking to horses away from his men. Horses are large riding animals assigned to the 12th house. Moon/Gemini signifies chatter.

ZRS. Releasing from LOS in Aquarius sets up two of Garfield's early academic career peaks and departures with L2-Leo (LB) timing study at Geuga Seminary and L2-Aquarius (CP) his position as President of Hiram College. Usually this type of event pairing would be seen at the FS and LB periods respectively, not the LB and CP periods. At least for Garfield, with the FS period occurring at the very young age of 9, the final completion period yields events that we might normally associate with loosing of the bond. L1-Pisces pushes Garfield to Civil War military service and his subsequent Congressional career. L1-Aries (angular from LOF) timed a recovery in political standing after the Credit Mobilier scandal and his rise to the Presidency under L2-Virgo.

L1 Aquarius 19 Nov 1831		
L2 Leo 01 Dec 1840	FS	
L2 Leo 19 Mar 1849	LB	Nov-1849, Taught school on Seminary break, encountered unruly students; 3-Mar-1850, religious conversion to Disciples of Christ; by end of period preparing to leave Geuga Seminary after disliking the institution.
L2 Aquarius 05 Jul 1857	CP	11-Nov-1858, married Lucretia Rudolph; 27/31-Dec-1858, in debate on Darwin vs Intelligent Design; JG takes Intelligent Design side and demolishes opponent; May-1859, position of President at Hiram College secured after trustees fired rival Norman Dunshee; however JG remained restless and considered other employment.
L1 Pisces 14 Jun 1861		Mid-Aug-1861, commissioned Lieutenant Colonel in 42nd Regiment Ohio.
L1 Aries 12 Apr 1873		Aug-1873, reputation recovered after taint from involvement with Credit Mobilier scandal.
L2 Virgo 04 Jun 1880		8-Jun-1880, nominated for President; 2-Jul-1881, mortally wounded; 19-Sep-1881, death.

Firdaria – Saturn major and minor periods

Firdaria according to Bonatti	Life Event
Moon **Saturn** 03 Mar 1833	1833 (no date), death of father.
Saturn 11 years Age 9 to 20	
Saturn Saturn 19 Nov 1840	Apr-1842, mother remarried and lived with Warren Belden only a year.
Saturn Jupiter 15 Jun 1842	No events found.
Saturn Mars 10 Jan 1844	No events found.
Saturn Sun 06 Aug 1845	No events found.
Saturn Venus 03 Mar 1847	16-Aug-1848, first job on canal, fell into canal 14 times.
Saturn Mercury 27 Sep 1848	Oct-1848/Jan-1849, ill with ague; 6-Mar-1849, entered Geuga Seminary; Nov-1849, taught school; 3-Mar-1850, conversion to Disciples of Christ.
Saturn Moon 24 Apr 1850	End-1850, left Geuga Seminary; Aug-1851, enrolled Hiram Eclectic Institute (Disciples of Christ) and flourished.
Jupiter **Saturn** 03 Mar 1862	14-Mar-1862, led successful raid near Piketown, JG's last independent command; 30-Jul-1862, sick leave for 2 months; 2-Sep-1862, selected Congressional candidate; end-Feb-1863, Chief of Staff for Rosecrans; 20-Sep-1863, Battle of Chickamauga + logistical resupply feat + promotion to Major General.
Mars **Saturn** 18 Nov 1868	Dec-1868, chair of Committee on Banking and Currency.
Sun **Saturn** 06 Aug 1881	2-Nov-1880, elected President; 19-Sep-1881, death.

Saturn as Victor. As Major Firdaria ruler for nocturnal horoscopes, Saturn's major years are between the ages of 9-20, a very young age to time events central to the native's life history. Nevertheless, Garfield's religious conversion and enrollment in Hiram Institute, a Disciples of Christ organization led directly to his first career as teacher and principal of Hiram. As a student, he also gained expertise in languages and public speaking central to his later political career. During Civil War service, his oversight of logistics at the Battle of Chickamauga was considered one of the most successful logistics operations during the entire Civil War, a major career milestone. As Congressman, his Committee Chair appointment to Banking and Currency is consistent with the command and control nature of Saturn/Virgo with Mercury-ruled Virgo a business significator. Finally Sun-Saturn timed his Presidential election and assassination.

As a specific delineation of Saturn/Virgo/3rd, consider that civil service reform is consistent with Saturn overcoming Mercury in the 6th of government employees, e.g., by derived houses, the 3rd is 10th from the 6th.

Profections

The first three events exemplify the *seasonality* of annual profections:

<u>8-Apr-1861</u>. *prof ASC sextile Mars*. Civil War outbreak, 12-Apr.

<u>8-Apr-1862</u>. *prof ASC square Mars*. Battle of Shiloh, 6/7-Apr.

<u>8-Apr-1865</u>. *prof ASC opposed Mars*. Lincoln Assassination, 14-Apr.
Note Mars in 5th, 8th from 10th, death of King.

<u>16-Jun-1881</u>. *prof ASC conj. Saturn*. Guiteau's first planned assassination attempt, 18-Jun; Saturn rules the 8th of death.

Transits

<u>23-Mar-1850</u>. *tr Saturn conj MC*.
Religious Conversion to Disciples of Christ, 3-Mar-1850.

<u>26-Oct-1850</u>. *tr Jupiter conj IC*.
Became disgusted with Geuga Seminary; left end of term, Oct-1850.

<u>12-Jul-1851</u>. *tr North Node conj ASC*.
Entered Hiram Eclectic Institute (Disciples of Christ), Aug-1851.

<u>21-Apr-1854</u>. *tr Jupiter conj DSC*.
Garfield and Lucretia Rudolph declared their love, Spring-1854.

<u>18-Jan-1857</u>. *tr North Node conj MC*.
Spoke as preacher in Great Awakening revivals in Ohio, early-1857.

<u>13-Jun-1860</u>. *tr Jupiter conj ASC*.
Speech at State Republican Convention raised prominence as a successful stump speaker, mid-Jun-1860.

<u>8-Dec-1863</u>. *tr North Node trine ASC*.
Resigned Army position to take House seat, 6-Dec.

<u>18-Mar, 10-May, 10-Nov-1866</u>. *tr Jupiter conj DSC*.
Asked to argue Milligan case before Supreme Court, Mar-1866; decided in Garfield's favor 17-Dec-1866.

<u>16-May, 22-Nov, 16-Dec-1880</u>. *tr Jupiter conj MC*.
Made final speech to House on 25-May; Presidential Nomination 8-Jun; Elected President 2-Nov; Blaine's acceptance of Secretary of State, mid-Dec-1880.

Solar Arc Directions

25-Oct-1861. *dsa ASC square Sun*.
24-Feb-1862. *csa Sun square ASC*.
   42nd Ohio Regiment under JG's command reached full strength, Nov-1861. Struggled with fame as military commander between Sandy Creek flood (22-Feb-1862), epidemic following flood, and victorious raid at Piketown (14-Mar-1862) which was last independent command. Promoted to brigadier general at height of the epidemic.

LOCK 19-Jan-1863. *dsa Mars trine MC*.
LOCK 8-Jun-1863. *csa MC trine Mars*.
   Received commission as General to Rosecrans, mid-Jan-1863.
   Presented attack plan to Rosecrans which undercut Rosecrans' excuses for not advancing, 12-Jun-1863. Biographer Peskin states this may have been Garfield's biggest contribution to the Union military effort (Peskin 189).

9-Mar-1879. *csa Saturn conj ASC*. Congress adjourned without signing Appropriations Bill, 3-Mar. Initiated heavy handed floor tactics as President Hayes recalled Congress in special session. Saturn in 3rd of communications rules the 7th of open enemies.

Primary Direction Sequences

PT	D	Mercury/Taurus	P	dex trine Saturn (SA) d. => MC	21-Sep-1863
PT	D	Mercury/Taurus	P	dex trine Saturn (0) d. => MC	7-Apr-1864

LOCK Battle of Chickamaugua (20-Sep) triggered Garfield's telegram to Washington with a request for massive troop support. Washington responded with 20,000 soldiers and equipment within 7 days, the greatest logistical feat of the entire Civil War. Notice how *logistical feat* is similar in delineation to *census data* in the next sequence. As this sequence finished, JG made a dramatic floor speech on 8-Apr-1864 in response to Ohio Democrat Long who suggested an end to war and recognition of the Confederacy. Garfield's speech included charges of treasonable correspondence with the enemy against two Indiana Democrats. Note Saturn rules 7th of open enemies and in the 3rd is tied to communication, including the alleged correspondence JG charged. It turns out these alleged correspondences were forgeries (showing impact of Mercury/Sag – exaggeration – disposing Saturn/3rd).

REG	D	Venus/Leo	P	sin trine MC c. => Saturn (0)	27-Jun-1869
REG	D	Venus/Leo	P	sin trine MC c. => Saturn (SA)	8-Jul-1869

Timed JG's passion for statistics in role as head of Census Committee. Saturn/Virgo/3rd house fits well with Census: Saturn/control-containment + Virgo/details + 3rd/neighborhood.

Longevity, 49y 10m 1d

Death in office: Garfield is fatally wounded by an assassin on 2-Jul-1881. Because of poor medical care, he eventually died from complications including blood poisoning on 19-Sep-1881, 10:35 PM, Elveron, New Jersey.

Hīlāj: **Sun/LOF**. Figure is nocturnal and Moon is preferred but ruled out for placement in the 12th house. Sun/5th/feminine qualifies. Empirically, LOF participates as Hīlāj. Episodes of dysentery during Civil War service (1862/63) appear timed by transits of Mars and the Nodes to the LOF. Death in 1881 is clearly marked by directions and transits of Mercury to the LOF.

Respective solar returns for the years 1847, 1862, and 1880 show various afflictions to the Sun and/or LOF. In the 1862 return, the LOF is combust the Sun and besieged by Sun, Venus, and Mercury; all disposed by Mars on the IC. The LOF is also similarly besieged by Sun and Mars in the 1880 return for the year of death.

Al-kadukhadāh: If Sun is the hīlāj, then **Mars** in the sign of rulership and co-present with the Sun is the al-kadukhudāh. Mars grants 66 major years. He lived fewer years. An argument can be made that Mars near the bendings and close to the antiscia of the South Node triggers a 25% haircut from the Nodes. 66 * 0.75 = 49.5 years which is accurate.

If the LOF is the hīlāj, while Mars receives the LOF by exaltation, consider **Saturn** as al-kadukhadāh keeping in mind Saturn is the Victor of the Horoscope. If so, then Saturn grants 57 major years. Mercury receives by square aspect and is justifiably classified as an accidental malefic for rulership of the 12th and empirical evidence that Mercury timed poor medical care which facilitated death. If Mercury deducts 20 minor years the net projection is 37 which is too short. Nevertheless, Mercury does suggest a deduction from Saturn's major years by delineation.

Victor of the Horoscope: **Saturn**

Killing Planets: **Mercury (54), Jupiter (48), Saturn (46)**

Arcus Vitae

2-Jul-1881. trMercury 1LE00 opposed LOS 1AQ03.

| PT | D | Mercury/Gemini | P | opposition Mercury (0) d. => MC | 11-Jul-1881 |
| PT | D | Mercury/Gemini | P | opposition Mercury (ME) d. => MC | 19-Sep-1881 |

LOCK Timed poor medical care, short-term travel, and death. Mercury rules 3rd house of short-term transportation.

1880 Solar Return for year of Death

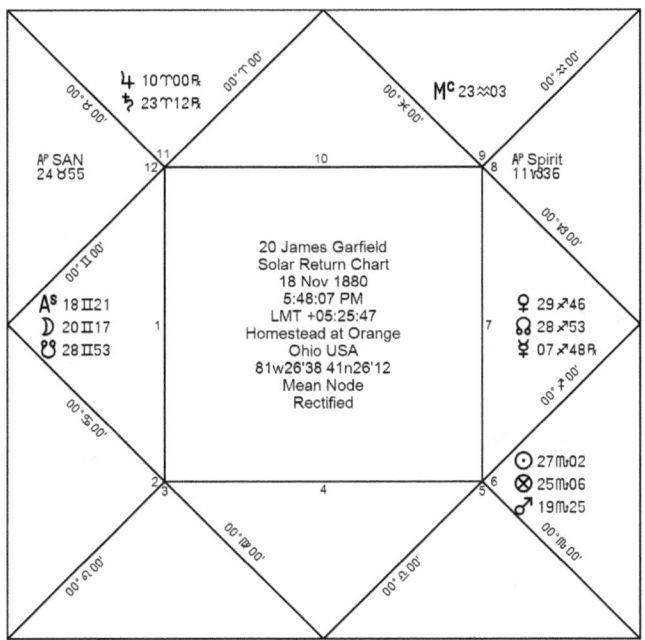

Ascendant Distributor: Mercury/Virgo since 6-Aug-1874
Profected Ascendant: 26LE40, 2nd house; SR Victor: Saturn
Lords: LOY – Sun; LOP – Jupiter
Firdaria: Sun-Saturn
Moon separates from sextile of Jupiter and applies to sextile of Saturn
Return Ascendant falls in natal 12th; natal Ascendant falls in return's 2nd.

This figure shows numerous indications of death with Mercury trumping as the high scoring killing planet. Both luminaries and Lot of Fortune are afflicted by malefics for starters. Return Ascendant falling in the 12th of secret enemies emphasizes the importance of enemies, errors, and hospitalization this year. Garfield suffered all three. Mercury, the return's Ascendant ruler, is given power to act by the return to his natal bound and is further amplified by the conjunction to the North Node. Mercury placed in the 7th is no longer a secret enemy; he is an open enemy with power to act in the angle of the West.

| PT | D | Jupiter/Sagittarius | P | Mercury (0) d. => ASC | 20-Jun-1881 |

The directed Ascendant reached Mercury midway between Guiteau's first two unsuccessful assassination attempts on 18 and 27-Jun. Mercury retrograde means Guiteau kept trying until successful.

556   A RECTIFICATION MANUAL

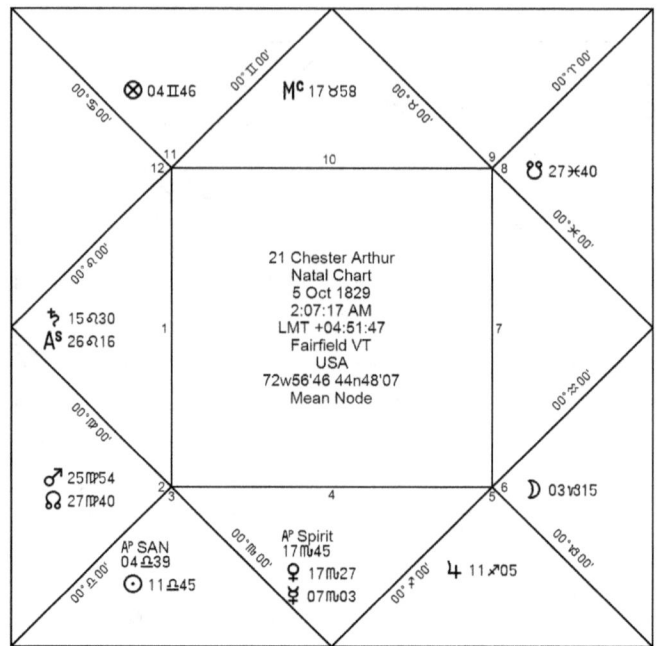

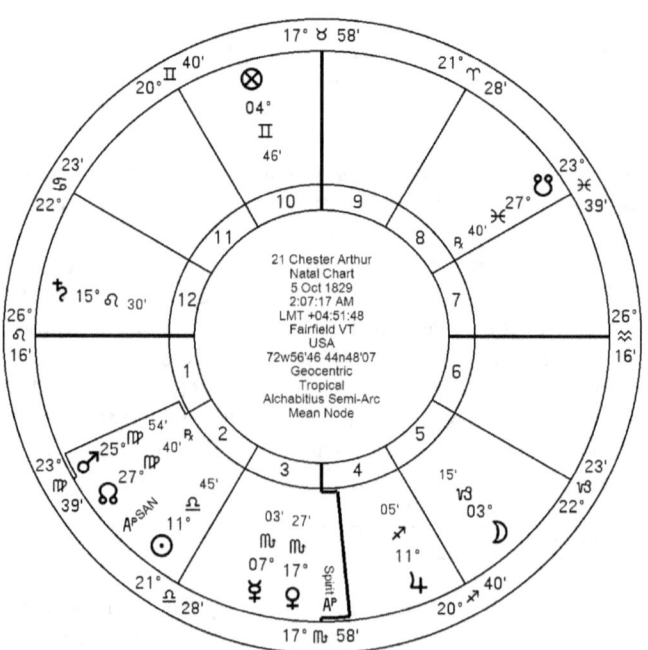

21. CHESTER ARTHUR

Moon's Configuration

Moon applies to **Mercury**, nocturnal, conjunctional.
Prenatal syzygy is 4LI39. Eclipse? **YES**. Annular Solar Eclipse.

Cognitive Assessment Model (Rulers of Moon and Mercury)

Sign rulers: **Saturn, Mars**
Bound rulers: **Mercury, Venus**

Victor Soul Models

Ibn Ezra Victor Model (1507), in-sect triplicity ruler, triplicity decans.

	Position	☉	☽	☿	♀	♂	♃	♄
Sun	11 LI 45			5	5			5
Moon	03 CP 15		3	2		4		6
Asc	26 LE 16	5				3	3	
Pars Fortuna	04 GE 46			11				
Syzygy	04 LI 39 (SE)			3	6			6
Oriental						3	0	3
Houses			6	7	3	9	6	9	2
Score		0	11	10	**24**	20	16	12	22

Porphyry's Expanded Victor Model (2022)

Mars rules the Lot of Spirit by sign; the ASC by bound. Sect: in-favor. Solar phase: oriental rising to waxing sextile. Position: 4th from Lot of Fortune. Dignity: participating triplicity and bound; mutual reception with Mercury by sign. Conjunct North Node.

Victor Table for Killing Planets

			☉	☽	☿	♀	♂	♃	♄
ASC		26LE16	5,3				2,1	3	3
Rul ASC	☉	11LI45			3,2	5		3	4,3,1
L.Death		5SC54		3		3	5,3,2,1		
Rul L.Death	♂	25VI54		3	5,4	3,1	3,2		
H8 Cusp		23PI39		3		4,3	3,2,1	5	
Rul H8	♃	11SA05	3				1	5,3,2	3
T-Rul H8	♂	25VI54		3	5,4	3,1	3,2		
SN in 8th	SN	27PI40		3		4,3	3,2,1	5	
8th from ☽		3LE11	5,3,1					3,2	3
Rul 8th fr ☽	☉	11LI45			3,2	5		3	4,3,1
TOTAL			20	15	28	**35**	37	34	25

2007 Proposed Rectification: 2:08:40 AM, ASC 26LE32'06"
2009 Revised Rectification: 2:00:35 AM, ASC 25LE00'31"
2022 Revised Rectification: 2:07:17 AM, ASC 26LE16'20"

Horoscopes of the U.S. Presidents lists Arthur's birth date as 5-Oct-1830 with a birth time of 4:33 a.m. Research has shown during Arthur's lifetime he changed his birth year from 1829 to 1830 presumably for reasons of vanity to pass himself off as a younger man. The correct birth year is 1829. ADB currently gives the correct 1829 birth year with a birth time of 6:07 based on a sunrise recollection.

The revision continues to focus on directions of the Moon to the IC as measurements which timed the end of Arthur's reign at the New York Custom House. They are listed as a primary directions sequence. The real haggling between the various 2:00 AM birth times I have proposed reflects the discovery that transits of the Lunar Nodes – not just to the angles themselves – but to the 10th positional degree from the angles – are capable of timing significant life events. This is a refinement of transiting Lunar Nodes since publication of ARM 3rd edition. The transit section includes six transits of the Lunar Nodes to the angles; two of which are transits to the 10th positional degrees of the MC and LOF. Given the accuracy of Lunar Nodes transits observed over the years, I judged these measurements significant enough to move the birth time 7 minutes.

ZRS. L1-Capricorn timed with great accuracy Arthur's political career.

L1 Scorpio 05 Oct 1829		
L1 Sagittarius 18 Jul 1844		30-Jul-1844, father/family moved to Schenectady, NY. briefly served as principal of Academy for Boys in Vermont (1850). by end of L1 finished legal studies, admitted to the bar, and made partner with Erastus Culver.
L1 Capricorn 16 May 1856		1856, met wife-to-be Nell Herndon; 12-Sep-1857, Nell's father died in sinking ship.
L2 Cancer 28 Jul 1865	FS	No major events, was in continuous law practice with Henry Gardner to 1867.
L2 Cancer 14 Sep 1873	LB	22-Jun-1874, Anti-Moiety Act limited CA's income.
L2 Sagittarius 06 Nov 1880		2-Jul-1881, Garfield shot; 20/22-Sep-1881, Presidential succession after JG died 19-Sep-1881; late-Oct-1881, Conkling disappointed that CA would not appoint a Stalwart to NY Custom House and Conkling to Secretary of State.
L2 Capricorn 01 Nov 1881	CP	26-June-1882, Pendleton spoke on behalf of Civil Service Reform in the Senate.
L1 Aquarius 26 Dec 1882		27-Dec-1882, Senate passed Pendleton Act; 4-Jan-1883, House passed Pendleton Act; 16-Jan-1883, signed Pendleton Act into law; 3-Mar-1883, Mongrel Tariff Act passed, increased Navy funding.
L2 Aries 08 Jun 1886		18-Nov-1866, death.

Firdaria – Mars major and minor periods

Firdaria according to Bonatti	Life Event
Moon **Mars** 13 Aug 1833	No events found.
Saturn **Mars** 26 Nov 1841	No events found.
Jupiter **Mars** 23 Jun 1851	1851 (no date), principal of academy for boys at North Pownal, Vermont.
Mars 7 years Age 32 to 39	
Mars Mars 04 Oct 1861	10-Feb-1862, appointed Brigadier General; 10-Jul-1862, appointed Quartermaster General for NY state.
Mars Sun 05 Oct 1862	31-Dec-1862, left quartermaster post; 8-Jul-1863, death of son William.
Mars Venus 05 Oct 1863	20-Aug-1864, brother William shot in face, survived but was badly disfigured.
Mars Mercury 04 Oct 1864	May-1865, purchased home 123 Lexington Ave, NYC; 25-Jul-1865, birth of son Chester Alan Arthur.
Mars Moon 04 Oct 1865	No events found.
Mars Saturn 05 Oct 1866	4-Mar-1867, Conkling elected to Senate (Saturn/Leo significator of Conkling).
Mars Jupiter 05 Oct 1867	No events found.
Sun **Mars** 01 May 1882	6-May-1882, signed revised Chinese Exclusion Act; 15-May-1882, appointed Tariff Commission; 11-Sep-1882, Star-Route trial concluded; 7-Nov-1882, Republicans suffered large losses in midterm elections; 16-Jan-1883, signed Pendleton Civil Service Reform Act; 3-Mar-1883, Mongrel Tariff Act passed; 3-Mar-1883, increased Navy funding.

Mars as Victor. Mars captured his first professional position as principal, his Civil War service, and the election of Roscoe Conkling to the Senate with whom Arthur's political fortunes were closely tied. Sun-Mars timed a portion of Arthur's presidential term, specifically passage of the Pendleton Civil Service Reform Act which ranked among the top events of Arthur's presidency.

Transits

29-Jan-1855. *tr North Node conj MC.*
Judge ruled in favor of Lizzie Jennings represented by CA, 22-Feb-1855.

3-Jan-1961. *tr Jupiter-rx conj ASC.*
CA appointed Chief Engineer for New York, 1-Jan-1861.

8-Jul-1863. *tr South Node conj LOF.*
Death of son William Lewis Herndon Arthur, 8-Jul-1863.

14-Jan-1869. *tr South Node 10th from MC degree.*
Death of mother, 16-Jan-1869.

23-Jun-1877. *tr South Node 10th from LOF.*
President Hayes issued order forbidding involvement of federal officeholders in political campaigns; also prohibited assessments, 22-Jun.

16-Feb-1882. *tr South Node conj LOF.*
Star Route mail fraud captured public attention, 15-Jan-1882.

31-Dec-1882. *tr South Node conj MC.*
Pendleton Civil Service Reform Act passed by Senate, 27-Dec-1882.
Passed by House, 4-Jan-1883; CA signed into law, 16-Jan-1883.

Notable Ascendant Profection

24-Nov-1871. *Profected ASC conj Sun.*
CA appointed collector of the Port of New York by Grant, 20-Nov-1871.

Solar Arc Directions

13-Mar-1855. *dsa Sun con. Mercury.*
Fame as attorney after victory in Lizzie Jennings Case, early Mar-1855.

15-Apr-1861. *dsa ASC conj North Node.*
10-Nov-1861. *csa North Node conj ASC.*
Appointed Chief Engineer for NY, 1-Jan-1861 (see also trJup-rx conj ASC).
Outbreak of Civil War, 12-Apr-1861.
Consulted concerning defense of New York harbor, Dec-1861.

12-Jan-1880. *dsa South Node conj MC.*
9-Jun-1881. *csa MC conj South Node.*
Death of wife Nell Herndon, pneumonia, 12-Jan-1880.
Charles Guiteau made 1st unsuccessful assassination attempt, 18-Jun-1881.
Note: dynamic activity of malefics to the MC times problems for the King.

21. CHESTER ARTHUR

Primary Directions

| PT | D | Mars/Pisces | P | South Node c. => MC | 27-May-1877 |

First Report of Jay Commission harmed Arthur's reputation, 24-May.

| PT | D | Saturn/Libra | P | dex square Moon (0) d. => ASC | 10-Jul-1878 |
| PT | D | Mars/Leo | P | ASC c. => Sun | 11-Jul-1878 |

Hayes suspended CA from NY Customhouse position, 11-Jul-1878.

Primary Direction Sequence

PT	D	Mars/Cancer	P	opposition Moon (BI) d. => MC	29-Aug-1877
PT	D	Mars/Cancer	P	opposition Moon (0) d. => MC	18-Oct-1877
PT	D	Mars/Cancer	P	opposition Moon (MO) d. => MC	11-Dec-1877

LOCK Among the issues of the 1876 Presidential contest (won by Rutherford Hayes) was Civil Service Reform. At the center of the storm of the reform movement was Chester Arthur, head of the New York Custom House. Arthur's employees were political appointees who padded salaries by additional customs duties and seizures of imported goods levied in an ad hoc manner. In turn, the political party (to whom Custom House employees owed their 'plum' positions) deducted assessments from employee salaries which were funded party finances. Arthur's nativity fits this story very well. Moon/Capricorn/6th signifies employees interested in high prices (e.g., excessive import duties) which eventually flow through political organizations because of the Moon's configuration. Moon applies by sextile to Mercury who receives the Moon by bound. Mercury rules the 11th house of political alliances and the LOF by position in the 11th. As 12th house lord, Moon also has another claim on party finances because the 12th as 2nd from the 11th signifies wealth of political alliances. Read purely as a 12th house ruler, high import tax assessments by Custom House employees are a source of problem and enmity for Arthur. Directions of the Moon to the IC (same as directing opposition of the Moon to the MC) signify an end to these arrangements as the IC is the 4th house cusp whose affairs signify the end-of-the-matter.

On 14-Apr-1877, Hayes created the Jay Commission to investigate allegations of financial impropriety of the NY Custom House. The 4th and final report of the Jay Commission was released on 31-Aug as this sequence commenced. Hayes fired CA on 6-Sep though CA refused to resign. No specific event was found for the second 18-Oct direction but the entire period timed counterattacks on Haye's civil service reform by Arthur ally Roscoe Conkling. As the sequence closed, on 12-Dec Conkling maneuvered the Senate's Commerce Committee to reject Hayes' nomination of Theodore Roosevelt as Arthur's replacement.

Longevity, 57y 1m 14d

Death: 18-Nov-1886, 5:00 AM, New York City, at home.

Arthur died from Bright's disease, a historical catch-all term for kidney disease no longer in use. Cardiovascular disease was a contributing factor. In final days, he suffered a fatal stroke the evening of 16/17-Nov-1886.

Hīlāj: **Sun/LOF**. Chart is nocturnal and Moon is preferred. Moon/5th/feminine sign qualifies; yet 6th house placement by whole signs is a disqualifier. Sun/2nd/masculine qualifies but 3rd house placement by whole signs also raises questions. Empirically both Sun and Moon test well as Hīlāj at times of critical illness. Yet Saturn the empirical Al-kadukhadāh tightly aspects the Sun, not the Moon. This shifts the weight of evidence to the Sun. LOF also appears to participate.

Al-kadukhadāh: **Saturn**. Saturn is oriental, in its own bound, and is powerfully placed in the Ascendant. Saturn is the Sun's Al-mubtazz and placed 60 degrees away from the Sun as a morning star is the strongest solar phase according to Ibn Ezra. Saturn grants 57 major years. Jupiter receives Saturn by nocturnal triplicity and decan in a trine aspect and should add 12 minor years for a net projection of 69 years. Instead, Arthur lived Saturn's 57 major years.

Victor of the Horoscope: **Mars**

Killing Planets: **Mars (37), Venus (35), Jupiter (34)**

Arcus Vitae

| REG | D | Saturn/Scorpio | P | dex trine South Node d. => Sun | 11-Oct-1882 |

Arthur's illness dates from 1882 when Bright's Disease was diagnosed by the Surgeon General during Oct-1882. Following 1882, his health never truly recovered.

| PT | D | Saturn/Cancer | P | sin trine South Node d. => LOF | 11-Oct-1886 |
| REG | D | Saturn/Cancer | P | sin trine South Node d. => LOF | 21-Oct-1886 |

In support of the 8th house South Node as a killer, see during the 1886 solar return the South Node returns to its natal sign giving it power to act. Also the return's LOF is conjunct natal South Node within 2 degrees; another piece of evidence that the LOF participates as Hīlāj.

1886 Solar Return for year of Death

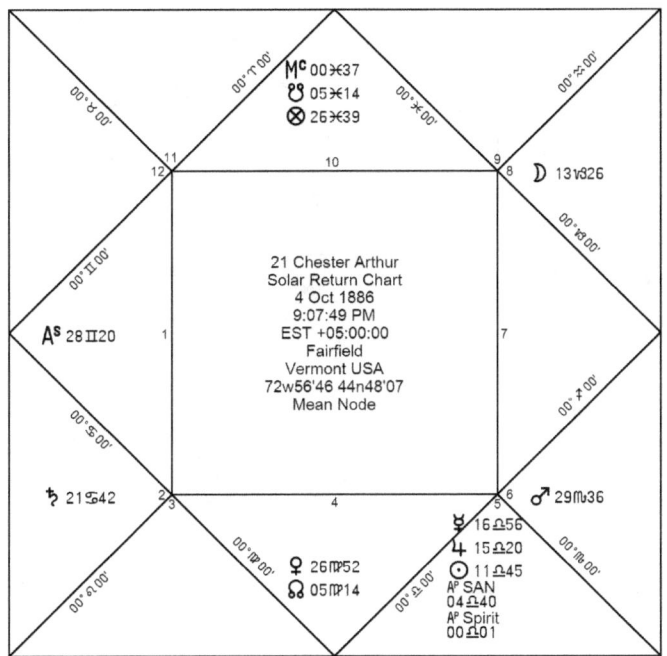

Ascendant Distributor: Mercury/Libra since 16-Feb-1882
Profected Ascendant: 26TA16, 10th house; SR Victor: Saturn
Lords: LOY – Venus; LOP – Sun
Firdaria: Venus-Moon
Moon: separates from square of Sun and applies to square of Jupiter
Return Ascendant falls in natal 11th; Natal Ascendant falls in return's 3rd

Lord of Year Venus falls in the 4th house end-of-life; she is received by Mars by bound in the 6th of illness and is conjunct natal Mars within a degree. Moon in the 8th of death squares Jupiter which rules the natal 8th and the return's 7th. Return's Saturn afflicts both luminaries.

Return's Ascendant squares natal Nodes within a degree.

Arthur died 18-Nov-1886 between the following two participating directions:

| PT | D | Saturn/Cancer | P | dex trine Mars (0) d. => ASC | 12-Nov-1886 |
| PT | D | Saturn/Leo | P | dex sextile Sun d. => ASC | 28-Nov-1886 |

564 A RECTIFICATION MANUAL

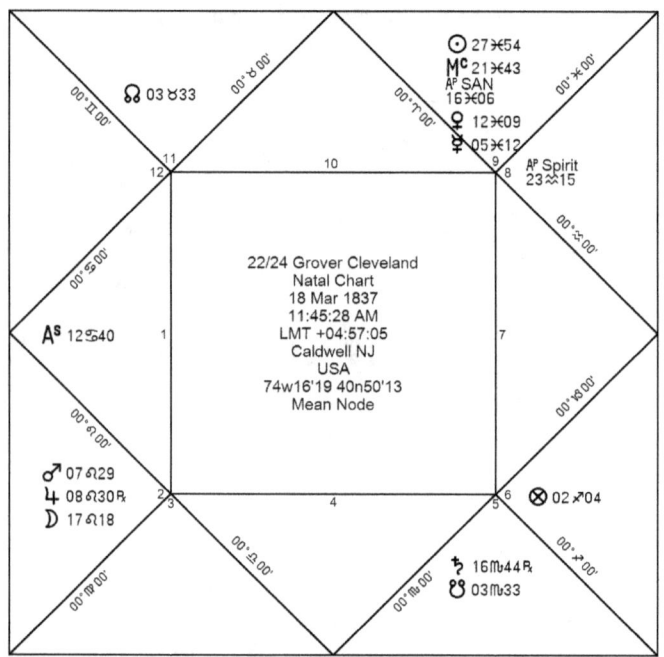

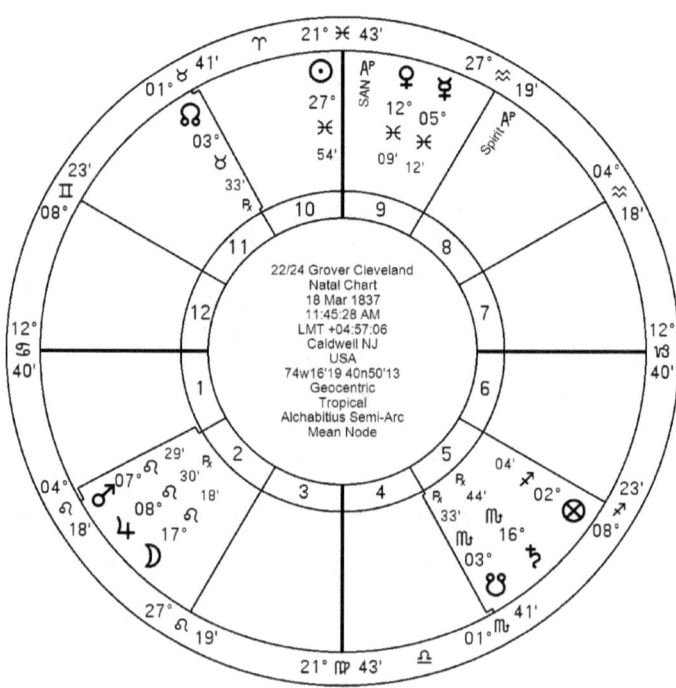

Moon's Configuration

Moon separates from **Saturn** and is **VOC** (Medieval) or applies to **Mercury** (Hellenistic), diurnal, conjunctional.
Prenatal syzygy is 16PI06. Eclipse? No.

Cognitive Assessment Model (Rulers of Moon and Mercury)

Sign rulers: **(Sun)/Mars, Jupiter**
Bound rulers: **Saturn, Venus**

Victor Soul Models

Ibn Ezra Victor Model (1507), in-sect triplicity ruler, triplicity decans.

	Position	☉	☽	☿	♀	♂	♃	♄
Sun	27 PI 54				7	3	5	
Moon	17 LE 18	8					1	2
Asc	12 CA 40		5		5	1	4	
Pars Fortuna	02 SA 04	3					8	
Syzygy	16 PI 06		1	2	7		5	
Oriental						0	0	1
Houses		11	6	4	4	6	6	7
Score	0	22	12	6	23	10	**29**	10

Porphyry's Expanded Victor Model (2022)

Mars rules the MC, Sun, and Lot of Spirit by bound. Sect: out-of-favor. Solar phase: occidental 2nd station to waning square. Position: 7th from Lot of Spirit. At the bending of the Nodes.

Victor Table for Killing Planets

			☉	☽	☿	♀	♂	♃	♄
ASC		12CA40		5,3		3,2	3,1	4	
Rul ASC	☽	17LE18	5,3					3,1	3,2
L.Death		3TA44		4,3		5,3,2,1	3		
Rul L.Death	♀	12PI09		3,1		4,3	3	5,2	
H8 Cusp		4AQ18			3,2			3	5,3,1
Rul H8	♄	16SC44		3	2	3	5,3	1	
T-Rul H8	♄	16SC44		3	2	3	5,3	1	
8th from ☉		27LI54			3,1	5,2		3	4,3
Rul 8th fr ☉	♀	12PI09		3,1		4,3	3	5,2	
TOTAL			8	29	13	**43**	29	30	21

2007 Proposed Rectification: 11:45:30 AM, ASC 12CA40'26"
2022 Proposed Rectification: 11:45:28 AM, ASC 12CA40'02"

Astrodatabank reports an X-rated birth date with no time. The proposed rectification is similar to other rectifications listed by ADB.

ZRS. The 2007 rectification holds up well with the ZRS overlay. Similar to James Garfield with LOS in Aquarius, the usual linkage between foreshadowing (FS) and loosing of the bond (LB) periods for L1-Aquarius is not obvious. Instead, GC's decision to stay in Buffalo NY (LB) is directly linked to his first political election victory during (CP). If Garfield and Cleveland are representative, this suggests individuals with horoscopes which release from Aquarius at birth may be too young to generate sufficient life events during L2 FS (age 9) which can be linked to the subsequent L2 LB period (age 17). Instead, link LB (age 17) to CP (age 25).

The proposed rectification is also consistent with LOF in Sagittarius making mutable signs angular from Fortune. Gemini subperiods are notable for GC's peak career periods. If correct, then the birth time cannot be prior to 11:36 AM for LOF to remain in Sagittarius.

L1 Aquarius 18 Mar 1837		
L2 Leo 31 Mar 1846	FS	5-Sep-1846, Father's health began to fail, father found another job with higher wages.
L2 Leo 17 Jul 1854	LB	21-May-1855, visited Uncle Allen who persuaded him to stay in Buffalo, NY; 3-Dec-1855, first paycheck for clerking position at Rogers, Bowan, and Rowan.
L2 Aquarius 02 Nov 1862	CP	Nov-1862, won first election for Supervisor of the 2nd ward, Buffalo, NY; 6-Jul-1863, paid George Benninsky $150 to substitute for Cleveland as a Civil War soldier; Nov-1863, appointed Assistant District Attorney.
L1 Pisces 12 Oct 1866		1866 (no date), formed law partnership with Isaac K Vanderpoel. part of new generation of corporate lawyers which started to flourish after Civil War. during L2-Gemini, was elected to Sheriff of Erie County.
L1 Aries 10 Aug 1878		His most politically active L1 period, elected Buffalo Mayor during L2-Gemini; elected to 1st Presidential term during L2-Leo; elected to 2nd nonconsecutive Presidential term during L2-Aquarius.
L1 Taurus 23 May 1893		L1-Taurus began with a stock market crash on 27-Jun-1893 which ushered in a depression; coincident was a secret emergency operation to remove throat cancer from the roof of his mouth. L2-Gemini timed the most active portion of his 2nd Presidential term with various bailouts arranged with J. P. Morgan to stabilize the nation's gold reserves.
L1 Gemini 12 Apr 1901		15-Oct-1901, elected trustee of Princeton University; 4-Oct-1901, suggested to TR that amidst the miner strike that miners should produce enough coal for consumers while negotiations continued.
L2 Libra 06 Mar 1908		24-Jun-1908, death.

Firdaria – Mars major and minor periods

Firdaria according to Bonatti	Life Event
Sun **Mars** 13 Oct 1845	1846, birth of sister Ruth who was later to become White House hostess; 1846/1847 (no exact date), father's health declined but his father found another job at higher salary.
Venus **Mars** 04 Dec 1852	3-Feb-1853, organized debating society at Fayetteville Academy; Mar-1853, traveled to Clinton to attend sister Anna's wedding and learned of father's illness; 1-Oct-1853, father's death, peritonitis; 5-Oct-1853, teacher at NY Institution for the Blind, worked for 1 year "unquestionably the bleakest in GC's whole life."
Mercury **Mars** 22 Aug 1862	Nov-1862, won first election for public office - Supervisor of the 2nd Ward; 6-Jul-1863, hired George Benninsky as Civil War army substitute.
Moon **Mars** 25 Jan 1872	6-Sep-1872, criminal Patrick Morrissey hanged; 22-Oct-1872, death of two younger brothers on a Missouri steamer; 14-Feb-1873, criminal Jack Gaffney hanged.
Saturn **Mars** 09 May 1880	25-Oct-1881, nominated for Mayor of Buffalo, Nov-1881, elected Mayor.
Jupiter **Mars** 03 Dec 1889	12-Dec-1889, delivered address on ballot reform; 10-Feb-1891, wrote letter to Reform Club opposing free coinage of silver in the Sherman Act, considered by some to be a 'start' to GC's re-election campaign.
Mars 7 years Age 63 to 70	
Mars Mars 18 Mar 1900	9-Apr-1900, lectured on "Independence of the Executive" at Princeton; 12-Oct-1900, did not condone formation of 3rd Party.
Mars Sun 18 Mar 1901	15-Oct-1901, elected trustee of Princeton University; 4-Oct-1901, suggested to TR that amidst the miner strike that miners should produce enough coal for consumers while negotiations continued.
Mars Venus 19 Mar 1902	No events found.
Mars Mercury 19 Mar 1903	14-Apr-1903, address on industrial education of Southern Negro; 30-Apr-1903, address on importance of conservation and forestry; 7-Jan-1904, death of daughter Ruth.
Mars Moon 18 Mar 1904	2-May-1904, address on Chicago strike; 26-Jun-1904, declined Presidential nomination; Oct-1904, "Presidential Problems" published; 29-Jan-1905, address on morality for the nation.
Mars Saturn 18 Mar 1905	10-Jun-1905, Trustee for Equitable Life Assurance; 19-Dec-1905, accepted referee position for three life insurance companies.
Mars Jupiter 19 Mar 1906	Feb-1907, head of 'Presidents' Association of Life Insurance Companies.'

Mars as Victor. As minor Firdaria ruler, Mars timed Cleveland's entry to political office as Ward Supervisor, high profile executions under his tenure as Buffalo Sheriff, Election to Mayor of Buffalo, and the launch of his Presidential re-election campaign in late 1889. Major Mars occurs post-Presidency. Notable events include trustee positions for Princeton University and Equitable Life as well as lectures and publications on Presidential power.

Transits

12-Nov-1870. *tr North Node conj ASC.*
Elected Sheriff of Erie County, Nov-1870 (no exact date).

27-Oct-1884. *tr South Node 10th from ASC.*
Dr. Samuel Burchard's comment that the Democrats were a party of *Rum, Romanism, and Rebellion* on 29-Oct insulted the Catholic Church and the Democratic Party, hurt the Republican party, and tipped NY in favor of Cleveland who won the Presidential election days later.

23-Jul-1890. *tr North Node 10th from MC.*
Benjamin Harrison signed the Sherman Silver Purchase Act, opposed by Cleveland, 14-Jul.

Solar Arc Directions

19-Oct-1872. *dsa Saturn square MC.*
Death of two younger brothers forced GC to manage their substantial estates including real estate (Saturn rules 8th of investments), 23-Oct.

7-Oct-1882. *csa Mars square MC.*
30-Nov-1883. *dsa MC square Mars.*
GC nominated Democratic candidate for Governor of NY, 22-Sep-1882.
Kelley letter published which effectively severed all ties with Tammany Hall. Propelled Cleveland towards the Presidency by his firmness against corruption, 23-Nov-1883.

27-Jun-1893. *dsa MC opposed Saturn.*
Stock market crash 27-Jun; Secret operation to remove oral cancer, 1-Jul.

2-Sep-1901. *csa MC sextile Saturn.*
McKinley Assassination, 6-Sep.

Primary Directions

| PT | D | Mercury/Taurus | P | sin sextile Sun c. => ASC | 4-Jan-1882 |

LOCK Began term as Mayor of Buffalo, 1-Jan.

| PT | D | Venus/Leo | P | Mars (0) c. => dexter sex LOF | 20-May-1887 |

Endorsed proposal to return Confederate flags (in storage at War Department), 25-May. Caused significant uproar. Mars/Leo is the significator of Confederate rebels.

| PT | D | Jupiter/Taurus | P | dexter sq Moon (MO) c.=> ASC | 7-Jul-1896 |

William Jennings Bryan made famous 'Cross of Gold' Speech at Democratic National Convention, 9-Jul-1896; Moon is exalted ruler of 11th house of currency and political affiliations. That the Free Silver Democrats have taken over his own party caused GC grief; GC did not support Bryan.

| PT | D | Mercury/Taurus | P | dexter dex ASC d. => Mercury (ME) | 6-Jan-1904 |

Death of daughter Ruth, 7 January. Mercury rules 12th (8th from 5th).
See also tr Saturn 8AQ12 conj Lot of Daughters 7AQ31.

Primary Direction Sequences

| REG | D | Venus/Aquarius | P | opposition Jupiter (0) c. => Sun | 20-Oct-1882 |
| REG | D | Venus/Aquarius | P | opposition Jupiter (JU) c. => Sun | 21-Feb-1883 |

This sequence corresponded with GC's election victory for the Governorship of New York on 7-Nov-1882 with the largest majority in state history. Also with his 1-Jan-1883 inauguration.

| PT | D | Jupiter/Taurus | P | opposition Saturn (0) c. => ASC | 9-Jul-1890 |
| PT | D | Jupiter/Taurus | P | opposition Saturn (SA) c. => ASC | 6-Sep-1893 |

This sequence timed Cleveland's battle with attempts by his political opposition to back the US currency with silver, which under Harrison's Presidency led to the Panic of 1893.

LOCK It began with President Benjamin Harrison's signing of the Sherman Silver Purchase Act on 14-Jul-1890 and concluded with GC's Special Session of Congress on 7-Aug-1893 to repeal the same Silver Purchase Act which Congress did so in late August; on 1-Nov the repeal took effect.

How Saturn signifies this: If the 11th house signifies the king's money or currency, then by derived houses the 5th, as 11th from 7th, can be read as currency of open enemies. Saturn falls in the 5th. Saturn/Scorpio/retrograde is paranoid, rebellious, and defiant. As Saturn's ruler, Mars/Leo is the cause of Saturn's behavior. While Mars/Leo works well for Cleveland as a professional significator for law enforcement; it works against him on the currency question. Mars/Leo dislikes gold and by default likes silver. Cleveland's own favoritism for the gold standard is signified by Moon/Leo ruling both his Ascendant and the 11th of currency by exaltation. Mars afflicts the Moon by conjunction and as ruler of Saturn influences the currency platform of the Free Silver Movement, his political opposition.

Longevity, 71y 3m 6d

Death: 24-Jun-1908, 8:40 AM, Princeton, NJ, at home. In his last years Cleveland's health was poor. He suffered from gout and indigestion which required use of a stomach pump. He lapsed into a coma the evening of the 23rd and died the next day of probable heart failure.

Hīlāj: **Sun**. Figure is diurnal. Sun in a feminine sign qualifies in the 10th by Alchabitius houses but is disqualified in the 9th by whole sign houses. Arcus vitae confirms Sun as Hīlāj. Sun is also very close to the MC, though just past the 5-degree cutoff rule.

Al-kadukhadāh: **Mars**. In the place of the Sun, Venus is the Al-mubtazz but moving fast into the sunbeams she is rejected. Bound and decan ruler Mars is the more logical Al-kadukhadāh candidate. Mars does not aspect the Sun yet is received by the Sun. Mars has also just made its second direct station and applies to Jupiter. Mars grants 66 major years. Jupiter is co-present and adds 12 minor years.

MA (66) + JU (12) = 78 years.

On first glance, it appears Saturn should deduct its 30 minor years by square aspect reducing longevity to 48 years taking Cleveland to the year 1885. Cleveland did have major surgery to remove cancer from his mouth in 1893 and it is possible that the cancer began in 1885. If so this is a good example of how planets received by the al-kadukhadāh maim but do not kill. Also consider that Al-Biruni's planetary orbs (Saturn=9; Mars=8) makes the Mars-Saturn square at 9deg 15min which falls slightly outside the 8 ½ degree orb of influence.

4th edition comment: Since Mars is the victor, it is easier to estimate longevity by Mars' 66 major years with no adjustments. Vitality declined after age 66. For example, at age 66 between Nov-1903 and Feb-1904 he only left his house five times (Nevins 1933, 755).

Victor of the Horoscope: **Mars**

Killing Planet: **Venus (43)**

Arcus Vitae

PT	D	Venus/Gemini	P	sin square Venus (0) d. => Sun	8-Jun-1908
PT	D	Venus/Gemini	P	sin square Venus (VE) d. => Sun	21-Sep-1908

1908 Solar Return for year of Death

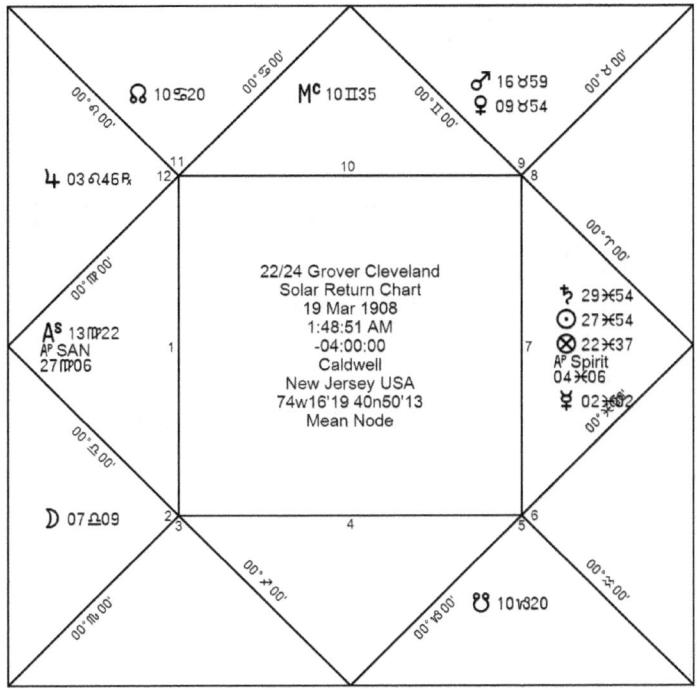

Ascendant Distributor: Venus/Virgo since 19-Sep-1905
Prof. Ascendant: 12GE40, 12th house; SR Victor: Mercury
Lords: LOY – Mercury; LOP – Moon
Firdaria: North Node
Moon: separates from sextile of Jupiter and is void of course
Return Ascendant falls in natal 3rd; Natal Ascendant falls in return's 11th

In this 12th house year, LOY Mercury is co-present with the Sun, ruler of the 12th of the return, and falls in the angle of the West in the 7th house. Saturn, ruler of the natal 8th, is closely conjunct the Hīlāj Sun. Moon is afflicted by the square from the Nodes and separates from Jupiter (ruling the return's 7th) to VOC.

No relevant Ascendant directions were found for the day of death. Health problems were reported in April 1908 prior to death on 24-Jun-1908.

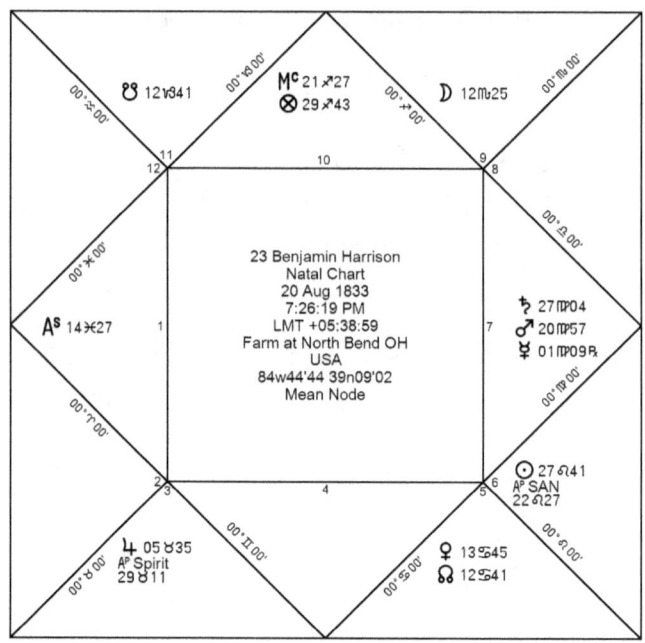
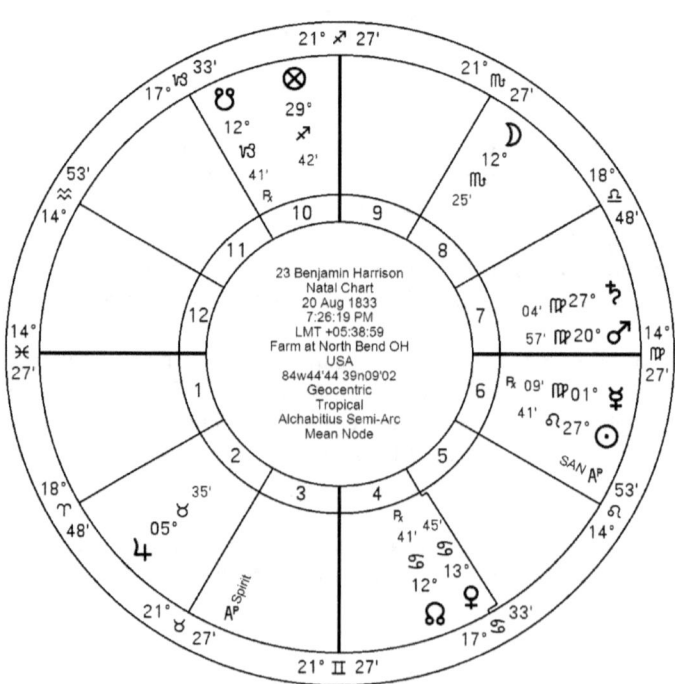

Moon's Configuration

Moon separates from **Jupiter** and applies to **Venus**, nocturnal, conjunctional. Prenatal syzygy is 22LE27. Eclipse? No.

Cognitive Assessment Model (Rulers of Moon and Mercury)

Sign rulers: **Mars, Mercury**
Bound rulers: **Mercury** (both)

Victor Soul Models

Ibn Ezra Victor Model (1507), in-sect triplicity ruler, triplicity decans.

	Position	☉	☽	☿	♀	♂	♃	♄
Sun	27 LE 41	5				3	3	
Moon	12 SC 25			2		8	1	
Asc	14 PI 27		1		4	3	7	
Pars Fortuna	29 SA 42	1				2	8	
Syzygy	22 LE 27	5		2		1	3	
Oriental						0	1	0
Houses		1	5	1	7	10	6	10
Score	0	12	6	5	11	27	**29**	10

Porphyry's Expanded Victor Model (2022)

Mars rules the Moon by sign; the Sun, Lot of Fortune, and Lot of Fortune by bound. Sect: in-favor. Solar phase: occidental sextile to sinking. Position: 7th from ASC, 10th from Lot of Fortune. Dignity: participating triplicity ruler.

Victor Table for Killing Planets

			☉	☽	☿	♀	♂	♃	♄
ASC		14PI27		3,1		4,3	3	5,2	
Rul ASC	♃	5TA34		4,3		5,3,2,1	3		
L.Death		3VI27		3	5,4,2,1	3	3		
Rul L.Death	☿	1VI09		3	5,4,2,1	3	3		
H8 Cusp		18LI48			3	5		3,2	4,3,1
Rul H8	♀	13CA45		5,3	2	3	3,1	4	
T-Rul H8	☿	1VI09		3	5,4,2,1	3	3		
8th from ☽		12GE25			5,3	2,1		3	3
Rul 8th fr ☽	☿	1VI09		3	5,4,2,1	3	3		
TOTAL			0	31	**56**	41	22	19	11

2007 Proposed Rectification: 7:26:19 PM, ASC 14PI27'31"
2022 Pro posed Rectification: 7:26:19 PM, ASC 14PI27'14"

Astrodatabank reports a DD-rated birth time of 3:17 AM, conflicting/unverified, citing Doane's *Horoscopes of the U.S. Presidents*. The proposed rectification is substantially different.

ZRS. Mentioned in the discussion of the choice of Mars/Virgo as victor is Mars' placement in the 10th sign from the LOF. This is a rare configuration because it supercharges life effects for Virgo because Virgo is the angular 10th house from LOF, the most important of angular signs for predicting career peaks by ZR methodology. With Mars as victor and the bound lord of the LOF effects for Virgo are doubly emphasized. To wit, Harrison was nominated and elected President under L2-Virgo in 1888. Not shown below is BH's first L2-Virgo active in 1841 when his grandfather William Henry Harrison was elected President.

Yet with LOF angles in mutable signs, mutable signs are skipped over during the otherwise dramatic FS-LB subperiods for L1 Cancer (cardinal) and L1 Leo (fixed) active during Harrison's political career. This leads to an awkward advancement of BJ's career which does not follow a straight path.

L1 Taurus 20 Aug 1833		
L1 Gemini 09 Jul 1841		
L2 Sagittarius 23 Apr 1850	FS	15-Aug-1850, death of mother; Summer-1850, death of two younger siblings; Fall-1850, transferred to Miami U to be in same town as Caroline Scott; Dec-1850, converted to Presbyterian faith.
L2 Sagittarius 07 Nov 1858	LB	No major events found.
L1 Cancer 26 Mar 1861		11-Apr-1861, Civil War outbreak; Aug-1862, entered Union Army.
L2 Capricorn 13 May 1869	FS	1869, President Grant appointed BH to represent US in civil suit filed by Milligan for damages in controversial 1864 Civil War treason case; 30-May-1871, BH lost the case in Milligan v. Hovey but limited damages to $5 plus court fees; increased status among local politicians.
L2 Capricorn 25 Jul 1878	LB	Summer-1878, made speech at Indiana Republican State Convention; Fall-1878, Indiana Republicans lost legislative elections; 1879, President Hayes appointed BH to Mississippi River Commission.
L1 Leo 15 Nov 1885		1885/1887, gained prominence during final two years in Senate.
L2 Virgo 08 Jun 1887		5-Jun-1888, nominated for President; 6-Nov-1888, won Presidential Election.
L2 Aquarius 03 Mar 1894	FS	1894/1895, active as lawyer; 3-Feb-1896, declined to run again as President; 6-Apr-1896, 2nd Marriage concerned children who worried about their inheritance; BH is permanently estranged from his children as a result.
L2 Cancer 25 Feb 1901		13-Mar-1901, death

Firdaria – Mars major and minor periods

Firdaria according to Bonatti	Life Event
Moon **Mars** 29 Jun 1837	8-Mar-1838, death of brother George.
Saturn **Mars** 11 Oct 1845	No events found.
Jupiter **Mars** 08 May 1855	Spring 1855, invited into legal partnership with attorney William Wallace.
Mars 7 years Age 32 to 39	
Mars Mars 20 Aug 1865	Following Civil War service, returned to role as Supreme Court reporter in addition to his own private law practice.
Mars Sun 20 Aug 1866	Spring-1867, suffered physical collapse.
Mars Venus 21 Aug 1867	No events found.
Mars Mercury 20 Aug 1868	13-Sep-1868, double homicide occurred; 1-Dec-1868, led prosecution; 29-Mar-1869, obtained conviction described as BH's "greatest courtroom triumph"
Mars Moon 20 Aug 1869	No events found.
Mars Saturn 20 Aug 1870	30-May-1871, increased reputation as lawyer after defending the US in Milligan v. Hovey even though he lost the case.
Mars Jupiter 21 Aug 1871	23-Feb-1872, made concession speech for Gubernatorial race in Indiana.
Sun **Mars** 17 Mar 1886	Fall-1886, lost Senate seat by one vote; 3-Mar-1887, ended six year Senate Career.
Venus **Mars** 07 May 1893	Summer-1893, Panic of 1893 in full swing; Aug-1893, Bering Sea arbitration ended.

Mars as Victor. Mars' periods captured BH's early legal career and his post-Civil War return to his legal practice. Mars' placement in the 7th house of open enemies and conflict is consistent with BH's legal and military careers.

Major Mars captured two career peaks: conviction for double homicide in 1869 and increased reputation after *Milligan v Hovey* in 1871. Venus-Mars timed the conclusion of a lengthy dispute over seal hunting in the Bering Sea initially brought up during BH's presidential administration.

Transits

13-May-1858. *tr North Node conj ASC*. Birth of daughter Mary Scott, 3-Apr.

27-Aug-1862. *tr North Node conj MC*. Joined Union Army, Aug-1862.

9-Sep-1890. *tr Mars conj MC*.
23-Sep-1890. *tr Mars conj LOF*.
   Senate passed McKinley tariff amendments, 10-Sep-1890.
   House passed McKinley tariff, 27-Sep-1890.
   Senate passed final version McKinley tariff and BH signed, 1-Oct-1890.

3-Mar-1891. *tr Jupiter 28AQ58 10th from LOS 29TA11*.
   Forest Reserve Act of 1891 was passed, 3-Mar-1891.
   Jupiter/Taurus is the significator for environmental protection.

Solar Arc Directions

7-Jan-1864. *dsa MC trine Mars*.
26-May-1864. *csa Mars trine MC*.
   First direction no exact event found, but BH was in the field at the time.
   Daring charge at New Hope Church, 26/28-May-1864; Appointed Chief of 1st Brigade, 29-May-1864.

LOCK 15-Jan-1865. *dsa Mars sextile MC*.
LOCK 14-Jun-1865. *csa MC sextile Mars*.
   Ordered to proceed to Savannah to rejoin his proper command, 16-Jan-1865. Brevetted Brigadier General near this date.
   Discharged, 8-Jun; Speaker at festivities for Indiana regiments, 16-Jun.

Primary Directions

| REG | D | Venus/Virgo | P | DSC c. => Saturn (0) | 27-Mar-1841 |
| REG | D | Jupiter/Scorpio | P | sin sextile Mars (MA) d. => Moon (0) | 5-Apr-1841 |

Death of Grandfather, 4-Apr. Saturn sign ruler of 11th; Mars by exaltation.

| PT | D | Mercury/Taurus | P | opposition Moon (MO) d. => ASC | 13-Apr-1864 |

Rebel chaplain deserted Johnston's forces and reported to Union forces the location of his Confederate army. Moon/Scorpio/9th signifies a rebel chaplain, late Apr-1864.

| REG | D | Saturn/Sagittarius | P | MC d. = > Moon (MO) | 4-Feb-1865 |

Contracted scarlet fever (Moon/Scorpio signifies illness) while on a furlough (furloughs are one example of 9th house sabbaticals/retreats/pilgrimages). Later learned by letter he was confirmed Brigadier General by the Senate, 18-Feb-1865.

23. BENJAMIN HARRISON

| PT | D | Mars/Taurus | P | dex trine Saturn (SA) d. => ASC | 29-May-1878 |

Death of father, 25-May.

| PT | D | Jupiter/Capricorn | P | South Node c. => ASC | 17-Jun-1880 |

At Republican National Convention, persuaded Indiana delegation to switch support from himself to Garfield as President on 30th ballot, 8-Jun.

| REG | D | Jupiter/Scorpio | P | sin sextile Mars (0) d. => Sun | 4-Mar-1887 |
| REG | D | Jupiter/Pisces | P | ASC d. => South Node | 16-Mar-1887 |

Ended Senate career, 3 March.

Primary Direction Sequences

| REG | D | Venus/Sagittarius | P | dex square ASC d. => Mars (MA) | 11-Jul-1891 |
| REG | D | Venus/Sagittarius | P | dex square ASC d. => Mars (0) | 9-Jun-1892 |

LOCK Mars/Virgo/7th ruling the 2nd and 9th by sign and the 11th by exaltation shows its effects powerfully during this period. 11th house is political alliances. As the sequence started, Republican National Chair Quay severed ties with BH on 29 July. As the sequence ended, BH was so angry about Secretary of State Blaine's threat to compete with him for the Presidential nomination, BH announced his intent to be the Republican candidate for President late in the game on 23-May-1892. BH was nominated during the convention held 7-10 June 1892.

Second house is death of the wife and during this period, Caroline Harrison's health deteriorated significantly. She suffered coughing spasms and a lung hemorrhage during May-1892.

Finally the 9th house signifies foreign lands/foreign policy. Between 18-Oct-1891 and 26-Jan-1892 there was a threat of war with Chile after several US troops were killed in a saloon fight.

| REG | D | Saturn/Sagittarius | P | MC d. => Mars (MA) | 13-Jun-1898 |
| REG | D | Saturn/Sagittarius | P | MC d. => Mars (0) | 13-May-1899 |

LOCK This sequence of 11 months closely matched the 15-month period during 1898/1899 when Venezuela retained BH as chief counsel in a boundary dispute with British Guyana. BH prepared the printed case by 15-Mar-1898, exchanged printed cases with England on 27-Feb-1899, was covered in an extensive newspaper article on 6-May-1899, and on 17-May-1899 booked passage for Europe to present his case before an arbitration panel culminating on 27-Sep. Note his booked trip on 17-May matches the concluding direction of the sequence; his foreign trip spurred by a legal dispute matches the delineation of Mars in 7th of legal disputes ruling the 9th of foreign travel.

Longevity, 67y 6m 22d

Death: 13-Mar-1901, 4:45 PM., Indianapolis, Indiana, at home. In early March, Harrison developed a cold which progressed to flu then pneumonia. He fell into unconsciousness on 12 March and died the afternoon of the 13th.

Hīlāj: **Moon**. Figure is nocturnal. Moon in a feminine sign is allowed in the 8th Alchabitius house but disallowed in the 9th by whole sign houses. Empirically, the Moon is confirmed as hyleg by measurements during illness. For example, Harrison's case of ptomaine poisoning on 24-Nov-1862 was timed by a Mars square Moon direction (not shown). See also the arcus vitae.

Al-kadukhadāh: **Mars**. Mars receives the Moon, is the Moon's Al-mubtazz, and is angular in the 7th. Mars grants 66 major years. Additions from Jupiter and Venus and a deduction from Saturn do not occur because of reception and aspect orb/configuration.

Jupiter's separating trine aspect with reception by bound does not add years. The Jupiter-Mars aspect is outside moiety of orb. Venus's applying sextile with reception by diurnal triplicity and decan does not add years. The applying sextile aspect does not perfect before Mars leaves Virgo. Also, Mars receives Venus by nocturnal triplicity and decan which mitigates the quality of years Venus can add. Saturn is co-present and should deduct 30 minor years. Mars receives Saturn by bound which appears sufficient testimony to prevent Saturn from reducing years.

Victor of the Horoscope: **Mars**

Killing Planets: **Mercury (56), Venus (41)**

Arcus Vitae:

PT	D	Mercury/Taurus	P	opposition Moon (0) c. => Venus (VE)	2-Jan-1900
PT	D	Mercury/Taurus	P	opposition Moon (MO) c. => Venus (VE)	19-Feb-1900

REG	D	Mercury/Taurus	P	opposition Moon (MO) c. => Venus (VE)	22-Apr-1900
REG	D	Mercury/Taurus	P	opposition Moon (0) c. => Venus (VE)	11-Jan-1901

REG	D	Mercury/Scorpio	P	Moon (0) c. => North Node	3-Apr-1901

The arcus vitae directs the opposition of the Moon located at 12TA25 by converse motion to the North Node - Venus conjunction in the 5th house. Moon is the Hīlāj; Venus is the 8th house ruler and 2nd high scoring killing planet. Listed are various latitude combinations for the Moon-Venus arcus vitae computed by both Ptolemy and Regiomontanus methods.

1900 Solar Return for year of Death

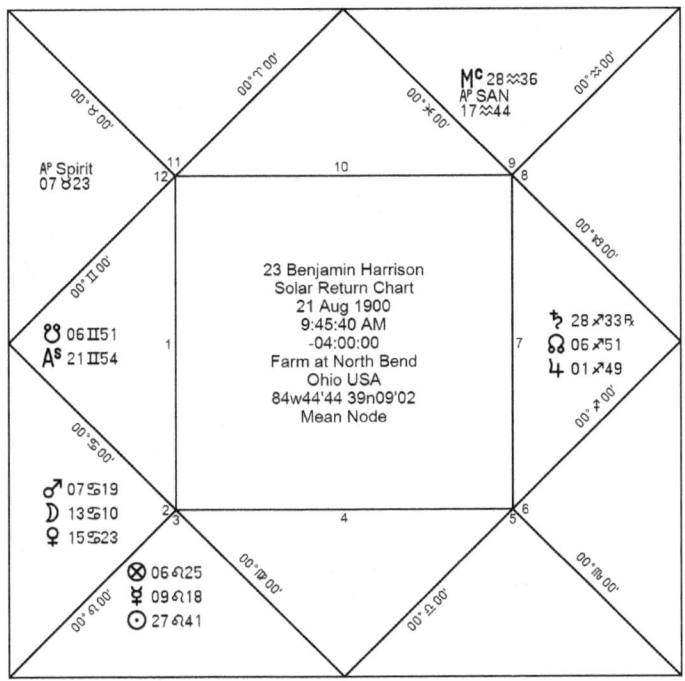

Ascendant Distributor: Mars/Gemini since 9-Oct-1898
Profected Ascendant: 14LI27, 8th house; SR Victor: Jupiter
Lords: LOY – Venus; LOP – Venus
Firdaria: Venus-Mars
Moon: separates from Mars and applies to Venus
Return Ascendant is conjunct natal 4th; Natal Ascendant falls in return's 10th

A profected 8th house year risks death. Venus has enormous power to act: she returns to her natal sign and bound; is Lord of the Year, Period, and Major Firdaria ruler; Hīlāj Moon also applies to her. Venus causes death.

Harrison died 204.69 days or <u>201deg 45min</u> after his return.

| PT | D | Jupiter/Capricorn | P | opposition Moon (MO) d. => Venus (0) | <u>201deg 13min</u> |

I have so far limited directions for solar returns to Ascendant directions. In this case I present an interplanetary direction because this Moon opposed Venus primary direction recapitulates the same primary direction computed for the natal horoscope, presented as the arcus vitae on the prior page.

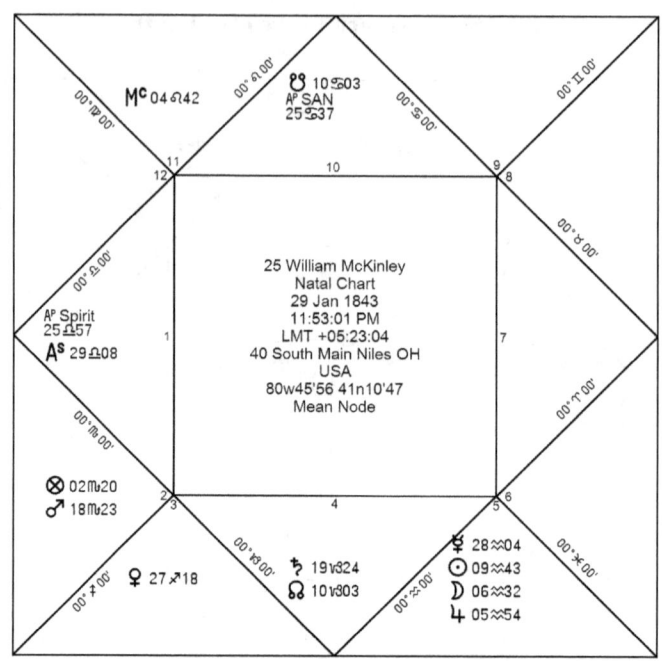

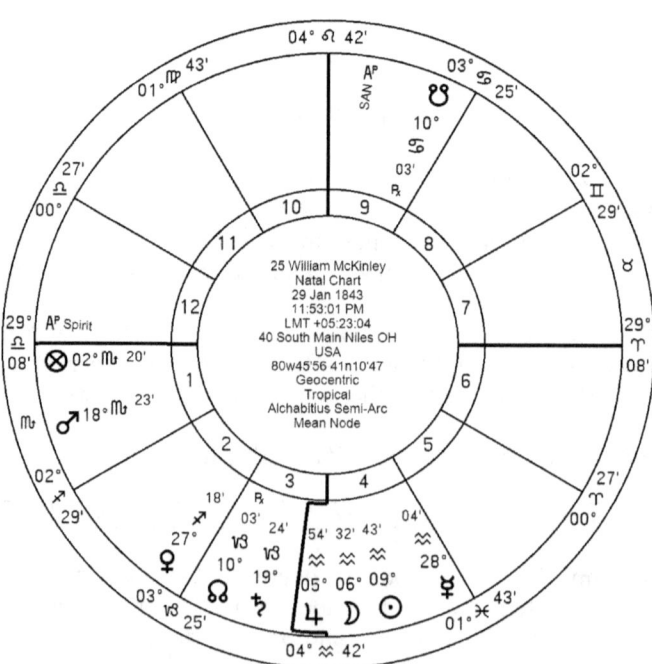

Moon's Configuration

Moon separates from **Jupiter** and applies to the **Sun**, nocturnal, preventional. Prenatal syzygy is 25CA37. Eclipse? **YES**. Appulse Lunar Eclipse.

Cognitive Assessment Model (Rulers of Moon and Mercury)

Sign rulers: **Saturn** (both)
Bound rulers: **Mercury, Saturn**

Victor Soul Models

Ibn Ezra Victor Model (1507), in-sect triplicity ruler, triplicity decans.

	Position	☉	☽	☿	♀	♂	♃	♄
Sun	09 AQ 43			3	2			6
Moon	06 AQ 32			5				6
Asc	29 LI 08			4	5	2		4
Pars Fortuna	02 SC 20					11		
Syzygy	25 CA 37 (LE)		5			3	7	
Oriental						2	0	3
Houses		9	9	7	3	12	9	3
Score	0	9	14	19	10	**30**	16	22

Porphyry's Expanded Victor Model (2022)

Jupiter rules the MC and syzygy by bound. Sect: out-of-favor. Solar phase: oriental combust. Position: 4th from Lot of Fortune. Dignity: participating triplicity. Moon's separation.

Victor Table for Killing Planets

			☉	☽	☿	♀	♂	♃	♄
ASC		29LI08			3,1	5	2	3	4,3
Rul ASC	♀	27SA18	3,1				2	5,3	3
L.Death		15TA21		4,3	1	5,3	3	2	
Rul L.Death	♀	27SA18	3,1				2	5,3	3
H8 Cusp		2GE29			5,3,2,1			3	3
Rul H8	☿	28AQ04			3	1		3	5,3,2
T-Rul H8	☿	28AQ04			3	1		3	5,3,2
8th from ☽		6VI32		3	5,4,2,1	3		3	
Rul 8th fr ☽	☿	28AQ04			3	1		3	5,3,2
TOTAL			8	10	37	19	9	36	46

2007 Proposed Rectification: 7:14:12 AM, ASC 7AQ15'39"
2022 Revised Rectification: 11:53:01 PM, ASC 29LI08'58"

Astrodatabank reports an A-rated birth time of 11:43 PM. The 2022 revised rectification is within 10 minutes of this time.

In truth, McKinley's horoscope has proven difficult to tackle; in my initial 2007 rectification it was not clear to me whether the Moon should be Capricorn or Aquarius. My initial choice was to choose Moon/Capricorn placed in the 12th house consistent with his invalid wife. This approach did not hold up under further scrutiny. ZRS proved helpful in returning closer to the ADB birth time, but McKinley's career timeline is best matched by releasing from Scorpio, which for the proposed rectification is the LOF not the LOS. This Scorpio influence is the same discerned by astrologer Luke Broughton (1906, 296-305) who rectified McKinley's horoscope to 2:00 AM, Scorpio rising. He used this rectification to predict McKinley would win the election contest against William Jennings Bryan in 1896 (in a published account from *The Baltimore American* dated 26-Jul-1896).

L1 Scorpio 29 Jan 1843		
L1 Sagittarius 11 Nov 1857		Period featured Civil War service, law studies, and first law practice. Supported Rutherford Hayes for Ohio Gubernatorial race, which Hayes won. Hayes' Presidential election occurred in 1877.
L1 Capricorn 9 Sep 1869		October-1869, elected Stark County prosecutor in upset victory.
L2 Cancer 21 Nov 1878	FS	Oct-1880, won re-election to House seat (3rd term)
L2 Cancer 8 Jan 1887	LB	16-Mar-1887, death of father-in-law yields inheritance which significantly improved finances; 6-Dec-1887, Cleveland anti-tariff address; 2-Apr-1888, Mills Tariff Bill introduced; 23-Jun-1888, name put into play for Republican Presidential candidate but opted to remove his name from the ballot; 6-Nov-1888, Benjamin Harrison elected President; Fall 1888, Re-elected House seat (6th term)
L2 Capricorn 25 Feb 1895	CP	8-Apr-1895, 'McKinley for President' club formed; 13-Jan-1896, Last day as Ohio Governor; returned to home in Canton, Ohio which he turned into his Presidential campaign headquarters.
L1 Aquarius 20 Apr 1896		30-Apr-1896, significant turning point in Republican primary season-backed by Illinois Republicans; 16/18-Jun-1896, nominated Republican Presidential candidate; 3-Nov-1896, won Presidential election; 1898, entire Spanish American War fought and won during this time period.
L2 Gemini 23 Aug 1901		31-Aug-1901, Czolgosz checked into Nowak's Saloon in Buffalo in prep for assassination; 5-Aug-1901, in last address McKinley argued broad policy of commercial reciprocity at Pan American Exposition; 6-Sep-1901, fatal gunshot wound; 15-Sep-1901, Died.
L2 Cancer 15 Apr 1903		

Firdaria – Jupiter major and minor periods

Firdaria according to Bonatti	Life Event
Moon **Jupiter** 25 Aug 1845	26-Jan-1846, death of infant sister Abbie.
Saturn **Jupiter** 25 Aug 1853	No events found. attended public school.
Jupiter 12 years Age 20 to 32	
Jupiter Jupiter 28 Jan 1863	7-Feb-1863, promoted to 1st Lieutenant; 24-Jul-1864, acclaimed for gallantry in battle at Kernstown;
Jupiter Mars 16 Oct 1864	19-Oct-1864, Battle of Cedar Creek; 13-Mar-1865, breveted Major of Volunteers for service at Battle of Cedar Creek; Autumn 1865, read law.
Jupiter Sun 04 Jul 1866	Mar-1867, admitted to bar; 8-Oct-1867, Hayes won Ohio gubernatorial election with McKinley's support.
Jupiter Venus 21 Mar 1868	Mid-1868, formed US Grant-for-President clubs; Oct-1869, elected prosecuting attorney of Stark County in upset election.
Jupiter Mercury 07 Dec 1869	1869-1871 (no exact dates), as prosecutor successfully fought illicit liquor sales; 25-Jan-1871, married Ida Saxton.
Jupiter Moon 25 Aug 1871	25-Dec-1871, daughter Katherine born; 31-Mar-1873, daughter Ida born.
Jupiter Saturn 12 May 1873	22-Aug-1873, death of daughter Ida McKinley.
Mars **Jupiter** 28 Jan 1881	4-Mar-1881, congressional term began after was unexpectedly given assignment to Ways and Means committee to help President Garfield with tariff legislation.
Sun **Jupiter** 21 Mar 1894	27-Aug-1894, Wilson-Gorman Tariff Act into force; 6-Nov-1894, Republicans claim significant victory in midterm elections, considered re-alignment election which paved the way for 1896; 9-Apr-1895, first McKinley Club formed.
Venus **Jupiter** 25 Aug 1901	5-Sep-1901, recommended broad policy of commercial reciprocity at Pan American Exposition; 6-Sep-1901, fatal gunshot; 15-Sep-1901, death.

Jupiter as Victor. Jupiter periods captured Civil War service, entry to politics with WM's support of Rutherford Hayes' successful gubernatorial campaign, first electoral victory in Stark County attorney race; marriage, birth of two daughters and death of the first. Though Jupiter did not identify passage of the famous McKinley tariff, Jupiter did highlight two congressional terms which focused on the tariff. Finally, Jupiter was active during WM's assassination.

Combination Transit/Solar Arc Direction for key Life Event

On 13-Mar-1865, McKinley was breveted Major of volunteers for Civil War battle service at Cedar Creek. After this event, McKinley was content to be called 'Major' the rest of his life despite any other title he earned.

Computed for 13-Mar-1865: *csa Mars 25LI53 conj LOS 25LI57*; also
12-Mar-1865. *tr North Node conj LOF.*
17-Mar-1865. *tr Saturn-rx conj ASC.*

This event represents an *AHA!* Moment in rectification as it links an event to the Ascendant, the LOF, and the LOS.

Transits

21-Sep-1869. *tr North Node conj IC.*
Elected Stark County prosecutor in an upset victory, Oct-1869.

18-Mar-1890. *tr Jupiter conj IC.*
19-Aug-1890. *tr Jupiter-rx conj IC.*
6-Nov-1890. *tr Jupiter conj IC.*
After named Chairman of the House Ways and Means Committee, WM introduced two bills – customs reform and a tariff bill the latter of which was his signature issue, early-Dec 1889.
Debate began on tariff legislation, 8-May-1890.
Death of sister Anna McKinley, 29-Jul-1890. (Jupiter rules 3rd WH house).
Over 400 amendments to the legislation accepted, 26-Sep-1890.
WM lost re-election to House seat because of gerrymandering and an anti-tariff campaign, 4-Nov-1890.

10-Feb-1893. *tr South Node conj LOF.*
Financial loss threatened WM with bankruptcy, 17-Feb-1893.

1-Oct-1895. *tr Jupiter conj MC.*
19-Jan-1896. *tr Jupiter-rx conj MC.*
12-Feb-1896. *tr Jupiter-rx 10th from LOF.*
27-May-1896. *tr Jupiter conj MC.*
WM headlined campaign kickoff, with 30-40K attendees, 10-Oct-1895.
Last day as OH Governor, returned home to start campaign, 13-Jan-1896.
Outlined "McKinleyism" in Marquette Club speech, 12-Feb-1896.
WM had 479 convention votes, enough for nomination, 1-Jun-1896.

Notes: The two sets of Jupiter transits offer compelling support for the proposed rectification. Collectively each transit set shows a series of events which push WM out of power (when Jupiter transits the IC) and back in power (when Jupiter transits the MC).

25. WILLIAM MCKINLEY

Solar Arc Directions

2-Mar-1862. *csa Ascendant trine Sun.*
9-Apr-1862. *dsa Sun trine Ascendant.*
   Promoted to commissary sergeant; regiment ordered to Washington D.C. and attached to the Army of the Potomac, 14-Apr-1862.

28-Jan-1897. *csa Midheaven trine Sun.*
13-Nov-1897. *csa Sun trine Midheaven.*
   Announced cabinet following Nov-1896 electoral victory, Feb-1897.
   1st Annual Message to Congress. Stated Spain must reform its Cuban policies; also admonished Americans to refrain from factionalism which is a delineation match to the humanitarian Sun/Aquarius, 6-Dec-1897.

Primary Directions

| PT | D | Mercury/Scorpio | P | Mars (MA) c. => LOF | 27-Sep-1862 |

Commissioned 2nd Lieutenant after Antietam, 24-Sep-1862.

| PT | D | Mercury/Scorpio | P | Mars (0) d. => ASC | 16-Oct-1867 |

Ally Rutherford Hayes won Ohio Gubernatorial election, 8-Oct-1867.
Learned importance of perseverance in hard fought elections.

| PT | D | Jupiter/Capricorn | P | North Node c. => Moon (0) | 24-Feb-1871 |

Marriage to Ida Saxton, 25-Jan-1871.

| PT | D | Jupiter/Sagittarius | P | dex sextile Sun d. => ASC | 20-Sep-1894 |

LOCK Campaigned in 16 states for Republican congressional candidates making 371 speeches, Sep/Oct-1894.

| PT | D | Jupiter/Aries | P | dex trine MC d. => Sun | 1-Feb-1896 |

LOCK Outlined "McKinleyism" in Marquette Club speech, 12-Feb-1896. Compare to trJupiter 10th from LOF.

| REG | D | Jupiter/Aries | P | dex trine MC d. => Sun | 16-Jun-1896 |

LOCK Received Republican Presidential Nomination, 18-Jun-1896.

Primary Direction Sequence

PT	D	Mercury/Aquarius	P	dex trine Jupiter (JU) d. => MC	6-Apr-1901
PT	D	Mercury/Aquarius	P	dex trine Jupiter (0) d. => MC	16-Jun-1901
PT	D	Mercury/Aquarius	P	dex trine Jupiter (BI) d. => MC	21-Jul-1901

National tour planned to win support for trust-busting and extending commercial reciprocity, 19-Apr to 13-Jun.
Dismissed talk of 3rd Presidential term, 11-Jun.
Left Washington to spend summer at home in Canton, Ohio, 5-Jul-1901.

Longevity, 58y 7m 15d

Shot. 6-Sep-1901, 4:07 PM, Buffalo, NY. McKinley was shot and fatally wounded by the unemployed wire millworker and anarchist Leon Czolgosz as he was standing in a receiving line at the Temple of Music at the American Exposition.

Death: 14-Sep-1901, 2:15 AM, Buffalo, NY. McKinley died from infection from the bullet, believed to have entered his pancreas.

Hīlāj: **Sun**. Figure is nocturnal. Moon/5th is preferred but combustion raises questions. Next candidate is the Sun/5th in a masculine sign.

Al-kadukhadāh: **Saturn**. In the place of the Sun, bound lord Venus makes a sextile aspect but has no essential dignity. Sign ruler Saturn is inconjunct but hard to ignore as the ruler of a four planet Jupiter-Moon-Sun-Mercury Aquarius stellium. In addition, Saturn is amplified by conjunction to the North Node. Saturn grants 57 minor years; North Node amplifies by 25%; Mars receives Saturn by sextile aspect by exaltation and participating triplicity and deducts 15 minor years.

SA (57) * NN (1.25) – MA (15) = 56.25

Note at death both Saturn and Mars make returns to their natal signs.

Victor of the Horoscope: **Jupiter**

Killing Planets: **Saturn (46), Mercury (37), Jupiter (36)**

Arcus Vitae:

| PT | D | Venus/Aries | P | dex sq South Node d. => Sun | 7-Feb-1901 |
| REG | D | Venus/Aries | P | dex sq South Node d. => Sun | 8-Jul-1901 |

South Node in the 10th is a traditional signature for career problems or, in the case of the head of state, removal from office. Direction of the South Node to the Sun is consistent with removal from office, not necessarily an assassination, but removal. The direction computed by either Ptolemy's or Regiomontanus' methods is early but near the time of Czolgosz's radicalization.

During the summer of 1901, the assassin Leon Czolgosz heard Emma Goldman lecture during May 1901 and briefly met her in Chicago on 12-Jul-1901 where she referred him to local anarchists. This date is 4 days after the Regiomontanus calculation method for the South Node – Sun direction.

1901 Solar Return for year of Death

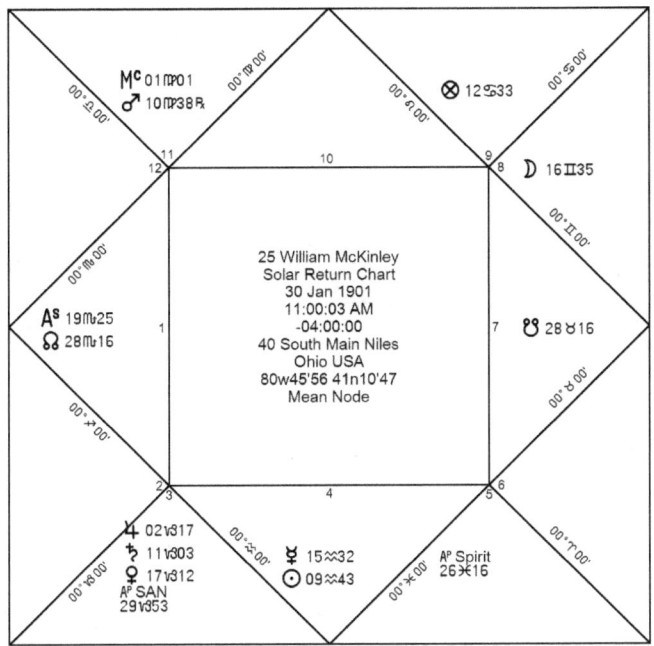

Ascendant Distributor: Venus/Sagittarius since 29-Jun-1897
Profected Ascendant: 29LE09, 11th house; SR Victor: Venus
Lords: LOY – Sun; LOP – Jupiter
Firdaria: Venus-Jupiter
Moon: separates from Mercury and is VOC.
Return Ascendant falls in natal 2nd; Natal Ascendant falls in return's 12th

Besides McKinley's assassination, this return marked his 2nd inauguration and the capture of Philippine resistance leader Emilio Aguinaldo, ending the active phase of the Philippine-American War. Return's Ascendant is conjunct natal Mars; return's LOF is conjunct natal South Node. This synastry raises flags. High scoring killing planets Saturn and Mercury return to their natal signs increasing their power to act. Czolgosz is better signified by Mercury in the return. Mercury rules Mars which signifies the actual bullets. Mars retrograde means 2 shots are required to kill because the first is deflected.

No relevant Ascendant directions were found for the day of death.

26 Theodore Roosevelt

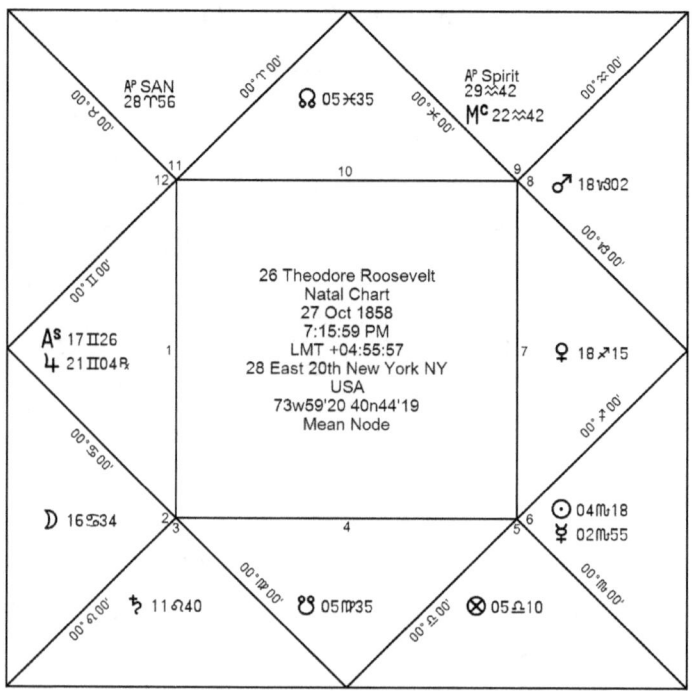

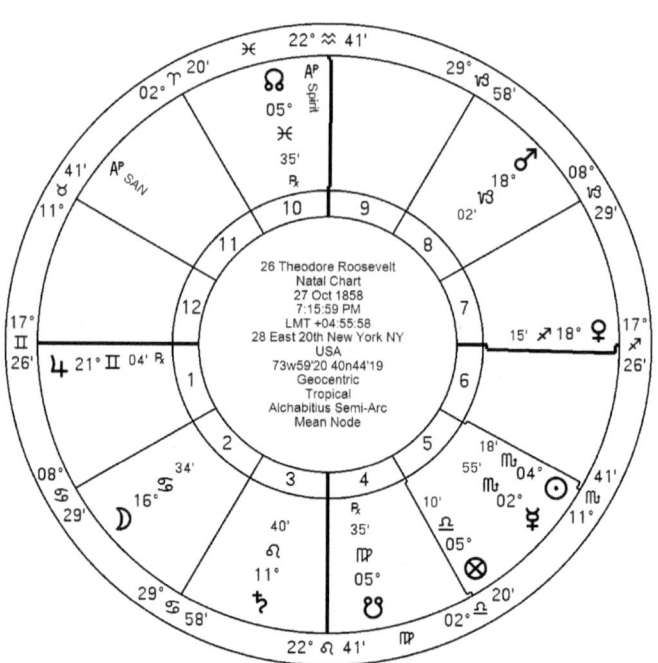

26. THEODORE ROOSEVELT

Moon's Configuration

Moon separates from the **Sun** and applies to **Mars**, nocturnal, preventional. Prenatal syzygy is 28AR56. Eclipse? No.

Cognitive Assessment Model (Rulers of Moon and Mercury)

Sign rulers: **(Moon) Mercury, Mars**
Bound rulers: **Mercury, Mars**

Victor Soul Models

Ibn Ezra Victor Model (1507), in-sect triplicity ruler, triplicity decans.

	Position	☉	☽	☿	♀	♂	♃	♄
Sun	04 SC 18					11		
Moon	16 CA 34		5	2		4	4	
Asc	17 GE 26			8	1	2		
Pars Fortuna	05 LI 10			3	6			6
Syzygy	28 AR 56	4				5	4	2
Oriental						0	1	2
Houses		7	6	7	10	5	12	3
Score		0	11	11	20	17	**27**	21	13

Porphyry's Expanded Victor Model (2022)

Mars rules the Sun and syzygy by sign; the MC, ASC, and Sun by bound. Sect: in-favor. Solar phase: occidental waning square to sextile. Position: 4th from Lot of Fortune. Dignity: exaltation and participating triplicity. Moon's application.

Victor Table for Killing Planets

			☉	☽	☿	♀	♂	♃	♄
ASC		17GE26			5,3	1	2	3	3
Rul ASC	☿	2SC55		3		3	5,3,2,1		
L.Death		3AQ35			3,2			3	5,3,1
Rul L.Death	♄	11LE40	5,3					3,1	3,2
H8 Cusp		8CP29		3		3	4,3	2	5,1
Rul H8	♄	11LE40	5,3					3,1	3,2
T-Rul H8	☽	16CA34		5,3	2	3	3,1	4	
Planets in 8th	♂	18CP02		3		3,2,1	4,3		5
8th from ☽		16AQ34			3,1			3,2	5,3
Rul 8th fr ☽	♄	11LE40	5,3					3,1	3,2
TOTAL			24	17	19	16	**31**	29	46

2007 Proposed Rectification: 7:15:58 PM, ASC 17GE25'07"
2022 Proposed Rectification: 7:15:59 PM, ASC 17GE26'30"

Astrodatabank reports a B-rated birth time of 7:45 PM with an Ascendant of 24GE37. The proposed rectification is 30 minutes earlier. The biggest difference between the two times is LOS moves from Pisces (ADB) to Aquarius (proposed rectification). LOS 29AQ41 in the bound of Saturn/Aquarius makes TR interested in science. The lot was active as recently as 19-Jan-2022 when the removal process started for TR's statue at the American Museum of Natural History. For this event transiting South Node 28SC32 was 10th from the LOS.

ZRS from Aquarius works well for Roosevelt. Notable was his political rise during L1-Pisces stopping just short of the Presidential ticket. A few weeks after the start of L1-Aries he was nominated VP. This is consistent with ZR methodology as Aries is angular from LOF; moreover, its ruler Mars/Capricorn is the victor of the horoscope.

L1 Aquarius 27 Oct 1858		
L2 Leo 9 Nov 1867	FS	12-May-1869, Roosevelt family set sail for Europe.
L2 Leo 25 Feb 1876	LB	12-Jun-1876, Father made pro-reform speech at RNC in attempt to unseat James Blaine with a reform candidate; 27-Sep-1876, left home for Harvard College, end of asthma.
L2 Aquarius 12 Jun 1884	CP	9-Jun-1884, returned to Badlands; 19-Jul-1884, political announcement stated TR would remain in Republican Party but not to campaign for office during the upcoming election season; Spring-1885, won battle against ill health, called 'rugged;' Aug-1886, engaged to Edith Carow.
L1 Pisces 22 May 1888		L1-Pisces timed the rapid political ascent of TR which stopped just short of the Presidency. 13-May-1889, appointed to Civil Service Commission by Grover Cleveland; May-1895, appointed NY Police Commissioner; 5-Apr-1897, nominated for Assistant Secretary of the Navy; 6-May-1898, resigned from Navy position and organized Rough Riders division to participate in the Spanish-American War; 8-Nov-1898, won NY Gubernatorial election; 6-Feb-1900, stated would not run for VP slot on Republican ticket.
L1 Aries 21 Mar 1900		21-Jun-1900, TR nominated VP slot on ticket with WM; 15-Sep-1901, assumed presidency after death of McKinley; 1905, arbitrated Russian/Japanese conflict at Portsmouth Conference; 3-Nov-1908, Taft won Presidency as TR's protégé; 1912, unsuccessful 3rd party Presidential run as leader of Progressive Party.
L1 Taurus 2 Jan 1915		Jan-1915, first suggestion made that TR should lead a division in WWI. attempts to return to the battlefield were stymied and denied by US military and political leadership over the next two years.
L2 Cancer 21 Apr 1917		6-Jan-1919. death from coronary embolism.

26. THEODORE ROOSEVELT

Firdaria – Mars major and minor periods

Firdaria according to Bonatti	Life Event
Moon **Mars** 05 Sep 1862	No events found.
Saturn **Mars** 18 Dec 1870	17-Jul-1871, death grandfather; Summer-1872, given gun and a large pair of glasses.
Jupiter **Mars** 14 Jul 1880	27-Oct-1880, married Alice Lee; about the same time, decided to take up law; Nov-1880, bought first land at Oyster Bay; 9-Nov-1881, elected State Assembly; 29-Mar-1882, called for investigation/impeachment of Justice Westbrook (Jay Gould ally).
Mars 7 years Age 32 to 39	
Mars Mars 27 Oct 1890	Jul-1891, TR felt that GC was not giving TR support for civil service reform following GC's appointment of TR to the Civil Service Commission on 13-May-1889.
Mars Sun 27 Oct 1891	No events found.
Mars Venus 27 Oct 1892	3-Jan-1893, GC asked TR to stay on in Civil Service position.
Mars Mercury 27 Oct 1893	No events found.
Mars Moon 27 Oct 1894	May-1895, appointed NYC Police Commissioner.
Mars Saturn 27 Oct 1895	Fall-1896, campaigned for McKinley.
Mars Jupiter 27 Oct 1896	3-Nov-1896, McKinley won election; 5-Apr-1897, McKinley nominated TR for Ass Sec of Navy; 2-Jun-1897, Made hawkish speech at Naval War College.
Sun **Mars** 25 May 1911	24-Oct-1811, AG suit against US Steel severed ties between TR and Taft; 22-Feb-1912, TR began Presidential campaign; 20-Jun-1912, split from Republicans and started own 3rd party bid; 6-Aug-1912, nominated by President by Progressive Party.
Venus **Mars** 15 Jul 1918	6-Jan-1919, death from coronary embolism.

Mars as Victor. Mars' periods captured his first marriage and entry to politics with TR's election to the NY assembly, tenure on Cleveland's Civil Service Commission, role as NYC Police Commissioner, appointment as Assistant Secretary of the Navy, his failed 3rd party bid in 1912, and death. While Mars does not highlight TR's presidency, consider his Presidency occurred during the Major Sun Firdaria period. With the Sun in the bound of Mars, Mars does in fact show through as a driving force during TR's presidency as the Sun's bound lord.

Transits

6-Feb-1878. *tr South Node conj IC*.
  Death of father, 9 February.

11-Mar-1898. *tr Mars conj MC*.
13-Aug-1898. *tr Mars conj ASC*.
  TR offered to raise a regiment for Spanish American War, 9-Mar-1898.
  Fighting ceased in Spanish American War, 12-Aug-1898.

2-Feb-1900. *tr South Node conj ASC*.
  TR Stated would not run for office of Vice President, 6 February.

30-Oct-1903. *tr North Node conj LOF*.
  Panamanian conspirators arrived in Colon, Columbia, 27-Oct-1903.
  Panama declared Independence, supported by Panama Canal Company and the Roosevelt administration, 3-Nov-1903.

1-Sep-1913. *tr Saturn conj ASC*.
29-Oct-1913. *tr Saturn-rx conj ASC*.
10-May-1914. *tr Saturn conj ASC*.
  Traveled to South America, 4-Oct-1913.
  Injured leg against a rock while attempting to extricate two canoes on River of Doubt, 27-Mar-1914.
  Developed jungle fever, 4-Apr-1914.
  Returned from South American trip, 19-May-1914.

Solar Arc Directions

10-Feb-1884. *csa Saturn conj Moon*.
  Death of wife and mother, 14-Feb.

3-Dec-1902. *dsa Mercury opposed ASC*.
  Refused to shoot tied up bear in Mississippi, 14-Nov, "Teddy Bear" origin.

17-Nov-1903. *dsa ASC square Mercury*.
  US and Panama signed Hay-Bunau-Varilla Treaty, 18-Nov.

LOCK 25-Sep-1906. *dsa Sun sextile MC*.
  Appointed Taft military governor of Cuba, 29-Sep. Cuba = Scorpio.

18-Jun-1912. *dsa ASC conj. Saturn*.
  Statement: "*I am as strong as a Bull Moose*" timed origin of TR's third party movement, 20/22-Jun-1912.

26. THEODORE ROOSEVELT

Primary Direction Sequences

PT	D	Mars/Pisces	P	dex square Jupiter (0) d. => MC	29-Jul-1885
PT	D	Mars/Pisces	P	dex square Jupiter (JU) d. => MC	3-Nov-1885

This sequence timed Roosevelt's dispute with the cattle baron Marquis de Mores. On 26-Aug-1885 de Mores was indicted for an 1883 murder. In a 3-Sep letter to TR, de Mores accused some of Roosevelt's employees/colleagues of rumor mongering which facilitated his indictment. TR misinterpreted de Mores' angry letter of 3-Sep to mean that de Mores had challenged TR to a duel. That was not de Mores' intent; after de Mores made his intent clear, the matter was dropped. These events conform to the position of Jupiter ruling the 7th of open enemies in the 1st. Roosevelt attracts open enemies by exaggerating the facts. Jupiter's ruler Mercury shows the cause: Mercury/Scorpio/6th – combust – hidden lies and rumors.

REG	D	Mercury/Leo	P	IC d. => Mercury (0)	14-Jan-1905
REG	D	Mercury/Leo	P	IC d. => Mercury (ME)	27-Jul-1905

LOCK While this sequence opened with a restatement of the Roosevelt Corollary in his 6-Dec-1904 Annual Message to Congress and a hemorrhage in his left eye following a boxing match, the most apparent continuous set of events matching the delineation of combust Mercury/Scorpio as hidden lies and intrigue are TR's lengthy involvement in setting up the Portsmouth Conference to negotiate the end of the Russo-Japanese War. TR set negotiations into motion by ordering Italian ambassador George Meyer to St. Petersburg as his own special representative on 26-Dec-1904. What followed were a series of evasive maneuvers by the Russians who believe they could still win and are not interested in peace talks. Following Japan's decisive naval victory on 27-May, all parties agreed to talks on 7/8-Jun with diplomatic parties arriving in Portsmouth on 5-Aug-1905 as the sequence ended. This sequence does not time the Portsmouth Conference itself, only the intrigue and delays involved in setting it up.

REG	D	Mars/Gemini	P	sinister trine MC c. => Saturn (0)	30-May-1912
REG	D	Mars/Gemini	P	sinister trine MC c. => Saturn (SA)	9-Jun-1912

LOCK This sequence comprised the climax of delegate selection when Roosevelt nearly garnered sufficient delegate seats to secure a victory. Roosevelt's strong showing in President Taft's home state of Ohio on 22-May gave Roosevelt a temporary surge in popularity. As the sequence closed, Roosevelt's luck ran out as he was unable to outmaneuver the Republican National Party. See NYT '48 More Votes Awarded to Taft; Roosevelt's Contests Collapse,' June 9, 1912, p. 1.

Longevity, 60y 2m 9d

Death: 6-Jan-1919, approx. 4:00 AM, Sagamore Hill estate, Oyster Bay, New York, at home. Roosevelt died from a coronary embolism in his sleep. Illnesses towards the end of his life, including malaria and leg infection, arthritis, and deafness in one ear, had taken their toll. Yet his actual death was a surprise.

Hīlāj: **Moon.** Figure is nocturnal and Moon/2nd/feminine sign qualifies.

Al-kadukhadāh: **Mars.** In the position of the Moon, Mars is the nocturnal triplicity and decan ruler. Mars is in the sign of exaltation in Capricorn; he is also the victor. Mars grants 66yrs. All benefics and malefics are inconjunct Mars and cannot modify years. Roosevelt lived fewer years.

Victor of the Horoscope: **Mars**

Killing Planets: **Saturn (46), Mars (31), Jupiter (29)**

Arcus Vitae:

| PT | D | Mars/Pisces | P | dexter square Jupiter (JU) c. => ASC | 18-Mar-1918 |
| PT | D | Mars/Pisces | P | dexter square Jupiter (0) c. => ASC | 6-Jan-1919 |

Fatal stroke and death, 6-Jan-1919, exact date.

| REG | D | Mercury/Taurus | P | dexter square Saturn (0) d. => Moon (MO) | 10-Jul-1918 |
| REG | D | Mercury/Taurus | P | dexter square Saturn (SA) d. => Moon (MO) | 15-Feb-1919 |

Death of son Quentin Roosevelt in WWI dogfight, 14-Jul-1918, 4 days error.
TR was depressed after the death of his son with some biographers going so far as to suggest it was a contributing factor to his own death. This primary direction sequence supports that thesis.

Note for primary directions students: the dexter square of Saturn is 11TA40 which is partile to the degree and minute of the 12th house cusp whose life affairs include the death of children, fear, and loneliness.

26. THEODORE ROOSEVELT

1918 Solar Return for year of Death

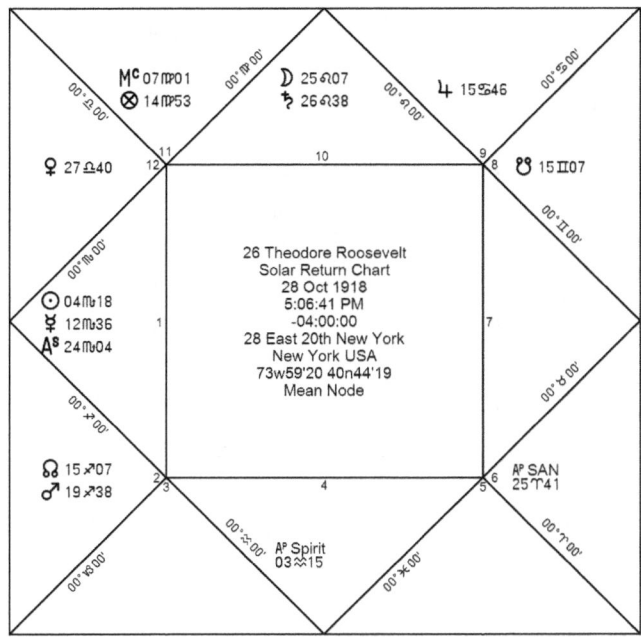

Ascendant Distributor: Venus/Leo since 10-Feb-1915
Profected Ascendant: 17GE25, 1st House; Victor: SR Mars
Lords: LOY – Mercury; LOP – Mars
Firdaria: Venus-Mars
Moon: separates from trine of Mars and applies to conjunction of Saturn
Return Ascendant falls in natal 6th; Natal Ascendant falls in return's 8th

The separation of the Moon from the trine of Mars to the conjunction of Saturn afflicts the Hīlāj with two high scoring killing planets. A profected 1st house year emphasizing the physical body places the solar return ascendant in the natal 6th of illness. Mercury returns to his natal sign, is Lord of the Year, and rules the 8th of death in the return. Note the South Node in the return's 8th house falls in the natal Ascendant. These configurations favor death during the 1918 return.

This is another example of an interplanetary solar return direction which kills. Roosevelt died 69.83 days or 68deg 49min following his return.

| PT | D | Mercury/Scorpio | P | Mercury (ME) d. => Moon (MO) | 69deg 54min |

Mercury kills by stroke.

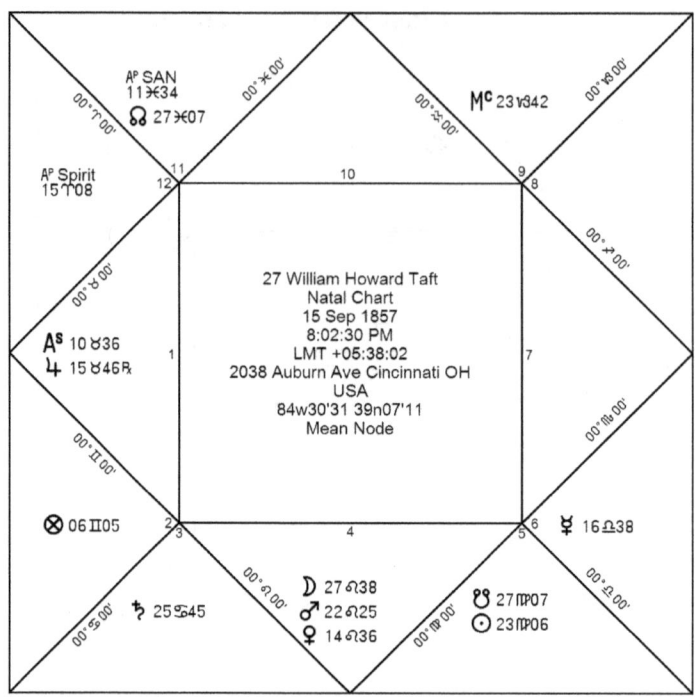

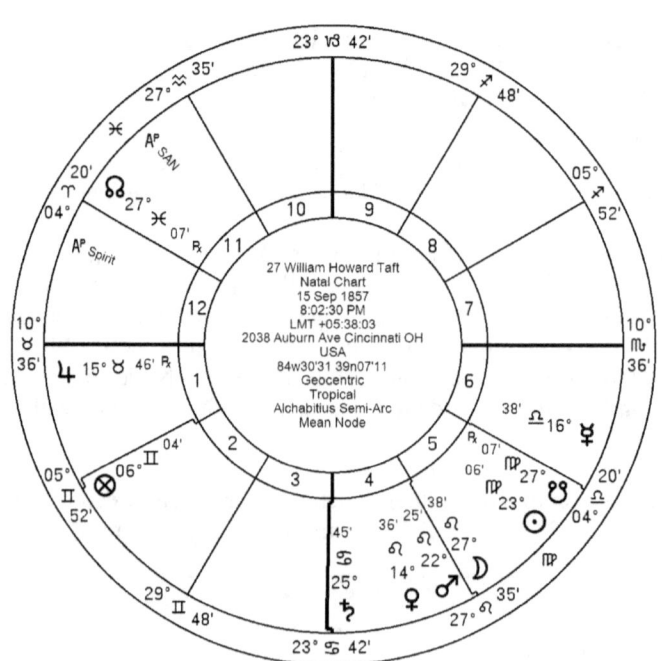

Moon's Configuration

Moon separates from **Mars** and is **VOC** (Medieval) or applies to **Jupiter** (Hellenistic), nocturnal, preventional.
Prenatal syzygy is 11PI34. Eclipse? **YES**. Appulse Lunar Eclipse.

Cognitive Assessment Model (Rulers of Moon and Mercury)

Sign rulers: **(Sun) Mars, Venus**
Bound rulers: **Mars, Jupiter**

Victor Soul Models

Ibn Ezra Victor Model (1507), in-sect triplicity ruler, triplicity decans.

	Position	☉	☽	☿	♀	♂	♃	♄
Sun	23 VI 06		3	9	1	2		
Moon	27 LE 38	5				3	3	
Asc	10 TA 38		7	3	5			
Pars Fortuna	06 GE 06			9			2	
Syzygy	11 PI 34 (LE)		1		6	3	5	
Oriental						3	1	3
Houses			7	7	1	9	9	12	9
Score		0	12	18	22	21	20	**23**	12

Porphyry's Expanded Victor Model (2022)

Jupiter rules the syzygy by sign; the Lot of Fortune by bound. Sect: out-of-favor. Solar phase: oriental retrograde to acronycal rising. Position: Angular in ASC. Dignity: bound.

Victor Table for Killing Planets

			☉	☽	☿	♀	♂	♃	♄
ASC		10TA36		4,3	2,1	5,3	3		
Rul ASC	♀	14LE36	5,3					3,1	3,2
L.Death		3SC59		3		3	5,3,2,1		
Rul L.Death	♂	22LE25	5,3		2		1	3	3
H8 Cusp		5SA52	3					5,3,2,1	3
Rul H8	♃	15TA46		4,3	1	5,3	3	2	
T-Rul H8	♃	15TA46		4,3	1	5,3	3	2	
8th from ☽		27PI38		3		4,3	3,2,1	5	
Rul 8th fr ☽	♃	15TA46		4,3	1	5,3	3	2	
TOTAL			19	34	8	**42**	30	29	11

2007 Proposed Rectification: 10:14:21 AM, ASC 16SC24'53"
2009 Proposed Rectification: 8:02:26 PM, ASC 10TA36'52"
2017 Revised Rectification: 8:02:29 PM, ASC 10TA36'29"

Astrodatabank reports an A-rated birthtime of 8:00 PM, ASC 9TA45. The proposed rectification is 2-3 minutes later. The initial 2007 rectification for Scorpio rising was a rookie mistake. The slight difference between the 2009 and 2017 rectifications is driven by a greater reliance on solar arc directions over primary directions for a horoscope with a Leo emphasis. Taft's horoscope has Ascendant ruler Venus/Leo in a stellium with Mars/Leo and Moon/Leo.

ZRS. Taft's horoscope exemplifies the ZR technique in one of the cleanest applications of the methodology. L1-Gemini encapsulates his private legal career. L1-Cancer launches Taft's career in public service with a stint in the Philippines. Linkage between L2-Capricorn FS and LB periods is dramatic and unmistakable: during FS Taft started to diverge from TR on matters of public policy which led to a split between both men. During LB, TR died. While WT was appointed Chief Justice of the Supreme Court while still in L1-Cancer (L2-Aquarius), the changeover to L1-Leo timed passage of the Judiciary Act which was a significant milestone in the history of the Court.

L1 Aries 15 Sep 1857		
L1 Taurus 28 Jun 1872		
L1 Gemini 17 May 1880		Summer 1880, graduated law school, admitted to Ohio bar; 25-Oct-1880, appointed assistant prosecutor of Hamilton County to start 3-Jan-1881.
L2 Sagittarius 1 Mar 1889	FS	4-Jun-1889, death of half-brother Peter Taft; 8-Sep-1889, birth of son Robert Taft; 14-Feb-1890, sworn in as Solicitor General of the United States.
L2 Sagittarius 15 Sep 1897	LB	20-Sep-1897, son Charles born; 8-Feb-1898, revived Sherman Antitrust Act by handing down decision that Ohio Pipe and Steel Company was guilty of combining to restrain interstate commerce.
L1 Cancer 2 Feb 1900		late-Jan-1900 (just before), summoned by President McKinley to run the Philippine Commission.
L2 Capricorn 22 Mar 1908	FS	16-Jun-1908, won Republican Presidential nomination; 3-Nov-1908, won election contest; 7-Jan-1910, WT fired Forest Service chief Gifford Pinchot in the first action which would eventually lead to the split from TR.
L2 Capricorn 3 Jun 1917	LB	5-Jan-1919, TR died.
L1 Leo 24 Sep 1924		13-Feb-1925, Judiciary Act passed. Gave Supreme Court greater power to decide which cases to hear.
L2 Sagittarius 28 Oct 1929		31-Dec-1929, half-brother Charles died; 3-Feb-1930, resigned Supreme Court because of deteriorating health; 8-Mar-1930, Death.

Firdaria – Jupiter major and minor periods

Firdaria according to Bonatti	Life Event
Moon **Jupiter** 12 Apr 1860	No events found.
Saturn **Jupiter** 11 Apr 1868	No events found.
Jupiter 12 years Age 20 to 32	
Jupiter Jupiter 15 Sep 1877	27-Jun-1878, graduated Yale, gave senior oration which discussed political corruption; Fall-1878, entered Cincinnati Law School.
Jupiter Mars 03 Jun 1879	Summer-1880, graduated from Law School and admitted to Ohio bar; 25-Oct-1880, appointed Assistant Prosecutor.
Jupiter Sun 18 Feb 1881	Jan-1882, appointed US collector of internal revenue for 1st district of Ohio.
Jupiter Venus 07 Nov 1882	Dec-1882, formed law partnership with Major Harlan Page Lloyd after resignation as collector.
Jupiter Mercury 25 Jul 1884	1-Jan-1885, appointed Assistant County Solicitor.
Jupiter Moon 12 Apr 1886	19-Jun-1886, married Nellie Herron; Mar-1887, appointed Judge of the Superior Court.
Jupiter Saturn 29 Dec 1887	Apr-1888, elected to full term as Superior Court Judge.
Mars **Jupiter** 16 Sep 1895	1896 (no date), Dean and Professor of Property at Cincinnati Law School.
Sun **Jupiter** 07 Nov 1908	4-Mar-1909, Presidential Inauguration.
Venus **Jupiter** 12 Apr 1916	15-May-1916, Democratic party used Taft's pleas for support of Wilson in the war crisis as political ammunition against the Republican party. Taft became critical and questioned the administration's preparedness program and policies.
Mercury **Jupiter** 12 Apr 1925	Oct-1926, In *Myers vs United States*, WT wrote what he considered one of his most important decisions. Taft said that senatorial agreement was not necessary for the dismissal of Frank Myers, an appointed postmaster of Portland Oregon. It was reversed by the Supreme Court in 1935.

Jupiter as Victor. WT's Major Jupiter period from age 20 to 32 timed his most important career development from entry in Law School to his election as Superior Court Judge. His Presidential inauguration occurred soon after Sun-Jupiter. In final years on the Supreme Court, *Myers v US* was heard during Mercury-Jupiter, considered one of his most important cases.

Transits

14-May-1891. *tr North Node conj LOF.*
  Death of father, 21-May-1891. North Node in 11th, death of the father.

29-Dec-1901. *tr South Node conj ASC.*
  Returned to US from Philippines to recover from surgery, 24 December.

5-Mar-1912. *tr South Node 10th from MC.*
  Resignation of Dr. Harvey Wiley, Agriculture Department, Mar-1912. Wiley was a proponent of safe food and drug laws, e.g., part of the progressive political faction associated with TR. Consumer advocates were disappointed with the resignation, this became an issue in fall elections.

25-Jun-1921. *tr North Node 10th from MC.*
  Named Chief Justice of the Supreme Court, 30-Jun-1921.

Solar Arc Directions

24-Feb-1884. *dsa Venus trine ASC.*
13-Jul-1884. *csa ASC trine Venus.*
  Began attending Hellen "Nellie" Herron's Sunday salons, Mar-1884.

20-Sep-1900. *dsa ASC square Sun.*
19-Sep-1901. *csa Sun square ASC.*
  Philippines policy document became effective, 1-Sep-1900.
  McKinley assassination, 8-Sep-1901.

LOCK 9-Sep-1901. *dsa North Node conj ASC.*
23-Sep-1902. *csa ASC conj North Node.*
  TR's accession to the Presidency on McKinley's death, 14-Sep-1901.
  TR and WT became close allies.
  WT declined appointment to Supreme Court by TR, 27-Oct-1902.

13-Sep-1905. *dsa Sun opposed ASC.*
  Food poisoning, 24-Sep-1905.

15-Nov-1907. *dsa LOF conj Saturn.*
LOCK 16-Mar-1909. *csa Saturn conj LOF.*
  Death of mother, 7-Dec-1907.
  Presidential inauguration marred by howling blizzard, 5-Mar-1909.

LOCK 11-Jul-1921. *dsa MC conj North Node.*
10-Aug-1923. *csa North Node conj MC.*
  Sworn in as Chief Justice of Supreme Court, 11-Jul-1921.
  Death of President Harding, 2-Aug-1923.

27 WILLIAM HOWARD TAFT

Primary Directions

| REG | D | Venus/Scorpio | P | DSC d. => Sun | 21-May-1889 |
| REG | D | Mars/Leo | P | Moon (0) d. => Saturn (SA) | 28-May-1889 |

Death of half-brother Peter Taft, 4-Jun.

| REG | D | Jupiter/Libra | P | Mercury (ME) d. => Moon (0) | 14-Sep-1889 |

Birth of son Robert, 8-Sep.

| REG | D | Jupiter/Cancer | P | IC d. => Sun | 23-Sep-1901 |

Death of McKinley, 14-Sep.

| PT | D | Venus/Scorpio | P | DSC d. => Moon (MO) | 17-Dec-1907 |

Death of Mother, 7-Dec.

| REG | D | Jupiter/Taurus | P | Jupiter (0) c. => IC | 26-Dec-1929 |

Death of half-brother Charles P. Taft, 31-Dec.

Primary Direction Sequences

| PT | D | Jupiter/Aquarius | P | dex square Jupiter (0) d. => MC | 13-May-1880 |
| PT | D | Jupiter/Aquarius | P | dex square Jupiter (JU) d. => MC | 13-Oct-1880 |

Following graduation from law school and admission to the Ohio bar during summer 1880, Taft was appointed assistant prosecutor of Hamilton County on 25-Oct-1880.

| PT | D | Jupiter/Pisces | P | dex sextile Jupiter (0) d. => MC | 13-Jan-1909 |
| PT | D | Jupiter/Pisces | P | dex sextile Jupiter (JU) d. => MC | 24-Jul-1909 |

LOCK Following his November 1908 Presidential election, Taft selected his cabinet on the basis of improving the fortunes of the National Republican Party. This was a rebuff to the referee system of patronage distribution in Southern States linked to local political bosses. Taft announced his decision to abandon the referee system on 12-Jan. Following inauguration, Taft signed the Aldrich-Payne Tariff Act into law on 5-Aug. By whole sign houses, Jupiter rules the 11th of political alliances and the 8th of foreign trade.

| PT | D | Mars/Pisces | P | dexter trine Saturn (0) d. => MC | 25-Mar-1918 |
| PT | D | Mars/Pisces | P | dexter trine Saturn (SA) d. => MC | 7-Apr-1918 |

LOCK On 28-Mar-1918, Taft and Lowell (Harvard) discussed with President Wilson a convention for a precursor group to the League of Nations. Both Taft and Wilson share natal Saturn/Cancer. On 8-Apr-1918, WT was named Joint Chairman of National War Labor Board.

Longevity, 72y 5m 21d

Death: 8-Mar-1930, late afternoon, Washington DC, at home. Taft suffered a steady deterioration in health primarily from heart disease, complicated by obesity. He died in his sleep after being semi-conscious for several days.

Hīlāj: **Moon**. Moon/5th qualifies in a nocturnal figure though placement in a feminine sign is preferred. Empirical arcus vitae confirms Moon as Hīlāj.

Al-kadukhadāh: **Jupiter**. Jupiter falling within 6 degrees of the Ascendant is the logical Al-kadukhadāh. He is also the Victor of the Horoscope. Jupiter grants his 79 major years. Venus adds 8 minor years by square aspect with reception by sign and diurnal triplicity; Mars deducts 15 minor years by square aspect.

JU (79) + VE (8) - MA (15) = 72 years.

Accurate. Note the simplification compared to the 3rd edition which added Venus' middle years as months. I no longer advocate using middle years.

Victor of the Horoscope: **Jupiter**

Killing Planets: **Venus (42)**

Arcus Vitae:

PT	D	Venus/Gemini	P	dexter sextile Venus (0) c. => Moon (0)	27-Feb-1930
PT	D	Venus/Gemini	P	dexter sextile Venus (VE) c. => Moon (0)	4-Mar-1930

REG	D	Venus/Gemini	P	dexter sex Venus (0) c. => Moon (MO)	9-Mar-1930
REG	D	Venus/Gemini	P	dexter sex Venus (BI) c. => Moon (MO)	17-Mar-1930

Taft resigned from the Supreme Court because of ill health, 3-Feb-1930. The third direction is the most accurate timer of death, error 1 day.

Research since the 3rd edition suggests when the Moon is the significator, the Moon's full latitude should be used. These results are consistent with that observation.

1929 Solar Return for year of Death

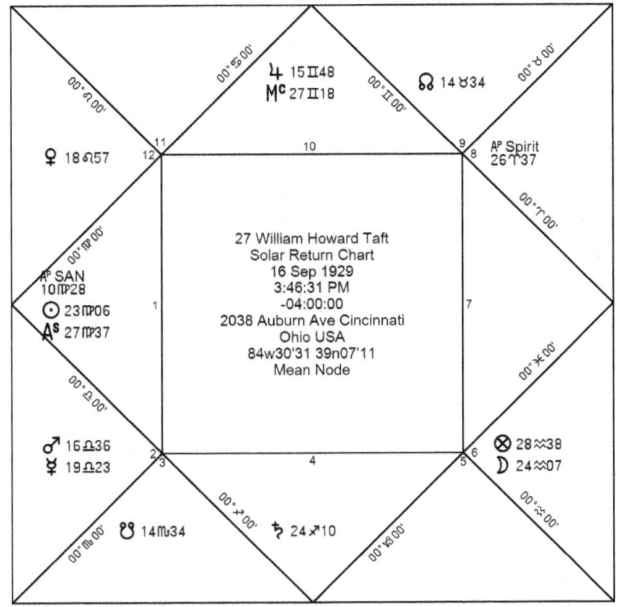

Ascendant Distributor: Jupiter/Cancer since 28-May-1923
Profected Ascendant: 10TA38, 1st House; SR Victor: Mercury
Lords: LOY – Venus; LOP – Venus
Firdaria: Mercury-Sun
Moon: separates from trine of Mercury and applies to sextile of Saturn
Return Ascendant in natal 5th; Natal Ascendant in return's 9th

High scoring killer Venus returns to her natal sign and has ample power to kill through her power as Lord of the Year.

Note natal South Node 27VI07 is partile conjunct the return's Ascendant. In addition, the return's North Node 14TA36 is conjunct the natal Ascendant by four degrees. Nature of North Node is to increase; here the physical body through eating (ruler Venus/Leo). Moon separates from Mercury (return's Ascendant ruler) and applies to Saturn in the 4th (end-of-life).

Taft died 173.88 days or 171deg 23min following his solar return.
This direction recapitulates the same planets in the proposed arcus vitae.

| PT | D | Mercury/Leo | P | Venus (VE) c. => Moon (MO) | 170deg 6min |

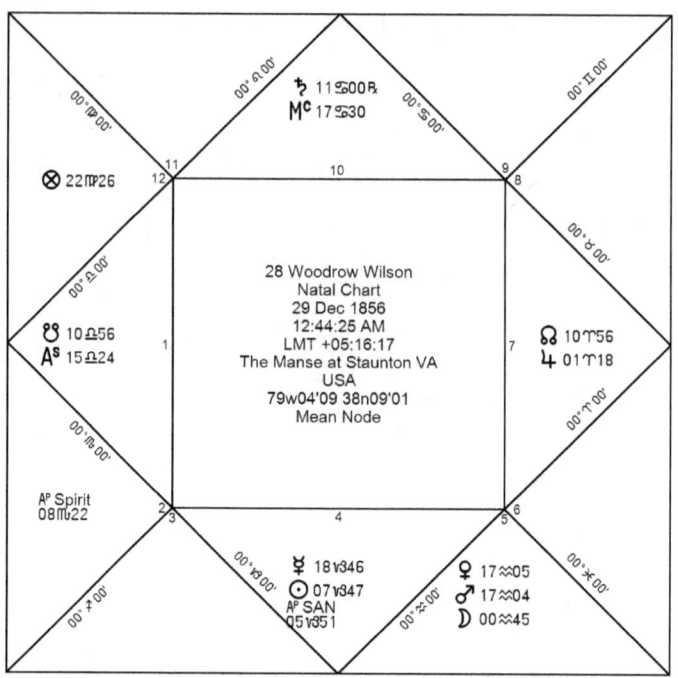
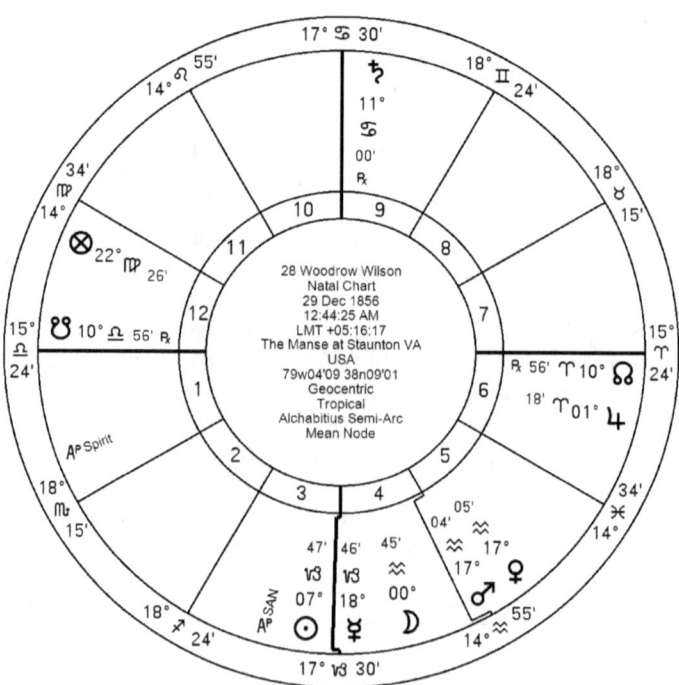

Moon's Configuration

Moon applies to **Jupiter**, nocturnal, conjunctional.
Prenatal syzygy is 5CP52. Eclipse? No.

Cognitive Assessment Model (Rulers of Moon and Mercury)

Sign rulers: **Saturn** (both)
Bound rulers: **Mercury, Venus**

Victor Soul Models

Ibn Ezra Victor Model (1507), in-sect triplicity ruler, triplicity decans.

	Position	☉	☽	☿	♀	♂	♃	♄
Sun	07 CP 47		3			4	2	6
Moon	00 AQ 45			5				6
Asc	15 LI 24			3	5		2	5
Pars Fortuna	22 VI 26		3	9	1	2		
Syzygy	05 CP 52		3	2		4		6
Oriental						0	0	1
Houses		3	9	9	7	7	1	4
Score	0	3	18	**28**	13	17	5	**28**

Porphyry's Expanded Victor Model (2022)

Jupiter rules the ASC and Sun by bound. Sect: out-of-favor. Solar phase: occidental waning square to sextile. Position: 7th from ASC. Dignity: nocturnal triplicity and bound. Moon's application. Conjunct North Node.

Victor Table for Killing Planets

			☉	☽	☿	♀	♂	♃	♄
ASC		15LI24			3	5		3,2	4,3,1
Rul ASC	♀	17AQ05			3,1			3,2	5,3
L.Death		28LI30			3,1	5	2	3	4,3
Rul L.Death	♀	17AQ05			3,1			3,2	5,3
H8 Cusp		18TA15		4,3	1	5,3	3	2	
Rul H8	♀	17AQ05			3,1			3,2	5,3
T-Rul H8	☽	00AQ45			3,2			3	5,3,1
8th from ☽		00VI45		3	5,4,2,1	3	3		
Rul 8th fr ☽	☿	18CP46		3		3,2,1	4,3		5
TOTAL			0	13	**37**	27	15	28	**53**

2007 Proposed Rectification: 12:44:25 AM, ASC 15LI24'44"

Astrodatabank reports a B-rated birth time of 12:45 AM. The proposed rectification is within one minute. I consider Wilson's horoscope a Rosetta stone for its ability to time similar events, linked in history, for ASC-Venus and ASC-Mars when computed by solar arc and primary directions. (See Chapter 10). **ZRS** works well with L1-Capricorn timing his academic career and L1-Aquarius his political career.

L1 Scorpio 29 Dec 1856		
L1 Sagittarius 12 Oct 1871		1872 (no exact date), entered Davidson College to prepare for the ministry. L-2 Aquarius, Fall 1875 transferred to Princeton.
L1 Capricorn 10 Aug 1883		Fall 1883, Entered Johns Hopkins, Dept of History, Politics and Economics, enabled WW to study politics and government; 16-Sep-1883, proposed marriage to Ellen Axson who accepted; 24-Jan-1885, book on Congressional Government accepted, very successful; same day 24-Jan-1885, accepted offer to teach history and political science at newly established Bryn Mawr College; 24-Jun-1885, Married Ellen Louise Axson.
L2 Cancer 21 Oct 1892	FS	Princeton Professor throughout L1-Cancer. 1893, Published: *Division and Reunion. American history leading up to Civil War*. Claimed Civil War was fought more over states' rights and not over slavery, a popular theme at time of publication; 1893, Started writing *A Short History of the United States*.
L2 Cancer 9 Dec 1900	LB	9-Jun-1902, chosen President of Princeton University. 26-Oct-1902, inauguration as President of Princeton.
L2 Capricorn 26 Jan 1909	CP	10-May-1909, Wilson received letter announcing a $500K gift to the graduate school by Proctor with the gift contingent on a site satisfactory to Proctor, a blow to Wilson; end-May-1909, made speech stating that wealth was a danger to education; Dec-1909, proposed graduate college locations not acceptable to Proctor; 14-Apr-1909; trustees defeated Wilson's Graduate School plan in favor of Proctor.
L1 Aquarius 22 Mar 1910		18-May-1910, death of Chauncey Wyman with gift of $2-4 million sealed Graduate College plans in mold of West's design. Wilson stayed on 'to prevent the demoralization of Princeton but made gracious surrender. Sep-1910, nominated Democratic candidate for Governor; 8-Nov-1910, elected Governor of NY in a Progressive electoral sweep; 2-Jul-1912, Democratic Presidential Nominee.
L2 Leo 4 Apr 1919	FS	3-Apr-1919 (day before) violently ill with vomiting, diarrhea, severe pain, stroke speculated; 4-Apr-1919, yielded to British and French demands that no monetary or time limit be placed on German reparations. This is the point where the Peace Conference turned nasty and vindictive; 28-Jul-1919, Treaty of Versailles signed; 10-Jul-1919, submitted Treaty of Versailles and proposed League of Nations to the Senate; 19-Nov-1920, League of Nations Treaty voted down in the Senate.
L2 Scorpio 12 Feb 1923		3-Feb-1924, death.

Firdaria – Jupiter major and minor periods

Firdaria according to Bonatti	Life Event
Moon **Jupiter** 26 Jul 1859	6-Nov-1860, Lincoln elected President, WW's earliest recollection that after the election that 'there will be war.'
Saturn **Jupiter** 26 Jul 1867	1868, election of James McCosh as Princeton President brought great changes.
Jupiter 12 years Age 20 to 32	
Jupiter Jupiter 28 Dec 1876	Jan-1877, won 2nd prize for oratorical contest, Princeton; 1877/1878, managing editor for Princetonian newspaper.
Jupiter Mars 16 Sep 1878	Fall-1879, entered UVA Law School; Apr-1880, won Orator's Medal.
Jupiter Sun 03 Jun 1880	25-Dec-1880, quit UVA and returned home suddenly.
Jupiter Venus 19 Feb 1882	Oct-1882, admitted to the Georgia bar; Feb-1883, decided to give up law practice and seek an academic career; 8-Apr-1883, met wife-to-be Ellen Axson; Fall-1883, entered Johns Hopkins Department of History.
Jupiter Mercury 07 Nov 1883	24-Jan-1885, *Congressional Government* published, accepted offer to teach history and political science at Bryn Mawr College; 24-Jun-1885, married Ellen Axson.
Jupiter Moon 25 Jul 1885	15-Sep-1885, began teaching at Bryn Mawr College.
Jupiter Saturn 12 Apr 1887	Jun-1888, left Bryn Mawr for Wesleyan.
Mars **Jupiter** 29 Dec 1894	1895/1896, worked punishing schedule for extra income to pay for house for which he miscalculated the mortgage interest; 10-Oct-1895, began 1st of 18 trips to deliver popular lectures under the auspices of the Brooklyn Institute of Arts and Sciences and the American Society for the Extension of University Teaching.
Sun **Jupiter** 20 Feb 1908	Oct-1908, preached New Morality to American Bankers Association; end-May-1909, Wilson's speech on danger of wealth to education became national sensation; followed Proctor's gift of 500,000 to the graduate college.
Venus **Jupiter** 26 Jul 1915	6-Oct-1915, engagement to Edith Bolling; 15-Mar-1916, Pershing invaded Mexico after Pancho Villa killed 17 Americans; 1-May-1916, Marines landed in Dominican Republic; 3-Jun-1916, National Defense Act; 16-Jun-1916, Nominated for President.

Jupiter as Victor. Jupiter's Major Firdaria period captured Wilson's academic student days, his teaching career at Bryn Mawr, Wesleyan, and public lectures in 1895/96. Sun-Jupiter turned Wilson into a moral crusader. He was nominated for President under Venus-Jupiter at the time when the Progressive Movement favored reformers in elected office.

Transits

26-May-1906. *tr South Node trine ASC*.
Major stroke, 28-May.

30-Jun-1912. *tr North Node 10th from MC*.
Nominated for President, 2-Jul.

15-Sep-1915. *tr North Node trine ASC*.
Confessed affair to Edith Bolling, 19-Sep.

23-Feb-1917. *tr South Node conj MC*.
Received Zimmerman letter, 25-Feb.

4-Apr-1917. *tr South Node 10th from ASC*.
War Declaration, 2-Apr; Congress passed war measure, 4/6-Apr.

Solar Arc Directions

16-Jun-1902. *dsa Jupiter sextile MC*.
Selected President of Princeton University, 9-June.

21-Jun-1914. *dsa Venus opposed ASC*.
Kaiser reopened Kiel Canal, 23-Jun.

LOCK 28-Jun-1914. *dsa Mars opposed ASC*.
Assassination of Archduke Ferdinand triggered outbreak of WWI, 28-Jun.

23-Nov-1914. *dsa Mercury trine MC*.
Evacuation of US troops from Vera Cruz, Mexico, 23-Nov.

6-Feb-1915. *dsa Vertex conj Saturn*.
Film *Birth of a Nation* released, favorable to KKK, 7-Feb.

Primary Direction Sequences

PT	D	Jupiter/Taurus	P	dexter sextile MC c. => Saturn (SA)	8-Mar-1914
PT	D	Jupiter/Taurus	P	dexter sextile MC c. => Saturn (0)	7-Apr-1914
REG	D	Jupiter/Taurus	P	dexter textile MC c. => Saturn (SA)	21-Apr-1914
REG	D	Jupiter/Taurus	P	dexter textile MC c. => Saturn (0)	25-May-1914

This pair of sequences covered the climax of American military intervention in Mexico under the military rule of Huerta. In early March 1914, civil unrest in Mexico had reached an action point. On 9-Mar, New Mexico Senator Albert Fall advocated in the Senate to send Army and Navy forces into Mexico to protect American and foreign interests. The Tampico Incident of 9-Apr, when Mexican authorities mistakenly detained US

Marines on the mainland looking for provisions, triggered President Wilson's decision to send US Naval forces to Tampico Bay where they arrived 19-Apr. Huerta severed diplomatic ties with the US on 22-Apr. As the sequence concluded, Pancho Villa's victories had sufficiently weakened Huerta's forces that news reports were rife with Huerta's departure. Huerta resigned on 15-Jul-1914.

| PT | D | Jupiter/Taurus | P | sinister trine Mercury (ME) c. => MC | 18-Jan-1919 |
| PT | D | Jupiter/Taurus | P | sinister trine Mercury (0) c. => MC | 1-Sep-1919 |

LOCK This sequence timed the exact start of the Paris Peace Conference on 18-Jan and the beginning of Wilson's American tour to support the League of Nations on 3-Sep. Mercury signifies negotiations and speeches; in the sign of Capricorn related to class and status; in the 4th of real estate Mercury is first tied to establishing territorial boundaries at the end of WWI; in the 4th of the homeland, a US speaking tour.

REG	D	Mercury/Aries	P	DSC d. => Venus (0)	25-Jan-1919
REG	D	Mercury/Aries	P	DSC d. => Mars (0)	31-Jan-1919
REG	D	Mercury/Aries	P	DSC d. => Venus (VE)	10-Feb-1919
REG	D	Mercury/Aries	P	DSC d. => Mars (MA)	10-Feb-1919

LOCK This sequence is an example of how a solar arc direction marking an *external* event is ultimately fed through the nativity through the same direction by primary motion. (See Chapter 10, pps. 161-162). As stated earlier, on 28-Jun-1914, solar arc Mars opposed natal ASC timed the outbreak of WWI. Now by primary direction, Wilson now faces the same set of belligerents across the table at the Paris Peace Conference. As before, the results are unfavorable. On 25-Jan, the Conference voted for a League of Nations. But as the sequence closed on 11-Feb, Wilson was asked by the Yugoslavians to arbitrate a dispute with the Italians over the Adriatic question. The Italians rejected Wilson's authority in this issue on 18-Feb and later threatened to withdraw from the Conference on 21-Mar in a dispute over Fiume. The situation was so bad the entire Conference nearly broke up on 28-Mar as each man threatened to resign.

PT	D	Mercury/Taurus	P	Vertex c. => Saturn (SA)	17-Sep-1919
PT	D	Mercury/Taurus	P	Vertex c. => Saturn (0)	17-Oct-1919
REG	D	Mercury/Taurus	P	Vertex c. => Saturn (SA)	13-Nov-1919
REG	D	Mercury/Taurus	P	Vertex c. => Saturn (0)	17-Dec-1919

Saturn/Cancer/10th ruling the 5th signifies uncompromising diplomacy which ruined Wilson's career and reputation. These directions timed Wilson's crippling stroke (25-Sep), a secondary stroke (2-Oct), and the US Senate's rejection of the League of Nations Treaty (19-Nov). As the sequence closed, the Supreme Council sent Germany its ultimatum about acceptance of the Conference's protocol. Ultimately, harsh terms accorded to Germany sowed the seeds for WWII.

Longevity, 67y 1m 5d

Death: 3-Feb-1924, 11:15 AM, Washington DC, at home. After his crippling strokes suffered in the fall of 1919, Wilson was a functional invalid. He suffered indigestion on 31-Jan-1924, grew weaker, and died soon after.

Hīlāj: **Sun**. Figure is nocturnal but Moon/5th/masculine sign is disqualified because of the sex of her sign. Sun/4th/5th/feminine sign qualifies. Empirical evidence supports the Sun as Hīlāj:

REG	D	Venus/Pisces	P	dexter trine Saturn (0) d. => Sun	23-Feb-1919
REG	D	Venus/Pisces	P	dexter trine Saturn (SA) d. => Sun	4-Jun-1919

Influenza and speculation of minor stroke, 3/7-Apr-1919.

A similar Saturn-Sun primary direction sequence was active in the time leading up to death (see below).

Al-kadukhadāh: **Jupiter**. Jupiter is the Sun's bound ruler, is the most dignified planet in the figure, and aspects the Sun by square aspect. Jupiter gives his 79 major years, augmented an additional 25% by conjunction to the North Node. Saturn squares and deducts his 30 minor years. The aspect from Mars and Venus is tricky because of competing receptions and a sextile aspect which is outside the moiety of orb. In particular, Jupiter receives both Mars and Venus by bound which appears to nullify the ability of either planet to modify years despite the fact that (1) Mars receives Jupiter by sign and (2) Venus's classification as a benefic and should allow Venus to add years by sextile aspect without the requirement of reception.

JU (79) + NN (+25%) - SA (30) = 68.75 years

Victor of the Horoscope: **Jupiter**

Killing Planets: **Saturn (53), Mercury (37)**

Arcus Vitae:

PT	D	Mars/Pisces	P	opposition LOF d. => Mercury (ME)	3-Sep-1919
REG	D	Mars/Pisces	P	opposition LOF d. => Mercury (ME)	13-Oct-1919

Mercury signifies speech and kills by stroke. On 3-Sep, Wilson began his speaking tour in support of the League of Nations. He suffered strokes on 25-Sep and 2-Oct. (See also Saturn-Vertex and Mercury-MC directions, prior page).

PT	D	Venus/Taurus	P	sinister trine Sun c. => Saturn (SA)	22-Dec-1923
PT	D	Venus/Taurus	P	sinister trine Sun c. => Saturn (0)	20-Jan-1924

The arcus vitae joins the high scoring killing planet with the Hīlāj. The same directions computed via Regiomontanus fall a few months later.

1923 Solar Return for year of Death

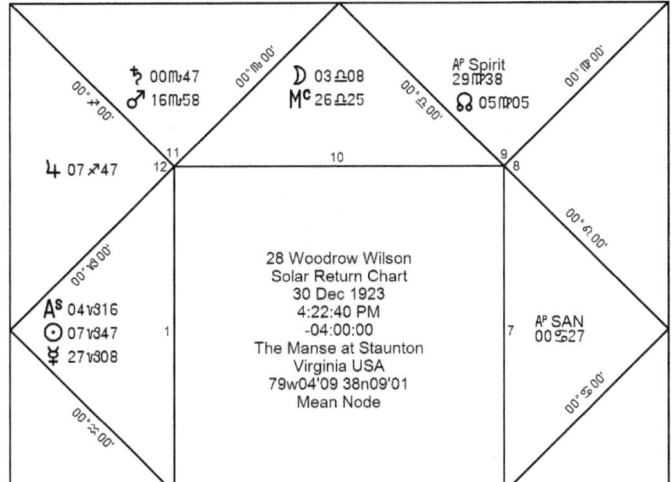

Ascendant Distributor: Jupiter/Sagittarius since 4-Aug-1912
Profected Ascendant: 15TA24, 8th House; Victor: Mars
Lords: LOY – Venus; LOP – Venus
Firdaria: Mercury-Saturn
Moon: applies to trine of Venus
Return Ascendant falls in natal 4th; Natal Ascendant falls in return's 10th

Both profected Ascendant in the 8th of death and the return's Ascendant falling in the natal 4th end-of-life are two configurations which suggest risk of death. Sun, Lord of the 8th of death, falls in the return's 1st of the physical body. Lord of Year Venus returns to her natal sign as does Mercury who is the second high scoring killer after Saturn. Primary killer Saturn transits natal Moon at the superior square, exact within 2 minutes of degree. On day of death, tr Mercury 18CP12 was just a few minutes shy of a perfect Mercury return at 18CP46.

Wilson died shortly after these two directions which link high scoring killers Saturn and Mercury to the solar return Ascendant.

| PT | D | Mars/Capricorn | P | Mercury (0) d. => ASC | 21-Jan-1924 |
| PT | D | Mercury/Aquarius | P | sin square Saturn (0) d. => Saturn | 24-Jan-1924 |

612 A RECTIFICATION MANUAL

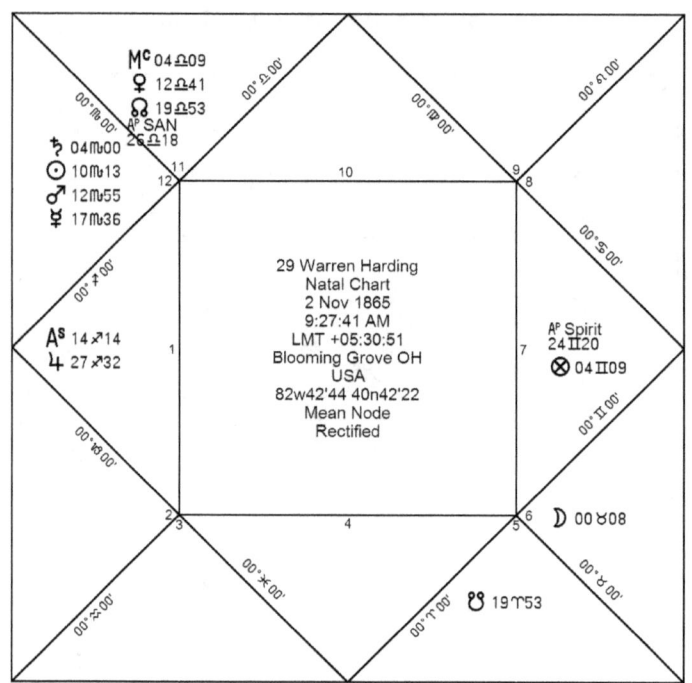

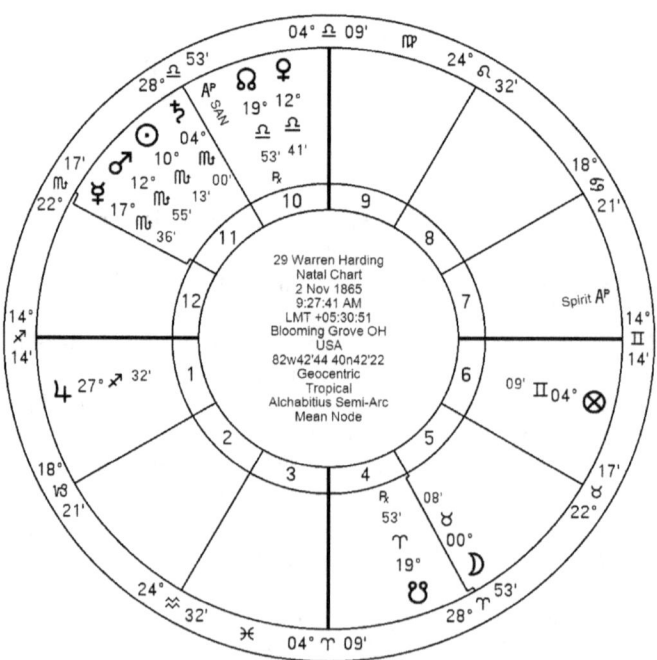

Moon's Configuration

Moon applies to **Saturn**, diurnal, conjunctional.
Prenatal syzygy is 26LI18. Eclipse? **YES**. Annular Solar Eclipse.

Cognitive Assessment Model (Rulers of Moon and Mercury)

Sign rulers: **Venus, Mars**
Bound rulers: **Venus, Mercury**

Victor Soul Models

Ibn Ezra Victor Model (1507), in-sect triplicity ruler, triplicity decans.

	Position	☉	☽	☿	♀	♂	♃	♄
Sun	10 SC 13				5	5	1	
Moon	00 TA 08		4		11			
Asc	14 SA 14	3			2	1	5	
Pars Fortuna	04 GE 09			8				3
Syzygy	26 LI 18 (SE)			1	7			7
Oriental						0	0	0
Houses			8	7	2	11	8	12	8
Score		0	11	11	11	**36**	14	18	18

Porphyry's Expanded Victor Model (2022)

Venus rules the MC, Moon, and syzygy by sign; the ASC, Moon, Sun, and syzygy by bound. Sect: out-of-favor. Solar phase: oriental from 1st direct station to sinking. Dignity: sign. Conjunct North Node.

Victor Table for Killing Planets

			☉	☽	☿	♀	♂	♃	♄
ASC		14SA14	3			2	1	5,3	3
Rul ASC	♃	27SA32	3,1				2	5,3	3
L.Death		22CP13		3	1	3	4,3		5,2
Rul L.Death	♄	4SC00		3		3	5,3,2,1		
H8 Cusp		18CA21	5,3	2		3	3,1	4	
Rul H8	☽	00TA08		5,4		5,3,2,1	3		
T-Rul H8	♀	12LI41		3,2	5			3	4,3,1
8th from ☉		10GE13		5,3	1			3,2	3
Rul 8th fr ☉	☿	17SC36		3	2	3	5,3	1	
TOTAL			7	24	18	**31**	**36**	29	24

2007 Proposed Rectification: 9:27:41 AM, ASC 14SA14'56"
2022 Proposed Rectification: 9:27:41 AM, ASC 14SA14'58"

Astrodatabank reports an A-rated birth time of 2:30 PM based on a secondhand account from a Harding personal letter. The time is consistent with a horoscope described by biographer Carl Anthony (1998, 173-176) in his study of the President's wife, Florence Harding, who used astrology actively and obtained several readings from Marcia Champney. Based on Anthony's recreated conversation between Harding and Champney, the description of Warren Harding's figure with Sun and Mars conjunct in the 8th house is consistent with the 2:00 p.m. time. DeGregorio (2001, 433) differs by stating Harding was born in the morning but with no attribution.

Despite a substantial departure from ADB, the 2007 proposed rectification continues to hold up well. New highlights: (1) The sweep of the natal profected Ascendant in a 12-year cycle accurately identified key revelations of Harding administration scandals in the year 1924 following Harding's death when the profected Ascendant contacted the Scorpio stellium in the 12th house. (2) **ZRS**. Both sets of L2 Capricorn and Aquarius FS-LB subperiods link related events as they should in ZR. See Chapter 9, Zodiacal Releasing, for a detailed case study of ZR using Warren Harding's horoscope, (pp. 151-155).

L1 Cancer 2 Nov 1865		
L2 Capricorn 20 Dec 1873	FS	Summer 1875, father acquired local newspaper, Harding taken in as printer.
L2 Capricorn 3 Mar 1883	LB	18-May-1884, father acquired half-interest in Marion STAR newspaper; May-1884, WH assumed editorship position of STAR newspaper.
L1 Leo 24 Jun 1890		During early L1-Leo years, WH's STAR newspaper expanded operations; 3-Jun-1893, STAR took over the city printing contract from a rival paper; 15-Jun-1895, STAR printed Industrial Edition, a successful 32-page supplement with lithographs of city landmarks and businesses.
L2 Aquarius 10 Oct 1898	FS	5-Jul-1899, announced bid for State Senator; 7-Nov-1899, won District election; 1-Jan-1900, inauguration.
L2 Aquarius 24 Oct 1907	LB	20-Nov-1907, endorsed Foraker for President; 22-Jan-1908, reversed and endorsed Taft over Foraker; 17-Sep-1908, Hearst published evidence of Foraker's improper relationship with Standard Oil; 3-Nov-1908, Taft won Presidential election; 29-Dec-1908, WH endorsed for Senator (does not win until 1914).
L1 Virgo 17 Mar 1909		L1-Virgo began with WH's promising bid for the 1910 Ohio gubernatorial race which he lost within the context of a 1910 Democratic political sweep which favored Progressive Movement politicians. Harding finally won a Senate seat in 1914 but is not remembered for any legislative achievements during WWI. L2-Aries included his 12-Jun-1920 Presidential nomination and L2-Taurus timed his Presidential election.
L2 Cancer 4 Dec 1922		2-Aug-1923, death.

Firdaria – Venus major and minor periods

Firdaria according to Bonatti	Life Event
Sun **Venus** 08 Apr 1867	Jun-1867, WH and sister Charity contracted whooping cough; 26-Apr-1868, sister Mary Clarissa born.
Venus 8 years Age 10 to 18	
Venus Venus 02 Nov 1875	Summer 1875, hired by father as printer for newly acquired newspaper Caledonia; 1876 (no date), sister Daisy born.
Venus Mercury 24 Dec 1876	
Venus Moon 14 Feb 1878	9-Nov-1878, death of siblings Charles & Persilla from childhood illness; jaundice possible cause.
Venus Saturn 08 Apr 1879	
Venus Jupiter 29 May 1880	1880 (no exact date), father Tryon lost money in speculations, forced to sell home and move to a farm; Autumn 1880, attended Iberia College.
Venus Mars 20 Jul 1881	Feb-1882, WH and classmate Frank Miller published college newspaper *Iberia Spectator* for 6 issues; Spring-1882, Graduated Iberia College; 1-Jul-1882, left home for Marion, starting out on his own.
Venus Sun 11 Sep 1882	Fall-1882, employed as teacher; also joined Huber Silver Band playing the cornet; 23-Feb-1883, Quit teaching job and tried reading law and insurance sales.
Mercury **Venus** 24 Dec 1894	1-Apr-1895, hired George H. Van Fleet to run advertising unit at STAR newspaper; 15-Jun-1895, STAR printed Industrial Edition, a successful 32-page supplement with lithographs of city landmarks and businesses.
Moon **Venus** 08 Apr 1903	4-Apr-1903 (4 days before period), selected Lieutenant Governor candidate by party bosses; Nov-1903, won election for Ohio Lieutenant Governor.
Saturn **Venus** 15 Feb 1912	14-Nov-1912, after Wilson Presidential win, WH received notice from Taft saying Harding's requested position as Japanese ambassador had already been filled.
Jupiter **Venus** 25 Dec 1921	1922, multiple events related to Teapot Dome scandal unfold; 18-Aug-1922, condemned butchery at Herrin Massacre (21-Jun); 1-Feb-1923, Charles Cramer resigned; 20-Jun-1923, Began western 'Voyage of Understanding'; 2-Aug-1923, death.

Venus as Victor. Venus captured Harding's entry to the newspaper business as an apprentice for his father, his first newspaper published during college years, and later with his own STAR newspaper launching its Industrial Edition in 1895. Moon-Venus timed Harding's first elected office. Saturn-Venus timed no significant event – in fact it timed a lost career opportunity (nature of Saturn as major ruler to inhibit ability of Venus as minor Firdaria ruler because Saturn and Venus are enemies). Finally, Jupiter-Venus captured the final two years of his Presidency marked by the Teapot Dome scandal and his sudden death from heart disease.

Venus/Libra is consistent with Harding's reputation as a harmonizer, cited as the reason for his 1920 Republican Presidential nomination.

Transits

<u>6-Apr-1885</u>. *tr North Node conj MC.*
Launched Weekly edition of *STAR*, Jun-1885.

<u>18-Nov-1903</u>. *tr North Node conj MC.*
Left for Kellogg Battle Creek Sanitarium, 19-Nov. Stayed one week.

<u>18-May-1910</u>. trSaturn conj Moon.
Death of mother, 20-May-1910.

<u>20-Mar-1914</u>. *trSouth Node 10th from ASC.*
Ohio Senator Burton announced no re-election bid, open to Harding, 8-Apr.

<u>13-Nov-1918</u>. *trSouth Node conj DSC.*
Wife ill with kidney inflammation, 11-Nov to end of month.

Solar Arc Directions

LOCK <u>7-Aug-1891</u>. *dsa MC opposed Moon*
Marriage to Florence King, 8-Jul-1891.

LOCK <u>10-Jul-1899</u>. *dsa Sun conj ASC*
<u>3-Feb-1900</u>. *csa ASC conj Sun*
  Announced candidacy for State Senator, 5-Jul-1899.
  Won local Caucus, 15/16-Jul-1899.
  Won District election, 7-Nov-1899 [see Sun-MC primary direction below].
  Inaugurated State Senator for Ohio, 1-Jan-1890.

<u>21-Jul-1901</u>. *dsa MC conj Sun*
<u>10-Mar-1902</u>. *csa Sun conj MC*
  Renominated for State Senate position by acclamation, rare event, most senators were not re-elected, Jul-1901 (no exact date).
  Inaugurated State Senator, selected as Republican floor leader, 6-Jan-1902.

LOCK <u>22-May-1910</u>. *csa Moon opposed ASC*
Death of mother Phoebe Dickerson, 20-May-1910.

<u>29-Jan-1919</u>. *dsa Sun sq MC*
LOCK <u>11-Jun-1920</u>. *csa MC sq Sun*
  Unexpected death of TR left void in Republican Party, 6-Jan-1919.
  Ohio Republican machine supported WH for President; he is more interested in Senate seat, Jan-1919.
  Nominated as Republican candidate for President, 12-Jun-1920.

29. WARREN HARDING

Primary Directions

| PT | D | Venus/Scorpio | P | Sun d. => MC | 3-Nov-1899 |

LOCK Won first political election, Ohio state Senator, 3-Nov.

| REG | D | Venus/Sagittarius | P | ASC d. => Sun | 13-Jan-1906 |

LOCK Boss Cox supported Herrick as candidate for Governor in order to squash to Harding's 6-Jan-06 comment that he would only be a candidate for Governor; not Lieutenant Governor, 15-Jan.

| REG | D | Venus/Aquarius | P | sin square Sun d. => ASC | 20-Aug-1920 |

Received Fellowcraft degree from Mason Lodge of Marion, 13-Aug.

Primary Direction Sequences

| PT | D | Venus/Aquarius | P | sin trine Venus (VE) d. => ASC | 2-Jun-1920 |
| PT | D | Venus/Aquarius | P | sin trine Venus (0) d. => ASC | 12-Jun-1922 |

LOCK Nominated for President as a harmonizer, 12-Jun-1920.
LOCK Received honorary doctorate degree from Princeton, 6-Jun-1922.

| PT | D | Venus/Aquarius | P | sin square Mars (MA) d. => ASC | 10-Jul-1922 |
| PT | D | Venus/Aquarius | P | sin square Mars (0) d. => ASC | 13-Aug-1922 |

UMW leader Lewis rejected Harding's request for UMW to work temporarily under terms of prior labor contracts, 10-Jul.
Herrin Massacre of strike-breakers in coal industry, 21-Jun.
Condemned Herrin butchery and growing lawlessness of UMW and other strikes, 18-Aug.

| PT | D | Jupiter/Leo | P | dex sq Saturn (SA) c. => MC | 3-Oct-1922 |
| PT | D | Jupiter/Leo | P | dex sq Saturn (0) c. => MC | 27-Apr-1923 |

LOCK Veteran's Administration scandal under Forbes broke.
Doc Sawyer publicly criticized Forbes, Oct-1922.
WH ordered Perryville shipments stopped, 24-Nov-1922.
Veterans Department reorganized, 31-Jan-1923.
Charles Cramer resigned, 1-Feb-1923.
Charles Forbes resigned, 15-Feb-1923.
Charles Cramer committed suicide, 14-Mar-1923.

Longevity: 58y 8m 27d

Death: 1-Aug-1923, 7:32 PM, San Francisco, CA. Harding died from heart disease complicated by pneumonia. Reports of either ptomaine food poisoning and/or poisoning by his wife have been proposed and disputed.

Hīlāj: **Sun/SAN**. This is a strange case with both luminaries are succedent by quadrant signs yet cadent by whole signs. More unusual is recognition that the SAN was a solar eclipse. Recent research shows when the SAN is an eclipse it usually trumps all other candidates as the Hīlāj.

Evidence for the Sun as Hīlāj: The configuration of killing planets in the solar return for year of death favor the Sun as Hīlāj.

Evidence for the SAN as Hīlāj: Three examples of Harding's trips to the Battle Creek Sanitarium for nervous disorders consistently demonstrate the conjunctional degree as Hīlāj:

7-Nov-1889. c. prog. Mars 26LI29 – conjunct SAN.
7-Jan-1894. tr. Saturn 24LI33 conjunct SAN; tr. Nodes opposed natal Nodes.
19-Nov-1903. c. tr. Sun-Venus-Jupiter all conjunct SAN.

In addition, the solar returns preceding each of these events show the conjunctional degree afflicted by malefics or emphasized in other ways.

Al-kadukhadāh: **Moon**. If the SAN is hīlāj, then Venus should be the giver of years. Yet Venus' years amplified by the North Node are too many. If the Sun is the hīlāj, there are two options. One is to take the Moon in her exaltation as the Sun's triplicity ruler. Moon grants her 108 years, conjunction to South Node just inside 12 degrees deducts 25%, opposition from Saturn deducts 30 years; net projection is 51 years. A second approach is unconventional. Consider the Sun as giver of years and deduct minor years for Mercury, Mars, and Saturn which besiege the Sun. Net projection is 55 years.

Victor of the Horoscope: **Venus**

Killing Planets: **Mars (36), Venus (31), Jupiter (29)**

Arcus Vitae:

| PT | D | Mercury/Sagittarius | P | dex trine SN d. => SAN | 29-Jul-1923 |

Arrived San Francisco, met by heart specialist, fever 102, pulse 120. Died, 2-Aug-1923, 7:32 PM.

| REG | D | Venus/Scorpio | P | Sun c. => Jupiter (JU) | 19-Aug-1923 |

Recapitulates the Sun-Jupiter conjunction in the solar return for death.

1922 Solar Return for year of Death

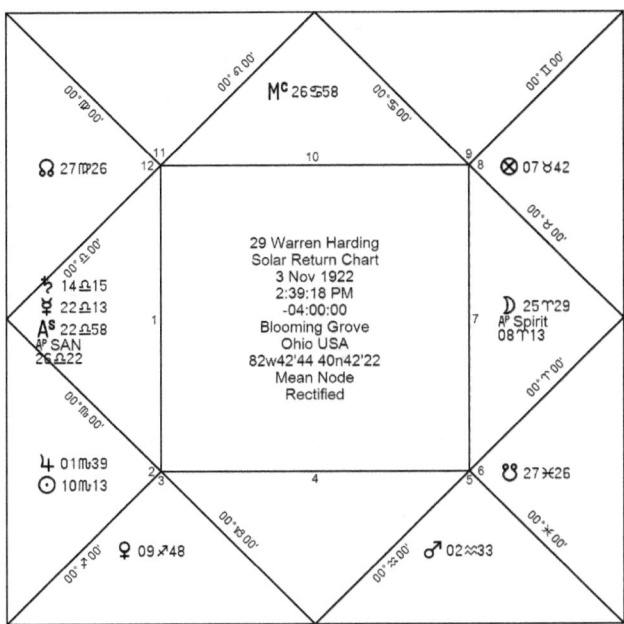

Ascendant Distributor: Jupiter/Aquarius since 2-Sep-1922
Profected Ascendant: 14VI18, 10th house; SR Victor: Venus
Lords; LOY – Mercury; LOP – Mercury
Firdaria: Jupiter-Venus
Moon: separates from opposition to Mercury and is void of course
Return Ascendant falls in natal 11th; Natal Ascendant falls in return's 3rd

Ascendant 22LI58 is near the Conjunctional degree (26LI18) and falls in the natal 10th house. Mercury & Saturn are conjunct the return's Ascendant and fall in the natal 10th. Mercury & Saturn are combust in the natal – they are hidden – in the return they are out in the open. Shows revelation of secret dealings by friends/alliances/Cabinet members which caused depression (sr 1st house placement) and a damaged reputation (natal 10th house transit).

High scoring killers Jupiter and Mars afflict the Sun by conjunction and square. They suggest the Sun participates with the conjunctional degree as Hīlāj. The Jupiter-Sun conjunction in the return recapitulates the arcus vitae. The following directions link the two high scoring killers with the Ascendant.

| PT | D | Mars/Capricorn | P | opposition Mars d. => ASC | 22-Jul-1923 |
| PT | D | Jupiter/Sagittarius | P | dexter trine Venus d. => ASC | 1-Aug-1923 |

620 — A RECTIFICATION MANUAL

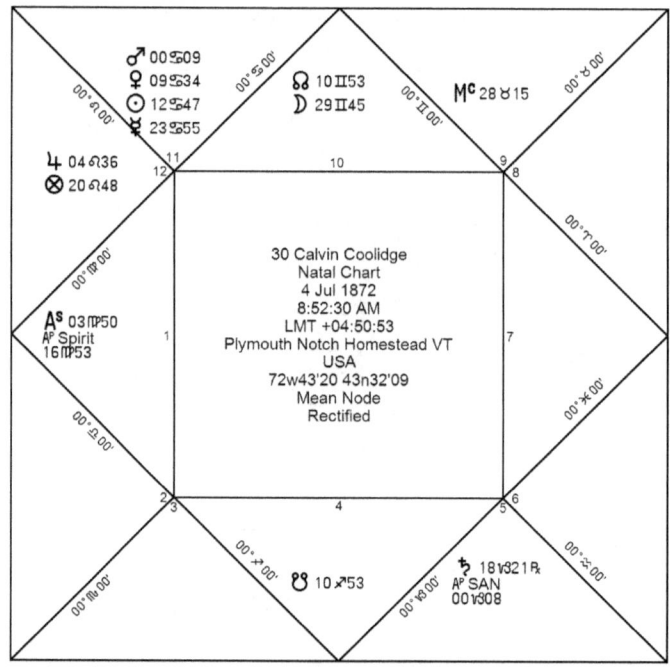
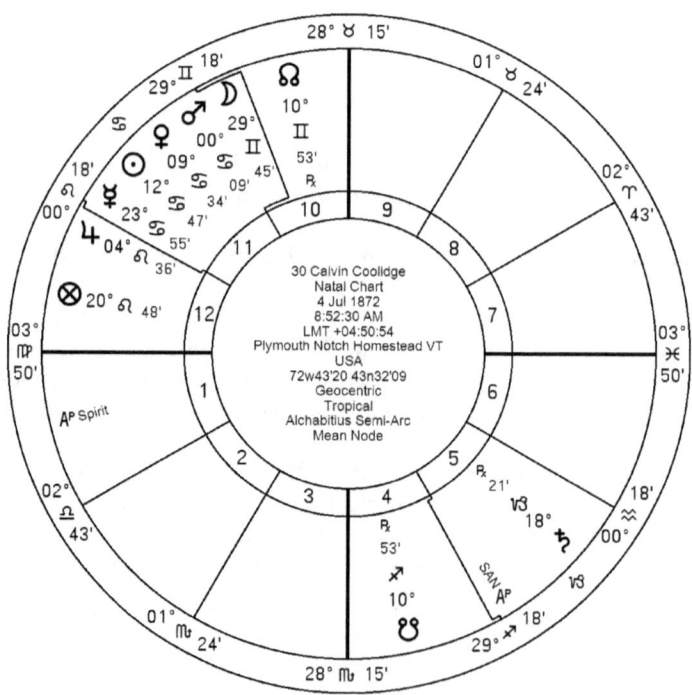

30. CALVIN COOLIDGE

Moon's Configuration

Moon separates from **Jupiter** and is **VOC** (Medieval) or applies to **Mars** (Hellenistic), diurnal, preventional.
Prenatal syzygy is 00CP08. Eclipse? No.

Cognitive Assessment Model (Rulers of Moon and Mercury)

Sign rulers: **Mercury, (Moon), Saturn**
Bound rulers: **Saturn, Jupiter**

Victor Soul Models

Ibn Ezra Victor Model (1507), in-sect triplicity ruler, triplicity decans.

	Position	☉	☽	☿	♀	♂	♃	♄
Sun	12 CA 47		5		5	1	4	
Moon	29 GE 45			5				6
Asc	03 VI 50			12	3			
Pars Fortuna	20 LE 48	8		2		1		
Syzygy	00 CP 08			2	3	4		6
Oriental						0	0	1
Houses			8	8	8	8	8	2	7
Score		0	16	13	**29**	19	14	6	20

Porphyry's Expanded Victor Model (2022)

Mercury rules the ASC, Moon, and Lot of Spirit by sign; the ASC, Lot of Fortune, and syzygy by bound. Sect: of-favor. Solar phase: occidental direct under the sunbeams.

Victor Table for Killing Planets

			☉	☽	☿	♀	♂	♃	♄
ASC		03VI50		3	5,4,2,1	3	3		
Rul ASC	☿	23CA55		5,3		3	3	4,2,1	
L.Death		21LI19			3,1	5,2		3	4,3
Rul L.Death	♀	9CA34		5,3,1		3,2	3	4	
H8 Cusp		2AR43	4,3				5,1	3,2	3
Rul H8	♂	00CA09		5,3,1		3	3,2	4	
T-Rul H8	☉	12CA47		5,3		3,2	3,1	4	
8th from ☉		12AQ47			3,1	2		3	5,3
Rul 8th fr ☉	♄	18CP21		3		3,2,1	4,3		5
TOTAL			7	**40**	20	**34**	**31**	30	23

2007 Proposed Rectification: 8:52:30 AM, ASC 3VI50'39"

Astrodatabank reports a C-rated birth time of 9:00 AM. The proposed rectification is 8 minutes earlier.

In reviewing this rectification for the 4th edition, transits to the angles for the Boston Police strike which elevated Coolidge to national attention remain one of the most important examples of transits in the Presidential database. As for directions, I have chosen to present a slightly different set of primary directions which focus on the Sun as significator for national political leaders.

ZRS. Other than the final L1-Capricorn period which timed Coolidge's decision to not run for re-election, other L1 periods do not provide overwhelming evidence in favor of ZR's ability to divide Coolidge's life into chapters. Coolidge's political rise was slow and steady with few setbacks.

L1 Virgo 4 Jul 1872		
L2 Pisces 15 Sep 1881	FS	No events found.
L2 Pisces 2 Nov 1889	LB	6-Mar-1890, sister Abigail died, probable cause: appendicitis; 23-May-1890, graduated from High School; Autumn 1890, took Amherst entrance exam.
L1 Libra 21 Mar 1892		L1-Libra began with the spring term of CC's freshman year at Amherst. It included his Amherst years, his legal studies, and election as City Solicitor on 18-Jan-1900 as the period closed.
L1 Scorpio 8 Feb 1900		L1-Scorpio timed a slow and steady political progression which concluded with his 3-Nov-1914 re-election as State Senator and President of the State Senate.
L1 Sagittarius 22 Nov 1914		L1-Sagittarius marked an unabated rise to national political office: 2-Nov-1915, elected MA Lieutenant-Governor; 11-Sep-1919, elected MA Governor; 2-Nov-1920, elected Vice-President; 3-Aug-1923, accession to Presidency on the death of Harding.
L1 Capricorn 20 Sep 1926		L1-Capricorn included CC's 2-Aug-1927 decision to not run for re-election and his life as a private citizen, author, and newspaper columnist.
L2 Aries 21 May 1932		5-Jan-1933, death.

Firdaria – Mercury major and minor periods

Firdaria according to Bonatti	Life Event
Sun **Mercury** 13 May 1875	No events found.
Venus **Mercury** 26 Aug 1883	No events found.
Mercury 13 years Age 18 to 31	
Mercury Mercury 04 Jul 1890	17-Sep-1891, entered Amherst College.
Mercury Moon 13 May 1892	No events found.
Mercury Saturn 22 Mar 1894	26-Jun-1895, graduated Amherst College; 23-Sep-1895, read law with Hammond & Field.
Mercury Jupiter 29 Jan 1896	2-Jul-1897, admitted to bar in Northampton.
Mercury Mars 07 Dec 1897	1-Feb-1898, opened private law practice; 6-Dec-1898, won first election, City Council.
Mercury Sun 17 Oct 1899	18-Jan-1900, elected City Solicitor.
Mercury Venus 26 Aug 1901	4-Jun-1903, appointed Clerk of Courts of Hampshire County.
Moon **Mercury** 23 Mar 1911	7-Nov-1911, elected State Senator, Chair of Committees on Legal Affairs and Agriculture.
Saturn **Mercury** 13 May 1920	18-May-1920, death of stepmother Carrie, great loss; 12-Jun-1920, nominated as VP for Republican ticket; 2-Nov-1920, elected VP; 4-Mar-1921, inauguration.
Jupiter **Mercury** 14 May 1930	1-Jul-1930, debut of syndicated newspaper column.

Mercury as Victor. Mercury captured Coolidge's early legal career, successful entry to elected politics, Vice Presidential inauguration, and launch of his syndicated newspaper column following his presidency.

Coolidge's nickname 'Silent Cal' is consistent with traditional aphorisms that classify Mercury in water signs as mute.

Transits

15-Jun-1897. *tr Jupiter conj ASC.*
Applied to Bar 29-Jun, admitted 2-Jul.

2-Oct-1914. *tr South Node conj ASC.*
After re-election to State Senate and President of same body, became more conservative in legislative goals, 3-Nov.

11-Sep-1919. *tr Mercury conj ASC.*
11-Sep-1919. *tr Saturn conj ASC.*
12-Sep-1919. *tr South Node conj MC.*
Following the Boston Police strike of 9 September, Coolidge called out the National Guard to assume control of the force on 11 September. On 13 September, a telegram published in newspapers stated *"There is no right to strike against the public safety by anybody, anywhere, anytime"* (Sobel 1998, 144). This elevated Coolidge to national fame. See Chapter 15: *Transits* for further discussion.

22-Jan-1924. *tr North Node conj ASC.*
Doheny testified on Albert Fall bribe in Teapot Dome scandal, 24-Jan.

1-Jan-1929. *tr North Node conj MC.*
Signed Kellogg-Briand Pact, 17-Jan.

Solar Arc Directions

10-Jan-1919. *dsa ASC square Saturn.*
Death of Theodore Roosevelt, 6-Jan.

24-Jan-1919. *dsa MC conj Sun.*
Death of TR left Republican void which favored Coolidge as a rising star.

28-Oct-1924. *dsa MC opposed Saturn.*
Death of Agriculture Secretary Henry Wallace, 25-Oct.

31-Jul-1930. *dsa MC conj Mercury.*
Syndicated newspaper column *Calvin Coolidge Speaks* appeared on 1-Jul.

Primary Directions

| REG | D | Mars/Taurus | P | MC c. => Sun | 21-Jun-1918 |

LOCK Announced candidacy for Governor, 23-Jun.

30. CALVIN COOLIDGE

| PT | D | Mars/Taurus | P | MC c. => Sun | 25-Nov-1918 |

Elected Governor of Massachusetts, 5-Nov.

| PT | D | Venus/Cancer | P | Sun d. => MC | 2-Jun-1920 |

LOCK Nominated for Vice President at RNC, 12-Jun.

| PT | D | Mercury/Libra | P | sin square Sun d. => ASC | 9-Feb-1923 |

Charles Cramer resigned, counsel for Veterans Bureau, 1-Feb.
This action set into motion the unraveling of the 'Harding Scandals' which were a key stressor in the time period leading up to President Harding's unexpected death in office on 2-Aug.

This direction is a reminder the Sun rules the 12th of secret enemies and mistakes. Based on primary directions, this is the most powerful direction which led to Coolidge's ascent to the Presidency after Harding's death. Beyond directions, the Firdaria time lord changeover to Major Jupiter on 4-Jul-1923 is also a key time lord change. Jupiter/Leo signifies moral authority and as Mercury's bound lord extends its influence via the Cognitive Assessment Model. Jupiter/Leo conjunct the Lot of Fortune in the 12th can be delineated as the purification of scandal though Jupiter's moral authority which is one interpretation of the Coolidge presidency.

| PT | D | Mercury/Virgo | P | ASC d. => Sun | 9-Mar-1930 |

Coolidge dedicated the Coolidge Dam, 4-Mar.

Primary Direction Sequences

| PT | D | Mercury/Taurus | P | dex sextile Sun c. => Mars (MA) | 20-Jun-1919 |
| PT | D | Mercury/Taurus | P | dex sextile Sun c. => Mars (0) | 5-Sep-1919 |

This sequence timed the period leading up to the Boston Police Strike of 9-Sep. One of the precursor events was formation of a union for police officers on 15-Aug-1919. The police, like many workers throughout the country, protested low real wages which were a consequence of high inflation caused by the WWI commodity boom.

| PT | D | Venus/Pisces | P | DSC d. => Saturn (SA) | 10-Jul-1924 |
| REG | D | Venus/Pisces | P | DSC d. => Saturn (SA) | 12-May-1926 |

LOCK Death of son, 7-Jul-1924.
Death of father, 18-May-1926. Or consider the next direction:

| PT | D | Venus/Capricorn | P | Saturn (0) d. => IC | 25-May-1926 |

Longevity, 60y 6m 2d

Death: 5-Jan-1933, about 12:45 PM, Northampton, Massachusetts, at home. Discovered dead on floor in home, unexpected heart attack.

Hīlāj: **Sun**. Figure is diurnal and Sun in 11th qualifies.

Al-kadukhadāh: **Mercury**. In the position of the Sun, Venus scores +6 in essential dignities, beating out Jupiter with a score of +5; yet Venus is combust moving fast into the beams and unusable. Jupiter's major 79 years do not match Coolidge's longevity. Mercury as victor, occidental and moving fast away from the Sun's beams, is the logical Al-kadukhadāh candidate. Mercury grants his 76 major years. Opposition from Saturn deducts Saturn's 30 minor years. Net projection of 46 years is too short.

ME (76) - SA (30) = 46

For Coolidge, the longevity model fails.

Consider as an alternate al-kadukhadāh the Sun with Coolidge living out 60 years, which is one-half the Sun's 120 major years.

Victor: **Mercury**

Killing Planets: **Moon (40), Venus (34), Mars (31)**

Arcus Vitae:

With death from a sudden heart attack, the obvious track is to determine how the Sun is afflicted on a dynamic basis. For Coolidge, the easiest solution is the following solar arc pair with the first arc triggered by transit at death:

25-Jan-1933. *dsa Sun square Nodes.*
20-Feb-1933. *csa Nodes square Sun.*

5-Jan-1933. *tr South Node 10VI39 square natal Nodes.*

Note by direct solar arc, the 25-Jan-1933 measurement moves the directed Sun to 10VI49. This is very close to the position of tr South Node at death.

By comparison, the same Sun square Node measurement computed by primary direction is either too early or too late depending on whether direct or converse motion is assumed.

1932 Solar Return for year of Death

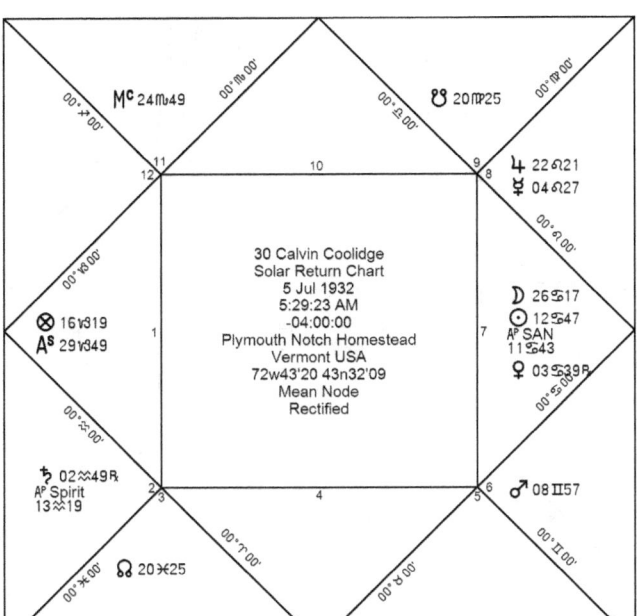

Ascendant Distributor: Jupiter/Libra since 1-Sep-1924
Profected Ascendant: 3VI50, 1st House; SR Victor: Moon (bound is Saturn)
Lords: LOY – Mercury; LOP – Jupiter
Firdaria: Jupiter-Moon
Moon: separates from Sun to void of course
Return Ascendant falls in natal 5th

Both luminaries in the 7th and killer Jupiter in the 8th are the strongest indications of death this year. In addition, natal Ascendant ruler Mercury at 4LE27 makes a partile conjunction to natal Jupiter at 4LE36; falling in the 8th of the return with Jupiter is also bad. Return's South Node falls in the natal Ascendant and further weakens Coolidge. The LOF may be a factor with the return's Jupiter conjunct natal LOF and the return's LOF conjunct natal Saturn.

At death, transiting South Node, Mars, and Jupiter fall in the natal Ascendant with the Nodes making a partile square to their natal position.

There are no relevant Ascendant directions at the time of death.

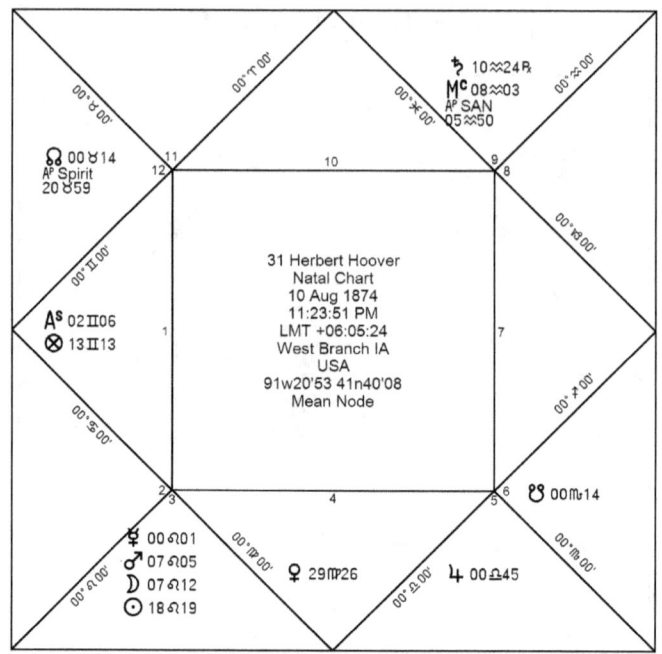

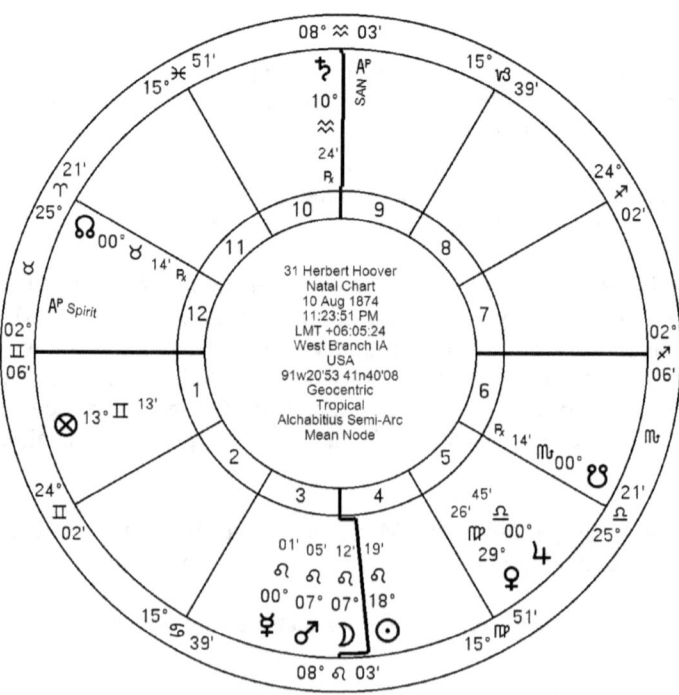

Moon's Configuration

Moon separates form **Mars** and applies to **Saturn**, nocturnal, preventional. Prenatal syzygy is 5AQ50. Eclipse? No.

Cognitive Assessment Model (Rulers of Moon and Mercury)

Sign rulers: **(Sun) Mercury** (both)
Bound rulers: **Venus, Jupiter**

Victor Soul Models

Ibn Ezra Victor Model (1507), in-sect triplicity ruler, triplicity decans.

	Position	☉	☽	☿	♀	♂	♃	♄
Sun	18 LE 19	5		2			4	
Moon	07 LE 12	6			2		3	
Asc	02 GE 06			11				
Pars Fortuna	13 GE 13			8	3			
Syzygy	05 AQ 50			5				6
Oriental						0	0	0
Houses		9	9	3	7	9	7	11
Score		0	20	9	29	12| 9	14	17

Porphyry's Expanded Victor Model (2022)

Saturn rules the MC and syzygy by sign. Sect: out-of-favor. Solar phase: opposition to 2nd station. Position: 10th from Lot of Spirit. Dignity: sign and diurnal triplicity. Moon's application.

Victor Table for Killing Planets

			☉	☽	☿	♀	♂	♃	♄
ASC		2GE06			5,3,2,1			3	3
Rul ASC	☿	00LE01	5,3,1					3,2	3
L.Death		27GE14			5,3			3	3,2,1
Rul L.Death	☿	00LE01	5,3,1					3,2	3
H8 Cusp		24SA02	3,1					5,3	3,2
Rul H8	♃	00LI45			3	5,1		3	4,3,2
T-Rul H8	♃	00LI45			3	5,1		3	4,3,2
8th from ☽		7PI12		3		4,3,2	3	5,1	
Rul 8th fr ☽	♃	00LI45			3	5,1		3	4,3,2
TOTAL			22	3	28	27	3	39	47

2007 Proposed Rectification: 11:23:45 PM, ASC 2GE04'52"
2022 Revised Rectification: 11:23:50 PM, ASC 2GE06'39"

Astrodatabank reports a C-rated birth time of 11:15 PM, rectified from an approximate time, with an Ascendant of 29TA24. The proposed rectification is slightly later with early Gemini rising.

ZRS. LOF Gemini makes mutable signs angular for LOF. Hoover is elected President under L2-Virgo with L1-Virgo timing his extensive post-presidential role as leader of the Republican Party in opposition to FDR.

L1 Taurus 10 Aug 1874		
L1 Gemini 29 Jun 1882		25-Feb-1893, mother died from pneumonia.
L2 Sagittarius 13 Apr 1891	FS	1-Oct-1891, entered Stanford as geology major, this year also the formal opening of Stanford.
L2 Sagittarius 28 Oct 1899	LB	May-1900, employees outlined the world's largest field of anthracite coal in China but the Boxer Rebellion during summer 1900 caused most Americans and the Hoovers to flee China; Aug-1900, reorganized Chinese contracts.
L1 Cancer 17 Mar 1902		
L2 Capricorn 4 May 1910	FS	HH and wife Lou completed the English translation of *De Re Metallica*, a project started in 1907 and completed in 1912 (no exact completion date).
L2 Capricorn 16 Jul 1919	LB	Very active political period with HH considered as Presidential nominee, continued work in private relief efforts, extensive contact with WW over League of Nations treaty; 2-Nov-1920, WH elected President; 24-Feb-1921; appointed Secretary of Commerce.
L1 Leo 6 Nov 1926		1926/1927, Great Mississippi Flood allowed Hoover another chance to show his ability to handle disasters. During the 1928 Presidential Campaign, the campaign film *Master of Emergencies* was produced which included scenes of WWI famine relief efforts and work HH did during the Great Mississippi Flood.
L2 Virgo 29 May 1928		14-Jun-1928, nominated as Republican Party Presidential Candidate; 6-Nov-1928, elected President; October 1929, Stock market crash and onset of Great Depression.
L2 Aquarius 22-Feb-1935	FS	10-Jun-1936, RNC address with anti-New Deal theme. For this entire L2 period, HH is known for anti-FDR speeches. HH did not support Alf Landon for President.
L2 Aquarius 6 Mar 1944	LB	Republicans lost to FDR in Nov 1944 election; 12-Apr-1945, FDR died; 24-May-1945, HT invited HH to White House, 1st time in 12 years.
L1 Virgo 29 Jul 1945		25-Feb-1946, HH asked to lend his name to a national committee for domestic food conservation to avert mass starvation in Europe.
L2 Pisces 10 Oct 1954	FS	May-1955, final Report of 2nd Hoover Commission published.
L2 Pisces 27 Nov 1962	LB	No events found.
L2 Aries 22 Nov 1963		20-Oct-1964, death.

31. HERBERT HOOVER

Firdaria – Saturn major and minor periods

Firdaria according to Bonatti	Life Event
Moon **Saturn** 23 Nov 1875	1876 (no exact date), almost died from croup.
Saturn 11 years Age 9 to 20	
Saturn Saturn 11 Aug 1883	1884, moved to Oregon to live with Uncle after both parents died in 1880 and 1883.
Saturn Jupiter 07 Mar 1885	
Saturn Mars 02 Oct 1886	
Saturn Sun 28 Apr 1888	end-1888, reunited with siblings; introduced to schoolteacher who opened world of creative literature; approx. 1889, learned how to use typewriter as office boy.
Saturn Venus 22 Nov 1889	1889/1890, enrolled in business college, night school; taught math.
Saturn Mercury 19 Jun 1891	1-Oct-1891, entered Stanford as geology major, this was the first year of Stanford's operations.
Saturn Moon 13 Jan 1893	No events found.
Jupiter **Saturn** 23 Nov 1904	late/1904-mid-1905, reorganized Burmese lead/copper mine; spectacular turnaround.
Mars **Saturn** 11 Aug 1911	1912, with wife Lou completed English translation of *De Re Metallica*; 1912, elected to Stanford Board of Trustees; Summer-1912, supported 3rd party Presidential bid of TR with Bull Moose party.
Sun **Saturn** 28 Apr 1924	28-Apr-1925, UK resumed pre-WWI gold-sterling parity, overvaluing the pound; 23-Sep-1925, lobbied for Bureau of Civil Aviation.
Venus **Saturn** 15 Jan 1932	22-Jan-1932, Reconstruction Finance Corporation funded with $2 bln created to lend to financial institutions; 27-Feb-1932, Glass-Steagall Banking Act passed; 29-May to 29-Jul-1932, Bonus Army marchers arrived in Washington and eventually forcibly driven out by MacArthur; 21-Jul-1932, expanded RFC with Relief and Reconstruction Act.
Mercury **Saturn** 28 Apr 1940	5-Nov-1940, FDR's victory over Willkie marked turning point with HH selling Washington DC home and moving into suite at Waldorf Towers in NYC; ear-1942, after Pearl Harbor, 1942, published *America's First Crusade* which proposes that Europeans (not American isolationism) were responsible for the current geopolitical situation.
Moon **Saturn** 23 Nov 1950	20-Dec-1950, in radio address opposed HT's plan to send four divisions of American soldiers to Europe to fulfill US duties in NATO alliance; 27-Feb-1951, testimony before Foreign Relations Committee echoed comments in 20-Dec-1950 radio address with HH sounding very bitter.
Saturn 11 years Age 84 to 95	
Saturn Saturn 11 Aug 1958	No events found.
Saturn Jupiter 07 Mar 1960	25-Jul-1960, bid farewell at Republican National Convention where Nixon is nominated for President.
Saturn Mars 02 Oct 1961	
Saturn Sun 29 Apr 1963	20-Oct-1964, Death.

Saturn/Aquarius-rx made Hoover reject New Deal command and control socialist policies in favor of the rugged individualism of the mid-20th century Republican Party for which he was a standard bearer.

Solar Arc Directions

<u>17-Jul-1900</u>. *dsa Mars square ASC*.
American Marines landed in China to quell Boxer Rebellion, 16-Jul.

<u>30-Nov-1902</u>. *dsa ASC square Venus*.
Company fraud uncovered, 26-Dec.

<u>30-Jun-1927</u>. *dsa MC opposed Venus*.
Scandal regarding treatment of African Americans during Great Mississippi Flood relief efforts. Additional charges of theft and profiteering made against Red Cross food/medical relief efforts, May-1927.

<u>23-Mar-1940</u>. *csa ASC opposed Venus*.
Surrender of Finland to Russia effectively ended relief efforts, 12-Mar.

<u>9-Jun-1946</u>. *csa MC sextile Venus*.
Met with Argentina's Peron to ask for 1.6 million tons of foodstuffs to close gap in worldwide supplies, 5-Jun.

<u>4-Jul-1952</u>. *dsa ASC conj. Sun*.
<u>14-May-1954</u>. *csa Sun conj ASC*.
Protégé Robert Taft lost Republican Presidential nomination to Dwight Eisenhower, 7-Jul-52.
In alumni address at West-Town Friends School, stated optimism and religious faith key to civilization, 29-May-1954.

Primary Directions

| PT | D | Venus/Leo | P | Moon (MO) d. => Mercury (ME) | 1-Mar-1883 |

Death of Mother, 24-Feb. Mercury rules 5th, or 8th from 10th.

| PT | D | Mercury/Capricorn | P | dex trine NNode c. => MC | 29-Oct-1914 |

LOCK Becomes head of Belgian Food Relief Commission, 19-Oct.

| REG | D | Mercury/Libra | P | dexter trine MC d. => Sun | 14-Apr-1917 |

Wilson to head US Food Administration during WWI, 6-Apr.

| REG | D | Venus/Aries | P | sin sextile MC d. => Saturn (SA) | 6-Aug-1927 |

Report to Coolidge on necessity for revision of government flood control measures, 20-Jul.

| REG | D | Mercury/Aries | P | sin trine Sun d. => Saturn (0) | 6-Nov-1929 |

Stock market crash, 'Black Tuesday,' 29-Oct.

31. HERBERT HOOVER

| PT | D | Venus/Aquarius | P | MC d. => North Node | 16-Dec-1930 |

Bank of the United States closed, 11-Dec. Largest of bank closings in the US during the Great Depression up to that point in time.

| REG | D | Venus/Aquarius | P | opp Mars (MA) c. => ASC | 22-Aug-1949 |

Gallbladder attack, 14-Aug.

| PT | D | Mercury/Gemini | P | ASC c. => Sun | 16-Aug-1954 |

LOCK President Eisenhower appointed Hoover's son Herbert Hoover Jr. to be Under Secretary of State, 17-Aug-1954. Note: Sun = son.

Primary Direction Sequences

| PT | D | Jupiter/Aries | P | opp Jupiter (0) c. => ASC | 28-Aug-1914 |
| PT | D | Jupiter/Aries | P | opp Jupiter (JU) c. => ASC | 25-Jan-1916 |

Began Belgium relief effort 3-Aug-1914. Late 1915/early 1916 resigned from business ventures (except Burma Lead Mines) to focus on relief.

| PT | D | Saturn/Virgo | P | opp Venus (VE) d. => MC | 21-Jun-1923 |
| PT | D | Saturn/Virgo | P | opp Venus (0) d. => MC | 16-Aug-1923 |

LOCK This sequence timed President Warren Harding's "Voyage of Understanding" – beginning 20-Jun, Hoover's acceptance of Harding's invitation to join the trip 3-Jul, Harding's admission to Hoover of scandal in his administration, and Harding's death 2-Aug. In his Memoirs, Hoover said: "one day after lunch when we were a few days out, Harding asked me to come to his cabin. He plumped me with the question: "If you knew of a great scandal in our administration, would you for the good of the country and the party expose it publicly or would you bury it?" My natural reply was, "Publish it, and at least get credit for integrity on your side." (Hoover 1952, 49). Venus in Virgo signifies financial fraud. She exerts influence in the 5th by position (QS) or rulership (WS).

| REG | D | Venus/Sag | P | opp LOF d. => Venus (VE) | 5-Mar-1930 |
| REG | D | Venus/Sag | P | opp LOF d. => Venus (0) | 31-Aug-1930 |

This sequence timed Hoover's Congressional negotiations and passage of the Smoot-Hawley Tariff bill. HH began negotiations on 24-Feb and signed the legislation on 16-Jun. With tariffs assigned to a Jupiter ruled 8th house, the connection is not immediately obvious. Venus applies to Jupiter which ties Venus to the 8th. Note also Venus rules the 12th house of self-undoing. This tariff was one of his major errors. The Smoot-Hawley legislation is one of the most common actions remembered about Hoover since his death.

Longevity, 90y 2m 10d

Death: 20-Oct-1964, 11:34 AM, New York City. After gallbladder surgery in 1958 and removal of a cancerous intestinal tumor during 1962, Hoover's health deteriorated. He was almost blind and deaf in final days. Official cause of death was internal bleeding which started on 17-Oct.

Hīlāj: **Sun**. Figure is nocturnal and Moon is preferred and acceptable in the 3rd house. Yet in her final quarter and under the beams she is ruled out. Sun/4th/masculine sign is the next choice and is acceptable. Empirically the Sun shows afflictions by transit during Hoover's major health crises. They include a gallbladder attack, 14-Aug-1949, gallbladder surgery, Apr-1958; gastrointestinal bleeding/pneumonia, Feb-1964. Sun was also afflicted at death by a transiting Mars-Saturn opposition.

Al-kadukhadāh: **Sun**. Sun in his sign of rulership trumps all other choices. Sun grants his major 120 years. Opposition from Saturn deducts Saturn's 30 minor years. Net projection of 90 years is accurate.

SU (120) - SA (30) = 90 years.

Victor: **Saturn**

Killing Planets: **Saturn (47), Jupiter (39)**

Arcus Vitae:

REG	D	Venus/Scorpio	P	dex square Saturn (SA) d. => Moon (MO)	9-Oct-1960
PT	D	Venus/Scorpio	P	dex square Saturn (SA) d. => Moon (MO)	8-Jan-1961
REG	D	Venus/Scorpio	P	dex square Saturn (0) d. => Moon (MO)	27-Jan-1961
PT	D	Venus/Scorpio	P	dex square Saturn (0) d. => Moon (MO)	26-Apr-1961

Despite arguments favoring the Sun as hīlāj, Moon still appears to participate as evidenced by the deterioration of Hoover's health in his final years timed by the Saturn-Moon directions listed above (both Ptolemy and Regiomontanus methods). Health problems included surgery for removal of cancer in 1962 and multiple attacks of gastrointestinal bleeding; the first in June 1963.

REG	D	Jupiter/Sag	P	sin sextile Jupiter (0) d. => Sun	22-Sep-1964
REG	D	Jupiter/Sag	P	sin sextile Jupiter (JU) d. => Sun	1-Apr-1965

This is the most accurate arcus vitae. It is similar to the Jupiter square Sun aspect in the solar return for the year of death.

1964 Solar Return for year of Death

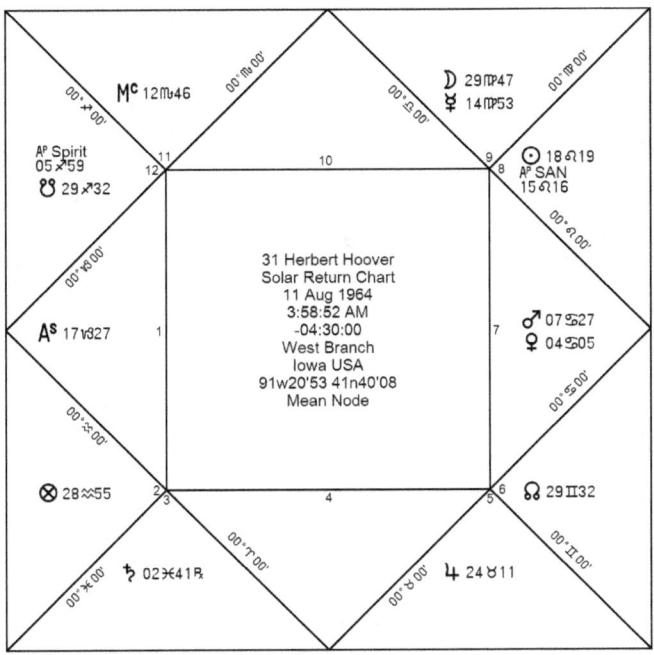

Ascendant Distributor: Mercury/Leo since 4-May-1960
Profected Ascendant: 2SA06, 7th House; SR Victor: Saturn
Lords: LOY – Jupiter; LOP – Jupiter
Firdaria: Major – Sun; Minor – Saturn
Moon: separates from trine of Jupiter to void of course
Return Ascendant falls in natal 8th

Hīlāj Sun falls in the return's 8th. High scoring killer Saturn at 2PI41 afflicts the natal Ascendant-Descendant axis by partile square. Secondary killer Jupiter is partile conjunct the Lot of Killing Planet and square the Hīlāj Sun. Jupiter also rules the natal 8th of death and has ample power to act because he is Lord of the Year and Lord of the Period.

The following direction links the high scoring killer to the Ascendant.

| PT | D | Venus/Taurus | P | sin sextile Saturn (0) d. => ASC | 19-Oct-1964 |

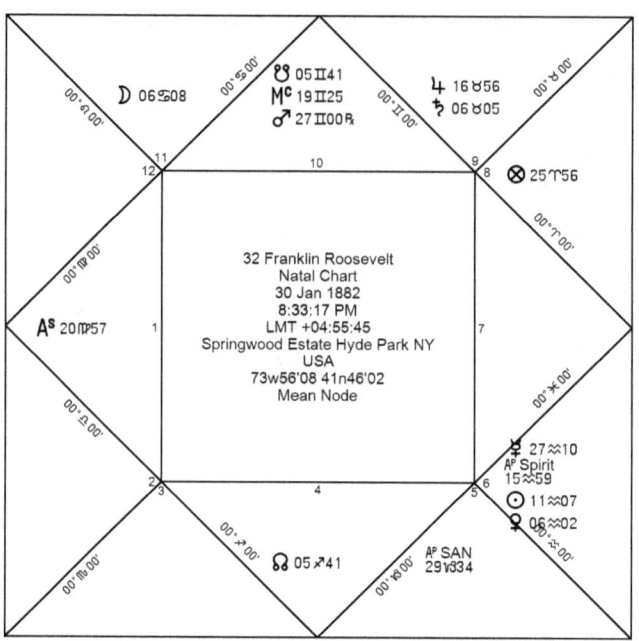
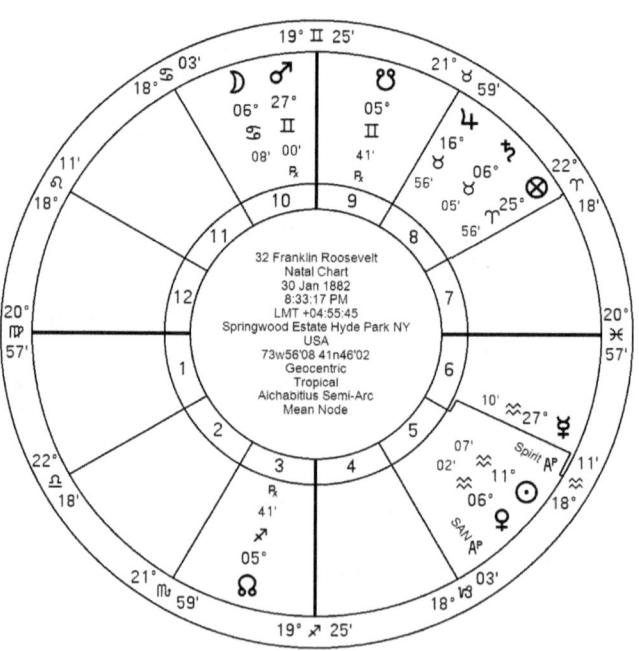

32. FRANKLIN ROOSEVELT

Moon's Configuration

Moon separates from **Saturn** and applies to **Jupiter**, nocturnal, conjunctional. Prenatal syzygy is 29CP34. Eclipse? No.

Cognitive Assessment Model (Rulers of Moon and Mercury)

Sign rulers: **(Moon)/Mars, Saturn**
Bound rulers: **Mars, Saturn**

Victor Soul Models

Ibn Ezra Victor Model (1507), in-sect triplicity ruler, triplicity decans.

	Position	☉	☽	☿	♀	♂	♃	♄
Sun	11 AQ 07			4	2			5
Moon	06 CA 08		6			5	4	
Asc	20 VI 58		3	9	1		2	
Pars Fortuna	25 AR 56	4				5	4	2
Syzygy	29 CP 34			3	1	6		5
Oriental						0	0	0
Houses			7	11	1	7	11	5	5
Score		0	11	23	15	10	**27**	15	17

Porphyry's Expanded Victor Model (2022)

Jupiter rules the ASC and Lot of Spirit by bound. Sect: out-of-favor. Solar phase: occidental from 2nd station to waning square. Position: 4th from Lot of Spirit. Dignity: bound; mutual reception with Moon by exaltation. Moon's application.

Victor Table for Killing Planets

			☉	☽	☿	♀	♂	♃	♄
ASC		20VI57		3	5,4	3,1	3	2	
Rul ASC	☿	27AQ10			3	1		3	5,3,2
L.Death		22AQ14			3	1	2	3	5,3
Rul L.Death	♄	6TA05		4,3		5,3,2,1	3		
H8 Cusp		22AR18	4,3				5,2	3,1	3
Rul H8	♂	27GE00			5,3			3	3,2,1
T-Rul H8	♃	16TA56		4,3	1	5,3	3	2	
8th from ☽		6AQ08			3,1			3	5,3,1
Rul 8th fr ☽	♄	6TA05		4,3		5,3,2,1	3		
TOTAL			7	24	**29**	**36**	21	20	**36**

2007 Proposed Rectification: 8:33:17 PM, ASC 20VI57'52"
2022 Proposed Rectification: 8:33:17 PM, ASC 20VI57'56"

Astrodatabank reports an AA-rated birth time of 8:45 PM, Ascendant 23VI16. The proposed rectification is 13 minutes earlier.

FDR's horoscope is an excellent example of how directions of the Sun to the angles, whether by solar arc or primary directions, can lock down a rectification. With zero latitude, directions of the Sun avoid choice of latitude assumptions over which traditional astrologers disagree.

ZRS. LOS 15AQ59, bound of Jupiter/Aquarius with Jupiter as victor 4th from the LOS, accentuates FDR's humanitarian philosophy as his central driving force, even though he often used deceit and half-truths to achieve his aims via Mars/Gemini-rx.

Following FDR's initial battle with polio 1920-1923, he entered the national stage with L2 subperiods in cardinal signs consistently timing political milestones. LOF in Aries makes cardinal signs angular from LOF.

L1 Aquarius 30 Jan 1882		
L2 Leo 12 Feb 1891	FS	Demonstrated evidence of mental 'juggling' by absorbing books read to him by his mother 'verbatim' while FDR worked on his stamp collection.
L2 Leo 31 May 1899	LB	1899/1900, more successful at Groton senior year, dorm prefect, generous and helpful to younger boys.
L2 Aquarius 17 Sep 1907	CP	Early 1910, offered nomination for NY state assembly seat.
L1 Pisces 27 Aug 1911		3-Mar-1912, in People's Forum address in Troy, NY; FDR attempted formulation of social and political views which anticipate limits of individual liberty and the necessity for cooperation ("intervention") at the community level to achieve societal objectives.
L1 Aries 25 Jun 1923		L1-Aries timed FDR's political activities at the national level. FDR emerged from polio to nominate Al Smith for President in 1924 (L2-Aries) and 1928 (L2-Cancer), was elected President (L2-Libra), and introduced 2nd phase of New Deal (L2-Capricorn).
L1 Taurus 07 Apr 1938		L1-Taurus began shortly after Germany's takeover of Austria on 11-Mar-1938 which triggered a cascading series of events leading up to US involvement in WWII. Pearl Harbor occurred during L2-Cancer, the only angular sign from LOF for the entirety of L1-Taurus for the remaining years of FDR's life.
L2 Virgo 06 Mar 1944		12-Apr-1945, death.

Firdaria – Jupiter major and minor periods

Firdaria according to Bonatti	Life Event
Moon **Jupiter** 27 Aug 1884	No events found.
Saturn **Jupiter** 26 Aug 1892	No events found.
Jupiter 12 years Age 20 to 32	
Jupiter Jupiter 31 Jan 1902	24-Jun-1903, graduated Harvard MBA.
Jupiter Mars 19 Oct 1903	Oct-1904, Columbia Law School, poor performance; 17-Mar-1905, married Eleanor.
Jupiter Sun 06 Jul 1905	19-Jun-1906, passed NY bar exam and began legal career.
Jupiter Venus 25 Mar 1907	No events found.
Jupiter Mercury 10 Dec 1908	Early-1910, offered NY state assembly seat.
Jupiter Moon 28 Aug 1910	9-Nov-1910, won election to NY state assembly; 16-Jan-1911, challenged Tammany Hall.
Jupiter Saturn 15 May 1912	24-Aug-1912, advanced in NY State Assembly; Jan-1913, chaired Agriculture Committee in Assembly; 4-Mar-1913, accepted appointment as Assistant Secretary of Navy.
Mars **Jupiter** 01 Feb 1920	2-Feb-1920, Secretary of Navy Daniels blew up at FDR after FDR made false allegations; 6-Jul-1920, nominated as VP; 13-Jul-1920, resigned Assistant Secretary of the Navy.
Sun **Jupiter** 24 Mar 1933	16-Jun-1933, Congress completed 'Hundred Days' legislation including NIRA, PWA, NRA, and FDIC; 30-Jan-1934, Gold Reserve Act.
Venus **Jupiter** 27 Aug 1940	3-Sep-1940, deal with Britain to trade US WWI destroyers for leases on British bases announced; 5-Nov-1940, re-elected to 3rd term; 6-Jan-1941, State of Union address proposed Lend-Lease program and espoused Four Freedoms.

Here is a case where reasonable people may disagree on the choice of victor. **Mars/Gemini-rx** conjunct the MC defines FDR's life as a deceitful, tricky politician and a wartime President. However as time lord, whether by Firdaria or by transit to the angles, I advocate **Jupiter/Taurus** as the empirical victor which signifies FDR's role of providing abundance during the depression and wartime years. The Moon's application to Jupiter is a significant factor which favors Jupiter as victor.

Jupiter as Victor. For FDR, Jupiter as Major Firdaria ruler captures the start of his legal career, marriage, entry to NY electoral politics, and first Federal appointment as Assistant Secretary of the Navy. Mars-Jupiter times his unsuccessful 1920 VP campaign. Sun-Jupiter times FDR's first 100 days in office. Venus-Jupiter captures the runup to US involvement in WWII which featured the Lend-Lease program.

Transits

30-Nov-1932. *tr Jupiter conj ASC.* 30-Nov-1932.
15-Feb-1933. *tr Jupiter-rx conj ASC.* 15-Feb-1933.
26-Jul-1933. *tr Jupiter conj ASC.* 26-Jul-1933.
    Elected President for 1st term, 8-Nov-1932.
    Unsuccessful assassination attempt by Guiseppe Zangara, 15-Feb-1933.
    End of London Economic Conference; rejected gold standard, 26-Jul-1933.

4-Sep-1941. *tr Jupiter conj MC.*
14-Nov-1941. *tr Jupiter-rx conj MC.*
21-Apr-1942. *tr Jupiter conj MC.*
    FDR maintained oil embargo against Japan, despite war warnings, 5-Sep-41
    Intercepted Tokyo message stated in the event of US involvement in a European war that Japan would fulfill her treaty obligations, 14-Nov-41
    Major General Doolittle headed bombing raid on Tokyo, 18-Apr-42

4-Nov-1944. *tr Jupiter conj ASC.*
    Re-elected President for 4th term, 7-Nov-1944.

Solar Arc Directions

LOCK 27-Aug-1921. *dsa Sun opposed ASC.*
    Press release on FDR's contraction of polio, 27-Aug. (contracted 10-Aug).

4-Oct-1926. *dsa Venus opposed ASC.*
    Traveled to Warm Springs, 4-Oct; spent most of next two years there.

31-Aug-1931. *dsa Moon trine LOF.*
    Proposed workfare, 28-Aug.

22-Sep-1931. *dsa Saturn sextile LOF.*
    UK devalued Sterling 21-Sep.

14-Jan-1932. *dsa ASC square Sun.*
    Announced Presidential bid, 22-Jan.

LOCK 4-Aug-1933. *dsa MC opposed Sun.*
    Created National Labor Board, 5-Aug.

26-Nov-1937. *dsa ASC opposed Jupiter.*
    Took sojourn after operation for tooth abscess, 27-Nov.

17-Jan-1942. *dsa Saturn conj. Moon.*
    Ordered all foreigners to register with government 14-Jan; Hitler outlined plan for Jewish extermination, 20-Jan.

Primary Directions

| REG | D | Mars/Pisces | P | DSC d. => Sun | 11-Mar-1929 |

LOCK Achieved fame for hydroelectric power proposal, 12-Mar.

| REG | D | Saturn/Leo | P | opposition Sun c. => ASC | 16-Apr-1933 |

LOCK Ended Gold Standard, 19-Apr.

| REG | D | Mercury/Sagittarius | P | IC c. => Sun | 20-Mar-1941 |

LOCK Authorized first appropriations under Lend-Lease Act, 27-Mar.

Primary Direction Sequences

| REG | D | Mars/Gemini | P | MC d. => Saturn (0) | 7-Aug-1932 |
| REG | D | Mars/Gemini | P | MC d. => Saturn (SA) | 21-Feb-1933 |

LOCK This sequence timed the depths of the Great Depression as measured by the Dow Jones Industrial Index which bottomed on 8-Jul-1932 and made a retest low on 27-Feb-1933. Central to the Depression were numerous bank failures in the United States (and elsewhere) which propelled both FDR and Hitler to power. By the end of the sequence the banking crisis reached its climax with FDR's declaration of a Bank Holiday starting on 5-Mar-1933, the day after his inauguration. Regarding Hitler's rise to power, the Nazi Party electoral victory on 31-Jul-1932 secured Nazi control of the Reichstag. As the sequence concluded, Hitler was appointed Chancellor on 30-Jan-1933 and on 27-Feb-1933 the Reichstag was burned.

| PT | D | Venus/Leo | P | sin square Saturn (SA) d. => MC | 16-Jun-1931 |
| PT | D | Venus/Leo | P | sin square Saturn (0) d. => MC | 22-Jan-1932 |

LOCK This Saturn sequence again dealt with the destruction of wealth (Saturn=destruction in financial sign of Taurus). It precisely timed Hoover's failed measures to shore up the financial system. Following the default of the Austrian Bank Credit Anstalt in May-1931, Hoover proposed a one-year moratorium on debt payments owed to the US by European nations on 20-Jun-1931. As the sequence culminated, Hoover formed the Reconstruction Finance Corporation (RFC) Act into law on 22-Jan-1932 designed to provide liquidity to financial institutions.

| REG | D | Saturn/Leo | P | sin square Jupiter (JU) d. => MC | 13-Sep-1942 |
| REG | D | Saturn/Leo | P | sin square Jupiter (0) d. => MC | 24-Dec-1942 |

LOCK This sequence timed favorable turnarounds on all fronts for the Allies. Plans for Operation Torch under Eisenhower were finalized 5-Sep; the second Battle of El Alamein was won 23-Oct/4-Nov; Russian General Chuikov was promoted at Stalingrad on 12-Sep and helped turn the tide against the Germans.

Longevity, 63y 2m 11d

Death: 12-Apr-1945, 3:45 PM; Warm Springs, Georgia. Roosevelt died of a cerebral hemorrhage following a lengthy deterioration in health from high blood pressure and arteriosclerosis.

Hīlāj: **Moon**. Figure is nocturnal. Moon qualifies in either 10th or 11th.

Al-kadukhadāh: **Moon**. In her own sign the Moon trumps all other candidates. If so, Moon grants 108 major years. Sextile aspect from Saturn cannot deduct years because Saturn does not receive the Moon. Moon applies to Jupiter by sextile aspect, outside moiety of orb, with both planets in mutual reception by exaltation. This type of reception should limit the ability of Jupiter to add years. With neither Jupiter or Saturn capable of modifying years, FDR's longevity estimate remains 108 years which is too long.

Alternate: **Mars** near the MC degree is a viable al-kadukhadāh. Mars grants 66 major years with actual longevity slightly less.

Victor of the Horoscope: **Jupiter**

Killing Planets: **Saturn (36), Venus (36), Mercury (29)**

Arcus Vitae:

PT	D	Mercury/Virgo	P	sin trine Saturn (SA) d. => Moon (MO)	22-Sep-1944
PT	D	Mercury/Virgo	P	sin trine Saturn (0) d. => Moon (MO)	7-Apr-1945

REG	D	Mercury/Virgo	P	sin trine Saturn (SA) d. => Moon (MO)	29-Jul-1945
REG	D	Mercury/Virgo	P	sin trine Saturn (0) d. => Moon (MO)	24-Dec-1946

Both Ptolemy and Regiomontanus directions are presented. The set of Ptolemy directions is more accurate; Regiomontanus directions are late.

1945 Solar Return for year of Death

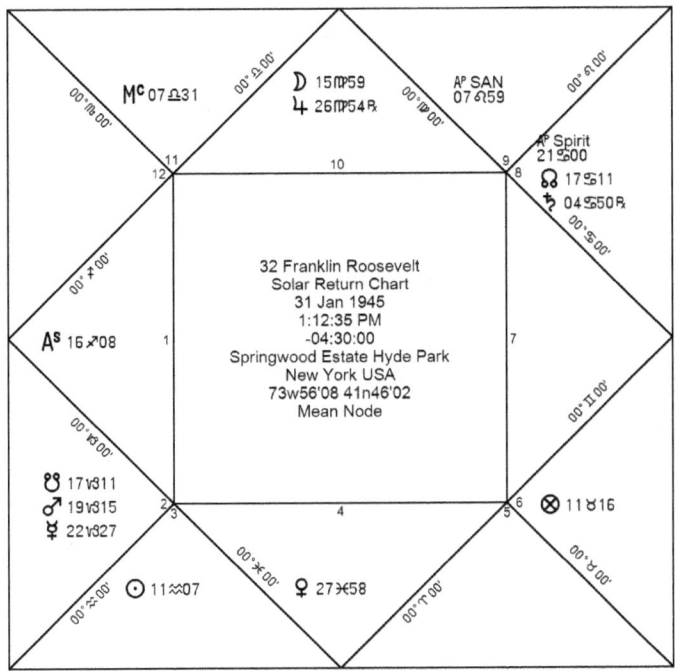

Ascendant Distributor: Venus/Scorpio since 22-Dec-1940
Profected Ascendant: 20SA57, 4th House; SR Victor: Venus
Lords: LOY – Jupiter, LOP – Saturn
Firdaria: Mercury-Mercury
Moon: separates from the sextile of Saturn to the trine of Mars
Return Ascendant falls in natal 4th

Hīlāj Moon separating from the sextile of Saturn to the trine of Mars is the first indication of death in this figure. Saturn is the high scoring killing planet and Mars rules the natal 8th house of death. Moon in the return herself rules the return's 8th of death. A profected 4th house year, with solar return Ascendant falling on the natal 4th cusp also ties this year to FDR's end-of-life.

The following direction links the high scoring killer to the return's Ascendant. The direction precedes death by two days.

| PT | D | Venus/Pisces | P | dexter trine Saturn (0) d. => ASC | 10-Apr-1945 |

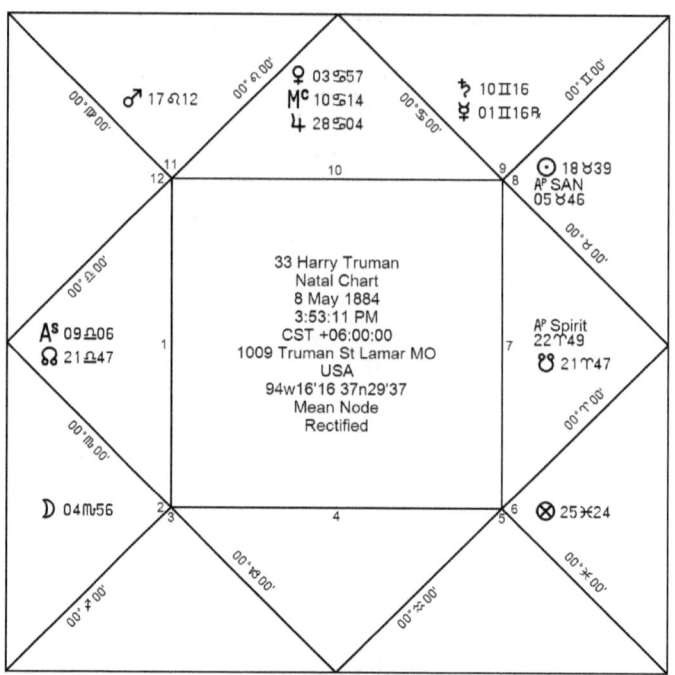
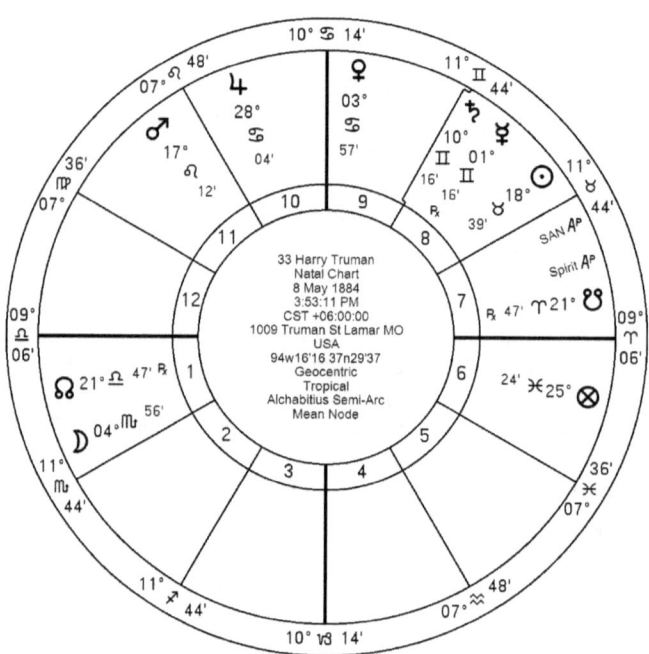

Moon's Configuration

Moon separates from **Venus** and applies to **Mars**, diurnal, conjunctional. Prenatal syzygy is 5TA46. Eclipse? **YES**. Partial Solar Eclipse.

Cognitive Assessment Model (Rulers of Moon and Mercury)

Sign rulers: **Mars, Mercury**
Bound rulers: **Mars, Mercury**

Victor Soul Models

Ibn Ezra Victor Model (1507), in-sect triplicity ruler, triplicity decans.

	Position	☉	☽	☿	♀	♂	♃	♄
Sun	18 TA 39		4	1	8		2	
Moon	04 SC 56				3	8		
Asc	09 LI 06			2	6			7
Pars Fortuna	25 PI 24				7	3	5	
Syzygy	05 TA 46 (SE)		4		11			
Oriental						0	0	0
Houses			5	12| 5	4	8	11| 4
Score		0	5	20	8	39	19	18	11

Porphyry's Expanded Victor Model (2022)

Mars rules the Moon and Lot of Spirit by sign; the Moon, Lot of Fortune, and Lot of Spirit by bound. Sect: out-of-favor. Solar phase: occidental waning square to sextile. Moon's application.

Victor Table for Killing Planets

			☉	☽	☿	♀	♂	♃	♄
ASC		9LI06			3,2	5,1		3	4,3
Rul ASC	♀	3CA57		5,3,1		3	3,2	4	
L.Death		17SA04	3		2		1	5,3	3
Rul L.Death	♃	28CA04		5,3		3	3	4,1	2
H8 Cusp		11TA44		4,3	2,1	5,3	3		
Rul H8	♀	3CA57		5,3,1		3	3,2	4	
T-Rul H8	♀	3CA57		5,3,1		3	3,2	4	
☉ in 8th	☉	18TA38		4,3	1	5,3	3	2	
8th from ☉		18SA38	3		2		1	5,3	3
Rul 8th fr ☉	♃	28CA04		5,3		3	3	4,1	2
TOTAL			6	57	13	37	29	43	17

2007 Proposed Rectification: 3:34:50 PM, ASC 5LI21'01"
2009 Revised Rectification: 3:53:12 PM, ASC 9LI06'45"
2022 Revised Rectification: 3:53:11 PM, ASC 9LI06'46"

Astrodatabank reports an A-rated birth time of 4:00 PM, ASC 10LI30. The proposed rectification is 7 minutes earlier.

ZRS. LOS 22AR49 falls the 7th house, bound of Mars/Aries. Bound lord Mars/Leo grants Truman a martial spirit in confronting open enemies. This configuration is a delineation match to Truman's slogan "The buck stops here." As a consideration for judgment, it is consistent with Truman's controversial termination of General Douglas MacArthur for insubordination during the Korean War. Mars/Leo is the victor of the horoscope.

Weakness of Mercury/Gemini-retro is clear during L1-Gemini and both FS and LB Sagittarius L2 subperiods. L1-Cancer is a standout with both benefics in Cancer and the Lunar Nodes in the Libra-Aries axis. Changeover to L1-Leo occurs within 18 months of the end of Truman's presidency. At this time the Korean War offensive operations diminished as a negotiated settlement was contemplated.

L1 Aries 8 May 1884		
L1 Taurus 19 Feb 1899		
L1 Gemini 9 Jan 1907		L1-Gemini is a mixed period with multiple failed business ventures, WWI service at the tail-end of the war, and his first political victory as Judge though he lost re-election during LB.
L2 Sagittarius 24 Oct 1915	FS	Sep-1916, Zinc mine closed, another failed business venture.
L2 Sagittarius 9 May 1924	LB	4-Nov-1924, lost re-election campaign during a Republican election sweep.
L1 Cancer 26 Sep 1926		Nov-1926, won election for Presiding Judge - served two terms from Jan-1927 to Jan-1935.
L2 Capricorn 13 Nov 1934	FS	3-Jan-1935, sworn in as Senator following 1st successful Senate bid.
L2 Capricorn 25 Jan 1944	LB	21-Jul-1944, selected as Vice President on FDR's ticket; 7-Nov-1944, elected VP; 12-Apr-1945, upon death of FDR accedes to Presidency; 7-May-1945, WWII German surrender; 14-Aug-1945, WWII Japanese surrender.
L1 Leo 18 May 1951		25-Jun-1951, prepared to negotiate Korean War settlement at the 38th parallel.
L2 Aquarius 3 Sep 1959	FS	2-Jul-1960, lashed out against JFK at convention, against the advice of Dean Acheson.
L2 Aquarius 15 Sep 1968	LB	No major events found.
L1 Virgo 7 Feb 1970		
L2 Scorpio 27 May 1972		26-Dec-1972, death.

Firdaria – Mars as major and minor periods

Firdaria according to Bonatti	Life Event
Sun **Mars** 03 Dec 1892	1893 (no date), grandfather Solomon Young's house burned to the ground.
Venus **Mars** 25 Jan 1900	No events found.
Mercury **Mars** 13 Oct 1909	Autumn 1909, appointed deacon in Masonic Lodge; Dec-1909, maternal grandmother Young died, dispute over will; Apr-1911, broke leg below the knee after knocked over by calf; Jun-1911, marriage proposal to Bess turned down.
Moon **Mars** 18 Mar 1919	Apr/May-1919, sailed home and discharged after WWI service; 8-May-1919, fight with Bess Wallace; 28-Jun-1919, married Bess Wallace; late-Nov-1919, opened haberdashery; Spring 1920, Bess suffered 1st miscarriage.
Saturn **Mars** 01 Jul 1927	8-May-1928, political victory as bond issue for roads and a hospital passed.
Jupiter **Mars** 25 Jan 1937	20-Dec-1937, made 2nd speech on impact of corporate greed and corruption on railroad business, NYT page 1 coverage.
Mars 7 years Age 63 to 70	
Mars Mars 09 May 1947	5-Jun-1947, Marshall Plan proposed; 20-Jun-1947, vetoed Taft-Hartley Act, 23-Jun-1947, Congress overrode veto; 25-Jul-1947, National Security Act passed; 2-Feb-1948, introduced Civil Rights legislation.
Mars Sun 09 May 1948	14-May-1948, State of Israel created; 28-Jun-1948, ordered Berlin Airlift; 17-Jun-1948, Dixiecrat revolt; 26-Jul-1948, Executive Order to bar segregation in US armed forces; 2-Nov-1948, won re-election in surprise victory against Thomas Dewey; 7-Jan-1959, Dean Acheson appointed Secretary of State; 1-Mar-1949, asked Sec Defense Forrestal for resignation; 4-Apr-1949, NATO treaty signed.
Mars Venus 09 May 1949	12-May-1949, Soviets ended Berlin Blockade; 21-May-1949, Federal Republic of Germany established; 15-Jul-1949, signed Housing Act; 21-Jul-1949, NATO treaty approved; 10-Aug-1949, National Security Act signed into law; 29-Aug-1949, Russia detonated first atomic bomb; 1-Oct-1949, PRC formed; 31-Jan-1950, approved hydrogen bomb production.
Mars Mercury 09 May 1950	24-Jun-1950, Korean War outbreak; 1-Nov-1950, assassination attempt at Blair House; 28-Nov-1950, Chinese counterattack in Korea; 16-Dec-1950, declared national emergency; 11-Apr-1951, fired Douglas MacArthur.
Mars Moon 09 May 1951	25-Jun-1951, prepared to negotiate settlement of Korean War at 38th parallel; 21-Dec-1951, appointed George Kennan Ambassador to Soviet Union; 7-Jan-1952, Eisenhower announced he would accept Republican nomination; 29-Mar-1952, announced would not run for re-election; 8-Apr-1952, announced seizure of steel mills.
Mars Saturn 09 May 1952	2-Jun-1952, Supreme Court declared HT's seizure of steel mills illegal; steel strike starts same day lasting 7 weeks; 4-Nov-1952, Eisenhower won election; 5-Dec-1952, death of mother-in-law.

Mars as Victor. Mars/Leo signified Truman's 'straight-shooter' reputation as a decision maker who operated without regret. This was essential as American transitioned from WWII to the Cold War.

Transits

28-Mar-1922. *tr North Node conj ASC.*
Campaign launched for Judge, 8-Mar.

30-Oct-1926. *tr North Node conj MC.*
Won election for Judge, November.

6-Nov-1940. *tr North Node conj ASC.*
Won Senate election, 5-Nov.

Solar Arc Directions

1-Apr-1922. *csa Mars conj MC.*
19-Nov-1922. *dsa MC conj Mars.*
This pair of directions captured Truman's first run for political office following his selection by Missouri political boss Tom Pendergast. Truman started his campaign 8-Mar and was elected November 1922.

10-Jul-1927. *csa MC sextile Jupiter.*
5-May-1928. *dsa Jupiter sextile MC.*
No exact event match for 1st direction.
Voters accepted HT's plan for large bond issue for roads and hospitals, considered an upset victory for HT by political bosses, 8-May-1928.

21-May-1934. *csa Jupiter trine ASC.*
22-Jun-1935. *dsa ASC trine Jupiter.*
Senate bid announced, 14-May-1934.
Won primary, 7-Aug-1934; Won Senate election, 6-Nov-1935.

Primary Directions

| REG | D | Venus/Virgo | P | sin sextile MC c. => North Node | 3-Nov-1934 |

Won Senate election, 6-Nov.

| PT | D | Jupiter/Taurus | P | Sun c. => MC | 23-Apr-1939 |

LOCK *LIFE* Magazine published article on political fortunes of Missouri Governor Lloyd C. Stark which included disclosure of financial irregularities of Truman's political ally Tom Pendergast, 24-Apr.

| PT | D | Jupiter/Sagittarius | P | sin sextile ASC d. => NNode | 10-Feb-1941 |

Proposed committee to investigate military spending, 10-Feb.

33. HARRY TRUMAN

PT	D	Venus/Cancer	P	MC d. => Sun	15-Jan-1942
REG	D	Venus/Cancer	P	MC d. => Sun	21-Nov-1942

LOCK Delivered first of 'Truman Reports' to Senate, 15-Jan.
Truman asked Justice Department to investigate shoddy construction of military housing at Winfield, New Jersey, 19-Nov.

Primary Direction Sequences

PT	D	Venus/Aries	P	DSC c. => Saturn (SA)	30-Jan-1949
PT	D	Venus/Aries	P	DSC c. => Saturn (0)	27-Mar-1949

This sequence captured the culminating dispute between Truman and Defense Secretary James Forrestal who supported Truman's opponent Dewey in the 1948 Presidential Campaign. The first rumor of Forrestal's departure was publicized on 15-Jan (see NYT, 'Denies Forrestal Quits,' January 15, 1949, p. 15.). Truman forced Forrestal to resign on 28-Mar. On 2-Apr Forrestal entered a hospital for treatment of depression and committed suicide on 22-May-1949.

Though Saturn does not rule the 11th of political alliances which includes cabinet members like Forrestal, Saturn/Gemini does rule the 4th of the homeland and can be read as older males who defend the homeland. Forrestal's mental problems are consistent with Mercury ruling both Saturn and the 12th of evil spirit.

REG	D	Venus/Aries	P	DSC c. => Saturn (SA)	23-Sep-1950
REG	D	Venus/Aries	P	DSC c. => Saturn (0)	27-Dec-1950

LOCK In a veto override, Congress passed the Internal Security Act on 23-Sep as this sequence began. Also known as the McCarran Internal Security Act or ISA, this Act required registration of persons and organizations suspected with Communist ties. Its primary investigating mechanism was the Subversive Activities Control Board (a.k.a. "Red Control Board"). All aliens were required to report addresses with the Immigration Service during the first 10 days of 1951 though problems in production and shipment of address cards delayed alien reporting past the original deadline.

Saturn/Gemini signifies the control (Saturn) of information (Gemini). Addresses were one type of information sought (Gemini - details of communication methods). The Act applied to alien residents (Saturn - placed in 9th house of foreign lands). Finally, not only does Mercury-retrograde (signifier of information details - with the retrograde condition matching delays in production of address cards) fall in the 9th but Mercury rules the 12th of secret enemies. For further research: Both sequences also time events in the Chinese Civil War (1949) and the Korean War (1950).

Longevity, 88y 7m 18d

Death: 26-Dec-1972, 7:50 AM, Kansas City, Missouri, at home. Truman was hospitalized for lung congestion on 5-Dec, stopped talking on 14-Dec, and died on 26-Dec, 7:50 AM CST. Cause of death was heart failure with lung and kidney complications.

Hīlāj: **Moon**. Chart is diurnal and Sun is preferred yet disqualified by placement in a feminine sign in the 8th. Moon in 2nd qualifies and aspects Al-kadukhadāh Venus.

Al-kadukhadāh: **Venus**. Venus in her triplicity, aspects and receives the Moon, and conjunct the MC by just over 2 degrees makes her the clear choice. Venus gives her 82 major years. While Jupiter is co-present with and receives Venus by exaltation, the separation by 25 degrees appeasrs sufficiently wide to prevent Jupiter from adding years.

Truman lived 6 years beyond Venus' major 82 years. Truman's health did decline as he approached 82. On 13-Oct-1964 he tripped on stairs leading to his bathroom, cracking his head and fracturing ribs. He stopped going to his office at the Truman Presidential Library on a regular basis in 1967 at age 83.

Victor of the Horoscope: **Mars**

Killing Planets: **Moon (57), Jupiter (43), Venus (37)**

Arcus Vitae:

4-Jan-1970. *csa Moon sextile Saturn.*
7-Nov-1972. *dsa Saturn sextile Moon.*

14-Mar-1970. *csa Venus opposed ASC.*
19-Jan-1973. *dsa ASC opposed Venus.*
   Both solar arc pairs occur at end-of-life.
   Saturn is a malefic and the Moon is the Hīlāj.
   Venus rules the 8th of death and is one of three high scoring killing planets.

REG	D	Merc/Cancer	P	dex sextile Sun c. => Mercury (0)	9-Oct-1964

Suffered fall and injury, 13-Oct. Mercury/retrograde rules the 12th.

REG	D	Merc/Gemini	P	Mercury (ME) d. => dex sextile Sun	8-Dec-1972

Lung congestion, 5-Dec. See similarity to above direction for fall/injury.

REG	D	Mars/Cancer	P	dex trine Moon (MO) d. => SN	9-Dec-1972

South Node falls in the 7th, angle of the West.
In addition: *tr Mercury 16SA46 conj. Lot of Death 17SA04.*

1972 Solar Return for year of Death

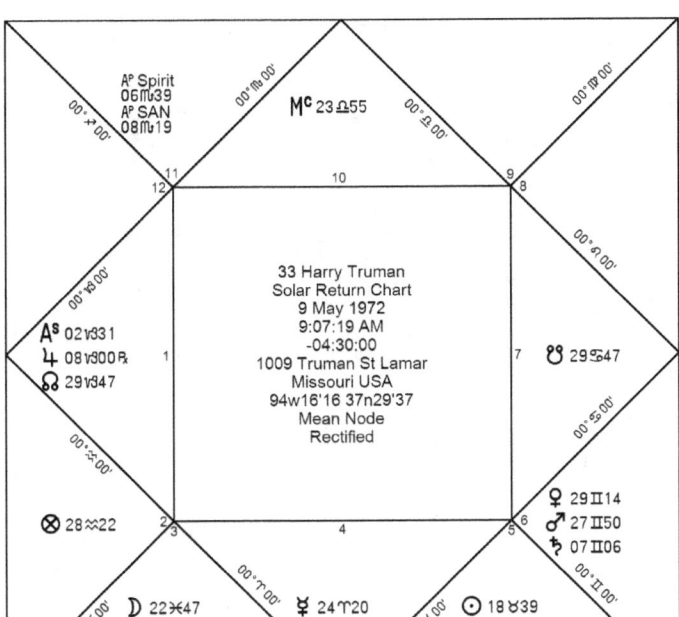

Ascendant Distributor: Saturn/Sagittarius since 21-July-1972
Profected Ascendant: 9AQ06, 5th House; SR Victor: Jupiter
Lords: LOY – Saturn; LOP – Moon
Firdaria: Venus-Saturn
Moon: separates from sextile of Sun and applies to trine of Mars
Return Ascendant falls in natal 4th; natal Ascendant falls in return's 10th.

Jupiter, third high scoring killer, falls in the return's Ascendant. High scoring killer Moon (also hīlāj) at 22PI36 is conjunct natal Lot of Fortune 25PI24 within 3 degrees.

The following direction pair occurs between 14-Dec-1972 when Truman stopped talking and his death on 26-Dec-1972. Jupiter is the 2nd high scoring killer planet, the victor of the return, and placed in the return's Ascendant.

| PT | D | Venus/Virgo | P | sinister square Saturn (0) d. => ASC | 17-Dec-1972 |
| PT | D | Venus/Virgo | P | dexter trine Jupiter (0) d. => ASC | 18-Dec-1972 |

652 A RECTIFICATION MANUAL

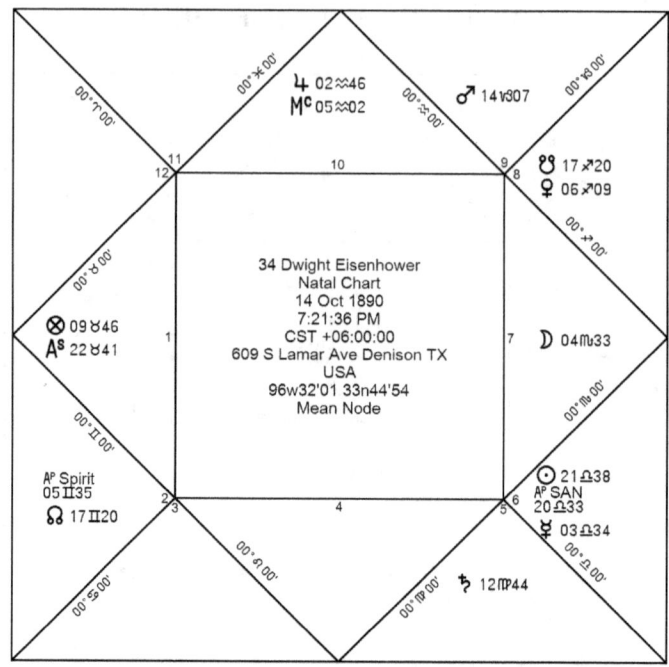

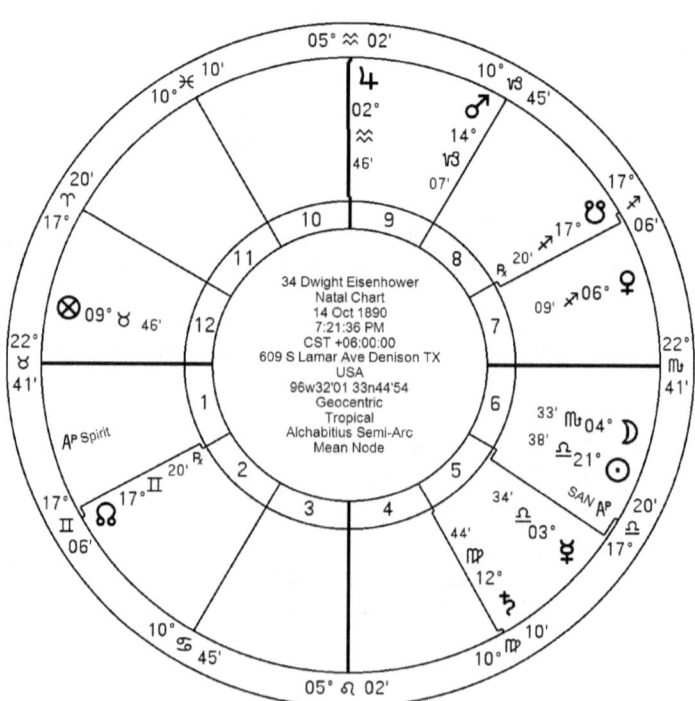

Moon's Configuration

Moon separates from **Jupiter** and applies to **Saturn**, nocturnal, conjunctional. Prenatal syzygy is 20LI33. Eclipse? No.

Cognitive Assessment Model (Rulers of Moon and Mercury)

Sign rulers: **Mars, Venus**
Bound rulers: **Mars, Venus**

Victor Soul Models

Ibn Ezra Victor Model (1507), in-sect triplicity ruler, triplicity decans.

	Position	☉	☽	☿	♀	♂	♃	♄
Sun	21 LI 38			4	7			4
Moon	04 SC 33					11		
Asc	22 TA 41			7	5			3
Pars Fortuna	09 TA 46			7	2	6		
Syzygy	20 LI 33			4	5		2	4
Oriental						0	0	3
Houses		1	1	7	10	4	11	7
Score	0	1	15	17	**33**	15	13	21

Porphyry's Expanded Victor Model (2022)

Jupiter rules the syzygy by bound. Sect: out-of-favor. Solar phase: occidental from 2nd station to waning square. Position: 10th from ASC and Lot of Fortune. Dignity: participating triplicity. Moon's separation.

Victor Table for Killing Planets

			☉	☽	☿	♀	♂	♃	♄
ASC		22TA41		4,3		5,3	3		2,1
Rul ASC	♀	6SA09	3					5,3,2,1	3
L.Death		25LI17			3,1	5,2		3	4,3
Rul L.Death	♀	6SA09	3					5,3,2,1	3
H8 Cusp		17SA06	3		2		1	5,3	3
Rul H8	♃	2AQ46			3,2			3	5,3,1
T-Rul H8	♃	2AQ46			3,2			3	5,3,1
♀ in 8th	♀	6SA09	3					5,3,2,1	3
SN in 8th	SN	15SA56	3		2		1	5,3	3
8th from ☽		4GE33			5,3,2,1			3	3
Rul 8th fr ☽	☿	3LI34			3	5,1		3	4,3,2
TOTAL			15	7	32	21	5	**64**	55

2007 Proposed Rectification: 7:21:44 PM, ASC 22TA43'47"
2022 Proposed Rectification: 7:21:36 PM, ASC 22TA41'24"

Astrodatabank reports a DD-rated birth time of 3:00 AM, dirty data. The proposed rectification is substantially later. The 2022 revised rectification was driven by a slight change to improve timing for Directing through the Bounds. Occurring during the early part of Eisenhower's 2nd term on 22-Jul-1956, the Ascendant distributor changed from the bound of Jupiter/Cancer to Saturn/Cancer. The next day the Civil Rights bill died in the Senate (but passed the following year). Also on 26-Jul-1956, Nasser nationalized the Suez Canal which proved a significant geopolitical headache for the next 6 months. The full Cancer Ascendant Distribution from 16-Jul-1926 to 14-May-1961 timed the bulk of his public service.

ZRS. For Ike, ZRS works like clockwork, most likely because Mars/Capricorn and Jupiter/Aquarius both occupy signs highlighted by FS/LB pairings during L1-Cancer and L1-Leo. Very powerful with Mars/Capricorn in its sign of exaltation and Jupiter/Aquarius the victor of the horoscope.

L1 Gemini 14 Oct 1890		
L2 Sagittarius 29 Jul 1899	FS	
L2 Sagittarius 13 Feb 1908	LB	No events recorded.
L1 Cancer 2 Jul 1910		4-Oct-1910, entrance exam for West Point; 14-Jun-1911, reported to West Point.
L2 Capricorn 19 Aug 1918	FS	Aug-1918, had 10,000 men under his command; 14-Oct-1918, Promoted Lieutenant Colonel, one of youngest lieutenant colonels in the Army; 10-Nov-1918, notice of armistice foiled chance of wartime service.
L2 Capricorn 31 Oct 1927	LB	Jun-1928, graduated from War College, top of class; Aug-1928, France posting to write expanded guidebook for the American Battlefield Monuments Commission. This exercise proved helpful in familiarizing DE with European geography later put to practical use as WWII commander.
L1 Leo 21 Feb 1935		In the Philippines with Douglas MacArthur (through 1939)
L2 Aquarius 9 Jun 1943	FS	10-Jul-1943, Allied invasion of Sicily; 3-Sep-1943. Italy surrendered to Allies; 6-Jun-1944, D-Day invasion of Europe; 20-Dec-1944, promoted to five-star general; 7-May-1945, accepted German surrender; 19-Nov-1945, named Army Chief of Staff.
L2 Aquarius 21 Jun 1952	LB	11-Jul-1952, Republican Presidential nomination; 4-Nov-1952, elected President; 27-Jun-1953, Korean Armistice signed; 3-Oct-1953, Earl Warren sworn in as Chief Justice Supreme Court.
L1 Virgo 13 Nov 1953		Followed 30-Oct-1953 "New Look" military strategy designed to balance military strategy with economic reality; emphasized Strategic Air Command and 'Massive Retaliation' nuclear attack strategy.
L2 Cancer 2 Aug 1967		28-Mar-1969, died.

Firdaria – Jupiter major and minor periods

Firdaria according to Bonatti	Life Event
Moon **Jupiter** 11 May 1893	No events found.
Saturn **Jupiter** 11 May 1901	Fall 192, started classes at Garfield.
Jupiter 12 years Age 20 to 32	
Jupiter Jupiter 15 Oct 1910	14-Jun-1911, reported to West Point.
Jupiter Mars 02 Jul 1912	16-Nov-1912, football injury.
Jupiter Sun 20 Mar 1914	11-Jun-1914, received infantry commission from War Secretary; 14-Feb-1915, engaged to Mamie Doud.
Jupiter Venus 07 Dec 1915	1-Jul-1916, married Mamie Doud; Jul-1916, promoted to 1st Lieutenant; 1-Apr-1917, left for Camp Wilson; 2-Apr-1917, Wilson asked for war declaration; May-1917, promoted to Captain.
Jupiter Mercury 24 Aug 1917	Jun-1918, temporary wartime promotion to Captain; 6-Jun-1918, received 1st tank; 14-Oct-1918, promoted to Lieutenant colonel; 11-Nov-1918, Armistice foiled chance of wartime service; Mar-1919, returned to Camp Meade commanding tank battalion.
Jupiter Moon 12 May 1919	7-Jul-1919, began trip East to West to promote military hardware to the public - Renault 'Whippet' tank; Jun-1920, promoted to Major; 2-Jan-1921, death of son Ikky from scarlet fever.
Jupiter Saturn 27 Jan 1921	Feb-1921, asked to run a brigade in Panama; 7-Jan-1922, sailed for Panama; 3-Aug-1922, son John born.
Mars **Jupiter** 15 Oct 1928	In France with Mamie working on WWI guidebook during this subperiod.
Sun **Jupiter** 06 Dec 1941	7-Dec-1941, Pearl Harbor; 11-Dec-1941, death of Col Bundy of War Plans Division (plane crash) opened spot for DE; 14-Feb-1942, made Chief of War Plans Division; 11-Jun-1942, given command of European Theatre of Operations; 6-Aug-1942, named commander of Operation Torch; 10-Feb-1943, promoted to 4-star general.
Venus **Jupiter** 11 May 1949	25-Jun-1950, Korean War outbreak.
Mercury **Jupiter** 11 May 1958	1-Jul-1958, Geneva Conference met to examine means of monitoring nuclear test ban; 1-Jan-1959, Castro came to power in Cuba; 13-Apr-1959, proposed nuclear test ban; 10-Sep-1959, Congress overrode DE's public works bill veto, first such defeat; 17-Mar-1960, approved covert action against Castro.
Moon **Jupiter** 11 May 1968	28-Mar-1969, death.

Jupiter as Victor. Were Mars/Capricorn the victor, Eisenhower would be remembered as a distinguished military leader. However Jupiter/Aquarius provides Eisenhower with administrative abilities which allows him to manage European alliances during WWII years (Jupiter is placed in the bound of Mercury/Aquarius with bound lord Mercury/Libra the sign of diplomacy). As President, Eisenhower occupied the center right position on the political scale, drawing on politicos like Thomas Dewey (also Jupiter/Aquarius) to build a centrist political coalition.

Transits

<u>29-Feb-1944</u>. *tr South Node conj. MC.*
Aerial bombings of Germany began last week of February. Note: natal South Node in Sagittarius, sign of flight.

<u>24-Oct-1948</u>. *tr Nodes square MC.*
Installed as President of Columbia University, 12-Oct.

<u>22-Jul-1952</u>. *tr Nodes square ASC.*
Presidential Nomination, 11-Jul.

<u>20-Jun-1953</u>. *tr North Node conj. MC.*
Julius and Ethel Rosenberg executed in the electric chair, 19-Jun.

<u>17-Jan-1961</u>. *tr Mercury conj. MC.*
Warned of rise of military industrial complex, 17-Jan.

Solar Arc Directions

<u>2-Jan-1921</u>. *dsa Saturn 12LI57 conj L.Children 12LI43*
Death of son Ikky.

<u>22-Dec-1941</u>. *dsa ASC opposed Mars.*
<u>29-May-1943</u>. *csa Mars opposed ASC.*
Pearl Harbor, 7-Dec-1941.
Arcadia strategy meeting with British and American commanders in Washington DC decided to create combined Chiefs of Staff, 22-Dec/7-Jan-42. DE is named Chief of War Plans Division, 14-Feb-1942.
Axis troops surrender at Tunisia ended North Africa Campaign, 13-May-43.
Churchill and Marshall met with DE to plan Italian campaign, 27-May-43.

<u>17-Dec-1942</u>. *dsa Nodes sq LOF.*
<u>10-Jun-1944</u>. *csa LOF square Nodes.*
D-Day invasion of France, 5-Jun-1944.

<u>7-Dec-1949</u>. *csa Jupiter sextile MC.*
<u>15-Aug-1952</u>. *dsa Jupiter sextile MC.*
In response to rumors that DE was unhappy at Columbia, the Dean said DE was not interested in running for President, 9-Dec-1949. (NYT p. 6).
Selected as Republican Presidential candidate, 11-Jul-1952.

35. DWIGHT EISENHOWER

Primary Directions

| PT | D | Venus/Taurus | P | opp Moon (0) c. => ASC | 22-Oct-1904 |

Scratched knee/blood poisoning/near death medical emergency, Fall 1904

| PT | D | Venus/Capricorn | P | Mars (0) c. => MC | 3-Nov-1912 |

Football knee injury ended chances for a football career, 16-Nov.

| PT | D | Merc/Sagittarius | P | South Node c. => MC | 12-Dec-1941 |

LOCK Death of Colonel Bundy in War Plans Division from plane crash opened position for DE, 11-Dec-1941. South Node/Sagittarius = air crash.

| REG | D | Jupiter/Leo | P | IC c. => Sun | 14-Nov-1945 |
| PT | D | Jupiter/Leo | P | IC c. => Sun | 21-Dec-1948 |

Named Army Chief of Staff, 19-Nov-1945.
Installed as President of Columbia University, 12-Oct-1948.
Eisenhower wanted neither of these positions with the Columbia position a widely agreed upon bad fit for his abilities. Sun-IC directions signify career problems or spiritual crisis (see Reagan for example of the latter).

| PT | D | Jupiter/Sagittarius | P | Venus (0) c. => MC | 26-Nov-1953 |

Unveiled *Atoms for Peace* proposal at United Nations, 8-Dec.
Venus 6SA09 is the antiscia of 23CP51 which is the nuclear degree area.
Examples: Regulus USA National Horoscope; also Edward Teller.

Primary Direction Sequences

| PT | D | Mercury/Cancer | P | opp Mars (0) d. => ASC | 2-Jul-1942 |
| PT | D | Mercury/Cancer | P | opp Mars (MA) d. => ASC | 26-Jan-1944 |

LOCK This sequence emphasized the 9th house signification of foreign travel tied to Eisenhower's WWII service. On 11-Jun-1942 Eisenhower was promoted to head the European Theatre of Operations. He arrived in London on 24-Jun and beginning on 7-Jul was given a series of promotions ahead of D-Day: 7-Jul-1942, Lieutenant General (temporary); 11-Feb-1943, 4-star General (temporary); 30-Aug-1943, Brigadier General and Major General (permanent); 7-Dec-1943, Supreme Commander of Allied Expeditionary Forces. He returned to in London on 13-Jan-1944 as the sequence ended. During this time Eisenhower led the Operation Torch invasion of North Africa. For a time he was stationed at the Rock of Gibraltar. Now used as a marketing logo by Prudential Financial, the Rock of Gibraltar demonstrates the influence of Mars placed in the bound of Venus/Capricorn (Venus=finance) in addition to the Rock's wartime staging operations consistent with: War (Mars) + Rock (Capricorn).

Longevity, 78y 5m 13d

Death: 28-Mar-1969, 12:35 PM, Walter Reed Army Medical Center, Washington, DC. Eisenhower suffered a series of heart attacks towards the end of his life and was hospitalized at Walter Reed during April 1968 and remained there until his death 11 months later. The official final cause of death was pneumonia following surgery for the removal of intestinal scar tissue.

Hīlāj: **Ascendant**. Figure is nocturnal and Moon is preferred yet falling more than 5 degrees below the cusp of the 7th is disqualified. Sun in 6th is disqualified. Chart is conjunctional; Ascendant qualifies and is confirmed by a trine aspect to Mars, the planet with the highest dignities in the Ascendant.

Al-kadukhadāh: **Jupiter**. Despite the logic in choosing Mars as an Al-kadukhadāh; Jupiter falls within 3 degrees of the MC and trumps Mars as the empirical Al-kadukhadāh. Jupiter gives his major 79 years which matches Eisenhower's lifespan. Though Mercury receives Jupiter by triplicity and bound, he does not add years. Nor does Venus add years by sextile aspect.

Victor: **Jupiter**

Killing Planets: **Jupiter (64), Saturn (55)**

Arcus Vitae:

| PT | D | Mercury/Aquarius | P | Jupiter (JU) c. => ASC | 10-Aug-1968 |
| PT | D | Mercury/Aquarius | P | Jupiter (0) c. => ASC | 25-May-1969 |

Sequence links the high scoring killing planet (Jupiter) with the Hīlāj.

1968 Solar Return for year of Death

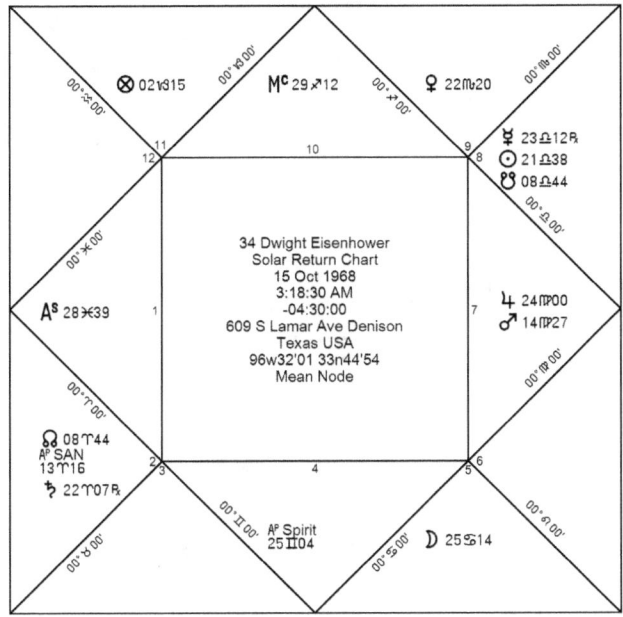

Ascendant Distributor: Venus/Leo since 19-Aug-1968
Profected Ascendant: 22SC43, 7th House; SR Victor: Mars
Lords: LOY – Mars; LOP – Mars
Firdaria: Moon-Jupiter
Moon: separates from sextile of Jupiter and is void of course
Return Ascendant falls in natal 11th; Natal Ascendant falls in return's 3rd.

High scoring killing planet Jupiter opposes the Ascendant. Secondary killer Saturn opposes the Sun and squares the Moon. Both high scoring killing planets afflict the luminaries and the return's Ascendant.

Jupiter is given further power to act because of his placement in the return's 7th house which is the profected natal house for the year. LOY and LOP Mars is also given power to act by falling in the return's 7th. Mars is tied to death because Eisenhower is weakened after surgery to remove scar tissue from the intestines. Intestines are assigned to Virgo; Mars in that sign signifies cutting.

Eisenhower dies on the day Mars meets the solar return Ascendant. The Jupiter direction is late.

PT	D	Venus/Virgo	P	Mars (0) d. => ASC	28-Mar-1969
PT	D	Venus/Virgo	P	Jupiter (0) d. => ASC	8-Apr-1969

660 — A RECTIFICATION MANUAL

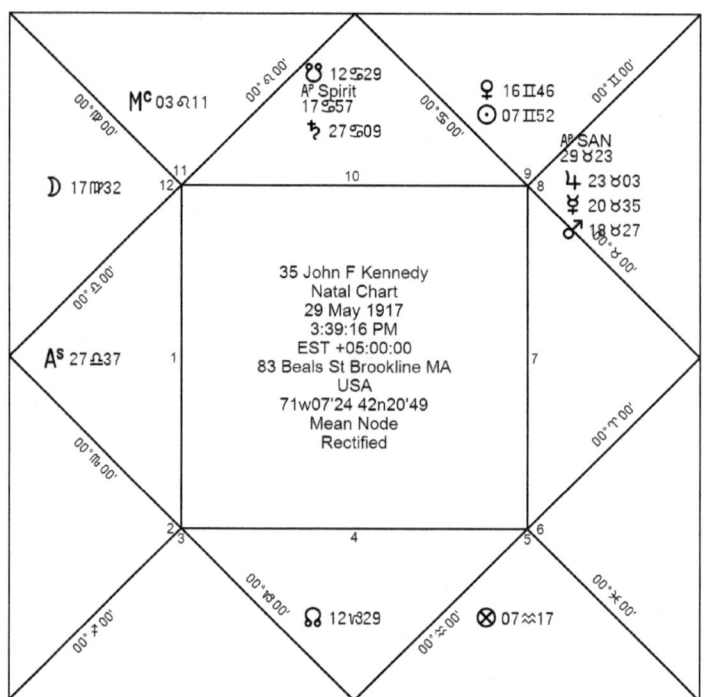

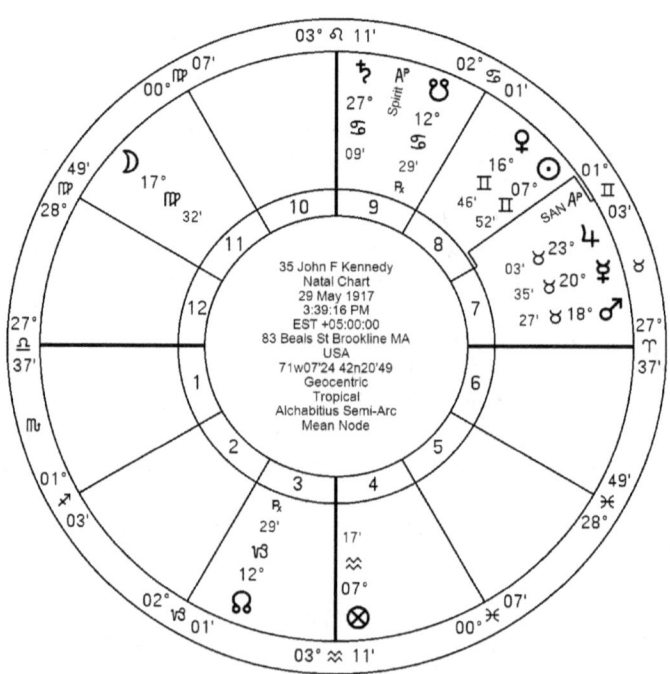

Moon's Configuration

Moon separates from **Venus** and applies to **Mars**, diurnal, conjunctional.
Prenatal syzygy is 29TA23. Eclipse? No.

Cognitive Assessment Model (Rulers of Moon and Mercury)

Sign rulers: **Mercury, Venus**
Bound rulers: **Jupiter** (both)

Victor Soul Models

Ibn Ezra Victor Model (1507), in-sect triplicity ruler, triplicity decans.

	Position	☉	☽	☿	♀	♂	♃	♄
Sun	07 GE 52			6			2	3
Moon	17 VI 32			9	3		2	1
Asc	27 LI 36			1	7			7
Pars Fortuna	07 AQ 16				2			9
Syzygy	29 TA 23		4		8	2		1
Oriental						3	0	0
Houses		5	8	10	5	10	10	4
Score		0	5	12	26	25	15	14	25

Porphyry's Expanded Victor Model (2022)

Jupiter rules the MC, Moon, and Sun by bound. Sect: in-favor. Solar phase: oriental under the sunbeams. Position: 4th from Lot of Fortune.

Victor Table for Killing Planets

			☉	☽	☿	♀	♂	♃	♄
ASC		27LI36			3,1	5,2		3	4,3
Rul ASC	♀	16GE46			5,3,1	2		3	3
L.Death		10AR40	4,3,1			2	5	3	3
Rul L.Death	♂	18TA27		4,3	1	5,3	3	2	
H8 Cusp		1GE03			5,3,2,1			3	3
Rul H8	☿	20TA35		4,3		5,3	3	2	1
T-Rul H8	♄	27CA09		5,3		3	3	4,1	2
♃ in 8th	♃	23TA03		4,3		5,3	3,2		1
☿ in 8th	☿	20TA35		4,3		5,3	3	2	1
♂ in 8th	♂	18TA27		4,3	1	5,3	3	2	
8th from ☉		7CP52		3		3	4,3	2	5,1
Rul 8th fr ☉	♄	27CA09		5,3		3	3	4,1	2
TOTAL			8	54	26	60	35	32	29

2007 Proposed Rectification: 3:39:14 PM, ASC 27LI36'55"
2022 Proposed rectification: 3:39:16 PM, ASC 27LI37'02"

Astrodatabank reports an A-rated birth time of 3:00 PM, ASC 20LI00. The proposed rectification is 40 minutes later. One key difference between the ADB time and the proposed rectification is the Lot of Fortune's sign placement: for the ADB time, LOF falls in the last degree of Capricorn; for the proposed rectification, the LOF advances to early Aquarius.

ZRS. L1-Leo opened with JFK's military service deemed necessary as a future political cred. L2-Aquarius (FS) links his Senate bid to L2-Aquarius (LB) his successful Presidential nomination. JFK was elected President a month after the start of L1-Virgo.

L1 Cancer 29 May 1917		
L2 Capricorn 16 Jul 1925	FS	20-Nov-1925, birth of brother Robert F. Kennedy; 1926, Kennedy family moved to NYC
L2 Capricorn 27 Sep 1934	LB	Feb-1935, threatened with expulsion at Choate for 'Choate Muckers Club' incident but allowed to stay. Graduated from Choate. Summer 1935, traveled to London to study at London School of Economics, forced to return home because of jaundice; Fall 1935, entered Princeton but dropped out because of jaundice; Sep-1936, entered Harvard.
L1 Leo 18 Jan 1942		Jan-1943, ordered to take four PT boats to Florida, then South Pacific; 24-Apr-1943, received his own command; 1-Aug-1943, PT boat attacked and hit; 6/7-Aug-1943, JFK and crew rescued.
L2 Aquarius 6 May 1950	FS	11-Jan-1951, Visited London to assess whether the US should send more troops to NATO; 6-Feb-1951, returned to Boston and made isolationist comments about Europe; late Oct/ear-Nov-1951, near death from Addison's disease (read late rites 2nd time); 7-Apr-1952, announced Senate bid.
L2 Aquarius 19 May 1959	LB	2-Jan-1960, announced Presidential Bid; 13-Jul-1960, nominated for President; 12-Sep-1960, stated independence from Catholic Church; 26-Sep-1960, surprise TV debate victory over Richard Nixon.
L1 Virgo 10 Oct 1960		13-Oct-1960, proposed concept of Peace Corps; 8-Nov-1960, won Presidential election.
L2 Scorpio 28 Jan 1963		8-Feb-1963, resumed underground nuclear tests; 26-Jun-1963, Berlin 'Ich bin ein Berliner!' speech; 25-Jul-1963, Nuclear Test Treaty agreement; 7-Aug-63, son Patrick born premature and died; Aug-1963, Vietnam conflict between Diem and Buddhist monks spirals out of control; 22-Sep-1963, Nuclear test-ban treaty ratified by Senate; 1-Nov-1963, Diem assassination; 22-Nov-1963, JFK assassination.

Firdaria – Jupiter major and minor periods

Firdaria according to Bonatti	Life Event
Sun **Jupiter** 20 Jul 1924	20-Nov-1925, birth of brother Robert.
Venus **Jupiter** 24 Dec 1931	22-Feb-1932, birth of brother Edward.
Mercury **Jupiter** 23 Dec 1940	5-Aug-1941, passed Navy physical, commissioned ensign; 7-Dec-1941, Pearl Harbor; 13-Jan-1942, transferred to Charleston SC to get JFK away from girlfriend Inga Arvad; Jul-1942, attended Navy training program for reserve officers at Northwestern University.
Moon **Jupiter** 24 Dec 1950	11-Jan-1951, arrived in London to assess US troop deployment to NATO; 6-Feb-1951, upon return to Boston makes isolationist comments about Europe; Feb-1951, met political consultant about possible senatorial or gubernatorial run; Spring-1951, met Jackie for first time; Summer-1951, traveled to Tehran just after oil fields nationalized; late/Oct-ear/Nov-1951, major illness with Addison's disease, given last rites 2nd time.
Saturn **Jupiter** 24 Dec 1958	4-Nov-1958, re-elected Senator by largest margin in history of Massachusetts; 2-Jan-1960, announced Presidential bid; 13-Jul-1960, nominated for President.

Jupiter as Victor. Kennedy did not live long enough for the major Jupiter Firdaria period to activate. In addition to the birth of two of his brothers which were also politically active, Jupiter subperiods captured initial WWII service, a key foreign tour prior to his Senate bid, and his Presidential nomination.

Transits

20-Apr-1952. *tr North Node trine ASC.*
Announced Senate Bid, 7-Apr.

31-Aug-1956. *tr North Node trine MC.*
DNC appearance elevated reputation and fame, 13/17-Aug-1956.

10-Aug-1961. *tr South Node trine ASC.*
Construction of Berlin Wall began, 13-Aug; followed Khrushchev's 9-Aug boast of Soviet ability to construct a one-hundred-ton hydrogen bomb.

14-Nov-1962. *tr North Node conj. MC.*
Brother Ted Kennedy elected to Senate Seat, 6-Nov-1962; Improved reputation following diffusion of Cuban Missile Crisis, 16/28-Oct-1962.

Solar Arc Directions

10-Jun-1931. *dsa Mars conj. Vertex.*
Austrian bank riots, 7-Jun; Hoover proposed debt moratorium, 20-Jun.

14-Apr-1933. *csa Mars square MC.*
FDR took US off gold standard, Value of dollar fell, 19-Apr.

19-Jan-1939. *csa Mars opposed ASC.*
14-Mar-1939. *dsa ASC opposed Mars.*
Test pilot crashed Douglas A-20; exposed clandestine plane deal under negotiation with France, 19-Jan. JFK is not directly connected to this event; yet see the 5-Jun/15-Aug-1944 primary direction sequence for similar events which did impact him directly.
Germany invaded remainder of Czechoslovakia, 15-Mar.

9-Jan-1944. *dsa ASC opposed Jupiter.*
Arrived San Francisco for recuperation after Pacific tour, 7-Jan.

10-Nov-1963. *dsa MC conj. Moon.*
Prisoner release of Yale Professor Frederick Barghoorn, 16-Nov.

Primary Directions

PT	D	Venus/Cancer	P	South Node c. => MC	29-Apr-1939

Followed Germany's 15-Mar takeover of the balance of Czechoslovakia, making mockery of Munich.

35. JOHN F. KENNEDY

| REG | D | Mercury/Pisces | P | dex sex Mars (MA) d. => LOF | 9-Dec-1957 |

Kennedy planned to threaten journalist Drew Pearson with $50 million suit on 9-Dec following Person's 7-Dec accusation that JFK's *Profiles in Courage* was a ghostwritten book.

| REG | D | Saturn/Aquarius | P | sin trine ASC d. => NNode | 22-Sep-1960 |

First Nixon-Kennedy debate where Nixon performed poorly, 26-Sep.

Primary Direction Sequences

| PT | D | Jupiter/Leo | P | MC d. => Saturn (SA) | 20-Jun-1923 |
| PT | D | Jupiter/Leo | P | MC d. => Saturn (0) | 4-Aug-1923 |

LOCK Harding left Washington on 20-Jun for a fateful vacation ending with death on 2-Aug. Saturn rules the 5th (WS) – death of the King. Similar to same sequence by method of Regiomontanus (17-Jun/25-Jul).

| REG | D | Saturn/Aries | P | DSC c. => Mars (MA) | 5-Aug-1943 |
| REG | D | Saturn/Aries | P | DSC c. => Mars (0) | 2-Oct-1943 |

LOCK This sequence timed Kennedy's most significant action under fire while a PT boat captain in the South Pacific. His PT-109 was attacked and destroyed on 1-Aug. Two men died. Following 6/7-Aug rescue, he assumed command of PT-59, added armaments to the boat in a lengthy conversion project and was bombed (but took no hits) on 18-Oct-1943.

| PT | D | Mercury/Scorpio | P | opp Mars (0) d. => ASC | 5-Jun-1944 |
| PT | D | Mercury/Scorpio | P | opp Mars (MA) d. => ASC | 15-Aug-1944 |

LOCK This sequence timed not only the D-Day invasion of 6-Jun but also his Brother Joe's death on 12-Aug-1944. Joe Kennedy died as pilot on a volunteer mission after his bomb payload detonated midair. Mars/Taurus is consistent with extremely large explosions. Note above 19-Jan-1939 solar arc direction which timed another aircraft explosion.

| PT | D | Jupiter/Virgo | P | sin trine Mars (MA) d. => MC | 11-Mar-1961 |
| PT | D | Jupiter/Virgo | P | sin trine Mars (0) d. => MC | 20-Apr-1961 |

LOCK Timed disastrous Bay of Pigs episode. Original Trinidad plan proposed 11-Mar; revised attack plans presented 16-Mar after JFK said that Trinidad was too bombastic – JFK wanted something on a smaller scale with less chance of the actions traceable to the United States; actual invasion 17/19-Apr; JFK debriefed Eisenhower on 22-Apr; Castro verbally attacked JFK on 23-Apr; JFK admitted full responsibility on 24-Apr.

| REG | D | Jupiter/Taurus | P | Mercury (0) d. => LOF | 18-Oct-2017 |

National Archives released main batch of 1963 assassination documents, 26-Oct-2017.

Longevity, 46y 5m 24d

Death: 22-Nov-1963, 12:30 PM, Dallas Texas. Assassinated by gunfire.

Hīlāj: **LOF**. Chart is diurnal and Sun 8th/9th in a masculine sign qualifies yet there is no ruler with dignity that aspects. Moon in 12th is disqualified. The Ascendant qualifies with Venus occidental making a trine. Yet the longevity projection for Venus fails. Empirically, the Lot of Fortune/Jupiter combination produces better results. Jupiter is in the contra-antiscion of the Lot of Fortune and the Victor of the Horoscope.

Key events for testing Hīlāj
1-Aug-1943. Attacked while leading PT Boat crew in South Pacific.
22-Jun-1944. Back surgery – did not go well.
Mid-Sept 1947. Diagnosed with Addison's disease – given last rites.
Late-Oct/early-Nov 1951. Lapsed into coma, fever to 106 degrees, Addison's disease – given last rites 2nd time.
24-Oct-1954. Vital signs failed following back surgery on 21-Oct – given last rites 3rd time. Additional surgery 15-Feb-1955.
22-Nov-1963. Assassination.

Evidence for Lot of Fortune as Hīlāj. For the 22-Jun-1944 back surgery, dsa North Node 7AQ06 conj LOF at 7AQ17. On 15-Sep-1947, tr Jupiter 22SC56 conj LOF's antiscia 22SC43; tr South Node 25SC23 also active. On 1-Nov-1947, tr Mercury 20SC27 conj LOF's antiscia. On 24-Oct-1954, tr Mars ingressed to Aquarius, sign of LOF. On 15-Feb-1955, tr Saturn 21SC01 conj LOF's antiscia (error=2 degrees).

Al-kadukhadāh: **Jupiter**. From Jupiter's 79 major years, Saturn's sextile receives Jupiter by bound and decan and deducts 30 minor years. JU (79) – SA (30) = 49 years. Mars is co-present with Jupiter and deducts 15 minor years yet Jupiter receives Mars so the 15-year deduction is one which maims but does not kill. Mars' deduction of 15 years reduces longevity to 34, the year 1951 when JFK was given last rites for the 2nd time.

Victor of the Horoscope: **Jupiter**
Killing Planets: **Venus (60), Moon (54)**

Arcus Vitae:

REG	D	Venus/Taurus	P	sin sq LOF c. => Venus (0)	23-Jul-1963
REG	D	Venus/Taurus	P	sin sq LOF c. => Venus (VE)	21-Sep-1963

Sequence joins high scoring killing planet with Hīlāj.

PT	D	Saturn/Gemini	P	dex trine ASC d. => Mars (0)	8-Nov-1963
PT	D	Saturn/Gemini	P	dex trine ASC d. => Mars (MA)	27-Dec-1963

Sequence includes assassination (bullet through the throat).

PT	D	Saturn/Aries	P	DSC c. => Sun	2-Dec-1963

Sun on 8th cusp promises famous death; arc is mirrored in solar return.

1963 Solar Return for year of Death

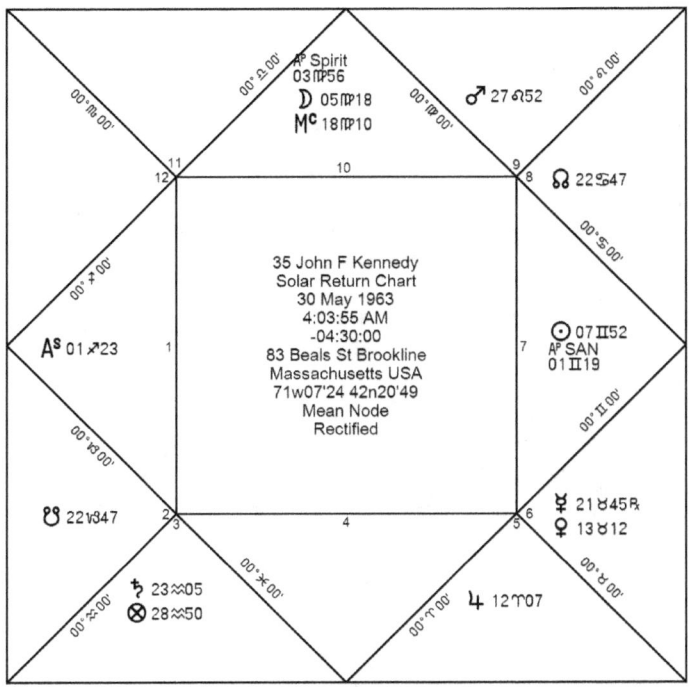

Ascendant Distributor: Jupiter/Sagittarius since 14-Apr-1959
Profected Ascendant: 27LE36, 11th House; SR Victor: Mercury
Lords: LOY – Sun; LOP – Jupiter
Firdaria: Saturn-Venus
Moon: applies to square of Sun
Return Ascendant falls in natal 2nd; Natal Ascendant falls in return's 11th

Hīlāj Lot of Fortune is afflicted by the destructive Saturn-Mars-Mercury T-square. Natal 8th cusp 1GE13 falls on the return's 7th cusp at 1GE24 which is the angle of the West. Sun is Lord of the Year and falls in the 7th. High scoring killer Moon also afflicts the Sun by square. Moon is given power to act in several ways in the return. First the Moon returns to her same sign of Virgo. Second the Moon's natal position of 17VI32 is within one degree of the return's MC. Third the Moon is the most elevated planet in the return. Fourth the Moon rules the 8th of death in the return.

Kennedy is assassinated 176.75 days or 174deg 12min following his return.

| PT | D | Mars/Leo | P | Mars (MA) d. => LOF | 175deg 19min |

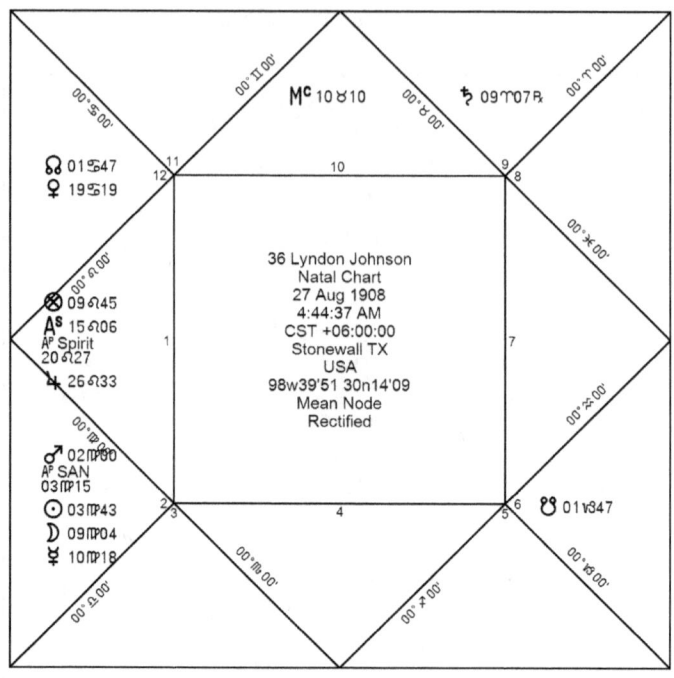
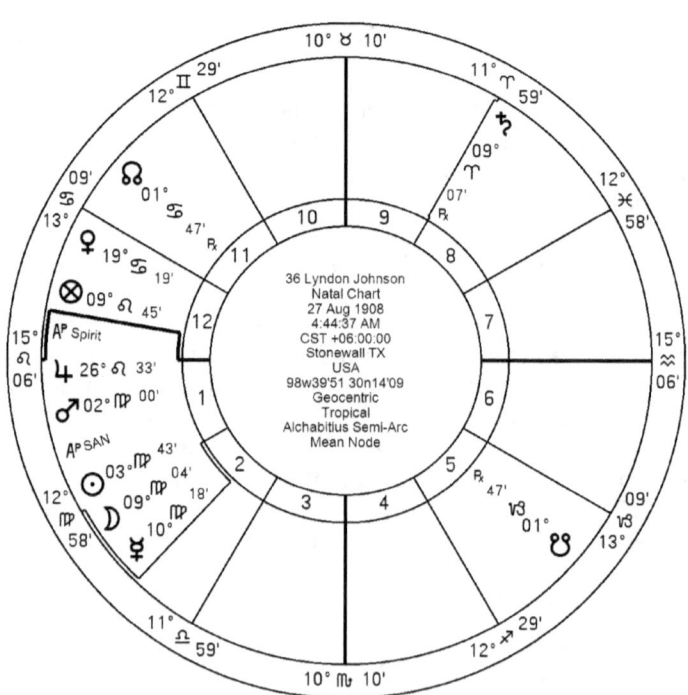

Moon's Configuration

Moon separates from **Sun** and applies to **Mercury**, nocturnal, conjunctional. Prenatal syzygy is 3VI15. Eclipse? No.

Cognitive Assessment Model (Rulers of Moon and Mercury)

Sign rulers: **Mercury** (both)
Bound rulers: **Venus** (both)

Victor Soul Models

Ibn Ezra Victor Model (1507), in-sect triplicity ruler, triplicity decans.

	Position	☉	☽	☿	♀	♂	♃	♄
Sun	03 VI 43		3	12				
Moon	09 VI 04		3	10	2			
Asc	15 LE 06	5					4	2
Pars Fortuna	09 LE 45	6			2		3	
Syzygy	03 VI 15		3	12				
Oriental						0	0	1
Houses		12	6	6	2	12	12	4
Score	0	23	15	**40**	6	12	19	7

Porphyry's Expanded Victor Model (2022)

Mercury rules the Moon, Sun, and syzygy by sign; the MC, Sun, and syzygy by bound. Solar phase: occidental direct combust. Sect: in-favor. Dignity: sign and exaltation. Moon's application.

Victor Table for Killing Planets

			☉	☽	☿	♀	♂	♃	♄
ASC		15LE06	5,3					3,1	3,2
Rul ASC	☉	3VI43		3	5,4,2,1	3	3		
L.Death		13LI01			3,2	5		3	4,3,1
Rul L.Death	♀	19CA19		5,3		3	3,1	4,2	
H8 Cusp		12PI58		3,1		4,3	3	5,2	
Rul H8	♃	26LE33	5,3				2,1	3	3
T-Rul H8	☿	2VI00		3	5,4,2,1	3	3		
8th from ☽		9AR04	4,3			2	5,1	3	3
Rul 8th fr ☽	☿	2VI00		3	5,4,2,1	3	3		
TOTAL			23	21	**41**	26	25	**26**	19

2007 Proposed Rectification: 4:47:37 AM, ASC 15LE06'39"

Astrodatabank reports a C-rated birth time of 5:40 AM, accuracy in question. The proposed rectification is an hour earlier. Both times feature Leo rising. The ADB time casts the LOF in Leo and the LOS in Virgo. The proposed rectification casts both lots in Leo. Because of Valens' rule that ZRS shall begin from the following sign when both lots are in the same sign, both ADB and rectified times will release from Virgo, e.g., no difference.

ZRS. Beginning with L1 Scorpio, L2 periods angular from LOF are included.

L1 Virgo 27 Aug 1908		
L2 Pisces 08 Nov 1917	FS	Feb-1918, father elected to TX legislature in special election.
L2 Pisces 26 Dec 1925	LB	Mar-1926, after returning home from CA, went to work on a road gang, driving bulldozers and pickup trucks.
L1 Libra 14 May 1928		5-Sep-1928, forced to withdraw from college because of financial difficulties.
L1 Scorpio 02 Apr 1936		10-Apr-1937, won special election for Texas 10th Congressional district after sudden death of Rep James Buchanan.
L2 Aquarius 08 Sep 1940		9-Oct-1940, FDR placed LBJ in charge of Democratic Congressional campaigns where LBJ excelled. Biographer Dallek says this is a key turning point where after this event LBJ played a significant part in national politics; 2-Jul-1941, defeated in Senate election but kept House seat; 27-Dec-1942, LBJ and Lady Bird purchased KTBC radio station.
L2 Taurus 15 May 1945		14-May/12-Jun-1945, Congressional junket to Europe; LBJ's takeaways were excessive military spending and the 'Communist threat'; 1-Jan to mid-Feb-1946, hospitalized for flu/pneumonia/exhaustion.
L2 Leo 21 Sep 1949		25-Jun-1950, Korean War; 2-Jan-1951, elected Majority Whip of Senate.
L1 Sagittarius 14 Jan 1951		
L2 Aquarius 29 Mar 1954		8-May-1954, French surrendered to North Vietnamese; 17-May-1954, Brown v Board of Education; 2-Nov-1954, re-elected to Senate; Jan-1955, elected Majority leader of the Senate.
L2 Taurus 03 Dec 1958		7-Jan-1959, re-elected Senate Majority Leader.
L1 Capricorn 12 Nov 1962		22-Nov-1963, acceded to Presidency after assassination.
L2 Aquarius 30 Jan 1965		13-Feb-1965, Operation 'Rolling Thunder' began in Vietnam; 8/9-Mar-1965, committed 1st US ground forces to Vietnam; 15-Mar-1965, promoted Voting Rights Act; 21-Jul-1965, decision made to escalate war in Vietnam; 30-Jul-1965, Medicare Act of 1965 signed; 6-Aug-1965, Voting Rights Act of 1965; by end of 1966, LBJ's Vietnam strategy turned disastrous; 5-Jun-1967, Six Day War in Israel.
L2 Taurus 06 Oct 1969		1-Mar-1970, hospitalized w/severe chest pains; problem with angina, hardening of arteries.
L2 Cancer 24 Jan 1972	FS	22-Jan-1973, death.

Firdaria – Mercury major and minor periods

Firdaria according to Bonatti	Life Event
Moon **Mercury** 14 May 1916	Jan-1917, family moved back to the farm near Stonewall; LBJ sent to one-room Junction School.
Saturn **Mercury** 06 Jul 1925	Mar-1926, went to work on a road gang, driving bulldozers and pickup trucks for one dollar a day.
Jupiter **Mercury** 06 Jul 1935	15-Aug-1935, opened National Youth Administration headquarters in Austin, TX.
Mars **Mercury** 27 Aug 1943	13/17-Jan-1944, met with FDR at White House to discuss politics; 22-Jul-1944, defeated Buck Taylor in Congressional primary.
Sun **Mercury** 06 Jul 1955	7-Aug-1955, released from hospital; 21-Nov-1955, made one of most effective political speeches of career, attempt to disarm the anti-southern bias; 22-May-1956, named Chair of Texas delegation to National Convention; 13/17-Aug-1966, attended DNC; 16-Aug-1956, nominated for President by John Connally, lost to Adlai Stevenson.
Venus **Mercury** 18 Oct 1963	22-Nov-1963, acceded to Presidency after assassination of JFK; 2-Jul-1964, signed Civil Rights Act of 1964.
Mercury 13 years Age 62 to 75	
Mercury Mercury 27 Aug 1970	22-May-1971, attended dedication of LBJ library.
Mercury Moon 05 Jul 1972	22-Jan-1973, death.

Mercury as Victor. Mercury periods captured the National Youth Administration launch in Austin while working as a New Dealer for FDR, his first successful electoral victory, an unsuccessful Presidential nomination attempt, accession to the Presidency on the death of JFK, and dedication of the LBJ Library.

A solid alternative to Mercury as victor is **Jupiter/Leo** near the Ascendant degree which signifies LBJ's grasp of political power. But consider that without Mercury/Virgo/2nd of wealth ruling the 11th of the King's treasury LBJ would have no political power. Slush funds helped built political alliances and once in office, LBJ spent liberally on programs to fight the War on Poverty, also Vietnam. Mercury rules the Sun which rules Jupiter in turn e.g., without Mercury working in the background the ability of Jupiter to harness political power on its own would be curtailed compared to LBJ's lived experience.

Transits

<u>7-May-1942</u>. *tr North Node trine MC.*
Arrived New Zealand to begin WWII fact finding mission, 21-May.

<u>20-Jul-1948</u>. *tr North Node conj. MC.*
Lost first Senate Primary to Stevenson; won second primary, 24-Jul. Declared winner of second disputed primary on 15-Sep.

<u>3-Apr-1962</u>. *tr North Node conj ASC.*
Hailed by JFK and Congress on 25 years of public service, 10-Apr.

<u>23-Jan-1964</u>. *tr North Node sextile MC.*
Met with Canadian PM for conservation agreements on Columbia River Basin and Roosevelt Campobello Park, 21/22-Jan.

Primary Directions

| PT | D | Venus/Aries | P | Saturn (SA) c. => MC | 28-Dec-1936 |

FDR issued statement denouncing an arms exporter who sold aircraft to the Republican government in Spain during the Spanish Civil War, 29-Dec.

| REG | D | Venus/Pisces | P | opp Sun c. => Saturn (0) | 30-Mar-1945 |
| REG | D | Venus/Pisces | P | opp Sun c. => Saturn (SA) | 27-Jul-1945 |

Death of mentor FDR, 12-Apr.

| PT | D | Venus/Cancer | P | sin square Saturn (0) c. => ASC | 23-Nov-1950 |

Chinese launched counteroffensive in Korean War, 26-Nov.

| REG | D | Venus/Leo | P | sin square MC d. => North Node | 2-Jan-1952 |

Elected Majority Whip of Senate for a second time, 3-Jan.

| PT | D | Mars/Pisces | P | dex trine Venus (VE) c. => MC | 7-Aug-1954 |

Eisenhower approved Housing Act of 1954, 2-Aug.

| REG | D | Saturn/Leo | P | ASC d. => North Node | 2-Aug-1957 |

Watered down Civil Rights legislation by eliminating Title III on 24-Jul and adding the Jury trial amendment on 2-Aug. (North Node in bound of Mars/Cancer in 12th signifies Dixiecrat enemies of Civil Rights.

| PT | D | Jupiter/Cancer | P | Venus (0) c. => Sun | 21-Jan-1959 |
| PT | D | Mars/Cancer | P | North Node c. => ASC | 3-Feb-1959 |

Proposed extending Civil Rights Commission for two years, provoked controversy, 20-Jan.

| PT | D | Mercury/Libra | P | opp Saturn (SA) d. => ASC | 11-Oct-1971 |

Members of the U.S. 1st Air Cavalry Division refused an assignment to go out on patrol. This was one of several examples of combat refusal.

Primary Direction Sequences

REG	D	Saturn/Leo	P	ASC c. => Mars (MA)	22-Feb-1928
REG	D	Saturn/Leo	P	ASC c. => Mars (0)	30-Apr-1928
PT	D	Mercury/Virgo	P	Mars (MA) d. => ASC	26-Apr-1928
PT	D	Mercury/Virgo	P	Mars (0) d. => ASC	19-Jul-1928

Mars in the 2nd house reduces wealth from high expenses. Beginning in February 1928, LBJ experienced high expenses which forced him to borrow money to pay for college expenses. He had to do this several times during 1928 until he withdrew from college on 5-Sep-1928 because of financial difficulties. Mars rules the 9th of higher education.

REG	D	Jupiter/Libra	P	sin sextile ASC d. => Mars (0)	15-Oct-1957
REG	D	Jupiter/Libra	P	sin sextile ASC d. => Mars (MA)	28-Dec-1957

This sequence timed LBJ's push for an accelerated space program following the launch of Sputnik on 4-Oct and the start of hearings conducted by the Subcommittee on Preparedness on 25-Nov whose proceedings LBJ dominated.

REG	D	Venus/Virgo	P	sin trine MC d. => Venus (VE)	10-Sep-1965
REG	D	Venus/Virgo	P	sin trine MC d. => Venus (0)	22-May-1967

LOCK Timed the creation of the Department of Housing and Development (HUD) which LBJ signed into law on 9-Sep. Robert Weaver, 1st black American to hold a cabinet seat, was confirmed on 11-Jan; LBJ attended his swearing in ceremony on 18-Jan. End of sequence: In a move labeled a major defeat for the Johnson Administration, the House of Representatives voted to terminate rent subsidies administered through HUD on 18-May-1967. Matches problems of Venus in the 12th.

REG	D	Jupiter/Aquarius	P	DSC c. => Saturn (0)	11-Feb-1965
REG	D	Jupiter/Aquarius	P	DSC c. => Saturn (SA)	2-Jun-1965

LOCK Saturn/Aries/retrograde in the 9th signifies repeated disruptions in overseas military operations. This delineation matches the failed strategy of periodic bombing halts to secure peace negotiations. As the sequence opened, Operation Rolling Thunder began on 13-Feb. Biographer Dallek (1998, pp. 251-253) notes LBJ's doubted the bombing strategy immediately after it started. Towards the end of the sequence, LBJ implemented the first bombing halt 13/19-May. Apart from Vietnam, a civil war in the Dominican Republic erupted on 24-Apr-1965. In response, LBJ deployed American troops on 28-Apr and 1-May to prevent a communist takeover. The troops were ordered withdrawn on 1-Jun as the sequence closed.

Longevity, 64y 4m 27d

Death: 22-Jan-1973, about 4:00 PM; LBJ Ranch, at home. Following a long history of arteriosclerosis, Johnson suffered a heart attack.

Hīlāj: **Moon**. Figure is nocturnal and Moon/2nd/feminine sign qualifies. While the Moon is combust, she is waxing and about to leave combustion. The Moon also tests well as the empirical Hīlāj.

Al-kadukhadāh: **Mercury**. Mercury grants 76 major years. Mercury approaches heliacal rising as an evening star. Mars is co-present with Mercury and deducts 15 minor years; however Mercury's reception of Mars means Mars should maim but not kill. Nevertheless, the projection of ME (76) – MA (15) = 61 years takes LBJ to August 1969 the month following the Apollo Moon landing. Other than dedication of the LBJ library in 1971, there were no major career milestones after age 61.

Victor of the Horoscope: **Mercury**

Killing Planets: **Mercury (41), Jupiter (26), Venus (26)**

Arcus Vitae:

Johnson lived an unhealthy lifestyle which included heavy smoking and overeating. Venus/Cancer/12th suggests a preference for high starch 'comfort' foods with high sugar content. Following an undiagnosed minor heart attack on 18-Jun-1955, LBJ had his first major heart attack on 2-Jul-1955.

PT	D	Jupiter/Taurus	P	dex square ASC d. => North Node	29-Jun-1955

Besides the ASC-Node direction which most accurately timed the heart attack, also active were a series of Venus square Moon primary directions ranging from 1951 to 1957. The role of Venus in these directions confirms the effect of a poor diet on cardiovascular health.

Johnson's second series of heart problems occurred at the end of his life. He was hospitalized on 1-Mar-1970 because of chest pain. While visiting his oldest daughter, LBJ suffered a major heart attack during June 1972 (no exact date available). Death on 22-Jan-1973 was sudden.

Death occurs near two primary direction sequences: (1) direction of the sinister square of Saturn to the Sun by converse motion and (2) direction of the dexter square of the Moon to Saturn by direct motion. Directions for the latter:

REG	D	Jupiter/Gemini	P	dex square Moon (0) d. => Saturn (SA)	28-Jul-1972
REG	D	Jupiter/Gemini	P	dex square Moon (MO) d. => Saturn (SA)	17-Apr-1973

1972 Solar Return for year of Death

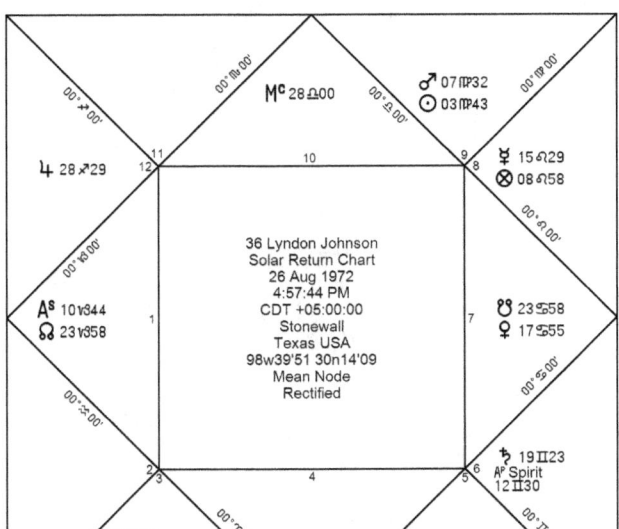

Ascendant Distributor: Mercury/Libra since 19-Oct-1967
Profected Ascendant: 15SA06, 5th House; Victor: Mars
Lords: LOY – Jupiter; LOP – Saturn
Firdaria: Mercury-Moon
Moon: applies to trine of Mercury
Return Ascendant falls in natal 6th; Natal Ascendant in return's 8th

Natal ascendant falling in the return's 8th house of death is the first sign of death in this return. Solar return Ascendant also falls in the natal 6th of illness. More telling is high scoring killing planet Mercury at 15LE29 partile conjunct the natal Ascendant 15LE06. Hīlāj Moon falls in the 4th house of the end-of-life and applies by trine to Mercury in the 8th. This Moon-Mercury aspect echoes the theoretical natal arcus vitae and times death by primary direction in the return (see below). Firdaria also reinforces the power of Moon and Mercury to act. Finally, the Sun is afflicted by a conjunction to Mars, whose power to act is increased by its natal return.

Death occurs between these two Ascendant directions.

| PT | D | Mars/Cancer | P | dex sextile Mars (0) d. => ASC | 19-Jan-1973 |
| PT | D | Venus/Cancer | P | dex sextile Sun d. => ASC | 23-Jan-1973 |

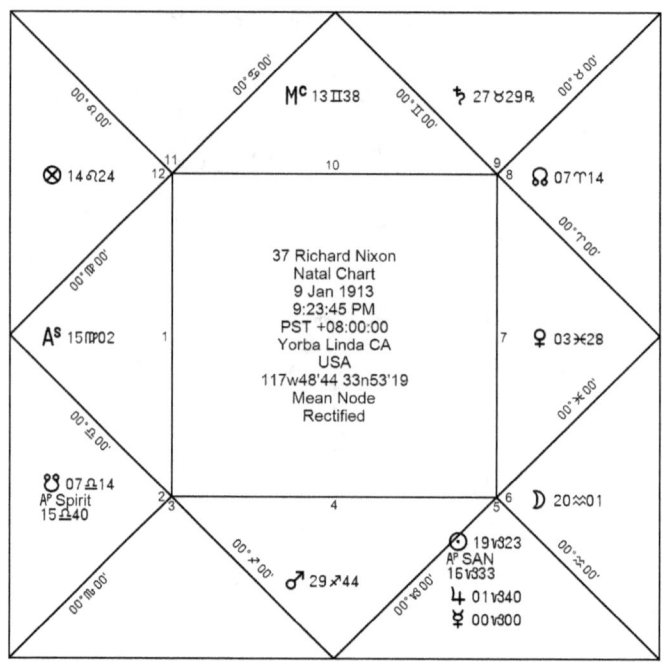
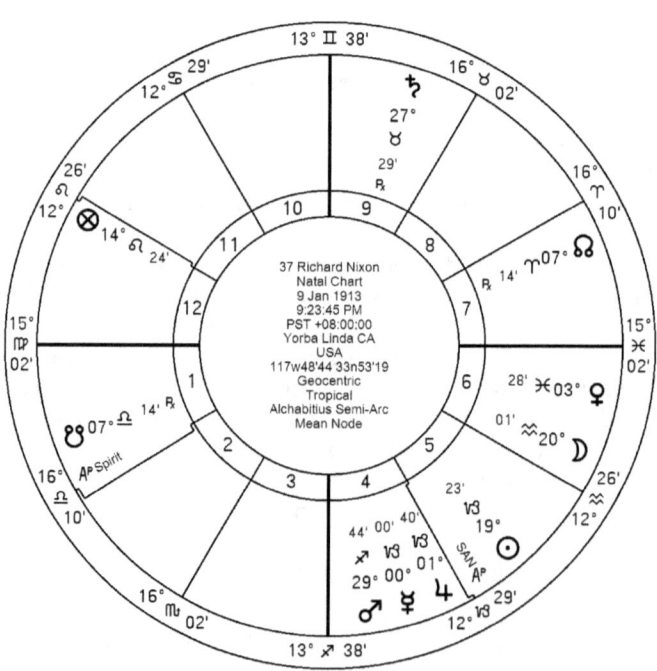

Moon's Configuration

Moon applies to **Saturn**, nocturnal, conjunctional.
Prenatal syzygy is 16CP33. Eclipse? No.

Cognitive Assessment Model (Rulers of Moon and Mercury)

Sign rulers: **Saturn** (both)
Bound rulers: **Mars, Mercury**

Victor Soul Models

Ibn Ezra Victor Model (1507), in-sect triplicity ruler, triplicity decans.

	Position	☉	☽	☿	♀	♂	♃	♄
Sun	19 CP 23		3		3	4		5
Moon	20 AQ 01			3	1	2		5
Asc	15 VI 02			3	9	2		1
Pars Fortuna	14 LE 24	5					4	2
Syzygy	16 CP 33		3		3	4		5
Oriental						3	3	0
Houses		7	1	9	1	9	9	4
Score		0	12	10	21	10	**22**	16	**22**

Porphyry's Expanded Victor Model (2022)

Venus rules the Lot of Spirit by sign; the MC, ASC, Sun, and syzygy by bound. Sect: in-favor. Solar phase: occidental rising to 2nd retrograde station. Position: 7th from ASC. Dignity: exaltation, diurnal triplicity, and bound.

Victor Table for Killing Planets

			☉	☽	☿	♀	♂	♃	♄
ASC		15VI02		3	5,4	3,2	3		1
Rul ASC	☿	00CP00		3	2	3	4,3		5,1
L.Death		23CA38		5,3		3	3	4,2,1	
Rul L.Death	☽	20AQ01			3	1	2	3	5,3
H8 Cusp		16AR10	4,3,1		2		5	3	3
Rul H8	♂	29SA44	3,1				2	5,3	3
T-Rul H8	♃	1CP40		3	2	3	4,3		5,1
NN in H8	NN	7AR14	4,3			2	5,1	3	3
8th from ☽		20VI01		3	5,4	3,1	3	2	
Rul 8th fr ☽	☿	00CP00		3	2	3	4,3		5,1
TOTAL			19	23	29	24	**45**	26	36

2007 Proposed Rectification: 9:09:18 PM, ASC 12VI00'15"
2009 Revised Rectification: 9:23:45 PM, ASC 15VI02'41"
2022 Revised Rectification: 9:23:46 PM, ASC 15VI02'38"

Astrodatabank reports an AA-rated birth time of 9:35 PM, ASC 17VI25. The proposed rectification is 12 minutes earlier.

ZRS. L1-Capricorn defined RN's active political career beginning with the Chambers-Hiss case and ending with the Watergate scandal.

L1 Libra 09 Jan 1913		
L1 Scorpio 28 Nov 1920		
L1 Sagittarius 11 Sep 1935		
L2 Cancer 17 Nov 1945		3-Nov-1946, won election to House.
L1 Capricorn 10 Jul 1947		late-Oct-1947, HUAC hearings on Hollywood 10; Aug-1948/Dec-1948, established anti-Communist credentials during Chambers-Hiss case.
L2 Cancer 20 Sep 1956	FS	6-Nov-1956, Eisenhower/Nixon re-elected; 25-Nov-1957, DE suffered stroke; 13-May-1958, RN mobbed in Venezuela.
L2 Cancer 07 Nov 1964	LB	Nov-1964, Goldwater Republican Presidential bid led to significant Republican losses in LBJ landslide; Nixon stayed out of the fray and not blamed for results; 1966, RN campaigned for Republicans in midterm elections who did well, RN shared credit.
L2 Capricorn 25 Dec 1972	CP	After landslide re-election in Nov-1972, Watergate picks up with Judge Sirica overseeing the trial of the Watergate Seven on 8-Jan-1973; 6-Apr-1973, John Dean began cooperation with Watergate investigation; 27-Jan-1973, Paris Peace Accords signed on Vietnam though many violations of cease fire occurred; Cambodia bombing halted; Nov-1973, Congress passed War Powers Act to limit power of Executive Branch to wage war; 18/21-Oct-1973, Arab oil embargo followed US support of Israel in Yom Kippur War + Saturday Night Massacre with firing of Watergate Special Prosecutor Cox.
L1 Aquarius 18 Feb 1974		1-Mar-1974, named unindicted co-conspirator in indictment against 7 former aides in Watergate; 3-Apr-1974, forced to pay back taxes; 24-Jul-1974, Supreme Court ruled Nixon must turn over tapes; 8-Aug-1974, resignation.
L2 Leo 03 Mar 1983	FS	1-Jan-1984: published: *Real Peace*.
L2 Leo 19 Jun 1991	LB	15-Jan-1992: published: *Seize the Moment*.
L2 Virgo 09 Jan 1993		22-Apr-1994, death.

Firdaria – Venus major and minor periods

Firdaria according to Bonatti	Life Event
Moon **Venus** 15 Jun 1919	No events found.
Saturn **Venus** 23 Apr 1928	No events found.
Jupiter **Venus** 03 Mar 1938	29-Jun-1938, improperly bought real estate in foreclosure auction, started series of problems which took years to resolve; 15-Aug-1939, Citra-Frost venture collapsed, RN opened branch of law office in La Habra.
Mars **Venus** 10 Jan 1947	18-Feb-1947, in maiden House speech, made communist charges against Gerhart Eisler; Jun-1947, chosen for House Select Committee on Foreign Aid; Sep/Oct-1947, European tour to witness WWII devastation, upon return made tour of speeches justifying support of Marshall Plan Aid.
Sun **Venus** 15 Jun 1958	24-Jul-1959, kitchen debate with Khrushchev.
Venus 8 years Age 54 to 62	
Venus Venus 09 Jan 1967	2-Feb-1968, announced Presidential bid.
Venus Mercury 02 Mar 1968	5-Nov-1968, won Presidential election in narrow margin.
Venus Moon 23 Apr 1969	4-May-1970, Kent State Massacre sparked nationwide protests and marked major change in national social mood.
Venus Saturn 15 Jun 1970	7-Oct-1970, proposed five-point peace plan; 16-Feb-1971, Taping system installed in White House; 6-Apr-1971, Taping system installed in Executive Office Building; 13-Jun-1971, NYT began publishing *Pentagon Papers*.
Venus Jupiter 06 Aug 1971	21-Feb-1972, China visit; 17-Jun-1972, Watergate break-in; 29-Aug-1972, denied Watergate involvement.
Venus Mars 27 Sep 1972	7-Nov-1972, won re-election in landslide but with Congress in Democratic hands; 13-Jul-1973, hospitalized for viral pneumonia; 7-Aug-1973, Spiro Agnew bribery scandal broke; 6-Oct-1973, Yom Kippur War and subsequent oil embargo; 20-Oct-1973, Saturday Night massacre.
Venus Sun 18 Nov 1973	6-Dec-1973, Ford confirmed as VP; 3-Apr-1974, IRS judgment for $432,787 in back taxes and $33,000 in interest; 8-Aug-1974, resignation.
Mercury **Venus** 02 Mar 1986	1-Nov-1987. published: *No More Vietnams*.

Venus as Victor. While many will find assigning Venus/Pisces as the victor for Richard Nixon is ridiculous (considering Venus/Pisces is also the victor for Martin Luther King Jr.), I suggest Nixon is a good example of the limits of the Victor model and why astrologers need to integrate Victor and Cognitive Assessment models to achieve a complete delineation of the soul. The Moon's application to Saturn together with Mercury/Mars as bound rulers of Moon and Mercury overwhelmed RN with paranoia and criminal activity and destroyed his presidency – so says the Cognitive Assessment model.

Consider after Watergate, Nixon largely rehabilitated his reputation and credentials as a foreign policy expert and was actively involved in communicating with all Presidents of both parties until his death (Gibbs and Duffy, 2013). His gravestone marker reads "The greatest honor history can bestow is the title of peacemaker." On the day he died, the galley proofs for his final book *Beyond Peace* arrived for Nixon to review. He lived just 9 months short of Venus' major 82 years.

Transits

<u>26-Oct-1946</u>. *tr North Node conj MC.*
House of Representatives election victory, 2-Nov.

<u>15-Sep-1960</u>. *tr North Node conj ASC.*
First Presidential debate with JFK, 26-Sep-1960.

<u>6-Aug-1971</u>. *tr South Node conj LOF.*
Initiated wage and price controls, severed the link between the US Dollar and gold. Value of dollar declined in response, 15-Aug.

<u>27-Sep-1974</u>. *tr South Node conj MC.*
Fallout after 8-Aug resignation and 8-Sep pardon.

Primary Directions

| PT | D | Venus/Capricorn | P | sin trine ASC c. => Moon (MO) | 24-Sep-1952 |

Checkers speech, 23-Sep.

| PT | D | Mercury/Capricorn | P | Jupiter (JU) c. => Moon (0) | 20-Mar-1968 |
| PT | D | Mercury/Capricorn | P | Jupiter (0) c. => Moon (0) | 4-May-1968 |

Period of revived political fortunes after LBJ announced he would not run again for the Presidency, 31-Mar.

| PT | D | Jupiter/Pisces | P | DSC d. => Sun | 2-Aug-1972 |
| REG | D | Jupiter/Pisces | P | DSC d. => Sun | 23-Mar-1974 |

As 12th house lord, Sun in the 5th of election contests promises infamy from criminal activities related to elections. Directed to the 7th cusp of legal conflict, also the western angle where the Sun sets, these directions timed an end to Nixon's public career during the Watergate Scandal. The 1-Aug-1972 report that a $25,000 check earmarked for the Nixon campaign found its way into the bank account of a Watergate burglar demonstrates the power of the Sun's rulership of the Lot of Fortune in the 12th of criminality. Besides the controversy over secret tapes prior to impeachment hearings in early 1974, Nixon also faced scrutiny over personal finances with an IRS audit of his 1968 tax returns at the time of the second Sun direction ('Nixon 1968 Audit Denied by Ziegler,' NYT, 26-Mar-1974, p. 26). As a result, Nixon was forced to pay over $400,000 in back taxes and interest.

37. RICHARD NIXON

Primary Direction Sequences

PT	D	Venus/Capricorn	P	sin trine ASC c. => Venus (VE)	5-Oct-1969
PT	D	Venus/Capricorn	P	sin trine ASC c. => Venus (0)	17-Jan-1970

PT	D	Mars/Scorpio	P	dex trine Venus (0) d. => ASC	16-Sep-1970
PT	D	Mars/Scorpio	P	dex trine Venus (VE) d. => ASC	24-Feb-1971

The War Protest Movement. Venus/Pisces placed in the 7th of open enemies ruling the 9th of higher education signifies college students who protested escalation of the Vietnam War under the Nixon Presidency. The first sequence opened with an editorial in the Wall Street Journal ('Uniting for Peace,' 2-Oct-1969, p. 46) which recognized the need for Americans to be united for peace but complained that in his first year of office Nixon had done little besides token withdrawals of American forces from Vietnam. One example of an early campus protest was the vote for a complete troop withdrawal held at Princeton University on 14-Nov-1969. As the sequence closed, Nixon took the conciliatory and forgiving quality of Venus/Pisces as a method of solving 7th house disputes by emphasizing world peace, settlement of Vietnam, and repair of the environment in his 22-Jan-1970 first State of the Union address. At this time, preparations were also underway for the Nonproliferation of Nuclear Weapons Treaty signed later 5-Mar-1970, one of the earliest diplomatic efforts in the detente period.

The Kent State shootings of 4-May-1970 marked an abrupt change in attitude toward the Nixon administration by college students. As the second sequence started on 12-Sep-1970, the National Peace Coalition announced war protests in 20 cities to be held on 31-October. As the sequence closed, war protests in the form of 'teach-ins' were held on 22-Feb-1971 ('War Protests Set for 12 Campuses Beginning Monday,' NYT, 20-Feb-1971, p. 11).

Examining the Distributor of both sequences is key to understanding why the level of protest during the first was relatively mild compared to events timed by the second sequence. For sequence #1, the sinister trine of the Ascendant falls at 15CP02 in the bound of Venus/Capricorn. Telling is the editorial from the Wall Street Journal, the voice of conservative (Capricorn) moneyed (Venus) interests, which opined war protest sentiments. For sequence #2, the dexter trine of Venus falls at 3SC38 in the bound of Mars/Scorpio. Placed in a sign he rules, Mars in Scorpio is capable of long-lasting military action driven by revenge. This matches the tone of student protests following the Kent State shootings when student militancy increased. Finally note the first sequence was formed by a sinister aspect; the second, by a dexter aspect. In accordance with theory, the dexter aspect produced the stronger effect of the two.

Longevity, 81y 3m 12d

Death: 22-Apr-1994. 9:09 PM New York City. Nixon suffered a stroke on 18-April and died in the hospital.

Hīlāj: **LOF**. Figure is nocturnal; both Moon and LOF in cadent houses should be ruled out in favor of the Sun in the 5th. Yet the LOF tests well as the empirical Hīlāj. This is a violation of the rules. Evidence in support:

| PT | D | Mars/Virgo | P | sin trine Saturn (SA) d. => LOF | 19-Sep-1960 |
| PT | D | Mars/Virgo | P | sin trine Saturn (0) d. => LOF | 23-Sep-1960 |

Nixon's performance in his televised debate against JFK on 26 September was hampered by a staphylococcal infection. This is consistent with the delineation of Saturn/Taurus as an affliction to the throat.

| REG | D | Saturn/Leo | P | LOF c. => South Node | 2 -Nov-1974 |

In mid-1974, Nixon developed swelling in the left leg. After his resignation, a blood clot was removed on 29-Oct-1974. Nixon faced a difficult hospital stay marked by various post-operative complications.

Al-kadukhadāh: **Venus**. Though the LOF tests well as the empirical Hīlāj, no workable al-kadukhadāh from a LOF ruler can be found. Instead, if one reverts to the Sun as the theoretical hīlāj, taking Venus as the Sun's triplicity and bound ruler gives solid results. Venus is also oriental and angular in the 7th by whole sign houses. Nixon lived just shy of Venus' 82 major years. Jupiter sextiles and receives Venus by triplicity and should add his 12 minor years. That Jupiter does not may be symptomatic of Jupiter's weakness in the sign of Capricorn, sign of his fall.

Victor: **Venus**

Killing Planet: **Mars (45), Saturn (36)**

Arcus Vitae:

| PT | D | Saturn/Leo | P | LOF d. => Saturn (0) | 23-Apr-1994 |

1994 Solar Return for year of Death

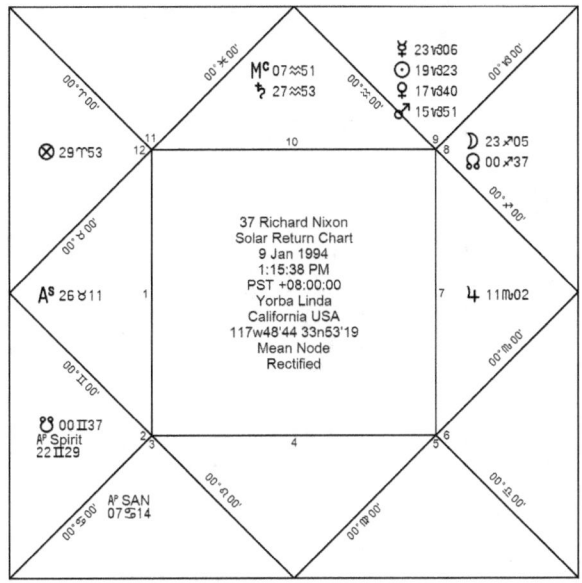

Ascendant Distributor: Jupiter/Scorpio since 11-Jul-1989
Profected Ascendant: 15GE02, 10th House; Victor: Saturn
Lords: LOY – Mercury; LOP – Moon
Firdaria: Moon-Sun
Moon: applies to sextile of Saturn
Return Ascendant falls in natal 9th; Natal Ascendant falls in return's 5th

Moon in the 8th of death applies to high scoring killer Saturn who in turn forms a sextile aspect to the LOF as Hīlāj. Saturn times death in the return when directed to the 7th cusp. Though Jupiter is not a high scoring killing planet, he does rule the 8th of death in the return, is placed in the 7th, and recapitulates Jupiter/Scorpio as bound ruler of the directed Ascendant. The Mercury-Sun-Venus-Mars Capricorn stellium includes high scoring killer Mars and focuses the energy on the knees which is Nixon's weak spot. As ruler of the stellium, Saturn is indicative of blood clots because Saturn's nature is to compress. This is reinforced by the association of Aquarius (significator of waterways) with the circulatory system. Saturn causes blood clots and stroke.

| PT | D | Mars/Leo | P | opp Saturn (SA) d. => ASC | 22-Apr-1994 |

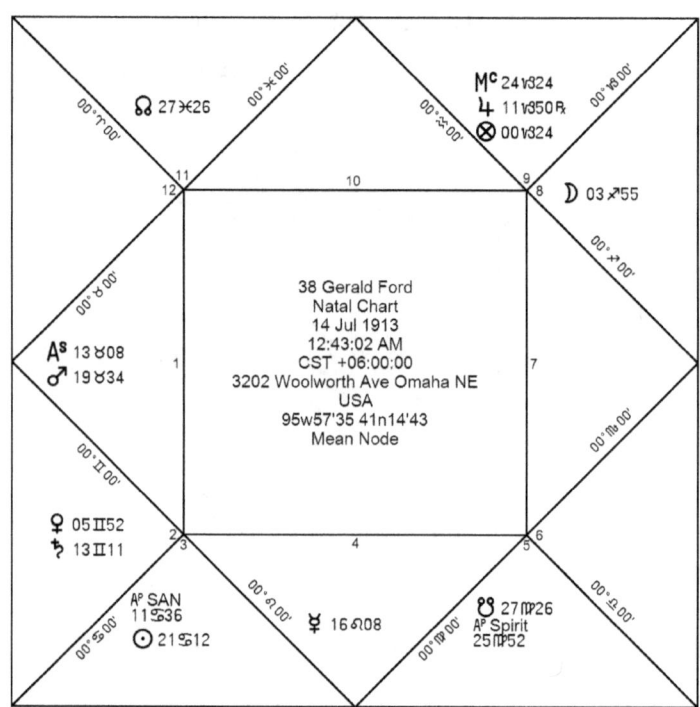

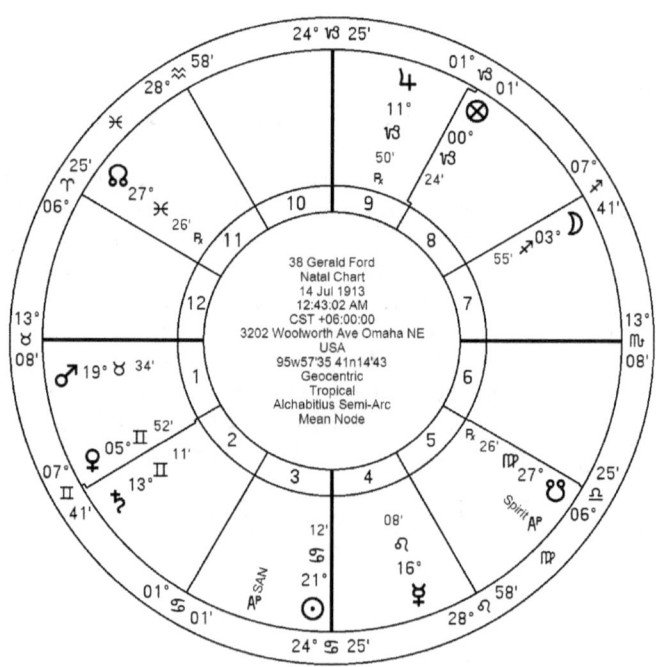

Moon's Configuration

Moon applies to **Venus**, nocturnal, conjunctional.
Prenatal syzygy is 11CA36. Eclipse? No.

Cognitive Assessment Model (Rulers of Moon and Mercury)

Sign rulers: **Jupiter, (Sun)/Jupiter**
Bound rulers: **Jupiter, Saturn**

Victor Soul Models

Ibn Ezra Victor Model (1507), in-sect triplicity ruler, triplicity decans.

	Position	☉	☽	☿	♀	♂	♃	♄
Sun	21 CA 12		5			3	7	
Moon	03 SA 55						11	
Asc	12 TA 40		7	3	5			
Pars Fortuna	29 SA 57	1				2	8	
Syzygy	11 CA 36		5		2	4	4	
Oriental						2	0	3
Houses		9	5	9	6	12	4	6
Score		0	10	22	12	13	23	**34**	9

Porphyry's Expanded Victor Model (2022)

Jupiter: rules the Moon and Lot of Fortune by sign; the Moon and Sun by bound. Sect: out-of-favor. Solar phase: occidental opposition to 2nd station. Dignity: bound. Debility: fall.

Victor Table for Killing Planets

			☉	☽	☿	♀	♂	♃	♄
ASC		13TA08		4,3	2,1	5,3	3		
Rul ASC	♀	5GE52			5,3,2,1			3	3
L.Death		16GE57			5,3	2,1		3	3
Rul L.Death	☿	16LE08	5,3					3,1	3,2
H8 Cusp		7SA41	3					5,3,2,1	3
Rul H8	♃	11CP50		3		3,1	4,3	2	5
T-Rul H8	♃	11CP50		3		3,1	4,3	2	5
☽ in 8th	☽	3SA55	3					5,3,2,1	3
8th from ☽		3CA55		5,3,1		3	3,2	4	
Rul 8th fr ☽	☽	3SA55	3					5,3,2,1	3
TOTAL			17	21	22	22	22	**51**	25

2007 Proposed Rectification: 12:53:31 AM, ASC 16TA54'02"
2009 Revised Rectification: 12:44 AM, ASC 13TA31'48"
2022 Revised Rectification: 12:43:02 AM, ASC 13TA08'39"

ZRS. The 2021 revision is a slight change based on a slightly different choice for matching directions to life events. Briefly, I considered moving the time earlier to shift the LOF late in Sagittarius but ultimately decided to maintain the LOF in early Capricorn.

L1 Virgo 14 Jul 1913		
L2 Pisces 25 Sep 1922	FS	No events found.
L2 Pisces 12 Nov 1930	LB	Dec-1930, car caught fire in garage; won contest as most popular high school senior in Grand Rapids; won trip to White House; elected captain of HS football team; named all-state center and captain of all-state team.
L1 Libra 31 Mar 1933		College years at Michigan and Yale Law School.
L1 Scorpio 17 Feb 1941		7-Dec-1941, Pearl Harbor compelled GF to enlist in Navy; military service influenced GF away from Midwest isolationism to an internationalist philosophy; 15-Oct-1948, married Betty Bloomer Warren; 2-Nov-1948, won House seat.
L1 Sagittarius 01 Dec 1955		1956, began to carve out legislative role in appropriations; 4-Jan-1956, chosen House Minority Leader.
L1 Capricorn 29 Sep 1967		Aug-1968, turned down offer of VP on Nixon ticket, preferred to try for House Speaker (unsuccessful).
L2 Aries 30 May 1973		6-Dec-1973, confirmed as VP.
L2 Taurus 23 Aug 1974		9-Aug-1974, Presidential swearing in (slightly before).
L2 Gemini 20 Apr 1975		30-Apr-1975, fall of Saigon; 14-May-1975, Mayaguez incident; entire balance of Presidential term; 2-Nov-1976, lost election to Jimmy Carter.
L2 Cancer 10 Dec 1976	FS	15-Dec-1976, announced formation of strategic oil reserve; 1978, family confronted Betty Ford with chemical dependency; 3-Dec-1978, GOP poll placed GF in lead over Reagan for 1980.
L2 Cancer 27 Jan 1985	LB	No events found.
L2 Capricorn 16 Mar 1993	CP	1-Jan-1994, biography published: *Time and Chance: Gerald Ford's Appointment with History*.
L1 Aquarius 10 May 1994		
L2 Leo 23 May 2003	FS	
L2 Libra 05 Aug 2006		25-Dec-2006, death.

Firdaria – Jupiter major and minor periods

Firdaria according to Bonatti	Life Event
Gregorian Calendar System Dates	
Moon **Jupiter** 08 Feb 1916	No events found.
Saturn **Jupiter** 08 Feb 1924	No events found.
Jupiter 12 years Age 20 to 32	
Jupiter Jupiter 13 Jul 1933	1934/35, awarded MVP for Michigan football team; 1-Jan-1935, played in East-West all-star football game, turned down offer to play professional football.
Jupiter Mars 01 Apr 1935	1-Aug-1935, began football coaching job at Yale; 3-Dec-1965, name legally changed to Gerald Ford Jr; Summer-1936, park ranger at Yellowstone.
Jupiter Sun 17 Dec 1936	Summer-1937, enrolled Michigan Law School; Spring-1938, admitted to Yale Law School; 1938, relationship with Phyllis Brown.
Jupiter Venus 04 Sep 1938	No events found.
Jupiter Mercury 22 May 1940	Summer-1940, worked for Wendell Willkie Presidential campaign; Jan-1941, graduated Yale Law; May-1941, began legal practice; 7-Dec-1941, Pearl Harbor.
Jupiter Moon 07 Feb 1942	13-Apr-1942, commissioned as Ensign in US Naval Reserve; 17-Jun-1943, USS Monterey commissioned.
Jupiter Saturn 26 Oct 1943	19-Nov-1943, USS Monterey saw action in Gilbert Islands; 18-Dec-1944, narrowly escaped death during typhoon.
Mars **Jupiter** 14 Jul 1951	Feb-1952, one of 18 in House who sent message to Eisenhower asking him to run for President.
Sun **Jupiter** 03 Sep 1964	4-Jan-1965, chosen as House Minority Leader.
Venus **Jupiter** 07 Feb 1972	Jun-1972, won House battle on Revenue sharing; 17-Jun-1972, Watergate Break-in.
Mercury **Jupiter** 06 Feb 1981	Spring-1981, Gerald Ford library dedicated.
Moon **Jupiter** 07 Feb 1991	No events found.
Saturn **Jupiter** 07 Feb 1999	Aug-1999, received Medal of Freedom award; Oct-1999, GF and BF received Congressional Gold Medal for dedicated public service.

Jupiter as Victor. Gerald Ford opened his inaugural speech with the phrase "Our long national nightmare is over." Historians remember Ford kindly as a politician who restored ethics to the Presidency by reversing corrupt practices of the Nixon White House. Jupiter/Capricorn placed in the sign of detriment signifies naked ambition and a leadership style which cares only for results no matter if results are obtained illicitly. Nixon's Jupiter/Capricorn is in stark contrast to Ford's Jupiter/Capricorn-rx which reverses the ill-gotten gains Nixon's Presidency. For more on retrograde planets producing opposite effects when compared to planets in direct motion, see Chapter 1, p. 22.

As Major Firdaria ruler, Jupiter identified Ford's career peak as a college football athlete, start of first job as football coach, Yale law degree, start of first law practice, and WWII military service. As Minor Firdaria ruler, Jupiter identified Ford's political association with Eisenhower, his peak Congressional position as House Minority Leader, the Watergate burglary, his library dedication, and receipt of national awards.

Transits

29-May-1935. *tr North Node conj MC.*
Played in Chicago Tribune College All-Star football game, Summer-1935.

25-May-1948. *tr North Node conj ASC.*
Announced bid for Republican Congressional seat, June-1948.

18-Aug-1972. *tr North Node conj MC.*
Republican National Convention, 21/23-Aug.

15-Nov-1973. *tr North Node conj LOF.*
Senate confirmed GF's nomination for VP, 29-Nov.

25-Apr-1976. *tr* South Node conj ASC.
Ford trailed Reagan during primary season with Reagan's Texas victory on 1-May and wins in Alabama, Georgia, and Indiana on 4-May.

Solar Arc Directions

14-Mar-1939. *dsa Venus opposed LOF.*
5-Apr-1939. *csa LOF opposed Venus.*
Appeared with Phyllis Brown in *Look* magazine, as a part of Brown's modeling career in NYC, 12-Mar-1939.

1-Apr-1946. *dsa Jupiter square ASC.*
7-May-1946. *csa ASC square Jupiter.*
Joined Butterfield law firm, trained under Julius Amberg, Spring 1946.

25-Dec-1947. *dsa North Node trine LOF.*
4-Feb-1948. *csa LOF trine North Node.*
Traveled alone on ski vacation to Sun Valley, discovered he missed Betty, Christmas 1947; Proposed to Betty Warren, Feb-1948.

27-Jul-1974. *dsa ASC opposed Jupiter.*
25-Nov-1974. *csa Jupiter opposed ASC.*
 LOCK House Judiciary Committee voted for impeachment against Nixon, 27-Jul; SALT II Agreement signed with Brezhnev, 24-Nov.
Ford stated 24-Nov was his high-water mark, next 5 ½ months most difficult of his presidency if not his entire life.

8-Nov-1975. *dsa Saturn square ASC.*
11-Mar-1976. *csa ASC square Saturn.*
House Intelligence subpoenaed HK documents on contempt charges, 7-Nov. Chevy Chase parodied GF for 1st time on Saturday Night Live, 8-Nov. Campaign manager Callaway resigned after financial impropriety, 12-Mar.

38. GERALD FORD

Primary Directions

| PT | D | Jupiter/Cancer | P | IC d. => Sun | 28-Dec-1916 |

Mother remarried to Gerald R. Ford, 1-Feb-1917.

| PT | D | Mercury/Taurus | P | ASC d. => North Node | 26-Jan-1946 |

End of WWII service, sent to Separation Center, Great Lakes, IL to be processed out, Jan-1946.

| PT | D | Saturn/Gemini | P | sin square North Node d. => ASC | 1-Feb-1952 |

GF one of 18 House Reps who asked DE to run for President, Feb-1952.

| PT | D | Jupiter/Aquarius | P | dex square Mars (MA) c. => ASC | 8-Jan-1963 |

Defeated Charles Hoeven for Chair House Republican Conference, 8-Jan.

| PT | D | Saturn/Capricorn | P | MC d. => Moon (0) | 7-Sep-1967 |

Mother died in church with her boots on, 17-Sep.

| PT | D | Mars/Capricorn | P | sin sextile South Node c. => MC | 12-Sep-1974 |

GF pardoned Nixon, 8-Sep.
Press Secretary terHorst resigned in protest of pardon, 8-Sep.

| PT | D | Mars/Virgo | P | dex trine MC d. => Sun. | 25-May-1976 |

GF defeated RR in Kentucky, Tennessee, and Oregon primaries, 25-May.
US and Russia signed 5yr limited nuclear test ban, 28-May.

| PT | D | Jupiter/Cancer | P | Sun d. => ASC | 12-Aug-1979 |

Memoir published: *A Time to Heal*, 1-Aug-1979.

Primary Direction Sequences

REG	D	Venus/Virgo	P	dex trine Jupiter (JU) d. => Sun	3-Feb-1965
REG	D	Venus/Virgo	P	dex trine Jupiter (0) d. => Sun	16-Feb-1965
REG	D	Venus/Virgo	P	dex trine Jupiter (BI) d. => Sun	22-Feb-1965

GF announced challenge to Halleck for Minority Leader, 19-Dec-1964.
GF selected as House Minority Leader, 4-Jan-1965.

| REG | D | Mercury/Scorpio | P | DSC c. => Jupiter (JU) | 14-Feb-1973 |
| REG | D | Mercury/Scorpio | P | DSC c. => Jupiter (0) | 28-Feb-1973 |

Senate created Select Committee on Presidential Campaign Activities to determine if campaign laws had been broken, 7-Feb.

| REG | D | Jupiter/Cancer | P | Sun d. => Mars (0) | 9-Jan-1975 |
| PT | D | Jupiter/Cancer | P | Sun d. => Mars (0) | 11-Apr-1975 |

North Vietnamese took Phuoc Long City, violated Paris Peace Accords, 6-Jan; Cambodia fell to Khmer Rouge, 11-Apr; Fall of Saigon, 30-Apr.

Longevity: 93y 5m 13d

Death: 25-Dec-2006, 6:45 PST, Rancho Mirage, California, at home. As the President with one of the longest life spans recorded, Ford suffered few problems until his last few years when he was hospitalized on several occasions for pneumonia, shortness of breath, and heart problems. A pacemaker was installed August 2006 three months before he died.

Hīlāj: **Moon**. Figure is nocturnal and Moon is preferred, placement in either 7th by quadrant houses or 8th by whole sign houses qualifies.

Al-kadukhadāh: **Jupiter**. The 4th edition replaces a convoluted longevity projection from earlier editions based on Saturn as al-kadukhadāh with Venus and Mercury adding minor years and middle years as months. Consider Jupiter as Victor of the Horoscope the al-kadukhadāh. Jupiter grants 79 major years. In a separating trine Mars receives Jupiter by exaltation and should deduct 15 minor years, but Jupiter's reception of Mars by bound suggests an injury which maims but does not kill.

JU (79) – MA (15) = 64 years.

Age 64 takes Ford to July 1977 which is six months after he left office. There are no reports of reduced vitality at that time but in the following year 1978 he and his family confronted his wife Betty Ford with substance abuse which initiated a long path to recovery. With Mars ruling the 7th of the spouse in the 1st, it is possible to interpret the negative influence of Mars on Ford's vitality as stress surrounding his wife's recovery. Ford's continued lifespan until his 90s may be tied to the vitality of Mercury/Leo in the 4th house end-of-life which corresponded to Ford's active career as a speaker, consultant, and corporate board member.

Victor of the Horoscope: **Jupiter**

Killing Planet: **Jupiter (51)**

Arcus Vitae:

REG	D	Venus/Cancer	P	opp Jupiter (0) c. => Moon (MO)	17-Nov-2005
REG	D	Venus/Cancer	P	opp Jupiter (JU) c. => Moon (MO)	7-Jan-2006

Joins high scoring killing planet with the Hīlāj. Jupiter signifies pneumonia for which Ford was hospitalized on 15-Jan-2006.

REG	D	Mercury/Virgo	P	dex square Moon (0) d. => Saturn (SA)	12-Jul-2006
REG	D	Mercury/Virgo	P	dex square Moon (MO) d. => Saturn (SA)	6-Apr-2008

Saturn is not the high scoring killing planet but does rule killer Jupiter and opposes the 8th house cusp. The first direction occurred two months prior to insertion of a pacemaker.

2006 Solar Return for year of Death

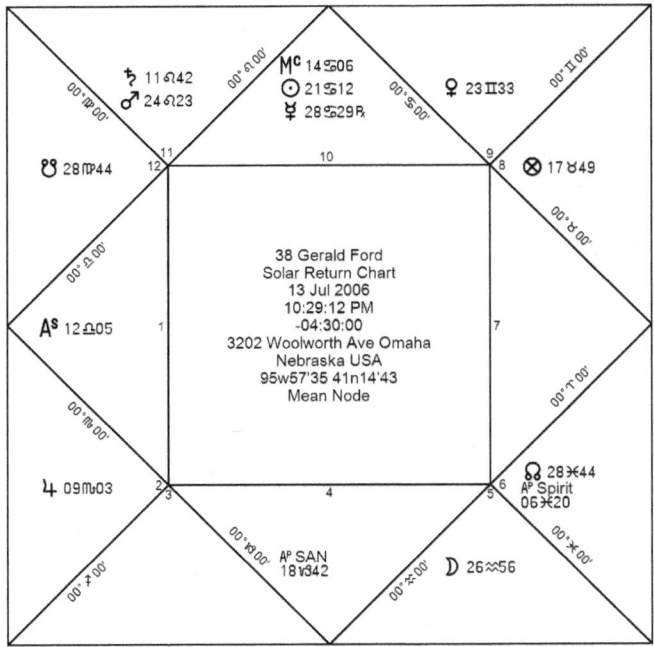

Ascendant Distributor: Saturn/Leo since 19-Aug-2004
Profected Ascendant: 13AQ08, 10th house; Return Al-mubtazz: Saturn
Lords: LOY – Saturn; LOP – Sun
Firdaria: Saturn-Moon
Moon: separates from opposition to Mars to void of course
Return Ascendant falls in natal 6th

Moon falls in the antiscion of Jupiter, linking the Hīlāj with the high scoring killing planet. Jupiter transits the natal 7th at the time of the return and transits the natal Moon at death. Moon forms a grand square with Jupiter, Mars, Saturn, and LOF in the 8th. Note LOF 17TA55 is within two degrees of natal Mars 19TA54 placed in the Ascendant.

| PT | D | Venus/Scorpio | P | Jupiter (0) d. => ASC | 17-Aug-2006 |

Pacemaker installed, Aug-2006.

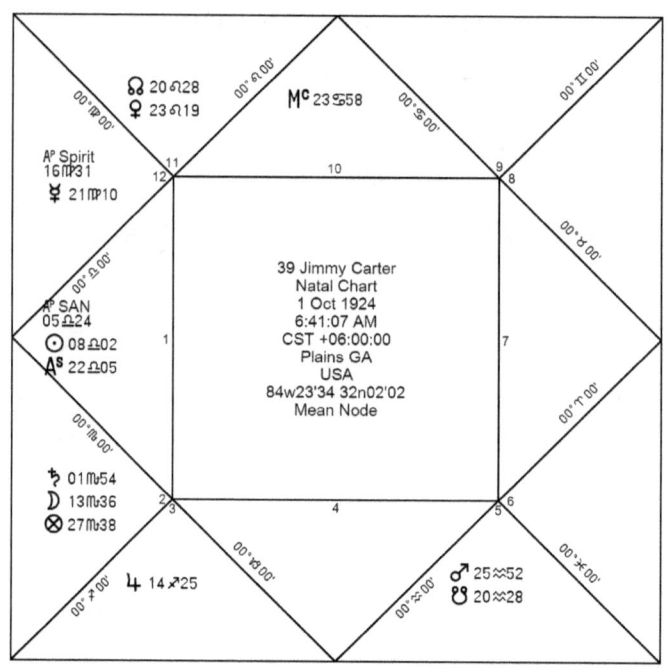
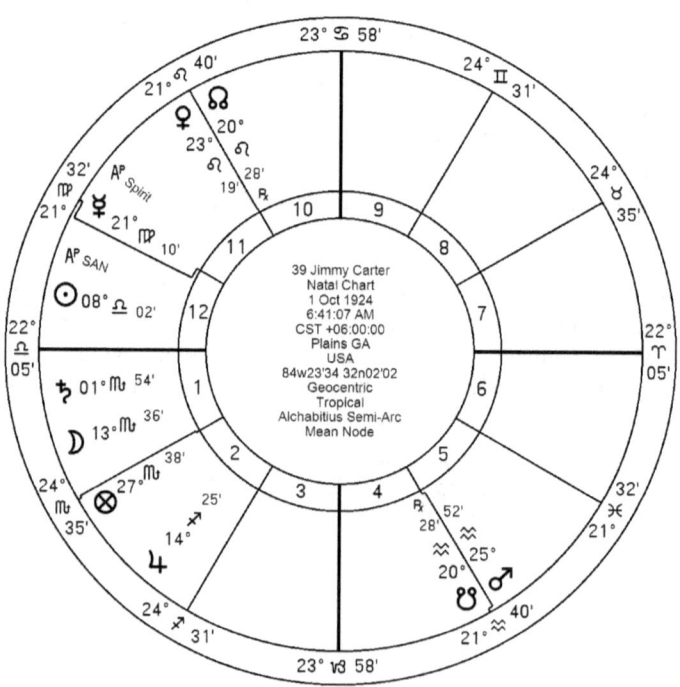

Moon's Configuration

Moon separates from **Saturn** and applies to **Mercury**, diurnal, conjunctional. Prenatal syzygy is 5LI24. Eclipse? No.

Cognitive Assessment Model (Rulers of Moon and Mercury)

Sign rulers: **Mars, Mercury**
Bound rulers: **Mercury, Mars**

Victor Soul Models

Ibn Ezra Victor Model (1507), in-sect triplicity ruler, triplicity decans.

	Position	☉	☽	☿	♀	♂	♃	♄
Sun	08 LI 02			2	6			7
Moon	13 SC 36			2	3	5	1	
Asc	22 LI 05			1	7			7
Pars Fortuna	27 SC 38		1		3	5		2
Syzygy	05 LI 24				6			9
Oriental						0	0	0
Houses			2	12| 2	8	7	6	12
Score		0	2	13	7	33	17	7	37

Porphyry's Expanded Victor Model (2022)

Venus rules the ASC, Sun, and syzygy by sign; the ASC, and Lot of Spirit by bound. Sect: out-of-favor. Solar phase: oriental from 1st direct station to sinking. Position: 10th from Lot of Fortune. Dignity: mutual reception with the Sun by sign. Conjunct North Node.

Victor Table for Killing Planets

Not published for the living.

2007 Proposed Rectification: 6:41:12 AM, ASC 22LI06'22"
2009 Revised Rectification: 6:41:07 AM, ASC 22LI05'19"
2022 Revised Rectification: 6:41:07 AM, ASC 22LI05'23"

Astrodatabank reports an AA-rated birth time of 7:00 AM, ASC 26LI05. The proposed rectification is 19 minutes earlier. This does shift the LOF from Sagittarius (ADB) back to Scorpio (proposed).

ZRS

L1 Virgo 01 Oct 1924		
L2 Pisces 13 Dec 1933	FS	
L2 Pisces 30 Jan 1942	LB	Summer 1942, appointment to Naval Academy.
L1 Libra 18 Jun 1944		L1-Libra timed JC's graduation from the Naval Academy, Jun-1946; and submarine qualification, 4-Feb-1950.
L1 Scorpio 07 May 1952		JC was accepted into Admiral Hyman Rickover's elite nuclear submarine program on 1-Jun-1952 on his way to a successful naval career. However, after the sudden death of his father on 22-Jul-1953, JC decided to return to Georgia to run the family farm. During the 1960s, JC became more active in civil rights, running unsuccessfully for GA Governor during the final L2-Leo subperiod.
L1 Sagittarius 18 Feb 1967		During L2-Capricorn, JC had a born-again Christian experience. Soon after he launched his 2nd Georgia gubernatorial bid and won the race during L2-Aquarius. JC launched his Presidential bid during L2-Taurus and won during L2-Gemini. The period concluded with the Camp David Accords.
L1 Capricorn 17 Dec 1978		On the exact day of the shift to L1-Capricorn the Camp David accords began to unravel. Although JC was able to save the peace agreement resulting with the Egypt-Israel Peace Treaty on 26-Mar-1979, a cascading series of problems would end his presidency: Iranian revolution and hostage crisis, the energy crisis, his 'crisis of confidence' speech, and his election loss 4-Nov-1980.
L2 Cancer 28 Feb 1988	FS	1-May-1988, published *An Outdoor Journal*; 26-Sep-1988, brother Billy dies from pancreatic cancer; 9-May-1989, monitored Panamanian elections with President Ford; Jul-1989, Democracy in Africa initiative; 23/28-Feb-1990, observed Nicaraguan elections and convinced loser Ortega to concede; 5-Mar-1990, sister Gloria died of cancer.
L2 Cancer 16 Apr 1996	LB	5-Mar-1997, met with Arafat in Plains; 18-Dec-1997, observed elections in Jamaica; 27-Apr-1998, Submarine USS Jimmy Carter christened.
L2 Capricorn 03 Jun 2004	CP	26-Jul-2004, endorsed John Kerry in DNC speech; 24-Mar-2005, JC and RC resigned Chair and Vice Chairwoman positions at Carter Center.
L1 Aquarius 28 Jul 2005		1-Nov-2006, published: *Palestine: Peace not Apartheid*; 12-Jan-2007, 14 of 200 members of Carter Center's advisory board resigned in protest of Palestine book.
L2 Leo 10 Aug 2014	FS	7-Jul-2015, published: *A Full Life*; 12-Aug-2015, cancer diagnosis; 6-Dec-2015, cancer-free diagnosis.
L2 Leo 26 Nov 2022	LB	18-Feb-2023, announced hospice care at home.

Firdaria – Venus major and minor periods

Firdaria according to Bonatti	Life Event
Sun **Venus** 07 Mar 1926	No events found.
Venus 8 years Age 10 to 18	No events found.
Venus Venus 01 Oct 1934	No events found.
Venus Mercury 23 Nov 1935	No events found.
Venus Moon 13 Jan 1937	No events found.
Venus Saturn 06 Mar 1938	No events found.
Venus Jupiter 28 Apr 1939	No events found.
Venus Mars 18 Jun 1940	2-Jun-1941, High School graduation, spoke on 'The Building of a Community'
Venus Sun 10 Aug 1941	Summer-1942, Annapolis Naval Academy appointment contingent on completion of additional science courses.
Mercury **Venus** 22 Nov 1953	17-May-1954, Brown v Board of Education.
Moon **Venus** 06 Mar 1962	26-Mar-1962, Supreme Court decided *Baker v Carr* establishing the 'one man, one vote' rule; 6-Nov-1962, won first political office as GA state senator.
Saturn **Venus** 13 Jan 1971	15-Feb-1971, signed bill which allowed him to propose government reorganization.
Jupiter **Venus** 22 Nov 1980	20-Jan-1981, Reagan inauguration and hostage release; 6-Oct-1981, Sadat assassinated.
Mars **Venus** 01 Oct 1989	23/28-Feb-1990, monitored Nicaragua presidential elections and convinced Ortega to accept the results and step down; 5-Mar-1990, sister Gloria died; 4-Apr-1990, met Yasser Arafat for first time; 16-May-1990, monitored elections in Dominican Republic.
Sun **Venus** 06 Mar 2001	12-May-2002, first visit by American President to Cuba in over 40 years.
Venus 8 years Age 85 to 93	
Venus Venus 30 Sep 2009	26-Aug-2010, secured release for US citizen held by North Korea.
Venus Mercury 22 Nov 2010	30-Nov-2010, visited White House and met with BO and National Security Adviser Thomas E Donilon; 12-Dec-2011, published: *366 Daily Meditations from the 39th President*.
Venus Moon 13 Jan 2012	No events found.
Venus Saturn 06 Mar 2013	25-Mar-2014, published: *A Call to Action: Women, Religion, Violence, and Power*; 3-Apr-2014, attended opening of play "Camp David."
Venus Jupiter 27 Apr 2014	No events found.
Venus Mars 18 Jun 2015	7-Jul-2015, published: *A Full Life*; 12-Aug-2015, cancer diagnosis; 23-May-2016, announced plans for Baptist Conference for Unity.
Venus Sun 09 Aug 2016	No events found.

Venus as Victor. Venus/Leo in mutual reception by sign with Sun/Libra is a powerful configuration which elevates Venus/Leo to the role of victor. Venus/Leo itself signifies the love of power and vitality; Sun/Libra signifies compromise. The reception allows JC to be one of the best negotiators of the recent political era. Many of his key diplomatic successes are captured by Venus as Firdaria ruler, including the release of Iranian hostages after Reagan was elected President.

Transits

<u>27-May-1968</u>. *tr Jupiter 27LE43 10th from LOF 27SC38*.
Christian born-again experience at Lock Haven, Pennsylvania, 27-May.

<u>26-Jul-1975</u>. *tr North Node conj LOF*.
Qualified for federal matching funds for 1976 campaign, 18-Aug.

<u>28-May-1977</u>. *tr North Node conj ASC*.
Made Human Rights foreign policy speech at Notre Dame, 22 May.

<u>7-Jan-1996</u>. *tr North Node conj ASC*.
Jimmy and Rosalynn Carter led 40-member delegation from 11 countries to Jerusalem to observe Palestinian elections, 18/21-Jan-1996.

<u>28-Jul-2000</u>. *tr North Node conj MC*.
Carter Center observed elections in Venezuela, 30-Jul.

Solar Arc Directions

<u>26-Jun-1946</u>. *dsa ASC conj Moon*.
<u>3-Oct-1946</u>. *csa Moon conj ASC*.
   Commissioned ensign in Navy, 5-Jun.
   Marriage to Rosalynn Smith, 7-Jul.
   Naval duty began on USS Wyoming, 8-Aug
   Moon rules the 10th of career and reputation/marriage; Scorpio is the significator for naval warfare because Scorpio is a water sign.

<u>20-Jun-1974</u>. *dsa Sun conj LOF*.
<u>3-Nov-1975</u>. *csa LOF conj Sun*.
   Meet the Press appearance, 2-Jun-1974.
   First of three rock concerts held as fundraisers, 31-Oct-1975.

LOCK <u>6-Mar-1977</u>. *dsa ASC conj Jupiter*.
LOCK <u>12-Sep-1978</u>. *csa Jupiter conj ASC*.
   Nine million people call "Ask President Carter" radio broadcast, 5-Mar.
   Camp David Accords, 17-Sep.

Primary Directions

| PT | D | Saturn/Leo | P | dex square Moon (MO) d. => MC | 13-Jul-1946 |

Duty aboard USS Wyoming, 8-Jul. Compare to ASC-Moon solar arc.

| PT | D | Jupiter/Gemini | P | dex trine Sun c. => MC | 27-Apr-1974 |

LOCK Carter upstaged Ted Kennedy in an impassioned speech about the use of politics as a vehicle for social justice, 4-May. Described as '*A King*

Hell Bastard of a Speech' (Bourne 1977, 242). Made strong impression on *Rolling Stone* journalist Hunter S. Thompson.

PT	D	Jupiter/Scorpio	P	sin trine MC d. => Sun	22-Apr-1977
REG	D	Jupiter/Scorpio	P	sin trine MC d. => Sun	18-Oct-1978

LOCK Carter proposed his energy legislation on 20-Apr-1977 and Congress passed a version of the legislation on 15-Oct-1978. The Distributor for this pair of directions is Jupiter/Scorpio which may prove a relevant significator for energy policy issues.

PT	D	Saturn/Scorpio	P	dex square Mars (0) d. => Sun	16-Jul-1979

Crisis of Confidence or 'malaise' speech, 15-Jul-1979.

PT	D	Jupiter/Sagittarius	P	sin sextile Sun d. => ASC	26-Jul-1979

Signed *Trade Agreements Act of 1979*, 26-Jul.
For the 4th edition, I re-assigned this direction from the malaise speech to the trade legislation. Libra is the mundane signature for trade liberalization. Sun/Libra in mutual reception with Venus/Leo pushes effects of Sun directions to signs that Venus rules and where Venus resides. Venus/11th of political alliances ruling the 8th of partner's moveable wealth, or 'traded goods' based on my research, is the basis of linking this direction to trade.

REG	D	Venus/Libra	P	ASC c. => Jupiter (JU)	16-Sep-1982

Carter began to teach at Emory University, September 1982.

Primary Direction Sequences

PT	D	Venus/Libra	P	ASC c. => dex square Mars (0)	29-Mar-1962
PT	D	Venus/Libra	P	ASC c. => dex square Mars (MA)	17-Dec-1962

LOCK In what is arguably the single most important sequence in understanding Carter's victory over voting segregation, this sequence included not only the Supreme Court's *Baker v Carr* decision of 26-Mar-1962 which established the 'one man, one vote' rule but Carter's first and successful election for public office, fought against ballot-box stuffing segregationists. Carter won his election on 6-Nov-1962 after a disputed primary recount and was last challenged by his opponents on 13-Nov as the sequence ended. See Carter (1992) for a full account. Here Mars/Aquarius signified those fighting against humanitarian or universal principles which seek a level playing field for all. South Node weakens Mars by conjunction; this indicates the failure of the opposition.

REG	D	Venus/Sag	P	Jupiter (JU) d. => Sun	6-Oct-2002
REG	D	Venus/Sag	P	Jupiter (0) d. => Sun	16-Dec-2002

LOCK Awarded Nobel Peace Prize, 11 October; accepted, 10 December.

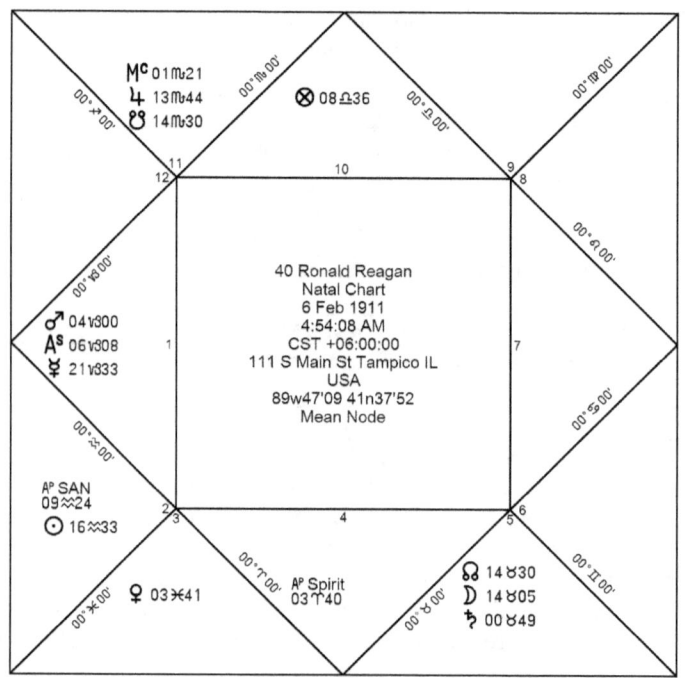
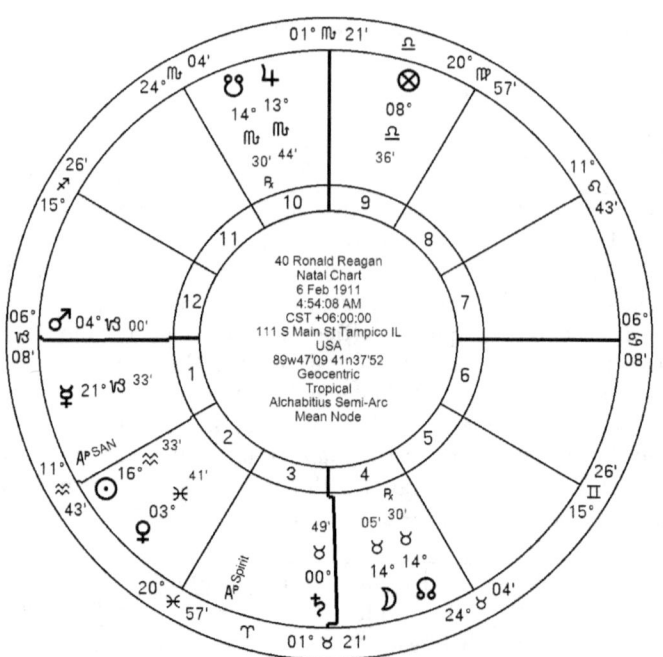

Moon's Configuration

Moon separates from **Jupiter** and applies to the **Sun**, nocturnal, conjunctional. Prenatal syzygy is 9AQ24. Eclipse? No.

Cognitive Assessment Model (Rulers of Moon and Mercury)

Sign rulers: **Venus, Saturn**
Bound rulers: **Jupiter, Venus**

Victor Soul Models

Ibn Ezra Victor Model (1507), in-sect triplicity ruler, triplicity decans.

	Position	☉	☽	☿	♀	♂	♃	♄
Sun	16 AQ 33			4			2	5
Moon	14 TA 05		7	1	5		2	
Asc	06 CP 08		3	2		4		6
Pars Fortuna	08 LI 36			5	6			4
Syzygy	09 AQ 24			3	2			6
Oriental						3	1	0
Houses		6	9	12	6	12	11	9
Score	0	6	19	27	19	19	16	**30**

Porphyry's Expanded Victor Model (2022)

Mars rules the MC and Lot of Spirit by sign; the MC by bound. Sect: of-favor. Solar phase: oriental rising to waxing sextile. Position: Angular in ASC, 4th from Lot of Fortune, 10th from Lot of Spirit. Dignity: exaltation and participating triplicity.

Victor Table for Killing Planets

			☉	☽	☿	♀	♂	♃	♄
ASC		6CP08		3		3	4,3	2	5,1
Rul ASC	♄	00TA49		4,3		5,3,2,1	3		
L.Death		28CA27		5,3		3	3	4,1	2
Rul L.Death	☽	14TA05		4,3	1	5,3	3	2	
H8 Cusp		11LE43	5,3					3,1	3,2
Rul H8	☉	16AQ33			3,1			3,2	5,3
T-Rul H8	♃	13SC44		3	2	3	5,3	1	
8th from ☽		14SA05	3			2	1	5,3	3
Rul 8th fr ☽	♃	13SC44		3	2	3	5,3	1	
TOTAL			11	**31**	9	**33**	**33**	28	24

2007 Proposed Rectification: 4:54:08 AM, ASC 6CP08'29"
2022 Revised Rectification: 4:54:08 AM, ASC 6CP08'21"

Astrodatabank reports a DD-rated birth time of 4:16 AM, conflicting/unverified dirty data. Reagan's birth time has been the subject of many debates within the astrological community. Since proposed in 2007, the proposed rectification has stood up well when tested against ZRS and Directing through the Bounds, the latter an especially difficult test to pass.

ZRS. LOS 3AR30, bound Jupiter/Aries, works well for ZRS. Reagan climbs the political ranks until his 2nd Presidential term when L2 Aquarius brings out the Iran-Contra scandal. Jupiter/Scorpio positioned 10th from Aquarius takes him down because Jupiter is the 12th house lord and signifies covert military activities which work against his political career.

L1 Aries 06 Feb 1911		
L1 Taurus 19 Nov 1925		
L1 Gemini 08 Oct 1933		Began film career with Warner Bros in 1937.
L2 Sagittarius 23 Jul 1942	FS	Worked in Army Air Force Motion Picture Unit.
L2 Sagittarius 06 Feb 1951	LB	15-Feb-1951, film premiere *Bedtime for Bonzo*.
L1 Cancer 25 Jun 1953		9-Jul-1953, *General Electric Theatre* debut; 26-Sep-1954, Reagan debut on *General Electric Theatre*.
L2 Capricorn 12 Aug 1961	FS	26-Aug-1962, fired by GE after RR's opposition to the TVA as example of 'big government' made him a political liability; 25-Jul-1962, death of Mother Nelle.
L2 Capricorn 24 Oct 1970	LB	1970, won re-election as CA Governor; 3-Apr-1971, NYT op-ed *Welfare is a Cancer*; 13-Aug-1971, California Welfare Reform Act became law.
L1 Leo 14 Feb 1978		13-Jun-1978. NYT "Ronald Reagan's Magic" discussed Reagan in context of his top ranking for Republican Presidential Nominee in 1980.
L2 Virgo 07 Sep 1979		4-Nov-1980, won Presidential election.
L2 Aquarius 02 Jun 1986	FS	29-May-1986 (just before), Oliver North told McFarlane that profits from Iran weapon sales were diverted to the Contras; after this point the Iran-Contra scandal quickly unfolded; 20-Jun-1986, two polyps removed from Reagan's large intestine.
L2 Aquarius 15 Jun 1995	LB	18-Jul-1995, Lesion on neck removed during annual physical.
L1 Virgo 06 Nov 1996		
L2 Aquarius 02 Aug 2003		5-Jun-2004, death

Directing through the Bounds.

Date	ASC Distributor	Event
15-Feb-1933	ME/AQ (00AQ)	Staff announcer for radio station WOC, 10-Feb-1933.
20-May-1954	VE/PI (00PI)	Debut as motivational speaker for GE Theatre, 26-Sep-1954
23-Nov-1971	JU/AR (00AR)	No specific event, 2nd term as CA Governor.
28-May-1989	VE/TA (00TA)	Bucked off horse, 4-Jul-1989; other injuries followed.
27-May-2004	SA/TA (22TA)	Death, 5-Jun-2004.

Firdaria – Mars major and minor periods

Firdaria according to Bonatti	Life Event
Moon **Mars** 15 Dec 1914	2-Nov-1915, moved to Chicago South Side, contracted bronchial pneumonia.
Saturn **Mars** 30 Mar 1923	1924 (no date), entered Dixon's Northside High School.
Jupiter **Mars** 24 Oct 1932	10-Feb-1933, formally took position as staff announcer for WOC; 29-Mar-1933, fired from WOC, ear-May-1933, rehired as Sports Director for WOC.
Mars 7 years Age 32 to 39	
Mars Mars 05 Feb 1943	22-Jul-1943, promoted to Captain.
Mars Sun 06 Feb 1944	22-Aug-1944, began work on relief model of Japan for Motion Picture Unit; 2-Feb-1945, recommended for promotion to Major.
Mars Venus 05 Feb 1945	18-Mar-1945, adopted son Michael; 5-Oct-1945, labor protest at Burbank; 9-Dec-1945, officially discharged from Army; 17-Jan-1946, Warner Bros downgraded RR film project to B&W.
Mars Mercury 05 Feb 1946	15-Feb-1946, guest column in AVC Bulletin railed against Native Fascism; 26-Apr-1946, noted that AVC appeared to have been taken over by Communists; 11-Sep-1946, tried to talk Herb Sorrell out of another strike; Sep-1946, recruited by FBI as informant; 30-Oct-1946, SAG speech; Nov-1946, asked to mediate dispute between rival unions; 19-Dec-1946, SAG speech indicated final conservative catharsis.
Mars Moon 05 Feb 1947	10-Mar-1947, President SAG; 10-Apr-1947, named six SAG members as suspected Communists to FBI; Jun-1947, contracted viral pneumonia; 26-Jun-1947, birth of Christine Reagan who lived only a day; 23-Oct-1947, HUAC testimony; 5-Dec-1947, media reported Wyman breakup.
Mars Saturn 06 Feb 1948	10-Feb-1948, repeated names of SAG members suspected to be Communists; 6-Jun-1948, divorced Jane Wyman; 29-Nov-1948, arrived England to film *The Hasty Heart* with Patricia Neal.
Mars Jupiter 05 Feb 1949	28-Jun-1949, divorce from Wyman finalized; 15-Nov-1949, met Nancy Davis for first date.
Sun **Mars** 02 Sep 1963	27-Oct-1964, "A Time for Choosing" speech at Goldwater nominating convention puts Reagan on the political map.
Venus **Mars** 24 Oct 1970	Nov-1970, won re-election as CA Governor; 13-Aug-1971, CA Welfare Reform Act became law.
Mercury **Mars** 11 Jul 1980	17-Jul-1980, nominated for President; 4-Nov-1980, won Presidential election; 30-Mar-1981, shot by Hinckley; 5-Aug-1981, broke air traffic controller strike; 13-Aug-1981, signed budget and tax laws; 2-Oct-1981, proposed military buildup; 26-Jan-1982, New Federalism speech.
Moon **Mars** 15 Dec 1989	16-Feb-1990, provided testimony for John Poindexter; Feb-1990, Marxist Sandinistas voted out of power in Nicaragua.

Mars as Victor. By nature, Mars cuts and divides; placed in Capricorn which signifies centralized authority makes Reagan a purveyor of reduced government power. At the same time Mars/Capricorn signifies military power, so what power the government does possess should be directed towards military endeavors. These two themes remain consistent during RR's career.

Transits

30-Jul-1981. *tr North Node 10th from MC.*
Won congressional approval for program of tax cuts, 29-Jul.

18-Nov-1982. *tr South Node conj ASC.*
USSR Leader Leonid Brezhnev died, 10-Nov.

Solar Arc Directions

21-Aug-1945. *csa Jupiter conj. LOF.*
Signed million-dollar contract with Warner Brothers, 21-Aug.

2-Oct-1981. *dsa Venus conj. Moon.*
Volunteerism Initiative, 5-Oct.

9-Aug-1982. *csa Moon trine MC.*
Launch of 1980s bull stock market, 9-Aug (exact day of low).

5-Jun-1984. *csa ASC square Mercury.*
Made speech on 50th anniversary of D-Day, 6-Jun.

11-Nov-1986. *csa LOF opposed Mercury.*
Poorly received press conference on Iran-Contra, 13-Nov.
Address to US & USSR on Geneva Summit, 14-Nov.

2-Feb-1987. *csa MC square Moon.*
Veto of Water Quality Act, 30-Jan.

24-Jul-1988. *dsa Mercury opposed LOF.*
Canadian free trade agreement sent to Congress, 25-Jul.

Primary Directions

| REG | D | Venus/Taurus | P | IC d. => Venus (VE) | 17-Dec-1948 |

Began filming *The Hasty Heart*, one of last films, 16-Dec.

| PT | D | Saturn/Leo | P | opposition Sun c. => MC | 17-Apr-1981 |
| PT | D | Mercury/Aries | P | sin sextile Sun d. => ASC | 27-Apr-1981 |

LOCK Following an assassination attempt on 30-Mar-1981, Reagan asked to speak with a minister on Good Friday (17-Apr). Following his session with NY Cardinal Cooke, Reagan stated 'I have decided that whatever time I have left is left for him' (Morris 1999, 435). The next day he began to draft a conciliatory letter to Brezhnev filled with humanitarian comments consistent with the nature of Sun in Aquarius. A revised letter was sent on 24-Apr which included cancellation of a grain embargo.

40. RONALD REAGAN

Primary Direction Sequences

REG	D	Jupiter/Aquarius	P	Sun d. => Mars (MA)	10-Apr-1947
REG	D	Jupiter/Aquarius	P	Sun d. => Mars (0)	14-Oct-1947

LOCK Beginning with Reagan's naming of six Screen Actors Guild members as suspected Communists on 10-Apr, this sequence timed Reagan's fame as a staunch anti-Communist, culminating with testimony before the House Un-American Activities Committee on 23-Oct-1947.

PT	D	Mars/Aries	P	sin square Mercury (ME) d. => ASC	3-Jan-1984
PT	D	Mars/Aries	P	sin square Mercury (0) d. => ASC	8-Apr-1984

Following the Democratic Congress' passage of the 2nd Borland Amendment on 8-Dec-1983 designed to reign in Reagan's Central American military activity, Reagan faced increasing pressure to maintain the Nicaraguan contras. On 10-Apr-1984 the Senate formally rebuked Reagan for his CIA/Nicaraguan activities.

PT	D	Mars/Scorpio	P	dex sextile Mars (MA) c. => ASC	6-Aug-1986
REG	D	Mars/Scorpio	P	dex sextile Mars (0) c. => ASC	2-Nov-1986

LOCK This sequence timed Oliver North's 8-Aug London meeting to begin discussions for the second arms-for-hostages deal. On 28-Oct, 500 TOW missiles were delivered to Iran; on 2-Nov hostage David Jacobsen was released; on 3-Nov the Lebanese weekly *Al-Shiraa* paper broke the scandal with an extensive detailing of the arms-for-hostages program.

REG	D	Mercury/Virgo	P	dex sextile MC c. => Jupiter (0)	17-Oct-1985
REG	D	Mercury/Virgo	P	dex sextile MC c. => Jupiter (JU)	24-Nov-1985

PT	D	Jupiter/Capricorn	P	dex trine Jupiter (JU) d. => MC	6-Sep-1986
PT	D	Jupiter/Capricorn	P	dex trine Jupiter (0) d. => MC	25-Oct-1986

LOCK Jupiter/South Node/11th ruling the 12th cusp signifies botched alliances as the cause of enmity and mistakes. Here is the cause of the failed arms-for-hostages program read through Reagan's figure. Jupiter ruled by Mars/Capricorn shows armaments as the cause of the American alliance with Hezbollah, whose geographic-astrological sign correspondence is most likely Scorpio. The strong power of Mars/Capricorn ruling Jupiter shows armaments perfecting captive release; yet the South Node conjunct Jupiter shows the alliance is botched. Referencing the 1st sequence, Rev. Weir was released on 15-Sep-1985, yet as the sequence ended there was a miscarriage of an attempt to deliver missiles to Iran during 18-25 November, referred to as a 'horror story' by historical accounts. The 2nd sequence timed the kidnapping of Frank Reed on 9-Sep and the delivery of 500 TOW missiles to Iran on 28-Oct.

Longevity, 93y 3m 29d

Death: 5-Jun-2004, 1:09 PDT, Bel-Air, California, at home. Reagan died from pneumonia following a lengthy battle with Alzheimer's disease.

Hīlāj: **Sun/LOF**. This is a difficult case. Figure is nocturnal and Moon/5th/feminine sign qualifies yet the Moon conjunct the North Node raises questions (see Polk for another example where this condition invalidates the Moon as Hīlāj). Sun/2nd/masculine also qualifies by position and sex, tests well in the arcus vitae calculations, yet all the Sun's rulers are peregrine. The LOF shows the best fit to a wider range of health crises.

Empirical Findings in support of Lot of Fortune as Hīlāj
- 17/25-Jun-1947. Viral pneumonia. c tr Jupiter conj LOF.
- 30-Mar-1981. Assassination attempt. tr Sun-Venus-Mars opposed LOF.
- 8-Sep-1989. Surgery to remove water on the brain following fall from horse. tr Merc conj LOF, tr Saturn conj ASC, tr Jupiter conj DSC.
- 5-Jun-2004. Death. Venus and LOF are conjunct in the 7th of the solar return, with return's LOF conjunct natal Venus within 4 degrees.

Al-kadukhadāh: **Mars**. Mars within 3 degrees of the Ascendant is the Al-kadukhadāh. Mars gives his 66 major years; Venus adds 8 minor years by sextile aspect; Jupiter adds 12 minor years by sextile aspect.

MA (66) + VE (8) + JU (12) = 86 years.

Projected lifespan is 6-Feb-1997. He lived longer though by this time Reagan's battle with Alzheimer's disease was very advanced. The public announcement of Alzheimer's disease was made 5-Nov-1994. Note also that Jupiter closely conjunct the South Node is highly afflicted. This suggests Jupiter's contribution of 12 years were low quality. Ignoring Jupiter's contribution dials the longevity projection back to 1985 when Reagan began having problems during his 2nd term of office. Son Ron Jr. suspected Alzheimers as early as 1984 (Reagan 2011).

Victor of the Horoscope: **Mars**

Killing Planets: **Mars (33), Venus (33), Moon (31)**

Arcus Vitae:

D	Changeover	Bound Saturn/Taurus => ASC	27-May-2004

Death occurred nine days after the Distributor changed from the bound of a benefic (Jupiter/Taurus) to the bound of a malefic (Saturn/Taurus).

40. RONALD REAGAN

2004 Solar Return for year of Death

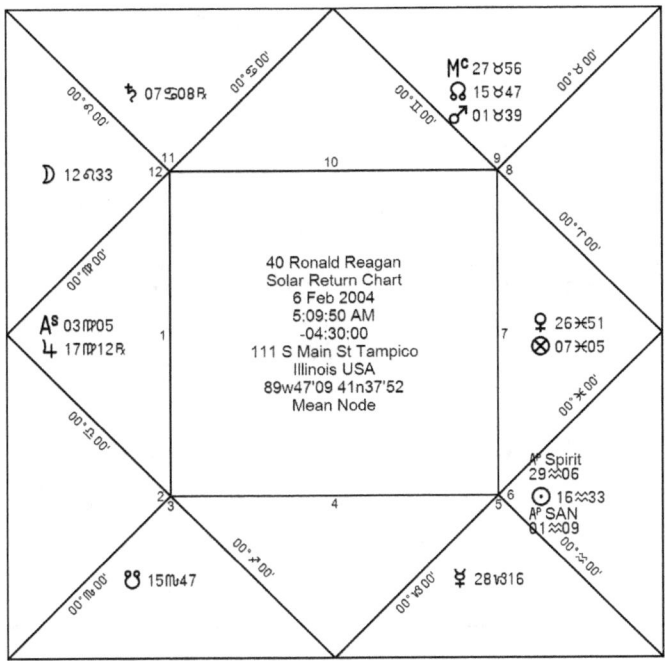

Ascendant Distributor: Saturn/Taurus since 27-May-2004
Profected Ascendant: 6LI08, 10th House; Victor: Jupiter
Lords: LOY – Venus; LOP – Moon
Firdaria: Saturn-Mercury
Moon: separates from square of Mars and applies to opposition of Sun
Return Ascendant falls in natal 9th; Natal Ascendant falls in return's 5th

LOY Venus returns to her natal sign and is placed together with the LOF in the return's 7th house. Venus is a high scoring killer and her conjunction with the empirical Hīlāj in the 7th is one indication of death. The return's victor Jupiter/Virgo, significator of pneumonia, falls in the return's 1st and rules the Venus-LOF conjunction in the 7th. Other solar return – natal connections include return's Mars and Saturn conjunct the natal IC and DSC respectively. There is also a Nodal return.

Reagan died 120.77 days or 119deg 1min following his return.

| REG | D | Mercury/Scorpio | P | South Node d. => Moon (MO) | 118deg 44min |

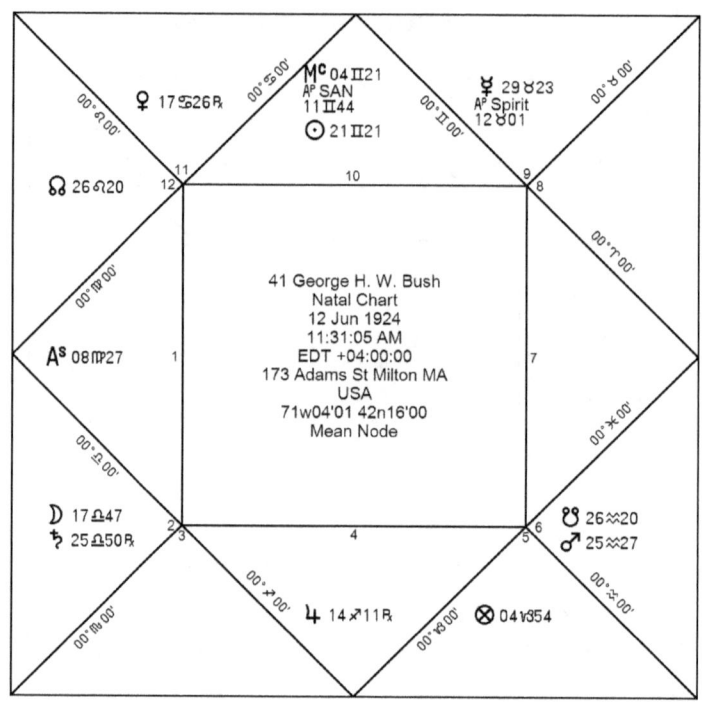
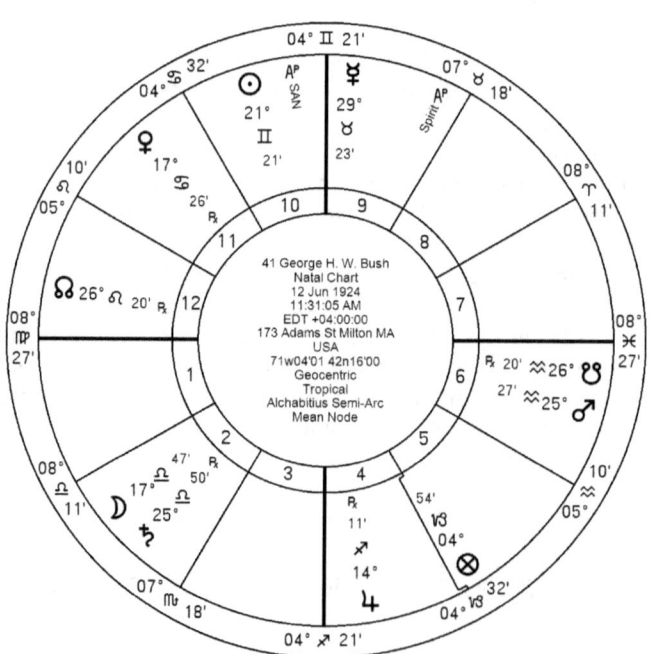

Moon's Configuration

Moon separates from **Venus** and applies to the **Sun**, diurnal, conjunctional. Prenatal syzygy is 11GE44. Eclipse? No.

Cognitive Assessment Model (Rulers of Moon and Mercury)

Sign rulers: **Venus (both)**
Bound rulers: **Jupiter, Mars**

Victor Soul Models

Ibn Ezra Victor Model (1507), in-sect triplicity ruler, triplicity decans.

	Position	☉	☽	☿	♀	♂	♃	♄
Sun	21 GE 21			5		2		4
Moon	17 LI 47				5		2	8
Asc	08 VI 27			10	5			
Pars Fortuna	04 CP 54			2	3	4		6
Syzygy	11 GE 45			5	1		2	3
Oriental						1	0	0
Houses			11	6	11	8	1	9	6
Score		0	11	6	**33**	22	8	13	27

Porphyry's Expanded Victor Model (2022)

Mercury rules the MC, ASC, Sun, and syzygy by sign; the MC, Lot of Fortune, and Lot of Spirit by bound. Sect: in-favor. Solar phase: oriental from 1st direct station to sinking. Position: Angular with Lot of Spirit. At the bending of the Nodes.

Victor Table for Killing Planets

			☉	☽	☿	♀	♂	♃	♄
ASC	8VI27			3	5,4,1	3,2	3		
Rul ASC	29TA23	☿		4,3		5,3	3,2		1
L.Death	16AR14		4,3,1		2		5	3	3
Rul L.Death	25AQ27	♂			3	1	2	3	5,3
H8 Cusp	8AR11			4,3		2	5,1	3	3
Rul H8	25AQ27	♂			3	1	2	3	5,3
T-Rul H8	21GE21	☉			5,3		2	3	3,1
8th from ☉	21CP21			3	1	3,2	4,3		5
Rul 8th fr ☉	25LI50	♄			3,1	5,2		3	4,3
TOTAL			15	13	31	29	**32**	18	**39**

2007 Proposed Rectification: 11:31:05 AM, ASC 8VI27'29"
2022 Proposed Rectification: 11:31:05 AM, ASC 8VI27'43"

Astrodatabank reports a B-rated birth time of 10:30 AM, ASC = 26LE36. The proposed rectification is an hour later. Based on life affairs, I reject Leo rising out of hand. Celebrity culture was an anathema to GHWB.

ZRS: L1-Gemini/Sagittarius emphasized family/home themes; L1-Cancer/Capricorn captured his father's Senate career milestones and an unsuccessful Senate bid; L1-Leo/Aquarius captured his active political career. GHWB won the Presidential election under L2 Aries, angular from LOF, but is somewhat out of synch with an ideal L2 pattern which links FS and LB.

L1 Taurus 12 Jun 1924		
L1 Gemini 01 May 1932		
L2 Sagittarius 13 Feb 1941	FS	7-Dec-1941, Pearl Harbor triggered desire for military service among Bush family; Dec-1941, met wife-to-be Barbara Pierce at a Christmas dance.
L2 Sagittarius 30 Aug 1949	LB	Living in California temporarily as salesman for Dresser Industries; 20-Dec-1949, daughter Robin Bush born; Jan-1950, moved back to Midland and purchased house on Easter Egg Row.
L1 Cancer 17 Jan 1952		4-Nov-1952, father PB won special election to Senate; Mar-1953, started Zapata Petroleum as learned of Robin's leukemia diagnosis.
L2 Capricorn 05 Mar 1960	FS	30-Dec-1960, father PB announced re-election bid for Senate seat (lost race).
L2 Capricorn 17 May 1969	LB	13-Jan-1970, announced Senate bid; 3-Nov-1970, lost race to Lloyd Bentsen; 16-Feb-1971, appointed to UN Ambassador.
L1 Leo 07 Sep 1976		2-Nov-1976, Carter won Presidential election; 19-Nov-1976, JC spurned GHWB's offer to stay on as CIA head.
L2 Aquarius 24 Dec 1984	FS	20-Jan-1985, VP inauguration under Reagan's 2nd term; 5-Oct-1986, Iran-Contra scandal unraveled; 27-May-1987, GHWB ignored Iran-Contra Independent Counsel Lawrence Walsh's request for records and diaries.
L2 Aries 06 Jun 1988		9-Jun-1988, opened Presidential campaign at Texas Republican Convention; 8-Nov-1988, won Presidential Election.
L2 Aquarius 06 Jan 1994	LB	Son GWB elected TX Governor; son Jeb lost Florida gubernatorial bid; 3-May-1995, ripped up NRA membership card and resigned, angry after the NRA's did not support his 1992 re-election campaign.
L1 Virgo 31 May 1995		
L2 Pisces 11 Aug 2004	FS	14-Sep-2004, published: Kitty Kelley's hatchet biography on the Bush family.
L2 Pisces 28 Sep 2012	LB	7-May-2013, published: Richard Ben Cramer's biography *Being Poppy: A Portrait of George Herbert Walker Bush* which was excerpted from previously published *What it Takes: The Way to the White House* (1993).
L1 Libra 15 Feb 2015		30-Nov-2018, death.

Firdaria – Mercury major and minor periods

Firdaria according to Bonatti	Life Event
Sun **Mercury** 22 Apr 1927	No events found.
Venus **Mercury** 04 Aug 1935	No events found.
Mercury 13 years Age 18 to 31	
Mercury Mercury 12 Jun 1942	12-Jun-1942, enlisted in Navy; 9-Jun-1943, completed basic flight training course; 12-Dec-1943, engaged to Barbara.
Mercury Moon 21 Apr 1944	Summer-1944, Operation Snapshot; 2-Sep-1944, shot down in air raid; 6-Jan-1945, married Barbara Pierce; 18-Sep-1945, discharged from Navy; moved to New Haven and attended accelerated Yale program.
Mercury Saturn 28 Feb 1946	6-Jul-1946, birth of son GWB Jr; 1947/48, led Yale fund-raising for United Negro College Fund.
Mercury Jupiter 07 Jan 1948	Spring-1948, moved to Odessa; April-1949, salesman for Dresser oil services company.
Mercury Mars 16 Nov 1949	20-Dec-1949, birth of daughter Robin Bush; late-1950, decided to leave Dresser and form his own firm; 1951 (no exact date), started Bush-Overbay Oil Development Co.
Mercury Sun 25 Sep 1951	4-Nov-1952, grandfather PB won special election to Senate; Mar-1953, started Zapata Petroleum as learned of Robin's leukemia diagnosis.
Mercury Venus 03 Aug 1953	11-Oct-1953, death of daughter Robin Bush; 22-Jan-1955, birth of Neil Bush.
Moon **Mercury** 28 Feb 1963	11-Sep-1963, announced Senate bid.
Saturn **Mercury** 20 Apr 1972	8-Oct-1972, death of grandfather PB; 20-Nov-1972, Chair of RNC; 18-Jan-1973, last day as UN ambassador.
Jupiter **Mercury** 21 Apr 1982	VP under Reagan, dealt with various issues including funding for Contras and nerve gas production, the latter of which was not approved.
Mars **Mercury** 12 Jun 1990	26-Jun-1990, broke 'no new taxes' pledge; 2-Aug-1990, Iraq invaded Kuwait; 17-Jan-1991, Operation Desert Storm; 27-Feb-1991, Cease fire in Gulf War.
Sun **Mercury** 21 Apr 2002	No events found.
Venus **Mercury** 03 Aug 2010	No events found.
Mercury Mercury 12 Jun 2017	30-Nov-2018, death.

Mercury as Victor. Mercury/Taurus, the Venus-ruled sign associated with earth-bound commodities, makes GHWB a businessman involved in oil. He specialized in contracts and relationships rather than the wildcatter side of the business even though Zapata's initial wildcat wells were successful.

Note that both Mars and the South Node overcome Mercury which itself is placed in the bound of Mars. While usually adhering to the 'kinder and gentler' diplomacy which was a hallmark of GHWB's political capital, he could be swayed otherwise by hawkish employees such as political operative Lee Atwater who used negative campaign ads to secure Bush's 1988 Republican Presidential victory. Mars/Aquarius also appears to signify nerve gas which was an issue which GHWB dealt with during the Reagan administration (see Mercury primaries).

Transits

8-Jun-1942. *trNorth Node conj ASC.*
  Enlisted in Navy, 12-Jun.

17-Jan-1961. *trNorth Node conj ASC.*
  Father Prescott Bush announced re-election bid for Senate seat, 30-Dec.

9-May-1970. *trSouth Node conj DSC.*
  Challenger Bentsen won Democratic primary, May-1970.

19-Dec-1988. *trSouth Node conj ASC.*
  Regulators seized assets of son Neil Bush's Silverado S&L, 9-Dec.
  South Node falls in 6th house, 2nd from 5th, or children's money.

3-Aug-1990. *trMercury conj ASC.*
18-Jan-1991. *trMercury conj LOF.*
  Following the Iraqi invasion, GWHB says "This will not stand," 5-Aug-90.
  Operation Desert Storm is launched, 17-Jan-1991.

Solar Arc Directions

11-Jul-1964. *csa MC opposed Saturn.*
2-Nov-1964. *dsa Saturn opposed MC.*
  Barry Goldwater nominated as GOP candidate on 1st ballot, 15-Jul.
  GHWB lost Senate race to Yarborough, 3-Nov.

20-Aug-1973. *csa Saturn conj ASC.*
3-Feb-1974. *dsa ASC conj Saturn.*
  Kissinger appointed Secretary of State, 22-Aug.
  House Judiciary Committee started to investigate grounds for Richard Nixon's impeachment, 6-Feb.

14-Aug-1991. *csa MC sextile Mercury.*
6-Jun-1992. *dsa Mercury sextile MC.*
  Signed bill on covert ops, to avoid another Iran-Contra, 15-Aug-1991.
  At Earth Summit in Rio, stated US will not sign treaty to protect rare and endangered animals and plants, saying it would retard development of technology, 12-Jun-1992.

14-Sep-2004. *csa Nodes square ASC.*
  Kitty Kelley's *The Family: The Real Story of the Bush Dynasty* appeared in newsstands. Very uncomplimentary to Bush family, 14-Sep.

Primary Directions

PT	D	Saturn/Cancer	P	sin sex Mercury (ME) d. =>MC	19-Jan-1983
PT	D	Saturn/Cancer	P	sin sex Mercury (BI) d. =>MC	1-May-1983
PT	D	Saturn/Cancer	P	sin sex Mercury (0) d. =>MC	13-Aug-1983

Reagan administration reopened drive for nerve gas production, 19-Feb.
Senate Armed Services Committee authorized nerve gas, 30-Jun.
GHWB cast tie breaking Senate vote for nerve gas production, 13-Jul.
GHWB cast 2nd tie breaking Senate vote for nerve gas production, 8-Nov.
Mars/Aquarius signifies nerve gas. Mars overcomes Mercury which it receives by bound. Interaction between Mercury and Mars is integrated.

PT	D	Venus/Libra	P	Saturn (SA) d. => ASC	19-Nov-1983
PT	D	Venus/Libra	P	Saturn (0) d. => ASC	23-Mar-1985

Congressional conferees rejected Reagan's plan to resume production of nerve gas and chemical weapons, 17-Nov-1983.
Followed GHWB's 8-Nov Senate vote (see above).
Ohio S&Ls open following emergency bank closure 15/21-Mar-1985.

PT	D	Saturn/Pisces	P	dex sex Mercury (ME) c. =>MC	10-May-1986
PT	D	Saturn/Cancer	P	sin sex Mercury (BI) c. =>MC	14-Nov-1986
PT	D	Saturn/Cancer	P	sin sex Mercury (0) c. =>MC	21-May-1987

McFarlane told Reagan: arms for hostage swap was not working, 29-May.
Reagan press conference: he had authorized arms sales to Iran, 13-Nov.
Iran-Contra Independent Counsel Lawrence Walsh requested all GHWB's personal records and diaries, 27-May. GHWB ignored the request.

Primary Direction Sequences

REG	D	Venus/Pisces	P	DSC d. => Mars (0)	23-Jan-1941
REG	D	Venus/Pisces	P	DSC d. => Mars (MA)	10-Nov-1942

This sequence marked Bush's entry into WWII service with Pearl Harbor on 7-Dec-1941, his enlistment on 12-Jun-1942, and his 6-Aug-1942 date for reporting for duty at Chapel Hill's preflight training center. Bush later joined Operation Snapshot, an aerial photography intelligence program.

PT	D	Saturn/Gemini	P	dex trine Saturn (SA) d. => MC	8-Jun-1947
PT	D	Saturn/Gemini	P	dex trine Saturn (0) d. => MC	12-Jul-1947

LOCK Bush's Saturn/Libra – Venus/Cancer combo recapitulates the same combination in the USA figure. Saturn/Libra is the *New World Order* significator. For Bush, Saturn/Libra/2nd is expenditures (and loss – see Ohio S&L direction above) on structures (Saturn/2nd) designed to support alliances through development of consumer spending (Venus/Cancer/11th) as a driver of foreign policy (Venus ruling 9th). Sequence timed Marshall Plan proposal on 5-Jun and negotiations on the structure of the Marshall Plan in Paris talks between 12-Jul and 12-Sep-1947 as the sequence ended.

Longevity, 94y 5m 18d

Death: 30-Nov-2018, 10:10 PM CST, Houston, TX, at home. Bush died following a long battle with Parkinson's disease.

Hīlāj: **Sun/LOF**.

Sun. Figure is diurnal and Sun/Gemini/10th qualifies as the Hilaj on an initial review. Sign lord Mercury is inconjunct but is the Victor. Bound lord Mars does aspect by trine but is afflicted in the 6th house by conjunction to the South Node. Any longevity workout with Mars would produce a solution significantly less than GHWB's actual longevity.

LOF. Empirical evidence suggests the LOF may be the Hīlāj.
2-Sep-1944. Shot down during WWII. tr Mars 10th from LOF.
30-Nov-2018. Solar return for year of death shows sr Saturn opposed sr LOF. On day of death tr Saturn 7CP48 was widely conjunct the LOF 4CP53.

Al-kadukhadāh: This is a difficult case where virtually any choice will produce a solution with too few years. Consider **Mercury** as the Sun's sign ruler and the Victor of the Horoscope. Mercury grants 76 major years; Mars at the superior square deducts 15 minor years, Venus receives Mercury by sign and sextile aspect and adds 8 minor years. Note Mercury receives Venus by bound (not sure of effect).

ME (76) – MA (15) + VE (8) = 69 years.

Bush lived considerably longer but in 1985 at age 61 Bush was injured in a tennis accident; he was knocked unconscious after falling and hitting his head on concrete. This accident demonstrates the negative influence of Mars on vitality since age 61 corresponds to Mars' deduction of 15 minor years from Mercury's major 76 years. The same year their dog Millie was born. There has been speculation about a linkage between Millie's lupus and Grave's disease which afflicted both GHWB and wife Barbara (with Millie a possible source). Radiation treatment in 1991 for hyperthyroidism significantly reduced Bush's vitality which speculatively may be linked to Millie's acquisition in 1985.

Victor of the Horoscope: **Mercury**

Killing Planets: **Saturn (39), Mars (32)**

Arcus Vitae:

REG	D	Mercury/Taurus	P	dex trine ASC d. => Mars (MA)	28-Nov-2018
PT	D	Mars/Gemini	P	Sun c. => ASC	15-Feb-2019

2018 Solar Return for Year of Death

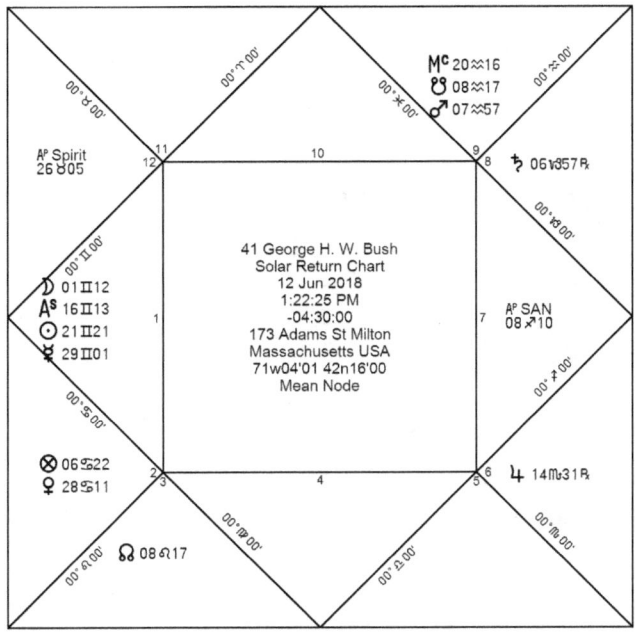

Ascendant Distributor: Jupiter/Scorpio since 27-Mar-2015
Profected Ascendant: 8CA27, 11th House; Victor: Mars
Lords: LOY – Moon; LOP – Mars
Firdaria: Major – Mercury; Subperiod – Mercury
Moon: applies to Mars
Return Ascendant falls in natal 10th; Natal Ascendant falls in return's 4th

Natal Mars-South Node conjunction in Aquarius is recapitulated in the return within a degree. srSaturn is conjunct nLOF and opposes srLOF.

GHWB died 171.7 days or 174deg 15min following his return.

| REG | D | Mercury/Gemini | P | Moon (MO) d. => Saturn (SA) | 175deg 50min |

714 · A RECTIFICATION MANUAL

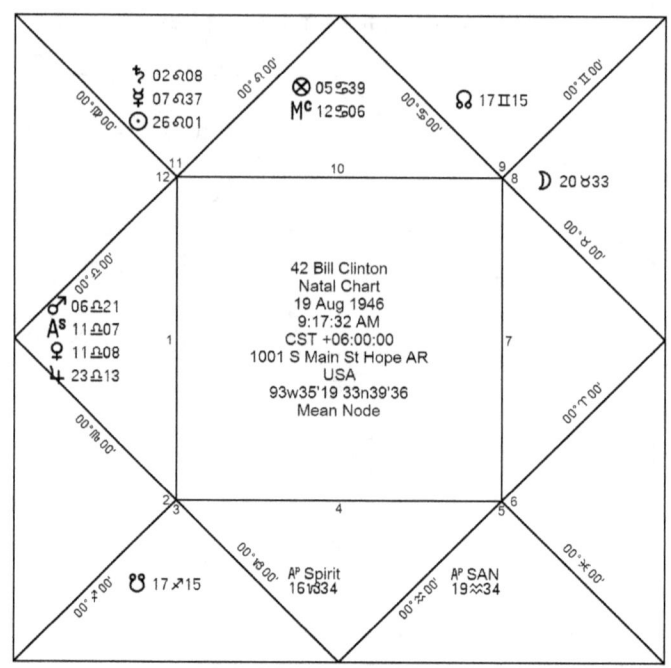

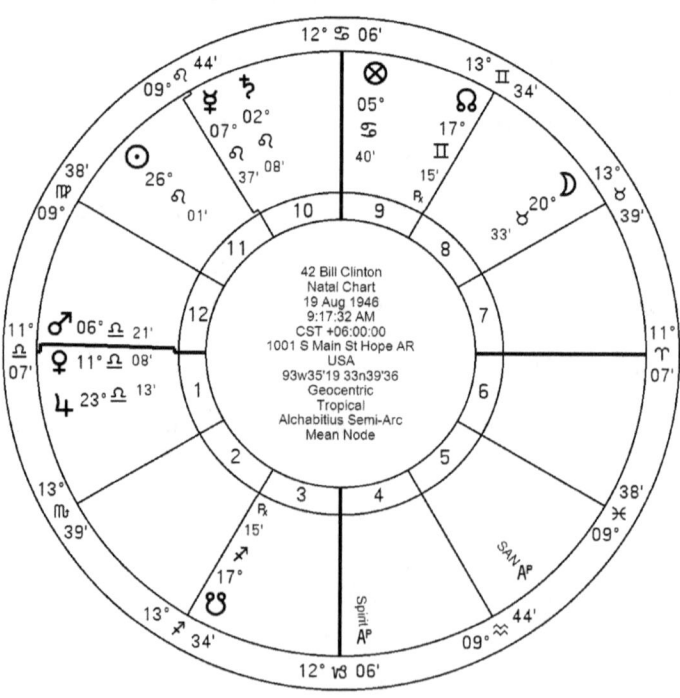

Moon's Configuration

Moon separates from **Mercury** and applies to the **Sun**, diurnal, preventional. Prenatal syzygy is 19AQ34. Eclipse? No.

Cognitive Assessment Model (Rulers of Moon and Mercury)

Sign rulers: **Venus, (Sun)/Mars**
Bound rulers: **Jupiter, Venus**

Victor Soul Models

Ibn Ezra Victor Model (1507), in-sect triplicity ruler, triplicity decans.

	Position	☉	☽	☿	♀	♂	♃	♄
Sun	26 LE 01	8				3		
Moon	20 TA 33		4		8		2	1
Asc	11 LI 07			2	5			8
Pars Fortuna	05 CA 40		6		3	2	4	
Syzygy	19 AQ 34			1			2	8
Oriental						0	0	3
Houses			8	5	8	12	12	11
Score		0	16	15	11	28	17	20	31

Porphyry's Expanded Victor Model (2022)

Jupiter rules the Moon and syzygy by bound. Sect: in-favor. Solar phase: occidental sextile to sinking. Position: Angular in ASC, 4th from Lot of Fortune, 10th from Lot of Spirit. Dignity: participating triplicity.

Victor Table for Killing Planets

Not published for the living.

2007 Proposed Rectification: 9:17:29 AM, ASC 11LI06'31"
2022 Revised Rectification: 9:17:32 AM, ASC 11LI07'26"

Astrodatabank reports an A-rated birth time of 8:51 AM, ASC 5LI31. The proposed rectification is later. The rectification advances the LOF from the 30th degree of Gemini to the 6th degree of Cancer, making the cardinal signs angular from the LOF. The rectification also advances the Ascendant from the 1st decan of Libra (ruled by Venus/Libra) to the 2nd decan of Libra (Aquarius, ruled by Saturn/Leo). I favor the 2nd decan for Saturn/Leo's penchant for BC's flashy neckties and gaudy colors which are a delineation match to the fashion flair of Leo.

The slight revision in the 2022 rectification was driven by the observation that solar arc directions time events more reliably than primary directions for horoscopes with a strong Leo emphasis. BC has Saturn, Mercury, and the Sun all in Leo. Accordingly, in this revision I selected the solar arc Sun-MC over the similar primary direction for BC's 1992 launch of his Presidential campaign. The converse solar arc Sun-MC direction timed the launch of his 'magical bus tour' during Summer '92.

ZRS. BC's political career is entirely contained by L1 Aquarius.

L1 Capricorn 19 Aug 1946		
L2 Cancer 31 Oct 1955	FS	Aug-1956, eagerly watched political conventions on TV; 24-Sep-1957, Federal troops quelled Little Rock school integration violence.
L2 Cancer 18 Dec 1963	LB	Apr-1964, Accepted to Georgetown; 29-May-1964, graduated from High School; 19-Aug-1964, draft registration, later deferred his draft status; Fall-1964, began classes at Georgetown; 1964/65, won election for Freshman class president.
L2 Capricorn 04 Feb 1972	CP	28-Mar-1972, competed with HRC in annual Barristers Union trial competition, won semi-final found; 29-Apr-1972, lost final round.
L1 Aquarius 30 Mar 1973		Spring 1973, graduated Yale Law School; 12-May-1973, received offer for law faculty at University of Arkansas; 1974, unsuccessful Congressional campaign, returned to teaching.
L2 Leo 12 Apr 1982	FS	2-Nov-1972, won AK Gubernatorial race.
L2 Leo 29 Jul 1990	LB	Nov-1990, won last AK Gubernatorial race; 3-Oct-1991, announced US Presidential Bid; 23-Jan-1992, Gennifer Flowers sex scandal broke.
L2 Aquarius 14 Nov 1998	CP	20-Jan-2001, George W Bush presidential inauguration.
L1 Pisces 24 Oct 2002		
L1 Aries 22 Aug 2014		3-May-2015, HRC announced Presidential bid.

Notable Ascendant Distributor Changeover

D	Changeover	Bound Jupiter/Scorpio => ASC	11-Feb-1992

Dubbed "the Comeback Kid" after New Hampshire 2nd place win, 18-Feb.

Firdaria – Jupiter major and minor periods

Firdaria according to Bonatti	Life Event
Sun **Jupiter** 10 Oct 1953	No events found.
Venus **Jupiter** 15 Mar 1961	14-Apr-1962, Virginia Cassidy filed for divorce.
Mercury **Jupiter** 15 Mar 1970	late-May-1970, accepted to Yale; Spring-1971, met Hillary at Yale Law library.
Moon **Jupiter** 15 Mar 1980	May/Jun-1980, Cuban refugee crisis in Arkansas while during term as Governor; 4-Nov-1980, lost re-election bid; 1981, returned to Wright, Lindsey & Jennings as lawyer.
Saturn **Jupiter** 15 Mar 1988	14-Jul-1988, decided against Presidential bid; 20-Jul-1988, bad nominating speech for Dukakis at DNC (too long); late-Oct-1988, released "Moving Arkansas Forward into the 21st Century" as legislative platform; 9-Jan-1989, presented platform to legislature.
Jupiter 12 years Age 51 to 63	
Jupiter Jupiter 18 Aug 1997	31-Oct-1997, ordered US to participate in financial bailout of Indonesia ($3 bln of $22 bln total); 19-Jan-1998, Lewinsky scandal broke; 10-Apr-1998, Good Friday Peace Accords signed in Northern Ireland; 7-Aug-1998, African embassy bombing by Al Qaeda; Aug/Oct-1998, collapse of Russian Ruble and Long Term Capital Management financial crisis; 23-Oct-1998, Wye River Memorandum; 12-Feb-1999, acquitted on impeachment charges by the Senate.
Jupiter Mars 06 May 1999	7-May-1999, NATO accidental bombing of Chinese embassy in Belgrade; 12-May-1999, Rubin left Treasury; 15-Nov-1999, trade agreement with China; 11-Jul-2000, Mideast peace summit at Camp David, talks collapsed afterwards; 7-Nov-2000, disputed election results; 13-Dec-2000, Supreme Court ruled in favor of Bush in disputed election.
Jupiter Sun 21 Jan 2001	20-Jan-2001, GWB inaugurated President.
Jupiter Venus 10 Oct 2002	1-Jun-2004, published autobiography: *My Life*.
Jupiter Mercury 27 Jun 2004	7-Sep-2004, quadruple bypass open heart surgery.
Jupiter Moon 15 Mar 2006	No events found.
Jupiter Saturn 01 Dec 2007	No events found.
Mars **Jupiter** 19 Aug 2015	Sep-2015, HRC ratings slumped regarding private email usage while at the State Department.

Jupiter as Victor. Clinton was so active as a politician that nearly every chapter of his life has been notable in some manner. Therefore, to make the counterfactual argument that Jupiter as Firdaria ruler outlines key events is a more difficult strategy to pursue in support of the correct Firdaria sequence.

As presented, Jupiter captured his Yale Law School acceptance and first meeting with Hillary Rodham, a lost Arkansas gubernatorial re-election bid after the Cuban refugee crisis, his DNC nominating speech for Dukakis; and as President the Northern Ireland Good Friday Peace Accords and the China trade deal. Post-presidency, his published memoir *My Life* and his open-heart surgery have been key personal milestones.

Transits

30-Aug-1968. *tr South Node conj ASC.*
  Witnessed Grant Park violence at DNC, 22-Aug.

7-Aug-1973. *tr South Node conj LOF.*
  Hillary rebuffed Bill's first marriage proposal, Summer-73.

27-Nov-1982. *tr North Node conj LOF.*
  Won race for AK Governor, 2-Nov-82; Took office, 11-Jan-83.

18-Mar-1992. *tr South Node conj LOF.*
  HRC "could have stayed home and baked cookies" comment, 16-Mar-92.

Solar Arc Directions

20-Apr-1972. *dsa North Node conj MC.*
  BC and HRC in Yale Barristers Union trial competition. Won semi-finals, 28-Mar; Lost finals, 29-Apr.

13-Mar-1974. *dsa Moon conj NNode.*
  Filed candidacy for Congress, 22-Mar.

3-Oct-1991. *dsa MC conj Sun.*
17-Jul-1992. *csa Sun conj MC.*
  LOCK Announced Presidential Bid, 3-Oct-1991.
  LOCK Campaign launched "magical bus tour," 17-Jul-1992.

19-Jan-1992. *dsa Mars opposed Moon.*
4-Nov-1992. *csa Moon opposed Mars.*
  Gennifer Flowers story broke, 23-Jan; appeared in *Star*, 4-Feb.
  Elected President, 3-Nov.

15-Apr-1998. *dsa LOF conj Sun.*
19-Apr-1999. *csa Sun conj LOF.*
  Good Friday Peace Accords signed, 10-Apr-1998.
  Jury acquitted Susan McDougal on obstruction of justice, 12-Apr-1999.

8-Jan-2018. *dsa Saturn square MC.*
  House fire at Chappaqua (bedroom), 3-Jan-18.

Primary Directions

PT	D	Jupiter/Leo	P	Saturn (0) d. => MC	14-Nov-1967

Death of stepfather Roger Clinton on 8-Nov is the most logical event for this direction because Saturn rules the 4th and is in the 11th (8th from the

4th). Yet the UK Sterling devaluation on 19-Nov from 2.80 to 2.40 also fits because currency (King's money) is also an 11th house affair.

| PT | D | Mars/Scorpio | P | sin square Saturn (0) d. => ASC | 20-Sep-1971 |

Clinton learned his friend Frank Aller committed suicide, 14-Sep.

| PT | D | Mars/Leo | P | Sun d. => MC | 26-Sep-1991 |

Announced Presidential Bid, 3-Oct. I prefer the solar arc measurement.

| PT | D | Jupiter/Scorpio | P | opposition Moon (0) d. => ASC | 3-Jan-1994 |

LOCK Washington Post called for Whitewater investigation, 4-Jan.
LOCK Mother Virginia Cassidy died, 6-Jan.
AG Janet Reno announced Independent Counsel for Whitewater, 12-Jan.
Moon/Taurus/8th signifies real estate investments.

| REG | D | Venus/Virgo | P | sin sextile MC d. => Jupiter (JU) | 20-Oct-1994 |

Israel/Jordan peace treaty, 26-Oct.
North Korea agreement to end nuclear proliferation signed, 21-Oct.

| REG | D | Mercury/Libra | P | sin square MC d. => Sun | 31-Jan-1997 |

2nd Presidential Inauguration, 20-Jan-1997.

| PT | D | Saturn/Scorpio | P | sin square Sun d. => ASC | 15-Aug-2000 |

Spoke at DNC; Al Gore nominated for President, 14-Aug.

| PT | D | Jupiter/Taurus | P | Moon (MO) c. => MC | 7-Jan-2001 |

HRC sworn in as US Senator, New York, 3-Jan-2001.

Primary Direction Sequences

| PT | D | Venus/Cancer | P | MC d. => Saturn (SA) | 30-May-1968 |
| REG | D | Venus/Cancer | P | MC d. => Saturn (SA) | 8-Aug-1968 |

This sequence timed Bobby Kennedy's assassination on 5-Jun and announcement of McGovern's Presidential bid, 10-Aug.

| REG | D | Venus/Cancer | P | dex square ASC c. => Saturn (0) | 7-Sep-1969 |
| REG | D | Venus/Cancer | P | dex square ASC c. => Saturn (SA) | 9-Sep-1969 |

This sequence timed one of Clinton's most difficult struggles with the Vietnam-era draft. As he was making the decision to enroll with the draft, a local newspaper leaked a story on 14-Sep that Nixon was planning a draft suspension; later announced on 19-Sep after Nixon faced turmoil on college campuses. On 1-Oct Nixon announced that anyone in graduate school could complete the full year; this left Clinton safe from the draft through Jun-1970.

A RECTIFICATION MANUAL

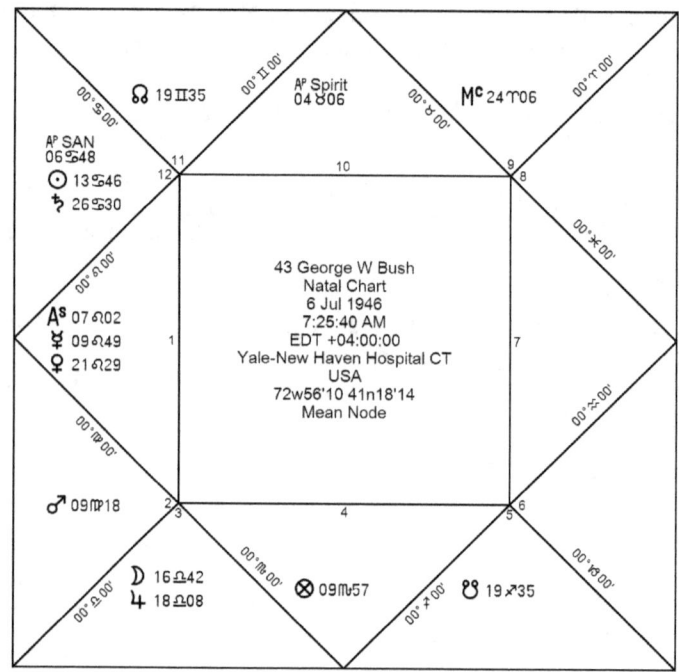

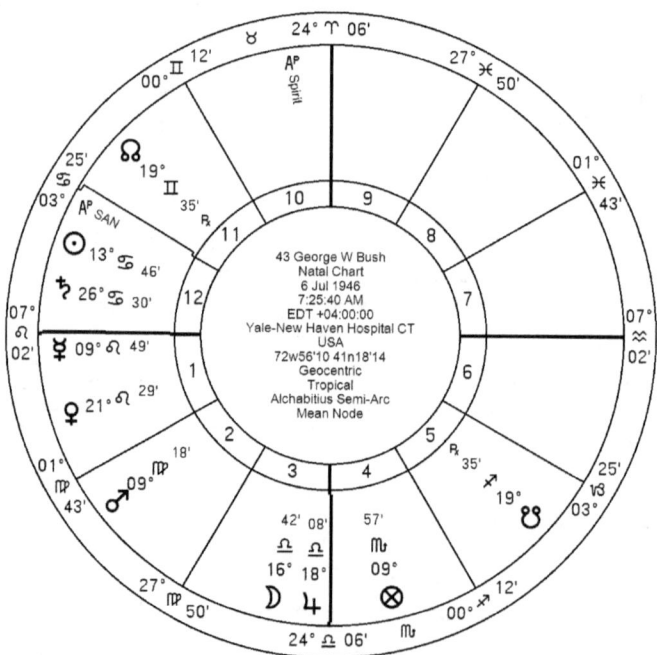

43. GEORGE W. BUSH

Moon's Configuration

Moon separates from the **Sun** and applies to **Jupiter**, diurnal, conjunctional. Prenatal syzygy is 6CA48. Eclipse? **YES**. Partial Solar Eclipse.

Cognitive Assessment Model (Rulers of Moon and Mercury)

Sign rulers: **Venus, (Sun)/Mercury**
Bound rulers: **Jupiter, Venus**

Victor Soul Models

Ibn Ezra Victor Model (1507), in-sect triplicity ruler, triplicity decans.

	Position	☉	☽	☿	♀	♂	♃	♄
Sun	13 CA 46		5	2	3	1	4	
Moon	16 LI 42				5		2	8
Asc	07 LE 02	9			2			
Pars Fortuna	09 SC 57				5	6		
Syzygy	06 CA 48 (SE)		6		3	2	4	
Oriental						0	0	0
Houses			2	3	12	12	6	3	2
Score		0	11	14	14	**30**	15	13	10

Porphyry's Expanded Victor Model (2022)

Venus rules the Moon and Lot of Spirit by sign; the ASC, Lot of Fortune, and Lot of Spirit by bound. Sect: out-of-favor. Solar phase: occidental rising to 2nd retrograde station. Position: Angular in ASC, 10th from Lot of Fortune, 4th from Lot of Spirit.

Victor Table for Killing Planets

Not computed for the living.

2007 Proposed Rectification: 7:25:37 AM, ASC 7LE02'07"
2022 Proposed Rectification: 7:25:40 AM, ASC 7LE02'13"

Astrodatabank reports a 7:26 AM birth time. The proposed rectification is less than a minute earlier. A fresh review using an expanded event database shows several directions off by a few weeks which suggests a slight tweak in the time. But it's a fine-tuning exercise best left for the next edition.

ZRS. Textbook case of FS-LB life changing events during L1-CA and L1-LE.

L1 Taurus 06 Jul 1946		
L1 Gemini 25 May 1954		
L2 Sagittarius 09 Mar 1963	FS	Fall 1963, grandfather Prescott Bush retired from Senate; 11-Sep-1963, father GHWB announced Senate candidacy, ran as Goldwater candidate and lost Senate race in November 1964.
L2 Sagittarius 23 Sep 1971	LB	During L2-Sagittarius, father GHWB served as UN ambassador; 23-Oct-1971, report of GWB interest in running for office, later decides against; 27-May-1972, began year of 'missing service' at Montgomery National Guard; 8-Oct-1972 (3 weeks after end of L2-Sagittarius), grandfather Prescott Bush died of lung cancer.
L1 Cancer 09 Feb 1974		7-Aug-1974, GHWB advised Nixon to resign; 12-Aug-1974, GHWB advocated for VP slot to Ford, was crushed when Ford appointed Nelson Rockefeller instead; 3-Sep-1974, GHWB took Ambassador to China position; 12-Jun-1975, GWB graduated from Harvard and moved to Midland, TX.
L2 Capricorn 29 Mar 1982	FS	April-1982, GWB offered public drilling partnerships for Bush Exploration but had difficulty in raising subscriptions; 29-Feb-1984, Bush Exploration merged with Spectrum 7, with GWB appointed Chairman and CEO; 3-Apr-1984, made born-again conversion to Christianity.
L2 Capricorn 10 Jun 1991	LB	21-Aug-1991, SEC cleared GWB of insider trading charges on Harken stock; 30-Oct-1991, groundbreaking ceremony for Arlington baseball field; 3-Nov-1992, father lost Presidential re-election bid to Clinton.
L2 Aquarius 28 Aug 1993		8-Nov-1993, announced TX Gubernatorial bid; 8-Nov-1994, elected TX Governor.
L1 Leo 01 Oct 1998		9-Nov-1998, re-elected as TX Governor; 12-Jun-1999, announced Presidential bid; 19-Feb-2000, defeated John McCain in SC primary; 7-Mar-2000, won Super Tuesday.
L2 Aquarius 17 Jan 2007	FS	10-Feb-2007, General David Petraeus took over in Iraq; 1-May-2007, vetoed troop removal, approval dropped to new lows; 2007/2009, Great Financial Crisis; Nov-2008, Obama elected President.
L2 Aquarius 30 Jan 2016	LB	8-Nov-2016, Donald Trump won Presidential election; 28-Feb-2017, published: *Portraits of Courage: A Commander in Chief's Tribute to America's Warriors*.
L1 Virgo 23 Jun 2017		30-Nov-2018, death of father GHWB.

Firdaria – Venus major and minor periods

Firdaria according to Bonatti	Life Event
Sun **Venus** 10 Dec 1947	Spring-1948, family moved to Odessa; Apr-1949, family temporarily moved to CA, GHWB salesman for Dresser oil services company.
Venus 8 years Age 10 to 18	
Venus Venus 05 Jul 1956	6-Nov-1956, grandfather PB won re-election to Senate; 20-Jun-1957, PB front page NYT photo shown playing golf with President Eisenhower.
Venus Mercury 27 Aug 1957	
Venus Moon 18 Oct 1958	Jul-1959, role as 'campfire lighter' at Longhorn Camp; Aug-1959, Scotland vacation.
Venus Saturn 09 Dec 1959	No events found.
Venus Jupiter 30 Jan 1961	No events found.
Venus Mars 23 Mar 1962	No events found.
Venus Sun 15 May 1963	Fall-1963, grandfather PB left Senate; 11-Sep-1963, father GHWB announced Senate bid.
Mercury **Venus** 27 Aug 1975	31-Jan-1976, father GHWB began 12-month tenure as CIA head; 4-Sep-1976, arrested for DUI; Jun-1977, incorporated Arbusto oil company.
Moon **Venus** 09 Dec 1983	29-Feb-1984, appointed Chair and CEO of the merged companies Bush Exploration and Spectrum 7; 3-Apr-1984, GWB made born-again conversion to Christianity; 6-Nov-1984, father re-elected VP under Reagan.
Saturn **Venus** 17 Oct 1992	3-Nov-1992, father GHWB lost Presidential re-election bid to Bill Clinton; 8-Nov-1993, announced TX Gubernatorial bid; 1-Apr-1994, first exhibition game played by Texas Rangers (GWB part-owner).
Jupiter **Venus** 27 Aug 2002	8-Jul-2002, called for new laws on corporate abuse after Enron bankruptcy; 4-Sep-2002, Identified Saddam Hussein as a 'serious threat'; 19-Mar-2003, Operation Iraqi Freedom; 8-Mar-2004, Iraq created interim constitution.

Venus as Victor. Venus captured key political milestones of his grandfather Prescott Bush and his father George Herbert Walker Bush, GWB's DUI arrest, his born-again conversion to Christianity, announcement of his Texas Gubernatorial bid, and the launch of Operation Iraqi Freedom.

Venus/Leo co-present with Mercury/Leo (both planets in each other's bounds) makes GWB a cheerleader and promotor for a variety of causes including the Jupiter/Libra-signified 'freedom agenda' which was a fundamental driver of Operation Iraqi Freedom as well as operations in Afghanistan. Venus' rulership of Jupiter makes the Venus-Jupiter connection. One cannot argue against **Jupiter/Libra** as a reasonable alternate to Venus/Leo as the victor but it is not an obvious model choice.

Transits

25-Jul-2000. *tr South Node 10th from MC.*
Chose Cheney as VP running mate, 24-Jul; made speech at Republican National Convention speech, 3-Aug.

12-Feb-2002. *tr North Node sextile MC.*
Axis of Evil speech, 29-Jan. This is also a Nodal return.

Solar Arc Directions

4-Oct-1952. *csa MC opposed Jupiter.*
7-Oct-1952. *dsa Jupiter opposed MC.*
Grandfather Prescott Bush won election to Senate, 4-Nov.

18-Nov-1970. *dsa Sun conj ASC.*
21-Nov-1970. *csa ASC conj Sun.*
Father GHWB lost Senate race to Lloyd Bentsen, 3-Nov.
Demonstrates weakness of Sun in 12th house.

13-Apr-1994. *dsa MC trine Mercury.*
25-Apr-1994. *csa Mercury trine MC.*
First exhibition game of Texas Rangers in Arlington Stadium, 1-Apr.

2-Mar-1998. *dsa ASC sextile Saturn.*
17-Mar-1998. *csa Saturn sextile ASC.*
Controversial Texas execution of Karla Faye Tucker who had born-again religious conversion while in prison, 3-Feb-1998.

15-Sep-2006. *dsa Mars square ASC.*
6-Oct-2006. *csa Mars square ASC.*
Vetoed stem cell research, 19-Jul.
Abortion and related issues, such as stem cell research, are signified by Mars/Virgo because Mars cuts and Virgo is the intestinal tract.
Approved border fence, 26-Oct.
Mars/Virgo signifies conflict over immigration with Virgo the best sign match to many Latin American countries, dating back to revolutions in the 1820s which followed the 17-Jun-1802 Jupiter Saturn conjunction in Virgo.

Primary Directions

| PT | D | Saturn/Aries | P | dex square Saturn (SA) d. => MC | 15-Sep-1948 |

Death of paternal grandfather, Samuel Prescott Bush, 8-Sep.

43. GEORGE W. BUSH

| PT | D | Saturn/Cancer | P | Saturn (SA) c. => ASC | 9-Jan-1960 |

Prescott Bush denounced Air Force for suggesting Communists had infiltrated the National Council of Churches, Feb-1960.

| REG | D | Mercury/Leo | P | dex sextile Jupiter (0) d. => Sun | 8-Nov-1988 |

Father GHWB elected President, 8-Nov.

| PT | D | Mercury/Taurus | P | sin sextile Sun d. => MC | 9-Aug-1993 |

GWB announced Texas gubernatorial bid, 8-Nov.

| REG | D | Mars/Aries | P | MC c. => North Node | 20-Dec-1993 |

Queen Elizabeth II bestowed knighthood on father GHWB, 22-Dec.

| PT | D | Mars/Gemini | P | North Node d. => MC | 16-Nov-2002 |

Appeared on TIME magazine cover after midterm victory, 18-Nov.

Primary Direction Sequences

| PT | D | Jupiter/Taurus | P | dex square Venus (VE) d. => MC | 12-Oct-1972 |
| PT | D | Jupiter/Taurus | P | dex square Venus (0) d. => MC | 4-Apr-1973 |

LOCK The death of Bush's grandfather Prescott Bush, 8-Oct-1972, marked the beginning of this direction. Venus rules the 4th of ancestors. Of greater interest is the coincidence of this direction with Bush's missing year of National Guard service which has been hotly disputed. According to some reports, Bush was not observed on duty between May-1972 and Apr-1973. In addition, the middle period of this sequence was punctuated by GWB's drinking & driving over Christmas holidays spent with family in Washington DC. As a result of a holiday incident, GHWB arranged for GWB to perform community service work for the Houston inner-city youth program PULL during Jan/Aug-1973. Bush's life of the party instinct – including his alcoholism – stems from Venus/Leo conjunct the Ascendant.

| PT | D | Jupiter/Gemini | P | dex square Mars (MA) d. => MC | 27-Aug-1991 |
| PT | D | Jupiter/Gemini | P | dex square Mars (0) d. => MC | 24-Oct-1991 |

LOCK On 21-Aug, GWB was cleared by the SEC of insider trading charges regarding sales of Harken common stock. Mars in 2nd shows financial losses; ruling the 10th shows losses attract attention from regulators. Despite his clean slate by the SEC, this incident remained fodder for Bush opponents in future campaigns. As this sequence ended, groundbreaking for the new Texas Rangers stadium occurred on 30-Oct. Mars rules the 4th house of real estate (WS); in the earth sign of Virgo Mars signifies digging dirt.

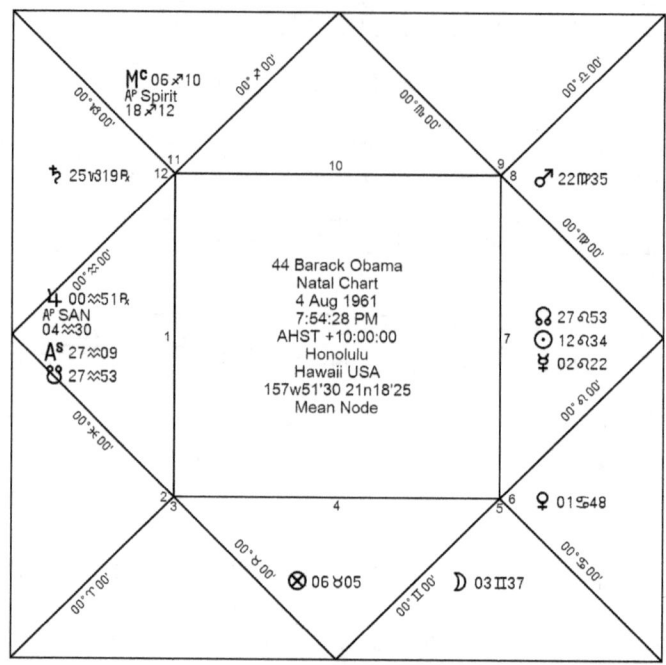
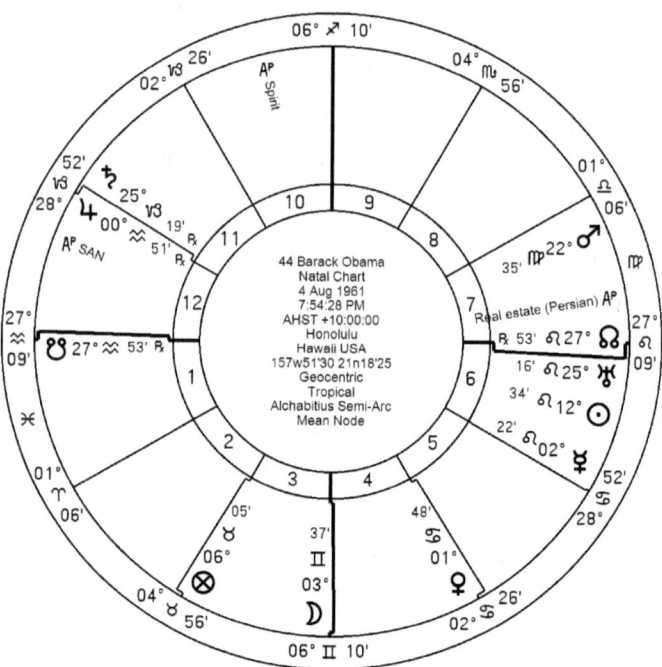

44. Barack Obama

Case Study: Testing a rectification with no available time.

The question of whether rectification works can be tested by comparing a proposed rectified time to an actual birth certificate time. This requires the official birth certificate time is not available to researchers prior to rectification. These tests are difficult to perform because of the unlikelihood of both conditions occurring in the proper sequence to satisfy disinterested parties and skeptics.

Between publication of the 2nd and 3rd editions of *A Rectification Manual*, on 20-Nov-2007 I published a proposed rectification of Barack Obama's birth time of 7:54:28 PM, ASC = 27AQ09'17". Subsequently, the Obama presidential campaign published his birth certificate on 13-Jun-2008 with a birth time of 7:24 PM. This was 30 minutes earlier than my rectification but agreed with my choice of Aquarius rising.

As Chris Brennan documented in a blogpost dated 6-Aug-2008, I was the only western astrologer to correctly identify Aquarius rising for Obama. Brennan did mention several Indian astrologers who indicated Obama must have a nocturnal horoscope which varied considerably from a 1:06 PM birth time, Scorpio rising, obtained by the astrologer Frances McEvoy and commonly used by the astrological community prior to publication of Obama's birth certificate. (Brennan, 2008).

In the interest of maintaining this historical record, the following 4th edition rectification details for Obama varies slightly from other listings in the Presidential database. The presentation begins with the original writeup made in 2007. The only changes are format adjustments in how directions are presented so they are comparable to other directions in this book.

While revelation of an official birth time date supplied on a birth certificate usually always settles the debate on what birth time astrologers should use – especially in Obama's case since the time is not rounded to the nearest 5, 15, 30, or 60 minute mark – my approach still demands that birth time data be subjected to testing against actual life events no matter what the source.

For the 2022 4th edition, I read David Garrow's 1000+ page biography: *Rising Star: The Making of Barack Obama*. Compared to my initial event database of 28 events (see next page), my current Obama database has nearly 1000 events. In making a slight tweak in my rectification by 3 minutes, I relied on the principal that for horoscopes with prominent Leo signatures solar arc directions are more reliable for rectification than primary directions. The solar arc direction of Sun to the DSC for the death of Obama's grandfather proved the *AHA!* moment. In fact, I submit that solar arc directions of the Sun to the angles alone are sufficient to lock down Obama's proposed rectification.

The Original Proposed Rectification published 20-Nov-2007

Event Database

30-Sep-65	Indonesia Coup against Sukarno harms father's profession.
11-Mar-66	Indonesia Coup: Suharto takes power.
1982	Death of father, auto accident.
25-Nov-87	Death of Chicago Mayor Howard Washington.
6-Feb-90	**Elected President Harvard Law Review.**
8-Feb-92	Death of maternal grandfather.
19-Oct-92	**Marriage.**
18-Jul-95	Book: Dreams for my Father published, hardback.
7-Nov-95	**Death of mother.**
21-Mar-00	Loses primary race to unseat Bobby Rush.
16-Apr-03	Chicago Republican Senator Peter Fitzgerald announced would not seek 2nd term.
16-Mar-04	**Wins Democratic Primary for Senate.**
22-Jun-04	**Republican Opponent Jack Ryan's custody files unsealed, sex scandal with wife is revealed.**
25-Jun-04	Republican Opponent Jack Ryan drops out of race.
27-Jul-04	**Speech at Democratic National Convention brings Obama national attention.**
10-Aug-04	Book: Dreams for my Father published, paperback.
4-Nov-04	**Elected Senate.**
30-Apr-06	Save Darfur Rally.
17-Oct-06	Book: Audacity of Hope published, hardback.
1-Nov-06	Chicago Tribune reports possible Conflict of interest dealings on Real estate with Tony Rezko.
20-Nov-06	Called for reduction of US forces from Iraq.
6-Dec-06	Endorsed for President by the Chicago Tribune.
11-Dec-06	New Hampshire visit marked by rock star comment by Gov. Lynch.
5-Jan-07	Stated the Iraq troop surge planned by Bush was a mistake.
10-Feb-07	Announced Presidential Bid.
5-Mar-07	www.thestreet.com questioned conflict of interest in stock transactions.
2,8-Jun-07	Obama campaign gave charities dollar-for-dollar amounts matching contributions received from associates of Tony Rezko.
6-Nov-07	Book: Audacity of Hope published, paperback.

Stage I: Determine the Ascending Sign

This is a case with unknown birth time.

Moon's sign. Moon's range is from 23TA00 to 5GE46. Is the Moon Taurus or Gemini? Moon in Taurus desires money, land, and food. Moon in Gemini desires information. Obama past legal training and the absence of finance, real estate, or culinary arts in his professional background suggest Moon in Gemini is a better match. Significator of his wife, Moon in Gemini matches Michelle Obama's specialization in marketing and intellectual property law prior to her public service activities. Moon is in Gemini.

Moon's range = 00GE00 to 5GE46; 1:03:52 PM to 12:00 midnight

Firdaria. With sunset not until 7:05 p.m. the day of Obama's birth, choice of diurnal or nocturnal Firdaria sequence can reduce the possible birth time range by a factor of two. Two factors favor the nocturnal sequence and a birth time after 7:05 p.m. If nocturnal,

Major Saturn Firdaria = 4-Aug-1970 to 3-Aug-1981; age 11 to 20. This is a reasonable match for Obama living with his maternal grandparents from the 5th to 12th grade. Saturn is the universal significator for the grandfather. If the figure were diurnal, Saturn's major period would range from 4-Aug-2001 to 3-Aug-2012; arguably Obama's most successful career period. This doesn't make much sense considering Saturn's delineation (below).

South Node period = 4-Aug-2003 to 3-Aug-2005; age 42-44. During this time Obama made his show stopping speech at the Democratic National Convention on 27-Jul-2004. Does this fit the South Node Firdaria period for the nocturnal series or the Saturn-Mars period for the diurnal series? For Firdaria selection, this is a make-or-break delineation. So what do Saturn, Mars, and the South Node signify in Obama's figure?

Saturn/Capricorn signifies the containment of social wealth and privilege through the construction of castles, walls, legal maneuvers, corporate and investment trusts. Consider on 13-Aug-1961, nine days after Obama was born, construction on the Berlin Wall. A wall indeed. At Obama's birth, Mars applied to the trine of Saturn. At the start of the Berlin Wall's construction, Mars separated from Saturn and applied to Jupiter which by this time had retrograded back to Capricorn with Saturn. Saturn receives Mars by exaltation and triplicity. At the very least, Mars/Virgo signifies the digging of earth used to construct the Berlin Wall. The more important delineation is the Saturn-ruled South Node/Aquarius. If Aquarius signifies the humanitarian principle of equality among people, then South Node in Aquarius is the negation of this principle. If Saturn rules the South Node/Aquarius, then for Obama, Saturn/Capricorn is the cause of this disruption. How so? Consider these excerpts from his 27-Jul-2004 DNC speech:

And fellow Americans – Democrats, Republicans, Independents – I say to you tonight: we have more work to do. More to do for the workers I met in Galesburg, Illinois, who are losing their union jobs at the Maytag plant that's moving to Mexico.....

John Kerry believes in America where hard work is rewarded. So instead of offering tax breaks to companies shipping jobs overseas, he'll offer them to companies creating jobs here at home (Barack Obama, Keynote Address at the 2004 Democratic National Convention, 27-Jul-2004).

Saturn/Capricorn signifies corporations who export jobs overseas in order to shield their future income streams from increased wage claims made by American employees (health care and other expenses). Exporting jobs overseas helps corporations contain their accumulated wealth and social status.

I suggest Obama's DNC speech is a better match to the nocturnal Firdaria's South Node period. Remember too that any Mars-Saturn periods are considered difficult. While at this point in the rectification we have to stick with universal significations of planets because house positions and rulerships are unknown, the configuration of Mars applying to the trine of Saturn raises questions. Considering the translation of Mars from Saturn to Jupiter was capable of triggering the Berlin Wall only 11 days after Obama's birth, Mars applying to Saturn for Obama has to be pretty nasty. Obama's meteoric rise to the national political stage is inconsistent with a possible match to the diurnal Firdaria's Mars-Saturn subperiod.

Conclusion: Nocturnal Firdaria Sequence. Birth time is 7:05 PM or later. Capricorn Ascendant ruled out. Ascendant is either Aquarius, Pisces, Aries, or early Taurus.

Physiognomy – Configuration of Chart. With a birth time of 7:05 p.m. or later, the Ascendant is either Aquarius, Pisces, Aries, or early Taurus. What clues does physiognomy suggest about the rising sign? Obama's facial profile matches the egg, or oval shape, of Libra (Hill 1993, 84). Yet Libra is not an Ascendant choice. However, Libra *does* rule the third decanate of Aquarius. Consider 25 Aquarius rising as a trial Ascendant, the midpoint of the 3rd decanate. This places 4SA30 on the MC, or an 11th house Midheaven.

Next step is to review the basic configuration of the chart against Obama's life patterns,

Moon/Gemini within 1 degree of the 4th cusp of father and family. Obama's Father attended the University of Hawaii at Manoa (where Obama's parents met) and later Harvard University. A strong hunger for knowledge was clearly evident. As a youth, Obama's unsettled home/family live was a direct result of his father's educational studies. Direction of Moon to the 4th cusp is logical to consider for his parent's separation at age 2 or their later divorce.

Jupiter/Aquarius in the Ascendant (WS) rules the MC and 11th of politics (WS). Obama builds political alliances from his humanitarian philosophy based on hope.

Saturn/Capricorn, Ascendant ruler, falls in the 12th. Delineated as corporate and investment trusts, these entities can be considered Obama's secret enemies.

Note for Sagittarius to fall on the MC, the Ascendant must be 19AQ24 or later. This confirms the 3rd decanate of Aquarius as the Ascendant.

Stage II: Narrow the Ascendant to within 1-4 degrees

Beginning Stage II with a trial Ascendant of 25 Aquarius, rectification can proceed to testing dynamic measurements to the angles.

Consider the following events:

Date	Event	Data type	Measurement
30-Sep-1965	Indonesia: coup against Sukarno	d. transit	South Node 7SA30
		c. transit	Saturn 10SA28
11-Mar-1966	Indonesia: Suharto takes power	c. transit	North Node 26SC51
		d. transit	South Node 28SC55
		c. transit	Saturn 9SA00
6-Feb-1990	Appointed President of Harvard Law Review	c. transit	North Node 9PI18
		d. solar arc	Jupiter 28AQ18
		d. solar arc	Mercury 29LE48
7-Nov-1995	Death of Mother	d. transit	Venus 5SA59
		c. transit	Saturn 6SA02
1-Nov-2006	Chicago Tribune reports possible Conflict of interest dealings on Real estate with Tony Rezko	d. transit	Mars 6SC28
		d. transit	Saturn 24LE01

The 1965-1966 coup which established Suharto as Indonesia's military strongman destroyed the political standing of Obama's father in the new regime. Transit of South Node to the MC area on 30-Sep-1965 is a match because in mundane astrology South Node-MC contacts signifies a King falling from power. Suharto's actual ascension on 11-Mar-1966 was marked by transits of the Nodes which would are square to the Ascendant. Obama's 1990 appointment as President of the Harvard Law Review was marked by the Jupiter-Mercury opposition moving to the ASC-DSC axis. Death of his mother was marked by the transit of Venus to the MC; see that Venus falls on the 5th cusp (by Alchabitius houses) which signifies death of the mother. By converse transit, Saturn moves to the MC. Saturn rules the 8th position from the Moon.

Finally there is the transit of Mars and Saturn, conjunct by antiscia, on 1-Nov-2006 when the Chicago Tribune broke the story of shady real estate dealings with Tony Rezko. Compared to a 4TA00 Lot of Fortune based on an Ascendant of 25AQ00, the Mars & Saturn transits suggest a Lot of Fortune between 5TA59 and 6TA28. Taking the midpoint, or 6TA15, moves the Ascendant to 27AQ19 and the MC to 6SA18. This change moves the angles close to most measurements above and will be the stopping place for Stage II.

Trial Ascendant: 27AQ19'30"

Stage III: Narrow the Ascendant to the exact Degree and Minute

Further study of conflict-of-interest charges relating to Obama's investments transactions was a breakthrough which allowed the identification of the first primary direction sequence required to lock down the rectification.

Proposed Stage III rectified Ascendant: 27AQ09'17"

5-Mar-2007. *csa Lot of Fortune opposed Mars*.

| REG | D | Mars/Gemini | P | dex square Mars (MA) d. => LOF | 10-Mar-2007 |
| REG | D | Mars/Gemini | P | dex square Mars (MA) d. => LOF | 2-Jun-2007 |

On 5-Mar-2007, thestreet.com broke a story that questioned the ethics of Obama's purchase of two small cap stocks whose activities benefited from Obama's legislative actions. Obama was forced to make a press conference on 7-March regarding his activities. This event opened up a sequence of events which forced the Obama campaign to scrutinize its campaign donations. As the sequence ended, on 2-June and 8-Jun-2007, the campaign gave charities dollar-for-dollar amounts matching campaign contributions received from associates of Tony Rezko. Recall that Rezko had damaged Obama's reputation from prior real estate transactions reported on 1-Nov-2006; timed by the Mars & Saturn transits to the POF identified in Stage II.

What is also important to this set of directions is the initial story broke by thestreet.com was timed by a solar arc direction; matching findings that solar arc events have a greater publicity component to them than similar primary directions.

| REG | D | Mercury/Libra | P | dex sextile MC d. => Sun | 7-Aug-2004 |
| REG | D | Saturn/Gemini | P | sin trine ASC c. => Sun | 9-Dec-2006 |

Both directions timed periods of fame for Barack Obama. The first direction followed his wildly successful 27-Jul-2004 speech at the Democratic National Convention and fell immediately before the 10-Aug-2004 reprint of his 1995 memoir *Dreams from my Father*.

The second direction timed the 6-Dec-2006 endorsement by the Chicago Tribune and his 11-Dec-2006 visit to New Hampshire where Governor John Lynch uttered his memorable line: "We originally scheduled the Rolling Stones. But then we canceled them when we realized Sen. Obama would sell more tickets." These remarks match the dynamism of the Leo Sun.

| PT | D | Saturn/Aries | P | sin square Saturn (0) d. => ASC | 24-Nov-2006 |
| PT | D | Saturn/Aries | P | sin square Saturn (0) d. => ASC | 11-Jan-2007 |

Besides a 'wait and see' period preceding Obama's official announcement of his Presidential bid on 10-Feb-2007, this period marked controversy over Bush administration proposals for an Iraq troop surge. On 20-Nov-06 as the sequence started, Obama called for a reduction of US forces from Iraq starting four to six months later. As the sequence culminated, Obama stated his opinion that the troop surge was a bad idea on 5-Jan-2007. Bush's troop surge plan was announced on 11-Jan-2007. How does Saturn/Capricorn/12th match these events? Saturn rules the 9th whole sign house of foreign affairs. Mars rules the 9th quadrant sign of foreign affairs. Mars applies to Saturn by trine who receives Mars by exaltation and triplicity. Saturn falls in the 12th of mistakes. Writing as of November 2007, so far the troop surge has curtailed violence in Iraq, suggesting that Obama's statements timed by this sequence were incorrect.

End of Text for Original Proposed Rectification published 20-Nov-2007

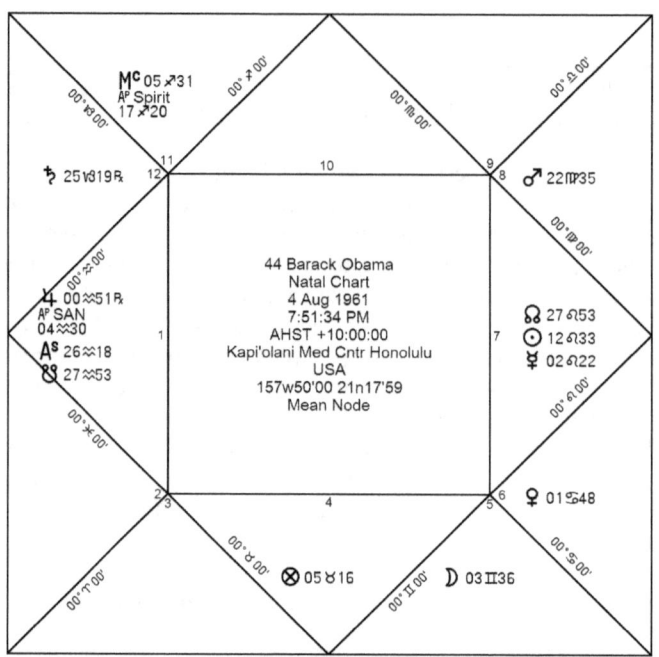
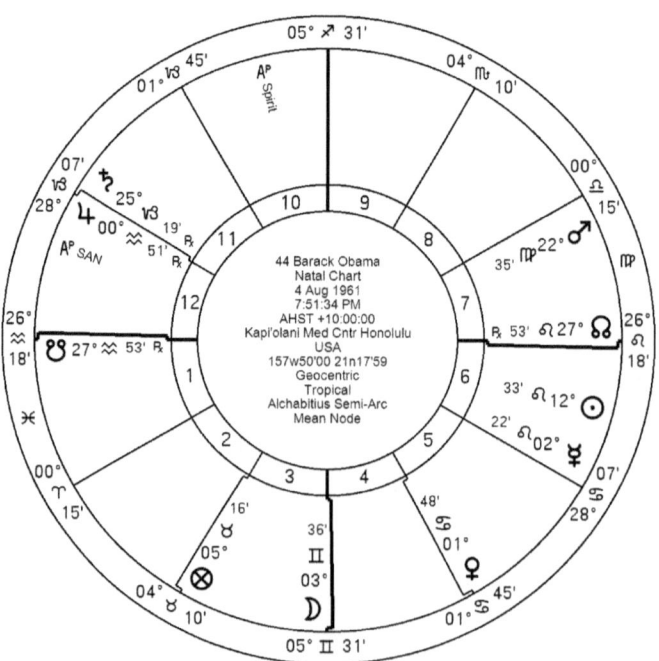

44. Barack Obama

Moon's Configuration

Moon separates from **Mercury** and applies to the **Sun**, nocturnal, preventional.
Prenatal syzygy is 4AQ30. Eclipse? No.

Cognitive Assessment Model (Rulers of Moon and Mercury)

Sign rulers: **Mercury, Sun (Saturn)**
Bound rulers: **Mercury, Jupiter**

Victor Soul Models

Ibn Ezra Victor Model (1507), in-sect triplicity ruler, triplicity decans.

	Position	☉	☽	☿	♀	♂	♃	♄
Sun	12 LE 33	5					4	2
Moon	03 GE 36			11				
Asc	26 AQ 18			3	1			7
Pars Fortuna	05 TA 16		7		8			
Syzygy	04 AQ 30			5				6
Oriental						0	0	0
Houses		1	9	1	7	10	2	2
Score		0	6	16	20	16| 10	6	17

Porphyry's Expanded Victor Model (2022)

Jupiter rules the MC and Lot of Spirit by sign; the MC by bound. Sect: out-of-favor. Solar phase: occidental opposition to 2nd station. Position: Angular in ASC, 10th from Lot of Fortune. Dignity: participating triplicity. Conjunct South Node.

Victor Table for Killing Planets

Not published for the living.

2007 Proposed Rectification: 7:54:28 PM, ASC 27AQ09'17"
2021 Proposed Rectification: 7:51:34 PM, ASC 26AQ18'16"

ZRS. The largest difference between the 7:24 PM birth certificate time and the proposed rectification is the Lot of Fortune moves from late Aries (birth certificate) to early Taurus (proposed rectification). From a ZR perspective there is an easy way to examine whether this choice is correct. First, the Lot of Spirit is placed in Sagittarius for both alternatives so there is no confusion that ZRS begins in Sagittarius. The difference occurs because ZR theory states signs which are angular from the LOF are more active and therefore generate events which are more likely to be career milestones than events which occur in other signs. For the proposed rectification, the angular houses are the fixed signs of Taurus (LOF1), Leo (LOF4), Scorpio (LOF7), and Aquarius (LOF10). When the LOS profects to these signs, career milestones should be obvious.

In fact, Obama's national political career is contained entirely during L1 Aquarius which is a delineation match that LOF10 milestones should be career peaks. Moreover within L1 Aquarius the angular L2 subperiods timed these milestones: US Senate election, start of 1st Presidential term (missing inauguration by only 4 days), ACA passage, start of 2nd Presidential term, and final midterm victory with Democrats retaking the House. This evidence favors LOF in Taurus which precludes a birth time any earlier than 7:33 PM.

L1 Sagittarius 04 Aug 1961		
L1 Capricorn 02 Jun 1973		Summer-1973, family tour of the American West.
L2 Cancer 14 Aug 1982	FS	24-Nov-1982, death of father from auto accident/drunk driving; 17-May-1983, graduated Columbia.
L2 Cancer 01 Oct 1990	LB	28-Nov-1990, signed publishing contract with Poseidon; Apr/Oct-1992, Illinois State Director of Project VOTE!; 3-Oct-1992, married Michelle Robinson.
L2 Capricorn 18 Nov 1998	CP	3-Nov-1998, won re-election to Illinois State Senate; May-1999, became disillusioned about political process in State Senate; 28-Jul-1999, mailed "Statement of Candidacy" to FERC.
L1 Aquarius 12 Jan 2000		21-Mar-2000, lost primary race to unseat Bobby Rush.
L2 Taurus 17 Sep 2004		2-Nov-2004, elected to US Senate.
L2 Leo 24 Jan 2009	FS	(four days after) 20-Jan-2009, inauguration; 23-Mar-2010, Affordable Care Act became law.
L2 Scorpio 04 Dec 2012		2-Jan-2013, American Taxpayer Relief Act extended tax breaks; 21-Jan-2013, 2nd Inauguration.
L2 Leo 12 May 2017	LB	6-Nov-2018, Democrats took back the House on strategy based on anger over Republicans trying to end Obamacare.
L2 Scorpio 22 Mar 2021		9-Aug-2021, extravagance of 60th birthday party on Martha's Vineyard in year following pandemic sparked controversy.
L2 Aquarius 28 Aug 2025	CP	
L1 Pisces 07 Aug 2029		

Firdaria – Jupiter major and minor periods

Firdaria according to Bonatti	Life Event
Moon **Jupiter** 01 Mar 1964	20-Mar-1964, mother's divorce decree granted, granted custody of BO; 15-Mar-1965, mother remarried Lolo Soetoro.
Saturn **Jupiter** 29 Feb 1972	Summer 1973, family tour of American West; Ann, Madelyn, Barry, and Maya.
Jupiter 12 years Age 20 to 32	
Jupiter Jupiter 04 Aug 1981	Aug-1981, started college at Columbia after transfer from Occidental; 24-Nov-1982, death of father.
Jupiter Mars 22 Apr 1983	1983/1984, worked as financial researcher/writer for Business Intl Corporation.
Jupiter Sun 07 Jan 1985	Jan/May-1985, worked for NY Public Interest Group; ear-Jul-1985, hired for Developing Communities Project (community organizer, Chicago); introduced to Sheila Jager; 18-Jul-1986, LTV filed for bankruptcy.
Jupiter Venus 26 Sep 1986	2-Mar-1987, stepfather Lolo died; 25-Nov-1987, death of Chicago Mayor Howard Washington; soon after decided to go to law school.
Jupiter Mercury 13 Jun 1988	6-Sep-1988, Harvard Law School, first day; 30-Jun-1989, first date with Michelle; mid-summer-1989, accepted to Law Review; 6-Feb-1990, elected President Law Review.
Jupiter Moon 01 Mar 1990	9-Mar-1990, Black Law School Association Conference; 28-Nov-1990, signed publishing contract with Poseidon; 31-Jul-1991, finished taking Illinois bar exam and proposed marriage to Michelle.
Jupiter Saturn 17 Nov 1991	Apr/Oct-1992, Project VOTE!'s Illinois state director; 3-Oct-1992, married; 20-Oct-1992, Simon & Schuster cancelled book contract; Mar-1993, returned to Chicago: (1) full-time work at law firm (2) worked on his book (3) taught at U Chicago Law School starting end of March.
Mars **Jupiter** 05 Aug 1999	21-Mar-2000, lost primary race to unseat Bobby Rush.
Sun **Jupiter** 25 Sep 2012	6-Nov-2012, re-elected President.
Venus **Jupiter** 29 Feb 2020	19-Aug-2020, made virtual address for Democratic National Convention; 3-Nov-2020, former VP Biden elected President; 17-Nov-2020, published memoir: *A Promised Land*.

Jupiter as Victor. For Obama, Jupiter/Aquarius-rx is a good example of the behavior of retrograde planets, a doctrine which I have developed since publication of the 3rd edition of ARM. My finding that retrograde planets function like they are placed in the opposite sign applies here. Jupiter/Aquarius when in direct motion is a delineation match to Obama's early career as a community organizer. But quickly, Obama learned the limits of community organizing as a method for making changes to improve outcomes. This is why he turned to politics which is a delineation match to Jupiter/Aquarius-rx functioning like Jupiter/Leo in the opposite sign. Among the most dramatic transits in support of this delineation is trJupiter 17VI50 occupying the 10th sign and degree from the LOS 17SA20 on 27-Jul-2004 when Obama spoke at the 2004 Democratic National Convention. This event brought him instant political capital which he used to build his 2008 Presidential campaign.

Transits

15-Apr-1980. *tr South Node conj ASC.*
Wisconsin Steel suddenly shut down Chicago operations, 28-Mar.
First in a long wave of shutdowns which increased unemployment in Chicago neighborhoods. BO later worked as community organizer in these same neighborhoods. Garrow opens his biography with this saga.

5-Aug-1989. *tr North Node conj ASC.*
At Michelle Robinson's request, played basketball with her brother Craig as part of Michelle's due diligence on BO as possible spouse, ear-Aug.

2-Aug-1995. *tr Jupiter direct station conj MC.*
Published: *Dreams from my Father*, hardback edition, 18-Jul.
Received first campaign contributions for Il State Senate bid, 31-Jul.

7-Nov-1995. *tr Venus conj MC.*
Death of mother Ann Dunham, 7-Nov.
Note: Venus is positioned on the 5th cusp which is death of the mother.

11-Jun-2002. *tr South Node 17SA46 conj LOS 17SA20.*
In the Illinois Senate, BO threatened Rickey Hendon with physical violence after a dispute over veto overrides of measures in their districts. Biographer Garrow states "Then, for the first and only time in his entire life, Barack Obama completely fucking lost it" 11-Jun (Garrow 767).

29-Jan-2003, *tr South Node conj MC.*
Chicago Defense stated "Obama has no relationship with the Black community and is a product of the white lakefront community. He is a white liberal in blackface," 22-Jan (Garrow 793).

27-Jul-2004. *tr Jupiter 17VI50 10th from LOS 17SA20.*
DNC speech brought Obama national attention, 27-Jul.

22-Aug-2004. *tr North Node conj LOF.*
Published: *Dreams from my Father*, paperback edition, 10-Aug.

16-Mar-2008. *tr North Node conj ASC.*
Jeremiah Wright sermons appeared on the internet including "God Damn America!" 13-Mar; Obama made damage control speech, 18-Mar.

20-May-2012. *tr North Node conj MC.*
Obama announced support for gay marriage, 9-May.
Note: natal North Node is placed in the 7th house of marriage.

Solar Arc Directions

25-Nov-1975. *dsa Sun opposed ASC.*
LOCK Death of paternal grandfather Hussein Onyango Obama, 25-Nov. Note: for the 4th edition, this was the most important direction which caused me to make a slight tweak in the rectification.

24-Nov-1982. *dsa North Node 18VI22 10th from LOS 18SA12.*
Death of father Barack Obama Sr, auto accident, drunk driving.

16-Jun-1985. *dsa Sun square MC.*
15-Aug-1985. *csa MC square Sun.*
Applied for Chicago community jobs position, mid-June.
Offered Chicago position, ear-July.
Arrived Chicago, 27-Jul.

22-Jun-1986. *dsa Mercury opposed ASC.*
Introduced to Sheila Miyoshi Jager, June.

2-Mar-1987. *dsa Jupiter 21AQ20 conj L.Death of Father 21AQ37.*
Death of stepfather Lolo Soetoro from liver failure, 2-Mar.

8-Feb-1992. *dsa Mercury 1VI45 conj L.Grandfathers 1VI50.*
Death of maternal grandfather Stanley Dunham, 8-Feb.

6-Jun-2009. *dsa ASC trine Sun.*
23-Jan-2010. *csa Sun trine ASC.*
LOCK Cairo University speech called for 'new beginning' of Mideast-US political relations, 4-Jun-2009.
LOCK Announced Volcker Rule, financial regulation, in response to the financial crisis of 2007-2009, 21-Jan-2010.

9-May-2017. *dsa South Node 21AR55 conj L.Marriage 22AR30.*
Published: *Rising Star: The Making of Barack Obama* by David Garrow.
Biography reveals that Obama had proposed marriage to, and was turned down twice for, by Sheila Miyoshi Jager. This fact was omitted in Obama's previous memoirs. Obama did write of a female love interest, but this was a composite of several different women including Jager.

Notable Ascendant and Midheaven Distributor Changeover

D	Changeover	Bound Mercury/Capricorn => ASC	28-Dec-1987
D	Changeover	Bound Saturn/Libra => ASC	28-Dec-1987

Following death of Chicago Mayor Howard Washington, 25-Nov, Obama decided to leave Chicago for Law School. Note: These ASC/MH changeovers to cardinal signs will happen the same date for all nativities.

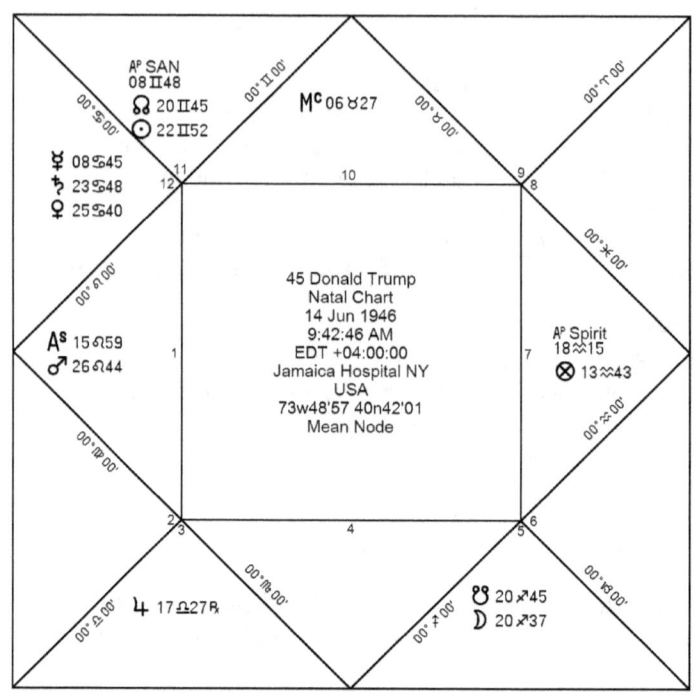
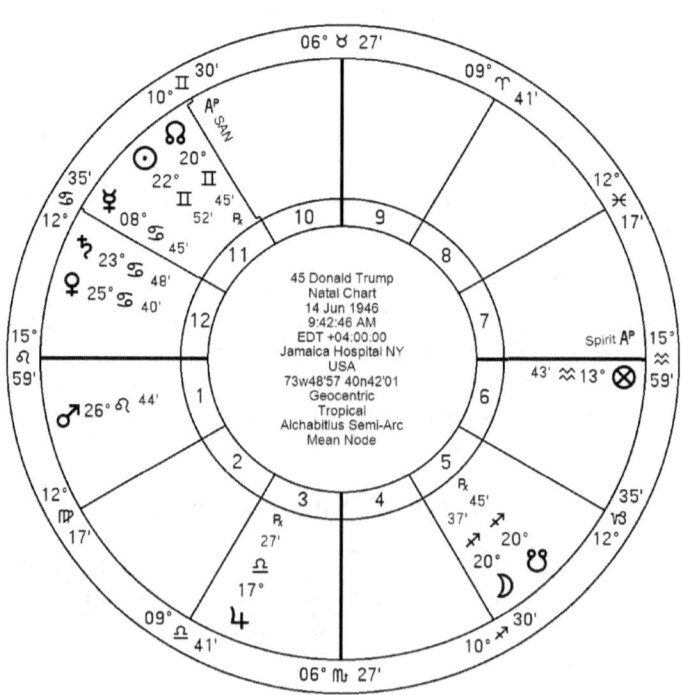

Moon's Configuration

Moon separates from **Jupiter** and applies to the **Sun**, diurnal, conjunctional. During the Moon's translation of light, Jupiter makes its direct station. Prenatal syzygy is 8GE48. Eclipse? **YES**. Partial Solar Eclipse.

Cognitive Assessment Model (Rulers of Moon and Mercury)

Sign rulers: **Jupiter, (Moon)/Mercury**
Bound rulers: **Mercury, Venus**

Victor Soul Models

Ibn Ezra Victor Model (1507), in-sect triplicity ruler, triplicity decans.

	Position	☉	☽	☿	♀	♂	♃	♄
Sun	22 GE 52			5		2		4
Moon	20 SA 37	4		2			5	
Asc	15 LE 59	8					1	2
Pars Fortuna	13 AQ 43				1		2	8
Syzygy	08 GE 48 (SE)				6		2	3
Oriental						0	0	0
Houses		8	7	2	2	12	3	2
Score	0	20	7	16	2	14	13	19

Porphyry's Expanded Victor Model (2022)

Jupiter rules the Moon by sign; the Lot of Fortune, Lot of Spirit, and syzygy by bound. Sect: in-favor. Solar phase: occidental 2nd direct station. Dignity: participating triplicity and bound; mutual reception with Saturn by exaltation. Moon's separation.

Victor Table for Killing Planets

Not published for the living.

2017 Proposed rectification: 9:42:46 AM EDT, ASC 15LE59'24"

Astrodatabank reports an AA-rated birth time of 10:54 AM, ASC 29LE58, taken from an official birth certificate available online. Prior to the 10:54 AM time, ADB reported an A-rated 9:51 AM birth time, from mother's memory. The proposed rectification is closer to the initial A-rated ADB time.

ZRS. For the proposed rectification, both Lots of Fortune and Spirit are cast in Aquarius making Pisces the first sign to release a/c Valens. This avoids the necessity to flip the lots, e.g., to release from LOF in Pisces for the later 10:54 AM birth time which features LOS in Aquarius and LOF in Pisces (procedure advocated by astrologer Patrick Watson).

Note the helicopter crash and the failure of Taj Mahal during L2-Sagittarius (26-Sep-1989). South Node/Sagittarius signifies an airplane crash as well as smashing unrealistic expectations.

L1 Pisces 14 Jun 1946		
L1 Aries 12 Apr 1958		L1-Aries included attendance at NY Military Academy (1959-64), attendance at Wharton Business School, and employment under his father Fred Trump.
L1 Taurus 23 Jan 1973		L1-Taurus period timed DT's first successful real estate development project - the Grand Hyatt hotel. A parallel West Side Rail Yard development project was started and abandoned at roughly the same time period.
L1 Gemini 12 Dec 1980		L1-Gemini period timed Trump's most active period as a real estate developer with casinos a particular focus.
L2 Sagittarius 26 Sep 1989	FS	10-Oct-1989, Helicopter crash killed top management of Taj Mahal casino; 11-Feb-1990, announced separation from Ivana Trump as Marla Maples affair was made public; 3-Apr-1990, Taj Mahal opens and immediately loses money; Summer-1990, casino debt restructuring after inability to pay interest on debt.
L2 Sagittarius 12 Apr 1998	LB	29-Apr-1988. FAI cancelled St. Moritz redevelopment plan; Sep-1988, met Melania Knauss; 15-Oct-1998, demolition began for site prep for Trump World Tower.
L1 Cancer 29 Aug 2000		L1-Cancer period saw DT move away from real estate and casino development towards branding. This included beefing up the value of his own celebrity brand through *The Apprentice* television series.
L2 Capricorn 16 Oct 2008	FS	4-Nov-2008, Barack Obama elected President; 17-Feb-2009, Trump Entertainment Resorts filed for bankruptcy; 1-Mar-2009, Celebrity Apprentice Debut Season 8.
L2 Gemini 07 May 2016		8-Nov-2016. won USA Presidential election.
L2 Capricorn 28 Dec 2017	LB	22-Dec-2017, tax cuts passed (6 days early); 23-Jan-2018, trade War begun with China; 8-May-2018, withdrawal from Iran nuclear deal; 11-Mar-2020, WHO declared coronavirus a global pandemic.
L2 Aquarius 17 Mar 2020		3-Nov-2020, Lost Presidential re-election bid.
L1 Leo 20 Apr 2025		

Firdaria – Jupiter major and minor periods

Firdaria according to Bonatti	Life Event
Sun **Jupiter** 05 Aug 1953	13-Jul-1954, father's firm suspected of wartime profiteering.
Venus **Jupiter** 08 Jan 1961	No specific events found. Attended Military Academy.
Mercury **Jupiter** 08 Jan 1970	1971, moved to Manhattan, part of plan to escape father's circle, joined Le Club in order to mix with rich and famous.
Moon **Jupiter** 09 Jan 1980	15-Mar-1980, began demolition of Bonwit building, future site of Trump Tower; 25-Sep-1980, Grand Hyatt official opening; Feb-1981, first meetings with NJ Attorney General on Casino permit; Early 1981, purchased 100 Central Park South (renamed Trump Parc East) and Barbizon Plaza Hotel (renamed Trump Park).
Saturn **Jupiter** 09 Jan 1988	Significant over-expansion wave which led to eventual bankruptcy; 26-Mar-1988, purchased Plaza Hotel for $390 mln including personal guarantee of $125 mln; 27-Jun-1988, arranged Tyson-Spinks boxing match; 15/16-Aug-1988, attended RNC; 1-Nov-1988, raised $675 mln in junk bonds to purchase Taj Mahal casino; 15-Jan-1989, *Art of the Deal* paperback made NYT Best Seller list for first time; 15-Apr-1989, purchased Atlantic Casino Hotel; 23-Apr-1989, Construction started on Trump Palace; 5-May-1989, cycling race Tour de Trump; 23-Jun-1989, Trump Shuttle airline.
Jupiter 12 years Age 51 to 63	
Jupiter Jupiter 13 Jun 1997	15-Oct-1998, demolition began on site to prepare for construction of Trump World Tower.
Jupiter Mars 01 Mar 1999	25-Jun-1999, death of father; 8-Oct-1999, left Republican party for Reform party; 3-Nov-1999, name change to Trump Organization LLC; 15-Jan-2000, published campaign book *The America we Deserve*; 14-Feb-2000, ended exploratory run for President; 7-Aug-2000, death of mother.
Jupiter Sun 17 Nov 2000	2001 (no exact date), construction completed for Trump World Tower; 17-Feb-2002, announced cancellation of plans to build golf courses in Westchester but moved ahead with Briarcliff Manor and Bedford courses.
Jupiter Venus 05 Aug 2002	26-Jan-2003, NJ Casino Control Commission approved refinancing of $375 mln in casino debt; 8-Jan-2004, debut of *The Apprentice*.
Jupiter Mercury 22 Apr 2004	26-Apr-2004, proposed to Melania Knauss; 18-Aug-2004, official unveiling ceremony of Trump "The Game", 9-Sep-2004, *The Apprentice* Season 2; Oct-2004, Trump University incorporated; 21-Nov-2004, Trump Hotels & Casino Resorts filed for bankruptcy; 20-Jan-2005, *The Apprentice* Season 3; 22-Jan-2005, married Melania Knauss; 23-May-2005, Trump University launch; 22-Sep-2005, *The Apprentice* Season 4.
Jupiter Moon 08 Jan 2006	27-Feb-2006, *The Apprentice* Season 5; 20-Mar-2006, Birth of son Barron; 7-Jan-2007, *The Apprentice* Season 6; 1-Apr-2007, WrestleMania 23; 19-May-2007, Announced was moving on from *The Apprentice* to another TV venture; 6-Jul-2007, *The Apprentice* rebranded *Celebrity Apprentice*.
Jupiter Saturn 26 Sep 2007	17-Feb-2009, Trump Entertainment Resorts filed for bankruptcy (3rd bankruptcy); 7-Mar-2009, Trump Ocean Resort Baja collapsed after could not get financing, buyers lost $32 in deposits.
Mars **Jupiter** 14 Jun 2015	16-Jun-2015, announced Presidential bid; 9-Jul-2016, first poll showed DT as frontrunner.

2022 Proposed Rectification:

Transits

29-Aug-1976. *tr South Node conj MC.*
Father arrested for housing code violations, 30-Sep.

27-Oct-1980. *tr North Node conj ASC.*
Grand Hyatt opened, 25-Sep; NYT profile, 19-Oct.

19-Dec-1985. *tr* North Node conj MC.
Announced West Side Yard development with 150-story building (never completed), 18-Nov; Mar-A-Lago purchased, 27-Dec.

16-Feb-1990. *tr South Node conj ASC.*
Announced separation from Ivana Trump, 11-Feb; *NY Post* headline "Best Sex I Ever Had" with Marla Maples, described as "media circus," 16-Feb. Contrast to the 8-Jun-1999 transit for Maples' divorce.

11-Apr-1995. *tr South Node conj MC.*
NYT: Jay Pritzker and Trump settled Grand Hyatt lawsuit, 5-May.

8-Jun-1999. *tr North Node conj ASC.*
Divorce proceedings finalized with Marla Maples, 8-Jun.

31-Jul-2004. *tr North Node conj MC.*
Trump "The Game" re-released, Jul-2004 (no exact date).

My *AHA!* moment for the Trump rectification was finding Nodal transits to the ASC-DSC axis for relationship events with Marla Maples on 16-Feb-1990 and 8-Jun-1999. Both were opposite in nature consistent with how the Nodes function. As the 16-Feb-1990 event was described as a 'media circus,' I was drawn to this set of transits to justify the proposed rectification for the ability of transits of Lunar Nodes to the angles to time public events for which documentary evidence exists.

Solar Arc Directions

17-Mar-1976. *csa ASC sq Jupiter.*
15-May-1976. *dsa Jupiter sq ASC.*
Penn Central announced the Commodore hotel would close in 6 days, 12-May. NYC Board of Estimate voted to give Trump Organization full tax-abatement program for the Commodore hotel, 20-May. Trump later transformed the Commodore Hotel into the Grand Hyatt Hotel, his first major Manhattan real estate venture.

LOCK <u>10-Nov-1984</u>. *csa Sun sq ASC*.
LOCK <u>15-Feb-1985</u>. *dsa ASC sq Sun*.
Donated to Mario Cuomo political committee to curry favor for proposal to build a football stadium in Queens for the NJ Generals, 13-Nov-1984. Baron Hilton turned down for AC casino license, leaving an opening for DT, 14-Feb-1985.

LOCK <u>5-Feb-1989</u>. *csa Jupiter trine MC*.
LOCK <u>4-Jun-1989</u>. *dsa MC trine Jupiter*.
Trump: *The Game*, Unveiled, 7-Feb.
Purchased Atlantis Casino (renamed Trump Regency), 15-Apr.
Construction started on Trump Palace, 23-Apr.
Cycling race Tour de Trump started, 5/14-May.
Bankruptcy judge approved purchase of Northeastern air shuttle from Eastern airlines, 24-May.

LOCK <u>20-Sep-2003</u>. *csa ASC conj North Node*.
LOCK <u>14-Apr-2004</u>. *dsa North Node conj ASC*.
The Apprentice started shooting first season, Sep-2003.
The Apprentice debut, 8-Jan-2004.
The Apprentice ended first season, 15-Apr-2004.

LOCK <u>14-Oct-2004</u>. *csa LOF sextile Jupiter*.
LOCK <u>16-May-2005</u>. *dsa Jupiter sextile LOF*.
Trump University incorporated, Oct-2004.
Trump University launched, 23-May-2005,

LOCK <u>4-Oct-2015</u>. *csa North Node sextile LOF*.
LOCK <u>23-Jul-2016</u>. *dsa LOF sextile North Node*.
Published: *Crippled America: How to Make America Great Again*, 3-Nov-2015. RNC Presidential Nomination, 21-Jul-2016.

Primary Directions

PT	D	Jupiter/Cancer	P	Venus (0) c. => ASC	18-Mar-1972
PT	D	Jupiter/Cancer	P	Venus (VE) c. => ASC	12-Oct-1973

LOCK Trump apt complex agent refused to rent to Alfred Hoyt, African American, while his white wife was able to rent the following day, 18-Mar-1972. US Justice Department filed discrimination suit against Fred Trump for incident above incident, 15-Oct-1973.

| REG | D | Venus/Taurus | P | MC c. => North Node | 21-Feb-1987 |
| PT | D | Venus/Taurus | P | MC c. => North Node | 18-May-1988 |

John O'Donnell began employment as SVP of marketing at Trump Plaza Hotel, 4-Feb-1987.

Announced Ivana would no longer manage Castle Hotel and Casino, would move to NY and manage the Plaza Hotel, 19-May-1988.

| REG | D | Venus/Taurus | P | MC c. => Sun | 18-Feb-1989 |
| PT | D | Venus/Taurus | P | MC c. => Sun | 7-Jun-1990 |

Trump: The Game, unveiled, 7-Feb-1989

Purchased incomplete project from Penthouse to add property around Trump Plaza, 19-Mar-1989.

NYT: "A Haze of Debt Clouds the Plaza Hotel's Gleam," 5-Jun-1990.

| PT | D | Mercury/Aries | P | dex trine ASC c. => NNode | 17-Jan-2005 |

Married Melania Knauss, 22-Jan.

| REG | D | Merc/Libra | P | dex trine LOF d. => Mars (0) | 24-May-2005 |

Trump University launched, 23-May.

| PT | D | Jupiter/Aquarius | P | LOF d. => South Node | 28-May-2005 |

NY State Dept of Education gave notice of violation for using word "university" when it was not chartered as one. Trump University lacked a license to offer student instruction or training in NY state, 27-May.

| PT | D | Saturn/Leo | P | ASC d. => Sun | 29-Oct-2005 |

LOCK Published: *Trump Nation*, 29-Oct.

| REG | D | Jupiter/Aquarius | P | LOF d. => South Node | 1-Apr-2006 |
| PT | D | Venus/Taurus | P | MC d. => Mercury (0) | 17-Apr-2006 |

DT said on CNBC "I think it's a great time to start a mortgage company" on his new business venture named Trump Mortgage. Started at the peak of the housing bubble, April 2006.

| PT | D | Mercury/Sagittarius | P | SNode c. => LOF | 7-Feb-2009 |
| REG | D | Mercury/Sagittarius | P | SNode c. => LOF | 11-Apr-2009 |

Trump Entertainment Resorts filed for bankruptcy, 17-Feb.

Lawsuit against Irongate, developer of failed Trump Ocean Resort Baja, 14-Apr.

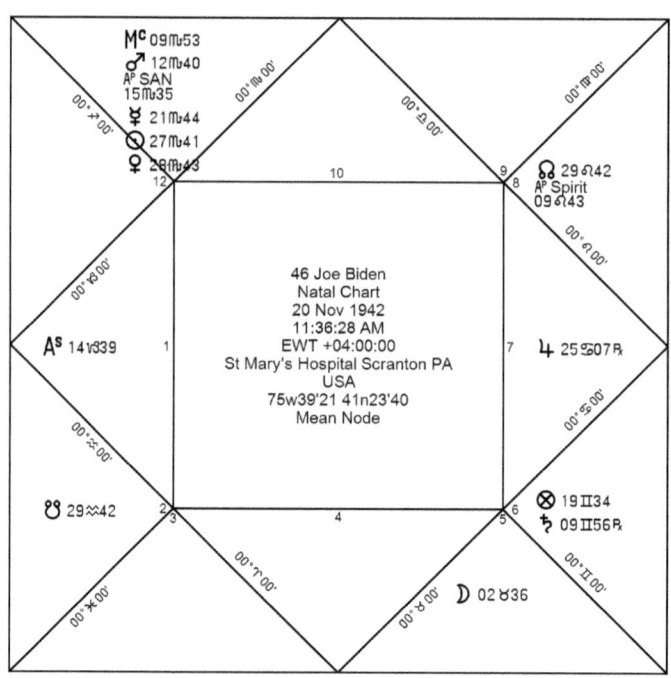
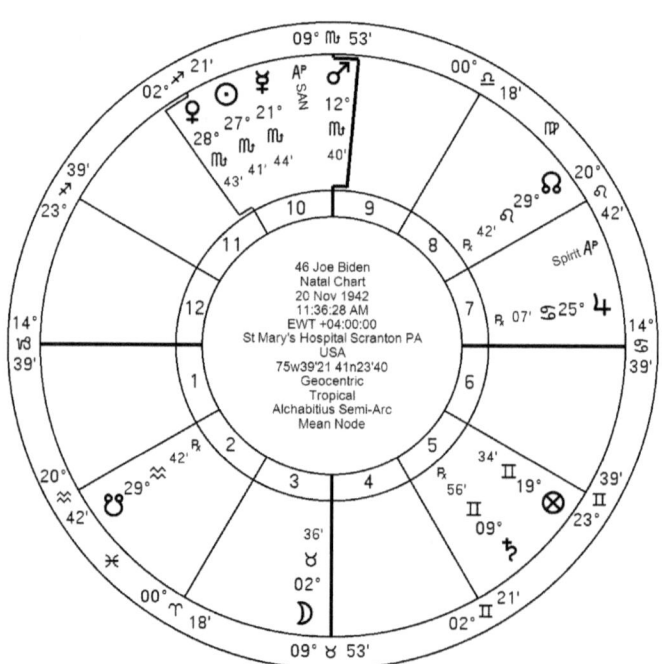

Moon's Configuration

Moon applies to **Mars**, diurnal, conjunctional.
Prenatal syzygy is 15SC35. Eclipse? No.

Cognitive Assessment Model (Rulers of Moon and Mercury)

Sign rulers: **Venus, Mars**
Bound rulers: **Venus, Jupiter**

Victor Soul Models

Ibn Ezra Victor Model (1507), in-sect triplicity ruler, triplicity decans.

	Position	☉	☽	☿	♀	♂	♃	♄
Sun	27 SC 41		1		3	5		2
Moon	02 TA 36		4		11			
Asc	14 CP 39				6	4		5
Pars Fortuna	19 GE 34			5	1	2		3
Syzygy	15 SC 35			2	3	5	1	
Oriental						3	1	1
Houses		8	3	11	8	11	10	7
Score		0	8	8	18	**32**	30	12	18

Porphyry's Expanded Victor Model (2022)

Venus rules the Moon by sign; the MC, ASC, Moon, and Lot of Spirit by bound. Sect: out-of-favor. Solar phase: occidental direct combust. Dignity: diurnal triplicity. At the bending of the Lunar Nodes.

Victor Table for Killing Planets

Not published for the living.

ZRS

L1 Leo 20 Nov 1942		
L1 Virgo 12 Aug 1961		Broadly speaking, L1-Virgo outlined JB in college, law school, brief tenure as trial lawyer and public defender, marriage, tragic car accident and death of first wife and daughter, and the start of his Senate career. L2-Pisces FS timed JB's first electoral victory and L2-Pisces LB timed his first overseas trip. Pisces is LOF10
L2 Pisces 24 Oct 1970	FS	Nov-1970. Elected New Castle County Council.
L2 Pisces 11 Dec 1978	LB	1979. First overseas trip to Yugoslavia, accompanied by Averill Harriman.
L1 Libra 29 Apr 1981		Birth of daughter Ashley on 8-Jun-1981 opened L1-Libra. By far the most active subperiod was L2-Aquarius (10th from Aquarius is Scorpio with a stellium that includes the Sun). During this subperiod, JB chaired the Senate Judiciary Committee where he pushed through Supreme Court confirmation of Anthony Kennedy after defeating Bork; ran and withdrew as a Presidential contender because of plagiarism charges, and suffered two life threatening brain aneurysms which he survived.
L1 Scorpio 18 Mar 1989		On 6-Dec-1989 the spree shooter Marc Lepine killed 14 women, wounded 10 women, and wounded and 4 men in an attack purposely targeting women. This action triggered JB to pursue legal protections for battered women through his signature Violence Against Women Act signed into law 13-Sep-1994. Other key events for L1-Scorpio included the Clarence Thomas Supreme Court nomination and JB's role in managing the Bosnia conflict under the Clinton administration.
L1 Sagittarius 30 Dec 2003		Compared to other L1 periods, activities for L1 Sagittarius took some time to develop. With Sagittarius angular from LOF, the L1 period was active with JB's eight-year service as VP under Obama, a position Obama offered JB after JB withdrew from another failed Presidential bid. If we apply the ZRS rule that the purpose of the period is not revealed until the L2 subperiod reaches the ruler of the L1 period, look no further to the final L2-Cancer subperiod beginning 7-Mar-2014 which includes the tragic death of son Beau Biden from brain Cancer. Yes the sign of Cancer is related to Cancer the disease. Jupiter/Cancer-rx is positioned in the sign of Cancer which is activated by the L2 ZRS subperiod.
L1 Capricorn 28 Oct 2015		L1-Capricorn begins seven days after JB announced he would not run for the 2016 Presidential campaign because of lingering loss from the tragic death of his son Beau. Later JB did win the Democratic nomination and Presidential election during L2-Pisces which is 10th from LOF.

Firdaria – Venus major and minor periods

Firdaria according to Bonatti	Life Event
Sun **Venus** 25 Apr 1944	No events found.
Venus 8 years Age 10 to 18	No events found.
Venus Venus 19 Nov 1952	No events found.
Venus Mercury 11 Jan 1954	No events found.
Venus Moon 04 Mar 1955	No events found.
Venus Saturn 25 Apr 1956	No events found.
Venus Jupiter 16 Jun 1957	No events found.
Venus Mars 08 Aug 1958	No events found.
Venus Sun 29 Sep 1959	No events found.
Mercury **Venus** 11 Jan 1972	7-Nov-1972, elected to Senate; 18-Dec-1972, car accident killed wife and daughter, injuring two sons.
Moon **Venus** 24 Apr 1980	8-Jun-1981, birth of daughter Ashley.
Saturn **Venus** 03 Mar 1989	28-Jun-1989, Bosnia: 600th Anniversary of Battle of Kosovo; 6-Dec-1989, Marc Lepine spree shooting; 19-Jun-1990, VAWA of 1990 Act introduced by JB.
Jupiter **Venus** 11 Jan 1999	7-Jun-1999, death of father-in-law; 15-May-2000, VAMA of 1994: Supreme Court struck down section that gave victims of gender-motivated violence the right to sue their attackers in federal court.
Mars **Venus** 20 Nov 2007	3-Jan-2008, withdrew from 2008 Presidential race after winning less than 1% of Iowa caucus; 22-Aug-2008, Barack Obama named JB running mate; 5-Oct-2008, death of mother-in-law; 4-Nov-2008, re-elected to Senate and elected Vice President.
Sun **Venus** 25 Apr 2019	25-Apr-2019, launched Presidential Bid; 13/16-Jul-2020, nominated Democratic Presidential Nominee.

Venus as Victor. Venus just past the superior conjunction to the Sun elevates the specific Venusian style in Biden's horoscope as a favored social convention. Venus placed in Scorpio, sign of her detriment, and in the bound of Saturn are both debilities and consistent with battered women Biden sought to bring out of the shadows and lift up within the broader society with his signature Violence Against Women Act legislation. During the 2020 Presidential campaign, Venus/Scorpio as Biden's victor allowed Biden to function as 'comforter-in-chief' during the COVID pandemic. The fact that Venus/Scorpio rules the bound of the LOS directly links Biden's Venusian style with his political career. LOS 9LE43 is placed in the sign of Leo (politics, power, the King) and in the bound of Venus/Leo (peace, love, vitality, entertainment).

2009 Proposed Rectification: 11:36:06 EWT, ASC 14CP32'11"
2022 Revised Rectification: 11:36:28 EWT, ASC 14CP39'13"

Rectification Notes

Like my presentation for Obama, I will present the original proposed rectification for then Vice-President Biden published 2009 in the 3rd edition of *A Rectification Manual*. Unlike Obama, Biden's birth time was known and published as 8:30 AM, Rodden Rating A, from memory, with an Ascendant of early Sagittarius.

My proposed rectification for Joe Biden is three hours later and features Capricorn rising. Among recent Presidents, it is only one of two where my rectification differs substantially from published birth times (the other is George H. W. Bush which I have proposed Virgo rising rather than Leo rising).

Next follows a discussion of how I tracked the 2009 proposed rectification as an out-of-sample test. I give reasons why I made a slight change in the rectification.

Key technical points for Biden's nativity:

1. How I used Uranus to time the 1972 tragic car accident but used other traditional techniques to identify the car accident in the revised rectification without recourse to Uranus.

2. How the Lot of Sons was crucial in timing the death of Beau Biden. This is one of the best examples in this entire manual which, like the Chapter 6 case study of Andrew Jackson's house fire, demonstrate that major life events can be timed by dynamic activity to Lots without dynamic activity to the angles.

3. How the Sun-MC solar arc direction which timed Marc Lepine's spree shooting is linked to the similar Sun-MC primary direction which timed passage of the Violence Against Women Act. This is an excellent example of linking solar arc and primary directions proposed in Chapter 10's *Proposition on The Relationship between Solar Arcs and Primary Directions*. The low odds of this occurrence significantly increase the probability the proposed rectification is correct.

The Original Proposed Rectification published 1-Sep-2009
(with format changes to directions for compatibility with 4th edition format).

Compared to a published birth time of 8:30 AM EWT with an Ascendant in early Sagittarius, the proposed rectification features Capricorn rising and a time of 10:36:06 AM EST (or 11:36:06 AM EWT).

Configuration of Chart - Car Accident

While Saturn transiting the 7th cusp for the 8:30 AM EWT chart is consistent with the fatal car accident of his first wife on 18-Dec-1972, it is not the only configuration which fits with that tragedy. In the proposed figure, Saturn falls on the cusp of the 5th house of children, and like the 8:30 AM chart, rules the 2nd, or 8th from the 7th (death of wife). In addition to losing his wife, Biden lost his daughter and both sons sustained broken bones and other injuries. Saturn/Gemini on the 5th is consistent with broken limbs of children, a configuration which does not appear in the 8:30 AM chart.

In addition to Saturn, the modern planet Uranus was helpful in locking down the rectification, first taking the step of adjusting the Moon to meet csa Uranus at 2TA36 the day prior to the accident. There are a total of four measurements which time the car accident on 18-Dec-1972:

17-Dec-1972. *csa Uranus conj Moon.*
17-Dec-1972. *tr Jupiter conj ASC.*
18-Dec-1972. *csa Saturn conj IC.*

Uranus (2GE46 – not shown) falls in the 5th of children which signifies an unexpected event for children. Jupiter, ruler of 12th of death of children (8th from 5th), matches death of Biden's daughter. Though a benefic, Jupiter is conjunct the fixed star Procyon whose nature is Mercury/Mars. Saturn in the 5th of children ruling the 2nd of death of wife breaks up Biden's family when directed to the IC (4th house of family) by converse motion. Finally, compared to the *Lot* of Marriage of Men a/c Hermes computed for 3CA18, Uranus moved to 3CA17 by direct solar arc conjunct the part within a minute of degree on the day of the accident. The probability that Uranus by direct solar arc hit the Lot of Marriage *and* Uranus by converse solar arc hit the Moon within a few days is extremely low.

Bork Hearings and Plagiarism Charges

| PT | D | Mars/Virgo | P | dex sextile Mercury (ME) c. => MC | 16-Sep-1987 |
| PT | D | Mars/Virgo | P | dex sextile Mercury (0) c. => MC | 7-Nov-1987 |

This sequence timed key events in the 1987 Bork hearings, charges of plagiarism levied against Biden, and his withdrawal from the 1988 Presidential race.

12-Sep. Plagiarism charges made against Biden's campaign speeches.
15-Sep. Bork Supreme Court nomination hearings started
17-Sep. Charges of plagiarism from Law School revived.
18-Sep. New York Times labeled events Biden's 'Waterloo'.
23-Sep. Withdrew from 1988 Presidential race.
23-Oct. Senate rejected Bork Supreme Court nomination.

See also converse tr Mars conj ASC on 16-Sep-1987 and converse tr Mercury conj ASC (6-Sep, 1-Oct, and 21-Oct-1987).

Brain Aneurysm and Surgery. Biden's unsuccessful 1988 Presidential bid and oversight of the Bork hearings coincided with Biden's life-threatening brain aneurysm.

23-Mar-1987. Serious head pain while campaigning in New Hampshire.
9-Feb-1988. Collapsed from brain aneurysm.
11-Feb-1988. Emergency surgery for two brain aneurysms.
4-May-1988. Second follow-up surgery.

| PT | D | Jupiter/Pisces | P | sin trine Mars (0) c. => Moon (0) | 30-Sep-1987 |
| PT | D | Jupiter/Pisces | P | sin trine Mars (MA) c. => Moon (MO) | 24-Jan-1990 |

| REG | D | Venus/Pisces | P | dex square Saturn (SA) c. => Moon (0) | 12-Feb-1988 |
| REG | D | Venus/Pisces | P | dex square Saturn (0) c. => Moon (MO) | 24-Oct-1991 |

The first direction of this sequence times surgery within 24 hours as do the following solar arc directions:

12-Feb-1988. *csa South Node conj. ASC.*
16-Sep-1987. *csa Mars 27VI54 conj Lot of Death 27VI54.*

Delineation: Moon/Taurus in sign of the Moon's exaltation may trump the Sun as Hīlāj. Mars is the high scoring killing planet. Saturn falls in the 6th of illness and rules the South Node/Aquarius. Aquarius is assigned to blood vessels; South Node in Aquarius signifies their rupture.

Congressional Legislation

Violence Against Women Act. Signed same time as crime bill.

<u>12-Sep-1994</u>. *dsa Saturn square Moon.* Bill Clinton signed the *Violence Against Women Act of 1994*, 13-Sep-1994.

Bosnia. Biden is remembered for his early Congressional support for military intervention against Bosnian Serbs. These Mars directions confirm the validity of Biden's own Mars/Scorpio/11th as political alliances designed for military reprisals. Mars/Scorpio is Biden's Al-mubtazz Figurae.

| REG | D | Saturn/Leo | P | dex square Mars (MA) d. => LOF | 30-May-1994 |

Visited Balkans with Bob Dole after D-Day celebration 6-Jun-1994.

<u>19-Jan-1999</u>. *dsa Mars sextile MC.* Račak Massacre, 15 January.
<u>7-Mar-2006</u>. *csa Mars sextile MC.* Death of Milosevic, 11-March.

2022 Revised Rectification: 11:36:27 EWT, ASC 14CP39'13"

Revised notes made Sep-2019 during the 2020 Presidential campaign. Revised slightly in 2022 using St Mary's Hospital Scranton PA as the exact birthplace.

The purpose of this discussion is to test the proposed rectification I made in 2009 against actual life events.

1. Apart from Joe Biden's tenure as Vice President under Barack Obama, the most important life event which happened since 2009 was the tragic death of his oldest son Beau Biden of brain cancer on 30-May-2015. I stated in *A Rectification Manual* that attempts to rectify horoscopes of political leaders based on mundane events are very problematic since other mundane horoscopes are involved making it difficult to link a political leader's natal horoscope to mundane events. It's possible to do but more difficult to prove. For this reason, I prefer events of a personal nature, such as the death of Beau Biden, to constitute a legitimate out-of-sample rectification test.

2. For the 2009 rectification, the Lot of Sons is computed as 7AR03. Beau Biden died on 30-May-2015 with tr South Node at 7AR00 within 3 minutes of degree. This precision is even more striking considering that for Joe Biden's 1968 solar return for the year of Beau Biden's birth on 3-Feb-1969, solar return North Node is 6AR50 which is 180 degrees opposite the Nodal placement at the time of death.

3. On a general delineation basis, for the birth of Hunter Biden on 4-Feb-1970, tr Mars 7AR56 (12:00 Noon, untimed birth chart) is also conjunct the Lot of Sons. Both Nodal placements for Beau and the Mars transit for Hunter are closely conjunct the Lot of Sons. This confirms a key principle outlined in *A Rectification*

Manual: that the modern rectification approach which relies on solar arc directions, progressions, and transits measurements to the angles is woefully underspecified. Major events can be timed by measurements to the lots with no dynamic activity to the angles whatsoever.

4. In a minor tweak which advances my 2009 rectification by just under 30 seconds, a connection is made between the 6-Dec-1989 spree shooting by Marc Lepine targeting women and passage of the Violence Against Women Act on 13-Sep-1994. The spree shooting was timed by the solar arc of Sun = ASC; VAMA was passed when the same measurement is recomputed using primary directions. The ability of a public event timed by solar arc directions to be mirrored by a personal event using primary directions is a proposition I made in *A Rectification Manual* (pp. 138-139). The low odds of such a linkage greatly increase odds of an accurate rectification.

5. During Fall 2019, transiting South Node was conjunct Biden's natal Ascendant on 1-Sep-2019 just 3 days before his poor performance in a Climate Debate during which a blood vessel burst in his left eye which raised questions of medical fitness for Presidential office. Natal South Node in the bound of Saturn/Aquarius promises blockage and/or breakage of blood vessels in the circulatory system. Prior South Node – ASC dynamic activity confirms this with dsa ASC conj South Node on 23-Mar-1987, an exact match for Biden's serious head pain, an early warning sign of two brain aneurysms the following year [the 23-Mar-1987 solar arc for the 2019 revised time and the 2022 revised location]. For an out-of-sample rectification test, this is an extremely precise event match based on delineation and timing.

6. The 2009 proposed rectification makes use of Uranus in timing the 18-Dec-1972 car crash which killed his first wife, his daughter, and injured his two sons. I no longer use modern planets. Within the traditional model, Biden's 1972 solar return shows injuries to his wife and daughter without resorting to modern planets.

September 2019 Update: Out-of-sample Rectification Tests

Death of Beau Biden, 30-May-2015
Age 72, Profected Ascendant = 1st house, Lord of Year = Saturn

Comment: In the proposed rectification, Lord of natal 5th of children is Venus; in the 2014 solar return (outer wheel) Venus transits the natal 12th house (death of children) and is placed in the return's 5th house (children) linking the two topics. This configuration does not exist for the ADB birth time. [Whole Sign houses].

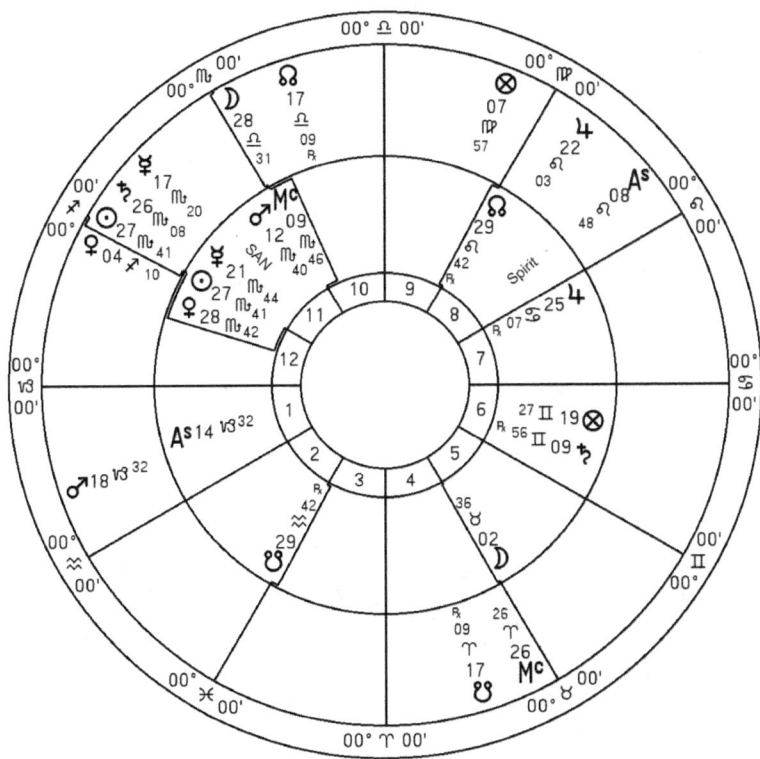

Revisiting the 1972 car accident without Uranus

18-Dec-1972. Death of wife Neilia, daughter Naomi, and injuries sustained by sons Beau and Hunter in car accident.

Age 30, Profected Ascendant = 7th house, Lord of Year = Moon.

Comment: The natal Moon-Mars opposition is replicated in the solar return with partile oppositions to natal counterparts. This is a highly unusual configuration and accentuates the harm to individuals signified by the natal Moon, in this case Biden's wife and daughter. Both sons lived.

srMoon 12TA48 opposed nMars 12SC40, difference = 8 minutes of degree.
srMars 2SC38 opposed nMoon 2TA36, difference = 2 minutes of degree.

A second problematic configuration is Biden's Saturn return with solar return Saturn conjunct natal Lot of Fortune, solar return Ascendant conjunct natal Saturn, and solar return MC conjunct natal 2nd cusp (death of wife).

There is no need for recourse to Uranus to identify the accident.

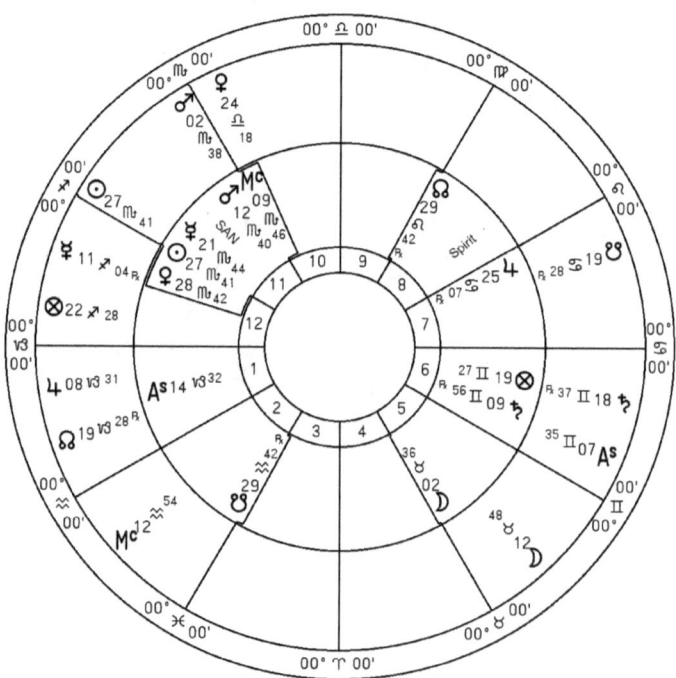

Revisiting the Violence Against Women Act suggests a revision

As Senator, Joe Biden's career highlight was passage of the Violence Against Women Act on 13-Sep-1994. This stemmed from his personal revulsion following Marc Lepine's spree shooting in Montreal on 6-Dec-1989 that targeted women, killing 14 women, injuring 10 women, and injuring 4 men.

> *8-Dec-1989. csa ASC conj Sun.*
> Marc Lepine shooting spree, 6-Dec-1989.
> (adding another 2 seconds makes this exact)
>
> | REG | D | Venus/Capricorn | P | ASC d. => Sun | 16-Sep-1994 |
> |---|---|---|---|---|---|
>
> VAMA passage, 13-Sep-1994.

The ability of Lepine's public spree shooting timed by solar arc directions later mirrored by VAMA passage timed by primary directions is an excellent example of my *Proposition: The Relationship between Solar Arcs and Primary Directions* (Chapter 10 Directions, p. 179). The low odds of this linkage greatly increases odds of an accurate rectification. As a result of this fine tuning, I identified the following measurements which also offer excellent fits to life events.

23-Mar-1987. dsa ASC conj South Node
30-Dec-1987. csa South Node conj ASC
   Serious head pain while campaigning in New Hampshire, early warning of aneurysm, 23-Mar-1987
   Collapsed from brain aneurysm, 9-Feb-1988.

REG	D	Venus/Leo	P	dex square MC c. => Sun	25-Jun-1990

VAWA of 1990 first introduced by Joe Biden, 19-Jun-1990.

REG	D	Mars/Pisces	P	sin trine Sun d. => ASC	4-Feb-1994

Wall Street Journal op-ed "A Million Mrs. Bobbitts" favors VAWA passage citing Biden's 1992 Judiciary Committee report *Violence against Women: a Week in the Life of America*, 28-Jan-1994.

REG	D	Venus/Aquarius	P	sin square MC d. => Sun	27-Dec-2018
PT	D	Venus/Aquarius	P	sin square MC d. => Sun	24-Apr-2019

New York Times: "How Biden has Paved the Way for a Possible Presidential Run," 1-Jan-2019.
Launched 2019 Presidential Bid, 25-Apr-2019.

2023 Update: Having revised the 2009 rectification in early September 2019, here are my out-of-sample observations on the revision.

Medical

tr North Node conj Lot of Fortune. 18-Dec-2020. Actual event: On 29-Nov-2020, Biden suffered a hairline fracture in his foot after playing with one of his dogs. He had to wear a boot for several weeks. This occurred during the heat of the Presidential transition following the 3-Nov-2020 Presidential election.

Among the measurements used to time Biden's life-threatening brain aneurysm in 1988 was a South Node – ASC solar arc direction. Research in *A Rectification Manual* demonstrated when the Lunar Nodes occupy the 2nd-8th house axis the Lunar Nodes take precedence over other possible planets and points as the functional killer at the time of death. In this case the North Node timed a fracture, not an aneurysm.

Afghanistan Withdrawal

PT	D	Mercury/Taurus	P	opp Mars (MA) d. => ASC	13-Dec-2020
PT	D	Mercury/Taurus	P	opp Mars (0) d. => ASC	6-May-2021
PT	D	Mercury/Taurus	P	opp Mars (BI) d. => ASC	27-Sep-2021

These three Mars primary directions direct Mars to the Descendant, or 7th house cusp. As the 7th house cusp signifies open enemies and conflicts Mars-DSC directions often time conflict; at the same time, the DSC is the angle of the west where the Sun sets so conflicts can also end at this time. Taken together, both of these configurations are an exact delineation match to the end of the Afghanistan conflict. Compare these directions to:

Talks between Afghan govt and Taliban began in Doha, 12-Sep-20.
Biden administration announced troop withdrawal, 13-Apr-21.
Taliban began last major offensive, 1-May-21.
Fall of Kabul, 15-Aug-21.
Final flight of US troops out of Kabul, 30-Aug-21.

Secret Service Vehicle Fleet Fire

tr Mercury 18SA39 separates from tr Mars 19GE27 and applies to Saturn 19AQ45. Actual event: on 29-Nov-2022 the day after the Biden family ended their Thanksgiving holiday in Nantucket, five cars rented by the Secret Service burst into flames first observed at 5:22 AM EDT. Natal LOF in 6th is beneficial for employees, here the Secret Service. But not for these transits (!) with Mercury lord of the 6th in the 12th separating from Mars and applying to Saturn. *Note tr Mars is conjunct the LOF by 7 minutes of degree !*

REFERENCES

Astrology

Abū Ma'shar al-Balhi. *The Abbreviation of the Introduction to Astrology.* Edited and Translated by Charles Burnett, KeijiYamamoto, and Michio Yano. Leiden: E.J. Brill, 1994.
_____. *The Great Introduction to the Science of the Judgments of the Stars.* Edited and Translated by Benjamin N. Dykes. Minneapolis, Minn.: The Cazimi Press, 2020.
_____. *On Historical Astrology: The Book of Religions and Dynasties (On the Great Conjunctions)*, 2 Vols. Edited and Translated by Keiji Yamamoto and Charles Burnett. Leiden: E.J. Brill, 2000.
_____. *On the Revolutions of the Years of Nativities.* The Complete Arabic Edition. Translated and Edited by Benjamin Dykes. Minneapolis, Minn.: The Cazimi Press, 2019.
_____. *On Solar Revolutions.* Part II. Translated by Robert Schmidt. Cumberland, Md.: The Phaser Foundation, Inc., 1999.
Al-Biruni, Muhammad ibn Ahmad. *The Book of Instruction in the Elements of the Art of Astrology.* Translated by R. Ramsay Wright. London: Luzac & Co, 1934.
Al-Khayyat, Abu 'Ali. *The Judgments of Nativities.* Translated by James Holden. Tempe, Ariz.: American Federation of Astrologers, 1988.
Al-Qabīsī. *The Introduction to Astrology.* Edited and Translated by Charles. Burnett, K. Yamamoto, and Michio Yano. London: The Warburg Institute, 2004.
Anrias, David. *Man and the Zodiac.* George Routledge & Sons, 1938. Reprint, New York: Samuel Weiser Inc. 1970.
Barrett, Gloria. *Astrological Physiognomy: a Key to the Ascending Sign and Decanate.* Chicago: The Aries Press, 1941.

Blaschke, Robert P. *Astrology: A Language of Life. Volume I: Progressions*. Lake Oswego, Oreg.: Earthwalk School of Astrology, 1998.

Bonatti, Guido. *Book of Astronomy*. Translated by Benjamin Dykes. Minneapolis, Minn.: The Cazimi Press, 2007.

Brennan, Chris. *Hellenistic Astrology: The Study of Fate and Fortune*. Denver, CO.: Amor Fati Publications, 2017.

Broughton, L.D. *The Elements of Astrology*. New York: Ray Boughton, 1906.

_____. Broughton's Monthly Planet Reader and Astrological Journal, 1860-1869. Available online: http://iapsop.com/archive/materials/monthly_planet_reader/ Last accessed: November 4, 2022.

Cornell, Howard Leslie. *The Encyclopaedia of Medical Astrology*. Abingdon, MD: Astrology Classic Publishing, reprint edition, 1972.

Dorotheus of Sidon. *Carmen Astrologicum*. Translated and Edited by Benjamin Dykes. Minneapolis, Minn.: The Cazimi Press, 2017.

Erza, Ibn. *The Beginning of Wisdom*. Translated by Meira Epstein. Reston, Va.: Arhat Publications, 1998.

Friedlander, Joel. *Body Types: The Enneagram of Essence Types*. Marin Bookworks, 2009.

Gadek, Peter. *History of the Astrological Technique of Solar Arc Directions*. 2017. Available online: http://www.friendsofastrology.org/peter-gadek-blog/history-of-the-astrological-technique-of-solar-arc-directions-by-peter-gadek. Last accessed: October 2, 2022.

Gansten, Martin. *Primary Directions: Astrology's Old Master Technique*. Bournemouth: The Wessex Astrologer, 2009.

Hand, Robert. *Horoscope Symbols*. Atglen, Pa.: Schiffer Publishing Company, 1981.

_____. *Night & Day: Planetary Sect in Astrology*. Reston, Va.: Arhat Publications, 1995.

_____. *Whole Sign Houses*. Reston, Va.: Arhat Publications, 2000.

Hermann of Carinthia. *The Search of the Heart*. Translated and Edited by Benjamin Dykes. Minneapolis, Minn.: The Cazimi Press, 2011.

Hill, Judith. *The Astrological Body Types: Face, Form, and Expression*. 2d ed. Bayside, Calif.: Borderland Sciences Research Foundation, 1997.

Kolev, Rumen. *Primary Directions II: Classic Placidian Interplanetary Directions*. Varna, Bulgaria.: Zenith Publishing House. 2005[?].

_____. "Robert Zoller & the Alchabitius Primary Direction Method," *Considerations* XVIII, no. 3 (2003): 81-89.

Labbān, Kūshyār Ibn. *Introduction to Astrology*. Edited and Translated by Michio Yano. Institute for the Study of Languages and Cultures of Asia and Africa. Tokyo, Japan, 1997.

Lilly, William. *Christian Astrology. Book Three: Nativities*. London, 1647. Reprint, Abingdon, Md.: Astrology Classics (page references are to the reprint edition), 2004.

Makransky, Jerry. "Primary Directions," *NCGR Journal*, Winter 1988-1989.

Maternus, Firmicus. *Ancient Astrology: Theory and Practice*. Translated by J. R. Bram. Park Ridge, N.J.: Noyes Press, 1975.

De Montulmo, Antonius. *On the Judgment of Nativities*. Parts 1 and 2. Translated by Robert Hand and Edited by Robert Schmidt. Berkeley Springs, WV: Golden Hind Press, 1995.

Morin, Jean-Baptiste. *Astrologia Gallica. Book Twenty-Two: Directions*. Translated by James H. Holden. Tempe, Ariz.: American Federation of Astrologers, 1994.

————. *Astrologia Gallica. Book Twenty-Three: Revolutions*. Translated by James H. Holden. Tempe, Ariz.: American Federation of Astrologers, 2002.

Omar of Tiberias. *Three Books on Nativities*. Translated by Robert Hand and Edited by Robert Schmidt. Berkeley Springs, W.Va.: Golden Hind Press, 1997.

Pearce, Alfred John. *The Textbook of Astrology*, 2d ed. Washington, D.C.: American Federation of Astrologers, 1911; Reprint, 1970.

Plato. *The Republic of Plato*. Translated by Allan Bloom. New York: Basic Books, 1968.

Porphyry. *Porphyry the Philosopher: Introduction to the Tetrabiblos and Serapio of Alexandria: Astrological Definitions*. Translated by James Holden. Tempe, Arizona: American Federation of Astrologers, 2009.

Ptolemy, Claudius. *Tetrabiblos*. Edited and Translated by F. E. Robbins. Harvard University Press. 1940.

Regulus. *America is Born: Introducing the Regulus USA National Horoscope*, Princeton, NJ.: Regulus Astrology LLC, 2008.

Regulus. *Working Paper on Astrological Physiognomy: History and Sources*, Princeton, NJ.: Regulus Astrology LLC, 2011.

Saunders, Hamish. *Solar Arc Directions*. 1996. Available online: https://www.astrology-house.com/content/docs/articles/Solar_Arc.pdf. Last accessed: October 2, 2022.

Schmidt, Robert. *Definitions and Foundations. The Astrological Record of the Early Sages, Vol.* 2. Golden Hind Press, 2009.

Schoener, Johannes. *Opusculum Astrologicum*. Translated and Edited by Robert Hand, 2d ed. Berkeley Springs, W.Va.: Golden Hind Press, 1996.

———. *On the Judgments of Nativities: Book I*. Translated by Robert Hand. Reston, Va.: Arhat Publications, 2001.

Scofield, Bruce. *Signs of Time: An Introduction to Mesoamerican Astrology*. Amherst, Mass.: One Reed Publications, 1994.

———. *Astrological Chart Calculations: An Outline of Conventions and Methodology*. Amherst, Mass.: One Reed Publications, 2002.

Sellar, Wanda. *The Consultation Chart*. Bournemouth, England: The Wessex Astrologer Ltd., 2000.

Shea, Mary. *Planets in Solar Returns: Yearly Cycles of Transformation and Growth*. Twin Stars Unlimited, 1999.

Simmonite, W.J. *The Arcana of Astrology*. London: W. Foulsham, 1890.

Stein, Madeleine G. *Heads & Headlines: The Phrenological Fowlers*. Norman: University of Oklahoma Press, 1971.

Trivedi, Prash. *The Key of Life: Astrology of the Lunar Nodes*. Twin Lakes, Wis.: Lotus Brands, Inc., 2002.

Tyl, Noel. *Solar Arcs: Astrology's Most Successful Predictive System*. St. Paul, Minn.: Llewellyn Publications, 2001.

Valens, Vettius. *The Anthology*. Translated by Mark T. Riley and Edited by Chris Brennan. Amor Fati Publications, 2022.

Ventura, João. "The Animodar Effect," The Tradition, Number 3, Autumn 2009. Available online: www.thetraditionajournal.com. Last accessed September 1, 2022.

Willner, John. *The Rising Sign Problem: A Series of Essays on the Physical Characteristics and Personality Traits of Individuals for the Twelve Astrological Signs on the Ascendant*. American Federation of Astrologers, 1991.

Zoller, Robert. *The Arabic Parts in Astrology: The Lost Key to Prediction*. Rochester: Inner Traditions International, 1980.

———. *Tools and Techniques of the Medieval Astrologer. Book One: Prenatal Concerns and the Calculation of the Length of Life*. London: New Library Limited, 2001.

———. *More Light on Primary Directions*. Privately printed, 2002.

———. *Tools and Techniques of the Medieval Astrologer. Book Two: Astrological Prediction by Direction and the Subdivision of the Signs*, 2d electronic edition. London: New Library Limited, 2003.

_____. *Diploma Course in Medieval Astrology.* London: New Library Limited, 2002.

Presidents and First Ladies – Surveys

Boller, Paul F. *Presidential Wives: An Anecdotal History.* New York: Oxford, 1988.

Bumgarner, John R. *The Health of the Presidents.* Jefferson, N.C.: McFarland & Company, Inc., Publishers, 1994.

Carlson, Brady. *Dead Presidents: Am American Adventure into the Strange Deaths and Surprising Afterlives of Our Nation's Leaders.* W. W. Norton & Company. 2016.

Cohen, Jared. *Accidental Presidents: Eight Men who Changed America.* Simon & Schuster. 2019.

Cramer, Richard Ben. *What it Takes: The Way to the White House.* New York: Random House. 1992.

DeGregorio, William A. *The Complete Book of U.S. Presidents.* New York: Gramercy Books, 2001.

Gibbs, Nancy and Michael Duffy. *The Presidents Club: Inside the World's Most Exclusive Fraternity.* New York: Simon & Schuster, 2013.

Leo, Leonard and James Taranto, eds. *Presidential Leadership: Rating the Best and the Worst in the White House.* New York: Free Press, 2004.

Rubenzer, Steven J. and Thomas R. Faschingbauer. *Personality, Character, and Leadership in the White House.* Washington D.C.: Brassey's, Inc., 2004.

Schlesinger, Arthur M. Jr., *The Almanac of American History.* New York: Barnes & Noble Books, 1993.

Smith, Carter. *Presidents: Every Question Answered.* New York: Hylas Publishing, 2004.

The National First Ladies Library. *Biographies: First Ladies of the United States* [article on-line]. Canton, Ohio; accessed 1 May 2007. Available from http://www.firstladies.org/biographies/; Internet.

Wead, Doug. *All the Presidents' Children.* New York: Atria Books, 2003.

Whipple, Chris. *The Gatekeepers: How the White House Chiefs of Staff Define Every Presidency.* Crown Publishing. 2017.

Presidents and First Ladies - Individual

Ammon, Harry. *James Monroe: The Quest for National Identity*. Charlottesville: University of Virginia Press, 1971.

Anderson, Judith Icke. *William Howard Taft: An Intimate History*. New York: W. W. Norton & Company, 1981.

Anthony, Carl Sferrazza. *Florence Harding*. New York: William Morrow, 1998.

Balcerski, Thomas J. *Bosom Friends: The Intimate World of James Buchanan and William Rufus King*. Oxford, 2019.

Bauer, K. Jack. *Zachary Taylor: Soldier, Planter, Statesman of the Old Southwest*. Baton Rouge: Louisiana State University Press, 1985.

Beschloss, Michael R. *Mayday: The U-2 Affair*. New York: Harper & Row, 1986.

Bemis, Samuel Flagg. *John Quincy Adams and the Foundations of American Foreign Policy*. New York: Alfred A. Knopf, 1950.

Bergeron, Paul H. *The Presidency of James K. Polk*. Lawrence: University Press of Kansas, 1987.

Bernstein, R. B. *Thomas Jefferson*. Oxford: Oxford University Press, 2003.

Black, Conrad. *Franklin Delano Roosevelt: Champion of Freedom*. New York: Public Affairs, 2003.

Blumenthal, Sidney. *The Clinton Wars*. New York: Penguin Books, 2004.

Bourne, Peter G. *Jimmy Carter: A Comprehensive Biography from Plains to Post Presidency*. New York: Scribner, 1997.

Bourneman, Walter R. *Polk: The Man who Transformed the Presidency and America*. New York: Random House, 2008.

Brennan, Chris. Reflections on the United Astrology Conference – UAC 2008, August 6, 2008. Available online:
https://horoscopicastrologyblog.com/2008/08/06/reflections-on-the-united-astrology-conference-uac-2008/

Bruce, Philip Alexander. *History of the University of Virginia 1819 – 1919*. Vol. I. New York: The MacMillan Company, 1920.

Burton, David H. *William Howard Taft: Confident Peacemaker*. Philadelphia: Saint Joseph's University Press, 2004.

Bush, George H. W. and Brent Scowcroft. *A World Transformed*. New York: Alfred A. Knopf, 1998.

Bush, George W. *Decision Points*. Crown Publishers, 2010.

Cannon, James. *Time and Change: Gerald Ford's Appointment with History*. New York: Harper Collins Publishers, 1994.

Carter, Jimmy. *Keeping Faith: Memoirs of a President.* London: William Collins Sons & Co Ltd., 1982.
_____. *Turning Point: A Candidate, a State, and a Nation Come of Age.* New York: Random House, 1992.
Chernow, Ron. *Washington: A Life.* New York: The Penguin Press, 2010.
_____. *Grant.* New York: The Penguin Press, 2017.
Cleaves, Freeman. *Old Tippecanoe: William Henry Harrison and His Time.* New York: Charles Scribner's Sons, 1939.
Clinton, Bill. *My Life.* New York: Alfred A. Knopf, 2004.
Clinton, Hillary Rodham. *Living History.* New York: Scribner, 2003.
Coletta, Paolo E. *The Presidency of William Howard Taft.* Lawrence: University Press of Kansas, 1973.
Crapol, Edward P. *John Tyler, the Accidental President.* University of North Carolina Press, 2006.
Cunningham, Noble E., Jr. *In Pursuit of Reason: The Life of Thomas Jefferson.* Baton Rouge: Louisiana State University Press, 1987.
D'Este, Carlo. *Eisenhower: A Soldier's Life.* New York: Henry Holt and Company, 2002.
Dallek, Robert. *One Star Rising: Lyndon Johnson and His Times 1908-1960.* New York: Oxford University Press, 1991.
_____. *Flawed Giant: Lyndon Johnson and His Times 1961-1973.* New York: Oxford University Press, 1998.
Damms, Richard V. *The Eisenhower Presidency 1953-1961.* London: Pearson Education Limited, 2002.
Dickey, J. D. *American Demagogue: The Great Awakening and the Rise and Fall of Populism.* New York: Pegasus books, 2019.
Donald, David Herbert. *Lincoln.* New York: Simon & Schuster, 1995.
Douglass, James W. *JFK and the Unspeakable. Why he died & Why it matters.* New York: Orbis Books, 2008.
Downes, Randolph C. *The Rise of Warren Gamaliel Harding.* Columbus: Ohio State University Press, 1970.
Dusinberre, William. *Slavemaster President: The Double Career of James Polk.* Oxford: Oxford University Press, 2003.
Eisenhower, Dwight D. *Mandate for Change 1953-1956.* Garden City, N. Y.: Doubleday & Company, 1963.
_____. *Waging Peace 1956-1961.* Garden City, N. Y.: Doubleday & Company, 1965.

Eisenhower, Susan. *Mrs. Ike: Portrait of a Marriage.* Herndon, Va.: Capital Books, Inc., 1996.

Ferrell, Robert H. *Woodrow Wilson and World War I.* New York: Harper & Row, 1985.

Freeman, Douglas Southall. *Washington.* Abridged by Richard Harwell. New York: Charles Scribner's Son, 1968.

Ford, Gerald. *A Time to Heal.* New York: Harper & Row, 1979.

Gordon-Redd, Annette. *Andrew Johnson: The American Presidents Series: The 17th President, 1865-1869.* New York: Times Books, 2011.

Guelzo, Allen C. *Lincoln's Emancipation Proclamation: The End of Slavery in America.* New York: Simon & Schuster, 2004.

Gara, Larry. *The Presidency of Franklin Pierce.* Lawrence: University Press of Kansas, 1991.

Garrison, Webb. *The Lincoln No One Knows.* Nashville: Rutledge Hill Press, 1993.

Goodwin, Doris Kearns. *Team of Rivals: The Political Genious of Abraham Lincoln.* New York: Simon & Schuster, 2005.

_____. *The Bully Pulpit: Theodore Roosevelt, William Howard Taft, and the Golden Age of Journalism.* New York: Simon & Schuster, 2013.

Hamilton, Nigel. *Bill Clinton: An American Journey.* New York: Random House, 2003.

Hargreaves, Mary W. M. *The Presidency of John Quincy Adams.* Lawrence: University Press of Kansas, 1985.

Heilemann, John and Mark Halperin. *Game Change: Obama and the Clintons, McCain and Palin, and the Race of a Lifetime.* New York: Harper. 2010.

Holzer. Harold. *Lincoln at Cooper Union: The Speech That Made Abraham Lincoln President.* New York: Simon & Schuster, 2004.

Hoogenboom, Ari. *Rutherford B. Hayes: Warrior and President.* Lawrence, University Press of Kansas, 1995.

Hoover, Herbert. *The Memoirs of Herbert Hoover: Years of Adventure 1874-1920.* New York: MacMillan Company, 1951.

_____. *The Memoirs of Herbert Hoover: The Cabinet and the Presidency 1920-1933.* New York: MacMillan Company, 1952.

_____. *The Memoirs of Herbert Hoover: The Great Depression 1929-1941.* New York: MacMillan Company, 1952.

Horn, Miriam. *Rebels in White Gloves: Coming of Age with Hillary's Class – Wellesley '69.* New York: Random House, 1999.

Hughes, Emmet John. *The Ordeal of Power: A Political Memoir of the Eisenhower Years.* New York: Antheneum, 1963

Irving, Washington. *Life of George Washington.* Edited and Abridged by Jess Stein. Tarrytown, N.Y.: Sleepy Hollow Restorations, 1975.

Jefferson, Thomas. *The Papers of Thomas Jefferson.* Vol. 1, ed. Julian Boyd. Princeton: Princeton University Press, 1950. Quoted in Garrett Ward Sheldon. *The Political Philosophy of Thomas Jefferson*, 45-49. Baltimore: The Johns Hopkins University Press, 1991.

Kaufman, Scott. Ambition, *Pragmatism, and Party. A Political Biography of Gerald R. Ford.* Lawrence: University Press of Kansas, 2017.

Kelley, Kitty. *The Family: The Real Story of the Bush Dynasty.* New York: Random House, 2004.

Ketcham, Ralph. *James Madison.* Charlottesville: University of Virginia, 1971.

Klein, Philip S. *President James Buchanan.* University Park, Pa.: Penn State University Press, 1962. Reprint, Newtown, Conn.: American Political Biography Press, 1995.

Lacayo, Richard. "The Making of America – Theodore Roosevelt," *TIME.* June 25, 2006.

Lemay, J. A. Leo. 1997. *Benjamin Franklin: A Documentary History.* Newark, Del.: University of Delaware, 1997; accessed 3 April 2007. Available from http://www.english.udel.edu/lemay/franklin/introduction.html; Internet.

Lewis, McMillan. *Woodrow Wilson of Princeton.* Narberth, Pa.: Livingston Publishing Company, 1952.

Link, Arthur. ed., *The Papers of Woodrow Wilson.* Princeton: Princeton University Press, 1966-1994.

Leech, Margaret. *In the Days of McKinley.* New York: Harper & Brothers, 1959.

Lincoln, Abraham. *The Collected Works of Abraham Lincoln.* Vol. 5. Edited by Roy P. Basler. New Brunswick: Rutgers University Press, 1953.

Long. E. B. *The Civil War Day by Day. An Almanac: 1861 – 1865.* Garden City: Doubleday & Company, Inc., 1971.

Longstreet, James. *The Battle of Fredericksburg.* [article on-line]. Accessed 1 September 2007; available from http://www.civilwarhome.com, 1997; Internet.

Luthin, Reinhard H. *The Real Abraham Lincoln.* New Jersey: Prentice-Hall, Inc., 1960.

MacMillan, Margaret. *Paris 1919: Six Months That Changed the World.* New York: Random House, 2001.

Marsden, George M. *Jonathan Edwards: A Life.* New Haven, CT: Yale University Press, 2003.

McCullough, David. *Mornings on Horseback.* New York: Simon & Schuster, 1981.

_____. *Truman.* New York: Simon & Schuster, 1992.

_____. *John Adams.* New York: Simon & Shuster, 2001.

McElroy. Robert. *Grover Cleveland: The Man and the Statesman.* New York: Harper & Brothers Publishers, 1923.

McFeely, William S. *Grant.* New York: W. W. Norton & Company, 1981.

McKinley, Silas Bent. *Woodrow Wilson.* New York: Frederick A. Praeger, 1957.

Meacham, Jon. *American Lion: Andrew Jackson in the White House.* New York: Random House, 2008.

Merry, Robert W. *President McKinley: Architect of the American Century.* New York: Simon & Schuster, 2017.

Miller, William Lee. *Lincoln's Virtues: An Ethical Biography.* New York: Random House, 2003.

Minutaglio, Bill. *First Son: George W. Bush and the Bush Family Dynasty.* New York: Three Rivers Press, 1999.

Morgan, H. Wayne. *William McKinley and his America.* Syracuse: Syracuse University Press, 1963.

Morris, Edmund. *The Rise of Theodore Roosevelt.* New York: Coward, McCann & Geoghegan, Inc., 1979.

_____. *Dutch: A Memoir of Ronald Reagan.* New York: Random House, 1999.

_____. *Theodore Rex.* New York: Random House, 2001.

_____. *Colonel Roosevelt.* New York: Random House, 2010.

Morris, Roger. *Richard Milhous Nixon: The Rise of an American Politician.* New York: Henry Holt and Company, 1990.

Nevins, Allan. *Grover Cleveland: A Study in Courage.* New York: Dodd, Mead & Company, 1933.

Nixon, Richard. *Six Crises.* New York: Simon & Schuster, 1962.

Novak, Michael and Jana Novak. *Washington's God: Religion, Liberty, and the Father of Our Country.* New York: Basic Books. 2006.

O'Donnell, Lawrence. *Playing with Fire: The 1968 Election and the Transformation of American Politics.* Penguin Press, 2017.

Olcott, Charles. *The Life of William McKinley.* 2 vols. Boston: Houghton Mifflin Company, 1916.

Parmet, Herbert S. *George Bush: The Life of a Lone Star Yankee.* New Brunswick: Transaction Publishers, 2001.

Rick Perlstein. Before the Storm: *Barry Goldwater and the Unmaking of the American Consensus*. Hill and Wang, 2001.

_____. Nixonland: *The Rise of a President and the Fracturing of America*. New York: Scribner, 2008.

_____. The Invisible Bridge: *The Fall of Nixon and the Rise of Reagan*. New York: Simon & Schuster. 2014.

_____. Reaganland: *America's Right Turn 1976-1980*. Simon & Schuster. 2020.

Perret, Geoffrey. *Eisenhower*. New York: Random House, 1999.

_____. *Jack: A Life Like No Other*. New York: Random House, 2001.

Peskin, Allan. *Garfield*. Kent: Kent State University Press, 1978.

Philbrick, Nathaniel. *Valiant Ambition: George Washington, Benedict Arnold, and the Fate of the American Revolutions*. Viking Books. 2016.

_____. *In the Hurricane's Eye: The Genius of George Washington and the Victory at Yorktown*. Viking Books. 2018.

_____. *Travels with George: In Search of Washington and His Legacy*. Viking Books. 2021.

Pringle, Henry F. *Theodore Roosevelt*. New York: Harcourt, Brace and Company, 1931.

Rayback, Robert J. *Millard Fillmore: Biography of a President*. Buffalo: Buffalo Historical Society, 1959.

Reagan, Ron. *My Father at 100: A Memoir*. New York: Viking. 2011.

Reeves, Richard. *President Nixon: Alone in the White House*. New York: Simon & Schuster, 2001.

Reeves, Thomas C. *Gentleman Boss: The Life of Chester Alan Arthur*. New York: Alfred A. Knopf, 1975.

Rejai, Mostafa and Kay Phillips. *The Young George Washington in Psychobiographical Perspective*. Lewiston, N.Y.: Edwin Mellen Press, 2000.

Remini, Robert V. *Andrew Jackson and the Course of American Empire, 1767-1821*. New York: Harper & Row, 1977.

_____. *Andrew Jackson and the Course of American Freedom, 1822-1832*. New York: Harper & Row, 1981.

_____. *Andrew Jackson and the Course of American Democracy, 1833 – 1845*. New York: Harper & Row, 1985.

_____. *John Quincy Adams*. New York: Henry Holt and Company, 2002.

Rove, Karl. *The Triumph of William McKinley. Why the Election of 1896 Still Matters*. New York: Simon & Schuster, 2015.

Russell, Francis. *The Shadow of Blooming Grove: Warren G. Harding in His Times*. New York: McGraw-Hill Book Company, 1968.

Sandburg, Carl. *Abraham Lincoln: The Prairie Years*, 2 vols. New York: Harcourt, Brace & Co., 1926.

_____. *Abraham Lincoln: The War Years*, 4 vols. New York: Harcourt, Brace & Co., 1939.

Scarry, Robert J. *Millard Fillmore*. Jefferson, N.C.: McFarland, 2001.

Schlesinger, Arthur M. Jr., *The Age of Jackson*. New York: Little, Brown and Company, 1945.

_____. *The Age of Roosevelt: The Crisis of the Old Order 1919-1933*. Boston: Houghton Mifflin Company, 1957.

Schulman, Bruce J. *Lyndon B. Johnson and American Liberalism*. Boston: Bedford/St. Martins, 1995.

Sievers, Harry J. *Benjamin Harrison*, vol. I & II. New York: University Publishers, 1952, 1959; vol. III. Indianapolis: Bobbs-Merrill, 1968.

Smith, Elbert B. *The Presidency of James Buchanan*. Lawrence: University Press of Kansas, 1975.

Smith, Richard N. *An Uncommon Man: The Triumph of Herbert Hoover*. New York: Simon and Schuster, 1984.

_____. *Patriarch: George Washington and the New American Nation*. New York: Houghton Mifflin, 1993.

Sobel, Robert. *Coolidge: An American Enigma*. Washington, D.C.: Regnery Publishing, Inc., 1998.

Socolofsky, Homer E. and Allan B. Spetter. *The Presidency of Benjamin Harrison*. Lawrence: University Press of Kansas, 1987.

Sotos, John G. *The Physical Lincoln Complete 1.1a*. Mt. Vernon: Mt Vernon Book Systems. 2008.

Stout, Harry S. *The Divine Dramatist: George Whitefield and the Rise of Modern Evangelicalism*. Grand Rapids, MI: William B. Eerdmans Publishing Company, 1991.

Styron, Arthur. *The Last of the Cocked Hats: James Monroe and the Virginia Dynasty*. Norman: University of Oklahoma Press, 1945.

Thompson, Hunter S. *Fear and Loathing on the Campaign Trail '72*. New York: Simon & Schuster, 1973.

_____. *Better Than Sex: Confessions of a Political Junkie (The Gonzo Papers series Book 4)*. New York: Random House, 1994.

Tomkins, Stephen. *John Wesley: A Biography*. Grand Rapids, MI: William B. Eerdsmans Publishing Company, 2003.

Trefousse, Hans L. *Andrew Johnson*. New York: W. W. Norton & Company, 1989.

_____. *Rutherford B. Hayes*. New York: Henry Holt & Company, 2002.

Unger, Craig. *House of Bush, House of Saud. The Secret Relationship Between the World's Two Most Powerful Dynasties*. New York: Scribner & Sons, 2004.

Wallner, Peter A. *Franklin Pierce: New Hampshire's Favorite Son*. Concord: Plaidswede Publishing, 2004.

_____. *Franklin Pierce: Martyr for the Union*. Concord: Plaidswede Publishing, 2007.

Weinstein, Edwin A. *Woodrow Wilson: A Medical and Psychological Biography*. Princeton: Princeton University Press, 1981.

White, Ronald C. Jr. *Lincoln's Greatest Speech: The Second Inaugural*. New York: Simon & Schuster, 2002.

White, Theodore H. *The Making of the President 1960: A narrative history of American politics in action*. Atheneum Publishers, 1961.

Widner, Ted. *Martin Van Buren*. New York: Henry Holt and Company, 2005.

Wilson, Joan Hoff. *Herbert Hoover: Forgotten Progressive*. Boston: Little, Brown and Company, 1975.

Withey, Lynne. *Dearest Friend: A Life of Abigail Adams*. New York: Simon & Schuster, 1981.

Woodward, Bob and Carl Bernstein. *All the President's Men*. New York: Simon & Schuster, 1974.

_____. *The Final Days*. New York: Simon & Schuster, 1976.

INDEX (Parts 1-3)

All Presidents are included in the following tables (not included in individual entries below)

Table 4. House Skewness: Ascendant-Midheaven Degree Difference, p. 29
Table 6. Physiognomy Significators, p. 45
Table 9. Victor Soul Model, p. 58
Table 11. Cognitive Assessment Model: Rulers of the Moon and Mercury, p. 62
Table 13. Longevity Model: Predicted vs Actual, p. 79
Table 15. Arcus Vitae: Model vs Empirical Results, p. 93
Table 16. Lifespan, Midpoint, Syzygy ante Navitatem, and Lunar Phase, p. 105
Table 17. Moon's Separation and Application, p. 115
Table 33. Transits of the Lunar Nodes to the Angles, p. 269
Table 37. Comparison of Reported and Proposed Birth Times, p. 379
Table 38. Presidential Birthplace Database, p. 380

George Washington. 4th edition revised rectification, xii; primary directions format, xii-xiv; 3rd edition notation style, xv; physiognomy, 46; al-mubtazz table for manners (old format), 59; implication for manners when bound and sign rulers differ for Moon and Mercury, 63; arcus vitae and primary directions, 85-87; distributor changeover as arcus vitae, 91-92; preventional degree, 106; Moon's configuration and presidential greatness, 114-118; directing by triplicity, 129-132; rectification with firdaria, 142-144; ZR/notable FS-LOB linkages, 155; delineation of lot of spirit by bound placement, 157; GW as military commander read through J. Monroe's 1788 solar return, 188, 194; planets placed in 30th or 1st degrees of signs, 330.

John Adams. Dedication, xxix; defense of British troops in Boston Massacre read through Saturn primary directions of T. Jefferson, 33; Alien & Sedition Acts read through Saturn primary directions of Jefferson, 35; implication for al-kadukhadah when SAN is eclipse, 78; distributor changeover as arcus vitae, 91-93; conjunctional degree, 106; presidential inauguration read through Washington's horoscope using directing by triplicity; ZR L1 period as timer of start of presidency, 155; delineation of lot of spirit by bound placement, 157; lots, 240, 242, 254; diplomatic dispute with Benjamin Franklin read through Franklin's South Node Firdaria period, 370.

Thomas Jefferson. Uranus transit for DNA results of Hemmings family, x, 370; house system comparison, xxiv, 25-37, 183; Mars/Leo as significator for states' rights philosophy, xxv; observations on James Monroe's soul, 63; when killing planet-Ascendant directions kill, 92; preventional degree, 106; Moon's application to Mars, 116, 118; Hamilton-Jefferson feud read through Washington's horoscope using directing by triplicity, 132; Jefferson's undeclared naval war read through James Madison's horoscope using directing by triplicity, 134; Louisiana purchase read through James Monroe's 1802 solar return, 192-193; recapitulation of 1802 Jupiter-Saturn conjunction in horoscope, 215; Jupiter/Virgo as significator of constitutional law, 227; hidden nature of 12th house planets – Venus/Taurus/12th, 241, 335; incidence of Mercury-Jupiter opposition aspect, 283; influence of John Locke on text of Declaration of Independence, 339; Uranus and release of DNA evidence in support of sexual union with Sally Hemings, 374.

James Madison. 4th edition revised rectification, xii; lunar nodes as killers, 92; preventional degree, 106; Moon's application to Mars, 116; directing by triplicity, 133-134; ZR/notable FS-LOB linkages, 155; Mars/Capricorn signification as opposition to centralized government power, similar to Theodore Roosevelt's opposition to corporate trusts, 173; correct day of birth, 329.

James Monroe. Cognitive Assessment Model: when bound rulers better signify morality than sign rulers, 63; preventional degree, 106-107; ZR/notable FS-LOB linkages, 155; Chapter 11 case study: Profections as a Planetary Period Method, 181-195.

John Quincy Adams. Implication for al-kadukhadah when SAN is eclipse, 78; multiple arcus vitae and death, 89; Ascendant-hīlāj direction as arcus vitae, 89, 92; distributor changeover as arcus vitae, 91-93; preventional degree, 107; Moon's application to out-of-sign aspect to Mars as signification of civil unrest, 116; ZR L1 period as timer of start of Presidency, 155.

Andrew Jackson. SAN as empirical Hīlāj, xvi; evaluation of house systems by testing transits to Lot of Death, 27; when lifespan exceeds al-kadukhadāh projection, 78; Chapter 6 The Problem of Under Specification, relevance of lot of real estate and directing through the bounds for timing Andrew Jackson's house fire, 97-102; conjunctional degree, 107; ZR/notable FS-LOB linkages, 155; delineation of lot of spirit's bound placement, 157; lots, 240, 242, 252; use of lots in Stage II rectification, 332.

Martin Van Buren. Physiognomy, 44; al-mubtazz calculation for killing planet, 83-84; conjunctional degree, 87; Ascendant-hīlāj direction as arcus vitae, 89, 92; conjunctional degree, 107; Moon's application to out-of-sign Saturn aspect, 116; ability of ZRS L1 to time start of presidential term, 155.

William Harrison. Solar arc directions as arcus vitae, 90; recapitulation of arcus vitae in solar return preceding death, 91; killing planet directed to the MC for arcus vitae, 92; preventional degree, 107; lots, 240, 242, 251, 255.

John Tyler. Mars/Leo as significator of states' rights philosophy, xxv; physiognomy, 43, 37; ability of Sun to add minor years in Al-kadukhadāh computation, 77; killing planet – Ascendant direction as arcus vitae, 92; conjunctional degree, 107; ability of ZRS L1 to time end of political career, 155; read through Lincoln's 1862 solar return, 233.

James Polk. 4th edition revised rectification, xii; cognitive assessment model, 63; preventional degree, 108; Moon's application to Mars, 116; zodiacal releasing from lot of courage as timer of Mexican War, 149; delineation of lot of spirit's bound placement, 157; 1845 solar eclipse, 272; ability of natal chart to time mundane events, 321.

Zachary Taylor. House skewness of Moon's placement, 28; role of distributor changeover in timing death, 91-92; conjunctional degree, 108; Moon's application to Mars, 116; 1845 and 1849 solar eclipses, 272-273; ability of natal charts to time mundane events, 321; exhumation of remains timed by posthumous dynamic measurements, 375.

Millard Fillmore. 4th edition revised rectification, ix, xii; LOF primary directions, xxiii; conjunctional degree, 108; ability of ZRS L1 to time end of political career, 155; transit recapitulation prior to death, 281-283.

Franklin Pierce. Preventional degree, 108; rectification with Moon's aspects, 119-123, 330; ZR/notable FS-LOB linkages, 155; lots and religious conversion, 239, 242, 246; 1854 solar eclipse, 274; planets in the 30th or 1st degrees of signs, 330.

James Buchanan. 4th edition revised rectification, xii; when killing planet – Ascendant directions kill, 92; preventional degree, 108; Jupiter in Virgo as significator for legal profession, 227; 1857 solar eclipse, 275; planets in the 30th or 1st degrees of signs, 330.

Abraham Lincoln. Ascendant profections, xxiii, 9-23; preventional degree, 108; Moon's aspects and Presidential greatness, 114, 116-118; planetary hours, 145; ZR/notable FS-LOB linkages, 155; relative importance of profections and directions, 195; 1862 solar return, 197, 202-236; 1854 solar eclipse, 274; Mercury-Jupiter opposition, 283; assassination read through James Garfield's Ascendant profections, 333; transits, 286; 2007 Mercury return and composition of Chapter 10, 336; display of relics after death, 376.

Andrew Johnson. LOF directions, xxiii; open carry gun as physiognomy significator for national security, 44; Ibn Ezra Victor Model, 54-57; nodes as killers, 92; conjunctional degree, 108; ZR/notable FS-LOB linkages, 155; Jupiter-Saturn waxing square, 213.

Ulysses Grant. Mars/Leo as significator for states' rights philosophy, xxv; effect of Jupiter in Ascendant sign on physiognomy, 43; when al-kadukhadāh does not give its major years, 73; when many directions kill, 89; when Hīlāj - Ascendant directions kill, 89, 92; conjunctional degree, 109, 113; Moon's application to out-of-sign aspect of Saturn, 116; ZR L1 ability to time end of Presidency, 155; case study for testing relocated solar return charts based on difference between birthplace and death locations, 199; influence on Lincoln's 1862 solar return, 228.

Rutherford Hayes. Preventional degree, 109; ability of ZR L1 period to time start of Presidential term, 155; Jupiter-Saturn waning square.

James Garfield. Killing planet direction to MC as arcus vitae, 92; preventional degree, 109; ZR/notable FS-LOB linkages, 155; debility of Moon's application to Saturn, 115-116; lots and religious conversion, 239, 242, 247; nomination read through Benjamin Harrison's lunar node transit, 266-267; planets in the 30th or 1st degrees of signs, 330; Mars-Ascendant profections, 333, 381.

Chester Arthur. 4th edition revised rectification, xii; 3rd edition revised rectification, xvi; nodes as killers, 92; conjunctional degree, 109; ZR L1 period as timer of reversal on Civil Service Reform, 155; deceit surrounding date of birth, 329.

Grover Cleveland. Physiognomy significators for large weight, 43; precision of theoretical arcus vitae, 89; conjunctional degree, 109; appointment of Theodore Roosevelt to Civil Service Commission, 166, 173; lot of adultery, 240, 242, 256.

Benjamin Harrison. Distributor changeover as arcus vitae, 91; nodes as killers, 92; conjunctional degree, 109-110; lot of grandparents, 240, 242, 251; mean versus true Node assumption, 266-267.

William McKinley. 4th edition revised rectification, ix, xii; 3rd edition revised rectification, xvi; LOF Directions, xxiii; nodes as killers, 92; preventional degree, 110; flipping the lots in ZR, 149; ZR/notable FS-LOB linkages, 155.

Theodore Roosevelt. Directing the Ascendant through the Bounds, xi, xxiii, 159, 163-179, 334; impact of exact birthplace location on computed primary directions, xii; Jupiter in Ascendant sign as physiognomy significator, 43; killing planet – Ascendant directions which kill, 92; preventional degree, 110; Moon's application to Mars, 116; delineation of lot of spirit by bound placement, 147, 156-157; death as read through Warren Harding's ZRS, 154; ZR L1 period which timed Vice-Presidential nomination, 155; reversal of environmental degradation in wake of 1861 Jupiter-Saturn conjunction, 218; mean versus true node calculation, 266-267.

INDEX 777

William Taft. 3rd edition revised rectification, xvi; Jupiter in the Ascendant as physiognomy significator, 43; preventional degree, 110; endorsement by Harding read through Harding's ZRS, 153; rejection of Harding's requested diplomatic post read through Harding's ZRS, 154; ZR/notable FS-LOB linkages, 155; 1912 electoral challenge by Theodore Roosevelt read by Roosevelt's primary directions, 163; Taft's appointment as Governor of Philippines as read by Roosevelt's Saturn/Cancer Ascendant Distributor, 168; Roosevelt's final break from Taft as read by Roosevelt's primary directions, 175; lot of parents, 239, 242, 250.

Woodrow Wilson. Vertex, x, xxiv; conjunctional degree, 110; Jupiter-Saturn aspect and WWI, 113, 117; ZR/notable FS-LOB linkages, 155; linkage between Solar Arc and primary directions, 160, 178-179; Wilson's Presidential election following T Roosevelt's splitting of the Republican Party, 163, 175; attacks made by T. Roosevelt against Wilson's initial WWI neutrality, 169; influence of natal figure on mundane affairs, 321; incorrect birth date, 329.

Warren Harding. ZRS case study, xi, 147, 151-155; role of SAN as hīlāj when SAN is an eclipse, xvi, 78; Jupiter in the Ascendant as a physiognomy significator, 43; nodes as killers, 92; conjunctional degree, 110-111; Herbert Hoover as Commerce Secretary under Harding administration, 125; ZR/notable FS-LOB linkages, 155; solar return relocation, 199; posthumous settlement of Phillips estate, 378.

Calvin Coolidge. When actual longevity is more than the al-kadukhadāh projection, 79; capacity for solar arc directions to time death, 90; nodes as killers, 92; preventional degree, 111; Moon's application to out-of-sign Mars aspect as significator of 1920s Communist Red Scare, 116; giving Herbert Hoover nickname "The Wonder Boy," 125; multiple planets in a single sign, 126; cases where ZRS was unimpressive as timer of Presidential elections, 155; transits to the angles, 282, 284; planets in the 30th or 1st degrees of signs, 330.

Herbert Hoover. LOF directions, xxiii-xxiv; preventional degree, 111; Mercury's separation and application, 124; multiple planets in a single sign, 125; ZR/notable FS-LOB linkages, 155; solar return relocation, 199; LOF activated in solar return, 239, 242, 244; mean versus true node assumption, 264-266; LOF delineation in the 1st house, 323; Mercury in 1st degree of Leo, 329-330.

Franklin Roosevelt. Precision of rectified Ascendant, xvii, xxi; influence of bound and dwad on Moon in Cancer xxiii, 3, 7-8, 23; LOF directions, xxiii; uncertainty whether Victor of the Horoscope is Jupiter/Taurus or Mars/Gemini-rx, 57; killing planet – Ascendant directions, 92; conjunctional degree, 111; Jupiter-Saturn and WWII, 111, 113; Moon's configuration and presidential greatness, 114, 117-118; directing through the bounds, 130; directing by triplicity, 132, 294; transit case study, 277, 282, 285, 289-313; death read through LBJ's figure, 321; LOF delineation based on 8th house placement, 323; magical times for rectification, 336.

Harry Truman. 3rd edition revised rectification, xvi; small ovate shape of Cancer as physiognomy significator for shape of face, 48; Nodes as killers, 92; conjunctional degree, 111; Moon's application to Mars, 116-117; Hoover Commission under auspices of Truman administration, 125; ZR/notable FS-LOB linkages, 155; availability of diary entries for testing monthly and daily profections, 206.

Dwight Eisenhower. Malefic sign placement as significator of injured body part, 40; conjunctional degree, 111; exception to rule that Moon's application to Saturn predicts calamity, 116; Hoover Commission under auspices of Eisenhower administration, 125; ZR/notable FS-LOB linkages, 155; linkage between solar arcs and primary directions, 178-179; solar return relocation, 199-200; Saturn/Virgo as significator of tank warfare, 217; opposition to Churchill's Italian invasion plans as read through FDR's transits, 292, 297; ability of Mars in natal horoscope to time mundane conflict, 321; bias of memoirs, 322.

John F. Kennedy. When hīlāj-ascendant directions kill, 89, 92; conjunctional degree, 112; Moon's application to Mars as significator for war, 116; Moon's application to Mars as significator for death from gunshot, 117; ability of ZR L1 period to time beginning of Presidential term, 155; variance of birthplace location and place of death location as case study for effectiveness of solar return relocation, 199.

Lyndon Johnson. Jupiter in the Ascendant as significator for large body mass, 43; choice of victor of the horoscope between Jupiter/Leo or Mercury/Virgo, 57; thwarted 1968 Vietnam peace deal from Nixon's back channel Annna Chennault, 64; combustion and hīlāj viability, 76; lot of life and longevity, 78; conjunctional degree, 112; ZR/notable FS-LOB linkages, 155; death of FDR read through LBJ's Sun, 321.

Richard Nixon. Interplay of Victor and Cognitive Assessment Models on the soul, xi, 64, 66; 3rd edition revised rectification, xvi; evidence against Ptolemy's day-only LOF calculation, xxiii-xxiv; signification of Jupiter/Capricorn as naked ambition and corruption, 22; conjunctional degree, 112; directing by triplicity, 132, 135-136; as read through directing by triplicity via G.H.W. Bush's horoscope, 139; ZR L1 as timer of Nixon's legal liability from Watergate, 155; variance of birthplace location and place of death location as case study for effectiveness of solar return relocation, 199; lots, 239-240, 242-243, 245, 253, 323; transits, 282, 286; Ford's accession to Presidency after Nixon's resignation, 287.

Gerald Ford. Transit of Uranus to 10th positional degree of MC for accession to Vice President and Presidential offices, x, 287, 332; 3rd edition revised rectification, xvi; Jupiter/Capricorn-rx as significator for the restoration of morality and the rule of law, 22; when longevity exceeds al-kadukhadāh projection, 78; conjunctional degree, 112; ZRS as unimpressive timer of presidential elections, 155; 4th house planets as significator of the opposition political party, 321.

Jimmy Carter. 3rd edition revised rectification, xvi; similarity of Mars/Aquarius conjunct South Node to horoscope of G. H. W. Bush, 138; as read through G. H. W. Bush's horoscope through directing by triplicity, 139; lots, 241-242, 257; effect of South Node on conjunction with Mars, 262-263.

Ronald Reagan. Precision of Ascendant: Directing through the bounds, xi; controversy over Reagan's birthtime, xxi; LOF directions, xxiii; 11th house Midheaven, 28; Ascendant distributor changeover as arcus vitae, 91-92; conjunctional degree, 112-113; variance of birthplace location and place of death location as case study for effectiveness of solar return relocation, 199; lots, 241-242, 258-259; 1986 solar eclipse, 276.

George H. W. Bush. Use of physiognomy to reject Astrodatabank Ascendant, x, 49, 331; when longevity exceeds al-kadukhadāh projection, 78; when hīlāj-ascendant directions kill, 89, 92; conjunctional degree, 113; synastry to USA mundane horoscope as significator of mundane conflict, 117; directing by triplicity, 132, 137-139; ZR/notable FS-LOB linkages, 155; lots, 239, 242, 248.

Bill Clinton. Jupiter in the Ascendant as significator for large body mass, 43; ZR/notable FS-LOB linkages, 155; transits, 282, 288.

George W. Bush. Jupiter/Libra contrasted to Jupiter/Libra-rx for Trump, 22; when Victor and Cognitive Assessment Models differ, 65; Jupiter-Saturn square as significator of mundane conflict, 117; lots, 239, 242, 249; mean versus true node assumption, 266-267.

Barack Obama. When the SAN is an eclipse, 78; management of Iraq war assigned to Joe Biden, 116; ZR/notable FS-LOB linkages, 155; transit of Jupiter to the 10th position degree from the Lot of Spirit, 332.

Donald Trump. Jupiter/Libra-rx contrasted to Jupiter/Libra for George W. Bush, 22-23; how the Moon's degree can be narrowed by its bound position in the context of the cognitive assessment model, 65; when the SAN is an eclipse, 78.

Joe Biden. Uranus transit as timer of fatal car crash for 1st wife and daughter, x; rising decan as physiognomy significator, 43; Moon's application to Mars, 116; delineation of bound placement of Lot of Spirit, 157; linkage between solar arc and primary directions, 160, 334.

LAUS DEO

For updates, errata, and further information, please visit:

www.regulus-astrology.com

www.ingramcontent.com/pod-product-compliance
Lightning Source LLC
Chambersburg PA
CBHW052106010526
44111CB00036B/1486